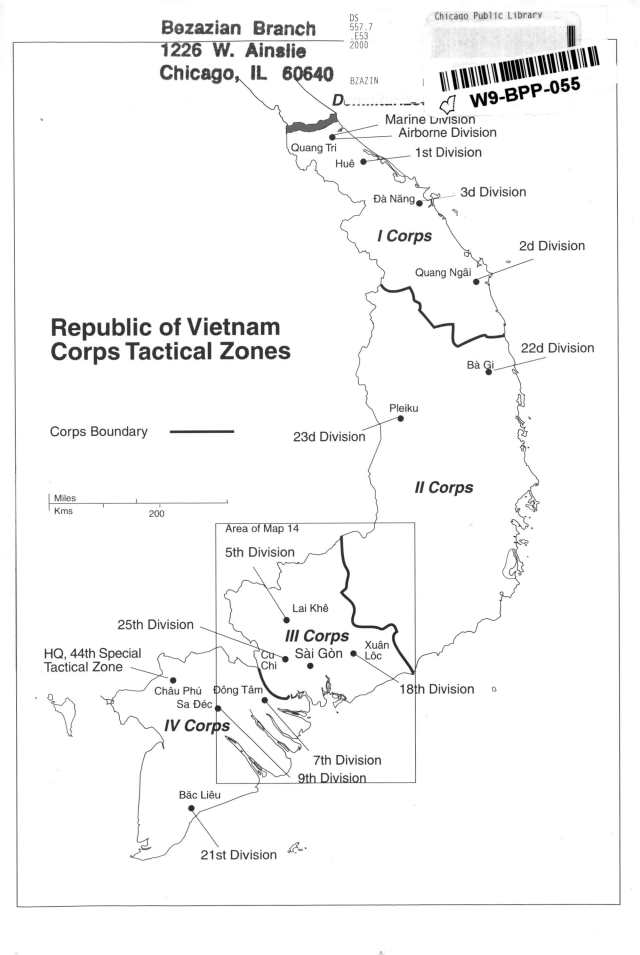

Marine Division
Airborne Division
1st Division

Quang Tri
Huê

3d Division

Đà Nẵng

I Corps

2d Division

Quang Ngãi

Republic of Vietnam
Corps Tactical Zones

22d Division

Bà Gi

Pleiku

Corps Boundary

23d Division

Miles
Kms
200

II Corps

Area of Map 14

5th Division

Lai Khê

25th Division

III Corps

Xuân
Lôc

HQ, 44th Special
Tactical Zone

Củ
Chi

Sài Gòn

Châu Phú

Đông Tâm

18th Division

Sa Đéc

IV Corps

7th Division
9th Division

Bắc Liêu

21st Division

Encyclopedia of the Vietnam War

A Political, Social, and Military History

Encyclopedia of the Vietnam War

A Political, Social, and Military History

Spencer C. Tucker
Editor

David Coffey
Nugyên Công Luân
Mike Nichols
Sandra Wittman
Associate Editors

OXFORD
UNIVERSITY PRESS

OXFORD
UNIVERSITY PRESS

Oxford   New York
Athens   Auckland   Bangkok   Bogotá   Buenos Aires   Calcutta
Cape Town   Chennai   Dar es Salaam   Delhi   Florence   Hong Kong   Istanbul
Karachi   Kuala Lumpur   Madrid   Melbourne   Mexico City   Mumbai
Nairobi   Paris   São Paulo   Singapore   Taipei   Tokyo   Toronto   Warsaw

and associated companies in
Berlin   Ibadan

Library of Congress Cataloging-in-Publication Data is available
Encyclopedia of the Vietnam War: a political, social, and military history/
Spencer C. Tucker [editor].
p.   cm.
Originally published: Santa Barbara, Calif.: ABC-CLIO, ©1998
Includes bibliographical references and index.
ISBN 0-19-513524-5
1. Vietnamese Conflict, 1961-1975 Encyclopedias.
I. Tucker, Spencer, 1937- .
DS557.7.E53   2000
959.7'003—dc21   99-36873

1 3 5 7 9 0 8 6 4 2
Printed in the United States of America
on acid-free paper

The Contributors

Betsy Alexander
Department of History
Texas Christian University

Kevin Arceneaux
Department of History
Texas Christian University

Lacie Ballinger
Department of History
Texas Christian University

Capt. Pat Barker
U.S. Air Force Academy

John Barcus
Department of History
Louisiana State University

Dr. Mark Barringer
Department of History
Texas Tech University

Dr. Harry Basehart
Department of Political Science
Salisbury State University

Dr. John L. Bell, Jr.
Department of History
Western Carolina University

Dr. David M. Berman
Department of Curriculum and
Education
University of Pittsburgh

Dr. Ernest C. Bolt
Mitchell-Billikopf Professor of History
University of Richmond

Walter Boyne
Smithsonian Institution, Retired

Dr. Robert Brigham
Department of History
Vassar College

Dean Brumley
Department of History
Texas Christian University

Peter Brush
Central Library
Vanderbilt University

Dr. Hum Dac Bui
Redlands, California

Dr. Robert J. Bunker
Claremont, California

Dr. Paul R. Camacho
The William Joiner Center
University of Massachusetts—Boston

J. Nathan Campbell
Department of History
Texas Christian University

Dr. Ralph Carter
Department of Political Science
Texas Christian University

Thomas R. Carver
Seymour, Texas

Rajesh H. Chauhan
Claremont, California

Dr. Edwin Clausen
Department of History
Pacific Lutheran University

David Coffey
Department of History
Texas Christian University

Matthew Crump
Department of History
Texas Christian University

Dr. Cecil B. Currey
University of South Florida
Lutz, Florida

Dr. Paul Daum
Department of History
New England College

Dr. Arthur J. Dommen
The Indochina Institute
George Mason University

Timothy G. Dowling
Department of History
Louisiana State University

Benjamin Dubberly
Department of History
Texas Tech University

Dr. Joe P. Dunn
Department of History and Politics
Converse College

Blake Dunnavent
Department of History
Lubbock Christian College

Dr. Bruce Elleman
History Department
Texas Christian University

Dr. Mark A. Esposito
Department of History
West Virginia University

Lt. Col. Peter Faber
Department of History
U.S. Air Force Academy

Dr. Will E. Fahey, Jr.
Haverhill, Massachusetts

Dr. Charles Fasanaro
Santa Fe, New Mexico

Dr. Arthur Thomas Frame
Lansing, Kansas

James Friuglietti
Department of History
Montana State University—Billings

Dr. Peter K. Frost
Department of History
Williams College

1st Lt. Noel Fulton
Department of History
U.S. Air Force Academy

George J. Gabera
Claremont, California

Charles J. Gaspar
Department of Humanities and
Communication Arts
Brenau University

John Gates
Department of History
Wooster College

Capt. Larry Gatti
Department of History
U.S. Air Force Academy

Laurie Geist
Department of Humanities
Illinois Institute of Technology

Dr. Marc J. Gilbert
Department of History
North Georgia College

Dr. Mark Gilderhus
Department of History
Texas Christian University

Dr. James Gilliam
Spellman College

Tim Grammer
Dallas, Texas

Professor John Robert Greene
Department of History
Cazenovia College

Capt. John Grenier
Department of History
U.S. Air Force Academy

Dr. Charles J. Gross
Departments of the Army and
the Air Force
National Guard Bureau

Debra Hall
Department of History
Cazenovia College

Dr. Mitchell K. Hall
Department of History
Central Michigan University

Dr. William Head
Chief, Office of History
Warner Robins Air Logistics Center

Glenn E. Helm
Naval Historical Center
Department of the Navy

Pia C. Heyn
Lexington, Kentucky

2nd Lt. Joel Higley
Department of History
U.S. Air Force Academy

2nd Lt. Lincoln Hill
Department of History
U.S. Air Force Academy

Anh Dieu Hô
Madison, Connecticut

Dr. Richard Hunt
Center for Military History

Dr. Arnold Isaacs
Pasadena, Maryland

Dr. Eric Jarvis
Department of History
King's College

Susan G. Kalaf

Mary Kelley
Department of History
Texas Christian University

Ann Kelsey
Whippany, New Jersey

Dr. Gary Kerley
Brenau Academy

Dr. Jeff Kinard
Greensboro, North Carolina

Lt. Col. Richard L. Kiper
Leavenworth, Kansas

2nd Lt. Brent Langhals
Department of History
U.S. Air Force Academy

Capt. Alex R. Larzelere
U.S. Coast Guard, Retired

Dr. Clayton D. Laurie
Conventional Warfare Studies Branch
United States Army Center of Military
History

Dr. William M. Leary
Department of History
University of Georgia

Dr. Jack McCallum, M.D.
Fort Worth, Texas

Dr. Stanley McGowen
Department of History
Texas Christian University

James McNabb
Claremont, California

Dr. Robert G. Mangrum
Department of History
Howard Payne University

Justin Marks
Department of History
Cazenovia College

Dr. Edward J. Marolda
Senior Historian
Naval Historical Center

Dr. (Col.) Joseph Martino
U.S. Air Force, Retired

Jay Menzoff
Department of History
Texas Christian University

Dr. Edwin E. Moise
Department of History
Clemson University

Louise Mongelluzo
Department of History
Cazenovia College

Dr. Malcolm Muir, Jr.
Department of History
Austin Peay State University

Mike Nichols
Department of History
Texas Christian University

Ngô Ngoc Trung
Institute for East Asian Studies
University of California

Nguyên Công Luân
Santa Clara, California

Stephen R. Maynard
Denton, Texas

Dr. Long Ba Nguyen
Viet Business Publications

Dr. Edward McNertney
Department of Economics
Texas Christian University

Cynthia Northrup
Department of History
Texas Christian University

Dr. Michael G. O'Loughlin
Department of Political Science
Salisbury State University

Eric Osborne
Department of History
Texas Christian University

Edward Page
Department of History
Texas Christian University

Greg Perdue
Department of History
University of Texas

Delia Pergande
Department of History
University of Kentucky

Dr. Pham Cao Duong
Huntington Beach, California

Thomas Phu
Alexandria, Virginia

Dr. Charlotte A. Power
Department of History
Black River Technical College

Dr. John Clark Pratt
Department of English
Colorado State University

Dr. Michael Richards
Department of History
Sweet Briar College

Dr. Priscilla Roberts
Department of History
University of Hong Kong

Dr. John D. Root
Lewis Department of Humanities
Armour College
Illinois Institute of Technology

Dr. Rodney J. Ross
Harrisburg, Pennsylvania

Mr. Harve Saal
MACV, Studies and Observations Group
MACV-SOG History Project

Dr. David C. Saffell
Department of History and Political
Science
Ohio Northern University

Dr. Stanley Sandler
JFK Special Warfare School
Fort Bragg

Dr. Claude R. Sasso
Kansas City, Missouri

Captain Carl Otis Schuster
HQ USCINCPAC, J-22
Kailua, Hawaii

Dr. Michael Share
Department of History
University of Hong Kong

Dr. Lewis Sorley
Potomac, Maryland

Dr. James Southerland
Brenau University

Dr. Phoebe Spinrad
Columbus, Ohio

Richard Starnes
Auburn, Alabama

Dr. Kenneth R. Stevens
Department of History
Texas Christian University

Leslie-Rahye Strickland
Stephenville, Texas

1st Lt. Tracy Szczepaniak
Department of History
U.S. Air Force Academy

Dr. Brenda Taylor
Department of History
Texas Wesleyan University

Capt. John Terino
U.S. Air Force Academy

Dr. Francis H. Thompson
Department of History
Western Kentucky University

Dr. Earl H. Tilford, Jr.
Army War College

Dr. Vincent Transano
Naval Facilities Engineering Command
Naval Construction Battalion Center

Zsolt Varga
Department of History
Texas Christian University

Dr. John F. Votaw
The Cantigny First Division Foundation

Hieu Dinh Vu
Dallas, Texas

Wes Watters
Department of History
Texas Christian University

Dr. James M. Welsh
English Department
Salisbury State University

Mike Werttheimer
Naval Historical Center
Department of the Navy

Donald Whaley
Department of History
Salisbury State University

Lt. Col. James H. Willbanks
Department of Joint and Combined
Operations
U.S. Army Command and General Staff
College

Professor Sandra Wittman
Library Services
Oakton Community College

Dr. Laura M. Wood
Department of Social Sciences
Tarrant County Junior College, Northwest

Lee Ann Woodall
Department of History
McMurry University

Colonel David T. Zabecki
Freiburg, Germany

Admiral Elmo R. Zumwalt, Jr.
U.S. Navy, Retired

Contents

Encyclopedia of the Vietnam War

A Political, Social, and Military History

Foreword

My own experience with Vietnam began in 1962 when I became Director of Arms Control in the Office of the Assistant Secretary of Defense for International Security Affairs. The Assistant Secretary, Paul H. Nitze, a brilliant and experienced statesman, made use of his staff without bureaucratic regard for their assigned titles so that I began, among other assignments, to be involved in analyses of the Vietnam situation. In late 1963, Paul Nitze became Secretary of the Navy and took me with him as his executive assistant, where our involvement with Vietnam intensified, until my departure for sea duty in 1965. From 1966 to 1968 I served as the Navy's director of systems analyses, where Paul Nitze, by then deputy secretary of defense, involved me almost weekly in discussions of Vietnam. From 1968 until 1970, I served as commander, U.S. Naval Forces, Vietnam. From 1970 to 1974, as chief of naval operations and a member of the Joint Chiefs of Staff (JCS), I was involved in the assignment of forces, analyses of strategic and tactical issues, and, subject to presidential direction, in the overall conduct of the war.

The development of consensus concerning U.S. strategy for Vietnam was made much more difficult by virtue of the personality of Secretary of Defense Robert S. McNamara, who demonstrated essential contempt for military leaders, frequently bypassed the JCS by using his secretaries of Air Force, Army, and Navy and his assistant secretaries of defense to do operational analyses, and often provided military advice to the president without the attendance of the chairman of the JCS to ensure military input directly to the commander in chief.

For me this inappropriate system provided the opportunity to participate with Paul Nitze for the three years of increased involvement, 1962–1965, in the development of national strategy.

In 1962 Dr. Walt Rostow in discussions with Department of Defense officials, espoused on behalf of President John F. Kennedy a theory of reprisal attacks by U.S. forces against North Vietnam. The North Vietnamese were to be given warnings that if their support of the war in the South continued, the United States would initiate a "punishing" strike. After a pause, if their action continued or increased, greater "punishment" would be administered. The military view was strongly against such a strategy. We believed that the "punishment" would not deter the Communist regime, that pauses between strikes would allow the them to rebuild, learn lessons as to how better to deal with such strikes, and thus would be totally counterproductive. Regrettably, this strike and pause theory within the White House continued under both Kennedy and Lyndon Johnson; and pauses in military action against North Vietnam, while building up U.S. forces in the South, greatly hampered the opportunity for a favorable outcome in the war.

While this overall strategy of reprisal and pause against the North persisted throughout the war, the strategy with South Vietnam developed in several phases.

Initially those of us preparing discussion papers for Paul Nitze to use with McNamara, reflecting Nitze's guidance, advocated that Vietnam was not the place to maintain the U.S. policy of containment of communism. We believed in the policy of containment of Communist expansion by the Soviet Union (USSR) and People's Republic of China (PRC), North Korea, and North Vietnam. But we held that South Vietnam was not a viable national entity, that the conditions for nation-building did not exist, and that containment should be achieved by building the economies and military capabilities of Thailand, Malaysia, Singapore, Indonesia, and the Philippines. Under this concept our efforts in South Vietnam would be limited to modest logistic support and military advisory personnel. This advice was not acceptable to McNamara, who insisted that the uncertainty of a favorable outcome for South Vietnam using the above strategy made it mandatory to do more.

The second phase of U.S. involvement, resulting from McNamara's rejection of the "contain elsewhere" policy, flowed from consideration of another two alternative views. Those of us working with Paul Nitze presented the view that for South Vietnam to have a high probability of survival as a non-Communist regime upon commitment of U.S. forces, U.S. forces would have to be brought to bear against North Vietnam by air and naval surface ship bombardment and by blockade against the North. If this did not cause Hà Nội to cease its infiltration of the South, amphibious landings to seize Hai Phòng and Hà Nội would have had to follow. In that later eventuality we estimated that on the order of 5,000 U.S. casualties would result and that, with all logistic lines by land and sea cut off, only limited efforts by the Communists could continue. We held that Chinese forces would not intervene against such U.S. action. U.S. forces had improved by an order of magnitude over PRC forces since they had last fought each other in Korea. U.S. nuclear superiority over the PRC was apparent to both sides. These facts plus assurances to Beijing that U.S. forces would not operate in the vicinity of the PRC borders, we judged adequate to neutralize the PRC. We further believed that if our calculations were proven inaccurate, U.S. forces would defeat invading PRC forces—as did the North Vietnamese military forces (who were good but not as formidable as U.S. forces) in the subsequent invasion of North Vietnam by the Chinese after the U.S. war ended.

We advocated that U.S. Army forces in South Vietnam be limited to major advisory efforts to equip and train South Vietnamese forces to fight their own war against indigenous Communist forces as the United States contained the threat in the North as outlined above.

McNamara was unwilling to depart from his grand strategy of reprisal and pause in the North, accepting the view that a PRC invasion was highly likely and that the risks to the United States were too great. His alternative was almost the exact opposite of our proposals—no invasion in the North, no all-out use of air and sea power in the North, reprisal against limited target systems followed by pauses, and ultimately a massive buildup of U.S. ground forces in the South.

Having been overruled by McNamara's decision, the Nitze school of thought maintained that we were in for a long, drawn-out war, that the U.S. public support would weaken as American casualties mounted in such inconclusive operations, and that we must therefore move to Vietnamize the war as rapidly as possible. This strategy was not to be fully implemented until Richard Nixon became president. By that time, it was judged to be politically necessary to begin withdrawals of U.S. forces, which meant that Vietnamization had to be accomplished in a much shorter than optimal time frame.

Having been ordered in September 1968 to Vietnam, to accomplish the Vietnamization of naval forces, which I had been advocating, I told my staff that if Hubert Humphrey were to be elected that November, we would probably have one year to complete Vietnamization; and, if Nixon were elected, we would probably have three years. We drew up a one-year plan with an alternatively more efficient three-year option.

In fact we were able to follow the three-year plan. U.S. naval forces set up a river/canal blockade along the Cambodian border. Communist logistic support of their forces in the Mekong Delta was greatly curtailed, Vietnamese sailors were trained and replaced U.S. sailors, one sailor at a time, on each boat, ship, and shore facility. By the time of the fall of Sài Gòn, the Delta had been so completely pacified and the people had become so supportive of U.S. objectives, that it took a considerable time for the Communist forces to take control there after the fall of Sài Gòn. As an interesting footnote, the South Vietnamese Navy never surrendered. They loaded their families on board their ships and steamed to Subic Bay in the Philippines where they turned the ships over to the U.S. Navy.

Despite all obstacles, despite a far less than optimal strategy, by the time of the truce in 1973, U.S. forces had turned the war-fighting successfully over to the South Vietnamese. These forces proved their steadfastness in defeating and driving back the North Vietnamese invasion by People's Army of Vietnam regular units after U.S. forces had departed.

Had the United States been politically capable of carrying out in 1974 and 1975 President Nixon's two secret commitments to President Nguyên Van Thiêu—i.e., to replace attrited equipment and to retaliate vigorously against truce violations—in my judgment, a successful two-Vietnam solution would have been achieved. The balance of forces between the two sides was much more favorable to the South than in the case of South Korea after the Korean War. With continuing U.S. support, as occurred in the Korean case, over time the South's burgeoning economy would have achieved a superiority over the Communist forces as had happened in Korea.

In my meetings with former North Vietnamese leaders in 1994, there was general agreement on their part that they always knew that they had to win the war in the United States and that the great constitutional crisis brought on by Watergate, superimposed upon the efforts of the antiwar faction in the United States, was responsible for their victory.

One additional point needs to be made to put the Vietnam War into historical context. Despite the great loss of political support for strong foreign policy initiatives by the United States as a result of Watergate and the defeat of South Vietnam that followed, despite the tragic loss of 58,000 lives versus the 5,000 or so that would likely have been lost with an aggressive early strategy against the North, despite the success the USSR was able to achieve in such places as Angola, Mozambique, and Ethiopia as the United States lay prostrate in the post-Vietnam environment, the U.S. actions in Vietnam gave Southeast Asia time to gain an economic and defense posture to survive Communist penetration.

As I left Vietnam in 1970 to become a member of the JCS, I visited Lee Quan Yew in Singapore and General Jiang Jieshi (Chiang Kai-shek) in Taipei. Both of these leaders made the point to me then and again in later years that the U.S. stand in Vietnam had given Southeast Asian nations the time to prosper and survive.

In the long light of history, the disastrous, grossly inefficient, incompetently conceived U.S. strategy in Vietnam caused a breakdown in containment in Africa but did contain Communist expansion in Southeast Asia with the result that, coupled with the resurgence of U.S. power and influence during the Reagan/Bush years, the free world's global containment policy proved successful.

—Admiral Elmo R. Zumwalt, Jr., U.S. Navy (Retired)

Acknowledgments

I would like to thank my associate editors. Texas Christian University (TCU) graduate student David Coffey made a significant contribution to the encyclopedia, both as an editor and as a writer. Mike Nichols, another TCU graduate student, was of immense assistance in running down elusive sources and scanning the documents into the computer. Former Army of the Republic of Vietnam (ARVN) officer Nguyên Công Luân helped with diacritical marks, spelling of Vietnamese words, writing, and editing. Sandy Wittman oversaw the bibliographies, assisted with the glossary, and read much of the manuscript. Virginia Military Institute Cadet Brad Arnold helped proofread documents and checked sources.

I would also like to thank the Lyndon Baines Johnson Presidential Library, Austin, Texas, which made available some documents for our use. I am also grateful to former TCU History Department Office Manager Barbara Pierce for her assistance, and Lacie Ballinger and Rita Marta Pálvölgy also helped in many ways. And, as always, I am especially grateful to my wife, Beverly, for her often tested patience and her support.

Preface

I first became involved in the Vietnam War while a captain in the U.S. Army between 1965 and 1967. I graduated from the Virginia Military Institute in 1959 with a B.A. in History and an Army commission but secured a delay in my military service while studying on a Fulbright scholarship in France and pursuing a doctorate in History at the University of North Carolina. In the fall of 1965, I entered the Army and, after completing officer basic training, I became the desk officer for North Vietnam and Laos in the Intelligence Support Facility (ISF) working under the U.S. Army assistant chief of staff for intelligence (ACSI). My responsibilities included writing intelligence analyses on the area and preparing daily briefing materials for the Army's chief of staff. Fate kept me from Vietnam, but many of my friends went there and some did not return. My first trip to Vietnam was not until in 1992, when I participated in a two-week seminar sponsored by the Council on International Educational Exchange (CIEE). It was an extraordinary experience that enhanced my own understanding of the war and Vietnam, and greatly aided me in teaching a course on the conflict.

This encyclopedia is an ambitious project and the largest such undertaking to date. It traces the long history of Vietnam and details early U.S. involvement in that country. It also brings Vietnamese history up to date, with discussions of the Socialist Republic of Vietnam from 1975 through the late 1990s. Contained herein are more than 900 separate entries; descriptions of warfare and weapons systems; biographies, including many more from the Communist side than are available in comparable reference works; analyses of the involvement and contributions of the various nations in the conflict; analyses of the U.S. domestic front, including the antiwar movement, to put in context the full impact of the war; significant information on early Vietnamese history, in order to place the Vietnam War in its proper historical contex; and analyses of Vietnam-related literature and film.

We have generally used the Vietnamese spellings and diacritical marks for individuals and place names. One exception is *Viêt Nam*. For ease of reading by Americans, for whom this volume is largely intended, *Viêt Nam* has throughout been Americanized to *Vietnam*.

For Vietnamese personal names we have chosen to use the Vietnamese system of family name first, followed by middle name, then given name. Subsequent references are to the given name only. Thus, in the case of Ngô Đình Diêm, Ngô is the family name, Đình the middle name, and Diêm the given name. After the first reference we refer to him only as Diêm. This follows the common Vietnamese practice of using the first name with the title, no matter how exalted the individual. The two exceptions to this among Vietnamese are Hô Chí Minh and Tôn Đuc Thang, both of whom are referred to as "Uncle" before their family name.

We have also elected to use the 24-hour military time throughout. Thus 6:00 A.M. is written as 0600, and 6:00 P.M. is expressed as 1800.

We have worked very hard to minimize mistakes and hope that they are few, but I take full responsibility for those that may appear.

—Spencer C. Tucker
John Biggs Professor of Military History
Virginia Military Institute, Lexington, Virginia

One cannot understand the Vietnam War without first studying the Indo-China conflict. This in turn cannot be understood without probing Vietnamese nationalist attitudes during the period of French rule. This in turn was conditioned by the long Vietnamese opposition to China. This reveals the truism that history cannot be understood in isolation. If any war clearly demonstrates the need to study history, it is the Vietnam conflict.

Geography—specifically the country's proximity to China—has conditioned Vietnam's history. It is no coincidence that warfare in Vietnam begins and ends with fighting against China. U.S. strategists failed to understand this strong historical antipathy; most could see only the play of ideology. Although China and Vietnam have been at loggerheads politically through most of their shared history, China was to exert great ideological and cultural influence on Vietnam.

In 111 B.C. the Chinese Han emperor sent an expeditionary corps into the northern part of what is now the Socialist Republic of Vietnam and added this kingdom to his empire. For the next thousand years, present-day northern Vietnam was, save for a few brief but glorious rebellions, a Chinese province.

With victory in the 938 Battle of the Bach Đang River, the Vietnamese freed themselves from Chinese rule. Nonetheless, the thousand years of Chinese domination produced a permanent Chinese cultural imprint, although over time something of a Sino-Vietnamese synthesis emerged.

Although China exercised nominal suzerainty over Vietnam until the 1885 Treaty of Tientsin, the Vietnamese in fact now controlled all the territory from the foothills of Yunan to the 17th parallel. From 938 through 1884, they built a new country—to use their own term, a Southern nation (Nuoc Nam or Nam Quôc)—facing China, the Northern nation (Bac Quôc). Chinese attempts to reconquer Vietnam failed, except for a 20-year period (1407–1427) during the Ming dynasty.

At the same time, the Vietnamese expanded their territory south of Đeo Ngang (Ngang Pass) to Cà Mâu. "Resisting the North" (Bac cu) and "Conquering the South" (Nam chinh) became major themes of Vietnamese history as did the development of an original culture and civilization. Nam chinh (or Nam Tiên), the effort to expand the national territory to the south, was accomplished at the expense first of the Chams and later of the Khmers. By 1658 the Vietnamese had taken all of South Vietnam north of Sài Gòn, which itself fell to the Vietnamese in 1672. The lower plain of the future Cochin China (southern Vietnam) came under Vietnamese control in the last decades of the eighteenth century. Vietnam, by then expanded to the full extent of its present shoreline, also took advantage of Cambodian weakness to intervene in the affairs of that neighboring state.

But at the same time, Vietnam itself was falling apart. Civil war raged intermittently from the mid-sixteenth to the late-eighteenth centuries, with the country divided between the Trinh and Nguyên families. In 1773 three brothers, the Tây Son, led a rebellion against the Nguyên. One brother, Nguyên Huê, proved to be a military genius. He defeated in turn the Nguyên rulers in the South, an invading Siamese army, and the Trinh in the North. In 1789 he won one of the most important of Vietnamese military victories by defeating an invading Chinese Army. Unfortunately Nguyên Huê did not live long, and the Tây Son were then defeated by a surviving member of the Nguyên, who in 1802 proclaimed himself emperor as Gia Long. His descendants ruled until 1945.

Meanwhile, Europeans had arrived. Although contacts between Vietnam and the West began in Roman times, the first lasting ties between Vietnam and Europe resulted from the 1535 arrival of Antônio da Faria, a Portuguese explorer. Europeans were attracted to Vietnam by the desire to secure trade, gain naval facilities, and attract religious converts. The Dutch and then the French followed.

The attempt by Gia Long's immediate successors to root out Christianity provided an excuse for French intervention. In 1847 French warships arrived at Tourane and sank three Vietnamese vessels. In 1858 the French returned with a naval squadron and land troops, taking Tourane and then Sài Gòn. In 1862 the French forced Emperor Tu Đuc to sign a treaty that gave France three treaty ports in Annam (central Vietnam) and Tonkin (northern Vietnam) and possession of the eastern provinces of Cochin China, including Sài Gòn.

French holdings in Indo-China expanded by fits and starts, but by 1867 France had secured all of Cochin China. French attentions then shifted to the north. In 1874 the emperor was forced not only to recognize French control of Cochin China but to grant concessions in Hà Nôi and Hai Phòng. French designs on the North brought Chinese military intervention in the Black Flag or Tonkin Wars (1882–1885).

Although their effort followed a zigzag course, France by the end of the nineteenth century ruled Indo-China. Only Cochin China was an outright colony, but France controlled Annam and Tonkin, as well as Laos, and Cambodia as protectorates.

French reforms barely touched most of the population and, when they did, had contradictory results. The discussion of French values of "liberty, equality, and fraternity," although circulated in a limited milieu, would contribute to the demise of French power in Vietnam. Also important in the rise of Vietnamese nationalism were the defeat of Russia by Japan (1905), the 1910 Chinese revolution (the Vietnamese National Party, or VNQDD, was modeled on Sun Yat-sen's party in China), and the World War I (especially U.S. President Woodrow Wilson's 1917 proclamation of the "self determination of peoples").

In the aftermath of the World War I, the French refused to recognize a historic cue and begin a dialog with moderate nationalist leaders for meaningful concessions in Indo-

China. This led directly to a military clash. The French defeat of the VNQDD opened the door for the more militant Communists headed by Hồ Chí Minh, easily the most powerful figure in modern Vietnamese history. Was Hồ simply a Communist or rather a nationalist first and a Communist second? Might he have become an Asian Tito? We will never know for certain, but it is true that Hồ tried to reach accommodation with the French, who rejected his efforts.

World War II had a major impact on Vietnam. Ironically, Washington's decision to make Indo-China its figurative line in the sand regarding Japanese expansion brought about the attack on Pearl Harbor and U.S. entry in the war. Japan's humbling of the French and its occupation of Vietnam were important in the spread of nationalist sentiment, especially the Japanese proclamation in March 1945 of an independent Vietnam.

In August 1945 Japan surrendered. Thanks in part to British assistance, the French reestablished their control in Indo-China, easily brushing aside the Việt Minh, which had been formed by Hồ Chí Minh during the war to fight for Vietnamese independence against both the Japanese and French.

Paris lost an opportunity to craft a stable, evolving relationship with Indo-China when it failed to implement the March 1946 Hồ-Sainteny Agreement. This recognized the independence of the Democratic Republic of Vietnam (DRV) in the North (publicly proclaimed by Hu on September 2 in Hà Nôi) and provided for a plebiscite in the South to determine whether it wanted to join the North. French Governor General Admiral Thierry d'Argenlieu torpedoed this agreement simply by proclaiming an "independent" Republic of Cochin China in the South. The failure of Paris to repudiate its proconsul—partly the result of political paralysis in France—also precluded meaningful compromise with Vietnamese nationalists. In November 1946 fighting broke out in the North between the Việt Minh and the French. The first Indo-China War (1946–1954) had begun.

Although the French easily established their control over the larger cities and towns, the Việt Minh relocated in the countryside and held increasingly more territory as the war wound on. Efforts to resolve differences failed because of French insistence on terms that were tantamount to surrender.

French forces in the war were led by professional officers and NCOs. No draftees were sent to Indo-China. Volunteers, the Foreign Legion, colonial troops, and native levies formed the French fighting forces that fought the Việt Minh.

Paris sought to mask the colonial nature of the struggle by playing up ideological aspects. In 1949 Paris concluded the Elysée Agreements, which created the State of Vietnam. France claimed to have given Vietnam its independence and that the war was a contest between democracy and international Communism. This played to U.S. opinion and the anti-Communist hysteria that had swept that country in the wake of the Communist victory in China. Vietnam became bound up in Cold War diplomacy. Washington considered French manpower vital to NATO and the security of Western Europe

and believed it needed to keep France as an ally at all costs. The price of this was Washington's support for Paris's Southeast Asian policies. Meanwhile France claimed to be merely "aiding" a loyal and "independent" ally. In fact, Paris closed the door to Vietnamese nationalism and therefore compelled virtually all genuine nationalists to join the Communists. Many joined reluctantly, only because France had left them no other choice.

The 1949 Communist victory in China was immensely important to the Việt Minh because it opened a source of resupply and provided ready sanctuaries. In effect this doomed the French military effort in the North by the end of 1950. The war continued, in part under pressure from the United States, which from 1950 to 1953 fought on a "interconnected front against communism" in Korea and was now bearing the brunt of the cost of the French military effort. The final act of the Indo-China War was played out at Điên Biên Phu, where French commander General Henri Navarre had hoped to lure a limited number of Vo Nguyên Giáp's troops into battle and defeat them. Giáp took the bait and attacked, relying on an army of coolies who dragged artillery to the hills surrounding the French fortress. On 7 May 1954, Điên Biên Phu surrendered. This defeat, which coincided with a meeting in Geneva to discuss Asian problems, allowed French politicians to shift blame to the generals and end an unpopular war.

During the resulting July 1954 Geneva Accords, the Việt Minh—winners on the battlefield—were forced to make most of the concessions. The agreements temporarily divided Vietnam at the 17th parallel with a demilitarized zone (DMZ) between the North and South but provided that Vietnam was one state and that national elections would be held in both halves in 1956 to reunite the country.

That these elections were never held made inevitable the renewal of fighting. This time the Americans replaced the French. Gradually and almost imperceptibly, the U.S. commitment to Vietnam deepened. The war ended up being a traumatic event for the United States and one of the greatest crises in its history. Ironically, the Vietnamese have done much better at putting it into perspective. In his 410-page "official history" of Vietnam (1993), Nguyên Khac Viên devotes only one chapter—"Building the Foundations of Socialism and the Struggle against U.S. Neo-Colonialism"—to the entire period of 1954–1973.

In the South, from 1955 to 1963, Ngô Đình Diêm controlled the new Republic of Vietnam. Hồ Chí Minh continued to dominate the northern Democratic Republic of Vietnam. Washington considered Diêm the best alternative to Hồ Chí Minh and Communist rule and supported Diêm in his refusal to hold the elections provided for by the Geneva Accords. Diêm was certainly not a puppet of the United States, and his regime was not as corrupt as many of his successors, who were, however, largely inept politically.

Meanwhile, Hồ and the rest of the DRV leadership could hardly be displeased with Diêm's consolidation of the South, including the suppression of its religious sects and minorities. Dissatisfaction with Diêm's policies, however, brought renewed fighting by Southern insurgents, which the North then supported. In May 1959 the DRV formed an infiltration group to move supplies into the South and fuel the growing insurgency. The resulting infiltration network became known as the Hô Chí Minh trail.

Growing disaffection in the South and in Washington over Diêm and his policies led to his overthrow and assassination in November 1963. His successors lacked his political acumen and his prestige. It seemed that the United States could not win the war with Diêm or without him.

Up to this point there were only U.S. military advisers in the South. In August 1964, however, came the Tonkin Gulf Incidents and Tonkin Gulf Resolution, which gave President Lyndon Johnson wide latitude in waging war in Southeast Asia. Direct Communist assaults against U.S. military personnel in the South led to the beginning of the air war against the North (ROLLING THUNDER) and the arrival of the first U.S. combat troops. The DRV also sent units of its regular army (the People's Army of Vietnam, or PAVN) south. An escalating military stalemate followed as the United States sought to achieve military victory.

Over Tết 1968 the Communists launched a massive offensive throughout South Vietnam that changed everything. The United States was caught off guard, not by the offensive (which was expected) but by its timing and scale. The magnitude of the offensive came as a shock to the American people, especially as their leaders had been telling them that the war was being won. The Communist offensive was defeated at great cost to their side, but this battlefield failure turned into a political triumph when the American public turned against the war. Meanwhile, the bombing of the North slowed the flow of supplies and men to the South but never halted them completely. It certainly did not sap morale or resolve in the North.

Beginning in 1968 Washington looked increasingly for a way out of the Vietnam quagmire. Vietnam was by this point a major, divisive issue, with growing antiwar demonstrations dominating the domestic scene. Acrimony at home led Johnson to abandon his 1968 reelection bid, suspend the bombing of North Vietnam, and enter into peace talks with the DRV. Richard Nixon, unable as was Johnson to come to grips with being "the first U.S. president to lose a war," actually widened the war in his bombing (Operation MENU) and ground invasions of Cambodia. These actions, designed to protect U.S. troop withdrawals and buy time for "Vietnamization" begun under Johnson, in fact helped to bring the Khmer Rouge to power in Cambodia.

Vietnamization was tested in the 1971 all-RVN invasion of Laos, Operation LAM SON 719. It was extremely costly in terms of the loss of junior officers and revealed serious RVN military weaknesses. In 1972 Há Noi launched its Spring or Easter Offensive, a conventional invasion of South Vietnam across the DMZ. Nixon responded with LINEBACKER (I), massive air strikes against the North. Finally the Paris peace talks bore fruit, but RVN President Nguyên Van Thiêu torpedoed the agreement. Nixon then resumed massive bombing of the North (LINEBACKER II), at the same time threatening Thiêu with loss of US support. At Paris, an agreement finally was signed in January 1973.

The peace barely survived the signing of the documents. Soon a "third" Vietnam War erupted. Meanwhile the U.S. Congress curtailed presidential war making authority and cut back U.S. aid to the RVN. The 1975 Communists spring offensive, the Ho Chi Minh Campaign, rapidly gained momentum and culminated in their military victory of April 1975.

In 1976 Vietnam was officially reunited in a Communist whole as the Socialist Republic of Vietnam (SRV). Relations between the United States and SRV remained acrimonious, with Washington imposing an economic embargo, the justification for which was the MIA issue. The reality was that many Americans found it difficult to accept the fact that they had lost a war in which so much blood and treasure had been expended.

Meanwhile, the SRV wrestled with difficult problems, including the task of knitting two very different regions together into one nation, a deteriorating economy, the flight of the "boat people," the SRV invasion of Cambodia, and a brief war in 1979 with China. Vietnam's situation improved in the 1990s after it withdrew from Cambodia, adopted a new economic model, and normal relations with the United States were restored.

Although the SRV still faces difficult times, we can assume that, if the past is any indication, the Vietnamese future will at the least be interesting.

—Spencer Tucker

A Shau Valley

Valley in northwestern South Vietnam running northwest to southeast in I Corps, southwest of Huê; location of some of the fiercest fighting of the Vietnam War. The long, narrow valley is bordered by Laos on the west and south. The eastern and western sides of the valley are mountainous and thickly forested, with a few isolated hamlets. Route 548, a loose-surface road, runs most of the valley's length. The northernmost of the two western fingers of the valley was the site of the May 1969 Battle of Âp Bia Mountain, better known as Hamburger Hill.

—Paul R. Camacho

References: U.S. Army military maps: Sheet 6441 II (1970).
See also: Geography of Indo-China and Vietnam; Hamburger Hill (Battle of Âp Bia Mountain); Vietnam, Climate of.

ABILENE, Operation (30 March–15 April 1966)

U.S. Army search-and-destroy operation 40 miles east of Sài Gòn. Operation ABILENE involved the 2d and 3d Brigades of the 1st Infantry ("Big Red One") Division, reinforced by the 1st Battalion of the Royal Australian Regiment and the 161st New Zealand Artillery Battery.

On 11 April, south of Cam My village, Company C, 2d Battalion, 16th Infantry ("Rangers") fought a pitched battle with the well-trained D800 main force Viêt Công (VC) battalion, which the infantry flushed during a search-and-destroy operation. The Americans killed five VC soldiers, then pursued the fleeing survivors toward Cam My in heavy jungle, not realizing that the VC platoon was falling back on its battalion base. The VC reacted near in late afternoon with heavy mortar and automatic weapons fire and mounted three successive human-wave assaults against defensive positions during the night. On the morning of 12 April, CH-47 Chinook helicopters brought medics and engineers to create a landing zone. Charlie Company was then evacuated by helicopter to the 2d Brigade's operational base at Bên Cát.

Company B reached the battle area before dawn and linked up at 0715. Other brigade units searched for the enemy without further major contacts. Charlie Company's battle was the significant action of Operation ABILENE, costing the Viêt Công 41 dead; perhaps an additional 100 dead or wounded were not found. The Americans suffered 36 killed and 71 wounded from a company team of 134 men that had taken the field the day before. During the balance of Operation ABILENE, U.S. forces killed another 40 VC soldiers in action, captured some supply caches, and destroyed more than 50 bases in aggressive search-and-destroy activities by the 2d and 3d Brigades of the 1st Division. Allied forces had penetrated a major Viêt Công sanctuary, but the jungle still belonged to the Communists. Following the battle, General Harold K. Johnson, Army Chief of Staff, told Maj. Gen. William E. DePuy that the American public would stop supporting the war if such high casualties continued.

—John F. Votaw

References: Haldane, Robert, ed. *First Infantry Division in Vietnam* (1993); Wilson, George C. *Mud Soldiers: Life Inside the New American Army* (1989).
See also: DePuy, William E.; Johnson, Harold K.; JUNCTION CITY, Operation; Military Assistance Command, Vietnam (MACV); Search and Destroy; United States: Army.

Abrams, Creighton (1914–1974)

Commander, U.S. Military Assistance Command, Vietnam (MACV), 1968–1972. When U.S. involvement in Vietnam intensified in mid-1964, Abrams was promoted to four-star general from far down the list of lieutenant generals and was made the Army's vice chief of staff. In that assignment (1964–1967) he was deeply involved in the Army's troop buildup, a task complicated by President Johnson's refusal to call up reserve forces. In May 1967 Abrams was assigned to Vietnam as deputy commander, where he devoted himself primarily to improving South Vietnamese armed forces. Abrams received much of the credit when Army of the Republic of Vietnam (ARVN) forces performed far better than was expected during the 1968 Têt Offensive.

Soon after the start of the Têt Offensive, Abrams was sent north to Phú Bài to take command of fighting in I Corps. Operating from a newly established headquarters designated MACV Forward, Abrams concentrated on retaking Huê, in the process forming a close relationship with ARVN General Ngô Quang Truong, commander of the 1st ARVN Division. Abrams coordinated the efforts of a growing assortment of U.S. Army and Marine elements and ARVN forces while working to improve the logistical system. After a month of hard fighting, Truong's forces cleared Huê and raised the Republic of Vietnam (RVN) flag over the Citadel.

Abrams formally assumed command of MACV on 3 July 1968, having been in de facto command since shortly after the Têt Offensive. As commander of MACV, Abrams changed the war's conduct in fundamental ways. His predecessor's attrition strategy, search-and-destroy tactics, and reliance on body count as the measure of merit were discarded. Stressing population security as the key to success, Abrams directed a "one-war" approach, pulling together combat operations, pacification, and upgrading of South Vietnamese forces into a coherent whole. Under him, combat operations had as their ultimate objective providing security for the population so that pacification, the most important thing, could progress.

Abrams was a consummate tactician with a feel for this kind of war. He urged his commanders to drastically reduce harassment and interdiction fires, unobserved artillery fire that he thought did little damage to the enemy and a good deal of harm to innocent villagers. He also reduced the multi-battalion sweeps that gave Communist forces the choice of terrain, time, and duration of engagement. He replaced these with multiple small-unit patrols and ambushes that blocked the enemy's access to the people, interdicting their movement of forces and supplies.

Abrams's analysis of the enemy "system" was key to this approach. He had observed that to function effectively, the enemy needed to extensively prepare the battlefield, pushing forward a logistics "nose" instead of being sustained by a logistics "tail," as in common military practice. Thus, many enemy attacks could be preempted if their supply caches could be discovered and captured or destroyed. Abrams also discerned that Communist main forces depended heavily on guerrillas and the Việt Công infrastructure in the hamlets and villages, not the other way around, and that digging out that infrastructure could deprive the main forces of the wherewithal they needed to function effectively.

By April 1970 Abrams's staff had developed a briefing, "The Changing Nature of the War." Change had been under way since Tết, said the study, but the significant aspect was what Abrams had done about acting on that realization: "For the first time in the war, the enemy's traditional bases of power are being directly challenged—his political organization and his control of the population." That, it appeared, was where the outcome of the war would be decided, because "both sides are finally fighting the same war."

Abrams's personality and character were at the heart of the U.S. effort in Vietnam. During his years in command, his army was withdrawn progressively until he was, in a symbolic sense, almost the last man left. A diplomat, observing the skill with which Abrams orchestrated the complex endeavor, once remarked that he "deserved a better war." Abrams viewed it differently, recalled his eldest son: "He thought the Vietnamese were worth it."

Abrams left Vietnam in June 1972 to become Army Chief of Staff and set about dealing with the myriad problems of an army that had been through a devastating ordeal. He concentrated on readiness and on the well-being of the soldier. Abrams had set a course of reform and rebuilding that General John W. Vessey later recalled: "When Americans watched the stunning success of our armed forces in Desert Storm, they were watching the Abrams vision in action. The modern equipment, the effective air support, the use of the reserve components and, most important of all, the advanced training which taught our people how to stay alive on the battlefield were all seeds planted by Abe."

—Lewis Sorley

References: Buckley, Kevin. "General Abrams Deserves a Better War" (1969); Colby, William, with James McCargar. *Lost Victory: A Firsthand Account of America's Sixteen-Year Involvement in Vietnam* (1989); Davidson, Phillip B. *Vietnam at War: The History, 1946–1975* (1988); Palmer, Bruce, Jr. *The 25-year War: America's Military Role in Vietnam* (1984); Sorley, Lewis. *Thunderbolt: General Creighton Abrams and the Army of His Times* (1992).
See also: Body Count; Clear and Hold; Huê, Battle of (1968 Tết Offensive); Johnson, Harold K.; Military Assistance Command, Vietnam (MACV); Ngô Quang Truong; Provincial Reconaissance Units (PRUs) (Đon Vi Thám Sát Tinh); Tết Offensive: Overall Strategy; Tết Offensive: the Sài Gòn Circle; United States: Involvement in Vietnam, 1969–1973; Vietnam, Republic of: Army (ARVN); Vietnamization.

Acheson, Dean G. (1893–1971)

U.S. secretary of state, 1949–1953. At a speech before the National Press Club on 12 January 1950, Acheson defined the U.S. "defense perimeter" in Asia as a line extending along the Aleutians to Japan, through the Ryukyu Islands, to the Philippines. Critics charged that Acheson's omission of South Korea from the defensive perimeter encouraged North Korea's invasion that June.

Although critical of French colonialism in Southeast Asia, Acheson presumed the Communist-led Vietnamese independence movement was dominated by China and the Soviet Union. He believed the collapse of Vietnam to communism would result in the fall of all of Southeast Asia. Thus, by the end of 1950, the United States supported the French effort in Vietnam with more than $130 million in aid, plus military equipment. In late 1952, Acheson tried unsuccessfully to convince Britain and France to join the United States in a program to develop and support an indigenous Vietnamese force to combat the Communist movement. After leaving office in 1953, Acheson continued in an advisory role and from 1965 to 1968 was one of the "Wise Men," President Johnson's group of senior advisors. In 1968 he joined other Wise Men in advising Johnson to deescalate the Vietnam War.

—Kenneth R. Stevens

References: Acheson, Dean. *Present at the Creation: My Years at the State Department* (1969); Brinkley, Douglas, ed. *Dean Acheson and the Making of U.S. Foreign Policy* (1993); McLellan, David S. *Dean Acheson: The State Department Years* (1976); Smith, Gaddis. *Dean Acheson* (1972).
See also: Ball, George W.; Bundy, McGeorge; Clifford, Clark M.; Containment Policy; Domino Theory; European Defense Community (EDC); Johnson, Lyndon Baines; McNamara, Robert S.; Rusk, Dean; Truman, Harry S.

ACTIV (Army Concept Team in Vietnam) (1962–1966)

Gen. Edward L. Rowny's team of 30 military and 25 civilian personnel, which was to evaluate "new or improved operational and organizational concepts, doctrine, tactics, techniques and procedures, and to gain further information on materiel." The major emphasis was on airmobility, but ACTIV also looked at armor, communications, logistics, civic action, scout dogs, and snipers. The Air Force opposed ACTIV's mission because airmobility would impinge on its troop transport and close air support missions.

ACTIV first experimented with armed UH-1 Huey helicopters, which were found to be essential in escorting H-21 Shawnee helicopters loaded with ARVN troops and in providing suppressive fire at landing zones (LZs). Survivable in combat, Hueys could also be used for reconnaissance and surveillance, were acceptable troop carriers, and were useful for night illumination. The Army's armed OV-1 Mohawks, allowed by the Air Force to fire only defensively, were found to have infrared, radar, and photography capabilities that could provide effective intelligence on the Việt Công. ACTIV also tested the CV-2 Caribou light transport plane, which was found to be adaptable in radio relay, command and control, air support operations, troop carrier, low-level extraction, and general supply functions. A short-takeoff-and-landing (STOL) aircraft, the Caribou could fly into 77 percent of all landing strips in Vietnam; the Air Force C-123 could use only 11 percent. In 1966 the Army gave up the armed Mohawks and Caribous to the Air Force in return for the Air Force dropping its opposition to the armed helicopter. ACTIV also tested CH-47 Chinook helicopters armed with various machine guns and grenade launchers. The 1st Cavalry troops liked its massive firepower, but the Army decided it needed the Chinook more for lift capability.

These experiments conducted by ACTIV improved counterinsurgency warfare in Vietnam and also contributed to the development of airmobility back in the United States.

—John L. Bell

References: Krepinevich, Andrew F., Jr. *The Army and Vietnam* (1986); Rowny, Edward L. *It Takes One to Tango* (1992); Tolson, John J. *Airmobility, 1961–1971* (1973).
See also: Airmobility; Airplanes, Allied and Democratic Republic of Vietnam; Helicopters, Allied and Democratic Republic of Vietnam; Helicopters, Employment of in Vietnam; Vance, Cyrus Roberts.

Adams, Samuel A. (1934–1988)

Central Intelligence Agency (CIA) analyst during the Vietnam War. Adams's duties included developing accurate estimates of Viêt Công (VC) troop strengths in South Vietnam. Adams believed that U.S. officials conspired to conceal the actual number of VC and North Vietnamese soldiers from Congress and the public to convey a favorable impression of the military situation in Vietnam, particularly from 1967 to 1968. He first publicly stated this belief in a May 1975 *Harper's Magazine* article, noting that senior-level CIA personnel consistently rejected information that contradicted their presentation of the situation. Adams, charging that this "groupthink" led to misleading intelligence reports, constructed his own estimates based on an analysis of captured documents and interviews with individuals in the field.

Adams discovered high desertion rates among the VC, which he took to be the result of poor morale. This, coupled with casualty rates and other factors, gave the impression of success of the Allied forces, but agents in the field revealed that this was not the case. Adams's findings indicated that U.S. estimates were much lower than those documented in captured Communist reports and directives. Adams brought these discrepancies to the attention of his superiors, who rejected his conclusions. Only after the 1968 Tết Offensive did various intelligence agencies reopen discussions of VC troop strength estimates. The problem was that acceptance of higher estimates implied greater U.S. participation.

Adams found himself increasingly isolated within the CIA, especially after he and a colleague charged that there were approximately 20,000 Communist agents within the South Vietnamese military and government. As a result, Adams was transferred to a Cambodian research post, where he found the same techniques of troop strength estimation. Adams argued stubbornly for an upgrading of Communist troop strength estimates and charged that General Westmoreland might have been involved in a conspiracy to conceal true Communist troop strengths.

Adams testified at the trial of Daniel Ellsberg in connection with the numbers controversy. He left the CIA in 1973. In 1975, following publication of his *Harper's* article, Adams was denounced by former deputy director of the CIA Adm. Rufus Taylor and others. Adams's work formed the basis for the 1982 CBS documentary, "The Uncounted Enemy: A Vietnam Deception," which accused Westmoreland of ordering intelligence officers to manipulate enemy troop strengths to give the appearance of battlefield success. Westmoreland sued CBS, and the case was later settled out of court. Adams's book concerning the affair was published posthumously in 1994.

—Paul R. Camacho

References: Adams, Sam. "Vietnam Cover-Up: Playing War With Numbers (1975); —. *War of Numbers: An Intelligence Memoir* (1994); Janis, Irving L. *Groupthink* (1982).
See also: Central Intelligence Agency (CIA); Ellsberg, Daniel; Order of Battle Dispute; Westmoreland, William Childs.

African American Personnel in U.S. Forces in Vietnam

In 1948 President Truman ordered the military establishment to desegregate. The Navy and Air Force accomplished integration by 1950. The Army, with the vast majority of African American servicemen, did not achieve desegregation until after the Korean conflict. Vietnam, then, marked the first major combat deployment of an integrated military and the first time since the turn of the century that African American participation was actually encouraged.

In 1962 President Kennedy reactivated the President's Committee on Equal Opportunity in the Armed Forces, chaired by attorney Gerhard Gesell, to explore ways to draw qualified African Americans into military service. In 1964 African Americans represented approximately 13 percent of the U.S. population, but less than 9 percent of the nation's men in arms. The committee found uneven promotion, token integration, restricted opportunities in the National Guard and Reserves, and discrimination on military bases and in their surrounding communities. Before the government could react to the report, U.S. involvement in Southeast Asia changed the situation. An expanded military, a discriminatory draft, and other government programs brought not only increased African American participation, but accusations of new forms of discrimination.

The alleged misuse of African American troops brought charges of racism. Dr. Martin Luther King, Jr., maintained that black youths represented a disproportionate share of early draftees and that African Americans faced a much greater chance of seeing combat. Most draftees were poor, under-educated, and urban. African Americans were woefully under-represented on local draft boards; in 1966, seven state boards had no black representation.

"Project 100,000," launched in 1966 to offer underprivileged youths more lenient military entrance requirements, largely failed. Casualty rates among Project 100,000 inductees were twice those of other entry categories, and few received training that would aid their military advancement or create opportunities for civilian life.

Although African American troops made up less than 10 percent of U.S. men in arms between 1961 and 1966, they accounted for almost 20 percent of combat-related deaths in Vietnam during that period. Army and Marine commanders worked to lessen black casualties after 1966; by the end of the conflict, African American combat deaths amounted to approximately 12 percent. African Americans did bear a heavy share of the fighting burden early in the conflict, but final casualty estimates do not support the assertion that they suffered disproportionate losses.

Violent reaction to the 1968 King assassination brought racial turmoil to the armed forces. Racial strife, rarely an issue among combat units because of shared risk and responsibility, became most evident in rear areas and on domestic installations. The Marine base at Camp Lejeune and the Army's Fort Benning were among the important domestic posts to witness racial problems.

African Americans played a major role in Vietnam and, in the process, changed the complexion of the U.S. Armed Forces. Many African American servicemen were highly motivated professionals; 20 received the Medal of Honor, and several became general officers. Despite the likelihood of seeing hazardous duty, they reenlisted at substantially higher rates than whites. Although the percentage of African American officers doubled between 1964 and 1976, they still accounted for less than 4 percent of the total.

—David Coffey

References: Binkin, Martin, Mark J. Eitelberg, et al. *Blacks in the Military*; Dougan, Clark, Samuel Lipsman, et al. *A Nation Divided. The Vietnam Experience*, edited by Robert Manning; Goff, Stanley, and Robert Sanders, with Clark Smith. *Brothers: Black Soldiers in the Nam*; Nalty, Bernard C. *Strength for the Fight: A History of Black Americans in the Military*.

See also: Antiwar Movement, United States; Casualties; Desertion, Allied and Communist; Draft; James, Daniel "Chappie," Jr.; Kennedy, John Fitzgerald; King, Martin Luther, Jr.; Powell, Colin L.; Project 100,000; Truman, Harry S; United States: Air Force; United States: Army; United States: Marine Corps; United States: Navy.

Agency for International Development (AID). *See* U.S. Agency for International Development (USAID).

Agnew, Spiro T. (1918–1996)

Vice-president of the United States, 1969–1974. Agnew faithfully served as a battering ram for Richard Nixon and the Republican Party despite exclusion from the president's inner circle. In speeches crafted by Patrick J. Buchanan and William Safire, Agnew polarized the nation. He frequently attacked the media, which he accused of lacking neutrality and blamed for undermining the U.S. effort in Vietnam. He also attacked the student protest movement, stating that educational pursuits on college campuses had been replaced by drug use. He referred to the intellectual community as "impudent snobs" and blamed them for campus unrest.

As vice-president, Agnew consistently favored any option that might win an outright victory in Vietnam. While on a second inspection tour of Asia in February 1973, Agnew met in Sài Gòn with President Nguyên Van Thiêu to assure him that the United States would not abandon the Republic of Vietnam.

Agnew resigned the vice-presidency on 10 October 1973 following allegations of bribery and income tax evasion while governor of Maryland. In a negotiated settlement with the Justice Department, he pleaded no contest. The deal plunged Agnew into political obscurity and denied him the opportunity to become president following Nixon's resignation.

—Dallas Cothrum

References: Agnew, Spiro T. *Go Quietly ... or Else* (1980); Cohen, Richard M., and Jules Witcover. *A Heartbeat Away: The Investigation and Resignation of Vice President Spiro T. Agnew* (1974); Lucas, Jim Griffing. *Agnew: Profile in Conflict* (1970).

See also: Amnesty; Antiwar Movement, United States; Ford, Gerald R.; Hardhats; Media and the War; Nixon, Richard Milhous.

Agricultural Reform Tribunals (1953–1956)

Democratic Republic of Vietnam (DRV) land reform campaign. The December 1953 Land Reform Law called for confiscation of the land and property of most of the landlord class, which Hô Chí Minh described as "a class struggle in the countryside." The program was preceded by a rent reduction program. During this phase, cadre were trained, and selected poor peasants were introduced to thought reform: Landlords were their enemy, the Party their guide. Those successfully indoctrinated, called *côt cán*, were expected to be the backbone of land reform.

The population was divided into five categories: landlords, rich peasants, middle peasants, poor peasants, and farm workers. Cadre and *côt cán* teams surveyed village land holdings and dragged those classified as "landlords" before "peasant struggle" meetings, where they were denounced and sentenced. In 1955 these trials gave way to more formal agricultural reform tribunals or people's courts of six to ten members, drawn mostly from the *côt cán*, which continued to denounce even greater numbers of "landlords," about 25 percent of whom were labeled "despots." The tribunals zealously fulfilled the quotas they had been given. Many peasants trumped up charges against their neighbors. Anyone who worked for the French or had merely showed insufficient ardor for the Viêt Minh might be a victim. Tens of thousands were executed, sent to forced labor camps, or starved to death.

Mass psychology was exploited in the Rectification of Errors campaign, during which 12,000 victims were released from labor or reeducation camps. Employing the Marxist cathartic of criticism and self-criticism, after the reform ended in August 1956, Hô apologized to the people, admitting that errors had been committed and that those wrongly classified as landlords or rich peasants would be reclassified. The government allowed the relatives of many victims to take revenge on Land Reform Group members and *côt cán*. Many who had recently carried out government orders now became secondary victims of the campaign. But this was not enough to prevent several peasant revolts, the most serious of which occurred in Nghê An and was crushed by the crack 325th Division.

Those who had served on the tribunals or supported the process were now committed to the Party's leadership by their complicity, and many took positions in the Party. The rest of the population was shocked into submission, thus ensuring that collectivization would not meet with the popular resistance encountered in the Soviet Union. In June 1958 the Party acknowledged that the ultimate objective of land reform had not been confiscating land of landlords, but "motivating the masses" to suppress the landlord class.

—Claude R. Sasso

References: Bain, Chester A. *Vietnam: The Roots of the Conflict* (1967); Gheddo, Piero. *The Cross and the Bo Tree: Catholics and Buddhists in Vietnam* (1970); Hoang Van Chi. *From Colonialism to Communism: A Case History of North Vietnam* (1970); Moise, Edwin, E. *Land Reform in China and North Vietnam: Consolidating the Revolution at the Village Level* (1983).
See also: Hô Chí Minh; Land Reform; Lao Đông Party; Vietnam, Democratic Republic of: 1954–1975; Võ Nguyên Giáp.

Agroville Campaign (1959)

Plan for strategically located, fortified settlements into which entire rural villages could be relocated. The Agroville campaign was launched by Republic of Vietnam President Ngô Đình Diêm in mid-1959 in response to mounting Viêt Công (VC) attacks throughout the south. Agrovilles theoretically offered security to peasants while denying VC access to recruits, information, and logistical support. Administered by Diêm's brother Nhu, the campaign called for construction of more than eighty Agrovilles, each offering water, electricity, health care, and security to several thousand peasants.

Doomed from its inception, the plan required peasants to abandon their ancestral homelands and frequently demanded substantial sacrifice with few governmental incentives. The Agrovilles more resembled concentration camps than protected havens. The peasants largely resisted relocation, and many came to view the Diêm government as a greater menace than the Viêt Công. Plagued from the beginning by governmental corruption, the program was abandoned by 1961. Less than twenty of the proposed communities were constructed, and most were in ruin within months of completion.

The Ngô brothers retained their belief in the Agroville concept, but more as a means of extending their influence than of winning the hearts and minds of the peasants. British counterinsurgency expert Sir Robert Thompson advanced the idea of "strategic hamlets," but Diêm remained noncommittal until a similar proposal by Eugene Staley, the Strategic Hamlet program, brought a favorable response from the Kennedy administration.

—David Coffey

References: Asprey, Robert B. *War in the Shadows: The Guerrilla in History* (1994); Karnow, Stanley. *Vietnam: A History* (1983).
See also: Staley, Eugene; Strategic Hamlet Program; Thompson, Sir Robert.

Aiken, George D. (1892–1984)

U.S. senator, 1941–1975. Despite expressed misgivings, Aiken voted for the Tonkin Gulf Resolution on 7 August 1964. By April 1965, however, he had become a critic of the Vietnam War. Following a fact-finding mission to the Republic of Vietnam (RVN) in November 1964, Aiken concluded that the United States should seek a political rather than a military settlement of the war. However, he continued to vote for war appropriations because he believed troops in Vietnam should be supported. In May 1967 Aiken argued that the Johnson administration could not achieve an "honorable peace" in Southeast Asia and called for the Republican party to develop an alternative policy. In May 1969 he called for U.S. withdrawal, and the next year he voted for the Cooper-Church Amendment barring the president from sending funds to support U.S. troops in Cambodia.

—Kenneth R. Stevens

References: Lichtenstein, Nelson, ed. *Political Profiles: The Johnson Years* (1976); Sherman, Michael. *The Political Legacy of George D. Aiken: Wise Old Owl of the U.S. Senate* (1995).
See also: Cooper-Church Amendment; Morse, Wayne Lyman; Tonkin Gulf Resolution.

Air America

In August 1950 the Central Intelligence Agency (CIA) secretly purchased the assets of Civil Air Transport, an airline started in China after World War II by General Claire L. Chennault and Whiting Willauer. Civil Air Transport continued to fly commercial routes but at the same time, under the guise of CAT Incorporated, it provided airplanes and crews for secret U.S. intelligence operations from Tibet to Indonesia. On 26 March 1959, the name was changed to Air America.

Air America took an increasingly prominent role in Southeast Asia as the United States became more deeply involved in the growing conflict in the region. Although the airline developed extensive operations in South Vietnam, it played a more important role in Laos as a key element in U.S. assistance to the Royal Lao government.

Air America's growth in Laos began early in 1961 following a CIA recommendation to arm and train Hmong tribesmen as a counterweight to Communist forces. With the Hmong scattered on mountainous terrain around the strategic Plaine des Jarres, CIA paramilitary specialist James W. Lair recognized that effective communications would be essential for successful operations. Air America, he believed, would have to develop both rotary-wing and short-takeoff-and-landing (STOL) capability to assist Laotian guerrilla forces. Air America's helicopter fleet was expanded in March 1961 when President Kennedy ordered the Marine Corps to transfer 14 UH-34s to the CIA's airline. At the same time, Air America acquired a small fleet of single-engine Helio Courier aircraft that were able to use short, primitive airstrips in the mountainous areas of Laos.

Air America quickly became involved in the war in Laos, supplying arms and ammunition to CIA-trained Hmong tribesmen and airdropping rice to displaced refugees. Its operations declined sharply following the Declaration of the

Neutrality of Laos on 23 July 1962. The truce in Laos, however, proved temporary. Full-scale fighting resumed in March 1964 as Communist forces attacked government positions on the Plaine des Jarres. Washington, declining to commit U.S. combat forces, instead expanded the CIA's role in Laos in an effort to avoid a major confrontation with North Vietnam in an area of clearly secondary importance. Although Hà Nôi had the capability of overrunning most of Laos in short order, the North Vietnamese were mainly interested in protecting their supply routes to South Vietnam and did not wish to destroy the general framework of the 1962 Geneva settlement. Within this general context of restraint, a guerrilla war took place in Laos over the next four years. Air America embarked upon an expansion program as it assumed a paramilitary role in support of CIA-led forces. Besides providing air transport for the Hmong, it also took responsibility for search-and-rescue operations as the U.S. Air Force began to fly combat sorties in the country.

Air America's role continued to grow as North Vietnam introduced major new combat forces into Laos in 1968–1969, and its operations became increasing hazardous as the enemy launched major offenses in the early 1970s. CIA-led forces delayed a final Communist victory but could not prevent it. A February 1974 cease-fire agreement led to the formation of a coalition government for Laos, and on 3 June the last Air America aircraft crossed from Laos into Thailand. Enemy action and operational accidents had cost the lives of 97 crew members.

Air America continued to fly in South Vietnam. On 21 April 1972 CIA director Richard Helms, after lengthy debate within the CIA over the continued need for a covert airlift capability, ordered the agency to divest itself of ownership and control of Air America and related companies. Air America took a major part in the final evacuation of April 1975, then on 30 June 1976 closed its doors and returned $20 million to the U.S. Treasury.

—William M. Leary

References: Air America Archives, University of Texas at Dallas; Robbins, Christopher. *Air America* (1979).
See also: Bird & Sons (Birdair); Central Intelligence Agency (CIA); Continental Air Services; Geneva Accords; Helms, Richard McGarrah; Kennedy, John Fitzgerald; Laos; Plain of Jars.

Air Defense, Democratic Republic of Vietnam

Air defenses of the Democratic Republic of Vietnam (DRV) expanded rapidly during the conflict in Southeast Asia and became one of the most formidable integrated air defense systems (IADS) yet seen in modern warfare. When U.S. air strikes began against North Vietnam in 1964, DRV air defenses resembled those of North Korea in 1950. By the end of 1968, however, DRV air defenses included 8,050 antiaircraft artillery (AAA) pieces, 152 fighter aircraft (106 safely based in China), 40 "active" SA-2 missile battalions, and more than 400 radars of all types.

The DRV's IADS consisted of detection, communication, and response elements. Detection elements provided warning of an imminent air attack by active or passive means, including early warning radars, radar detection devices, and observers with binoculars. Communication elements tied this system together by telephone or radio. DRV air defenses operated under strict Soviet-style centralized control and were highly dependent on fast, efficient communications. Three basic types of response elements available: AAA, airborne interceptors, and surface-to-air missiles (SAMs).

AAA, responsible for 80 percent of U.S. aircraft losses over Southeast Asia, fired unguided shells based on the gunner's judgment or on radar-based predictions. Smaller-caliber weapons (7.62 mm, 20 mm, 37 mm) had higher rates of fire and threw a high volume of projectiles into the air. Medium-caliber (57 mm) and heavy-caliber (85 mm, 100 mm) weapons had relatively slower rates of fire and often relied on fire control radars for target data. AAA fire was exceptionally deadly at lower altitudes, simply because of the amount of bullets flying in the air.

The DRV had no interceptor force at the time of the 1964 Gulf of Tonkin incident. Two days later, however, the Chinese sent MiG-15 and MiG-17 aircraft to an airfield near Hà Nôi. By 1966 the newer, more capable Soviet MiG-21 entered the DRV inventory. These operated sporadically throughout the conflict, working in concert with the other elements of the air defense system. On some days the MiGs assumed primary responsibility for the air defense; on others the SAMs assumed the role. Interceptor pilots might entice American pilots to pursue them into an area well defended by SA-2s, or SA-2s might be fired to force U.S. air formations into a MiG ambush. DRV pilots practiced the Soviet doctrine of strict positive control. Soviet radar operators—and North Vietnamese operators under close Soviet supervision—directed every action of fighter pilots other than takeoffs and landings. Radar operators would typically vector MiGs to the rear of U.S. formations, where they would strike either early in a mission (forcing U.S. F-105s to jettison their bombs) or after the bomb run, when escorting F-4s would be low on fuel. These guerrilla-style tactics were often effective, especially throughout Operation ROLLING THUNDER, when DRV airfields were declared off-limits to U.S. airstrikes.

SAMs, primarily the radar-guided SA-2 and the infrared-guided SA-7, constituted the third response element of the IADS. SA-2s were most effective at higher altitudes. Of more than 9,000 SA-2s fired from 1965 to 1972, fewer than 2 percent brought down aircraft. However, SAMs were a constant threat to aircraft formations and, in the early stages of ROLLING THUNDER, SA-2s denied U.S. aircraft the opportunity to operate at medium and high altitudes until the advent of Wild Weasels, AGM-45 Shrikes, and ALQ-71 jamming pods.

—Patrick K. Barker

References: Lavelle, A. J. C., ed. *The Tale of Two Bridges and the Battle for the Skies over North Vietnam* (1976); Momyer, William W. *Airpower in Three Wars* (1978); Morrocco, John. *Thunder from Above: Air War, 1941–1968* (1984); Nordeen, Lon O., Jr. *Air Warfare in the Missile Age* (1985).
See also: Aircraft Carriers; Airplanes, Allied and Democratic Republic of Vietnam; ROLLING THUNDER, Operation; Surface-to-Air Missiles (SAMs).

Air Force. See by country.

Air Power, Role in War
More than half of the $200 billion the United States expended to wage war in Vietnam went to support air operations, including Air Force, Navy, Army, Marines, Allied aviation, and civilian contract airlines. Although occasionally pivotal, especially in supporting ground operations, air power was never decisive. The role of air power in the war remains subject to controversy and myth. Air power enthusiasts perpetuate the myth that if U.S. air forces had been unleashed, quick and decisive victory would have followed, pointing to the "Christmas Bombing" of LINEBACKER II in December 1972. At the other extreme, some in the antiwar movement claimed that North Vietnam's cities were carpet bombed and that napalm was used indiscriminately throughout the war. Many such claims are the result of ignorance or shoddy scholarship.

From 1962 through 1973 the United States dropped nearly 8 million tons of bombs on Vietnam, Laos, and Cambodia. South Vietnam received about half that tonnage, making it the most bombed country in the history of aerial warfare. U.S. Air Force, Navy, Marines, and Army lost a total of 8,588 fixed and rotary-wing aircraft during that period.

Although missions against North Vietnam inspired the most controversy, the focus of air operations was South Vietnam. Nearly 75 percent of all sorties (one aircraft on one mission) were flown in support of U.S. and Army of the Republic of Vietnam (ARVN) ground forces, but air power played a larger role than dropping bombs. Helicopters provided unprecedented mobility to U.S. and Allied forces by hauling troops and artillery to and from battle. Medical evacuation helicopters carried wounded—many of whom otherwise would not otherwise have survived—to modern rear-area medical facilities. Air Force transports kept far-flung outposts such as Khâm Đuc and Khe Sanh supplied even when surrounded by Communist forces and cut off from land lines of communications. Twin-engine, propeller-driven, side-firing gunships, such as the AC-47 (and later the AC-119) went aloft at night to keep the enemy from overrunning isolated Special Forces outposts. B-52 ARC LIGHT missions pounded supply caches and sometimes obliterated entire Communist regiments when they massed for attack. They were particularly effective during the siege of Khe Sanh in 1968 and at An Lôc in 1972.

Air power's primary role in Vietnam was support of ground operations, running counter to U.S. Air Force doctrine which held that air power could be better used in a strategic air campaign against North Vietnam. It can be argued that air power played a strategically counterproductive role in South Vietnam, since images of napalm bursting over villages and forests denuded by Agent Orange fed the claims of the antiwar movement. On a more rational level, it can be argued that the Air Force's ability to provide support for troops actually prolonged the war by making it possible for the Army and Marines to stay engaged in a conflict they really did not know how to win.

Air power used outside South Vietnam in "out-country" operations accounted for nearly another 4 million tons of bombs. Out-country operations included three major air campaigns over North Vietnam, a series of interdiction campaigns along the Hô Chí Minh Trail in Laos, and various air operations over Cambodia. Of all out-country campaigns, only Operation LINEBACKER I, the air response to North Vietnam's Spring Offensive of 1972, was an unmitigated success. The rest either failed or are subject to conflicting interpretations.

Nevertheless, air power did some remarkable things. Noteworthy technical and tactical innovations introduced during the Vietnam War included aerial defoliation; the development and employment of propeller-driven, side-firing gunships; and the use of forward air controllers to coordinate air strikes in South Vietnam and northern Laos. Among the U.S. Air Force's greatest success stories was the development of a superb long-range combat aircrew search-and-rescue (SAR) capability.

The United States was the first major power to lose a war in which it controlled the air. What Vietnam indicated for air power is that winning or losing in warfare is much more than a function of sortie generation and firepower on targets. It incorporates many factors, including politics, national resolve, geography, time, and weather. U.S. air power leaders in Vietnam may have been masters of air power, but they were not masters of the art of war.

—Earl H. Tilford, Jr.

References: Berger, Carl, ed. *The United States Air Force in Southeast Asia, 1961–1973: An Illustrated Account* (1984); Clodfelter, Mark. *The Limits of Air Power: The American Bombing of North Vietnam* (1989); Momyer, William W. *Airpower in Three Wars: World War II, Korea and Vietnam* (1978); Morrocco, John. *Thunder from Above: Air War, 1941–1968* (1984); —. *Rain of Fire: Air War, 1969–1973* (1986).

See also: Airplanes, Allied and Democratic Republic of Vietnam; COMMANDO HUNT, Operation; Helicopters, Allied and Democratic Republic of Vietnam; Helicopters, Employment of, in Vietnam; LINEBACKER I, Operation; LINEBACKER II, Operation; LORAN; MENU, Operation; Raven Forward Air Controllers (FACs); ROLLING THUNDER, Operation; Search-and-Rescue (SAR) Operations; Yankee Station.

Airborne Operations
Operations involving troops parachuting into battle. During the Indo-China War, elite French paratroopers jumped to relieve isolated posts, carry out raids, gather intelligence, and support infantry units during ground operations. During Operation CASTOR, begun on 20 November 1953 at the village of Điên Biên Phu, France conducted its largest airborne operation of the war. By 22 November 1953 the French had deployed six airborne battalions to Điên Biên Phu. During the 1954 Siege of Điên Biên Phu, parachute reinforcements insisted on dropping into a battle that was already lost so that they might be with their comrades.

Airborne operations were not a major factor during the Vietnam War because of the difficult terrain and the development of air mobile-air assault tactics. However, the first major U.S. Army ground combat unit sent to Vietnam was the 173rd Airborne Brigade (Separate) ("Sky Soldiers"), the U.S. Pacific Command's quick-reaction strike force. Arriving in Vietnam on 7 May 1965, initially on temporary assignment, the 173rd was to provide security for the Biên Hòa air base complex until elements of the 101st Airborne Division could be deployed from the United States. It remained in Vietnam for six years.

The 2nd Battalion, 503rd Regiment of the 173rd conducted the only major U.S. airborne operation of the war while attached to the 1st Infantry Division, during Operation JUNCTION CITY (February 1967). On the morning of 22 February, lifted by 16 C-130 transports, the 2nd Battalion carried out the first major U.S. airborne assault since the Korean War. The 101st Airborne Division also served in Vietnam but did not conduct airborne operations there.

The U.S. Marines had parachute-qualified reconnaissance battalions in Vietnam, and in June 1966 a Marine reconnaissance company conducted a combat jump near Chu Lai. Other military formations possessing an airborne capability and conducting limited airborne operations were the U.S. Military Assistance Command, Vietnam Studies and Observation Group (MACV-SOG), the Vietnamese Strategic Technical Directorate, and the Australian Special Air Service (SAS). All members of U.S. Army Special Forces in Vietnam were airborne qualified. Other U.S. units, including the Navy Seals and Army Rangers, were airborne qualified but generally used riverine craft and air assault (helicopters) during the war.

Airborne units also developed within the Army of the Republic of Vietnam (ARVN), beginning in 1955 with the Airborne (or Parachutist) Group. In 1960 it was reorganized as the Airborne Brigade and on 1 December 1965 officially became the Airborne Division, with three brigades. A fourth brigade was added in early 1975. Between 1962 and 1966 ARVN airborne units conducted various parachute assaults. In 1966, with the infusion of U.S. helicopters, these elements adopted air mobile-air assault tactics. In 1968 the battalions were assembled into an airborne division headquartered in Sài Gòn to serve as a helicopter-borne reaction force. ARVN airborne units made a combat parachute jump on 4 May 1972, during an operation near Pleiku.

During 1966 to 1968, U.S. Army Special Forces units trained six airborne-qualified battalions of Montagnards, as well as other ethnic groups. Led by American Special Forces advisors, these battalions conducted four airborne operations during 1967 and 1968 and established Special Forces camps in Communist-held territory.

Neither the Viêt Công nor the People's Army of Vietnam developed airborne capabilities during the Vietnam War.

—James McNabb

References: Arkin, William M., et al., eds. *Encyclopedia of the U.S. Military* (1990); Davidson, Phillip B. *Vietnam at War: The History, 1946–1975* (1988); Galvin, John R. *Air Assault: The Development of Airmobile Warfare* (1969); Hoyt, Edwin F. *Airborne: The History of American Parachute Forces* (1979); Simpson, Howard R. *Dien Bien Phu: The Epic Battle America Forgot* (1994).

See also: Airmobility; CASTOR, Operation; Điên Biên Phu, Battle of; JUNCTION CITY, Operation; Military Assistance Command, Vietnam (MACV); Montagnards; Studies and Observation Group (SOG).

Aircraft Carriers

French and U.S. aircraft carriers played a prominent role in the struggle in Southeast Asia. On 2 April 1947, the *Dixmude*, an ex-American escort carrier, sent its SBD Dauntless dive bombers into action supporting French forces in central Vietnam. Ferrying additional French planes to the war, the *Dixmude* returned to launch strikes near Hà Nôi in October, the *Dixmude* set a pattern of aircraft transport and strike operations that French carriers would follow until 1954. In November 1948 the light carrier *Arromanches* joined the fray.

The operations of U.S. aircraft carriers overlapped with those of France and closely paralleled U.S. involvement in Southeast Asia. U.S. carriers first appeared in the theater in March 1950, when aircraft from the *Boxer* overflew Sài Gòn in a show of support for the French. Soon thereafter, the U.S. Navy transferred to France two light aircraft carriers, renamed the *LaFayette* and the *Bois Belleau*. During the Điên Biên Phu crisis, the Eisenhower administration deployed several carriers to the South China Sea, as did President Kennedy in 1961 during the Laotian crisis.

Full-fledged carrier operations began in 1964 with reconnaissance flights over the Plain of Jars from Seventh Fleet warships deployed on "Yankee Station" in the Gulf of Tonkin. On 6 June an RF-8A from the *Kitty Hawk* became the first U.S. carrier plane lost to enemy fire. Two months later, carrier planes initiated combat strikes during the Tonkin Gulf episode, followed by the PIERCE ARROW, BARREL ROLL, and FLAMING DART retaliatory raids. In March 1965 the carriers *Hancock* and *Ranger* joined the Air Force in opening the episodic Operation ROLLING THUNDER. By the end of that year U.S. carriers had launched 31,000 sorties; their planes would strike targets in North Vietnam until 1973. The ships also operated on "Dixie Station" to the south, their aircraft flying one-third of the missions directed at Communist forces in South Vietnam over a 16–month period beginning in April 1965.

From 1964 to 1975 carriers averaged three on station at a time, but they reached peaks of seven in June 1972 and January 1973. Except for the *John F. Kennedy*, all of the Navy's large attack carriers (*America, Constellation, Enterprise, Forrestal, Independence, Kitty Hawk, Ranger,* and *Saratoga*) made at least one tour, as did the three carriers of the Midway class (*Coral Sea, Franklin D. Roosevelt,* and *Midway*). Six ships of the smaller Essex class also participated: four attack carriers (*Bon Homme Richard, Hancock, Oriskany,* and *Ticonderoga*) and two antisubmarine carriers with air groups configured for attack purposes (*Intrepid* and *Shangri-La*). Individual tours lasted about nine months, and most carriers returned repeatedly to the war.

U.S. carriers off Vietnam remained in action day after day for months at a time. During summer 1972, carriers launched an average of 4,000 sorties monthly and accounted for 60 percent of all missions supporting ground operations in South Vietnam. Techniques such as vertical replenishment and at-sea transfer of munitions and stores made possible such lengthy time on station.

Air groups on the largest carriers numbered about 90 planes each and on the three Midway-class ships, about 75. The smaller Essex-class carriers were quite crowded with their complements of 70. The carriers operated several aircraft types. For attack, the propeller-driven A-1 Skyraider and jet-powered A-3 Skywarrior and A-4 Skyhawk were gradually supplanted by the A-7 Corsair II and the A-6 Intruder. Fighter coverage was provided by the F-8 Crusader and increasingly by the F-4 Phantom II, which also conducted attack missions. Reconnaissance tasks fell to the RA-5 Vigilante, the RA-3B, and specially configured fighters. The E-1 Tracer and E-2 Hawkeye provided air control and early warning capabilities. A few EA-6 Prowler electronics countermeasures aircraft saw service beginning in 1972. Helicopters such as the SH-3 Sea King and the UH-2 Seasprite were employed primarily for antisubmarine patrols and search-and-rescue missions. Unlike their Air Force counterparts, most Navy planes retained their light colors (for ease of deck spotting at night) and vivid squadron insignia.

Despite restrictions imposed by Washington, carrier strike aircraft successfully hit important North Vietnamese targets, such as the Uông Bí thermal power plant in December 1965 and oil tank farms in 1966. Efforts to interfere with North Vietnamese lines of communication proved less productive.

Although Communist forces never confronted carriers directly, North Vietnamese fighters often challenged Navy planes that flew from them. Following an unacceptably high loss rate early in the war, in 1969 the Navy instituted its Top Gun program and then enjoyed a 12–to-1 kill ratio. Enemy antiaircraft fire downed 345 planes, 91 aircraft fell victim to surface-to-air missiles, and 79 were lost to "other causes." Operational losses totaled 329 aircraft, and accidental fires claimed 39 additional planes aboard the *Oriskany, Forrestal*, and *Enterprise*.

The Nixon administration kept a large carrier presence in the theater, but the number of attack sorties dropped. By the end of 1972, most missions were reconnaissance flights. Carriers remained on station following the 23 January 1973 cease-fire, and four of the ships participated in Operation FREQUENT WIND, the final evacuation of Sài Gòn. On 15 May 1975, planes from the *Coral Sea* helped cover the *Mayaguez* rescue operations.

U.S. Navy aircraft carriers provided one of the strong arms of the U.S. war effort. Essentially invulnerable to enemy countermeasures, the carriers gave policy makers flexibility, mobility, and power. In return, the war validated the large carrier.

—Malcolm Muir, Jr.

References: Francillon, René J. *Tonkin Gulf Yacht Club: U.S. Carrier Operations off Vietnam* (1988); Friedman, Norman. *U.S. Aircraft Carriers: An Illustrated Design History* (1983); Marolda, Edward J., and Oscar P. Fitzgerald. *The United States Navy and the Vietnam Conflict.* Vol. 2: *From Military Assistance to Combat, 1959–1965* (1986); Nichols, John B., and Barrett Tillman. *On Yankee Station: The Naval Air War over Vietnam* (1987); Rausa, Rosario. *Gold Wings, Blue Sea: A Naval Aviator's Story* (1980).

See also: BARREL ROLL, Operation; FLAMING DART, Operation; FREQUENT WIND, Operation; *Mayaguez* Incident; PIERCE ARROW, Operation; Plain of Jars; ROLLING THUNDER, Operation; United States: Navy; Yankee Station.

Airmobility

Tactical doctrine developed by the U.S. Army in the 1960s entailing the use of helicopters to find the enemy, carry troops to battle, provide them with gunship support, position artillery, and provide communications and resupply. In Vietnam the U.S. Army's 1st Cavalry and 101st Airborne Divisions were designated airmobile divisions, but most other Allied combat units used airmobility to some degree.

The Kennedy administration was receptive to airmobility because it promised increased combat power through greater mobility. Despite opposition from the Army staff, Secretary of Defense Robert S. McNamara ordered the Army to experiment with airmobility. The result was the 1962 Howze Board, which recommended the organization of airmobile units. The need for such a division in Vietnam led to the redesignation of the 11th Air Assault Division (Test) as the 1st Cavalry Division (Airmobile) and its deployment there in 1965.

Before the 1st Cavalry arrived in Vietnam, the Army had been experimenting there with airmobile concepts. In 1962 Army H-21 and Marine H-34 helicopters began lifting Army of the Republic of Vietnam (ARVN) troops into battle. Using ground troops or air reconnaissance to locate Việt Công (VC) units, Army and Marine advisors developed quick-reaction "Eagle Flights" of ARVN troops to be flown into pursuit or blocking positions. Starting in 1962 the Army used the Army Concept Team in Vietnam (ACTIV) to test airmobile concepts. The team tested many workable ideas, including armed helicopters, UH-1 helicopters as troop ships, reconnaissance helicopters, and better communications and navigation.

In Vietnam the 1st Cavalry Division consisted of eight maneuver battalions controlled by three brigades. Other units included four artillery battalions, an air cavalry squadron, an engineer and signal battalion, and an aviation group. Artillery was organized into three 105-mm howitzer battalions and an aerial artillery battalion. The aviation group included two UH-1 Huey battalions and a CH-47 Chinook battalion, enough lift for a third of the division's troops at one time.

After organizing at An Khê, the 1st Cavalry entered battle near the Ia Drang. The tactics used were typical of later operations. Teams of H-13 scouts and UH-1 gunships from the 9th Cavalry Squadron sought and found People's Army of Vietnam (PAVN) forces near the Ia Drang. Then CH-47s lifted artillery to landing zones (LZs) Columbus and Falcon to cover infantry landing sights near the Chu Pong Massif. After suppressive fire at the LZ, UH-1s lifted infantry to LZ X-Ray on the Chu Pong, where they made contact with the PAVN troops. Soon Hueys carried reinforcements and supplies and evacuated the wounded. As PAVN troops hurled themselves at the infantry, forward observers called in artillery and air strikes, the latter delivered by the Air Force and the division's own aerial artillery battalion. The area outside the infantry's perimeter became a killing zone. When the battle ended, UH-1s lifted the troops to home base. These airmobile tactics were repeated in fast-paced actions that emphasized attrition rather than holding ground. Later tactics featured airlifted platoons or companies to contact the enemy while other units were inserted in blocking positions.

Operations in which the 1st Cavalry and 101st Airborne divisions used airmobile tactics included the Ia Drang, MASHER/WHITE WING, CRAZY HORSE, LEJEUNE, PER-SHING, PEGASUS-LAM SON 207A, DELAWARE-LAM SON 216, and the Cambodian incursion. These operations showed that airmobile units could make long moves on short notice and were capable of many types of missions, including scouting, search and destroy, pursuit, raiding, and cordon.

While the 1st Cavalry and 101st Airborne had dedicated aircraft, other combat units had helicopters attached to make them airmobile for short periods. For this reason the Army located aviation units in every corps tactical zone. Units using these aircraft developed their own procedures, so aviation units could not easily be switched from one combat unit to another. The Army thus created the 1st Aviation Brigade in 1966 and named Brig. Gen. George P. Seneff its commander. He quickly established training schools, enforced safety regulations, and standardized operating procedures throughout Vietnam. Seneff allocated one aviation battalion headquarters to each division. By 1968 the 1st Aviation Brigade managed four combat aviation groups containing a total of 14 aviation battalions and three air cavalry squadrons.

Airmobility proved itself in Vietnam. Airmobile divisions were proficient in airmobile operations because artillery, aviation, cavalry, and infantry units worked together. Their men had a different concept of combat because terrain was not a major obstacle. These units were more flexible in responding to enemy initiatives and had shorter reaction time. Troops could go into battle rested and carrying less weight. While helicopters proved survivable in battle, they still required the air superiority and close air support provided by the Air Force.

—John L. Bell

References: Stanton, Shelby. *Anatomy of a Division: 1st Cav in Vietnam* (1987); Tolson, John J. *Airmobility, 1961–1971* (1973).
See also: Army Concept Team in Vietnam (ACTIV); Gavin, James; Helicopters, Allied and Democratic Republic of Vietnam; Helicopters, Role in the War; Ia Drang, battle of; Kinnard, Harry W. O.; McNamara, Robert.

Airplanes, Allied and Democratic Republic of Vietnam

Aerial warfare over Indo-China began in 1941, when Japanese land-based bombers took off from airports near what is now Hô Chí Minh City to sink the British capital ships *Repulse* and *Prince of Wales*. During the Indo-China War,

French aircraft were obsolete and insufficient in number to contain the enemy. Most French aircraft were of World War II vintage, except for a few jet fighters.

When the United States began assisting the Republic of Vietnam (RVN) in October 1954, the initial aviation equipment supplied was of similar limited capability. By the end of the war, the United States had made a large commitment in aircraft and associated necessary equipment. Unfortunately, the level of strategy and political leadership did not measure up to the quantity of aircraft or the quality of technology employed.

The principal aircraft used in the Vietnam War follow.

Allied Forces: Bombers

Boeing B-52 Stratofortress ("Buff") Eight-engine heavy jet bomber originally designed as an intercontinental weapon system; converted to duties equivalent to World War II artillery bombardments. B-52s usually flew ARC LIGHT strikes in three-ship cells and dropped their bombs on cue from special equipment such as the Combat Skypot. Used for carpet bombing, B-52s were eventually called upon for close air support, bombing near perimeters of fortified camps.

Douglas A-1 Skyraider ("Spad") Originally developed as a U.S. Navy single-place, carrier-based dive bomber and torpedo plane; served in the Korean and Vietnamese wars, in the latter with Navy, Marine, Air Force and RVN Air Force units. Several versions were developed, but most bombing was carried out by the single-seat A-1 version. A-1s were prized for their accuracy in close support, particularly in air-rescue operations, and for the ability of their rugged fuselage and engine to sustain damage and keep flying.

Douglas B-26 Invader (RB-26) (Counter-Invader) First flown in July 1942 as the XA-26. Redesignated the B-26 after World War II, the basic design was extensively modified by On Mark Engineering as the B-26K Counter-Invader. In Vietnam it was redesignated the A-26A. This twin-engine light bomber was a delight to fly and was among the first U.S. combat aircraft introduced in Operation FARM GATE. Some RB-26s were used for reconnaissance.

Douglas A-4 Skyhawk First flown in 1954; in continuous production longer than any other combat aircraft. Small and rugged, the A-4 was a favorite workhorse of Navy and Marine crews in Vietnam. The Skyhawk carried a wide variety of weapons during tens of thousands of sorties against enemy targets.

Douglas EB/RB-66 Destroyer, A-3 Skywarrior First flown in October 1952 as the Navy XA3D-1 Skywarrior, a twin-jet carrier-based nuclear bomber. This durable aircraft served in Vietnam with the U.S. Navy as the KA-3B tanker and EKA-3B tanker/ECM aircraft. Its principal use there was by the U.S. Air Force as the EB-66 electronic countermeasures aircraft. Operating with or without fighter escort, EB-66s probed deep into enemy territory.

Martin B-57/RB-57 Canberra The only non-U.S. design adopted by the U.S. Air Force since World War II. The B-57 was originally built by England's English Electric as the Canberra, with its first flight in May 1949. The first USAF example was English-built, but Martin was awarded a contract to redesign the aircraft and produce it. A Martin B-57B was the first American jet to be employed in Vietnam. Canberras were subsequently used in bombing, flak suppression, night interdiction, and reconnaissance roles. The Viêt Công called the B-57 the "*con sâu*" (caterpillar) and dreaded its long time on station and its great bomb capacity. The Republic of Vietnam Air Force (RVNAF) also operated a few B-57s for a brief period. B-57s and RB-57s flew almost 38,000 sorties in Southeast Asia.

Grumman A-6, EA-6A Intruder, EA-6B Prowler (also KA-6D Tanker) The innocuous-looking Grumman A2F-1 (later designated A-6) first flew on 19 April 1960 and served an increasingly important role as an attack, reconnaissance, electronic warfare, and tanker aircraft. Intruders began operations in Vietnam in 1965 and were in the forefront of battle until the end of the war. They remain in active service. The Intruder/Prowler's versatility has won wide popularity.

Vought A-7 Corsair II Designed to replace the McDonnell Douglas A-4 and based heavily on the Vought F-8 design. The Vought A-7 was a highly successful attack bomber for the Navy and, later, the Air Force. Built for a ground-attack role with armor and damage-resistant systems, the Corsair II proved to be as rugged as its World War II namesake.

Allied Forces: Fighters/Fighter-Bombers

Convair F-102 Delta Dagger ("Deuce") First flown in October 1953. This delta-wing aircraft was modified to have an "area-ruled" fuselage and became a missile-carrying supersonic interceptor. The F-102 flew air defense missions in Vietnam from 1962 to 1969, was phased out of the USAF inventory in 1976, and had a second career as a drone aircraft (PQM-102A).

General Dynamics F-111 Aardvark, EF-111A Raven Among the most controversial of warplanes, the F-111 derived from Robert McNamara's quest for the TFX tri-service fighter. The variable-geometry F-111 overcame early problems to become an extraordinarily capable long-distance, low-level fighter-bomber and, as the EF-111A, a remarkable electronic countermeasures aircraft. The first deployment of F-111s to Thailand for the Vietnam War ended in disaster, but the second deployment allowed the F-111A to perform brilliantly, flying more than 4,000 missions at night and in bad weather.

Lockheed F-104 Starfighter A product of Lockheed's famous "Skunk Works," the F-104 was far more successful in foreign service than with the USAF. A lightweight air superiority fighter, the F-104 set numerous speed and altitude records. It was transferred from Air Defense Command squadrons to National Guard units when the Air Force decided that it lacked the endurance and all-weather capability required for the interceptor role. It proved more useful in its foreign F-104G ground support role. USAF F-104s, despite their inability to carry an adequate weapons load, were deployed to Vietnam in 1965 and to Thailand in 1966–1967 for operations over North and South Vietnam,

where heavy losses eventually forced their replacement by McDonnell F-4s.

McDonnell F-101 (RF-101) Voodoo Originally designed to the concept of "penetration fighter," an outgrowth of the earlier XF-88. First flown in September 1954, the F-101 was subsequently developed in various roles, including interceptor, tactical bomber, nuclear bomber, and, in the RF-101, as a reconnaissance aircraft. RF-101s flew most USAF reconnaissance missions in Vietnam until replaced by RF-4C Phantoms.

McDonnell Douglas F-4 (RF-4) Phantom Most successful Western fighter produced during the Vietnam War period. The Phantom was versatile and rugged, performing well for all three USAF services. Originally designed as a missile-equipped all-weather fleet defense fighter for the U.S. Navy, the Phantom was adopted by the USAF initially as an interceptor and later served in various roles, including air-superiority fighter, fighter-bomber, reconnaissance, fast forward air control (FAC), and Wild Weasel. Not an aesthetic triumph but continually modified and upgraded, the Phantom earned a formidable reputation in Vietnam.

North American F-100 (RF-100) Super Sabre The world's first operational fighter capable of supersonic speed in level flight. The F-100 first flew in May 1953. Distinguished by its 45–degree swept wings, the Super Sabre had a troubled early development followed by widespread service, first as an air-superiority fighter, then in Vietnam as a ground attack, Wild Weasel, reconnaissance, and fast FAC aircraft. As many as 13 squadrons of F-100s served in Vietnam, prolonging the F-100's life in service.

North American T-28 (RT-28) Trojan Used for training, ground attack, and reconnaissance, the T-28 was among the first USAF aircraft to participate in the Vietnam conflict.

Northrop F-5 Tiger Lightweight fighter sold aggressively to nations approved by the United States under the Military Assistance Program. In 1965 the USAF took twelve F-5A's (modified with aerial refueling equipment to F-5C status) to Vietnam in the Skoshi Tiger program. These aircraft were later transferred to the RVNAF. A later version, the F-5E, with more powerful engines, was called the Tiger II and was used subsequently for dissimilar air combat training.

Republic F-105 Thunderchief Originally designed as a supersonic fighter-bomber to deliver nuclear weapons. The F-105 distinguished itself by carrying the brunt of the aerial offensive against the DRV. Familiarly known as the "Thud" and first flown in October 1955, the F-105 went through a troublesome development period that marred its reputation, which was redeemed over Vietnam. The Thud served brilliantly in fighter-bomber and Wild Weasel roles.

Vought F-8 (RF-8A) Crusader Often called "the last of the gunfighters." The Vought F-8 Crusader was beloved by its pilots and ground crew members. Designed as a supersonic air-superiority fighter, it exceeded Mach 1 on its maiden flight in March 1955. Unusual with its variable-incidence wing, the Crusader had the great advantage in Vietnam of carrying four 20-mm cannons at a time when F-4s had only missiles. The F-8 was credited with downing 19 MiGs in

Vietnam. The RF-8 served equally well in the reconnaissance role, although suffering heavy losses.

Allied Forces: Other Aircraft

Cessna A-37 Dragonfly ("Tweetie-Bird") The Cessna T-37 trainer first flew on 12 October 1954. The design was modified to the A-37A attack plane that was sent to Vietnam for evaluation in 1967. An advanced version with in-flight refueling provisions and a reinforced airframe was placed into production as the A-37B. Many of these were delivered to the RVNAF and to U.S. Air National Guard units. It was used in Vietnam for forward air control and designated the OA-37B.

Douglas C-47 (AC-47, HC-47, EC-47, RC-47, SC-47) Skytrain ("Gooneybird") First flown in December 1935, the Douglas DC-3 gained a reputation more as a civilian transport than as the military jack-of-all trades C-47. The faithful Gooneybird was adapted to the gunship role in Vietnam, where, known as "Puff the Magic Dragon" it proved invaluable outfitted with three General Electric 7.62 Miniguns. It also did well in electronic reconnaissance, photographic reconnaissance, and psychological warfare roles.

Curtiss C-46 Commando Another World War II design, the Commando was first flown in March 1940. It served in World War II and the Korean War and received a brief new period of service with the 1st Air Commando Group of the Tactical Air Command in Vietnam in 1962. Many Commandos were also used by civil and paramilitary airlines in the area.

Fairchild C-119 (AC-119, RC-119) Flying Boxcar Outgrowth of the Fairchild C-82 Packet. The C-119 first flew in November 1947 and was used extensively in the Korean War. In Vietnam it was a troop and cargo transport but came into its own as the AC-119 gunship, of which there were several variants. AC-119Ks had the added power of two J85 jet engines slung under the wing.

Fairchild C-123 (UC-123K, NC-123K, AC-123K) Provider Developed from a Chase XG-20 cargo glider. The C-123 had first two and then four engines installed to undertake various roles in Vietnam. The most controversial was on Operation RANCH HAND. These aircraft were fitted with spray bars and two additional J85 jet engines.

Douglas C-54 Skymaster Among the most beloved transports, the C-54 distinguished itself in World War II and Korea. In Vietnam, a few served as an early airborne command post; the Marines also used some as transports.

Douglas C-124 Globemaster II ("Old Shakey") The portly Douglas C-124 was a workhorse, carrying tons of supplies into Vietnam. Called "Old Shakey" because of its vibrations, it nonetheless was a dependable aircraft with a great capacity for outsize cargo.

Lockheed EC-121 (RC-121) Super Constellation Considered by many to be the most beautiful piston-engine airliner ever built, the Super Constellation served in Vietnam to provide air defense control and as an airborne communication relay aircraft.

Lockheed C-130 (DC-130, WC-130, RC-130, AC-130, EC-130, HC-130) Hercules Among the most efficient, longest-lived aircraft. The Lockheed C-130 served well in multiple roles in Vietnam. First flown in August 1954, and still in production four decades later, the "Herky-bird" distinguished itself as a troop carrier, gunship, electronic reconnaissance craft, and drone launcher and various other roles. Rugged, reliable, and able to endure flak damage, the C-130 was, and remains, indispensable.

Lockheed C-141 Starlifter Based on the experience gained with the C-130 but much larger and with more advanced systems. The C-141 brought jet power to the cargo transport age and did yeoman service transporting large cargo and personnel to Vietnam, especially during emergencies.

Lockheed C-5 Galaxy Designed to carry cargo as wide and heavy as the largest Army tanks, the C-5 was destined for a turbulent introduction to a skeptical Congress and public. Despite early difficulties, it proved itself during the Vietnam War where, in conjunction with the Starlifter, it was able to rush supplies in emergencies. Its inflight refueling capability made it especially valuable.

Boeing KC-135 (EC-135, RC-135) Stratotanker Developed in parallel with the Boeing 707 transport. The KC-135 became a true force multiplier, enabling bombers and fighters to extend their range and increase their sortie rate and permitting them to take off with larger loads of ammunition. KC-135s served dangerously near enemy positions and, amazingly, none were lost to DRV fighters. Many a returning fighter pilot owed his life to the persistence and daring of KC-135 crews.

de Havilland C-7 (CV-2) Caribou Originally developed for the U.S. Army, the Caribou served the Air Force well in Vietnam with its short-takeoff-and-landing characteristics. After U.S. forces departed, some Caribous were turned over to the RVNAF and presumably were later of use to the Air Force of the Socialist Republic of Vietnam.

McDonnell Douglas C-9 Nightingale Appearing in Vietnam in 1972, the C-9 aeromedical evacuation plane was a welcome sight for sick and wounded military personnel leaving the country. A straightforward development of the standard Douglas DC-32CF, the C-9 supplemented the venerable C-118s also used for the task.

Douglas C-118 (R6D-1) Liftmaster Military version of the Douglas DC-6, the Liftmaster was used both by the Army and the Navy. Rugged, dependable, and comfortable, the C-118s gave good service in Vietnam.

Douglas F-10 (F-3D) Skyknight First flown in 1950 and used effectively in the Korean War, where it destroyed more enemy aircraft than any other Navy or Marine aircraft. Aging and difficult to exit in an emergency, the Skyknight was pressed into service in Vietnam as an electronic countermeasures aircraft.

Cessna O-1 (L-19) Bird Dog The Cessna O-1 played an essential forward air control (FAC) role in Vietnam. Unarmed and unarmored, O-1s were constantly in the thick of the battle spotting enemy targets.

Cessna O-2A (O-2B) A militarized version of the standard Cessna 337 "Push-Pull" Skymaster, the O-2A supplemented the Bird Dog in the Forward Air Control role. The O-2B version was used for psychological warfare.

Grumman OV-1 Mohawk The Mohawk served the Army well in Vietnam as a night reconnaissance and battlefield surveillance aircraft. It was modified continually with equipment such as Side-Looking Airborne Radar (SLAR).

North American Rockwell OV-10 Bronco Product of a competition for a "COIN" aircraft—an armed reconnaissance plane for counterinsurgency work—the Bronco was delivered to the USAF and the Marine Corps. It served as an FAC and in reconnaissance.

Lockheed P-3 Orion A development of the ill-starred Lockheed Electra civil transport, the Orion was originally intended for antisubmarine warfare work but was adapted for various other roles.

Lockheed P-2 (RB-69A, OP-2E) Neptune From its first flight in May 1945, the Neptune proved to be an aircraft of exceptional ability. It filled the Navy's requirement for a long-range land-based patrol and antisubmarine warfare plane. The Air Force used it in Vietnam as the RB-69A for electronic countermeasure tests and training.

de Havilland U-6 (RU-6A, TU-6A, L-20) Beaver Known as "the General's jeep" in Korea, the Beaver served equally well in Vietnam. Simple and easy to maintain, it was popular with its pilots.

de Havilland U-1 Otter Built in Canada for the U.S. Army, U.S. Navy, and Royal Canadian Air Force. Capable of short-takeoff-and-landing (STOL) performance, it was rugged and versatile.

Lockheed U-2C and U-2R Another of the Lockheed Skunk Works' great triumphs, the U-2 first gained international prominence when one was shot down over the Soviet Union in 1960. U-2s operated out of Vietnam and Thailand.

Lockheed SR-71 Blackbird An aircraft that excited public imagination since it was first announced, the Blackbird's performance outstripped all other aircraft for a period of more than 20 years.

Helio U-10 Super Courier A six-seat long-range STOL aircraft with the capability to get into and out of primitive airstrips.

Beech QU-22B Bonanza An adaptation of a conventionally tailed A-36 Bonanza with drone capability, the QU-22B usually was flown in Vietnam as a radio-relay aircraft in IGLOO WHITE operations (see McNamara Line).

Democratic Republic of Vietnam: Principal Aircraft

Antonov AN-2 Colt Outstanding light transport built in large numbers. The biplane Colt appeared anachronistic but possessed exactly the performance needed for a transport in North Vietnam.

Ilyushin IL-28 Beagle The twin-jet Ilyushin bomber was reportedly a delightful aircraft to fly and easy to maintain. Although only a threat in the Vietnam War, it was a significant one, for it could have done damage to U.S. airfields.

Mikoyan-Gurevich MiG-15 Fagot Classic fighter of the Korean war. Chinese-built versions of the MiG-15 were the first jet fighters delivered to the DRV Air Force. They were used primarily for training.

Mikoyan-Gurevich MiG-17 Fresco A development of the famous MiG-15 of the Korean war. The MiG-17 began equipping front-line Soviet units in 1953 and more than a decade later was still a formidable opponent in Vietnam because of its maneuverability and firepower.

Mikoyan-Gurevich MiG-19 Farmer (J-6) Built in large numbers in the Soviet Union, and in China as the Shenyang J-6. The MiG-19 was a formidable supersonic fighter with an effective armament package centered around three 30-mm cannon.

Mikoyan-Gurevich MiG-21 Fishbed Interceptor designed for high speeds and a swift climb. The tiny delta-wing MiG-21 was a formidable opponent to the heavier F-4s and F-105s it faced in Vietnam.

—Walter J. Boyne

References: Berger, Carl, ed. *The United States Air Force in Southeast Asia, 1961–1973; An Illustrated Account* (1984); Bowers, Peter M., and Gordon Swanborough. *United States Military Aircraft since 1909* (1989); —. *United States Navy Aircraft since 1911* (1968); Bowers, Ray L. *The United States Air Force in Southeast Asia: Tactical Aircraft* (1983); Francillon, René J. *Lockheed Aircraft since 1913* (1982); —. *McDonnell Douglas Aircraft since 1920* (1979); Littauer, Raphael, and Norman Uphoff, eds. *The Air War in Indochina* (1971); Van Vleet, Clarke, and William J. Armstrong. *United States Naval Aviation, 1910–1980* (1980).

See also: Air Power, Role in War; FARM GATE, Operation; McNamara Line; RANCH HAND, Operation; Raven Forward Air Controllers (FACs); Search-and-Rescue (SAR) Operations.

ALA MOANA, Operation

(1 December 1966–14 May 1967)
Military operation conducted by elements of the 25th Infantry Division, principally in Hậu Nghĩa Province. Its goal was to push the Việt Cộng (VC) away from a major rice-producing area near Sài Gòn.

During December 1966, 25th Division troops made sporadic contact with VC forces near Đức Hòa. In early 1967, units of the 25th operated principally along Highway 1 east of their base camp at Cu Chi and also in the area to the northeast. Concurrent with ALA MOANA, in January the division's 2nd Brigade, serving temporarily as a blocking force north of Cu Chi as part of CEDAR FALLS, collided with a company of the 165th VC Regiment and killed 50 VC soldiers.

The heaviest action in ALA MOANA occurred in late February, when the 4th Battalion, 9th Infantry, and the 3rd Squadron, 4th Cavalry, ran into a tough fight in the Filhol Rubber Plantation northeast of Cu Chi. After the conclusion of CEDAR FALLS, the heaviest action shifted to the area around Đức Hòa, south of Cu Chi, as elements of the 2nd Brigade swept along the banks of the Vàm Co River. While ALA MOANA continued, elements of the 25th Division participated in another multidivision operation, JUNCTION CITY, in War Zone C. During most of ALA MOANA, several battalions of the 25th Division also were assigned to clearing operations between Cu Chi and Trang Bàng District but made little contact. After ALA MOANA officially ended, the

25th Division's 1st and 2nd Brigades began an all-out pacification effort in Hâu Nghia Province, a longtime Communist stronghold, for the remainder of 1967.

—John D. Root

References: Bergerud, Eric M. *The Dynamics of Defeat: The Vietnam War in Hau Nghia Province* (1991); Stanton, Shelby L. *The Rise and Fall of the American Army: U.S. Ground Forces in Vietnam, 1965–1973* (1985).
See also: CEDAR FALLS, Operation; Iron Triangle; JUNCTION CITY, Operation.

Alessandri, Marcel (1895–1968)

French Army general, second in command to General Gabriel Sabattier during the French retreat into Yunnan following the Japanese coup of 9 March 1945. During the retreat, Alessandri disarmed his Indo-Chinese riflemen, most of whom were loyal to the French, and left them behind. Later, the Viêt Minh used this as an example of French perfidy.

Regarded as anti-American and anti-Chinese, Alessandri became commissioner to Cambodia in October 1945. In March 1946 he led French troops into Laos to replace the Chinese, then commanded French Army units in Tonkin. He left Indo-China in August 1946 but returned in 1948 as commander of French ground forces. Commander of the Expeditionary Corps General Marcel Carpentier, who had little knowledge of Indo-China, deferred to Alessandri's judgment. Alessandri opposed General Army Chief of Staff Georges Revers's May 1949 recommendation that France evacuate its outposts along Route Coloniale (RC) 4. Following the disastrous French defeat in the battles for RC 4 and the evacuation of Cao Bang, Alessandri was relieved of command and recalled to France. He left Indo-China on 2 December, 1950, returned in September 1952 as military advisor to the Bao Ðai government, then returned to France in June 1955.

—Spencer C. Tucker

References: Dalloz, Jacques. *The War in Indo-China, 1945–1954* (1990); Gras, Yves. *Histoire de la Guerre d'Indochine* (1992); Marr, David G. *Vietnam 1945: The Quest for Power* (1996); Patti, Archimedes L. A. *Why Viet Nam? Prelude to America's Albatross* (1980).
See also: France: Army; French Indo-China; Sabattier, Gabriel.

Ali, Muhammad (1942–)

Prizefighter, born Cassius Marcellus Clay, Jr., who lost his title after refusing to be drafted and serve in Vietnam. Clay captured the heavyweight title in 1964 and in 1965 joined the Nation of Islam and changed his name. Previously deferred by the Selective Service as a slow reader, Ali was reclassified and called for service in 1966. He sought conscientious objector (CO) status on religious grounds. Denied the exemption, Ali was called to service in April 1967 but refused induction. He was stripped of his title and boxing license and on 20 June 1967 was found guilty of violating the Selective Service Act. In June 1970 the Supreme Court overturned Ali's conviction. Speaking against injustice and oppression, Ali called for social change in America and became a focal point for the peace movement and disenchanted African Americans.

—Laura Matysek Wood

References: Ali, Muhammad, with Richard Durham. *The Greatest: My Own Story* (1975); Hauser, Thomas. *Muhammad Ali: His Life and Times* (1994).
See also: Antiwar Movement, United States; Conscientious Objectors (COs); Draft.

Alsop, Joseph W. (1910–1989)

Journalist; prominent and outspoken supporter of the Vietnam War. His influential column, "Matter of Fact," appeared in *The Washington Post* from 1958 to 1974. Alsop defended Ngô Ðình Diêm against increasing attacks by other American journalists until September 1963, when he advised Kennedy that Diêm had lost his ability to govern. Arthur Krock of *The New York Times* asserted that Alsop, along with Walt Rostow, talked President Kennedy into escalating U.S. committment in Vietnam. Alsop was highly critical of President Johnson's policy of gradual escalation and goaded him, privately and in print, to commit more troops or be prepared to preside over America's first military defeat.

Alsop was accorded VIP status during his visits to Vietnam and was given complete access to the highest U.S. military and civilian officials. McGeorge Bundy told Johnson in October 1967 that one favorable report from Alsop was worth ten official spokesmen. Consequently, he was fed classified information that allegedly demonstrated the precariousness of the enemy position. Although suspicious of President Nixon and worried that "Vietnamization" might be a cover for surrender, Alsop heartily approved of the Cambodian and Laotian invasions and developed an intimate relationship with Henry Kissinger.

Alsop's increasingly bitter feuds with liberals and other jounalists left him isolated by the time of his 1974 retirement, leading John Kenneth Galbraith to declare that, next to Johnson, Alsop was "the leading noncombatant casualty of Vietnam."

—John D. Root

References: Almquist, Leann G. *Joseph Alsop and American Foreign Policy: The Journalist as Advocate* (1993); Alsop, Joseph W., with Adam Platt. *"I've Seen the Best of It": Memoirs* (1992); Andrews, Deborah. *The Annual Obituary, 1989* (1992); Merry, Robert W. *Taking on the World: Joseph and Stewart Alsop-Guardians of the American Century* (1996); Yoder, Edwin M., Jr. *Joe Alsop's Cold War: A Study of Journalistic Influence and Intrigue* (1995).
See also: Bundy, McGeorge; Galbraith, John Kenneth; Halberstam, David; Johnson, Lyndon Baines; Kennedy, John Fitzgerald; Kissinger, Henry Alfred; Lippmann, Walter; Media and the War; Nixon, Richard Milhous; Rostow, Walt Whitman; Sheehan, Cornelius Mahoney (Neil).

Alvarez, Everett, Jr. (1937–)

Navy lieutenant; first U.S. pilot taken prisoner by the North Vietnamese. On 5 August 1964, Alvarez's A-4 Skyhawk was shot down over Hòn Gai during the first bombing raids against North Vietnam following the Gulf of Tonkin incidents. Alvarez spent eight and a half years in captivity, the first six months as the only U.S. prisoner in North Vietnam. Although he was among the more junior-rank prisoners of war, his conduct helped establish a model emulated by other American POWs.

—Joe P. Dunn

References: Alvarez, Everett, Jr., and Anthony S. Pitch. *Chained Eagle* (1989); Hubbell, John G., et al. *P.O.W.: A Definitive History of the American Prisoner of War Experience in Vietnam, 1964–1973* (1976).

See also: Prisoners of War, Allied; Tonkin Gulf Incidents.

Amerasians

Children born of American fathers and Vietnamese mothers between 1962 and 1975. Vietnamese called Amerasian children *con lai* (half-breed) and *bui doi* (dust of life). Despite social ostracism and rumors of retribution against the children and their mothers, no national policy sanctioned discrimination. However, many families with Amerasian children were moved into New Economic Zones, unimproved land intended for settlement by surplus urban population. Some families abandoned their Amerasian children, and although orphanages took a few, many grew up on city streets. Children of African American soldiers usually suffered the most discrimination.

Some men left Vietnam never knowing they had fathered children there. Those who hoped to bring their Vietnamese families to the states were stymied by red tape. Between 1975 and 1982, refugee organizations attempted to identify fathers, who were then asked to have their state governments recognize the children as legitimate so the children could be declared U.S. citizens. Even with citizenship, immigration from Vietnam required mastery of U.S. and Vietnamese bureaucracies.

In 1982 Congress passed the Amerasian Immigration Act to expedite immigration of half-American children from Asian countries. Unfortunately, this law required a consular interview for the Amerasian immigrant at a time when the United States had no official diplomatic contact with Vietnam. Other provisions, intended to keep the refugees from overwhelming the U.S. welfare system, required American sponsors who agreed to support each child to age 21 or for five years, whichever came first. Despite these restrictions, in September 1982, under the auspices of the United Nations' Orderly Departure Program (ODP), a few Amerasian children left Vietnam for the United States.

Two years later Secretary of State George Shultz announced a special Amerasian subprogram within the ODP, but departure rates remained low. In 1986, citing a backlog of 25,000 applicants, the Vietnamese government stopped processing new cases. Congress responded by passing the Amerasian Homecoming Act, which took effect on 21 March 1988. Allowing Vietnamese Amerasians and specified family members to enter the United States as immigrants, and providing for resettlement assistance, the act had an immediate effect. By 1991, 67,028 Amerasians had arrived. Refugee aid societies estimated in 1994 that only a few thousand Amerasians remained in Vietnam, mostly by choice.

Resettled Amerasian children faced formidable obstacles, including discrimination. Those who identified themselves as American in Vietnam found that, in all ways but appearance, they were Vietnamese in America. Many mothers of Amerasians hoped to find the fathers of their children, but even with assistance from the American Red Cross, only about two percent of father searches ended positively. Nevertheless, there were sucess stories. Those who came to America with their relatives, especially their mothers, seemed to fare best. Big Brother and Big Sister organizations were especially important in locating mentors for Amerasian children, and studies indicated their effectiveness. When the youngest members of this legacy of the Vietnam War reached adulthood in the mid-1990s, programs to assist their assimilation ended.

—Elizabeth Urban Alexander

References: Bass, Thomas A. *Vietnamerica: The War Comes Home* (1996); DeBonis, Steven. *Children of the Enemy: Oral Histories of Vietnamese Amerasians and Their Mothers* (1995); Montero, Darrel. *Vietnamese Americans: Patterns of Resettlement and Socioeconomic Adaptations in the United States* (1979).

See also: United Nations and the Vietnam War; Vietnam: Socialist Republic of, 1975 to the Present.

American Friends of Vietnam (1955–1975)

Private association promoting U.S. interests in Vietnam. American Friends of Vietnam (AFV), announced to the press in December 1955, had its roots in an earlier network that vigorously promoted U.S. support for Ngô Đình Diêm. International Rescue Committee members Leo Cherne and Joseph Buttinger founded AFV with Harold Oram and Elliot Newcombe, employees of a public relations firm hired by Diêm. AFV attracted support from politically diverse figures, including Cardinal Francis Spellman, Henry Luce, Justice William O. Douglas, and Senators John F. Kennedy, Mike Mansfield, Hubert Humphrey, and William Knowland.

AFV's specific goal was to save Vietnam from communism. U.S. government provided information, speakers, and fund-raising assistance to help AFV counter criticism of American Vietnam policy. In the early 1960s AFV activities dwindled when members divided over how to respond to Diêm's autocratic rule. AFV revived after Diêm's 1963 ouster and, working closely with the Johnson administration, supported military escalation and countered criticism of U.S. policy with government help and funds. These official connections made AFV a frequent target of policy critics and antiwar protesters. By the 1970s financial and administrative problems had undermined AFV operations, and by 1975 it had all but ceased to exist.

Contemporary critics of the AFV charged that it purposely distorted Diêm's capabilities and set the ideological stage for U.S. intervention in Vietnam. AFV's first two presidents, Generals William Donovan and John O'Daniel, were intimately connected to U.S. covert operations, leading some scholars to suggest that the group likely had the endorsement, if not the veiled support, of the Central Intelligence Agency. However, most historians argue that AFV's influence was marginal because the Eisenhower,

Kennedy, and Johnson administrations were always strongly committed to Vietnam.

—Delia Pergande

References: Anderson, David. *Trapped by Success: The Eisenhower Administration and Vietnam, 1953–1961* (1991); Kahin, George McT. *Intervention: How America became Involved in Vietnam* (1986); Morgan, Joseph G. "The Vietnam Lobby: The American Friends of Vietnam, 1955–1975" (1992).

See also: Humphrey, Hubert H.; Kennedy, John Fitzgerald; Mansfield, Michael Joseph; Ngô Đình Diêm; O'Daniel, John W.; Spellman, Francis Joseph.

Amnesty

Pardon or exemption from prosecution granted to groups or individuals convicted or accused of violations of law. Amnesty was first proposed during the Vietnam War when the American Civil Liberties Union (ACLU) asked President Nixon to grant amnesty to draft evaders, deserters, exiles, and less-than-honorable discharges. Both Nixon (who stated that amnesty was "the most immoral thing [he] could think of") and Vice-President Agnew were opposed to the idea.

The ACLU was the strongest advocate of amnesty. Its records showed that 7,400 draft evaders had been convicted by federal courts; 39,000 were referred to the Department of Justice for prosecution; 5,700 draft evaders still had indictments pending. Between August 1964 and December 1972 there were 495,689 cases of desertion, 450,000 less-than-honorable discharges, and 37,000 to 40,000 exiles who resisted prosecution by fleeing the country.

Public support for amnesty grew as the Vietnam War came to an end, and the antiwar movement reconstituted itself into an amnesty lobby. In 1971 Senator Robert Taft sponsored a bill providing that draft resisters could gain amnesty if they worked for four years at a public service job. The bill was defeated.

President Gerald Ford, seeking to restore confidence in the federal government following the Watergate scandal, announced a clemency program that offered leniency to offenders, rather than a full pardon. It required that draft resisters, exiles, and deserters meet with a U.S. attorney and sign an agreement to work for 24 months in alternative service, after which charges would be dismissed. Ford's clemency program failed—only 6 percent of 350,000 offenders applied for the program, and of those only a few completed their terms—but the program worked as a symbol of forgiveness and disarmed the amnesty issue. The ACLU abandoned its amnesty project in 1975.

On his first full day in office, President Carter offered a blanket pardon to draft resisters but granted no relief to deserters. In March 1977 the Defense Department announced a Special Discharge Review Program that offered 432,000 veterans the opportunity to apply for upgrades from undesirable/clemency discharges and to receive medical benefits. However, the program excluded more than 22,000 Vietnam veterans. Neither the Carter nor the Defense Department program was successful, leading to a public perception that both programs were unfair and that the Carter

Administration, like its predecessors, had failed to resolve this issue. The amnesty issue faded in importance as many Americans lost interest.

—Lacie Ballinger

References: Baskir, Lawrence M., and William A. Strauss. *Chance and Circumstance* (1978); Schardt, Arlie, et al. *Amnesty? The Unsettled Question of Vietnam* (1973).

See also: Agnew, Spiro T.; Carter, Jimmy; Ford, Gerald R.; Nixon, Richard Milhous.

Amphibious Warfare

Military activity involving landing from ships, either directly or by means of landing craft or helicopters. The Vietnam War posed challenges to the conventional amphibious operations elaborated in LFM-01 *Doctrine for Amphibious Operations*. It did not offer the hostile shore environment this doctrine was directed toward. Instead, Vietnam was an endemic "semi-hostile" place stemming from a guerrilla war, a situation that resulted in unanticipated problems for the more than 50 amphibious operations conducted during the war.

Marine support elements were sent to Vietnam in mid-February 1965, ahead of Marine combat units. The traditional absolute authority of the Amphibious Task Force commander within the Amphibious Objective Area (AOA) came into question. Civilians loyal to the RVN government resided in this area, and Allied air operations and commercial flights were being conducted within it. Commercial flights had to be warned of no-fly zones for impending amphibious operations, causing potential security breaches .

The Seventh Fleet's amphibious task force, designated Task Force 76, was composed of the Amphibious Ready Group/Special Landing Force (ARG/SLF). An ARG initially comprised three to four (later, five) ships, an amphibious assault ship (LPH), attack transport (APA), landing platform dock (LPD), landing ship dock (LSD), and tank landing ship (LST). Each 2,000–man SLF was composed of a Marine Battalion Landing Team (BLT) and a helicopter squadron.

Four types of amphibious operations took place in Vietnam: those including operations such as DECKHOUSE I and BEAU CHARGER, based solely on Fleet Marine Force (FMF) and Seventh Fleet forces; those composed of FMF and Seventh Fleet forces as part of an in-country operation, of which Operation BEAVER TRACK was representative; amphibious operations utilizing in-country, FMF and Seventh Fleet forces, of which Operation DOUBLE EAGLE is a prime example; and those based on in-country and Seventh Fleet forces, of which Operation BLUE MARTIN is an example.

Two debates raged over amphibious forces during this period. The initial one dealt with the deployment of the SLF. The Commander in Chief, Pacific Fleet (CinCPacFlt) viewed this force as a naval contribution to the war effort and, for that reason, under its direct authority. The Commander, U.S. Military Assistance Command, Vietnam (COMUSMACV), however, viewed it as a ready manpower reserve that circumvented Pentagon-mandated troop ceilings. The second debate concerned the needs of "brown water" (riverine) versus "blue water" operations. The Marine Corps was criticized for not adapting its amphibious doctrine to operations suited for the Mekong Delta.

One of the final amphibious operations in South Vietnam was conducted by the 31st Marine Amphibious Unit (MAU) in 1971 during Operation LAM SON 719. Thereafter, Marine amphibious forces did not deploy ashore in Vietnam until the April 1975 Operations EAGLE PULL and FREQUENT WIND that evacuated U.S. personnel from Phnom Penh and Sài Gòn, respectively. The final employment of U.S. amphibious forces in the Vietnam War came during the May 1975 *Mayaguez* incident.

Although some Marine officers considered amphibious warfare doctrine adequate, others viewed it as inappropriate to the overall counterinsurgency effort in Vietnam, noting that air space and landing sites were already controlled by U.S. forces. Some have suggested that most SLF operations were contrived simply to protect the future of the Marine Corps. In 1972 Marine Corps Commandant General Robert E. Cushman, Jr. wryly observed, "we are pulling our heads out of the jungle and getting back into the amphibious business."

—Robert J. Bunker

References: Alexander, Joseph H., and Merrill L. Bartlett. "Amphibious Warfare and the Vietnam War" (1994); Hilgartner, Lt. Col. P. L. "Amphibious Doctrine in Vietnam" (1969); Marolda, Edward J., and G. Wesley Pryce III. *A Short History of the United States Navy and the Southeast Asia Conflict, 1950–1975* (1984); Shulimson, Jack, and Maj. Charles M. Johnson, USMC. *U.S. Marines in Vietnam, 1965, The Landing and the Buildup* (1978); Simmons, Edwin H. "Marine Corps Operations in Vietnam, 1965–66, 1967, 1968, 1969–72" (1974).

See also: Cushman, Robert Everton, Jr.; DOUBLE EAGLE, Operation; EAGLE PULL, Operation; FREQUENT WIND, Operation; MARKET TIME, Operation; *Mayaguez* Incident; McNamara Line; PIRANHA, Operation; United States:Marine Corps.

An Lôc, Battle of (April 1972)

Southernmost prong of the 1972 People's Army of Vietnam (PAVN) Easter Offensive, a large-scale, conventional three-pronged attack designed to confuse and defeat Army of the Republic of Vietnam (ARVN) defenders. Its architect, General Võ Nguyên Giáp, divided his assault force of more than 120,000 troops into three separate operations.

The offensive began with a multidivisional PAVN attack across the Demilitarized Zone (DMZ) toward Huê and Đà Nang, with other forces pressing in from the A Shau valley in the west. Giáp wanted to force President Nguyên Van Thiêu to commit reserves to protect his northern provinces, after which Giáp planned to launch a second assault from Cambodia to threaten Sài Gòn. Then Giáp would launch the third attack in the Central Highlands to take Kontum and aim for the coast in Bình Đinh Province, thus splitting South Vietnam in two. This would lead to an RVN collapse, or at least a peace agreement on Hà Nôi's terms.

Giáp launched the offensive on 30 March 1972. PAVN forces routed ARVN defenders in Quang Tri Province. On 2 April Giáp launched the second prong when PAVN troops crossed the Cambodian border into III Corps area of operations and threatened Tây Ninh City. This proved to be a feint; the main attack followed on 5 April against Lôc Ninh, which was quickly overwhelmed, opening a direct route down Highway QL-13 to Sài Gòn. After the fall of Lôc Ninh, VC/PAVN Divisions moved to attack An Lôc itself. Thiêu ordered the 5th ARVN Division to An Lôc to assume control of defense of the city. By 7 April PAVN forces had surrounded An Lôc, effectively cutting off ground reinforcement and resupply. On 12 April PAVN troops began shelling the city.

On 13 April, PAVN troops began a massive infantry attack supported by T-54 and PT-76 tanks and increased artillery fire on An Lôc. AH-1G Cobra helicopter gunships and continuous tactical air support from U.S. Air Force, Navy, and Marine fighter-bombers and Air Force AC-130 Spectre gunships enabled the defenders to hold out against the initial assault, but not before they were pushed into an area less than a mile square. B-52 "ARC LIGHT" strikes ringed the city and precluded the Communists from massing their forces and completely overrunning the defenders. An attack by the 21st ARVN Division to relieve the city from the south failed, and An Lôc remained cut off and besieged, suffering repeated ground attacks and round-the-clock heavy shelling. ARVN forces, aided by U.S. Army advisors and U.S. air power, held their ground against overwhelming odds, sustaining heavy casualties in the process. Air support was vital; B-52s flew 252 missions, and there were 9,023 tactical air strikes. The siege was finally lifted in June and the 5th ARVN Division was replaced in July by the 18th ARVN Division. During the siege, the three attacking PAVN divisions sustained an estimated 10,000 casualties and lost most of their tanks and heavy artillery. The ARVN had 5,400 casualties, including 2,300 dead or missing.

Although An Lôc was in ruins, the ARVN defenders had stopped a direct assault on Sài Gòn and effectively blunted the PAVN Easter Offensive in the South.

—James H. Willbanks

References: Ngô Quang Truong. *The Easter Offensive of 1972* (1980); Pimlott, John. *Vietnam: The Decisive Battles* (1990); Willbanks, James H. *Thiet Giap! The Battle of An Loc, April 1972* (1993).

See also: Air Power, Role in War; ARC LIGHT (B-52 Raids); Easter Offensive (Nguyên Huê Campaign); Nguyên Van Thiêu; Vietnamization; Võ Nguyên Giáp.

An Nam

Middle "state" of the three former French possessions that make up present-day Vietnam. From 1883 the French divided Vietnam into three administrative states: Tonkin, An Nam (or Annam), and Cochin China. Under the French, the Vietnamese people became known as "Annamese" and even referred to themselves as such over time. An Nam and Tonkin were ruled by titular Vietnamese emperors under the imposed protectorate; Cochin China was administered directly as a French colony.

—Arthur T. Frame

References: Buttinger, Joseph. *Vietnam: A Political History* (1968); Karnow, Stanley. *Vietnam: A History* (1984).

See also: Cochin China; French Indo-China; Minh Mang; Nguyên Phúc Ánh (Gia Long); Tonkin; Tu Đuc; Vietnam: Prehistory to 938; Vietnam: from 938 through French Conquest.

Antiaircraft Artillery, Allied and Democratic Republic of Vietnam

During the Vietnam War, the Democratic Republic of Vietnam (DRV) developed the most sophisticated antiaircraft defense network in the world. This included antiaircraft artillery (AAA), MiG interceptors, surface-to-air missiles (SAMs), and extensive communications and radar links. In contrast, the United States and the Republic of Vietnam (RVN) did not require or develop robust air defenses against the DRV, which used its air force in a purely defensive role and restricted it to its own airspace.

Through late 1964 the DRV air defense system was very primitive, with no more than 700 AAA weapons. However, the Chinese quickly supplied air defense equipment after the United States began Operation ROLLING THUNDER against the DRV in early 1965. After China subsequently refused to supply additional AAA weapons to Hà Nôi, the Soviet Union became the primary supplier. Moscow provided guns ranging from the 8-mm M1944 to the ZU-23. AAA rapidly became the pilots' primary fear, and the situation worsened in 1968, when the DRV married radar tracking to many of its 8,000 AAA weapons. Prior to radar tracking, U.S. pilots sacrificed bombing accuracy for safety, operating above 5,000 feet to avoid lethal, low-altitude 12-mm and 40-mm guns. With radar tracking, however, the DRV AAA's effective range covered 1,500 to over 40,000 feet. Only in the 1972 LINEBACKER campaigns did U.S. air forces finally neutralize the DRV air defense system.

North Vietnamese AAA batteries performed multiple roles, including air-base defense and the protection of the Hà Nôi and Hai Phòng areas. AAA units often operated in residential areas and near hospitals and dikes, in violation of international law, since the rules of engagement as defined by the United States protected these areas from attack. As a result, U.S. pilots had two basic options to neutralize the AAA threat. They could jam radar-equipped AAA batteries (although low-flying aircraft were still vulnerable to line-of-sight fire) or make radical random changes in speed, altitude, and/or direction to confuse the radar ("jinking"). However, pilots approaching a target had to fly straight and steady, leaving them vulnerable to enemy fire.

In contrast to the very limited air defense system of the RVN, which included two Hawk Missile battalions from 1965 to 1968 and three AAA battalions used to support ground combat, the DRV's system was exceptionally well equipped. One simple but effective DRV antiaircraft device against low-flying aircraft was the "People's Air Defense," private citizens in urban areas who concentrated rifle and machine gun fire on one selected aircraft.

By requiring time, resources, and technology to neutralize their air defense system, the DRV denied the United States total control of its airspace until 1972. The DRV air defense system, of which AAA was a major component, thus became a model for other nations during and after the Vietnam War.

—Adam J. Stone

References: Lavalle, A. J. C. *The Tale of Two Bridges* (1985); Morrocco, John. *Rain of Fire: Air War, 1969–1973* (1985); Nordeen, Lon O., Jr. *Air Warfare in the Missile Age* (1985); Sharp, U. S. G., and W. C. Westmoreland. *Report on the War in Vietnam* (1969).
See also: Air Power, Role in War; Air Defense, Democratic Republic of Vietnam; LINEBACKER I, Operation; LINEBACKER II, Operation; ROLLING THUNDER, Operation.

Antiwar Movement, United States

The antiwar movement consisted of independent interests, often only vaguely allied and contesting each other on many issues, united only in opposition to the Vietnam War. The movement gained national prominence in 1965, peaked in 1968, and remained powerful throughout the duration of the conflict. It exposed a deep schism within 1960s American society.

A small, core peace movement had long existed in the United States, largely based in Quaker and Unitarian beliefs, but failed to gain popular currency until the Cold War era. The National Committee for a Sane Nuclear Policy (SANE), a middle-class organization founded in 1957 whose goal was reduction of nucleur weapons, represented traditional liberal peace activism. The Student Peace Union (SPU), which emerged in 1959 on college campuses, was more liberal than radical. Never an effective interest group, the SPU faded away in 1964, its banner taken up by a more active assemblage, Students for a Democratic Society (SDS).

SDS formed in 1960 as the collegiate arm of the League for Industrial Democracy, an Old Left institution with an impressive heritage. Within a year, however, SDS was taken over by University of Michigan student radicals Al Haber and Tom Hayden. In June 1962, 59 SDS members met at Port Huron, Michigan, in a conference sponsored by the United Auto Workers. From this meeting materialized the Port Huron Statement, called the manifesto of the New Left. Written by Hayden, the document expressed disillusionment with the military-industrial-academic establishment. Throughout the first years of its existence, SDS focused on domestic concerns and actively supported Lyndon Johnson in his 1964 campaign. Not yet an antiwar organization, SDS actively participated in the Civil Rights struggle and proved an important link between the two defining causes of the decade.

Another bridge between Civil Rights and the antiwar crusade was the Free Speech Movement (FSM) at the University of California, Berkeley, begun in December 1964 by students who had participated in Mississippi's "Freedom Summer." In several skirmishes with University President Clark Kerr, the FSM and its dynamic leader Mario Savio publicized the close ties between academic and military establishments.

By the beginning of 1965, the antiwar movement base had coalesced on campuses and lacked only a catalyst to bring wider public acceptance. That catalyst appeared early in February, when the U.S. began bombing North Vietnam. In

February and March 1965, SDS organized marches on the Oakland Army Terminal, departure point for many troops bound for Southeast Asia. SDS escalated the scale of dissent to a national level, calling for a march on Washington to protest the bombing. On 17 April 1965, between 15,000 and 25,000 people gathered at the capital, a turnout that surprised even the organizers. Buoyed by the attendance at the Washington march, movement leaders, still mainly students, expanded their methods and gained new allies over the next two years.

"Vietnam Day," a symposium held at Berkeley in October 1965, drew thousands to debate the moral basis of the war. The Underground Press Syndicate (1966), Liberation News Service (1967), and other networks disseminated information related to the antiwar movement. In spring 1967, more than 1,000 seminarians wrote to Secretary of Defense Robert McNamara advocating recognition of conscientious objection on secular, moral grounds. In June, 10,000 students wrote the secretary to suggest a program of alternative service for those who opposed violence. A two-day march on the Pentagon in October 1967 attracted nationwide media attention, while leaders of the "Fort Hood 3" gained acclaim among dissenters for their refusal to serve in Vietnam. Draft evaders were funneled by underground railroads to Canada or Sweden or given sanctuary in churches.

A significant development between 1965 and 1968 was the emergence of Civil Rights leaders as active proponents of peace in Vietnam. In a January 1967 article written for the *Chicago Defender*, Martin Luther King, Jr. openly expressed support for the antiwar movement on moral grounds. In April he asserted that the war was draining resources from domestic programs and voiced concern about the percentage of African American casualties. His statements rallied African American activists to the antiwar cause and established a new dimension to the moral objections of the movement.

As the movement's ideals spread beyond college campuses, doubts about the wisdom of escalation also began to appear within the administration, but widespread opposition within the government did not appear until 1968. The 1968 Têt Offensive led many to question the administration's veracity and contributed to President Johnson's decision to retire. After Têt American public opinion shifted dramatically, with fully half of the population opposed to escalation. Dissent escalated to violence. In April police used force to evict protesters occupying the Columbia University administration building. Raids on draft boards, in which activists smeared blood on records and shredded files, soon followed in Baltimore, Milwaukee, and Chicago. Offices and production facilities of Dow Chemical, manufacturers of napalm, were targeted for sabotage. Brutal clashes between police and activists at the August 1968 Democratic National Convention in Chicago typified the divided nature of American society and foreshadowed a rise in domestic conflict.

The antiwar movement became more powerful but less cohesive between 1969 and 1973. In November 1969 a second march on Washington drew an estimated 500,000 participants. At the same time, much of the public disapproved of the counterculture that had arisen alongside the antiwar movement. Clean-cut SDS members who had tied their hopes to McCarthy in 1968 were being subordinated as movement leaders. Their replacements, tagged with the label "hippie," faced mainstream opposition from middle-class Americans uncomfortable with long hair, casual drug use, and promiscuity. Protest musicians, typified by Joan Baez and Bob Dylan, contributed to the gulf between young and old. Cultural and political protest became inextricably intertwined. The new leaders became increasingly strident, taunting and harrassing returning soldiers. A unique situation arose in which most Americans supported the cause but opposed the leaders, methods, and culture of protest.

The movement regained solidarity in 1970, after news of the My Lai massacre became public and Nixon, who had previously committed to a planned withdrawal, announced that U.S. forces had entered Cambodia. On 4 May, Ohio National Guardsmen fired on student protesters at Kent State University, killing four and wounding sixteen. More groups openly called for withdrawal, and Congress began threatening the Nixon administration with challenges to presidential authority. Publication of the Pentagon Papers beginning 13 June 1971 made Americans aware of the true nature of the war. Reports of drug trafficking, political assassinations, and indiscriminate bombings led many to believe that military and intelligence services had lost all accountability. Antiwar sentiment, previously tainted with an air of anti-Americanism, now dominated America; the antiwar cause had become institutionalized. Nixon's 1973 announcement of the effective end of U.S. involvement in Vietnam came in response to a mandate unequaled in modern times.

—Mark Barringer

References: DeBenedetti, Charles. *An American Ordeal: The Antiwar Movement of the Vietnam Era* (1990); Garfinkle, Adam. *Telltale Hearts: The Origins and Impact of the Vietnam Antiwar Movement* (1995); Halstead, Fred. *Out Now! A Participant's Account of the American Movement Against the Vietnam War* (1978).

See also: Ali, Muhammad; Baez, Joan Chandos; Ball, George W.; Clark, William Ramsey; Conscientious Objectors (COs); Democratic Party National Convention, 1968; Dylan, Bob; Federal Bureau of Investigation (FBI); Fort Hood Three; Ginsberg, Allen; Goldman, Eric F.; Hardhats; Hayden, Thomas E.; Hoover, J. Edgar; Huston Plan; International War Crimes Tribunal; Jackson State College; Johnson, Lyndon Baines; Kennedy, Robert Francis; Kent State University; King, Martin Luther, Jr.; Levy, Howard B; May Day Tribe; McCarthy, Eugene Joseph; McCarthy, Joseph Raymond; McGovern, George S.; McNamara, Robert S.; My Lai Massacre; Pentagon Papers and Trial; Seale, Bobby; Spock, Benjamin M.; Students for a Democratic Society (SDS); *Tinker v. Des Moines*; United States: Department of Justice; University of Wisconsin Bombing.

Âp Bac, Battle of (2 January 1963)

Fierce battle on 2 January 1963 at the small village of Âp Bac, approximately 40 miles southwest of Sài Gòn. Stung by the October 1962 loss of a South Vietnamese Ranger platoon and concerned about the ease with which the Viêt Công were recruiting support in the Mekong Delta region, Lt. Col. John

Vann, senior advisor to the 7th Division of the Army of the Republic of Vietnam (ARVN), hoped for a quick victory at Âp Bac and its sister hamlet, Âp Tân Thoi.

Aware that an ARVN attack was imminent, the Communist 261st Main Force Battalion of 320 men, augmented by about 30 regional guerrillas, assumed strong defensive positions in tree lines and along canals. They demonstrated superior weapons discipline throughout the day. Conversely, the 7th Division exhibited cowardice, confusion, and incompetence, and the mission quickly disintegrated as ARVN soldiers refused to advance under fire. By noon, five U.S. helicopters carrying ARVN soldiers were downed. Intermediate ARVN commanders refused to act. Finally, hoping to contain the Communist forces, ARVN paratroopers dropped into the battle zone. The greatly outnumbered Communist troops outfought ARVN forces, then escaped into the night.

General Paul Harkins, senior-ranking military officer in South Vietnam, stated that the mission was successful because Âp Bac had been secured. He didn't mention that this occurred after the enemy had escaped. However, reporters David Halberstam, Neil Sheehan, and Malcolm Brown, covering the battle at the site, revealed a debacle. Even with U.S. technology and planning, the ARVN was an inferior fighting force. Communist forces lost 18 men killed and 39 wounded; the ARVN suffered about 80 dead and more than 100 wounded.

The battle at Âp Bac became symbolic of the ARVN's difficulties. Furthermore, the U.S. military damaged its credibility with the press corps, a problem that increased as the war continued.

—Charles J. Gaspar

References: Halberstam, David. *The Making of a Quagmire* (1987); Karnow, Stanley. *Vietnam: A History* (1991); Sheehan, Neil. *A Bright Shining Lie: John Paul Vann and America in Vietnam* (1988).

See also: Halberstam, David; Harkins, Paul D.; Mekong Delta; Sheehan, Cornelius M. (Neil); Taylor-McNamara Report; Vann, John Paul.

Âp Bia Mountain. *See* Hamburger Hill (Battle of Âp Bia Mountain).

APACHE SNOW, Operation (10 May–7 June 1969)
U.S. military operation designed to keep pressure on People's Army of Vietnam (PAVN) units and base camps in the A Shau Valley. The A Shau was a PAVN base area and terminus for replacements and supplies sent south by the Democratic Republic of Vietnam along the Hô Chí Minh Trail. A monsoon-season bombing cessation allowed the Communists to move and stockpile materiel throughout their infiltration network in the A Shau, and in February 1969 Military Assistance Command, Vietnam (MACV) Intelligence reported bunker and way-station construction in the valley. Several Army of the Republic of Vietnam (ARVN) and U.S. operations were conducted to disrupt the activity and destroy PAVN units to prevent attacks on the coastal provinces.

APACHE SNOW involved the 3rd Brigade, U.S. 101st

Airborne Division (Airmobile), the U.S. 9th Marine Regiment, and the ARVN 3rd Regiment, 1st Infantry Division. Although most elements met with some resistance, the 3rd Battalion, 187th Infantry "Rakassans," became embroiled in heavy contact on the second day of the operation as they approached Âp Bia Mountain (Hill 937).

Having engaged the 7th and 8th Battalions of the 29th PAVN Regiment who were dug into heavily fortified positions on the hill, the 3rd/187th was reinforced with two more 101st Airborne Division battalions and a battalion of the 3rd ARVN Regiment. The battle for Âp Bia Mountain ("Hamburger Hill") was the major event of APACHE SNOW, forcing PAVN forces out of the A Shau and into Laotian sanctuaries. Despite this success, PAVN troops returned to the area as soon as U.S. and ARVN forces withdrew. Official U.S. casualty figures for the operation were 56 Americans and 5 South Vietnamese killed in action; enemy losses were estimated at 630. Samuel Zaffiri gives U.S. casualties as 70 dead and 372 wounded.

—Arthur T. Frame

References: Stanton, Shelby L. *The Rise and Fall of An American Army: U.S. Ground Forces in Vietnam, 1965–1973* (1985); Zaffiri, Samuel. *Hamburger Hill* (1988).

See also: Attrition; Hamburger Hill (Battle of Âp Bia Mountain).

ARC LIGHT (B-52 Raids) (1965–1973)
General term and code name for U.S. Air Force B-52 Stratofortress operations in Vietnam flown out of Guam and Thailand from 18 June 1965 to 15 August 1973. ARC LIGHT missions were flown above 30,000 feet in South Vietnam and Laos to support ground troops or interdict enemy infiltration. B-52s, originally designed to carry nuclear weapons, were modified to carry nearly 30 tons of conventional bombs each.

ARC LIGHT operations were most often close air support (CAS) carpet bombing raids of enemy base camps, troop concentrations, or supply lines. An unusual CAS operation because it was carried out at high altitudes by strategic bombers, it was welcomed by the ground forces, who called the raids "aerial excavations." Most ARC LIGHT sorties were flown south of the 17th parallel; only 141 missions were flown north, mostly near the Demilitarized Zone.

On 28 June 1965, 27 B-52Fs of the 7th and 320th Bomb Wings in Guam made the first ARC LIGHT raid against a Viêt Công (VC) jungle redoubt. No VC were killed, and two B-52s were lost in a midair collision. One newspaper report compared ARC LIGHT to a housewife "swatting flies with a sledge-hammer," but General William Westmoreland was convinced of the B-52s' potential effectiveness. From June through December 1965, the 7th, 320th, and 454th Bomb Wings flew more than 100 missions with F-model B-52s. Most were saturation attacks, but some were tactical support missions, such as for the USMC's Operation HARVEST MOON campaign and the Army's Ia Drang Valley operations. The need for greater payload led to the "Big Belly" program for B-52Ds, which increased internal 500-pound-bomb capacity from 27 to 84 and 750-pound-bomb capacity from 27 to 42. They still carried 24 500-pound or 750-pound-bombs externally.

Between 12 and 16 April 1966, B-52s raided outside South Vietnam for the first time, bombing Mu Gia Pass in Laos to stop PAVN infiltrations. Later they also attacked PAVN infiltration routes along the Hô Chí Minh Trail. By the end of 1967, B-52 units in Southeast Asia had been augmented by elements of the 306th, 91st, 22nd, 454th, 461st, and 99th Bomb Wings.

Operations in support of U.S. Marines at Khe Sanh began in late January 1968, and crews used ground-based radar to direct their aircraft to the targets. B-52s continued to pound areas in northern South Vietnam throughout the year. Targets of particular importance were the A Shau Valley, the Kontum-Dak To tri-border area, and the PAVN/VC infiltration area in southeastern War Zone C. The attacks on PAVN supply and troop concentrations were among the greatest ARC LIGHT successes.

Although President Johnson halted bombing of the North in March 1968, B-52 strikes continued throughout 1969. In 1970 President Nixon's Vietnamization program led to a reduction of ARC LIGHT raids, although significant missions were flown against Laotian infiltration routes and Cambodian supply dumps, base areas, and troop concentrations. From November 1969 to April 1970, B-52s flew in COMMANDO HUNT III in Laos. In April and May they supported ground operations in both Laos and Cambodia.

In 1972, in an effort to stem the tide of the PAVN's Easter Offensive and to force the Democratic Republic of Vietnam and the National Liberation Front back to the Paris Peace Talks, Nixon twice ordered B-52 raids on Hà Nôi and Hai Phòng. LINEBACKER I (10 May–23 October 1972) was composed of ARC LIGHT missions, raids on infiltration routes, and some attacks on Hà Nôi and Hai Phòng. LINEBACKER II (18–29 December 1972) focused on 24 military targets. On 30 December 1972 Hà Nôi agreed to return to negotiations, but because of cease-fire violations in South Vietnam, Laos, and Cambodia, B-52 raids continued until 15 August, when the last ARC LIGHT raid was carried out over Cambodia.

Between 18 June 1965 and 15 August 1973 SAC launched 126,615 sorties, of which 125,479 actually reached their targets and 124,532 released their bombs. More than 55 percent of these sorties were flown in South Vietnam, 27 percent in Laos, 12 percent in Cambodia, and 6 percent in North Vietnam. The USAF lost 31 B-52s, 18 to enemy fire over North Vietnam, and 13 due to operations problems.

—William Head

References: Berger, Carl, ed. *The United States Air Force in Southeast Asia, 1961–1973: An Illustrated Account* (1984); Hopkins, J. C., and Sheldon A. Goldberg. *The Development of the Strategic Air Command, 1946–1986: The Fortieth Anniversary History* (1986); Schlight, John. *The Air War in South Vietnam: The Years of the Offensive, 1965–1968* (1988); Tilford, Earl H., Jr. *Setup: What The Air Force Did in Vietnam and Why* (1991); U.S. Air Force Special Study, Headquarters Strategic Air Command. "Activity Input to Project Corona Harvest-Arc Light Operations, 1 Jan 65–31 Mar 68" (Declassified 1990).

See also: Air Power, Role in War; Airplanes, Allied and Democratic Republic of Vietnam; HARVEST MOON, Operation; Ia Drang, Battle of; Johnson, Lyndon Baines; LINEBACKER I, Operation; LINEBACKER II, Operation; Nixon, Richard Milhous; Westmoreland, William Childs.

Argenlieu, Georges Thierry de. *See* d'Argenlieu, Georges Thierry.

Armor Warfare

Allied tanks were deployed offensively and defensively during the Vietnam War. Offensive employment of Allied tanks made good use of their mobility, heavy firepower, defensive armor, and shock effect. Communist tanks were deployed mostly late in the conflict, primarily in an offensive role.

The U.S. high command initially held that Vietnam was not appropriate tank country, a perception eventually dispelled by the M48 Patton. The "jungle-busting" Patton was used to create paths through dense vegetation and to assault Viêt Công (VC) bunkers. M48 crews often sandbagged the turrets for crew protection, and the bulldozer variant commonly had claymore mines attached to its working blade for added firepower. In its counterinsurgency support role, tanks helped clear out enemy strong points, patrol secure areas, and engage in sweeps and ambushes.

On the defensive, night laagers (defensive perimeters) were systematically employed, with fighting positions between each vehicle. Concertina wire and claymore mines surrounded the perimeter, and listening posts were also established. Harassment and interdiction (H&I) missions kept enemy forces off balance and away from the night laager positions.

Tanks were prime targets for VC and People's Army of Vietnam (PAVN) forces. They attacked tanks indirectly with mines or directly with rocket-propelled grenades, Sagger antitank missiles, satchel charges, and antitank grenades. Mines, ranging from TNT demolition blocks and converted dud bombs to conventional Soviet and Chinese antitank munitions, caused the principal U.S. armor losses in Vietnam. They were placed in road junctions, networks, and likely night laager positions; thus, armor units normally rarely used the same static position two nights in a row. M48 crews had good chances of surviving a mine detonation, but crews of lighter vehicles had a much lower survival rate.

Attacks on tanks with rocket-propelled grenades— Soviet RPG2 (Vietnamese B40) and RPG7V (Vietnamese B41)—were a common problem, especially when tanks were in static positions. Cyclone fencing was found to defeat these grenades, causing premature detonation in the RPG2 while rendering RPG7 detonation circuitry inert from the initial impact. A second fencing screen was usually established by command elements to protect vehicles in static positions.

The Sagger (9M14M Malyukta) antitank guided missile was first used in Vietnam in April 1972. Armor units soon learned to counter this missile by firing at the smoke plume at the launch site, causing the gunner (who controlled the wire-guided missile with a joystick) to flinch and miss the target. In the meantime, the crew of the target vehicle maneuvered it violently, in hopes of disrupting the missile's flight path, or attempted to confuse the missile's control system by throwing flares.

Tank crews used two methods to repel suicide groups with satchel charges or antitank grenades: a "tanker's grenade" (two pounds of wire- or chain-wrapped TNT lobbed over the side), and "back-scratching" (small-caliber fire by one tank at another, buttoned-up, tank that was being assaulted).

PAVN tank crews tended to be undertrained, and their tanks were inferior to their U.S. counterparts. The T-54 and T-55 used optic systems inferior to the M-48s', and their side-mounted gasoline tanks and ammunition storage were vulnerable to enemy fire. PAVN tanks initially were not well integrated with infantry and artillery units, in contrast to such highly decorated Allied units as the U.S. Army's Company A, 1st Battalion, 69th Armor.

Communist armor forces were seen only sporadically in South Vietnam and Laos before 1973. However, tanks were critical to minor Communist victories at the Lang Vei Special Forces camp (February 1968) and at LZ31, north of A Luoi, during Operation LAM SON 719 (February 1971). At An Lôc during the 1972 Easter Offensive, the PAVN employed approximately 100 tanks, 80 of which fell prey to ARVN tank-hunter teams armed with M72 light antitank weapons (LAWs) and Allied air assets. Tube-fired, optically tracked, wire-guided (TOW) missiles, mounted on UH-1B helicopters, only recently deployed, registered a remarkable number of kills.

With the U.S. military withdrawal from Vietnam in January 1973, military and material support for ARVN forces began to evaporate. In the final 1975 offensive, PAVN armor units, now better trained and integrated with infantry and artillery, proved integral in the swift conquest of South Vietnam.

—Robert J. Bunker

References: Dunstan, Simon. *Vietnam Tracks: Armor in Battle, 1945–1975* (1982); Hay, John H., Jr. *Tactical and Materiel Innovations. Vietnam Studies* (1974); Pimlott, J. C. "Armour in Vietnam" (1990); Starry, Donn A. *Armored Combat in Vietnam* (1980); Zumbro, Ralph. *Tank Sergeant* (1988).

See also: Easter Offensive (Nguyên Huê Campaign); Grenades, Launched, Allied and Democratic Republic of Vietnam; LAM SON 719, Operation; Mines, Antipersonnel and Antitank; Tanks, Allied and Democratic Republic of Vietnam

Armored Personnel Carriers (APCs)

Armored vehicles used for transporting personnel and equipment, used widely and successfully in Vietnam. Based on studies conducted by the Military Assistance and Advisory Group (MAAG), two companies of Armored Personnel Carriers (APCs) were organized in April 1962 and assigned to the Army of the Republic of Vietnam (ARVN) 7th and 21st Infantry Divisions, operating in the Mekong Delta. By January 1968 more than 2,100 APCs were operating with ARVN and American units.

Most APCs in Vietnam were variants of the M-113, the most successful and widely used APC in the non-Communist

world. The M-113, introduced in 1960 to replace the bulky M-59, carried 11 infantrymen plus a driver and was constructed from aluminum armor welded over a watertight hull. Its 1.5– to 1.75-inch armor provided ballistic protection only from shell fragments, flash burns, and small arms fire of less than .50 caliber. Not intended as a fighting platform, it was designed to carry troops to combat, where they would dismount and fight, supported by the APC's machine gun. Thus, the M-113 was a personnel carrier, not a true infantry fighting vehicle (IFV).

The first version of the M-113 was powered by highly combustible gasoline, which soon caused serious problems in combat. The diesel-powered M-113A1, introduced in 1964, reduced the combustible fuel hazard and increased the M-113's cruising range by 50 percent. The amphibious M-113 was fitted with a hinged breakwater plate (a trim vane) to maintain the vehicle's balance in water, but conditions had to be almost perfect for the M-113 to swim properly. Swamped M-113s were not uncommon.

More than 150 variants of the M-113 appeared worldwide, most based on the M-113A1. Those commonly used in Vietnam included the M-125A1, a self-propelled platform for an 81-mm mortar; the M-106A1, a self-propelled 4.2-inch mortar; and the M-132, a self-propelled flame thrower that GIs called the "Zippo." Another outstanding variant, the M-577A1 command post carrier, had a large armored box added behind the driver's compartment to provide 15 inches of additional headroom. Equipped with extra radios but no armament, M-577s were used as mobile command posts, fire direction centers, and even ambulances.

Several other APC models saw service in Vietnam. The light, underpowered M-114A1, intended as a reconnaissance vehicle, was withdrawn from service after several years. The thin-skinned M-548 tracked cargo carrier was based on the M-113 drive train. In northern South Vietnam, the Marines used their huge LVTP-5 as an APC.

Troops in Vietnam modified their newly issued M-113. Rubber mud guards, which made quick track repairs difficult in tense situations, were removed, and troop seats were replaced with more practical wooden benches. The most significant local modifications converted the M-113 to an ACAV (armored cavalry assault vehicle) by mounting an armor shield in front of the M2 machine gun, installing extra plating around the gunner's cupola, and mounting the extra 7.62-mm M60 machine gun (intended for the troops to use while dismounted) behind a small armor plate on one side of the top deck cargo hatch. Another M60 was mounted on the other side of the hatch. Thus, the M-113 evolved into the IFV it was never intended to be.

VC and PAVN quickly learned how to engage the APCs. Weapons of choice against the M-113 were the 57-mm and later the 75-mm recoilless rifle; the RPG-2 (rocket-propelled grenade) and later the more powerful RPG-7; and the antivehicular mine. All could easily destroy or cripple an M-113 with a solid hit. Chances of survival were slim inside an APG that hit a mine or was hit by an RPG, so troops often rode on the top, preferring to take their chances with small arms fire.

Only the driver usually rode inside, and casualty rates for drivers were high.

In the final analysis, the M-113 did not provide much protection, but it offered significant increases in firepower, speed, and mobility. Soldiers in the mechanized infantry and armored cavalry units grew attached to their own "tracks" and painted wild designs on them reminiscent of World War II aircraft nose art. Improved versions of the M-113 remained in U.S. Army service until they were replaced in the 1990s by the M-2 Bradley IFV. In other western armies, M-113s and variants are expected to remain in service well into the twenty-first century.

—David T. Zabecki

References: Crimson, Fred W. *U.S. Military Tracked Vehicles* (1992); Stanton, Shelby. *Vietnam Order of Battle* (1981); Starry, Donn A. *Mounted Combat in Vietnam* (1978).

Arnett, Peter (1934–)

New Zealand-born correspondent who covered the Vietnam War from 26 June 1962. Arnett's war coverage established him as high-profile reporter, but his candor created controversy. In 1963 Premier Ngô Đình Diêm, upset with Arnett's coverage of the Republic of Vietnam government's treatment of Buddhist monks, threatened to expel him from the country; on 23 July 1963, South Vietnamese secret police beat Arnett on a Sài Gòn street. Only after the Kennedy administration intervened did the Diêm regime allow Arnett to remain in South Vietnam. Arnett's forthright style also caused tension with the U.S. military establishment. Because he refused to compromise the accuracy of his stories, Arnett was targeted by the Johnson administration for surveillance. Military officials sought to limit his access to combat, but Arnett's connections with men in the field negated those efforts.

Arnett's penchant for covering difficult and revealing stories earned him a Pulitzer Prize for International Reporting in 1966. During the 1968 Têt Offensive, he reported an American officer's now-infamous statement that that U.S. forces had to destroy the village of Bên Tre in order to save it. That same year he quoted John Paul Vann's opinion that the initial U.S. troop withdrawals would consist of "nonessentials," leading readers to question the veracity of Nixon's promised troop reductions. In 1972 Arnett witnessed the release of the first U.S. prisoners of war in Hà Nôi and in 1975 covered the 1975 fall of Sài Gòn. Arnett maintains that journalists merely reported the events and did not make policy decisions.

—Dean Brumley

References: Arnett, Peter. *Live From The Battlefield: From Vietnam to Baghdad, 35 Years in the World's War Zones* (1994); Halberstam, David. *The Best and the Brightest* (1983); Karnow, Stanley. *Vietnam: A History* (1984); Sheehan, Neil. *A Bright Shining Lie: John Paul Vann and America in Vietnam* (1988).
See also: Halberstam, David; Media and the War; Ngô Đình Diêm; Vann, John Paul.

Art and the Vietnam War

Following formal U.S. troop committement to the Republic of Vietnam, New York artists collectively known as the Artists and Writers Protest (AWP) group on 18 April 1965 published the first of two open-letter advertisements in the *New York Times* intended to arouse the attention of the art community. Similarly, The Artists Protest Committee (APC) in Los Angeles began orchestrating a series of "whiteout" demonstrations in front of local museums to close down the galleries. This group later oversaw construction of the Peace Tower in Los Angeles. Designed by Mark di Suvero and erected with the help of Mel Edwards, it was decorated with 400 uniformly sized panels contributed by artists worldwide and was intended to stand from 26 February 1966 until the end of the war.

More than 600 artists gathered from 29 January to 5 February 1966 for Angry Arts Week, a series of well-received dance, art, film, poetry, and music exhibitions that served as the catalyst to a more comprehensive protest movement among artists. Included was the 10' x 150' *Collage of Indignation*, a collaborative work of more than 150 artists organized by critics Dore Ashton and Max Kozloff at New York University Student Center. Although such nascent attempts at protest aroused public consciousness, the art itself, as Leon Golub notes, was largely "not political art, but rather a popular expression of popular revulsion." Although desire to speak out against the war quickly surfaced within the artistic community, the artists had not yet perfected means of expressing through art their outrage and opposition to U.S. involvement in Vietnam. Imbued with the self-reflective values that governed the predominant art movements of the time, artists in 1967 rarely touched on social issues, convinced that political art was old-fashioned. Few possessed the prescience to break from this dominant view. As in many other aspects of American life, the Vietnam War sparked a revolution of sorts within the art world, marking the return of political art.

A few artists, most notably Wally Hedrick, produced serious responses to the Vietnam conflict as early as the late 1950s. A Korean War veteran, Hedrick knew of the troubles brewing in Vietnam under French and U.S. presence. His *Anger/Madam Nhu's Bar-B-Q* depicts a black sun with a brown penis penetrating into a red vagina, readable as a heart and a mushroom cloud, and bears the inscription "Madam Nhu Blows Chiang." A reaction to the self-immolation of Vietnamese Buddhist monks and the U.S. presence, Hedrick's early works resemble the grotesque expressions of rage common to the late 1960s, particularly evidenced in the works of Peter Saul.

Such productions were exceptions, however, as artists focused on group antiwar actions. On 2 April 1969 the Art Workers Coalition (AWC) and AWP engineered a "Mass Antiwar Mail-In" in which mailable artworks, including a papier-mâché bomb, were marched in procession to the Canal Street Post Office in New York and mailed to Washington. Public "Events" or "Happenings" also became popular during the war, especially under the guise of the Guerrilla Art Action Group (GAAG), a group consisting mainly of Jon Hendricks and Jean Toche that often performed unannounced. In October 1969 the two entered the

Museum of Modern Art and replaced Malevich's *White on White* with a manifesto denouncing poverty, war, and the enjoyment of art during wartime. At the Whitney in November 1969 they dropped a list of written demands on the floor while ripping at each other's clothes and screaming "Rape!"

By 1969 artists were beginning to produce individual pieces of protest. Jasper Johns's subtly critical poster *Moratorium* (1969)—black stars and stripes on an orange and green field with a bullet hole in the middle—stands in stark contrast to his late 1950s flag series. *Moratorium*'s colors produce an afterimage of the American flag, with the bullet hole possibly referencing lines from a Yevtushenko poem: "The stars / in your flag America / are like bullet holes." Among the most successful poster images to emerge from this period was the AWC's Poster Committee's *Q: And Babies? A: And Babies* (1970). Picturing Ronald Haeberle's graphic color photo of the My Lai massacre and titled after a Mike Wallace interview with My Lai participant Paul Meadlo, this collaborative effort of Irving Petlin, Jon Hendricks, and Fraser Dougherty was reproduced more than 50,000 times. A second version of *Q: And Babies?* surfaced in 1972, this time captioned "Four More Years?" in reference to President Nixon's reelection campaign.

By the early 1960s artists were beginning to incorporate war images into paintings, as evidenced by James Rosenquist's gigantic 10' x 86' *F-111* (1965), completed as U.S. involvement in the war was escalating. Rosenquist admitted in a 1994 interview that Vietnam influenced this work, with its dominant image of an Air Force F-111 fighter-bomber against a montage that includes a mushroom cloud shaded by a beach umbrella, a small girl seated under a hair dryer, and a large tire preparing to crush a light bulb. The red tip of the plane penetrates a field of spaghetti and tomato sauce, a clear reference to entrails. Rosenquist's 1968–1969 *Horse Blinders* dealt with the war as well. Both paintings are powerful critiques of the war and the U.S. military-industrial complex of the 1960s.

Other large works ("installations") emerged in the 1960s. Claes Oldenburg's sarcastic *Lipstick Monument* (1969), a 24'-high lipstick mounted on a red tractor-tank, was a biting commentary on how the U.S. munitions industry maintained the affluence of the 1960s. Duane Hanson's installation *War* or *Vietnam Scene* (1969) presented the gross brutality of war by contrasting realistic scenes of muddy, dead, and wounded U.S. soldiers to the clean, white galleries. Ed Kienholz contributed two major installations. In his *Portable War Memorial* (1968), a television showing the classic "I Want You" Uncle Sam poster provides the background for a group of Iwo Jima soldiers raising the American flag over an overturned cafe chair. The cafe furniture serves to link the "war" side of the work with the "peace" side, a hot dog stand emerging from a blackboard containing the names of 475 extinct countries. The two scenes are further linked by a tombstone cross in the middle of the work that commemorates "V__ Day, 19__." A young smiling couple sits at the hot dog stand, oblivious to the action. Kienholz's *Eleventh Hour*

Final (1968) denounced the media's rosy approach to the Vietnam conflict, especially criticizing the daily body-count. In an average American TV room, a television encased in a tombstone displays the daily body-count numbers over the watchful eyes of an Asian child. The remote control stretches to the couch, implicating the viewer in the televised carnage.

Reporters in South Vietnam brought home images of combat and war. Leon Golub had incorporated these combat scenes into his works since the early 1960s. In 1969 Golub did a variation on his earlier "Gigantomachy" series—monstrous, nude heroic figures engaged in battle—draping molten-looking paint across the chest of a fallen, wounded giant (subsequently titled "Napalm (I)"). In 1972 Golub expanded on this theme in his "Assassins" series (later entitled "Vietnam"), three oversized canvases, that represented a modernization of sorts for the classical Golub. The figures here were clothed in modern military garb, and the gestures, stances, and bodies of the figures moved toward naturalism. Influenced by media photos and military handbooks, Golub included machine guns and an armored car in his works. In addition, Golub cut large chunks out of his canvases to demonstrate the savage brutality of war. Although the first two works in the series depict actual battle scenes as U.S. soldiers massacre Vietnamese civilians, there remains a curious timelessness as Golub depicts the moments before the conflict, when the impending violence is being drifted into—just as the U.S. gradually drifted into Vietnam. The void between the Americans and the Vietnamese in the paintings further heightens the sense of blankness and desperation.

Peter Saul's approach was geared more toward shock. *Saigon* (1967), one of his earliest "social consciousness" canvases, demonstrates an affinity for racist and sexist pornography. The writhing, active work centers around a yellow Vietnamese prostitute labeled "innocent virgin." Also included are "her father," "her mother," and "her sister," grotesquely contorted and in the act of being severely abused by Coke-guzzling American GIs. Further confusing the canvas are eyeballs, mines, helmets, palm trees, and oriental inscriptions reading "White Boys Torturing and Raping the People of Saigon" and "High Class Version." *Typical Saigon* (1968) and *Pinkville* (1969–1970) present similar repulsive scenes in inexhaustible detail. In Saul's view, "the entire conflict was more of an opportunity for robust American farm boys to give their libidos healthy exercise than any serious attempt to resolve global political instability." *Fantastic Justice* (1968) depicts a disfigured Lyndon Johnson crucified on a yellow palm tree cross with live firecrackers in his rectum. Saul sought to evince the unabashed spectacle of a national consciousness focused on destruction.

Sam Wiener made his appeal through American dead in his 1970 work originally entitled *45,391 ... and counting*. His work is a small, open-topped box sculpture filled with six American-flag-draped coffins and lined with mirrors that cause the coffins to stretch into infinity. Following U.S. involvement in Central America, this work was retitled and resurrected in poster form.

African American artists spoke out against the war and

against racism. Cliff Joseph's 1968 *My Country, Right or Wrong* presented black and white Americans blindfolded with American flags and drifting through a sea of bombs, bones, skulls, and blood. In the periphery of the painting a cross, the star of David, and an upside-down flag reference different historical and militaristic chauvinisms.

Michael Aschenbrenner sustained a leg injury during the Têt Offensive, an experience that obviously affected him, as evidenced in his *Damaged Bone Series: Chronicle 1968* (1982). Like Aschenbrenner's art, works by John Wolfe focus less on laying blame for his experiences than on the experiences themselves. His 1986 *Incident near Phu Loc* depicts three GIs standing above a nude, spread-eagled Vietnamese woman. At least one soldier is contemplating rape; at least one other looks skeptical. Three Buddhists stand at the woman's head, proselytizing to the soldiers, while a South Vietnamese soldier arbitrates the developing confrontation. Taken as a whole, *Incident near Phu Loc* passes no judgment on the players but merely presents in unflinching sincerity events as they occurred.

Other veteran art is gentler and even somewhat regretful. Michael Page's wooden sculpture *Pieta* (1980) beautifully represents a despairing GI holding a dead Vietnamese baby in his arms. The work is particularly distinguished by the face of the soldier, who seems to be at the point of realization of what has happened, what is happening, and what lies ahead for him and his enemies. Not all veteran art bears this self-reflective quality, however. Combat artists like Leonard Cutrow and William Linzee Prescott were commissioned by the U.S. to create images to commemorate the conflict for the Armed Forces museums. In response, other veterans, such as Kim Jones, commemorated the war on their own terms. With mud-caked boots, body-stockinged face, and a bundle of bound sticks jutting from his back and head, Jones adopts the persona of the Mudman to help the public remember the legacy of the Vietnam War. Appearing unannounced at art galleries and the Vietnam Veterans Memorial in Washington, the Mudman exists as the Lazarus who reminds us not of the political maelstrom surrounding the Vietnam conflict, but instead of harsh reality, resisting any popular effort to sanitize the war in retrospect.

No piece of artwork, however, better captures the spirit of conflict and controversy surrounding the war than does the Vietnam Veterans Memorial in Washington, D.C. Heated debate over the extent to which memorials should combine war and politics marred Maya Lin's effort to honor American casualties, and eventually Frederick Hart was commissioned to supplement Lin's work with a statue of three soldiers. There is nothing heroic about the monument, and the memorial makes no reference to the political turmoil of the era. Instead, it merely honors the patriotic service of the veterans themselves. Contemplative in nature, the Memorial's main purpose is therapeutic. Thus the artwork is apolitical, leaving viewers to come to their own conclusions regarding the Vietnam War.

—John Gregory Perdue, Jr.

References: Cameron, Dan. "The Trials of Peter Saul" (January 1990). Castelli, Leo. *James Rosenquist: The Big Paintings* (1994);

Castleman, Riva. *Jasper Johns: A Print Retrospective* (1986); Lippard, Lucy R. *A Different War: Vietnam in Art* (1990); Marzorati, Gerald. "Leon Golub's Mean Streets" (1985); Mitchell, W. J. T., ed. *Art and the Public Sphere* (1990); Norris, Margot. "Painting Vietnam Combat: The Art of Leonard Cutrow" (1989); Safer, Morley. "Prescott's War" (1991); Walsh, Jeffrey, and James Aulich, eds. *Vietnam Images* (1989). **See also:** Drama and the Vietnam Experience; Film and the Vietnam Experience; Goldman, Eric F.; Media and the War; Poetry and the Vietnam Experience; Prose Narrative and the Vietnam Experience; Vietnam Veterans Memorial.

Artillery, Allied and People's Army of Vietnam

The U.S. Army used towed and self-propelled artillery in Vietnam. The vast majority of the U.S. weapons were howitzers. The most widely used U.S. artillery piece in Vietnam was the venerable M101A1 towed 105-mm howitzer, a slightly modified version of the U.S. mainstay in World War II and Korea. Probably the most widely used artillery piece in history, the M101A1 was finally phased out of U.S. service in the early 1990s but will remain in the inventory of other armies well into the twenty-first century.

The M102 towed 105-mm howitzer, a new design particularly suited to the Vietnam environment, arrived in March 1966. At almost a ton lighter than the M101A1, more ammunition could be carried when the gun was helicopter lifted. Its much lower silhouette made it a more difficult target for enemy ground fire. Rather than being stabilized by conventional spades and trails as with the M101A1, the M102 used a firing platform mounted in the center of its undercarriage. This gave the M102 the ability to traverse 360 degrees. The M101A1 could traverse only about 25 degrees right and left, and firing on targets outside the arc of traverse required pulling the spades out of the ground and relaying the gun, all of which took time.

The M109 155-mm howitzer saw its first combat service in Vietnam and has since become the most widely used self-propelled (SP) weapon in the world. With upgrades, it will remain in the U.S. arsenal for many years to come. The M107 SP 175-mm gun was the longest-range artillery weapon of the war, but it was fairly inaccurate. The M110 SP 8-inch howitzer had the same motor carriage and gun mount as the M107. With its 200-poundshell, the M110 packed the heaviest punch of all U.S. artillery and was amomg the most accurate artillery pieces in the world.

The U.S. Army used two semiobsolete air defense systems in a ground fire role in Vietnam. The M42A1 SP twin 40-mm automatic cannon and the truck-mounted M55 .50–caliber quad-machine gun were widely used for perimeter defense and convoy escort. Not in the active Army inventory at the start of the war, the weapons were recalled from National Guard and Army Reserve units. During the Vietnam War, an air defense artillery battalion armed with the M42A1 "Duster" was usually augmented with an additional air defense artillery battery armed with the M55 "Quad 50."

The Việt Công (VC) generally did not have conventional artillery and relied on mortars and rockets for their fire support. Occasionally the VC used U.S.-made 75-mm pack howitzers, which Communist forces had captured from the French years earlier. The People's Army of Vietnam (PAVN) was well equipped with Soviet-designed artillery and some captured U.S. weapons. The American M101A1 was used by both sides at Ðiên Biên Phu, where the Viêt Minh overwhelmingly out-gunned the French artillery. Some older Soviet-designed guns, such as the M46 and M38, were actually Chinese made. During the early part of the Vietnam War, PAVN artillery was deployed mostly along the Demilitarized Zone. Later in the war the PAVN moved more of its big guns into the south. The PAVN/VC used some 400 artillery pieces in their 1975 final offensive. During the final attack in the Central Highlands, PAVN artillery had a two-to-one superiority over the Army of the Republic of Vietnam (ARVN).

The basic shell for all artillery is the high-explosive (HE) round. It produces both blast and fragmentation effects, the latter usually being the most lethal to troops. Different fuzes produce different effects. The most commonly used fuze is the point detonating fuze (called "Fuze Quick"). The time (TI) fuze is used to achieve air bursts of varying heights. The fragmentation pattern from an air burst is always much more deadly than from a ground burst. The variable time (VT) fuze is a proximity fuze that produces a 20–meter-high air burst, generally considered the optimal height of burst. Concrete piercing (CP) fuzes are effective against bunkers, and delay (D) fuzes are used to penetrate thick jungle canopy.

The 8-inch and 175-mm guns fired mostly HE projectiles. The 105-mm howitzers had the widest range of ammunition types. Although not designed as an antitank gun, the 105-mm did have high-explosive antitank (HEAT) ammunition, which were very effective against bunkers. Other specialized shells included the smoke round, for signaling and screening; the white phosphorus round, for quickly establishing a smoke screen and for incendiary effect; and the illumination round, which deposited a parachute flare 600 feet above the target. The 105-mm howitzer also had a leaflet scattering round, which was rarely used in Vietnam. Not used at all in Vietnam were various types of gas rounds and nuclear rounds.

Two new types of artillery ammunition were introduced in Vietnam, both old ideas wrapped in new technology. The antipersonnel (APERS) round fired 8,000 one-inch-long steel flechettes. It was designed to defend fire bases from ground attack by firing almost point-blank into attacking enemy formations. Code-named the BEEHIVE round, it was simply a revival of the old canister round that had proved so deadly in the days of muzzle-loading artillery. The first major use of BEEHIVE came on 21 March 1967, during the 2nd Battalion, 77th Artillery's defense of Fire Support Base Gold. The improved conventional munition (ICM) round was a new application of the World War I shrapnel round. An artillery-fired version of a cluster bomb, the shell itself is little more than a cargo carrier that transports the bomblets and ejects them into the air over the target. Code named FIRECRACKER, the 105-mm ICM round carried 18 bomblets, the 155-mm round carried 60, and the huge 8-inch round carried 104. The first ICM round was fired in combat by Battery C, 1st Battalion, 40th Artillery on 12 February 1968 in the northern I Corps Tactical Zone.

Every U.S. division normally had one battalion of direct support (DS) artillery for each maneuver brigade, and a battalion of general support (GS) artillery for the entire division. DS battalions had 105-mm howitzers, with three batteries of six guns each. GS battalions normally had 155-mm howitzers. In some cases divisional GS battalions were composite units of 155-mm towed howitzers and 8-inch SP howitzers, or 175-mm guns and 8-inch howitzers. The heavy 8-inch and 175-mm batteries had only four guns each. During the war the U.S. Army put 68 artillery battalions into Vietnam to support 93 maneuver battalions. The total figure included 32 105-mm towed and two 105-mm SP battalions; seven 155-mm towed and five 155-mm SP battalions; five composite battalions of 155-mm and 8-inch; twelve composite battalions of 175-mm and 8-inch; two aerial rocket artillery battalions; and three 40-mm Duster battalions. Five separate target acquisition batteries provided survey control, meteorological data, and radar support; and four separate searchlight batteries provided battlefield illumination. Two of the 155-mm battalions—the 2nd Battalion, 138th Artillery, and the 3rd Battalion, 197th Artillery—were National Guard units. The nondivisional artillery units, for the most part larger than 105 mm, were organized into five artillery groups. The 41st and 52nd Artillery Groups supported I Field Forces; the 23rd and 54th Artillery Groups supported II Field Forces; and the 108th Artillery Group supported IV Corps.

The U.S. Marine Corps 1st Field Artillery Group consisted of the 11th and 12th Marine Regiments, totaling ten artillery battalions. The Marines also had five separate batteries and a searchlight battery. Among the Allied forces, New Zealand had one artillery battery; Australia and the Philippines had an artillery battalion each; Thailand had a three-battalion artillery brigade; and South Korea had six 105-mm battalions and two 155-mm battalions.

In 1972 the ARVN had 44 battalions of 105-mm howitzers; 15 battalions of 155-mm howitzers; and 5 battalions of 175-mm SP guns. By 1975 most of these weapons had passed into the PAVN arsenal. During the 1972 Easter Offensive alone, the ARVN lost 117 guns and howitzers, enough to arm six and a half battalions.

—David T. Zabecki

References: Caruthers, Lawrence H. "Characteristics and Capabilities of Enemy Weapons" (1970); Ott, David E. *Field Artillery, 1954–1973* (1975); Scales, Robert H., Jr. *Firepower in Limited War* (1995); Stanton, Shelby. *Vietnam Order of Battle* (1981).

See also: Ðiên Biên Phu, Battle of; Harassment and Interdiction (H&I) Fires; Mortars, Allied and Democratic Republic of Vietnam; Rockets; Rules of Engagement (ROE); Vessey, John W.

Artillery Fire Doctrine

The two basic elements of combat power are maneuver and firepower. Maneuver is the movement of combat forces to gain positional advantage, psychological shock, physical momentum, and massed effects. Firepower is the destructive force essential to defeating an enemy's ability and will to fight. As a revolutionary war, Vietnam might have seemed like an ideal environment for maneuver to dominate. The U.S. military, however, had a longstanding tradition of heavy reliance on firepower, and Vietnam was no exception. Until the twentieth century, artillery was almost the sole source of battlefield firepower. During the Vietnam War firepower support also came from helicopters and tactical aircraft. The challenge for ground commanders was to integrate these forms of firepower with the scheme of maneuver to produce the desired tactical effect.

Most field artillery units had a mission of either direct support (DS) or general support (GS). A division normally had one DS artillery battalion for each maneuver brigade, plus a GS battalion to provide fires for the whole division. Nondivisional artillery units were organized into artillery groups, which had a mission of providing general support to an entire corps (called "field forces" in Vietnam). For some specific operations, nondivisional artillery could be given the mission of reinforcing the fires of a divisional unit. In the absence of large divisional operations in Vietnam, most nondivisional artillery units were used to provide support for a specific geographical area.

When supporting a brigade, the DS artillery battalion normally had three firing batteries of six guns each. In Vietnam, however, operations tended to be fragmented and dispersed, and the guns had to disperse, a violation of the time-proven principle that artillery is effective only when fired in mass. During the Vietnam War the enemy rarely presented massed targets for Allied artillery.

Starting at the company level, every echelon in the maneuver chain of command had a fire support coordinator (FISCOORD). The company FISCOORD was the company commander, but he was assisted in this task by a forward observer (FO) from the DS artillery battalion. FOs generally were the most junior lieutenants in the artillery. Nonetheless, good FOs were highly prized by their infantry units, and a company commander usually kept his FO within arm's reach. The enemy also appreciated the extra combat power the FO represented and made special efforts to identify and kill him quickly if possible.

At the maneuver battalion, the FISCOORD was the artillery liaison officer (LNO), a more senior captain also supplied by the DS artillery battalion. Quite often, the artillery LNO worked from a command and control (C2) helicopter, along with the supported maneuver battalion commander and his operations officer (S-3). The LNO was responsible for coordinating all fires for the battalion, not just artillery-delivered fires. Thus the LNO had to ensure that artillery, helicopters, and tactical air were synchronized on the target, yet separated from each other in time and space to preclude midair collisions. Making the task more complicated, radios in Army and Air Force strike aircraft were incompatible. Operating a bank of radios in the C2 helicopter, the LNO had to pass messages and commands back and forth between FOs on the ground, Army helicopters in the air, and Air Force forward air controllers (FACs) on the ground or in the air, who then talked to the Air Force aircraft.

The commander of the DS artillery battalion was the designated FISCOORD for the brigade, and the division artillery (DIVARTY) commander was the FISCOORD for the division. In practice, assistant FISCOORDs at the brigade and division fire support coordination centers (FSCCs) performed the day-to-day tasks.

When a company FO called for fire on the radio, his request went directly to the battery or battalion (depending on the situation) fire direction center (FDC). The LNO at the maneuver battalion monitored the call and had the authority to cancel or modify the request. If the LNO failed to intervene, his silence implied consent and the mission continued. The fire direction officer (FDO) made the final determination and issued the fire order. The FDC crew then computed the data and sent the fire commands to the gun crews.

Most FDCs in Vietnam, especially in the later years, were equipped with FADAC, the U.S. Army's first digital fire direction computer, a notoriously cranky piece of equipment that was often inoperable. It also was slow, requiring two-thirds of the projectile time of flight for an initial solution. Where FADAC excelled was in handling multiple fire missions simultaneously.

Artillery was (and still is) the fastest of the fire support means. Under ideal conditions, a well-trained battery had the technical capability of placing rounds on the target within two to three minutes of the FO's initial request. In Vietnam, however, the actual average was approximately six minutes for light artillery and thirteen minutes for heavy guns, which often had to shift their trails to fire. Even longer delays were caused by the political nature of the war itself. In populated areas, the local Vietnamese sector headquarters had to approve the mission before it could be fired. Later in the war, Air Warning Control Centers (AWCCs) were established to broadcast warnings to all friendly aircraft in the area, adding another element of delay. Still, artillery was much more responsive than tactical air.

Vietnam warped the traditional relationships between firepower and maneuver in subtle ways. On the strategic level, the front line of the war may have been the DMZ and the Cambodian border, but on the operational and tactical levels there were no front lines. The war was circular, not linear; the enemy could be anywhere. This, combined with the dense jungle in which actions were fought, reduced the effectiveness of envelopments, turning movements, and the other classical forms of tactical maneuver.

Company commanders quickly learned that adding more friendly infantry to a fight often led to more friendly casualties, concern over which was another factor inhibiting maneuver in Vietnam. The preservation of soldiers' lives was the overriding tactical imperative, driven by shaky political support for the war at home, close media scrutiny, and the lack of clearly defined objectives. Faced with these tactical, social, and political imperatives, the only alternate course of action was to give massive firepower primacy over maneuver. The prevailing philosophy became "bullets, not bodies." The United States, with its abundant materiel resources, could do this easily. But in so doing, it provided the worst sort of role model for the Army of the Republic of Vietnam (ARVN), which lacked resources but knew no other way of operating once it had to fight on its own. Thus, infantry units in Vietnam maneuvered to first find the enemy, and then to take up the best position from which to call in and direct overwhelming fire assets to finish the job. The automatic response to bring in heavy firepower meant that infantry units had to stay at least 200 to 300 meters from the enemy to avoid becoming casualties of their own supporting fires. The Viêt Công (VC) and People's Army of Vietnam (PAVN) quickly recognized this weakness and developed "hugging tactics," which brought them in so close that Allied firepower became unusable. Some U.S. commanders decried the overdependence on firepower and the corresponding loss of infantry maneuver skills. They advocated the adoption of guerrilla tactics, but even these minority voices recognized that U.S. firepower was the final trump card.

The VC and PAVN most feared the cordon, an operation that began with multiple helicopter assault landings to isolate and encircle an enemy unit in its base camp. Once on the ground, Allied troops formed a perimeter, and when the cordon was sealed, everything inside was systematically pounded with air and artillery firepower. Slow and methodical to avoid casualties from friendly fire, it became even more careful as infantry moved toward the center, shrinking the circle and the target area. If set up properly and sprung quickly, cordon operations were very effective.

Early in the war, fire bases were little more than temporary artillery emplacements established to support infantry operating in a given area. But after Communist forces drastically scaled back operations after the 1968 Têt Offensive, the Allies began using fire bases as a means to lure the enemy into firepower traps.

Fire bases thus became semipermanent fortresses with dug-in gun pits, bunkers, and sandbags. Although this basic tactic had failed the French on a grand scale at Điên Biên Phu, it was a success for the Americans (on the tactical level at least) because they had the artillery and air assets to overwhelmingly reinforce any fire base that came under attack. As a result, many infantry units were reduced to little more than perimeter security guards for the fire bases, and U.S. artillery positions routinely came under direct ground attack more than at any other time since the Civil War. Artillerymen devised ways to defend themselves, including the flechette-firing "Beehive" round and "Killer Junior," a high-explosive round set to detonate 30 feet off the ground at ranges between 200 and 1,000 meters. Communist forces never overran a U.S. fire base.

Operating from fire bases required new ways of thinking. In Vietnam the "front" was in all directions, and only 50 or 100 meters away. The solution was to position the guns on a fire base in either a diamond (four-gun battery) or a star (six-gun battery) formation so the guns could fire in any direction and the pattern of rounds (a "sheaf") would be the same. Setting up to fire in all directions also required special preparations in the gun pits and modifications to the firing charts in the FDC. The fire base concept led to a sharp increase in worth-

less harassment and interdiction (H&I) fire, random rounds fired at suspected enemy locations and routes. H&I became slightly more effective later in the war with the introduction of sophisticated remote sensors, which served as firing cues, but in general H&I fire was largely a waste of ammunition, accounting for some 60 percent of all artillery fire during the war.

From a systems analysis standpoint, artillery fire in Vietnam was rather ineffective. But these results were no different than in other wars. Artillery is effective only when used in conjunction with maneuver to produce a synergistic effect. This did not happen during the Vietnam War. Early in the war, U.S. policy makers opted for a war of attrition based in part on unrealistic expectations of the ability of American firepower to send a persuasive message. Robert H. Scales, Jr., best summarized the principal firepower lesson of the Vietnam War: "Overwhelming firepower cannot compensate for bad strategy."

—David T. Zabecki

References: Bailey, Jonathan B. A. *Field Artillery and Firepower* (1987); Ott, David E. *Field Artillery, 1954–1973* (1975); Scales, Robert H., Jr. *Firepower in Limited War* (1995); U.S. Department of the Army. *FM 6–40 Field Artillery Cannon Gunnery* (1967).
See also: Artillery, Allied and People's Army of Vietnam; Điên Biên Phu, Battle of; Rules of Engagement (ROE).

Assimilation versus Association

Terms used to describe conflicting French colonial policies. Assimilation professed the universality of French civilization and attempted to bridge the gap between humanitarianism and the actualities of French colonial role. It was bound up in the term *mission civilisatrice* (civilizing mission), a kind of generous cultural imperialism that suggested the French government should make the colonies carbon-copies of France in institutions and in culture. The pull of assimilation was strongest in the late nineteenth century.

By 1905 association rather than assimilation held sway in France. Association held that France should work with native leaders and concentrate on economic policies, leaving cultural patterns largely untouched. Associationists attacked assimilationists on pragmatic grounds, believing that volume of trade mattered more than the number of civilized souls. Associationists believed that Franco-native cooperation was indeed possible. After the Russo-Japanese War (1904–1905) the idea of association also received support in some military circles that saw Japan as endeavoring to control all of south Asia.

—Spencer C. Tucker

References: Buttinger, Joseph. *The Smaller Dragon: A Political History of Vietnam* (1968); Thompson, Virginia. *French Indo-China* (1968).
See also: Beau, Jean-Baptiste-Paul; Cochin China; Doumer, Paul; Ferry, Jules; Le Myre de Vilers, Charles Marie.

Association of Foreign Correspondents in Vietnam (AFCV)

The Association of Foreign Correspondents in Vietnam (AFCV) represented foreign journalists from all media with the South Vietnamese government, foreign embassies, and international organizations such as the International Press Institute and the International Committee of the Red Cross. In 1970 AFCV membership totaled 66. To draw attention to the disappearance in Cambodia of a large number of foreign journalists, the AFCV distributed a list of the missing, dates and places of disappearance, and their credentials, which was circulated to the various parties to the conflict.

—Arthur J. Dommen

See also: Media and the War.

ATLAS WEDGE, Operation (18 March–2 April 1969)

Joint military operation conducted along Highway 13 north of Sài Gòn in the Michelin Rubber Plantation area. ATLAS WEDGE was part of the larger TOÀN THANG III Operation that began on 17 February 1969. For ATLAS WEDGE, the 1st Infantry ("Big Red One") Division exercised operational control of the 11th Armored Cavalry ("Blackhorse") Regiment (ACR) and worked with the 25th Infantry ("Tropic Lightning") and 1st Cavalry ("The First Team") Divisions. Combat activities consisted of reconnaissance in force, night ambush patrols, land clearing, and route security. The U.S. was poised to enact the Vietnamization program with emphasis on securing the local hamlets from Viêt Công (VC) and People's Army of Vietnam (PAVN) infiltration and control, while providing support to Army of the Republic of Vietnam (ARVN) units that ultimately had to manage the operational area.

The 1st Division's 3rd Brigade committed one armor and two infantry battalions, plus the division's cavalry squadron (1st Squadron, 4th Cavalry, the "Quarterhorse"). The Blackhorse Regiment provided two cavalry squadrons and its air cavalry troop to give a heavy, armored punch to ATLAS WEDGE.

The operation's target was the 7th PAVN Division. The Blackhorse Regiment's air cavalry troop had effectively engaged large PAVN groups in the Michelin Plantation on 18 March. A major contact was developed by the Quarterhorse on 30 March at the southern end of the Michelin's heavily wooded area. Hit by rocket-propelled grenades, the cavalrymen pursued a platoon-sized PAVN force northward until coming under fire from both sides of the road. The mounted column reacted to the ambush by maneuvering their armored personnel carriers (APCs) into a "herringbone" formation so that all automatic weapons could be fired at the attackers. Charlie Troop, supported on its left flank by a company of tanks, began to move on line to the south when the left flank came under fire from low, heavily fortified bunkers. Bravo Troop moved through Charlie Troop to continue the attack. This armored force, supported by artillery and air strikes, exacted a heavy toll on PAVN soldiers boxed in the killing zone in fierce close combat.

U.S. forces killed 421 PAVN soldiers, captured tons of rice, and seized large quantities of small arms and ammunition. U.S. losses were 20 soldiers killed and 100 wounded. Operation ATLAS WEDGE was followed on 10 April by Operation ATLAS POWER, which featured armor and

infantry attacks into the same operational area after it had been pounded by B-52 strikes.

—John F. Votaw

References: Haldane, Robert, ed. First Infantry Division in Vietnam (1993); Summers, Harry G., Jr. Vietnam War Almanac (1985).

See also: Airborne Operations; TOÀN THANG (Complete Victory), Operation; United States: Army.

Atrocities during the Vietnam War

Situations in which an unarmed, nonresisting noncombatant or prisoner died as the result of small-arms fire, beating, or other corporal assault. The Viêt Công (VC) practice of seeking refuge in the guise of civilians frustrated and infuriated U.S. troops and led to misdirected reprisals. Likewise, the VC perpetrated a number of massacres to achieve political ends.

Most U.S. atrocities occurred because of the nature of the American response to guerrilla tactics. Small units patrolled the countryside in pursuit of the VC, who left mines or punji pits in their wake. Viciously efficient, these booby traps killed or maimed many GIs, leaving their frightened and angry comrades with no means for revenge. Veterans regaled newly arrived soldiers with tales of buddies who had been blown up while buying soft drinks or cigarettes from children. Although only a small minority of U.S. soldiers in Vietnam experienced an ambush or encountered mines or booby traps, the stories created an atmosphere of distrust toward all Vietnamese civilians.

Retribution, or "payback," took several forms; mutilation was by far the most prevalent. A horrific U.S. atrocity occurred in 1966, when members of an off-duty battery support unit staked a young Vietnamese girl to the ground. and set fire to her. Some GIs took target practice on farmers or their stock. The torture of captured VC suspects ranged from bare-knuckle beatings to forcible ejection from airborne helicopters. Members of the Republic of Vietnam (RVN) police accompanying U.S. units in the field occasionally served as executioners. U.S. forces also committed atrocities in a more organized fashion. Phoenix teams, introduced in 1967 to weaken the VC infrastructure and cripple its capacity for espionage and terrorism, became known as "heads and ears guys" for the decapitations that were their trademark.

Some routine operations degenerated into massacres. Early in 1967, after a three-day engagement that resulted in heavy U.S. casualties, Marines entered the village Thuy Bo and, by their own account, shot anything that moved. In 1968 three companies of the American Division committed the best-known atrocities of the war at My Lai. Although U.S. forces met with little or no resistance, estimates of Vietnamese civilian dead ranged from 100 to 400 women, children, and elderly men.

As support for the war waned, and pressure for some indication of success mounted, body counts became increasingly inflated, and some commanders offered extra R&R to units with the highest counts. Many GIs interpreted the incentive as tacit approval for indiscriminate killings. In this context, such horrendous practices as counting the pregnant dead as two kills became a sort of morbid "bargain."

The VC engaged in atrocities as well, but in different situations and for different reasons. Emotional outbursts triggered U.S. atrocities and, excluding some Phoenix operations, few were planned as such. In contrast, the Vietnamese communists killed systematically, most often with a political end in mind. The VC assassinated village leaders, disemboweling and decapitating them in full view of the village to demonstrate their primacy in a given area. They also used terror tactics during the 1968 Tết offensive, most notably in Huê. Communist operatives abducted "enemies" and clubbed, shot, or buried them alive. VC units skinned or eviscerated captured GIs and hung the the defiled corpses in the paths of American patrols.

Little evidence exists to suggest that the VC committed rape as a matter of course. The same cannot be said of American soldiers. As early as 1966, a reconnaissance patrol in the Central Highlands embarked on a mission with explicit orders to kidnap a Vietnamese girl. The team commander gave the men instructions to carry the girl along for some "boom-boom," and then kill her when the operation was completed. In 1968 a company commander in the American division reportedly stood 60 feet away from a group of soldiers who raped and sodomized two Vietnamese nurses. Seven Marines stationed at a hospital in Đà Nang murdered a South Vietnamese nurse after raping her repeatedly. Women suspected of collaborating with the VC had their vaginas sewn shut or their breasts branded with heated bayonets.

Allied Republic of Korea (ROK) units also contributed to the gruesome litany of human suffering. A surprise mine detonation triggered the 1968 action at Phong Nghi in which the Koreans leveled the village. Evidence suggested they shot women and children at point-blank range. It is unclear whether the Korean troops involved in the Phong Nghi massacre received disciplinary action.

At least some war crimes did not go unpunished. Between 1965 and 1971, courts-martial convicted 201 Army personnel and 77 Marines of murder, rape, and assault. More than three-quarters of these came after public revelation of the My Lai massacre in September 1969. More enlisted men served time than did officers, and few of either group served their entire sentences.

The Vietnam conflict was especially "dirty." The U.S. Army may have conducted ground operations with less concern for the civilian population than in the two world wars or Korea. The perception of the Vietnam war as "atrocity-ridden," however, owes as much to the various sociopolitical contexts of American wars in this century as to any illegal military action.

—Benjamin C. Dubberly

References: Caputo, Philip. *A Rumor of War* (1977); Ebert, James R. *A Life in a Year* (1993); Karnow, Stanley. *Vietnam: A History* (1991); Lewy, Guenter. *America in Vietnam* (1978); MacPherson, Myra. *Long Time Passing* (1984).

See also: Body Count; Booby Traps; My Lai Massacre; Search and Destroy.

ATTLEBORO, Operation (5–25 November 1966)

Major military operation in War Zone C. ATTLEBORO had modest beginnings in September 1966 as a single battalion air assault followed by a search-and-destroy mission in a tactical area of operations north and west of Tri Tâm (Dâu Tiêng). By the end of November it had gradually expanded into a confrontation between the resurgent 9th Viêt Công (VC) Division and more than 22,000 Allied troops. The U.S. 196th Light Infantry Brigade conducted battalion-sized operations in the area with very few VC contacts until late October, when the 1st Infantry ("Big Red One") Division encountered a battalion of the 9th VC Division's 273rd Regiment just east of the ATTLEBORO area. The 196th expanded the operation to include the entire brigade, reinforced by a battalion from the 25th Infantry ("Tropic Lightning") Division.

In early November contacts with units of the 9th VC Division near Dâu Tiêng and the Special Forces camp at Suôi Đá led to expansion of the operation, with command passing first to the Big Red One Division, then to II Field Force, the U.S. corps-sized headquarters near Sài Gòn. ATTLEBORO had become the largest U.S. joint operation of the war to date.

The Allies destroyed the 9th VC Division's extensive base area, including shops and factories. ATTLEBORO reduced the effectiveness of one of the first-echelon VC divisions for about six months, but did not knock it out of the war. More importantly for the U.S. and its allies, ATTLEBORO suggested that large numbers of battalions could arrive quickly in an operational area to confront major VC and PAVN troop concentrations and bring them to battle. ATTLEBORO set the scene for Operations CEDAR FALLS and JUNCTION CITY.

Several pitched battles occurred between Allied forces and the Communist forces, but the fight at Âp Cha Đo on 8 November was perhaps the most significant of the operation. On 4 November, II Field Force (IIFFV) commander Lt. Gen. Jonathan O. Seaman committed the Big Red One to ATTLEBORO. The division's 3d Brigade closed into Suôi Đá and its 1st Battalion, 28th Infantry moved by helicopter to a landing zone north of Suôi Đá on 6 November. The landing zone had been cleared by the 2d Battalion, 28th Infantry, which was located nearby. Both battalions were in defensive positions by nightfall on 7 November after a day of vigorous patrolling and small skirmishes.

Early on 8 November, the 1st Battalion's commander commenced a reconnaissance-by-fire using mortars, which prematurely triggered intense small arms fire from VC units that had assembled during the night. The first Communist assault fell on the defensive perimeter at 0620, followed by others in rapid succession. The 1st Battalion brought withering artillery fire and air strikes on the attacking VC soldiers. By 1130 the battle was over.

The 2d Battalion swept through the battle area and discovered an enormous Communist base camp, large enough to support the 9th VC Division's operations. Captured documents revealed that the 101st PAVN Regiment and the 272d VC Regiment, both assigned to the 9th VC Division, had been engaged in the battle at Âp Cha Đo. They lost nearly

400 soldiers killed, compared with 21 Americans killed and 42 wounded.

This battle demonstrated that in a stand-up fight between large U.S. units and equivalent VC and PAVN units, the advantage lay with the Allies because of their maneuverability and firepower. Operations CEDAR FALLS and JUNCTION CITY, both of which followed ATTLEBORO by several months, again demonstrated that disparity. But a string of successful battles did not necessarily guarantee strategic victory in Vietnam.

—John F. Votaw

References: Haldane, Robert, ed. *First Infantry Division In Vietnam* (1993); Krepinevich, Andrew F., Jr. *The Army and Vietnam* (1986); Palmer, Bruce, Jr. *The 25-year War: America's Military Role in Vietnam* (1984); Rogers, Bernard William. *Cedar Falls-Junction City: A Turning Point* (1974).

See also: CEDAR FALLS, Operation; JUNCTION CITY, Operation; Palmer, Bruce, Jr.; War Zone C and War Zone D.

Attrition

Military strategy adopted by General William Westmoreland to win the Vietnam War. Also referred to as the "body count" syndrome, attrition became the measure of progress of a war in which neither conquering enemy territory nor winning total victory were U.S. objectives. To Westmoreland and his supporters, the attrition strategy appeared to be the quickest way to end hostilities, and it also preserved the traditional mission of the U.S. Infantry—to find, fight, and destroy the enemy. Its goal was to cajole the Viêt Công (VC) and People's Army of Vietnam (PAVN) to fight a midintensity war. U.S. forces would then destroy their opponents at a rate faster than the Democratic Republic of Vietnam (DRV) or VC could replace them. Despite its elegant logic, the attrition strategy suffered from four basic problems.

First, it did not account for the American people's historical antipathy toward long, drawn-out conflicts, especially in the absence of a formal declaration of war. This hostility collided with two revealing statistics: The DRV had 13 million people available for military service during the war and, unlike other nations that historically capitulated when they lost 2 percent of their prewar population, Hà Nôi consistently accepted losses closer to 3 percent and showed no signs of surrender. Given these numbers, U.S. military analysts determined by 1969 that the attrition strategy had failed, concluding that the DRV could have continued the war until 1981.

A second problem was that the attrition strategy tried to turn what was largely a jungle insurgency into a conventional, European-style war. In other words, Westmoreland and his staff assumed that the DRV had objectives, strategies, and tactics similar to their own. But Vietnam was a war unlike anything the United States had ever fought. The U.S. Army's emphasis on body counts and conventional warfare did not match the DRV's Maoist, largely unconventional strategy.

A third problem was that attrition was not compatible with the U.S. Army's pacification program. Not only did it pull U.S. troops away from the people, it typically allowed Hà Nôi to determine when and where combat would occur.

Communist commanders could control their own attrition rates to a level low enough to sustain the war indefinitely and fatigue U.S. forces to the point of defeat.

Lastly, the attrition strategy indirectly eroded the moral fiber of U.S. forces. As it became increasingly difficult to distinguish insurgents from civilians, some U.S. units became less concerned about inflicting civilian casualties. Field commanders began padding reports of enemy dead to make themselves appear more promotable in what they saw as a dead-end war. The attrition strategy severely damaged a once-proud force by fostering careerism and criminality.

—Adam J. Stone

References: Krepinevich, Andrew F., Jr. *The Army and Vietnam* (1986) Lewy, Guenter. *America in Vietnam* (1978); Palmer, Bruce, Jr. *The 25-year War: America's Military Role in Vietnam* (1984).

See also: Body Count; Casualties; Westmoreland, William Childs.

August Revolution (1945)

Proclamation of a sovereign Vietnamese government in August 1945. When Japan surrendered at the end of World War II, Hô Chí Minh stepped into the vacuum and on 16 August declared himself president of the provisional government of a "free Vietnam." On 19 August the Viêt Minh seized power in Hà Nôi. Five days later in Sài Gòn, Trân Van Giàu declared the insurrection under way in the South. Hô held his first cabinet meeting on the 27th, at which time it was decided to fix 2 September as National Independence Day. On that day Hô publicly announced the formation of a Provisional Government of the Democratic Republic of Vietnam with its capital at Hà Nôi.

—Spencer C. Tucker

References: Marr, David G. *Vietnam 1945. The Quest for Power* (1995); Patti, Archimedes L. A. *Why Viet Nam? Prelude to America's Albatross* (1980).

See also: Hô Chí Minh; Viêt Minh (Viêt Nam Độc Lâp Đông Minh Hôi [Vietnam Independence League]); Vietnam, Democratic Republic of: 1945–1954.

Australia

Charter member of the Southeast Asia Treaty Organization (SEATO), Australia had long been concerned that a Communist victory in Vietnam would threaten democracies throughout Asia. In 1962 Australia sent the Australian Army Training Team Vietnam (AATTV), a 30–man team of jungle warfare experts, to assist in training the Republic of Vietnam Army. In 1964 Australia increased its commitment to the Republic of Vietnam (RVN) in response to President Johnson's call for "Free World Military Forces" to forge an alliance of "Many Flags" in South Vietnam. Australia joined 40 nations in providing support to the RVN. By 1964 the AATTV had been increased to 80 personnel, many of whom worked with U.S. Special Forces and accompanied ARVN units in active operations. For command purposes, the Australians were integrated into the U.S. advisory framework.

In April 1965, the Australian government agreed to send combat troops to South Vietnam. In June 1965 the 1st Battalion, Royal Australian Regiment (RAR), augmented by the 79th Signal Troop and a logistical support company, was deployed to South Vietnam. This force of approximately 1,400 troops was attached to the U.S. 173d Airborne Brigade. Operating from Biên Hòa, the 1st Battalion was limited primarily to local security operations during the rest of 1965 but gained invaluable experience in a series of helicopter-borne operations in War Zone D. That same year New Zealand sent a 105-mm howitzer battery to South Vietnam, also attached to the 173d Airborne Brigade, with the primary mission of supporting the Australians. This force became known as 1RAR Group.

In March 1966 the Australian government agreed to increase its troop commitment in South Vietnam. The 1st Battalion, RAR, returned to Australia in June 1966 and was replaced by the First Australian Task Force (ATF), formed from the newly arrived 5th and 6th Battalions, RAR, and associated logistical support elements. The senior military headquarters for Australian forces in South Vietnam was a joint command known as Headquarters, Australian Forces Vietnam in Sài Gòn. The Australians were anxious for the ATF to have its own operational area in which it could conduct semi-independent operations, rather than as a subordinate of a U.S. command. Accordingly, the ATF was placed under the operational control of II Field Force and given its own tactical area of responsibility in Phuoc Tuy Province southeast of Sài Gòn. The ATF commenced full offensive combat operations shortly after it was formed and moved to Bà Ria. It was eventually bolstered by a Special Air Service squadron of commandos, a medium tank squadron, a helicopter squadron, artillery, engineer, signal, supply, and other support forces, to include a field hospital. Additionally, a New Zealand unit, including two infantry companies and a Special Air Service troop, was subsequently added. The Australian ground forces used unit rotation and, during the course of the war, nine battalions of the RAR rotated through Vietnam.

The ATF fought a major battle at Long Tân on 18 August 1966, inflicting a major defeat on the VC and giving the ATF the initiative within the province. It then instituted a counterinsurgency campaign, a mixture of military operations and civic aid designed to simultaneously protect the civilian population and give them an interest in preserving the political status quo. This campaign proved very successful and gradually extended control over the entire province. There were no more major battles, but the ATF ran constant patrols, cordon and search operations, and civic action projects.

The Australian–New Zealand force was made up initially of highly trained and experienced volunteers who were particularly effective in the field. Eventually, however, Australian Prime Minister Harold Holt had to turn to conscription to supply Australia's troop commitment, leading to an antiwar movement in Australia. This brought pressure to bear on the Australian government, which began in 1970 to gradually reduce its forces in South Vietnam. By December 1971, all Australian forces had been withdrawn from the RVN, except for the Australian Army Assistance Group Vietnam, a small contingent that continued to work with ARVN forces until it was withdrawn in 1973. After South Korea and Thailand, Australia provided the most extensive military support to the United States in the conflict. In addition to the ATF, Australian forces in South Vietnam included a squadron of B-57 Canberra bombers, which operated with U.S. Air Force units, and a guided missile destroyer, the *Hobart*, which operated with the U.S. Navy. Australian forces suffered 423 men killed and 2,398 wounded in action.

—James H. Willbanks

References: King, Peter, ed. *Australia's Vietnam: Australia in the Second Indo-China War* (1983); Larsen, Stanley Robert, and James Lawton Collins, Jr. *Allied Participation in Vietnam* (1975); McNeill, Ian. *The Team: Australian Army Advisors in Vietnam 1962–1972* (1984).

See also: Free World Assistance Program; Korea, Republic of; New Zealand; Order of Battle; Thailand.

B

BABYLIFT, Operation (1–14 April 1975)
Plan to bring 2,000 Vietnamese orphans to the United States for adoption by American parents, announced by President Ford on 3 April 1975. The first flight, on 4 April, crashed soon after takeoff from Sài Gòn's Tân Son Nhut Air Base, killing 138, mostly Vietnamese children. Subsequent flights took place without incident, and BABYLIFT ferried orphans across the Pacific until its conclusion on 14 April, 16 days before the fall of Sài Gòn.

More than 2,600 children were adopted. Questions were raised regarding how these children were selected and whether some were not orphans at all, but children whose parents wanted them safely out of South Vietnam. Subsequent critics of the operation pointed to its excessive public relations aspect, with its oft-repeated predictions of a "bloodbath" once North Vietnam conquered the South, or focused on possible political motives behind the airlift. There were accusations, for instance, that the Ford Administration hoped the flights would create public sympathy for the embattled Thiêu government, thus pressuring Congress into rushing emergency aid to the Republic of Vietnam. As with U.S. involvement in the war, BABYLIFT was a combination of humanitarianism and political manipulation.

—Eric Jarvis

References: Burkard, Dick J. *Military Airlift Command: Historical Handbook, 1941–1984* (1984); DeBenedetti, Charles. *An American Ordeal: The Antiwar Movement of the Vietnam Era* (1990).
See also: Ford, Gerald R.

Baez, Joan Chandos (1941–)
American musician and protestor. Baez severely criticized U.S. involvement in Vietnam and often made significant financial donations to antiwar movements and draft resistance groups. While performing at a reception to honor President Johnson, Baez performed Bob Dylan's "The Times They Are A-Changin'" and voiced her opposition to the Vietnam War. In 1964 she refused to pay that portion of her taxes going to the armed forces. The following year Baez gained international recognition when she established the School for the Study of Nonviolence to examine the concept, history, and various applications of nonviolence. Her 1967 activities included an antiwar performance in Tokyo, a draft card turn-in and concert for 30,000 people at the Washington Monument, and her arrest along with her mother and sister for demonstrating at an induction center in California. At the 1969 Woodstock Festival, Baez, the most experienced protest singer of the performers, brought an intellectual and political element to the reckless nature of the proceedings.

In 1972 Baez visited Hà Nôi as a guest of the Committee for Solidarity with the American People and was there during the "Christmas Bombings." Upon her return home she produced "Where Are You Now, My Son?," a bitter antiwar album that included recordings from her time in Hà Nôi.

—Dallas Cothrum

References: Baez, Joan. *And a Voice to Sing With: A Memoir* (1987); Garza, Hedda. *Joan Baez* (1991); Scadato, Anthony. *Bob Dylan* (1971).
See also: Antiwar Movement, United States; Dylan, Bob; Music and the Vietnam War.

Ball, George W. (1909–1994)
American lawyer, government official, and opponent of the Vietnam War. Ball was named under secretary of state for economic affairs and later under secretary of state in the Kennedy administration. A close advisor to the president, he became an early opponent of American military involvement in Vietnam. In November 1961 he privately warned Kennedy that committing troops there would prove a tragic error.

After Kennedy's assassination, Ball continued as "devil's advocate" in the Lyndon Johnson administration, arguing against escalation on the grounds that Southeast Asia was diverting attention from more important European affairs. Ball sought deescalation and a political settlement with Hà Nôi. In 1966 he resigned and returned to private practice. Ball criticized Preident Nixon's Vietnam policies until the conflict finally ended.

—James Friguglietti

Reference: Ball, George W. *The Past Has Another Pattern: Memoirs* (1982).
See also: Johnson, Lyndon Baines; Kennedy, John Fitzgerald; Nixon, Richard Milhous; "Wise Men."

Ban Mê Thuôt, Battle of (March 1975)
First major battle of the final People's Army of Vietnam (PAVN) offensive in the Vietnam War. The battle took place at Ban Mê Thuôt, capital of Darlac Province. Encouraged by the failure of the United States to respond militarily to their seizure of Phuoc Long Province in early January 1975, two months later the PAVN undertook an offensive, code-named Campaign 275. Under the direct supervision of Senior General Van Tiên Dung, the operation was to prepare the way for a decisive general offensive the following year.

Campaign 275 began with small diversionary attacks north of Ban Mê Thuôt, followed on 4 March by the isolation of the Central Highlands from the coast with the blocking of Route 19 east of Pleiku. Route 21 was cut a day later. Army of the Republic of Vietnam (ARVN) II Corps commander Maj. Gen. Pham Van Phú ignored mounting evidence of the forthcoming attack on Ban Mê Thuôt, convinced that the main blow would fall on or near his Pleiku headquarters.

On 8 March Dung's forces blocked Route 14 between Pleiku and Ban Mê Thuôt. Attacks in Quang Ðuc Province, south of Ban Mê Thuôt, began on 9 March. On 10 March three PAVN divisions moved against Ban Mê Thuôt, sidestepping outlying defenses to attack command posts and supply depots. Initially the ARVN put up a stout resistance, particularly at the Phung Duc airfield east of the city.

Destruction of the ARVN sector command post ended

defensive coordination and ARVN attempts to reinforce the city from Buôn Hô to the north failed. By 12 March Dung's forces had secured the city, although fighting continued on its periphery and around the Phung Duc airfield. An ARVN attempt to mount a counterattack from Phuoc An to the east failed as airlifted soldiers deserted to save their families. With many of the city's defenders and their dependents already fleeing in disarray toward the coast, resistance ended entirely on 18 March.

On 14 March President Thiêu made the situation worse when he ordered the withdrawal of regular ARVN forces from the Central Highlands in an attempt to bolster defenses around Sài Gòn and along the coast. A debacle ensued. Neither regional forces nor civil administrators were informed of Thiêu's plan, and when Phú's units began to withdraw, thousands of civilians, many already in flight from Kontum, joined the exodus. Phú flew to Nha Trang, literally abandoning his command.

Although the RVN forces surprised the enemy by withdrawing along Route 7B, an abandoned provincial highway, General Dung soon had units moving to engage them. PAVN troops struck the fleeing column at Cheo Reo on 18 March, and from that time onward the commingled mass of disorganized military and civilian refugees suffered almost constant attack. They sustained heavy casualties, and only a small fraction reached the coast.

The withdrawal from the Highlands dealt a devastating blow to RVN morale and furthered the disintegration of its military. PAVN forces occupied Kontum and Pleiku on 18 March, and two days later the Hà Nôi Politburo began to reevaluate its timetable for the final offensive, sensing that it need not wait until 1976 to achieve complete victory. By 3 April all of the major coastal cities in the RVN II Corps area except Phan Rang had fallen to Dung's rapidly advancing troops.

—John M. Gates

References: Dougan, Clark, David Fulghum, and the editors of Boston Publishing Company. *The Fall of the South* (1985); Hosmer, Stephen T., Konrad Kellen, and Brian M. Jenkins. *The Fall of South Vietnam: Statements by Vietnamese Military and Civilian Leaders* (1980); Isaacs, Arnold R. *Without Honor: Defeat in Vietnam and Cambodia* (1983); Le Gro, William E. *Vietnam from Cease-Fire to Capitulation* (1981); Van Tiên Dung. *Our Great Spring Victory* (1977). **See also:** Ban Mê Thuôt, Battle of; Van Tiên Dung.

Bao Đai (1913–1997)

Last of the Nguyen emperors. Born Nguyen Phuoc Vinh Thuy, he was educated in France and lived with a wealthy dignitary's family. He did not return to Vietnam until the death of his father. On 8 January 1926 he was crowned emperor, taking the imperial name Bao Đai ("Keeper or Preserver of Greatness" or "Protector of Grandeur") before returning to France. The French government did not permit him to return to Vietnam until 10 September 1932. Enthusiastic about forming a loyal alliance between the colonial power and his own government, Bao Đai was left with little maneuvering room. The "Agreement of 1925" stripped the Vietnamese

Court of most of its remaining authority, leaving emperors with little to do save issue ritual decrees. All other matters would be left to the French Résident Supérieur.

Undaunted, Bao Đai began a series of reforms, hoping to erect a modern imperial government and convince France to establish a framework allowing limited independence for Vietnam under his rule. He fired most of his francophile Mandarin advisors, established a Commission of Reform, and dissolved his official harem. In 1933 he prohibited requisitioned labor except in time of public emergency. The French stymied his zeal at every turn. As Bao Đai's enthusiasm for reform waned, he settled into a sedentary life. With little else to do, he traveled around Vietnam on ceremonial visits and became a playboy governor, interested primarily in gambling, women, and hunting.

Bao Đai cooperated with the Japanese during their World War II occupation and, in March 1945, at their behest, he declared independence from France in proclaiming the "Empire of Viet Nam." In the few months allotted to this government Bao Đai tried to deal with northern famine, supported extensive press freedoms, and called on his people for support. It was not to be. With the collapse of the Japanese government, the Viêt Minh took control during the August Revolution and called on Bao Đai to abdicate. He did so on 25 August, becoming First Citizen Vinh Thuy. Elected to a seat in the new Viêt Minh legislature from his dynasty's ancestral home in Thanh Hóa Province, Vinh Thuy quickly became dissatisfied with his Communist overlords and left his country as part of an official diplomatic delegation to China. He remained in Chungking until September 1946 and then moved to Hong Kong, where he remained through late 1947, when he returned to Europe.

In June 1946 French High Commissioner for Indo-China Admiral Georges Thierry d'Argenlieu created the Autonomous Republic of Cochin China as a means to limit Viêt Minh power and called on Bao Đai to serve as its head. Unenthusiastic, Bao Đai called instead for real Vietnamese independence. Emile Bollaert, d'Argenlieu's replacement, continued to urge Bao Đai to return to Vietnam as chief of state. Bao Đai did so, somewhat reluctantly, after signing the Elysée Agreements with French President Vincent Auriol on 8 March 1949. Now designated as an Associated State within the French Union, the State of Vietnam received official acknowledgement on 29 January 1950 when the Elysée Accords were ratified by the French National Assembly. Bao Đai took up residence in Sài Gòn and remained head of this government through the partitioning of Vietnam by the Geneva Conference and the first year of existence of the new southern Republic of Vietnam. In this capacity, Bao Đai institutionalized corruption by his dealings with Lê Van "Bay" Vien, leader of the Bình Xuyên gang, the illicit activities of which included control of opium trafficking, gold smuggling, racketeering, prostitution, and gambling in the southern republic.

Following the Geneva Accords, Bao Đai named Ngô Đình Diêm as his premier. Later regretting this move, Bao Đai tried to regain control, finally authorizing one of his generals to lead a coup against Diêm. This failed, and Diêm then called for an election to determine whether the nation should be a monarchy or a republic. Held on 23 October 1955, the voting was supervised by Diêm's henchmen; Diêm won handily and became president of the Republic of Vietnam. Bao Đai spent much of the remainder of his life at his chateau near Cannes.

—Cecil B. Currey

Reference: Currey, Cecil B. "Bao Dai: The Last Emperor" (1994).

See also: Bình Xuyên; Bollaert, Emile; d'Argenlieu, Georges Thierry; Elysée Agreement; French Indo-China; Lê Van "Bay" Viên; Vietnam, Republic of: 1954–1975.

Barker, Frank A., Jr. (1927–1968)

Commander of Task Force Barker, a battalion-sized strike force of the 11th Light Infantry Brigade. On 16 March 1968 this strike force killed Vietnamese civilians in Son My village in what became known as the My Lai Massacre.

Barker conceived and planned the My Lai operation against an area allegedly occupied by a large Việt Công force. Whether or not Barker directly ordered the deliberate killing of noncombatants, Company C commander Capt. Ernest Medina later testified that Barker had instructed him to destroy the hamlet of My Lai. After the dimensions of the massacre and its cover-up became known, the Peers Inquiry concluded that Barker (who died in a helicopter crash in June 1968) had planned and directed an unlawful operation and created a belief that his men were authorized to kill noncombatants; the artillery preparation violated the intent of Military Assistance Command, Vietnam (MACV) regulations; he intentionally or negligently told his commanders that no civilians would be present; he conspired to conceal the number of civilians killed, falsely attributing most to artillery fire; he submitted a false and misleading after-action report; and he failed to investigate indications of war crimes that were reported to him. Barker's report, which describes the operation as "well-planned, well-executed, and successful," is a sad and dishonorable epitaph to what had been a promising career.

—John D. Root

References: Bolton, Michael, and Kevin Sim. *Four Hours in My Lai* (1992); Goldstein, Joseph, et al. *The My Lai Massacre and Its Cover-up: Beyond the Reach of the Law?* (1976).

See also: Calley, William Laws, Jr.; Medina, Ernest L.; My Lai Massacre; Peers Inquiry.

BARREL ROLL, Operation (1964–1973)

Allied air campaign carried out in northern Laos primarily to support ground forces of the Royal Laotian Government (RLG) and the CIA-trained Hmong irregular forces of General Vang Pao. Their area of operation stretched from Vientiane on the border of Thailand north to the strategic Plain of Jars and then northeast to the Pathet Lao capital of Sam Neua bordering North Vietnam.

BARREL ROLL was born out of the failure to implement the July 1962 Geneva Accords, which declared Laos an independent and neutral state. In June 1964, in response to a Pathet Lao/People's Army of Vietnam (PAVN) spring offensive in the Plain of Jars, Allied air forces with President Johnson's approval commenced Operation BARREL ROLL in support of RLG forces. The first attacks were on 9 June by U.S. Air Force (USAF) F-100s against enemy antiaircraft artillery (AAA). Throughout its nine years, BARREL ROLL operated under a strange set of rules of engagement; all air assets were controlled by the U.S. ambassador in Vientiane.

The three U.S. ambassadors during this time—Leonard Unger, William H. Sullivan, and G. McMurtrie Godley—were responsible for directing all air operations in northern Laos. Although they did not develop the details, they did validate targets, usually with Laotian government approval. No enemy target could be bombed without their permission. Attacks were often limited to specific areas to avoid hitting irregular units operating beyond the control of Allied authorities.

At the outset, the USAF established Headquarters 2d Air Division/Thirteenth Air Force at Udorn, Thailand, 45 miles from Vientiane, to support the Royal Lao Air Force (RLAF). This command was headed by a major general who reported directly to the Thirteenth Air Force commander and the 2d Air Division commander in Sài Gòn, as well as to the U.S. ambassadors in Thailand and Laos, and established actual directives for daily BARREL ROLL missions. The Udorn headquarters unit was redesignated Seventh Air Force/Thirteenth Air Force in April 1966 when the Seventh Air Force was established at Tân Son Nhut Air Base.

The U.S. embassy in Vientiane also had an air staff that by the end of 1969 had grown to 125 personnel. There were also air operations centers in each of the five military regions of Laos. In turn, American-flown forward air controllers (FACs), known as "Ravens," were also assigned to support Hmong units as well as Royal Lao air and ground forces. Ravens flew O-1s, U-17s, and T-28s during their six-month tours of duty. They also employed C-47s as airborne battlefield command and control centers (ABC&CCs). These tours were hazardous and unofficial, since the United States and Laos maintained the illusion of adhering to the 1962 Geneva Accords that forbade belligerent forces of any nation in Laos.

Between 1965 and 1973 the war in Laos assumed a regular pattern tied to the region's weather. The makeup of the warring forces in Laos was nearly the opposite of those in Vietnam. The Communists had the regular army troops and equipment, while the Hmong, who did most of the fighting for the Allies, usually operated as guerilla or irregular units. Indeed, since Royal Lao Army (RLA) troops were generally poor fighters, U.S. interests increasingly depended on General Vang Pao's youthful soldiers. However, attrition soon took its toll, and by the 1970s the United States was also depending on Thai "volunteer" forces.

Given the relative size and firepower of Hmong and Communist forces (increasingly PAVN regulars), the Hmong used the monsoon season (April–August) to take to the offensive; the Pathet Lao/PAVN, needing open roads, used the dry season (September–March) to launch counterattacks. Vang Pao's forces usually were outnumbered and outgunned, but with significant support from U.S. and RLAF air power they held their own and often launched highly successful offensives deep into Communist territory.

By August 1966 Hmong forces had pushed to within 45 miles of North Vietnam, only to be countered by 14,000 PAVN regulars and 30,000 Pathet Lao. By April 1967 the enemy counteroffensive had overrun several key Royal Lao and Hmong villages and defensive positions, including several Lima sites (LSs)—mountaintop strong-point bases. By diverting significant numbers of aircraft from Operation ROLLING THUNDER in North Vietnam, intensive U.S. air strikes halted Communist advances and allowed Vang Pao's forces to go on the offensive during the 1967 monsoon season.

However, the 1967–1968 dry season witnessed another counterattack led by PAVN regulars using Soviet tanks and Soviet AN-2 Colt aircraft to overrun several Allied towns and bases, including the key LS85 position only 25 miles from Sam Neua. LS85 had an important 700–foot runway and tactical air navigation system built by USAF personnel in 1966. In late 1967 this system was augmented with an all-weather unit manned by 19 USAF personnel. PAVN forces captured and destroyd the site in March 1968, killing seven U.S. airmen.

The Communists employed more and better Soviet tanks and artillery throughout 1968–1969. Despite these additions, RLA and Hmong forces enjoyed their greatest victories in the summer of 1969. By September 1969, supported by hundreds of BARREL ROLL sorties, they had taken nearly all of the Plain of Jars, including Xieng Khouang, and had captured enormous caches of ammunition, supplies, food, and fuel, as well as vehicles. However, the Communist counteroffensive that began in December 1969 retook all the lost territory. So great was the disaster that in February 1970, Ambassador Godley was forced to beg President Nixon for B-52 strikes to save the situation. On 17–18 February 1970, B-52s flew 36 sorties and dropped 1,078 tons of bombs. During the first battle of Skyline Ridge, B-52s supported by truck-killing night-raiding T-28s, AC-47s, AC-119s, and AC-130s, flew nearly 3,000 sorties. By 18 March Communist forces had been beaten back from Vang Pao's base camp at Long Tieng.

In 1971 the Communists repeated their successes during SKYLINE II only to be pushed back again by determined Hmong defenders and 1,500 U.S. air sorties. Between August and November 1972, a third PAVN offensive pushed to within 16 miles of Long Tieng, only to be halted by massive B-52 and F-111 strikes.

On 10 November 1972, cease-fire talks began between the Pathet Lao and Royal Lao Government of Souvanna Phouma. Anticipating a cease-fire, Communist forces used the negotiation period to mop up RLG outposts on the Plain of Jars. On 21 February 1973, Washington signed the cease-fire agreement and all but abandoned their Laotian allies. While B-52 sorties were flown on 23 February followed by tactical aircraft sorties in April, because of potential cease-fire violations they were futile gestures. The last BARREL ROLL sortie was flown on 17 April 1973. Before the end of the war Allied aircraft dropped more than 3 million tons of bombs on Laos, three times the tonnage dropped on North Vietnam. From 1965 to 1968, Allied aircraft flew fewer than 100 sorties per day on average over northern Laos. In 1969 this jumped to approximately 300, then fell back to 200 in 1970. From 1971 to 1973 it returned to pre-1969 levels. As with other Laotian air operations, the numbers and performance were impressive, but in the end it proved fruitless.

—William Head

References: Berger, Carl, ed. *The United States Air Force in Southeast Asia, 1961–1973: An Illustrated Account* (1984); Momyer, William H. *Airpower in Three Wars* (1978); Morrocco, John. *Rain of Fire: Air War, 1969–1973* (1986); —. *Thunder from Above* (1984); Schlight, John. *The Air War in South Vietnam: The Years of the Offensive, 1965–1968* (1988); Tilford, Earl H., Jr. *Crosswinds: The Air Force's Setup in Vietnam* (1994).

See also: Air Power, Role in War; Geneva Accords (1962); Godley, G. McMurtrie; Hmong; Johnson, Lyndon B.; Laos; Lima Site 85; Nixon, Richard M.; Plain of Jars; Raven Forward Air Controller (FAC); ROLLING THUNDER, Operation; Souvanna Phouma; STEEL TIGER, Operation; Sullivan, William H.; TIGER HOUND, Operation; Vang Pao; Vietnam, Democratic Republic of: Army (People's Army of Vietnam [PAVN]).

Beau, Jean-Baptiste-Paul (1857–1927)

Governor general of French Indo-China, 1902–1908. In contrast to his predecessor, Paul Doumer, Beau fostered assimilation. He believed that France's duties were to bring about material change and to reform Vietnamese customs and institutions. Beau reorganized the administrative system in the first serious attempts at a form of representative government, creating provincial councils and advisory chambers at the regional level in An Nam and Tonkin. These had both fiscal and administrative responsibilities. He created a public educational system, although even after World War I only 10 percent of Vietnamese of school age attended Franco-Vietnamese schools. Beau also greatly improved the quality of local medical care, worked to reduce the opium trade, and ended certain corporal punishments. He was instrumental in railroad construction and made Sài Gòn very much a European city. He negotiated with Siam the 1907 demarcation of the borders between that country and Cambodia that saw the retrocession of the provinces of Angkor and Battambang to Cambodia.

Beau's hopes that his reforms would make the Vietnamese grateful to France proved fleeting. Many French in Vietnam considered them dangerously radical; Vietnamese patriots, such as Phan Chu Trinh, considered them totally insufficient. With the example of an Asian nation defeating a European power in the Russo-Japanese War and resentment of heavy taxes resulting from poor harvests during the Beau years, the French administration had to deal with rising Vietnamese nationalism. Beau forfeited what confidence he had gained from the Vietnamese by ordering the 1907 exile of Emperor Thành Thái after the latter demanded political reforms. The necessity of maintaining order co-opted Beau's policy of cooperation. He was recalled to France in February 1908.

—Spencer C. Tucker

References: Beau, Paul. *Situation de L'Indo-Chine de 1902 à 1907* (1908); Buttinger, Joseph. *The Smaller Dragon: A Political History of Vietnam* (1968); Duiker, William J. *The Rise of Nationalism in Vietnam, 1900–1911* (1976); Prevost, M., and Roman D. Amat, eds. *Dictionnaire de Biographie Française* (1951); Thompson, Virginia. *French Indo-China* (1968).

See also: An Nam; Assimilation versus Association; Doumer, Paul; Franco-Thai War; French Indo-China; Phan Chu Trinh; Quôc Ngu; Thành Thái; Tonkin.

Bên Súc

Village along the Sài Gòn River at the southwestern boundary of the Iron Triangle; site of the blocking position in Operation CEDAR FALLS (8–26 January 1967) directed against the Iron Triangle and headquarters of Viêt Công (VC) Military Region IV. Operation CEDAR FALLS, the first corps-sized search-and-destroy operation of the war, was a "hammer-and-anvil" attack. The anvil, or blocking position, was along the Sài Gòn River at the southwestern boundary of the Iron Triangle. Bên Súc and three nearby villages housed a VC base responsible for moving supplies by sampan along the river. At 0800 on 8 January, without preparatory artillery fire, 60 transport helicopters protected by ten armed helicopters lifted 500 men of the 2d Brigade of the 1st Infantry Division directly into Bên Súc itself. The assault achieved tactical surprise. Artillery fire was then directed north of the village to prevent escape by that route, and at 0830 men from the 2d Brigade were airlifted south of the village to block escape in that direction. There were no U.S. casualties, and by midmorning the village was secured. An Army of the Republic of Vietnam (ARVN) battalion that had been driven out of the area by the VC months earlier then returned to conduct a methodical search of Bên Súc.

The village was bulldozed, and VC tunnels beneath the village were collapsed. By 26 January engineers had cleared 2,711 acres of jungle. Most VC forces avoided battle and escaped. Nearly 6,000 villagers, two-thirds of them children, were removed to a resettlement camp at Phú Loi. Villagers were allowed only those personal possessions they could carry, and for security reasons no advance preparations were made to receive them at Phú Loi.

For all of CEDAR FALLS, U.S. Military Assistance Command, Vietnam (MACV) reported 750 VC/People's Army of Vietnam (PAVN) killed, 280 captured, and 540 defectors. Allied losses were 83 killed and 345 wounded. Although a setback for the VC, the operation was hardly what Maj. Gen. William DePuy, commander of the 1st Infantry Division, characterized as "a blow from which the VC in this area may never recover." Communist forces soon returned.

—Spencer C. Tucker

Reference: Schnell, Jonathan. *The Village of Ben Suc* (1967).
See also: CEDAR FALLS, Operation; Iron Triangle; Search and Destroy.

Bên Tre (1968)

Capital of the island province of Kiên Hòa attacked during the 1968 Têt Offensive. During the month before Têt, tensions remained high in the province as intelligence reports indicated Viêt Công (VC) units moving into staging areas prior to launching ground attacks. VC units began to infiltrate Bên Tre during the night of 30–31 January. Gunfire broke out at 0400, followed by a mortar barrage and small arms fire that lashed the downtown Republic of Vietnam administrative bunker complex. After fierce fighting, Army of the Republic of Vietnam forces secured the vicinity of the provincial hospital and reinforced the local radio station. Beginning in the afternoon and continuing through the next morning, two battalions of the U.S. 9th Infantry Division were deployed by air to prevent the town from being overrun. Until fighting subsided on 2 February, Allied infantry supported by airstrikes successfully battled to clear the VC from the urban area. During the fighting, nearly 1,000 civilians were killed, more than half of the town's houses were destroyed, and many other structures were badly damaged. An unidentified U.S. Army officer attempted to explain the destruction in Bên Tre, saying, "It became necessary to destroy the town to save it."

—Glenn E. Helm

References: Braestrup, Peter. *The Big Story* (1977); Oberdorfer, Don. *Tet!* (1971); Pham Van Son and Le Van Duong, eds. *The Viet Cong Tet Offensive* (1969).
See also: Têt Offensive: Overall Strategy; Têt Offensive: the Sài Gòn Circle.

Berger, Samuel David (1911–1980)

U.S. diplomat and deputy ambassador to the Republic of Vietnam (RVN). From 1968 to 1972, Berger served as deputy ambassador to the RVN, where he supported President Nguyên Van Thiêu as the best means of establishing a stable South Vietnamese government. In 1970 he stated that Vietnamization was working and that the Army of the Republic of Vietnam (ARVN) was "developing a healthy professional quality." Graenum Berger, the diplomat's brother and biographer, disagreed and doubted "the government's ability to create and sustain the popular support and morale necessary" to make Vietnamization successful. Nevertheless, in 1973 Berger received an appreciative letter from President Nixon thanking him for helping to "achieve the honorable peace we fought for."

—Paul S. Daum, with B. J. Rogers

References: Berger, Graenum. *Not So Silent an Envoy: A Biography of Ambassador Samuel David Berger* (1992); Dougan, Clark, Stephen Weiss, and the editors of Boston Publishing Company. *Nineteen Sixty-Eight* (1983).
See also: Bundy, William P.; Harriman, W. Averell; Nguyên Van Thiêu; Nixon, Richard Milhous;

Berrigan, Daniel (1921–)

Antiwar activist, poet, and
U.S. involvement in Vietnam
helped found the Catholic P
firsthand the effects of U.S. b
he traveled to Hà Nôi and s
tured American pilots. On 1
brother Philip and seven ot

napalm to burn draft cards from the Selective Service office in Catonsville, Maryland. Sentenced to three years in prison for this action, he went underground for several months before being apprehended in August 1970. Poor health led to his parole on 26 January 1972.

—James E. Southerland

References: Berrigan, Daniel. *No Bars to Manhood* (1970); Zinn, Howard. *The Twentieth Century: A People's History* (1984).

See also: Antiwar Movement, United States; Berrigan, Philip.

Berrigan, Philip (1923–)

Antiwar activist. In 1964 Philip Berrigan founded the Emergency Citizens' Group Concerned about Vietnam and helped found the Catholic Peace Fellowship. On 27 October 1967 Berrigan and three others poured blood on draft records at the Selective Service office in Baltimore. Brought to trial, he became the first Roman Catholic priest in the United States to be sentenced to prison for a political crime. On 17 May 1968, before his sentencing, Berrigan participated in burning draft files in Catonsville, Maryland, for which he was sentenced to federal prison for conspiracy and destruction of private property, to be served concurrently with his earlier sentence. While in prison Berrigan was unsuccessfully prosecuted for conspiring to kidnap Henry Kissinger and blow up the heating systems of federal buildings in Washington, D.C. He was paroled in December 1972.

—James E. Southerland

References: Meconis, Charles. *With Clumsy Grace: The American Catholic Left, 1961–1975* (1979); Zaroulis, Nancy, and Gerald Sullivan. *Who Spoke Up: American Protest Against the War in Vietnam, 1963–1975* (1985); Zinn, Howard. *The Twentieth Century: A People's History* (1984).

See also: Antiwar Movement, United States; Berrigan, Daniel.

Bidault, Georges (1899–1983)

French politician, Resistance leader, premier, and foreign minister. In colonial matters Bidault was a staunch defender of the French Empire. He was premier on 23 November 1946 when the French cruiser *Suffren* bombarded the port of Hai Phòng, and he approved Admiral Thierry d'Argenlieu's request to "teach the Vietnamese a lesson." He left office the next month.

—Spencer C. Tucker

Reference: Bell, David S., Douglas Johnson, and Peter Morris. *Biographical Dictionary of French Political Leaders since 1870* (1990).

See also: d'Argenlieu, Georges Thierry; Hai Phòng, Shelling of.

Bình Gia, Battle of (28 December 1964–1 January 1965)

Village southeast of Sài Gòn in coastal Phuoc Tuy Province. In 1964 the 271st and 272d Regiments of the Viêt Công [...]th Division moved in small groups from War Zones C [...] coast to receive supplies sent by sea from North [...] regrouped to train on rubber plantations sur[...]ia.

[...]ning of 28 December 1964, a battalion of [...]d Bình Gia, which was defended by

two platoons of regional Republic of Vietnam (RVN) forces. Never before in the war had VC troops attacked in such a large number. After their successful attack the Communists were reinforced, as were the RVN regional forces. Army of the Republic of Vietnam (ARVN) Military Region III headquarters sent the 30th Ranger Battalion by helicopter. The VC laid an ambush and attacked the Rangers in the landing zone; surviving Rangers sought refuge in the village church.

The next day the 33d Ranger Battalion was lifted by helicopter to a point south of Bình Gia and counterattacked toward it. The fight lasted all day, but the Rangers could not clear the VC from their dug-in positions. On the morning of 30 December, the RVN 4th Marine Battalion was also sent into the battle. The VC had already moved to the northeast, and the Marines were able to retake the village. At night the VC returned and attacked but were pushed back. On the 31st the 4th Marine Battalion was ordered to retrieve a downed helicopter and its crew on the Quang Giáo rubber plantation near Bình Gia. In trying to reach the helicopter the 2d Company of the Marines fell into an enemy ambush. The remainder of the battalion then arrived but took heavy casualties and was forced to retreat to Bình Gia. On 1 January 1965 the 1st and 3d Airborne Battalions were airlifted to the eastern side of the battlefield, but the Communists had already left.

On 4 January 1965 the Viêt Công held a press conference and announced that during the battle for Bình Gia they had killed 2,000 ARVN and 28 Americans and destroyed 37 military vehicles and 24 airplanes. Actual casualties were some 200 killed, including five U.S. advisors. Probably 250 VC died in the battle.

Bình Gia was a warning for ARVN and the United States that VC forces, when supplied with modern weapons, were capable of fighting large battles. It also signaled a mix of guerilla and conventional warfare.

—Hieu D. Vu

References: Pham, Kim Vinh. *The ARVN: A Stoic Army. How They Victimized the Army of Free Vietnam* (1983); Nguyen, Duc Phuong. *Nhung tran danh lich su trong chien tranh Viet Nam 1963–1975* (1993).

See also: National Front for the Liberation of South Vietnam (NFLSV); Vietnam, Republic of: Army (ARVN); Vietnam, Republic of: Marine Corps (VNMC).

BÌNH TÂY I–IV, Operations (May–June, 1970)

Northernmost operations of the 1970 Cambodian Incursion. *Bình Tây* means "Taming the West." While the principal Allied thrusts were in the Fishhook and Parrot's Beak areas abutting III and IV Corps (Operations Toàn Thang 43 and 44), BÌNH TÂY was a four-stage operation, primarily by the Army of the Republic of Vietnam (ARVN), directed at logistical support complexes of the People's Army of Vietnam (PAVN) B-3 Front in northeastern Cambodia.

The U.S. 4th Infantry Division and the 40th Regiment of the ARVN 22d Division initiated BÌNH TÂY I on 4 May. U.S. participation was poorly executed and relatively brief. Maj. Gen. Glen D. Walker's 4th Division was overextended, having only recently relocated to Bình Định Province. Having no forward installations and only limited logistical support, Walker planned to place artillery at the Plei D'Jereng Special Forces camp. A convoy of 4th Division mechanized infantry and the 40th Regiment, 22d ARVN Division, moved down Highway 19, reaching Plei D'Jereng on 4 May before the artillery arrived and before C-130 cargo planes could supply sufficient helicopter fuel.

Despite preparation by six B-52 sorties, the U.S. 3d Battalion, 506th Infantry (3/506th) encountered heavy machine gun fire while attempting to land at densely vegetated landing zones (LZs), and the insertions were aborted. By late the following day, the 3/506th and the 1st Battalion, 14th Infantry (1/14th) were on the ground, but under heavy fire and with several helicopters downed. Joined by the 2d Battalion, 8th Infantry (2/8th) on 6 May, during the next few days 1st Brigade troops discovered an abandoned People's Army of Vietnam (PAVN) training camp and large amounts of supplies.

As his battalions took significant casualties without making substantial contact with PAVN units, Walker decided to turn the operation over to the ARVN. All 4th Division units had left Cambodia by 16 May. Supported by U.S. air and artillery from inside south Vietnam, the ARVN 22d and 23d Divisions, 2d Ranger Group, and 2d Armored Brigade moved into Ratankiri Province. When BÌNH TÂY I terminated on 25 May, Allied forces claimed 212 PAVN dead. Allied casualties were 43 killed and 118 wounded. Captured documents revealed that the PAVN B-3 Front had anticipated the Allied incursion and had orders to avoid direct contact.

BÌNH TÂY II began on 14 May along the border with Darlac Province in Vietnam and was directed at Enemy Base Area 701, from which three known PAVN regiments had operated. Following air strikes, U.S. helicopters inserted the 40th and 47th Regiments of the 22d ARVN Division, while the 3d Armored Cavalry Squadron drove across the border. The ARVN troops discovered caches of hundreds of weapons and tons of ammunition and medical supplies. Contact was made only with enemy security forces. When BÌNH TÂY II ended on 27 May, the ARVN claimed to have killed 73 PAVN soldiers and captured 6 at the cost of only 1 killed and 4 wounded.

BINH TÂY III was conducted by the 23d ARVN Division in three phases from 20 May until 12 June. Its objective was Enemy Base Area 740, in Cambodia west of Ban Mê Thuôt. In the first phase, supported by U.S. artillery and gunships, 23d Division troops were inserted into the area to search for the PAVN 33d Regiment and 251st Transportation Battalion. The most dramatic event was the destruction of a ten-truck convoy by U.S. gunships and ARVN infantry. ARVN forces killed 98 PAVN troops while suffering 29 killed and 77 wounded. During the second and third phases, conducted in the Nam Lyr Mountains area, tactical air and gunship attacks inflicted heavy casualties on company-sized PAVN units on the move. Together, Operations BÌNH TÂY I–III accounted for 434 PAVN troops killed, 1,900 weapons captured, and more than 1,000 tons of rice destroyed.

A final, unplanned operation, BÌNH TÂY IV, took place from 23 to 27 June. An ARVN 22d Division task force of military and civilian vehicles, protected by U.S. artillery and air cavalry, moved deep into Cambodia along Highway 19 to reach a Khmer army garrison and hundreds of refugees threatened by PAVN forces at Labang Siek. On 25 June the ARVN forces transported the Khmers east to Ba Kev, where U.S. helicopters flew them to Đuc Co in Pleiku Province. Several hundred more refugees who arrived in Ba Kev by foot were transported to Đuc Co in ARVN vehicles. BÌNH TÂY IV ended on 27 June, with six PAVN killed and only two ARVN killed and eight wounded. By then, all II Corps ARVN troops had left Cambodia and a total of 7,571 Khmer soldiers, dependents, and refugees had been evacuated to Camp Enari at Pleiku.

—John D. Root

References: Nolan, Keith William. *Into Cambodia: Spring Campaign, Summer Offensive, 1970* (1990); Tran Dình Thô. *The Cambodian Incursion* (1979).

See also: Cambodia; Cambodian Incursion; Vietnam, Democratic Republic of: Army (People's Army of Vietnam [PAVN]); Vietnam, Republic of: Army (ARVN); Vietnamization.

Bình Xuyên

Bandit political sect that operated in Sài Gòn, 1945–1955. The Bình Xuyên originated as a band of river pirates operating along the Sài Gòn River. Headquartered in the Cho Lon district of Sài Gòn under the leadership of Lê Van Viên, alias Bay Viên, it became a political force after World War II when it entered into an alliance with the Viêt Minh. In 1947 the Bình Xuyên switched loyalties. Recognized as a legal sect by the French and the Bao Đai regime, the Bình Xuyên offered monetary, military, and political support in exchange for governmental protection of their illegal activities. Bay Viên gained total control of the region's gambling, prostitution, money laundering, and opium trafficking and by the early 1950s controlled a private army of 40,000 soldiers.

In 1955 Ngô Đình Diêm launched a crackdown on his political and religious opposition, but the Bình Xuyên posed a major obstacle. On 27 April Bay Viên refused Diêm's order to move his army out of Sài Gòn. Diêm ordered an attack that initiated a bloody battle in the Sài Gòn streets and left 500 dead and 25,000 homeless. A vicious month-long civil war followed. Within a month Diêm's forces had scattered the Bình Xuyên army, and Bay Viên escaped to France, taking most of his personal fortune with him. Some survivors joined the Viêt Công, but the Bình Xuyên ceased to exist as an organized entity.

—David Coffey

Reference: Buttinger, Joseph. *Vietnam: A Dragon Embattled* (1967).
See also: Lê Van "Bay" Viên; Ngô Đình Diêm.

Bird & Sons (Birdair)

Air carrier that operated in Southeast Asia for the U.S. government, 1960–1965 and 1970–1975. Bird & Sons was owned by William H. Bird, who in 1960 acquired a Twin Beechcraft and began an air division of his construction company. Bird & Sons grew in response to the expanding American role in Laos. By 1965 the company was operating 22 aircraft, flying primarily short-takeoff-and-landing (STOL) airplanes into tiny airstrips in Laos under contract with the U.S. Agency for International Development. Bird & Sons introduced to Southeast Asia the Swiss-manufactured Pilatus Porter, the most capable STOL aircraft used during the war.

Bird & Sons also flew clandestine missions for the Central Intelligence Agency (CIA). CIA operations personnel valued the flexibility offered by Bird & Sons, which often responded more promptly to urgent requests than the CIA's proprietary airline, Air America, a much larger and more bureaucratic organization. The CIA admired the piloting skill and personal discretion of Robert L. Brongersma, Bird & Sons' operation manager, who flew many of the most sensitive covert missions.

In September 1965, Bird sold his air division to Continental Air Lines for $4.2 million. The agreement included a five-year no-competition restriction. After the restriction lapsed, Bird's new company, Birdair, flew helicopters in northern Thailand and Laos, mainly for the USAID medical program, until 1975.

—William M. Leary

Reference: Seagrave, Sterling. *Soldiers of Fortune* (1981).
See also: Air America; Central Intelligence Agency (CIA); Laos; U.S. Agency for International Development (USAID).

Black Flag Pirates

Chinese pirates who devastated North Vietnam in the late nineteenth century. Remnants of the Taiping Revolt who fled into Vietnam after their failure in the 1860s, the Black Flags (in Vietnamese, Giac Co −Den) at first were located in mountainous areas in upper North Vietnam, in Lào Cai, on the Hông Hà (Red River), and in the Lô River basin. They descended to the plain, exacting ransom and terrorizing the population, after the Nguyên Court in Huê called on them to cooperate with the imperial army in fighting against the French invasion of the early 1870s. The situation became so serious that people abandoned farming and commercial activities, and villages became empty. The Black Flags killed French Lt. Francis Garnier in 1873 and Capt. Henri Rivière in 1882. The French were able to eliminate the Black Flags after they established their protectorate over the country, thanks to their material superiority and support from the inhabitants. Mopping-up operations, however, were very costly. They required means of transportation and communications beyond the capability of the premodern Vietnamese dynasties.

—Pham Cao Duong

References: McAleavy, Henry. *Black Flags in Vietnam. The Story of a Chinese Intervention* (1968); Pham Cao Duong. *Vietnamese Peasants under French Domination* (1985).
See also: Garnier, Francis; Nguyên Dynasty.

Blacks in the U.S. Military. *See* African American Personnel in U.S. Forces in Vietnam.

Blaizot, Roger (1891–1981)

General and commander of French forces in Indo-China, 1948–1949. After the liberation of France in 1944, the provisional government authorized creation of a Far East Army of 60,000 men with Blaizot commanding the French Far East Expeditionary Forces (FEFEO). Blaizot reached Ceylon that October, but for months he had nothing to command; even at the end of the war, he had only 1,000 men. He remained head of the French military mission with the South-East Asia Command from 6 October 1944 until 16 June 1945. In June 1945, the French government created an expeditionary corps of two divisions for Indo-China and gave command to General Jacques-Philippe Leclerc.

On 22 April 1948 Blaizot replaced General Etienne Valluy as commander of French forces in Indo-China. He arrived in Sài Gòn on 15 May. Blaizot favored concentrating on the northern part of the country and, within it, he wanted ambitious operations against enemy strongholds in the highlands to retake parts of Tonkin abandoned by the French the previous year. The major French military effort that fall was in the North, although the tardy arrival of reinforcements caused Blaizot to push back his plans. Operation DIANE, begun in October 1948 and extended into mid-February 1949, was to expand French military control of the Red River Valley upstream in order to control the Tonkin redoubt. Largely unsuccessful, this operation had to be scaled back. Blaizot soon found himself in disagreement with High Commissioner Léon Pignon, who wanted the main military effort to be in the South.

During May and June 1949, French Army Chief of Staff General Georges Revers made a fact-finding trip to Indo-China. He recommended the evacuation of vulnerable French military positions in northern Tonkin to concentrate on the vital Red River Delta. Just as Blaizot was about to evacuate Cao Bang and Route Coloniale 4, General Marcel Carpentier replaced him as French military commander in Indo-China. Hounded by those who opposed the evacuation, Carpentier put it on hold. Ironically, the outcry over the French loss of Cao Bang the next year led to Carpentier's replacement.

Blaizot left Indo-China on 2 September 1949 and retired in 1950.

—Spencer C. Tucker

References: Dalloz, Jacques. *The War in Indo-China, 1945–54* (1990); Gras, Général Yvres. *Histoire de La Guerre d'Indochine* (1992); Porch, Douglas. *The French Foreign Legion. A Complete History of the Legendary Fighting Force* (1991).
See also: Carpentier, Marcel; de Gaulle, Charles André Marie Joseph; France: Army; Indo-China War; L HÔNG PHONG II, Operation; Pignon, Léon; Revers Report.

BLUE LIGHT, Operation

(23 December 1965–23 January 1966)
First major U.S. Air Force airlift operation of the Vietnam War. Two Military Airlift Command units, the 60th and 61st Military Airlift Wings (MAW), demonstrated U.S. ability to deploy large numbers of men and materiel on short notice.

The units transported 2,841 troops and 6,087 tons of equipment from Hawaii to Pleiku, Republic of Vietnam (RVN), which presented several challenges to Twenty-Second Air Force planners. The runway there was an asphalt-covered, pierced steel plate design only 6,000 feet long. Combat engineers did not know whether the runway surface could withstand the strain of heavy aircraft loads. Landing C-141s would be difficult since 6,000 feet was the minimum runway length the aircraft required, and BLUE LIGHT missions would complicate an already heavy transport schedule.

Twenty-Second Air Force planners decided that a combination of C-141 and C-133 aircraft would cause the least interference with other operations. The Twenty-Second Air Force also used experienced flight examiners on all missions into Pleiku to assist C-141 crews during the difficult landings.

BLUE LIGHT had two phases. The first involved transporting the 25th Infantry's advance deployment team to Pleiku between 23 and 26 December and used four C-133 and two C-141 missions to transport men and equipment required for the advance team. The second phase involved transporting the remainder of the 3d Brigade of the 25th Infantry Division.

BLUE LIGHT was the first impromptu test of the new Lockheed C-141 Starlifter, which had entered service in 1964 as the Air Force's first turbojet transport aircraft. The operation also highlighted the older turboprop McDonnell-Douglas C-133's ability to deliver oversized cargo to forward locations. By conducting 231 missions into a marginal airfield without incident, the Air Force demonstrated it could project military power into once inaccessible areas.

—Larry Gatti

References: Gunston, Bill. *The Illustrated Encyclopedia of the World's Modern Military Aircraft* (1978); U.S. Department of the Air Force. *Military Airlift Command History, Jul 65–Jan 66* (n.d.); U.S. Department of the Air Force. *61st Military Airlift Wing History, Dec 65–Jan 66* (n.d.).

See also: Airplanes, Allied and Democratic Republic of Vietnam.

Blum, Léon (1872–1950)

French political leader, premier, and man of letters. Blum made his mark in literary criticism and law before abandoning both on the eve of World War I to enter politics. In 1919 he won election to the Chamber of Deputies as a Socialist and soon drafted the Socialist Party (SFIO) program. By the mid-1930s the SFIO was the leading party in the leftist Popular Front (with the Radical Socialists and Communists), and the 1936 election victory catapulted Blum into the premiership in June. The Popular Front was not a success, and Blum lasted barely a year as premier, the coalition collapsing under economic pressures and the Spanish Civil War. The liberal labor laws of the Popular Front government did, however, directly influence the 1937 labor code in Vietnam that reduced hours of work for women, prohibited labor by children younger than 12, and provided for an obligatory one day's rest per week and minimum wages.

Blum's second premiership, March–April 1938, was even less successful. The defeat of France in 1940 splintered the SFIO. Taken to Buchenwald in 1943, Blum was welcomed back to France after the war, although his role was then that of an elder statesman. From December 1946 to January 1947 he headed an all-socialist government as events in Indo-China came to a crisis. A week before heading the government, Blum had written in *Le Populaire* that independence (later qualified to read "independence within the French Union") was the only solution for Vietnam. A hopeful Hô Chí Minh sent Blum proposals to relieve Franco-Vietnamese tensions, but French military censors in Sài Gòn held the cable until it was too late to do any good.

There was a certain irony that a long-standing critic of French colonialism should be premier when the Indo-China War began. In responding to the events of 19 December 1946, Blum reacted very much as a leader of the center or right would have. He told the Assembly that France was using military force in self-defense, certain of the justness of its cause. In January fellow Socialist Paul Ramadier replaced Blum as premier.

—Spencer C. Tucker

References: Blum, Léon. *Léon Blum, chef de gouvernement* (1967); Colton, Joel. *Léon Blum. Humanist in Politics* (1966); Hammer, Ellen J. *The Struggle for Indochina* (1954); Hutton, Patrick H., ed. *Historical Dictionary of the Third French Republic, 1870–1940* (1986); Logue, William. *Léon Blum: The Formative Years, 1872–1914* (1973); Thompson, Virginia. *French Indo-China* (1968).

See also: De Gaulle, Charles; French Indo-China, 1860s to 1956; Hai Phòng, Shelling of; Hô Chí Minh.

Boat People. *See* Refugees and Boat People.

Body Armor

Body armor in Vietnam was known primarily by the terms *flak jacket* and *flak vest*. *Flak* is a term derived from the German word for antiaircraft gun, *fliegerabwehrkanone*. The American soldier, sleeveless in his flak jacket, became a common media image.

Flak suits, in widespread use by the U.S. Army Air Forces in 1945, evolved into infantry body armor during the Korean War. The Marine Corps' M1955 armored vest and the Army's M69 fragmentation protective vest, fielded in 1962, both offered neck protection. These two vests, along with the earlier M1951 and M1952 models, were standard for Marine and Army forces in Vietnam. The M1955 armor weighed about 10 pounds; the M69 armor weighed about 8.5 pounds. These sleeveless vests were composed of Nylon filler and inserts enclosed in cloth. Although they were against regulations, slogans such as "LBJ's hired gun" typically adorned such flak jackets.

Until late 1968 helicopter crewmen generally wore infantry body armor. Hard face composite (HFC) kits were commonly used to provide seat ballistic protection. HFC chest protectors also existed but were never used because of design problems. They were reengineered as T65–1 frontal torso armor.

Aviator body armor was introduced in 1970. Sarcastically referred to as "chicken plate," its official classified designation was Body Armor, Small Arms Protective, Aircrewmen. Gunners wore full armor; pilots and copilots generally wore only frontal armor. Torso armor, composed of aluminum oxide ceramics, was able to defeat high-velocity small arms projectiles. Leg armor was made from composite steel. Full armor weighed about 25 pounds; however, new variants incorporated lighter, stronger ceramics based on boron carbide. Body Armor, Fragmentation-Small Arms Protective, Aircrewmen—introduced in 1968—became the standard-issue body armor.

Later infantry body armor developments were directly inspired by advances in aircrewmen armor. In 1968, a "variable body armor" was introduced that used boron carbide ceramics. Special body armor was also used by naval and riverine forces. Naval and Coast Guard forces were issued floating body armor, while many riverine troops wore a light flak jacket composed of a special titanium-nylon composite that offered better protection against flechettes.

—Robert J. Bunker

References: Dean, Bashford. *American and German Helmets and Body Armor of World War I and Body Armor in Modern Warfare* (1980); Dunstan, Simon. *Flak Jackets: 20th Century Military Body Armor* (1984); Katcher, Philip. *The American Soldier: U.S. Armies in Uniform, 1755 to the Present* (1990); Kennedy, Stephen J. *Battlefield Protection of the Soldier through his Clothing/Equipment System* (1969); U.S. Army. *Body Armor for the Individual Soldier. DA PAM 21–54* (1965).

Body Count

Calculation of the number of enemy troops killed in battle. As Lt. Gen. William R. Peers observed, in Vietnam "with improper leadership, 'body count' could create competition between units, particularly if these statistics were compared like baseball standings and there were no stringent requirements as to how and by whom the counts were to be made."

Preoccupation with body count during the Vietnam War was fueled by Secretary of Defense Robert McNamara's obsession with statistical indicators. General Westmoreland pushed commanders to achieve the "crossover point" at which more of the enemy were being killed than could be replaced by infiltration or recruitment, essential to success in his strategy of fighting a war of attrition. That goal was never reached, but in striving for it considerable corruption was introduced into the reporting of body counts. The unreliability of body counts was well documented by Brig. Gen. Douglas Kinnard in his book *The War Managers*.

Body count was important in Vietnam because of the absence of the usual indicators of progress, such as seizing and holding enemy terrain and advancing the front lines. Ultimately, however, body count was irrelevant since, as General Kinnard wrote, "there was no way of really comparing the number of enemy against his manpower potential because the manpower base varied with the effectiveness of his political apparatus and losses never approached his absolute limit to sustain them."

As became evident when General Creighton Abrams assumed command in 1968, the security of the populace of South Vietnam, not slaughter of enemy main forces, was the real determinant of progress. Abrams made this clear early in his tenure. "Body count is really a long way from what's involved in this war," he told his commanders, a radical change in outlook on what mattered in this complex war.

—Lewis Sorley

References: Kinnard, Douglas. *The War Managers* (1977); Peers, William R. *The My Lai Inquiry* (1979).

See also: Abrams, Creighton; Attrition; Casualties; McNamara, Robert S.; Peers, William R.; Westmoreland, William Childs; Wheeler, Earle G.

BOLD MARINER, Operation (January–July 1969)

U.S. Marine Corps and Army and operation known by the Army as RUSSELL BEACH. It employed two battalions of the Army's 23d Division (Americal) and two Marine Corps battalion landing teams. The operation began in January 1969 in the Batangan Peninsula in Quang Ngãi, one of the least secure provinces of the Republic of Vietnam (RVN). Previous efforts by U.S., Army of the Republic of Vietnam (ARVN), and Republic of Korea (ROK) forces had failed to clear the Việt Công (VC) from the peninsula. The operation's basic objective was to support the pacification of the peninsula by clearing out VC forces and converting the Communist stronghold into an area of government control.

In RUSSELL BEACH/BOLD MARINER, U.S. forces helped to cordon the peninsula and round up VC forces. The operation involved deliberate destruction of property and relocation of civilians, who were moved to a tent encampment, screened for VC cadres, and then returned home. Because the operation envisioned the return of the villagers to their homes in about a month, the government and CORDS approved the relocation.

The operation began on 13 January. Two U.S. Marine Corps battalions were landed on the peninsula and met little resistance, while Task Force Cooksey, composed of units from the U.S. 23d Division, sealed off the southern boundary. The cordon lasted until 6 February and the operation ended in July. Army engineers destroyed more than 13,000 yards of underground passages and hiding places, and all houses in the area of operation were destroyed to preclude VC use and to facilitate identification of tunnel entrances. The Americans suffered 56 combat deaths; Việt Công losses were put at 158. Most casualties resulted from concealed mines and booby traps.

Of the 1,000 people detained for screening, the 23d Division asserted that 256 belonged to the Việt Công Infrastructure (VCI). Other reports placed the number of confirmed members of the VCI captured at fewer than 50. By late February, province officials had begun to resettle refugees in new settlements south of the peninsula but refused to let them rebuild on their original home sites. The new camps proved inaccessible by land and difficult to expand because of mines and booby traps in surrounding areas. Not until 1971 did security improve enough to permit all refugees displaced during RUSSELL BEACH to return to the areas where their homes once stood.

RUSSELL BEACH bestowed little political advantage on the RVN government, which mishandled the relocation of people and alienated them. No lasting military gains accrued; the area remained insecure for another two years. Allied forces had failed to eliminate a Communist stronghold, and VC forces continued to levy taxes and abduct local officials. During NANTUCKET BEACH, a February 1970 operation in the same area, numerous GIs were killed by booby traps and mines, and Army engineers destroyed new bunkers and tunnels in nearly the same sites as during the previous operation. By January 1971, the VC 48th Battalion was back in action on the peninsula.

—Richard A. Hunt

References: Hunt, Richard A. *Pacification: The American Struggle for Vietnam's Hearts and Minds* (1995); Lewy, Gunter (1978); Wiesner, Louis. *Victims and Survivors* (1988).

See also: Civilian Operations and Revolutionary Development Support (CORDS); My Lai Massacre; Refugees and Boat People.

Bollaert, Emile (1890–1978)

French High Commissioner for Indo-China, March 1947–October 1948. Bollaert, a member of the Radical Socialist Party, presided over the beginning of the "Bao Đai solution," the French attempt to build up the former emperor as an alternative to Hô Chí Minh and the Việt Minh. Bollaert tried to keep the door open to negotiations with Hô as well as with Bao Đai for a time, but he lacked boldness and authority.

Bollaert succeeded Admiral Thierry d'Argenlieu as High Commissioner. Treading a thin line between the advocates of improved Franco-Vietnamese relations and the military, who favored a hard-line policy, Bollaert prepared a plan for announcing an offer of independence tied to a unilateral cease-fire on 15 August 1947. However, news of the plan alarmed opponents of concessions to the Việt Minh, and Bollaert was forced to delay the announcement and tone down its political content considerably. In the end, it came to naught.

Instead of engaging the Việt Minh in a dialogue, Bollaert approached Bao Đai, in exile in Hong Kong, and signed a preliminary agreement with him in the Bay of Ha Long on 7 December 1947 to assuage his nationalist supporters. This agreement was formalized in a second meeting in the Bay of Ha Long on 5 June 1948, by which Vietnam was to be granted a carefully circumscribed independence as an Associated State within the French Union. The "Bao Đai solution," in the hands of Bollaert's successor, Léon Pignon, became a pretext for waging all-out war against the Việt Minh, and it ultimately failed to win the struggle for allegiance of the Vietnamese people.

—Arthur J. Dommen

Reference: Hammer, Ellen. *The Struggle for Indochina* (1954).

See also: Bao Đai; d'Argenlieu, Georges Thierry; Pignon, Léon; Việt Minh (Việt Nam Độc Lập Đông Minh Hôi [Vietnam Independence League]).

BOLO, Operation (2 January 1967)

Ruse designed by the U.S. Air Force (USAF) to engage North Vietnamese MiG-21s on an equal footing. Since the Johnson administration prohibited U.S. aircraft from bombing Democratic Republic of Vietnam (DRV) airfields until April 1967, the Air Force neededed another way of reducing increasingly dangerous levels of MiG activity in the North. Consequently, in December 1966 Seventh Air Force Headquarters planned a trap for the MiGs by exploiting deception and the weaknesses of DRV ground radar network.

Normally U.S. Air Force strike packages flew in standard formations, which included refueling F-105 fighter-bombers at lower altitudes than their F-4 escorts. In Operation BOLO, F-4s imitated F-105 formations to convince DRV ground controllers that their radars showed a normal F-105 strike mission. However, when controllers vectored MiG interceptors against their enemies, the MiG 21s found F-4s, equipped for air-to-air combat, rather than the slower F-105s. To maximize fighter coverage over Hà Nôi and deny North Vietnamese MiGs an exit route to airfields in China, Operation BOLO called for 14 flights of USAF fighters to converge over the city. Aircraft from the 8th Tactical Fighter Wing (TFW) based at Ubon Air Base in Thailand would fly into the Hà Nôi area from Laos; fighters from the 366th TFW based at Đà Nang would arrive from the Gulf of Tonkin.

Marginal weather on 2 January 1967 delayed the start of the mission, and only three flights of F-4s reached the target area. Col. Robin Olds, 8th TFW commander, led the first of these flights; Lt. Col. Daniel "Chappie" James, the second; and Capt. John Stone, the third. Olds's flight passed over the Phúc Yên airfield twice before MiG-21s popped out of the clouds. The intense air battle that followed lasted less than 15 minutes but was the largest single aerial dogfight of the Vietnam War. Twelve F-4s destroyed seven MiG-21s and claimed two more probable kills. There were no USAF losses.

Operation BOLO destroyed almost half of the DRV's inventory of MiG-21s. Although bad weather prevented full execution of the plan, it achieved its primary objective of reducing U.S. aerial losses. Because of the reduced number of MiG-21s, the DRV Air Force had no choice but to stand down their operations.

—John G. Terino, Jr.

References: Bell, Kenneth H. *100 Missions North* (1993); Middleton Drew, ed. *Air War—Vietnam* (1978); Momyer, William W. *Airpower in Three Wars* (1980); Nordeen, Lon O. *Air Warfare in the Missile Age* (1985); Pimlott, John. *Vietnam: The Decisive Battles* (1990).

See also: Airplanes, Allied and Democratic Republic of Vietnam; Air Defense, Democratic Republic of Vietnam; Olds, Robin.

Bombs, Dumb

Class of unguided munitions dropped by aircraft. Dumb bombs used by U.S. forces during the Vietnam War can be principally classified into standard bomb and cluster bomb types, although such classification is at times misleading. Standard bombs tend to be more effective against troops in fortified bunkers or in dense vegetation. Cluster bombs tend to be more useful against troops in open ground.

Standard (conventional) bombs used in Vietnam were larger and more streamlined than earlier conventional bombs because of advances in aircraft and bomb design.

General purpose (GP) bombs, such as the Mk82, M-117, Mk84, and M-118 weighed 500, 750, 2,000 and 3,000 pounds, respectively. These bombs had equal proportions of high-explosive filler and fragmenting steel casing. Variants of the GP bomb were fragmentation bombs, with a higher percentage of steel casing, and concussion bombs, with a higher percentage of explosive filler. Cluster bombs are a more recent development than standard bombs and, as the name implies, are groups of bombs released together in a cluster. This allows a larger area to be targeted than with single conventional munitions.

An extensive series of dispensers and cluster bombs were employed in the Vietnam War. A dispenser (suspension and release unit [SUU]) carried a large number of submunitions (bomblet units [BLUs]). Later modifications to both dispensers and cluster bombs resulted in the development of almost indecipherable designations. To add to this confusion, many BLUs, such as the 500-pound BLU-57 fragmentation bomb, are actually conventional bombs. A wide range of munitions were thus used in BLU designations. These ranged in weight from about a pound for bomblets up to 15,000 pounds.

Such munitions were based on blast, antipersonnel fragmentation, antiarmor shaped charge, white phosphorus, smoke, napalm, fuel air explosive, and chemical warfare types. Specific bombs of note are the BLU-82B, MK20, and BLU-73. The BLU-82B, the renowned "Daisy Cutter," was first employed in early 1970. This 15,000-poundbomb is filled with DBA-22M, a slurry of ammonium nitrate, aluminum powder, and a binding agent. The result is an explosive filler with about twice the power of TNT, which for this bomb produced casualties out to a radius of almost 400 meters. The Daisy Cutter, which relied on a parachute to slow its descent, was used against enemy troop concentrations and to create helicopter landing zones and cause landslides for road interdiction.

The MK20 "Rockeye" was a common 500-pound antitank cluster bomb. It dispensed 247 Mk118 nine-inch antiarmor/antipersonnel bomblets shaped like darts and could discriminate between hard and soft targets. The BLU-73 was a 100-pound fuel-air explosive (FAE) bomblet. Three of them were contained within a CBU-55 and relied on a parachute for a controlled descent. These bomblets burst on impact with the ground and sprayed out an ethylene oxide vapor cloud. After a few seconds' delay, the cloud was detonated, producing an immense and violent explosion. This bomb became operational in Vietnam in October 1970.

Cluster bombs, while considered dumb, should still be considered highly advanced from a technical perspective. To stress this point, the number of bomblets a B-52 bomber could drop is almost unimaginable. In one sortie, 25,488 BLU-26B or BLU-36B submunitions could be dispersed. A BLU-26B "Guava" fragmentation bomblet was 6 cm in diameter, and upon impact each projected 300 steel pellets. The BLU-36B variant had a random delay fuze. A single B-52 loaded with these bomblets could thus saturate an area of approximately 629 acres, slightly less than a square mile, with over 7.5 million steel pellets.

—Robert J. Bunker

References: Doleman, Edgar D. *Tools of War* (1984); Naval Air Systems Command. *Antitank Bomb Cluster Mk 20, Mods 2, 3, 4 and 6 and Antipersonnel/Antimateriel Bomb Cluster CBU-59/B* (1975); Stockholm International Peace Research Institute (1978); U.S. Army. *Bombs and Bomb Components* (1966).
See also: ARC LIGHT (B-52 Raids); Bombs, Smart (PGMs); Napalm.

Bombs, Smart (PGMs)

Class of guided munitions dropped by aircraft. The origins of the smart bomb can be traced to development of the German Fritz X and Hs-293 visually guided bombs and U.S. Azon and Razon radio-guided bombs during World War II. Smart bombs allows for precision accuracy in the engagement of a target so planes can fly less vulnerable attack profiles. Fewer sorties and munitions are required to destroy a target, and logistical demands are reduced. Thus both human and economic costs are lowered in the attainment of a military objective.

In Vietnam several factors further stimulated the need for such precision guided munitions (PGMs). Supplies were brought into South Vietnam at night, evading U.S. air superiority. Moral concerns dictated that vital military targets in or near population centers be destroyed without harming innocent civilians. Finally, many North Vietnamese targets were protected by highly effective antiaircraft defense zones around Hà Nôi and Hai Phòng.

Two types of smart bombs were developed for use in this war: the laser-guided bomb (LGB) and the electro-optical guided bomb (EOGB). The LGB program, the product of the U.S. Army's Missile Command (MiCom) in the early 1960s, was based on the use of a pulsed laser beam to "spot" a target. The reflected light could then be homed in by a seeker system attached to a missile. This program was abandoned by the Army but was resurrected by the Air Force's Detachment 5 research group in 1965. Prototype testing for the "Paveway" bomb, based on laser seeker/guidance kits attached to M117 (750-pound) and Mk-84 (2,000-pound), began in summer 1966. The cheaper but riskier design won out and was field tested in Vietnam in May 1968. Early 1970s computer simulations estimated that target kill was improved by a factor of 200 when laser guidance was added to the manually released 2000-pound bomb. The GBU-2 "Pave Storm" variant was a cluster bomb that released 1,800 BLU-63 fragmentation bomblets.

The EOGB program, led by the U.S. Navy, was vastly smaller than the LGB program. It was based around a specially built bomb known as the "Walleye" (AGM-62) fitted with a nose camera that the pilot aimed at the target. After release, the bomb's internal computer system took it to the aim point. This 850-lb bomb was first used over North Vietnam in 1967. The 2,000-lb Walleye II version was introduced in 1972. It was later modified with a data link that allowed an air crew to correct the aim point or manually take the bomb to the target once it had been released. The Air Force also produced a homing bomb system (HOBOS), based on a modified Mk-84, that was first used in combat in February 1969.

Smart bombs allowed much flexibility in the use of air-power tactics. The designator for a LGB could either be in the aircraft dropping the bomb or in a second combat aircraft outside the range of enemy threats. The advantage of having a second aircraft designate a target was that it allowed the first aircraft to exit the target area immediately and head for safety. Toward the end of the war, the Walleye II could be dropped up to 32 miles from a designated target, toward which it would then glide. Such targets had to be very large and provide enough contrast to allow for seeker lock-on.

In Vietnam the Air Force and Navy dropped 26,690 smart bombs. LGBs represented 94 percent of this total, with the Mk-84 LGB representing 84 percent of that total or 79 percent of all PGMs used. Although they represent less than 1 percent of all bombs of more than 500 pounds dropped by U.S. forces, smart bombs had an influence on target destruction far out of proportion to their limited numbers. Their average circular error probability (CEP) was 30 feet; conventional (dumb) bombs had an average CEP of 420 feet. Smart bombs were used with devastating effect in LINEBACKER II.

—Robert J. Bunker

References: Blackwelder, Donald I. *The Long Road to Desert Storm and Beyond: The Development of Precision Guided Bombs* (1993); Deleon, Peter. *The Laser-Guided Bomb: Case History of a Development* (1972); Doleman, Edgar D. *Tools of War* (1984).
See also: Bombs, Dumb; LINEBACKER I, Operation; LINEBACKER II, Operation.

Booby Traps

Concealed devices used to inflict casualties. Booby traps were an integral component of the war waged by Viêt Công and People's Army of Vietnam (PAVN) forces in Vietnam. Between January 1965 and June 1970, 11 percent of the fatalities and 17 percent of the wounds among U.S. Army troops were caused by booby traps and mines. These devices were used to delay and disrupt the mobility of U.S. forces, divert resources toward guard duty and clearance operations, inflict casualties, and damage equipment. They were a key component in pre-arranged killing zones. Booby traps had a lasting psychological impact on Marines and soldiers and further alienated them from civilian populations that could not be distinguished from combatants. Many of the materials used in mines and booby traps were of U.S. origin or indigenous resources.

Booby traps were divided into explosive and nonexplosive antipersonnel devices and antivehicle devices. Antipersonnel booby traps were concentrated in commonly traveled routes. Antivehicle booby traps were deployed primarily on road networks, bridges, potential laager positions, and riverine choke points. Nonexplosive antipersonnel devices included punji stakes, bear traps, crossbow traps, spiked mud balls, double-spike caltrops, and scorpion-filled boxes. Punji stakes—sharpened lengths of bamboo with fire-hardened, needle-like tips that were often coated with excrement to cause infection—were a common booby trap. Explosive antipersonnel devices included the powder-filled coconut, mudball mine, grenade-in-tin-can mine, bounding fragmentation mine, cartridge trap, and bicycle booby trap. The mud ball mine was a clay-encrusted grenade with the safety pin removed. Stepping on the mud ball released the safety lever, resulting in detonation. Antivehicle devices included the B-40 antitank booby trap, concrete fragmentation mine, mortar shell mine, and oil-drum charge. The oil-drum charge, a 5–gallon drum filled with explosives and triggered by a wristwatch firing device, had immense sabotage applications for use against fuel dumps.

These devices were used on a scale never before encountered by U.S. military forces. As casualties stemming from booby traps mounted, U.S. forces employed numerous countermeasures. The most effective focused on destruction of underground VC/PAVN mine and booby trap factories and elimination of raw materials used in such devices. Tactical countermeasures included use of electronic listening devices and ground surveillance radar; patrolling; deploying scout-sniper teams and Kit Carson Scouts; booby trapping trash left by a unit; and employing artillery ambush zones. Principal individual countermeasures were wearing body armor, sandbagging the floors of armored personnel carriers (APCs), and abstaining from the collection of souvenirs.

—Robert J. Bunker

References: Doleman, Edgar D. *Tools of War* (1984); U.S. Army Foreign Service and Technology Center. *Mines and Booby Traps* (1969); U.S. Marine Corps Base, Quantico. *Vietcong Mine Warfare* (1966); Wells, Robert, ed. *The Invisible Enemy: Boobytraps in Vietnam* (1992).
See also: Kit Carson Scouts; Mines, Antipersonnel and Antitank.

Bowles, Chester B. (1901–1986)

U.S. under secretary of state. A New Deal Democrat who preferred economic aid and development to military coercion, Bowles opposed the growing U.S. troop commitment to Laos and Vietnam and argued that it might provoke Chinese intervention. Fired from the State Department in November 1961, he received a largely meaningless appointment as the president's special representative for foreign policy. In this capacity he called for a "Peace Charter for Southeast Asia," a continuation of his earlier neutralization schemes, together with massive economic aid for the region. He resigned in January 1963 and served as ambassador to India, where he stayed until 1969. Privately he continued to advocate similar economic policies and supported a halt to bombing and the opening of peace negotiations; publicly he remained silent. The Johnson administration ignored his dissenting advice.

In January 1968 Bowles represented the United States in talks with Prince Norodom Sihanouk of Cambodia. His intended objectives were to deny Cambodian sanctuary to Viêt Công and People's Army of Vietnam forces and to limit U.S. military incursions into Cambodian territory to preserve that country's neutrality and integrity. The talks failed to prevent a full-scale American invasion of Cambodia.

—Priscilla Roberts

References: Bowles, Chester B. *Promises to Keep: My Years in Public Life, 1941–1969* (1971); Schaffer, Howard B. *Chester Bowles: New Dealer in the Cold War* (1993).
See also: Cambodia; Kennedy, John Fitzgerald; Sihanouk, Norodom.

Bradley, Omar Nelson (1893–1981)

U.S. Army general; first chairman of the Joint Chiefs of Staff, 1949–1953. In February 1948 Bradley succeeded Eisenhower as Army Chief of Staff, and in August 1949 he became the first chairman of the Joint Chiefs of Staff, a post he held throughout the Korean War until August 1953. Bradley was promoted to General of the Army (five-star rank) in September 1950.

During the Korean War Bradley sought to keep Europe as the top U.S. military priority, something that General Douglas MacArthur could not appreciate. This was exemplified in Bradley's well-known characterization of that conflict as the "wrong war, in the wrong place, and with the wrong enemy." Bradley supported U.S. military aid for the French in Indo-China. He characterized the Navarre Plan as "a marked improvement in French military thinking," but added a cautionary note that, based on "past performances" by the French, there could be no predictions regarding the effects of increased U.S. assistance. In U.S. contingency planning, Bradley doubted that American air and naval attacks could alone bring victory, although he accepted these as preferable to U.S. involvement in another Asian ground war.

Bradley retired from the service in August 1953. In 1968 he was one of the "Wise Men" who advised President Johnson against a withdrawal from Vietnam.

—Spencer C. Tucker

References: Arnold, James R. *The First Domino. Eisenhower, The Military, and America's Intervention in Vietnam* (1991); Bradley. Omar N. *A Soldier's Story* (1951); Dupuy, Trevor N., Curt Johnson, and David L. Bongard. *The Harper Encyclopedia of Military Biography* (1992); Prados, John. *The Sky Would Fall. Operation Vulture: The U.S. Bombing Mission in Indochina, 1954* (1983).
See also: Eisenhower, Dwight David; Johnson, Lyndon Baines; MacArthur, Douglas; Navarre Plan; "Wise Men."

Brady, Patrick H. (1936–)

U.S. Army officer, considered by many the top helicopter pilot of the Vietnam War. Brady first reported to Vietnam in January 1964 and was assigned as a medical evacuation pilot to the 57th Medical Detachment (Helicopter Ambulance), under the command of Maj. Charles L. Kelly. After Kelly was killed in action on 1 July, Brady assumed command of the 57th's Detachment A, operating out of the Mekong Delta. In August 1967 Brady returned to Vietnam for a second tour of duty, this time as the operations officer and later commander of the 54th Medical Detachment. Brady instilled in his new unit the ethos of his old mentor Kelly: "No compromise. No rationalization. No hesitation. Fly the mission. Now!" Patients came above all else.

On 5 January 1968, piloting "Dust Off 55," Brady flew an incredible series of nine medevac missions in the fog-wrapped mountains near Chu Lai, under intense enemy fire. For his actions, Brady was awarded the Medal of Honor. By the time he finished his second tour in Vietnam, Brady also had the Distinguished Service Cross and the Distinguished Flying Cross with five Oak Leaf Clusters.

—David T. Zabecki

References: Brady, Patrick H. "When I Have Your Wounded" (1989); Dorland, Peter, and James Nanney. *Dust Off: Army Aeromedical Evacuation in Vietnam* (1982).
See also: Helicopters, Employment of, in Vietnam; Kelly, Charles L.; Medevac.

BRAVO I and BRAVO II, Operations
(29 October–2 November 1963)

The two stages of the 1963 South Vietnamese "pseudocoup" devised by Ngô Đình Nhu to preempt an anticipated generals' revolt and preserve the regime of his brother, Ngô Đình Diêm. In early October 1963, a cabal of Army of Republic of Vietnam (ARVN) generals conspired with U.S. approval to overthrow the government of Ngô Đình Diêm. Led by General Trân Van Đôn, the plotters included Generals Duong Van Minh, Lê Van Kim, Nguyên Van Vy, Mai Huu Xuân, Tôn Thât Đính, and Colonel Pham Ngoc Thao. U.S. Ambassador Henry Cabot Lodge, Jr., and CIA officer Lt. Col. Lucien Conein provided crucial support and encouragement to the conspirators.

The generals' coup was first scheduled for 26 October—Armed Forces Day in the RVN—so that insurgent ARVN units could be deployed in the capital without attracting undue attention. Uncertainties, however, caused the date to be pushed back to 2 November. The generals proceeded cautiously, anxious about U.S. policy and unsure of themselves in the complex and turbulent world of South Vietnamese politics, which seethed with murky plots within plots.

A thorny problem for the plotters was the recruitment of Sài Gòn region commander General Tôn Thât Đính, whose cooperation was essential if the coup was to succeed. Adroitly playing to his ego, Đôn advised Đính to demand that Diêm appoint him minister of the interior. When Diêm refused—as Đôn knew he would—Đôn promised Đính the same post in the successor regime if he joined the conspiracy, and Đính accepted. Although now officially a conspirator, Đính was far from a trusted partner.

Đôn used Đính's position to neutralize General Huynh Van Cao, a Diêm loyalist commanding ARVN forces in the Mekong Delta. Cao's three divisions, deployed near Sài Gòn, could easily thwart the coup if allowed into the city. To avert this, Đôn and Đính planned to have Đính's deputy, Col. Nguyên Huu Có, take temporary command of Cao's nearest division at My Tho on the eve of the coup. Có would then use these troops to block any rescue attempts by Cao's other forces. News of this supposedly secret maneuver, however, reached Nhu, who confronted Đính with his knowledge of Có's role. Feigning astonishment, Đính flew into such a theatrical rage at his deputy's "duplicity" that he convinced Nhu of his complete loyalty to the regime. Nhu then took Đính into his confidence, advised him of his knowledge of the rest of the generals' plot, and proposed an elaborate "phony coup" to trap them in their betrayal.

Nhu divided his scheme into two phases—designated BRAVO I and BRAVO II—and assigned Đính a pivotal role in each. In early November Đính would begin BRAVO I by ordering Col. Lê Quang Tung's loyalist Special Forces out of the city on the pretext of hunting guerillas. During their absence loyalist police and other soldiers disguised as rebels and hoodlums would stage a "spontaneous" revolt, murdering selected Vietnamese and U.S. officials and spreading terror throughout the city. During the uproar, Diêm and Nhu would "flee" to a secure refuge. Sài Gòn radio would then issue a false proclamation announcing the creation of a "revolutionary government" dedicated to the eviction of all Americans and conciliation with the Communists. BRAVO II would follow a few days later. Spearheaded by Tùng's Special Forces, Đính would sweep back into Sài Gòn, crush the "uprising," "rescue" the Diêm brothers, and triumphantly return the rightful government to power. His legitimacy reaffirmed, Diêm would emerge stronger than ever.

The problem with Nhu's plot was his reliance upon Đính. Đính promptly informed Đôn of Nhu's scheme, prompting the generals to move up their own coup to 1 November to preempt that of Nhu. In turn, when he learned through more informants of the generals' change of schedule—although astonishingly not of Đính's treachery—Nhu moved BRAVO I up to 29 October. Believing that he could now turn his phony coup into a real countercoup, Nhu instructed Đính to order Colonel Tùng's Special Forces out of the city to begin BRAVO I. Đính obeyed but insisted on command of General Cao's Mekong Delta divisions to ensure the smooth unfolding of BRAVO II. Despite all his informants, Nhu was still unaware of Đính's true purpose and agreed. Thus, at the start of the coup, Đính personally controlled most military forces in and around Sài Gòn.

During the last days of October, Đính freely deployed troops inside the capital and positioned them to attack key government installations. The Ngô brothers, sequestered in the Presidential Palace and still believing Đính to be on their side, confidently awaited news of their countercoup. On 1 November the coup leaders summoned Colonel Tùng and Capt. Hô Tân Quyên, Diem's loyalist Navy commander, to "a routine meeting." Both men were killed, along with Tùng's brother, Maj. Lê Quang Triêu.

Still believing that BRAVO I was unfolding smoothly, Diêm and Nhu rejected the generals' initial demands that they surrender. They began to have doubts when Đính would not return their calls. At about 1500 on 1 November Diêm telephoned Đôn and attempted to initiate conciliatory talks. When calls for resistance failed, the Ngô brothers fled to Cho Lon, where they were arrested and murdered on 2 November.

—Edward C. Page

References: Berman, Larry. *Planning a Tragedy: The Americanization of the War in Vietnam* (1982); Davidson, Phillip B. *Vietnam at War: The History: 1946–1975* (1988); Kahin, George M. *Intervention: How America Became Involved in Vietnam* (1986); Karnow, Stanley. *Vietnam: A History* (1984); Morrison, Wilbur H. *The Elephant and the Tiger: The Full Story of the Vietnam War* (1990).

See also: Conein, Lucien Emile; Duong Van Minh; Huynh Van Cao; Lê Quang Tung; Lê Van Kim; Lodge, Henry Cabot, Jr.; Ngô Đình Diêm; Ngô Đình Nhu; Nguyên Huu Có; Pham Ngoc Thao; Taylor, Maxwell Davenport; Tôn Thât Đính; Trân Van Đôn.

Brezhnev, Leonid Ilyich (1906–1982)

Soviet Communist Party general secretary. After Khrushchev's ouster in 1964, Brezhnev became the Communist Party general secretary, the Soviet Union's most important position. Under his leadership the Soviet Union achieved strategic military parity with the United States, but at the cost of an ever-deepening economic crisis that would eventually engulf the Soviet Union.

Brezhnev viewed American involvement in Vietnam as a windfall for the USSR. He reversed Khrushchev's policy of disengagement and increased economic and military aid to the Democratic Republic of Vietnam (DRV), hoping to entice it from its pro-Chinese stance. Yet he discouraged a further escalation of the war, fearing a direct confrontation with the United States. Thus Soviet assistance was carefully calculated to allow the DRV to hold its own and to tie up American forces. Vietnam, however, was never high on Brezhnev's list of priorities, and he would not allow the war to destroy his emerging détente with the United States.

After the DRV's 1975 military victory Brezhnev continued the close relationship and extensive aid. The DRV/Socialist Republic of Vietnam (SRV) leadership held Brezhnev in higher regard than any other Soviet leader, believing he best understood their goals. In 1980 the SRV awarded Brezhnev its highest decoration, the Order of Golden Star.

—Michael Share

References: Edmonds, Robin. *Soviet Foreign Policy: The Brezhnev Years* (1983); Gelman, II. *The Brezhnev Politburo* (1984).

See also: Khrushchev, Nikita Sergeyevitch; Union of Soviet Socialist Republics (USSR; Soviet Union); Vietnam, Socialist Republic of: 1975 to the Present.

Brown, George Scratchley (1918–1978)

U.S. Air Force general and chairman of the Joint Chiefs of Staff. In 1968 Brown assumed command of the Seventh Air Force and was also designated deputy commander for air operations for Military Assistance Command, Vietnam (MACV). In these dual capacities Brown emphasized his role as General Creighton Abrams's primary advisor on air operations, while delegating great authority over daily operations to his staff. Brown felt air power was underutilized, and he sought to integrate air operations fully into all tactical and strategic plans. Abrams agreed with this approach, and the two men worked well together to manage joint operations effectively.

After two successful years in South Vietnam, Brown left there in 1970. In June 1974 he was appointed chairman of the Joint Chiefs of Staff and successfully led the services through the initial crises of the post–Vietnam War era. His tenure was somewhat tarnished by comments he made that were interpreted to be anti-Semitic.

—Richard D. Starnes

References: Puryear, Edgar F., Jr. *George S. Brown. General, U. S. Air Force: Destined For Stars* (1983); Tilford, Earl H. *Crosswinds: The Air Force's Setup in Vietnam* (1993).

See also: Abrams, Creighton; Military Assistance Command, Vietnam (MACV); United States: Air Force.

Brown, Samuel Winfred, Jr. (1943–)

Political activist/organizer; cofounder and coordinator of the Vietnam Moratorium Committee. While at Redlands University, Brown participated in the National Student Association, met Allard Lowenstein, and became an antiwar activist. In 1966 Brown enrolled at Harvard Divinity School, where Lowenstein recruited him to organize seminarians against the war. Brown directed the "Children's Crusade," student volunteers in Eugene McCarthy's 1968 New Hampshire presidential primary campaign. Responding to the concept for a nationwide strike against the war, on 30 June 1969 Brown and others established the Vietnam Moratorium Committee. His genius for organizing contributed in large measure to the success of the October and November demonstrations, the largest public protests to that time in U.S. history.

In 1970 Brown coedited *Why Are We Still in Vietnam?*, an examination of U.S. policy in Southeast Asia, and cofounded Operation Pursestrings to lobby for the McGovern-Hatfield end-the-war amendment. In 1972 he actively supported George McGovern's presidential campaign.

On 4 May 1994 the Senate Foreign Relations Committee approved President Clinton's nomination of Brown as ambassador to the Conference on Security and Cooperation in Europe. Senate Republicans led an opposition filibuster, citing Brown's anti–Vietnam War activities and knowingly misrepresented him as an unrepentant 1960s radical. The nomination failed when the Senate twice failed to break the filibuster.

—Paul S. Daum, with Francis Ryan

References: Brown, Sam, and Len Ackland, eds. *Why Are We Still in Vietnam?* (1970); DeBenedetti, Charles. *The Antiwar Movement of the Vietnam Era* (1990); Rosenbaum, David E. "Moratorium Organizer" (1969); Zaroulis, Nancy, and Gerald Sullivan. *Who Spoke Up? American Protest against the War in Vietnam, 1963–1975* (1984). **See also:** Hatfield-McGovern Amendment; McCarthy, Eugene Joseph; McGovern, George S.; Moratorium to End the War in Vietnam.

Bruce, David K. E. (1898–1977)

American diplomat; head of the U.S. delegation to the Paris Peace Talks, 1970–1971. From the late 1940s onward, Bruce, who did not share the anticolonialist leanings of many Americans, paid much attention to French Indo-China, initially enthusiastically urging greater U.S. military and economic assistance for French efforts to subdue the Việt Minh and promote Emperor Bao Đai, to whom he thought his own government too unsympathetic. He was, however, somewhat relieved by the final French defeat at Điên Biên Phu, which he believed ended an increasingly pointless and expensive commitment to an unwinnable war.

Doubting the wisdom of U.S. involvement in South Vietnam, Laos, and Cambodia, and unconvinced that U.S. military efforts were likely to succeed, Bruce in the 1960s nonetheless believed that, having pledged itself to these states, the United States should keep its commitments. As ambassador to Great Britain, he was frequently obliged to defend U.S. policies in public, even as private skepticism led him to question the accuracy of reports of the Tonkin Gulf incident. He was repelled by growing public protests against the war. Bruce's growing private doubts as to the likelihood of an American victory in Southeast Asia and concern over the war's domestic and international political implications for the United States led him to hope for a negotiated settlement. To this end, Bruce supported various proposals, particularly an abortive attempt to end the war mounted in 1967 by British Prime Minister Harold Wilson in collaboration with visiting Soviet Premier Aleksei Kosygin. He therefore welcomed President Johnson's 1968 decision to seek peace and U.S. withdrawal. From 1970 to 1971 he headed the U.S. delegation at the Paris peace talks. There he frequently was frustrated by lengthy North Vietnamese propaganda harangues and came to regard his assignment as an empty charade, in which each side's rhetoric was designed for public consumption rather than to further genuine negotiations.

Bruce served as the first head of the new U.S. Liaison Office to the People's Republic of China (1973–1974), a largely symbolic position. His seniority, ability, and charm proved important assets at a crucial stage in the reopening of Sino-American relations. In poor health, he retired after a final stint as ambassador to NATO (1974–1975).

—Priscilla Roberts

Reference: Lankford, Nelson D. *The Last American Aristocrat: The Biography of Ambassador David K. E. Bruce* (1996).
See also: Kosygin, Alexei Nikolayevich; Paris Negotiations.

Brzezinski, Zbigniew Kazimierz (1928–)

U.S. assistant to the president for national security affairs, 1977–1981. Noted throughout his political career as a hardline anti-Communist, Brzezinski was an early advocate of U.S. involvement in Vietnam. An academic by profession, he served as a foreign policy advisor to Presidents Kennedy and Johnson. In the 1960s and 1970s Brzezinski saw Communist expansion in Asia as the greatest threat to world peace and worked to oppose it. His antiexpansionism persisted during his tenure on the National Security Council under President Carter, although the focus shifted. Brzezinski played a key role in the 1978 Camp David meetings and received the Presidential Medal of Freedom in 1981.

—Timothy C. Dowling

References: Brown, Seyom. *The Faces of Power: United States Foreign Policy from Truman to Clinton* (1994); Brzezinski, Zbigniew. *Power and Principle: Memoirs of the National Security Advisor, 1977–1981* (1983).
See also: Carter, Jimmy; Johnson, Lyndon Baines; Kennedy, John Fitzgerald.

Buddhists

Buddhism was introduced to Vietnam from China in the second and third centuries. During the French control of Vietnam in the nineteenth century, Buddhism faced some restrictions as the French tried to spread Catholicism. In 1951 Vietnamese Buddhists formed the General Association of Buddhists (GAB) to reorganize their religious activities. In the mid-1960s only three million Vietnamese considered themselves active Buddhists, but 15 million (80 percent of the population) were nominally associated with the religion.

Republic of Vietnam President Ngô Đình Diêm, raised a Catholic, granted high-level administrative and military positions to Catholics and refused to repeal anti-Buddhist restrictions remaining from the French occupation. Following the 8 May 1963 gathering in Huê to celebrate Buddha's birthday, at which nine people were killed by police, a Buddhist delegation presented Diêm with five demands calling for an end to religious persecution. Diêm claimed the deaths were from a Communist terrorist's grenade. This blatantly false statement outraged the Buddhists, who publicized their complaints and called for Diêm's resignation.

On 11 June 1963 a Buddhist monk, Thích Quang Đuc, committed self-immolation at a busy Sài Gòn intersection. During the next few months, more protests and self-immolations took place. In August 1963 special troops disguised as regular soldiers attacked Buddhists in Sài Gòn and Huê, jailing more than 1,000 monks, nuns, and students. Citizens rioted in protest. Washington demanded that Diêm deal with the unrest, but he refused to capitulate. Madame Nhu exacerbated the situation by calling the self-immolations "barbecues."

The Buddhist protests were religious in nature. Recognizing that the Democratic Republic of Vietnam (DRV) would use them to denounce Diêm and the United States, the leaders wanted to keep political grievances separate. No evidence existed to support Diêm's accusation of Communist intervention. His stubbornness led Buddhist leaders to the conclusion that religious freedom would be achieved only with a new government. Although they did not take part in the actual coup, Buddhists were partly responsible for Diêm's overthrow. Their unrest had diverted much of his government's attention from counterinsurgency operations and created a schism in his supporters. Three cabinet officials and 80 to 90 percent of the military forces were Buddhist.

Following Diêm's assassination, General Nguyên Khánh, his successor, lifted some restrictions and appointed Buddhists to high-level positions. The Venerable Thích Tâm Châu, recently elected leader of the growing GAB, cooperated with the government. Later, when Khánh reneged, Thích Trí Quang organized more protests in Huê, citing the United States as an accomplice in the repressive regime. The American Library and Consulate in Huê, as well as the American Embassy in Sài Gòn, were burned.

The Buddhists' unified strength forced Nguyên Cao Ky to place political power in elected representatives. In May 1966, after Ky was accused of harboring pro-Diêm sentiments, ten monks and nuns set themselves afire. But Ky was able to win back the allegiance of military leaders who had been supporting the Buddhists and jailed Thích Trí Quang, who was in the middle of a hunger strike. Since Washington strongly supported Ky, the protest movement soon died.

—Charles N. Fasanaro

Reference: Vietnam Archives, Texas Tech University.
See also: Ngô Đình Diêm; Ngô Đình Nhu, Madame; Nguyên Cao Ky; Thích Quang Đuc; Thích Trí Quang.

BUFFALO, Operation (2–14 July 1967)

Military operation conducted just south of the Demilitarized Zone (DMZ) at Côn Thiên. A small rise two miles south of the DMZ, Côn Thiên was considered by many on both sides as the most important natural observation post along the entire DMZ. Washington saw it as a critical element in the McNamara Line, the purpose of which was to impede the movement of People's Army of Vietnam (PAVN) regiments across the DMZ into South Vietnam. Côn Thiên overlooked the crucial "Leatherneck Square" area, a quadrilateral defined by Marine strong points at Côn Thiên, Gio Linh, Đông Hà, and Cam Lô.

By the end of June 1967 some 35,000 PAVN troops were positioned above the DMZ. Their mission was to launch a major invasion into Quang Tri Province and score an important propaganda victory. PAVN forces were organized into the 304th, 320th, 324B, and 325C Divisions.

Operation BUFFALO began on 2 July 1967 when Companies A and B of Lt. Col. Richard Schening's 1st Battalion, 9th Marines (1/9), went out to sweep an area east of Côn Thiên. The battalion's primary mission was defense of the Côn Thiên combat base. Constraints imposed by Washington allowed PAVN troops to use the northern half of the DMZ for regrouping and employment of heavy artillery, and Companies A and B immediately came under fire from two PAVN battalions in prepared positions. Schening alerted Company C in Đông Hà to prepare for lifting by helicopter into Company B's area. To support Companies A and B he also dispatched four tanks and a platoon from Company D, under Assistant S-3 Capt. Henry Radcliffe. As Company C arrived by helicopter, Captain Radcliffe ordered the platoon of Company D to secure the landing zone (LZ) and evacuate casualties. The battle grew in intensity, and Capt. Albert Slater's Company A remained under heavy fire. Enemy forces got within 50 meters of his lines before artillery and small arms broke their attack.

Late in the afternoon, commander of the 9th Marines Col. George Jerue ordered Maj. Willard Woodring's 3d Battalion, 9th Marines to move by helicopter to assist 1/9. During the next three days there was constant contact, especially with heavy mortar and artillery fire. On 3 July Lt. Col. Peter Wickwire's battalion landing team (BLT) 1/3 from Special Landing Force (SLF) Alpha joined the 9th Marines. The regiment planned to drive north and push the PAVN troops out of the Lang Sòn area to the northeast of Côn Thiên by 4,000 meters. Maj. Wendell Beard's BLT 2/3 from SLF Bravo joined the operation on 4 July. The next day all units came under heavy artillery fire while recovering Company B's dead. On 6 July, following preparatory artillery fire, all units continued their drive north.

By late afternoon on the 6th both Wickwire's and Woodring's battalions were taken under heavy PAVN artillery fire and were unable to move. Some 500 to 600 rounds hit the 3d Battalion's position and over 1,000 rounds fell on BLT 1/3. Providing security on the left flank, Major Woodring's forces were able to move into position without opposition and establish a strong outpost.

By early evening heavy enemy probes, including small

arms and mortar fire, were directed at Slater's unit. Throughout the night PAVN units maintained pressure on the Marines. On 7 July Woodring ordered Captain Slater's Company A to pull back into the battalion perimeter.

Late in the afternoon on 7 July the Marines countered with supporting arms, attack aircraft, flare ships, naval gunfire, and artillery. By 8 July the Marines had repelled the assault and reported that the Communists had pulled back across the Bên Hai River. The Marines could not give an accurate count of PAVN losses because they could not continue north of the river. Based on documents recovered, the 90th PAVN Regiment had borne the brunt of the attack. The last major engagements of Operation BUFFALO took place on 8 July when Companies F and G came under small arms fire. The Marines responded with both artillery and air strikes.

Operation BUFFALO ended on 14 July 1967. The Marines reported 1,290 PAVN dead and losses of their own totaling 159 killed and 345 wounded. Côn Thiên had held, and the fighting affirmed the importance of the Marine Corps doctrine with regard to close coordination between elements of the ground and air commands. Two ominous developments were evident, however: the ability of PAVN gunners to employ accurate long-range artillery and the increased use of surface-to-air missiles (SAMs).

—W. E. Fahey, Jr.

References: Nolan, Keith William. *Operation Buffalo: U.S.M.C. Fight for the DMZ* (1991); Tefler, Gary L., Lane Rogers, and V. Keith Flemming, Jr. *U.S. Marine in Vietnam: Fighting the North Vietnamese* (1984).
See also: Côn Thiên; Demilitarized Zone (DMZ); United States: Marine Corps; Vietnam, Democratic Republic of: Army (People's Army of Vietnam [PAVN]).

Bùi Diêm (1923–)

Republic of Vietnam (RVN) ambassador to the United States, 1967–1972. Bùi Diêm participated in the 1954 Geneva Conference, but he then remained outside of politics until after the November 1963 coup that toppled Ngô Đình Diêm. New efforts to create a democracy in the Republic of Vietnam soon failed, and a succession of military leaders followed Diêm. In 1965 Phan Huy Quát became prime minister, but he had no real power. Bùi Diêm became his chief of staff and, in 1966, secretary of state for foreign affairs. From 1967 to 1972 Bùi Diêm was RVN ambassador to Washington; between 1973 and 1975 he was ambassador at large and special envoy to the Paris Peace Talks. In April 1975 Bùi Diêm settled in the United States. Since then he has been president of the executive board of the National Congress of Vietnamese in America. In 1987 he published his autobiography, *In The Jaws of History*.

—William Head

References: Bùi Diêm. "Reflections on the Vietnam War: The Views of a Vietnamese on Vietnamese-American Misconceptions" (1993); Bùi Diêm and David Chanoff. *In The Jaws of History* (1987).
See also: Bao Đai; Đai Viêt Quôc Dân Đang (National Party of Greater Vietnam); Geneva Conference and Geneva Accords; Ngô Đình Diêm; Paris Negotiations; Phan Huy Quát.

Bùi Phát

Refugee slum in Sài Gòn. Bùi Phát was created by peasants, many of them Catholic, who migrated from the northern dioceses of Phát Diêm and Bùi Chu after the signing of the 1954 Geneva Accords. As a result of their religion, these refugees offered a political power base for President Ngô Đình Diêm and actively supported his regime. Other such shanty towns formed as the war expanded and increasing military operations in the South displaced thousands of people. Eventually, the people residing in such slums represented 40 to 50 percent of the South's total population. These refugees became so dependent on the U.S. presence in South Vietnam that they actively resisted efforts by the Viêt Công and Buddhists to organize protests against the growing American presence.

—Robert G. Mangrum

Reference: FitzGerald, Francis. *Fire in the Lake: The Vietnamese and the Americans in Vietnam* (1973).
See also: Ngô Đình Diêm; Search and Destroy; Vietnam, Republic of: 1954–1975.

Bùi Tín (1924–)

North Vietnamese officer, correspondent, and, later, opposition figure. Bùi Tín joined the Viêt Minh struggle against the French in 1945, for a time served as one of Hô Chí Minh's bodyguards, then fought with Viêt Minh forces in 1951 battles in the Red River Delta area and at Điên Biên Phu in 1954. A trusted member of the Communist Party in the years that followed, Bùi Tín was sent by foot down the Hô Chí Minh trail in 1963 to assess the situation in the Republic of Vietnam (RVN). He returned to Hà Nôi in spring 1964 to inform his government that the Viêt Công would have to have northern help.

Over the next ten years Bùi Tín rose to the rank of colonel. During the final People's Army of Vietnam (PAVN) thrust into the South in 1975, he covered the battles as a newspaper correspondent. He rode a tank into the grounds of the South Vietnamese presidential palace on 30 April 1975 and, as senior available officer, accepted Duong Van ("Big") Minh's surrender of the RVN.

Bùi Tín served in Hà Nôi as deputy editor of the *Quân Đôi Nhân Dân* (*People's Army*) newspaper and as deputy editor in chief of the *Nhân Dân* (*People's Daily*) newspaper. Often using the pseudonym of Thành Tín, Bùi Tín argued that the Socialist Republic of Vietnam (SRV) must not turn its back on the Viêt Kiêu (overseas Vietnamese), as there was great potential for the state if all two million of them could be mobilized, as were overseas Chinese, to help build their fatherland with modern technology, science, and management. Slowly frustrated by the conservative intransigence of his government, Bùi Tín went to Paris, ostensibly for health reasons, where he chose to remain in exile. In 1991 and 1993 he published his memoirs under the pseudonym of Thành Tín, *Hoa Xuyên Tuyêt* (*Snowdrop*) (1991) and *Mat Thât* (*The Real Face*) (1993), in which he called for significant changes in his country's government.

—Cecil B. Currey

References: Bùi Tín. Interview with author (1988). Karnow, Stanley. *Vietnam: A History* (1983).
See also: Duong Van Minh; Vietnam, Socialist Republic of: 1975 to the Present; Viêt Minh (Viêt Nam Đôc Lâp Đông Minh Hôi [Vietnam Independence League]).

Bundy, McGeorge (1919–1996)

Special assistant to the president for national security affairs, 1961–1966; key figure in the development of U.S. Vietnam policy. Known for his intelligence (although some thought him arrogant), Bundy was among the most powerful and influential advisors in the Kennedy and Johnson administrations. During five years as special assistant, Bundy was intimately involved in critical decisions on the Vietnam War. He was part of Kennedy's inner circle during the 1963 Buddhist crisis and the coup against President Ngô Đình Diêm. He sought to ensure the survival of a democratic, independent South Vietnam but did not want the United States to take over the fight against the Communist insurgents.

By the end of 1964, however, Bundy favored an enlarged U.S. role, including a graduated bombing campaign against North Vietnam and the buildup of U.S. troops in South Vietnam. He was in Vietnam when the Viêt Công attacked the U.S. barracks and helicopter base at Pleiku in February 1965, killing nine Americans and destroying five aircraft, an event that helped to confirm his belief that the U.S. military had to intervene. He supported retaliatory air raids on North Vietnam and believed that a strong military presence would strengthen the United States and the Republic of Vietnam in peace negotiations. Yet even in the midst of the 1965 troop buildup, Bundy feared that the Americanization of the war would overwhelm civil reform programs and pacification efforts in South Vietnam. During 1965 he urged Johnson to enhance the pacification effort by allocating more resources and improving its management. By that year he also began to question the continuing military escalation.

Bundy resigned from government service because he questioned continuing escalation in Vietnam. He had played an influential role in centralizing U.S. management of pacification programs in Washington under Robert Komer and in Sài Gòn under Ambassador William Porter. As one of the Johnson's "Wise Men," Bundy continued to advise the president. During the critical post-Têt 1968 meeting with Johnson that March, he supported deescalation and a new approach to the war.

—Richard A. Hunt

References: Barrett, David M. *Uncertain Warriors: Lyndon Johnson and his Vietnam Advisors* (1993); Halberstam, David. *The Best and the Brightest* (1972); Hunt, Richard A. *Pacification: The American Struggle for Vietnam's Hearts and Minds* (1995).
See also: Bundy, William P.; Johnson, Lyndon Baines; Kennedy, John Fitzgerald; Komer, Robert W.; McNamara, Robert S.; Ngô Đình Diêm; Ngô Đình Diêm, Overthrow of; Pacification; Porter, William James; Read, Benjamin Huger; Rostow, Walt Whitman; Rusk, Dean; Tonkin Gulf Resolution; "Wise Men."

Bundy, William P. (1917–)

Vietnam policymaker, 1961–1969; brother of McGeorge Bundy. A devoted yet unheralded bureaucrat, Bundy knew Southeast Asia and, as a supporter of U.S. objectives in the region, helped to frame policy for the Republic of Vietnam (RVN). He favored covert operations, questioned President Kennedy's firmness, and endorsed U.S. troop deployments to South Vietnam. He supported President Ngô Đình Diêm and thought that the Communist threat warranted a U.S. response.

By 1964 Bundy bore much of the responsibility for Vietnam policy-making. Intolerant of in-house dissent, he labored to stave off doubters while proposing to strike the Democratic Republic of Vietnam through interdiction of the Hai Phòng port and air attacks on transportation systems, industrial areas, and military bivouac areas. Such action required congressional authorization in the form of a resolution, the rough draft of which Bundy coauthored by late May. Once Congress ratified the Tonkin Gulf Resolution, Bundy again recommended forceful measures against the Hà Nôi government until its leadership decided to disengage.

In November 1964 President Johnson created a unit of eight intermediate-level State Department, Defense Department, and CIA functionaries chaired by Bundy. Instructed to examine U.S. policy choices for Southeast Asia, the group offered three approaches. Option A advanced limited bombing, additional reprisals, and greater resort to clandestine operations; Option B pleaded an all-out air campaign from the outset; Option C, which Bundy backed, called for graduated pressure and discouraged retreat, but was noncommittal regarding the use of U.S. combat troops. However, disenchantment with the president's management style and the poor coordination of the war effort contributed to a growing pessimism about escalation that brought Bundy to the brink of hopelessness after the 1968 Têt Offensive.

—Rodney J. Ross

References: Halberstam, David. *The Best and the Brightest* (1973); Herring, George C. *LBJ and Vietnam: A Different Kind of War* (1994); Sheehan, Neil, et al. *The Pentagon Papers as Published by* The New York Times (1971).
See also: Acheson, Dean G.; Buddhists; Bundy, McGeorge; Harriman, W. Averell; Johnson, Lyndon Baines; Ngô Đình Diêm; Nguyên Cao Ky; Nguyên Van Thiêu; Taylor-McNamara Report; Tonkin Gulf Resolution; "Wise Men."

Bunker, Ellsworth (1894–1984)

U.S. ambassador to the Republic of Vietnam, 1967–1973. Arriving in Sài Gòn as U.S. ambassador in April 1967, Bunker established the practice of sending periodic reporting cables to the president. These constitute an impressive record of sound judgment and wise counsel, including his insight into military matters. After General Creighton Abrams took command, Bunker often emphasized, as he did in an October 1968 cable, that "there is only one war—not a separate war of big battalions, a separate war of pacification, a separate war of territorial security; these are all integral parts of the same war."

Bunker's reporting was both practical and timely. In May 1968 he cabled that most Vietnamese regarded peace negotiations "with more apprehension than hope." Bunker consistently urged that the United States not cease bombing North Vietnam "without specific commitments from Hà Nôi with respect to activity in the south." The wisdom of this approach was demonstrated when, on the representations of Averell Harriman, the U.S. accepted vague assurances that reciprocity would be demonstrated, only to see the enemy subsequently deny that there had been any "understandings" while simultaneously violating their supposed terms.

Bunker developed great regard for the South Vietnamese during his years in their country. He appreciated and stressed how the Vietnamese were taking on a growing share of the financial burden of prosecuting the war and thought they "reacted with great stoicism and courage and patience" to the war. Bunker's regard for President Nguyên Van Thiêu also grew yearly, and in turn he enjoyed the wide respect of Republic of Vietnam (RVN) government leaders. However, Bunker did draw criticism from some quarters for his open support of Thiêu in the 1967 and 1971 elections.

Ellsworth Bunker served as ambassador to the RVN for six years, longer than any other senior American official, military or civilian, had been in continuous service there. He continued to believe that America's effort to help the Vietnamese "was in line with our history, our traditions, our view about individual liberty, about self-determination."

—Lewis Sorley

References: Bunker, Ellsworth. *The Bunker Papers: Reports to the President from Vietnam, 1967–1973* (1990); Johnson, Lyndon Baines. *The Vantage Point* (1971); Kissinger, Henry. *White House Years* (1979); Nixon, Richard M. *RN: The Memoirs of Richard Nixon* (1978).

See also: Abrams, Creighton; Harriman, W. Averell; Nguyên Van Thiêu; Palmer, Bruce, Jr.; United States: Involvement in Vietnam, 1965–1968; United States: Involvement in Vietnam, 1969–1973.

Burchett, Wilfred (1911–1983)

Australian journalist and author. Burchett first went to Vietnam in March 1954, where he met Hô Chí Minh in his jungle encampment. For more than 20 years, Vietnam preoccupied Burchett's writing. From *North of the Seventeenth Parallel* (1956), which examined land reform, to the overtly polemical *Vietnam Will Win!* (1968), to *Grasshoppers and Elephants* (1977), which depicted the Paris peace talks, Burchett steadfastly proselytized the Communist struggle against the evils of capitalism. Even his best book, *Vietnam: Inside Story of the Guerrilla War* (1965), which presents in firsthand immediacy the experiences of a National Liberation Front (NLF) cadre, is politicized to his purposes. Burchett's affiliation with leftist political and military causes alienated him from Western governments, but his works influenced antiwar sympathizers. He continued to write about politics in Cambodia (with Prince Norodom Sihanouk), Portugal, and elsewhere until his death.

—Charles J. Gaspar

References: Burchett, Wilfred. *At the Barricades* (1981); Kiernan, Ben. *Burchett Reporting the Other Side of the World, 1939–1983* (1986); Maclear, Michael. *The Ten Thousand Day War* (1981).

See also: Australia; Fall, Bernard B.; Media and the War; National Front for the Liberation of South Vietnam (NFLSV); Sihanouk, Norodom.

Bush, George Herbert Walker (1924–)

Director of the Central Intelligence Agency, 1976–1977; vice-president of the United States, 1981–1988; president of the United States, 1989–1992. Bush avoided much of the rancor of the Vietnam War in his public service. In 1991, during the Persian Gulf conflict, Bush pledged that "this will not be another Vietnam." After the U.S. victory he exclaimed, "we've kicked the Vietnam syndrome once and for all." While the Bush administration conducted talks with the Socialist Republic of Vietnam (SRV) concerning diplomatic recognition, Bush pleased U.S. conservatives by refusing to lift the trade embargo or establish diplomatic relations. The first retired or sitting president to visit Vietnam since the war, Bush in September 1995 traveled to Hà Nôi and Hô Chí Minh City and spoke on behalf of Citibank, reportedly for a six-figure fee. He welcomed the new relationship between the United States and the SRV, established by President Clinton, but mildly criticized the Vietnamese government on its human rights record. In Hà Nôi Bush said he had delayed establishing diplomatic relations because of the issue of Americans missing in action.

—Brenda J. Taylor

Reference: Bush, George, with Victor Gold. *Looking Forward* (1987).

See also: Central Intelligence Agency (CIA); Clinton, William Jefferson; Reagan, Ronald.

C

Calley, William Laws, Jr. (1943–)

U.S. Army lieutenant and platoon leader found guilty in the My Lai Massacre. Calley's school years were characterized by mediocrity, a trait that continued to haunt him as an adult. Calley graduated 120th in his officer candidate school class of 156 and was commissioned a second lieutenant in September 1967.

In Vietnam, Calley commanded a platoon in Capt. Ernest Lou Medina's Company C of the 1st Battalion, 20th Infantry Regiment, 23d Infantry (Americal) Division. On 16 March 1968 he participated, as part of Task Force Barker, in an assault on the hamlet of My Lai 4 in Quang Ngãi Province. The Americans believed My Lai was the headquarters of the Việt Công (VC) 48th Light Force Battalion, which had inflicted heavy losses on Charlie Company in the previous weeks. However, the attack force encountered mainly women, children, and elderly persons. During the next several hours more than 100 civilians were killed; some women were raped and then murdered. Charlie Company's official report listed 128 VC killed and three weapons captured. In April 1969 Vietnam veteran Ronald L. Ridenhour exposed the massacre in letters to the Pentagon, the White House, and members of Congress.

Upon recommendation of the Peers-MacCrate Commission, in September 1969 the Army indicted Calley for the murder of 109 Vietnamese civilians. After a four-month court-martial, the longest in U.S. history, Calley was convicted and sentenced in March 1971 to life imprisonment. After Calley had served only three months in the stockade, President Nixon freed him and ordered him confined to quarters pending review of the case. Calley's punishment was subsequently reduced to 20 years, and then to 10. Finally, in November 1974 Federal District Court Judge J. Robert Elliott ruled that Calley was convicted unjustly, citing "prejudicial publicity." Although the Army disputed civil court jurisdiction, Calley was paroled for good behavior after serving 40 months, most of them in the relative comfort of his own quarters.

—Brenda J. Taylor

Reference: Hersh, Seymour. *Cover-Up* (1972).
See also: COWIN Report; Medina, Ernest L.; My Lai Massacre; Peers, William R.; Peers Inquiry.

Cam Ranh Bay

Protected natural harbor in Khánh Hòa Province south of Nha Trang in II Corps. An important way station for navigators since the days of Marco Polo, Cam Ranh Bay was developed into one of the largest seaports in South Vietnam.

The U.S. military buildup in the 1960s increased the need for another deep-water port to relieve pressure on Sài Gòn, South Vietnam's only modern facility. In May 1965 the U.S. Army's First Logistical Command established a support unit at Cam Ranh to provide defense for U.S. and Allied troops in the southern half of II Corps. In June 1965 the U.S. Army Corps of Engineers began constructing roads, warehouses, fuel tanks, and larger cargo-handling facilities. A new pier allowed six large vessels to be handled simultaneously. These facilities were turned over to the Republic of Vietnam in June 1972, as was the airfield that had served as a base for the U.S. Air Force's 12th Tactical Fighter Wing and 483d Tactical Air Wing.

Security was provided by the Republic of Korea's 9th Infantry Division. The port was considered so safe that President Johnson visited twice. Nevertheless, in 1969 the Việt Công raided Cam Ranh Bay, killing two Americans and wounding 98. Security was tightened, and Cam Ranh Bay remained a key logistical base even after the port fell to the Communists in April 1975. The Soviet Union used it as a naval base after signing a "treaty of friendship and cooperation" with the Socialist Republic of Vietnam in 1978.

—J. Nathan Campbell

References: Dunn, Carroll. *Base Development in South Vietnam, 1965–1970* (1972); —. *Building the Bases: The History of Construction in Southeast Asia* (1975); Karnow, Stanley. *Vietnam: A History* (1983); Ploger, Robert R. *U.S. Army Engineers, 1965–1970* (1974); Smith, Harvey H., et al. *Area Handbook for South Vietnam* (1967); Stanton, Shelby L. *Vietnam Order of Battle* (1981).

Cambodia

The last Indo-China nation to be drawn into the Vietnam War, Cambodia ultimately endured an even greater tragedy than its neighbors. Wedged into the Indo-China peninsula between southeastern Thailand and southern Vietnam, it resembles a nut held in the jaws of a giant wrench, an image that accurately reflects Cambodians' historic fears of being extinguished by their larger, more powerful neighbors.

Rimmed by the Cardamom and Elephant Mountains in the southwest, the Dangrek Hills in the northwest, and rocky ridges in the east along the Vietnam border, Cambodia's heartland is a flat expanse of forests and alluvial fields watered by streams that flow into the Mekong, Bassac, and Tonle Sap rivers. With well-watered fields and rivers teeming with fish, Cambodians were traditionally well fed in peacetime.

Cambodia's first major civilization, Funan (Kingdom of the Mountain, according to ancient Chinese chronicles), arose from the Mon-Khmer tribes that had migrated to the Mekong basin from Asia's interior. Funan, which flourished from the first to the sixth centuries A.D., was essentially Indian in culture, influenced by Indian traders and priests. So were its successors, the state of Chenla and the Angkor kingdom, which represented the high point of Khmer civilization.

Ruling from the ninth to the fifteenth centuries, the Angkor kings at the height of their power dominated most of present-day Cambodia, Thailand, Laos, and Vietnam. At Angkor, the seat of their realm, they built temples in the shape of hills, symbolizing Mount Meru, the sacred mountain at the center of the universe. (Later, the design symbolized Mount Kailasa, abode of the god Shiva.) The older temples honor Shiva, the Hindu deity worshipped by the earlier Angkor rulers. Later temples, although still bearing Hindu symbols, reflect the Angkor kings' twelfth-century conversion to Buddhism. Angkor Wat, the greatest of the temples, was built during the reign of Suryavarman II (ruled 1113–1150 A.D.). Stone friezes depicted gods and mythical creatures as well as grisly executions and torture, glimpses of the violence and cruelty that also ran through Khmer tradition.

The Theravada branch of Buddhism, which teaches that every person must seek his or her own enlightenment through meditation, austerity, humility, and poverty, eventually became the majority religion in Cambodia. Except when it was brutally suppressed by the Khmer Rouge regime between 1975 and 1979, Buddhism and the *sangha* (clergy) have remained pervasive and powerful influences in the country's life and beliefs.

The Khmer kingdom declined in the thirteenth and fourteenth centuries. Thai invaders destroyed Angkor in 1431. In succeeding centuries, as the Thais seized more Cambodian territory, an expanding Vietnam pressed into Cambodia from the east, gradually occupying the fertile lands of the Mekong Delta. The Khmers at least shared a common religion and cultural heritage with the Thai. The Vietnamese, whose culture and political structures were essentially derived from China, were more alien; their encroachments aroused among Cambodians a lasting legacy of hatred and racial fear. By the mid-nineteenth century, the Cambodian monarchy was a virtual vassal of Thailand, which chose and crowned the Khmer kings.

Cambodia appeared in danger of losing its national identity altogether until France, in the process of establishing colonial rule over Vietnam, made Cambodia a protectorate in 1864. Cambodia's King Norodom welcomed French protection, but not France's later moves that gave ever greater powers to its colonial administrators. Although Norodom and his successors remained on the throne, within 20 years Cambodia became a de facto colony, with all real governing power in French hands. It did, however, survive as an identifiable state—a status it might well have lost had France not intervened.

French rule lasted 90 years, with little benefit for the Cambodians. The French built roads and a railway as the infrastructure for a colonial economy based chiefly on rubber plantations, rice exports, and small-scale timber and gem mining industries. However, there was no real development of a modern economy or of an educated population. Instead of training Cambodians, the French customarily imported Vietnamese to fill civil service jobs; traders and shop owners were also predominantly Vietnamese. Thus, when Cambodia recovered its independence in November 1953 under Norodom Sihanouk, it lacked resources, infrastructure, and the trained technicians, managers, and administrators needed in a modern state.

Cambodia's independence was part of a larger regional upheaval that spanned five years of Japanese occupation (1940–1945) and nine additional years of conflict between France and Viêt Minh revolutionaries. The July 1954 Geneva Accords ended French rule in all of Indo-China but also left Vietnam divided, with the Viêt Minh ruling in the North and an anticommunist government under Ngô Đình Diêm ruling in the South. Within a few years violence began to mount again in South Vietnam. Sihanouk's chief concern was to prevent his country from becoming involved in the violence that was engulfing its larger neighbor. In 1955 he had abdicated the throne in favor of his father, Norodom Suramarit, to take more direct control of the government as prime minister. (After Suramarit died in 1960, Sihanouk was given the title Chief of State; the throne remained vacant.) Outside Cambodia, the prince was widely regarded as erratic, but his frequent policy reversals did have a consistent goal: to keep Cambodia neutral.

After first cultivating relations with the United States, in 1963 Sihanouk abruptly ordered U.S. military and economic aid programs canceled and two years later broke off relations completely. Believing that the Vietnamese revolutionaries would ultimately win, he then entered into a fateful compromise that allowed the Vietnamese Communists to set up bases on Cambodian territory along the border and to receive arms shipments that came by sea to Cambodia's main port of Sihanoukville (later renamed Kompong Som) and were then transported overland to the border region. Underlying this accommodation was Sihanouk's calculation that if Cambodia helped the Vietnamese win their revolution, they might respect Cambodian independence after their victory. As an additional benefit for Sihanouk, the Vietnamese would give no help to the small Khmer Rouge insurgency that was opposing the prince's regime.

After the United States entered the Vietnam War, resentment of Sihanouk's policies and Vietnamese encroachments grew among military leaders, students, and other segments of the population. Sihanouk's authority, meanwhile, was weakening as the result of economic strains, corruption, and abuses of power in his regime. By the late 1960s, the prince was still balanced on his diplomatic and political tightrope, but his position was more precarious than ever—as was peace in Cambodia.

In March 1969 the United States began secretly bombing Vietnamese Communist positions on the Cambodian side of the border. In August Sihanouk named army commander General Lon Nol to head a new right-wing Government of National Salvation. The secret U.S. bombings, meanwhile, encouraged Cambodian army commanders in the border region to conduct harassing operations against Communist Vietnamese bases. In November, reinforcements were sent to the area and attacks were stepped up. Then in March 1970, after violent, government-orchestrated anti-Vietnamese demonstrations in Phnom Penh, Lon Nol publicly demanded a complete Vietnamese withdrawal from all Cambodian territory within 72 hours.

Prince Sihanouk, then traveling abroad, denounced the demand, but Lon Nol and his allies sent troops to surround the National Assembly and government ministries and obtained a unanimous Assembly vote on 18 March deposing Sihanouk as chief of state. Five days later in Beijing, Sihanouk sealed an alliance with his former mortal enemies, the

Khmer Rouge, against Lon Nol's "reactionary and pro-imperialist" government. A month later he formally allied with the Lao and Vietnamese Communists as well.

The new leaders in Phnom Penh, having inflamed Cambodia's traditional anti-Vietnamese feelings for their own political purposes, now called for national mobilization against the estimated 40,000 Vietnamese Communist troops on Cambodian territory. Thousands of young men and women enthusiastically flocked to recruiting stations to join the crusade against the *Yuon*, the pejorative Khmer term for Vietnamese. Legally, the new government's policy was indisputably justified; the Vietnamese were flagrantly in violation of Cambodian sovereignty. Whether the policy was prudent was another matter. The Vietnamese easily defeated the poorly armed and inexperienced Cambodian soldiers whenever an engagement took place. In their ambition and naiveté, Lon Nol and his associates marched blindly into a war they could not win, with catastrophic consequences.

The new Cambodian leaders were also naive about the United States, which they assumed would come unstintingly to their defense as it had come to the aid of the Republic of Vietnam (RVN). But after years of frustrating stalemate in Vietnam, the American public had no appetite for a wider war. U.S. military leaders perceived Cambodian events almost entirely in terms of their own tactical needs in Vietnam. Seeing a chance to disrupt the Communist logistical network on the Cambodian side of the border, the U.S. command supported several sizable operations by RVN forces in Cambodia during April 1970. Then on 30 April 1970, 32,000 U.S. troops rolled across the border. This "incursion," as U.S. officials called it, aroused such a storm of protest at home that President Nixon quickly promised to withdraw all U.S. troops from Cambodia by the end of June.

Although the United States continued to provide air support after its troops left, Cambodia's Army suffered a series of disastrous defeats. In less than four months the Communists took the entire region east of the Mekong River and large areas in the rest of the country. Those early defeats set a pattern that would never be reversed. Over the next five years, Lon Nol's troops steadily lost ground while Cambodia's economy disintegrated and its people sank into defeat, hunger, and despair.

When the war began, the forces opposing Lon Nol's army were chiefly Vietnamese Communists. The Vietnamese moved quickly, however, to build up a Khmer resistance movement. A group known as "Khmer Viet Minh," Cambodian veterans of the Viêt Minh war living in Vietnam, were sent back to Cambodia to manage the armed struggle. The Khmer Rouge, now allies (if uneasy and mistrustful ones) of the Vietnamese Communists, were also expanding their strength. Also joining the insurgent side were soldiers, officials, and others loyal to Sihanouk. Gradually, Cambodians took over most of the fighting, although still with guidance and some direct combat support from the Democratic Republic of Vietnam (DRV).

Led by two French-educated Cambodian Communists, Saloth Sar (better known as Pol Pot) and Ieng Sary, the Khmer Rouge emerged during the 1970s as the most extreme and violent Indo-China revolutionary movement. Sary and his colleagues bitterly resented the Vietnamese, at least partly because of the Vietnamese Communists' failure to support their struggle when it was young and weak.

Cooperation between Vietnamese and Cambodians against Lon Nol ended after the DRV and the United States concluded a peace agreement in January 1973. The Khmer Rouge regarded the cease-fire as a betrayal and secretly demanded that the Vietnamese leave Cambodia. Meanwhile, they carried out a bloody purge inside the insurgent ranks that killed hundreds of Khmer Viêt Minh cadres and Sihanouk's loyalists, although Sihanouk remained the titular head of the revolution. From 1973 to 1979 the Khmer Rouge imposed the violent and fanatical doctrines they had nursed through years of isolation, hatred, and a war that was spiraling deeper into savagery. Meanwhile, the war-weary U.S. Congress ended U.S. bombing in Cambodia on 15 August 1973.

On 17 April 1975 Lon Nol's decrepit government surrendered. In five years of war approximately 10 percent of Cambodia's seven million people had died. The economy was in ruins, and half of the population had been uprooted, but worse was to come. The Khmer Rouge, bent on extirpating all traces of the old society, emptied the cities and forced millions of Cambodians into slave labor camps, murdered hundreds of thousands of real or imagined opponents, and caused more hundreds of thousands of deaths from exhaustion, hunger, and disease.

Khmer Rouge rule ended in January 1979 when Vietnamese forces, who had invaded Cambodia after months of escalating border clashes, occupied Phnom Penh and installed a new pro-Vietnamese government. Falling back to the countryside, Khmer Rouge guerrillas—eventually joined by two smaller groups backed by the United States and the non-Communist Southeast Asian states—mounted a stubborn resistance against the Vietnamese and their Cambodian allies. Although the Khmer Rouge terror had ended, the new war brought new miseries. A third of a million Cambodians spent years in dismal refugee camps along the Thai border, and millions of others struggled to survive in a devastated country.

Vietnamese troops withdrew in 1989, but war continued between the Khmer Rouge and its allies and the Vietnamese-sponsored Phnom Penh government headed by Prime Minister Hun Sen. A peace agreement was finally signed under United Nations (UN) auspices on 23 October 1991. All sides agreed to give up their arms, but the Khmer Rouge never fully complied. It also refused to participate in UN-supervised elections for a new government. Despite widespread Khmer Rouge attacks meant to disrupt the voting, the election was held in May 1993. Prince Sihanouk's party, the United Front for an Independent, Neutral, Peaceful and Cooperative Cambodia (FUNCINPEC), won a narrow plurality over Hun Sen's Cambodian People's Party. Following the election a new constitution restored the monarchy.

On 24 September 1993 Sihanouk resumed the throne he had abdicated 38 years before. His son, Prince Norodom

Ranariddh, and Hun Sen shared leadership as co–prime ministers of the new government. Ranariddh nominally ranked first among the two, reflecting the election results. Hun Sen's loyalists, however, controlled most of the army and police and judiciary, and much of the press. Openly or in secret, Hun Sen's network also owned a huge part of the Cambodian economy and largely controlled the flow of international aid, which reached more than $3 billion in the next three years. This power-sharing arrangement did not lead to a new era of compromise and multiparty democracy, as international peace brokers had hoped. Instead, Ranariddh and Hun Sen and their followers broke into two hostile camps, each with its own armed bands of supporters. Violence became so frequent that one foreign diplomat compared the two factions to "rival mafias competing for territory and assets." Free-market policies and foreign dollars brought prosperity to some, but corruption, abuses of power, and incompetent administration sapped the government's moral authority.

The coalition's final destruction was precipitated in late spring 1997 when representatives of the disintegrating Khmer Rouge, defying their long-time leader Pol Pot, began negotiating with associates of Ranariddh on the possible surrender of their remaining forces. The Khmer Rouge offered to join Ranariddh's alliance in opposition to Hun Sen, whom they still regarded as a puppet of the Vietnamese. Khmer Rouge soldiers would change into government uniforms and pledge allegiance to the king, government, and constitution, but would not be disbanded or disarmed and would remain in the territory they previously occupied.

After Pol Pot and his few remaining followers were captured by the new Khmer Rouge leaders, the two sides were only a day away from announcing the surrender when Hun Sen, fearing that a Khmer Rouge alliance with Ranariddh's forces would tilt the military balance against him, seized power in Phnom Penh on 6 July. Hun Sen, insisting that Ranariddh's troops had started the fighting, called the coup a "counteroffensive." But the United States and most other countries condemned him for overturning the elected government. Whoever actually fired the first shots, it was evident that both sides shared the blame for the climate of violence, revenge, and fear that had overtaken Cambodian political life. During the fighting, Ranariddh fled the country, while Hun Sen's forces hunted down his political allies and armed supporters. Captured Ranariddh loyalists were tortured and then killed in mass executions.

The coup left Hun Sen seemingly in firm control of Phnom Penh and most of the country. Sihanouk—who by ironic coincidence was receiving medical treatment in Beijing on the day of Hun Sen's coup, exactly as he had been when he was overthrown 27 years before—was once again pushed to the sidelines. He was unable to protect his son's position, just as he had been unable to protect his own in 1970. It seemed unlikely that the consequences would be as horrendous as the bloodbath of the 1970s, but once again Cambodia's destiny had been determined by force instead of the peaceful choice of its citizens. For Cambodians the dream of democratic development and true national reconciliation seemed as far from realization as ever.

—Arnold R. Isaacs

References: Becker, Elizabeth. *When the War Was Over* (1986); Hardy, Gordon, Arnold R. Isaacs, MacAlister Brown, and the editors of Boston Publishing Company. *Pawns of War: Cambodia and Laos* (1987); Isaacs, Arnold R. *Without Honor: Defeat in Vietnam and Cambodia* (1983); Mazzeo, Donatella, and Chiara Silvi Antonini. *Monuments of Civilization: Ancient Cambodia* (1978).

See also: Cambodian Incursion; Khmer Rouge; Lon Nol; Parrot's Beak; Pol Pot; Sihanouk, Norodom; United States: Involvement in Vietnam, 1969–1973; Vietnam, Socialist Republic of: 1975 to the Present; Vietnamese Invasion and Occupation of Cambodia; Washington Special Actions Group (WSAG).

Cambodian Airlift (1974–1975)

U.S. government-funded airlift to keep supply lines open to Phnom Penh. In July 1974 William H. Bird, a longtime air transport operator in Southeast Asia, submitted an "unsolicited proposal" to conduct an airlift from Thailand to Cambodia. The U.S. Air Force (USAF) would supply five C-130s, fuel, and required maintenance; Bird would furnish the necessary aircrews and operations personnel. Within five months, Bird's company, Birdair, would have the capability of flying 450 hours per month. A letter contract for $1.4 million was issued on 28 August despite U.S. Air Force (USAF) opposition to using civilian crews to fly USAF aircraft into combat conditions.

Birdair mobilized five crews in September. After airmen passed USAF ground and flight checks, they began operations from U-Tapao Royal Thai Air Force Base, 100 miles south of Bangkok. By the end of 1974, Birdair had flown more than 1,000 hours, carrying 450,000 tons of supplies to Cambodia. In February 1975 military pressure against Phnom Penh intensified after the Communists blocked the Mekong River supply route to the beleaguered capital. The U.S. government turned over to Birdair seven additional C-130s, ordered daily sorties doubled to twenty by the end of the month, and added $1.9 million to the original contract. At the same time Washington awarded contracts to World Airways, Airlift International, and Trans-International Airlines to fly rice from Sài Gòn to Phnom Penh. Carriers would be paid $30,000 a day for every DC-8–60 used on the airlift, with full indemnification of $9 million if an aircraft was lost due to an act of war. As Communist troops neared the capital, flight operations often took place in the midst of rocket and artillery fire. Several aircraft were damaged, but no crew members were injured.

Although the airlift prolonged the life of the Lon Nol government, it could not affect the outcome of the conflict in Cambodia. On 12 April 1975 U.S. Marine Corps helicopters evacuated American personnel from Phnom Penh. Five days later, Khmer Rouge troops entered the city, bringing the airlift—and the war—to an end.

—William M. Leary

References: Bird, William H. *Papers*, San Leandro, CA; Isaacs, Harold R. *Without Honor: Defeat in Vietnam and Cambodia* (1983).

See also: Bird & Sons (Birdair); Cambodia; EAGLE PULL, Operation; Khmer Rouge.

Cambodian Incursion (May–June 1970)

Joint U.S. Army/Army of the Republic of Vietnam (ARVN) invasion of officially neutral Cambodia. Following the overthrow of Cambodia's neutralist Prince Norodom Sihanouk on 18 March 1970, pro-U.S. Prime Minister General Lon Nol closed the port of Sihanoukville and sent his small army against 60,000 Vietnamese Communist troops entrenched in three border provinces. People's Army of Vietnam (PAVN) and Viêt Công (VC) forces counterattacked, occupying two more Cambodian provinces and threatening Phnom Penh itself.

The Cambodian incursion actually began in early April when Republic of Vietnam (RVN) forces, ostensibly with Lon Nol's assent and unaccompanied by U.S. advisors, mounted multibattalion raids against Communist bases in the Parrot's Beak next to the III Corps border. Surprised PAVN and VC forces withdrew deeper into the Cambodian jungles. By 20 April the ARVN claimed to have killed 637, while losing 34.

U.S. leaders viewed these raids with alarm, emphasizing to Republic of Vietnam (RVN) President Nguyên Van Thiêu the need to keep Cambodia neutral. But when Communist forces seriously threatened the new government in Cambodia, U.S. Military Assistance Command, Vietnam (MACV) commander General Creighton Abrams argued for a full ARVN intervention with U.S. combat support. On 25 April, despite opposition from Secretary of Defense Melvin Laird and Secretary of State William Rogers, President Nixon ordered ARVN and U.S. ground forces into Cambodia to relieve pressure on the National Khmer Armed Forces (FANK), destroy Communist sanctuaries, and perhaps capture the elusive headquarters of the Central Office for South Vietnam (COSVN), assumed to be in the Fishhook area. Broader goals included demonstrating the progress of Vietnamization, buying time for additional U.S. troop withdrawals, and breaking the bargaining stalemate.

The Cambodian incursion, involving 50,000 ARVN and 30,000 U.S. troops, was the largest series of Allied operations since Operation JUNCTION CITY in 1967. Troops were divided among three groups of operations: TOÀN THANG (Total Victory), conducted by ARVN III Corps and U.S. II Field Force; CUU LONG (Mekong), conducted by ARVN IV Corps; and BÌNH TÂY (Tame the West), conducted by ARVN II Corps and U.S. I Field Force. The ARVN would operate more than 60 kilometers inside Cambodia; U.S. forces would penetrate only 30 kilometers. Ordered by Abrams to be ready to move into the Fishhook on 72 hours' notice, Lt. Gen. Michael S. Davison, II Field Force commander, met with Lt. Gen. Đô Cao Trí, ARVN III Corps commander, and Maj. Gen. Elvy Roberts, commander of the U.S. 1st Cavalry Division (Airmobile), to select areas of operation. Roberts quickly assembled a joint task force but lacked clear guidance about operation's real objectives and duration as well as hard intelligence about the Communist situation.

Set for 30 April, the hastily planned Fishhook invasion was delayed to allow ARVN forces to initiate Phase I of Operation TOÀN THANG 42 on the 29th, which was aimed at clearing Communist base areas in the Parrot's Beak. Run entirely by the ARVN, this operation attracted little media attention. Phase II began on 2 May, with ARVN III Corps forces attacking south of Route 1 into the Parrot's Beak, while an ARVN IV Corps task force pushed north. The Communists broke contact after losing 1,043 killed and 238 captured; hundreds of weapons and tons of ammunition were captured. In Phase III, which began on 7 May, ARVN forces killed 182 retreating Communist soldiers near Prasot and discovered a hospital and several supply caches. The Allies also rushed small arms and ammunition to Lon Nol's army, which quickly expanded to more than 100,000 men but retreated into urban areas and never launched a real offensive. When the ARVN linked up with FANK forces, it discovered that Khmer soldiers had murdered hundreds of ethnic Vietnamese. ARVN troops avenged these acts by looting several Cambodian towns.

In Phase IV, as ARVN forces began clearing Route 1 up to 50 kilometers inside Cambodia, President Thiêu began assembling an armed flotilla to sail up the Mekong to repatriate as many as 50,000 ethnic Vietnamese. Ironically, while the ARVN was concerned with rescuing ethnic Vietnamese, the Cambodians asked them to relieve a FANK garrison under siege at Kompong Cham northeast of Phnom Penh. In Phase V of TOÀN THANG 42, General Trí rushed a column of 10,000 men to accomplish this mission, but ARVN forces would have to retake Kompong Cham in June, inflicting and absorbing significant losses. When the Communists overran Kompong Speu on 13 June, a 4,000–man ARVN mechanized force quickly advanced to retake the town. ARVN and FANK troops then cleared Route 4 from Phnom Penh to Sihanoukville, which had been blockaded by the RVN Navy. TOÀN THANG 42 had upset Communist plans to overthrow the Lon Nol regime and accounted for 3,588 Communist killed or captured and the seizure of more than 2,000 weapons, 308 tons of ammunition, and 100 tons of rice.

The second stage of the Cambodian Incursion, called TOÀN THANG 43–46, was a series of joint U.S.-ARVN operations aimed at clearing Communist sanctuaries in the Fishhook area. Commanded by Brig. Gen. Robert H. Shoemaker, deputy commander of the 1st Cavalry Division, the initial task force consisted of the 1st Cavalry's 3d Brigade (reinforced by a mechanized infantry battalion), the 11th Armored Cavalry Regiment (ACR), and the 3d ARVN Airborne Brigade. TOÀN THANG 43 began early on 1 May, coinciding with Nixon's televised announcement that the incursion would "guarantee the continued success of our withdrawal and Vietnamization program." Following extensive preparatory support by B-52 bombing, tactical air strikes, and artillery fire, an armada of U.S. helicopters inserted the ARVN Airborne troops into three landing zones to block escape routes. The 1st Cavalry's 3d Brigade and the 11th ACR then advanced across the border.

General Davison then ordered the 11th ACR to move north to capture the Communist-occupied town of Snoul. Sporadic fire greeted the armored column, and the town was leveled in two days of bombardment. No dead PAVN soldiers were found, and as expectations of open-battlefield victories faded, TOÀN THANG 43's mission largely became one of seizing and destroying supply depots. After entering the Fishhook on 2 May, the 1st Cavalry's 2d Brigade stumbled into a massive but lightly defended supply, which they dubbed "The City." Alhough not the COSVN, it contained large weapons and ammunition caches and a training base, including a surgical hospital. Captured materials included more than two million rounds of ammunition; by mid-June, Allied forces in the Fishhook also captured or destroyed more than 300 vehicles. TOÀN THANG 43 accounted for 3,190 Communist soldiers killed or captured.

TOÀN THANG 44 began on 6 May as the U.S. 25th Division's 1st Brigade drove across the border west of Tây Ninh to search for Enemy Base Area 354. On 6 May, the 1st Cavalry's 2d Brigade initiated TOÀN THANG 45, aimed at Enemy Base Area 351 located north of Phuoc Long Province. Facing only sporadic contact, the brigade uncovered the largest depot captured during the war, so huge that it was dubbed "Rock Island East." By June, the entire 1st Cavalry Division was inside Cambodia and, amidst frequent contact with Communist forces, uncovered more weapons and supply caches, a vehicle maintenance depot, and an abandoned communications depot. 1st Cavalry units repelled harassing attacks as they rushed to meet the withdrawal deadline. Their last fire base in Cambodia was dismantled by 27 June, and all troops were back inside South Vietnam by 29 June.

Simultaneously with TOÀN THANG 45, an ARVN 5th Division regiment and a squadron of the ARVN 1st Armored Cavalry Regiment launched TOÀN THANG 46 against Enemy Base Area 350, north of Bình Long Province. ARVN forces discovered another surgical hospital and several major caches of supplies and ammunition. By 20 June, increased Communist activity forced the termination of TOÀN THANG 46.

ARVN IV Corps troops initiated Operation CUU LONG I on 9 May to open the Mekong River. Within two days the ARVN 9th and 21st Divisions, augmented by five armored cavalry squadrons, cleared both banks of the river, allowing a 100–ship convoy to reach Phnom Penh and proceed north to Kompong Cham. By 18 May the convoy had repatriated nearly 20,000 Vietnamese held in refugee camps. Simultaneously, ARVN III Corps forces cleared Route 1 as far as Neak Luong. In CUU LONG II, from 16 to 24 May, ARVN IV Corps troops joined FANK forces in recapturing Takeo, 40 kilometers south of Phnom Penh, and cleared Routes 2 and 3. IV Corps forces then launched CUU LONG III, again joining with FANK forces to reestablish control over towns south of Phnom Penh and to evacuate more ethnic Vietnamese.

Two days after the Parrot's Beak and Fishhook incursions began, the Allies decided to expand operations to attack Communist base areas in northeastern Cambodia facing II Corps. In this operation, designated Operations BÌNH TÂY I–IV, Allied forces included the ARVN 22d and 23d Infantry Divisions, the 2d Ranger Group, the 2d Armor Brigade, and two brigades of the U.S. 4th Infantry Division. U.S. participation was relatively brief and poorly executed. In fairness, Maj. Gen. Glen D. Walker's 4th Division was overextended, having recently relocated to Bình Định Province, leaving the ARVN

in control of the western Highlands. Having no forward installations and only limited logistical and artillery support, the 3d Battalion, 506th Infantry (3/506th) had to abort its initial insertion into Cambodia on 4 May. The next day, the 1st Battalion, 14th Infantry (1/14th) joined them in a successful insertion, but heavy hostile fire downed several helicopters. Joined by the 2/8th on 6 May, 4th Division troops uncovered an abandoned PAVN training camp. After his understrength battalions took significant casualties without making direct contact with the Communists, Walker decided to turn the operation over to the ARVN. All 4th Division troops left Cambodia by 16 May.

In BÌNH TÂY II, from 14 to 27 May, battalions of the 22d ARVN Division swept across the border from Darlac Province, searching for Enemy Base Area 701. Contact was limited, but the ARVN uncovered several more caches of weapons and supplies. In BÌNH TÂY III, from 20 May to 12 June, the 23d ARVN Division searched for Enemy Base Area 740, located west of Ban Mê Thuôt. The most dramatic event was the destruction of a ten-truck convoy. In BÌNH TÂY IV, from 23 to 27 June, a 22d ARVN Division task force of military and civilian vehicles, supported by U.S. artillery and helicopter gunships, moved deep into Cambodia along Route 19 to reach a beleaguered FANK garrison at Labang Siek and evacuated more than 7,000 Khmer soldiers and dependents across the border to Pleiku Province. All II Corps ARVN troops left Cambodia by 27 June.

Although all U.S. ground forces had left Cambodia by 30 June, President Thiêu considered the survival of Lon Nol's regime vital to Sài Gòn and would not be bound by the deadline. ARVN units continued operating up to 60 kilometers inside Cambodia into 1971, supported by U.S. long-range artillery, tactical air support, and B-52 bombings.

During the Cambodian incursion the amount of supplies uncovered was ten times more than that captured inside Vietnam during the previous year: The total was enough to supply fifty-four Communist main force battalions for up to a year. The human cost also was great: officially, at least 11,349 Communist, 638 ARVN, and 338 U.S. killed; 4,009 ARVN and 1,525 U.S. wounded; and 35 ARVN and 13 U.S. missing. In addition, 2,328 Communist soldiers rallied or were captured.

Henry Kissinger believed that the Cambodian incursion dealt a stunning blow to the Communists, drove main force units away from the border, damaged their morale, and bought up to a year for the RVN's survival. During 1970 and 1971, the ARVN held the initiative on all battlefields in South Vietnam. The incursion temporarily reduced pressure on Lon Nol, lessened the dangers to withdrawing U.S. troops, and showcased ARVN improvement. But the operations also exposed critical tactical and organizational deficiencies in the ARVN and their complete dependence on U.S. air support. The facade of renewed ARVN strength became evident during the disastrous Laotian incursion in February 1971.

The short-term gains from the Cambodian incursion may have boomeranged. Knowing that U.S. intervention would be limited in time and scope, the Communists avoided open confrontation and quickly returned to reclaim their sanctuaries and reestablish complete control in eastern Cambodia. The PAVN compensated for their temporary losses in Cambodia by seizing towns in southern Laos and expanding the Hô Chí Minh Trail into an all-weather network capable of handling tanks and heavy equipment, eventually enabling them to overrun the South with massive conventional assaults. Furthermore, continued withdrawal of U.S. combat units from III Corps forced the ARVN to deploy an excess of troops there, thus reducing their strength in the north where the Communist threat grew incessantly. In the long run, the Cambodian incursion posed only a temporary disruption of the march of Communist forces toward the domination of all of Indo-China.

The incursion gave the antiwar movement in the United States a new rallying point. Dissent, no longer limited to campus confrontations, led to a series of congressional resolutions and legislative initiatives to severely limit the executive power of the president. By the end of 1970, Congress had prohibited expenditures for U.S. forces operating outside of South Vietnam.

The widening of the battlefield in 1970 eventually left Cambodia the most devastated nation in Indo-China. To avoid massive Allied bombings, Communist forces spread deeper inside Cambodian territory and, receiving only minimal U.S. assistance, Lon Nol's army struggled futilely for five more years against the Khmer Rouge and the PAVN. The Cambodian invasion had turned the war into one for all of Indo-China, and the departure of U.S. troops left a void too great for the ARVN or the FANK to fill.

—John D. Root

References: Davidson, Philip B. *Vietnam at War: The History, 1946–1975* (1988); Nolan, Keith William. *Into Cambodia: Spring Campaign, Summer Offensive, 1970* (1990); Stanton, Shelby L. *The Rise and Fall of an American Army: U.S. Ground Forces in Vietnam, 1965–1975* (1985); Tran Dinh Thô. *The Cambodian Incursion* (1983).

See also: Abrams, Creighton; Cambodia; Cambodian Airlift; Cao Van Viên; COSVN (Central Office for South Vietnam or Trung Uong Cuc Miên Nam); Đô Cao Trí; FANK (Forces Armées Nationale Khmer); Fishhook; Hardhats; JUNCTION CITY, Operation; Kent State University; Kissinger, Henry Alfred; Laird, Melvin R.; Lake, William Anthony Kirsopp; Lon Nol; Nguyên Van Thiêu; Nixon, Richard Milhous; Rogers, William Pierce; Sihanouk, Norodom.

Cân Lao Nhân Vi Cách Mang Đang (Revolutionary Personalist Labor Party)

Political party and intelligence apparatus on which Republic of Vietnam (RVN) President Ngô Đình Diêm relied in his early years in power. When Diêm left Vietnam in 1950, his brother Ngô Đình Nhu sought to establish a doctrine to counter communism. In 1952 Nhu began promoting "socialist personalism," which sought to combine social reform with respect for personality. In 1953 Nhu and five others formed the Revolutionary Party of Workers and Peasants, which soon changed its name to the Cân Lao Nhân Vi Cách Mang Đang (Revolutionary Personalist Labor Party, usually

known simply as the Cân Lao). Nhu became its secretary general and leader.

Cân Lao ideology drew on the writings of Emmanuel Mournier, a leftist Catholic writer. It espoused a virulent anti-communism (especially important in enlisting U.S. support), respect for the dignity of the individual, a community life in which the common good took precedence over that of the individual, and a democratic structure that allowed pluralism within certain bounds. The relationship between individualism and the community and democracy were expounded in the regime's doctrine of personalism, or *nhân vi*, which stressed human dignity and the value of humanism in modern society in contrast to communism's treatment of human beings as "the masses." But the Vietnamese also sought to incorporate elements from Confucianism, placing emphasis on *thanh* (acute consciousness and clear vision) and *tin* (sincere and courageous practice of all duties). In this way cultivation of individuality became compatible with duty and obedience in Confucianism. Diêm championed strong control as necessary to foster the solid moral basis over a pluralistic bourgeois democracy. This opened the way for a cult of personality, which was very much at odds with the pluralistic and democratic society favored by Americans. Personalism thus became a useful cloak for the authoritarianism that was so much a part of the Diêm regime.

Appointed premier by State of Vietnam Chief of State Bao Đai in June 1954, Diêm returned to South Vietnam the next month. Support for his regime was at first quite narrow, resting primarily on Catholics and northerners who had fled to the south following the 1954 Geneva Accords. To create a wider base of support, Diêm and Nhu built up the Cân Lao as a political organization. In September 1954 the government authorized the Cân Lao Party.

The Cân Lao was organized along the lines of the French Sûreté into four *bureaux*: Premier Bureau, administration; Deuxième Bureau, intelligence; Troisième Bureau, operations; and Quatrième Bureau, finances. The party came to have immense influence, largely because all government officials assumed its omnipotence. Nhu used the Cân Lao as an instrument of power to strike down real and imagined opponents. The party existed publicly, but its members and activities were secret. The party's small active membership was to be supported by the Phong Trào Cách Mang Quôc Gia (National Revolutionary Movement), founded in October 1954 with Diêm as leader and Nhu as advisor. Intended to provide mass support for the regime, it also supported the Republican Youth.

At its height, the Cân Lao had about 50,000 members, mostly high-ranking government employees and military officers. Government officials were pressured to join and to submit to an initiation ceremony that reportedly involved kissing a picture of Diêm and swearing loyalty to him. The party used terror and intimidation against its opponents and was closely linked to a secret police force, headed by Dr. Trân Kim Tuyên, that also answered to Nhu. It also controlled an efficient intelligence network, Service des Etudes Politiques, Economiques et Sociales (SEPES), was involved in shady financial dealings, and reportedly siphoned off some U.S. aid to the RVN.

Lt. Col. Edward Lansdale soon recognized the threat that the Cân Lao posed to democratic institutions and a pluralistic society and stated his opposition to Diêm and the U.S. government. U.S. Ambassador George F. Reinhardt, the Central Intelligence Agency (CIA), and the Eisenhower administration were unsympathetic to Lansdale's arguments. They believed that Diêm needed his own political party and ordered U.S. officials in Vietnam to support the Cân Lao.

Nhu's doctrine should not be confused with that espoused by Bishop Ngô Đình Thuc, Diêm's oldest brother and bishop of Vinh Long Diocese, who advocated a Catholic form of "personalism" that differed from the Cân Lao line. Although this displeased Nhu, he did not interfere with his brother. The Cân Lao was strongest before Diêm came to power and immediately afterward. As dissatisfaction with the Ngô family increased, Diêm came under pressure to make public the activities of the Cân Lao or to dissolve it. After 1960 the party played an increasingly smaller role in the government. After General Nguyên Khánh took power, the Cân Lao and many other political parties were officially dissolved in March 1964. Enough Cân Lao influence remained, however, for it to play a role in deposing General Khánh in 1965. The end of the Cân Lao contributed to instability in the RVN because it removed restraints on labor unions and student associations, which were now free to agitate against the government.

—Ho Diêu Anh, Nguyên Công Luân (Lu Tuân),
and Spencer C. Tucker

References: Currey, Cecil B. *Edward Lansdale. The Unquiet American* (1988); Duncanson, Dennis J. *Government and Revolution in Vietnam* (1968).
See also: Lansdale, Edward Geary; Ngô Đình Diêm; Ngô Đình Diêm, Overthrow of; Ngô Đình Nhu; Ngô Đình Thuc; Nguyên Khánh; Reinhardt, George Frederick.

Canada

Canada never played a direct role in the Vietnam War. The Canadian government was generally sympathetic to Washington's concerns regarding the containment of communism and support for a democratic South Vietnam. However, it was often anxious about the degree of U.S. involvement in Southeast Asia and about what it saw as the excesses of American military strategy there. Canadian leaders were generally unsuccessful in their attempts to influence U.S. policy toward a more restrained approach. Washington's response was to view Canada as unsupportive and somewhat sanctimonious. This attitude surfaced following Prime Minister Lester Pearson's 2 April 1965 call for a brief cessation of the bombing of North Vietnam. President Johnson was furious over the speech and soon let Pearson know of his displeasure in person.

Canada participated in two peacekeeping organizations during the war. The first was the International Commission for Supervision and Control, or International Control

Commission (ICC). In 1954 Canada became a member of the ICC, along with Poland and India. Canada clearly represented Western, non-Communist interests and used its position to feed intelligence about Communist activities to the United States. The second, actually a reconstituted version of the first, was the International Commission of Control and Supervision (ICCS) formed in 1973 to oversee the Paris peace accords that ended U.S. military involvement in Vietnam. Canada reluctantly joined alongside Hungary and Indonesia but soon left that body, in July 1973, when it was obvious that the accords were not being honored.

Canada had other indirect connections to the war. Many Canadian companies profited from the sale of materials to the United States that were later used in the war effort. Approximately 10,000 to 12,000 Canadians served in the U.S. military in Vietnam, although nearly half were Canadian citizens living in the United States. Seventy-eight Canadians are listed at the Vietnam Veterans Memorial in Washington, D.C. Pierre Trudeau, Pearson's successor, eased immigration laws and allowed a significant number of American draft resisters and a small number of deserters into Canada. In January 1973 the Canadian Parliament passed a resolution condemning U.S. prolongation of the war, an action strongly denounced by the Nixon administration.

By the late 1960s, growing U.S. involvement in Vietnam and the domestic problems that it caused tended to enhance many Canadians' belief that their country was different from, and perhaps better than, the United States. Ironically, the war that tore apart American society created an increased sense of national identity in Canada in the short term.

—Eric Jarvis

References: Gaffen, Fred. *Unknown Warriors: Canadians in the Vietnam War* (1990); Granatstein, J. L., with Norman Hillmer. *For Better or For Worse: Canada and the United States to the 1990s* (1991); Levant, Victor. *Quiet Complicity: Canadian Involvement in the Vietnam War* (1986); Ross, Douglas. *In the Interests of Peace: Canada and Vietnam, 1954–1973* (1984).
See also: Draft; International Commission for Supervision and Control (ICC); Pearson, Lester Bowles; Vietnam Veterans Memorial.

Canines (K-9 Corps)

In 1960 the Military Assistance and Advisory Group (MAAG), Vietnam, recommended establishment of a military dog program for the Army of the Republic of Vietnam (ARVN). In April 1962 four U.S. instructors arrived to provide tactical training for the ARVN at Gò Vâp, the old French dog compound near Sài Gòn. Later they moved to a new ARVN dog training center at Thành Tuy Ha. Although authorized at 1,000 dogs, the ARVN dog program had only 130 by 1966. Cultural differences, a shortage of Vietnamese veterinarians, and practical problems thwarted U.S.-ARVN plans.

U.S. canine efforts were more successful. Following enemy penetration at Đà Nang air base in July 1965, the U.S. Air Force launched Project TOP DOG, calling for four-month deployment of 40 handlers and 40 dogs. These sentry dog teams, sent to Tân Son Nhut, Biên Hòa, and Đà Nang air bases, proved an effective deterrent against attacks and led to an expanded program. In August 1965 the U.S. Army began deploying its sentry dogs to Vietnam. Organized in 1966, the 212th Military Police Company (Sentry Dog), along with the 981st and 595th Military Police Companies (Sentry Dog), which arrived in Vietnam in November 1967 and January 1970 respectively, brought the total number of sentry dogs to about 300, a wartime high. In 1965 the Army also reactivated its program of scout dogs trained to give a silent alert based on airborne scent.

The Marines began tactical dog training in winter 1965 and deployed two Scout Dog platoons to Vietnam in February 1966. Kenneled near Đà Nang at Camp Kaiser, the two platoons had by November participated in 11 major operations and had saved an estimated 2,000 lives. The Navy, with the smallest canine program, had 37 sentry dogs and four aqua (swimmer) dogs. Begun in October 1969 as an Air Force project, the aqua dog program aimed at interdicting enemy swimmers and scuba divers. Although it received a positive evaluation in 1970, Vietnamization prevented any further use in Vietnam. The Air Force, in its effort to develop a quick reaction force that included scout dogs, in 1966 created Operation SAFE SIDE, which never developed beyond an interim program utilizing 14 dogs. In 1969 the Air Force discarded the entire Combat Security Police concept.

The Army expanded its use of dogs to include trackers. Using ground scent, the teams sought to reestablish contact with a fleeing enemy. The first teams, trained at the British Jungle Warfare School in Malaysia in 1966, were designated the 63d Infantry Platoon–Combat Tracker (IPCT), 23d "Americal" Division, and the 65th IPCT, 9th Infantry Division. Each platoon consisted of three teams of five men and a single tracker dog each, mainly black and golden Labrador retrievers. In November 1967 the United States began its own Combat Tracking Team Center at Fort Gordon, Georgia. The Army deployed 11 tracker teams to Vietnam in 1968–1969. The Australians also employed two combat tracker teams near Vung Tàu and Núi Đât.

In 1968 the Army contracted with the civilian Behavior Systems, Inc., to develop dogs to detect booby traps, mines, trip wires, and tunnels. A positive initial evaluation of these M-Dogs led to the 1968 activation of the 60th Infantry Platoon (Scout Dog) (Mine/Tunnel Detector Dog), which arrived at Cu Chi in April 1969. Only the Army and the Marines used these specialized dogs.

Approximately 3,000–4,000 dogs served with U.S. forces; an additional 639 were delivered directly to the ARVN. At Tân Son Nhut, the Army's 936th Medical Detachment and Seventh Air Force Hospital served as war dog hospitals, and there were veterinary detachments in each corps. Yet, only about 500 dogs survived, of which 190 returned to the United States. Hostile action accounted for less than 3 percent of canine deaths. Many fell victim to accidents, but probably most died from illnesses endemic to the region. Under Vietnamization the military either euthanized the dogs or handed over to the ARVN hundreds whose final disposition remains unknown.

Poor record keeping and missing reports make the exact number of handlers—estimated at 12,000 to 14,000—diffi-

cult to determine. Army after-action reports reveal 83,740 missions (although undoubtedly there were many others) and credit scout and mine/tunnel dog teams with more than 4,000 Communist troops killed, 1,000 captured, over 1 million pounds of rice and corn recovered, 3,000 mortars located, and at least 2,000 tunnels and bunkers exposed. Such successes led the enemy to place bounties on the handlers and their dogs. The Vietnam Veterans Memorial includes the names of at least 211 dog handlers.

The number of Allied lives saved certainly was in the thousands; sentry dogs prevented penetration of Allied perimeters, frequently because the enemy specifically avoided facilities with these assets. The United States does not have specific military decorations, a museum, or a national memorial for canines. The Vietnam Dog Handlers Association (VDHA) and Military Police–Vietnam–Sentry Dogs Alumni, both founded in 1993, honor this military occupational specialty and stand as testimony to the lasting relationships between these men and their dogs.

—Paul S. Daum, with Elizabeth Daum

References: Hayes, Howard. Interviews with the author (1996); Langley, John. Interviews with the author (1996); Lemish, Michael G. *War Dogs: Canines in Combat* (1996); Miller, Kenn. *Tiger the Lurp Dog* (1983); Mitchell, Tom, ed. *DogMan* (1994, 1996).

See also: Cu Chi, Tunnels of.

Cao Bang. *See* Blaizot, Roger; Indo-China War; Pignon, Léon; Revers Report.

Cao Đài

Religion founded in Vietnam in 1926. The principle of Cao Đàism, also called Đài Đao Tam Ky Phô Đô (Third Revelation of the Great Way), is "all religions are one." Cao Đài ("high palace") is the symbolic name of God. Followers of Cao Đài believe the history of religion is divided into three major periods of revelation. In the first two, figures chosen by God were given the mission to serve humanity by founding the Way and its five branches: Confucianism, Geniism, Christianity, Taoism, and Buddhism. As the revelations from these prophets were "truth" in their pristine form, these five religions were deemed to impound all aspects of human spirituality; but human weakness brought conflicts instead of peace and love. In the third period, God gave the world a final amnesty, saying, "I have decided to unite all these religions into one to bring them to primordial unity."

Cao Đàism believes that God created the universe, mankind, animals, and plants, and to each he has given a share of his Spirit. All human beings are brothers and sisters from the same father and have God's Spirit: "I am each of you and you are Me." Cao Đàists worship God in the form of an Eye shining over a pantheon consisting of Buddhas, Immortals, Saints, and Genies, representing universal consciousness of which man is a part. Cao Đàism believes in the existence of the spirit, its survival from the physical body, and its successive reincarnations in accordance with Karma laws. Cao Đàism commends people to remember their duties toward themselves, their families, their neighbors, and nature; prescribes the renouncement of prestige, riches, and luxury and the control of greed, anger, and desires; advocates eschewing materialism for spirituality; and teaches meditation and self-cultivation as the way to spiritual elevation.

A Cao Đài leader, Ho Phap Pham Công Tac, was involved in the struggle for independence of Vietnam from French domination. In 1941 the French deported Tac to Madagascar. During his absence another Cao Đai leader, Trân Quang Vinh, cooperated with the Japanese and formed a Cao Đài army to resist the French. During the Indo-China War, Cao Đài forces joined in a loose alliance with the French against the Viêt Minh. Later, many Cao Đài became high-ranking officials in the Republic of Vietnam (RVN) government, including Lê Van Hoach, General Nguyên Thành Phuong, General Trình Minh Thê, and Chief of State Phan Khac Suu. But Cao Đaism had no active role in politics.

In 1975 the end of the RVN led many Cao Đàists to flee abroad. At the present time there are perhaps six million Cao Đàists in the world.

—Bui Dac Hum

References: Hue Luong. *Đài Đao Tam Ky Phô Đô, Cao Đài Giáo So Giai* (1963); Tòa Thánh Tây Ninh. *Thanh Ngôn Hiep Tuyen. Tân Luât Pháp Chánh Truyên* (1972); Wallace, Anthony. *Religion: An Anthropological Review* (1966).
See also: Buddhists; Pham Công Tac.

Cao Van Viên (1921–)

Army of the Republic of Vietnam (ARVN) general; chief of the Joint General Staff, 1965–1975. General Viên completed advanced paratroop and helicopter pilot training in the United States and studied at the U.S. Army Command and General Staff College. In 1957 he returned from the United States and became chief of staff to President Ngô Đình Diêm, who he admired. Viên refused to participate in the 1963 overthrow of the Diêm regime. Condemned to death, he was later released and returned to command. In fall 1965 he was appointed chief of staff to the ARVN Joint General Staff and subsequently commanded III Corps. He was later appointed chief of the Joint General Staff, concurrently acting as minister of defense for much of the time.

Viên was a close friend of President Nguyên Van Thiêu, but Thiêu's close control over the Republic of Vietnam armed forces left Viên with little direct influence in military matters. Viên attempted to resign several times in protest of U.S. military primacy and steadfastly refused to carry out military reforms urged by the United States.

During the 1968 Têt Offensive, Viên used nearly all his staff and service personnel as combat troops and took personal command of them. Colonels and majors commanded platoons; junior officers filled the ranks as privates. Viên later held that the United States and South Vietnam missed an opportunity to win the war immediately after Têt by not going on the offensive with large-scale attacks. He also complained of not being consulted by the Johnson administration on its "expedient" policy of Vietnamization, for which he considered Vietnamese armed forces neither psychologically nor physically prepared. He was an enthusiastic advocate

of the 1971 ARVN invasion of Laos, having in 1965 proposed a "strategy of isolation involving a fortified zone along the 17th parallel running through Laos and an amphibious landing at Vinh."

Viên last appeared in public on 27 April 1975 at a joint session of Congress, to which he reported the deteriorating situation in South Vietnam. The next day he and his family secretly left Vietnam for the United States, where they settled and he became a citizen. Viên summed up the 1975 defeat by saying that ARVN had "fought well until undercut by events beyond its control." After his arrival in the United States, Viên worked at the U.S. Army Center of Military History and produced two monographs on his experiences in the war.

—Ho Diêu Anh and Spencer C. Tucker

References: Cao Van Viên. *The Final Collapse* (1982); Cao Van Viên and Dong Van Khuyen. *Reflections on the Vietnam War* (1980); Kiêm Đat. *Chiên Tranh Viêt Nam* (1982); Nguyên Khac Ngu. *Nhung Ngày Cuôi Cung Cua Viêt Nam Công Hòa* (1979); Post, Ken. *Revolution, Socialism and Nationalism in Viet Nam* (1989–1994); Westmoreland, William C. *A Soldier Reports* (1976); *Who's Who in Vietnam* (1967–1968).
See also: Joint General Staff; LAM SON 719, Operation; Military Assistance Command, Vietnam (MACV); Ngô Đình Diêm; Ngô Đình Diêm, Overthrow of; Ngô Đình Nhu; Nguyên Van Thiêu; Vietnam, Republic of: Army (ARVN).

Caravelle Group (26 April 1960)

Group of 18 South Vietnamese professionals who, at a press conference at the Hotel Caravelle in Sài Gòn on 26 April 1960, made public a manifesto addressed to President Ngô Đình Diêm. Couched in moderate terms, it charged that Diêm had isolated himself from his people by delegating power to family cronies; that repressive measures against religious sects had turned these into allies of the Viêt Công; that public opinion and the press had been silenced; and that election fraud had been committed. The manifesto called for total reorganization of the administration and the armed forces and for liberalization of the economy.

The signatories included several former ministers and high officials, lending credibility beyond that of an ordinary political tract. Although in 1960 such open dissent risked imprisonment, the government at first ignored its Caravelle critics, only later quietly arresting several of them. Frank Gonder, an American businessman living in Sài Gòn, acted as the Caravelle group's spokesman with the American Embassy, which accpeted much of the criticism as valid but maintained a hands-off position.

—Arthur J. Dommen

Reference: Fall, Bernard B. *The Two Viet-Nams. A Political and Military Analysis* (1967).
See also: Ngô Đình Diêm; Vietnam, Republic of: 1954–1975.

Carpentier, Marcel (1895–1977)

French general and commander of French forces in Indo-China, 1949–1950. In August 1949 Carpentier replaced General Roger Blaizot as commander in chief of French forces in Indo-China, shortly before the Communist victory in China. Carpentier used this event to justify U.S. military aid, referring to the French Army on the Chinese border as the "last bulwark against Communism."

Carpentier's military strategy was cautious. Rather than seeking out the Viêt Minh, he garrisoned northern Vietnamese frontier posts to defend against a Chinese invasion. The previous March the French government had concluded the Elysée Agreement, which provided for the creation of a Vietnamese National Army (VNA). Carpentier welcomed the expanded military support but wanted it firmly in French hands, believing that Vietnamese troops were unreliable, would not make good soldiers, and were not to be trusted on their own. He steadfastly refused to allow U.S. military aid to be channeled directly to the Vietnamese and threatened to resign within 24 hours if this were done.

By late 1949 the French Army had lost the initiative in the war. General Blaizot had planned the evacuation of Cao Bang and Route Coloniale 4; but, on pressure from his subordinate General Marcel Allesandri, Carpentier had put it off. Later Carpentier was blamed for the disastrous October 1950 French withdrawal from Cao Bang. In November 1950 Paris formally named General Jean de Lattre de Tassigny to replace Carpentier as commander of French forces in Indo-China.

—Spencer C. Tucker

References: Davidson, Phillip B. *Vietnam at War. The History 1946–1975* (1988); Gras, Général Yvres Gras. *Histoire de La Guerre d'Indochine* (1992); Hammer, Ellen J. *The Struggle for Indochina* (1954); Spector, Ronald H. *Advice and Support: The Early Years, 1941–1960* (1983); *Who's Who, 1974–1975* (1975).

See also: Blaizot, Roger; de Lattre de Tassigny, Jean Joseph Marie Gabriel; Elysée Agreement; France: Army; Indo-China War; L HÔNG PHONG II, Operation; Vietnamese National Army.

Carter, Jimmy (1924–)

President of the United States, 1977–1981. As late as 1971 Carter supported increased military aid to the Republic of Vietnam and did not oppose U.S. action there. During his 1976 presidential campaign, however, Carter was especially critical of secrecy in foreign policy and insisted that the pall cast by Vietnam and Watergate called for a candidate who could restore integrity and faith in government. Position papers released by Carter campaign headquarters in 1976 promised a pardon (rather than outright amnesty) for those "outside our country, or in this country, who did not serve in the armed forces." Deserters would be treated on a case-by-case basis.

Although prepared to establish normal relations with the Socialist Republic of Vietnam (SRV) in 1977, the Carter administration ended negotiations until Hà Nôi dropped demands for reparations in summer 1978. Talks did not proceed, however, because of what Washington saw as Hà Nôi's callous disregard for refugees and because of intelligence reports revealing SRV preparations to invade Cambodia. The U.S. State Department announced on 9 August 1979 that normalization was impossible for these reasons.

The United States restored diplomatic relations with the People's Republic of China on 1 January 1979. The potential for widening conflict between China and the Soviet Union, who had signed a "friendship treaty" with Hà Nôi, was at the center of Carter's talks with Chinese Vice-Chairman Deng Xiaoping that month. The president disapproved of Chinese intentions to invade Vietnam in retaliation for its strikes against Cambodia; subsequent to the Chinese attack he warned the Soviets against escalation. During the June 1979 Tokyo Economic Summit, Carter doubled the U.S. Indo-Chinese refugee quota, which led to openings for resettlement in other countries, a policy described by Secretary of State Cyrus Vance as among the most significant acts of the Carter administration.

Since leaving office, Carter has been one of America's most active former presidents, offering his services as mediator and negotiator in several major conflicts.

—Brenda J. Taylor

References: Adee, Michael J. "American Civil Religion and the Presidential Rhetoric of Jimmy Carter" (1994); Carter, Jimmy. *Keeping Faith: Memoirs of a President* (1982); Vance, Cyrus. *Hard Choices: Critical Years in America's Foreign Policy* (1983).

See also: Amnesty; Draft; Ford, Gerald R.; Habib, Philip Charles; Nixon, Richard Milhous; Reagan, Ronald; Refugees and Boat People; Vance, Cyrus Roberts.

Case, Clifford P. (1904–1982)

U.S. Senator, 1955–1979. Case won election to the U.S. Senate in 1954, defeating the extreme-right McCarthyites in the New Jersey Republican party. Known as a champion of social and civil rights programs, in 1967 he became a strong critic of U.S. policy in Southeast Asia and remained so through the Nixon administration. He condemned the war as an unconstitutional extension of executive power. With Senator Frank Church, he authored the 1973 Case-Church Amendment that severely restricted U.S. expenditures in Southeast Asia. He opposed U.S. military aid to Laos and Cambodia and was particularly hostile to the manner in which Presidents Johnson and Nixon used the military assistance program to enlarge U.S. military commitments overseas without Congressional consent.

—Priscilla Roberts

Reference: Schoenebaum, Eleanora W. *Political Profiles: The Nixon/Ford Years* (1979).

See also: Case-Church Amendment; Church, Frank Forrester; Fulbright, J. William; Goldwater, Barry Morris; Johnson, Lyndon Baines; McCarthy, Joseph Raymond; Nixon, Richard Milhous.

Case-Church Amendment

Congressional legislation to end U.S. military involvement in Indo-China. President Nixon's decision to continue heavy bombing of Cambodia in early 1973 and his 27 June veto of a bill to immediately terminate that bombing provoked a strong reaction in the U.S. House of Representatives and Senate.

Senators Clifford P. Case and Frank Church, authors of several end-the-war measures, introduced an amendment to the State Department authorization bill in June 1973 to bar appropriations from being used to finance U.S. military forces in North Vietnam, South Vietnam, Laos, or Cambodia unless specifically authorized by Congress. The amendment also blocked assistance "of any kind, directly or indirectly, to or on behalf of North Vietnam, unless specifically authorized hereafter by Congress." The amendment was added to the bill in committee and slipped through the full Senate without debate. Modified in a House-Senate conference to conform to a 15 August 1973 cutoff compromise favored by the Nixon administration, it then was endorsed by the House.

In response to suggestions that the Case-Church Amendment might undermine peace talks, an aide to Senator Church said, "It seems that the administration is always sending Kissinger off somewhere when these [antiwar] votes are coming up, but that tactic is pretty much finished."

—David C. Saffell

References: Karnow, Stanley. *Vietnam: A History* (1991); *Congressional Quarterly Weekly Reports* (1973).

See also: Cambodia; Case, Clifford P.; Church, Frank Forrester; Cooper-Church Amendment; Hatfield-McGovern Amendment; Nixon, Richard Milhous; Watergate.

CASTOR, Operation (20 November 1953)

Operation initiated by French General Henri Navarre that led to the Battle of Điên Biên Phu. CASTOR was Navarre's response to General Vô Nguyên Giáp's plans to invade northern Laos. Although not enthusiastic about the idea, Navarre decided to establish an airhead in northwestern Tonkin (North Vietnam), astride the main Viêt Minh invasion route into Laos, to prevent an outright enemy invasion of that country. The key position would be at Điên Biên Phu.

Contrary to Navarre's statement in his memoirs, many well-placed French officers in the north opposed CASTOR. Nonetheless, in November 1953 Navarre gave orders for CASTOR to proceed. On 20 November 1953 the entire French transport lift of 65 C-47s dropped 1,500 "paras," the cream of the French Expeditionary Corps, into the valley north and south of Điên Biên Phu, with its small Viêt Minh garrison. Some paras landed outside the drop zone, where they were ambushed. French B-26s assisted the operation by strafing Viêt Minh positions. A second lift later that day brought 700 additional French troops. By the end of the day Điên Biên Phu was in French hands.

Controversy surrounds Navarre's exact motives in CASTOR. There were Montagnard tribesmen in the area around Điên Biên Phu, and some maintain that he merely intended to use the base as a blocking position or mooring point from which the French and their auxiliaries could assault Viêt Minh rear areas. Others hold that Navarre saw this as his best chance of inflicting serious losses on the Viêt Minh by engaging them in conventional warfare. Inserting a force at Điên Biên Phu would tempt Giáp and allow Navarre, with his artillery, airpower, and trained troops, to inflict a serious defeat on his adversary. At most he expected Giáp to commit one division. Giáp, however, took the bait and put all available resources into what would become the Battle of Điên Biên Phu.

—Spencer C. Tucker

References: Fall, Bernard. *Hell in a Very Small Place: The Siege of Dien Bien Phu* (1967); Navarre, Général Henri. *Agonie de*

l'Indochine, 1953–1954 (1956); Roy, Jules. *The Battle of Dienbienphu* (1965); Simpson, Howard R. *Dien Bien Phu: The Epic Battle America Forgot* (1994).

See also: Điên Biên Phu, Battle of; Navarre, Henri Eugène; Navarre Plan.

Castries, Christian M. de. *See* de Castries, Christian M.

Casualties

In the Indo-China War the French and their allies sustained 172,708 casualties (94,581 dead or missing; 78,127 wounded). These include 140,992 French Union casualties (75,867 dead or missing; 65,125 wounded), with the allied Indo-China states losing 31,716 (18,714 dead or missing; 13,002 wounded). Viêt Minh losses are estimated at perhaps three times the French losses. Vietnamese civilian deaths from the fighting are estimated at 250,000.

In the Vietnam War, estimates of Republic of Vietnam war losses vary. A low figure is 110,357 killed in action and 499,026 wounded. The number of civilians killed in the war will never be known with any accuracy; estimates vary widely, but the lowest figure given is 415,000.

U.S. forces had 47,382 killed in action, 10,811 noncombat deaths, 153,303 wounded in action (some 74,000 survived as quadriplegics or multiple amputees), and 10,173 captured and missing in action. Between 1961 and 1975, 30,868 soldiers died in Vietnam as the result of hostile action; 7,193 died from other causes. Of those killed, 65.8 percent were Army, 25.5 percent Marine, 4.3 percent Navy, 4.3 percent Air Force, and 0.1 percent Coast Guard. Of ranks (including Navy equivalents), 88.8 percent were enlisted men and warrant officers, 8.6 percent lieutenants and captains, and 2.6 percent majors and colonels. Twelve U.S. generals died in Vietnam. In April 1995 the U.S. Department of Defense listed 1,621 Americans missing in Vietnam and 2,207 for all of Southeast Asia. On 13 November 1995 the Department of Defense announced that the remains of more than 500 American servicemen missing in Southeast Asia would never be recovered. It held out hope for the recovery of the other 1,500.

Other Allied casualties included Republic of Korea (4,407 killed in action); Australia (423 killed; 2,398 wounded in action); Thailand (351 killed); and New Zealand (83 killed).

Previous estimates had placed total Communist losses at 666,000 dead, but in April 1995 Hà Nôi announced that 1.1 million Communist fighters had died; 600,000 were wounded between 1954 and 1975. This casualty total included Viêt Công guerrillas in South Vietnam and People's Army of Vietnam personnel and presumably includes 300,000 missing in action. Hà Nôi estimated civilian deaths in the war in the same period at 2 million. The U.S. government estimate for civilians killed in the bombing of the North is 30,000.

—Spencer C. Tucker

References: Fall, Bernard. *Street with Joy* (1961); —. *The Two Viet Nams* (1964); Larson, Stanley Robert, and James Lawton Collins, Jr. *Allied Participation in Vietnam* (1975).

See also: Fragging; Friendly Fire.

Catholicism in Vietnam. *See* Roman Catholicism in Vietnam.

Catroux, Georges (1877–1969)

French soldier, civil servant, and governor-general of Indo-China. Named governor-general of Indo-China in August 1939, Catroux was an outstanding advocate of a liberal policy toward nationalism in the colonies. In summer 1940 Tokyo demanded the closing of the Sino-Vietnamese border and an end to transportation of war materials from Indo-China to Chungking. Catroux tried to stall for time but was forced to accept Tokyo's demands, including a Japanese control commission to oversee French compliance. Catroux's refusal to submit to the conditions of the armistice between the French government and the Germans, and his independent actions in dealing with the Japanese, led the Vichy government to replace him with the commander of French naval forces in the Far East, Vice-Adm. Jean Decoux. No more able to resist the Japanese, Decoux in September 1940 was forced to grant Japan the right to transport troops across northern Vietnam to south China, build airfields, and station 6,000 men in Tonkin.

—Spencer C. Tucker

References: Catroux, Général [Georges]. *Deux Actes du Drame Indochinois* (1959); Hammer, Ellen. *The Struggle for Indochina* (1954).

See also: de Gaulle, Charles André Marie Joseph; French Indo-China.

CEDAR FALLS, Operation (8–26 January 1967)

U.S. military operation against the Iron Triangle. In the early summer of 1966 Military Assistance Command, Vietnam (MACV) commander General William Westmoreland directed II Field Force (IIFFV) to develop an operation in War Zone C shortly after the Christmas holiday period. Lt. Gen. Jonathan O. Seaman's IIFFV staff added as a preliminary to Operation JUNCTION CITY a strike into the Iron Triangle to interdict Viêt Công (VC) control of the transportation and communications network emanating from that base area. A coordinated intelligence-gathering plan tracked and analyzed VC movements and contacts over several months to identify patterns. The target of Operation CEDAR FALLS was the headquarters of the VC Military Region IV and its support units.

The tactical technique chosen was a "hammer-and-anvil" attack. The anvil was to be positioned along the Sài Gòn River at the southwestern boundary of the Iron Triangle, with the hammer to swing through the triangle. Local residents were then evacuated and the triangle area stripped of vegetation. To preserve security for the operation, the plan was known only to a small group at IIFFV headquarters. The Army of the Republic of Vietnam (ARVN) III Corps commander was not briefed until 6 January 1967, two days before the operation commenced.

Operation CEDAR FALLS consisted of two phases. Phase I was the stealthy positioning of forces (the anvil) from 5 to 8 January with an air assault on the village of Bên Súc on the 8th. Phase II began on 9 January with two squadrons of the 11th Armored Cavalry ("Blackhorse") Regiment and elements of the 173d Airborne Brigade (Task Force Deane) making the hammer-like penetration from east to west beginning near Bên Cát, and the 3d Brigade, 1st Infantry ("Big Red One") Division, making airmobile assaults into the jungle of the Thanh Điên forest to the north of the triangle to seal off the area, then sweep south toward the junction of the Sài Gòn and Thi Tình Rivers. Two U.S. and one ARVN infantry divisions, supported by extensive artillery, engineer, and aviation units, were committed to the operation, the largest of the war to date.

Bên Súc, at the northwest corner of the Iron Triangle, was the headquarters of the VC secret base area, Long Nguyên. About 6,000 Vietnamese residents had been organized into four service units charged with moving supplies by sampan on the Sài Gòn River. Bên Súc and three smaller villages nearby were to be attacked by the 1st Battalion, 26th Infantry Regiment ("Blue Spaders"), commanded by Lt. Col. Alexander M. Haig, Jr., then evacuated and demolished.

A reinforced VC battalion defended Bên Súc. Accordingly, without preparatory artillery fires, the U.S. infantry battalion was lifted swiftly in 60 transport helicopters directly into the village. Ten armed helicopters protected the troops on the closely coordinated route into Bên Súc. Within minutes an entire infantry battalion of more than 400 men was landed, achieving complete tactical surprise. By midmorning the village was secured and an ARVN battalion that had been driven out of the area by the VC months earlier returned to conduct a methodical search of Bên Súc. VC tunnels beneath the village were collapsed, while bulldozers knocked down trees and brush. Nearly 6,000 villagers, along with their livestock and food, were moved to a resettlement camp near Phú Cuong.

The five infantry battalions, two cavalry squadrons, and one artillery battalion of the 3d Brigade of the Big Red One had commenced operations in the heavily wooded and entrenched area of the Thanh Điên forest north of the Iron Triangle on the morning of 9 January. They formed the hammer, along with the 173d Airborne Brigade, reinforced by the Blackhorse Regiment, striking into the triangle from the east. Despite the large number of Allied units engaged in the operation, the actual work of search and destroy was done by small infantry squads and fire teams. Search by day and ambush by night became the routine. The absence of strongly held VC defensive positions and counterattacks confirmed that the VC were trying to slip away from the attacking forces and exfiltrate the Iron Triangle to fight another day.

Gradually the forces committed to CEDAR FALLS wound down their search-and-destroy activities in the Iron Triangle, with the 1st Squadron, 4th Cavalry ("Quarterhorse") providing security for the engineer work parties who completed their work on 26 January. By the end of CEDAR FALLS, 2,711 acres of jungle had been cleared and 34 landing zones were chopped out of the jungle in the Iron Triangle.

CEDAR FALLS provided important tactical lessons about engineers and infantry working in unison to deny cover to the VC and about the preparation of helicopter landing zones and artillery fire bases. Procedures for clearing VC tunnel systems were refined, and the "tunnel rat" was introduced to the American reading public. VC documents recovered from the Military Region IV headquarters told the Allies a great deal about their Communist antagonists. The conventional statistics showed 750 VC/PAVN killed, 280 prisoners, and 540 Chiêu Hôi converts, compared with Allied losses of 83 killed and 345 wounded.

The VC suffered a significant setback with the penetration of their previously safe base areas close to Sài Gòn, but they avoided the destruction of their major combat forces in the area. Maj. Gen. William E. DePuy judged the operation "the most significant operation thus far conducted" by his division but less prophetically called it "a blow from which the VC in this area may never recover."

—John F. Votaw

References: Rogers, Bernard William. *Cedar Falls–Junction City: A Turning Point* (1974); Summers, Harry G., Jr. *Vietnam War Almanac* (1985).

See also: Bên Súc; DePuy, William E.; Haig, Alexander Meigs, Jr.; Iron Triangle; JUNCTION CITY, Operation; Search and Destroy; Tunnel Rats; United States: Army; United States: Involvement in Vietnam, 1965–1968.

Cédile, Jean (1908–1983)

French commissioner for Cochin China immediately after World War II. Cédile parachuted into Indo-China on 24 August 1945 and was immediately captured by the Japanese, who, although the war had ended, interrogated him under torture. A few days later he escaped and, with the help of Loyalists, reasserted French control over the governor's palace in Sài Gòn by outwitting Japanese soldiers and Viêt Minh militia guarding the building. In 1946 Cédile served as advisor to the French delegations in the Đà Lat negotiations between the French and Viêt Minh. He left Indo-China in 1947.

—Arthur J. Dommen

Reference: Gras, General Yves. *Histoire de la Guerre d'Indochine* (1992).

See also: French Indo-China.

Central Highlands

Important geographical feature at the southern terminus of the Truong Son Mountains in remote west-central South Vietnam. The northern part consists mainly of bamboo and tropical forests, with peaks ranging up to more than 8,000 feet in Ngoc Linh, the highest elevation in South Vietnam. The southern portion mostly lies above 3,000 feet. The area's sparse population consists of tribes of Austroasiatic (related to Khmer) and Austronesian (related to Cham, Malay, and Indonesian) peoples, whom the Vietnamese call *moi* ("savages") and the French called *Montagnards* ("mountain people"). The Montagnards did not adopt Chinese tradition or writing and are considered backward by the Vietnamese, with whom there is a natural antipathy. Principal ethnic groups include the Rhade, Jarai (Austronesian), and Bahnar (Austroasiatic).

In 1953 the Viêt Minh attempted to unify the disparate tribal groups into the National Union Front, and in 1954 the North Vietnamese took about 1,000 disgruntled minority cadres with them to North Vietnam for training and subsequent use in their homelands. After the Indo-China War, Republic of Vietnam (RVN) President Ngô Đình Diêm settled thousands of poor peasants from overpopulated coastal lowland villages in the area, and by 1958 the Montagnards were demanding autonomy. In 1961 U.S. Special Forces set up Civilian Irregular Defense Groups (CIDGs) in an effort to block North Vietnamese infiltrations, which used the Central Highlands as the southern terminus of the Hô Chí Minh Trail. A short-lived Montagnard rebellion in 1964, organized by the United Front of Liberation of the Oppressed Races (FULRO), was settled peacefully with U.S. assistance. FULRO subsequently led resistance to the Communists in the Central Highlands, but the Montagnards turned against the RVN government because of the exploitation of Montagnards by Army of the Republic of Vietnam (ARVN) officers and favoritism shown to Vietnamese soldiers.

The Central Highlands, or Cao Nguyên Trung Phân, have been called the "strategic fulcrum" of South Vietnam because RVN independence hung in the balance each time the North Vietnamese attacked the area and aimed toward the coast. Important battles here include attacks on the French in 1953 and 1954, the 1965 Ia Drang Valley campaign, the 1967 Battle of Đak Tô , the defense of Kontum during the 1972 Easter Offensive, and the 1975 fall of Ban Mê Thuôt to People's Army of Vietnam forces. Although Communist cadre speaking for the North Vietnamese had promised the Montagnards autonomy after the war, the promise was unfulfilled. Many were instead sent to reeducation camps, and approximately one million Vietnamese were forcibly resettled on their lands. FULRO led an armed resistance against the Communists after the fall of South Vietnam.

—Claude R. Sasso

References: Duiker, William J. *The Communist Road to Power in Vietnam* (1981); Hickey, Gerald C. *Sons of the Mountains: Ethnohistory of the Vietnamese Central Highlands to 1954* (1982); Nguyên Van Canh. *Vietnam under Communism, 1975–1982* (1983); Palmer, Bruce C. *The 25-year War: America's Military Role in Vietnam* (1984).

See also: Ban Mê Thuôt, Battle of; Đak Tô, Battle of; FULRO (Le Front Unifié de Lutte des Races Opprimées); Geography of Indo-China and Vietnam; Ia Drang, Battle of; Montagnards.

Central Intelligence Agency (CIA)

U.S. government foreign intelligence agency established in 1947 to oversee all foreign intelligence operations. During World War II its predecessor, the Office of Strategic Services (OSS) allied itself with Hô Chí Minh's Viêt Minh to oppose the Japanese. After World War II the CIA supported France in its war against the Viêt Minh.

Following the 1954 Geneva peace conference, the CIA strongly supported Ngô Đình Diêm's effort to create a new state in South Vietnam and provided money to bribe the leaders of South Vietnam's religious sects so that he could consolidate his control. One of Diêm's strongest American backers, Lt. Col. Edward Lansdale, came to Sài Gòn as CIA station chief in 1954 and used his expertise in countersubversion and guerrilla warfare to combat the Democratic Republic of Vietnam (DRV) and the Việt Minh. Operation EXODUS, Lansdale's black propaganda campaign in the North, portrayed forthcoming conditions under Communist rule as grimly as possible. It helped stimulate the mass migration of some 900,000 people, mostly Roman Catholics, from the North in 1954.

Yet even Lansdale recognized that Diêm's repressive techniques were proving counterproductive and driving opposition into the hands of the Communists. Gradually, Lansdale and the CIA turned against Diêm. During a 1960 abortive coup against Diêm the CIA was in touch with the plotters but did not aid them. Following massive Buddhist demonstrations in 1963, several senior Army of the Republic of Vietnam (ARVN) officers plotted another coup against Diêm. CIA Director John McCone instructed his Sài Gòn station not to prevent it. Influential CIA agent Lucien Conein went further and assured the generals that they had U.S. support in implementing the November 1963 coup that toppled Diêm.

After the coup, CIA station chief William Colby sought to foster a guerrilla war in the North with CIA-trained South Vietnamese infiltrators. The idea was to frighten the DRV leaders into abandoning the Việt Cộng (VC). CIA-conducted air drops and coastal raids on targets in the North had little effect in halting the escalating war.

Within the RVN the CIA supported U.S. Special Forces units (Green Berets), who were sent into rural areas to conduct unconventional warfare and political-psychological activities. The Special Forces were very successful in setting up paramilitary units, especially among the Montagnards of the Central Highlands. Some 80 base camps were set up, all under Special Forces leadership, with the goal of sealing the border and cutting VC supply lines. By 1964, 60,000 tribesmen were armed and trained. This effort was among the most successful campaigns of the Vietnam War. In 1969, when U.S. troops started withdrawing from Vietnam, Special Forces in the Highlands were also withdrawn.

At the height of the Vietnam War the CIA built an extensive network of 400 agents and officials, making the Vietnam station its largest in the world. Intelligence gathering was an essential task, and throughout the war the CIA issued regular reports to Washington to assist in policy decisions. These reports make sobering reading, detailing the political chaos, factionalism, and corruption within the RVN government that would only contribute to a Communist victory. As early as 1965 the CIA concluded that the war was stalemated and that the United States could not win. Washington thus always had the information to allow policymakers to make accurate decisions based on facts.

In Laos the United States engaged in a secret but extensive war. Beginning in 1960 the CIA trained and equipped mountain tribesmen, mostly from the Hmong tribe, to fight the Communist Pathet Lao and to sever the Hô Chí Minh Trail into South Vietnam. The CIA flew in food, supplies, and personnel on their proprietary airline, Air America. A secret army of 40,000 men led by General Vang Pao fought the CIA's secret war in Laos.

Throughout the 1960s the CIA sought to destroy VC cadres and infrastructure with pacification operations. The most controversial and brutal of these campaigns was the Phoenix Program, begun in 1968 to identify individual VC and then neutralize them through arrests, "conversion," or assassination. Although basically an RVN operation, the CIA provided essential advice and personnel. Its most ferocious section, the Provincial Reconnaissance Unit (PRU), was under direct CIA command. Interrogation centers were set up in every district and provincial capital. Monthly quotas of 3,000 people to be killed or captured were then sent to these centers. Altogether, 20,000 to 40,000 people died, 28,000 were imprisoned, and 20,000 were "reeducated" or "converted." Torture was routinely employed. Many were innocent victims of personal vendettas or of corruption. Phoenix's impact is difficult to estimate. Although the VC infrastructure was definitely hurt, many peasants were alienated by the number of casual arrests.

Early in the 1970s the CIA came under tremendous pressure from congressional critics in response to revelations concerning the Phoenix Program and Operation CHAOS, a program of wiretapping and surveillance of American opponents to the war that violated the CIA's charter. Next came revelations of indirect CIA's involvement in drug operations within the RVN and Laos that contributed to a booming heroin market in the United States. These abuses led Congress in 1974 to amend the Foreign Assistance Act to require that the CIA be involved only in intelligence activities outside the United States. Both houses of Congress established permanent oversight committees to monitor CIA activities.

When the end came for the RVN in 1975, the CIA was forced into a frantic evacuation that included flying President Thiêu with two suitcases full of gold to Taiwan. Many CIA employees and agents were left behind, along with key documents identifying them for the Communists to capture when they took Sài Gòn. Thus, the CIA record in Vietnam was indeed mixed.

—Michael Share

References: Kolko, Gabriel. *Anatomy of a War: Vietnam, the United States, and the Modern Historical Experience* (1985); Prados, John. *Presidents' Secret Wars: CIA and Pentagon Covert Operations Since World War II* (1986); Sheehan, Neil. *A Bright Shining Lie: John Paul Vann and America in Vietnam* (1988).

See also: Adams, Samuel A.; Air America; Colby, William Egan; Conein, Lucien Emile; Federal Bureau of Investigation (FBI); Hmong; Hoover, J. Edgar; Huston Plan; Lansdale, Edward Geary; Laos; McCone, John Alex; Montagnards; Nguyên Van Thiêu; Office of Strategic Services (OSS); Phoenix Program; Provisional Reconnaissance Units (PRUs) (Đon Vi Thám Sát Tinh); Quach Tom; United States: Special Forces; Vietnam, Republic of: Commandos.

Central Office for South Vietnam. *See* COSVN (Central Office for South Vietnam or Trung Uòng Cuc Miên Nam).

Champa, Kingdom of, and Cham People

Former kingdom in Vietnam and present ethnic minority there. Chams are descendants of the ancient kingdom of Champa that evolved from the Hindu civilizations of India as early as the second century. Cham civilization flourished across central Vietnam from the second to fifteenth centuries and, at its height, stretched from Vinh southward along the central coast to Phan Rang. The Vietnamese eventually subdued the Cham kingdom in 1471, although the Cham still retained lands south of the Cù Mông pass. Vestiges of the kingdom lived on until the late eighteenth century, when the end of the Tây Son Rebellion saw the final suppression of Cham autonomy as well.

There were four major Cham centers: Amaravati (Quang Bình to Quang Nam–Đà Nang); Vijaya (Nghia Bình); Kauthara (Khánh Hòa); and Panduranga (Bình Thuân/Thuân Hai). The most prominent archaeological remains, dating to the fourth century, are found at My Son, southwest of Đà Nang. The inscriptions of stelae at My Son suggest the division of Cham society into four castes akin to the Hindu caste system of India. Buddhism also flourished in Champa as early as the fourth century. The Cham settled in coastal enclaves and engaged in seafaring and maritime trade as far as China and islands in Southeast Asia. The Cham are also wet-rice farmers. In the plains around Phan Rang, remains of ancient hydraulic works attest to the height of Cham civilization.

Today many Chams still derive their livelihood from the sea. Along the central coast, Chams practice both Hinduism and Buddhism; in the south, they are Muslim. Cham society is organized into two clans ("areca" and "coconut"), which are broken down into subclans, each of which include ten to 15 families organized by matrilineal descent patterns and matrilocal residence. The Cham language is Malayo-Polynesian, and the ancient heritage is also seen in the written Sanskrit language as a vestige of their Hindu origins.

—David M. Berman

References: Hickey, Gerald Cannon. *Sons of the Mountains: Ethnohistory of the Vietnamese Central Highlands to 1954* (1982); Lebar, Frank M., Gerald C. Hickey, and John Musgrave. *Ethnic Groups of Mainland Southeast Asia* (1964).
See also: Lê Loi (Lê Thái Tô); Lê Thánh Tông; Tây Son Uprising; Vietnam: from 938 through the French Conquest.

Chapman, Leonard Fielding, Jr. (1913–)

General and commandant of the U.S. Marine Corps, 1968–1972. Chapman was Marine Corps chief of staff from 1964 to 1967; in July 1967 President Johnson appointed him commandant with the rank of full general. Though some saw Chapman's appointment as a "dark horse" compromise among factions within the Corps, he was soon recognized as an expert in military logistics and communications. At the time of his four-year appointment, more than one-fourth of the 300,000 Marines were on combat duty in Vietnam. Chapman's main task was to use his considerable management skills to aid in their systematic withdrawal. Chapman

retired from public service in 1977. Both of his sons, also Marines, saw active duty in Vietnam.

—Gary Kerley

References: *Current Biography Yearbook 1968* (1969); Jessup, John E., and Louise B. Ketz, eds. *Encyclopedia of the American Military* (1994); *Webster's American Military Biographies* (1978).
See also: Johnson, Lyndon Baines; United States: Marine Corps.

Charner, Léonard Victor Joseph (1797–1869)

Vice-admiral and commander of French forces in Cochin China in 1861. In 1861 Charner fought a brief but highly successful campaign against the Vietnamese, and by the end of the year the French were in control of much of Biên Hòa, Gia Đinh, and Đinh Tuong provinces. Charner returned to France in 1862 and became a senator. The French named a principal boulevard in Sài Gòn after him.

—Arthur J. Dommen

Reference: Whitfield, Danny J. *Historical and Cultural Dictionary of Vietnam* (1976).
See also: French Indo-China.

CHECO, Project (1963–1975)

In-depth studies of operations in Vietnam. Created by the U.S. Air Force in Sài Gòn in 1964, the Contemporary Historical Examination of Combat Operations (CHECO) project was to provide top-level commanders with classified book-length analyses of significant events and operations. The first title was *The History of the War in Vietnam, October 1961–December 1963* (1964). The project produced in all more than 200 major studies. In 1967 CHECO's mission was expanded to include microfilming of all pertinent documents. In addition, a Thailand office was opened at Udorn Royal Thai Air Force Base to cover operations in Laos. Key personnel creating the project included Joseph Angell, Office of Air Force History; Melvin Porter; and Kenneth Sams, chief in Sài Gòn from 1964 to 1971. Numerous U.S. Air Force Academy faculty members wrote reports on subjects ranging from rules of engagement to psychological operations. Some CHECO reports have been declassified. The complete collection, including millions of frames of microfilmed documents, is deposited in the archives of the U.S. Air Force Historical Research Center at Maxwell Air Force Base, Alabama.

—John Clark Pratt

Reference: "Projects CHECO and Corona Harvest: Keys to the Air Force's Southeast Asia Memory Bank" (1986).
See also: United States: Air Force; United States: Involvement in Vietnam, 1954–1965; United States: Involvement in Vietnam, 1965–1968; United States: Involvement in Vietnam, 1969–1973; United States: Involvement in Vietnam, 1973–1975.

Chemical Warfare. *See* Defoliation, Herbicides; RANCH HAND, Operation.

Chennault, Anna (1925–)

Chinese-born widow of U.S. General Claire Chennault, commander of the Flying Tigers during World War II. A friend of Jiang Jieshi (Chiang Kai-shek) and other Asian and American right-wing politicians, Chennault in 1968 served as the chairperson of the Republican Women for Nixon. Just days before the 1968 election, Chennault worked secretly to undermine Democratic efforts to halt the bombing of North Vietnam. She recommended to Republic of Vietnam President Nguyên Van Thiêu that he object to the last-minute halt of the bombing of the Democratic Republic of Vietnam and stall on the Paris peace talks, embarrassing the Democrats and helping Nixon in the election. She also urged Thiêu to make it clear that his support for U.S. policy hinged on Nixon's election as president.

President Johnson, however, had Chennault's telephone bugged. Chennault's contact was RVN Ambassador to the United States Bùi Diêm, and the Federal Bureau of Investigation and Central Intelligence Agency monitored his telephone conversations. Johnson warned Nixon not to depend on Chennault's maneuvering to win the election for him, but her efforts to stall the peace talks may have had an impact on the close presidential race, which Nixon won with 43.3 percent of the vote to Democrat Hubert Humphrey's 42.7 percent.

—Charlotte A. Power

References: Karnow, Stanley. *Vietnam: A History* (1983); Young, Marilyn B. *The Vietnam Wars, 1945–1990* (1991).

See also: Bùi Diêm; Elections, U.S.: 1968; Humphrey, Hubert H.; Johnson, Lyndon Baines; Nguyên Van Thiêu; Nixon, Richard Milhous.

Chiang Kai-shek. *See* Jiang Jieshi (Chiang Kai-shek).

Chicago Eight

Group charged with criminal responsibility for violent demonstrations in Chicago during the August 1968 Democratic National Convention. Defendants in the Chicago Conspiracy Trial, which began 24 September 1969, included David Dellinger, Rennie Davis, Thomas Hayden, Abbie Hoffman, Jerry Rubin, Lee Weiner, John Froines, and Bobby Seale, all charged with conspiracy to cross state lines with intent to cause a riot.

In the federal courtroom of Judge Julius Hoffman, attorneys William Kunstler and Leonard Weinglass represented all except Seale. Throughout the raucous trial the judge and lawyers exchanged insults while the defendants used disruptive tactics, trying to make the Vietnam War, racism, and repression the real issues. To blunt Seale's outbursts, Hoffman ordered him gagged and strapped to a chair, eventually separating his trial and imposing a four-year sentence for contempt. At trial's end in February 1970, Hoffman found the seven defendants and their lawyers guilty of 175 counts of contempt and sentenced them to terms from two (Weinglass) to four years (Kunstler). Although declaring the defendants not guilty of conspiracy, the jury found all except Froines and Weiner guilty of intent to riot. Each was sentenced to five years and fined $5,000, but none served time. In 1972 a Court of Appeals overturned the criminal convictions. Eventually most of the contempt charges were dismissed. The cantankerous Hoffman retired soon after the trial.

—John D. Root

References: Epstein, Jason. *The Great Conspiracy Trial* (1970); Schultz, John. *The Chicago Conspiracy Trial* (1993); Zaroulis, Nancy,

and Gerald Sullivan. *Who Spoke Up? American Protests Against the Vietnam War, 1963–1975* (1984).

See also: Antiwar Movement, United States; Dellinger, David; Democratic Party National Convention, 1968; Ginsberg, Allen; Hayden, Thomas E.; Hoffman, Abbie; May Day Tribe; Rubin, Jerry; Students for a Democratic Society (SDS); Youth International Party ("Yippies").

Chicago Seven. *See* Chicago Eight.

Chiêu Hôi (Open Arms) Program

Republic of Vietnam (RVN) amnesty program. The Chiêu Hôi program, also known as the Great National Solidarity or Open Arms program, was a decade-long campaign initiated by RVN President Ngô Đình Diêm in April 1963 to subvert the Communist military effort and convince their troops to desert or rally to the RVN cause. Its basic theme was that both sides were brothers in the same family. Since all wanted to end the war, the best and least costly way to do so was to renounce internecine bloodletting, forsake hatred, and cooperate in rebuilding the nation. The campaign promised clemency, financial aid, free land, job training, and family reunions to Communists who stopped fighting and returned to live under RVN authority. The program was intended as a meaningful and humanitarian effort that provided real opportunities for those the government considered wrongdoers to mend their ways and begin a new life. To this end the government and its allies used family contacts, radio and loudspeaker broadcasts, and propaganda leaflets to convince Communists to defect.

The Chiêu Hôi Program produced an encouraging number of ralliers at first but soon faltered and fell short of its 1964 goal of 40,000 defectors. Beginning in September 1964 the government offered financial rewards to defectors who surrendered with weapons or who volunteered to lead Allied forces to guerrilla arms caches or sanctuaries. This campaign uncovered a significant number of Communist arsenals and revived the program, aided in no small part by the arrival of U.S. combat forces in March 1965. During 1965 more than 11,100 Viêt Công (VC) defected, followed by 20,000 more in 1966. Another reward campaign, the Third Party Inducement Program, was started in mid-1967 in the IV Corps tactical zone, whereby people who induced a Communist to defect received a financial reward commensurate with the rallier's rank and importance. Although most ralliers during the life of the program were of relatively low rank, evidence suggests that the Communists were hurt in limited ways by Chiêu Hôi–induced manpower shortages.

The reward programs and increased Allied military activities provided the entire Chiêu Hôi Program with a needed boost, and in 1969 the number of defectors shot up to 47,000. It was soon discovered, however, that many ralliers— up to 30 percent in some ares—were not Communist defectors, but peasants who had been organized by corrupt RVN officials to surrender in return for a part of the reward or for one year's deferred conscription. When evidence of corruption became manifest in 1969 the financial reward aspects of the Chiêu Hồi Program were terminated, causing a sharp drop in the number of defectors to about 16,400 by mid-1970.

The Open Arms program was run by the RVN Government Chiêu Hồi Ministry. It controlled a country-wide system of offices at the provincial, district, and village levels. Ralliers were initially collected at provincial Chiêu Hồi Centers, or in Sài Gòn, where they underwent reeducation and rehabilitation. During the early years ralliers were well treated and were given access to vocational training. Government policy was to help ralliers acquire a skill to earn a living when they were released after 45 to 60 days. Ralliers who wanted to return to their home villages were provided with an allowance to do so. The government also constructed Chiêu Hồi villages, one for each province, and provided free housing to ralliers who had no place to go.

Depending on their success at reeducation and rehabili-tation, defectors were allowed to apply for civil service jobs; enlist in RVN regular, territorial, or paramilitary forces; or seek jobs in private industry. Of the ralliers who volunteered for government service as of 1970, 27 percent were employed in some capacity by the RVN government or armed forces; 20 percent were in private industry. More than 50 percent returned to their villages and lived as farmers on land pro-vided by the government. Efforts to reintegrate ralliers into society through government service had drawbacks. By late 1970 and early 1971, for example, evidence indicated a con-certed Communist effort to use the various Chiêu Hồi Programs to infiltrate VC cadres into RVN territorial and paramilitary forces and pacification programs.

U.S. military forces employed many ralliers, especially in units such as the Kit Carson Scouts, where their knowledge of terrain and Communist tactics proved useful. Other defec-tors were used for intelligence work against VC infrastructure throughout South Vietnam and made up the bulk of the membership of the Provincial Reconnaissance Units (PRUs) that operated as part of the Phoenix Program after 1968. They also participated in long-range reconnaissance opera-tions in Communist-controlled areas, including those north of the 17th parallel.

From 1963 to 1973 the Chiêu Hồi Program produced more than 159,700 Communist defectors, of whom 30,000 were positively identified as members of the VC infrastruc-ture. The program also netted 10,699 individual weapons and 545 crew-served weapons. The Chiêu Hồi Program's most successful year was 1969, when more than 47,000 cadres, VC, and People's Army of Vietnam soldiers defected, primarily because of setbacks suffered during the 1968 Têt Offensive and the increasing pressures being placed on the VC infra-structure by Republic of Vietnam pacification programs.

—Clayton D. Laurie

References: Andrade, Dale. *Ashes to Ashes: The Phoenix Program and the Vietnam War* (1990); Dinh Tan Tho. *Pacification* (1980); Lewy, Guenther. *America in Vietnam* (1978).

See also: Kit Carson Scouts; National Front for the Liberation of South Vietnam (NFLSV); Ngô Dình Diêm; Phoenix Program; Vietnam, Republic of: Army (ARVN).

China, People's Republic of (PRC)

The People's Republic of China (PRC) has had a long and tumultuous history with Vietnam. Despite intensive Chinese influence and more than 1,000 years of Chinese rule, in A.D. 939 the Vietnamese claimed their independence from China and expanded south of the Red River valley. This new state, called Đai Viêt (Great Viet), remained a tributary state of China and adopted many Chinese customs and practices. It retained its political autonomy, however, until the end of the nineteenth century, when it was conquered by France and joined with the French protectorates of Laos and Cambodia into the Union of Indo-China. After World War II, the Chinese Communists supported Hô Chí Minh's Viêt Minh guerrillas against France. Chinese aid, which increased following the 1949 revolution in China, was vital to the Viêt Minh and played a key role in the French defeat at Điên Biên Phu.

At the 1954 Geneva Conference, PRC premier Zhou Enlai pressured Hô Chí Minh to accept both the "temporary" divi-sion of Vietnam at the 17th parallel and the two-year wait before national elections. Zhou Enlai also agreed to recognize the states of Cambodia and Laos, since the PRC did not want Vietnam to take control over all of Southeast Asia. The promised elections were not held, however, and Hà Nôi adopted the "people's war" strategy favored by Chinese Communist leader Mao Zedong.

The PRC was the first Communist state to recognize the National Liberation Front (NLF) in South Vietnam. The PRC also provided substantial material support to the insurgents, including large quantities of arms and help in moving sup-plies. Mao was determined to keep the Democratic Republic of Vietnam (DRV) in the fight and, after the 1964 Tonkin Gulf incidents, China sent a squadron of MiG-15 and MiG-176 jets to the DRV. PRC leadership expressed outrage over U.S. esca-lation of the war in 1965, and in April of that year it signed an agreement with the DRV providing for the introduction into North Vietnam of Chinese air defense, engineering, and rail-road troops to help maintain and expand lines of communi-cations within the DRV. China later claimed that 320,000 of its troops served in the DRV from 1965 to 1971 and that 1,000 died there. The PRC probably provided three-quarters of the total military aid given to the DRV during the war, although this represented only about one-quarter of its total value. PRC aid to the DRV between 1949 and 1970 is estimat-ed at $20 billion. The PRC refused to allow Soviet aircraft to overfly its airspace to Vietnam but did permit the Soviets to ship military assistance to the DRV over its railroad net.

The PRC took a hard line toward negotiations between Hà Nôi and Washington. In 1971, however, the Chinese did for the first time endorse a DRV peace plan for ending the war. Worsening Sino-Soviet diplomatic relations and warm-ing Sino-American friendship played a role, however, in end-ing the Vietnam War during the early 1970s. Certainly President Nixon's February 1972 visit to China shocked the DRV leadership.

Soured diplomatic relations between the PRC and the Socialist Republic of Vietnam (SRV) led to military clashes during the late 1970s. In November 1978 the SRV signed a treaty of friendship and cooperation with the Soviet Union, and in early 1979 Vietnamese forces invaded Cambodia and installed a pro–Hà Nôi government. In response, on behalf of the ousted Khmer Rouge government, PRC troops invaded Vietnam the same year. This short but costly border war left the Sino-Vietnamese border virtually unchanged. During this period an estimated 1.4 million Vietnamese, many of them ethnic Chinese, fled Vietnam by boat. Approximately 50,000 of these "boat people" perished at sea; about a million settled abroad, including some 725,000 in the United States.

Sino-Vietnamese relations entered a new phase in the 1990s as the two governments apparently put aside inherent conflicts and past confrontations to maintained as smooth a relationship as they could manage.

—Bruce Elleman and Spencer C. Tucker

References: Butterfield, Fox. *China: Alive in the Bitter Sea* (1982); Chen, King G. *China's War with Vietnam, 1979* (1987); Fairbank, John King. *The Great Chinese Revolution 1800–1985* (1992); Hsü, Immanuel C. Y. *The Rise of Modern China* (1995); Spence, Jonathan D. *The Search for Modern China* (1990).

See also: Mao Zedong (Mao Tse-tung); Refugees and Boat People; Union of Soviet Socialist Republics (USSR; Soviet Union); Vietnam: Prehistory to 938; Vietnam: from 938 through the French Conquest; Zhou Enlai (Chou En-lai).

China, Republic of (ROC; Taiwan)

Although the Republic of China (ROC) made several offers to the United States to provide combat troops during the Vietnam War, Taiwanese military contributions to the war effort remained limited. Washington did not want to offend the Nationalist Chinese government by declining its offers but feared provoking overt retaliation by the People's Republic of China. Anti-Chinese attitudes among the Vietnamese were also factors in U.S. considerations. Consequently, the U.S. sought to channel ROC aid into the area of civic action.

ROC assistance to South Vietnam began with the dispatch of a military assistance advisory group in 1964. Taiwan gave aid in such areas as political warfare, health care, refugee relief, logistics, electrical power generation, and agriculture. In all, ROC economic and technical assistance totaled $3 million. Taiwan also sent 31 military advisors, and approximately 300 Vietnamese technicians received training in Taiwan. During the 1968 Têt Offensive, the ROC was among the first countries to provide emergency assistance to South Vietnam, in the form of 5,000 tons of rice. The ROC also provided prefabricated warehouses, agricultural implements, seeds, fertilizers, and textbooks. Improved Taiwanese agricultural techniques were much appreciated by South Vietnamese farmers.

—Peter W. Brush

Reference: Larsen, Stanley R., and James L. Collins, Jr. *Allied Participation in Vietnam* (1975).

See also: China, People's Republic of (PRC); Civic Action; Free World Military Forces; Jiang Jieshi (Chiang Kai-shek); Order of Battle; Têt Offensive: Overall Strategy; Têt Offensive: the Sài Gòn Circle.

Chinese in Vietnam

In 1960 Chinese made up the largest single minority group in the Republic of Vietnam (RVN), numbering one million people (about 8 percent of the total population). The first mass migration of Chinese to Vietnam occurred in the late seventeenth century, when defeated Ming dynasty generals and their followers received large landholdings in the Sài Gòn area and in the Mekong Delta. Ultimately, 85 percent of all Chinese lived in the Sài Gòn–Cho Lon area. Cho Lon became Vietnam's greatest commercial city, and soon the Chinese community dominated Vietnam's economy.

The Chinese organized themselves according to their origins into five groups (*bangs*), known as "congregations" by the French. These *bangs* were responsible to the government for the good behavior of their members and payment of taxes. In return each *bang* had substantial autonomy. The compartmentalization and segregation from the local Vietnamese population set the Chinese on a collision course with Vietnamese nationalism in its first attempts to seek assimilation by all minority groups in an independent Vietnam.

Under French administration, Chinese in Vietnam acquired a commanding position in rice processing, marketing, transport, and meat slaughtering. Their privileges in Vietnamese society were ratified through a series of bilateral treaties between France and China. Eventually the Chinese had the same privileges as the French. The Vietnamese resented these special privileges, Chinese domination of the economy, and Chinese isolation from the rest of the Vietnamese community. During the Indo-China War the Chinese were not clearly allied with either side. Taking advantage of the conflict, they continued to prosper economically. Close relations developed between the Chinese community and the Chinese Nationalist government, located after 1949 in Taiwan. Vietnamese nationalists questioned whether the Chinese were loyal to Vietnam or to Taiwan.

In fall 1956, President Ngô Đình Diêm launched an attack against the Chinese community on the political and economic fronts. His intention was to assert his nationalist credentials and to curb Chinese economic power. One decree required that all Chinese become Vietnamese citizens and adopt Vietnamese names. Another barred Chinese nationals from various occupations. A third required that the Vietnamese language be used exclusively in Chinese schools, which would come under direct Vietnamese government control. A final decree in 1960 ordered the dissolution of all five Chinese *bangs*.

Had these decrees been fully enforced they would have destroyed the Chinese community politically, economically, and culturally. But the Chinese reacted immediately to the decrees, refusing to become Vietnamese citizens. Furthermore, Taiwan vigorously protested the decrees, bringing relations between these two anti-Communist states and U.S. allies to a new low. The Chinese demonstrated their great economic power by withdrawing their bank deposits, causing a collapse of the piaster. In 1957 the RVN plunged into a near-depression as commercial transactions virtually ceased. The United States pressured both sides to negotiate face-saving measures so that the effects of these assimilationist measures were at best limited. At the same time, government discrimination against Chinese nationals provoked more resentment by the Chinese.

During the Vietnam War the Chinese continued to control most RVN commerce, industry, and trade, including 80 to 90 percent of the wholesale and retail trades. Cho Lon remained the economic hub of the RVN. "Crony capitalism" was prevalent in South Vietnam, and for Chinese merchants, bribes were an integral part of business. In the absence of effective legal and judicial mechanisms to protect wealth and property, business leaders were forced to develop relations with political patrons to gain protection. Corruption pervaded South Vietnam to the end of the war despite occasional government campaigns against it. These campaigns were often for show and were directed against the Chinese as obvious scapegoats.

The Chinese community was represented in only token numbers in the upper and middle ranks of the RVN government and army. Few Chinese played an active role militarily. Many Chinese were middle or upper class, and virtually all were urban. Although apolitical and aloof from South Vietnam's turbulent political life, they were deeply conservative. Thus, the Chinese were a natural constituency for the rightist RVN government. But Diêm's policy of forced assimilation, a seemingly endless war, economic depression, corruption, discrimination, and persecution all caused this group to become essentially neutral. Above all, the Chinese were pragmatists who were never ideologically motivated in Vietnam.

During the 1968 Têt Offensive Cho Lon was badly damaged in heavy street fighting. After Têt, inflation increased, causing popular resentment among the mostly Chinese merchants. The government arrested and executed many Chinese to assure the population that the government was cracking down on corruption. The 1972 Spring offensive by the People's Army of Vietnam (PAVN) worsened the economy, plunging the RVN into an economic depression. Numerous Chinese-owned factories and businesses closed, and people held their money. As they controlled the bulk of imports to the RVN, the Chinese suffered the most. Thus in April 1975 when PAVN troops entered the Sài Gòn area, thousands of Chinese in Cho Lon welcomed them, hoping economic prosperity could resume.

As relations between Vietnam and China worsened in the post-reunification period, however, Chinese in both the North and the South became hostages. In 1976 virtually all southern Chinese were forced to become Vietnamese citizens, an action contrary to all prior DRV and Việt Công pledges. The Vietnamese government nationalized some 30,000 Chinese businesses, impoverishing the Chinese community and ending their livelihoods. Many Chinese were forced by the government to leave Cho Lon for harsh New Economic Areas, recently created in underpopulated and poor regions. As a result, thousands of Chinese sought to leave Vietnam. In May 1978 China charged Vietnam with deliberate persecution and sent a few ships to rescue the Chinese.

Vietnam's reaction was sharp and harsh. Government officials expelled hundreds of thousands of Chinese, demanding exorbitant fees in hard currency or gold. More than 250,000 Chinese fled, often in tiny, poorly equipped boats; between 30,000 and 40,000 drowned under horrible circumstances. Thousands of others crossed the northern border into China. As tensions mounted between the People's Republic of China (PRC) and the Socialist Republic of Vietnam (SRV), the SRV government sent to internment camps at least 6,000 Vietnamese suspected of being Chinese moles or sympathizers. With the expulsion of the skilled Chinese, the South's economy sank even lower. But Vietnam had solved its "China problem."

Since the institution of free-market reforms and the opening of the SRV to foreign investment, those Chinese remaining in Cho Lon have resumed their commercial roles, this time with the support of compatriots in Taiwan and the United States. Some suggest that the Chinese are now a greater influence in the Vietnamese economy than before 1975.

—Michael Share

References: Pao-min Chang. *Beijing, Hanoi, and the Overseas Chinese* (1982); Schrock, J. L. *Minority Groups in the Republic of Vietnam* (1966); Share, Michael. "The Chinese Community in South Vietnam during the Second Indochina War" (1994); Tsai Maw-Kuey. *Les Chinois au Sud-Vietnam* (1968).

See also: China, People's Republic of (PRC); China, Republic of (ROC; Taiwan); Ngô Đình Diêm; Refugees and Boat People; Vietnam, Republic of: 1954–1975; Vietnam, Socialist Republic of: 1975 to the Present.

Chomsky, Noam A. (1928–)

Massachusetts Institute of Technology (MIT) professor; leading critic of the Vietnam War. A major contributor to the development and progress of linguistic theory, Chomsky was also a leading intellectual critic and political activist in the antiwar movement. His critiques emphasized the immorality of the war and the institutional culpability of the state, mass media, corporations, universities, and other institutions. He was particularly critical of what he called the "new mandarins," elite intellectuals whom he believed provided an ideological defense for an indefensible war. Chomsky argued that U.S. policy in Vietnam had an imperial strategic objective, and he rejected the view that U.S. policy was largely the result of well-intentioned but misguided leaders. He defended the courage and moral commitment of antiwar protestors and was respected in turn. Antiwar activist Fred Halstead commented that Chomsky's writing on the war "earned him the respect of virtually all sections of the movement."

—Michael O'Loughlin

References: Chomsky, Noam. *American Power and the New Mandarins* (1969); —. *The Chomsky Reader* (1987); Halstead, Fred. *Out Now! A Participant's Account of the American Movement Against the Vietnam War* (1978).

See also: Antiwar Movement, United States; LINEBACKER II, Operation; Spock, Benjamin M..

Chu Van Tân (1909–ca. 1983)

People's Army of Vietnam (PAVN) general; key Democratic Republic of Vietnam (DRV) political figure. In 1934 Tân joined the Indo-Chinese Communist Party (ICP), and over the next six years he organized protest demonstrations, strikes, and secret self-defense groups. In 1941 Tân received a field command in the newly formed Army of National Salvation. He held out for eight months against French military raids but in March 1942 was forced to withdraw to the Chinese border. In February 1943, when the French concentrated to the south, he returned to his old Bac Son–Vu Ninh area base, then over the next two years built up his military strength. In March 1945 he joined Vô Nguyên Giáp in the Cao Bang area to form the Vietnam Army of Liberation.

Elected to the ICP Central Committee in 1945, Tân continued in that capacity into the mid-1970s. He was minister of defense in Hô Chí Minh's first cabinet and held various other posts in the Democratic Republic of Vietnam government. Suspected of being pro-Chinese, in August 1979 Tân was removed from his posts and reportedly placed under arrest. He is said to have died in a prison in a Sài Gòn suburb in 1983.

—Spencer C. Tucker

References: Marr, David G. *Vietnam 1945: The Quest for Power* (1996); Patti, Archimedes L. A. *Why Viet Nam? Prelude to America's Albatross* (1980).

See also: Vietnam, Democratic Republic of: 1945–1954; Vietnam, Socialist Republic of: 1975 to the Present.

Church, Frank Forrester (1924–1984)

U.S. senator and opponent of U.S. involvement in Southeast Asia. An early critic of U.S. involvement in Vietnam, in 1963 the liberal Church opposed U.S. aid to the Diêm regime. In June 1965 Church called for direct negotiations with the Viêt Công, free elections in the South, and a scaling down of the U.S. effort there. During the remainder of 1965 and throughout 1966 Church voted against supplemental appropriations for the war. In May 1967 he drafted a letter, signed by 16 antiwar senators, warning the Democratic Republic of Vietnam that the U.S. objective was to settle the war at the conference table, but not at the expense of U.S. commitments or unilateral withdrawal.

In spring 1970 Church and Senator John S. Cooper introduced an amendment to the foreign military sales bill that barred funding for future military operations in Cambodia. Although the bill eventually passed the Senate, the House rejected it. A scaled-down version, passed in December 1970 as part of the defense appropriations bill, imposed limits on the president's power. In 1973 Congress passed a bill sponsored by Church and Senator Clifford Case that authorized a complete cutoff of all funding of American combat operations in Indo-China.

—Robert G. Mangrum

References: Karnow, Stanley. *Vietnam: A History* (1984); Summers, Harry G. *Vietnam War Almanac* (1985).

See also: Case, Clifford P.; Case-Church Amendment; Cooper, John Sherman; Cooper-Church Amendment; Fulbright, J. William; Kennedy, Edward Moore; McGovern, George S.

Civic Action

General term for civilian assistance programs and projects of U.S. military units within the Republic of Vietnam (RVN). Sometimes referred to as military-civic action, civic action was viewed as one component of pacification. Civic action projects were to promote social and economic development as well as identification with, and support for, the Sài Gòn government. This process was commonly known as "winning the hearts and minds" of the Vietnamese people. The pacification effort was also known as "the other war," hence the common references to two wars being fought in parallel—one to destroy the enemy who threatened the nation, and the other to build the nation itself. Other terms used in reference to civic action programs were "revolutionary development" and "rural reconstruction."

Civic action projects included construction of schools, health centers, wells, roads, bridges, and canals; distribution of food, clothing, and medical supplies to orphanages; and medical civic action programs (MEDCAPs) that brought military doctors and medics to rural areas. U.S. military personnel conducted English classes for Vietnamese; agricultural advisors under the protection of military patrols introduced new strains of rice to villagers in contested areas; and Montagnard and Vietnamese refugees were placed in refugee resettlement centers. Some civic action projects were viewed as an extension of the role of military units. Others became the primary mission of many units operating in the Vietnamese countryside.

The MEDCAP was perhaps the best-known form of civic action project. U.S. military units, often with their medics or corpsmen and sometimes escorting doctors from nearby field or evacuation hospitals, offered medical assistance to villages in their area of operations. In many cases, villagers were brought back to military or civilian hospitals for treatment. MEDCAPs also provided inoculations, established local dispensaries, and trained villagers to treat minor conditions.

Such civic action projects served two purposes. First, they addressed the primary mission of the pacification effort, to "win the hearts and minds" of the people for the RVN government in the face of Viêt Công (VC) opposition. Unfortunately, these projects were usually carried out by U.S. forces without the involvement of the Sài Gòn government or Army of the Republic of Vietnam (ARVN). Second, civic action projects also served military objectives. In the process of these operations, patrols often gathered intelligence through their own observations and discussions with local villagers. Over time, patrols developed intelligence on the movement of villagers, VC infiltration, executions or kidnappings, and the allegiance of the village to either the government or the VC.

U.S. Marine Corps civic action programs were of particular note. They evolved out of the tactical situation in I Corps, where in March and April 1965 Marine Corps combat operations began against the VC in heavily populated areas along the coast. As the Marines moved inland, they created tactical areas of responsibility (TAOR), enlarging the coastal enclaves through "clear-and-hold" operations that deprived the VC of perhaps 90 percent of the population base of the I Corps tactical zone. The Marines instituted pacification programs to gain the allegiance of the estimated two million people living in the coastal area. This approach was in direct opposition to more conventional search-and-destroy operations conducted by the U.S. Army.

The advocates of this strategy were Lt. Gen. Victor H. Krulak, commanding general of Fleet Marine Force Pacific, and Lt. Gen. Lewis W. Walt, commanding general of III Marine Amphibious Force (III MAF). They believed that military civic action programs were the key to the pacification effort. Because haphazard civic action programs proved ineffective in gaining the allegiance of the local population, during August 1965 the Marines developed the combined action company (CAC) to integrate RVN Popular Forces (PF) soldiers into Marine tactical units. By placing these units into Vietnamese hamlets and relying on indigenous PFs, "combined action" operations began to achieve success against the VC. By spring 1966, 40 CACs were operating throughout the I Corps area.

By February 1967 the combined action platoon (CAP) became the means to wage what the Marines termed "the other war." The CAP combined a Marine rifle squad of 14 men and one Navy corpsman with three ten-man PF militia squads, and a five-man platoon headquarters into a combined platoon of 50 American and Vietnamese soldiers to provide security at the local level and initiate civic action programs as part of the pacification effort. The CAP mission was to destroy the VC infrastructure within the village or hamlet area of responsibility; protect public security and help maintain law and order; protect the friendly infrastructure; protect bases and communication axes within the villages and hamlets; organize people's intelligence nets; and participate in civic action and conduct propaganda against the VC. Civic action programs were an integral part of the CAP mission. From 1965 to 1971, 114 Marine CAPs operated throughout the five I Corps provinces to implement the Marine counterinsurgency strategy.

U.S. Army civic action programs developed within a somewhat different tactical situation. Army combat operations began against regular People's Army of Vietnam (PAVN) units in the Central Highlands with the October–November 1965 battle of the Ia Drang Valley. The Army's primary mission was to hunt down and destroy PAVN main force units; pacification was a secondary emphasis. With their military bases more segregated from the indigenous population than those of the Marines along the coast, Army civic action programs tended to emphasize specific civic action projects rather than the ongoing military civic action programs of the Marines that were integrated with indigenous units at the village or hamlet level. One notable exception was the 25th Infantry Division's Operation LANIKAI in Long An Province. Begun in September 1966 by the 4th Battalion, 9th Regiment, in conjunction with ARVN units, it sought to secure a district with a dense population. Battalion units lived with the indigenous population to devel-

op cooperation with local forces and provide security for the local population. The operation lasted only two to three months, until the battalion was pulled out to participate in Operation FAIRFAX.

MEDCAPs were perhaps the most common form of civic action. The 25th Infantry Division initiated the "Helping Hand" program with the distribution of thousands of parcels of goods to villages along Highway 1, along with various self-help projects, such as the construction of public works. The 1st Cavalry Division out of An Khê distributed healthcare supplies to villages along Highway 14 and sponsored Boy Scout jamborees. Most Army units had a G-5 and/or S-5 civil affairs officer, whose primary responsibility was to coordinate civic action programs within the unit's area of operations.

Civil affairs teams were the closest Army analogy to the Marine Corps combined action platoons. By 1968, three Army civil affairs companies and one detachment, totalling 439 men, were operating in the RVN in conjunction with the Refugee Division of the Civilian Operations and Revolutionary Development Support (CORDS). The 29th Civil Affairs Company operated in I Corps and worked exclusively on refugee assistance. The 41st Civil Affairs Company in II Corps and the 2d Civil Affairs Company in III Corps also worked on refugee resettlement but had other civic action responsibilities.

In the short term, civic action projects had positive benefits, including improved medical care for the local population, resettlement of Vietnamese and Montagnard refugees, construction of housing and public works, establishment of short-term good will toward the government, and the gathering of intelligence information. In the long term the results were at best minimal. Except for the Marine Corps CAPs and Army civil affairs teams, few U.S. military personnel lived with the Vietnamese long enough to learn their language and their culture in order to win their allegiance to a government that failed to heed their concerns.

—David M. Berman

References: Corson, William R. *The Betrayal* (1968); Hunt, Richard A. *Pacification: The American Struggle for Vietnam's Hearts and Minds* (1995); West, F. J. *The Village* (1985); Wiesner, Louis A. *Victims and Survivors: Displaced Persons and Other War Victims in Viet-Nam, 1954–1975* (1988).

See also: Clear and Hold; Krulak, Victor H.; Marine Combined Action Platoons (CAPs); Montagnards; Pacification; Refugees and Boat People; Search and Destroy; U.S. Agency for International Development (USAID); Walt, Lewis W.

Civilian Irregular Defense Group (CIDG)

In 1961 and 1962 U.S. Army Special Forces (Green Berets) on temporary duty established several isolated camps in remote areas in South Vietnam. These camps served to extend the influence of the Republic of Vietnam (RVN) government, to provide security for the local population, and to isolate the people from Communist influence and intimidation. Volunteers recruited from local populations were trained as soldiers. Known as the Civilian Irregular Defense Group

(CIDG) and paid by the Central Intelligence Agency's Combined Studies Division/Group through the U.S. Special Forces (USSF), they played a significant role in securing sparsely populated highland areas. At its peak the CIDG numbered 45,000 men.

U.S. Special Forces first operated around Ban Mê Thuôt in the Central Highlands with Rhade and Jarai Montagnards. Most CIDG personnel throughout Vietnam were Montagnard tribesmen, although there were also Cambodians and Vietnamese. The initial USSF approach was to organize the Montagnards, place them under government control, and train them to fight the Viêt Công (VC). The Green Berets organized CIDG personnel into combat units that were assigned specific missions: border surveillance and interdiction of Communist infiltration, communications, and supply routes; offensive operations against VC units and sanctuaries; identification and destruction of VC infrastructure; and establishment of area security. Another CIDG concept was to organize and train tactical reserve reaction forces to serve as mobile strike force units.

Army of the Republic of Vietnam (ARVN) Special Forces (Luc Luong Đac Biêt, or LLDB) placed officers in each camp to serve as its commander and staff; USSF assumed the CIA mission and served as advisors. Camps were organized into three companies of 132 men each, three reconnaissance platoons, a heavy weapons section with two 105-mm howitzers, and a political warfare section. Each camp was authorized 530 men.

Many of the isolated CIDG camps came under attack or siege. In 1965 People's Army of Vietnam (PAVN) forces besieged the CIDG camp at Đuc Co in the Central Highlands for more than two months. In June 1965 Viêt Công units overran the CIDG camp at Đông Xoài but failed to take the town because of fierce CIDG resistance. In March 1966 two PAVN regiments attacked the A Shau CIDG camp, forcing U.S. and ARVN Special Forces to withdraw. Other CIDG camps were abandoned because of insufficient manpower. The CIDG program also experienced problems with fraud and corruption, and in March 1970 U.S. and RVN military leaders agreed to convert the CIDG camps to ARVN Ranger camps. The last two CIDG border camps were officially converted on 4 January 1971.

—Vu Đinh Hiêu and Harve Saal

References: Kelly, Francis J. *The Green Berets in Vietnam 1961–71* (1991); Westmoreland, William C. *A Soldier Reports* (1981).

See also: Central Intelligence Agency (CIA); Montagnards; United States: Special Forces; Vietnam, Republic of: Special Forces (Luc Luong Đac Biêt [LLDB]).

Civilian Operations and Revolutionary Development Support (CORDS)

Umbrella organization for U.S. pacification efforts in the Republic of Vietnam (RVN). Civilian Operations and Revolutionary Development Support (CORDS) organized all civilian agencies involved in the pacification effort in South Vietnam under the military chain of command. Established under the Military Assistance Command, Vietnam (MACV)

on 10 May 1967, CORDS was placed under the direction of Robert Komer, an MACV civilian deputy commander. Komer, special assistant to President Johnson, held the rank of ambassador and the military equivalent of three-star general, and he reported directly to General William Westmoreland. Upon Komer's departure in November 1968, William Colby, who had been the assistant chief of staff (ACS) for CORDS, took direction of CORDS.

CORDS succeeded the Office of Civilian Operations (OCO), originally created to assume responsibility over all civilian agencies working in the South under the jurisdiction of the U.S. Embassy in Sài Gòn. CORDS integrated U.S. aid programs targeting the social and economic development of South Vietnam. These were viewed as the basis upon which to build the Vietnamese nation and win the "hearts and minds" of the Vietnamese people in the face of Communist political and military opposition. CORDS activities were primarily directed toward the 80 percent of the South Vietnamese population who lived in the rural villages and hamlets most vulnerable to the Viêt Công (VC). In this way the Communists would be deprived of their traditional population base.

CORDS was organized into six operational divisions: Chiêu Hôi (Open Arms), Revolutionary Development, Refugees, Public Safety, Psychological Operations, and New Life Development. The Chiêu Hôi program was designed to induce VC and People's Army of Vietnam (PAVN) soldiers to turn themselves in to the RVN government as *hôi chánh* ("returnees") through government propaganda campaigns and monetary payments. Returnees were given job training, welfare services, and resettlement assistance and were also integrated into Army of the Republic of Vietnam (ARVN) military units.

The Revolutionary Development (RD) division was organized into 59–member teams designed to provide security and promote economic development at the village level. RD teams were trained at the National Training Center in Vung Tàu and assigned to villages throughout the country. Working through the U.S. Agency for International Development (USAID), the refugee program was designed to resettle millions of displaced villagers across the country, often through the establishment of refugee resettlement centers, and to provide them security.

CORDS integrated all military and civilian personnel into a single chain of command by assigning them to the same missions through the establishment of CORDS advisory teams at the province level. During 1968, for example, in the 12 II Corps provinces some 4,000 CORDS personnel served under the operational command of James Megellas, CORDS deputy, who held the military equivalent of major general and reported directly to Lt. Gen. William R. Peers, commander of I Field Force, Vietnam. CORDS teams at the province level consisted of State Department, USAID, U.S. Information Agency (USIA), and U.S. Public Health Service personnel. In Khánh Hòa Province, for example, Team 35 had 87 military and 23 civilian personnel, including foreign service officers, public health nurses, rural health, and agricultural advisors.

Priority projects in 1968 were the resettlement of Montagnard tribesmen and improving the quality and effectiveness of Regional Forces/Popular Forces (RF/PF) units to provide security at the village level.

With the war intensifying and the increasing vulnerability of civilian aid efforts in the countryside, providing security for pacification became a military priority. In September 1969 there were 6,464 U.S. military advisors assigned to CORDS, 5,812 of whom served in the field. Major efforts were made within the U.S. Army in particular (which had 95 percent of CORDS military advisors) to assign qualified military advisors to CORDS advisory teams. Three Army civil affairs companies (the 2d, 29th, and 41st) were directly involved in pacification programs under CORDS administration. Major efforts were also made under both Komer and Colby to improve the effectiveness of RF/PF units by increasing both their manpower and their firepower equivalent to local Viêt Công units. By the end of 1969 RF/PF units numbered 475,000 men. Their effectiveness was a major factor in providing security at the village level in support of pacification efforts.

With the January 1973 Paris Peace Accords and the withdrawal of American armed forces, the rationale for the existence of CORDS was removed. CORDS ceased operations on 27 February 1973, and selected functions were assumed by the office of the special assistant to the ambassador for field operations (SAAFO), a civilian operation headed by George Jacobson, who had been ACS of CORDS under William Colby.

—David M. Berman

References: Hickey, Gerald Cannon. *Free in the Forest: Ethnohistory of the Vietnamese Central Highlands, 1954–1976* (1982); Hunt, Richard A. *Pacification: The American Struggle for Vietnam's Hearts and Minds* (1995); Wiesner, Louis A. *Victims and Survivors: Displaced Persons and Other War Victims in Viet-Nam, 1954–1975* (1988).

See also: Chiêu Hôi (Open Arms) Program; Civic Action; Colby William Egan; Komer, Robert W.; Marine Combined Action Platoons (CAPs); Pacification; Psychological Warfare Operations (PSYOP); Refugees and Boat People; Territorial Forces; U.S. Agency for International Development (USAID); Vann, John Paul; Westmoreland, William Childs.

Clarey, Bernard A. (ca. 1911–1996)

U.S. Navy admiral; commander of U.S. Navy forces in the Pacific, 1970–1973. In 1970, when Admiral Elmo R. Zumwalt became chief of naval operations and chose his own aides, Clarey became commander of the Pacific Fleet (CINCPACFLT) in Hawaii. As such Clarey had command of all U.S. Navy vessels in the Pacific, including those off Vietnam, and naval air operations against the Democratic Republic of Vietnam DRV. Racial unrest in the Pacific fleet led Clarey to order his unit commanders to be more sensitive to minority grievances. Clarey retired from the Navy in October 1973.

—Spencer C. Tucker

Reference: Personnel File, Naval History Division, U.S. Navy, Washington, DC.

See also: United States: Navy; Zumwalt, Elmo R, Jr.

Clark, William Ramsey (1927–)

U.S. attorney general under President Johnson. In 1960 Clark campaigned for John F. Kennedy, who in 1961 appointed Clark assistant attorney general in charge of the Lands Division of the Justice Department. Clark also supervised several other projects, mainly in the civil rights area, and for his diligent work he was appointed deputy attorney general in 1965. In this post he helped to draft the 1965 Voting Rights Act.

In 1966, President Johnson appointed Clark acting attorney general and five months later made the promotion permanent. As attorney general from 1967 to 1969, Clark strongly supported civil rights for all Americans, opposed the death penalty, criticized police violence toward citizens, and steadfastly refused to use wiretaps except in cases of national security. These positions, in addition to his lenient stance on antiwar activities, attracted criticism from within the Johnson administration and from conservatives, who labeled him soft on crime. After leaving office in 1969, Clark actively opposed the Vietnam War, and in 1972 he visited North Vietnam to investigate U.S. bombing of civilian targets.

—Laura Matysek Wood

References: Clark, William Ramsey. *Crime in America: Observations on Its Nature, Causes, Prevention and Control* (1970); *Who's Who in America, 1968–1969* (1969).

See also: Antiwar Movement, United States; Johnson, Lyndon Baines; Katzenbach, Nicholas.

Claymore Mines. *See* Mines, Antipersonnel and Antitank.

Clear and Hold

Designation for Allied military efforts to eradicate the Communist presence in selected areas of South Vietnam. Part of the pacification program, the clear and hold concept was an attempt to solve the unconventional problems of a guerrilla conflict with a conventional solution of traditional land warfare—the effective garrisoning of territory after it was taken.

The dilemma in Vietnam lay in holding, not clearing. Although massive sweep operations against areas controlled by the People's Army of Vietnam (PAVN) or the Viêt Công (VC) were generally successful, these effects were temporary. Communist guerillas simply reasserted themselves once clearing forces departed. The civilian population fully understood that any cooperation with Allied soldiers during the sweeps could well prove fatal to them after the guerillas returned. The clear and hold concept envisioned the permanent stationing of garrison troops in selected areas after their clearing to prevent a Communist return.

The clear and hold solution required large numbers of personnel to succeed. The Allies did not have enough reliable soldiers both to conquer the countryside and to control it. General William Westmoreland stated that the main goal was to seek out and destroy PAVN/VC forces rather than to pacify the countryside. He later argued that he believed the clear and hold concept could have worked had he received enough U.S. troops to perform both functions. The numbers he wanted, however, would have required the mobilization of U.S. reserve forces, an option that was unacceptable to President Johnson and the American people. Consequently, while U.S. combat troops pursued an attrition strategy against Communist main force units, MACV was forced to use unreliable soldiers from the Army of the Republic of Vietnam, the Popular Forces, and the Regional Forces to hold the cleared areas. The combination proved unsuccessful.

—Edward C. Page

References: Summers, Harry G., Jr. *On Strategy: A Critical Analysis of the Vietnam War* (1982); Westmoreland, William C. *A Soldier Reports.*

See also: Civic Action; Marine Combined Action Platoons (CAPs); Pacification; Search and Destroy; United States: Marine Corps; Westmoreland, William Childs.

Cleland, Joseph Maxwell (1942–)

U.S. Army officer; head of the Veterans Administration (VA), 1977–1981. After successfully completing jump school, in 1967 Cleland volunteered for duty in Vietnam with the 1st Cavalry Division (Airmobile). The next year, Captain Cleland lost both legs and his right arm as a result of a grenade blast. He received numerous citations, including the Bronze Star and the Silver Star. Not released from the hospital until 1970, he wasted little time in resuming a productive life. In 1971 he won a seat in the Georgia Senate and used his position to promote issues related to veterans and the handicapped. From 1975 to 1977 he served on the professional staff of the U.S. Senate Veterans Affairs Committee.

In February 1977 President Carter nominated Cleland to head the VA. Speedy Senate confirmation followed, and Cleland, at age 34, became the youngest person to head the VA and the first Vietnam veteran to hold that position. He launched a vigorous expansion of VA programs, including drug and alcohol treatment and counseling services, and worked to improve the public image of the VA and Vietnam veterans. His tenure at the VA ended in 1981 with the election of Ronald Reagan.

In November 1996 Cleland won election to the U.S. Senate, joining such prominent Vietnam veterans as John Kerry, Robert Kerrey, and John McCain. He has written extensively on veterans' issues and the plight of Vietnam veterans.

—David Coffey

Reference: *Who's Who in America, 1997* (1996).

See also: Kerry, John Forbes; Khe Sanh, Battles of; McCain, John S., III.

Clemenceau, Georges (1841–1929)

French politician and premier. Clemenceau was a strong opponent of French imperial efforts in Indo-China and elsewhere, believing that these detracted from France's real interests in Europe and inhibited military preparedness against Germany. Clemenceau first served as premier of France from 1906 to 1909. On 16 November 1917, following wide-scale French Army mutinies, he again became premier. He thoroughly dominated the government, and his leadership helped infuse the French with the will to fight through to final victory. Much criticized in Britain and the United States for his role at the Paris peace conference,

Clemenceau was seen as a vengeful Shylock determined to keep Germany in subjection, but his goal was simple security. He also opposed concessions to native nationalism in the French colonies. In 1920 he resigned the premiership and went into embittered retirement.

—Spencer C. Tucker

References: Brunn, Geoffrey. *Clemenceau* (1943); Jackson, John Hampden. *Clemenceau and the Third Republic* (1948); Watson, David R. *Georges Clemenceau: A Political Biography* (1974).

See also: French Indo-China.

Clergy and Laymen Concerned about Vietnam (CALC, CALCAV, CLCV)

Organization founded in October 1965 by New York religious leaders, including Rev. Richard Neuhaus, Rabbi Abraham Heschel, and Father Daniel Berrigan. Founded as Clergy Concerned about Vietnam, the organization underwent several name changes: National Emergency Committee of Clergy Concerned about Vietnam (January 1966); Clergy and Laymen Concerned about Vietnam—A National Emergency Committee (April 1966); Clergy and Laymen Concerned about Vietnam (1967); and Clergy and Laity Concerned (1973). Building on interfaith cooperation in the civil rights struggle, it evolved in 1966 into a national organization with Revs. John Bennett, Martin Luther King, Jr., and William Sloane Coffin assuming leadership roles.

CALC sought an indefinite halt to U.S. bombing of North Vietnam and a negotiated settlement. Under Executive Director Richard Fernandez (1966–1973), CALC broadened its base by recognizing lay people's interest in its moderate forms of protest that avoided the stigma of radical antiwar organizations. In February 1967, with King as chairman, CALC initiated the "Fast for Peace." In that year, the federal government targeted CALC for investigation as a threat to national security. In February 1968 CALC released *In the Name of America*, accusing the United States of war crimes and violations of international law. CALC protested at the 1968 Democratic Party National Convention in Chicago and, in 1972, it had representatives at the World Assembly for Peace and Independence of the Peoples of Indo-China. By August 1973 the founders had changed the name to Clergy and Laity Concerned, enabling the group to address a wider range of issues.

—Paul S. Daum, with Francis Ryan

References: DeBenedetti, Charles. *An American Ordeal: The Antiwar Movement of the Vietnam Era* (1990); Hall, Mitchell Kent. "Clergy and Laymen Concerned about Vietnam: A Study of Opposition to the Vietnam War" (1987); Zaroulis, Nancy, and Gerald Sullivan. *Who Spoke Up? American Protest against the War in Vietnam* (1984).

See also: Antiwar Movement, United States; Berrigan, Daniel; Coffin, William Sloane, Jr.; Democratic Party National Convention, 1968; Fellowship of Reconciliation (FOR); Fernandez, Richard; King, Martin Luther, Jr.

Clifford, Clark M. (1906–)

U.S. secretary of defense, 1968–1969. By 1960 Clifford was widely regarded as the most influential and well-connected

Democratic lawyer in Washington. After handling several delicate legal matters for John F. Kennedy, in late 1960 he headed the president-elect's transition team but refused any formal office for himself. However, both Kennedy and his successor, Lyndon Johnson called upon Clifford for advice on various issues.

In the early 1960s Clifford did not oppose the relatively small-scale incremental increases in U.S. economic and military aid to Vietnam. In May 1965, though, Johnson consulted Clifford on the proposed major escalation of U.S. ground forces in Vietnam. With George W. Ball, Clifford argued forcefully but unsuccessfully against this. He urged a negotiated settlement, even if it was unsatisfactory, rather than entering into a potentially dangerous open-ended commitment. Having lost this argument, Clifford then felt that the United States should prosecute the war strongly, without being diverted from its aims. Until 1967, therefore, he opposed bombing halts and pauses and recommended that the United States make an intensive effort to win the war. In November 1967, Clifford joined the other "Wise Men" in urging Johnson to stand firm in Vietnam. Later that month, he spoke against Robert McNamara's memorandum calling for determined U.S. efforts to make peace.

In late January 1968 Clifford was confirmed as Secretary of Defense, replacing the now-dovish McNamara. Almost immediately, the Têt Offensive occurred, after which General William Westmoreland requested an additional 206,000 U.S. troops. Clifford set up a Vietnam Task Force to reassess the situation in Vietnam and learned that U.S. military leaders could offer no plan for victory or assurance of success. In early March, therefore, he recommended to Johnson that the United States commit only the forces necessary to meet immediate needs in Vietnam and not embark on another major buildup.

Fearing that victory was impossible, Clifford summoned another meeting of the Wise Men. After extensive briefings from State and Defense Department officials, most of this group concluded that the United States could not attain its ends in Vietnam and should begin peace negotiations. Throughout 1968 Clifford battled National Security Advisor Walt W. Rostow, Secretary of State Dean Rusk, and other administration hawks in pushing for a bombing halt and negotiations with the Democratic Republic of Vietnam (DRV) and in publicly putting pressure on the Republic of Vietnam (RVN) to join in peace talks. He left office in 1969 with the rest of the Johnson administration.

In the early months of the Nixon administration, Clifford approved of the new president's intention to withdraw American troops. But Clifford alienated both Nixon and Johnson in summer 1969 when he published an article in *Foreign Affairs* calling for the withdrawal of 100,000 U.S. troops by December 1969 and all U.S. ground forces by December 1970. He believed that only this prospect would impel the RVN to enter into serious negotiations. Clifford repeated these suggestions in an article in *Life* magazine the following summer, in which he also condemned the May 1970 invasion of Cambodia.

—Priscilla Roberts

References: Barrett, David. *Uncertain Warriors: Lyndon Johnson and His Vietnam Advisors* (1994); Berman, Larry. *Lyndon Johnson's War* (1989); Clifford, Clark, with David Holbrooke. *Counsel to the President: A Memoir* (1991); Frantz, Douglas, and David MacKean. *Friends in High Places. The Rise and Fall of Clark Clifford* (1995); Hoopes, Townsend. *The Limits of Intervention* (1969); Schandler, Herbert Y. *Lyndon Johnson and Vietnam: The Unmaking of a President* (1977).

See also: Acheson, Dean G.; Ball, George W.; Harriman, W. Averell; Johnson, Lyndon Baines; Kennedy, John Fitzgerald; McNamara, Robert S.; Nixon, Richard Milhous; Rostow, Walt Whitman; Rusk, Dean; Têt Offensive: Overall Strategy; Têt Offensive: the Sài Gòn Circle; Truman, Harry S; Warnke, Paul C.; Westmoreland, William Childs; "Wise Men."

Climate. *See* Vietnam, Climate of.

Clinton, William Jefferson (1946–)

U.S. President since 1993. As a draft-age male, Clinton was determined to keep his deferment by entering law or graduate school; a Rhodes Scholarship proved the solution. While studying in England, he protested U.S. involvement in Vietnam. Clinton's avoidance of the draft became a major issue in the 1992 presidential campaign. The "draft-dodger" label continued to follow Clinton into the presidency and temporarily poisoned his relationship with the military. In 1995 Clinton normalized relations with Vietnam and appointed Douglas "Pete" Peterson the first U.S. ambassador to the Socialist Republic of Vietnam.

—Brenda J. Taylor.

Reference: Oakley, Meredith L. *On the Make: The Rise of Bill Clinton* (1994).

See also: Bush, George Herbert Walker; Draft; Embargo; Fulbright, J. William; Peterson, Douglas "Pete"; United States: Involvement in Vietnam, 1975 to the Present; Vietnam, Republic of: Commandos.

Cluster Bomb. *See* Bombs, Dumb.

Coast Guard, United States. *See* United States: Coast Guard.

Coastal Surveillance Force. *See* MARKET TIME, Operation.

Cochin China

Cochin China (or Cochinchina) was the southernmost of the three former French colonies that make up present-day Vietnam. The name originated from "Cauchichina," a title given to all of Vietnam by sixteenth-century Portuguese explorers and traders.

The French established their first trading post in Vietnam in 1680, but Vietnamese persecution of French Catholic missionaries provided the excuse for French military intervention. Cochin China was the first to fall to French control, in 1862. France completed its conquest of Vietnam in 1883, after which Vietnam was divided into three administrative "states": Cochin China, An Nam, and Tonkin. Although

Colby, William Egan 79

Tonkin had larger numbers of Vietnamese Catholics, Cochin China was the initial focus of French colonization because it constituted the "rice bowl" of the nation. The French also believed that the city of Sài Gòn would become an important commercial center once it was opened to Europeans.

—Arthur T. Frame

References: Buttinger, Joseph. *Vietnam: A Political History* (1968); Karnow, Stanley. *Vietnam: A History*. New (1984).

See also: An Nam; French Indo-China; Minh Mang; Nguyên Phúc Ánh (Gia Long); Tonkin; Vietnam: Prehistory to 938; Vietnam, from 938 through French Conquest.

Coffin, William Sloane, Jr. (1924–)

Anti–Vietnam War activist. Ordained a Presbyterian minister in 1956, Coffin in 1958 became chaplain of Yale University. Active in the civil rights movement, he came to hold a prominent position in the antiwar movement, both as a moral leader and as a political strategist. He was particularly active in the efforts to resist the military draft. In September 1967 Coffin cosigned with 319 other ministers, writers, and professors "A Call to Resist Illegitimate Authority," which pledged aid to draft resisters. That same year he played an important role in a national "Stop the Draft" week. On 20 October he and others attempted to deliver more than a thousand draft cards to the Justice Department in Washington, which refused them. He was also active in the organization Clergy and Laymen Concerned about Vietnam. Throughout, Coffin emphasized the immorality of the war. At the October 1967 rally in Washington, D.C., Coffin asked, "If what the United States is doing in Vietnam is right, what is there left to be called wrong?"

—Michael O'Loughlin

References: Halstead, Fred. *Out Now! A Participant's Account of the American Movement against the Vietnam War* (1978); Mailer, Norman. *The Armies of the Night* (1968); "320 Vow to Help Draft Resisters" (1967).

See also: Antiwar Movement, United States; Clergy and Laymen Concerned about Vietnam (CALC, CALCAV, CLCV); Conscientious Objectors (COs); Draft.

Cogny, René (1904–1968)

General and commander of French forces in northern Vietnam during the final phase of the Indo-China War. In 1950 Cogny went to Indo-China, where he served as director of General Jean de Lattre de Tassigny's military cabinet. Virtually alone among senior officers who had accompanied him to Indo-China, Cogny stayed on after de Lattre's departure. In May 1953 he became commander of ground forces in northern Vietnam. After advocating the occupation of Điên Biên Phu as a means of controlling Viêt Minh movements threatening Laos, Cogny oversaw the hasty abandonment of Lai Châu in December 1953, which led to the loss of most of the airborne battle groups based there. They were left to their own devices, remaining on the sidelines as the Viêt Minh encircled the camp at Điên Biên Phu in preparation for the climactic battle of the war. After the fall of Điên Biên Phu, Cogny waged a punishing campaign against the Viêt Minh

that succeeded in preserving French control of the Hà Nôi–Hai Phòng axis. By then, however, the fate of Indo-China was being decided in the armistice negotiations at Geneva.

—Arthur J. Dommen

References: Fall, Bernard B. *Hell in a Very Small Place* (1966); Gras, Yves. *Histoire de la Guerre d'Indochine* (1992); Roy, Jules. *The Battle of Dienbienphu* (1965).

See also: Điên Biên Phu, Battle of; France: Army; Geneva Conference and Geneva Accords; Indo-China War; Navarre, Henri Eugène; Salan, Raoul Albin Louis.

Colby, William Egan (1920–1996)

U.S. ambassador; Central Intelligence Agency (CIA) station chief in Sài Gòn; deputy to the commander of U.S. Military Assistance Command, Vietnam (COMUSMACV). Colby joined the CIA in 1950 and in 1959 became CIA station chief in Sài Gòn. For the next three years Colby and other CIA officials experimented with various forms of security and rural development programs for the Republic of Vietnam (RVN). From their endeavors, the Citizens' (later Civilian) Irregular Defense Groups (CIDGs), the Mountain Scout program, and the Strategic Hamlet project emerged in 1961. In 1962 Colby became chief of the CIA's Far East Division, a position he held until 1968. This new appointment forced him to concentrate not only on Southeast Asia, but also on China and other areas, such as the Philippines. In this new office he began to stress pacification as the key to overcoming Communist aggression in Vietnam. In 1965 CIA analysts established the Hamlet Evaluation System (HES) to measure certain factors in the villages in South Vietnam that would identify the progress of pacification in the countryside. However, an aggressive pacification strategy did not emerge until 1968.

In 1968 Colby returned to Vietnam and, with ambassadorial rank, succeeded Robert Komer as deputy to COMUSMACV for Civil Operations and Revolutionary (later changed to Rural) Development Support (CORDS). While serving in this post, Colby oversaw the accelerated pacification campaign (APC), initiated in November 1968, which focused on enhanced security and development within South Vietnam's villages and included such components as the Phoenix program and the People's Self-Defense Force.

From 1969 to 1970, planning for the pacification and development shifted from the Americans to the South Vietnamese in accordance with the Nixon administration's policy of Vietnamization. In 1971 the program shifted to a more self-oriented role for the villages of South Vietnam. A year later, Colby returned to Washington, D.C., to become executive director of the CIA. From May 1973 until his retirement in November 1976 he served as director.

Colby assumed leadership of the CIA during the worst crisis in its history, triggered by that agency's assistance of E. Howard Hunt in his Watergate-related break-ins. Colby revealed to Congress a list of CIA actions that might have violated its charter, including agency involvement in domestic surveillance, plots to kill foreign leaders, and use of humans in mind-control experiments. He believed that revealing the agency's unsavory side helped to save it from congressional abolition. This action earned Colby admiration from many in Congress and the public, but the enmity of many Cold War warriors and an end to his tenure as director in 1976.

In retirement Colby maintained that the United States and the Republic of Vietnam might have won the war if only they had fought the CIA's kind of war and countered Communist guerrilla tactics. He claimed that in the early 1970s Vietnamization was succeeding and pacification was building the base for an RVN victory, culminating in the defeat of the 1972 Communist offensive, with U.S. air and logistical support, but no ground assistance. He believed this chance for victory was thrown away when the United States sharply reduced its military and logistical support and then sold out the RVN government during negotiations in Paris.

—R. Blake Dunnavent

References: Andrade, Dale. *Ashes to Ashes: The Phoenix Program and the Vietnam War* (1990); Colby, William. *Honorable Men: My Life in the CIA* (1978); Colby, William, with James McCargar. *Lost Victory: A Firsthand Account of America's Sixteen-Year Involvement in Vietnam* (1989).

See also: Air America; Civilian Operations and Revolutionary Development Support (CORDS); Hamlet Evaluation System (HES); Komer, Robert W.; Pacification; Phoenix Program; Psychological Warfare Operations (PSYOP); Schlesinger, James R.; Strategic Hamlet Program; Taylor-McNamara Report.

Collins, Joseph Lawton (1896–1987)

U.S. general and special representative of President Eisenhower. Collins was sent to Vietnam in 1954 to assess the situation following the French defeat at Điên Biên Phu and the Geneva Accords and to determine the size and scope of future U.S. assistance. In sending Collins to Vietnam, Eisenhower gave him the rank of ambassador and, in his letter of introduction, "broad authority to direct, utilize and control all agencies and resources of the U.S. government with respect to Vietnam."

Upon his arrival in Sài Gòn in November 1954, Collins found the government under challenge from the Cao Đài and Hòa Hao religious sects and from the Bình Xuyên gang, as well as a threatened coup by Vietnamese Armed Forces Chief of Staff General Nguyên Van Hinh. After Collins reached agreement with the French authorities, combined French and U.S. pressure induced General Hinh to go to France for "consultations" with State of Vietnam titular head of state Bao Đai. Although Collins personally agreed with the French that Ngô Đình Diêm was not capable of leading the State of Vietnam, his instructions were to support the Diêm government by assisting it to establish a military training program and agrarian reforms, which he did.

—Arthur T. Frame

References: Collins, J. Lawton. *Lightning Joe: An Autobiography* (1979); Spector, Ronald H. *Advice and Support: The Early Years, 1941–1960* (1983).

See also: Bình Xuyên; Cao Đài; Dulles, John Foster; Eisenhower, Dwight David; Ely, Paul Henri Romuald; Hòa Hao; Military Assistance and Advisory Group (MAAG), Vietnam; Ngô Đình Diêm; Nguyên Van Hinh.

Combined Action Platoons. *See* Marine Combined Action Platoons (CAPs).

COMMANDO HUNT, Operation
(15 November 1968–10 April 1972)

Series of aerial interdiction campaigns aimed at the Hô Chí Minh Trail logistical corridor in southeastern Laos. Each campaign lasted approximately six months, covering either a dry or a wet season as dictated by the monsoonal climate. The objectives of COMMANDO HUNT were first to reduce the flow of People's Army of Vietnam (PAVN) troops and supplies from North Vietnam into South Vietnam and Cambodia; and second, to destroy trucks, supply caches, storage bases, the trail support structure, and even the topography around the trail. Of the nearly three million tons of bombs that fell on Laos from 1962 to 1973, approximately 95 percent were dropped on the Hô Chí Minh Trail. Laos became the third most bombed country in the history of warfare.

The U.S. Air Force conducted most of these attacks, although U.S. Navy, Marine, and Royal Laotian Air Force planes also participated. During the day, jet fighters and B-52s attacked suspected truck parks and storage areas. Passes leading from the Democratic Republic of Vietnam (DRV) into Laos were bombed to cause landslides. Into 1969 occasional RANCH HAND jungle defoliation missions were also flown. At night, when the most traffic moved on the trail, Air Force AC-130 and AC-119 gunships, specially modified B-57Gs, and other aircraft attacked trucks. Meanwhile, up to 30 B-52 sorties a day were flown to bomb predetermined "interdiction boxes" located around Tchépone, a key transshipment point leading into the Republic of Vietnam (RVN), and in each of the four passes leading from the DRV into Laos.

Although it was intensive and sophisticated, COMMANDO HUNT failed for two reasons. First, PAVN forces controlled the tempo of the war in the South, and their consumption of supplies was easily regulated according to their ability to receive those supplies. Second, the Hô Chí Minh Trail possessed no easily spotted and targeted railroad marshaling yards or difficult-to-repair steel and concrete bridges. It consisted of 200 miles of paved roads and 6,000 miles of dirt roads, pathways, and waterways down which supplies could move.

The "truck count," a statistical compilation of trucks destroyed or damaged, was the measure of success. But statistics became meaningless estimates based on faulty assumptions for determining whether or not a truck had been destroyed. During COMMANDO HUNT V, the Air Force claimed 16,266 vehicles destroyed and 4,700 damaged. The Central Intelligence Agency countered that, according to their estimates, there were only 10,000 trucks in all the DRV and Laos. The figures, although adjusted, were never rectified because COMMANDO HUNT became an exercise in the compilation of statistics, which became an end unto themselves.

On 20 April 1972, as the DRV Spring Offensive got under way and 14 PAVN divisions streamed into South Vietnam, COMMANDO HUNT VII came to an end and the operation was canceled. Concerted bombing of the Hồ Chí Minh Trail continued, however, until February 1973.

—Earl H. Tilford, Jr.

References: Berger, Carl, ed. *The United States Air Force in Southeast Asia: An Illustrated Account* (1984); Gibson, James William. *The Perfect War: Technowar in Vietnam* (1986); Littauer, Raphael, and Norman Uphoff, eds. *The Air War in Indochina* (1971).

See also: Air Power, Role in War; Hồ Chí Minh Trail; Laos; RANCH HAND, Operation; STEEL TIGER, Operation; TIGER HOUND, Operation.

Commandos, Vietnamese. *See* Vietnam, Republic of: Commandos.

Côn Thiên (September–October 1967)

Site of a battle 14 miles from the coast of Vietnam and two miles south of the Demilitarized Zone (DMZ). A low hill 160 meters in elevation, Côn Thiên overlooked a principal People's Army of Vietnam (PAVN) infiltration route into South Vietnam.

In spring 1967 the U.S. Military Assistance Command, Vietnam (MACV) ordered construction of an anti-infiltration barrier across the DMZ. Manned strongpoints would occupy prominent terrain features overlooking infiltration routes. Artillery positions would provide fire support and house reaction forces needed to man the strongpoint system. Côn Thiên was to be an important component of this anti-infiltration barrier. By mid-1967 U.S. Marines had established a formidable presence in the area. Côn Thiên provided a clear view of Đong Hà, the major logistics base in the region. If the PAVN could seize Côn Thiên, they would be able to bring the Đông Hà base under artillery and rocket fire.

Côn Thiên remained a primary target for PAVN artillery. During September 1967 the PAVN subjected the Marines at Côn Thiên to one of the heaviest shellings of the war. Côn Thiên's defenders came to expect incoming artillery fire daily. On 25 September more than 1,200 rounds fell there, and PAVN ground activity increased under this artillery umbrella. On 4 and 7 September Marines located and fought PAVN forces south of Côn Thiên. On 10 September the 3d Battalion, 26th Marines (3/26) engaged a PAVN regiment in battle near Côn Thiên, spoiling a major attack. On 13 September a PAVN company attacked the perimeter at Côn Thiên but failed to breach the defensive wire. When the Marines sent two additional battalions to reinforce Côn Thiên, the PAVN response was to blast the defenders with 3,000 incoming rounds during 19–27 September. The U.S. reacted to these attacks with one of the greatest concentrations of firepower during the Vietnam War.

The constant combat took a heavy toll. In a one-month period, 2d Battalion, 4th Marines (2/4), saw its strength reduced from 952 to 462 men. On 14 October a PAVN ground force attacked 2/4's position, overran a company command post, and engaged the Marines in hand-to-hand combat. By the end of October, 2/4's strength was down to about 300 men. Although fighting around Côn Thiên fell off after October, it remained a harsh place. The monsoon's endless drizzle turned roads into quagmires, and the threat of Communist artillery fire was constant, as was the possibility of massed infantry attacks. Neuropsychiatric ("shell shock") casualties were not unusual.

MACV estimated PAVN deaths around Côn Thiên in this period at 1,117, while Marine casualties totaled over 1,800 killed and wounded. General Westmoreland described the fighting around Côn Thiên as a "crushing defeat" for the PAVN, but it had exacted a heavy toll on the Americans as well.

—Peter W. Brush

Reference: Tefler, Gary L., Lane Rogers, and V. Keith Fleming, Jr. *U.S. Marines in Vietnam: Fighting the North Vietnamese* (1984).

See also: Artillery, Allied and People's Army of Vietnam; Clear and Hold; United States: Marine Corps.

Conein, Lucien Emile (1919–)

Office of Strategic Services (OSS) and Central Intelligence Agency (CIA) officer in Vietnam. Conein received his commission as a second lieutenant in July 1943 and was recruited by the OSS. After the OSS was abolished at the end of World War II, Conein served on various classified assignments in Europe and in Southeast Asia. Between 1954 and 1956 he served in Vietnam as a vital part of Col. Edward Lansdale's Military Mission team, working on sabotage and destabilization activities north of the 17th parallel. After returning to the United States Conein joined the Special Forces but was still occasionally used by the CIA.

Conein retired from the Army in 1961. The next year he was called back by the CIA, given the cover of an Army lieutenant colonel, and sent to Sài Gòn ostensibly assigned to the Interior Ministry. His real mission was to maintain CIA contacts with senior Vietnamese generals, many of whom he had known in North Vietnam when they were junior officers. Conein was one of the few Americans they were willing to trust. Operating under the code names Lulu or Black Luigi, he served as liaison between Ambassador Henry Cabot Lodge and such Vietnamese generals as Trân Van Đôn and Duong Van Minh at the time of the 1963 coup against President Ngô Đình Diêm. Conein let the generals know that the United States would not look unfavorably on a change in their government. After the coup Conein departed Vietnam and shortly thereafter left CIA work.

—Cecil B. Currey

References: Conein, Lucien, and Joseph Baker. Interviews with the author; Grant, Zalin. *Facing the Phoenix: The CIA and the Political Defeat of the United States in Vietnam* (1991); Prados, John. *Presidents' Secret Wars: CIA and Pentagon Covert Operations from World War II through Iranscam* (1988).

See also: Central Intelligence Agency (CIA); Duong Van Minh; Lansdale, Edward Geary; Lodge, Henry Cabot, Jr.; Ngô Đình Diêm, Overthrow of; Office of Strategic Services (OSS); Richardson, John H.; Trân Van Đôn.

Confucianism

Confucianism (in Vietnamese, Không Giáo) is not so much a religion as a way of life. Founded in China by the disciples of Confucius (551–449 B.C.) almost 2,500 years ago, it has had a pervasive influence on China, Japan, Korea, Mongolia, and Vietnam. In Vietnam the traditional social structure was largely based on the Confucian model, which binds subject to ruler, son to father, wife to husband, younger brother to older brother, and friend to friend. Since Confucius supported the rights of the ruler over his subjects, Confucianism was later used in the service of autocratic governments to justify strong central states. Thus, Vietnam's traditional government was extremely hierarchical, with a large class of Mandarin bureaucrats trained in the Confucian classics. These bureaucrats acted as emissaries of the emperor all the way down to the village level.

Confucian literature consists of Five Canonical Books and Four Books. The Five Canonical Books are the Book of Rites, the Book of Change, the Book of History, the Book of Poetry, and the Book of Spring and Autumn Annals (Kinh Lê, Kinh Dich, Kinh Thu, Kinh Thi, and Kinh Xuân Thu). The Four Books are the Analects, the Golden Mean, the Great Learning, and the Book of Mencius (Luân Ngu, Trung Dung, Ðai Hoc, Manh Tu). The Book of Change, in particular, promotes a belief in the cyclical movement of history. In the sense that history is thought to move forward by stages, this aspect of Confucianism was not radically different from the Marxist concept of dialectical materialism. Although oriental Marxists have generally accused Confucianism of supporting feudalism and so have sought to destroy it, many elements of Confucianism—such as unquestioned loyalty to the ruler and the state—have been successfully incorporated into the revolutionary philosophy of these new Communist regimes.

—Tho Van Nguyen

References: Legge, James. *Four Books of the Chinese Classics* (1885); —. *The Chinese Classics* (1861–1876); *The I Ching, or Book of Changes* (1977).
See also: Buddhists; Vietnam: Prehistory to 938.

Conscientious Objectors (COs)

U.S. classification for active-duty or draft-eligible individuals opposed to war or combatant participation in war on certain moral or religious grounds. This status, normally restricted to members of historically pacifist groups such as Mennonites, Quakers, and Jehovah's Witnesses, was not open to all persons who sought exemption on matters of conscience. Recognized conscientious objectors (COs) endured ridicule, isolation, and, frequently, hard labor; but those without official sanction faced harsh punishments, including prison terms.

As U.S. involvement in Southeast Asia deepened in the early 1960s, more than 20 million young American men faced the increasing possibility of being drafted and sent to Vietnam. Many sought to avoid military service by taking advantage of the numerous deferment and exemptions available. Conscientious objection became a popular avenue of draft avoidance, but rules limited the scope of conscientious objection. Applicants had to present convincing pacifist credentials, such as letters from clergy, and declare opposition to all war. Selective aversion, such as moral opposition to U.S. involvement in Vietnam, did not justify CO eligibility.

Applicants were subject to inconsistent review from local draft boards. A study of three boards in one southern city found that one granted CO exemptions to almost every applicant, another granted no CO exemptions, and one reviewed the merits of each case.

Growing opposition to the draft brought challenges to traditional interpretations of conscientious objection. A barrage of law suits and court decisions continually expanded the criteria. *United States v. Seeger* (1965) held that neither church affiliation nor belief in God were required for CO status; a "sincere and meaningful belief that occupies in the life of its possessor a place parallel to that filled by God" would suffice if the applicant met all other requirements. This left with draft boards the ill-defined task of establishing sincerity. Pacifist Muslims tested the law on grounds that they could fight only if called to do so by Allah. Since they could not claim opposition to all wars, most were denied CO exemptions. Consequently, many Muslims went to prison for refusing military service.

Selective Service System (SSS) classifications listed three CO categories: I-A-O, conscientious objector available for noncombatant military service only; I-O, conscientious objector available for civilian work contributing to the maintenance of the national health, safety, or interest; and I-W, conscientious objector performing civilian work contributing to the maintenance of the national health, safety, or interest. By far, I-O status was the most sought after. Between 1960 and 1973, more than 170,000 men received I-O status, which became I-W upon entering alternative service. Almost 100,000 men accepted two years of alternative service as hospital orderlies or in other low-paying public-service positions. The monitoring of I-W COs usually fell to overburdened local draft boards who exercised little supervision. More than 70,000 I-O COs never completed alternative service; a third were later excused because of high lottery numbers. Of the remaining 40,000 who faced prosecution, only 1,200 were convicted.

COs granted I-A-O status were included with I-As (available for military service) in the group most likely to be drafted. These COs were just as likely to be sent to Vietnam as any draftee but were assigned noncombatant duties (not required to carry or fire weapons) as cooks, orderlies, and drivers. A significant number were trained as medics and, while most worked in field hospitals and rear-area medical facilities, others went into combat units. Although no accurate statistics exist, COs did see combat, and many were killed or wounded in action.

Active-duty personnel could also apply for CO status. Between 1965 and 1973 almost 20,000 active-duty personnel from all branches of service applied for discharges or noncombatant assignments as COs. Active-duty applicants confronted a more rigorous examination process. Potential COs applied through company or base commanders and had to be interviewed by an officer, a chaplain, and a psychiatrist. A unanimous finding was required to receive CO status. Many active-duty COs received discharges but others worked in noncombatant capacities and often saw hazardous duty as combat medics. Between 1966 and 1969 the military granted fewer than twenty percent of all CO applications processed, but by 1975 almost all were being confirmed. Disapproved CO applicants were required to return to duty without any restrictions. Those who refused faced court-martial and imprisonment.

—David Coffey

References: Baskir, Lawrence M., and William A. Strauss. *Chance and Circumstance: The Draft, The War, and The Vietnam Generation* (1978); Dougan, Clark, Samuel Lipsman, et al., eds. *A Nation Divided* (1984); Gioglio, Gerald R. *Days of Decision: An Oral History of Conscientious Objectors in the Military during the Vietnam War* (1989).

See also: African American Personnel in U.S. Forces in Vietnam; Antiwar Movement, United States; Draft; Project 100,000.

Containment Policy

U.S. government strategy to limit the expansion of communism during the Cold War. The doctrine of containment originated in the antagonism that developed between the United States and the Soviet Union during World War II and in the immediate postwar period. The doctrine gained potency from the lesson American policymakers learned from the prewar era—that appeasement of aggression merely fueled increasingly more strident and unreasonable demands from dictators—and from the "domino theory," the belief that the fall of one country to communism would lead to a chain reaction in neighboring nations.

George F. Kennan, a career foreign service officer stationed in Moscow from July 1944 to April 1946, was the architect of containment. On 22 February 1946 he sent the State Department what has since been called the Long Telegram, an 8,000–word analysis of Soviet actions and ideology. The Soviet Union, Kennan said, represented a political force fanatically committed to the destruction of capitalist society. The Long Telegram received a positive reception in Washington, and the next year Kennan was selected to head the newly created State Department Policy Planning Staff, a study and reporting group charged with advising the secretary of state on policy.

Kennan's containment doctrine was cogently expressed in his essay "The Sources of Soviet Conduct," published under the pseudonym "Mr. X" (although his authorship was soon revealed) in the July 1947 issue of *Foreign Affairs*. In the article Kennan suggested "long-term, patient but firm and vigilant containment of Russian expansive tendencies." The Soviets, he believed, would eventually mellow or break up, but in the meantime the United States should "confront the Russians with unalterable counterforce, at every point where they show signs of encroaching upon the interests of a peaceful and stable world." Kennan's views did not go unchallenged. Journalist Walter Lippman wrote 12 critiques of the article (later published as *The Cold War*), and Kennan himself acknowledged deficiencies in the piece, including the failure to show clearly that he meant "political containment of a political threat" rather than containment by military means. Kennan's views were readily adopted by U.S. policymakers suspicious of Soviet actions and intentions.

Containment, along with the domino theory, became the touchstone of U.S. Cold War policy, and its implementation through military as well as political and economic means can be seen in conflicts with the Soviet Union and, after 1949, the People's Republic of China. Examples of containment in action include the Marshall Plan for European economic recovery, the North Atlantic Treaty Organization (NATO), the Berlin airlift, the refusal to recognize the People's Republic of China, the Korean War, and the Vietnam War.

Containment in Vietnam initially was linked with checking communism in Europe. Postwar American leaders supported French colonialism because they needed France as a military ally to contain the Soviet Union in Europe. They also believed that since Hô Chí Minh was a Communist, he was controlled by Moscow and Beijing. Starting in 1950, the United States provided France with military and economic assistance to defeat Hô. Containment of communism seemed jeopardized by the 1954 French defeat at Điên Biên Phu and the de facto division of Vietnam at the Geneva Conference later that year. To contain the Communist threat, U.S. Secretary of State John Foster Dulles took the lead in establishing the Southeast Asia Treaty Organization (SEATO) in 1955, which included the United States, France, and Britain in a defense alliance with Asian nations. In 1956 the United States assumed responsibility for training and supporting the South Vietnamese military.

President Kennedy continued the policy of Communist containment and increased the U.S. presence in Vietnam. In May 1961 he authorized commando raids against North Vietnam and sent Special Forces advisors to South Vietnam. In the following years, under Lyndon Johnson, the number of U.S. troops increased to more than 500,000. The war destroyed Johnson's presidency, and in the end the United States was unable to contain communism in Vietnam.

Kennan regarded U.S. involvement in Vietnam as a tragic mistake. He believed Vietnam was a marginal area in the Cold War and that involvement there kept the United States from taking advantage of divisions within the Communist world. In 1966 he testified before Senator J. William Fulbright's hearings on the war that containment was designed for Europe and did not fit Asia. In the judgment of many historians, Kennan was right.

—Kenneth R. Stevens

References: Gaddis, John Lewis. *Strategies of Containment: A Critical Appraisal of Postwar American National Security Policy* (1982); Kennan, George F. *Memoirs, 1925–1950* (1967); Lippman, Walter. *The Cold War: A Study in U.S. Foreign Policy* (1947).

See also: China, People's Republic of (PRC); Domino Theory; Johnson, Lyndon Baines; Kennan, George Frost; Kennedy, John Fitzgerald; Munich Analogy; Roosevelt, Franklin Delano; Southeast Asia Treaty Organization (SEATO); Stevenson, Adlai E.; Truman, Harry S; Union of Soviet Socialist Republics (USSR; Soviet Union).

Continental Air Services

Airline that flew for the U.S. government in Southeast Asia. Continental Air Services (CAS), a wholly owned subsidiary of Continental Air Lines, began flight operations in

Southeast Asia on 1 September 1965. Robert Six, president of the parent company, had acquired the assets of Bird & Sons for $4.2 million. CAS continued to fly under U.S. government contracts, especially for the Agency for International Development. In addition to routine commercial business, CAS often functioned (as had Bird & Sons) as a paramilitary adjunct to CIA-led guerrilla forces in Laos. Robert E. Rousselot, former head of flight operations for Air America, served as president of CAS.

After the civilian version of the military's C-130 failed to live up to Rousselot's expectations, de Havilland Twin Otters and Pilateus Porters became the CAS's workhorses. These planes carried rice, ammunition, and personnel throughout Southeast Asia. The airline's 50 aircraft averaged 4,000 hours per month, transporting 20,000 passengers and 6,000 tons of cargo. CAS and Air America performed identical tasks in support of the U.S. war effort, and both airlines suffered losses due to enemy action and the difficult operating conditions. More than a dozen CAS aircrew members were killed in Laos, Cambodia, and South Vietnam. The airline's business declined as the war in Southeast Asia drew to a conclusion. On 19 December 1975, Six terminated the company.

—William M. Leary

References: Air America Archives, University of Texas at Dallas; Davies, R. E. G. *Continental Air Lines: The First Fifty Years, 1934–1984* (1985).

See also: Air America; Bird & Sons (Bird Air); Cambodian Airlift; Central Intelligence Agency (CIA); Laos; U.S. Agency for International Development (USAID).

Cooper, Chester A. (1917–)

National Security Council assistant for Asian affairs, 1964–1966. From 1945 to 1964 Cooper worked for the Central Intelligence Agency, specializing in Far Eastern affairs in the Office of National (Intelligence) Estimates. He served on the U.S. delegations to the 1954 Geneva Conference, the 1954 Manila Conference that established SEATO, and the 1961–1962 Geneva Conference on Laos. From 1964 to 1966 he served on McGeorge Bundy's staff as assistant for Asian affairs, where he was one of the few policymakers genuinely knowledgeable on Indo-China. Throughout the Vietnam conflict, Cooper recommended it be resolved by political rather than military means. Unlike many who supported this approach, he stood by the U.S. commitment to Ngô Đình Diêm. In 1966 Cooper left the National Security Council but shortly thereafter became chief of staff to the group of would-be peace negotiators surrounding W. Averell Harriman. Disillusioned by their lack of progress, in fall 1967 he again resigned. Cooper opposed the American invasion of Cambodia, which he feared would make any peace settlement impossible. By 1972 he was convinced that the Indo-Chinese states should be left to work out their own futures free from interference by the major powers.

—Priscilla Roberts

References: Cooper, Chester A. *The Lost Crusade: America in Vietnam* (1973); Gibbons, William Conrad. *The U.S. Government and the Vietnam War* (1989).

See also: Bundy, McGeorge; Harriman, W. Averell; Ngô Đình Diêm.

Cooper, John Sherman (1901–1991)

U.S. senator and opponent of American involvement in Southeast Asia. During the 1960s Cooper became a vocal critic of U.S. policy in Vietnam. With Senator George McGovern he expressed reservations about the power that the Tonkin Gulf Resolution (1964) provided the president. Under pressure from Senator J. William Fulbright, Cooper voted for the resolution. He expressed confidence in the Johnson administration but urged the president to keep in mind the "distinction between defending our forces, and taking offensive measures in South Vietnam."

After the 1970 invasion of Cambodia, Cooper and Senator Frank Church sponsored the Cooper-Church Amendment. It barred funds for U.S. ground combat forces and advisors in Cambodia after 30 June 1970 and prohibited any combat activity in the air above Cambodia in support of Cambodian forces unless approved by Congress. The amendment passed in the Senate but met failure in the House of Representatives. A revised version passed in December 1970 as part of the defense appropriations bill.

—Charlotte A. Power

References: Olson, James S., ed. *Dictionary of the Vietnam War* (1987); Young, Marilyn B. *The Vietnam Wars, 1945–1990* (1991).

See also: Case, Clifford P.; Case-Church Amendment; Church, Frank Forrester; Cooper-Church Amendment; Fulbright, J. William; McGovern, George S.; Tonkin Gulf Resolution.

Cooper-Church Amendment

Amendment introduced by Senators John Sherman Cooper and Frank Church to bar funds for the support and maintenance of U.S. ground combat forces and advisors in Cambodia after 30 June 1970 and prohibit any combat activity in the air above Cambodia in support of Cambodian forces unless Congress approved such operations. It also would have barred U.S. support for third-country (Republic of Vietnam, or RVN) forces in Cambodia. Debate from 13 May through 30 June on the amendment, and the military appropriations bill to which it was attached, brought about heated discussion of the Nixon administration's Asian policy and blocked Senate action on other major legislation. After numerous amendments were introduced to weaken it, the Senate approved the Cooper-Church Amendment by a vote of 58 to 37 on 30 June 1970.

During the debate, Senator Robert Dole, a leader of the anti–Cooper-Church forces, introduced an amendment to repeal the 1964 Gulf of Tonkin Resolution that was overwhelmingly approved. The Nixon administration opposed the Cooper-Church Amendment but was neutral on the Gulf of Tonkin matter.

House and Senate conferees remained deadlocked for six months over the Cooper-Church Amendment. Eventually the amendment was attached to the supplementary foreign aid authorization bill but was later dropped from the bill. A revised Cooper-Church Amendment, added to the fiscal 1971 foreign aid authorization bill, cleared Congress on 22

December 1970. Unlike the earlier amendment passed by the Senate, the final version did not prohibit U.S. air activity over Cambodia. Its approval came about six months after U.S. ground troops had withdrawn from Cambodia.

Nixon denounced the Cooper-Church Amendment and other antiwar amendments as harmful to his bargaining position with the Democratic Republic of Vietnam. In February 1971 the Nixon administration supported the RVN invasion of Laos and it eventually rode out the political storm over Cambodia. Still, the Cooper-Church Amendment and the proposal of even more restrictive amendments in the Senate put increasing pressure on the Nixon administration to end the war in Indo-China. Senate debate also encouraged increased antiwar sentiment among the media, clergy, and other opinion leaders in the United States.

—David C. Saffell

References: Herring, George C. *America's Second Longest War: The United States and Vietnam 1950–1975* (1986); Morris, Roger. *Uncertain Greatness: Henry Kissinger and American Foreign Policy* (1977).

See also: Cambodia; Case, Clifford P.; Case-Church Amendment; Church, Frank Forrester; Cooper, John Sherman; Fulbright, J. William; McGovern, George S.; Nixon, Richard Milhous; Tonkin Gulf Resolution.

CORDS. *See* Civilian Operations and Revolutionary Development Support (CORDS).

COSVN (Central Office for South Vietnam or Trung Uong Cuc Miên Nam)

Democratic Republic of Vietnam title for the headquarters controlling all Viêt Công military forces in the South. It represented the Lao Đông Party Central Standing Committee in South Vietnam and had charge of the war efforts on all fronts. Located in a corner of Tây Ninh Province, III Corps area of operations, near the Cambodian border, the Central Office for South Vietnam (COSVN) was a continual target of U.S. ground and air operations. Although it was the specific objective in Operation JUNCTION CITY in 1967 and the 1970 Cambodian incursion, COSVN eluded capture or destruction throughout the war. In terms of organization or structure, it was no more than what the U.S. Army would describe as a forward command post, consisting of a few senior officers and key staff personnel. As a result, it was extremely mobile and moved frequently to avoid capture or destruction. Many contend that the U.S. pursuit of COSVN was symbolic of the myriad difficulties of fighting a guerrilla war.

—Robert G. Mangrum

References: Davidson, Phillip B. *Vietnam At War: The History 1946–1975* (1988); Herring, George C. *America's Longest War: The U.S. and Vietnam, 1950–1975* (1986); Karnow, Stanley. *Vietnam: A History* (1984); Olson, James S. *Dictionary of the Vietnam War* (1988); Palmer, Bruce, Jr. *The 25 Year War: America's Military Role in Vietnam* (1984); Reinberg, Linda. *In the Field: The Language of the Vietnam War* (1991); Summers, Harry G. *Vietnam War Almanac* (1985).

See also: Cambodia; Cambodian Incursion; Fishhook; JUNCTION CITY, Operation; National Front for the Liberation of South Vietnam

(NFLSV); Vietnam, Democratic Republic of: Army (People's Army of Vietnam [PAVN]).

Counterinsurgency Warfare

Insurgency is an armed or unarmed rebellion against an established authority with the ultimate goal of undermining and/or overthrowing the ruling party or government. Insurgencies in recent history have come to be known as guerrilla wars. However, modern insurgencies (also known as revolutionary wars) imply not merely fighting another force by guerrilla tactics but also trying to seize political power. Revolutionary war is perhaps best exemplified by the Communist struggle against the Nationalists in China and the post–World War II conflicts in Vietnam.

Counterinsurgency is the strategy whereby a government sets out to defeat an insurgency, guerrilla war, or revolutionary war. British counterinsurgency expert Robert Thompson, drawing on his experience in helping to defeat Communist guerrillas in Malaya, gave five rules for successfully defeating an insurgency: (1) the goal must be the establishment of a democratic, economically stable state; (2) this must be done within the law rather than outside of it, avoiding brutal methods; (3) there must be a coherent plan; (4) first priority must be the defeat of opposing political operatives rather than the guerrillas; and (5) making base areas secure must be the top priority. Those knowledgeable about insurgencies acknowledge that the key in defeating them is to win control of the people: the "sea" in which the guerrillas "swim," as Mao Zedong put it.

The French Army did not ignore what it called revolutionary war, although its theories for combating it were for the most part developed after the Indo-China War and were used in Algeria. Early theorists who wrote about revolutionary war during the Indo-China War included General Lionel-Max Chassin, who commanded the French Air Force against the Viêt Minh. His book *La conquête de la Chine par Mao Tsé-Toung (1945–1949)* was published in 1952. Others were Col. Charles Lacheroy and General J. M. Nemo (*En Indochine: Guérilla et contre-guérilla*, 1952), both of whom contributed articles to *Revue de Défense Nationale*. Their principal argument was that a numerically inferior military force can triumph over a larger one only if it has the support of the people in a particular area. The French theorists also came to appreciate the close marriage of the political and the military by both the Chinese Communists and the Viêt Minh. They were convinced that proper psychological measures could create cohesion among fighters and the civilian population.

The point missed by the French, and later the Americans, was that as foreigners in Southeast Asia they were operating at a tremendous disadvantage. Given the long history of Vietnamese resistance to foreign occupation, this was a serious, perhaps insurmountable, liability, especially for the French, who were seen as returning foreign masters. Despite appearances, Paris never granted Vietnam its independence. The State of Vietnam was always a sham with no real power, even over its own army. As such, the Viêt Minh, not the State of Vietnam, gained the loyalty of the people.

Although the lessons learned had largely been forgotten, the United States had more experience in guerrilla war than almost any other country, extending from wars against the American Indians to the Philippine Insurrection of 1899–1902. For all practical purposes, U.S. counterinsurgency doctrine came into being in the 1960s to counter Communist "wars of national liberation." On 6 January 1961, Nikita Khrushchev stated that although the Soviet Union and other Communist-bloc nations opposed world wars and local wars, they recognized and would support "just wars of liberation and popular uprisings." This led President Kennedy to seek solutions for countering Communist-supported insurgencies against vulnerable friendly nations.

Washington's interest in counterinsurgency predated U.S. involvement in Vietnam. In 1952 Congress gave the U.S. Army authority to create a new formation that would mirror American heritage in unconventional warfare. Known as the Special Forces, it would carry on the traditions of Roger's Rangers, Francis Marion, Darby's Rangers, Merrill's Marauders, the 1st Special Service Force, and the Office of Strategic Services (OSS). Special Forces came into being in June 1952 at Fort Bragg, North Carolina. Their training stressed infiltration and land navigation techniques and the use of parachutes and small boats. Specialized training followed and included sabotage, intelligence gathering, communications, medicine, and weaponry. U.S. Army volunteers who successfully completed the secret training were "detached" from the Army and assigned directly to Special Forces. This did not sit well with many in the Army's hierarchy.

Kennedy and his military advisor, General Maxwell D. Taylor, were strong advocates of counterinsurgency and an enhanced Special Forces capability. In his book *The Uncertain Trumpet* (1959), Taylor had argued that the United States should not place undue reliance on nuclear deterrence and should develop its own limited-war capability, including the ability to fight insurgencies. Kennedy, who strongly supported the development of counterinsurgency forces, relieved Army Chief of Staff General George Decker, who opposed anything apart from conventional warfare. In February 1962 he appointed U.S. Marine Corps Maj. Gen. Victor Krulak to a newly established position as a counter–guerrilla warfare specialist within the Pentagon's Joint Chiefs of Staff. In this position, identified as the special assistant for counterinsurgency and special activities (SACSA), Krulak was responsible for monitoring the use of unconventional warfare in Southeast Asia and reporting his findings to the Joint Chiefs and Secretary of Defense Robert McNamara.

The chief instrument of U.S. counterinsurgency policy was the Army Special Forces. Here the goal was not so much to destroy enemy armed forces as to win the allegiance of the people and inspire them to defend themselves. On 21 September 1961 the 5th Special Forces Group (Airborne), 1st Special Forces, was activated at Fort Bragg. Its mission was to train personnel in counterinsurgency methods to be employed in Vietnam. Under various guises, including "pacification" and "population control," the United States set out not only to destroy the Việt Cộng (VC) infrastructure but to "win the hearts and minds" of the Vietnamese people. Programs involved the Central Intelligence Agency (CIA), Special Forces (operating mainly with Montagnards), doctors, engineers, agricultural experts, and civilian advisors.

During January 1962 the Republic of Vietnam (RVN)'s Special Topographic Exploitation Service was given responsibility for internal security and operations outside South Vietnam. An activated element, the Special Branch for Clandestine Operations, had the mission of recruiting military and civilian personnel for intelligence operations against North Vietnam. To increase counterinsurgency initiatives in Vietnam, in August 1962 a paramilitary program, the Civilian Irregular Defense Group (CIDG), was established throughout South Vietnam under the control of the CIA's Combined Studies Division/Group (CSD/G). Its members were to defend villages and carry out interdiction operations, including ambushes, against the People's Army of Vietnam (PAVN) and VC guerrillas. They concentrated their efforts in areas where the Hô Chí Minh Trail entered South Vietnam.

Beginning in November 1962 the U.S. Military Assistance Command, Vietnam (MACV) gradually assumed operations of the CIA's paramilitary operations. The CIDG and border surveillance program were transferred to MACV (military) control. During December 1962, emphasis was placed on building and occupying border camps for the CIA's "Border Surveillance" program after intelligence reports indicated increased Communist activities. Initially, five Special Forces camps were built to hold the troops that performed the border surveillance mission.

During the Vietnam War it made little sense for U.S. forces, most of whom did not speak Vietnamese and did not understand the language, to be the chief instrument of counterinsurgency. By 1964 the vast majority of Special Forces, prior to being sent on temporary duty to Vietnam for six-month periods, were being schooled in the Vietnamese language at Fort Bragg.

In January 1962 Assistant Secretary of State for Far Eastern Affairs Roger Hilsman presented "A Strategic Concept for South Vietnam." It defined the war essentially as a political struggle and proposed policies aimed at the rural Vietnamese as the key to victory, leading to the Strategic Hamlets program. Hilsman also recommended that the Army of the Republic of Vietnam (ARVN) adopt guerrilla warfare tactics. President Johnson rejected the latter.

General William Westmoreland's priority was never pacification, and he left pacification and counterinsurgency largely up to the government of the Republic of Vietnam (RVN). The RVN leadership, however, was little interested in pacification. It saw the Strategic Hamlets program as a means of control rather than an exercise in materially aiding the peasants and winning their allegiance in the process. Established programs were riddled with corruption, including the CIDG program controlled by the RVN Luc Luong Đac Biêt (LLDB: Special Forces). In 1970 the CIDG camps were abandoned altogether and turned over to the ARVN Rangers.

In 1967 a great many U.S.-sponsored projects were brought together under one authority—Civilian Operations and Revolutionary Development Support (CORDS)—headed by Robert W. Komer. This also led to the controversial Phoenix program, which incorporated the use of counterterrorism.

It remains questionable whether earlier implementation of a fully developed pacification effort would have been successful. The principal U.S. effort in that regard came when the insurgency was already too well established for the pacification effort to have a chance at success.

—Harve Saal and Spencer C. Tucker

References: Bell, J. Bower. *The Myth of the Guerrilla: Revolutionary Theory and Malpractice* (1971); Blaufarb, Douglas S. *The Counterinsurgency Era: U.S. Doctrine and Performance 1950 to Present* (1977); Cable, Larry. *Conflict of Myths: The Development of American Counterinsurgency Doctrine and the Vietnam War* (1988); Johnson, Chalmers. *Autopsy on People's Wars* (1973); Kelly, Col. Francis J. *Vietnam Studies, U.S. Army Special Forces, 1961–1971* (1985); McClintock, Michael. *Instruments of Statecraft: U.S. Guerrilla Warfare, Counterinsurgency, and Counter-Terrorism, 1940–1990* (1992); Paret, Peter. *French Revolutionary Warfare from Indochina to Algeria. The Analysis of a Political and Military Doctrine* (1964); Saal, Harve. *MACV-Studies and Observations Group (SOG)* (1990); Shafer, D. Michael. *Deadly Paradigms: The Failure of U.S. Counterinsurgency Policy* (1988); Sutherland, Ian D. W. *1952/1982. Special Forces of the United States Army* (1990); Westmoreland, William C. *A Soldier Reports* (1976).

See also: Central Intelligence Agency (CIA); Civilian Operations and Revolutionary Development Support (CORDS); Eisenhower, Dwight David; Johnson, Lyndon Baines; Kennedy, John Fitzgerald; Komer, Robert W.; Krulak, Victor H.; McNamara, Robert S.; Montagnards; Pacification; Phoenix Program; Psychological Warfare Operations (PSYOP); Strategic Hamlet Program; Taylor, Maxwell Davenport; Thompson, Robert Grainger Ker; United States: Army; United States: Special Forces; Vietnam, Republic of, Special Forces (Luc Luong Đac Biêt [LLDB]); Westmoreland, William Childs.

COWIN Report (May 1971)

Report commissioned to explore General William Westmoreland's personal culpability for war crimes in the wake of public outrage over the My Lai massacre. In early 1971 Columbia University law professor Telford Taylor, who had been the chief U.S. prosecutor at Nuremberg, published *Nuremberg and Vietnam*, in which he argued that Westmoreland was culpable for war crimes committed at My Lai and would have been held responsible had World War II-era standards been in effect. Taylor lent a note of academic respectability to the sometimes sensational public criticism of the Army's handling of My Lai, which included the perceived cover-up and questionable dismissal of charges by Lt. Gen. Jonathan O. Seaman. Under increasing public pressure, and encouraged by Westmoreland, who wanted to clear his name, the Army commissioned a task force to prepare an investigative report of the allegations against him.

In May 1971, after an extensive 14-week investigation, the task force produced a report entitled "Conduct of the War in Vietnam" (COWIN). The task force had been instructed to examine how effectively the rules of engagement had been carried out; whether violations had occurred; if those violations had been properly reported; and, if so, whether appropriate disciplinary measures had been taken. The committee investigated whether the need to adhere strictly to the rules of engagement had been communicated to the troops involved at My Lai, or if they had been communicated with the tacit understanding that they were merely "window dressing." If the latter was true, those at the top of the chain of command should have been held culpable rather than individuals such as Lt. William Calley, who had previously been found guilty of the murder of 25 people at My Lai.

Westmoreland's critics, including Taylor, compared his situation to that of convicted Japanese General Tomoyuki Yamashita during World War II, who had denied knowledge of war crimes committed by troops in his command. The COWIN Report did not accept this comparison and exonerated Westmoreland. It concluded that the undeniable crimes against Vietnamese civilians had been investigated and prosecuted appropriately. The fact that the charges against many of those originally implicated had been dropped by high-ranking military officers held no sway with the task force. The report concluded that Westmoreland had, in fact, outlined clear and appropriate procedures for the proper treatment of civilians and had sufficiently communicated these guidelines to his immediate subordinates. In conclusion, the task force determined that there was no basis whatsoever for holding Westmoreland responsible for war crimes committed by the troops.

—John M. Barcus

References: Lewy, Guenter. *America in Vietnam* (1978); Taylor, Telford. *Nuremberg and Vietnam: An American Tragedy* (1970); Zaffiri, Samuel. *Westmoreland: A Biography of General William C. Westmoreland* (1994).

See also: Calley, William Laws, Jr.; My Lai Massacre; Westmoreland, William Childs.

Cronkite, Walter Leland (1916–)

Influential television news reporter and anchorman. Cronkite joined the CBS network in 1950 and in 1962 became anchor and editor of the "CBS Evening News." With his reputation for hard work, accuracy, competitiveness, and impartiality, Cronkite achieved great credibility, often ranking in polls as the most trusted man in America. In 1968 Cronkite, upon returning from a trip to Vietnam, publicly stated his belief that U.S. policy there would not win the war. Coming shortly after the Têt Offensive, and coupled with the public's growing doubts, this statement seemed to confirm that Americans wanted out of the Vietnam War. During his career Cronkite received two Peabody awards and an Emmy award; after retiring in 1981 he was honored with the Presidential Medal of Freedom.

—Laura Matysek Wood

References: Fensch, Thomas, ed. *Television News Anchors* (1993); James, Doug. *Cronkite: His Life and Times* (1991).

See also: Media and the War; Moyers, Bill; Television and the Vietnam Experience; Têt Offensive: Overall Strategy; Têt Offensive: the Sài Gòn Circle.

Cu Chi, Tunnels of (1966–1967)

Important Communist base area. In 1966 the village of Cu Chi, 25 miles north of Sài Gòn, was astride a prime Viêt Công (VC) line to Cambodian supply points. Thus, VC leaders decided to locate a headquarters complex there and fortify the surrounding area. Surprisingly to Americans, the VC constructed these positions underground. An interlocking series of tunnels and chambers, sometimes three or four levels deep, were a marvel of military engineering, made possible by dense clay soil. Stretching over hundreds of kilometers, the tunnels contained hospitals, armories, classrooms, kitchens, living quarters, and even munitions factories. Ventilation shafts allowed occupants to survive underground for months at a time. Trap doors at the surface were well concealed, and the tunnels had many hidden doors and passages that enhanced their tactical advantage. Although they did not find it pleasant duty, VC soldiers used the tunnel networks to considerable advantage.

On 7 January 1966, units of the U.S. 1st Infantry Division and 173d Airborne Brigade discovered this extensive network. Initial contact provided only a glimpse of the problems tunnel fortifications would pose for U.S. forces at Cu Chi and across Vietnam. When the 25th Infantry Division established its base camp at Cu Chi later that spring, it assumed the task of clearing the tunnels. For several weeks the rear areas of the division were attacked by VC soldiers emerging from the tunnels, a type of envelopment from below.

U.S. personnel took several approaches to clearing the tunnels, including tear gas, acetylene gas, and explosives, before U.S. commanders realized the only effective way to clear them was by hand. This task fell to a group of volunteers who became known as "tunnel rats." Because of the narrow passages, these men were almost uniformly small in stature and performed their duties with minimal equipment—usually a pistol, knife, and flashlight. Most tunnel rats served relatively short periods in this physically and psychologically draining assignment.

Tunnel networks were later discovered in other parts of Vietnam, but none were as extensive or as problematic as those at Cu Chi. By 1967 the tunnels had been cleared, but they served as an early example of the tactical ingenuity and tenacity facing U.S. forces in Vietnam.

—Richard D. Starnes

References: Bergerud, Eric M. *Red Thunder, Tropic Lightning: The World of a Combat Division in Vietnam* (1993); Mangold, Tom. *The Tunnels of Cu Chi* (1985); Stanton, Shelby L. *The Rise and Fall of an American Army: U.S. Army Ground Forces in Vietnam, 1965–1973* (1985).

See also: Clear and Hold; National Front for the Liberation of South Vietnam (NFLSV); Tunnel Rats.

Cunningham, Randall "Duke" (1941–)

U.S. Navy F-4 pilot and first pilot ace in Vietnam (five MiG kills). Cunningham joined the U.S. Navy in 1967 and received his wings the next year. During his second Vietnam tour, on 19 January 1972, Lieutenant Cunningham shot down a MiG-21 and, on 8 May 1972, a MiG-19. On 10 May 1972 he downed three MiG-17s. While returning to the carrier *Constellation*, his plane was downed by a surface-to-air missile, but Cunningham and his radar intercept officer, Lt. (jg) Bill Driscoll, were picked up at the mouth of the Red River by a search-and-rescue helicopter. In all, Cunningham flew 300 Vietnam combat missions. His decorations included the Navy Cross, two Silver Stars, and the Purple Heart. Many of Cunningham's experiences as both naval aviator and fighter pilot instructor were depicted in the film *Top Gun*. He retired from the Navy in 1988 and in 1990 was elected on the U.S. House of Representatives from California.

—James McNabb

References: Cunningham, Randy. *Fox Two* (1984); Duncan, Philip, and Christine Lawrence, eds. *Congressional Quarterly's Politics in America: The 104th Congress* (1995).

See also: Air Power, Role in War; Aircraft Carriers; Airplanes, Allied and Democratic Republic of Vietnam; Alvarez, Everett, Jr.; McCain, John S., III; Search-and-Rescue (SAR) Operations; United States: Navy.

Cuong Đê (1882–1951)

Prince of the Nguyên Dynasty and leader of an anti-French movement in the early twentieth century; also known as Ky Ngoai Hâu Cuong Đê. Cuong Đê was selected by Phan Bôi Châu and other Confucian scholars in central Vietnam to head their anti-French movement in 1903. In 1906 he left Vietnam for Japan and was elected President of the Viêt Nam Duy Tân Hôi (Association for Modernization of Vietnam). In 1910 the Japanese deported all Vietnamese students, and Cuong Đê moved to China where, with Phan Bôi Châu, he founded the Viêt Nam Quang Phuc Hôi (Association for the Restoration of Vietnam), of which he was elected president. During World War II the Japanese had a plan to support Cuong Đê as an alternative ruler (to replace Bao Đai) for Vietnam. This plan attracted many Vietnamese nationalists, including Ngô Đình Diêm, but never was realized.

—Pham Cao Duong

References: Nguyên Huyên Anh. *Viêt Nam Danh Nhân Tu Điên* (1990); Nguyên Thê Anh. *Viêt Nam Duoi Thoi Pháp Đô Hô* (1970).

See also: French Indo-China; Ngô Đình Diêm; Nguyên Dynasty.

Cushman, Robert Everton, Jr. (1914–1985)

U.S. Marine Corps general and commandant. General Cushman's most important combat assignment was as commander of the III Marine Amphibious Force in Vietnam (June 1967–March 1969). This was the largest force ever commanded by a Marine officer to that date, numbering over 172,000 troops.

Cushman was responsible for operations in I Corps Tactical Zone, a task that required him to manage assets from all arms and services. He distinguished himself directing operations during the 1968 Têt Offensive.

Cushman was first and foremost a Marine, and he clashed with the Military Assistance Command, Vietnam (MACV) staff, and even General William Westmoreland, over what he saw as mismanagement of Marine assets, particularly Air Force control of Marine air wings. Cushman left

Vietnam in March 1969 to become deputy director of the CIA. In 1972 he became commandant of the Marine Corps, then retired three years later.

—Richard D. Starnes

References: Smith, Charles R. *High Mobility and Standdown, 1969* (1988); Tefler, Gary L., Lane Rogers, and V. Keith Fleming, Jr. *Fighting the North Vietnamese, 1967* (1984).
See also: United States: Marine Corps; Walt, Lewis W.

da Faria, Antônio (sixteenth century)
Portuguese explorer who in 1535 became the first European to establish a lasting settlement in Vietnam. The village of Faifo, 15 miles south of present Đà Nang, offered a usable harbor that da Faria envisioned as a major Portuguese trade center. However, Faifo never prospered to the extent of other Portuguese settlements.

—David Coffey

Reference: Karnow, Stanley. *Vietnam: A History* (1983).
See also: Vietnam: from 938 through the French Conquest.

Đà Nang
Capital of Quang Nam Province; second largest city in South Vietnam. On 8 March 1965, the first U.S. combat units in Vietnam landed at Đà Nang, which soon became headquarters of the Army of the Republic of Vietnam (ARVN) I Corps. It was also the site of a major military base, port, and resupply area for ARVN and U.S. forces and headquarters for the U.S. III Marine Amphibious Force, the U.S. 1st and 3d Marine Divisions, and later the U.S. Army's XXIV Corps.

As the war progressed, Đà Nang was strangled with refugees fleeing their ancestral homes. During the 1966 "Buddhist Crisis," the city was the site of massive antigovernment demonstrations as rebellious ARVN troops joined the Buddhists against Prime Minister Ky's government. U.S. Marines secured the city and averted a confrontation by positioning themselves between belligerent troops.

In 1967, Communist forces mortared and rocketed Đà Nang's air base, destroying aircraft valued at $75 million. During the 1968 Tết Offensive, Đà Nang was attacked by People's Army of Vietnam (PAVN) and Việt Công forces. During the Communist 1975 Spring Offensive, refugees crammed into the city, which fell quickly to the PAVN onslaught, prompting a catastrophic retreat in which thousands of ARVN soldiers and civilians perished amid heavy fighting. After the Communist victory, Đà Nang became a major staging area for the mass flight of Vietnamese "boat people."

—J. Nathan Campbell

References: Dunn, Carroll H. *Base Development in South Vietnam, 1965–1970* (1972); —. *Building the Bases: The History of Construction in Southeast Asia* (1975); Fitzgerald, Frances. *Fire in the Lake: The Vietnamese and the Americans in Vietnam* (1972); Kahin, George McTurnan. *Intervention: How America Became Involved in Vietnam* (1986).
See also: Geneva Accords; Nguyễn Cao Ky; Tết Offensive: Overall Strategy; Tết Offensive: The Sài Gòn Circle; United States: Marine Corps.

Đai Viêt Quôc Dân Đang (National Party of Greater Vietnam)
Vietnamese nationalist party founded in 1936. The Đai Viêt adopted the theory of *dân tôc sinh tôn* (people's existence), which focused on economic development and the people's welfare. During World War II, the Đai Viêt Quôc Dân Đang (ĐVQDĐ) established bases in Viêt Trì, Đông Triêu, and other locations, as well as a training center. During 1945–1946, like other nationalist parties, it was subsumed by the Communists and its leaders, including Truong Tu Anh, were killed or kidnapped. In the early 1950s it was revived in areas controlled by Bao Đai's State of Vietnam. One leader stated that the ĐVQDĐ recruited up to 200,000 new members, mostly in North Vietnam, Quang Tri, Thua Thiên, and Quang Nam. Other Vietnamese nationalist parties incorporated Đai Viêt in their names, including the Đai Viêt Duy Dân, Đai Viêt Dân Chính, Đai Viêt Quôc Xã of Phan Quang Đán, and Đai Viêt Quôc Gia Liên Minh.

—Pham Cao Duong

References: Nguyên Khac Ngu. *Đai Cuong Vê Các Đang Phái Chính Tri Viêt Nam* (Overview of Political Parties in Vietnam). Montreal: Tu Sách Nghiên Cuu Su Đia, 1989; Nguyên Van Canh. "Thanh Niên Và Các Phong Trào Chông Pháp Thoi Cân Đai (1900–1945)." In *Tuyên Tâp Ngôn Ngo Và Van Hoc Viêt Nam—Essays on Vietnamese Language and Literature,* No. 2, Fascicle II. San Jose, CA: Mekong-Tynan, 1994, pp. 491–505.
See also: Viêt Minh (Viêt Nam Đôc Lâp Đông Minh Hôi [Vietnam Independence League]).

Đak Tô, Battle of (1967)
Series of battles at the U.S. Special Forces camp at Đak Tô. On 17 June, Đak Tô came under heavy mortar fire. During the next few days, the 2d Battalion, 503d Infantry Regiment, 173d Airborne Brigade searched Hill 1338 for the attackers. On 22 June, Company A encountered a battalion of the 24th People's Army of Vietnam (PAVN) Infantry Regiment but encountered difficulty in fighting in the jungle-covered mountains. U.S. losses were 76 killed in action and 23 wounded in action. PAVN losses were estimated at 475, which is disputed.

During July, companies from the 173d Airborne Brigade continued to patrol near Đak Tô. Documents found in PAVN camps indicated three PAVN regiments in the area with a mission to attack U.S. Army Special Forces camps blocking infiltration routes into South Vietnam. On 7 July, Company B, 4th Battalion, 503d Infantry met a strong PAVN force on Hill 830. Contacts continued throughout the month. In late 1967, the PAVN began moving more units south to prepare for the Tết Offensive. Units from the U.S. 4th Infantry and 1st Cavalry Divisions, units from the Army of the Republic of Vietnam (ARVN), and other battalions from the 173d Airborne Brigade deployed to Đak Tô.

During 1–9 November, companies from the 8th Infantry and 12th Infantry, 4th Division, and from the 173d Airborne engaged in savage fighting near Hill 823. Examination of PAVN dead revealed fresh, well-equipped troops. A major battle occurred on 11 November between the 66th PAVN Regiment and U.S. units on Hill 724, where the 1st Battalion, 8th Infantry, fought off a PAVN attack. On Hill 223,

Companies A, C, and D, 1st Battalion of the 503d Infantry, 173d Brigade, encountered a PAVN battalion. Hit by fire from the well-camouflaged PAVN, they were surrounded. Company C of the 4th Battalion of the 503d landed about 800 meters from the battle and relieved the 1st Battalion.

Between 12 and 15 November, units from the 1st and 2d Battalions, 503d Infantry encountered PAVN troops in bunkers and trenches. In the ensuing battles, U.S. troops lost numerous killed. PAVN rockets, meanwhile, destroyed the ammunition dump at the Đak Tô fire support base. On 19 November, the 2d Battalion of the 503d began moving up Hill 875, unaware that in front of them the 174th PAVN Regiment occupied bunkers and trenches connected by tunnels. PAVN troops closed behind the two advancing companies. Company A's command post was overrun and its remnants, plus Companies C and D, were surrounded. In late afternoon, a U.S. Air Force fighter dropped a 500-pound bomb in the middle of Company C, killing 42 Americans and wounding 45. Throughout 20 November, the survivors repelled numerous PAVN attacks. That night, three companies from the 4th Battalion of the 503d arrived to reinforce the defenders. Units from the 4th Division and 42d ARVN Infantry Regiment encountered PAVN troops west, south, and northeast of Đak Tô. The 4th Battalion, with two 4th Division companies, did not gain the crest of Hill 875 until 22 November.

In these engagements, known collectively as the Battle of Đak Tô, the PAVN failed to achieve one of their main objectives—the destruction of an American unit, although they had come close. However, three PAVN regiments scheduled to participate in the upcoming Tết Offensive were so mauled that they had to be withdrawn to refit.

—Richard L. Kiper

Reference: Murphy, Edward F. *Dak To* (1993).
See also: Central Highlands; Tết Offensive: Overall Strategy; Tết Offensive: The Sài Gòn Circle. United States: Involvement in Vietnam, 1965–1968; Vietnam, Democratic Republic of: Army (People's Army of Vietnam [PAVN]); Vietnam, Republic of: Army (ARVN).

Daley, Richard Joseph (1902–1976)

Mayor of Chicago, 1955–1976. Daley extended his control over Illinois voters to sway the 1960 presidential vote in favor of John F. Kennedy. In 1964 he again delivered the Illinois vote to Lyndon Johnson. Daley's heavy-handed response to rioting in Chicago following the assassination of Dr. Martin Luther King, Jr. was a preview of the 1968 Democratic National Convention riots. Daly made security the priority at the convention site by creating a fenced "fortress" there. He clearly tried to manipulate the convention in favor of Senator Hubert Humphrey. Chicago police clashed with antiwar demonstrators before the convention opened, and Daley's opening remarks to the convention included a promise to keep law and order. On his orders, Chicago police brutally attacked the crowds in what was dubbed a "police riot."

—Charlotte A. Power

References: Lichtenstein, Nelson, ed. *Political Profiles: The Johnson Years* (1976).
See also: Antiwar Movement, United States; Chicago Eight; Democratic Party National Convention, 1968; Elections, U.S.: 1968; Humphrey, Hubert H.

DANIEL BOONE, Project

Cross-border reconnaissance from South Vietnam into Cambodia by U.S. Special Forces authorized in June 1966 by the Joint Chiefs of Staff. Final approval for the conduct of these operations (code-named Project DANIEL BOONE) was not approved until May 1967, and then only for the small section of the Cambodian triborder area above the Se San River. Teams typically included two or three Americans and about ten indigenous personnel whose mission was to penetrate Cambodia on foot or by helicopter-borne insertion, conduct reconnaissance, plant mines, commit sabotage, and gather intelligence. Operations were expanded in October 1967 to cover Cambodia's border facing Vietnam to a depth of 20 (later 30) kilometers and was divided into two zones. Zone Alpha stretched approximately from Snoul north to Laos; Zone Bravo, from Snoul to the Gulf of Thailand. Missions in Zone Bravo required case-by-case presidential approval. In November 1967, Project SIGMA assets were transferred to DANIEL BOONE teams, which increased their efforts. During November and December 1967, DANIEL BOONE teams detected a large People's Army of Vietnam (PAVN) and Việt Công (VC) buildup in such areas as the Fishhook. General Westmoreland's urgent requests to launch spoiling attacks into the detected base areas were denied. DANIEL BOONE's successful strategic reconnaissance effort was not capitalized upon, and these areas later proved to be key PAVN/VC staging bases for the Tết Offensive.

Project DANIEL BOONE was renamed SALEM HOUSE in December 1968 and THOT NOT in 1971. In four years, 1,835 missions were conducted.

—James H. Willbanks

References: Shawcross, William. *Sideshow: Kissinger, Nixon, and the Destruction of Cambodia* (1979); Stanton, Shelby L. *Green Berets at War* (1985).
See also: Cambodia; Cambodian Incursion; SIGMA, Project; United States: Special Forces; Westmoreland, William Childs.

Đào Duy Tùng (ca. 1922–)

Key figure in the Vietnamese Communist Party (VCP). Deputy chief of the Propaganda and Training Department of the VCP Central Committee since the 1960s, Tùng was the editor of *Hoc Tap*, later renamed *Tap Chí Công San* (*Communist Review*), the political journal of the VCP. It is believed that he continues to supervise propaganda and training. Considered a hard-liner who tried to adhere to socialist ideology, Tùng was dropped from the Politburo at the 8th Communist Party Congress in June 1996.

—Ngô Ngoc Trung

Reference: Biographical Files, Indo-China Archives, University of California at Berkeley.
See also: Vietnam, Socialist Republic of: 1975 to the Present.

d'Argenlieu, Georges Thierry (1889–1964)

Commander in chief of Free French naval forces in World War II; High Commissioner of Indo-China, 1945–1947. In 1945 d'Argenlieu was appointed vice-president of the Supreme Naval Council and inspector general of French naval forces, and in mid-August de Gaulle named him high commissioner to Indo-China with instructions "to restore French sovereignty in the Indo-China Union."

d'Argenlieu's public service during the period was controversial. Correctly seen as a staunch defender of French colonialism, his appointment to the Indo-China post came over heated Socialist opposition. Bernard Fall, who wrote that d'Argenlieu's appointment was France's "major postwar blunder in Southeast Asia," describes d'Argenlieu as a man of narrow vision who saw the world as one of extremes in which evil was to be eradicated and lacked the patience and tact for negotiating with "natives." d'Argenlieu's 2 June 1946 proclamation of a Republic of Cochin-China, presented to Hô Chí Minh and Paris with a fait accompli, effectively torpedoed the Fontainebleau Conference and ended the possibility of working out accommodation with Hô and the Viêt Minh. d'Argenlieu, having succeeded in convincing French Premier Georges Bidault of the need to "teach the Vietnamese nationalists a lesson," cabled General Jean-Etienne Valluy, his deputy in Sài Gòn, who in turn ordered the French Commissioner in Tonkin, General Morlière, to use force in the north. This produced the 23 November 1946 shelling of Hai Phòng by the cruiser *Suffren*, leading directly to the 19 December outbreak of war. In February 1947, d'Argenlieu was recalled to France.

—Spencer C. Tucker

References: Alford, Elisée. *Le Père Louis de la Trinité, Admiral Thierry d'Argenlieu* (1969); Fall, Bernard. *The Two Viet Nams* (1964); Hammer, Ellen J. *The Struggle for Indochina* (1954).
See also: Bidault, Georges; de Gaulle, Charles André Marie Joseph; Fontainebleau Conference; Hai Phòng, Shelling of; Leclerc, Jacques-Philippe; Valluy, Etienne.

Đâu Tranh

Strategy reportedly devised by Vô Nguyên Giáp, Hô Chí Minh, and Truong Chinh. *Đâu tranh* has two elements—political struggle and armed struggle—jaws of the pincer movement that must work together against an enemy. Armed struggle involves military actions and other forms of bloodshed; political struggle is the systematic coercive activity involving individual and societal mobilization, organization, and motivation. Every action taken in war falls within the framework and scope of these two elements.

Đau tranh, which means "the people as instrument of war," has a threefold sequence of implementation: control the people, forge them into a weapon, and hurl the weapon into battle. Because *Đâau tranh* is a political strategy, violence is necessary but is not its essence. The goal is to seize power by disabling society through primarily organizational means; organization becomes more important than ideology or military tactics. A united front, an organization of organizations, is the basic instrument of control. Victory goes to the side that is best organized, stays best organized, and most successfully disorganizes the other.

Armed *dâu tranh* included military actions as well as assassinations, kidnappings, and other activities not usually associated with regular armed forces. Violence is always cast in a political context. Political *dâu tranh* consisted of three programs: action among the people, its most potent aspect being the village-level effort to gain support; action among the military, a proselytizing effort aimed at individual enemy soldiers and civil servants; and action among the people controlled by the National Liberation Front (Viêt Công).

This kind of struggle channels the enemy's response, in effect dictating his strategy and forcing him to fight under unfavorable terms. This aspect of the strategy confused Americans about the essential nature of the war, its conduct, and its outcome, as well as the nature of their enemy.

—T. R. Carver

References: Pike, Douglas. *PAVN: People's Army of Vietnam* (1986); *Truong-Chinh Selected Writings* (1994); Vô Nguyên Giáp. *People's War People's Army: The Viet Cong Insurrection Manual for Underdeveloped Countries* (1967).
See also: Hô Chí Minh; National Front for the Liberation of South Vietnam (NFLSV); Truong Chinh (Đang Xuân Khu); Vietnam, Democratic Republic of: Army (People's Army of Vietnam [PAVN]); Vô Nguyên Giáp.

Davidson, Phillip Buford, Jr. (1915–)

U.S. Army general in charge of military intelligence at Military Assistance Command, Vietnam, 1967–1969. As chief intelligence advisor to General Westmoreland, Davidson revamped and redirected U.S. military intelligence efforts, focusing on providing useful intelligence estimates and accurate predictions of future enemy activities. He played a prominent role in the controversial 1967 enemy order of battle estimates, then left Vietnam in 1969. In 1984, Davidson was a plaintiff's witness in the libel case brought by General Westmoreland against CBS. He testified as to the accuracy of 1967 estimates of enemy order of battle and claimed that possible political ramifications did not influence that process.

—Richard D. Starnes

References: Davidson, Phillip B. *Secrets of the Vietnam War.* (1990) — *Vietnam at War: The History, 1946–1975* (1988); Zaffiri, Samuel. *Westmoreland: A Biography of General William C. Westmoreland* (1994).
See also: Military Assistance Command, Vietnam (MACV); Order of Battle Dispute; Westmoreland, William Childs.

Davis, Raymond G. (1915–)

U.S. Marine general and commanding general, 3d Marine Division, Vietnam, May 1968–April 1969. Under Davis, Marine tactics changed from staffing fixed defensive positions to conducting highly mobile operations throughout western Quang Tri Province. Davis was also instrumental in reestablishing unit cohesion at battalion and regiment levels within the 3d Marine Division. For his Vietnam service, he received the Distinguished Service Medal. In March 1971,

Davis received his fourth star and appointment as assistant commandant of the Marine Corps. He retired in March 1972.

—W. E. Fahey, Jr.

Reference: Davis, Raymond G. Interview with author (1995).

See also: Bush, George Herbert Walker; United States: Marine Corps.

de Castries, Christian M. (1902–1991)

Commander of French forces in the 1954 Battle of Điên Biên Phu. During the battle, de Castries kept a high profile and at times showed reckless bravery under fire, but at other times he seemed detached and withdrawn. In retrospect, it is easy to question de Castries's defensive dispositions at Điên Biên Phu, but it is unlikely that anything he could have done would have changed the outcome. His appeals for reinforcements were rejected and after a siege of nearly two months, on 7 May 1954 he surrendered. He emerged from four months' imprisonment as a national hero.

—Spencer C. Tucker

References: Andrews, Deborah, ed. *The Annual Obituary, 1991* (1992); Fall, Bernard. *Hell in a Very Small Place: The Siege of Dien Bien Phu* (1967); Roy, Jules. *The Battle of Dienbienphu* (1965); Simpson, Howard R. *Dien Bien Phu: The Epic Battle America Forgot* (1994).

See also: Điên Biên Phu, Battle of; Indo-China War; Navarre, Henri Eugène.

de Gaulle, Charles André Marie Joseph (1890–1970)

French Army general; head of the French government-in-exile in World War II; provisional president of the Fourth Republic, 1944–1946; president of the Fifth Republic, 1958–1969. Determined to reestablish French influence in Asia, de Gaulle, acting with the National Defense Committee, on 4 June 1945 decided to create an expeditionary corps of two divisions for Indo-China. In mid-August the National Defense Committee decided to send the expeditionary force along with a naval squadron centered on the battleship *Richelieu*, already in the Far East, and three aviation groups of about 100 aircraft. In perhaps the most fateful decision in the coming of the Indo-China War, de Gaulle appointed Adm. Georges Thierry d'Argenlieu high commissioner to Indo-China and charged him with restoring French sovereignty over the Indo-China Union. The command arrangement placed General Jacques-Philippe Leclerc under d'Argenlieu.

De Gaulle later lectured the Americans on Vietnam and warned President Kennedy about involvement in Indo-China. "You will find," de Gaulle told him, "that intervention in this area will be an endless entanglement."

—Spencer C. Tucker

References: de Gaulle, Charles. *The War Memoirs of Charles de Gaulle* (1960); Gras, Yves. *Histoire de La Guerre d'Indochine* (1992); Lacouture, Jean. *De Gaulle. The Rebel, 1890–1944* (1990); Gras, Yves. *De Gaulle: The Ruler, 1945–1970* (1972).

See also: d'Argenlieu; Georges Thierry; Faure, Edgar; Kennedy, John Fitzgerald; Leclerc, Jacques-Philippe.

de Genouilly, Charles Rigault (1807–1873)

French Navy admiral and commander in chief of French forces in Indo-China, February–November 1859. He ordered the bombardment of Đà Nang in April 1847. In 1858 he was promoted to vice admiral and occupied Đà Nang that September. In February 1859, in concert with a Spanish force, he sailed up the Sài Gòn River and captured the port of Sài Gòn. Returning to Đà Nang in April, he found his troops decimated by disease and harassed by Vietnamese attacks. He despaired of being able to prevail, asked to be relieved of his command, and returned to France in 1860.

—Arthur J. Dommen

References: Buttinger, Joseph. *The Smaller Dragon: A Political History of Vietnam* (1958); Whitfield, Danny J. *Historical and Cultural Dictionary of Vietnam* (1976).

See also: French Indo-China; Vietnam: from 938 through the French Conquest.

de Lattre de Tassigny, Jean Joseph Marie Gabriel (1889–1952)

French general; high commissioner and commander of French forces in Indo-China, 1950–1951. In an effort to get the Vietnamese to fight on the French side, de Lattre created wholly Vietnamese units. This policy, known as "le Jaunissement," came too late in the war to succeed.

Viêt Minh commander Vô Nguyên Giáp played into de Lattre's hands by initiating Operation Hoàng Hoa Thám, which sought conventional battle with French forces. Defeat of the Viêt Minh in a series of battles in the first half of 1951 enabled de Lattre to make a forceful plea for additional U.S. military assistance during a much-publicized September 1951 trip to Washington. In meetings with President Truman and at the Pentagon, de Lattre stressed the interdependence of fronts in Vietnam and Korea against communism. Meanwhile, Giáp shifted attention to the Thái Highlands. The resulting December 1951–February 1952 fighting at Hòa Bình initiated by de Lattre became an inconclusive battle of attrition with high casualties for both sides. In December 1951, consumed by cancer, de Lattre left Indo-China.

—Spencer C. Tucker

References: Clayton, Anthony. *Three Marshals Who Saved France: Leadership after Trauma* (1992); Fall, Bernard. *The Two Viet Nams* (1964); Karnow, Stanley. *Vietnam: A History* (1991).

See also: French Indo-China; Hòa Bình, Battle of; Indo-China War; "Jaunissement, Le" (Yellowing); Truman, Harry S; Vô Nguyên Giáp.

de Rhodes, Alexandre (1591–1660)

French missionary to Vietnam who devised *quôc ngu,* the national alphabet. De Rhodes recorded baptized 6,700 Vietnamese into the Catholic faith, and his activities aroused great animosity and suspicion among traditional Confucianists when 18 members of the Trinh court nobility converted to Catholicism. In 1630, de Rhodes was banished from the North, but his missionary labors in the South were found unacceptable by the equally hostile Nguyên court. Between 1640 and 1645, de Rhodes lived in Macao but made repeated trips to Vietnam to continue his work. On one occasion he was sentenced to be beheaded but was expelled after three weeks' imprisonment. When the Vatican failed to support his work, he urged the French church to increase its efforts in Vietnam. In 1644, de Rhodes convinced the French church to organize the *Société des Missions Etrangères* (Society of Foreign Missions) to oversee mission endeavors in Vietnam. By 1700, there were hundreds of thousands of Vietnamese Catholics.

—Cecil B. Currey

Reference: Karnow, Stanley. *Vietnam: A History* (1983).

See also: Nguyên Dynasty; *Quôc Ngu*; Trinh Lords; Vietnam, from 938 through the French Conquest.

Dê Thám (real name, Truong Van Thám, aka Hoàng Hoa Thám) (1858–1913)

Vietnamese nationalist hero who led an uprising against the French. Thám centered his resistance activities in the Yên Thê area of Bac Giang Province. From 1886 he expanded his activities, chiefly to Bac Giang, Thái Nguyên, and Hung Hóa Provinces. In 1896, the French sent out Col. Joseph Galliéni to destroy his movement, with only partial success. In 1897 the French agreed to create an autonomous zone of six cantons containing 22 villages in the Phôn Xuong area in return for disarmament by Thám's group.

Thám did not disarm, and in 1905 he expanded his activities and established the Nghia Hung Party. During the next eight years, his forces battled the French and inflicted serious losses. Dê Thám was assassinated on18 March 1913 by his associate Luong Tam Ky, a Vietnamese agent working for the French and former member of the Black Flag. His death was a great blow to the Yên Thê resistance movement, which soon collapsed. Dê Thám was revered by Vietnamese nationalists; the 1951 Viêt Minh offensives, Operations HOÀNG HOA THÁM, were named after him.

—Ngô Ngoc Trung

References: Biographical Files, Indo-China Archives, University of California at Berkeley; Buttinger, Joseph. *The Smaller Dragon: A Political History of Vietnam* (1968); Nguyên Huyên Anh. *Viêt Nam Danh Nhân Tu Điên* (1990).

See also: French Indo-China; HOÀNG HOA THÁM, Operations.

Dean, John Gunther (1926–)

U.S. diplomat with lengthy service in South Vietnam, Laos, and Cambodia. Dean was regional director of Civilian Operations and Revolutionary Development Support (CORDS) in central Vietnam, 1970–1972. Between 1972 and 1974, he was deputy chief of mission at the embassy in Vientiane, Laos. There he was involved in efforts to recover U.S. prisoners of war and soldiers missing in action, thought at the time of the Vientiane Agreement to be in Pathet Lao hands. From Laos, Dean went to Phnom Penh as U.S. ambassador to Cambodia (1974–1975) and was involved in U.S. attempts to negotiate a settlement of the war between Lon Nol's forces and the Khmer Rouge. These efforts failed, and when the Khmer Rouge prepared to enter the capital, Dean oversaw the embassy evacuation, code-named Operation EAGLE PULL, in April 1975.

—Arthur J. Dommen

See also: Cambodia; Khmer Rouge; Laos; Lon Nol.

Dèbes, Pierre-Louis (1900–1947)

French commander at Hai Phòng in November 1946, when a bombardment of the town by naval gunfire—sometimes considered the opening shots of the First Indo-China War—caused serious damage and many casualties. At the end of five days, the French were in complete control at a cost of 23 dead and 86 wounded. Estimates of the number of dead among the Vietnamese civilian population range from the official 300 to 6,000, the latter a frequently published figure that some consider highly exaggerated. Although criticized later for his actions by General Morlière, the commander in Tonkin, Dèbes was not reprimanded and went on to take part in the clearing of the area around Hà Nôi.

—Arthur J. Dommen

Reference: Gras, Yves. *Histoire de la Guerre d'Indochine* (1992).

See also: French Indo-China; Hai Phòng, Shelling of; Indo-China War; Valluy, Etienne.

Decoux, Jean (1894–1963)

French Navy vice admiral; commander of the French Far Eastern Fleet, 1939; governor general of Indo-China, 1940–1945. Succeeding Georges Catroux as governor general in Indo-China in June 1940, Decoux was obliged to negotiate a series of agreements with the Japanese, who were endeavoring to take advantage of France's weakness to press for concessions in the region. Decoux was successful to a considerable degree in maintaining the symbols and substance of French sovereignty over Indo-China, but eventually his policies became controversial. His insistence on strict allegiance to Marshal Henri Philippe Pétain's Vichy government brought punishment for "dissidents," as Decoux called them, who followed General Charles de Gaulle. With difficulty, Decoux circumvented or delayed the Japanese occupiers' demands for war production, particularly of rice, and for measures to ensure the "common defense" of Indo-China.

As Decoux feared, the Japanese military police, the Kempeitai, soon discovered the too-open resistance activities. On 9 March 1945, Japanese authorities demanded that Decoux hand over command of all French forces to them. He refused and was immediately arrested. After the Japanese surrender to the Allied forces, Decoux was held incommunicado. His plea to be reinstated in office was ignored. In October 1945, Decoux was returned to France in humiliating circumstances and in May 1946 brought up for trial on a charge of treason. A mistrial was declared, although he was dismissed from the navy. But after charges of collaboration with the Vichy government were dropped, he was restored to his rank and prerogatives in February 1949.

—Arthur J. Dommen and Spencer C. Tucker

References: Buttinger, Joseph. *The Smaller Dragon: A Political History of Vietnam* (1968); Decoux, Jean. *A la Barre de l'Indochine* (1952); Devillers, Philippe. *Histoire du Viêt-Nam de 1940 à 1952* (1952); Marr, David G. *Vietnam 1945: The Quest for Power* (1996); Patti, Archimedes L. A. *Why Viet Nam? Prelude to America's Albatross* (1980).

See also: Catroux, Georges; de Gaulle, Charles André Marie Joseph; Franco-Thai War; French Indo-China; Mordant, Eugène.

Deer Mission (1945)
World War II U.S. Office of Strategic Services (OSS) operation in Indo-China. Conceived by OSS headquarters in Kunming, China, Deer Mission had two objectives: to support Operation CARBANADO, the possible landing of a U.S. expeditionary force in southern China; and to gather intelligence on Japanese forces in Vietnam for the 14th Air Force.

On 16 July 1945, the seven-man Deer Mission, led by Maj. Allison Kent Thomas, parachuted from Dakota airplanes along with containers of small arms and explosives sufficient to equip 100 guerrillas. When they arrived, they learned that Hô Chí Minh was extremely ill. Team medic Paul Hoagland treated the Việt Minh leader, possibly saving his life. In the following weeks, Deer Mission personnel trained guerrillas, observed them in the attack, and had many conversations with Hô and Võ Nguyên Giáp, both of whom gave assurances that they were friendly to the United States and were willing to assist the United States against the Japanese. They expressed hatred of the French and swore willingness to fight to the death to secure their independence. On 15 August 1945, the Japanese surrendered and Deer Mission team members ceased operations. They reached Hà Nội on 16 September 1945 and soon afterward were withdrawn.

—Cecil B. Currey

Reference: Thomas, Allison Kent. Interviews with author.
See also: Hô Chí Minh; Office of Strategic Services (OSS); Thomas, Allison Kent; Võ Nguyên Giáp.

DEFIANT STAND, Operation (7 September 1969)
Last of 62 Seventh Fleet Special Landing Force operations in Vietnam; first amphibious assault conducted in the 25-year history of the Republic of Korea (ROK) Marine Corps. On 7 September 1969, a battalion of ROK Marines, in conjunction with the U.S. 1st Battalion, 26th Marines, landed by amphibian tractor on Barrier Island, 34 miles south of Đà Nang. The Special Landing Force then swept inland while naval patrol craft cut off escape routes. The Việt Công offered only light resistance and successfully avoided the massive sweep.

—Edward C. Page

Reference: Stanton, Shelby. *The Rise and Fall of an American Army: U.S. Ground Forces in Vietnam 1965–1973* (1985).
See also: United States, Navy; United States, Marines Corps; Korea, Republic of.

Defoliation
Process of applying herbicides to plants to inhibit their growth. Defoliation in Vietnam had two primary objectives: to reduce the dense jungle foliage so that Communist forces might not use it for cover and to deny them use of crops needed for subsistence. Secondary objectives included spot clearing in sensitive areas such as around base perimeters.

About 19 million gallons of herbicides were applied in Vietnam from 1961 through 1970. Operation RANCH HAND aircrews, flying specially equipped C-123 aircraft, sprayed over 90 percent of that quantity; equipment for use in small-scale situations included backpacks, towed vehicles, and helicopters. The optimal application rate was three gallons per acre. Preferred herbicides to defoliate inland and mangrove forests were Agents Orange and White. Both caused drying of the foliage; leaves dropped several weeks after application and would not reappear for four to six months. Oil-soluble Agent Orange was preferred during the rainy season, since it would not wash away, and was the optimal herbicide for use on waxy leaves.

On crops the preferred herbicide was Agent Blue, which was most effective when applied during rapid crop growth. A fast-acting desiccant, it prevented fruit or grain from forming without killing the plant itself. Within two to four days, water-soluable Agent Blue would affect a wide range of crops, but it was less persistent than other agents.

Inland forest defoliation missions were the most extensive. Approximately 450,000 acres, mostly in III Corps north of Sài Gòn, were sprayed with Agents Orange and White over nine years. Inland forests near the Cambodian and Laotian borders and along the Demilitarized Zone were sprayed to prevent Communist troops from using these areas to mask their movements into South Vietnam. Agents Orange and White were also used on mangrove forests near Sài Gòn to discourage use of these areas to interrupt supplies coming to the city. Agent Blue was used on approximately 40,000 acres of crop land, primarily in the northern and eastern provinces of South Vietnam.

Initial results of defoliation missions were extremely positive. Field commanders surveyed in 1968 reported that horizontal visibility increased by up to 70 percent and vertical visibility increased by up to 90 percent, significant factors in increasing the safety and efficiency of their operations.

Long-term effects of defoliation on the ecosystem are difficult to assess. Certainly soil damage occurred; yet dioxin, the most dangerous contaminant of the herbicides, has only a three- to five-year half-life in the soil. Some animal species appear less frequently than before the war, but others have begun to reappear as the forests return. The forests themselves suffered after the war from inept reforestation techniques, such as annual burning, and from erosion by heavy rains.

By the late 1980s, evidence suggested that the environment was recovering more rapidly than originally expected. In the inland forests that were sprayed repeatedly, growth began to return when shade trees were planted first, followed later with native trees planted in the shade. In the mangrove forests, where extensive damage occurred to the sensitive coastal habitat, growth began when plantings were done in a dense pattern to allow interlocking root systems to develop. Despite these successes, in the 1990s some land still needed to be properly reforested to recapture it from nonproductive grass cover and bamboo.

—Charles J. Gaspar

References: Carlson, Elof Axel. "International Symposium on Herbicides in the Vietnam War" (1983); Gough, Michael. *Dioxin, Agent Orange* (1986); Irish, Kent R. *Information Manual for Vegetation Control in Southeast Asia* (1969).
See also: Herbicides; International War Crimes Tribunal; RANCH HAND, Operation.

DELAWARE–LAM SON 216, Operation
(19 April–17 May 1968)

Operation in the A Shau Valley to eliminate People's Army of Vietnam (PAVN) bases used in the 1968 Têt attack on Huê. U.S. Army Lt. Gen. William B. Rosson planned the operation, which called for his Provisional Corps of the 1st Cavalry Division and Army of the Republic of Vietnam (ARVN) 3d Regiment to air assault into the valley while the 1st Brigade of the 101st Airborne Division and ARVN Airborne Division troops blocked routes of escape. The 101st fire base of 175-mm guns would cover most of the valley, which was about 18 miles long and hedged in by 3,000–foot mountains. Lacking intelligence on the enemy, 1st Cavalry Division commander Maj. Gen. John J. Tolson used Lt. Col. Richard W. Diller's 1st Squadron, 9th Cavalry (1/9th) to conduct air reconnaissance. Diller uncovered heavy antiaircraft positions of 37-mm guns that were then attacked from the air. Still, PAVN fire destroyed 23 of Diller's helicopters.

Tolson attacked on 19 April, landing Lt. Col. James B. Vaught's 5th Battalion, 7th Cavalry (5/7th) and Lt. Col. Joseph E. Wasiak's 1st Battalion, 7th Cavalry (1/7th) on peaks at the northern end of the valley. Heavy antiaircraft fire downed ten U.S. helicopters. That night, PAVN forces probed U.S. defenses as a severe storm obscured visibility and forced Wasiak's men on a grueling three-day march to a lower elevation where resupply could reach them.

On 24 April, Col. John E. Stannard's 1st Brigade of the 1st Cavalry Division began an air assault near the A Luoi airstrip and quickly developed it into an airhead. CH-54 flying cranes lifted in engineering equipment while the men received airdropped supplies from C-130s, one of which was shot down. Soon Caribous and C-130s landed to resupply the men. The 1st Brigade attacked south and west, discovering a mile-long depressed storage area defended by a PAVN company. Dubbed the "Punchbowl," this area was secured on 3 May. It contained a large logistical center of the PAVN 559th Transportation Group.

On 29 April, the ARVN 3d Regiment landed and attacked southward along the Rao Lao River, uncovering a large supply cache. Operating to the east of A Shau, the 101st Airborne and ARVN Airborne troops made contact with the enemy and also uncovered large caches. Meanwhile, the troops came under heavy PAVN artillery and rocket attacks from Laos.

DELAWARE-LAM SON 216 resulted in the capture of a large quantity of supplies and vehicles. Although departing troops booby-trapped the area and left acoustic sensors, PAVN troops returned to the A Shau Valley within weeks and had to be cleared out again in 1969.

—John L. Bell

References: Stanton, Shelby. *Anatomy of a Division: 1st Cav in Vietnam* (1987); Tolson, John J. *Airmobility, 1961–1971* (1973).

See also: Airborne Operations; Airmobility; Airplanes, Allied and Democratic Republic of Vietnam; Antiaircraft Artillery, Allied and Democratic Republic of Vietnam; Geography of Indo-China and Vietnam; Helicopters, Allied and Democratic Republic of Vietnam; Têt Offensive: Overall Strategy; Têt Offensive: The Sài Gòn Circle.

Dellinger, David (1915–)

Pacifist and antiwar activist. In early 1965 Dellinger organized a coalition of groups to protest the bombing of North Vietnam. The August demonstrations in Washington, D.C., marked the first use of civil disobedience in the antiwar movement. In November 1966, Dellinger served as cochairman of the Spring Mobilization to End the War in Vietnam, which spent five months organizing churches, women's leagues, universities, and peace groups to show widespread opposition to the war. The 15 April 1967 marches were the largest demonstrations in U.S. history to that date. Dellinger was involved in the riots during the 1968 Democratic National Convention and was one of the "Chicago Eight" tried in 1969. In September 1972 he was part of an antiwar delegation admitted to North Vietnam to accept the early return of three U.S. prisoners of war.

—Clayton D. Laurie

References: Dellinger, David. *Revolutionary Non-Violence* (1971); Gitlin, Todd. *The Sixties: Years of Hope, Days of Rage* (1987); Maclear, Michael. *The Ten Thousand Day War: Vietnam, 1945–1975* (1981).

See also: Antiwar Movement, United States; Chicago Eight; Democratic Party National Convention, 1968.

DELTA, Project (1964–1971)

Long-range reconnaissance and intelligence collection missions within South Vietnam. Its forerunner was Project LEAPING LENA, which in October 1964 was redesignated as Project DELTA. U.S. Army Special Forces "A" detachments trained Vietnamese Civilian Irregular Defense Group (CIDG) and Vietnamese Special Forces (Luc Luong Đac Biêt, or LLDB) for combined reconnaissance operations. Initially there were six teams of two U.S. Special Forces (USSF) soldiers and eight Vietnamese each. The Army of the Republic of Vietnam (ARVN) 91st Ranger Battalion was the reaction force. Missions had to be approved by MACV and the RVN Joint General Staff. The teams operated throughout South Vietnam.

In June 1965, Detachment B-52 was created to provide a command and control headquarters for the project. Project DELTA eventually expanded to include 93 USSF soldiers, 121 Vietnamese, 187 CIDG, an ARVN Ranger Battalion of 836 men, a security company of 105 Nùng tribesmen, a 36–man mortar platoon, and a 36–man bomb damage assessment platoon.

The SF, LLDB, and CIDG composed the reconnaissance and roadrunner teams. Project DELTA's organization varied over time and was never formalized by official documents. Reconnaissance teams normally were inserted at dusk or at night by helicopter or on foot into areas of little Allied activity. Team missions were to collect intelligence, direct air or artillery strikes, lead a reaction force to a target, or capture prisoners. Roadrunner teams, composed entirely of LLDB and CIDG, posed as People's Army of North Vietnam (PAVN) or Viêt Công (VC) soldiers and openly traveled PAVN and VC routes.

In September 1965, DELTA began to train its replacements in patrolling techniques, and on 15 September 1966, Detachment B-52 opened the MACV Recondo School to train

Army personnel in reconnaissance techniques. Project DELTA was deactivated on 31 July 1970. It had identified more than 70 PAVN units, located numerous infiltration routes, captured valuable documents and prisoners, and inflicted extensive personnel losses upon PAVN and VC troops.

—Richard L. Kiper

References: Kelly, Francis J. *U.S. Army Special Forces, 1961–1971* (1973); Stanton, Shelby L. *Green Berets at War* (1985).

See also: Montagnards; United States: Special Forces; Vietnam, Republic of: Army (ARVN); Vietnam, Republic of: Special Forces (Luc Luong Đac Biêt, LLĐB).

Demilitarized Zone (DMZ)

Buffer zone between North and South Vietnam established at the 1954 Geneva Conference. The Geneva Accords established a "temporary" 39-mile-long demarcation line dividing Vietnam at roughly the 17th parallel with a five-mile-wide buffer zone—the Demilitarized Zone (DMZ). No military forces, supplies, or equipment were to be within the zone during its temporary existence. However, after scheduled elections were scuttled throughout Vietnam in 1956, the DMZ became, in Washington's eyes, the official boundary between North and South Vietnam. To the leaders of the Democratic Republic of Vietnam (DRV), it was no such thing.

During the Vietnam War, the United States and the DRV regularly violated the neutrality of the DMZ by moving troops and materiel in and out of the area. Despite its failure to fulfill its original charter, the DMZ remained politically intact until the 1972 Spring Offensive, when three PAVN divisions crossed the DMZ and overran 12 Army of the Republic of Vietnam (ARVN) bases and outposts in the area. The political integrity of the DMZ was never restored, and today the only remnants of the DMZ are the decaying outposts that once lined its borders.

—Brent Langhals

References: Fall, Bernard B. *Viet-Nam Witness 1953–66I* (1966); Karnow, Stanley. *Vietnam: A History* (1991); O'Ballance, Edgar. *The Wars in Vietnam, 1954–1980* (1981); Randle, Robert F. *Geneva 1954; The Settlement of the Indochinese War* (1969); Turley, William S. *The Second Indochina War* (1986); Young, Kenneth T. *The 1954 Geneva Conference* (1968).

See also: Geneva Conference and Geneva Accords.

Democratic Party National Convention, 1968

Controversy and civil unrest plagued the Democratic Party Convention in Chicago (26–29 August 1968). The party establishment, dominated by Lyndon Johnson and his loyalists, used political force to control official proceedings, while on the streets the Chicago police, directed by Mayor Richard Daley, physically suppressed unofficial opposition.

The Democrats had suffered through tumultuous times, with Johnson facing a challenge from antiwar Senator Eugene J. McCarthy, who upset Johnson in the New Hampshire primary. Senator Robert F. Kennedy then entered the contest, dividing the party's peace faction. Johnson withdrew from the race on 31 March 1968; Humphrey became a candidate on 27 April. Following Kennedy's 4 June assassina-

tion, his campaign organization transferred its loyalty to Senator George S. McGovern, who took up the antiwar crusade. Humphrey arrived in Chicago with a clear majority of committed delegates.

Adoption of a platform plank supporting administration Vietnam policies was introduced by Platform and Rules Committee Chairman Hale Boggs after midnight on 27 August, a move orchestrated to limit television coverage of the debate. Debate over the Vietnam plank highlighted the convention; the actual nominating process was anticlimactic. After four hours of heated exchange, the final vote favored the majority position supporting administration policy. By 29 August, Humphrey had become the Democratic Party candidate for president.

Meanwhile, Chicago police, assisted by Illinois state troopers and National Guardsmen, attempted to control far more contentious events outside, where thousands of antiwar protesters had converged. Although denied permits to demonstrate, they marched, sang, and lobbied in support of the antiwar candidates and platform. The convention site resembled an armed camp, surrounded with barbed wire and defended by combat vehicles. In violent clashes, thoroughly documented by the media and watched by a stunned nation, police arrested 668 demonstrators and injured an indeterminate number.

—Mark Barringer

References: Foote, Joseph, ed. *The Presidential Nominating Conventions 1968* (1968); Mailer, Norman. *Miami and the Siege of Chicago: An Informal History of the Republican and Democratic Conventions of 1968* (1968); Walker, Daniel. *Rights in Conflict: Chicago's Seven Brutal Days* (1968).

See also: Antiwar Movement, United States; Chicago Eight; Humphrey, Hubert H.; Johnson, Lyndon Baines; Kennedy, Robert Francis; McCarthy, Eugene Joseph; McGovern, George S.; Nixon, Richard Milhous.

Denton, Jeremiah A., Jr. (1924–)

U.S. Navy commander and pilot; among the first and most senior-ranking prisoners of war (POWs). Shot down over North Vietnam on 18 July 1965, Comdr. Jerry Denton spent seven and a half years in captivity. He was a key leader of the resistance movement. In April 1966 during a televised interview, he blinked the word "torture" in Morse code. During the infamous July 1966 Hà Nôi Parade, he ordered his fellow POWs to keep their heads up and walk with pride. Denton's *When Hell Was in Session*, among the best captivity accounts, was made into a television movie. Denton has stated that he believes the error in Vietnam was in not using decisive force early in the conflict.

—Joe P. Dunn

References: Denton, Jeremiah A., Jr., with Ed Brandt. *When Hell Was in Session* (1976); Howes, Craig. *Voices of the Vietnam POWs: Witnesses to Their Fight* (1994); Hubbell, John G., et al. *P.O.W.: A Definitive History of the American Prisoner of War Experience in Vietnam, 1964–1973* (1976).

See also: Hà Nôi Hilton (Hoa Lò Prison); HOMECOMING, Operation; McCain, John S., III; Prisoners of War, Allied.

DePuy, William E. (1919–1992)

U.S. Army general and commander of the 1st Infantry Division. In 1963 DePuy was requested to be in charge of operations on General Westmoreland's Military Assistance Command, Vietnam (MACV) staff. In March 1966, he took command of the 1st Infantry ("Big Red One") Division and was promoted to major general in April.

DePuy's command of the 1st Infantry Division was anything but tranquil. While on Westmoreland's staff, he had argued persuasively for more troops and an offensive strategy of attrition. Other units, notably the 25th Infantry ("Tropic Lightning") Division and U.S. Marine Corps units in I Corps Tactical Zone in the north, gave priority to supporting the Vietnamese by protecting them from Viêt Công (VC) harassment and recruiting, but DePuy's 1st Infantry Division pursued Communist troops in their own territory and sought to destroy them by maneuver and firepower. DePuy described his philosophy as going "after the Main [VC] Forces wherever they could be found…with as many battalions as I could get into the fight"—what was later called "pile-on."

As head of the Army's Training and Doctrine Command after the Vietnam War, DePuy fashioned the organization and cultivated a talented group of subordinates to lead the army out of the dark post-Vietnam days. His intellect and leadership helped resurrect the spirit, morale, and fighting efficiency of the U.S. Army. He retired from active duty in 1977.

—John F. Votaw

References: DePuy, William E. *Selected Papers of General William E. DePuy* (1994); Halberstam, David. *The Best and the Brightest* (1972); Herbert, Maj. Paul H. *Deciding What Has to Be Done: General William E. DePuy and the 1976 Edition of FM 100–5, Operations* (1988); Kinnard, Douglas. *The War Managers* (1985); Sheehan, Neil. *A Bright Shining Lie: John Paul Vann and America in Vietnam.* (1988).

See also: Military Assistance Command, Vietnam (MACV); United States: Army; Westmoreland, William Childs.

DEROS (Date of Estimated Return from Overseas)

Date for departure from Vietnam, established at the same time as the assignment date. Standard combat area tours were one year except for the Marine Corps, where they were generally 13 months. Assignments to nontheater areas in support of the war were also fixed-length, ranging from 12 to 24 months, again with the DEROS known before the assignment began. An individual might request an extension to the length of the tour; a shortened enlistment term was sometimes offered as an incentive for such extensions. The 12- or 13–month combat tour, an innovation in the Vietnam War, originally was intended to increase morale by letting combat troops know when their ordeal might end. However, in later years the fixed DEROS was blamed for creating a slackening of effort in anticipation of departure. Whether or not this was so, it was evident that consciousness of the DEROS was an important part of every soldier's life.

—Phoebe S. Spinrad

See also: United States: Army.

Desertion, Allied and Communist

By U.S. military definition, "absent with the intention to remain away permanently." Some 500,000 of the nearly 7.6 million Americans who served in the U.S. military during 1965–1973 deserted, although fewer than one-fifth remained away from their units more than 30 days. There were 32,000 reported cases of failure to report for duty in Vietnam, refusal to return from Rest and Relaxation (R&R), and desertion after service in Vietnam, with most of these in the latter category.

There were only 5,000 reported cases of desertion in Vietnam. Within the combat zone, there were only 24 cases related to avoidance of hazardous duty. Overall absent-without-leave (AWOL) rates during the Vietnam War were lower than those during World War II and not much higher than those of the Korean War. Long-term AWOL rates, however, were higher and corresponded with the growth of U.S. antiwar sentiment. Army desertion rate went from 1.49 percent in 1966 to a high of 7.35 percent in 1971. At the peak of the war, a U.S. soldier went AWOL every two minutes and deserted every six. This was a loss of roughly one million man-years of service, almost half the total man-years U.S. troops spent in Vietnam.

Those who deserted from the U.S. military during the Vietnam War generally tended to be younger, less educated, and less well off economically than the average soldier. Three-quarters of U.S. Army deserters were white, but African Americans were twice as likely to desert. Navy deserters also tended to be white; Air Force deserters tended to be African American and better educated. Most desertions were prompted by noncombat-related reasons.

Deserters who were located were given less-than-honorable discharges. Less than 9,000 of the 93,250 men and women who deserted during 1967–1971 were never caught and are listed as "fugitives." President Ford formed the Presidential Clemency Board (PCB), which reviewed individual cases and assigned specific sanctions or acquittal. Ford proposed two years of alternate service for draft resisters and deserters in return for "clemency discharges." President Carter, who in 1977 offered blanket pardons to draft resisters, succumbed to national outrage and offered almost nothing to deserters; they were ordered to apply in person to secure a change in their discharge status. The Ford and Carter administrations agreed to upgrade the discharges of the 20,000 who deserted after service in Vietnam.

The highest desertion rates of the Vietnam War occurred among soldiers of the Army of the Republic of Vietnam (ARVN). Desertion was primarily a problem in regular ARVN units. Regional Forces (RF) had a low desertion rate, and there were almost no deserters in the village-level Popular Forces (PF). ARVN desertions were prompted by low pay, homesickness, military corruption, dangerous field conditions, and various hardships. Only rarely did ARVN deserters join the Communists. An ARVN deserter could easily find his way to a populous area and live there with little risk of being found and arrested.

Between 1967 and 1971, only 87,000 People's Army of Vietnam (PAVN) and Viêt Công (VC) deserted within South

Vietnam. Desertion from the PAVN within the Democratic Republic of Vietnam (DRV) was virtually impossible because of rigid population control. Every citizen had to present food stamps to buy basic foodstuffs, and these were canceled on the date that a draftee was to report to local military authorities for basic training.

Ethnic South Vietnamese soldiers from the south deserted at a higher rate than native northerners. This grew during periods of intense Allied military activity. In 1967, 90 percent of two elite VC battalions, Phu Loi I and Phu Loi II in Bình Duong Province, deserted in a two-month period. Communist deserters who openly declared their intentions to become citizens of the RVN were given Chiêu Hôi (open arms) status and then citizenship in the RVN. The few who refused were sent to prisoner-of-war camps. Some elite ARVN units, especially the Rangers, contained a high percentage of Communist defectors. Perhaps the best known of these was former PAVN Lt. Bùi Ngoc Phep, a talented sapper who surrendered in 1968 and became the leader of Kit Carson Scouts working with the U.S. Army 11th Cavalry Brigade.

After the April 1975 Communist victory, almost all former Communist defectors were detained, and many were killed in the immediate aftermath. In 1978, Hà Nôi courts-martial handed down death sentences to former PAVN Col. Lê Xuân Chuyên and Capt. Phan Van Xuong; others were given lengthy prison sentences. In recent years, the Socialist Republic of Vietnam has allowed many former Chiêu Hôi to emigrate to the United States.

—Nguyên Công Luân (Lu Tuân) and Spencer C. Tucker
References: Baskir, Lawrence M., and William A. Strauss. *Chance and Circumstance: The Draft, the War, and the Vietnam Generation* (1978); Dong Van Khuyen. *The Republic of Vietnam Armed Forces* (1980); MacPherson, Myra. *Long Time Passing. Vietnam and the Haunted Generation* (1984); Olson, James, ed. *Dictionary of the Vietnam War* (1987).
See also: Carter, Jimmy; Chiêu Hôi Program (Open Arms Program); Conscientious Objectors (COs); Draft; Ford, Gerald R.; Kit Carson Scouts.

DeSoto Missions (1963–1964)

Naval intelligence program authorized by President Johnson. DeSoto was conceived as a four-month mission but was later extended for an additional year. Certain ships of the Seventh Fleet with electronic intelligence listening gear were to cruise the coast of the Democratic Republic of Vietnam (DRV). While commandos of the Republic of Vietnam (RVN) landed shore parties to harass radar installations, electronic intelligence (ELINT) ships would record resulting electronic transmissions.

The first DeSoto mission, assigned to the destroyer *Craig,* wac canceled because of inclement weather. The destroyer *Maddox* was then ordered to the Tonkin Gulf, where her captain was warned to go no closer than eight miles from the northern mainland and not to approach within four miles of coastal islands. Picking up its ELINT gear in Taiwan, it made its way into the Tonkin Gulf.

At the same time, another program, OPLAN 34–A, was in motion. It employed several U.S. Navy Patrol Torpedo (PT) boats stripped of their torpedo tubes; U.S.-built light craft called "Swifts," captained occasionally by Norwegian skippers; and Norwegian-built aluminum patrol boats nicknamed "Nasties," captained by Americans. Nasties transported South Vietnamese commandos from their base at Đà Nang to locations on the coast above the 17th parallel. These teams engaged in various covert actions ashore, including sabotage and kidnapping.

Early on 31 July 1964, one such mission raked the island of Hòn Mê while another OPLAN 34–A team fired at the island of Hòn Ngu. The *Maddox* monitored these activities, coming no closer to Hòn Mê than five miles. In reaction, on 2 August, North Vietnamese patrol boats from Vinh attacked the *Maddox*. They were driven off or sunk by aircraft from the carrier *Ticonderoga*. Commander of the Pacific Fleet, Adm. Ulysses Grant Sharp, Jr., then ordered the carrier *Constellation* and destroyer *C. Turner Joy* as reinforcement. A supposed second attack by North Vietnamese patrol boats against the *Maddox* and the *C. Turner Joy* was reported on 4 August, whereupon President Johnson temporarily suspended both DeSoto Missions and OPLAN 34–A activities. These Tonkin Gulf incidents paved the way for the passage of the Tonkin Gulf Resolution by the U.S. Congress and greater American involvement in the war in Vietnam.

—Cecil B. Currey
References: Karnow, Stanley. *Vietnam: A History* (1983); Mooney, James L., ed. *Dictionary of American Naval Fighting Ships* (1959).
See also: ELINT (Electronic Intelligence); Operation Plan 34A (OPLAN 34A); Sharp, Ulysses Simpson Grant, Jr.; Tonkin Gulf Incidents; Tonkin Gulf Resolution.

Devillers, Philippe (1920–)

French journalist and writer of the most influential political history of the French Indo-China War. His *Histoire du Viêt-Nam de 1940 à 1952* was published in Paris on 28 April 1952. By presenting a firmly nationalist point of view rooted in Vietnam's own history of struggle against outside domination, the book acted as a counterweight to the arguments of those who wanted to keep Indo-China in the French Empire at all costs and a foil to propagandistic portrayals of the Viêt Minh that had dominated the press up to that point. With the Vietnam War, Devillers experienced a renewal of his reputation as an expert on Vietnamese politics. His subsequent writings provided ammunition for antiwar writers in the United States.

—Arthur J. Dommen
Reference: Devillers, Philippe. Personal communication (n.d.).
See also: Fall, Bernard B.; French Indo-China.

Dewey, Albert Peter (1916–1945)

Office of Strategic Services (OSS) lieutenant colonel; first American killed in Vietnam. In August 1945 he was sent to Sài Gòn as head of a seven-man contingent to search for missing Americans and to gather information on conditions there. That portion of Vietnam was then under British control, and British commander Maj. Gen. Douglas D. Gracey was trying to cope with problems he found there.

In August, the Viêt Minh declared themselves the legitimate government for all of Vietnam. Dewey's sympathies lay with the Viêt Minh, and Gracey, unsympathetic to Viêt Minh claims, took this as an affront to his own authority. He had already come to despise this outspoken and abrasive U.S. officer and ordered him not to fly the American flag from his jeep. When Dewey ignored him, Gracey ordered him to leave Indo-China. Thus, no flag identified Dewey's vehicle as American on his way to the airfield. Encountering a roadblock staffed by three Viêt Minh soldiers, Dewey spoke to the men in French, then attempted to drive around the roadblock. The Viêt Minh, assuming Dewey to be French, opened fire, killing Dewey instantly. A tragic case of misidentity made Dewey the first American fatality in Vietnam.

—Cecil B. Currey and Scott Rohrer

Reference: Karnow, Stanley. *Vietnam: A History* (1983).

See also: Bình Xuyên; Cao Đài; Gracey, Douglas D.; Office of Strategic Services (OSS); Hòa Hao.

DEWEY CANYON I, Operation
(22 January–18 March 1969)

Military operation in the southwest corner of Quang Tri Province conducted by Maj. Gen. Raymond Davis's 3d Marine Division. The operation was conducted in response to a Communist buildup in Base Area 611 in the Da Krong Valley, an important location because it fed Route 548 through the A Shau Valley, from which troops and supplies went east into Huê and southeast to Đà Nang. DEWEY CANYON's mission was to deny the Communist forces access to the critical populated areas of the coastal lowlands. Military Assistance Command, Vietnam (MACV) believed it was critical to cut infiltration from the Laotian sanctuaries, eliminate antiaircraft capabilities, and destroy basic infrastructure capable of supporting another major Têt Offensive.

On 22 January General Davis sent three battalions of the 9th Marine Regiment commanded by Col. Robert Barrow into the Da Krong Valley. The Marines were completely dependent upon helicopters for logistical support, a challenge in the northwest monsoon season. General Davis and Colonel Barrow made skillful use of fire support bases (FSBs). Initially the 9th Marines developed FSBs Shiloh, Razor, and Riley. As the regiment advanced, other FSBs were opened in a leapfrog manner. Phase I of DEWEY CANYON involved getting the forces established in the operation area.

Phase II, designed to clear the area around the FSBs and move gradually into position for Phase III, commenced on 24 January as Colonel Barrow ordered the 2/9th and 3/9th to extend their perimeters north of the east-west axis of the Da Krong River. During the first week of February, with visibility and ceiling at zero, and rations and water a potential problem, Barrow ordered the commanders of 2/9th and 3/9th to pull their companies into areas from which they could be supported. Continued bad weather during 4–10 February permitted Communist forces to strengthen defenses to the south and better prepare to meet the attack.

In Phase III, each battalion had a three-mile-wide zone of action (ZOA); the total regimental ZOA was about nine miles east to west. From Phase Line Red—the regimental "jumping off point"—each battalion would have to cover about five miles to the regimental objective. On 11–12 February, as the battalions moved across Phase Line Red, they encountered People's Army of Vietnam (PAVN) units that fought from their fighting holes until destroyed.

From 16–23 February the Marine battalions pushed south toward their objectives. New FSBs were established, but remained under fire from reinforced PAVN units. The Americans uncovered large quantities of arms and ordnance, and Company C, 1/9th, overran a bunker complex and captured two 122-mm field guns. While the Marines experienced success, heavy PAVN mortar fire hampered resupply of rifle companies and casualty evacuation and replacement. By 1 March, the weather closed in again. FSBs and company positions were not always open for helicopters. Only Marine pilots had full instrumentation to fly in such weather. Despite difficulties, the pilots were generally able to accomplish their missions within three hours from demand.

On 18 March, with the extraction of 1/9th, DEWEY CANYON was terminated. On 19 March, MACV reported PAVN dead at 1,617 and 1,461 weapons recovered, along with tons of ammunition, equipment, and supplies. DEWEY CANYON claimed 121 Marines killed and 803 wounded. It arguably was the most successful high-mobility regimental-size action of the war.

—W. E. Fahey, Jr.

References: Davis, Gordon M. "Dewey Canyon: All Weather Classic" (1969); Simmons, Edward H. *The United States Marines, 1775–1975* (1976).

See also: Davis, Raymond G.; United States: Marine Corps.

DEWEY CANYON II, Operation (January–March 1971)

Operation in support of Operation LAM SON 719, the Army of the Republic of Vietnam (ARVN) invasion of Laos in early 1971; first major ARVN deployment unaccompanied by U.S. advisors. LAM SON 719 was a 20,000–man operation to interdict the Hô Chí Minh Trail, advance to Tchépone, and destroy People's Army of Vietnam (PAVN) supply dumps. DEWEY CANYON II technically lasted to 7 February, but U.S. involvement continued until the last ARVN troops departed Laos in late March. It was a special operation because in 1970 Congress prohibited U.S. ground troops from entering Cambodia or Laos. U.S. XXIV Corps Commander Lt. Gen. James Sutherland coordinated airmobile and aviation operations; Commanding General of the 101st Airborne Division Maj. Gen. Thomas Tarpley led the ground forces. The United States also supplied tactical air and B-52 bombing support.

On 30 January, an armored cavalry detachment from the 1st Brigade, 5th Infantry, moved down Route 9 to the Khe Sanh area, securing the road by 5 February. Meanwhile, the 101st Airborne launched a feint assault into the A Shau Valley to distract PAVN forces. Following B-52 strikes, the cross-border attack began on 8 February with U.S. helicopter gunships of the 2/17th Cavalry attacking PAVN weapons sites and troop columns and securing landing zones north and south of Route 9, ARVN armor proceeding into Laos, and U.S. helicopters inserting two ARVN divisions into the landing zones.

Intense antiaircraft fire hampered U.S. helicopter missions, and the ARVN advance came under heavy attack. In the next three weeks, the PAVN mauled three ARVN battalions, completely overrunning one fire base. Nevertheless, the offensive continued. On 3 March, an ARVN battalion air-assaulted to the outskirts of Tchépone, and three days later an ARVN regiment air-assaulted into the ruined ghost town.

After reaching Tchépone, Republic of Vietnam (RVN) and U.S. officials proclaimed Lam Son 719 a tactical and strategic success, but the continued presence in southern Laos of five PAVN divisions, a tank regiment, and 20 antiaircraft battalions ruled out any further advance by ARVN units. President Nguyên Van Thiêu claimed a victory and ordered a withdrawal that collapsed into a rout. The PAVN was hurt, but within days their base at Tchépone was back in service. The LAM SON 719 debacle proved that PAVN troops still could defeat the best ARVN units. President Nixon nevertheless proclaimed on 7 April 1971, "Vietnamization has succeeded."

—John D. Root

References: Nolan, Keith William. *Into Laos: The Story of Dewey Canyon II/Lam Son 719, Vietnam 1971* (1986). Tolson, John. *Airmobility, 1961–1971* (1973).

See also: Airmobility; Air Power, Role in War; LAM SON 719, Operation; Nguyên Van Thiêu; Nixon, Richard Milhous; Vietnamization.

Diêm, Overthrow of. See Ngô Đình Diêm, Overthrow of.

Điên Biên Phu, Battle of (April–May 1954)
Set-piece battle that ended the Indo-China War; most famous battle of the war and among the great battles of the twentieth century. In 1953, French military commander in Indo-China General Henri Navarre decided to establish an airhead in northwestern Tonkin at the village of Điên Biên Phu, astride the main Viêt Minh invasion route into Laos. In November 1953, Navarre gave orders for the operation, dubbed CASTOR, to proceed. On 20 November, 2,200 "paras," the cream of the French Expeditionary Corps, dropped into the valley north and south of Điên Biên Phu, easily defeated the few Viêt Minh there, then began establishing defensive positions.

Navarre totally underestimated his enemy. He assumed that Viêt Minh commander General Vô Nguyên Giáp would commit at most one division to such an effort. Should this belief prove incorrect, Navarre was confident the garrison could be evacuated. Điên Biên Phu was an obscure village surrounded by hills on all sides. To leave the enemy the opportunity to control the high ground was dangerous, but when the French arrived there, the Viêt Minh did not have artillery; thus, there was thus no danger at the time. Col. Christian Marie Ferdinand de la Croix de Castries commanded French forces at Điên Biên Phu. Although widely experienced in Indo-China and regarded as a capable commander, during the subsequent battle he at times showed signs of detachment.

By the end of the first week, the French had 4,500 men in the valley who were entirely dependent on air supply by a few transport aircraft. The Viêt Minh, on the other hand, relied on a primitive system of transport by human porters. Giáp's troops improved Route 41 leading to Điên Biên Phu to enable it to handle trucks and artillery pieces, but the porters remained the core of the Viêt Minh supply system and were critical to the battle's outcome.

The French central command post in Điên Biên Phu itself was surrounded by a series of strongpoints, supposedly all named for de Castries's lovers: Beatrice, Gabrielle, Anne-Marie, Dominique, Huguette, Françoise, Elaine, and Isabelle. Isabelle, separated from the others three miles to the south, was easily cut off and diverted a third of the French forces. de Castries had planned a wider defensive ring, but the problems of bringing everything in by air shrank the perimeter. Fortifications were also woefully inadequate. The French, contemptuous of Viêt Minh artillery capabilities, made no effort to camouflage their positions and placed their guns in open pits without protective cover. The Viêt Minh easily observed French work from the hills, but French light observation aircraft failed to detect the Viêt Minh buildup.

The Chinese directly supported the Viêt Minh by handling some artillery batteries and helping to draw up fire plans. Chinese General Vy Quôc Thanh was also at Điên Biên Phu as military advisor and to help plan the campaign.

The French flew in reinforcements, but these were negated because Giáp had called off his northern offensive to commit all available divisions to attack Điên Biên Phu. Thus the defenders would encounter a much larger force than the single division Navarre anticipated. Giáp also worked to cripple the French airlift capacity. In daring early March raids, Viêt Minh commandos attacked French air bases at Gia Lâm and Đô Son and Cát Bi airfields, destroying 22 aircraft.

At Điên Biên Phu, meanwhile, the French had started patrols, which were routinely mauled by the Viêt Minh. After de Castries's chief of staff was killed near one of the strongpoints, the French abandoned such patrolling.

Giáp now closed the ring on the French fortress. The 304th, 308th, 312th, and 316th Divisions were brought to the area. The French called in air power. F-8F Bearcats and B-26 bombers attacked Viêt Minh hill positions, which were well disguised by natural camouflage and difficult to identify. The French also flew in ten tanks by air and assembled them in the fortress under fire, but these had little impact on the battle.

By mid-February, de Castries had sustained casualties of almost 1,000 men while Viêt Minh continued to build their strength. Bernard Fall estimates that the Viêt Minh ultimately assembled at Điên Biên Phu 49,500 combat troops and 31,500 support personnel; an additional 23,000 troops maintained supply lines back to the China border. In mid-March, the French had 10,814 men in the valley, fully a third of them Vietnamese. The Viêt Minh thus enjoyed a superiority of approximately five to one in manpower. They also had greater firepower.

The siege of Điên Biên Phu officially began on 13 March with a heavy Viêt Minh bombardment. Giáp steadily improved the quantity and quality of his artillery. During the battle, the Viêt Minh fired 103,000 rounds of 75-mm or larger size, most of it by direct fire, simply aiming down their gun tubes at the French positions. Approximately 75 percent of French casualties came from artillery fire. By contrast, French artillery assets were totally inadequate. The French fired only 93,000 shells during the battle and, unlike the Viêt Minh, had difficulty identifying their targets.

On the first night of the siege, the Viêt Minh took Beatrice. Gabrielle fell two days later. Giáp's basic tactic was massive artillery fire followed by waves of infantry. The Viêt Minh also brought the airstrip under fire and destroyed an F-8F Bearcat fighter on the 13th; six more were destroyed on the ground the next day. The control tower was also badly damaged, and the radio beacon was knocked out.

Pessimism now began to spread in the French command. In Hà Nôi, General René Cogny, who was never enthusiastic about the operation, now began to consider the possibility of losing the fortress. His resources were stretched thin, as Giáp had sent the 320th Division, three autonomous regiments, and fourteen regional battalions to disrupt the vital transportation link between Hà Nôi and Hai Phòng and divert French resources by attacking French outposts in the Tonkin Delta. The Viêt Minh offensive there began on 12 March, the day before the battle began at Điên Biên Phu. Thus Cogny had to fight two battles at once. Navarre refused all reinforcements to Cogny. de Castries's pleas for reinforcements fell on deaf ears. Even ammunition was in short supply as Viêt Minh sappers blew up French stocks.

On 22 March, the French used their last four tanks to counterattack People's Army of Vietnam (PAVN) troops that had cut off Isabelle. This met up with units from Isabelle striking north. It was the first French success of the battle, but Giáp had a seemingly inexhaustible supply of manpower. The arrival of the rainy season further complicated French resupply problems. C-47 Dakotas still flew in supplies and evacuated wounded, but at great risk. On 26 March, one was shot down; two more were shot down on the 27th. Later that day, one landed and picked up 19 wounded, the last flight in or out of Điên Biên Phu.

On 26 March, Maj. Marcel Bigeard, who had parachuted into the fortress only ten days before, commanded a successful attack against Viêt Minh positions. Supported by artillery, fighter aircraft, and a tank platoon from Isabelle, the paras sallied from the fortress to assault the Viêt Minh. Bigeard later gave enemy losses at 350 enemy dead and more than 500 wounded, as well as 10 prisoners. The raiders also captured weapons and reclaimed ten prisoners.

Having already suffered about 6,600 killed and 12,000 wounded, Giáp's army suffered from low morale. Discussions led by political cadres about courage, right thinking, and dedication helped to restore morale, as did a change in tactics. Giáp abandoned the costly human wave attacks in favor of attrition warfare. He pushed forward trenches until the particular target strongpoint was cut off from outside support.

The last stage of the battle was fought without letup in an area around the airstrip. The Viêt Minh attacked on 29 April. By 4 May, French senior officers knew there was no longer any hope. The last French reinforcements, 165 men of the 1st Colonial Parachute Battalion, jumped into the garrison on 5 and 6 May, having come at their own insistence to share the fate of their comrades. By now, most airdropped supplies were falling into Viêt Minh hands. The final Viêt Minh assault occurred on 6 May; the last French troops surrendered on the evening of 7 May.

During the siege, the French suffered 1,600 dead, 4,800 wounded, and 1,600 missing. The Viêt Minh immediately sent their 8,000 prisoners off on foot on a 500-mile march to prison camps; less than half would return. Of the Vietnamese taken, only 10 percent would be seen again. The Viêt Minh had shot down 48 French planes and destroyed 16 others on the ground. Viêt Minh casualties were estimated at approximately 7,900 killed and 15,000 wounded.

The French had two plans to rescue the garrison: Operation CONDOR, an infantry thrust from Laos to link up with airborne forces sent from Hà Nôi; and ALBATROSS, a plan for the garrison to break out on its own. Navarre did not order Cogny to begin planning for this until too late, on 3 May. Not until May 7 did de Castries decide to attempt to execute the plan, but it was then too late. Another plan, codenamed VULTURE, was also considered. This envisioned massive U.S. intervention in the form of air strikes, but President Eisenhower could not secure British support, and the plan was dropped.

The battle of Điên Biên Phu was the death knell of the French in Asia. In Paris, Premier Joseph Laniel, dressed in black, gave the news to the National Assembly. The Geneva Conference was already in progress to discuss Asian issues, and the French defeat provided politicians with an excuse to shift blame for the Indo-China debacle to the military. Although France had not provided the troops or resources its military required to win the war, it could now blame the military for the defeat and extricate the nation from the Indo-China morass. A new government under Pierre Mendès-France came to power to carry out that mandate.

—Spencer C. Tucker

References: Bigeard, Marcel. *Pour une parcelle de gloire* (1975); Fall, Bernard. *Hell in a Very Small Place: The Siege of Dien Bien Phu* (1967); Porch, Douglas. *The French Foreign Legion. A Complete History of the Legendary Fighting Force* (1991); Roy, Jules. *The Battle of Dienbienphu* (1965); Simpson, Howard R. *Dien Bien Phu: The Epic Battle America Forgot* (1994).

See also: CASTOR, Operation; Cogny, René; de Castries, Christian M.; Eisenhower, Dwight David; Geneva Conference and Geneva Accords; Laniel, Joseph; Mendès-France, Pierre; Navarre, Henri Eugène; Navarre Plan; VULTURE, Operation.

Dikes

System of walls built along rivers in North Vietnam to protect the important Red River Delta and tributaries against flooding. The French consolidated and widened existing ancient dikes and raised their height around the Hà Nôi area to hold floods of more than nine meters. The total volume of the system reached 77 million cubic meters in 1930 compared with 20 million cubic meters in the late nineteenth century.

—Pham Cao Duong

Reference: *Bac Ky Hà Đê Su Tích* (History of Red River Dikes in North Vietnam).
See also: Geography of Indo-China and Vietnam; Red River Delta.

Dinassauts

French abbreviation for *divisions navales d'assaut;* integrated French tactical units composed of naval and army forces for riverine warfare during the Indo-China War. These units patrolled and, in the south, controlled the key rivers upon which Indo-China's inland commerce and communications so depended. Each Dinassaut had a permanently assigned light infantry battalion operating from a mix of landing craft, river patrol boats, and river transports. The units could also project power inland. Two companies of naval infantrymen constituted the ground element. Naval Brigade commanding officer Comdr. François Jaubert used barges to form combined arms units capable of operating even in small creeks and estuaries. Dinassauts were formidable fighting units that achieved a remarkable combat record.

Jaubert's first opportunity to prove his concept of combined arms riverine units came in October 1945 during Operation MOUSSAC, when the riverine force successfully relieved My Tho. A similar operation later retook Vinh Long. The lessons learned from these initial successes provided the doctrinal foundations for the Dinassauts. Permanent riverine units were not established until the arrival of French landing craft (acquired from British stocks) in December 1945. On 1 January 1947, the units were organized into two flotillas, one in the north and one in the south. Each flotilla included "river commandos," combined arms teams operating on the rivers. Designated Dinassauts in 1948, they became the primary French force on the rivers of Indo-China.

Dinassauts were employed whenever Việt Minh ground units were suspected of operating in a river area. They fought their way through to isolated French garrisons, relieved towns, paved the way for supply convoys, and rushed reinforcements to threatened outposts and provincial capitals. Operating as self-contained units, they proved imminently flexible in combat.

—Carl O. Schuster

References: Kilian, Robert. *Fusiliers-Marins d'Indochine* (1948); Koburger, Charles W., Jr. *The French Navy in Indochina* (1991); McClintock, Robert. "The River War in Indochina." (1954).
See also: French Indo-China.

Đô Cao Trí (1929–1971)

Army of the Republic of Vietnam (ARVN) general. During the administration of President Ngô Đình Diêm, Colonel Trí commanded at Huê, where he repressed the militant Buddhists. Diêm promoted him to general, but in 1963, as commander of the First Army Corps, he participated in the coup that removed Diêm from power. Informed that the coup was imminent, he arranged a meeting in Đà Nang with government officials to preclude their calling out the Republican Youth or other movements that might defend the government. Trí then received command of II Corps (the 12 central provinces), but was one of several Buddhist generals that General Nguyên Cao Ky exiled after became premier in 1965. After two years, Trí was invited to return to Vietnam and was appointed ambassador to the Republic of Korea. After the Têt Offensive, Trí was recalled from Korea and appointed commander of III Corps. General Westmoreland referred to the flambouyant Trí as "a tiger in battle, South Vietnam's George Patton."

—Claude R. Sasso

References: Palmer, Bruce, Jr. *The 25-year War: America's Military Role in Vietnam* (1984); Pike, Douglas, ed. *The Bunker Papers: Reports to the President from Vietnam, 1967–1973* (1990); Westmoreland, William. *A Soldier Reports* (1976).
See also: Ngô Đình Diêm; Nguyên Cao Ky; Cambodia; Vietnam, Republic of: Army (ARVN).

Đô Muoi (1917–)

Vietnamese Communist revolutionary; Việt Minh general; government official of the Democratic Republic of Vietnam (DRV) and Socialist Republic of Vietnam (SRV). Muoi assumed various posts at the provincial level during the Indo-China War, reaching the rank of brigadier general, and commanded the Việt Minh during the battle for Hai Phòng at the end of the war.

In 1960 Muoi became a full member of the Vietnamese Communist Party (VCP) Central Committee. In February 1961 he left politics because of poor health. He returned to government work in November 1967 as chairman of the Economy Board of the Premier's Office and in December 1969 became vice premier and minister of construction of the DRV. After the 1975 Communist victory, Muoi took charge of the unsuccessful effort to amalgamate the economies of the DRV and former Republic of Vietnam (RVN) by introducing socialism in the former capitalist South. Although this policy prompted a serious economic crisis and exodus of people from the country, Muoi survived politically and was the SRV's key economic liaison with Soviet bloc countries in the 1980s.

—Ngô Ngoc Trung

References: Biographical Files, Indo-China Archives, University of California at Berkeley; Vu Thu Hiên. *Đêm Giua Bn Ngày* (1997).
See also: Vietnamese Communist Party (VCP); Pham Hùng; Vietnam, Socialist Republic of: 1975 to the Present.

Đô Quang Thang (1927–)

Leader in the Vietnamese Communist Party (VCP) and Socialist Republic of Vietnam. Đô Quang Thang was active only at the local level during the Vietnam War. He became secretary of Nghia Bình Province's VCP committee in May 1983. In April 1991 Thang became secretary of the Quang Ngãi Province party committee. He was elected a full member of the national Central Committee during the 1986 Sixth Party Congress and became chairman of the party Control

Commission and secretary of the Secretariat. He was promoted to the Politburo in January 1994.

—Ngô Ngoc Trung

Reference: Biographical Files, Indo-China Archives, University of California at Berkeley.

See also: Vietnamese Communist Party (VCP); Vietnam, Socialist Republic of: 1975 to the Present.

Đoàn Khuê (1923–)

Key figure in the Vietnamese Communist Party (VCP); Socialist Republic of Vietnam (SRV) army general and minister of defense. During the Indo-China War, Khuê was known as an intelligence specialist, and he was once political commissar of a regiment in Interzone V of Central Vietnam. During the Vietnam War, Khuê returned to the South and fought there from 1964 to 1975. In August 1991, Khuê was appointed minister of defense by the Socialist Republic of Vietnam's National Assembly.

—Ngô Ngoc Trung

Reference: Biographical Files, Indo-China Archives, University of California at Berkeley.

See also: Lê Duân; Vietnam, Socialist Republic of: 1975 to the Present.

Dobrynin, Anatoly Fedorovich (1919–)

Soviet diplomat and politician. As Soviet ambassador during the Vietnam War, Dobrynin acted as a conduit for messages from the U.S. State Department to the Soviet government, most often regarding the sincerity of negotiations between the Democratic Republic of Vietnam and the United States. Dobrynin gave optimistic assessments that U.S. concessions would be positively received in Moscow and Hà Nôi. During two U.S. bombing pauses in May and December 1965, Dobrynin passed messages from the State Department to Moscow that sought Soviet support for negotiations, but nothing came of those attempts. At no time did Dobrynin have the power to play a substantive role in making or affecting Soviet foreign policy.

—Michael Share

References: Dobrynin, Anatoly. *In Confidence* (1995); Longmire, R. A. *Soviet Relations with Southeast Asia: An Historical Survey* (1989); Pike, Douglas. *Vietnam and the Soviet Union: Anatomy of an Alliance* (1987).

See also: Brezhnev, Leonid Ilyich; Khrushchev, Nikita Sergeyevitch; Union of Soviet Socialist Republics (USSR; Soviet Union).

Đôi Moi

Term, commonly translated as "renovation," signifying the liberalization of economic and, to a lesser extent, political policies of the Vietnamese government ratified by the Sixth National Congress in 1986. By 1981 the Socialist Republic of Vietnam ended some restrictions on rural trade and established a "contract system" whereby the government leased land to peasants for a set fee and the peasants could keep any surplus over that amount. Industries were given permission to break away from centrally planned allocations and buy and sell more on their own. Upset by increased inflation and

corruption after economic controls were lightened, conservatives stopped further change and dismissed the reformist Nguyên Van Linh as mayor of Hô Chí Minh City. Continued economic difficulties undermined the conservative position, however, as did the rise of Mikhail Gorbachev, Vietnam's chief patron, in the USSR. Reformers also gained power after the death of Party Secretary Lê Duân in July 1986.

The Vietnamese Communist Party and National Congress officially proclaimed *đôi moi* at the end of 1986. New regulations required that economic decisions be decentralized, government industry be profitable, workers be payed based on productivity, the contract system in agriculture be strengthened, and foreign investment be encouraged. Some relaxation in censorship and an effort to allow voters more choices in elections were soon cut back, however. Political pluralism, the regime declared, was not the proper system for Vietnam.

Đôi moi thus resembled policies in China. In both countries, the demands for a better life that had toppled Communist regimes in Eastern Europe and the former Soviet Union led to an effort to maintain a Communist government by liberalizing economically but not politically. *Đôi moi* represented not simply a risky political maneuver, but also an important change in basic Marxist theory.

—Peter K. Frost

References: Marr, David, and Christine White, eds. *Postwar Vietnam: Dilemmas in Socialist Development* (1988); Turley, William S., and Mark Selden, eds. *Reinventing Vietnamese Socialism: Doi moi in Comparative Perspective* (1993).

See also: Nguyên Van Linh (Nguyên Van Cúc); Refugees and Boat People; Vietnam, Socialist Republic of: 1975 to the Present.

Domino Theory

View held by U.S. policymakers during the Cold War that if one country fell to communism, its neighbors were threatened with a chain reaction of Communist takeovers. The domino theory arose from fear that the withdrawal of colonial powers from Southeast Asia would lead to the fall of Vietnam, then the rest of Southeast Asia. Remembering the failure of appeasement before the War II, policymakers believed that firmness might deter Communist takeovers. The phrase was first used by President Eisenhower on 7 April 1954, in anticipation of French defeat at Điên Biên Phu, but the idea was already in place in 1947.

A 1950 study commissioned by President Truman emphasized Vietnam's strategic importance as a natural invasion route into Southeast Asia and anticipated repercussions for other countries in the region if Vietnam became Communist. Entering office in 1953, Eisenhower accepted the domino theory without reservation. In August 1954, following the French defeat at Điên Biên Phu and the division of Vietnam along the 17th parallel, Eisenhower approved NSC 5429/2, which stated that the United States needed to prevent further losses to communism in Asia through all available means. Presidents Kennedy and Johnson also subscribed to the domino theory. In a speech at Johns Hopkins University in April 1965, Johnson said that retreat in Vietnam would not end conflict with communism in Southeast Asia.

The Communist victory in Vietnam in 1975 did not substantiate the domino theory. The neighboring states of Cambodia and Laos did fall to communism, but these nations were destabilized by the Vietnam conflict itself. Cambodia is no longer Communist, and other Asian nations have remained safely non-Communist.

—Kenneth R. Stevens

References: Berman, Larry. *Planning a Tragedy: The Americanization of the War in Vietnam* (1982); Herring, George C. *America's Longest War: The United States and Vietnam, 1950–1975* (1996).

See also: Central Intelligence Agency (CIA); Containment Policy; Điên Biên Phu, Battle of; Eisenhower, Dwight David; Johnson Lyndon Baines; Kennedy, John Fitzgerald; Laos; Munich Analogy; Southeast Asia Treaty Organization (SEATO); Stevenson, Adlai E.; Truman, Harry S.

Đôn Điên

Form of military settlement or colony widely used in traditional Vietnam as a strategy to increase the amount of land under cultivation and to protect the border from foreign infiltration. The *dôn diên* can be traced at least to 1343 under the Trân Dynasty. In the nineteenth century under Minh Mang, the *dôn diên* were used to improve peasant conditions in the South and in the North's coastal region. By the middle of that century, under the direction of Nguyên Tri Phuong, about 100 villages were created in the Mekong Delta through the *dôn diên* system. These later became centers of resistance against the French.

—Pham Cao Duong

Reference: Pham Cao Duong. *Vietnamese Peasants under French Domination (1861–1945)* (1985).

See also: Lê Thánh Tông; Minh Mang; Vietnam: from 938 through the French Conquest.

Đông Âp Bia. *See* Hamburger Hill (Battle of Âp Bia Mountain).

Đông Hà, Battle of (29 April–15 May 1968)

Battle between the People's Army of Vietnam (PAVN) and the Army of the Republic of Vietnam (ARVN) and U.S. Marines in northern I Corps. On 29 April, the PAVN 320th Division launched a widespread offensive throughout the Demilitarized Zone (DMZ). The 3d Marine Division labeled these engagements above the Bô Diêu and Cua Viêt Rivers collectively the Battle of Đông Hà.

A town in northeastern Quang Tri Province in I Corps, Đông Hà provided the southeast anchor of "Leatherneck Square," a defensive barrier along the DMZ. At the junction of Highways 1 and 9 (the only major north-south and east-west land lines) and accessible to the Cua Viêt River system, this proved to be an ideal site for the Đông Hà Combat Base (DHCB). DHCB served as 3d Marine Division headquarters and logistics center for III Marine Amphibious Forces units.

After the Têt Offensive, the Democratic Republic of Vietnam (DRV)/National Liberation Front's (NLF's) strategy to improve their bargaining position at the upcoming Paris peace talks was to prepare for successful military action that led to 119 attacks on civilian and military targets. As the 3d Marine Division was preparing a counteroffensive to attack PAVN units along the DMZ, on 29 April elements of the PAVN 320th Division were spotted about four miles north of the DHCB. The 1st and 2d Battalions, 2d Regiment, 1st ARVN Division made contact with a PAVN regiment along Route 1. The 2d Battalion, 4th Marines engaged the PAVN main force in fierce fighting at Đai Đo hamlet northeast of Đông Hà. After three days of hard fighting, the 1st Battalion, 3d Marines, relieved the 2d Battalion, 4th Marines for an additional three days at Đai Đo. The 3d Battalion, 21st Infantry, 196th Light Infantry Brigade, American Division (under the operational command of the 3d Marines) shared in taking the brunt of the PAVN attack in a bitter battle at Nhi Hà, northeast of Đông Hà. On 16 May, the PAVN 320th Division broke off contact.

Other Marine units (in order of insertion: 3/3d, 1/9th, 3/9th, 1/26th) saw significant combat, as did the ARVN 1st Division. The 1st and 2d Battalions, 5th Cavalry, 1st Cavalry Division (Airmobile), with its units positioned from northeast of Nhi Hà to north of Đông Hà, operated under the 3d Marines 6–17 May and called its participation Operation CONCORDIA.

Total casualties in units under operational control of the 3d Marines numbered 233 killed, 821 wounded, and 1 missing in action. ARVN casualties were estimated at 42 killed and 124 wounded. The PAVN reportedly lost 2,366 dead and 43 prisoners. Đông Hà retained its role as command and logistics center until being turned over to the ARVN in November 1969.

—Paul S. Daum, with B. J. Rogers

References: Nolan, Keith William. *The Magnificent Bastards: The Joint Army-Marine Defense of Dong Ha, 1968* (1994); Olson, James S., ed. *Dictionary of the Vietnam War* (1988); Simmons, Edwin H. "Marine Corps Operations in Vietnam, 1968" (1974).

See also: Demilitarized Zone (DMZ); Têt Offensive: Overall Strategy; Têt Offensive: The Sài Gòn Circle; United States: Marine Corps; Vietnam: Democratic Republic of: Army (People's Army of Vietnam [PAVN]).

Đông Quan Pacification Project (1953)

U.S.-funded village regroupment plan developed by Governor of North Vietnam Nguyên Huu Trí in 1953; prototype for pacification of the Red River Delta. The Đông Quan Pacification Project was based on the successful model used by the British in Malaya, but Trí found little enthusiasm to fund it until he described his plans to the U.S. Special Technical and Economic Mission (STEM). With an estimated 40,000 Viêt Minh infiltrators in the Red River Delta, pacification held particular appeal to STEM Special Representative James P. Hendrick. The site selected for the first "Great Village" was 20 miles south of Hà Nôi in a region of destroyed villages and heavy Viêt Minh presence. Trí's plan called for regrouping peasant farmers of 25 surrounding villages into Đông Quan. To attract villagers to such an arrangement, the "Great Village" offered a handicraft and commercial area, subsidized housing, a hospital, and other facilities. Other pacification sites were set up in 1954 to house war refugees fleeing Viêt Minh areas.

Surrounded on three sides by water, Đông Quan appeared defensible. Since the French would not detach troops from the war effort to provide security, Trí used three companies of Bao Chính Đoàn (national guardsmen). The Viêt Minh targeted Đông Quan from the beginning, threatening and attacking workers and residents. A tri-nation committee made up of Vietnamese from Trí's government, Americans from STEM, and a French military representative met weekly to oversee the project and adopt countermeasures. Despite their efforts, the project never reached its full potential.

—Claude R. Sasso

Reference: National Archives. "Mission to Vietnam" (n.d.).
See also: Agroville Campaign; Đai Viêt Quôc Dân Đang (National Party of Greater Vietnam); Nguyên Huu Tri; Pacification; Strategic Hamlet Program; United States: Involvement in Indo-China through 1954; Vietnam, Democratic Republic of: 1945–1954.

Đông Xoài, Battle of (9–12 June 1965)

Viêt Công (VC) attack on a U.S. Special Forces camp. Beginning at 2330 on 9 June 1965, approximately 1,500 men of the 762d and 763d VC Regiments attacked the newly established U.S. Special Forces camp at Đông Xoài, which was staffed by approximately 400 Montagnard Civilian Irregular Defense Group (CIDG) troops and 24 U.S. Seabees. Unprepared for the attack, the defenders retreated to district headquarters in town.

Four VC assaults were pushed back. The next morning, Sài Gòn sent one infantry battalion by land and the Army of the Republic of Vietnam (ARVN) 52d Ranger Battalion into Đông Xoài by helicopter. Ambushed at Thuân Loi plantation, the infantry battalion was scattered. The 52d Ranger Battalion counterattacked, supported by U.S. and Republic of Vietnam aircraft, which dropped napalm and phosphorous bombs. On 11 June, the 52d Ranger Battalion was rested because of its casualties and pursuit of the VC went to the recently arrived ARVN 7th Airborne Battalion. Late on 12 June at the rubber plantation, the paratroopers were ambushed and quickly overrun, although some survivors made it back to Đông Xoài. Later the fatigued Americans were airlifted out.

Viêt Công propaganda claimed Đông Xoài as a major victory in which they proved that they were capable of fighting large battles and confronting ARVN elite units. The battle was important in undermining Washington's confidence in the ARVN and thus bolstered arguments for the commitment of large numbers of U.S. ground forces.

—Hieu D. Vu

References: Nguyên Đuc Phuong. *Nhung Trân Đánh Lich Su Trong Chiên Tranh Viet Nam 1963–1975* (1993); Westmoreland, William C. *A Soldier Reports* (1981).
See also: Civilian Irregular Defense Group (CIDG); Montagnards; Rifles; United States: Seabees; Vietnam, Republic of: Army (ARVN).

Donovan, William Joseph (1883–1959)

American lawyer, soldier, and diplomat; director of the Office of Strategic Services (OSS), 1942–1945. By autumn 1942, Donovan had developed plans for intelligence-gathering operations in China, Mongolia, and Indo-China. His base for operations in Indo-China was the southern China province of Yunnan, especially the city of Kunming. The OSS stepped up activities in Indo-China following the Japanese takeover in March 1945 and began contacting groups of Vietnamese living in exile in southern China, including the Viêt Minh. In summer 1945, with Japanese defeat imminent, the OSS dispatched teams into northern Indo-China to establish Vietnamese intelligence networks and train guerrillas to cut Japanese supply routes. The most famous of these was the Deer Mission. After the Japanese surrender, teams were also sent to Sài Gòn (Embankment Mission) and Vientiane (Raven Mission) to recover prisoners of war.

In August 1953, Donovan was named ambassador to Thailand by President Eisenhower and became a strong advocate of using Hô Chí Minh's guerrilla tactics against the Communists. He was instrumental in establishing Police Aerial Reconnaissance Units (PARUs), elite paramilitary units that later played a role in advising the Hmong in Laos. In accordance with his stipulation that financial constraints would allow him to serve in that post no longer than one year, he left Thailand in August 1954.

—Arthur J. Dommen

References: Brown, Anthony Cave. *The Last Hero: Wild Bill Donovan* (1982); Donovan, William Joseph. Papers (n.d.); Dunlop, Richard. *Donovan, America's Master Spy* (1982); Fineman, Daniel. *A Special Relationship; The United States and Military Government in Thailand, 1947–1958* (1997); Ford, Carey. *Donovan of the OSS* (1970); Troy, Thomas F. *Donovan and the CIA* (1981).
See also: Deer Mission; Dewey, Albert Peter; Office of Strategic Services (OSS); Patti, Archimedes L. A.

DOUBLE EAGLE, Operation (28 January–6 March 1966)

Unsuccessful attempt by U.S. Army and Marine Corps and Army of the Republic of Vietnam (ARVN) forces to trap Viêt Công (VC) and People's Army of Vietnam (PAVN) units in Quang Ngãi Province. In the fall of 1965, I Corps intelligence analysts concluded that Communist main force units were in Quang Ngãi and that their critical base areas were in the Tam Quan region. In response, the Marine Corps planned Operation DOUBLE EAGLE during December 1965 and January 1966, calling for the 4th and 7th Marine Regiments to join units of the 2d ARVN Division and deploy south. At the same time, units of the U.S. Army's 1st Cavalry Division (Airmobile) and the ARVN 22d Division would move north and attack suspected VC/PAVN base areas. The pincer movements were to crush the Communist forces caught between them.

Members of the III Marine Amphibious Force began the operation by assaulting "Red Beach," northeast of Đuc Phô. The Marines attempted to deceive their enemy into thinking that they would conduct only limited strikes against coastal areas. The buildup on the beach was intentionally slow and two Marine battalions remained at sea. On the second day, when the exploitation phase began, the Marines encountered problems. B-52 "Stratofortresses," plagued by poor visibility, battered a few targets, but rain and jungle terrain impeded Marine progress inland, and Communist forces evaded contact. The Marines moved toward Bình Định Province and the trap planned in conjunction with the Army's 1st Cavalry Division.

Unlike the Marines, the 1st Cavalry encountered heavy PAVN resistance when it moved north. With the Marines and 1st Cavalry poised to squeeze the 18th PAVN Regiment between them, especially after linking up on 4 February, PAVN forces evaded the trap and there were no real engagements. The VC and PAVN escaped, and DOUBLE EAGLE ended on 6 March 1966 with most of the reported 2,000 Communist casualties occurring in the first week of the operation.

DOUBLE EAGLE's early delays gave Communist forces the opportunity to escape. VC and PAVN units moved too fast for the slow, linear U.S. tactics. By the time U.S. helicopters finally entered the fray, their targets had already vanished. This scenario would repeat itself.

—Lincoln Hill

References: Shulimson, Jack. *U.S. Marines in Vietnam: An Expanding War, 1966* (1982); Stanton, Shelby L. *The Rise and Fall of an American Army: U.S. Ground Forces in Vietnam, 1965–1973* (1985); West, Francis J. *Small Unit Action in Vietnam, Summer 1966* (1967).

See also: National Front for the Liberation of South Vietnam (NFLSV); United States: Army; United States: Marine Corps; Vietnam, Democratic Republic of: Army (People's Army of Vietnam [PAVN]).

Doumer, Paul (1857–1932)

President of France; governor general of Indo-China, 1897–1902; key figure in the economic development of French Indo-China. Doumer set in motion the economic patterns that guided the colony throughout the French period. Interested in centralization, Doumer believed that the French government would have to take an active role in bringing about social change. He unified administration by replacing the emperor's mandarin advisory council with a new body containing French officials. He also worked to expand industrialization on the basis that the colony was to be exploited for France's benefit. Believing that Indo-China should pay for its own development, he transferred the financial burden from French taxpayers to the Vietnamese people and accelerated land policies that dispossessed many Vietnamese peasant proprietors. Doumer created official monopolies on sales of salt, opium, and rice alcohol, and he was an inveterate builder. In 1902 he returned to France.

—Spencer C. Tucker

References: Doumer, Paul. *L'Indochine française (Souvenirs)* (1930); *Historical Dictionary of the Third French Republic, 1870–1940* (1986); Karnow, Stanley. *Vietnam: A History* (1991); Thompson, Virginia. *French Indo-China* (1968).

See also: Assimilation versus Association; French Indo-China.

Draft

U.S. process of selecting men for service in the armed forces. President Johnson's 1965 decision to rely on the draft rather than reserves to provide the manpower for the Vietnam War resulted in a young man's war; 19 years of age became the most common in the field as compared to 26 in World War II. At the height of the conflict, more than 60 percent of Vietnam deaths were draftees, and 19– and 20–year-olds suffered the greatest number of casualties.

The Selective Training and Service Act was passed in 1940, and the draft in various forms was periodically extended until its demise in 1973. Rapid troop buildup, beginning in spring 1965 and continuing for four years, brought the draft to center stage. From 1964 to 1973, approximately 26.8 million male "baby boomers" reached draft age, becoming the largest manpower pool in U.S. history. More than 57 percent were deferred, exempted, or disqualified from military service; 2 percent committed draft violations. More than 8.7 million men and women served in the military services during 1964–1975, 2.7 million of them in Vietnam.

At the heart of the Selective Service System were nearly 4,000 local draft boards in the 1960s. Staffed by unpaid volunteers—predominantly middle-class white men, usually World War I or II veterans—most rubber-stamped the recommendations of the full-time civil service clerks. A 1966 study of 16,638 draft board members found that only 1.3 percent were African American. Women were not allowed to serve on the boards until 1967.

Demands for manpower grew dramatically as the war progressed. The numerous deferments and exceptions available helped to determine who would be called to meet the quotas. General Lewis B. Hershey, the head of the Selective Service, was proud of how the deferment system channeled young men into areas important to the national interest, but local boards had great discretion over what deferments were in the national interest. Agricultural deferments were paramount in some areas; cheese makers were even deferred in rural Wisconsin counties.

Discrimination and favoritism were the norm for precious slots in the National Guard and reserves, safe havens from Vietnam. In 1968, only 1 percent of Army National Guardsmen were African American. Slots often were made available for the sons of prominent individuals. This, and the inequities and corruption in gaining physical disqualification from the draft, as well as the class-biased deferment system, all contributed to the war's unpopularity. Some reforms came in the draft extension bill in 1967. Ending graduate school and teaching deferments raised the percentage of college-educated personnel in Vietnam from 6 percent in 1966 to 10 percent in 1970. A national lottery implemented at the beginning of 1970, as the manpower numbers were winding down, had marginal effect on who served in Vietnam. The day after the signing of the Paris Accords in January 1973, President Nixon ended the draft and inaugurated the all-volunteer military.

—Joe P. Dunn

References: Appy, Christian G. *Working Class War: American Combat Soldiers and Vietnam* (1993); Baskir, Lawrence M., and William A.

Strauss. *Chance and Circumstance: The Draft, the War and the Vietnam Generation* (1978); Flynn, George Q. *The Draft, 1940–1973* (1993); Flynn, George Q. *Lewis B. Hershey: Mr. Selective Service* (1985); Gerhardt, James M. *The Draft and Public Policy* (1971).

See also: African American Personnel in U.S. Forces in Vietnam; Antiwar Movement, United States; Conscientious Objectors (COs); Desertion, Allied and Communist; Johnson, Lyndon Baines; Nixon, Richard Milhous; Project 100,000.

Drama and the Vietnam Experience

Playwrights of the Vietnam War used noticeably similar subjects, themes, and techniques. Often using the war as a metaphor for the problems of the world of the 1960s and 1970s, more than 200 plays considered such common subjects as the loss of identity, drug use, the role of the individual, the morality of war, the draft, the returned veteran, the power of government, sexuality, the roles of men and women, and race issues. These plays present no traditional heroes and nothing heroic. Possibly excepting the TV drama *The Final War of Ollie Winter* (1967), they all contain definite, sometimes strident, antiwar themes.

With their dramatic styles varying widely, most of the plays use expressionistic or absurdist techniques and incorporate innovative character roles and narrators, sparse sets, music, and even puppets. Only about one-fourth to one-third of these plays were eventually published. Many, such as David Jones's *Saigon, Mon Ami Vieille* (1979) received a single production. Many were products of the burgeoning street theater scene in San Francisco and New York, written as protest statements in reaction to specific events.

Although most of the plays were written and produced in the United States, four foreign titles deserve notice. From Australia came Rob George's *Sandy Lee Live at Nui Dat* (1983), which attacks the actions of some Australian soldiers, entertainers, the antiwar movement, and elements of Australian society. Equally sardonic is Peter Brook's *US* (London, 1968), which condemns British citizens and institutions that supported what is portrayed as a U.S. imperialistic venture in Vietnam. David Hare's *Saigon: Year of the Cat* (London, 1983), set during the 1975 fall of Sài Gòn, shows the humanity and confusion of that time. And in a Russian stage version unavailable in English, Graham Greene's *The Quiet American* (1955) was produced later in the USSR.

Many of the major plays fall into three categories: those set in Vietnam, those that focus on racial issues, and those that feature returned veterans. Many playwrights used settings such as firebases, medical trauma rooms, or unspecified Vietnam locations. In-country plays include *The Secret War of Olly Winter* (1967), *Botticelli* (1968), *The Dramatization of 365 Days* (1972), *G. R. Point* (1975), *How I Got That Story* (1979), *Back to Back* (1981), *Dustoff* (1982), *Eleven Zulu* (1983), *Tracers* (1986), and *Five in the Killing Zone* (1989). Dramas that emphasize racial issues are *Indians* (1969), *Soldado Raso* (1971), *Vietnam Campesino* (1971), *Medal of Honor Rag* (1975), *Streamers* (1976), *Back to Back* (1981), *Dustoff* (1982), *Eleven Zulu* (1983), and *Wasted* (1983). Among those that feature the returned veteran are

Sticks and Bones (1969), *Kennedy's Children* (1973), *Medal of Honor Rag* (1975), *Still Life* (1980), *Strange Snow* (1980), and *Tracers* (1983).

The most distinguished playwright of the Vietnam War was David Rabe, who served with the U.S. Army for 11 months in Vietnam, then received his M.A. in theater from Villanova. His first Vietnam-related play, *Sticks and Bones* (1969) was followed by *The Basic Training of Pavlo Hummel* (1971). *Sticks and Bones* was later produced on Broadway and won the 1972 Tony Award for Best Play. In 1976, *Streamers*, produced by Mike Nichols, won the New York Drama Critics Circle Award for the best American play. *Hurlyburly*, also first produced in Chicago by Nichols, moved to Broadway in the mid-1980s and enjoyed a successful run. Rabe wrote numerous other plays and screenplays, winning other distinguished drama awards.

Megan Terry's *Viet Rock* (1966), the earliest play about the war, can be seen as an avant-garde musical. The most popularly acclaimed later production, Alain Boublil's and Claude-Michel Schoenberg's *Miss Saigon* (1988), is a more traditional, albeit high-tech, Broadway musical. Both use striking, expressionistic, dramatic and musical effects. In *Viet Rock*, actors play multiple roles in often surrealistic scenes that include basic training, U.S. Senate committee room proceedings, combat and death in Vietnam, and life in a Việt Cộng prison. There are numerous solo and choral numbers, as well as symbolic group dance scenes in this production that uses the Vietnam War as a modern example of the senselessness of all wars. *Miss Saigon*, a loose retelling of the story line of Puccini's opera *Madame Butterfly*, features a simulated helicopter evacuation during the fall of Sài Gòn, choral and dance production scenes, and dazzling sets and special effects.

Most of these plays should be appreciated more as social than historical documents.

—John Clark Pratt

References: Brecht, Stephan. *The Bread and Puppet Theatre* (1988); Bigsby, C. W. E. *A Critical Introduction to Twentieth-Century American Drama*, Vol. 3 (1985); *Coming to Terms: American Plays and the Vietnam War* (1985); DeRose, David J. "Drama" (1996); Fenn, Jeffery. "Vietnam: The Dramatic Response" (1988).

See also: Art and the Vietnam War; Fiction, U.S., and the Vietnam Experience; Film and the Vietnam Experience; Poetry and the Vietnam Experience; Prose Narrative and the Vietnam Experience.

Drugs and Drug Use

Drug use was a serious problem in Vietnam, especially from 1968 onward. By the time of U.S. withdrawal in 1973, the Department of Defense estimated that almost 70 percent of U.S. servicemen in Vietnam had used some type of illicit drug. Cheap and readily available, drugs provided an escape from the anxiety and boredom prevalent among combat soldiers.

After the 1968 Tết Offensive, drug use rose dramatically, with marijuana the drug of choice for most GIs. A marijuana cigarette cost a dime in Sài Gòn, but cost nothing when Vietnamese threw them into passing American jeeps and trucks. A soldier could buy an entire carton of prerolled marijuana cigarettes in resealed cigarette packs for $5 or a carton of American cigarettes. Smoking marijuana eventually became part of the standard initiation rite for those arriving in Vietnam.

Amphetamines were also popular. Liquid amphetamine, readily available on the black market, was used for staying alert on patrol or for parties in rear areas. Christian Appy noted in *Working-Class War* that some veterans remarked that coming down from an amphetamine high made them so edgy and extremely irritable that they felt like shooting children in the streets. Perhaps for that reason, amphetamines were not as commonly used as marijuana.

Narcotics, such as opium and heroin, ran a distant third behind marijuana and amphetamines for obvious reasons; no one wished to be caught nodding during an ambush. Binges were fairly common in the rear, however, because of low prices and remarkable purity. In Vietnam, soldiers could buy a gram of 95–percent pure heroin for $2. The same amount in the United States cost over $100 and was rarely more than 10–percent pure. Opiates produced more lasting addictions than marijuana or amphetamines and led some veterans to crime to support their habits back in the states.

The high incidence of drug use among GIs in Vietnam may be seen as either a predisposition to use of drugs or as a reaction to the environment. Easy access to the drugs may have been be a determining factor. Statistics show, however, that personnel in Vietnam were much more likely to use drugs than were personnel in Europe, where drugs were also easily accessible. Combat stress certainly accounts for a portion of the disparity. Still, men who had used drugs before entering the military composed the vast bulk of the user population. For the vast majority, this consequence of combat experience was not a lasting one: 93 percent of first-time narcotics users, and 86 percent of first-time marijuana users stopped completely upon returning to the United States.

—Benjamin C. Dubberly

References: Appy, Christian G. *Working-Class War* (1993); Boettcher, Thomas D. *Vietnam, The Valor and the Sorrow* (1985); Lewy, Guenter. *America in Vietnam* (1978).

See also: Draft; Drama and the Vietnam Experience; Film and the Vietnam Experience.

Dulles, Allen Welsh (1893–1969)

Diplomat and head of the Central Intelligence Agency (CIA). Following passage of the National Security Act of 1947, which established the CIA, Dulles headed a study on the role and structure of the agency, which was submitted to President Truman as National Security Council Paper 50 (NSC-50). From 1951 to 1953 Dulles was deputy director at the CIA, and during the Eisenhower administration he served as the agency's director. Because his brother, John Foster Dulles, was Eisenhower's secretary of state, Allen Dulles had more than usual influence on foreign policy.

During the Sect Crisis of 1955, in which South Vietnamese Prime Minister Ngô Đình Diêm challenged the power of the Cao Đài, Hòa Hoa, and Bình Xuyên, French officials and General J. Lawton Collins argued that Diêm was

ineffective and should be removed. The Dulles brothers convinced Eisenhower to continue support for Diêm. Shortly thereafter, the French began a withdrawal and the United States took on primary responsibility for Vietnam. Dulles left office in 1961.

—Kenneth R. Stevens

References: Dulles, Allen. *The Craft of Intelligence* (1963); Mosley, Leonard. *Dulles: A Biography of Eleanor, Allen, and John Foster Dulles and Their Family Network* (1978).

See also: Bình Xuyên; Cao Đài; Central Intelligence Agency (CIA); Collins, Joseph Lawton; Dulles, John Foster; Hòa Hao; McCone, John Alex; Ngô Đình Diêm.

Dulles, John Foster (1888–1959)

Lawyer and diplomat; secretary of state, 1953–1959. As secretary of state in the Eisenhower administration, Dulles criticized the Truman administration's policy of containment as "negative, futile, and immoral." Republican rhetoric promised the "rollback of the iron curtain" plus the prospect of massive nuclear retaliation against attacks by America's enemies.

Dulles's ideas were tested in Southeast Asia in spring 1954. With French military forces under attack by the Viêt Minh at Điên Biên Phu, the Laniel government requested U.S. military intervention. American officials debated Operation VULTURE, a plan for intervention that Dulles favored, but Eisenhower refused unless the plan was supported by the united action of Britain, France, Australia, and New Zealand and by support from the U.S. Congress. Both proved unobtainable. After Điên Biên Phu fell, Dulles helped establish the Southeast Asia Treaty Organization (SEATO) to resist Communist expansion in the region and undertook an increased program of military and economic aid to South Vietnam.

—Kenneth R. Stevens

References: Gerson, Louis L. *John Foster Dulles* (1968); Goold-Adams, Richard. *The Time of Power: A Reappraisal of John Foster Dulles* (1962); Guhin, Michael. *John Foster Dulles: A Statesman and His Times* (1972); Hoopes, Townsend. *The Devil and John Foster Dulles* (1973); Marks, Frederick W., III. *Power and Peace: The Diplomacy of John Foster Dulles* (1993).

See also: Containment Policy; Điên Biên Phu, Battle of; Dulles, Allen Welsh; Eisenhower, Dwight David; Faure, Edgar; Heath, Donald R.; Knowland, William F.; Laniel, Joseph; Murphy, Robert D.; Southeast Asia Treaty Organization (SEATO); VULTURE, Operation.

Duong Quynh Hoa (1930–)

South Vietnamese nationalist; founding member of the National Front for the Liberation of South Vietnam, or National Liberation Front (NLF). Joining the resistance to President Ngô Đình Diêm, Dr. Duong used her access to Sài Gòn social circles to gather information on the Diêm government and its U.S. supporters. In 1960 she became a founding member of the National Liberation Front, while continuing her clandestine activities.

During the Têt Offensive, Dr. Duong and her family slipped out of Sài Gòn to a Viêt Công jungle camp. Appointed deputy minister of health in the NLF's Provisional Revolutionary Government, she worked tirelessly for the remainder of the war, traveling abroad to garner support for the Communist effort. Following the 1975 fall of the Republic of Vietnam, Dr. Duong administered a children's hospital in Hô Chí Minh City (Sài Gòn).

Disillusioned with Socialist Republic of Vietnam leadership, Dr. Duong became a high-profile critic of Vietnamese communism. She observed that the Northerners did not understand local traits and conditions and alienated their Southern compatriots who still clung to their regional character despite attempts to forge a national identity.

—Robert G. Mangrum

References: Hiebert, Murray. "Ex-Communist Official Turns into Vocal Critic" (1993); Karnow, Stanley. *Vietnam: A History* (1991).
See also: National Front for the Liberation of South Vietnam (NFLSV).

Duong Van Đuc (1926–)

Army of the Republic of Vietnam (ARVN) general. He came to command paratroopers in the ARVN and was promoted to brigadier general in 1956. From 1956 to 1957 he served as minister to the Republic of Korea. In September 1964, he participated in an unsuccessful coup, prompted by his being relieved of command of ARVN forces in the Mekong Delta. The coup attempt collapsed within 24 hours.

—Charlotte A. Power

Reference: Karnow, Stanley. *Vietnam: A History* (1983).
See also: Vietnam, Republic of: 1954–1975; Vietnam, Republic of: Army (ARVN).

Duong Van Minh (1916–)

Army of the Republic of Vietnam (ARVN) general and politician. Considered a Diêm loyalist in the military, Minh in early 1956 helped subdue religious sects that were causing problems for the Diêm regime by capturing Hòa Hao guerrilla commander Ba Cut.

Diêm came to view the popular Minh as a threat and, in 1963, after Diêm demoted Minh to special advisor, Generals Trân Van Đôn and Lê Van Kim recruited him into their planned coup. On 5 October 1963, Minh met with Central Intelligence Agency (CIA) operative Lucien Conein at Camp Lê Van Duyêt, Sài Gòn garrison headquarters. He informed Conein that the conspirators did not expect U.S. assistance in the coup, but sought only assurances that the U.S. would not attempt to thwart it. He also asked for more military and economic aid after Diêm's overthrow. This gave Ambassador Henry Cabot Lodge, Jr., the situation he wanted; the United States could encourage the plot without directly assisting the plotters. Conein later told Minh that the United States would not attempt to stop the coup. Minh then assigned General Đôn to continue meeting with Conein.

Minh's bodyguard, Capt. Nguyên Van Nhung, was the executioner in the 1 November 1963 coup, shooting Col. Lê Quang Tung, Maj. Lê Quang Triêu and (along with Maj. Duong Hiêu Nghia) the two Ngô brothers. When news of the deaths reached shocked U.S. authorities, Lodge ordered Conein to meet with Minh who, in a lame alibi claimed that Diêm had committed suicide.

Following the coup, the ruling generals formed a 12–member Military Revolutionary Council. Minh publicly stated that this arrangement would prevent the excesses of the previous regime. In truth, he had created this body to increase his prestige without assuming more personal responsibility. Minh preferred his hobbies to tedious government meetings and business. Lodge tried to help Minh rule but concluded that the general was not strong enough to last long. On 30 January 1964, General Nguyên Khánh conducted a coup in which he had Nhung executed, made Minh the head of state in name only, and made himself prime minister. Khánh replaced Minh in the summer of 1964 when he promoted himself to the presidency. When Sài Gòn erupted in protest, Khánh resigned and the Military Revolutionary Council met to choose a new president. The council decided to install a compromise triumvirate of Khánh, Minh, and General Trân Thiên Khiêm, with Khánh as acting prime minister. In the fall, Khánh continued his plotting and sent Khiêm to Washington as the Republic of Vietnam (RVN) ambassador and assigned Minh to a goodwill tour abroad. When Minh returned to South Vietnam, he was arrested along with other political figures and taken to Pleiku by Khánh and his armed forces council. In the 1971 RVN presidential election, Minh challenged President Nguyên Van Thiêu, but dropped out of the race when he realized he would lose.

Minh played a final political role during the collapse of the RVN. Six days after Thiêu resigned on 21 April 1975, Minh became RVN president. He and his supporters mistakenly thought he would be an acceptable figure to the Communists. As People's Army of Vietnam (PAVN) forces took the presidential palace, they found Minh and his cabinet waiting to transfer the government to the Communists. Minh surrendered unconditionally to the North Vietnamese.

—Michael R. Nichols

References: Bain, Chester A. *Vietnam: The Roots of Conflict* (1967); Davidson, Phillip B. *Vietnam at War: The History: 1946–1975* (1988); Duncanson, Dennis J. *Government and Revolution in Vietnam* (1968); Karnow, Stanley. *Vietnam: A History* (1991); Olson, James, ed. *Dictionary of the Vietnam War* (1987).
See also: Conein, Lucien Emile; Ngô Đình Diêm, Overthrow of ; Hòa Hao; Hô Chí Minh Campaign; Lê Quang Tung; Lê Van Kim; Lodge, Henry Cabot, Jr.; Military Revolutionary Council; Ngô Đình Diêm; Ngô Đình Nhu; Nguyên Khánh; Nguyên Van Thiêu; Trân Thiên Khiêm; Trân Van Đôn.

Dupuis, Jean (1829–1912)

French arms merchant, explorer, and writer who demonstrated the navigability of the Red River for trade with China in 1870. In a daring move in December 1872, Dupuis with a heavily armed company of 150 Asians and 25 Europeans occupied a section of Hà Nôi and appealed for French military assistance. This was not forthcoming, and a few months later he was obliged to leave Hà Nôi without his ships and return to France.

—Arthur J. Dommen

Reference: Buttinger, Joseph. *The Smaller Dragon: A Political History of Vietnam* (1958).
See also: Garnier, Francis; Vietnam: from 938 through the French Conquest.

Durbrow, Elbridge (1903–1997)

U.S. Foreign Service officer; ambassador to the Republic of Vietnam (RVN), March 1957–April 1961. As ambassador to the RVN, Durbrow urged that military aid be conditioned on Sài Gòn's progress in political and economic reform, while Military Assistance and Advisory Group (MAAG) chief Lt. Gen. Samuel T. Williams placed greater emphasis on building the armed forces. Durbrow minimized the guerrilla threat and doubted the need to maintain an army of 150,000, but President Eisenhower's policy of giving priority to military strength remained unchanged.

In early 1960, Durbrow told Ngô Đình Diêm that the repressive actions of his brother, Ngô Đình Nhu, had damaged his regime. After this, Diêm and Durbrow rarely spoke. When the Army of the Republic of Vietnam (ARVN) forces suffered heavy casualties during Viêt Công attacks in mid-1960, even Durbrow supported increased military assistance, but he urged Diêm to relax controls over the press and conduct village elections, and he boldly suggested that Nhu be sent out of the country. Brig. Gen. Edward G. Lansdale called Durbrow's advice "misinformed and unfriendly." Durbrow was certain that without reforms, Diêm's government faced disaster; Lansdale was sure that undercutting Diêm would be counterproductive. Despite U.S. Embassy neutrality during the abortive November 1960 coup, Lansdale and others spread word that Durbrow had welcomed it, thus destroying his effectiveness. Durbrow's final report to the Eisenhower administration acquiesced in the MAAG's proposal for a 20,000–man increase in ARVN armed forces but advised withholding funds pending initiation of reforms.

Lansdale warned President Kennedy of the imminent danger of a Communist victory in Vietnam. Kennedy considered appointing Lansdale the new ambassador, which Dean Rusk rejected along with national security advisor Walt Rostow's attempt to have Lansdale appointed coordinator of Vietnam policy. To replace Durbrow, Kennedy eventually settled on Frederick E. Nolting, another career Foreign Service officer.

—John D. Root

References: Anderson, David L. *Trapped by Success: The Eisenhower Administration and Vietnam, 1953–1961* (1991); Newman, John M. *JFK and Vietnam* (1992); Spector, Ronald H. *Advice and Support: The Early Years of the U.S. Army in Vietnam, 1941–1960* (1985).
See also: Colby, William Egan; Eisenhower, Dwight David; Kennedy, John Fitzgerald; Lansdale, Edward Geary; Ngô Đình Diêm; Ngô Đình Nhu; Nolting, Frederick, Jr.; Rostow, Walt Whitman; Rusk, Dean; Williams, Samuel T.

Duy Tân (1900–1945)

Eleventh emperor of the Nguyên Dynasty; son of Emperor Thành Thái; real name Vinh San. French authorities placed Duy Tân on the throne at age eight. During his nine-year reign, Duy Tân proved to be intelligent and a staunch patriot. In 1915, with France occupied in World War I, he believed it a good opportunity for the Vietnamese to fight for their independence. He secretly contacted leaders of the Viêt Nam Phuc Quôc Hôi (Association for the Restoration of Viet Nam), including Thái Phiên and Trân Cao Vân, and planned an uprising in Thua Thiên, Quang Nam, and Quang Ngãi provinces. The plan was to spread the revolt throughout central Vietnam, and the date for the uprising was set for 3 May 1916. The uprising failed after a mandarin, Phan Liêu of Quang Nam, revealed the plans to the French. The emperor was arrested with his two lieutenants, detained in Mang Cá prison, and later exiled to Reunion Island. After World War II, the French reportedly considered him as a replacement for Emperor Bao Đai.

—Pham Cao Duong

References: Hoàng Trong Thuoc. *Hô So Vua Duy Tân (Thân Thê Và Su Nghiêp)* (1993); Lê Thanh Khoi. *Le Viet-Nam: Histoire et Civilisation* (1955); Nguyên Huyên Anh. *Viêt Nam Danh Nhân Tu Điên* (1990); Nguyên Thê Anh. *Viêt Nam Duoi Thoi Pháp Đô Hô* (1970).
See also: French Indo-China; Nguyên Dynasty.

Dylan, Bob (1941–)

American musician and social protester, born Robert Allen Zimmermann. Dylan was influenced by folk singer Woody Guthrie and the beat generation poetry of Allen Ginsberg. In the 1960s Dylan emerged as a symbol of the counterculture movement, radicalizing popular music and underscoring domestic tensions. The civil rights and antiwar movements adopted as anthems Dylan's "Blowin' in the Wind" and "The Times They Are A-Changin'." Dylan's songs frequently criticized the Vietnam War. "John Brown," performed for years but not officially released until 1995, tells of a young man sent to the war much to the delight of his mother, who represents the establishment; the soldier returns disabled but with medals to present to his mother. Dylan's "Masters of War" holds the older generation responsible for creating a situation in which military leaders could hide the horrors of war "while young people's blood runs out of their bodies and into the mud."

In 1965, Dylan unveiled a new blend of folk and rock incorporating electric instruments and broader subject matter. Folk purists criticized this change, but Dylan reached a larger audience and emerged as a rock star. His songs maintained their social commentary and helped change conceptions about popular rock music. Dylan's credibility and commercial success paved the way for other protest rock performers in the 1960s and beyond.

—Dallas Cothrum

References: Heylin, Clinton. *Bob Dylan: Behind the Shades* (1991); Scadato, Anthony. *Bob Dylan* (1971); Shelton, Robert. *No Direction Home: The Life and Music of Bob Dylan* (1986).
See also: Antiwar Movement, United States; Baez, Joan Chandos; Students for a Democratic Society (SDS); Weathermen.

E

EAGLE PULL, Operation (12 April 1975)
Air evacuation of Phnom Penh, Cambodia. On 27 June 1973, the U.S. Support Activities Group/Seventh Air Force (USSAG/7AF) at Nakhon Phanom Royal Thai Air Force Base (RTAFB), Thailand, published Contingency Plan 5060C (CONPLAN 5060C, code-named "EAGLE PULL) concerning the evacuation of Phnom Penh. Rescue units received the EAGLE PULL plan as Khmer Rouge units closed in on the capital and it seemed that Phnom Penh and all of Cambodia would fall. But when U.S. bombing stopped on 15 August 1973, the Cambodian Army repulsed the Khmer Rouge attack.

Over the next 20 months, USSAG/7AF changed EAGLE PULL to meet evolving circumstances. As one Cambodian town after another fell to the Khmer Rouge, EAGLE PULL focused only on evacuating Americans and a handful of others from Phnom Penh. A complex prioritization system that classified noncombatant evacuees by sex, age, and physical condition was developed, and a U.S. Marine Corps ground security force was added to the plan.

On 3 April 1975, as Khmer Rouge forces again closed in on Phnom Penh, EAGLE PULL forces were put on alert. An 11–man Marine element, flown into the city to prepare for the arrival of the evacuation helicopters, designated a soccer field near the American Embassy as "Landing Zone Hotel." On 10 April, Ambassador Gunther Dean asked that EAGLE PULL be executed no later than 12 April.

At 0850 on 12 April, an Aerospace Rescue and Recovery Service (ARRS) HH-53 landed a four-man Air Force combat control team to coordinate the operation. Three minutes later, it guided in a Marine Corps CH-53 with the first element of the Marine security force. Marine and Air Force helicopters carried 276 evacuees, including 82 Americans, 159 Cambodians, and 35 foreign nationals, to U.S. Navy assault carriers in the Gulf of Thailand. By 1000, the Marine contingency force, the advanced 11–man element, and the combat control team had been evacuated. There were no casualties.

—Earl H. Tilford, Jr.

References: Benjamin, Milton R., and Paul Rogers, Brinkley. "Farewell to Phnom Penh" (1975); Tilford, Earl H., Jr. *A History of U.S. Air Force Search and Rescue in Southeast Asia, 1961–1975* (1980).
See also: Cambodia; Search-and-Rescue (SAR) Operations.

Easter Offensive (Nguyên Huê Campaign) (1972)
Massive, coordinated three-pronged attack designed to strike a decisive blow against the Republic of Vietnam (RVN) government and its armed forces. Within two weeks of its beginning on 30 March, large conventional battles were fought simultaneously on three major fronts. The People's Army of Vietnam (PAVN) used conventional tactics and introduced weaponry beyond that of previous campaigns. The largest offensive ever launched by Hà Nôi, it was a radical departure from past Democratic Republic of Vietnam (DRV) strategy and methods of warfare.

DRV leaders decided to employ conventional tactics for this offensive for several reasons. They did not believe that the Americans, with only 65,000 troops left in Vietnam, could influence the strategic situation or that the political situation in the United States would permit President Nixon to commit new troops or combat support to assist ARVN. They hoped to discredit Nixon's Vietnamization and pacification programs and cause faster withdrawal of remaining U.S. forces. Additionally, a resounding DRV military victory would humiliate Nixon and perhaps help defeat his reelection bid, leaving the White House open to a more moderate president less disposed to further U.S. involvement in Vietnam.

General Vô Nguyên Giáp was the architect of the Nguyên Huê Campaign. According to seized documents and information obtained from PAVN prisoners of war after the invasion, the campaign was designed to destroy as many ARVN forces as possible, thus permitting the Communists to occupy key South Vietnamese cities and their forces to be in position to threaten the government of President Nguyen Van Thiêu directly. Giáp hoped to achieve a knock-out blow, but if that could not be achieved, he hoped to seize at least enough critical terrain to strengthen the North Vietnamese position in any subsequent negotiations.

Throughout 1971, Hà Nôi requested and received large quantities of modern weapons from the Soviet Union and China, including MiG-21 jets, surface-to-air (SAM) missiles, T-54 medium tanks, 130-mm guns, 160-mm mortars, 57-mm antiaircraft guns, and for the first time, heat-seeking, shoulder-fired SA-7 Strella antiaircraft missiles. Other war supplies were shipped to North Vietnam in unprecedented quantities.

The offensive plan called for a multidivisional attack across the Demilitarized Zone (DMZ), toward Huê and Dà Nang, with other forces pressing in from the A Shau Valley in the west. Giáp wanted to force Thiêu to commit reserves to protect his northern provinces, upon which he would launch a second assault from Cambodia to threaten Sài Gòn. Then Giáp would launch the third attack in the Central Highlands to take Kontum and aim for the coast in Bình Đinh Province, splitting the RVN in two and leading to its collapse or, at least, a peace agreement on Hà Nôi's terms.

The North Vietnamese offensive began on 30 March 1972, when three PAVN divisions, reinforced by T-54 medium tanks, attacked south across the DMZ and along Highway 9 out of Laos toward Quang Tri and Huê in I Corps. Three days later, three additional divisions pushed into Bình Long Province from Cambodian sanctuaries, capturing Lôc Ninh and surrounding An Lôc, the provincial capital, 65 miles from Sài Gòn. Additional PAVN forces attacked across the Cambodian border in the Central Highlands toward Kontum in II Corps. Finally, two more PAVN divisions took control of several districts in Bình Đinh Province, along the South China Sea. The PAVN assaults were characterized by human wave attacks backed by tanks and massive artillery support.

Fourteen PAVN infantry divisions and 26 separate regiments (including 120,000 troops and 1,200 tanks and other armored vehicles) participated in the offensive.

The PAVN thrusts initially were successful, particularly in northern South Vietnam, where they quickly overran the newly formed ARVN 3d Division in Quang Tri. The PAVN also threatened both Huê and Kontum, but ARVN forces were able to stiffen their defenses north of Huê while defenders at Kontum were also successful in halting the PAVN assault there. ARVN forces at An Lôc, besieged by the PAVN and sustaining repeated ground attacks and massive artillery and rocket fire, held out until the siege there was broken in July 1972.

Nixon resumed bombing North Vietnam on 8 May 1972 and ordered mining of Hai Phòng Harbor and other North Vietnamese ports. This took some pressure off ARVN forces, but intense fighting continued throughout the summer in South Vietnam. In June, ARVN forces in Military Region I launched a counteroffensive, and eventually recaptured Quang Tri Province. The Easter Offensive had failed.

Although the ARVN's combat performance had been uneven, it had held, supported by U.S. advisors and massive American air power, including B-52 strikes that repeatedly broke up attacking enemy formations. North Vietnam lost an estimated 100,000 or more killed and at least half of their large-caliber artillery and tanks. However, the PAVN controlled more territory in South Vietnam than before, and Hà Nôi believed it was in a stronger bargaining position at the Paris negotiations. Nevertheless, the success of South Vietnamese forces in confronting the North Vietnamese onslaught was touted as proof that Nixon's Vietnamization policy had worked.

—James H. Willbanks

References: Clarke, Jeffrey J. *Advice and Support: The Final Year* (1988); Lavalle, A. J. C., ed. *Airpower and the 1972 Spring Invasion* (1976); Ngo Quang Truong. *The Easter Offensive of 1972* (1980); Turley, G. H. *The Easter Offensive* (1985); Willbanks, James H. *Thiet Giap! The Battle of An Loc, April 1972* (1993).

See also: An Lôc, Battle of; Nixon, Richard Milhous; Nguyên Van Thiêu; Pacification; Quang Tri, Battle of; Vietnamization; Vô Nguyên Giáp.

Economy, U.S., and the War

To fight the Vietnam War, the Johnson administration had to increase defense expenditures. Because tax revenues did not keep pace with expenditure increases, and reductions in other spending did not occur, the war was partially financed by deficit spending.

From 1965 to 1969, as U.S. involvement in the war increased most dramatically, defense expenditures increased by $31.9 billion while total federal government outlays increased by $65.4 billion, indicating that the defense buildup was not being financed by reductions in other parts of the budget. Tax revenue increases did not keep pace with the increased spending; thus, the deficit reached $25.2 billion in fiscal year 1968.

An increased budget deficit results in increased overall price levels, a decreased unemployment rate, an increased output level, a deterioration in the international trade account, and increased interest rates. The impact of the increased deficits was as expected through 1969. The economy did well as measured by the real gross domestic product and unemployment rate, but the cost was felt in inflation, increased international trade deficit, and higher interest rates.

There is some evidence that private sector expenditures were adversely affected by the deficit spending associated with the war. Increased interest rates should reduce private-sector expenditures that are financed by borrowing, such as homes, business investments, and consumer durable goods. Construction of new private housing units, net fixed investment expenditures, and expenditures on consumer durable goods decreased during this period.

Another aspect of the war's impact was a massive rethinking of macroeconomic theory that occurred because of the difficulty encountered when the Nixon administration embarked on policies to decrease the inflation rate. A steady increase in the price level and a decrease in the unemployment rate occurred from 1965 through 1969, but then something curious happened. The price level continued to rise in 1970–1972 while the unemployment rate also increased. In 1972 the unemployment rate was 1.1 percentage points (24.4 percent) higher than in 1965, and the price level was still increasing.

Consider what we would expect the data to show, given macroeconomic theory at the time. The Vietnam War caused increased government expenditures not fully financed by tax increases, leading to a demand-side expansion during 1964–1969. Data for those years match what should happen in a demand-side expansion—increased price level and reduced unemployment. In response to increased inflation, the Nixon administration embarked on the standard policy response of a tight government budget and tight monetary policy. If all went according to theory, reduced inflation would result in some increased unemployment, but the increase should match the decrease in unemployment that occurred during the expansionary phase. Thus, an unemployment rate increase to 4.9 percent should have reduced the inflation rate to about 1.4 to 1.5 percent. If the policy further increased the unemployment rate to 5.9 percent, the inflation rate should have decreased further to under 1 percent. Instead, the inflation rate increased to 5.7 percent and then decreased to 4.4 percent. (The 1971 inflation rate was misleading, as the Nixon administration had imposed price and wage controls in August 1971.) Something had gone wrong.

There was a tradeoff between inflation and unemployment, leading policymakers to believe one could choose how much of each the economy should have. An increase in the inflation rate would be accompanied by a decrease in the unemployment rate, and a decrease in the inflation rate would be accompanied by an increase in the unemployment rate. The first aspect worked fine during 1965–1969, but the process did not reverse itself in 1970–1971.

The changes in macroeconomic theory spawned by the unreaction of the inflation rate resulted in the supply-side policies of the 1980s and 1990s. The only way that the inflation rate could continue to increase when unemployment was also increasing was if something was occurring on the supply side as well. The first attempt to analyze these "somethings" was with the role of expectations on labor supply. It was thought that inflation would not be expected when it had been historically low, so that wages were slow to catch up to price increases. Once inflation becomes expected, wage increases would match, or even precede, price increases. This would have the effect of raising production costs and the unemployment rate. This was called adaptive expectations. It had the side effect of implying that activist government demand-management policy would be ineffective, which led to the next step in the theory revamping. Why would people be slow to catch on to inflation? If it was known that expansionary policy would cause inflation, then as soon as an expansionary policy was "discovered," wages and prices would immediately adjust and no expansion could occur. Even more important, government attempts to stabilize the economy would only result in destabilization; thus, the government must cease all efforts at demand management and move to the supply side of the economy. What could be done on the supply side? Remove the impediments to work efforts and saving. These could be accomplished by lowering taxes and reducing regulations.

In summary, the deficit financing of the war led to a demand-side expansion that increased the Consumer Price Index, the international trade deficit, and interest rates. Increased interest rates decreased some private expenditures. The inflation that occurred did not respond to the traditional demand-side remedy, and therefore led to a massive rethinking of macroeconomic theory.

—Edward M. McNertney

References: Matusow, Allen J. *The Unraveling of America: A History of Liberalism in the 1960s* (1984); Stein, Herbert. *Presidential Economics: The Making of Economic Policy from Roosevelt to Reagan and Beyond* (1984); U.S. Council of Economic Advisors. *Economic Report of the President.*
See also: Great Society Program; Johnson, Lyndon Baines; Nixon, Richard Milhous; United States: Involvement in Vietnam, 1965–1968; United States: Involvement in Vietnam, 1969–1973.

Eden, Anthony (1897–1977)

British foreign minister who helped negotiate the 1954 Geneva Accords; British prime minister, 1955–1957. British foreign policy concerns in Southeast Asia centered on the well-being of investments in Thailand and Malaya and the potential spread of communism. Eden believed as early as 1953 that Communist expansion could be halted if their control of Vietnam was limited to the North. Eden cochaired the 1954 Geneva Conference and, despite U.S. Secretary of State John Foster Dulles's push for military intervention, worked to forge an alternative to a larger war. Acting as an intermediary between the Soviets, Chinese, and Americans, he brokered a political division of the area, conceding the North to the Communists.

—Laura Matysek Wood

References: Aster, Sidney, *Anthony Eden* (1976); Rothwell, Victor. *Anthony Eden: A Political Biography, 1931–57* (1992).
See also: Dulles, John Foster; French Indo-China; Geneva Conference and Geneva Accords; Great Britain; Molotov (née Scriabin), Vyacheslav Mikhailovich.

Eisenhower, Dwight David (1890–1969)

General of the Army; U.S. president, 1953–1961. During World War II, Eisenhower rose rapidly in rank and responsibility and commanded Operation TORCH, the November 1942 Allied invasion of North Africa. Later he commanded the cross-channel invasion of France and became Supreme Allied Commander in Europe. After the war, Eisenhower returned to the United States and in 1952, ran as Republican presidential candidate against Democrat Adlai Stevenson. He was easily elected and served two terms (1953–1961).

Eisenhower's defense policies placed emphasis on nuclear weapons at the expense of conventional forces. But at the end of his tenure in office, Eisenhower also warned the nation about the cost to society of unbridled military spending and the growth of a "military-industrial complex." Eisenhower endeavored to calm tensions arising from the Cold War. Early in his first term, an armistice was achieved in Korea partly through his pledge to "go to Korea" and his bluffing about the possible use of nuclear weapons. The latter so impressed Vice-President Richard Nixon that early in his own presidency he tried the same technique (the "Madman Strategy") against the Democratic Republic of Vietnam (DRV), but without success. Eisenhower's efforts to reduce international tensions with the Soviet Union's Nikita Khrushchev were stymied in part because of Central Intelligence Agency missteps such as the U-2 incident.

Eisenhower's Indo-China policies were cautious and measured. He followed the containment doctrine begun by Truman, and his administration subscribed to the domino theory that a Viêt Minh victory in Vietnam would soon bring Communists to power throughout Southeast Asia. He increased U.S. weapons and logistical support for the French in Indo-China, and by 1954 the United States was paying as much as 80 percent of the cost of the war there. Under Eisenhower, a Military Assistance Advisory Group (MAAG) was created for Indo-China, although the French insisted that all military aid be channeled through them. Publicly the Eisenhower administration supported the French line that they had turned over real political control in Vietnam to the Vietnamese and that the war was a Cold War struggle between democracy and communism, not a colonial war for independence. Privately, as late as 1953 Eisenhower was pushing U.S. Ambassador to France C. Douglas Dillon to insist that the French grant real independence to Vietnam.

In spring 1954, Eisenhower debated active U.S. military intervention, including possible use of nuclear weapons, to help rescue the French garrison at Điên Biên Phu. He resisted advocates of intervention, such as Nixon, Chairman of the Joint Chiefs of Staff Adm. Arthur Radford, and Secretary of State John Foster Dulles, because Army Chief of Staff General

Matthew B. Ridgway was firmly opposed and because the British government refused to participate. Eisenhower was, in any case, considering only air strikes and material support, not ground troops.

Eisenhower said he would not leave his party open to charges of having "lost" Vietnam. The State Department participated in the Geneva talks only as an observer, and the Eisenhower administration distanced itself from the resulting Geneva Accords. John Foster Dulles led the way in creating the Southeast Asia Treaty Organization (SEATO), which proved unsupportive of U.S. plans to create a separate state in southern Vietnam and, if need be, fight collectively to maintain it. The Eisenhower administration gave unqualified and substantial economic and political support to Republic of Vietnam President Ngô Đình Diêm's government and supported Diêm's refusal to hold the elections called for in the Geneva Accords.

After leaving office in 1961, Eisenhower continued to support U.S. involvement in Vietnam as a private citizen. He reportedly warned President Kennedy to stand firm there, although he disliked Kennedy's acceptance of a coalition government in Laos. Eisenhower also disapproved of President Johnson's failure to use sufficient military force to bring the war to a successful conclusion, but he insisted that the Vietnamese do the bulk of the fighting themselves. He opposed Johnson's bombing halt, and he considered some antiwar demonstrations tantamount to treason. In 1968 he enthusiastically Nixon for the presidency.

—Spencer C. Tucker

References: Alexander, Charles C. *Holding the Line: The Eisenhower Era, 1952–1961* (1975); Ambrose, Stephen E. *Eisenhower.* Vol. 2. *President and Elder Statesman* (1984); Billings-Yun, Melanie. *Decision against War: Eisenhower and Dien Bien Phu* (1988); Divine, Robert A. *Eisenhower and the Cold War* (1981); Eisenhower, Dwight D. *The White House Years* (1963–1965); Spector, Ronald H. *United States Army in Vietnam. Advice and Support: The Early Years, 1941–1960* (1983).

See also: Central Intelligence Agency (CIA); Điên Biên Phu, Battle of; Dulles, John Foster; Eden, Anthony; Kennedy, John Fitzgerald; Johnson, Lyndon Baines; Madman Strategy; Murphy, Robert D.; Ngô Đình Diêm; Nixon, Richard Milhous; Radford, Arthur W.; Ridgway, Matthew B.; Southeast Asia Treaty Organization (SEATO); Truman, Harry S; Twining, Nathan Farragut; United States: Involvement in Indo-China through 1954; VULTURE, Operation.

EL PASO, Operation (June–July 1966)

Military operation conducted by the U.S. 1st Infantry Division against the 9th Việt Công (VC) Division in Bình Long Province, War Zone C. EL PASO's objective was to open Route 13 and deter a VC offensive against An Lôc before the monsoon season. The first of four major encounters occurred on 8 June when the 272d VC Regiment ambushed Troop A, 1st Squadron, 4th Cavalry, north of the Ấp Tàu Ô bridge on Route 13, disabling several tanks and armored personnel carriers (APCs). The cavalry underestimated the size of the VC force. Although infantry arrived too late to be a factor, they claimed more than 100 of the enemy. Three days,

later the 2d Battalion, 28th Infantry (2/28th) battled an entrenched 273d VC Regiment northwest of Lôc Ninh.

On 30 June, the 271st VC Regiment ambushed Troop B, 1st Squadron, at Srok Dong on Route 13 south of Lôc Ninh, taking out four tanks and inflicting heavy casualties. Troop C advanced to evacuate the dead and wounded and clear a landing zone for the insertion of two companies of the 2d Battalion, 18th Infantry (2/18th). The VC initially offered stiff resistance but soon broke contact. Only U.S. air superiority prevented a major Communist victory. Maj. Gen. William E. DePuy, commanding the 1st Infantry Division, then developed a plan to lure the VC into attacking his armor.

Rumors circulated that a large U.S. column would move up Route 13 and a smaller one down Minh Thanh Road, running southwest from An Lôc. The opposite was true. Potential ambush sites were identified along Minh Thanh Road, and two armored cavalry troops and a company of mechanized infantry prepared to move. Two other companies were airlifted into counterambush positions and artillery was positioned at Minh Thanh village.

Early on 9 July, following artillery and air strikes, the task force passed the first checkpoint, but before reaching the second the 272d VC Regiment attacked Troop C, 1st Squadron, 4th Cavalry, knocking out the lead tank and destroying two M-113s. Air and artillery fire was called, and Troop B moved forward. When the VC was found to be west of the road, the pre-positioned infantry went into action, attacking the ambush force frontally and from both flanks. Well-timed air strikes ended the ambush.

EL PASO ended on 13 July. The VC had lost 855 dead and failed to seize An Lôc. Although U.S. forces suffered nearly 200 casualties, the operation was termed a success because Route 13 was reopened and secure. Learning from the near disasters of the two engagements before the battle of Minh Than Road, the 1st Division had developed an effective counterambush tactic by which armored cavalry with coordinated air and artillery support would be used as a fixing force against a numerically superior enemy until airmobile infantry could be inserted as encircling maneuver elements.

—John D. Root

References: Stanton, Shelby L. *The Rise and Fall of the American Army: U.S. Ground Forces in Vietnam, 1965–1973* (1985); Starry, Donn A. *Armored Combat in Vietnam* (1982).

See also: ATTLEBORO, Operation; DePuy, William E; United States: Army; War Zone C and War Zone D.

Elections, U.S.: 1968

Startling political developments in the 1968 U.S. presidential race included Lyndon Johnson's decision not to seek the Democratic Party's nomination and the election of Republican Richard Nixon, who was not expected to return to national politics after his 1960 and 1962 losses.

Opposition to Johnson's renomination started in late 1967 when Allard Lowenstein originated a "Dump Johnson" movement. Senator Eugene McCarthy, a Vietnam War opponent, announced his candidacy for the nomination in late 1967. In the first presidential primary (12 March), thousands of

"Clean for Gene" college students canvassed New Hampshire voters. McCarthy lost, but his unexpectedly strong showing against a sitting president (42.4 percent versus Johnson's 49.5 percent) exposed Johnson's vulnerability. Johnson's weakened position was not lost on Senator Robert Kennedy, who also opposed Johnson's war policies. Kennedy declared his candidacy a few days after the New Hampshire primary. In a nationally televised address on 31 March, Johnson announced a partial bombing halt of North Vietnam and then stunned the nation by stating, "I shall not seek, and I will not accept, the nomination of my party for another term as your president."

The Republican convention was held in August in Miami Beach, followed by the Democratic convention in Chicago. Only one-third of the delegates attending both parties' national conventions were selected at primary elections. Most delegates were controlled by state party leaders and were selected in state conventions and caucuses rather than primaries. The eventual nominee was determined by candidates bargaining with leaders of state delegations.

Richard Nixon spent much of 1966 cementing his ties with the Republican Party by raising money and campaigning for its candidates for Congress. Early 1968 polls of Republican voters showed Nixon almost a 2-to-1 favorite over Governor Nelson Rockefeller, with Governor George Romney a poor third. Nixon had the support of party regulars and used the primaries to demonstrate support among Republican voters.

The Democratic road to the convention was anything but smooth. Vice-President Hubert Humphrey announced his candidacy in late April, avoiding all primaries and dealing directly with delegates and state party leaders. Although McCarthy and Kennedy traded early primary victories, Kennedy won the last one in delegate-rich California, only to be assassinated minutes after his victory speech. His death ensured Humphrey's nomination.

Governor George Wallace formed a third party, the American Independence Party. He was on the ballot in all 50 states, but only after considerable work in gathering signatures on petitions and occasionally requesting and receiving help from federal courts.

At the start of the general election campaign, the Gallup poll showed Nixon (43 percent) with a clear lead over Humphrey (31 percent) and Wallace (19 percent). In opinion surveys, Americans saw the Vietnam War as the most important problem facing the country (51 percent); nearly half thought the United States was mistaken in sending troops to Vietnam; and nearly two-thirds disapproved of Johnson's handling of the war. The Vietnam War eclipsed civil rights and law-and-order issues by a more than 2-to-1 lead. There was little difference between Humphrey's and Nixon's stated positions on Vietnam policy. Both favored a gradual reduction of U.S. forces, replacing them with Republic of Vietnam soldiers. Neither had a timetable in mind; both opposed invading North Vietnam.

Nixon disparaged Johnson's war policies but avoided discussing specifics for fear of undermining efforts to get real negotiations started. In Salt Lake City on 30 September, Humphrey tried to disassociate himself from Johnson's policies by proposing a complete bombing halt of North Vietnam to improve the outlook for negotiations. Wallace said that if negotiations failed, he would ask the military for a plan to win. Voters perceived Humphrey and Nixon as occupying a middle position between hawk and dove, with Wallace closest to the hawk position. Most voters occupied the middle position, which might be described as "Don't pull out, but try to end the fighting."

Humphrey's standing in the polls was improved by the Salt Lake City speech and organized labor's efforts to bring back to the Democratic Party members who were leaning toward Wallace. Mid-October polls showed support for Nixon at 44 percent and Humphrey at 36 percent, but Humphrey continued to gain, and by Election Day the race was a tossup between him and Nixon.

In the weeks before the election, the Johnson administration searched for a way to make progress in the Paris peace talks that had begun in May. Johnson announced a complete bombing halt on 31 October, five days before the election, but RVN representatives did not attend the Paris negotiations until 25 January 1969. It is not certain whether the start of serious negotiations before the election would have affected its outcome. The voters' judgment was that the policies of Johnson and the Democrats had failed. In the popular vote, Nixon received 31,770,237, Humphrey 31,270,533, and Wallace 9,906,141. In the Electoral College, Nixon received 301 votes, Humphrey, 191, and Wallace, 46.

—Harry Basehart

References: Asher, Herbert B. *Presidential Elections & American Politics* (1992); Clifford, Clark. *Counsel to the President* (1991); Converse, Philip E., Warren E. Miller, Jerrold G. Rusk, and Arthur C. Wolfe. "Continuity and Change in American Politics: Parties and Issues in the 1968 Election" (1969); Page, Benjamin I., and Richard A. Brody. "Policy Voting and the Electoral Process: The Vietnam War Issue" (1972); White, Theodore H. *The Making of the President, 1968* (1969).

See also: Antiwar Movement, United States; Democratic Party National Convention, 1968; Humphrey, Hubert H.; Johnson, Lyndon Baines; Kennedy, Robert Francis; Lowenstein, Allard K.; McCarthy, Eugene Joseph; Nguyên Van Thiêu; Nixon, Richard Milhous; Paris Peace Accords; Rockefeller, Nelson A.; Romney, George W.; Wallace, George Corley, Jr.

Elections, U.S.: 1972

Richard Nixon's reelection was not a foregone conclusion at the beginning of 1972. A Gallup survey of voters in January found a close contest. Nixon was favored by 43 percent; Senator Edmund Muskie, the likely Democratic nominee, polled 42 percent; and George Wallace, as a third-party candidate, had 12 percent. The remaining 3 percent of voters polled were undecided.

By late 1971 Nixon's Vietnam policies had reduced the number of U.S. soldiers in Vietnam to 156,800 men. In January 1972 Nixon announced that, in addition to ongoing formal peace talks in Paris, secret negotiations between the

United States and North Vietnam had started in August 1969. Neither had made any progress. The Gallup poll and other surveys showed voters still identified the Vietnam War as the most important issue facing the country, but the percentage holding this view (25 percent) was about half as large as it had been in 1968. Fifty-two percent of the public approved of Nixon's handling of the Vietnam War; 39 percent disapproved, and 9 percent had no opinion. Inflation and unemployment were on voters' minds as much as the Vietnam War.

Nixon announced that he would seek reelection in early January. Facing little opposition within his party, he won the New Hampshire primary with nearly 70 percent of the vote. Nixon was renominated by the Republican National Convention at Miami Beach in August.

In addition to McGovern and Muskie, serious candidates for the Democratic nomination were Hubert Humphrey and George Wallace. Wallace planned to enter several Democratic primaries and also kept open the option of a third-party candidacy. The road to capturing the nomination at the 1972 Democratic Convention was much different than previous ones.

Almost overlooked at the tumultuous 1968 convention was the adoption of resolutions authorizing creation of a commission to reform the national convention delegate selection process. The McGovern-Fraser Commission, as it was informally called, adopted guidelines that, among other changes, encouraged each state to have minority groups, women, and people between ages 18 and 30 in their delegation in "reasonable relationship to their presence in the population of the state." This was not to be interpreted as a quota system, the commission said, but it was widely perceived as one. Also important, but less noticed, was the elimination of ex-officio delegates. To comply with the recommendations, many states simply switched to primaries to select delegates. In the 1972 convention, 60 percent of the delegates were chosen in primaries, up from only 38 percent in 1968. These new rules angered party regulars who lost influence, as they saw it, to individuals who were committed to a candidate or issue but not to the party.

George McGovern thundered from obscurity with a strong second-place finish in the New Hampshire primary, much as Eugene McCarthy had done in 1968. Muskie faded in subsequent primaries and ceased to be a viable candidate. Wallace won the Florida primary and went on to win alternating primary victories with Humphrey and McGovern. An assassination attempt on Wallace while campaigning in Maryland forced him from the race. The showdown between Humphrey and McGovern was in California, where McGovern emerged victorious; because of California's "winner-takes-all" law, all of the delegates were bound to vote for McGovern. In a crucial procedural vote at the Democratic Convention in Miami Beach, the unit rule was allowed for California although it went against commission guidelines. McGovern was nominated on the first ballot.

The general election campaign began with the Gallup poll showing Nixon had 64 percent to McGovern's 30 percent; 6 percent remained undecided. The full story of what would become the Watergate scandal was contained by the White House, and Nixon's involvement in the cover-up was kept secret during the election. Most voters were satisfied with Nixon's policy of gradual withdrawal, and McGovern's proposals for defense spending cuts and a controversial welfare program were viewed as extreme. Voters also questioned McGovern's competence, a problem underscored when the media disclosed that his vice-presidential nominee, Senator Thomas Eagleton, had suffered from mental exhaustion and undergone electric-shock treatments. Initially McGovern said that he backed Eagleton, but he soon dropped his beleaguered running mate in favor of Sargent Shriver.

Still, the Vietnam War was more than a backdrop issue. The war dramatically reasserted itself on 26 October, when the Democratic Republic of Vietnam unexpectedly revealed that secret negotiations had produced an agreement to end the war. National Security Advisor Henry Kissinger, despite difficulty in gaining Sài Gòn's acceptance of the agreement, announced "Peace is at hand."

Nixon's landslide victory may have been more a rejection of McGovern than a mandate for president. In the popular vote, Nixon received 47,169,911 votes; McGovern received 29,170,383. The Electoral College vote was 521 for Nixon to only 17 for McGovern.

—Harry Basehart

References: Asher, Herbert B. *Presidential Elections & American Politics* (1992); Isaacs, Arnold R. *Without Honor* (1983); Miller, Arthur H., Warren E. Miller, Alden S. Raine, and Thad A. Brown. "A Majority Party in Disarray: Policy Polarization in the 1972 Election" (1976); Ranney, Austin. *Curing the Mischiefs of Faction* (1975); White, Theodore H. *The Making of the President, 1972* (1973).

See also: Elections, U.S.: 1968; Humphrey, Hubert H.; Kissinger, Henry Alfred; McGovern, George S.; Nixon, Richard Milhous; Wallace, George Corley, Jr.; Watergate.

Elections (National), Republic of Vietnam: 1955, 1967, 1971

Accruing political legitimacy was a principal difficulty facing all Republic of Vietnam (RVN) governments. Development of a politically viable electoral system was seen as one way of bolstering support. Such an effort would provide legitimacy, accountability, and stability and would help develop interest-group and political-party participation in the government. Declassified Defense Department, State Department, and security agency documents reveal an ethnocentric pattern combining desire for true reform and democratic institution-building with determination to reject any results indicating that the South Vietnamese people favored choices differing from what the U.S. government thought they should seek. Washington undoubtedly demanded that the South Vietnamese recast themselves and their government in the U.S. image. Equally certain is that the United States helped President Ngô Đình Diêm consolidate his authority, prevented the unifying election called for by the 1954 Geneva Accords, assisted RVN President Nguyên Van Thiêu in eliminating opponents in 1967, and did the same in 1971.

Election of 1955 In 1954 the Eisenhower administration

supported Catholic anti-Communist Ngô Đình Diêm's efforts in establishing a pro–U.S. government in the southern half of the country. Washington favored Diêm over playboy Emperor Bao Đai, head of the State of Vietnam that had been established during the Indo-China War. The extent of U.S. support for Diêm became clear in October 1954, when Washington decided to channel all economic and military assistance directly to his government rather than through the French mission. Later, critics such as Edward S. Herman and F. Brodhead charged that the election process in South Vietnam produced the appearance of a democracy that did not exist there. Official documents bear out this assessment.

An excerpt of National Security Council draft 5519 (17 May 1955) summarizes the basic situation in South Vietnam with regard to the all-Vietnam elections called for by the 1954 Geneva Accords. Essentially, the United States and the Diêm administration weighed the dilemma of appearing undemocratic if they avoided or postponed the elections against the danger of losing to a better organized Communist Party apparatus if elections were held. In lieu of elections, Washington recommended a strategy whereby the Diêm government would engage in talks with the Việt Minh about preconditions for the elections to insure their integrity. It is clear from Secretary of State John Foster Dulles's memo that Washington's strategy was to make the conditions mirror those supported by the West in other areas. Dulles assumed that such conditions would be so difficult for the Communists that they would be refused. Although Dulles said that the Communists could never win a free election, memos from the State Department to the Sài Gòn embassy indicates that Washington was prepared to "review" the entire situation if the Communists did win an election.

The Communists sought the elections called for in the accords because they were confident of winning them. The Communists believed that they held the nationalist card from having led the fight against the Japanese and French. The Communists also believed that they benefited from Diêm's use of force to silence political opposition. In his efforts to crush opposition, Diêm abolished local (village level) elections and installed political friends and supporters.

In the end, Diêm refused to even discuss the unification election issue. In a radio broadcast of 16 July 1955, he rejected free elections while simultaneously promising freedom for all Vietnam. The implication was that the Communists would have to give up power in the North before there could be discussions of elections. Instead of an election, Diêm arranged a referendum in South Vietnam between himself and Bao Đai, held on 23 October 1955. There was rampant election fraud, and Diêm received 5.7 million votes to 63,000 for Bao Đai. Diêm would probably have won a free election easily, and the U.S. embassy thought that his total of 98.9 percent of the vote was excessive.

On 4 March 1956, the South Vietnamese elected a national legislative assembly of 123 members. The initial constitution for South Vietnam—described by Robert Scigliano as an "executive-drafted document ... by a handful of intimate advisors to Diem"—was developed. Diêm submitted only a general statement of basic principles to the assembly to provide the appearance that the finished product was of their making. The constitution was to have been ratified by the voting public, but Diêm later reconsidered and had the assembly ratify it. The constitution came into effect on 26 October 1956.

Election of 1967 Development of more meaningful national institutional structures continued after Diêm's assassination. The Republic of Vietnam's Constitution of 1967, ratified on 1 April 1967, reflected several improvements over the original 1956 constitution. It provided for a judiciary equal to the executive and legislative branches and called for establishment of an Upper House (Senate) to the National Assembly. It acknowledged the acceptability of political parties and opposition to the government, although neither of these provisions could be taken too far. The complex electoral law involved ten-member slates, and voters in 1967 had to choose from 48 such slates. This ensured that well-organized voting blocs could achieve electoral power.

In the 3 September 1967 election, Army General Nguyên Van Thiêu and Air Vice-Marshal and Vice-President Nguyên Cao Ky prevented a few of their most politically threatening opponents from participating as candidates. One was General Duong Van ("Big") Minh, who had piloted the coup against Diêm in 1963. Another, Âu Truong Thanh, advocated an immediate cease-fire and a negotiations platform. The Thiêu forces derailed these candidacies. Thiêu and Ky garnered only 34.8 percent of the vote, sufficient for victory because the remaining votes were split among ten sets of candidates. The runner up, Sài Gòn attorney Truong Đình Dzu, advocated a peace effort, but only after he was certified as an acceptable candidate. In Region I, the Buddhist vote was solidly in support of General Trân Van Đôn. His "Worker-Farmer-Soldier" slate included individuals respected by a wide spectrum of the population. Buddhist support also carried the Phan Khac Suu and Phan Quang Đán slate to victory in Đà Nang and Huê. Catholic candidates did well in Military Regions II, III, and IV.

Election of 1971 One of the most controversial actions of President Thiêu's administration was the passage of an election law requiring candidates to obtain the support of at least 40 national assembly members or 100 provincial/municipal councilors. Various minority opposition groups opposed this change, arguing its sole purpose was to exclude them from participation. Although the Senate rejected the law, it was reinstated by the Lower House. Critics charged this had occurred as a result of bribery and intimidation.

In the election, President Thiêu's chief rivals were General Duong Van Minh and Vice-President Nguyên Cao Ky. Minh secured enough support to become a certified candidate but Ky did not. Ky later charged that his efforts had been illegally thwarted by Thiêu's campaign apparatus. After an appeal to the entire Supreme Court, it certified Ky as a candidate. Shortly afterward, both he and Minh determined that the election would be unfair and withdrew from it.

Ky subsequently challenged Thiêu to resign with him in favor of a new election organized by the Senate chairman.

Thiêu rejected this but offered to resign if he did not receive 50 percent of the votes cast. All invalid ballots (blank, torn, improperly marked, etc.) would count as opposing votes in what became a referendum. Ky's efforts to encourage an election boycott were no match for the Thiêu administration's efforts to get out the vote. On 3 October 1971, a purported 87 percent of the electorate cast ballots. Thiêu won 90 percent in each of the four military regions, falling below this figure only in Huê and Đà Nang.

The 1971 election is generally conceded as a brilliant tactical success for Thiêu. The election was clearly rigged, although Thiêu probably would have won by a good margin even had it been fair. His actions significantly damaged the legitimacy of the election process, the National Assembly as a representative institution, and the government as a whole. They also compromised the RVN's credibility with the population, and antigovernment and Communist forces were able to capitalize on this. Donald Kirk quoted L″ Qu″ Chung, a deputy of the Lower House, as saying that, had the election been fair and free, the 1972 Democratic Republic of Vietnam offensive would not have occurred, because the people would have supported the government they freely elected.

—Paul R. Camacho

References: Buttinger, Joseph. *Vietnam: A Political History* (1968); Herman, Edward S., and F. Brodhead. *Demonstration Elections— U.S.—Staged Elections in the Dominican Republic, Vietnam, and El Salvador* (1984); Kirk, Donald. "Presidential Campaign Politics: The Uncontested 1971 Election" (1974); Porter, Gareth. *Vietnam: The Definitive Documentation of Human Decisions* (1979); —. *Vietnam: A History in Documents;* Tull, Theresa. "Broadening the Base: South Vietnamese Elections, 1967–71" (1974); Scigliano, Robert. *South Vietnam: Nation under Stress* (1964).

See also: Bao Đai; Dulles, John Foster; Duong Van Minh; Geneva Conference and Geneva Accords; Ngô Đình Diêm; Nguyên Cao Ky; Nguyên Van Thiêu; Trân Van Đôn; Truong Đình Dzu; Vietnam, Republic of: 1954–1975.

ELINT (Electronic Intelligence)

After 1964 the Democratic Republic of Vietnam's (DRV's) integrated air defense system (IADS) expanded rapidly. The primary method of obtaining information on types and capabilities of the growing DRV system was through electronic intelligence (ELINT).

ELINT provided the U.S. military an electronic order of battle, listing all known types of DRV radars, their projected capabilities, and their locations. The United States deployed special ELINT "collectors" to Southeast Asia to obtain this badly needed information. Specially configured U.S. Navy ships gathered ELINT data on North Vietnamese radars from the ships' stations in the Gulf of Tonkin. Various aircraft also performed ELINT duties. Two electronic warfare squadrons of RB-66Cs (B-66 bombers reconfigured for electronic intelligence) and their variants operated in Southeast Asia throughout most of the war. Airborne ELINT missions typically operated well beyond the range of North Vietnam's air defense weapons, high over the Republic of Vietnam, Laos, or the Gulf of Tonkin. Each RB-66C carried specialized avionics—including sensitive antennas, receivers, pulse analyzers, and recorders—and could display and record unique radar characteristics, such as the pulse width, scan pattern, frequency, and the rate at which DRV radars sent signals.

This information was crucial to the development of U.S. electronic countermeasures. For example, a typical radar jammer, designed to overpower a DRV radar, would have to match the DRV frequency to be effective. Since ELINT data could determine the range of frequencies within which hostile radar operated, the radar would remain jammed no matter what its transmission frequency. Accurate ELINT was particularly crucial to deceptive jammers that relied on finesse rather than brute strength. Such jammers were most commonly carried on fighter-bombers such as the F-4 or F-105. By mimicking the enemy's radar pulse exactly, these jammers would make DRV radar operators believe that the target aircraft were elsewhere.

One successful ELINT operation was UNITED EFFORT, implemented by the U.S. Air Force to determine the exact frequencies of the SA-2 missile's radar proximity fuse. Starting in late 1965, crewless drone aircraft flew at high altitude over DRV air defenses to provoke SA-2 launches. In 1966 a drone managed to relay the proximity fuse signal to a nearby orbiting Strategic Air Command RB-47H aircraft seconds before two missiles blew it apart. The collected signal was an important piece to the puzzle of how American electronic countermeasures (ECM) might defeat SA-2 air defenses. ELINT efforts were not always successful, however. During LINEBACKER II in December 1972, U.S. Air Force aircrews faced a nasty surprise when the North Vietnamese introduced a heretofore secret fire control radar to guide SA-2 launches over Hà Nôi and port facilities. Since aircrews could neither jam nor in many cases detect this new radar, several missiles exploded amid B-52 formations, downing 15 bombers and damaging more.

Vietnam drove the lesson home to U.S. military aviation that any advantage it enjoyed on the electronic battlefield was fleeting at best. ELINT data had to be continuously updated to prevent further losses.

—Patrick K. Barker

References: Eschmann, Karl. *Linebacker: The Untold Story of the Air Raids over North Vietnam* (1989); Francillon, Rene, and Mick Roth. *Douglas B-66 Destroyer* (1988).

See also: Air Power, Role in War; Airplanes, Allied and Democratic Republic of Vietnam; Antiaircraft Artillery, Allied and Democratic Republic of Vietnam; LINEBACKER II, Operation; LORAN; Surface-to-Air Missiles (SAMs).

Ellsberg, Daniel (1931–)

RAND Corporation and U.S. government intelligence analyst who helped compile the Defense Department's secret history of the Vietnam War, later known as the Pentagon Papers and leaked it to *The New York Times* in 1971. Ellsberg joined the RAND Corporation in 1959. In 1964 he took a staff position within the Defense Department and maintained a special interest in policymaking decisions related to Vietnam. Ellsberg traveled to Vietnam in July 1965 to evaluate the civilian pacification program and stayed on as assistant to Deputy Ambassador William Porter. The apparent failure of pacification, increasing civilian casualties, and widespread corruption within the Sài Gòn government began to erode his support for Washington's Vietnam policy, and he repeatedly communicated with Defense Secretary Robert McNamara about his views.

In late 1967, McNamara assigned 36 researchers to document and analyze the history of U.S. involvement in Vietnam since World War II. The study revealed the accuracy of many of the antiwar movement's criticisms: that U.S. policy developed with little concern for Vietnamese desires and that leading U.S. officials had deceived the public about their intent and actions. They clearly showed that the government was not the reluctant participant it had often claimed to be.

Ellsberg, now opposed to the war's escalation, returned to RAND in 1968 and worked within the system to influence policy. He read additional sections of the Pentagon study and concluded that U.S. aggression was the primary force behind the war. In fall 1969, with the help of RAND colleague Anthony Russo, Ellsberg copied parts of the study, hoping that public knowledge of its conclusions would speed the end of the war. Senator William Fulbright refused to act on the copies he received, and Ellsberg had no more success in approaching other government officials.

Tormented over the war's continuation, Ellsberg became increasingly involved in antiwar activities and resigned from RAND in early 1970. He leaked the Pentagon report to Neil Sheehan of *The New York Times*, which began publishing excerpts on 13 June 1971. After three days, the Nixon Justice Department temporarily blocked publication of the Pentagon Papers with an injunction, arguing that prior restraint was necessary to prevent damage to national security. The Supreme Court rejected this claim on 30 June, and publication continued.

When Ellsberg identified himself as the source of the leak, a grand jury indicted him on charges including illegal possession of government documents, conspiracy, theft, and violation of the Espionage Act. After an initial late 1972 mistrial, the second Pentagon Papers trial began on 18 January 1973 in Los Angeles. On 11 May 1973, Judge Matthew Byrne dismissed the charges prior to jury deliberations after government misconduct—the beginning of the Watergate scandal—became known. Determined to discredit Ellsberg, the White House had conducted illegal wiretapping, ordered a break-in of Ellsberg's psychiatrist's office, and offered Judge Byrne the FBI directorship. Ellsberg remained a target of White House animosity until Nixon resigned.

—Mitchell K. Hall

References: Ellsberg, Daniel. *Papers on the War* (1972); *The Pentagon Papers as Published by The New York Times* (1971); Schrag, Peter. *Test of Loyalty: Daniel Ellsberg and the Rituals of Secret Government* (1974); Ungar, Sanford J. *The Papers & the Papers: An Account of the Legal and Political Battle over the Pentagon Papers* (1988).

See also: Adams, Samuel A.; Fulbright, J. William; McNamara, Robert S.; Nixon, Richard Milhous; Pentagon Papers and Trial;

RAND Corporation; Russo, Anthony J., Jr.; Sheehan, Cornelius Mahoney (Neil); Watergate.

Ely, Paul Henri Romuald (1897–1975)

French Army chief of staff; high commissioner and commander in chief of French forces in Indo-China. Following a fact-finding mission to Indo-China that convinced that France could not win the war there without massive military assistance, Ely arrived in Washington on 20 March 1954 in an effort to secure that aid. He candidly informed his American counterpart, Adm. Arthur Radford, of the likely fall of Điên Biên Phu and the dire consequences this would have for the Indo-China War and perhaps all of Southeast Asia. It quickly became apparent to the Eisenhower administration that only massive U.S. military intervention, possibly including nuclear weapons, could save the French. With the British government opposed and the battle apparently too far gone, Eisenhower decided against U.S. intervention. He did agree, after Ely's return to Paris, to supply 25 additional B-26 bombers.

After the fall of Điên Biên Phu, Ely again went to Indo-China with Generals Raoul Salan and Pierre Pélissier to prepare a military report on which the French government might base requests to its allies for aid. Ely recommended that France immediately evacuate northern Vietnam and replace General Henry Navarre as commander in chief. On 3 June 1954, the French government named Ely to succeed Navarre as military chief and Maurice Dejean as French high commissioner. On 11 June, French and Vietnamese troops began Operation AUVERGE, the last major battle of the war, in which they fought their way toward the Hà Nôi-Hai Phòng lifeline. The 21 July 1954, Geneva Accords brought the Indo-China War to an end.

The pro-American Ely contributed much to Ngô Đình Diêm's consolidation of power, and training of the Vietnamese Army came under Ely's overall authority. But the presence of French troops wounded the nationalist sensibilities of the Diêm government, and the last of them departed Vietnam in April 1956.

—Spencer C. Tucker

References: Ely, Paul. *Mémoires. L'Indochine dans la Tourmente* (1964); Fall, Bernard. *The Two Viet Nams* (1964).

See also: Điên Biên Phu, Battle of; de Gaulle, Charles André Marie Joseph; French Indo-China; Mendès-France, Pierre; Navarre, Henri Eugène; Ngô Đình Diêm; Radford, Arthur W.; Salan, Raoul Albin Louis; VULTURE, Operation.

Elysée Agreement (8 March 1949)

Formal treaty signed at Elysée Palace, Paris, between French President Vincent Auriol and Emperor Bao Đai whereby France recognized Vietnam as an associated state within the French Union and promised to support its application for membership in the United Nations. According to the treaty, formally ratified by the French Chamber of Deputies in January 1950, France promised to incorporate the Republic of Cochin China within the State of Vietnam. Paris lauded the agreement as proof that Vietnam was "independent," and it no doubt helped convince Washington that the war in Indo-

China had been transformed into a civil war between Vietnamese "democrats" and Vietnamese "Communists," rather than a colonial conflict.

The reality was quite different. Under the constitutional framework of the French Union, Vietnam could not receive full independence, only autonomy. France recognized Vietnam's right to have diplomats in only China, Thailand, and the Vatican. (With the Communist victory in China, India was substituted, but India did not recognize the Bao Đai regime.) Proof that the new State of Vietnam was not independent was seen in its recognition of Paris's right to control its army and foreign relations. French economic domination of Vietnam was preserved. Stanley Karnow quotes Bao Đai as remarking, "What they call a Bao Đai solution turns out to be just a French solution." Thus, Bao Đai was unable to offer Vietnamese nationalists any alternative to the Communists. The French had, however, recognized the territorial unity of Vietnam. By the end of 1949, Laos and Cambodia signed treaties similar to the Elysée Agreement.

—Spencer C. Tucker

References: Buttinger, Joseph. *The Smaller Dragon: A Political History of Vietnam* (1958); Hammer, Ellen J. *The Struggle for Indochina* (1954); Karnow, Stanley. *Vietnam: A History* (1983).
See also: Bao Đai; French Indo-China; Indo-China War.

Embargo

U.S. trade embargo against the Democratic Republic of Vietnam (DRV) and, later, the Socialist Republic of Vietnam (SRV). Following the fall of Sài Gòn in April 1975, Washington soon extended its trade embargo, formerly affecting only the DRV, to include the reunited SRV. Using the 1917 Trading with the Enemy Act for authority, the embargo had originally prohibited trade with, or investment in, the Communist-controlled portion of Vietnam. With the capitulation of the South, Washington strengthened the sanctions to prohibit aid from multilateral organizations such as the International Monetary Fund, the Asian Development Bank, and the World Bank.

The purpose of the embargo was essentially punitive, and U.S. policymakers had no real expectation of influencing Vietnamese actions. Eventually, issues arose that hardened the U.S. position and led to increasing international support for the embargo, including the Vietnamese invasion and occupation of Cambodia. The embargo's effectiveness is difficult to access. Its most damaging aspect was the denial of access to international aid. During these years of Vietnamese economic isolation, the Soviet Union proved to be Vietnam's greatest source of aid. Ironically, the embargo's greatest effect may have been to drive Vietnam closer to the USSR.

The SRV withdrew its troops from Cambodia in September 1989, and foreign aid and investment soon began trickling in. Trade with the former Soviet Union fell significantly, but new relationships with Singapore, Japan, and Hong Kong proved fruitful. Economic assistance to the SRV also began to grow. As foreign investment in the SRV grew, U.S. firms pressed Washington to relax restrictions to prevent American companies from losing more opportunities there,

but the trade barriers fell slowly and in piecemeal fashion. In April 1992, the United States allowed reestablishment of direct telephone service with Vietnam, and in December the Bush administration responded to Hà Nôi's increased cooperation in recovering and identifying American remains by allowing U.S. businesses to enter into contracts with Vietnamese businesses and government. Although these contracts could not yet take effect, this action hinted at further relaxation of restrictions. In July 1993, President Clinton renewed Vietnamese access to international funds, and in February 1994 he formally lifted remaining trade restrictions. IBM, General Electric, and Citibank soon entered the newly opened market. U.S. investment in the SRV rose from only $3.3 million in 1993 to $1.2 billion in 1995, although the United States was only the sixth largest investor, trailing Taiwan, Japan, Hong Kong, Singapore, and the Republic of Korea. Complete normalization of relations between the United States and Vietnam occurred in 1997 with the arrival of the first U.S. ambassador in more than 20 years. That same year, the SRV agreed to assume debts of about $140 million incurred by the Sài Gòn government before its fall in 1975. Hà Nôi took this step to help pave the way for most-favored nation trading status.

—Matthew A. Crump

References: Abegglen, James C. *Sea Change: Pacific Asia as the New World-Industrial Center* (1994); Beresford, Melanie. *Vietnam: Politics, Economics and Society* (1988); Kim, Young C., ed. *The Southeast Asian Economic Miracle* (1995); Schultz, Clifford J., II, et al. "American Involvement in Vietnam, Part II: Prospects for U.S. Business in a New Era" (1995); U.S. House Select Committee on Hunger. *Three Asian Countries in Crisis: Afghanistan, Vietnam, and the Philippines* (1988).
See also: Clinton, William Jefferson; United States: Involvement in Vietnam, 1975 to the Present; Vietnam, Socialist Republic of: 1975 to the Present.

Enclave Strategy

Strategy adopted in early 1965 by the Johnson administration that restricted the movement of U.S. forces to Vietnam's coastal areas. The enclave strategy was suggested by U.S. Ambassador to Vietnam General Maxwell Taylor, who opposed introduction of large numbers of U.S. troops. Considered a "go slow" approach that would keep the Army of the Republic of Vietnam (ARVN) as a key player in the war, it was indicative of a larger struggle within the Johnson administration about how far commitment to Vietnam should go.

Inherent in the strategy was the idea that the war had to be won by the Republic of Vietnam (RVN) and that the most effective U.S. role was to aid ARVN forces by controlling the densely populated coast. The ARVN could then fight inland while U.S. troops protected rear areas. The enclave strategy would allow ARVN forces to recover and take control of the countryside while the government built credibility and legitimacy, secure in the knowledge that Americans held strategic points.

The enclave strategy was first applied to the 3,500 U.S. Marines who landed in Đà Nang in March 1965. Restricted to occupying and defending critical terrain around the airfield and to support and communications facilities, the Marines were not to engage the Việt Công.

The enclave strategy never had General William Westmoreland's support. He claimed it would induce a garrison mentality among U.S. troops, who would lose their combat edge and advantages in mobility and firepower if they sat by while the ARVN fought. ARVN's continued poor performance, coupled with increased Communist attacks in June, convinced U.S. leaders that their strategy was not working. Westmoreland on 7 June requested 44 U.S. battalions. On 27 June, U.S. forces began to engage the Communists in their own right along the coast and in the Central Highlands, effectively ending the enclave strategy.

—Clayton D. Laurie

References: Herring, George C. *America's Longest War: The United States and Vietnam, 1950–1975* (1986); Krepinevich, Andrew F., Jr. *The Army and Vietnam* (1986); Lewy, Guenther. *America in Vietnam* (1978).

See also: Ball; George W.; Geography of Indo-China and Vietnam; Johnson, Lyndon Baines; Taylor, Maxwell Davenport; United States: Involvement in Vietnam, 1954–1965; Vietnam, Republic of: Army (ARVN); Westmoreland, William Childs.

END SWEEP, Operation. *See* Mining and Mine Clearance in North Vietnam.

ENHANCE PLUS, Operation
(12 October–23 December 1972)
Massive short-term 1972 logistical aid to the Republic of Vietnam (RVN). On 8 October 1972, the Democratic Republic of Vietnam (DRV) delegation to the Paris Peace Conference offered the U.S. representatives a peace proposal timed to coincide with the 1972 U.S. presidential election and to pressure the Nixon administration to accept a peace treaty.

Operation ENHANCE PLUS was an outgrowth of Project ENHANCE, which began in March 1972 to replenish ARVN equipment lost during the Easter Offensive. On 12 October, the Nixon administration ordered the U.S. military to supply the RVN with billions of dollars in military supplies and equipment. Washington hoped that with replenished military stocks, the Army of the Republic of Vietnam (ARVN) would conduct successful offensive operations to strengthen the RVN position in negotiations following the signing of the Paris Peace Accords. This massive influx of aid was dubbed Operation ENHANCE PLUS. By January 1973, the United States had provided $2 billion worth of military equipment, and the RVN possessed the fourth largest air force in the world.

Material provided by ENHANCE and ENHANCE PLUS was important in securing Thiệu's eventual grudging support of the reworked Paris Peace Accords that followed the LINEBACKER II campaign.

—J. A. Menzoff

References: Clark, Jeffrey J. *Advise and Support: The Final Years, The U.S. in Vietnam* (1988); Karnow, Stanley. *Vietnam: A History* (1991); Snepp, Frank. *Decent Interval* (1977).

See also: Abrams, Creighton; Bunker, Ellsworth; Kissinger, Henry

Alfred; Lê Đuc Tho; LINEBACKER II, Operation; Nguyên Van Thiêu; Nixon, Richard Milhous; Paris Negotiations; United States: Involvement in Vietnam, 1973–1975; Vietnamization; Washington Special Actions Group (WSAG); Weyand, Frederick C.

Enoul, Y Bham (1913–ca. 1975)
Rhadé Montagnard and activist; president of the Bajaraka movement and of the United Struggle Front for the Liberation of Oppressed Races (FULRO). Y Bham Enoul was an activist in the ethnonationalist Bajaraka movements created in opposition to Republic of Vietnam (RVN) President Ngô Đình Diệm's program to resettle Vietnamese refugees on Montagnard lands in the Central Highlands and the forced resettlement of Montagnard villagers. Imprisoned in 1958 by the RVN government, he was released in 1964 and resumed his work as Deputy Province Chief for Highland Affairs in Darlac Province as well as his ethnonationalist activities.

In 1964 during an uprising at Special Forces camps around Ban Mê Thuôt, Y Bham Enoul delivered a "FULRO manifesto" calling for action to reclaim Montagnard lands. Threatened with imprisonment by Vietnamese authorities, he fled to Mondulkiri Province, Cambodia, where he assumed leadership of a FULRO army of 5,000 to 6,000 soldiers and their dependents. As FULRO president, Y Bham Enoul represented the Montagnards in negotiations with the Cambodian and South Vietnamese governments, the North Vietnamese, and the Việt Công.

With the increasing vulnerability of Montagnard villages after the 1968 Tết Offensive, Y Bham Enoul sought to return to Vietnam with his FULRO army to protect Central Highland villages from Communist attack. In negotiations with the Sài Gòn government, he was promised that FULRO army units would be integrated into Regional Force units to protect Highland villages and that FULRO leaders would receive government positions in exchange for their support. FULRO militants overthrew Y Bham Enoul, however, and exiled him to Phnom Penh, where he was placed under house arrest by the Cambodian government in 1970. Y Bham Enoul was last seen leading his Montagnard followers from the French embassy to surrender to the Khmer Rouge following the April 1970 fall of Phnom Penh.

—David M. Berman

References: Hickey, Gerald Cannon. *Free in the Forest: Ethnohistory of the Vietnamese Central Highlands, 1954–1976* (1982); —. *Shattered World: Adaptation and Survival among Vietnam's Highland Peoples during the Vietnam War* (1993); Wiesner, Louis A. *Victims and Survivors: Displaced Persons and Other War Victims in Viet-Nam, 1954–1975* (1988).

See also: Ban Mê Thuôt, Battle of; Cambodia; Civilian Irregular Defense Group (CIDG); FULRO (Le Front Unifié de Lutte des Races Opprimées); Hickey, Gerald Cannon; Khmer Rouge; Mobile Strike Force Commands; Montagnards.

ENTERPRISE, Operation (February 1967–March 1968)
Long-term operation, initiated south of Sài Gòn in Long An Province, involving the U.S. 9th Infantry Division, Army of the Republic of Vietnam (ARVN) units, and South

Vietnamese Regional and Popular Forces. The 3d Battalion, 39th Infantry, the first of the 9th Division's elements to arrive in Vietnam, reached Sài Gòn in January 1967. Moving south to Rach Kiên in February, it came under harassing fire almost immediately in undisputed Viêt Công territory. Commands venturing outside the camp were certain to meet heavy opposition. Other units of the 9th Division soon arrived. The entire 3d Brigade colocated at Rach Kiên, while the mechanized 2d Battalion, 60th Infantry established itself nearby at Bình Phuoc.

On 13 February 1967, these elements initiated Operation ENTERPRISE to clear Long An Province of Viet Công (VC) forces. Allied troops swept the area through 11 April, suffering considerable losses. Most VC scattered and escaped. Allied operations continued in the province for another six months, inflicting more than 2,000 VC casualties by the time ENTERPRISE ended on 11 March 1968. The operation failed to clear Long An Province, however, and the VC remained a popular and powerful presence throughout the area.

—Edward C. Page

Reference: Stanton, Shelby. *The Rise and Fall of an American Army: U.S. Ground Forces in Vietnam 1965–1973* (1985).
See also: Clear and Hold; LAM SON 719, Operation; Têt Offensive: Overall Strategy; Têt Offensive: The Sài Gòn Circle; Vietnamization; United States: Army; Vietnam, Republic of: Army (ARVN).

Enthoven, Alain (1930–)

U.S. Department of Defense official. In 1961, believing that airmobility had merit, Enthoven's office persuaded the secretary of defense to conduct tests that led to the organization of the 1st Cavalry Division (Airmobile) and the 101st Airborne Division (Airmobile) that fought in Vietnam. Starting in 1966, Enthoven examined the U.S. strategy of attrition in Vietnam and found it wanting. He concluded that Communist forces initiated most firefights and controlled their rate of attrition; thus, sending more troops would not achieve greater attrition. President Johnson and Secretary of Defense Robert McNamara agreed with this conclusion and rejected Military Assistance Command, Vietnam's (MACV's) request for 200,000 more troops. By 1968 Enthoven strongly opposed the bombing of North Vietnam.

—John L. Bell

References: *The Pentagon Papers as Published by The New York Times* (1971); Westmoreland, William C. *A Soldier Reports* (1976).
See also: Airmobility; Attrition; Johnson, Lyndon Baines; McNamara, Robert S.; Military Assistance Command, Vietnam (MACV).

European Defense Community (EDC)

Treaty that attempted to create a unitary West European army of German, French, Italian, and Benelux forces. Prolonged negotiations resulted in the signing of a treaty on 27 May 1952 for a European Defense Community (EDC). Inevitably, the EDC became linked with the war in Indo-China. Paris tried to tie French approval of the treaty to increased U.S. aid for the Indo-China War, bringing an accusation of blackmail from U.S. Secretary of State Dean Acheson. The French, who had first proposed the EDC, scuttled the agreement.

—Spencer C. Tucker

Reference: Le Prestre, P. "European Defense Community" (1992).
See also: Acheson, Dean C.; Faure, Edgar; Mendès-France, Pierre.

F

FAIRFAX, Operation (1966–1967)
U.S. military operation to improve security around Sài Gòn. Alarmed by deteriorating security so near the capital, General William Westmoreland decided to use U.S. battalions to inspire reluctant South Vietnamese regular and territorial units to action. FAIRFAX was essentially an advisory effort. The commander of II Field Force Vietnam Major General Johnathan Seaman assigned one U.S. Army battalion to each district in Gia Đinh. The South Vietnamese employed three Army of the Republic of Vietnam (ARVN) battalions, each linked to an American unit. The plan called for U.S. and South Vietnamese forces to operate jointly and restore security to the point where the South Vietnamese could manage the province themselves.

Security improved in Gia Đinh by the end of 1967, but confusion and duplication in collating intelligence led to little progress in identifying or eliminating the Viet Công Infrastructure (VCI). The presence of U.S. troops forced some VC forces to depart and the guerrillas to shift underground, but in 1967 the VC still collected taxes and recruited. FAIRFAX did not disrupt the web of interpersonal relations and institutions that allowed the VCI to function in Gia Đinh. U.S. operations achieved a stalemate.

Robert Komer, later head of the U.S. pacification effort, studied FAIRFAX and concluded that the anti-infrastructure effort needed better coordination. His search for a way to bring together at the district level all available intelligence information culminated in 1967 in the establishment of the Phoenix program.

—Richard A. Hunt

References: Clarke, Jeffrey J. *Advice and Support: The Final Years, 1965–1973* (1988); Hunt, Richard A. *Pacification: The American Struggle for Vietnam's Hearts and Minds* (1995).
See also: Civilian Operations and Revolutionary Development Support (CORDS); Komer, Robert W.; National Front for the Liberation of South Vietnam (NFLSV); Phoenix Program; Westmoreland, William Childs.

Fall, Bernard B. (1926–1967)
Analyst of the military and political situation in Vietnam. Fall wrote seven books and more than 250 magazine articles about Vietnam and Southeast Asia. His 1961 *Street without Joy* became a classic account of the Indo-China War. In 1966 he published *Hell in a Very Small Place, The Siege of Dien Bien Phu*, a definitive account of that battle. Fall was deeply critical of French and U.S. approaches to the war. The Vietnam War, he maintained, was first and foremost political—a fact that neither the Americans, nor the French before them, fully understood. Because Fall analyzed all sides of an issue with the same degree of penetrating criticism, his writings were often cited by supporters as well as opponents of the war. A believer in collecting information firsthand, Fall was killed by a Việt Công mine while accompanying a U.S. Marine patrol near Huê.

—David T. Zabecki

References: Fall, Bernard B. *Street without Joy* (1961); —. *Vietnam Witness: 1953–1966* (1966); —. *Hell in a Very Small Place, The Siege of Dien Bien Phu* (1966); —. *Last Reflections on a War* (1967).
See also: Điên Biên Phu, Battle of; Halberstam, David; Salisbury, Harrison E.

FANK (Forces Armées Nationale Khmer)
Training command established in April 1970 after President Nixon authorized military aid for Cambodia following the March collapse of Norodom Sihanouk's neutral government. It was staffed by U.S. Army Special Forces personnel who trained light infantry and marine fusilier battalions at Long Hai, Đông Bá Thìn, and Chi Lang (later Phuoc Tuy). After the 5th Special Forces departed Vietnam in spring 1971, the training sites were redesignated U.S. Army Individual Training Group. Australian and New Zealand jungle instructors were assigned to the group, which was redesignated FANK Training Command in May 1972. Redesignated Field Training Command on 1 December 1972, it was closed at the end of January 1973. As a result of these training actions, an entirely new national army was created for Cambodia; 86 infantry and marine battalions were cycled through the various training sites. In 1975 the FANK was defeated when Khmer Rouge troops captured Phnom Penh.

—Robert G. Mangrum

References: Dougan, Clark, David Fulghum, and the editors of Boston Publishing Company. *The Fall of the South* (1985); Olson, James S. ed. *Dictionary of the Vietnam War* (1988); Shawcross, William. *Sideshow: Kissinger, Nixon and the Destruction of Cambodia* (1979); Summers, Harry G. *Vietnam War Almanac* (1985).
See also: Cambodia; Khmer Rouge; Nixon, Richard Milhous; Sihanouk, Norodom; United States: Special Forces.

FARM GATE, Operation (1961–1967)
Extended U.S. air operation in Vietnam. Operation FARM GATE began on 11 October 1961, when President Kennedy ordered the U.S. Air Force (USAF) to send a combat detachment to South Vietnam to assist the Republic of Vietnam (RVN) in its struggle against an increasingly aggressive Communist foe. Kennedy earlier had asked the military services to develop a counterinsurgency capability. The Air Force had responded by forming the 4400th Combat Crew Training Squadron. Nicknamed "Jungle Jim," the unit relied on older, propeller-driven aircraft to train indigenous air forces and undertake limited combat missions in support of ground forces.

The 155 officers and airmen of Detachment 2A, 4400th Combat Crew Training Squadron, arrived at Biên Hòa Airfield in November 1961. The air commandos initially were restricted to training South Vietnamese airmen, but soon the mission's eight T-28s, four B-26s, and four C-47s became involved in other tasks. Shortly after the detachment's arrival, it started flying reconnaissance missions and providing logistical support to U.S. Army Special Forces. On 6 December, the Joint Chiefs of Staff authorized FARM GATE to undertake combat missions, provided that at least one Vietnamese national was carried on board strike aircraft for training purposes.

During 1962, FARM GATE's B-26s and T-28s became the nucleus of an expanding U.S. effort in Vietnam. The emphasis remained training of South Vietnamese airmen to bear the burden of combat, but FARM GATE aircraft also flew air strikes. However, they were restricted by rules of engagement to missions that the Vietnamese were unable to undertake. Poor facilities, inadequate supplies, and the lack of a clearly defined role contributed to FARM GATE morale problems.

Increasing requests for air support as the war intensified led Kennedy on 31 December to approve an expansion of FARM GATE. The growth of FARM GATE in 1963 brought organizational changes. In July the contingent at Biên Hòa became the 1st Air Commando Squadron (Provisional), part of the Pacific Air Force (PACAF). It contained two strike sections of ten B-26s and thirteen T-28s, plus support sections of four U-10s (for psychological warfare) and six C-47s. In addition, there were small detachments of B-26s at Pleiku and Sóc Trang.

The growing intensity of the ground war brought demands for combat sorties that the air commandos were unable to fulfill. Between May and August 1963, 431 requests for air support went unanswered. The sortie rate for FARM GATE aircraft suffered from shortages of spare parts and structural problems with the wings of the B-26s. Following several structural failures, in spring 1964 FARM GATE's B-26s and T-28s were replaced by more modern A-1Es. The growth of the U.S. role in the war also led to the establishment of a second squadron of A-1Es (the 602d Fighter Commando Squadron) at Biên Hòa in October.

In March 1965 Washington dropped the requirement that a South Vietnamese national be carried on combat missions. At the same time, Secretary of Defense Robert S. McNamara approved the replacement of South Vietnamese markings on the aircraft with regular U.S. Air Force markings. The two FARM GATE squadrons of A-1Es were now flying 80 percent of all sorties in support of the Army of the Republic of Vietnam (ARVN).

As USAF presence in South Vietnam increased in 1966, FARM GATE declined in importance. The last vestiges of FARM GATE disappeared at the end of 1967, by which time the war in South Vietnam had long since lost its counterinsurgency character and assumed a more conventional nature. The air commandos would find a more congenial environment for their special talents in Laos, where a different kind of war was being fought.

—William M. Leary

References: Futrell, Robert F. *The United States Air Force in Southeast Asia: The Advisory Years to 1965* (1981); Schlight, John. *The United States Air Force in Southeast Asia: The War in South Vietnam, The Years of the Offensive, 1965–1968* (1988).

See also: Airplanes, Allied and Democratic Republic of Vietnam; Air Power, Role in War; Kennedy, John Fitzgerald; McNamara, Robert S.; United States: Air Force.

Faure, Edgar (1908–1988)

French centrist politician and twice premier of France. In May 1955 in Paris, Faure had a confrontation with U.S. Secretary of State John Foster Dulles regarding French influence in Vietnam. Judging Ngô Đình Diệm to be "not only incapable but mad," Faure broke with Washington over its support of the South Vietnamese leader. This attitude helped pave the way for unilateral U.S. action in South Vietnam. Lessened French interest in Indo-China was also occasioned by unrest in Tunisia, Morocco, and Algeria. Defeated in 1958 for reelection to the National Assembly, Faure undertook a series of diplomatic assignments for Charles de Gaulle, including the establishment of diplomatic relations between France and the People's Republic of China.

—Spencer C. Tucker

References: Northcutt, Wayne. ed. *Historical Dictionary of the French Fourth and Fifth Republics, 1946–1991* (1992); Spector, Ronald H. *Advice and Support. The Early Years. The U.S. Army in Vietnam* (1983).

See also: de Gaulle, Charles André Marie Joseph; Dulles, John Foster; European Defense Community (EDC); Mendès-France, Pierre; Ngô Đình Diệm.

Federal Bureau of Investigation (FBI)

Branch of the U.S. Justice Department responsible for investigating violations of federal law in cases not specifically assigned to other federal agencies.

The antiwar movement concerned Presidents Johnson and Nixon, and for most of the Vietnam War period, FBI director J. Edgar Hoover was their willing accomplice. Hoover shared many of their concerns and obsessions, but his relationship with Nixon changed as the president's paranoia intensified. Nixon extended electronic surveillance to his own administration in an effort to plug information leaks and in 1970 attempted to create a covert, extralegal intelligence force that would include elements of the FBI, Central Intelligence Agency (CIA), and the National Security Council (NSC). The so-called Huston Plan found some favor in the Nixon administration, but Hoover reportedly killed the plan when Nixon refused to provide written authorization. The director also feared the loss of the FBI's long-standing autonomy in such an arrangement.

Hoover's death in 1972 opened the door for a more accommodating director, L. Patrick Gray. By this time, the Watergate scandal was unfolding and the FBI was involved in ongoing investigations that Gray could not control. Nixon and Chief of Staff H. R. Haldeman conspired to have the CIA derail the FBI investigation. Nixon's resignation largely ended the issue, but in the wake of the Watergate scandal and the Vietnam War, the FBI faced a major image crisis.

—David Coffey and Lee Ann Woodall

References: DeLoach, Cartha D. "Deke." *Hoover's FBI: The Inside Story by Hoover's Trusted Lieutenant* (1995); Woodward, Bob, and Carl Bernstein. *The Final Days* (1976); Ungar, Sanford J. *FBI* (1976).

See also: Antiwar Movement, United States; Central Intelligence Agency (CIA); Hoover, J. Edgar; Huston Plan; Johnson, Lyndon Baines; Kennedy, John Fitzgerald; Kennedy, Robert Francis; King, Martin Luther, Jr.; Nixon, Richard Milhous; United States: Department of Justice.

Fellowship of Reconciliation (FOR)

The Fellowship of Reconciliation (FOR) played an important, but not very public, role in the American antiwar movement. Its leading spokesperson was A. J. Muste, who in 1964 issued the first public statement advocating draft resistance to the Vietnam conflict.

In 1965 disparate groups began protesting as antiwar sentiments arose in response to the military buildup in Vietnam. FOR provided leadership and organization that helped focus these groups and guide the movement. Its actions remained consistent with its position that a freely elected government in Vietnam and a negotiated settlement would stop killing by both sides. The organization did not debate with radical antiwar leaders but acted as a moderating influence on radical groups, conducting nonviolent demonstrations that stressed education and peaceful solutions. Its "movement center," established for the November 1969 demonstration in Washington, D.C., served as a clearinghouse for information and a forum for discussion of nonviolent means. FOR advised and supported conscientious objectors and those opposed to military service. It also raised money for medical aid to Vietnamese victims of the war and assisted Buddhist groups in their peace efforts.

When the war ended in 1975, FOR protested mistreatment of Buddhist pacifists and other antimilitary activists in Vietnam and continued its activities of working for peace. It remains an active peace organization.

—Charles N. Fasanaro

Reference: Fellowship of Reconciliation Archives.
See also: Antiwar Movement, United States; Buddhists; Clergy and Laymen Concerned about Vietnam (CALC, CALCAV, CLCV); Conscientious Objectors (COs); Jackson State College; Kent State University; Moratorium to End the War in Vietnam; Nixon, Richard Milhous.

Felt, Harry D. (1902–1992)

Commander in chief, U.S. Pacific Command (CINCPAC), during the pivotal era from 1958 to 1964 who strongly influenced the direction of U.S. policy in Southeast Asia. Felt was an energetic supporter of the Kennedy administration's counterinsurgency strategy. He oversaw deployment to Laos and South Vietnam of increasing numbers of Army Special Forces (Green Berets), Navy SEAL teams, and Air Force Air Commandos. Felt also presided over the employment of the South Vietnamese-crewed fast patrol craft of Operation 34 ALPHA in the Democratic Republic of Vietnam (DRV) coastal waters.

Felt supported deployment to Southeast Asia of conventional U.S. military forces to stiffen the resolve and fighting ability of Royal Laotian and Republic of Vietnam (RVN) armed forces. During Felt's tour as CINCPAC, U.S. Army and Marine helicopter companies, Navy coastal patrol ships, and U.S. Air Force tactical squadrons operated in support of the Allied forces.

Felt recognized that indigenous Communists served as the foot soldiers in the struggle against the pro-U.S. governments of Laos and the RVN, but he believed that Hô Chí Minh and his Communist *Lao Đông* Party directed the effort from Hà Nôi. Hence, when the Communist Pathet Lao in Laos and the Việt Công in the RVN threatened to overwhelm government forces on several occasions between 1959 and 1964, Felt did not hesitate to recommend that aircraft carrier and amphibious task forces be used to deter North Vietnamese actions. The presence in Southeast Asia of counterinsurgency units and conventional forces did not cause the DRV to relent for long, however. When Felt turned over his command to Adm. Ulysses S. G. Sharp in June 1964, the specter of war loomed over the region.

—Edward J. Marolda

References: Marolda, Edward J. *By Sea, Air, and Land: An Illustrated History of the U.S. Navy and the War in Southeast Asia* (1994); Schreadley, Richard L. *From the Rivers to the Sea: The U.S. Navy in Vietnam* (1992).
See also: DeSoto Missions; FARM GATE, Operation; Operation Plan 34A (OPLAN 34A); United States: Involvement in Vietnam, 1954–1965; United States: Navy.

Fernandez, Richard (1934–)

Executive Director of Clergy and Laymen Concerned about Vietnam (CALCAV), America's largest religiously oriented antiwar organization. An effective fundraiser, Fernandez strengthened CALCAV by organizing local chapters and planning creative actions against the war. He joined Lee Webb in 1967 as codirector of Vietnam Summer, an effort to build a grassroots political base for deescalating the war. He also involved himself with the Committee of Liaison to facilitate communications between U.S. prisoners of war and their families. Despite his outreach, CALCAV rarely established formal ties to the antiwar coalitions out of concern that inflammatory rhetoric or radical leadership might alienate its primary constituency. Fernandez resigned from CALCAV in June 1973.

—Mitchell K. Hall

References: Hall, Mitchell K. *Because of Their Faith: CALCAV and Religious Opposition to the Vietnam War* (1990); Wells, Tom. *The War Within: America's Battle over Vietnam* (1994).
See also: Antiwar Movement, United States; Clergy and Laymen Concerned about Vietnam (CALC, CALCAV, CLCV); Fellowship of Reconciliation (FOR).

Ferry, Jules (1832–1893)

French politician and promoter of imperialism and educational reform; twice premier of France, 1880–1881 and 1883–1885. To many Frenchmen, Ferry's chief claim to greatness lay in expanding French colonial power, but he initiated almost none of the colonial enterprises of the 1880s, most of which were the work of officials on the spot. Ferry's conversion to imperialism seems to have been motivated by the desire to restore French greatness. During his premierships, the French consolidated their hold over Indo-China with the establishment of protectorates on An Nam and Tonkin. He fell from power in May 1885 following a minor French defeat at Lang Son in March.

—Spencer C. Tucker

References: Gaillard, Jean-Michel. *Jules Ferry* (1989); Guilhaume, Philippe. *Jules Ferry* (1992); Hutton, Patrick, ed. *Historical Dictionary of the Third French Republic, 1870–1940* (1986); Power, T. *Jules Ferry and the Renaissance of French Imperialism* (1944). **See also:** French Indo-China.

Fiction, U.S., and the Vietnam Experience

The major categories of American fiction about the Vietnam experience are the preinvolvement and early involvement period (pre-1965), combat experience, veterans' experiences, and the experience of Southeast Asian people during and after the war.

Two major works associated with the prewar and early war period are Graham Greene's *The Quiet American* (1955) and Eugene Burdick and William Lederer's *The Ugly American* (1958). Both novels examine the role played by U.S. advisors in Vietnam during and immediately after the French Indo-China War and portray American policy as ranging from misguided to inept to deliberately obscurantist. A central figure in each book appears to have been based on Colonel Edward Lansdale, who worked with the Central Intelligence Agency (CIA) in Sài Gòn during and after 1953. A later novel, Asa Baber's *The Land of a Million Elephants* (1970), carries the same air of futility into neighboring Laos during late 1960, depicting the U.S.- and Soviet-backed struggle for a power base as contributing to further confusion within the country and depicting the indigenous population as archetypal victims struggling for their own cultural autonomy. David Halberstram's *One Very Hot Day* (1967) continues the theme of American ignorance of Vietnamese culture, describing a battle (probably modeled on Ấp Bac) in which South Vietnamese forces are defeated and U.S. advisory efforts prove useless at best.

In contrast to these pessimistic views of U.S. involvement is Peter Derrig's *The Pride of the Green Berets* (1966), a traditional war novel about American Special Forces troops in the early 1960s. Here, Americans are presented as war heroes in the earlier mode of World War II fiction. This novel, published before the explosion of antiwar protests in America, inspired a film, a popular song, and even a syndicated comic strip.

Among the combat novels that form the core of well-known Vietnam War fiction, the most often cited are Larry Heinemann's *Close Quarters* (1977); Tim O'Brien's *Going after Cacciato* (1978); James Webb's *Fields of Fire* (1978); and John Del Vecchio's *The 13th Valley* (1982). The first two are more pervasively pessimistic than the second two, showing the war not only as futile but as something that destroys or at least brings out the worst in the character of those who participate in it, unless (especially in *Cacciato*) they can somehow escape, either to another place or into the imagination.

Close Quarters, set in an armored personnel carrier (APC) unit just before the Tết Offensive, mirrors the author's view of the war in the isolated, claustrophobic setting of the APC, where formerly idealistic young men discard their ideals and find meaning in drugs, sex, and harassment of the indigenous population. The novel follows the central figure back to the United States, where, although welcomed back into civilian society, he is unable to identify with it any longer and remains fixated on his combat experience.

Going after Cacciato is an exercise in surrealism that takes as its central premise the supposed pursuit by an infantry unit of one of its members who has deserted. The novel is divided into three interwoven parts: the "observation post" chapters in which the central figure, Paul Berlin, reflects on what happened and what might have happened during the course of one night on sentry duty; the "real" chapters, scenes from Berlin's experiences before and after Cacciato's desertion, told in flashback and out of chronological sequence; and the "what might have been" chapters, a surrealistic fictional narrative concocted by Berlin, following the men in their journey to Paris. They are accompanied in this fantasy by a Southeast Asian woman they meet early in the journey, who eventually tries unsuccessfully to persuade Berlin to desert like Cacciato from this senseless war. Significantly, Berlin's response that young men go to war out of cowardice and fear of being scorned by their families and friends who hold traditional values echoes O'Brien's similar statement in his memoir, *If I Die in a Combat Zone* (1973). The disjointed and surrealistic narrative pattern of *Going after Cacciato* reflects O'Brien's view of the war as futile and unreal.

Fields of Fire, although similarly ending on a seemingly futile note, portrays war as essentially bringing out the best in most of its participants. Although Webb does not minimize the failings of his characters, either before or during the war, their strengths are reinforced by crisis and camaraderie. A central figure in the novel, and one of the unit's few survivors, is both the "conscience" of the unit and an outcast within it. Nicknamed "Senator" because of his college background and continual philosophizing, he reports the killing of the civilians but also causes the death of many men in his unit by his ill-advised actions and occasional cowardice. He returns home disillusioned and remorseful about his own actions, but with a new admiration for his fallen comrades whom he once scorned. In the final chapter, he participates in an antiwar rally with his former college classmates, but, once again an outcast, he shouts from the rally podium that they don't know what they are talking about. The novel focuses attention on the combatants as individuals forming a cohesive society under pressure, rather than on the purpose of the war itself. In many ways, the combat society is seen as more viable than that of the civilian society from which the men have come.

The 13th Valley is more an epic than a novel. Like *Fields of Fire*, it follows one unit through a specific mission, focusing attention on the individuals and their cohesion as a unit. Interspersed among the combat chapters are official reports on the mission on which the novel is based. Also interspersed are flashbacks of the characters' backgrounds and their ongoing attempts to be reconciled with the lives of their civilian counterparts back home. In a neat reversal of the standard civilian novel, in which the war forms a background to other social issues, here the major social issues back home—especially racial conflicts emerging from the civil rights movement—impinge on the relationships of the men in combat. The unit is an exemplary one, despite its occasional internal conflicts, and in fact does finally take the hill that all the other units have failed to capture. However, at the culmination of this final battle, three of the strongest characters in the novel are killed when a helicopter on its way to pull the unit out is shot down on top of them. Another central figure, a new recruit who attempts to model himself on a war-jaded sergeant, misunderstands everything he attempts to learn and slowly loses his humanity. Despite the sometimes unresolved social issues in the novel, and portrayals of stereotypical "bad" soldiers and units, the overall sense of the novel is positive, both about combat troops and about the nature of the war itself.

Other combat novels of interest are Josiah Bunting's *The Lionheads* (1972), one of the first serious treatments of the U.S. Army in Vietnam; Robert Roth's *Sand in the Wind* (1973); John Clark Pratt's *The Laotian Fragments* (1974); Gustav Hasford's *The Short Timers* (1980); and Harrison Marshall's *Cadillac Flight* (1991), one of Marshall's several novels about the air war.

Following veterans back home is another staple of Vietnam War fiction Some combat novels, such as *Close Quarters* and *Fields of Fire*, end with the retrospective analysis of a returned combat participant. The veteran is usually portrayed as traumatized by his experiences, sometimes as an outcast in civilian society, and usually as someone who must come to terms with some kind of guilt, if only survivor guilt. Philip Caputo's *Indian Country* (1987) is typical of this genre. In a classic American wilderness motif, the central figure must go into the wild to repair his shattered spirits and is led through a spiritual healing by a wise Native American. In Larry Heinemann's *Paco's Story* (1986), the central figure is not only emotionally but physically (and symbolically) scarred by his wartime experience. In a state of mental upheaval, and covered with horrible welts and scars, he drifts around the country, taking odd jobs and never entirely being accepted by the civilian populace, to whom he is an ugly reminder of what the United States has suffered through during the war. Finally, in Bobbie Ann Mason's *In Country* (1985), among the few novels about the war written by a woman, a young woman whose father has died in the war attempts to help her uncle, a veteran with emotional and physical problems, recover from his experiences. The veterans in this novel seem to suffer from post-traumatic stress disorder, and a few have succumbed to the effects of Agent Orange. The young woman—the central figure in the novel—begins, like her counterparts in many of the combat novels, with an idealization of war and is then disillusioned by reading the diary of her deceased father. She is then able to communicate with her uncle's similar

disillusionment, and in the final scene, all are healed emotionally by a visit to the Vietnam Veterans Memorial in Washington.

One of the few exceptions to the format of the veteran novel is John Del Vecchio's *Carry Me Home* (1994). One central figures undergoes a severe case of post-traumatic stress disorder, another is stigmatized on his return home as a war criminal, and still another is a dishonest and unsuccessful criminal and traitor. Their recovery is based on regaining a sense of purpose and pride in what they have done and what they can now do. As in Del Vecchio's previous novel, *The 13th Valley*, the veterans have much to teach their civilian society. And in Robert Olen Butler's *On Distant Ground* (1985), the genres of combat narrative, veteran narrative, and Vietnamese aftermath are combined as a veteran still on active duty returns to Vietnam during the fall of Sài Gòn to attempt to find a child he had with a Vietnamese woman during his service there. Intermingled with this quest is another one: to find the North Vietnamese soldier he helped to escape because of what he thought was a heroic inscription the soldier had written in his cell. He discovers, on his return, that the soldier had not written the inscription at all. Despite the confusion symbolized by this mistaken action on his part, the equivocal nature of his Vietnamese and American family ties, and the scenes he observes as Sài Gòn falls, the overall sense of the book is one of continuity and hope—differences can eventually be reconciled.

Two other Butler novels cross the categories of Vietnam War fiction: *The Alleys of Eden* (1981), set in wartime and postwar Sài Gòn, and *The Deuce* (1989), a domestic novel in which a young American runaway meets the stereotypical Vietnam veteran. However, his collection of short stories, *A Good Scent from a Strange Mountain* (1992), deals specifically with the South Vietnamese experience, particularly that of the South Vietnamese who fled to the United States at the end of the war. Most of these stories reflect the attempt of the immigrants to build—or avoid building—an American life in lieu of (or as an overlay to) their cultural heritage. The stories often reflect the clash of cultures involved in this attempt at adaptation or the realization that too much has been lost in the attempt or that too much cannot be transplanted. In some stories, however, the adaptation is enriched by a realization, and most of the stories end on a hopeful note. The most striking story in the collection is "The American Couple," in which two couples who have won trips to Mexico confront the past and almost literally refight the war. At the end of the story, the Vietnamese American husband—a former South Vietnamese major who has become almost more American than the Americans—and the American husband—a stereotypical veteran who talks obsessively about the war—stage a mock battle that culminates in an actual fistfight. Meanwhile, their wives talk idly about the scenery but watch the battle and wonder at what is happening. Both marriages have had problems, but the refighting of the battle seems to have freed the husbands from their obsessive remembering or forgetting. Again the story ends on a note of hope, although it remains unclear who "the American couple" really is: the two Americans, the two Vietnamese Americans, the two wives, or the two husbands.

—Phoebe S. Spinrad

References: Beidler, Philip. *American Literature and the Experience of Vietnam* (1982); Gilman, Owen W., and Lorrie Smith, eds. *America Rediscovered: Critical Essays on Literature and Film of the Vietnam War* (1990); Helling, Philip H. *Vietnam in American Literature* (1990); Herzog, Tobey C. *Vietnam War Stories: Innocence Lost* (1992); Jason, Philip K., ed. *Fourteen Landing Zones: Approaches to Vietnam War Literature* (1991); Lomperis, Timothy. *Reading the Wind: The Literature of the Vietnam War* (1987); Newman, John. *Vietnam War Literature: An Annotated Bibliography of Imaginative Works about Americans Fighting in Vietnam* (1988); Searle, William, ed. *Search and Clear: Critical Responses to Selected Literature and Films of the Vietnam War* (1988); Wilson, James C. *Vietnam in Prose and Film* (1982); Wittman, Sandra M. *Writing about Vietnam: A Bibliography of the Vietnam Conflict* (1989).

See also: Film and the Vietnam Experience; Greene, Graham; Lansdale, Edward Geary; Poetry and the Vietnam Experience; Prose Narrative and the Vietnam Experience.

Film and the Vietnam Experience

The Vietnam War and its aftermath provided subjects for numerous television dramas and hundreds of dramatic films. Many of the significant productions portrayed graphic combat scenes and presented the standard themes of traditional literary and cinematic works about war: a young man's coming-of-age amid the horrors of war; the basic inhumanity and senselessness of war; the effects of war on innocent civilians, both in and away from the combat zone; and the destructive effects on veterans long after their combat experiences are over.

Of 36 French movies made from 1957 to 1992 that concern Indo-China, critic Jean-Jacques Malo notes only nine that depict significant combat action. Among the best of these are *Patrouille de Choc* (1957), *Le Facteur S'en Va-t-en* (1966), and *Charlie Bravo* (1980), all directed by war veteran Claude Bernard-Aubert. Another noted director who also served in Indo-China was Pierre Schoendoerffer, whose *The 317th Platoon* (*Le 317eme Section*, 1964) and *Dien Bien Phu* (1991) both center around the battle that precipitated French withdrawal from Vietnam. Schoendoerffer also directed two documentary films, *The Anderson Platoon* (1966) and *Reminiscence* (1989). *Indochine* (1992), based on the novel of the same name, has rightly been called a multigenerational soap opera in its attempt to cover so much of the period of French control in the twentieth century. Most of these French films are apolitical, preferring to emphasize the effects of war on individuals instead of examining causes or colonialism.

Quite different in intent and politicization are most of the nearly 200 Vietnamese films produced in Hà Nôi during and after the war. (No significant dramatic films were made in South Vietnam.) From the earliest title, *On the Same River* (1959) until the end of the war, the film industry of the Democratic Republic of Vietnam (DRV) produced movies that were designed to enlighten, reassure, and inspire audiences in their opposition to what the films described as imperialist Americans and their puppet government in the South. In *On the Same River,* an engaged couple is separated by the Bên Hai River, which has recently defined the 1954 division of North and South Vietnam. The woman chooses to forego marriage and remain in the South to fight the Americans and South Vietnamese. In *The A Phu Couple* (1961), only the help of Communist Party leaders permits a Meo minority couple to transcend traditional village persecution and achieve happiness. In *The Call to the Sea* (1967), a valiant North Vietnamese naval officer's death inspires his crew to fight even harder. Some postwar films, such as the four-part saga *The Pursued Woman* (1989–1990), addressed broader issues, such as the impossibility of achieving solace in the modern world. But even after the war, the overall emphasis of the Vietnamese film industry remained instructional in nature. Examples are the later films *White Flowers on the River* (1989) and *Fierce Childhood* (1990), which depict the heroic deaths of men and women at the hands of American and South Vietnamese enemies.

Productions from most other countries cannot be categorized and vary widely in content, accuracy, and applicability to the war. From Australia, which sent combat troops in support of the Republic of Vietnam (RVN), came a number of films that mainly showed the effects of the war on returning veterans. Three Australian TV miniseries are also notable: *Sword of Honor* (1986), *Vietnam* (1987), and *Frankie's House* (1992). The first two objectively present prowar and antiwar themes, contain realistic combat episodes, have accurate and sympathetically drawn Vietnamese characters, and end with a sense of reconciliation. *Frankie's House* is different, graphically portraying the experiences of British photographer Tim Page, who spent three years in Vietnam and was wounded four times. Also notable was *The Odd Angry Shot* (1979), which depicts the combat experiences of the Australian Special Air Service (SAS).

In the United States, more than 400 films and TV dramas were produced that derived major themes, characters, and subjects from the war. Differing from films about previous wars, however, many significant American productions presented variations on an antiwar theme: not only that the Vietnam War produced individual and group tragedies, but also that the United States was wrong to have entered the conflict at all. Some definite categories are recognizable: the antiwar protest films; the TV productions, the settings of which were more restricted and the political agendas of which were less obvious; films that depicted Vietnam veterans as criminal, suicidal, or otherwise disturbed; and the combat films (usually shot in Thailand or the American Southeast) that either attempted verisimilitude or eschewed it in favor of what many critics called "Ramboesque" exaggerations.

Three major protest films received wide recognition. *In the Year of the Pig* (1968), a collage documentary nominated for an Academy Award, blends combat scenes and news clips with statements by antiwar leaders. *Woodstock* (1970), an Academy Award winner, documents the August 1969 rock-and-drug festival that featured many antiwar songs. Using a similar documentary format was *Hearts and Minds* (1974), a carefully edited film that portrays U.S. forces in Vietnam committing atrocities and bombing hospitals and civilians. This film also won an Academy Award.

There were also two major postwar documentary productions, one by the Public Broadcasting Service, and a shorter series by the Canadian Broadcasting Corporation. Both vary in intensity and coverage; the war in Laos, for instance, is rarely mentioned. The Canadian series remains generally objective, but the American series becomes selectively antiwar as its historical episodes progress.

Forty Vietnam War–related dramas were produced for televsion. The series *Tour of Duty* (1987–1989) tracks a culturally diverse platoon through combat and behind-the-lines experiences. Restrained and realistic at first, this series began to incorporate more sexual subject matter as the competing *China Beach* (1988–1992) gained audience favor for its exploitive portrayal of female nurses. In HBO's *Vietnam War Story* (1989–1990), Patrick S. Duncan produced 12 short dramas on subjects ranging from a soldier's departure for Vietnam in 1963 to the problems of veterans in a VA hospital. Also notable is HBO's *Dear America: Letters Home from Vietnam* (1987), a poignant film that deftly superimposes combat footage with actual letters written by American men and women and read by Hollywood stars. An equally impressive TV movie was *Friendly Fire* (1979), in which Carol Burnett portrays the mother of an American soldier accidentally killed by his own artillery. Other TV films include *The Final War of Ollie Winter* (1967), *A Rumor of War* (1980), *Kent State* (1981), and two productions about U.S. prisoners of war, *When Hell Was in Session* (1979) and *In Love and War* (1987).

Critic Michael Lanning categorizes the more than 200 commercial films that feature Vietnam war veterans as follows: the crazed veteran (40); the not-so-welcome-home veteran (40); the criminal veteran (72); the disturbed veteran (53); and the suicidal veteran (22). This recurrent portrayal of veterans with severe problems helped maintain and reinforce a stereotype that applied to only a small percentage of former combatants. Of the few good returned-veteran films, Oscar-winning *Coming Home* (1978) and *In Country* (1989) are by far the best.

American films set during the war all have one major deficiency: none portrays Vietnamese characters with accuracy and understanding. Significant productions that consider the early years of U.S. involvement began with *The Quiet American* (1958). Although based on Graham Greene's novel, the movie version's changed ending attributes civilian deaths to the Communist Viêt Minh and considerably enhances, to Greene's later disgust, the image of Americans in Vietnam. *The Ugly American* (1963), starring Marlon Brando, satirized the actions of the U.S. Foreign Service. Also set before the massive force buildup was *Go Tell the Spartans* (1978), in which Burt Lancaster convincingly plays the commander of an ill-fated U.S. advisory unit. *Good Morning, Vietnam* (1987), billed as a comedy to showcase the talents of Robin Williams, accurately depicts many of the events and prevailing attitudes of the time.

From 1978 to 1989, seven significant movies were produced that featured the coming-of-age theme for Americans in full-scale combat. Of these, *84 Charlie Mo Pic* (1989), which depicts an American platoon on patrol, is the most accurate and poignant. Others were *The Deer Hunter* (1978), which received numerous Oscars; *Apocalypse Now* (1979); *Platoon* (1986), an Oscar winner for best picture and the first of Oliver Stone's Vietnam films; *Full Metal Jacket* (1987); *Hamburger Hill* (1987); and *Casualties of War* (1989). In these films, gruesome brutality and symbolic scenes often masquerade as realism, and they universally show the U.S. presence in Vietnam as tragically wrong. Also produced at this time was *Hanoi Hilton* (1987), which portrayed rather accurately the tribulations of American prisoners in North Vietnam.

Few films depicted pilots and their experiences. *Bat 21* (1988) concerns an Air Force pilot who is shot down and evades capture; *Flight of the Intruder* (1990) is a clichéed and unbelievable story of Navy airmen; and *Air America* (1990), a satiric study of Central Intelligence Agency operations in Laos, contains some startlingly accurate scenes and observations.

Perhaps the best film of all was not officially about the Vietnam War but depicted its aftermath in Cambodia. *The Killing Fields* (1984) starred Sam Waterston and Haing S. Ngor, who survived the genocidal events portrayed in the movie.

The best-known American writer/producer of films dealing with the Vietnam War is Oliver Stone, himself a war veteran. After *Platoon*, Stone produced *Born on the Fourth of July* (1989), adapted from the book by paralyzed veteran Ron Kovic; *JFK* (1991), which theorizes that President Kennedy was assassinated because he was becoming opposed to U.S. involvement in Vietnam; and *Heaven and Earth* (1993), the story of a Vietnamese woman who had two American husbands. Although demonstrating Stone's penchant for adapting fact to make a thematic point, his films are nevertheless stirring cinematic experiences.

—John Clark Pratt

References: Adair, Gilbert. *Hollywood's Vietnam* (1981); Dittmar, Linda, and Gene Michaud, eds. *From Hanoi to Hollywood: The Vietnam War in American Film* (1990); Lanning, Michael Lee. *Vietnam at the Movies* (1994); Malo, Jean Jacques, and Tony Williams. *Vietnam War Films* (1994); Walsh, Jeffrey, and James Aulich, eds. *Vietnam Images: War and Representation* (1989).

See also: Art and the Vietnam War; Drama and the Vietnam Experience; Music and the Vietnam War; Poetry and the Vietnam Experience; Prose Narrative and the Vietnam Experience.

Fishel, Wesley Robert (1919–1977)

American political science professor and influential advisor to Republic of Vietnam (RVN) President Ngô Đình Diêm. Fishel's professional career combined academic pursuits in the United States with work for the U.S. government in the Far East. He first met Ngô Đình Diêm in Japan in 1950. When Diêm took control of the Sài Gòn government in 1954, he arranged for Michigan State University to set up a program under which a faculty resident in South Vietnam would advise his government on a wide range of issues. Fishel served as chief administrator of the program, which was financed by the U.S. aid program in South Vietnam, from 1956 to 1958. He remained influential in the program until its termination by Diêm in 1962.

Fishel became a strong critic of Diêm after 1962 and served as an advisor to the Department of State in the critical weeks before Diêm's 1963 overthrow. He served as chairman of the American Friends of Vietnam, a public relations lobby for South Vietnam, from May 1964 until spring 1966.

Fishel's involvement in South Vietnamese affairs was controversial at home. The MSU program, especially its police training component, was accused of acting as a cover for Central Intelligence Agency activities. Fishel's continued advocacy of U.S. policy, and particularly his attempt to rally support for U.S. military intervention in 1965, made him unpopular with the antiwar movement, and he was pilloried in articles and at campus teach-ins.

—Arthur J. Dommen

References: Fishel, Wesley R., ed. *Problems of Freedom; South Vietnam Since Independence* (1961); —. *Vietnam: Anatomy of a Conflict* (1968); Morgan, Joseph G. *The Vietnam Lobby; The American Friends of Vietnam, 1955–1975* (1997).
See also: Michigan State University (MSU) Advisory Group; Ngô Đình Diêm; United States: Involvement in Vietnam, 1954–1965.

Fishhook

Densely forested region in Cambodia across the border from South Vietnam, 60 miles from Sài Gòn. Viêt Công (VC) and Peoples Army of Vietnam (PAVN) forces, infiltrating into War Zones C and D, maintained semipermanent installations in the area. One was believed to be the location of the Central Office for South Vietnam (COSVN), the headquarters that controlled all VC party activities and military forces in the South.

President Johnson prohibited American forces from pursuing Communist forces into these Cambodian sanctuaries, but beginning in March 1969 President Nixon authorized secret B-52 bombing strikes against Communist locations in Cambodia, especially in the Fishhook. Throughout 1969 and in early 1970, Allied forces drove main-force PAVN units into Cambodia, where they regrouped and expanded their support bases. Base Areas 350, 352, and 353, in the Fishhook area, became major objectives of the Cambodian incursion ordered by Nixon and begun on 1 May 1970. During the 60–day operation, the U.S. 1st Cavalry Division (Airmobile) and 25th Infantry Division, supported by the 11th Armored Cavalry Regiment and the Army of the Republic of Vietnam (ARVN) Airborne Division, pushed Communist forces deeper inside Cambodia and discovered two huge, but abandoned, fortified bases. 1st Cavalry units destroyed thousands of bunkers and captured massive amounts of military supplies.

Allied forces experienced significant casualties in continuous skirmishes and in mortar and rocket attacks on temporary firebases. Although the elusive COSVN was not found, destruction of huge supply caches effectively prevented sig-nificant main-force activity in War Zones C and D for more than a year, allowing the planned withdrawal of U.S. combat units to proceed. Nevertheless, when the Cambodian incursion ended, PAVN and VC units quickly reoccupied the Fishhook and, despite continued secret B-52 bombing, replenished their forces and reestablished their operational and supply bases. In spring 1972, War Zones C and D again became bloody battlegrounds.

—John D. Root

References: Coleman, J. D. *Incursion* (1991); Stanton, Shelby L. *The Rise and Fall of an American Army: U.S. Ground Forces in Vietnam: 1965–1973* (1985).
See also: Cambodian Incursion; COSVN (Central Office for South Vietnam or Trung Uong Miê Nam); MENU, Operation; Nixon, Richard Milhous; Parrot's Beak.

"Five O'Clock Follies"

Derisive epithet appended by the media to daily media briefings by the Military Assistance Command, Vietnam (MACV), Office of Information (MACOI) at the Joint U.S. Public Affairs Office (JUSPAO) in Sai Gòn. JUSPAO was essentially a resource and logistics center for news people, providing many services to media personnel to assist in their quest for news. MACOI was the interservice information office located at MACV headquarters at Tân Son Nhut air base. The MACOI staff compiled daily communiqués from operational reports received at the MACV operations center and monthly chronologies of U.S. military actions. Each day, members of the MACOI staff would travel to the JUSPAO building auditorium to present the military portion of the daily 5:00 P.M. briefing.

The "five o'clock follies" was so named because of reporters distrusted the information presented by those briefings. This distrust began during the Kennedy administration, when U.S. information sources in Sài Gòn were obligated to stress the positive side of the conflict. As the war escalated under the Johnson administration, with the Americanization of the war, pressure to stress damage done to the Communists, while limiting the impact of damage to the U.S. and its allies, led to what became known as a "credibility gap."

—Arthur T. Frame

References: Braestrup, Peter. *Big Story: How the American Press and Television Reported and Interpreted the Crisis of Tet 1968 in Vietnam and Washington* (1978); Hammond, William M. *Public Affairs: The Military and the Media, 1962–1968* (1990); ———. *Public Affairs: The Military and the Media, 1968–1973* (1996); Westmoreland, William C. *A Soldier Reports* (1976); Wyatt, Clarence R. *Paper Soldiers: The American Press and the Vietnam War* (1993).
See also: Joint U.S. Public Affairs Office (JUSPAO); Media and the War; Television and the Vietnam Experience.

FLAMING DART, Operation (February 1965)

Reprisal air raids signaling a sustained bombing campaign against the Democratic Republic of Vietnam (DRV). Early on 7 February 1965, the Viêt Công mortared the U.S. helicopter installation at Camp Holloway and the adjacent Pleiku airfield in South Vietnam's Central Highlands, killing 8 U.S. servicemen, wounding 109, and destroying or damaging 20 aircraft. President Johnson decided to order reprisals, hoping that quick and effective retaliation would persuade the North Vietnamese that their leadership could not rely on continued freedom from bombing while persevering in belligerent actions against South Vietnam. Johnson dismissed the possibility that a restricted attack would activate Russian or Chinese involvement.

With South Vietnamese agreement, the Johnson administration ordered air strikes against four targets in the DRV north of the 17th parallel. Carried out under a previously developed Joint Chiefs of Staff contingency labeled FLAMING DART, U.S. Navy jets from Seventh Fleet aircraft carriers rocketed and bombed North Vietnamese installations at Đông Hoi. Johnson ordered FLAMING DART II 48 hours later, after Việt Công killed 23 Americans at Qui Nhon, a second series of sorties explained as the onset of ROLLING THUNDER.

—Rodney J. Ross

References: Clodfelter, Mark. *The Limits of Air Power: The American Bombing of North Vietnam* (1989); Johnson, Lyndon Baines. *The Vantage Point: Perspectives of the Presidency 1963–1969* (1971); Kahin, George McT. *Intervention: How America Became Involved in Vietnam* (1986).

See also: Air Power, Role in War; BARREL ROLL, Operation; Johnson, Lyndon Baines; McNaughton, John T.; ROLLING THUNDER, Operation; Taylor, Maxwell Davenport.

Flexible Response

U.S. strategic defense policy developed in the 1960s by retired Army General Maxwell Taylor. The policy called for an end to the Eisenhower administration's policy of "massive retaliation," which had been contrived to curtail defense expenditures by threatening the Soviet Union with nuclear conflict rather than maintaining a large and costly conventional force. In 1959 Taylor wrote *The Uncertain Trumpet*, in which he called for a diversified military with counterinsurgency capability. Taylor stated that inflexible massive retaliation offered "only two choices, the initiation of general war or compromise and defeat." President Kennedy read *The Uncertain Trumpet,* and on 1 July 1961 Taylor became the president's military advisor.

Kennedy embraced the need for a new defense program, one in large measure shaped by Taylor, who was tired of seeing his service downsized, denigrated in budget considerations, and ill-prepared for ground war. Taylor contended that the Eisenhower doctrine of massive nuclear retaliation left the United States with no room to respond to localized or limited conflicts, especially in emerging Third World battlegrounds. Kennedy accepted Taylor's policy of "flexible response," namely a sizable increase in armed forces prepared to fight nonnuclear battles or "brushfire wars," including wars of counterinsurgency against Communist guerrillas. The adoption of flexible response helped to facilitate U.S. involvement in Vietnam.

—J. Nathan Campbell

References: Buzzanco, Robert. *Masters of War: Military Dissent and Politics in the Vietnam Era* (1996); Halberstam, David. *The Best and the Brightest* (1972); Karnow, Stanley. *Vietnam: A History* (1983); Kinnard, Douglas. *The Certain Triumph: Maxwell Taylor and the American Experience in Vietnam* (1991); Taylor, Maxwell. *The Uncertain Trumpet* (1960).

See also: Kennedy, John Fitzgerald; Taylor, Maxwell Davenport.

Fonda, Jane Seymour (1937–)

American actor and anti–Vietnam War activist; daughter of actor Henry Fonda. The Pentagon in 1962 named Fonda "Miss Army Recruiting," but as she became increasingly outspoken about the Vietnam War, the Federal Bureau of Investigation (FBI) hatched plots to discredit her. Fonda was accused of drug smuggling and assaulting a police officer, charges that were later dropped. In 1971 she met Students for a Democratic Society founder Tom Hayden at an antiwar rally. They married in 1972 and divorced in 1989.

In 1972 Fonda appeared with Donald Sutherland in *FTA* (*Free* [or *Fuck*] *the Army*), a collection of skits she described as "political vaudeville." Becoming increasingly radicalized, she flew to Hà Nôi, where she made ten propaganda broadcasts, a decision she would later regret. She was put on display with U.S. prisoners of war and met with Democratic Republic of Vietnam Vice Premier Nguyên Duy Trinh. To patriotic Americans she became "Hanoi Jane," the Vietnam equivalent of Axis Sally and Tokyo Rose.

The Justice Department ignored Fonda's actions to avoid making her an antiwar martyr, but her Hollywood career was temporarily compromised. In 1974, after a second trip to Vietnam with Hayden, Fonda made a 60–minute documentary, *Introduction to the Enemy.* Her last Vietnam-related picture, for which she garnered an Oscar, was *Coming Home* (1978), inspired by Ron Kovic, a paraplegic veteran she met at a 1972 antiwar rally. By 1981 she had reentered the American mainstream with *On Golden Pond,* but many Americans still despised her for her antiwar activities. To counter this backlash, Fonda in 1988 publicly apologized for her 1972 actions on ABC's "20/20." Fonda expressed regret if anyone who had served in Vietnam had been hurt "because of things I said or did." This performance closed the chapter on Vietnam for Jane Fonda.

—James Michael Welsh

References: Andersen, Christopher. *Citizen Jane: The Turbulent Life of Jane Fonda* (1990); Collier, Peter. *The Fondas: A Hollywood Dynasty* (1990); Guiles, Fred Lawrence. *Jane Fonda: The Actress in Her Time* (1982); Herman, Gary, and David Downing. *Jane Fonda: All-American Anti-Heroine* (1980).

See also: Antiwar Movement, United States; Film and the Vietnam Experience; Hayden, Thomas E.; Students for a Democratic Society (SDS).

Fontainebleau Conference (July–September 1946)

Conference between Democratic Republic of Vietnam (DRV) and French political leaders at the Chateau Fontainebleau south of Paris. The conference was an effort to work out implementation of the Hô-Sainteny Accord and a last chance for the French government to develop a working relationship with the DRV. It was undermined by High Commissioner Thierry d'Argenlieu's 2 June proclamation of a Republic of Cochin China in South Vietnam and by political developments in France. The French Socialist and Communist parties on which Hô Chí Minh had counted failed to support him.

When the DRV delegation, led by Hô, reached France, the government had fallen and the delegation was forced to wait while a new cabinet was formed under Popular Republican Movement (MRP) leader Georges Bidault. This represented a political shift to the right. The conference finally opened on 6 July, but two months of talks accomplished nothing. The French would make no meaningful concessions, and in the middle of the conference d'Argenlieu torpedoed the effort by calling his own conference at Đà Lat, to which he invited representatives of the Republic of Cochin China and "Southern Annam," in effect carving another chunk out of Vietnam. The sum of the conference's work was a draft accord reinforcing France's economic rights in northern Vietnam without solving the problem of Cochin China. Hô sent the DRV delegation home. On 14 September he signed the modus vivendi worked out with the French. On the 19th he left France by ship, never to return. The Indo-China War began that December.

—Spencer C. Tucker

References: Hammer, Ellen. *The Struggle for Indochina* (1954); Sainteny, Jean. *Histoire d'une Paix Manquée: Indochine, 1945–1947* (1953).

See also: d'Argenlieu, Georges Thierry; Hô Chí Minh; Hô-Sainteny Agreement; Indo-China War; Sainteny, Jean.

Ford, Gerald R. (1913–)

U.S. congressman, 1949–1973; vice-president, December 1973–August 1974; president, August 1974–January 1977. Throughout his years in Congress, a tenure that was highlighted by service as his party's minority leader (1965–1973), Ford developed an expertise in defense appropriations. He consistently supported U.S. commitment in Vietnam, differing with the Johnson administration only in recommending that more money and resources be allocated there. Appointed vice-president by Richard Nixon in October 1973 following Spiro T. Agnew's resignation, Ford publicly defended the administration's record on Vietnam.

Following Nixon's 9 August 1974 resignation, Ford presided over the final stage of the Vietnam War. As president, Ford moderated his earlier, hawkish views on the war. Only two weeks into his presidency, Ford ignored the advice of Secretary of State Henry Kissinger—who counseled a harsh policy against "draft dodgers" and combat personnel who were absent without leave—and formed the Presidential Clemency Board to review individual cases.

In January 1975, Ford faced the final offensives of the Cambodian Khmer Rouge and the North Vietnamese. The Ford administration took no serious steps to counter either attack. Having no treaty commitment to Cambodia, it was relatively easy for Ford to order Operation EAGLE PULL, the abandonment of the U.S. embassy in Phnom Penh on 11

April 1975. But in a secret correspondence delivered before his resignation, Nixon had promised RVN President Nguyên Van Thiêu that, if the Democratic Republic of Vietnam violated the 1973 truce, the United States would recommit troops to South Vietnam. Despite the advice of Kissinger and Ambassador Graham Martin, Ford refused to honor that pledge. Instead, after the North Vietnamese began their 1975 Spring Offensive, Ford made a half-hearted attempt to cajole Congress into appropriating monies for the RVN's defense. When it refused, the Ford administration ordered the evacuation of all remaining U.S. military and embassy personnel. The 28 April evacuation of Sài Gòn (Operation FREQUENT WIND) removed 1,400 Americans and 5,600 Vietnamese.

The evacuations from Phnom Penh and Sài Gòn, as well as the May 1975 *Mayaguez* crisis—America's final military engagements of the Vietnam War—were used against Ford in the 1976 presidential election. The evacuations were cited as evidence that the Ford administration did not adequately support U.S. allies, while the *Mayaguez* incident was cited to show that, by choosing force over diplomacy in a crisis, Republican administrations had learned nothing from Vietnam. In part because of his handling of the end of the Vietnam War, Ford was defeated by Governor Jimmy Carter.

—John Robert Greene

References: Ford, Gerald R. *A Time to Heal: The Autobiography of Gerald R. Ford* (1979); Greene, John Robert. *The Presidency of Gerald R. Ford* (1995).

See also: Agnew, Spiro T.; Amnesty; Cambodia; Carter, Jimmy; EAGLE PULL, Operation; FREQUENT WIND, Operation; Hô Chí Minh Campaign; Kissinger, Henry Alfred; Martin, Graham A.; Nixon, Richard Milhous; *Mayaguez* Incident; Nguyên Van Thiêu.

Foreign Legion. *See* France: Foreign Legion in Indo-China.

Forrestal, Michael V. (1927–1989)

Head of the Vietnam Coordinating Committee, National Security Council, 1962–1965. In late 1962, Forrestal and Roger Hilsman, director of intelligence for the State Department, visited Vietnam to review the situation there. Although initially committed to U.S. intervention in Vietnam, they produced a mixed report on the war that reinforced growing doubts about the viability of the Republic of Vietnam government. They pointed to ominous increases in Viêt Công strength, suggesting a longer and costlier war than had been predicted, and expressed doubts about the effectiveness of the Strategic Hamlet program while agreeing with it in principle. A secret annex to their report recommended that the United States exert additional pressure on President Ngô Đình Diêm to institute reforms and liberalize the "authoritarian political structure."

Working with Averell Harriman in late August 1963, Forrestal and Hilsman were central figures in obtaining presidential approval to dispatch a cable recommending the overthrow of the Diêm government. Forrestal remained in government until mid-1965, but his discontent with official policy steadily increased. He felt that military estimates were overoptimistic and supported a negotiated settlement, a position that won him President Johnson's disfavor. In mid-1965 he returned to the practice of law.

—Priscilla Roberts

References: Gibbons, William Conrad. *The U.S. Government and the Vietnam War* (1986, 1989); Halberstam, David. *The Best and the Brightest* (1973).

See also: Harriman, W. Averell; Hilsman, Roger; Hilsman-Forrestal Report; Johnson, Lyndon Baines; Taylor-McNamara Report.

Fort Hood Three

Collective name given U.S. Army privates James Johnson, Dennis Mora, and David Samas. Their case attracted national attention as the first highly publicized refusal of U.S. soldiers to accept duty in Vietnam. Members of the 142d Signal Battalion of the 2d Armored Division stationed at Fort Hood, Texas, Johnson, Mora, and Samas refused assignment to Vietnam and, to avoid forced shipment or arrest, contacted New York's Fifth Avenue Peace Parade Committee. Supported by the Parade Committee, the Fort Hood Three held a 30 June press conference to state their belief that the Vietnam War was immoral, illegal, and unjust. They also filed a lawsuit in a U.S. district court challenging their orders on the grounds that the Vietnam War was illegal and requesting an injunction to prevent the Army from sending them to Vietnam. Antiwar activists established a Fort Hood Three Defense Committee.

On 7 July, military authorities arrested them for making disloyal statements and placed them in "investigative detention" at Fort Dix, New Jersey, until 14 July. On 11 July, District Court Judge Edward Curran denied their lawsuit, affirming the president's authority in foreign policy and denying that civilian courts had jurisdiction in such a case. On 14 July, Johnson, Mora, and Samas refused orders to board transportation for Vietnam. On 15 August all were formally charged with insubordination. Separately court-martialed at Fort Dix in September, all were convicted after the military court refused to allow the defense to argue the war's illegality. On 6 February 1967 the Supreme Court refused to hear the case. Mora, Johnson, and Samas served most of their sentences at Fort Leavenworth, Kansas. Following release they became active supporters of the antiwar movement.

—Mitchell K. Hall

References: Bannan, John F., and Rosemary S. Bannan. *Law, Morality, and Vietnam: The Peace Militants and the Courts* (1974); Halstead, Fred. *Out Now! A Participant's Account of the American Movement against the Vietnam War* (1978); Lynd, Alice, ed. *We Won't Go: Personal Accounts of War Objectors* (1968).

See also: Antiwar Movement, United States.

Fortas, Abe (1910–1982)

Advisor to President Johnson; associate justice of the U.S. Supreme Court, 1965–1969. Fortas exerted great influence on Johnson's Vietnam policies. As a member of the "Wise Men," a group of senior advisors convened by Johnson, Fortas at first feared that the war's costs would bankrupt the social programs of the Great Society. But between 1965 and 1967, as Johnson's other advisors became disenchanted with

prospects for victory in Vietnam, Fortas hardened his support for U.S. involvement. Reasoning that "a long period of national self-doubt and timidity" would follow a unilateral U.S. withdrawal, Fortas saw no alternative but to proceed with the war until the Democratic Republic of Vietnam (DRV) agreed to end the fighting. Fortas's arguments impressed Johnson, but when the "Wise Men" met in March 1968 to advise that the United States should reduce its involvement in Vietnam, Fortas was almost alone in advocating further expansion of the conflict.

The lame-duck president nominated Fortas to succeed retiring Earl Warren as chief justice of the Supreme Court, but Republicans saw this as an attempt to replace Warren with another liberal chief justice, and a filibuster sent the nomination to defeat. The following year, Fortas resigned from the Supreme Court under allegations of impropriety for agreeing to accept a retainer from the Louis Wolfson Foundation for legal services while serving on the Supreme Court. Returning to his private law practice, Fortas continued to write and speak on U.S. involvement in Vietnam.

—Elizabeth Urban Alexander

References: Barrett, David M. *Uncertain Warriors: Lyndon Johnson and His Vietnam Advisors* (1993); Kalman, Laura. *Abe Fortas: A Biography* (1990); Karnow, Stanley. *Vietnam: A History* (1983); Murphy, Bruce Allen. *Fortas; The Rise and Ruin of a Supreme Court Justice* (1988).

See also: Johnson, Lyndon Baines; "Wise Men."

Four-Party Joint Military Commission (FPJMC)

Sài Gòn–based commission created 27 January 1973 by the Paris Peace Accords and consisting of representatives from the United States, the Republic of Vietnam (RVN), the Democratic Republic of Vietnam (DRV), and the Provisional Revolutionary Government of South Vietnam (PRG, Việt Công). Its mission was to establish a cease fire, supervise withdrawal of the remaining U.S. and Free World Military Forces, exchange prisoners of war (POWs), and resolve the status of those missing in action (MIAs). These missions were to be accomplished within 60 days of the signing of the peace accords.

On 29 March 1973, the FPJMC was disbanded with 587 U.S. POWs repatriated and the last of the U.S./Free World combat forces withdrawn. Less successful were efforts to enforce the cease-fire and to resolve the MIA issue. The latter was turned over to the Four-Power Joint Military Team (FPJMT), which had even less success after the Việt Công and People's Army of Vietnam, no longer threatened by U.S. military presence, refused further cooperation. The U.S. delegation to the FPJMT withdrew from Sài Gòn on 10 April 1975.

—Robert G. Mangrum

References: Cao Van Viên. *The Final Collapse* (1983); Olson, James S., ed. *Dictionary of the Vietnam War* (1988); Summers, Harry G. *Vietnam War Almanac* (1985).

See also: Hồ Chí Minh Campaign; HOMECOMING, Operation; Missing in Action, Allied; Missing in Action and Prisoners of War, Việt Công and People's Army of Vietnam; Provisional Revolutionary Government of South Vietnam (PRG).

Fragging

Intentional causing of friendly casualties from weapons in U.S. hands, directed primarily toward unit leaders, officers and noncommissioned officers (NCOs). This form of homicide gained its name from the use of fragmentation hand grenades (which left no finger prints) as the weapon of choice, but it was not limited to a single type of weapon. However, it is virtually impossible to determine how many officers and NCOs might have been shot by their own men during engagements with the enemy.

Fragging was practically unheard of early in U.S. involvement in ground combat. But as leadership and discipline declined, and the rapid turnover caused by the one-year rotation policy weakened unit cohesion, incidents of "combat refusal" (mutiny) and fragging increased. Fragging incidents in combat were attempts to remove leaders perceived to be incompetent and a threat to survival. Most fragging incidents, however, occurred in rear-echelon units. Unit leaders who were perceived as too stringent sometimes received warnings via a fragmentation grenade with their name painted on it or a smoke grenade discharged under their bunk. Most understood the message, and intimidation through threat of fragging far exceeded actual incidents. Toward the end of U.S. involvement, however, some fraggings took place without visible provocation or motive.

Although violence directed toward military superiors was not a phenomenon limited to the Vietnam War, reliable statistics are not available for any conflict, including Vietnam. The incidence of fragging took a dramatic upswing in 1969, coincident with the initiation of Vietnamization, and increased as a percentage of troop strength each year until final withdrawal.

—Arthur T. Frame

References: Neel, Spurgeon. *Medical Support of the U.S. Army in Vietnam, 1965–1972* (1973); Office of Information Management and Statistics. *Data on Vietnam Era Veterans* (1983).
See also: Attrition; Casualties; Drugs and Drug Use; Friendly Fire; Grenades, Hand, Allied and Democratic Republic of Vietnam.

France: Air Force (1946–1954)

The French Air Force in Indo-China was employed primarily as an Army support weapon. It was reconstituted in 1945 from personnel and aircraft already in Indo-China and included a mixture of Japanese, British, American, and German aircraft. The French built up their air assets as quickly as resources were available. Additional C-47s and British Mosquito fighter-bombers arrived in 1947. The fragile plywood Mosquito proved unsuitable for Indo-China's climate and was replaced with the American B-26 (Invader) light bomber as the United States began to supply the French in Vietnam. Late in the war, Washington sent modern F6F and F8F fighters and C-119 transports. The French also introduced their own "Bretagne" transports—twin-engine planes equipped with auxiliary wing-tip jet engines for short-terrain takeoff assistance—and experimented with American H-51 Sikorsky helicopters for medical evacuation and observation.

In 1950 General Jean de Lattre de Tassigny reorganized the Air Force and changed its doctrinal role, calling for increased massed tactical strikes and strategic objectives to work in conjunction with the Army rather than be subordinate to it. French fighter-bombers and light bombers flew numerous close air support missions, dropping napalm in support of ground units. French bomber pilots attempted strategic bombing of Viêt Minh targets but played only a small role in the war. As the French relied more on close air support, the Viêt Minh began to adopt tactics and acquire antiaircraft weapons that negated their opponent's air superiority.

The French suffered a chronic shortage of transport aircraft (which proved a factor in their defeat at Điên Biên Phu) and lacked sufficient experience in what would later be termed "airmobile" warfare to conduct effective helicopter operations. Equipment shortages and lack of effective doctrine doomed the French air effort to failure, despite the bravery of the aircrews and ground support personnel.

—J. A. Menzoff

References: Beckett, Brian. *The Illustrated History of the Viet Nam War* (1985); Bonds, Ray, ed. *The Viet Nam War: An Illustrated History* (1983); Christienne, Charles, and Pierre Lissarague. *A History of French Military Aviation* (1986); Spector, Ronald H. *Advise and Support, The Early Years: The U.S. Army in Vietnam* (1983).
See also: Airplanes, Allied and Democratic Republic of Vietnam; France: Army; Indo-China War; Order of Battle.

France: Army (1946–1954)

The French Army in Indo-China comprised Europeans, Vietnamese, Cambodians, Thais, North Africans, and the French Foreign Legion. After 1948, the French raised a colonial army from the indigenous peoples of Vietnam, supplemented with troops from other colonial possessions and France. French Union Forces were primarily a professional force that served under the direction of the colonial administrator. The commander in chief of the expeditionary force was the military advisor to the colonial administrator, responsible to the government in Paris. France's efforts in Indo-China suffered from a rapid changeover of military commanders and lacked a cohesive aggressive strategy. This frequent change at the top undoubtedly hurt overall efficiency and morale. Of the French commanders, only de Lattre was able to infuse a fighting spirit and successful cohesive military policy.

The conventional French Army in Vietnam consisted of infantry, armor, artillery, airborne, and support forces. Major troop concentrations were based near urban centers throughout Vietnam. As the war progressed, the French made the battalion rather than regiment the standard garrison unit. These battalions were then configured into mobile battle groups to respond to Viêt Minh attacks throughout the country. French armor was designated as cavalry and included all armored fighting vehicles. The armor battalion or cavalry squadron contained approximately 17 tanks; an infantry division had one cavalry regiment of nearly 60 tanks.

The initial French strategy was to establish a series of

forts garrisoned by small forces that would link the major population centers. These "postes" were linked by the major highways. French dependence upon the road networks led to disaster, however, as conventional mechanized forces were vulnerable to the Viêt Minh, who cut highways at will and destroyed French convoys attempting to resupply and reinforce beleaguered outposts. Consequently, the French placed increasing reliance upon parachute troops, raising a number of colonial parachute battalions.

During 1947–1950, the Viêt Minh carried out a concerted offensive to drive the French from northern Vietnam. The French effort to maintain their outposts was a failure. By the end of 1950, the Viêt Minh controlled most of north Vietnam; the French, only the cities. Paris sent the country's most illustrious army general, Jean de Lattre de Tassigny, to command in Indo-China. General de Lattre designed a new doctrine to use French forces in a conventional role. He embarked upon the "set-piece" battle. de Lattre established a fortified base, offering Viêt Minh commander General Vô Nguyên Giáp an irresistible target and an opportunity to destroy the French Army. In the 14–15 January 1951 Battle of Vinh Yên, French massed conventional forces, well-supported by air power, decisively defeated the Viêt Minh. French artillery fire and aircraft-dropped napalm turned the tide in favor of the French. de Lattre's "strategic enclave" policy, continued by his successors Generals Raoul Salan and Henri Navarre, culminated in the the Battle of Điên Biên Phu (13 March–8 May 1954). The French defeat at Điên Biên Phu was a testament to Giáp's battle planning and the endurance of Viêt Minh soldiers, but French mismanagement and command failures also contributed to the defeat.

The French also experimented with new tactics to combat the Viêt Minh's guerrilla warfare, raising several commando brigades for raids and other light infantry operations. The Groupement de commandos mixtes aéroportés (GCMA) was designed for long-range penetration missions into Viêt Minh territory. Their missions included intelligence gathering and training, equipping, and leading indigenous peoples in a counterguerrilla campaign against the Viêt Minh. The GCMAs were to enter Communist-controlled areas, live in the jungle, and receive supplies by air while attacking the Viêt Minh where they lived. GCM teams lacked sufficient radio communications, and shortages of air support left them virtually isolated in the jungle. The French high command failed to plan for extractions or reinforcements, and the Viêt Minh gradually eliminated the GCMA teams.

The bolt-action 7.5-mm MAS 36 rifle was the standard issue small arm until the 1956 adoption of the semiautomatic MAS 49. The submachine gun was popular for jungle combat, and the excellent French 9-mm MAT 49 was issued in large quantities to French Union Forces. As U.S. military aid began to reach Indo-China, .30–caliber M1 and M2 carbines were distributed to French units. Light automatic weapons used by the expeditionary force were the French Mitrailleuse 1931 7.5-mm light machine gun and the .303–caliber British Bren gun, which provided sustained firepower at the small-unit level. American .30–caliber light and M2 .50–caliber

heavy Browning machine guns were used in various roles. The American .45–caliber Colt was the official-issue handgun, but most known types of pistols were in evidence during the Indo-China War.

The expeditionary force's primary armor was the American M-26 Chaffee light tank. The French also used U.S. 81-mm and 4.2-inch mortars. Field artillery weapons were the U.S. 105-mm and 155-mm howitzers. French artillery battalions were divided and employed as separate batteries supporting isolated garrisons. Artillery batteries were also included as part of French mobile battle groups.

The French Army attempted to fight an unconventional war with conventional strategy and tactics, yet the French Expeditionary Force fought well in Indo-China. The French experimented with helicopter warfare, counterinsurgency warfare techniques, and psychological warfare. French operational doctrine and air employment were studied by the United States, which endeavored to improve on these during the subsequent Vietnam War.

—J. A. Menzoff

References: Beckett, Brian. *The Illustrated History of the Viet Nam War* (1985); Bonds, Ray, ed. *The Viet Nam War: An Illustrated History* (1983); Christienne, Charles, and Pierre Lissarag... *A History of French Military Aviation* (1986); Fall, Bernard B. *Hell in a Very Small Place: The Siege of Dien Bien Phu* (1966); Spector, Ronald H. *Advise and Support, The Early Years: The U.S. Army in Vietnam* (1983).
See also: Airplanes, Allied and Democratic Republic of Vietnam; Artillery, Allied and People's Army of Vietnam; Carpentier, Marcel; de Lattre de Tassigny, Jean Joseph Marie Gabriel; Điên Biên Phu, Battle of; France: Foreign Legion in Indo-China; Indo-China War; Leclerc, Jacques-Philippe; Navarre, Henri Eugène; Order of Battle; Salan, Raoul Albin Louis; Vô Nguyên Giáp.

France: Foreign Legion in Indo-China (1883–1954)

The French Foreign Legion first saw action in Indo-China in December 1883 during an operation to seize the town of Son Tây, beginning a 71-year presence that ended with the 1954 capture of Điên Biên Phu. For most of this period the French Foreign Legion was the backbone of French military presence in Indo-China. For the Legion, the Indo-China War posed familiar tactical problems. Fighting primarily a guerrilla war, the Legion perpetuated its superior combat reputation among friends and foes alike. By 1951 it created a new type of formation, called "groupes mobile," to meet the difficult tactical nature of the war. These formations consisted of motorized infantry battalions with attached support units that relied on tactical mobility to defeat the Viêt Minh. Initially effective, the groupes mobile grew less so as the war wore on. The Legion also organized battalions of Vietnamese volunteers led by Legionnaires, which met with varying degrees of battlefield success depending on the quality of volunteers, prejudice of the French, and demands of combat.

On 20 November 1953, Legion paratroopers established a presence at Điên Biên Phu. When the Viêt Minh attacked the following March, the Legion held its poorly chosen positions with characteristic tenacity. Despite the hopelessness of the situation, Legionnaires volunteered to parachute into the valley as reinforcements. When French positions were overrun on 7 May, hundreds of Legionnaires were taken prisoner. The loss of Điện Biên Phu and subsequent French withdrawal was a severe blow to Legion morale. Although not broken by Indo-China, the Legion was certainly changed by the experience.

—Richard D. Starnes

References: Davidson, Phillip B. *Vietnam at War: The History, 1945–1975* (1988); Dunn, Peter M. *The First Vietnam War* (1985); Porch, Douglas. *The French Foreign Legion: A Complete History of the Legendary Fighting Force* (1991).

See also: Điện Biên Phu, Battle of; France: Army; French Indo-China; Indo-China War; Order of Battle.

France: Navy (1946–1954)

In August 1945 the French government dispatched to Indo-China a naval squadron already in the Far East to support the planned invasion of Japan. Commanded by Admiral Auboyneau, it was centered on the battleship *Richelieu*, supported by the cruisers *Gloire* and *Suffren*, two destroyers, and the old aircraft carrier *Béarn*, in service since the 1920s and now used as an aircraft transport vessel. Additional naval assets had to be dispatched from France but were delayed by the U.S. refusal to provide logistical support. France's difficult postwar economic situation constrained the size and extent of its naval forces in the Indo-China War.

In 1945 French Indo-China depended heavily upon its river and coastal waters for the movement of people and commerce. Most of the region's population lived on the rivers or the coast. Controlling those waters thus became critical to both sides during the Indo-China War. The French Navy began operations in the Indo-China War with little in the way of assets conducive to riverine warfare: a handful of converted civilian barges and personnel recently released from Japanese prisoner of war camps. Those early units gained control of the lower Mekong Delta and eventually opened the river as far as Phnom Penh. The arrival of reinforcements in late 1945 enabled the Navy to conduct amphibious raids, interdict Việt Minh coastal traffic, and penetrate the Red River.

Given the Navy's low priority in the French defense budget and the lack of U.S. aid to support a war for recolonization, reduction in naval forces was inevitable. In 1950 only a single cruiser and several destroyers and sloops remained to carry the coastal war to the enemy, while riverine forces operated inland almost unsupported. This naval downscaling could not have come at a worse time. From 1950 the Việt Minh contested the rivers. As the level of coastal infiltration steadily increased, the reduced French naval presence was unable to prevent it.

The Indo-China War saw the rebirth of French naval aviation. The only modern carrier available was the *Arromanches*, which the British transferred in August 1946. In 1951 the United States supplied the light fleet carrier *Langley*, renamed the *Lafayette*; and in 1953, her sister ship the *Belleau Wood*, renamed *Bois Belleau*. The effectiveness of the French air arm declined even with the deployment of two French aircraft carriers to the theater. French naval air assets

were increasingly committed to supporting fighting ashore and few resources were left for coastal surveillance.

Much of the French success in riverine warfare can be credited to the innovative tactics and leadership of her first naval chief in Indo-China, Comdr. François Jaubert, commander of the Far East Naval Brigade. Realizing the importance of the rivers, in 1945 he formed the first combined naval-land river units and employed them around Sài Gòn. His objective was to regain control of the critical provincial cities and towns dominating the Mekong and Bassac Rivers. His first operation, MOUSSAC, in October 1945, used British landing craft and improvised French river gunboats to recapture the provincial capitals of My Tho and Cần Tho. By December, Jaubert had expanded his force by 14 LCAs (landing craft, assault) and 6 LCVPs (landing craft, vehicle and personnel). He also had two companies of naval infantry, supported by landing parties from the *Richelieu* and the *Béarn*. His force expanded again when the British withdrew from Sài Gòn in December and transferred their landing craft to the French.

One of the French Navy's first operations in 1946 was to expand its operations into the north. The most important of these was Operation BENTRE, in which 21,700 French troops were landed just outside Hà Nội after a brief firefight with Nationalist Chinese forces holding the city. The Nationalist Chinese were not convinced to withdraw until October. A French naval bombardment of Hai Phòng facilitated the driving of Hồ Chí Minh's forces from that key coastal city, but resulting civilian casualties led to local resentment against the French. French amphibious operations brought coastal towns and the main channel town of Nam Định under French control, and later operations opened the Red and Clear Rivers to French use, but a lack of resources prevented the French from retaining a continuous presence on those rivers.

As 1946 wore on, Jaubert noted that his units were best employed when they operated with army units familiar with naval and riverine operations. That realization led in January 1947 to the first permanent riverine organizations in Indo-China. Designated Dinassauts, these units consisted of a variable number of armored and unarmored landing craft, river monitors, gunboats, and approximately one battalion of either naval or light (army) infantry. Total unit strength was approximately 1,200 men. Two formal Dinassauts were formed, one in the north and one in the south. At various times in the war, other ad hoc Dinassauts were formed from local forces. The combined land-naval riverine force was the basis for all French riverine operations from 1947 to the end of the war.

The basic patrol craft operating in advance of these units was the 82–foot *vedette patrouille*—an unarmored motor launch equipped with two 20-mm cannon, two .50–caliber machine guns, a light mortar, and a .30–caliber machine gun. The troops themselves were transported in unarmored landing craft supported by armored landing craft mounting light cannon and heavy machine guns. The French also converted some craft by adding tank turrets and such weapons as the 40-mm Bofors and 20-mm Oerlikon antiaircraft guns.

French naval efforts in Indo-China reached their peak in 1951, following the introduction of U.S. assets. This U.S. equipment and financial support enabled the French to form four more Dinassauts and employ them against Viêt Minh offensives along the Red and Clear Rivers. The French also increased surveillance along the coast and intercepted more than 1,500 Viêt Minh junks and other transports. For the first time in the war, the Red River and its tributaries were firmly under French control. Facing a logistical shortfall, the Viêt Minh withdrew into the mountains and shifted their supply routes to the slower but now safer land lines from China.

The Navy supported French land offensives in late 1951, providing sea-based air support, transporting supplies and units up rivers, and conducting amphibious raids against suspected Viêt Minh coastal strongpoints. French casualties mounted on the river routes as convoys faced increasingly more powerful and numerous ambushes as the convoys worked their way north and as enemy strength grew along the waterways. By March 1952, river convoy escort had become the French Navy's primary mission in the north. River and coastal patrol (and thereby control) remained the primary mission only in the south.

The lack of a coordinated French strategy after 1950, a dearth of resources, the reluctance to transfer political control to Vietnamese officials, and a declining will to pursue the war all led to the French defeat. Nothing illustrates this more than the mounting losses sustained by French riverine units as they were increasingly committed to escorting convoys on the Red and Black Rivers after 1952. Lacking the resources to conduct both patrol and escort missions, the French essentially surrendered the coastal waters of the north to the Viêt Minh, who used them to great effect from mid-1952 until the war's end.

The French Navy's efforts in Indo-China were exemplary and yet ultimately unsuccessful. Growing from a force of 1,200 former POWs to nearly 12,000 men, it successfully transported and supported almost 200,000 troops in theater. The Navy provided strategic and tactical mobility to French forces on the ground prior to the advent of airmobile warfare.

—Carl O. Schuster

References: Jenkins, E. F. *A History of the French Navy. From Its Beginnings to the Present Day* (1973); Kilian, Robert. *History and Memories: Naval Infantryman in Indochina* (1948); Koburger, Charles W., Jr. *The French Navy in Indochina* (1991); McClintock, Robert. "The River War in Indochina" (1954).

See also: Dinassauts; French Indo-China; Geography of Indo-China and Vietnam; Indo-China War; Order of Battle; Riverine Warfare.

France and Vietnam (1954 to present)

During the Geneva Conference of 1954, the French government attempted to distance itself from the Indo-China conflict. The cease-fire agreement implied continued French responsibility for the administration of the south, but a French conference declaration recognized the independence of Vietnam without specifying the government. In September 1954 the French grudgingly reaffirmed official support for Premier Ngô Đình Diêm. Negotiations on 13 December 1954 between U.S. General J. Lawton Collins and French General Paul Ely produced an agreement to officially transfer responsibility for training and financing Vietnamese troops from France to the United States. This agreement went into effect on 12 February 1955; Paris gave formal notice of its withdrawal from Vietnam on 3 April 1956.

On 29 April 1963, Paris officially informed Laotian Prince Souvanna Phouma of its intention to withdraw immediately from its Seno base in Laos. The French departure gave the United States exclusive responsibility for Western military support of the Laotian government and removed the last elements of French military presence in Laos and Vietnam. It also permitted French President Charles de Gaulle to play a more independent role in trying to resolve the Vietnam quagmire.

On 29 August 1963, in the first of many such pronouncements, de Gaulle indicated French support for eventual neutralization of the Republic of Vietnam. In early January 1964, French Minister of Defense Pierre Messmer traveled to Phnom Penh and promised the Cambodian government some military equipment, reestablishing a military relationship between the two countries. Washington became concerned on 27 January 1964, when Paris announced that France was opening full diplomatic relations with Beijing. All future French efforts at neutralizing the Republic of Vietnam were based on the triangular relationship between Paris, Phnom Penh, and Beijing. President Johnson thoroughly resented what he regarded as meddling French diplomacy and regarded de Gaulle's statements concerning neutralization as unwanted intrusions. This did not bother the French leader, who continued to insist on the immediate withdrawal of American troops from Vietnam.

Relations between the United States and France became more cordial in 1968 with the beginning of Richard Nixon's presidency. De Gaulle (and later Georges Pompidou) got along well with Nixon, and these improved relations spilled over into France's attitude toward U.S. involvement in Vietnam. Pompidou and de Gaulle took U.S. deescalation efforts as a sign of that Nixon intended to withdraw from Vietnam. This belief kept France from speaking out against the 1970 Cambodian incursion, which took place during the Paris peace negotiations. Even when the U.S. bombing of Hà Nôi in 1972 killed the French delegate general to the DRV, Paris issued only routine protests. Although the government attempted to remain neutral, it could not prevent anti-U.S. demonstrations from taking place throughout France. The French government was particularly proud of its ability to keep the first two years of the Henry Kissinger–Lê Đuc Tho talks secret. This was done primarily by using Jean Sainteny to carry messages between Hà Nôi and Paris.

After the war's conclusion, France became the third largest foreign investor in the Socialist Republic of Vietnam (SRV), after Taiwan and Hong Kong. France normalized relations with the SRV in 1989 after Hà Nôi withdrew its troops from Cambodia, and French aid to Vietnam in that year totaled more than $30 million. In February 1993, French President François Mitterrand became the first Western leader to visit Vietnam since 1975. He promised to increase French aid to the SRV if the latter would improve human rights, and he criticized Washington for its continued economic embargo of Vietnam.

—Michael R. Nichols

References: Smith, R. B. *An International History of the Vietnam War* (1991); Sullivan, Marianna P. *France's Vietnam Policy: A Study in French-American Relations* (1978); Wilson, Harold K. *A Personal Record. The Labour Government, 1964–1970* (1971).

See also: Bao Dai; Cambodia; Cambodian Incursion; Collins, Joseph Lawton; de Gaulle, Charles André Marie Joseph; Ely, Paul Henri Romuald; Geneva Conference and Geneva Accords; Hô Chí Minh; Johnson, Lyndon Baines; Kissinger, Henry Alfred; Laos; Lê Duc Tho; Ngô Đình Diêm; Nixon, Richard Milhous; Paris Negotiations; Paris Peace Accords; Sainteny, Jean; Souvanna Phouma.

FRANCIS MARION, Operation (April–October 1967)

Last of a series of U.S. Army screening operations in 1967 along the Cambodian border of Pleiku Province. Operation FRANCIS MARION was intended to prevent the 1st and 10th People's Army of Vietnam (PAVN) Divisions from pushing into the Central Highlands. Conducted by the 1st and 2d Brigades of the 4th Infantry Division from 5 April to 12 October 1967, it followed Operation SAM HOUSTON. The 1st Brigade patrolled the area north from Đuc Co to the Plei D'Jereng Special Forces camp; the 2d worked south toward the Ia Drang Valley. By October there were eight major military engagements.

On 30 April, after ambushing a PAVN patrol north of Đuc Co and pursuing stragglers, Company A, 2d Battalion (Mechanized), 8th Infantry (2/8th) came under withering machine-gun fire from a battalion of the 95B PAVN Regiment. After a harrowing night, artillery, air strikes, and tanks allowed Company A's M113s to push into a bunker complex and inflict heavy PAVN casualties.

The tables turned on 18 May, when a 32d PAVN Regiment battalion entrapped a platoon of Company B, 1st Battalion, 18th Infantry (1/18th). Its remaining platoons broke through, but the company lost 21 killed. Two days later, the 1/18th repulsed a night attack on its hilltop positions by the same PAVN unit at heavy cost. On 22 May, as the 3d Battalion, 12th Infantry (3/12th) moved to link up with the 2/8th near Đuc Co, they were caught in a mortar barrage and attacked by the 66th PAVN Regiment. The PAVN troops broke contact only after being battered by artillery and air strikes. On 12 July, two companies of the 3/12th again fought the 66th PAVN Regiment, this time in the hills south of Đuc Co. On 23 July, in the same area, a 32d PAVN Regiment battalion nearly destroyed a platoon that had become separated from a company of the 3d Battalion, 8th Infantry (3/8th). The remaining platoons established a defensive line and repulsed two attacks. Slow to retreat, PAVN troops were pulverized by air strikes.

Contact with PAVN units in western Pleiku Province diminished by the early fall, and it became evident that the principal thrust was to be farther north in Kontum Province, where Operation GREELEY was under way. On 12 October, 4th Division commander Maj. Gen. William R. Peers consolidated FRANCIS MARION with GREELEY to create Operation MACARTHUR, which became the context for the pivotal struggle of the Central Highlands campaign, the Battle of Đak Tô. In 191 days, FRANCIS MARION accounted for 1,203 known PAVN dead but had not prevented the PAVN from moving large forces into the Central Highlands.

—John D. Root

Reference: Stanton, Shelby L. *The Rise and Fall of the American Army: U.S. Ground Forces in Vietnam, 1965–1973* (1985).

See also: Armor Warfare; Đak Tô, Battle of; GREELEY, Operation; Mortars, Allied and Democratic Republic of Vietnam; Peers, William R.; Vietnam, Democratic Republic of: Army (People's Army of Vietnam [PAVN]).

Franco-Thai War (November 1940–January 1941)

Undeclared war between Vichy France and Thailand. The Thais began the war to regain the rich rice-growing provinces of Battambang, Siemréap, and Sisophon that the French had forced them to restore to Cambodia in 1907. Thailand also claimed territory in Laos, the return of which the French had secured in 1904. In early June 1940 Thailand concluded nonaggression pacts with France and Britain but lost interest in ratifying them after the defeat of France by Germany. The pro-Japanese military government of Marshal Pibul Songgram sought to capitalize on France's weakness.

The French in Indo-China appeared vulnerable militarily and diplomatically, and Bangkok believed there was no better time to reassert its claims. From mid-November 1940, the Thais sent military units across the Mekong River into eastern Cambodia. These incursions led to skirmishes with the French, who were temporarily sidetracked by the 23 November Indo-China Communist Party uprising in Cochin China. The French crushed this uprising in the first week of December.

French High Commissioner Adm. Jean Decoux answered the Thai attacks with offensives on land and sea. The land offensive began on 16 January 1941, when a mixed French brigade attacked Thai positions at Yang Dom Koum. This effort failed for lack of manpower and an insufficient number of heavy weapons. The Thais, who had planned an attack for the same day, then counterattacked. Their offensive, supported by tanks, was beaten back by Legionnaires with grenades. Although Bangkok claimed a major victory, both sides then withdrew from the immediate area.

Simultaneously there was fighting at sea. The French Navy plan called for attacks on the Thai Navy detachment at Koh Chang and at the principal navy base at Sattahib. On 16 January the French force sailed for the Gulf of Siam to attack Koh Chang, which guarded the passage to Sattahib. French warships surprised the Thais there early on 17 January. In the ensuing 90–minute action, the French sank two Thai torpedo boats and a coast defense vessel and mortally damaged another coast defense ship. The French task force escaped with no direct hits or losses and returned to Sài Gòn on the

19th. There was little air action during the war, although the Thais did use their Curtiss Hawk III biplanes in a dive-bombing role. The French had a plan, not implemented, to fire-bomb Bangkok from the air.

On 31 January, a Japanese-dictated armistice was signed at Sài Gòn, and in March the Vichy government accepted Japanese mediation. By Japanese edict, on 9 May 1941 in Tokyo, France and Thailand signed a peace treaty whereby France transferred to Thailand three Cambodian and two Laotian provinces on the right bank of the Mekong, some 42,000 square miles of territory.

In September 1945 with the reintroduction of French forces into Indo-China, Thailand agreed to return this territory and accept the Mekong River as the boundary between their country and Laos and Cambodia. That the issue remained unsettled was seen in border skirmishes along the Mekong River in 1946, in clashes between May 1987 and February 1988 between Thailand and Laos, and in continuing Thai support of the Khmer Rouge in Cambodia.

—Spencer C. Tucker

References: Decoux, Adm. Jean. *A La Barre de L'Indochine* (1949); Meisler, Jurg. "Koh Chang. The Unknown Battle. Franco-Thai War of 1940–41" (1989); Mordal, Jacques. *Marine Indochine* (1953); Mordal, Jacques, and Gabriel Auphan. *La Marine Française pendant la Deuxième Guerre Mondiale* (1958).
See also: French Indo-China; Japan; Thailand.

Free Fire Zones

Early term used by the U.S. Department of Defense for bombing and artillery fire against purported Viêt Công (VC) personnel and strongholds. In 1965, after critical publicity, the term was changed to "specified strike zones." Designated areas were supposedly nearly uninhabited by noncombatants. This tactic was an effort to structure the conflict along conventional lines, with Communist and Allied forces separated and occupying distinct and identifiable zones. In actuality, such divisions seldom occurred.

Sài Gòn–appointed Vietnamese district and province chiefs charted these zones and authorized the use therein of unrestricted bombing and artillery fires. Rarely did such individuals come from the zones for which they approved targets. Following such approval, friendly inhabitants were to be warned by loudspeaker, leaflet drops, and infantry sweeps to leave their homes immediately to seek safety elsewhere, usually in "protected villages." Many had to be forcibly evacuated, usually by Army of the Republic of Vietnam (ARVN) troops. Some could not read the leaflets and so remained in the zone, soon to become hapless casualties of war. Many of those who were moved to new locations found the facilities either strange or insufficient and so returned home. These returnees were viewed by the Sài Gòn government and U.S. Military Assistance Command, Vietnam (MACV) as VC sympathizers. This human factor was rarely taken into account. Certainly, the loss of life among noncombatants was large. A U.S. Senate subcommittee released figures purporting to show 300,000 civilian casualties from such actions by 1968.

—Cecil B. Currey

References: Cincinnatus [Cecil B. Currey]. *Self-Destruction: The Disintegration and Decay of the United States Army during the Vietnam Era* (1981); Gibson, James William. *The Perfect War: Technowar in Vietnam* (1986); Littauer, Raphael, and Norman Uphoff, eds. *The Air War in Indochina* (1972).
See also: Artillery Fire Doctrine; Clear and Hold; Pacification; Strategic Hamlet Program.

Free Khmer. *See* Khmer Serai.

Free World Assistance Program

In 1964, prior to the buildup of U.S. combat forces, President Johnson called for "Free World Military Forces" to create an alliance of "Many Flags" to aid the Republic of Vietnam (RVN). The earlier decision to request support was confirmed in National Security Policy Memorandum No. 328 on 6 April 1965. Over time 39 nations, in addition to the United States, provided help to the RVN under the Free World assistance program. Australia, New Zealand, Thailand, and the Republic of Korea (ROK) participated with combat forces. The Philippines provided a Civic Action group. The Republic of China provided a Military Assistance Advisory Group, consisting primarily of political warfare advisors and medical personnel. Germany, Australia, Canada, Japan, the United Kingdom, New Zealand, and the Netherlands established continuing programs of economic, humanitarian, and technical assistance, either as part of bilateral agreements or under the Columbo Plan (a plan drafted in Columbo, Ceylon, in 1951, for the cooperative development of South and Southeast Asia). In all cases, military working agreements were signed between commanders of the various Free World forces and the commander, U.S. Military Assistance Command, Vietnam (MACV), that placed their combat forces under MACV operational control.

The Korean agreement required ROK forces to operate under parameters established by the Free World Military Assistance Council, composed of the chief of the Vietnamese Joint General Staff (JGS), the senior Korean officer in Vietnam, and the commander, MACV. This council provided operational guidance to, not control of, Free World forces through the annual Combined Campaign Plan, which broke the operational effort down geographically and functionally but did not assign tasks or goals. A combined command and staff arrangement was considered but was rejected because of ROK and RVN political sensitivities to their forces falling under U.S. military command.

Coordination of combat operations without the benefit of an integrated command at the top was provided through joint agreements between local Free World commanders and Army of the Republic of Vietnam (ARVN) ground commanders. While ARVN corps commanders retained overall responsibility for military actions in each corps tactical zone (CTZ, also known as military regions), U.S. and other Free World commanders accepted responsibility for tactical areas of responsibility (TAOR), arbitrary geographical areas in which American and Free World units conducted combat operations.

—Arthur T. Frame

References: Clarke, Jeffrey J. *Advice and Support: The Final Years, 1965–1973* (1988); Larsen, Stanley R., and James L. Collins, Jr. *Allied Participation in Vietnam* (1975).
See also: Australia; Canada; China, Republic of [Taiwan]; Civic Action; Germany, Federal Republic of; Great Britain; Japan; Korea, Republic of; New Zealand; Military Assistance Command, Vietnam (MACV); Philippines; Thailand.

French Indo-China (1860s through 1946)

European powers came to Vietnam in their quest for religious converts, trade, and naval facilities. The first lasting contact between Vietnam and Europe resulted from the 1535 arrival of Portuguese explorer Captain Antonio da Faria. Subsequently the Portuguese and Dutch established rival trading posts in Vietnam. Although Catholic missionaries might have come to Vietnam before da Faria, the first permanent Catholic mission was not established there until 1615. French priest Alexandre de Rhodes made Catholicism a cultural force as well as a religious one.

Steadily Southeast Asia began to attract more European attention. The term *Indo-China*, attributed to Danish cartographer Konrad Malte-Brun, was applied collectively to Burma, Thailand, Tonkin, Annam, Cochin-China, Laos, and Cambodia. Another Catholic priest, Pierre Pigneau de Béhaine, helped secure European mercenaries and military equipment crucial in enabling Nguyên Phúc Ánh (from 1802, Emperor Gia Long) to reunify Vietnam. The French mercenaries brought with them numerous Western technological advances, including improved engineering and metallurgical techniques.

Emperor Gia Long may have welcomed Western military and technological assistance, but he was not interested in advancing their religion. His successors, Minh Mang, Thiêu Tri, and Tu Đuc, lacked Gia Long's flexibility and appreciation of Western strengths and weaknesses and were much less successful than he in dealing with Western pressures. During Gia Long's reign, however, the European powers were too embroiled in the Napoleonic Wars to pay much attention to Vietnam. It fell to Gia Long's successors to deal with reawakened European imperialism.

The Vietnamese emperors regarded Catholicism as a threat to the Confucian concept of order and harmony, but the imperial court would persecute Buddhists and Taoists as well. The royal concubines, who saw Christian opposition to polygamy as a direct threat to their own position, were a powerful source of opposition to the Western religion. The attempt by the nineteenth-century Vietnamese emperors to root out Christian missionaries provided the excuse for French intervention. The Vietnamese had shown little interest in the vastly improved armaments that were introduced since the reunification of their country, so were at a great disadvantage when the inevitable collision with the West occurred.

Although trade was a more powerful force than missionary fervor in pushing the French to intervene in Vietnam, alleged mistreatment of Catholic missionaries was the excuse for French intervention. In 1845 and 1846, French warships were sent to Vietnam to secure the release of Monseigneur Dominique Lefèvre, who had been imprisoned on imperial order for refusing to leave the country. During the second intervention, French warships sank four Vietnamese warships that they regarded as presenting a hostile intent. On 31 August 1858, a Franco-Spanish squadron of 14 ships commanded by Adm. Charles Rigault de Genouilly anchored at Tourane (Đà Nang). The next day a landing party went ashore. Tourane proved no prize, and the expedition soon moved southward. On 18 February 1859, the French took Sài Gòn, a promising deep-water port.

In 1862 Emperor Tu Đuc was obliged to sign a treaty confirming the French conquest. From 1862 to 1887, France established control over Indo-China. It had conquered all of Cochin China, the southernmost part of Vietnam, by 1867. Guerrilla warfare continued in parts of the country for a time. Emperor Hàm Nghi led a brief rebellion until his capture in 1888. One last nationalist leader, Đê Thám, was killed in 1913.

In 1887 Paris formed French Indo-China, to which Laos was added in 1893. Technically, only Cochin China was an outright colony; the others were merely protectorates. In reality, all were ruled by a French governor-general responsible to the minister of colonies in Paris. The next 50 years of French rule in Indo-China would be as fateful for the country as the 1,000 years of Chinese domination.

French administration in Indo-China was haphazard. Ministers of colonies and governors-general changed frequently, and with each came policy changes. Indo-China did not attract the most capable civil servants, and many never learned the local language. French officials' salaries consumed the colonial budget, leaving little for education or public works. The small French community (40,000 to 50,000 people) dominated the economy of what was France's richest colony.

The educational ideal was to turn Vietnam into a cultural copy of mainland France, but even after World War I, only 10 percent of Vietnamese of school age attended Franco-Vietnamese schools. In 1940 there were only 14 secondary schools and a single university in Vietnam. This situation produced a small native elite aspiring to positions of influence that were closed to them by the colonial regime. Frustration eventually turned many of them against France.

Vietnamese nationalist hopes were raised by President Wilson's call for the self-determination of peoples. But at the Paris Peace Conference, Vietnamese nationalists discovered that this doctrine was limited to Europe. Moderate nationalists in Vietnam after World War I took China's Kuomintang as their model. Their organization, the Viêt Nam Quôc Dân Đang (Vietnam National Party), was not well-organized. It led to premature uprisings in 1930–1931 that were easily crushed by the authorities. This had the unfortunate effect for the French of opening the way for the more militant Indo-Chinese Communist Party (ICP), which by World War II was the dominant nationalist force in Indo-China.

The Japanese arrived in Indo-China in 1940; France was in no position to resist Tokyo's demands for bases. Ironically,

Japan's July 1941 move into southern Indo-China brought the United States into the war. With Japanese long-range bombers now able to reach Malaya, the Dutch East Indies, and the Philippines, the United States, Great Britain, and the Netherlands imposed an embargo on scrap iron and oil to Japan. This decision caused Tokyo to embark on a war with the United States. The Japanese left the Vichy French government in Indo-China in place, but the French were determined to liberate themselves as the conflict neared its end. With these plans an open secret, the Japanese struck first. On 9 March 1945, they arrested virtually all French administrators and military personnel. Tokyo created a further problem for France by declaring Vietnam independent under Emperor Bao Đai.

Under the July 1945 Potsdam agreements, the British took the surrender of Japanese troops south of the 16th parallel; the Chinese took the surrender north of it. The British released French troops from Japanese camps, and Paris sent reinforcements to reestablish its control over southern Vietnam, Cambodia, and Laos. The French also arranged a Chinese withdrawal from the North.

Hô Chí Minh moved into the vacuum left by the defeat of Japan, declaring himself president of a "free Vietnam" on 16 August 1945. On 2 September Hô proclaimed the independence of the Democratic Republic of Vietnam (DRV). Even before the end of the war, the French government had planned to make concessions and grant more freedom to Indo-China, but only if Paris retained ultimate authority. French leaders, however, failed to seek accommodation with nationalist leaders. In Indo-China the result was a missed opportunity for orderly transition to self-rule and a close relationship with France.

In January 1946, Hô held elections in the North which, although not entirely free, left no doubt that Hô had won. In March 1946 Hô worked out an agreement with French diplomat Jean Sainteny by which Paris recognized the DRV as a free and independent state within the French Union. France could send a limited number of troops into the North to protect her interests there, but all were to be withdrawn over five years. Paris also accepted the principle of a united Vietnam by agreeing to a plebiscite in the South that would allow a vote on whether it would join the North. However, French High Commissioner for Indo-China Thierry d'Argenlieu refused to allow the promised southern plebiscite. Hô led a delegation to appeal to directly to Paris, but by the time it arrived the French government had fallen. It was weeks before a new one was formed, and at the Fontainebleau Conference, Paris made no concessions to the Vietnamese nationalists. Meanwhile, d'Argenlieu had on his own initiative proclaimed the independence of the South as the Republic of Cochin China. His action clearly violated the Hô-Sainteny agreement and left Vietnamese leaders feeling betrayed. In September Hô left Paris. He forecast an early start of war and correctly predicted how it would be fought and how it would end.

The war began in Hà Nôi on 19 December 1946, following the 23 November shelling of the port of Hai Phòng by the French cruiser *Suffren* on d'Argenlieu's orders. This fighting, including its American phase, would be the longest war in the twentieth century: 29 years.

—Spencer C. Tucker

References: Duiker, William J. *The Communist Road to Power in Vietnam* (1981); —. *The Rise of Nationalism in Vietnam, 1900–1941* (1976); Fall, Bernard B. *The Two Vietnams* (1964); Hammer, Ellen J. *The Struggle for Indochina* (1954); Lacouture, Jean. *Ho Chi Minh: A Political Biography* (1968); Sainteny, Jean. *Ho Chi Minh and His Vietnam: A Personal Memoir* (1972); Thompson, Virginia. *French Indo-China* (1937).

See also: Bao Đai; d'Argenlieu, Georges Thierry; de Genouilly, Charles Rigault; de Rhodes, Alexandre; Fontainebleau Conference; Hai Phòng, Shelling of; Hàm Nghi; Hô Chí Minh; Hô-Sainteny Agreement; Minh Mang; Nguyên Phúc Ánh (Gia Long); Pigneau de Béhaine, Pierre; Potsdam Conference; Sainteny, Jean; Thiêu Tri; Tu Đuc; Viêt Nam Quôc Dân Đang (Vietnam National Party).

FREQUENT WIND, Operation (29–30 April 1975)

Final U.S. evacuation from the Republic of Vietnam (RVN). Operation FREQUENT WIND began at 1051 on 29 April 1975. Before dawn a heavy artillery and rocket barrage on Tân Son Nhut Air Base signaled the imminent assault on Sài Gòn. At first light, RVN aircrews jettisoned bombs and fuel tanks on the runways and fled in their planes. Maj. Gen. Homer D. Smith reported to Ambassador Graham A. Martin that with the runways unusable, Americans and endangered South Vietnamese would have to be helicoptered to ships off the Vietnamese coast—"Option IV" in the evacuation plan. Martin waited nearly two more hours before ordering the evacuation at 1051. Before the airlift could begin, however, a complicated series of ship-to-ship flights had to be carried out to load 865 Marines who were to provide security for the evacuation.

The first CH-53s landed at the DAO Tân Son Nhut compound at 1506. By evening, nearly 4,500 Vietnamese and 395 U.S. citizens had been flown out of the air base. The Marines began withdrawing at 2250. Last to leave were demolition teams who blew up secret communications gear and then the DAO building itself, along with barrels containing more than $3.6 million in U.S. currency.

No large-scale airlift was planned from the U.S. embassy. Accordingly, Marine commander Brig. Gen. Richard E. Carey was stunned when word came that several thousand people, about half Vietnamese, were stranded in the embassy compound. Carey issued new orders directing helicopters and additional Marines to the embassy. Only one CH-53 at a time could land in the embassy courtyard; the rooftop pad accommodated only the smaller CH-46s. Darkness and thunderstorms dispersed the gathering crowd outside the embassy walls but also made flying hazardous. An embassy officer used a slide projector to illuminate the landing area. A steady stream of flights continued until about 2300, paused while the Marines were evacuated from the DAO, then resumed after midnight. Fearing that the operation might go on indefinitely, task force commanders and White House officials ordered the refugee flights stopped. At 0430, Carey radioed his pilots that only Americans were to be flown out. Ambassador Martin boarded just before 0500, by presidential order, and the handful of remaining Americans followed.

About 420 Vietnamese were left waiting in the compund. Hundreds of other Vietnamese employed by the U.S. government were abandoned elsewhere in Sài Gòn. At daybreak, with only the Marine security force remaining, the last nine CH-46s loaded and left for the fleet. M.Sgt. Juan Valdez was the last to board; at 0753, the final helicopter lifted off. Altogether, 978 Americans and approximately 1,100 Vietnamese were flown out of the embassy.

—Arnold R. Isaacs

References: Herrington, Stuart A. *Peace with Honor?* (1983); Isaacs, Arnold R. *Without Honor: Defeat in Vietnam and Cambodia* (1983). **See also:** EAGLE PULL, Operation; Gayler, Noel Arthur Meredyth; Hồ Chí Minh Campaign; Martin, Graham A.; United States: Involvement in Vietnam, 1973–1975.

Friendly Fire

Human casualties (killed and wounded) incurred by military forces in active combat operations resulting from fire from their own or Allied forces. Fratricide, another term for this type of casualty-producing phenomenon, may be unintentional or intentional. Intentional production of friendly casualties ("fragging") and the related issue of civilian casualties are not considered here.

Casualties resulting from friendly fire were difficult to prevent in Vietnam, with the lack of defined front lines and units operating independently, sometimes overlapping within the same area of operations, in dense jungle, and often at night. U.S. losses to friendly fire in Vietnam do not appear to exceed those of previous modern wars. However, documented friendly fire cases in Vietnam exist for all forces engaged. Even so, exact figures for casualties caused by friendly fire in Vietnam are not available. Commanders failed to report the incidence of friendly fire out of concern for the possible loss of benefits and honors due the dead and wounded; the desire not to damage the reputation of the unit or personnel involved or the morale of surviving troops; or the inability to prove fratricide. If circumstances permit, a formal investigation and report are required in cases of recognizable fratricide. Casualty statistics published by the Department of Defense for Vietnam appear to include friendly fire losses in "Casualties not the Result of Hostile Forces," which are made up of "Deaths from aircraft accidents/incidents" and "From ground action," which total 18 percent of all casualties.

—Arthur T. Frame

References: Neel, Spurgeon. *Medical Support of the U.S. Army in Vietnam, 1965–1972* (1973); Office of Information Management and Statistics. *Data on Vietnam Era Veterans* (1983). **See also:** Attrition; Casualties; Fragging.

Fulbright, J. William (1905–1995)

U.S. senator and Vietnam War critic. Fulbright disagreed with the foreign policy of every president from Harry S Truman to Richard Nixon, but he especially attacked Lyndon Johnson on the Vietnam issue. Although Fulbright shepherded the 1964

Gulf of Tonkin Resolution through the Senate, by 1966 he had concluded that the war was primarily an insurgency against a corrupt and repressive Sài Gòn government. He believed that Vietnam had no bearing on U.S. vital interests and that U.S. involvement was undermining democracy and individual liberty at home and overseas. Hearings by Fulbright's Foreign Relations Committe, televised in 1966, helped turn popular opinion against the war and endeared him to antiwar activists.

—Brenda J. Taylor

References: Berman, William C. *William Fulbright and the Vietnam War: The Dissent of a Political Realist* (1988); Woods, Randall Bennett. "Dixie's Dove: J. William Fulbright, the Vietnam War, and the American South" (1994). **See also:** Church, Frank Forrester; Clinton, William Jefferson; Gruening, Ernest Henry; Johnson, Lyndon Baines; Kennedy, Edward Moore; McGovern, George S.; Morse, Wayne Lyman; Nixon, Richard Milhous; Proxmire, William; Tonkin Gulf Resolution; Truman, Harry S.

FULRO (Le Front Unifié de Lutte des Races Opprimées)

United Struggle Front for the Oppressed Races: the ethnonationalistic movement of Montagnard (Le Front pour la Libération des Montagnards [FLM], Khmer Krom [FLKK], and Cham [FLC]). FULRO evolved from the Bajaraka (consolidated Bahnar, Jarai, Rhadé, and Koho) movement created in opposition to Ngô Đình Diêm's Land Development Program, the confiscation of Montagnard lands, and the forced resettlement of Montagnard villagers.

FULRO made its presence known in 1964 through a military uprising at Civilian Irregular Defense Group (CIDG) camps around Ban Mê Thuôt. There Y Bham Enoul, a Rhadé, offered a "FULRO manifesto" calling for action to reclaim Montagnard lands. Although the Ministry for Development of Ethnic Minorities was created by the Sài Gòn government in response to the uprising in efforts to win Montagnard support, Y Bham Enoul and his followers fled to Cambodia under threat of imprisonment by the Republic of Vietnam (RVN). By 1965, FULRO maintained an army of 5,000 to 6,000, along with 15,000 of their dependents. As FULRO President, Y Bham Enoul represented the Montagnards in negotiations with the Cambodian and RVN governments, the North Vietnamese, and Viêt Công.

Following the 1968 Têt Offensive, Y Bham Enoul sought to return to the Central Highlands to protect Montagnard villages from Communist attacks. The Sài Gòn government promised that FULRO army units would be integrated into Regional Force units to protect Montagnard villages and that FULRO leaders would receive positions within the government. Upset by this arrangement, militant FULRO members overthrew Y Bham Enoul's leadership in December 1968 and exiled him and his followers to Phnom Penh. Nevertheless, the agreement to integrate FULRO forces into Regional Force units was upheld. With the return of FULRO soldiers to Vietnam and the exile of Y Bham Enoul, FULRO lost its position as an ethnonationalistic movement by early 1969.

FULRO resurfaced in opposition to Communist rule

around 1974–1975 as the Dega Highlands Provisional Government with its military arm, the Dega Highlands Liberation Front. Up to 2,000 Montagnard soldiers held out against superior Communist forces before giving up the struggle in 1984. Many Montagnards returned to the highlands, but 200 men who formed the core of the resistance fled to refugee camps along the Thai-Cambodian border in 1985. Found at Site 2 South by three Americans, they were brought to the United States and resettled in North and South Carolina.

—David M. Berman

References: Hickey, Gerald Cannon. *Free in the Forest: Ethnohistory of the Vietnamese Central Highlands, 1954–1976* (1982); ———. *Shattered World: Adaptation and Survival among Vietnam's Highland Peoples during the Vietnam War* (1993); Wiesner, Louis A. *Victims and Survivors: Displaced Persons and Other War Victims in Viet-Nam, 1954–1975* (1988).

See also: Ban Mê Thuôt, Battle of; Cambodia; Central Highlands; Civilian Irregular Defense Group (CIDG); Enoul, Y Bham; Hickey, Gerald Cannon; Mobile Strike Force Command; Montagnards; Territorial Forces.

G

Galbraith, John Kenneth (1908–)

Economist and critic of U.S. involvement in Vietnam. After his election to the presidency in 1960, John F. Kennedy appointed Galbraith ambassador to India (1961–1963). As early as the spring of 1961, Galbraith warned Kennedy of potential conflict in Vietnam, writing that "Diem has alienated his people to a far greater extent than we allow ourselves to know." Galbraith opposed sending troops to Vietnam, and Kennedy concurred, sending only helicopters and advisors. Galbraith became more outspoken against the Vietnam War during the Johnson administration, and he supported Eugene McCarthy's 1968 presidential candidacy. After the 1972 defeat of Democratic presidential candidate George McGovern, Galbraith eschewed active politics in favor of writing and publishing.

—Brenda J. Taylor

References: Galbraith, John Kenneth. *A Life in Our Times* (1981); Lamson, Peggy. *Speaking of Galbraith: A Personal Portrait* (1991).

See also: Kennedy, John Fitzgerald; Rostow, Walt Whitman; Taylor, Maxwell Davenport.

GAME WARDEN, Operation (1965–1970)

U.S. Navy operation in the Mekong Delta to halt Việt Công (VC) inland waterways logistics and military operations. On 18 December 1965, Chief, Naval Advisory Group (CHNAVAD-VGP) Rear Adm. Norvell G. Ward formed the River Patrol Force (Task Force 116). Known as Operation GAME WARDEN, it was to interdict VC activities along the major rivers of the Mekong Delta. The primary impetus for GAME WARDEN emerged in September 1965 when naval and military representatives from the Military Assistance Command, Vietnam (MACV), Naval Advisory Group (NAG), Chief of Naval Operations (CNO), Commander in Chief, Pacific (CINCPAC), and Commander in Chief, Pacific Fleet (CINCPACFLT) decided that Operation MARKET TIME, although successful at countering seaborne traffic, could not prevent enemy movement on inland waterways.

The River Patrol Force required a mission-designed, shallow-draft, high-speed boat to navigate the inland waterways. From December 1965 to March 1966, the U.S. Navy adopted and procured the fiberglass-hulled river patrol boat (PBR) to operate in South Vietnam. PBRs were placed into River Divisions (RIVDIVs), based either around landing ship, tanks (LTSs) anchored at the mouths of rivers or at shore installations.

In 1967 the Navy allocated 24 Bell UH-1B Iroquois helicopters to provide air support for the PBRs. This air component, designated HAL-3 (Helicopter Attack Light Squadron 3), or "Seawolves," was stationed aboard the LSTs with their PBR counterparts. Another air component, VAL-4 (Navy Attack Light Squadron 4), consisting of heavily armed OV-10 Broncos to bridge the gap between helicopter and jet and known as the "Black Ponies," arrived in Vietnam in April 1969 and provided additional air support for GAME WARDEN.

GAME WARDEN forces conducted day and night patrols, usually consisting of two boats, to inspect Vietnamese river craft, enforce curfews, establish ambushes, and support Allied troops ashore. GAME WARDEN forces also inserted SEALs (U.S. Navy Sea Air Land teams), who collected intelligence data and assaulted VC units in the Mekong Delta. Other responsibilities included minesweeping the vital Lòng Tào shipping channel.

In 1968, COMNAVFORV (Commander Naval Forces, Vietnam) combined elements of the River Patrol Force with other task forces to create and participate in the Navy's new strategy, SEALORDS. ACTOV (Accelerated Turnover to the Vietnamese), the Navy's Vietnamization program, began in the same year. GAME WARDEN material shifted to the Republic of Vietnam Navy, and Task Force 116 was disestablished by December 1970.

—R. Blake Dunnavent

References: Cutler, Thomas J. *Brown Water, Black Berets: Coastal and Riverine Warfare in Vietnam* (1988); Marolda, Edward J. *By Sea, Air, and Land: An Illustrated History of the U.S. Navy and the War in Southeast Asia* (1994); Schreadley, R. L. *From the Rivers to the Sea: The United States Navy in Vietnam* (1992).

See also: MARKET TIME, Operation; Mekong Delta; Riverine Craft; Riverine Warfare; SEAL (Sea, Air, Land) Teams; SEALORDS (South East Asia Lake Ocean River Delta Strategy); United States: Navy.

Garnier, Francis (1839–1873)

French naval officer, administrator, explorer, and writer. In 1873, Governor of Cochin China Adm. M. J. Dupré recruited Garnier to lead an expedition to extricate French arms merchant Jean Dupuis from Hà Nôi and to negotiate freedom of navigation on the Red River. Convinced of Emperor Tu Đuc's local weakness, Garnier dropped all pretense of negotiation and on 15 November 1873 proclaimed the Red River open for international trade. On 20 November, after receiving reinforcements from Sài Gòn, Garnier bombarded and stormed the Hà Nôi Citadel, then turned his artillery against all important and fortified places between the coast and Hà Nôi. Garnier's three-week campaign of terror culminated in the capture of Nam Đinh. However, he was killed on 21 December 1873, in an engagement with Black Flag pirates outside Hà Nôi.

—Arthur J. Dommen

References: Buttinger, Joseph. *The Smaller Dragon: A Political History of Vietnam* (1958); Garnier, Francis. *Voyage d'exploration en Indochine* (1985); Osborne, Milton. *River Road to China: The Mekong River Expedition, 1866–73* (1975); Whitfield, Danny J. *Historical and Cultural Dictionary of Vietnam* (1976).

See also: Black Flag Pirates; Cochin China; Dupuis, Jean; Vietnam: from 938 through the French Conquest.

Garwood, Robert "Bobby" Russell (1946–)

U.S. Marine Corps private; prisoner of war and alleged defector. Captured by the Việt Công (VC) in a village south of Đà

Nang, Garwood was treated roughly as a prisoner. However, he taught himself enough Vietnamese to converse with his guards, which made him useful to them. Garwood was not released in 1973 with other prisoners of war, but was moved to North Vietnam. After the Communists captured Sài Gòn, he worked in the motor pool of a reeducation camp for South Vietnamese prisoners.

Garwood occasionally made supply trips to Hà Nôi, and on one such trip in 1979 he passed a note identifying himself as an American to an English-speaking guest in a hotel. The guest reported the incident to the State Department, and publicity surrounding the case led to Garwood's release. He arrived in the United States in military custody on 22 March 1979. At his court-martial, Garwood was found guilty of serving as a guard for the VC, informing on his comrades, interrogating them on military and other matters, and assaulting a fellow American prisoner.

—Arthur J. Dommen

References: Grant, Zalin. *Survivors* (1975); Howes, Craig. *Voices of the Vietnam POWs: Witnesses to Their Fight* (1993); Hubbell, John G., et al. *P.O.W.: A Definitive History of the American Prisoner of War Experience in Vietnam, 1964–1973* (1976); Groom, Winston, and Duncan Spencer. *Conversations with the Enemy* (1983); Jensen-Stevenson, Monika. *Spite House; The Last Secret of the War in Vietnam* (1997); Jensen-Stevenson, Monika, and William Stevenson. *Kiss the Boys Goodbye: How the United States Betrayed Its Own POWs in Vietnam* (1990); *The Case of Pvt. Robert R. Garwood, USMC* (1993).
See also: Prisoners of War, Allied.

Gavin, James M. (1907–1990)

U.S. Army general; outspoken critic of the U.S. role in Vietnam. In 1954 Gavin strongly opposed committing U.S. forces to Indo-China to support the French. Early in 1958 he abruptly retired from the Army in frustration. In 1965 he wrote an article clearly pointing out that U.S. leadership had articulated no clear military objective in Vietnam. Rejected by *Infantry* magazine as too controversial, the article was published by *Harper's* in February 1966 as "Gen. James Gavin vs. Our Vietnam Strategy." Gavin spoke out against the war before the Senate Foreign Relations Committee in February 1966 and again in February 1967. At the invitation of General William Westmoreland, Gavin toured South Vietnam, but nothing he saw changed his mind. In 1968 Gavin published a book, *Crisis Now*, and he briefly flirted with the idea of running for president. Neither party was supportive, and he quietly dropped from the public scene.

—David T. Zabecki

References: Booth, Michael T. *Paratrooper: The Life of General James M. Gavin* (1994); Gavin, James M. *On to Berlin: Battles of an Airborne Commander, 1943–1946* (1978).
See also: Đà Nang; Eisenhower, Dwight David; Kennedy, John Fitzgerald; Ridgway, Matthew B.; Westmoreland, William Childs.

Gayler, Noel Arthur Meredyth (1914–)

U.S. Navy admiral; commander in chief, Pacific, during the final stages of the Vietnam War. In September 1972, Gayler was promoted to admiral and made commander in chief, Pacific. In this capacity, he directed Operation FREQUENT WIND, the 1975 airlift of Americans and South Vietnamese from Sài Gòn. He was also named U.S. military advisor to the Southeast Asia Treaty Organization (SEATO), U.S. military representative to the Australia–New Zealand–United States Council (ANZUS), and military advisor to the U.S.-Japanese Security Consultative Committee. Admiral Gayler continued in these posts until his retirement from the Navy in September 1976.

—Laura Matysek Wood

Reference: Reynolds, Clark G. *Famous American Admirals* (1978).
See also: FREQUENT WIND, Operation; United States: Navy.

Gelb, Leslie H. (1937–)

Deputy Director of the Policy Planning Staff of the U.S. Defense Department; director of the Defense Department's Vietnam Task Force, 1967–1968. In 1967 Gelb joined the Department of Defense as deputy director of the Policy Planning Staff. Outgoing Secretary of Defense Robert S. McNamara, who had come to doubt both the wisdom and morality of the Vietnam War, entrusted Gelb to undertake a secret comprehensive review of the origins of U.S. military involvement in Vietnam. The result was the 47–volume *History of the United States Decision-Making Process on Vietnam Policy*, based on Defense Department materials. Popularly known as the Pentagon Papers, it traced the deepening U.S. role in Vietnam from 1945 to 1968.

Intended as a secret study not to be shared with other government departments, the Pentagon Papers were leaked to the press in March 1971, and *The New York Times* and *Washington Post* published substantial portions of them. Publication of the Pentagon Papers further stoked the heated public debate over how the United States became involved in Vietnam and who should shoulder the blame. They revealed that from Eisenhower onward, all presidential administrations had been committed to aiding South Vietnam.

Gelb later wrote several books on U.S. foreign relations, including *The Irony of Vietnam: The System Worked* (1979), which suggested that a seriously flawed bureaucratic decision-making process led U.S. policymakers to deepen their commitment to Vietnam although they were well aware that success was highly unlikely.

—Priscilla Roberts

References: Gelb, Leslie H., with Richard K. Betts. *The Irony of Vietnam: The System Worked.* (1979); Olson, James, and Randy Roberts. *Where the Domino Fell: America and Vietnam, 1945 to 1990* (1991); Rudenstine, David. *The Day the Presses Stopped: A History of the Pentagon Papers Case* (1996).
See also: McNamara, Robert S.; Pentagon Papers and Trial.

Geneva Accords (1962)

Big-power agreement regarding Laos. Although Laotian neutrality had been guaranteed by the 1954 Geneva Accords, by 1961 the Communist Pathet Lao was threatening to convert Laos into a Communist satellite country and conduit for the export of wars of national liberation throughout Southeast Asia. The Kennedy administration rejected military intervention under Southeast Asia Treaty Organization (SEATO) Plan 5 in favor of neutralization and insisted on a cease-fire before convening a 14–nation conference on Laos. In the interim, the Pathet Lao seized key towns such as Tchépone, which subsequently became the center of People's Army of Vietnam (PAVN) supply activity serving the Hồ Chí Minh Trail.

The Geneva Conference, convened on 6 May 1961, dragged on despite a U.S. concession that provided for a weak International Control Commission (ICC), which could inspect only if all three factions in the proposed coalition government for Laos agreed. The Pathet Lao, whose offensive was often spearheaded by PAVN troops, exploited the lack of progress by extending the area under their control to support North Vietnamese use of the trail in southeastern Laos. When the Pathet Lao seized the key town of Nam Tha, Kennedy, in a successful bluff, sent 5,000 U.S. troops into northeast Thailand and the Seventh Fleet to the Gulf of Siam. This halted the Communist advance and permitted the formation of the neutralist government of Souvanna Phouma, recognized in the final accords of 23 July 1962.

The accords required removal of all foreign military personnel from Laos within 75 days, but the North Vietnamese removed only 40, and the Pathet Lao announced that they had no foreign troops. The North Vietnamese, with an estimated 10,000 troops inside Laos, continued to exploit southeast Laos as a corridor to South Vietnam, and the Soviets deflected U.S. pressure to adhere to their promises and responsibilities to ensure compliance.

The Kennedy administration removed its military and Central Intelligence Agency personnel from Laos, accepting a "tacit agreement" that, in effect, conceded southeast Laos as a corridor for guerrilla infiltration into South Vietnam in return for the continuation of a neutralist government in northeast Laos. Secretary of State Dean Rusk said that Communist noncompliance "bitterly disappointed" Kennedy and affected decision making on Vietnam. The facade of a neutral Laos during the Vietnam conflict restricted U.S. strategic options and enabled the transport of 500,000 troops and 45 million tons of war materials to the South on the Hồ Chí Minh Trail.

—Claude R. Sasso

References: Hannah, Norman, B. *The Key to Failure: Laos and the Vietnam War* (1987); Johnson, U. Alexis. *The Right Hand of Power* (1984); Rusk, Dean. *As I Saw It* (1990).

See also: Harriman, W. Averell; Kennedy, John Fitzgerald; Khrushchev, Nikita Sergeyevitch; Hồ Chí Minh Trail; Laos; Rusk, Dean; Souvanna Phouma.

Geneva Accords (1954). *See* Geneva Conference and Geneva Accords.

Geneva Conference and Geneva Accords (1954)
International conference that brought to an end the Indo-China War. The Geneva Conference began on 26 April 1954, with negotiations directed toward converting the previous year's armistice in Korea into a permanent peace. Those negotiations produced no result, however, and eparate negotiations over the war in Indo-China began on 8 May, a day after the fall of Điên Biên Phu to the Viêt Minh.

The Indo-China talks involved representatives of France, the Democratic Republic of Vietnam (DRV), the United States, the Soviet Union, China, Britain, Laos, Cambodia, and the State of Vietnam (later the Republic of Vietnam). The United States and the State of Vietnam proposed that DRV forces (the Viêt Minh) be disarmed and the State of Vietnam be left in control of all Vietnam. This proposal was simply ignored by those who were serious about an agreement— principally the representatives of France, the DRV, China, the Soviet Union, and Great Britain.

U.S. Secretary of State John Foster Dulles saw no likelihood of an agreement on Indo-China that Washington could approve, and he left the conference on 3 May. Following his departure, the U.S. delegation was headed at various times by Under Secretary of State Walter Bedell Smith or U.S. Ambassador to Czechoslovakia U. Alexis Johnson. Under orders from Dulles, Johnson was to listen to, but not participate in, the negotiations.

The accords were completed in the early morning of 21 July, but the clocks had been stopped to allow a pretense that it was still 20 July. This was a concession to Pierre Mendès-France, who had threatened to resign if he could not achieve an agreement by that date. During the conference, China and the Soviet Union had pressured the DRV to conclude a settlement. This pressure was instrumental in causing DRV leaders to accept an agreement under which the Viêt Minh gave up large amounts of territory and population then under its control in exchange for a promise of later reunification. There have also been assertions that Moscow obtained something more concrete in exchange for its pressure on the DRV to accept the Geneva Accords: a promise that France would refuse to join the proposed European Defense Community (EDC), an organization that would have considerably strengthened the North Atlantic Treaty Organization (NATO). DRV Foreign Minister Pham Van Đông, who was less than certain that reunification of North and South Vietnam would actually occur as promised in the accords, submitted to this pressure reluctantly.

The accords included separate peace agreements for Vietnam, Cambodia, and Laos (signed by French, DRV, and Cambodian officers) and an unsigned declaration of the conference. There were also unilateral declarations by several governments. The Laotian and Cambodian governments associated with the French Union were left in control of their respective countries, save for two provinces of northeast Laos where the Pathet Lao were to concentrate their forces pending a political settlement.

Vietnam was to be temporarily split, with a Demilitarized Zone (DMZ) along the 17th parallel separating the two areas. The North was to be governed by the DRV and the South by the French Union until 1956. The DRV had considerably less territory and population than the Viêt Minh controlled at the time the agreement was signed. Authorities in each zone were forbidden to take reprisals against people who had supported the other side in the recent war. The two zones were to be reunified following internationally supervised elections in 1956. Most conference participants assumed that the Communist leaders of the DRV would win such elections, were they held.

During the 300 days it would take for all DRV armed forces to leave the South and for all French Union forces to leave the North, civilians could move from one zone to the other. Many northerners, mainly Catholics, went south; far fewer southerners moved north.

The accords forbade Vietnam, Laos, and Cambodia from participating in military alliances; thus, none became members of the Southeast Asia Treaty Organization (SEATO). The accords also limited the introduction of foreign troops and weapons into Indo-China. As the Geneva Accord provisions for Vietnam collapsed over the following years, the restriction on foreign troops eventually became the only important part of the accords still taken seriously. Supervision of the implementation of the accords was left to an International Commission for Supervision and Control, usually referred to as the International Control Commission. India, Canada, and Poland each supplied one-third of the personnel, and India furnished its chairman.

Washington was not happy with the Geneva settlement. The widespread belief that the U.S. government pledged not to undermine the accords arose from a misreading of a U.S. declaration of 21 July 1954, which stated only that the United States would not go so far as to use force or the threat of force in undermining them. Washington certainly hoped to prevent the reunification of Vietnam as called for by the accords. Years later, after reunification had been blocked, Washington began claiming that the Geneva Accords had proclaimed South Vietnam an independent country.

Ngô Đình Diêm, who in June 1954 became premier of the State of Vietnam, also disliked the accords, but his position in his early months in office was weak. By mid-1955, however, Diêm had attained effective control of most of South Vietnam, and in July of that year he declared his refusal to discuss with the DRV the holding of the 1956 elections. Diêm endorsed the idea of reunification, but he rejected the procedures established by the accords for achieving reunification.

—Edwin E. Moise

References: Randle, Robert F. *Geneva 1954: The Settlement of the Indochinese War* (1969); U.S. Department of State. *Foreign Relations of the United States, 1952–1954*. Vol. XVI, *The Geneva Conference;* Young, Kenneth T. *The 1954 Geneva Conference* (1968).

See also: Canada; Dulles, John Foster; India; Johnson, U. Alexis; Knowland, William F.; Mendès-France, Pierre; Ngô Đình Diêm; Pham Van Đông; Poland; Smith, Walter Bedell; Zhou Enlai (Chou En-lai).

Genovese, Eugene Dominick (1930–)

U.S. historian, educator, and antiwar activist. A Marxist, Genovese stirred controversy when he declared at an antiwar teach-in, "I do not fear or regret the impending Viêt Công victory. I welcome it." Genovese's remarks quickly became an issue, with Richard Nixon calling for his ouster and Barry

Goldwater denouncing him for "treason." For his part, Genovese wanted a political rather than a military victory by the Democratic Republic of Vietnam (DRV) and had no wish for American troops to die in Vietnam. Genovese later taught in Canada, where he continued to denounce U.S. military involvement, commenting that American forces sought to fight the Vietnamese revolution by destroying the Vietnamese people. In 1969 he returned to the United States from his self-imposed exile.

—James Friguglietti

Reference: Beichman, Arnold. "Study in Academic Freedom" (1965).

See also: Antiwar Movement, United States; Goldwater, Barry Morris; Nixon, Richard Milhous.

Geography of Indo-China and Vietnam

Located in the northern hemisphere within the Southeast Asian realm between the 8th and 23d parallels and the 100th and 110th meridians, the Indo-Chinese peninsula is a crossroads with India to the west, China to the north, and a large archipelagic extension into the South China Sea to the southeast. A part of Indo-China, Vietnam is situated east of Laos and Cambodia along the Gulf of Tonkin and South China Sea littoral.

Indo-China's mountains overlay nearly as much territory as its plains, but the level lands house most of the population. Chinese mountain chains reach into the region and provide threadlike river valleys used as paths by migratory groups entering from the north. Consequently, the Indo-Chinese peninsula has been greatly affected by the contacts and cultures of outside civilizations.

The climate of northern Indo-China is controlled by tropical and polar air masses, creating a noticeable winter season. The South is regulated by equatorial and tropical air masses, resulting in warm temperatures during the entire year. Typhoons threaten recurrently, and with winds possibly surpassing 80 knots, the Vietnamese seacoast particularly is ravaged.

The Indo-China peninsula contains seven physical regions. To the southwest in Cambodia, the jagged Cardamom and Elephant Mountains, forested and agriculturally unyielding, is lightly settled and occupied by the tribal Pears. The Tonle Sap Basin, Mekong Lowlands, and Angkor region, a Cambodian area to the northeast of the Cardamom and Elephant Mountains, is bordered by the Dangrek Range to the north and the Annamite Cordillera to the east. It houses the ancient Khmer core at Angkor. To the north lies the Upper Mekong Valley and Laos, the heartland of the Lao people. Further eastward is the Annamite Cordillera and Northern Mountains and Plateaus, a highland region situated in parts of Cambodia, Laos, and Vietnam, and a local sanctuary for the Montagnards. The northeastern corner of Indo-China, or Tonkin, holds the productive Red River Delta, the center of Vietnamese civilization, while the narrow coastal plains and former Champa area connects the Red River Delta with the mainly Vietnamese region of the Mekong Delta and Funan to the south.

Vietnam is accessible by land and water to the People's Republic of China to the north. Its extensive coastline means vulnerability to invasion and exposure to typhoons, yet contributes to the country's food supply and promotes national unity via the sea.

Vietnam's two broad deltas are linked by a long, thin stretch of territory no more than 50 miles wide. This central section, called An Nam by the French (from the Chinese meaning "Pacified South"), is interspersed by rivers and mountains. A few touch the shoreline and inhibit north-south transportation. This narrow strip yields rice, salt, and fish and possesses Đà Nang (Tourane) and Cam Ranh Bays, as well as Huê.

The Red River delta is 250 miles wide and bracketed by hills and mountains. With fertile alluvium produced by numerous rivers, this is the agricultural heartland. With Hà Nôi, the national capital, it experiences average temperatures of 85 degrees in summer and 62 degrees in winter. Rainfall is heavy—averaging six feet in summer months—but variable. Influenced by monsoons that bring forth wet and dry periods, precipitation may vary from three to more than eight feet during the rainy season. Such extremes require the creation of a system of dikes, canals, and dams for water control. The north is Vietnam's core, acting as a market, manufacturing, and transportation hub served by the port of Hai Phòng at the mouth of the delta.

In the South, the Mekong Delta has temperatures averaging 86 degrees in the summer and 80 degrees in the winter. Mean precipitation during the rainy summer months is six feet but, like the north, can vary widely. The wide, fertile delta, interlaced by streams and canals, is a major rice-growing region interspersed with extensive forests, swamps, and jungle—what the Vietnamese refer to as the land of "bad water." Hô Chí Minh City (formerly Sài Gòn) remains the country's major urban area.

—Rodney J. Ross

References: Buttinger, Joseph. *Vietnam: A Political History* (1968); Dutt, Ashok J., ed. *Southeast Asia: Realm of Contrasts* (1985); Dwyer, Denis J., ed. *South East Asian Development* (1990); SarDesai, D. R. *Southeast Asia: Past and Present* (1989).
See also: Annam; Cambodia; Central Highlands; Champa, Kingdom of and Cham People; Cochin China; Dikes; Laos; Mekong Delta; Montagnards; Red River Delta; Tonkin; Vietnam, Climate of.

Germany, Federal Republic of

Under Chancellors Ludwig Erhard (1963–1966) and Kurt Kissinger (1966–1969), the government of the Federal Republic of Germany (FRG) supported the United States in Vietnam and contributed economic and humanitarian aid. In 1966 the FRG sent the hospital ship *S.S. Helgoland* and medical and technical personnel to the Republic of Vietnam (RVN). It also provided approximately $7.5 million annually in foreign aid to the RVN and gave $21.3 million in credits for capital projects and commodity imports. It constructed and staffed nine social centers in Sài Gòn, donated medical supplies and equipment, and in 1969 financed a 170–bed hospital in Đà Nang to replace the *S.S. Helgoland*. In March 1967,

the FRG's Maltese Aid Service program for refugees included doctors, dentists, and nurses to provide health care to Vietnamese civilians. German teachers taught at the high school and university level in Vietnam, and scholarships were awarded annually for Vietnamese students to study in the Federal Republic.

As the war dragged on, the German public, especially German youth, became critical of U.S. Vietnam policy. A protest movement, centered in the major German cities, peaked in 1968 with the eruption of violent demonstrations. In January 1973, Chancellor Willy Brandt and finance minister and Social Democratic Party colleague Helmut Schmidt criticized the Christmas bombing of North Vietnam in a speech in Washington. The end of the war, however, removed Vietnam as an impediment to FRG–U.S. relations.

—Pia C. Heyn and Spencer C. Tucker

References: Brandt, Willy. *People and Politics. The Years 1960–1973* (1978); Gatzke, Hans W. *Germany and the United States. "A Special Relationship?"* (1980); Larson, Stanley Robert, and James Lawton Collins. *Vietnam Studies: Allied Participation in Vietnam* (1975).
See also: Nguyên Phúc Ánh (Gia Long).

Gia Long. *See* Nguyên Phúc Ánh (Gia Long).

Giáp, Vô Nguyên. *See* Vô Nguyên Giáp.

Ginsberg, Allen (1926–1997)

Counterculture artist and poet. Ginsberg rose to prominence in the 1950s as a leader of the beat generation and shocked America with his celebration of drugs and alternative lifestyles. Equally at home in the protests of the 1960s, he was in the forefront of whatever movement was in vogue. He was arrested in 1967 in New York City for protesting against the war and in 1968 in Chicago for demonstrating during the Democratic Party National Convention. Ginsberg also testified at the trial of the Chicago Eight.

—Spencer C. Tucker

See also: Antiwar Movement, United States; Chicago Eight.

Godley, George McMurtrie (1917–)

U.S. diplomat. Posted to the Congo in 1964, Godley played a key role in suppressing the Chinese-backed rebellion there, coordinating Central Intelligence Agency (CIA)–sponsored air operations with Belgian-paid mercenaries. Godley's experience in the Congo made him a natural choice for Laos, where he became ambassador in April 1969. By presidential directive, Godley was responsible for "overall direction, coordination, and supervision" of all military operations in Laos.

In January 1970, the North Vietnamese expanded the war in Laos by sending two People's Army of Vietnam (PAVN) divisions to deal with CIA-led forces there. Godley secured Washington's approval to use B-52s against PAVN troop concentrations. U.S. airpower stopped the Communist offensive, but the fighting took a heavy toll of the Hmong, who shouldered most of the combat burden in Laos. To replace them, Godley arranged with Thai officials to recruit "volunteer" battalions to serve in Laos. Led by noncommissioned and regular officers, these units were funded by the U.S. government. The B-52s and Thai troops delayed a Communist victory in Laos, but could not prevent it. By the time Godley left his post in April 1973, a cease-fire agreement had been signed and a new coalition government formed. Within two years, the Communists gained complete control over Laos.

—William M. Leary

References: "Diplomat with Aggressive Style" (1973); "Our Man in Vientiane" (1972); Leary, William M. "The CIA and the 'Secret' War in Laos: The Battle for Skyline Ridge, 1971–1972."

See also: Central Intelligence Agency (CIA); Hmong; Laos; Vietnam, Democratic Republic of: Army (People's Army of Vietnam [PAVN]).

Goldberg, Arthur Joseph (1908–1990)

U.S. Secretary of Labor, 1961–1962; Supreme Court Justice, 1962–1965; ambassador to the United Nations, 1965–1968. As President Kennedy's Secretary of Labor, Goldberg was also often consulted on foreign affairs, including the Vietnam War. Kennedy appointed Goldberg to the Supreme Court in 1962; President Johnson asked him to leave the Court for the United Nations in 1965. Goldberg was a member of the "Wise Men," Johnson's informal advisors on Vietnam policy. A consistent critic of the war, Goldberg often urged Johnson to withdraw from the conflict. Goldberg maintained a good working relationship with United Nations Secretary-General U Thant, and the two men tried several times to initiate a negotiated peace in Vietnam. After the 1968 Tết Offensive, Goldberg became weary of his attempts at peace. He resigned in June 1968 and returned to his law practice.

—Debora Hall

Reference: *The Supreme Court Justices: Illustrated Biographies* (1993).

See also: Johnson, Lyndon Baines; Paris Negotiations; U Thant; "Wise Men."

Goldman, Eric F. (1915–1989)

Special consultant to President Johnson, February 1964–August 1966. One of Goldman's projects was to associate the White House with the arts community. In June 1966, he organized the White House Festival of the Arts. Artists were selected to participate in the event based on talent, with no consideration given to political ideology. Days before the festival, Robert Lowell, a prominent writer, wrote to the president to decline his invitation, since participation would give the impression that he condoned several of Johnson's recent foreign policy decisions, including U.S. bombing of North Vietnam. After his letter was published in *The New York Times*, the festival became a source of tension, and several participants used the opportunity to express antiadministration sentiments. Problems associated with the event ultimately led to Goldman's resignation in August 1966.

—Cynthia Northrup

Reference: Goldman, Eric F. *The Tragedy of Lyndon Johnson* (1969).
See also: Antiwar Movement, United States; Art and the Vietnam War; Johnson, Lyndon Baines.

Goldwater, Barry Morris (1909–1999)

U.S. Senator, 1952–1965, 1969–1984; Republican presidential candidate, 1964. During the 1964 presidential campaign, Goldwater advocated a strong military establishment and heavy reliance on air power. He was also steadfast in his commitment to halting the spread of communism, and he referred to Communist leaders as captors of enslaved peoples. Although Goldwater believed the United States should do whatever was necessary to support U.S. troops in the field, he also stated that the United States should withdraw if it was not prepared to make a major military commitment, including "carrying the war to North Vietnam." He discussed the use of low-level atomic weapons to defoliate infiltration routes but never actually advocated the use of nuclear weapons in Vietnam. The Democrats easily painted Goldwater as a warmonger, a key factor in his crushing defeat at the hands of Lyndon Johnson, who took about 61 percent of the vote to Goldwater's 39 percent. Goldwater remained a consistent critic of U.S. command decisions, blaming America's defeat in Vietnam on the bureaucracy and government officials who stood in the way of aiding the troops in the field. He retired from politics in 1986.

—Lauraine Bush

References: Goldwater, Barry N. *The Conscience of a Conservative* (1960); Shagegg, S. Stephen. *Whatever Happened to Goldwater?* (1965).
See also: Johnson, Lyndon Baines; Stevenson, Adlai E.

Gorbachev, Mikhail Sergeyevich (1931–)

General secretary of the Communist Party; president of the USSR, 1990–1991. Although Gorbachev continued Soviet support for the Socialist Republic of Vietnam (SRV), he played a crucial role in persuading the SRV to withdraw from Cambodia in 1989. Gorbachev instigated a period of more friendly relations with China and in 1989 renounced the "Brezhnev Doctrine," which had asserted the USSR's right to intervene militarily in Warsaw Pact countries. This action, in addition to Gorbachev's insistence that these former Soviet satellite states also adopt reforms, quickly led to the fall of the Eastern European Communist regimes. For his role in ending the Cold War, Gorbachev was awarded the Nobel Peace Prize in 1990. Forced to resign his position as Soviet president on 25 December 1991, he was succeeded by Boris Yeltsin as president of a new Russian federation.

—Bruce Elleman

References: Cohen, Stephen F. *Sovieticus* (1985); Dunlop, John B. *The Rise of Russia and the Fall of the Soviet Empire* (1993); Malia, Martin. *The Soviet Tragedy* (1994); Sakwa, Richard. *Gorbachev and His Reforms 1985–1990* (1991); Woodby, Sylvia. *Gorbachev and the Decline of Ideology in Soviet Foreign Policy* (1989).
See also: Brezhnev, Leonid Ilyich; Cambodia; Reagan, Ronald; Union of Soviet Socialist Republics (USSR; Soviet Union); Vietnam, Socialist Republic of: 1975 to the Present.

Gracey, Douglas D. (1894–1964)

British commander who led Allied land forces into Sài Gòn in September 1945. Gracey declared martial law on 12

September 1945, an act directed against the Viêt Minh, whom he held in disdain. Under the Potsdam Agreement, Gracey's troops were to disarm Japanese forces, but they instead triggered clashes with the Viêt Minh by rearming 1,400 French soldiers who had been imprisoned by the Japanese. French and British troops (and Japanese forces ordered by Gracey to assist them) were unable to prevent bloodshed, and civilians were killed on both sides. By 2 October, however, Viêt Minh resistance in Sài Gòn had been crushed. Gracey remained in Vietnam until March 1946 to direct British efforts to assist the French in subduing Viêt Minh opposition in the countryside.

—Clayton D. Laurie

References: Boettcher, Thomas D. *Vietnam: The Valor and the Sorrow* (1985); *Who Was Who* (1975).

See also: French Indo-China; Great Britain; Potsdam Conference; Viêt Minh.

Gravel, Maurice Robert (Mike) (1930–)

U.S. senator, 1969–1981. Considered hawkish in the late 1960s, Gravel did not gain major public attention until spring 1971, when he placed large portions of the Defense Department study of the Vietnam War (the Pentagon Papers) into the Senate record. In June 1971, after a federal grand jury indicted former Defense Department aide Daniel Ellsberg on charges of the theft of these documents, Gravel responded by reading aloud for three hours from these papers in a meeting of the Subcommittee on Public Buildings. Although the Supreme Court ruled the next day that senatorial immunity did not protect Gravel and his aides from prosecution for acquiring the papers, no action was taken against him, and in 1972 he oversaw their publication in a five-volume edition.

Gravel became an increasingly active and vocal opponent of U.S. involvement in Vietnam. He voted against the military appropriations bill of 1971 and in summer 1972 filibustered against extension of the draft. He opposed Nixon's 1972 resumption of bombing and the mining of Hai Phòng harbor and supported all attempts to cut off further funding for the war. He criticized Vietnamization as a means of extending indefinitely the U.S. commitment to South Vietnam, and he unsuccessfully attempted to bring to the Senate floor a vote on a declaration of war against North Vietnam. Gravel also called for major cuts in the defense budget and in troop levels and advocated an all-volunteer army. Gravel easily won reelection in 1974, but in 1980 he lost the Democratic senatorial primary.

—Priscilla Roberts

References: Gravel, Mike. *Citizen Power: A People's Platform* (1972); —. *Introduction to The Pentagon Papers: The Senator Gravel Edition* (1972); Schoenebaum, Eleanora. *Political Profiles: The Nixon/Ford Years* (1979).

See also: Ellsberg, Daniel; Gruening, Ernest Henry; Pentagon Papers and Trial; Russo, Anthony J., Jr.

Great Britain

Great Britain played a modest yet important role in the Indo-China and Vietnam Wars. During World War II, British com-mander in the Far East Lord Louis Mountbatten reached an informal agreement with Chinese leader Chiang Kai-shek whereby the Nationalist Chinese and Americans would be responsible for supporting resistance movements and intelligence operations in Indo-China north of the 16th parallel (Laos and North Vietnam), while the British would do the same south of that line (Cambodia and South Vietnam). This informal agreement and American antipathy toward the French formed the basis for British operations in Indo-China both during and immediately after World War II.

First British support to the French came in August 1940, when the British consul in Hà Nôi offered an informal agreement to the French colonial governor for an exchange of intelligence about Japanese forces in the area. The British also tried to enlist U.S. assistance for the French in resisting Japanese pressure for bases within Indo-China. Failing in that, British intelligence established links with anti-Vichy elements within the colony's French garrison. These operations escalated after the December 1941 Japanese invasion of Malaya, but the British were inhibited by the great distances involved and Japan's breaking of the French diplomatic code. Despite these difficulties, the Anglo-French resistance was able to provide better intelligence to Allied authorities. It also was able to rescue more Allied pilots than was the Viêt Minh, which enjoyed more support from the American Office of Strategic Services (OSS) station in China. Often at odds with their American allies, the British worked to sustain the French colonial structure and prevent the growth of a Marxist-dominated resistance movement.

In accordance with arrangements reached at the Potsdam Conference, Britain dispatched troops to restore Allied authority in southern Indo-China. Arriving in Sài Gòn on 12 September 1945, the British were lightly armed in anticipation of only a minor security role. Maj. Gen. Sir Douglas Gracey commanded the troops, which were drawn from his 20th Indian Division. Gracey initially limited himself to restoring order in Sài Gòn, releasing French officials and Allied POWs, disarming and repatriating Japanese troops, and reestablishing essential services. However, increasing Viêt Minh attacks against French citizens, along with seizures of Allied property, led him to attempt to constrain their activities.

Lacking sufficient troops to maintain order, Gracey employed recently released French POWs to augment his forces. Their poor discipline, combined with French resentment against the Viêt Minh, whom the Japanese had used to guard their POW camps, led to French excesses. On 23 September, these culminated in open conflict as Gracey attempted to bring the last remaining civil facilities under Anglo-French control. Facing expanded combat with limited forces and American denial of additional French troops, Gracey resorted to employing Japanese troops.

Neither Mountbatten nor London wanted British forces involved in the Indo-China fighting. Gracey tried to arrange negotiations between the French and their opponents, but the Viêt Minh did not adhere to the agreements they made. The arrival of 1,500 French troops in early October only reinforced French stubbornness and Vietnamese insecurity.

In October 1945, the Viêt Minh began offensive operations against the British garrison. Most of the early fighting was centered around Sài Gòn, with the city's river and road approaches coming under Viêt Minh attack. The remainder of the 20th Indian Division, supported by Royal Air Force contingents, arrived between 17 and 20 October. This enabled Gracey to conduct local counterattacks and strengthen his more isolated garrisons. On 20 October, Gracey decided to extend assistance to French naval forces.

Gracey used his reinforcements and Japanese troops to expand his control into the lower Mekong River Delta and over coastal ports, from which he intended to evacuate the Japanese troops. This operation took nearly six weeks and involved a combined force of British, French, and Japanese soldiers. As the towns were secured, the Japanese troops were replaced by French or local Vietnamese troops. The British turned over Sài Gòn to the French on 1 January 1946, and the last British troops were withdrawn on 7 February.

British policymakers also played a key role during the 1954 siege of Ðiên Biên Phu, when they rejected U.S. efforts to secure multinational military intervention to save the French. President Eisenhower made this a condition of U.S. military intervention.

British leaders did not believe in military intervention in Vietnam, and Britain did not provide any material support for the U.S. effort during the conflict. However, some British officers did serve unofficially with Australian forces in South Vietnam. London maintained contact and trade with both the Democratic Republic of Vietnam (DRV) and the Republic of Vietnam (RVN) during the war and attempted to facilitate communications between the two major antagonists to peacefully resolve the conflict. Britain's caution in Southeast Asia was related to the Communist insurgency in Malaya, Indonesian threats to Brunei and Malaya, and the maintenance of its links with Singapore and the rest of the region.

Although both the Labour and Conservative Parties supported U.S. bombing of North Vietnam following the 1964 Gulf of Tonkin incidents, privately Prime Minister Harold Wilson sought both an end to the bombing and a negotiated end to the war, and he so informed President Johnson. Wilson was constrained from publicly criticizing U.S. policy by the long-standing close relationship between the two countries and by Washington's support of the pound sterling. However, criticism of U.S. policy was evident among university student groups in Great Brtain. Although several British peace initiatives in 1965 failed, London did endeavor in early 1966 to act as intermediary in establishing talks between Washington and Moscow concerning Vietnam.

In 1970 the Labour Party lost the national elections to the Conservatives, and Edward Heath replaced Wilson. The Conservatives took a more sympathetic position toward U.S. involvement in Vietnam, a stance eased by Vietnamization. London fully supported that policy, but it also supported the Nixon administration's continued bombing of North Vietnam and its decision to mine DRV ports. Heath also refused to condemn the U.S. military incursion into Cambodia. London chose instead to call for a new Geneva Conference to discuss a peace settlement in Indo-China.

—Carl O. Schuster and Spencer C. Tucker

References: Alan, Louis. *The End of the War in Asia* (1976); Dunn, Peter M. *The First Vietnam War* (1985); Irving, R. E. M. *The First Indochina War* (1975); Maclean, Donald. *British Foreign Policy: The Years since Suez, 1956–1968* (1970); Wilson, J. Harold. *A Personal Record: The Labour Government, 1964–1970* (1971).
See also: Dinaussauts; Eisenhower, Dwight David; France: Navy; French Indo-China; Gracey, Douglas D.; Indo-China War; Johnson, Lyndon Baines; Kosygin, Aleksei Nikolayevich; Nixon, Richard Milhous; SUNFLOWER, Operation.

Great Society Program

President Johnson's domestic reform program for social justice, economic equity, and racial equality. Influenced by President Roosevelt's New Deal, the program developed along with the emerging civil rights movement, an increasing awareness of poverty, and a lessening of tension between the United States and the Soviet Union. Supported by such influential figures as Henry Luce and Martin Luther King, Jr., Johnson sent 63 messages to Congress that encompassed recommendations from 17 task forces. The resulting legislation included the Elementary and Secondary Education Act, granting federal aid to impoverished children; the Voting Rights Act of 1965, guaranteeing African American rights at the polls; and Medicare, providing medical assistance to the elderly. However, the war in Vietnam increasingly diverted dollars from the Great Society program, which in the end failed to significantly change American society.

—Brenda J. Taylor

References: Divine, Robert A., ed. *The Johnson Years* (1981); Kearns, Doris. *Lyndon Johnson and the American Dream* (1976).
See also: Economy, U.S., and the War; Johnson, Lyndon Baines; King, Martin Luther, Jr.

GREELEY, Operation (17 June–12 October 1967)

Operation more appropriately identified as the second battle for Ðak Tô. Operation GREELEY began on 17 June 1967 when two battalions of 173d Airborne Brigade were deployed to Kontum Province in anticipation of a People's Army of Vietnam (PAVN) attack on the Ðak Tô Special Forces camp. At the time, the 173d's 1st and 2d Battalions, 503d Infantry (1/503d and 2/503d) were under the operational control of the 4th Infantry Division. On 22 June, Alpha Company, 2/503d, met an entrenched battalion of the 24th PAVN Regiment while moving up thickly wooded Hill 1338 south of Ðak Tô. In one of the bloodiest single battles of the war, 76 paratroopers from Alpha Company were killed and another 23 wounded. The after-action report claimed 513 PAVN troops killed, but only 75 bodies were counted.

With indications that a full PAVN division was present, General William Westmoreland hoped to force a decisive battle for the Central Highlands. On 23 June the 1st Cavalry Division's 1st Battalion, 12th Infantry (1/12th) was airlifted from Bình Ðinh and immediately thrown into combat south of Ðak Tô. Within three days, the 1st Cavalry's entire 3d

Brigade arrived to begin search-and-destroy missions. The remaining units of the 173d Brigade also moved into Kontum.

Augmenting U.S. forces were the 5th and 8th Army of the Republic of Vietnam (ARVN) Airborne Battalions, and one battalion from the 42d ARVN Regiment. To coordinate the expanding operation, Maj. Gen. William R. Peers established the 4th Division's command post in Kontum City. On 10 July, while approaching the crest of Hill 830 southwest of Đak Tô, companies of the 4th Battalion, 503d Infantry (4/503d) encountered heavy mortar and machine gun fire and suffered devastating casualties in fighting that continued through the night. When enemy contact ebbed, the remnants of the 4/503d withdrew to Đak Tô. But in the next two months, both 4th Division and 173d Airborne troops continued to suffer heavy casualties while attacking heavily fortified bunker complexes. Also in July, the 1st Cavalry's 3d Brigade continued airmobile operations north of Kontum, and its artillery supported a Special Forces–Civilian Irregular Defense Group (CIDG) force as it successfully ambushed a PAVN unit. By 25 July, the 3d Brigade was recalled to Bình Định, but fighting around Đak Tô continued.

By early September, contact with the PAVN had so diminished that the bulk of the 173d Airborne departed to assume a new mission near the coastal city of Tuy Hòa. It was thought that the 4th Division, now at full strength, could handle the situation in Kontum. In fact, the Battle of Đak Tô was not over. On 12 October, Operation GREELEY was folded into Operation MACARTHUR, and the decisive battle began.

—John D. Root

References: Murphy, Edward F. *Dak Tô: The 173rd Airborne Brigade in South Vietnam's Central Highlands, June–November 1967* (1993); Stanton, Shelby L. *The Rise and Fall of the American Army: U.S. Ground Forces in Vietnam, 1965–1973* (1985).

See also: Civilian Irregular Defense Group (CIDG); Đak Tô, Battle of; HAWTHORNE, Operation; MACARTHUR, Operation; Peers, William R; Search and Destroy; Westmoreland, William Childs.

Greene, Graham (1904–1991)

British novelist and foreign correspondent. Greene visited Vietnam four times from 1951 to 1955, filing reports in *Spectator* and other magazines. His book *The Quiet American* (1955) fictionalizes Greene's observations, chronicling the faults of colonialism. In linking Alden Pyle, a composite character based on Colonel Edward Lansdale and Leo Hochstetter, a member of the American legation in Sài Gòn, with General Thê, Greene implicates the United States with violent covert operations. Increasingly engaged, the cynical Thomas Fowler, Greene's alter ego, becomes the novel's hero when he helps the Việt Minh murder Pyle. Greene's attraction to the Third World communism of Hô Chí Minh alienated many American readers. Nevertheless, his blending of fact into fiction, using a method he called *rapportage*, greatly influenced American writers such as Michael Herr and Gloria Emerson.

—Charles J. Gaspar

References: Adamson, Judith. *Graham Greene: The Dangerous Edge* (1990); Shelden, Michael. *Graham Greene: The Man Within* (1994).

See also: Cao Đài; Fiction, U.S., and the Vietnam Experience; Hô Chí Minh; Lansdale, Edward Geary; Prose Narrative and the Vietnam Experience.

Greene, Wallace M. (1907–)

U.S. Marine Corps general and commandant, 1964–1967. Under General Greene, the Marine Corps perfected its operational readiness, response time, and sustainability as the nation's primary strategic reinforcement outside of the North Atlantic Treaty Organization (NATO). Greene staunchly advocated combining new technology with traditional Marine tactics to make the Corps a more effective element of "flexible response." He saw the Communist insurgency in Southeast Asia as a direct challenge to U.S. Pacific interests and felt that U.S. military power and political credibility were too committed there to allow withdrawal without victory. Greene opposed the Johnson administration's limited air raids and graduated response, and he thought the idea of a negotiated settlement illusory. He was also critical of Secretary of Defense Robert S. McNamara's micro-management of the war. By the end of his tour as commandant in 1967, Greene feared that the war of attrition was not working and that, despite the excellent performance of the Marines in Vietnam, the war could not be won.

—W. E. Fahey, Jr.

Reference: Herring, George C. *LBJ and Vietnam: A Different Kind of War* (1994).

See also: Attrition; Pacification; McNamara, Robert S.; United States: Marine Corps.

Grenades, Hand: Allied and Democratic Republic of Vietnam

Hand grenades were used extensively by both sides in the Vietnam War and can be placed in several categories. High-explosive antipersonnel grenades can be either offensive or defensive in nature. Defensive hand grenades rely upon fragmentation of the outer casing to cause casualties; offensive hand grenades rely solely upon flash and blast effect because of the danger fragmentation would pose to an assaulting infantryman. Both types of grenades were used by Allied and Communist forces.

Communist forces employed a variety of grenades. The World War II Soviet F1 (Type1/M33 PRC) grenade, like the U.S. MK2 "Pineapple" grenade, was based upon the British No. 36 "Mills Bomb." This was a defensive grenade with a 20–meter casualty radius. It was later replaced by the Soviet RGD5 (Type 59/M32 PRC), a lighter egg-shaped model that could be thrown farther and produced a 15– to 20–meter casualty radius. The obsolete Soviet RG42 (Type 42 PRC) and RGD33 grenades were also used by Communist forces in Vietnam. The RG42 is a defensive antipersonnel grenade. The RGD33 can be used in either offensively (with a 5–meter casualty radius) or defensively (with a 25–meter casualty radius when a serrated fragmentation sleeve is attached). Homemade Việt Công (VC) grenades were also manufactured from unexploded U.S. munitions.

Free World forces initially relied upon the U.S. MK2 defensive grenade, similar to the Soviet F1. The MK2 was later replaced by the egg-shaped Korean War–vintage M26 series, which included the M61. The M26A2 variant was impact-detonated. The casualty radius of the M26 series grenade was 10 meters. Another series of defensive grenades, based on the American ball-shaped M33 "baseball" grenade, included the M33, M67, M59, and M68 variants and produced a casualty radius of 15 meters. An offensive grenade series based on the U.S. MK3 was used principally for clearing enclosed areas.

Antitank grenades were used by Communist forces in Vietnam but were unpopular with Free World forces because of the seemingly suicidal requirement of closing in with opposing armored fighting vehicles. The older Soviet RPG40, RPG43, and RPG6 series of grenades dated to World War II. The latter two grenades can penetrate from 75 to 100 mm of armor, respectively, and rely upon parachute cloth strips for stabilization after being thrown. These grenades could be thrown about 20 meters. The newer Soviet RKG3/3M (RKG3T PRC) drogue-stabilized grenade was introduced in the final stages of the Vietnam War. The RKG3 model could penetrate 125 mm of armor; the later RKG3M model could penetrate 165 mm of armor.

Irritant grenades were used almost exclusively by U.S.-backed forces for counterinsurgency operations. The M7 and M25 series were filled with CS (orthochloro-benzylidene malonoitrile), DM (diphenylamine chloroarcsine), and/or CN (chloroacetophenone) agents. CS and CN are riot control agents; DM is a sickening agent no longer used by the U.S. military because it can be fatal. CS-filled grenades were extensively used against VC tunnels at Cu Chi.

Incendiary grenades were used by Allied forces principally to destroy equipment. These grenades, of which the thermate-filled M14 is a standard example, burn for about 40 seconds at 4,300 degrees Fahrenheit and are meant to be placed directly on the object that is to be destroyed. The MK1 illuminating grenade, an incendiary variant that produced up to 55,000 candlepower for 25 seconds, could light up an area up to 200 meters in diameter. VC homemade incendiary grenades, composed of sodium, also existed.

Smoke grenades were employed by both sides for the signaling and screening of forces. The Soviet RDG1 and RDG2 grenades could be thrown 35 meters and produced white smoke; an RDG1 variant produced black smoke. The RDG1 could float and was used to cover river crossings. U.S. forces used both white and colored smoke for signaling, but used white smoke almost exclusively for screening purposes. The M8 grenade produced white smoke; the M18 series produced green, red, yellow, or violet smoke.

The U.S. M34 WP grenade was its own unique category. Although considered a smoke grenade, it also had antipersonnel and incendiary applications. Its bursting effect caused casualties within a radius of 25 meters as a result of its white phosphorus filler, which burned at slightly less than 5,000 degrees Fahrenheit for one minute and ignited any flammable material it contacted.

—Robert J. Bunker

References: Rosser-Owen, David. *Vietnam Weapons Handbook* (1986); U.S. Army Materiel Command. *Grenades (U). Engineering Design Handbook* (1967); U.S. Marine Corps Base Quantico. *Vietcong Mine Warfare* (1966); Weber, Mike. *Grenades!* (1979); Wells, Robert, ed. *The Invisible Enemy: Boobytraps in Vietnam* (1992).
See also: Booby Traps; Grenades, Launched, Allied and Democratic Republic of Vietnam.

Grenades, Launched: Allied and Democratic Republic of Vietnam

Two principal types of launched grenades were used in Vietnam. Those employed by Allied forces were based on the 40-mm grenade series; those employed by Communist forces were based on the PG2 (later PG7) grenade series.

Antitank and antipersonnel grenades had been developed for the U.S. M1 rifle that saw service from World War II to Vietnam. The need for such grenades was replaced by the M72 light antitank weapon (LAW) and the M79 grenade launcher, respectively. The M72 represents a 66-mm rocket launcher and so is not covered here.

Development of the M79 began in 1952, but it was not issued in quantity to combat units until 1961. The M79, a single-shot shotgun type of weapon, is shoulder-fired, has a break-open action, and fires a 40-mm grenade. The standard cartridge is the M406 high-explosive round, which produces a five-meter casualty radius. High-explosive bounding, antitank, canister, smoke, and tear gas (CS) rounds were also available. Area fire range is between 30 and 350 meters, covering the dead zone between the maximum throwing range of a hand grenade and the minimum range for mortar fire. Direct fire ranges are from 30 to 150 meters, while the maximum range is 400 meters. The M79 proved exceptionally useful in ambush and counterambush situations and could be used to mark targets for air strikes and as a secure signaling device between ground and air elements (a light source was placed in the weapon's breech).

The follow-up to the M79 was the XM148 launcher, later known as the M203, which attached under the M-16 rifle. Although possessing the same capability as the M79, this adaptation also allowed each grenadier to function as a rifleman. Another 40-mm grenade system based on the helicopter-mounted M75 fired high-velocity rounds that were incompatible with those of the shoulder-fired weapons.

The basis of the PG grenade series used by Communist forces was the German *Panzerfaust*, a World War II rocket-propelled grenade. These grenades have shaped-charged high-explosive antitank (HEAT) warheads and are percussion fired. Launchers are single-man operated and can fire up to six rounds per minute. Image-intensifier and infrared night sights were fitted to the various launchers. The performance attributes of the grenades fluctuated widely, depending on the country of origin.

The Soviet RPG2 (Czechoslovakian P27, Chinese Type 56, or Vietnamese B40) had an effective range between 100 and

150 meters. Armor penetration, depending on angle of impact, ranged from 150 mm to 265 mm; grenade caliber ranged from 80 mm to 120 mm. The Soviet RPG7V (Chinese Type 69 or Vietnamese B41) appeared in 1962 and represented an improved version of the RPG2 with a rocket assist motor that fired ten meters from the muzzle of the launcher. Effective range was increased to 500 meters and armor penetration up to 330 mm.

Although effective as weapons, these rocket-propelled grenades had several shortcomings. The black powder–based firing charge produced smoke upon ignition, giving away an attacker's firing position. In a crosswind the grenade's flight path tended to become erratic. The PG7's piezo-electric fusing system could be defeated by regular cyclone fencing emplaced eight to ten feet in front of a defensive position. This squeezed the grenade's two metal cones together, shorting out its fuse. Cyclone fencing also caused premature detonation of the B40. As a result, such fencing was commonly used by U.S. armor units.

—Robert J. Bunker

References: Doleman, Edgar D. Jr., and the editors of Boston Publishing Company. *Tools of War* (1984); Hay, John H., Jr. *Tactical and Materiel Innovations* (1974); Rosser-Owen, David. *Vietnam Weapons Handbook* (1986); U.S. Army. *40-mm Grenade Launchers M203 and M79* (1972); U.S. Army Materiel Command. *Grenades (U)* (1967).

See also: Artillery, Allied and People's Army of Vietnam; Grenades, Hand, Allied and Democratic Republic of Vietnam; Rockets.

Gruening, Ernest Henry (1887–1974)

U.S. Senator, 1959–1969; opponent of the Vietnam War. As a senator, Gruening was among the first critics of the Vietnam War, arguing in a 10 March 1964 speech that the United States should withdraw its military forces. On 7 August 1964, Gruening and Senator Wayne Morse were the only two members of Congress to vote against the Tonkin Gulf Resolution. For the rest of his political career, Gruening voted against appropriations for the war. In April 1965, he supported and spoke before antiwar demonstrators in Washington. He opposed bombing North Vietnam and called on President Johnson to open negotiations with Hà Nôi. On 1 March 1966, Gruening and Morse were again the only senators to vote for Morse's proposal to repeal the Tonkin Gulf Resolution and Gruening's proposal to send only volunteers to Vietnam. Gruening lost the 1968 Democratic primary to Mike Gravel but still received 15 percent of the vote in write-ins. In 1972 he supported antiwar presidential candidate George McGovern.

—Kenneth R. Stevens

References: Gruening, Ernest. *Many Battles: The Autobiography of Ernest Gruening* (1973); Lichtenstein, Nelson, ed. *Political Profiles: The Johnson Years* (1976).

See also: Antiwar Movement, United States; Gravel, Maurice Robert (Mike); Morse, Wayne Lyman; Tonkin Gulf Resolution.

Guam Conference (20–21 March 1967)

Third summit between U.S. and Republic of Vietnam (RVN) leaders. President Johnson, Secretary of State Dean Rusk, and Secretary of Defense Robert McNamara led the U.S. delegation. From Sài Gòn came Ambassador Henry Cabot Lodge and RVN leaders, headed by Premier Nguyên Cao Ky and Chief of State Nguyên Van Thiêu. In all, 22 U.S. and 10 RVN principal officials participated.

Johnson reaffirmed the U.S. commitment to its ally and personally introduced new appointments: Ellsworth Bunker, assuming Lodge's responsibilities, would have as his assistant Eugene Locke. General Creighton Abrams would become General William Westmoreland's deputy and eventually take over command from him. Robert Komer would become Westmoreland's deputy for Civilian Operations and Revolutionary Development Support (CORDS) and, as a civilian under Military Assistance Command, Vietnam (MACV), would direct the pacification effort. Johnson rejected Westmoreland's request for 200,000 additional troops (but agreed to 55,000) and Ky's proposal to step up bombing raids against People's Army of Vietnam/Viêt Công sanctuaries and supply routes in Cambodia and Laos.

The agenda consisted of a review of the war, United Nation Secretary-General U Thant's peace proposal, RVN political developments, and the pacification effort. Although Washington viewed U Thant's initiative with skepticism, its timing just before the conference convinced the Vietnamese public that the U.S. government was behind it. U.S. officials reassured their RVN counterparts by promising full consultation should there be developments. RVN leaders presented their new constitution to persuade Johnson that they were moving meaningfully toward democracy, which had been promised in February 1966, in Honolulu.

The Vietnamese, concerned about the faltering pacification program, responded positively to Komer's appointment. Journalists I. F. Stone and Frances FitzGerald reacted with less enthusiasm. Stone criticized Komer and the conference for omitting the issue of RVN shortcomings, such as land reform and freedom of the press. FitzGerald wrote that to put all pacification operations under the military "signified that Washington no longer gave even symbolic importance to the notion of a 'political' war waged by the Vietnamese government." U.S. officials tried to put a positive light on the conference, but indicated privately that it was "hasty and threadbare."

—Paul S. Daum, with Trevor Curran

References: Bùi Diêm. *In The Jaws of History* (1987); FitzGerald, Frances. *Fire in the Lake: The Vietnamese and the Americans in Vietnam* (1972); Olson, James S., ed. *Dictionary of the Vietnam War* (1988); Stone, I. F. *Polemics and Prophecies, 1967–1970: A Non-Conformist History of Our Times* (1989).

See also: Abrams, Creighton; Bùi Diêm; Bunker, Ellsworth; Honolulu Conference; Johnson, Lyndon Baines; Komer, Robert W.; Lodge, Henry Cabot, Jr.; McNamara, Robert S.; Nguyên Cao Ky; Nguyên Van Thiêu; Pacification; Rusk, Dean; U Thant; United States: Involvement in Vietnam, 1965–1968; Vietnam, Republic of: 1954–1975.

Guizot, François (1787–1874)

French statesman and historian. From 1840 to 1848, as minister of foreign affairs and de facto head of the ministry,

Guizot advocated conservative policies designed to maintain peace abroad and order at home and to restrict political rights to the wealthy. Under Guizot's influence, a new French concept of colonialism evolved. Colonies received new military and commercial significance. In the Far East, this began to supplant French traditional interest in missionary activities.

Guizot initially resisted suggestions that he send a naval squadron to the Far East but changed his mind following the 1841 British acquisition of Hong Kong. In 1843 he sent sizable French naval forces under the command of Admiral Cécille and Capt. Léonard Charner to Asian waters. Guizot instructed his naval commanders to acquire positions equal to those the British enjoyed in Hong Kong and Singapore, but to avoid operations along the coast of Vietnam. He thought the country too unhealthy and coastal positions there too difficult to defend.

—Spencer C. Tucker

References: Buttinger, Joseph. *The Smaller Dragon: A Political History of Vietnam* (1968); Guizot, François. *Mémoires pour servir à l'histoire de mon temps* (1872); Johnson, Douglas W. J. *Guizot: Aspects of French History, 1787–1874* (1963); Newman, Edgar L. *Historical Dictionary of France from the 1815 Restoration to the Second Empire* (1987); Woodward, Ernest L. *Three Studies in European Conservatism: Metternich, Guizot, the Catholic Church in the Nineteenth Century* (1963).
See also: French Indo-China.

H

Hà Nôi (Đông Đa), Battle of (30 January 1789)
Culminating military engagement of the 1771–1789 Tây Son rebellion, regarded as one of the greatest victories in Vietnamese history. What might be called the first Têt Offensive, the Battle of Hà Nôi (also known as the Battle of Đông Đa) was proof that the holiday was not always peacefully observed by warring Vietnamese factions.

In a brilliant campaign between May and July 1786, Nguyên Huê defeated the Trinh lords in North Vietnam, brought the Lê emperor under his control, then returned to the south to consolidate his authority there. Emperor Lê Chiêu Thông fled to China; his only hope of reclaiming his throne was with Chinese assistance. In December 1788 a Chinese expeditionary force commanded by Sun Shiyi took Hà Nôi, but events worked to undermine their authority. On 22 December, after learning of the Chinese invasion, Nguyên Huê proclaimed himself emperor Quang Trung and then raised an army, playing to Vietnamese nationalism. He ordered his soldiers to celebrate the Têt holiday early. His attack on the eve of Têt was a brilliant stroke, catching his enemy off guard celebrating the lunar new year. On the afternoon of the seventh day of the new year, Quang Trung entered Hà Nôi, a victory still celebrated in Vietnam as one of the nation's greatest military achievements.

Concentration of force and mobility, rather than numbers, were the keys in the Tây Son victory. The attackers were motivated by a desire to free their country from foreign domination, and thousands of civilians joined the Tây Son force as it moved north. Quang Trung also profited from Chinese errors. Sun Shiyi had taken virtually his entire army to Hà Nôi. Confident in his superior numbers, he underestimated his adversary and relaxed discipline.

—Spencer C. Tucker

References: Buttinger, Joseph. *The Smaller Dragon: A Political History of Vietnam* (1958); Truong Buu Lâm. *Resistance, Rebellion, and Revolution: Popular Movements in Vietnamese History* (1984); Viêt Chung. "Recent Findings on the Tay Son Insurgency" (1985).
See also: Nguyê Dynasty; Nguyên Huê (Quang Trung); Tây Son Rebellion; Trinh Lords.

Hà Nôi Hilton (Hoa Lò Prison)

Most notorious of the camps or prisons housing U.S. prisoners of war (POWs) in the Hà Nôi area. Hoa Lò Prison (named "Hà Nôi Hilton" by Bob Schumaker, the second U.S. POW there) was a fortress built by the French in 1886. Formerly a place of incarceration for high-ranking Vietnamese government officials, it covered a city block in Hà Nôi. Its twenty-foot-high outer walls were extended an additional five feet with electrified barbed wire. The prison itself was a series of cellblocks and administration buildings.

The Hà Nôi Hilton was one of several prisons located in or near Hà Nôi, including those known as the Zoo, Alcatraz, the Briarpatch, and Camp Hope (Son Tây). Some 700 American POWs were housed in these camps between August 1964 and February 1973. The exact number of POWs held in the Hà Nôi Hilton is unknown, but estimates are that by late 1970 up to 360 prisoners were housed in its "Camp Unity" cellblock. The prisoners gave each cellblock a name, such as "Heartbreak Hotel" and "Little Vegas." Almost all new prisoners were housed temporarily in "New Guy Village." Sanitation was poor, and the cells were insect- and rodent-infested. Much of the food was inedible, medical treatment was poor to nonexistent, and torture and isolation were commonplace. Prisoners were crowded 40 to 60 men per room.

Most knowledge of Hoa Lò Prison and other POW camps comes from prisoner debriefings and published personal accounts, many of them testimonials of faith and courage. The North Vietnamese constantly attempted to break captives psychologically, mostly to gain confessions or information for propaganda purposes. Prisoners were isolated, shackled, prohibited from communicating or bathing, and tortured in specially designed interrogation rooms. Despite deplorable conditions and inhumane treatment, prisoners maintained communication with each other and got news from the outside. They held regular church services, taught each other foreign languages and math, and reenacted their favorite movies. Some prisoners had been held since 1967 at Hoa Lò, which at one time held such notable POWs as Jeremiah A. Denton, Jr., John S. McCain III, and James B. Stockdale.

Two factors contributed to the increase in the POW population at Hoa Lò. A 21 November 1970 attempt to rescue POWs at Son Tây camp caused the North Vietnamese to move more than 200 American aircrew members there. And in 1972, as bombing raids of Hà Nôi continued, the North Vietnamese rounded up POWs from camps scattered throughout the north and moved them to downtown Hà Nôi. The prison was poorly equipped to handle the increasing number of American prisoners. Even before these events, however, conditions at the Hà Nôi Hilton improved. Some attribute this to a U.S. letter-writing campaign demanding more humane treatment of the prisoners; others cite the death of Hô Chí Minh in September 1969 or North Vietnamese propaganda statements that backfired.

POW releases began with the signing of the Paris peace accords on 23 January 1973. The first 116 of the 566 U.S. POWs released landed at Clark Air Force Base in the Philippines on 12 February 1973. First off the plane was Navy Capt. Jeremiah Denton, who, after seven and a half years in captivity, saluted the American flag.

In 1997 a Singapore company began turning the Hà Nôi Hilton into a block of luxury apartments and stores.

—Gary Kerley and Spencer C. Tucker

References: Olson, James S., ed. *Dictionary of the Vietnam War* (1988); Risner, Robinson. *The Passing of the Night: My Seven Years As a Prisoner of the North Vietnamese* (1973); Routledge, Howard, and Phyllis Routledge. *In the Presence of Mine Enemies, 1965–1973: A Prisoner at War* (1974); Rowan, Stephen A. *They Wouldn't Let Us*

Die: The Prisoners of War Tell Their Story (1973); Schemmer, Benjamin F. *The Raid* (1976).

See also: Denton, Jeremiah A., Jr.; HOMECOMING, Operation; McCain, John S., III; Missing in Action, Allied; Prisoners of War, Allied; Son Tây Raid; Stockdale, James B.

Habib, Philip Charles (1920–1992)

Career diplomat; U.S. minister-counselor at the Sài Gòn embassy, 1965–1966; subsequently the highest ranking State Department official specializing in Vietnamese affairs. As deputy assistant secretary of state, Habib accompanied Gen. Earle Wheeler on a fact-finding mission to Sài Gòn following the Têt Offensive. On 25 March 1968, Habib shocked President Johnson's senior policy advisors with his assessment that it would take five to ten years to make any substantial progress in Vietnam. This led to Johnson's famous remark that "somebody poisoned the well" and ultimately to a significant change in U.S. war policy. Habib served on the U.S. delegation to the Paris peace talks, and in November 1969 President Nixon appointed him to head that delegation. In 1974 Habib was appointed assistant secretary of state for East Asian and Pacific Affairs and went to Sài Gòn to determine the need for a $300 million supplemental aid package. In 1975 he worked to obtain military and economic aid for Cambodia.

—Claude R. Sasso

References: Bùi Diêm. *In the Jaws of History* (1987); Karnow, Stanley. *Vietnam: A History* (1983).

See also: Nixon, Richard Milhous; Johnson, Lyndon Baines; Paris Peace Accords; Wheeler, Earle G.; "Wise Men."

Hackworth, David H. (1931–)

Much-decorated soldier and strong critic of the war in Vietnam. In January 1965, Hackworth was assigned to the 101st Airborne Division. Sent to the Infantry Officer Advanced Course, he learned counterinsurgency doctrine. Discussions with Special Forces officers who had served in Vietnam led him to become highly critical of Army tactics that he viewed as failing to address basic issues of guerrilla warfare.

In July 1965, Hackworth arrived in South Vietnam with the 101st Airborne Division for a one-year tour. Assigned to the Pentagon upon his return, he spent much of that assignment accompanying Brig. Gen. S. L. A. Marshall on a research trip to Vietnam. A tour as commander of a training battalion at Fort Lewis, Washington, convinced Hackworth of the ineffectiveness of training given soldiers sent to Vietnam. In 1969 he returned to Vietnam, where various assignments further strengthened his disenchantment with the U.S. military effort, particularly its emphasis on body count, overly optimistic reports, and the awards system. He was also highly critical of the Army of the Republic of Vietnam and many of its officers. Hackworth departed Vietnam in June 1971.

Hackworth's disenchantment erupted in an interview aired by ABC on its 27 June 1971 "Issues and Answers." This broadcast led to an investigation of his conduct in Vietnam, which Secretary of the Army Robert F. Frohlke eventually directed be dropped. Hackworth retired from the Army in September 1971. His criticisms of the U.S. Army in the Vietnam War, shared by many of his contemporaries, helped bring about substantial military reform.

—Richard L. Kiper

Reference: Hackworth, David H., and Julie Sherman. *About Face: The Odyssey of an American Warrior* (1989).

See also: Body Count; HAWTHORNE, Operation; Marshall, Samuel Lyman Atwood; Rifles; Vann, John Paul; United States: Special Forces.

Hai Phòng, Shelling of (23 November 1946)

On 20 November, a French patrol vessel seized a Chinese junk attempting to run contraband into the port of Hai Phòng. Vietnamese soldiers fired on the French vessel, and shooting erupted in the city. A subsequent meeting between French and Vietnamese officials brought a French promise to respect Vietnamese sovereignty, and both sides agreed to separate their troops within Hai Phòng. By the afternoon of 22 November, fighting had ended, but French High Commissioner Georges Thierry d'Argenlieu proposed using the Hai Phòng clash to teach the Vietnamese a lesson. On 23 November, Col. Pierre-Louis Debès, commander of French troops at Hai Phòng, gave the Vietnamese two hours to withdraw from the French section, Chinese quarter, and port, then subjected them to air, land, and sea bombardment. The Vietnamese quarter was destroyed. Fighting in Hai Phòng halted on 28 November, but Franco-Vietnamese relations steadily deteriorated after the 23 November incident. On 19 December, the mutual fear and mistrust, fueled by bloodshed and broken promises, erupted into all-out war.

—Spencer C. Tucker

References: Fall, Bernard. *The Two Viet Nams* (1964); Hammer, Ellen J. *The Struggle for Indochina* (1954); Karnow, Stanley. *Vietnam: A History* (1983).

See also: Bidault, Georges; d'Argenlieu, Georges Thierry; Dèbes, Pierre-Louis; French Indo-China; Indo-China War; Valluy, Etienne.

Haig, Alexander Meigs, Jr. (1924–)

U.S. Army officer, deputy assistant to the president for national security affairs and vice-chief of staff of the U.S. Army. From 1965 to 1967, Col. Haig served in Vietnam with the 1st Infantry Division.

Haig's reputation was that of a diligent administrator, well-schooled in politics and diplomacy. When Henry Kissinger reorganized the foreign affairs staff for President Nixon in 1968, he chose Haig as military assistant to the assistant to the president for national security affairs, a position not well-defined at first. Haig acted as liaison between the Pentagon and State Department, screened intelligence information, prepared security reports for the president, and ran the National Security Council in Kissinger's absence.

Haig was promoted to brigadier general in October 1969 and in early 1970 went to Vietnam to assess the situation for Nixon and Kissinger. Made deputy assistant to the president for national security affair in June 1970, he gained direct access to Nixon. In September 1972, Nixon promoted Haig to four-star rank and the post of Army vice-chief of staff, bypassing 240 higher-ranking generals and prompting criticism from some who saw Haig as the president's "yes-man." He continued to work with Kissinger on secret peace negotiations and accompanied him on secret trips to Sài Gòn and Paris. In 1974 President Ford made Haig supreme Allied commander of North Atlantic Treaty Organization operations in Europe, a post he held until his retirement from the Army in 1979.

—Laura Matysek Wood

References: Haig, Alexander. *Inner Circles* (1992); Morris, Roger. *Haig* (1982).
See also: CEDAR FALLS, Operation; Ford, Gerald R.; JUNCTION CITY, Operation; Kissinger, Henry Alfred; Nixon, Richard Milhous; Watergate.

Halberstam, David (1934–)

Journalist and author of books on the Vietnam War. In September 1962, *The New York Times* dispatched Halberstam to Vietnam, where his honest, if impressionistic, reporting was criticized by those who wanted to portray the military situation in positive terms. In January 1963, Halberstam reported that the battle at Âp Bac had been a shattering defeat for the Army of the Republic of Vietnam, earning him the distrust of high-ranking military officials. In summer 1963 he covered the disintegrating political situation in the Republic of Vietnam with unflinching honesty. Claiming Halberstam's reporting was too subjective, President Kennedy asked for his reassignment from Vietnam. The *Times* did not honor his request, but Halberstam returned to New York in early 1964.

Halberstam continued to write on Vietnam. *The Making of a Quagmire* (1965, revised 1987), an astute early examination of the war, reflects Halberstam's desire to win a war that he feared was unwinnable. *The Best and the Brightest* (1972), Halberstam's lengthy biographical and psychological examination of those in the Kennedy and Johnson administrations whose search for power led the United States into Southeast Asia, won the 1973 National Book Award.

—Charles J. Gaspar

References: Misra, Kalidas. "Print-Journalism and Vietnam: Shifting Perspectives" (1985); Prochnau, William. *Once upon a Distant War: Young War Correspondents and the Early Vietnam Battles* (1995).
See also: Âp Bac, Battle of; Buddhists; Cronkite, Walter Leland; Fall, Bernard B.; Fiction, U.S., and the Vietnam Experience; Harkins, Paul D.; Kennedy, John Fitzgerald; Ngô Đình Diêm; Ngô Đình Nhu, Madam (Trân Lê Xuân); Prose Narrative and the Vietnam Experience; Salisbury, Harrison E; Sheehan, Cornelius Mahoney (Neil).

Halperin, Morton H. (1938–)

Deputy assistant secretary of defense, 1966–1969; senior staff member for planning, National Security Council, 1969. A Harvard protégé of Henry Kissinger, Halperin initially supported U.S. involvement in Vietnam. In December 1965 he was one of 190 American academics who signed a petition supporting President Johnson's conduct of the war.

In January 1969 Halperin followed Kissinger to the National Security Council (NSC) as senior staff member for planning. There he devised strategies whereby Kissinger essentially seized control of foreign policy from the State Department. However, H. R. Haldeman and others in the Nixon administration considered Halperin too liberal and accused him of leaking confidential information to the press. Halperin's telephone was tapped, and in September 1969 he resigned from the NSC. By then, Halperin had become highly critical of aspects of U.S. involvement in Vietnam, and he expressed his reservations in a series of books and articles. He particularly criticized the manner in which successive administrations' fears of appearing soft on communism led to escalation of the war. He also condemned the manner in which the imperatives of secrecy inhibited or precluded public discussion of such initiatives as the bombing of Cambodia and the use of herbicides and chemical weapons.

—Priscilla Roberts

References: Halperin, Morton H. *Bureaucratic Politics and Foreign Policy* (1974); —. *National Security Policy-Making* (1975); Halperin, Morton H., et al. *The Lawless State: The Crimes of the U.S. Intelligence Agencies* (1976); Isaacson, Walter. *Kissinger: A Biography* (1992).
See also: Clinton, William Jefferson; Johnson, Lyndon Baines; Kissinger, Henry Alfred; Nixon, Richard Milhous; Watergate.

Hàm Nghi (1872–1947)

Seventh emperor of the Nguyên Dynasty (1884–1885) and hero of the Vietnamese resistance movement against the French invasion of the late nineteenth century. After the failure of the Vietnamese army's heavy assault on the French at the fort of Mang Cá on 5 July 1885, Hàm Nghi fled to Tân So. There, he appealed for support in his fight against the French. Many people responded, opening a great anti-French movement, the Phong Trào Cân Vuong (Supporting the King Movement).

—Pham Cao Duong

References: Le Thanh Khoi. *Le Viet-Nam: Histoire et Civilisation* (1955); Nguyen Huyen Anh. *Viêt Nam Danh Nhân Tu Điên* (1990); Nguyên Thê Anh. *Viêt Nam Duoi Thoi Pháp Đô Hô* (1970).
See also: French Indo-China; Minh Mang; Thiêu Tri; Tu Đuc; Vietnam: from 938 through the French Conquest.

Hamburger Hill (Battle of Âp Bia Mountain) (11–20 May 1969)

One of the bloodiest military battles of the Vietnam War. The Battle of Âp Bia Mountain occurred as part of Operation APACHE SNOW. It was fought against entrenched People's Army of Vietnam (PAVN) regulars who, as they seldom did during the war, decided to stand against repetitive U.S. frontal assaults. This created the bloody "meat-grinder" battle that led U.S. participants to call it "Hamburger Hill."

On the second day of the operation, Company B of the 3d Battalion, 187th Infantry (3/187th) came under concentrated PAVN fire on Hill 937. After several assaults conducted over three days, the 3/187th was reinforced with two more 101st Airborne Division battalions and a battalion of the 3d ARVN Regiment. On 18 May, with the ARVN battalion posted to seal off the hill, a two-battalion assault nearly took the summit before torrential rain forced a withdrawal. Finally on 20 May, after ten previous tries, a four-battalion assault drove the PAVN from their mountain fortress and into Laos. Once the PAVN withdrew from the mountain, U.S. and ARVN forces abandoned it as well. As in previous operations, as soon as U.S. and ARVN forces withdrew, PAVN troops moved back into the area. U.S. casualty figures for the whole of Operation APACHE SNOW were 56 American and 5 South Vietnamese killed in action; enemy losses were estimated at 630.

Fanned by media attention to the battle, which seemed to symbolize the frustration of winning battles without ever consummating the strategic victory, a controversy arose over the cost in American lives of taking the hill only to abandon it for the Communists to reoccupy. This led to the limiting of U.S. military operations in the face of U.S. troop withdrawals and Vietnamization.

—Arthur T. Frame

References: Stanton, Shelby L. *The Rise and Fall of an American Army: U.S. Ground Forces in Vietnam, 1965–1973* (1985); Zaffiri, Samuel. *Hamburger Hill* (1988).

See also: A Shau Valley; APACHE SNOW, Operation; Attrition; United States: Involvement in Vietnam, 1969–1973; Vietnamization; Vietnam, Democratic Republic of: Army (People's Army of Vietnam [PAVN]).

Hamlet Evaluation System (HES)

Technique to measure the pacification process. The Hamlet Evaluation System (HES) began in January 1967. Some 250 U.S. Military Assistance Command, Vietnam (MACV) district advisors completed monthly evaluation worksheets for 9,000 of South Vietnam's 13,000 hamlets, using a matrix of 18 equally weighted indicators—9 for security and 9 for development. MACV assigned graduated decimal values (5 to 0) to conditions A (best) through E (worst) and determined averages. A-, B-, and C-rated hamlets were considered "relatively secure." D and E hamlets were considered "contested." Approximately 3,000 acknowledged Viêt Công hamlets were not evaluated. Beginning in October 1967, results appeared in a Monthly Pacification Status Report.

Critics noted that high development scores often offset low security scores, and that increases in the "secure" population often were the result of refugees moving to cities rather than an extension of government control into the hamlets. A frequent charge was that favorable HES data was used as propaganda to support the U.S. position in Vietnam. Robert Komer, who became director of Civilian Operations and Revolutionary Development Support (CORDS) in May 1967, insisted that HES was designed as a tool for pacification management and analysis, not progress reporting. But he conceded that Washington officials relied on HES output as an indicator of overall pacification progress, thereby contributing to the "credibility gap."

When William Colby replaced Komer as head of CORDS in late 1968, he initiated an accelerated pacification program to upgrade all hamlets. By late 1971 HES rated 97 percent of hamlets C ratings or above, with most gains in rural areas.

Much of this progress was due to a drop in the intensity of the war, increases in Regional and Popular Forces, and the success of the Phoenix program.

Retrospective studies show that HES figures suffered from inflation caused principally by command pressure and undervaluing security. Surveys of former district advisors revealed more realistic and pessimistic "'gut' HES" parallel reports, but these never got into the computer.

—John D. Root

References: Bole, Albert G., Jr., and K. Kobata. *An Examination of the Measurements of the Hamlet Evaluation System* (1975); Brigham, Col. Erwin R. "Pacification Measurement" (1970); Komer, Robert W. "Impact of Pacification on Insurgency in South Vietnam" (1971).

See also: Civilian Irregular Defense Group (CIDG); Civilian Operations and Revolutionary Development Support (CORDS); Colby, William Egan; Komer, Robert W.; Pacification; Phoenix Program; Strategic Hamlet Program; Territorial Forces.

Hanoi Hannah (Ngô Thi Trinh) (ca. 1929–)

Broadcaster on "Voice of Vietnam," a propaganda vehicle on Democratic Republic of Vietnam radio. Of several broadcasters known as "Hanoi Hannah," Trinh was the most important. She hosted an English-language program as part of the psychological war waged to discourage U.S. troops. She reported names of American casualties, praised the antiwar movement, appealed to class and racial differences, played tapes of Americans whose comments she thought helpful, and aired half-hour music segments. The broadcasts reportedly amused or angered their audience, although American prisoners of war at times found her broadcasts helpful as a connection to the outside world. Made less meaningful by the 1973 Paris peace accords, the show was canceled. Ngô Thi Trinh now works for Vietnamese television.

—Paul S. Daum, with B. J. Rogers

References: Doyle, Edward, Samuel Lipsman, Terrence Maitland, and the editors of Boston Publishing Company. *The North* (1986); Shenon, Philip. "Air Warfare: The Broadcaster Once Known to GIs as Hanoi Hannah Has No Regrets" (1994).

See also: Prisoners of War, Allied; Psychological Warfare Operations (PSYOP).

Hanoi Hilton. *See* Hà Nôi Hilton (Hoa Lò Prison).

Harassment and Interdiction (H&I) Fires

Harassment fire is defined in the U.S. Army Field Manual as "fire delivered for the purpose of disturbing rest, curtailing the movement and lowering the morale of enemy troops by the threat of casualties or losses in material." The same publication defines interdiction fire as "fire delivered for the purpose of denying the enemy the unrestricted use of an area or point. Interdiction fire is usually of less intensity than neutralization fire." Usually tactically combined, they are termed harassment and interdiction (H&I) fires. H&I fires are usually unobserved, of short duration, and delivered against likely enemy troop concentrations or routes of supply.

In 1965 U.S. field artillery doctrine in Vietnam changed to maximize the role of fire support. By 1967 firebases—semipermanent fortified locations containing one or two batteries of artillery and supporting infantry—dotted the landscape. Massive employment of field artillery in conjunction with air power was an essential American strategy for keeping casualties to a minimum while inflicting maximum losses on the Peoples Army of Vietnam (PAVN) or Viêt Công (VC). Despite the tremendous amounts of ammunition expended by artillery units during H&I missions, there was little confirmation of success when target areas were swept by infantry. In most cases, H&I missions were planned and executed without efforts to confirm targets.

In 1969 U.S. Army Vietnam (USARV) Deputy Commander Gen. Frank T. Mildren stated that "pure H&I fires in Vietnam environment have little, if any, value while doing practically no damage to the enemy." Mildren recommended that all USARV units drastically reduce H&I missions. U.S. 4th Infantry Division Commander Gen. Arthur "Ace" Collins, concerned that his division was substituting massive artillery fire for infantry closing with and destroying Communist units, instituted an intelligence and interdiction (I&I) program whereby those missions were permitted only if targets were confirmed by intelligence sources. In 1970, Commander of II Field Force Artillery Gen. H. Kalergis directed that artillery batteries relocate to areas of known contact rather than fire high numbers of H&I missions. However, most field commanders disagreed with Mildren, Collins, and Kalergis, and enthusiastically supported active H&I programs.

H&I did prove effective when enhanced by technology. AN/TPQ-4 countermortar radar could locate mortar fire by tracking projectiles back to their points of origin, and AN/TPS-25 ground surveillance radar could detect movement of vehicles and troops at a six-mile range within its sectors of search. If firing elements could respond to radar sightings within approximately five minutes, the effectiveness of H&I fires was greatly enhanced. In 1968 remote sensors, introduced into Southeast Asia as part of the Igloo White program, also increased the effect of H&I missions. Sensors, fired by artillery or dropped by aircraft, were radio-linked with fire direction centers at numerous firebases, allowing almost immediate response to confirmed targets. However, there were insufficient radar and other target acquisition assets to increase the overall effect of daily H&I missions.

H&I could be an effective tool when certain conditions were met (confirmed or fixed target locations and observed and adjusted artillery fires), but most U.S. use of H&I met neither parameter. Additionally, H&I accounted for almost 70 percent of all ammunition expenditures. In Vietnam, H&I did not achieve the kill ratios it might have, but it produced a morale-building factor for American and Allied forces engaged in ground operations.

Ironically, the PAVN began its 1972 offensive with H&I missions against the Army of the Republic of Vietnam from positions across the Demilitarized Zone.

—J. A. Menzoff

References: Dastrup, Boyd. *King of Battle: A Branch History of the U.S. Army's Field Artillery* (1982); Ott, David E. *Vietnam Studies: Field Artillery, 1954–1973* (1975); Scales, Robert H., Jr. *Firepower in Limited War* (1990).

See also: Artillery Fire Doctrine.

Hardhats

Construction workers organized to support President Nixon's Vietnam policies. The National Hard Hats of America mounted several, often brutal counterdemonstrations against antiwar protests. In New York City on 8 May 1970, 200 Hardhats attacked a group of students protesting the deaths at Kent State University and the Cambodian incursion. Using fists, crowbars, and metal wrenches, the construction workers forced the students to disperse, injuring 70. Nixon told New York union leaders that he found their expressions of the support for the war "very meaningful," which fueled speculation that the White House had helped to engineer Hardhat activities.

—J. Nathan Campbell

References: Dougan, Clark, Samuel Lipsman, and the editors of Boston Publishing Company. *A Nation Divided* (1984); Wells, Tom. *The War Within: America's Battle over Vietnam* (1994); Zaroulis, Nancy, and Gerald Sullivan. *Who Spoke Up? American Protest against the War in Vietnam, 1963–1975* (1984).

See also: Agnew, Spiro T.; Antiwar Movement, United States; Cambodian Incursion; Kent State University; Nixon, Richard Milhous.

Harkins, Paul D. (1904–1984)

U.S. Army general; commander, Military Assistance Command, Vietnam (MACV), 1962–1964. Harkins arrived in Sài Gòn on 13 February 1962. As part of "Project Beefup" in 1962, the Kennedy administration replaced the Military Assistance and Advisory Group with an expanded and remodeled MACV commanded by Harkins. Harkins expressed confidence about the war's course, stood firmly behind President Ngô Đình Diêm, and favored postponing political and social improvements until the military subdued the Viêt Công (VC) and secured the countryside. He endorsed the use of napalm against villages housing the VC, regardless of political effects, and believed that the Strategic Hamlet program was conceptually valid and impressive in implementation.

Harkins's tenacious support for Diêm nearly caused South Vietnamese generals to back off from their November 1963 coup. His insistence on retaining Diêm while eliminating the Nhus brought him into disagreement with Ambassador Henry Cabot Lodge, who urged Diêm's removal. From the beginning, Harkins and his aides were on bad terms with the successor junta headed by Duong Van Minh. MACV became uneasy with the new administration's endeavors to assert its independence and to restrict the U.S. advisory function. When the junta's leadership demonstrated little initiative against the Communists, Harkins, who admired Gen. Nguyên Khánh and was aware of his plot against Minh, promoted the former's coup, a move labeled "Harkins' Revenge" by some in the South Vietnamese military. In March 1964, President Johnson replaced Harkins with Gen. William Westmoreland.

—Rodney J. Ross

References: Hammer, Ellen J. *A Death in November: America in Vietnam, 1963* (1987); Kahin, George McT. *Intervention: How America Became Involved in Vietnam* (1986); Sheehan, Neil. *A Bright Shining Lie: John Paul Vann and America in Vietnam* (1989).
See also: Duong Van Minh; Lodge, Henry Cabot, Jr.; Military Assistance Command, Vietnam (MACV); Ngô Đình Diêm; Ngô Đình Diêm, Overthrow of; Ngô Đình Nhu; Nguyên Khánh; Sheehan, Cornelius Mahoney (Neil); Strategic Hamlet Program; Taylor-McNamara Report; Westmoreland, William Childs.

Harriman, W. Averell (1891–1986)

U.S. ambassador-at-large, 1960–1961; assistant secretary of state for Far Eastern affairs, 1962–1963; undersecretary of state for political affairs, 1963–1964; ambassador-at-large, 1965–1969. Harriman was among the most senior Democratic Party figures within the foreign policy establishment and was widely regarded as a leading architect of Cold War policy.

Harriman's involvement with Indo-China initially centered upon his 1961 and 1962 attempts to broker a settlement between warring factions in Laos that effectively would have neutralized that country and prevented Viêt Công (VC) passage through it to South Vietnam. Hawks in the Kennedy administration criticized Harriman's efforts as unrealistic, but after protracted negotiations at Geneva involving the Soviet Union, the United States, and the three warring Laotian factions, an agreement was reached in 1962. This understanding was rarely honored by the Communist Pathet Lao and their VC allies.

Harriman later claimed that he had always opposed U.S. intervention in Vietnam, an exaggeration. However, he was to become the most senior leader of the Vietnam doves, favoring reforms in Vietnam and a negotiated settlement. In the early 1960s Harriman visited Vietnam and warned that Diêm's government was corrupt and unstable. In summer 1963 he urged that Diêm be pressured to accept the demands of Buddhist monks to punish soldiers who had fired on Buddhist demonstrators in Huê that spring, or lose U.S. support. In late August 1963 Harriman, working with Roger Hilsman and National Security Council staffer Michael V. Forrestal, dispatched a cable to U.S. Ambassador Henry Cabot Lodge that implicitly authorized U.S. support for a coup against Diêm. Although this cable provoked bitter recriminations within the State and Defense Departments and the Central Intelligence Agency, whose secretaries and director had not seen it before its dispatch, it was never revoked.

Harriman never developed the close relationship with President Johnson that he had enjoyed with President Kennedy and his brother Robert. In February 1965 he was once more named ambassador-at-large, and in this capacity he vigorously defended administration Vietnam policy publicly; privately, he urged a bombing halt and the opening of negotiations with the Democratic Republic of Vietnam (DRV). Harriman was excluded from operational meetings on Vietnam and the Tuesday White House discussion luncheons of top policymakers and was generally restrained in expressing his criticism directly to Johnson. Many close to him ascribed his reticence to his fear of losing office. Even so, at a November 1967 meeting of the president's most senior advisors, Harriman dissented from the consensus that favored Johnson's bombing policy and called for the opening of negotiations.

After the Têt Offensive and consequent reassessment of U.S. policy goals in Vietnam, Johnson named Harriman his representative in peace negotiations at Paris. Several months of discussions finally succeeded in establishing procedural guidelines for the talks, at which the Soviet Union, United States, DRV, VC, and the Republic of Vietnam were to be represented. At this stage, Richard Nixon took office, and Harriman returned to Washington, completing his last formal government assignment.

—Priscilla Roberts

References: Abramson, Rudy. *Spanning the Century: The Life of W. Averell Harriman 1891–1986* (1992); Halberstam, David. *The Best and the Brightest* (1973); Isaacson, Walter, and Evan Thomas. *The Wise Men: Six Friends and the World They Made* (1986).
See also: Acheson, Dean G.; Forrestal, Michael V.; Hilsman, Roger; Johnson, Lyndon Baines; Kennedy, John Fitzgerald; Kennan, George Frost; Lodge, Henry Cabot, Jr.; Ngô Đình Diêm; Ngô Đình Diêm, Overthrow of; Paris Negotiations; Truman, Harry S; "Wise Men."

Harris, David (1946–)

With Dennis Sweeney, Lennie Heller, and Steve Hamilton, David Harris founded The Resistance in March 1967 to encourage opposition to the Selective Service System. On 16 October 1967, more than 2,000 men returned their draft cards, and The Resistance conducted three more national draft card returns by the end of 1968. Harris delivered hundreds of speeches promoting draft resistance, sometimes appearing with singer Joan Baez, whom he married on 26 March 1968. Two months later, a jury convicted Harris for refusing draft induction, a verdict upheld on appeal. He spent nearly two years in federal prison before being paroled in 1971.

—Mitchell K. Hall

References: Ferber, Michael, and Staughton Lynd. *The Resistance* (1971); Harris, David. *Dreams Die Hard* (1982); —. *I Shoulda Been Home Yesterday* (1976).
See also: Antiwar Movement, United States; Baez, Joan Chandos; Conscientious Objectors (COs); Draft.

Hartke, Vance Rupert (1919–)

U.S. Senator, 1958–1976. President Johnson counted Hartke as one of his most loyal supporters in Congress until January 1966, when Hartke drafted a letter sent by 15 other senators urging Johnson not to resume the bombing of North Vietnam. In February he delivered his first major speech opposing escalation of the war. He did, however, vote for a $13 billion arms appropriations bill that included funding for the war. In 1967 Hartke wrote *The American Crisis in Vietnam* but withheld publication for a year to prevent its damaging the Democratic Party in Indiana during a presidential election year.

—Charlotte A. Power

Reference: Lichtenstein, Nelson, ed. *Political Profiles: The Johnson Years* (1976).

See also: Case, Clifford P.; Church, Frank Forrester; Cooper, John Sherman; Fulbright, J. William; Great Society Program; Hatfield, Mark Odum; Johnson, Lyndon Baines; Kennedy, Edward Moore; McGee, Gale William; McGovern, George S.; Proxmire, William.

HARVEST MOON, Operation (8–20 December 1965)

Largest U.S. Marine combat effort in the Vietnam War to that point. Operation HARVEST MOON resulted from President Johnson's March 1965 decision to send U.S. ground troops to Vietnam. It was an early test of Gen. William Westmoreland's strategy of attrition through search-and-destroy missions and a violent and frustrating test of Marine tactics and equipment. It was carried out during the monsoon season, adding significantly to the operation's problems and to the misery of individual Marines.

HARVEST MOON was intended to find and attack Viêt Công (VC) units in the Phuoc Ha Valley, a Communist base area southwest of Đà Nang. It was a combined Marine and Army of the Republic of Vietnam (ARVN) expedition; however, the ARVN units involved were attacked en route on 8 December and sustained heavy casualties. On 9 December, the Marines moved into the area under a temporary command structure known as Task Force DELTA. Originally the plan called for the Marines to trap the VC from the flank and rear; now they also had to come to the aid of ARVN forces. On 10 December, the Marines counterattacked overland in the face of stiff VC resistance.

The Special Landing Force (SLF), a newly created unit stationed in reserve aboard an aircraft carrier off the coast, was brought in by helicopter. It came under heavy fire and had a difficult time securing its landing zones before the VC withdrew into the Phuoc Ha Valley. During 12–24 December, B-52 bombers attacked VC positions in the valley, but the VC had already pulled out. On 18 December, one last battle took place in the southern margin of the HARVEST MOON operating area.

The Marines learned a number of lessons, including the necessity for better air-to-ground coordination and the need for more advanced planning. Search-and-destroy had brought only mixed results, as had the use of B-52 bombers, the SLF, and the UH-1E (Huey) helicopters. Marine casualties numbered 51 dead and 256 wounded. VC dead were estimated at 407.

Following the operation, the Marines returned to their enclave base area, meaning that the Phuoc Ha Valley would be the scene of future battles.

—Eric Jarvis

References: Shulimson, Jack, with Maj. Charles M. Johnson. *U.S. Marines in Vietnam: The Landing and the Buildup, 1965* (1978); Stanton, Shelby L. *The Rise and Fall of an American Army: U.S. Ground Forces in Vietnam, 1965–1973* (1985); Walt, Lewis W. *Strange War, Strange Strategy* (1970).

See also: Ia Drang Valley, Battle of; Johnson, Lyndon Baines; Search and Destroy; United States: Marines; Westmoreland, William Childs.

HASTINGS, Operation (July 1966)

U.S. Marine reconnaissance operation in Quang Tri Province. U.S. Marines in Vietnam were deployed in I Corps, the northernmost of South Vietnam's four military regions. Its five provinces contained 2.6 million people and the important cities of Đà Nang and Huê.

Gen. Westmoreland did not approve of the Marine emphasis on counterinsurgency. He wanted them to conduct large-unit operations against Communist main forces. He was convinced that the People's Army of Vietnam (PAVN) was building up its strength in northern South Vietnam for a major offensive, possibly including an attack on Huê. In spring 1966, at Westmoreland's insistence, the Marines began conducting reconnaissance operations in Quang Tri Province to determine the extent of the PAVN buildup. On 7 July 1966, these reconnaissance operations were code-named Operation HASTINGS.

Fighting during HASTINGS took place across a broad front between Route 9 and the Demilitarized Zone (DMZ). The Marines' adversaries were well-armed, well-trained members of the PAVN 324B Division, who frequently ambushed Marine patrols from strongly fortified positions and were equipped with Chinese assault rifles, automatic weapons, and mortars. The heaviest fighting took place during 12–25 July, and the operation officially ended on 3 August. HASTINGS was the largest and most violent operation of the war to that point.

B-52 bombers from Guam carried out strikes to support the Marines, bombing the DMZ for the first time. Marine casualties were 126 killed in action and 498 wounded in action; more than 800 PAVN were killed. Fighting in the area continued after HASTINGS as the Marines continued their reconnaissance of the area and established permanent bases.

The Marine command was uncertain of the PAVN 324B Division's tactical goals. Perhaps it sought to shorten the long march down the Hô Chí Minh Trail through Laos, but it might also have been an attempt to disrupt successful Marine pacification programs in southern I Corps by drawing U.S. forces farther north, away from the more heavily populated areas.

HASTINGS did bring a realignment of Marine forces in I Corps. No longer would primary emphasis be on pacification. The North Vietnamese had expanded the war, and the U.S. military felt that it had little choice but to respond.

—Peter W. Brush

References: Pearson, Willard. *The War in the Northern Provinces, 1966–1968* (1975); Shulimson, Jack. *U.S. Marines in Vietnam, 1966. An Expanding War* (1982).

See also: Clear and Hold; Pacification; PRAIRIE, Operation; United States: Marines; Vietnam, Democratic Republic of: Army (People's Army of Vietnam [PAVN]); Westmoreland, William Childs.

Hatfield, Mark Odum (1922–)

U.S. senator and critic of American involvement in Vietnam. In June 1970, Hatfield proposed replacing the Nixon administration, since it had failed to deliver the 1968 campaign promise to end the war. Following the Cambodian incursion in May 1970, Hatfield and Senator George McGovern cosponsored an amendment to the arms appropriations bill calling for a cutoff of funds for the war after 31 December. Although defeated twice by the Senate, the Hatfield-McGovern Amendment became a rallying point for antiwar activists. Hatfield also proposed an end to the draft by substituting an all-volunteer force. Although this bill never passed, Nixon ended the draft in 1973.

—Robert G. Mangrum

References: Karnow, Stanley. *Vietnam: A History* (1984); Olson, James S., ed. *Dictionary of the Vietnam War* (1988); Summers, Harry G. *Vietnam War Almanac* (1985).

See also: Case, Clifford P.; Case-Church Amendment; Church, Frank Forrester; Cooper, John Sherman; Cooper-Church Amendment; Hatfield-McGovern Amendment; McGovern, George S.

Hatfield-McGovern Amendment

(August–September 1970)

Most significant U.S. Senate defiance of executive power between 1965 and 1970. Before ordering the Cambodian incursion in April 1970, President Nixon conferred with only a few supportive lawmakers. Senators, upset with his secrecy and enraged at his expansion of the conflict, discontinued the 1964 Tonkin Gulf Resolution and ratified a proposal of John Sherman Cooper and Frank Church calling for severing all financing for U.S. military activity in Cambodia beyond 30 June 1970. More restrictive was an amendment affixed to military procurement legislation sponsored by Senators George S. McGovern and Mark O. Hatfield, known as the "amendment to end the war," that required termination of U.S. military operations in the Republic of Vietnam by 31 December 1970 and withdrawal of American forces halfway through 1971. Rewritten to garner more favor, the revised version maximized troop levels at 280,000 men beyond 30 April and changed the removal deadline to the end of 1971. It also urged the Nixon administration to tender information concerning the difficulties of implementing disengagement.

The White House, joined by congressional allies, pounced upon the Hatfield-McGovern Amendment. Senators John C. Stennis and Cooper backed the administration, arguing that the amendment would impede the president's role as chief diplomat and the U.S. position at the Paris peace talks. The Hatfield-McGovern Amendment suffered defeat on 1 September 1970 by a vote of 55–39.

—Rodney J. Ross

References: Ambrose, Stephen E. *Nixon: The Triumph of a Politician 1962–1972* (1989); Herring, George C. *America's Longest War: The United States and Vietnam, 1950–1975* (1996); Sobel, Lester A., ed. *South Vietnam: U.S.-Communist Confrontation in Southeast Asia, Vol. 5, 1970* (1973).

See also: Agnew, Spiro T.; Church, Frank Forrester; Cooper, John Sherman; Cooper-Church Amendment; Hatfield, Mark Odum; McGovern, George S.; Nixon, Richard Milhous; Stennis, John Cornelius.

HAWTHORNE, Operation (2–20 June 1966)

The first battle for Đak Tô, an outpost in northern Kontum Province. HAWTHORNE began with the mission to rescue Vietnamese irregulars at the Tou Morong Special Forces camp, near Đak Tô, which was surrounded by units of the 24th People's Army of Vietnam (PAVN) Regiment. The 101st Airborne Division's 1/327th Infantry, commanded by Lt. Col. David H. Hackworth, and the Army of the Republic of Vietnam (ARVN) 1st Battalion of the 42d Regiment fought through moderate resistance to reach the hilltop garrison and evacuate its 150 inhabitants. The 1/327th then pursued the PAVN forces into the surrounding valleys.

On the night of 6 June, a large PAVN force attacked and partially overran an artillery position. The next day a company of the 1/327th was mauled as it wandered into the middle of a PAVN base camp and was saved only by artillery barrages and the insertion of additional infantry. It was apparent that a major PAVN force was present, and the 101st's 2/502d joined the fray. In a tragic episode, waves of PAVN attackers surrounded and nearly overran the night position of one of the companies. Headlines were generated at home when it was learned that the company commander, Capt. William S. Carpenter, an all-American football player at West Point, bravely called in napalm strikes on his own position to repel the attack.

Soon afterward, the remaining company of the 1/327th moved out of Tou Morong and encountered well-entrenched PAVN positions. Companies of the 2/502d immediately air-assaulted from Đak Tô as a blocking force. Hoping to entrap the entire 24th PAVN Regiment, II Corps command flew in the 1st Cavalry Division's 1/5th Infantry from An Khê and a company of the 101st's 2/327th Infantry from Tuy Hòa. U.S. forces were supported by air strikes and B-52 sorties that sometimes cut safety margins to a minimum, but accounted for more than 200 PAVN casualties. HAWTHORNE was nearing termination when, on 17 June, a company of the 1/327th engaged a small PAVN force in dense terrain. Responding to a call for support, 1st Cavalry gunships hit the company position itself.

On 20 June, the remaining PAVN forces withdrew, having suffered more than 500 dead. U.S. casualties were more than 50 dead and 200 wounded.

—John D. Root

References: Hackworth, Col. David H. *About Face: The Odyssey of an American Warrior* (1989); Marshall, S. L. A. *Battles in the Monsoon: Campaigning in the Central Highlands, South Vietnam, Summer, 1966* (1967); Stanton, Shelby L. *The Rise and Fall of an American Army: U.S. Ground Forces in Vietnam, 1965–1973* (1985).

See also: Airmobility; Đak Tô, Battle of; Friendly Fire; Hackworth, David H.

Hayden, Thomas E. (1939–)

Influential early leader of Students for a Democratic Society and antiwar activist associated with the demonstrations during the 1968 Democratic National Convention in Chicago. Hayden was among the founders of Students for a Democratic Society and was the primary author of the Port

Huron Statement. This extensive critique of U.S. society called for individuals to share in making the decisions that affected their lives and proved to be one of the defining documents of the New Left.

Hayden's opposition to the Vietnam War twice took him to Indo-China. In December 1965, he visited the Democratic Republic of Vietnam (DRV) with Herbert Aptheker and Staughton Lynd, and in 1967 he accompanied three released U.S. prisoners of war from Cambodia. As a leader of the National Mobilization Committee to End the War in Vietnam, Hayden acted as a key planner of demonstrations during the 1968 Democratic National Convention. These often violent confrontations between police and protesters led the government to charge Hayden and others with conspiracy to riot. As a defendant in the highly publicized trial of the Chicago Eight (later known as the Chicago Seven after defendant Bobby Seale's trial was separated), Hayden and six others initially were convicted in February 1970, but an appeals court overturned the verdict in November 1972 because of Judge Julius Hoffman's improper and antagonistic conduct.

—Mitchell K. Hall

References: Gitlin, Todd. *The Sixties: Years of Hope, Days of Rage* (1987); Hayden, Tom. *Reunion: A Memoir* (1988); Miller, James. *"Democracy Is in the Streets": From Port Huron to the Siege of Chicago* (1987); Sale, Kirkpatrick. *SDS* (1973).

See also: Antiwar Movement, United States; Chicago Eight; Fonda, Jane Seymour; Students for a Democratic Society (SDS).

Healy, Michael J. (1926–)

U.S. Army officer and last commander of the 5th Special Forces Group in Vietnam. In July 1963 Healy was reassigned to Headquarters, U.S. Army Special Forces, Vietnam, with duty initially as the operations officer and then as senior advisor to the Republic of Vietnam (RVN) Special Forces.

In August 1964, Healy returned to the United States and assumed command of the 1st Battalion (Airborne), 501st Infantry, 101st Infantry Division. After almost two years in command, he elected to deploy to Vietnam with his battalion, which was redesignated as the 4th Battalion (Airborne), 503d Infantry, 173d Airborne Brigade (Separate). After 30 consecutive months in command, he returned to the United States, then in March 1969 returned for his third tour of duty in Vietnam. In August 1969, Healy assumed command of the 1st Brigade, 9th Infantry Division, and redeployed the Brigade to Hawaii. After only three weeks in Hawaii, he was recalled to Vietnam to take over the 5th Special Forces Group, which he commanded for 20 months.

Healy supervised the conversion of the RVN Civilian Irregular Defense Group (CIDG) to Army of the Republic of Vietnam (ARVN) Rangers and the subsequent phasedown of the 5th Special Forces Group. This involved the conversion of the 38 remaining A-detachment camps to ARVN ranger battalions by the end of 1970. Special Forces strength in support of the CIDG program was reduced to zero by 31 March 1971. Col. Healy presided over the last 5th Special Forces Group formation on 28 February 1971. The Department of the Army officially closed 5th Special Forces Group out of the RVN effective 3 March 1971, and Healy returned to the United States.

In May 1972 Healy was again recalled to Vietnam, where he initially served as the deputy commanding general, 3d Regional Assistance Command, Military Region Three and III Corps. In June 1972 he replaced John Paul Vann, who had been killed in a helicopter crash, as commanding general, 2d Regional Assistance Command, Military Region Two, and II Corps. He remained in command until all U.S. forces were withdrawn in 1973.

—James H. Willbanks

Reference: Stanton, Shelby L. *Green Berets at War* (1985).

See also: Civilian Irregular Defense Group (CIDG); United States: Special Forces; Vann, John Paul; Vietnam, Republic of: Special Forces (Luc Luong Đac Biêt, LLĐB).

Heath, Donald R. (1894–1981)

U.S. minister to the Associated States of Indo-China (Cambodia, Laos, and Vietnam) from 1950 to 1952; ambassador to Vietnam and Cambodia from 1952 to 1955. In 1952 Heath became the first U.S. ambassador to Vietnam and Cambodia. Although devoted to the French cause in Southeast Asia, Heath met stern resistance from French officials who resented U.S. interference. When Ngô Đình Diêm emerged as the de facto leader of South Vietnam in 1954, Heath argued in favor of prompt U.S. support for the Diêm regime. Heath was sustained in his opinion by Secretary of State John Foster Dulles, and soon massive amounts of U.S. aid poured into Sài Gòn.

—David Coffey

References: Findling, John E. *Dictionary of American Diplomatic History* (1980); Karnow, Stanley. *Vietnam: A History* (1983); *Who Was Who in America with World Notables* (1989).

See also: Dulles, John Foster; Ngô Đình Diêm.

Helicopters, Allied and Democratic Republic of Vietnam

More helicopters were used for more purposes in the Vietnam War than in any previous war. Hardly an operation was executed without the use of helicopters. Poor roads and dense jungles made Vietnam ideal for guerrilla ambush. Troop-carrying helicopters avoided ambushes by avoiding roads, one factor that led the United States to send helicopters to South Vietnam in 1961. As the French discovered by 1950, helicopters could also evacuate the wounded quickly. They were also ideal for reconnaissance because of their good crew visibility and maneuverability.

Still in their infancy in the 1950s, helicopters improved greatly in the 1960s. Most important was the change from piston to turboshaft engines and from wooden to composition rotor blades. Improved parts allowed longer runs between overhauls, less downtime, and higher availability rates. Better helicopters led the U.S. Army in the 1960s to experiment with the concept of airmobility—flying troops into battle and supporting them with an air line of fire support and supply—and Vietnam provided the laboratory. U.S. forces used airmobility repeatedly.

Airmobility was not possible unless helicopters were able to survive in combat. From the first, they could survive against small arms fire. A dominant Democratic Republic of Vietnam (DRV) air force could have swept them from the skies, but Allied air arms enjoyed full air superiority in the South, and Allied helicopters flew under a friendly air umbrella. Initially Viêt Công (VC) and People's Army of Vietnam (PAVN) units lacked antiaircraft weapons. Later in the war, when the VC and PAVN did have these weapons, as in Operations DELAWARE and LAM SON 719, they shot down many helicopters. Defensive techniques such as treetop flying and suppressive fire at the landing zone (LZ) also helped helicopters survive.

The following are the various types of helicopters used in the Vietnam War.

Westland Sikorsky S-51 (R-6) Manufactured in Great Britain under license from Sikorsky, an improved version of the R-4. The French used it for medical evacuation and supply before 1954.

Hiller H-23 Raven Used by the French for medical evacuation, observation, and supply before 1954. The U.S. also used the H-23 for observation before it was replaced by the Hughes OH-6A Cayuse about 1968.

Bell H-13 Sioux First used by the French before 1954, the H-13 was the main U.S. light observation helicopter in Vietnam until it was replaced by the Hughes OH-6A Cayuse about 1968.

Sikorsky H-19 Chickasaw Used by the French for troop movement and supply before 1954, the H-19 found use as a utility helicopter in the early days of U.S. involvement.

Piasecki CH-21C Shawnee Used by the first U.S. Army units in Vietnam in 1961 as a troop carrier and for search-and-rescue operations. Its laminated wooden rotor blades came apart in the humid heat, and small exits made troop debarkation difficult. To afford better protection at LZs, some Shawnees were armed with machine guns and rockets. By 1964 the Shawnee was replaced as a troop carrier by the UH-1 Iroquois.

Sikorsky H-34 Choctaw The United States sent H-34s to Vietnam in 1961 for use in an ARVN strike force, but President Ngô Đình Diêm used them for administrative purposes. The U.S. Marines sent an aviation unit of H-34s to Vietnam in 1962. It was moved to the mountains below the DMZ because the H-34 had more lifting power at high altitude than the CH-21C. The H-34 was used for troop movement, supply, and artillery emplacement. In 1966 the Boeing-Vertol CH-46A Sea Knight replaced the H-34.

Sikorsky CH-37 Mojave The U.S. Army used the Mojave in Vietnam from 1962 until the late 1960s largely for recovering downed aircraft and for heavy lift. It was replaced by the Boeing-Vertol CH-47 Chinook.

Bell UH-1H Iroquois Known as the Huey, the UH-1 went through several design changes from 1962 until the end of the war. Especially notable were the A, B, and D models. The UH-1 was the main helicopter used by all Allied forces in Vietnam for many missions: troop carrying, gunship escort, supply, command and control, medical evacuation, rocket artillery, radio relay, reconnaissance, rescue, base security, and psychological warfare.

Boeing-Vertol CH-47 Chinook Referred to as the "Shithook" by troops, the Chinook was the U.S. Army's primary medium-lift helicopter in Vietnam, starting in 1965. ARVN forces also used it. Its major missions included troop transport, medical evacuation, artillery emplacement, aircraft retrieval, and supply. An external sling allowed transport of heavy objects.

Sikorsky CH-54 Tarhe The CH-54 provided heavy lift capability for the U.S. Army in Vietnam beginning in 1965. Known as the "Flying Crane" or "Skycrane," the CH-54 could lift externally slung objects weighing up to 12.5 tons, including vehicles, 155-mm artillery, disabled aircraft, and special command and troop transport modules. Downdraft from its blades could easily blow away tents and similar objects.

Bell AH-1 Huey Cobra Designed and developed by Bell Helicopter around UH-1 Iroquois components. Its two crew members had tandem seats in the sleek fuselage, and they controlled mixes of armaments: 7.62-mm miniguns, 40-mm grenade launcher, 20-mm cannon, antitank missiles, and various rockets. The AH-1 was designed to replace the slower armed UH-1B, called a "Hog," for suppressive fire at the LZ. Coming into service in 1967, the Cobra proved versatile in fire support for the Army and Marines.

Hughes OH-6A Cayuse Also called a "Loach" because it won the 1962 U.S. Army Light Observation Helicopter (LOH) competition. Coming into service in 1967, it replaced the Bell H-13 and Hiller H-23 observation helicopters. The Marines also used it beginning in 1969. A major tactic was to fly low to draw and then pinpoint enemy fire.

Bell OH-58 Kiowa The Kiowa won the 1968 U.S. Army Light Observation Helicopter competition. It replaced the OH-6A Cayuse.

Kaman H-43 Husky Introduced in 1958 and used by the U.S. Air Force mainly for air base crash-and-rescue functions in Vietnam. It had two counter-rotating rotors and tail fins on twin booms, but no tail rotor.

Kaman UH-2 Seasprite The U.S. Navy used the Seasprite mainly for rescue, firefighting, and antisubmarine warfare after its introduction in 1962.

Boeing-Vertol CH-46 Sea Knight The U.S. Navy and Marines used the Sea Knight for troop transport. During 1966, it replaced the H-34 Choctaw. Its design is similar to the CH-47 Chinook, having tandem rotors.

Sikorsky H-3 Sea King Used by the U.S. Air Force for search and rescue and by the U.S. Navy mainly for antisubmarine warfare. The Air Force HH-3E model was called the "Jolly Green Giant." By 1967 it had air refueling capability.

Sikorsky HH-53B Sea Stallion Known as the "Super Jolly Green Giant" or "Buff" for "Big Ugly Fat Fellow," the Sea Stallion replaced the Sea King in search and rescue. The U.S. Navy used one model for minesweeping, and the Marines used another for assault. Designers stretched the Sea King fuselage and used CH-54 Tarhe components.

Mil Mi-4 Hound The DRV used this Soviet helicopter, first produced in 1953, for transporting troops and cargo and carrying crews to repair roads and bridges.

Mil Mi-6 Hook Introduced by the Soviets in 1960, the Hook was used by the DRV as a heavy lift helicopter for emplacing heavy artillery and surface-to-air missiles (SAMs). It also transported insurgents into Thailand.

Sud-Est Alouette III Introduced by France in 1960, the Alouette III was a multipurpose helicopter used by the DRV to insert insurgents from Cambodia into Thailand.

—John L. Bell

References: *Aviation Week and Space Technology* (1961–1975); Bell, Dana. *Vietnam Warbirds in Action* (1986); Polmar, Norman, and Floyd D. Kennedy, Jr. *Military Helicopters of the World: Military Rotary-Wing Aircraft Since 1917* (1981).

See also: DELAWARE-LAM SON 216, Operation; Helicopters, Employment of, in Vietnam.

Helicopters, Employment of, in Vietnam

French forces introduced helicopters in Indo-China, using them in medical evacuation. Their small Hiller 360s were underpowered, and soon Sikorsky H-5s and H-19s bolstered French helicopter forces. By 1954, 42 U.S.-built helicopters served with French troops in Indo-China, compiling an impressive record in medical evacuation and in supplying isolated units.

On 11 December 1961, two companies of Piasecki CH-21 Shawnees arrived by carrier in the Republic of Vietnam (RVN). Twelve days later they lifted more than 1,000 Army of the Republic of Vietnam (ARVN) paratroopers in the first helicopter combat assault in Vietnam. From late 1961 to early 1965, U.S. helicopter crews, learning by trial and error, taught ARVN commanders tactical employment of helicopters.

U.S. Army CH-21 and Marine Sikorsky CH-34 Choctaws evacuated casualties, supplied outlying camps, and provided rapid disposition of units to meet Communist threats. By the end of 1964, the United States had more than 250 helicopters in Vietnam. The success of these units forced the Democratic Republic of Vietnam (DRV) to supply insurgent forces in the South with modern weapons and to escalate movement of regular People's Army of Vietnam (PAVN) troops and supplies south by the Hô Chí Minh Trail network.

Initially, tactical helicopter-borne transportation received little artillery or tactical air support, and U.S. advisors realized they needed additional firepower to conduct airmobile operations. In September 1962, 15 Bell UH-1 Iroquois (Hueys), modified to fire 2.75-inch folding-fin aerial rockets (FFAR) and 7.62-mm forward-firing machine guns, were deployed to Tân Son Nhut. By experimentation in combat, pilots developed tactical concepts governing gunship employment. Air assault operations included three phases: en route, approach, and landing.

Armed helicopters proved most effective during the landing phase. After a few missions, hits on transport helicopters dropped from 0.011 hits per flying hour to 0.0074 for escorted aircraft. Hits on unescorted helicopters doubled during

the same period. Suppressive fire delivered by armed helicopters proved effective in reducing the amount and effectiveness of fire on transport helicopters.

As a result of initial combat experience, a platoon of five to seven armed helicopters formed an escort for twenty to twenty-five troop-carrying helicopters. As transportation helicopters approached a landing zone (LZ), gunships began racetrack, or similar, patterns on each side of landing helicopters. Gunships directed rocket and machine-gun fire on hostile concentrations while their door gunners covered their breakaway from these positions.

U.S. forces also instituted Eagle Flights. These included an armed Huey, piloted by the U.S. aviation commander, carrying the ARVN troop commander. This command and control (C&C) aircraft flew at a safe altitude and directed seven to ten transport helicopters ("slicks") escorted by five gunships to provide fire support for the insertion. A medevac trailed the formation to extract any casualties. Eagle Flights provided immediate response to targets of opportunity and could easily be melded into one large airmobile operation. These became the bases for airmobile concepts employed by U.S. combat units arriving in Vietnam in 1965.

In August and September 1965, elements of the 1st Cavalry Division (Airmobile) (1st Cav), the first such division in the U.S. Army, began to arrive at An Khê. It departed radically from a standard infantry division, containing 434 helicopters divided into two battalions of assault helicopters, a battalion of attack helicopters, a battalion of assault support helicopters, an aerial rocket artillery (ARA) battalion (the first in the Army), and an air cavalry squadron. The division had the capability to move one-third of its combat power at one time into terrain inaccessible to normal infantry vehicles. To support the large number of aircraft in the division, an Aviation Maintenance Battalion augmented normal Division Support Command. In June 1968, the 101st Airborne Division, in Vietnam since 1965, received a change of organization and became the second airmobile division in the U.S. Army.

ARA units, in contrast to other gunships, operated under direction of artillery officers. Divisional or separate artillery commanders used these helicopters as an adjunct to tube (field) artillery. When called, ARA platoons communicated on fire direction frequencies, and their fires were adjusted much the same as with conventional artillery. ARA's great advantage lay in its long range and heavy firepower; it provided rocket support to units beyond the range of conventional artillery. The Bell AH-1G Cobra carried up to 76 rockets. With 17-pound warheads, these could deliver the same initial firepower as a battalion of 105-mm artillery.

Boeing CH-47 Chinooks and Sikorsky CH-54 Tarhees ("Skycranes") expanded the combat versatility of ground units in Vietnam. Chinooks lifted artillery pieces to forward positions to provide fire support for units moving into contact. Towed 155-mm and 8-inch artillery could be transported by the huge Skycrane. Chinooks unloaded large numbers of infantrymen on precarious mountaintop LZs and, employing a rope ladder that dangled through the trees, delivered infantrymen into triple-canopy jungle. Outlying firebases and Special Forces camps relied on frequent resupply from these workhorse helicopters. Airmobile units used the CH-47 to pre-position fuel and ammunition for future operations. Forward area refueling points (FARPs) cut down turnaround time for helicopters to return to their missions. The excellent lift capabilities of the CH-47 and CH-54 allowed U.S. forces to sling-load downed aircraft that would have been lost in other circumstances.

Marine helicopter operations followed much the same pattern, with a few exceptions. Beginning in March 1966, Boeing CH-46 Sea Knights and Sikorsky CH-53 "Super Jolly Green Giants" replaced older CH-34 and CH-37 Mojave helicopters. UH-1Es provided the Marines with gunships throughout their service in Vietnam. AH-1s began to augment the Hueys in April 1969.

In August 1965, Marine helicopter crewmen flew the first night assault in Vietnam, using CH-34s to insert infantry into the Elephant Valley northwest of Đà Nang. Marine medevacs extracted several severely wounded men. Radar operators guided the pilots to the wounded, while other aircraft dropped flares to illuminate LZs long enough for the medevac to evacuate casualties.

Radar guidance allowed the Marines to resupply units in inclement weather. During the siege of Khe Sanh and 1969 operations in the A Shau Valley, CH-46s and CH-53s made instrument climbs through the overcast at Quang Tri and Đà Nang and, with radar directions, flew to the beleaguered Marines. When an opening in the clouds appeared, they spiraled down to drop external loads of water, rations, ammunition, and medical supplies into small LZs hacked into the Central Highlands rainforests.

Triple-canopy jungle prevented conventional helicopter resupply or insertion of troops. Innovative commanders remedied this problem by training their men to rappel from ropes dangling from hovering Hueys. If time permitted, ground units used engineer demolitions to blast openings in the jungle, some so small that pilots could only hover over them and drop supplies to the waiting infantry. In some areas, the Air Force dropped a special 15,000-pound bomb ("daisy cutter") to blast clearings in the dense foliage large enough to accommodate several Hueys.

The Republic of Vietnam Air Force (RVNAF) controlled all RVN helicopters. In 1963 the United States began supplying the Vietnamese with H-34s and upgraded RVNAF utility and transport helicopters as newer types became available. RVNAF pilots received training by U.S. advisors on the same tactics and procedures implemented by U.S. forces. Because of U.S. need for helicopters, RVNAF units did not acquire enough aircraft to institute large airmobile operations.

Despite U.S. equipment and training, Vietnamese units on the whole did not deliver the same results as U.S. units. Interservice rivalry between Air Force and Army commands hampered cooperation with and support to ARVN units. Many RVNAF pilots seemed reluctant to press combat operations in support of their own ground troops in the face of heavy ground fire and often refused to reinforce or resupply government troops caught in ambushes or hot LZs. In most cases, ARVN troops received much better support from U.S. aviators.

Initially, transportation helicopter companies doubled as medical evacuation aircraft. In April 1962, the first five UH-1s arrived in South Vietnam, expressly modified for medical evacuation. The ARVN never established its own medevac organization.

Each medevac helicopter ("dustoff") carried trained medics, up to nine litters, and medical supplies to care for critically wounded soldiers. Crews waited on alert for a mission and could be airborne in less than three minutes. Because Việt Công (VC) and PAVN troops ignored the large red crosses painted on medevac helicopters (the U.S. Army even tried all-white helicopters in late 1972) and fired on medevac helicopters, armed helicopters were requested to provide suppressive fire for medevacs going into hot LZs. In many instances, medevac pilots violated standard operating procedure (SOP) by going into hot LZs without gunship cover. They flew day, night, and in inclement weather, sometimes hovering just over the trees to locate casualties.

Extracting wounded from the jungle proved almost impossible until the 1966 introduction of a rescue hoist and "jungle penetrator." The penetrator could be lowered to the jungle floor, where casualties were strapped to the device and hoisted to the hovering medevac. Daring crews endured heavy enemy fire while executing rescue hoist operations. Dedicated medevac crewmen accomplished hundreds of nearly impossible rescues during the Vietnam War. Wounded could expect to arrive at a hospital within 15 minutes of being lifted out of a pick-up zone (PZ). Only 1 percent of the wounded died if they survived the first 24 hours after their injury.

Some Hueys carried specialized equipment, including radio consoles to intercept communications and locate PAVN or VC headquarters. Others, known as "people sniffers," flew low over the jungle with chemical equipment that collected air samples and measured uric acid concentrations, high concentrations of which supposedly indicated latrines, but rumors abounded about water buffalo bombed because of "sniffer" reports. Psychological warfare units used Hueys to drop leaflets and broadcast Chiêu Hồi (open arms, amnesty program) messages to VC and PAVN troops.

Search-and-rescue tactics evolved from an operation developed by the German Luftwaffe during the Battle of Britain. Four A-1E or A-7 fixed-wing fighters, broken into a high and low section of two aircraft each, escorted two HH-3 or (after 1967) HH-53 rescue helicopters into the PZ. The helicopters and two escorts orbited out of range of antiaircraft fire. The high section of fighters reconnoitered the site to determine resistance and attacked antiaircraft weapons in the vicinity. With hostile fire diminished sufficiently, the leader then called in the first helicopter with its two escorts. The second helicopter remained available to act as a recovery vehicle if the first helicopter was shot down or damaged. Many times the alternate helicopter swooped in to rescue both the downed helicopter crew and the object of the rescue mission. However, on numerous occasions, several U.S. aircraft and men were lost attempting to rescue downed airmen.

From administrative assignments to combat and service operations, helicopters changed U.S. military doctrine forever. Used properly, helicopters proved much less fragile than some critics had predicted and flew thousands of hours for every aircraft lost or damaged. Many listed as destroyed in combat were lost to mortar and rocket fire as they sat in revetments.

During the Vietnam War, U.S. helicopters flew 36,125,000 sorties (one individual flight by one aircraft): 3,932,000 attack sorties; 7,547,000 assault (troop landing) sorties; 3,548,000 cargo sorties; and 21,098,000 observation, reconnaissance, search-and-rescue, and command and other sorties. U.S. forces lost 10 helicopters over North Vietnam and 2,066 in South Vietnam. An additional 2,566 were lost to nonhostile causes. Pilots killed in action totaled 564 (Army), 74 (Marines), 17 (Air Force), 12 (Navy), and 1 (Coast Guard); 1,471 aircrew members were also killed in action. An additional 401 pilots and 994 aircrew died from non–combat-related accidents. U.S. Army aviators suffered the highest per capita ratio of casualties of any contingent of U.S. combat troops participating in the Vietnam War.

—Stanley S. McGowen

References: Galvin, John R. *Air Assault: The Development of Airmobile Warfare* (1969); Gregory, Barry. *Vietnam Helicopter Handbook* (1988); Gurney, Gene. *Vietnam: The War in the Air* (1985); Johnson, Lawrence H., III. *Winged Sabers: The Air Cavalry in Vietnam, 1965–1973* (1990); Summers, Harry G., Jr. *Vietnam War Almanac* (1985); Tilford, Earl H., Jr. *The USAF Search and Rescue in Southeast Asia* (1992).

See also: Air Power, Role in War; Airmobility; Airplanes: Allied and Democratic Republic of Vietnam; Antiaircraft Artillery, Allied and Democratic Republic of Vietnam; Brady, Patrick H.; Chiêu Hôi Program (Open Arms Program); Helicopters, Allied and Democratic Republic of Vietnam; Kelly, Charles L.; Medevac; Psychological Warfare Operations (PSYOP); Rockets; Search-and-Rescue (SAR) Operations; Surface-to-Air Missiles (SAMs).

Helms, Richard McGarrah (1913–)

U.S. intelligence officer, ambassador, journalist, and consultant. In June 1966, President Johnson appointed Helms director of Central Intelligence, a position that made him an important and controversial figure during the U.S. involvement in Vietnam.

Helms was skeptical about the potential for U.S. success in Southeast Asia. As director of Central Intelligence, he did not directly formulate U.S. policy, but policy was often based on information his agency provided. As the Central Intelligence Agency's (CIA's) advocate at the highest government levels, Helms often clashed with the military services over the accuracy of intelligence. He battled the military establishment over issues such as the effectiveness of the bombing campaign in Vietnam, control of covert operations, and the 1970 Cambodian incursion. The most important

controversy occurred in 1967, when the CIA estimated Viêt Công (VC) and People's Army of Vietnam (PAVN) order of battle at nearly 600,000 troops. Military Assistance Command, Vietnam (MACV) put it at only 270,000. To avoid a schism in the U.S. intelligence community, Helms forwarded a compromise figure of 334,000 to President Johnson. The original report later resurfaced and, after debate, was adopted as the official U.S. estimate. Helms's capitulation on this and other estimates caused him to become increasingly unpopular within his own agency.

During Helms's directorship, the CIA engaged in domestic surveillance operations. Although a serious violation of the CIA charter, Helms launched Operation CHAOS, to investigate relationships between U.S. and foreign governments, and Projects MERRIMACK and RESISTANCE, which targeted Washington-based peace movements and radical college organizations, respectively. Helms also presided over agency paramilitary and intelligence operations, such as Air America, and supported active CIA covert action in Southeast Asia.

Helms enjoyed the confidence of President Johnson; the president considered Helms a bearer of information rather than a member of the inner circle, however. President Nixon felt that the CIA had an overt liberal bias and was always skeptical of information Helms brought him. Helms had limited access to Nixon and in 1973 was not reappointed to the directorship, allegedly because he refused to involve the CIA in the Watergate controversy.

—Richard D. Starnes

References: Ameringer, Charles D. *U.S. Foreign Intelligence: The Secret Side of American History* (1990); Powers, Thomas. *The Man Who Kept the Secrets: Richard Helms and the CIA* (1979); Ranelegh, John. *The Agency: The Rise and Decline of the CIA* (1986).

See also: Air America; Central Intelligence Agency (CIA); Colby, William Egan; Johnson, Lyndon Baines; Nixon, Richard Milhous; Pacification; Phoenix Program; Studies and Observation Group (SOG); Watergate; "Wise Men."

Heng Samrin (1934–)

Cambodian Communist revolutionary who became head of state of the Vietnamese-installed government in Phnom Penh after Vietnamese troops invaded and occupied Cambodia, driving out the Khmer Rouge.

Heng Samrin joined the Khmer Rouge when it started organizing resistance to Sihanouk from rural bases in 1967. He rose to second-echelon leadership in the Khmer Rouge during its war against the Lon Nol government (1970–1975) and became a top figure in the Eastern Zone, where Khmer Rouge policies were less draconian than in the rest of the country.

The growing anti-Vietnamese line followed by the top Khmer Rouge leaders in Phnom Penh induced Heng Samrin and other leaders to defect to the relative safety of Vietnam. They reappeared on 2 December 1978 with the announcement of formation of the Kampuchean United Front for National Salvation, which served as cover for the invasion of Cambodia by Vietnamese "volunteer force."

Heng became president of the Revolutionary People's Council, the new government formed after the 7 January 1979 capture of Phnom Penh. This was formalized in 1981 in the People's Republic of Kampuchea, with a State Council with Heng Samrin as president. On 5 December 1981, Heng Samrin also assumed the top post of secretary of the ruling Kampuchean People's Revolutionary Party (KPRP). Heng Samrin remained as head of state and the party until the changes made necessary by the 1991 Paris Agreement that finally ended the continuing guerrilla war against coalition forces including the Khmer Rouge. This agreement brought withdrawal of Vietnamese troops from Cambodia and interim institutions pending the May 1993 elections.

Abandoning its revolutionary name, the KPRP transformed itself into the Cambodian People's Party and contested the elections in which Prince Sihanouk's party won a narrow plurality over the Cambodian People's Party. Heng Samrin, as honorary chairman of the party, ceased wielding power.

—Arthur J. Dommen

Reference: Kiernan, Ben. *How Pol Pot Came to Power* (1985).
See also: Cambodia; Hun Sen; Khmer Rouge; Lon Nol; Sihanouk, Norodom; Vietnamese Invasion and Occupation of Cambodia.

Herbert, Anthony (1930–)

U.S. Army officer. Herbert won promotion to lieutenant colonel in August 1968 and volunteered for Vietnam service, becoming a battalion commander in the 173d Airborne Brigade.

Herbert later sharply criticized the wasteful employment of the brigade, charging that the 10,000-man brigade was sending, at most, only 800 men into the field. In 1970 Herbert publicly accused his immediate superiors in Vietnam, Maj. Gen. John Barnes and Col. J. Ross Franklin, of ignoring and subsequently covering up acts by U.S. soldiers in violation of the Geneva Convention. The official U.S. Army response was that no documentary evidence supported Herbert's claims of war crimes. Some time later, at least two of Herbert's charges were verified. Claiming the Army was harassing him, Herbert retired in February 1972 in a storm of controversy.

Herbert published his version of these events in 1973, the same year that CBS in a "60 Minutes" program questioned the veracity of his claims. In retaliation Herbert sued CBS. His attorneys pointed out that CBS selected the weakest of Herbert's claims and used it to attack all the claims as well as Herbert's credibility.

—Paul R. Camacho

References: Herbert, Anthony B., with James T. Wooten. *Soldier* (1973); Zito, Tom. "Old Soldier's Media Battle; Col. Herbert's War with CBS" (1979).
See also: Media and the War; United States: Army.

Herbicides

Chemicals designed to inhibit or destroy plant life. Herbicides act by inhibiting growth; by prematurely removing leaves; by drying the foliage; by neutralizing plant nutrients in the soil; or by causing chemicals to adhere to the plants. By using herbicides, the Republic of Vietnam (RVN) and U.S. governments hoped to deny the Communists a natural environment in which to hide and to deny easy access to food crops.

Beginning with a small test program in July 1961, more than 30 herbicidal chemicals were tested or used in Vietnam during the next nine years, mostly in small quantities. Six major herbicides were given military code names based on colored bands on the 55-gallon drums. Although each chemical is slightly different, and usage data varies slightly depending upon the source, certain important patterns emerge.

From 1962 to 1964, Agents Purple, Pink, and Green were applied in relatively modest amounts—less than 9,000 gallons of Green, about 123,000 gallons of Pink, and 145,000 gallons of Purple. Mixed with oil or diesel fuel, they generally were used to attack jungle vegetation. Unknown to those applying the chemicals or, apparently, to anyone in the Department of Defense, these herbicides contained significant amounts of dioxin (2,3,7,8-tetrachlorodibenzo-p-dioxin), a chemical that was later discovered to be highly toxic even in minuscule amounts.

Two other herbicides that did not contain dioxin were used. Agent Blue, preferred for crop denial missions, was manufactured in two varieties. Between 1962 and 1964, only 5,200 gallons of the first type were used; between 1965 and 1971, approximately 1 million gallons of a second variety were employed. About half of that amount was used on defoliation missions. Agent White was employed fairly extensively after 1966 and was used instead of Agent Orange after the toxic effects of that chemical became known. About 5.2 million gallons of Agent White were used. Water-soluble, Agents Blue and White were not particularly effective against the thickest jungle canopies or during the rainy season.

The military used Agent Orange from mid-1965 through 1970. Soluble in diesel fuel and organic compounds, Agent Orange was employed primarily for jungle defoliation. Toxicologically, Orange was much less potent than Agents Purple, Pink, and Green. Nevertheless, its extensive use, and its employment at the time when awareness of the toxicity of these herbicides became known, made Orange the most notorious of the group. About 11.2 million gallons of Agent Orange were used in Vietnam.

In 1992, after much controversy and studies by the U.S. Air Force, the National Cancer Institute, and the Centers for Disease Control, the Department of Defense decided officially to accept that Hodgkin's disease, non-Hodgkin's lymphoma, soft-tissue sarcoma, chloracne, and birth defects could be caused by exposure to dioxin in herbicides. Thus began closure for a legal debate begun in the late 1970s as veterans sought medical treatment for a number of illnesses of unknown origin. Dow Chemical Company and other manufacturers of Agent Orange agreed to an out-of-court settlement in 1984 and established a $180 million trust fund that may be dissolved in 2009, or when the monies are depleted.

In Vietnam, the medical effects of herbicide use are more difficult to verify, but the ecological impact is beginning to be understood. About 19 million gallons of herbicides were sprayed over approximately 10 percent of the landmass of South Vietnam. Although in the short term these defoliation missions affected all aspects of the ecosystem, studies in the late 1980s and early 1990s demonstrate significant recovery in this area.

—Charles J. Gaspar

References: Berman, Harvey P. "The Agent Orange Payment Program" (1990); Verger, Paul, et al. "Correlation between Dioxin Levels in Adipose Tissue and Estimated Exposure to Agent Orange in South Vietnamese Residents"(1994); Young, A. L., and G. M. Reggiani, eds. *Agent Orange and Its Associated Dioxin* (1988).

See also: Defoliation; International War Crimes Tribunal; RANCH HAND, Operation.

Hersh, Seymour Myron (1937–)

Investigative journalist. In 1968 Hersh published his first book, *Chemical and Biological Warfare: America's Hidden Arsenal,* which detailed the effects of such weapons and their use in Vietnam. Of his six nonfiction books, four address Vietnam issues. During 1969–1970, Hersh uncovered the story of the My Lai massacre and Lt. William L. Calley, Jr. This led to five articles and two books, including *My Lai 4: A Report on the Massacre and Its Aftermath* (1970), for which he received a Pulitzer Prize..

Hersh's years with *The New York Times*, 1972–1979, saw his distaste for secrets generate scoops, among them the Nixon administration's secret war in Cambodia and the unauthorized bombings of North Vietnam ordered by Air Force Gen. John D. Lavelle.

—Paul S. Daum, with Trevor Curran

References: Locher, Frances Carol, ed. *Contemporary Authors* (1978); Moritz, Charles, ed. *Current Biography Yearbook 1984* (1984); *Who's Who in America* (1994).

See also: Calley, William Laws, Jr.; Kissinger, Henry Alfred; Lavelle, John D.; McCarthy, Eugene Joseph; Media and the War; My Lai Massacre; Nixon, Richard Milhous.

Hickey, Gerald Cannon (1925–)

Anthropologist and principal ethnographer of the Montagnards of the Central Highlands of Vietnam. Hickey first went to Vietnam in 1956 to conduct research for the Michigan State University Vietnam Advisory Group. He spent more than 13 years in Montagnard villages, describing their cultural patterns and charting the course of their destruction through the fall of the country in 1975.

Hickey became the principal advocate for the Montagnard peoples in the face of impending threats to their traditional homelands. He wrote working papers on the effects of herbicides in the Central Highlands, spoke on the plight of refugees before the U.S. Senate Foreign Relations Committee, worked with government officials to protect Montagnard land rights, and intervened with military commanders to protect Montagnard villages. As a visiting researcher at Nam Đông Special Forces camp during July 1964, Hickey became an honorary member of Special Forces Team A-726 for his service during an assault there.

Hickey's works include a two-part ethnohistory of the Vietnamese Central Highlands: *Sons of the Mountains* (1982), an ethnohistory through 1954; and *Free in the Forest* (1982), charting the war years 1954–1976. His more recent *Shattered World: Adaptation and Survival among Vietnam's Highland Peoples during the Vietnam War* (1993), charts the destruction of indigenous Montagnard culture during the war.

—David M. Berman

References: Hickey, Gerald Cannon. *Free in the Forest: Ethnohistory of the Vietnamese Central Highlands, 1954–1976* (1982); —. *Shattered World: Adaptation and Survival among Vietnam's Highland Peoples during the Vietnam War* (1993); —. *Sons of the Mountains: Ethnohistory of the Vietnamese Central Highlands to 1954* (1982); —. *Village in Vietnam* (1964); Wiesner, Louis A. *Victims and Survivors: Displaced Persons and Other War Victims in Viet-Nam, 1954–1975* (1988).

See also: Civic Action; Civilian Irregular Defense Group (CIDG); Herbicides; Michigan State University (MSU) Advisory Group; Montagnards; Nam Đông, Battle of; Refugees and Boat People.

High National Council (HNC)

Political body created in 1964 to govern the Republic of Vietnam (RVN). On 30 January 1964, Army of the Republic of Vietnam (ARVN) Gen. Nguyên Khánh overthrew the regime headed by Gen. Duong Van Minh. Minh and his supporters had failed to rally public support following the November 1963 overthrow of Ngô Đình Diêm. They had also failed to deal effectively with the growing Communist insurgency. Gen. Minh was retained as figurehead head of state, and Khánh became premier.

In August 1964, after months of delay, Khánh moved to rid himself of his rival Minh. On 16 August, Khánh secured approval from the Military Revolutionary Council (MRC) for a new constitution that abolished the office of head of state and, in effect, made him president. This move triggered opposition and protests in the cities, especially from students and Buddhists. The MRC then reversed its decision, revoking the new constitution and announcing that a National Provisional Steering Committee comprising Generals Khánh, Minh, and Trần Thiên Khiêm would direct national affairs until a National Congress was established to elect a head of state. Khánh would continue as premier of an interim government.

Confronted with another attempted coup led by younger army officers, Khánh found it difficult to regain the power he had lost earlier, and a 17-member High National Council was established with members chosen by Gen. Duong Van Minh from among elderly personages.

The HNC proved more assertive than expected. It insisted on making Minh head of state with strong constitutional powers and chose a civilian premier. U.S. Ambassador Maxwell Taylor, who supported Khánh, blocked this. At the end of September the HNC produced a new constitution. Failing to get Minh to accept the office with reduced powers, it nominated as president Phan Khac Suu. To Khánh went the consolation prize of ARVN commander in chief.

The HNC's attempt to promote civilian rule in the RVN after a succession of military governments did not stabilize the political situation. The new government was divided and weak, the military threatened another coup against civilian rule, and there were popular demonstrations. The Huong government had to resort to martial law and government by decree.

When Buddhist leaders called on the HNC for a vote of no confidence in Huong, the government reacted by relying more heavily on the military and instituted repressive measures. Meanwhile, younger officers (the Young Turks) demanded that the HNC retire all officers with 25 years or more of service, including Minh. When the HNC refused, on 20 December 1964, the Young Turks arrested five HNC members and nearly 20 other politicians, student leaders, and government officials. They also formed a new Armed Forces Council.

Khánh, privy to the conflict between the HNC and the younger officers, attempted his own coup by announcing the dissolution of the HNC. The Huong government tried to hang on and insisted in carrying on repressive measures to keep order. After further student demonstrations, U.S. authorities concluded that increased military participation in the government was needed to restore order. Huong was then forced to accept Generals Nguyên Van Thiêu, head of the Armed Forces Council (AFC), and Linh Quang Viên as deputy premiers, along with U.S.-educated economist Nguyên Xuân Oánh. This was in fact a step toward a complete military takeover.

As Buddhists demonstrated in major cities on 27 January, the AFC called for ARVN commander Gen. Khánh to restore order. After this was accomplished, Suu remained as head of state, but Nguyên Xuân Oánh replaced Huong as acting premier.

—Ho Diêu Anh and Spencer C. Tucker

References: FitzGerald, Frances. *Fire in the Lake: The Vietnamese and the Americans in Vietnam* (1972); Nguyên Cao Ky. *Twenty Years and Twenty Days* (1976); Westmoreland, William C. *A Soldier Reports* (1976).
See also: Duong Van Minh; Ngô Đình Diêm; Ngô Đình Diêm, Overthrow of; Nguyên Khánh; Taylor, Maxwell Davenport; Trân Thiên Khiêm; Vietnam, Republic of: 1954–1975.

Hilsman, Roger (1919–)

U.S. State Department official and advisor on Vietnam policy. In 1961 President Kennedy appointed Hilsman director of the State Department's Bureau of Intelligence and Research. Charged with analyzing foreign developments to allow for long-term planning, Hilsman was a principal architect of U.S. Vietnam policy.

In January 1962, Hilsman presented "A Strategic Concept for South Vietnam." This plan defined the war as a political struggle, proposed policies aimed at the rural Vietnamese as the key to victory, and led to the Strategic Hamlets program. It also recommended that the Army of the Republic of Vietnam adopt guerrilla warfare tactics. In July 1963, following attacks on Buddhist dissidents by Ngô Đình Nhu's police, Hilsman recommended, along with Forrestal and Harriman, that new instructions be relayed to U.S. Ambassador Henry

Cabot Lodge in Sài Gòn. These led to at least tacit U.S. approval of the military coup that was carried out against Diêm and Nhu in November 1963.

Increasingly at odds with President Johnson and Secretary of State Rusk over U.S. Vietnam policy, Hilsman resigned in February 1964. In 1967 he wrote *To Move a Nation*, which praises the process of foreign policy formulation under Kennedy, while criticizing Johnson's escalation of the war.

—Robert G. Mangrum

References: Herring, George C. *America's Longest War: The United States and Vietnam, 1950–1975* (1986); Karnow, Stanley. *Vietnam: A History* (1984).
See also: Forrestal, Michael V.; Harriman, W. Averell; Hilsman-Forrestal Report; Johnson, Lyndon Baines; Kennedy, John Fitzgerald; Lodge, Henry Cabot, Jr.; Ngô Đình Diêm, Overthrow of; Rusk, Dean; Strategic Hamlet Program; Taylor-McNamara Report.

Hilsman-Forrestal Report

President Kennedy, concerned about contradictory reports from the news media and the U.S. military, sent a fact-finding mission to South Vietnam in December 1962. The State Department's Roger Hilsman and presidential aide Michael Forrestal were charged with determining whether the Republic of Vietnam (RVN) government could be salvaged. While arguing that U.S. Southeast Asian policies should be continued, the Hilsman-Forrestal Report exposed the weakness of the RVN government, which it contended was caused in part by corruption within the Ngô Đình Diêm regime. It further asserted that Diêm was increasingly isolated from his own people and that only those with close ties to the Diêm family actually supported Diêm and his brother, Ngô Đình Nhu. The report especially criticized the Strategic Hamlet program as it was being administered by Nhu. The report concluded that U.S. commitment to South Vietnam would be much longer than originally anticipated and that the war would be long and costly, but its overall optimistic tone contributed to a continued escalation of U.S. war efforts.

—Robert G. Mangrum

References: Herring, George C. *America's Longest War: The United States and Vietnam, 1950–1975* (1986); Olson, James S., ed. *Dictionary of the Vietnam War* (1988).
See also: Forrestal, Michael V.; Hilsman, Roger; Kennedy, John Fitzgerald; Ngô Đình Diêm; Ngô Đình Nhu; Strategic Hamlet Program.

Hmong

A principal ethnic minority of Laos. The Hmong live in the mountains surrounding the Plain of Jars. They migrated there in the nineteenth century from China, where large numbers of Hmong remain. Their present population in Laos is estimated at 200,000.

Hmong regard kinship patrilineally and identify 15 or 16 patrilineal exogamous clans, each tracing its descent to a common mythical ancestor. There are several subdivisions in Hmong society, usually named according to features of traditional dress. The White, the Striped, and the Green Hmong (sometimes called the Blue Hmong) are the most numerous. Their languages are somewhat different but mutually comprehensible. The Hmong practice polygamy. Divorce is possible but discouraged. Gender roles are strongly differentiated, with women responsible for child care and household chores. Farming tasks are the responsibility of men and women.

The Hmong use a swidden (slash-and-burn) farming system and are excellent hunters. They have traditionally grown opium in small quantities for medicinal and ritual purposes. Houses are built directly on the ground, with a stamped earthen floor, bamboo or wood planking walls, and thatch roofs. Interiors are divided into a kitchen/cooking alcove at one end and sleeping alcoves at the other, with beds or sleeping benches raised above the floor. In contrast with the lowland Lao, the Hmong share no temple or common house in their village. Hmong cultural norms are individualistic, and the household is more important than the village.

Most Hmong supported the French, first against the Japanese and then against the Viêt Minh. In 1961 Hmong leaders were enlisted by the United States and Thailand to fight against the Pathet Lao and North Vietnamese. The Hmong requested and received modern weapons that enabled them to defend their villages as the Plain of Jars became a major battleground. Many Hmong men fought almost continuously from 1961 until the 1973 cease-fire, and Hmong casualties were heavy.

The main Hmong base was Long Chieng. The U.S. Central Intelligence Agency provided support for the anti-Communist Hmong because of the prohibition against U.S. military personnel on the ground in Laos. Throughout their wars, the French and the Americans called the Hmong the *Meo*, a term later judged by some to be derogatory.

After 1975 the Hmong were left on their own. Many fled to Thailand; others organized resistance in their old mountain bases but were relentlessly pursued by the new government, which accused them of having committed "crimes against the people." Some began new lives in the United States, France, Australia, and other countries.

—Arthur J. Dommen

References: Hamilton-Merritt, Jane. *Tragic Mountains: The Hmong, the Americans, and the Secret Wars for Laos, 1942–1992* (1993); Quincy, Keith. *Hmong: History of a People* (1988); Savada, Andrea Matles, ed. *Laos: A Country Study* (1995); Warner, Roger. *Back Fire: The CIA's Secret War in Laos and Its Link to the War in Vietnam* (1995); Yang Dao. *Hmong at the Turning Point* (1993).

See also: Central Intelligence Agency (CIA); Laos; Long Chieng; Vang Pao.

Hô Chí Minh (1890–1969)

Leading Vietnamese revolutionary and president of the Democratic Republic of Vietnam (DRV) from 1945 until his death. In 1911 Hô, then called Van Ba, hired on to a French ship as a kitchen helper and traveled to the United States, Africa, and Europe. While in the United States, he supposedly developed an interest in the political rights outlined in the Declaration of Independence and the Constitution.

When World War I erupted, Hô moved to Paris, joining many Vietnamese nationals and changing his name to Nguyên Âi Quôc (Nguyen the Patriot). There he accepted Marxist Leninism because of its anticolonial stance and position on national liberation. In 1920, after the Paris Peace Conference failed to address Indo-Chinese independence, he helped found the French Communist Party, claiming that anticolonial nationalism and class revolution were inseparable.

In 1923 and 1924, Hô traveled to Moscow to attend the Fourth and Fifth Comintern Congresses and to receive formal theoretical and revolutionary training. In late 1924, Hô traveled to China, where he visited one of the most important Vietnamese nationalists of the modern period, Phan Bôi Châu. Hô stayed in Canton for two years, organizing what became the first Vietnamese Communist Party and writing his highly influential *Duong Cách Mang* (Revolutionary Path). In 1925 he founded the Viêt Nam Thanh Niên Cách Mang Đông Chí Hôi (Vietnam Revolutionary Youth League), commonly known as the Thanh Niên, an anticolonial organization that attempted to unite political and social issues for the ultimate liberation of Vietnam. Hô's efforts within the Thanh Niên led to the founding of the Indo-Chinese Communist Party in 1929, and Hô spent much of 1930 recruiting skilled organizers and strategists. He also carried out a fusion of three Communist parties that had emerged in Vietnam.

By the early 1940s, Nguyên Âi Quôc had changed his name to Hô Chí Minh (Hô the Bringer of Light). With the Japanese invasion of Vietnam during World War II, he moved his revolutionary group to the caves of Pac Bo in the northernmost reaches of Vietnam. In Pac Bo, at the Eighth Party Plenum of the Indo-Chinese Communist Party in May 1941, Hô supervised the organization of the Viêt Minh, a nationalist and Communist front organization created to mobilize the citizenry to meet party objectives.

During World War II, the Viêt Minh entered into an alliance with the American Office of Strategic Services (OSS), providing the Allies with tactical and logistical support and helping to rescue downed U.S. pilots. Some scholars have suggested that Hô's revolutionary army even received financial and military support from the OSS and that Hô himself was an "official agent."

After the Japanese surrender in 1945, the Viêt Minh seized power in Hà Nôi during the August Revolution. On 2 September 1945, with several Americans present, Hô declared Vietnamese independence from French colonial rule and announced the formation of the DRV. On 2 March 1946, he became president of the newly formed DRV.

The French and DRV soon clashed, and a nine-year war began. Most Soviet bloc countries quickly recognized the DRV, thus it was easy for the French to cast their colonial reconquest of Vietnam in Cold War terms. After years of bloody stalemate, in 1954 the French suffered a humiliating defeat at Điên Biên Phu and accepted the subsequent Geneva Accords that recognized the supremacy of Hô's Communists north of the 17th parallel. The Geneva Accords called for nationwide elections in 1956 to reunify the country, but these never took place.

Instead, the United States and southern Vietnamese nationals tried to build a counterrevolutionary non-Communist alternative, south of the 17th parallel.

The result was the creation of the Republic of Vietnam (RVN) with Ngô Đình Diêm as president. Diêm quickly went on the offensive, sending thousands of suspected Communists to prison. His anti-Communist sweeps devastated the party and led to a sharp decrease in the number of cadres operating in the South. Hô called these "the darkest days" for the revolutionary movement. He vowed to reunify the country and called the RVN a historical aberration because "Vietnam is one country, and we are one people with four thousand years of history."

In 1960 the Lao Đông, a national, united Communist party under Hô's leadership, approved the use of armed violence to overthrow Diêm and liberate Vietnam south of the 17th parallel. In December 1960, the National Front for the Liberation of South Vietnam (NFLSV) was established to unite former Viêt Minh activists with elements of southern society who opposed the U.S.–backed Diêm regime. The character and nature of the NFLSV and its relationship to the government in Hà Nôi remains one of the most controversial issues from the war. Some scholars have suggested that Hô Chí Minh and the Lao Đông Party (as the Communist Party was renamed in 1951) had little influence over the NFLSV and that the conflict in the South was essentially a civil war. Washington policymakers claimed that Hô himself had presided over the birth of the NFLSV and that the insurgency was an invasion by North Vietnam against South Vietnam. This provided the rationale for U.S. involvement in Vietnam. It appears that both explanations are wanting, since Hô Chí Minh's Communist Party was a nationwide, national organization with representation from all regions of Vietnam.

In March 1965, the United States intervened militarily in Vietnam, presenting Hô with the most difficult challenge of his life. He remained steadfast in his determination to see Vietnam reunified and refused to discuss any settlement with the United States that did not recognize this objective. He also demanded that any settlement of the war must recognize the political and military supremacy of the NFLSV in the South. Since this was not compatible with Washington's rationale for fighting the war, Hô was clearly outlining the parameters of a struggle with no clear or easy solution.

Hô was a skillful leader who knew how to adapt revolutionary strategy to meet changing conditions. In 1965 he supervised the transition from total battlefield victory to victory through a protracted war strategy. He believed from his experience with the French that Westerners had little patience for a long and indecisive conflict.

As the war dragged on, Hô used his leadership to mobilize the Vietnamese population. During preparations for the 1968 Têt Offensive, Hô threw his enormous prestige behind the effort, making his first public appearance in many months just weeks before the offensive to ensure universal support. Many scholars also credit Hô with ending several bitter inner-party disputes throughout the conflict with the United States. He was especially skillful at managing the con-flict between Lê Duân, secretary general of the Lao Đông Party, and his political rival, Truong Chinh, leader of the National Assembly.

Hô proved an able diplomat in the international arena as well. For years, he skillfully avoided taking sides in the Sino-Soviet dispute and successfully played one against the other to secure increased aid. Eventually, the Lao Đông Party moved closer to Moscow, and Hô accepted the Soviet-supported strategy of "fighting while negotiating." During the last year of his life, Hô worked closely with the Vietnamese negotiators in Paris, outlining the nuanced differences in the Lao Đông Party's strategy.

Hô did not live to see his country reunified. His death inspired a tremendous emotional outpouring in Vietnam, adding significantly to the powerful imagery surrounding his name. Throughout the war, the Lao Đông Party cultivated the image of Hô as the protector of the Vietnamese people and the label "Uncle Hô" was exploited to its fullest potential. Today, Hô Chí Minh is enshrined in central Hà Nôi in a public mausoleum that attracts thousands of visitors each year.

—Robert K. Brigham

References: Duiker, William J. *The Rise of Nationalism in Vietnam, 1900–1941* (1976); Fenn, Charles. *Ho Chi Minh: A Biographical Introduction* (1973); Halberstam, David. *Ho* (1971); Herring, George C. *America's Longest War: The United States and Vietnam, 1950–1975* (1986); Hemery, Daniel. *Ho Chi Minh: de l'Indochine au Vietnam* (1990); Hô Chí Minh. *Ho Chi Minh on Revolution: Selected Writings, 1920–1966* (1967); Karnow, Stanley. *Vietnam: A History* (1983); Lacouture, Jean. *Ho Chi Minh: A Political Biography* (1968); Sainteny, Jean. *Ho Chi Minh and His Vietnam: A Personal Memoir* (1972); Woodside, Alexander B. *Community and Revolution in Modern Vietnam* (1976); Young, Marilyn B. *The Vietnam Wars, 1945–1990* (1991);

See also: Agricultural Reform Tribunals; August Revolution; *Đâu Tranh*; Điên Biên Phu, Battle of; Lao Đông Party; Lê Duân; Ngô Đình Diêm; Office of Strategic Services (OSS); San Antonio Formula; Truong Chinh (Đang Xuân Khu); United Front; Viêt Minh (Viêt Nam Đôc Lâp Đông Minh Hôi [Vietnam Independence League]); Viêt Nam Thanh Niên Cách Mênh Hôi (Vietnam Revolutionary Youth Association).

Hô Chí Minh Campaign (April 1975)

April 1975 attack on Sài Gòn. The Hô Chí Minh Campaign gave the Democratic Republic of Vietnam (DRV) the decisive victory it had fought so long to achieve. Encouraged by the collapse of the Army of Republic of Vietnam (ARVN) in early 1975 in Military Regions I and II, the Hà Nôi Politburo revised its timetable, deciding late in March that Sài Gòn should be taken before the beginning of the 1975 rainy season rather than the following year. The plan was to achieve victory in the Hô Chí Minh Campaign before their dead leader's 19 May birthday.

In early April, People's Army of Vietnam (PAVN) units engaged ARVN forces around Sài Gòn, blocking roads and shelling Biên Hòa airfield. While cadres moved into the city to augment their already significant organization there, sappers positioned themselves to interrupt river transportation and attack Biên Hòa. At Xuân Lôc, 35 miles northeast of Sài Gòn, a hard-fought battle began on 8 April, the same day an RVN Air Force pilot attacked the presidential palace and then defected.

The U.S. evacuation of Cambodia on 12 April further reinforced the DRV assessment that Washington would do nothing to prevent the collapse of the RVN, although some members of the Sài Gòn government could not bring themselves to believe that they would be abandoned. Even after the fall of Military Regions I and II, U.S. officials in Vietnam and visitors from Washington continued to act as if the Sài Gòn government could successfully defend itself or, at worst, achieve some kind of negotiated settlement. Among South Vietnamese, however, opposition to President Nguyên Van Thiêu was growing, and talk of a coup was widespread.

As PAVN forces cut Route 1 to the east and prepared to prevent reinforcement from the Delta by blocking Route 4 and from Vuung Tàu by interdicting Route 15 and the Lòng Tàu River, the ARVN engaged in maneuvering of its own. On 21 April, Thiêu resigned in favor of Vice-President Trân Van Huong, but all attempts by Washington to support the Sài Gòn regime with increased aid failed in Congress.

Thiêu's resignation did nothing to stall the PAVN offensive or buoy RVN morale. While some ARVN units fought on, leaders began sending personal goods and money out of the country. Banks and foreign embassies began closing, and a steady stream of foreign nationals, including many Americans, left the country, often with their Vietnamese employees.

Xuân Lôc fell on 21 April, and by 25 April, ARVN forces around Sài Gòn were under pressure from all sides. The PAVN attack on Sài Gòn proper began on 26 April, with artillery bombardments and a ground assault in the east. PAVN forces also occupied Nhon Trach, southeast of Sài Gòn, enabling them to bring 130-mm artillery to bear on Tân Son Nhât airport. On 27 April, they cut Route 4, but ARVN forces fought back.

As an increasing number of ARVN military and civilian officials abandoned their posts, on 28 April President Huong resigned in favor of Duong Van Minh. That same day, a flight of captured A-37 aircraft struck the Tân Son Nhât airfield, and the Communists pushed forward their attack, positioning units for the final assault and successfully attacking ARVN units in bases surrounding the city. U.S. Ambassador Graham Martin delayed beginning a full evacuation, fearing its negative impact on morale. When the evacuation did begin on 29 April, the final U.S. pullout was chaotic, a poorly organized swirl of vehicles and crowds trying to connect with helicopters, ships, and planes. In the confusion, the Americans left many Vietnamese employees behind, and as few as a third of the individuals and families deemed to be at risk were evacuated or escaped.

Units around the Sài Gòn perimeter came under heavy attack on 29 April. While some PAVN units held outlying ARVN garrisons in check, other elements of Gen. Van Tiên Dung's large force moved toward the center of the city and key targets, including the presidential palace. On 30 April, President Minh ordered ARVN forces to cease fighting. The Hô Chí Minh Campaign had achieved its goal.

The Vietnam War ended as students of revolutionary warfare theory expected. Drawing upon the power developed in their DRV base area, the Communists combined regular units with southern guerrillas and cadres in a final offensive that grew in strength as it piled victory upon victory against a demoralized opposition. PAVN forces could sustain their momentum in part because they did not have to detach a significant portion of their strength to administer conquered areas. That task could be left to local forces and the political infrastructure already in place before the final offensive began. Against such a strong opponent, the Sài Gòn government proved incapable of continued resistance without active U.S. support.

—John M. Gates

References: Dougan, Clark, David Fulghum, and the editors of Boston Publishing Company. *The Fall of the South* (1985); Hosmer, Stephen T., Konrad Kellen, and Brian M. Jenkins. *The Fall of South Vietnam: Statements by Vietnamese Military and Civilian Leaders* (1980); Isaacs, Arnold R. *Without Honor: Defeat in Vietnam and Cambodia* (1983); Le Gro, William E. *Vietnam from Cease-Fire to Capitulation* (1981); Van Tiên Dung. *Our Great Spring Victory* (1977).
See also: Bùi Tín; Duong Van Minh; FREQUENT WIND, Operation; Martin, Graham A.; Nguyên Van Thiêu; Trân Van Trà; Van Tiên Dung; Vietnam, Democratic Republic of: Army (People's Army of Vietnam [PAVN]); Vietnam, Republic of: Army (ARVN); Xuân Lôc, Battle of.

Hô Chí Minh Trail

A network of roads stretching from North Vietnam through eastern Laos to South Vietnam, forming the main supply route for troops and materiel that supported Hà Nôi's war against the Sài Gòn government. The United States recognized the importance of this vital transportation and economic link and waged a massive air interdiction campaign against it.

On 19 May 1955, Hô Chí Minh's birthday, Maj. Gen. Nguyên Van Vinh of Hà Nôi's Central Military Committee instructed Maj. Vo Ban to open a supply route to the South. The Communist Party's Central Committee had decided to conduct a campaign of overt insurgency against South Vietnam, and troops and materiel would have to be moved south to support this new phase of the struggle against the Republic of Vietnam (RVN) government.

Assigned 500 troops for the task, Maj. Ban set to work building the necessary staging areas, depots, and command posts along the ancient system of footpaths and roads that connected North and South. In August, Ban's Unit 559 delivered the first supplies to Viêt Công insurgents in Thua Thiên Province. By the end of the year, 1,800 troops had used the Trail to infiltrate South Vietnam.

The need for secrecy led in 1960 to development of a new route along the western side of the rugged Truong Son Range in Laos. The Trail's segments gradually were widened, and bicycles were introduced to transport supplies. With strengthened frames, each bicycle could handle loads of 220 to 330 pounds, with loads in excess of 700 pounds on occasion.

Hà Nôi continued to expand the Trail over the next two years. Infiltration training centers were established at Son Tây and Xuân Mai, where soldiers underwent rigorous physical training and instruction in the use of camouflage. Once en route, infiltrators averaged six miles a day along the Trail. By winter 1962–1963, North Vietnam had 5,000 troops, plus an engineering regiment, assigned to the Trail. The road complex now stretched more than 600 miles, nearly all of it well hidden from aerial observation. Trucks began using portions of the route in summer 1962.

In October 1964, following a decision in Hà Nôi to expand the war in the South, the 95th People's Army of Vietnam (PAVN) Regiment completed its infiltration training and departed for Laos. This first large PAVN unit to hike down the Trail intact arrived in Kontum Province in South Vietnam's Central Highlands in December. Two additional regiments reached the South in January and February 1965.

The North Vietnamese in 1965 undertook a massive effort to improve the Trail to handle the increased traffic. Engineers, assisted by North Korean, Russian, and Chinese advisors, widened footpaths into roads, strengthened bridges, and piled rocks in streams and rivers to create fords. Truck convoys, covering 50 to 75 miles during the night, moved increasing amounts of materiel to the South.

Despite the beginning of heavy air attacks, the number of infiltrators increased from 12,000 in 1964 to 33,000, while truck traffic quadrupled. The tremendous expansion of the supply route led to a reorganization of the Trail command, with Unit 559's area of operation redesignated a military zone under the authority of the party's Central Committee. Brig. Gen. Phan Trong Tuê took charge of the new zone, with Ban as his deputy.

The war in the South during 1966 and 1967 saw heavy fighting between North Vietnamese regular army units and U.S. forces. The Trail, historian Richard Stevens has pointed out, became "a massive labyrinth of hundreds of paths, roads, rivers, streams, passes, caves, and underground tunnels burrowing through mountains, forests, and into the earth." By the end of 1966, according to U.S. intelligence estimates, the Hô Chí Minh Trail consisted of 820 miles of well-hidden fair-weather roads. Supplies moved mainly during the dry season (November to April) in southern Laos. It became clear to U.S. planners that a major effort had to be undertaken to cut this essential supply route.

In September 1966, Secretary of Defense McNamara wrote to President Johnson that the task of stopping the flow of troops and supplies from North Vietnam represented "one of our most serious unsolved problems." Attempts to use small ground units to disrupt the flow of supplies—Operations LEAPING LENA (1964), PRAIRIE FIRE (1965), and SHINING BRASS (1966)—had proved ineffective. The U.S. Air Force had first attacked the Trail in 1964 as part of Operation BARREL ROLL. Although air attacks had increased in 1965 with ROLLING THUNDER, operations against the Trail remained secondary to the air war against

North Vietnam. The bombing, including the introduction of B-52 strikes in December 1965, had not slowed the rate of infiltration.

A new study by the Jason Division of the Institute of Defense Analysis recommended the placement of an electronic barrier across the infiltration routes in Laos. McNamara ordered construction of what became known as the "McNamara Line." In December 1967 the electronic barrier, with its 20,000 sensors linked to computer arrays, was placed into operation.

The appearance of the McNamara Line coincided with a shift in the air campaign from North Vietnam to Laos. On 1 April 1968, Johnson announced a limitation on bombing North Vietnam. When the air war against the North ended in November, U.S. air assets focused on interdiction. Operation COMMANDO HUNT, formally begun on 15 November 1968, was directed in part against the Trail itself. Mountainsides were bombed so that landslides would block key passes, clouds were seeded in an effort to extend the rainy season, and chemicals were used to defoliate the jungle. None of these tactics proved effective.

COMMANDO HUNT's main target was the truck traffic along the Trail. Initially, propeller-driven fighter-bombers and jets were used against the growing number of trucks, but as time passed, the offensive burden shifted to gunships. By the late 1960s, AC-130s had replaced the earlier AC-47s and AC-119Ks. Equipped with 20-mm Gatling guns and 40-mm Bofors guns (later, computer-aimed 105-mm howitzers) that were combined with low-light television and infrared and ignition detections systems, the AC-130s proved a formidable truck-killer, at least until the North Vietnamese introduced surface-to-air missiles (SAMs) in the early 1970s. In 1970, the air campaign claimed 9,012 trucks destroyed. At the same time, however, the Central Intelligence Agency estimated the *total* of trucks in all of North Vietnam at only 6,000.

By late 1970, 70,000 PAVN soldiers defended the Trail in Laos. An estimated 8,000 men and more than 10,000 tons of war materiel moved monthly along the roads. Even the March 1970 closure of the port of Sihanoukville (which since 1966 had been a major source of supplies, carried through Cambodia on the Sihanouk Trail to link up with the Hô Chí Minh Trail) failed to stem the tide of troops and matériel.

In 1971, following an abortive attempt by the United States to cut the Trail (Operation LAM SON 719), the North Vietnamese seized Attopeu and Saravane in southern Laos, widening the Trail to the west. The Trail now had fourteen major relay stations in Laos and three in South Vietnam. Each station, with attached transportation and engineering battalions, served as a POL (petroleum-oil-lubricants) storage facility, supply depot, truck park, and workshop. Soviet ZIL trucks, with a capacity of five to six tons, traveled day and night on all-weather roads. Protected by nature and sophisticated antiaircraft defenses, the PAVN had become—to use Richard Stevens's phrase—"absolute masters" of a 2,700-mile network of roads.

On 31 March 1972, COMMANDO HUNT VII ended. It proved to be the last of the interdiction efforts waged by the

U.S. Air Force against the Trail. The North Vietnamese had won the battle of supply, a victory that spelled defeat for South Vietnam and its U.S. ally.

—William M. Leary

References: Staaveren, Jacob Van. *The United States Air Force in Southeast Asia: Interdiction in Southern Laos, 1960–1968* (1993); Stevens, Richard Linn. *The Trail: A History of the Ho Chi Minh Trail and the Role of Nature in the War in Viet Nam* (1993); Tilford, Earl H., Jr., *Crosswinds: The Air Force's Setup in Vietnam* (1993).

See also: Air Defense, Democratic Republic of Vietnam; Air Power, Role in War; BARREL ROLL, Operation; COMMANDO HUNT, Operation; Defoliation; Geography of Indo-China and Vietnam; Johnson, Lyndon Baines; Logistics, Allied and People's Army of Vietnam/Viêt Công; McNamara, Robert S.; ROLLING THUNDER, Operation SHINING BRASS, Operation; Surface-to-Air Missiles (SAMs); Transportation Group 559; Vietnam, Climate of; Vietnam, Democratic Republic of: Army (People's Army of Vietnam [PAVN]).

H.O. Program

Resettlement in the United States of former military officers, officials, and political leaders of the former Republic of Vietnam (RVN) who were detained by the Socialist Republic of Vietnam (SRV) in so-called reeducation camps. Although there were rumors of such a program in the early 1980s, the U.S. and SRV governments did not begin to exchange proposals until April 1984. In late 1988 official negotiations were begun to produce an agreement on the resettlement program.

The program was a part of the Orderly Departure Program (ODP) to assist in family reunification and resettlement of political refugees, including former political prisoners. Under the H.O. program, former RVN political prisoners are sponsored by their relatives or by private organizations involved in the ODP. The U.S. government provides assistance in the form of social security programs. This program has provided assistance in the immigration of tens of thousands of Vietnamese to the United States.

—Nguyên Công Luân (Lu Tuân)

See also: Reeducation Camps.

Hòa Bình, Battle of

(14 November 1951–24 February 1952)
Key Indo-China War battle initiated by the French. French military commander in Indo-China Gen. Jean de Lattre de Tassigny went on the offensive as a result of increasing U.S. military aid, the success of "meat-grinder" battles in the Korean War, and the need to secure a victory to influence the French National Assembly debate over the 1952–1953 Indo-China budget.

de Lattre chose as his objective the major Viêt Minh road connecting northeastern Viêt Minh strongholds on the southern edge of the Red River Delta redoubt with Viêt Minh–controlled areas north of central Vietnam. The battle's focus was the city of Hòa Bình. Another important consideration for de Lattre was maintaining the support of Muong Montagnards of the area, who thus far had remained staunch French supporters.

The Battle of Hòa Bình began when three French para-troop battalions dropped on the city. The ... Hòa Bình with almost no resistance. After h... HOÀNG HOA THÁM and HÀ NAM NINH O... Minh commander Gen. Vô Nguyên Giáp had ...voiding battle with the French except in conditions of his choosing; thus the Viêt Minh at Hòa Bình simply melted away. But the French position there seemed to offer an excellent opportunity for Giáp to repeat his 1950 successes along RC 4 (Route Coloniale 4). He ordered south the 304th, 308th, and 312th Infantry Divisions, along with artillery, antiaircraft, and engineer troops; and he called in Viêt Minh regional forces stationed to the west of the Red River Delta. Giáp also ordered his 316th and 320th Divisions to infiltrate French lines and disrupt their lines of communication feeding Hòa Bình.

Hòa Bình became a meat-grinder battle for both sides. de Lattre left Indo-China in December 1951, before the battle was over, but before his departure he stripped French outposts as far as Laos and Cambodia of manpower, making these more vulnerable to Viêt Minh attack. The Battle of Hòa Bình clearly showed the limitations imposed by the paucity of French manpower resources.

The French held Hòa Bình, to no advantage. The Viêt Minh simply built a bypass road around the town; and by the end of the battle on 24 February 1952 had succeeded in penetrating the Red River Delta as never before.

The French lost 894 killed and missing. Although the Viêt Minh sustained perhaps 12,000 casualties, their divisions gained firsthand experience in fighting the French and learned enemy strengths and weaknesses. This would be of immense benefit in the battles to come. Giáp rotated units in and out of the battle and those that were bloodied had merely to withdraw into the jungle to rest and regroup.

—Spencer C. Tucker

References: Fall, Bernard. *Street without Joy* (1961); —. *The Two Viet Nams* (1964); Gras, Yvres. *Histoire de La Guerre d'Indochine* (1992).

See also: de Lattre de Tassigny, Jean Joseph Marie Gabriel; Dinassauts; France: Air Force; France: Army; HOÀNG HOA THÁM, Operations; Indo-China War; Vô Nguyên Giáp.

Hòa Hao

Religious sect in South Vietnam. The Hòa Hao was founded in 1939 by Huynh Phú Sô in the South Vietnam hamlet that gave the religion its name. Sô, a native of Hòa Hao, preached a revised Buddhism targeting the impoverished peasantry.

Sô's flock increased to 2 million people before World War II. Without a formal ruling body of clergy or edifices for religious exercises, the Hòa Hao was less a church and more an impassioned sectarian crusade. Desiring to create a Buddhist community on earth rather than in heaven, Sô criticized the populace's extravagance, ceremony, and irrational beliefs, and he urged renunciation of drugs, alcohol, and gambling. Philosophically the Hòa Hao blamed Westernization for afflicting the Vietnamese with an immoderate urban lifestyle. Despite a program promoting equal treatment and the termination of special privilege, Sô opposed Marxism and the class struggle.

The growing anticolonial Hòa Hao soon menaced France's authority. In 1940 Sô was apprehended and institutionalized, then was freed but confined to the town of Bac Liêu, where he received pilgrims through whom he circulated religious inspiration and anti-French propaganda. In effect, the Hòa Hao subverted imperial administration in areas under its influence. It replaced colonial courts, converted French-led native soldiers, and later provisioned Japanese forces with rice.

Sô created the Dân Xã Ðang, or Social Democratic Party, which called for common land ownership on a voluntary basis. He continued to reject Marxist ideology and waged a brutal war against the Viêt Minh after 1945. Following Sô's death, the sect fragmented into four parts, each commanded by one of his former military subordinates. Thereafter, hamlet and provincial tiers administered welfare, while the military regions controlled political matters.

The Hòa Hao engaged in a power struggle with the Cao Ðài and other nationalist groups, even while it participated in various national coalitions and united fronts. The sect fought the efforts of both Emperor Bao Ðai and Premier Ngô Ðình Diêm to assert central government authority over its autonomous domain northwest of Sài Gòn. Diêm, through a combination of military action and bribery, finally broke the back of its resistance in 1954.

—Rodney J. Ross

References: Buttinger, Joseph. *Vietnam: A Political History* (1968); Kahin, George McT. *Intervention: How America Became Involved in Vietnam* (1986); Popkin, Samuel L. *The Rational Peasant: The Political Economy of Rural Society in Vietnam* (1979); Woodside, Alexander B. *Community and Revolution in Modern Vietnam* (1976). See also: Bao Ðai; Buddhists; Cao Ðà; Huynh Phú Sô; Ngô Ðình Diêm.

Hoàng Ðuc Nha (1941–)

Cousin of Republic of Vietnam (RVN) President Nguyên Van Thiêu and RVN minister of information, 1973–1974. Nha was unqualified for the positions he held. Except for his close links to Thiêu, he had little experience and no knowledge of how to deal with the Communists. As the author of the 007 Decree, which required all RVN newspapers and magazines to deposit at least 10 million dông with the government if they wanted to continue publication, he earned widespread scorn. This measure eliminated many critics who were too poor to pay and was correctly perceived as censorship. Nha also used his influence to place young and unqualified cronies in important government positions. Nha was forced to leave office in October 1974. U.S. Ambassador Graham Martin reportedly made Nha's dismissal a condition for continued aid to the Thiêu government. When the RVN collapsed, Nha fled to the United States.

—Ho Diêu Anh

References: Karnow, Stanley. *Vietnam: A History* (1983); Kiêm Ðat. *Chiên Tranh Viêt Nam* (1982); Nguyên Khac Ngu. *Nhung Ngày Cuôi Cung Cua Viêt Nam Công Hòa* (1979). See also: Nguyên Van Thiêu; Vietnam, Republic of: 1954–1975.

HOÀNG HOA THÁM, Operations (January–June 1951)

First set-piece battles of the Indo-China War. Following his 1950 victories that wrested northeastern Tonkin from the French, Viêt Minh Gen. Vô Nguyên Giáp believed that the time had come for a "general counteroffensive" against the main French defensive line in the flat lands of the Red River Delta. The prize was Hà Nôi itself, and Viêt Minh propagandists began to post leaflets with the inscription, "Hô Chí Minh in Hà Nôi for Têt."

By mid-January 1951, Giáp had assembled 81 battalions, and on 13 January he struck with two divisions against two French mobile groups defending the approaches to Vinh Yên, 30 miles from Hà Nôi, in an operation known as HOÀNG HOA THÁM. The Battle of Vinh Yên initially favored the Viêt Minh, but on 14 January, French commander Gen. Jean de Lattre de Tassigny took personal charge. In what became the most massive aerial bombardment of the Indo-China War, the French dropped large quantities of napalm on their attackers. On 17 January, de Lattre committed his last reserves, and by day's end the Viêt Minh withdrew.

Giáp was not prepared to concede defeat, and in Operation HOÀNG HOA THÁM II he used three divisions to try to cut the French in Hà Nôi from the port of Hai Phòng, which handled the bulk of French military sealift in the north. de Lattre misread Giáp's intentions, believing that he would next strike at Viêt Tri, northwest of Hà Nôi. As a result, de Lattre had the bulk of his heavy forces to the west of the capital.

The attack began on the night of March 23–24, with Gen. Raoul Salan commanding for de Lattre. One of the most incredible incidents of the Indo-China War occurred during the fight for Mao Khê (the location of a large coal mine) when a company of 95 Thô tribesmen, commanded by Vietnamese Lt. Nghiêm Xuân Toàn and three French noncommissioned officers, held off a Viêt Minh division for an entire day. Again Giáp had failed to pierce the French defensive Red River Delta ring.

Undaunted, Giáp tried again when three Viêt Minh divisions attacked from the south in an effort to secure important rice-producing areas of the southern part of the delta. One important Viêt Minh innovation in this battle was the coordination of the frontal attack with the infiltration beforehand of two entire regiments within the French battle line. This offensive, known as HÀ NAM NINH for Hà Nam and Ninh Bình Provinces, which were its objective, resulted in major battles at Ninh Bình and Phát Diêm. Giáp failed to realize the great demands of supplying conventional forces in battle, and the French were again able to bring superior firepower to bear.

These battles helped restore some French confidence and allowed Gen. de Lattre to go to Washington and press for additional U.S. assistance. They also revealed French shortcomings, such as inadequate cross-country mobility and lack of sufficient air power and manpower to exploit local victories.

On the Viêt Minh side, the battles caused Giáp to go back to phase-two guerrilla strategies. He refused to accept battle except on his own terms, while seeking out vulnerable French peripheral units and working to undermine French authority. He and the Viêt Minh leadership believed that a combination of factors would ultimately force the French to quit Indo-China.

—Spencer C. Tucker

References: Currey, Cecil B. *Victory at Any Cost. The Genius of Viet Nam's Gen. Vo Nguyen Giap* (1996); Fall, Bernard. *Street without Joy* (1961); —. *The Two Viet Nams* (1964); Gras, Yvres. *Histoire de la Guerre d'Indochine* (1992).

See also: de Lattre de Tassigny, Jean Joseph Marie Gabriel; Đê Thám (real name, Truong Van Thám, aka Hoàng Hoa Thám); Dinassauts; France: Air Force; France: Army; Indo-China War; Viêt Minh (Viêt Nam Đôc Lâp Đông Minh Hôi [Vietnam Independence League]); Vô Nguyên Giáp.

Hoàng Van Hoan (1905–)

Vietnamese revolutionary and influential official of the Lao Đông Party. Hoan joined the Viêt Nam Thanh Niên Cách Mang Đông Chí Hôi in 1926 and became a founding member of the Indo-Chinese Communist Party in 1930. In 1958 the delegates of the DRV's National Assembly elected Hoan as vice-chairman of the Standing Committee, a position he held throughout the Vietnam War. Hoan openly criticized the leadership of powerful Lao Đông Secretary Gen. Lê Duân and in 1979 defected to China. He remains the highest-ranking Vietnamese Communist official to leave Vietnam.

—Robert K. Brigham

References: Garver, John W. *Foreign Relations of the People's Republic of China* (1993); Hoàng Van Hoan. *A Drop in the Ocean: Hoang van Hoan's Revolutionary Reminiscences* (1988).

See also: Lao Đông Party; Lê Duân; Viêt Nam Thanh Niên Cách Mênh Hôi (Vietnam Revolutionary Youth Association).

Hoàng Van Thái (real name, Hoàng Van Xiêm) (1915–1986)

Prominent Vietnamese Communist Party official and People's Army of Vietnam general. Thái played a major role in the Indo-China and Vietnam Wars and participated in most of the major military campaigns and battles. In the Indo-China War, this included the Biên Gioi (border) operations and the battles of Hà Nam Ninh, Hòa Bình, Tây Bac, and Điên Biên Phu. During the Vietnam War, he saw action in the 1968 Têt Offensive, Chen-la I and Chen-la II, Operation NGUY N HU, and the 1975 Hô Chí Minh Campaign. After 1975, Thái, an in-law of Minister of Defense Vô Nguyên Giáp, became deputy minister of defense with responsibility for training and military technology research.

—Ngô Ngoc Trung

Reference: Biographical Files, Indo-China Archives, University of California at Berkeley.

See also: Điên Biên Phu, Battle of; Hòa Bình, Battle of; Hô Chí Minh Campaign; Lao Đông Party; Têt Offensive: Overall Strategy; Têt Offensive: The Sài Gòn Circle; Vietnam, Democratic Republic of: Army (People's Army of Vietnam [PAVN]); Vietnam, Socialist Republic of: 1975 to the Present; Vô Nguyên Giáp.

Hoffman, Abbie (1936–1989)

Anarchist and cofounder of the Youth International Party (Yippies). Hoffman designed protest demonstrations as entertainment so that the media would cover them and disseminate radical images to a mass audience.

Hoffman organized the "exorcism" of the Pentagon in 1967, and under his leadership in 1968, the Youth International Party nominated a pig for president. Following his indictment for activities during the 1968 Democratic Party National Convention, Hoffman transformed the Chicago Seven conspiracy trial into a piece of guerrilla theater that ridiculed the government by depicting the trial as a sporting event. Hoffman was convicted of crossing state lines for the purposes of inciting a riot and contempt of court; the convictions were subsequently overturned on appeal. Hoffman remained a radical until his death by suicide.

—Donald Whaley

References: Hoffman, Abbie. *Revolution for the Hell of It* (1968); —. *Soon to be a Major Motion Picture* (1980); Whitfield, Stephen J. "The Stunt Man: Abbie Hoffman (1936–1989)" (1992).

See also: Antiwar Movement, United States; Chicago Eight; Dellinger, David; Democratic Party National Convention, 1968; Hayden, Thomas E.; Rubin, Jerry; Youth International Party ("Yippies").

HOMECOMING, Operation
(12 February–29 March 1973)

Return of U.S. prisoners of war (POWs) held in Southeast Asia. On 27 January 1973, the Paris Agreement called for the release of U.S. POWs and the simultaneous final reduction in active U.S. forces (24,000) within 60 days.

The parties agreed to four stages, the first on 12 February and the last, which included nine Americans captured in Laos, ending on March 29, one day late. After an initial reception at Sài Gòn (for those held by the Viêt Công), Hà Nôi (for those held by the DRV), and Hong Kong (for the three to be freed from China), all U.S. POWs would be flown to Clark Air Force Base in the Philippines. At the Joint Homecoming Reception Center at Clark, the former POWs would go through processing, debriefing, and medical examinations. Those released could go to any of 31 U.S. military hospitals for recovery.

Of the 591 U.S. POWs returned, 497 were officers, 69 enlisted men, and 25 civilians. Not only had some former POWs survived the longest captivity of any prisoners in U.S. military history, but many had become the focus of widespread affection and respect. This important event gave many Americans, on a personal level, a "successful final chapter" to the POW story.

Operation HOMECOMING also represented a public relations event orchestrated by the White House and Pentagon. The POWs were among the few popularly recognized heroes of the war. After elaborate receptions at each stop along their journey home, POWs arrived in the United States to a heros' welcome. Although President Nixon proudly spoke of the return of "all" POWs, questions remained: Had any men been left behind, and when would there be an accounting of those missing in action?

—Paul S. Daum, with Joseph Ratner

References: Berger, Carl, ed. *The United States Air Force in Southeast Asia, 1961–1973: An Illustrated Account* (1984); Franklin, H. Bruce.

M.I.A. or Mythmaking in America (1992); Gruner, Elliott. *Prisoners of Culture: Representing the Vietnam POW* (1993); Isaacs, Arnold R. *Without Honor: Defeat in Vietnam and Cambodia* (1983); Lipsman, Samuel, Stephen Weiss, and the editors of Boston Publishing Company. *The False Peace, 1972–1974* (1985).

See also: Casualties; Denton, Jeremiah A., Jr.; Hà Nôi Hilton (Hoa Lò Prison); McCain, John S., III; Missing in Action, Allied; Paris Peace Accords; Prisoners of War, Allied; Stockdale, James B.

Honolulu Conference (7–9 February 1966)

Meeting between U.S. and Republic of Vietnam (RVN) leaders in February 1966. On 31 January, the United States resumed bombing of North Vietnam, and President Johnson's staff recommended that he meet with South Vietnamese leaders to discuss the RVN's economic and political future. Johnson believed that a renewed pacification and rural development program, coupled with the creation of a viable, democratic RVN government, were keys to the South's future security.

Chairman of the Senate Foreign Relations Committee J. William Fulbright had turned against the war and scheduled Congressional hearings for early 1966. Johnson believed that a meeting between himself and South Vietnamese leaders would defuse some criticism being leveled by Fulbright and others.

Accompanying Johnson to Honolulu were various cabinet members and the director of the Agency for International Development. They were joined in Honolulu by Ambassador Henry Cabot Lodge and commander of the Military Assistance Command, Vietnam (MACV), Gen. William Westmoreland. The South Vietnamese delegation included Prime Minister Nguyên Cao Ky and Gen. Nguyên Van Thiêu.

Meetings began on 7 February and concluded with a joint communiqué on 9 February. Social, political, and economic goals were to be as important as those for the military. Ky and Thiêu pledged to defeat the Viêt Công, eradicate social injustice, establish a stable economy, and build a true democracy with a constitution and elections. They also offered incentives to soldiers who defected from the Communists. Westmoreland was to continue to destroy Communist forces and was assigned percentage goals for securing the population and geographic areas of the country. To achieve these, two of Johnson's principal assistants developed a plan to increase U.S. troop strength in the RVN. Johnson established a White House office to coordinate the pacification program in South Vietnam, which later became Civil Operations and Revolutionary Development Support.

Ky returned to Vietnam to face a Buddhist crisis, during which he dispatched soldiers to suppress dissidents. Nevertheless, in 1967 the South Vietnamese government drafted a new constitution and held elections that September. Despite this, lack of coordination among U.S. and South Vietnamese military and civilian agencies precluded substantive progress in the rural pacification effort.

—Richard L. Kiper

References: Herring, George C. *America's Longest War: The United States and Vietnam, 1950–1975* (1986); Johnson, Lyndon Baines. *The Vantage Point: Perspectives of the Presidency, 1963–1969* (1971).

See also: Civic Action; Civilian Operations and Revolutionary Development Support (CORDS); Fulbright, J. William; Johnson, Lyndon Baines; Lodge, Henry Cabot, Jr.; Nguyên Cao Ky; Nguyên Van Thiêu; Pacification; Westmoreland, William Childs.

Hoopes, Townsend (1922–)

U.S. deputy assistant secretary of defense for international security affairs, 1965–1967, and undersecretary of the Air Force, 1967–1969. After joining the Johnson administration in 1965, Hoopes became convinced that the Vietnam War was unwinnable. In 1968 he put these views forcefully to Clark Clifford after the latter succeeded Robert McNamara as secretary of defense. Hoopes recommended a bombing pause and a less aggressive ground strategy. He helped convince Clifford that the United States must reverse its Vietnam policy. Hoopes was a source for *The New York Times* article of 22 March 1968 that revealed that Gen. Westmoreland was requesting 206,000 more troops for Vietnam.

—Priscilla Roberts

References: Clifford, Clark, with David Holbrooke. *Counsel to the President: A Memoir* (1991); Hoopes, Townsend. *The Limits of Intervention* (1969); Schandler, Herbert Y. *Lyndon Johnson and Vietnam: The Unmaking of a President* (1977).

See also: Clifford, Clark M.; Johnson, Lyndon Baines; McNamara, Robert S.; McNaughton, John T.; Media and the War; Warnke, Paul C.; Westmoreland, William Childs.

Hoover, J. Edgar (1895–1972)

Director of the U.S. Federal Bureau of Investigation (FBI), 1924–1972. In the 1960s, Hoover and the FBI began to draw criticism from a number of fronts, including the civil rights movement, antiwar activists, Congress, and the Supreme Court.

Antiwar groups were among the numerous targets of FBI domestic counterintelligence programs (COINTELPROs) during the 1960s and early 1970s. President John F. Kennedy and Attorney General Robert Kennedy strongly advocated wiretapping to expose domestic foes. Presidents Johnson and Nixon authorized massive FBI surveillance and infiltration of antiwar groups, but Hoover apparently recognized some limits. Former FBI Assistant Director Cartha "Deke" DeLoach credits Hoover with torpedoing the Nixon administration's so-called Huston Plan, which would have created, under White House direction, a highly illegal multiagency intelligence organization to attack perceived threats to domestic security such as the antiwar movement and information leaks within the government. This notwithstanding, Hoover's heavy-handed approach to domestic dissent was viewed by many as an attack on civil liberties and constitutional rights.

During his final years, Hoover faced repeated calls for his ouster, saw his methods curtailed by the Supreme Court, and dealt with an increasingly hostile Congress. Still, his power and public prestige held sway. Presidents Johnson and Nixon waived mandatory retirement after Hoover reached 70 years and continually sustained him in office. Hoover's death in 1972 freed Nixon to appoint a more cooperative director.

—David Coffey

References: DeLoach, Cartha D. "Deke." *Hoover's FBI: The Inside Story by Hoover's Trusted Lt.* (1995); Jackson, Kenneth T., ed. *Dictionary of American Biography* (1994); Ungar, Sanford J. *FBI* (1976).
See also: Antiwar Movement, United States; Central Intelligence Agency (CIA); Federal Bureau of Investigation (FBI); Huston Plan; Johnson, Lyndon Baines; Kennedy, John Fitzgerald; Kennedy, Robert Francis; King, Martin Luther, Jr.; Nixon, Richard Milhous; Spock, Benjamin M.

HOP TAC (1964)

Code name for a U.S.–sponsored combined military-political pacification plan for the Sài Gòn area. At a June 1964 Honolulu meeting, top U.S. political and military policymakers endorsed a plan by Gen. William Westmoreland, codenamed HOP TAC (cooperation), that called for pacification of guerrilla-held areas in six provinces around Sài Gòn. Col. Wilbur Wilson, advisor to the Army of the Republic of Vietnam (ARVN) commander of III Corps, developed the concept and organization; his successor, Col. Jasper Wilson, worked out the details.

Under HOP TAC, military forces were to drive Viêt Công (VC) guerrillas from selected provinces. Aggressive patrolling and ambushes would follow until security could be entrusted to local militia or an expanded police force. Civilian officials would then establish Republic of Vietnam (RVN) government agencies and provide protection, services, and amenities. As Westmoreland put it, "The idea was to provide a standard of living perceptibly higher than the Viet Công could provide." The essence of the plan was clearing, securing, and search-and-destroy.

HOP TAC incorporated elements of the French "oil slick" (*tache d'huile*) pacification method pursued during the Indo-China War, dividing the territory to be pacified into grids. Once this gridding (*quadrillage*) was accomplished, each square was to be "raked" (*ratissage*) by pacification forces, who knew the area well. Once accomplished in smaller areas, the program could expand over a much larger area, the way an oil slick spreads on water. Westmoreland saw HOP TAC as an experiment which, if successful, could be duplicated around other cities "until eventually all might merge."

HOP TAC also sought to incorporate lessons learned in the Strategic Hamlet program. The Vietnamese would carry the brunt of the effort against the VC. To coordinate the military and political agencies, the RVN government established a HOP TAC council that included Gen. Westmoreland and Premier Gen. Nguyên Khánh and local officials and representatives from the ministry of interior, national police, and intelligence agencies.

HOP TAC got off to a slow start in September 1964. Determined to keep the Army of the Republic of Vietnam (ARVN) at the center of efforts against the Viêt Công, Westmoreland informed the RVN that the United States would contribute only advice and commodities. He persuaded the ARVN to transfer its 25th Division from Quang Ngãi Province in II Corps to join the operation. This proved a mistake. Many of the division's soldiers deserted, and it was three years before the 25th Division recovered and became fully proficient.

Political instability in Sài Gòn was another negative factor. Gen. Khánh became so involved in political concerns that he was little interested in HOP TAC. He seemed more concerned with holding back troops to prevent a possible coup than allowing them to participate in the project. The RVN police failed to do their job, and the South Vietnamese government did not deliver the American supplies that were to be the economic leverage.

HOP TAC did give the ARVN experience in pacification. It increased the National Police by several thousand and made the capital more secure. But these positives did not outweigh the negatives, and the RVN formally ended HOP TAC in 1965. Even Westmoreland admitted it was a failure. It probably removed some illusions Westmoreland may have had about the ARVN and weakened his commitment to pacification. In 1965 he relied increasingly on U.S. troops to carry the war.

—Ho Diêu Anh and Spencer C. Tucker

References: Cable, Larry E. *Conflict of Myths: The Development of American Counterinsurgency Doctrine and the Vietnam War* (1988); FitzGerald, Frances. *Fire in the Lake: The Vietnamese and the Americans in Vietnam* (1972); Westmoreland, William C. *A Soldier Reports* (1976).
See also: Desertion, Allied and Communist; Pacification; *Quadrillage/Ratissage*; Strategic Hamlet Program; *Tache d'huile*; Westmoreland, William Childs.

Hope, Leslie Townes "Bob" (1903–)

Comedian who entertained U.S. troops in Vietnam. Starting in 1941 and continuing through World War II, Hope and many other Hollywood stars traveled overseas and near the fighting to entertain U.S. troops. Hope continued the tradition after the war, taking his humor to U.S. soldiers and sailors wherever they were stationed, including Vietnam. Although some antiwar protesters felt that Hope was supporting government policies in Vietnam, he saw his task as providing morale for the troops. His generosity and selflessness was rewarded with a Congressional Medal of Honor.

—Laura Matysek Wood

References: Morella, Joe, Edward Epstein, and Eleanor Clark. *The Amazing Careers of Bob Hope* (1973); Thompson, Charles. *Bob Hope* (1981).

Hô-Sainteny Agreement (6 March 1946)

Agreement signed on 6 March 1946 by Democratic Republic of Vietnam (DRV) President Hô Chí Minh and Vo Hông Khanh for the Viêt Nam Quôc Dân Đang (VNQDD, Vietnam National Party) and Jean Sainteny for France to set the future relationship between the DRV and France. The DRV leadership, abandoned by the United States and the Soviet Union and under pressure from China, agreed to a French military presence in the North. France was allowed to introduce 15,000 French and 10,000 Vietnamese troops under unified French command to protect French lives and property. France promised to withdraw 3,000 of its troops each year; all were to be gone by the end of 1951, with the possible exception of those guarding bases.

In return, France recognized the DRV as a "free state with its own government, parliament, army and finances, forming part of the Indo-Chinese Federation of the French Union." In a key provision, France also agreed to the holding of a plebiscite in the South to see whether it wanted to join the DRV in a unified state; however, no date for the vote was specified. France also agreed to train and equip units of the new Vietnamese Army. After the agreement was signed, Hô told Sainteny, "I am not happy about it, for basically it is you who have won."

The Hô-Sainteny Agreement, although much less than the Viêt Minh wanted, might have led to a working relationship between France and the DRV had it been allowed to stand. The agreement was undermined, however, by French High Commissioner Georges Thierry d'Argenlieu's 2 June 1946 proclamation in Sài Gòn of the "Republic of Cochin China," just after Hô's departure for Paris to negotiate implementation of the agreement. With an "independent" Republic of Cochin China, there would be no need of a plebiscite in the South.

—Spencer C. Tucker

References: Hammer, Ellen. *The Struggle for Indochina* (1954); Sainteny, Jean. *Histoire d'une Paix Manquée: Indochine, 1945–1947* (1953).

See also: d'Argenlieu, Georges Thierry; Fontainebleau Conference; Hô Chí Minh; Sainteny, Jean; Salan, Raoul Albin Louis; Vô Nguyên Giáp.

HOT PURSUIT Policy

Designation for 1965 U.S. Military Assistance Command, Vietnam (MACV) requests for authority to pursue Communist forces retreating from South Vietnam into sanctuaries in Cambodia. HOT PURSUIT was to be used in conjunction with a proposed blockade of the Cambodian port of Sihanoukville. The U.S. State Department opposed such plans, and President Johnson was reluctant to widen the conflict because Cambodia was officially neutral. Nonetheless, small Allied units did occasionally cross the border without official sanction. Although the HOT PURSUIT debate continued, it became academic in May 1970, when President Nixon ordered the military incursion into Cambodia.

—Edward C. Page

References: Karnow, Stanley. *Vietnam: A History* (1984); Maitland, Terrence, Peter McInerney, and the editors of Boston Publishing Company. *A Contagion of War* (1983); Stanton, Shelby. *The Rise and Fall of an American Army: U.S. Ground Forces in Vietnam 1965–1973* (1985).

See also: Cambodia; Cambodian Incursion; Johnson, Lyndon Baines; Military Assistance Command, Vietnam (MACV); Sihanouk, Norodom; Nixon, Richard Milhous.

Huê, Battle of (1968)

Longest and bloodiest of the Têt Offensive battles. Huê was the cultural and intellectual center of Vietnam. Its imposing Citadel, built in 1802, was surrounded by a zigzag moat and protected by an outer wall, and at its heart was the Imperial Palace of Peace. There were two key Allied military installations in Huê: the headquarters (HQ) of the Army of the Republic of Vietnam (ARVN) 1st Division and the U.S. Military Assistance Command, Vietnam (MACV) compound.

On the morning of 30 January 1968, Brig. Gen. Ngô Quang Truong, commander of the ARVN 1st Division, put his headquarters on alert after receiving reports of the premature Têt attacks against cities to the south. Truong's move was critical in preventing a complete Communist takeover of Huê.

Inside the city, Communist supporters had been preparing for several months. Two days before the actual attack, elements of the Viêt Công (VC) 12th and Huê City Sapper Battalions slipped into Huê and began preparations. At 0200 on 31 January, ARVN patrols reported battalion-sized People's Army of Vietnam (PAVN) elements advancing on the city from the west. Aided by dense fog, these forces made their approach march unhindered. Less than two hours after the first reports, the 1st Division HQ compound came under attack from 122-mm rocket fire.

The main attack on Huê was made by two regiments. The 6th PAVN Regiment, commanded by Lt. Col. Nguyên Trong Dan, attacked north of the river from the west. Its objective was the Citadel. The 4th PAVN Regiment, commanded by Lt. Col. Nguyên Van, approached from the south and east. Initially delayed by an ARVN ambush, it finally attacked the southern part of the city and the MACV compound. By dawn, Communist forces held much of Huê south of the river, all of Gia Hôi, and the southern half of the Citadel. At 0800, they hoisted the Viêt Công flag in front of the Palace of Peace.

ARVN troops, however, still held the northern half of the Citadel, while inside the MACV compound, approximately 200 Americans and a few Australian advisors continued to hold out. These two Allied enclaves unhinged Communist plans for holding the city. The U.S. Marine Corps base at Phú Bài received the distress call from the MACV compound and dispatched a relief column, but this force was far too small to accomplish the mission. With additional augmentation, the Marines eventually reached the MACV compound and were ordered to move across the river and link up with Gen. Truong's ARVN forces, but were beaten back. Over the next few days, the Marine 1st Division continued to send units piecemeal into the action without clearing the city.

When the Communists first stormed the city, they captured the jail and freed 2,500 inmates, about 500 of whom joined the attacking forces. The PAVN troops also captured an ARVN depot stocked with U.S. weapons and ammunition. For most of the next three weeks, the main Communist supply line into the city from the A Shau Valley remained open, ensuring that attackers were well-armed and supplied. Eventually, five PAVN reinforcing battalions joined the nine that made the initial assault.

The U.S. high command underestimated the size and nature of the PAVN threat until well into battle. MACV Commander Gen. William Westmoreland believed that the Communists would attempt to overrun Khe Sanh; thus, for several weeks he kept tight rein on Allied strategic reserve forces in that area. The nature of the urban fighting considerably neutralized U.S. advantages in mobility, and the desire to minimize damage to Huê itself hamstrung the Allies' enormous firepower assets. ARVN I Corps commander Lt. Gen. Hoàng Xuôn Lãm on 12 February finally authorized Allied forces to use whatever weapons were necessary to dislodge the Communists.

In an attempt to cut the Communist supply lines into Huê, on 2 February the 2d Battalion, 12th Cavalry of the U.S. 1st Cavalry Division began an air assault into a landing zone six miles northwest of the city. Instead of cutting the supply lines, the Americans ran into a strong Communist blocking force. Meanwhile, another unit from the 1st Cavalry Division, the 5th Battalion, 7th Cavalry, approached from the west and attempted to link up with their sister battalion, but were prevented from doing so until 9 February.

PAVN blocking forces were much stronger than the Allies had anticipated. Units opposing the 1st Cavalry Division consisted of elements of the PAVN 304th, 325C, and 324B Divisions, all of which U.S. intelligence had placed at Khe Sanh massing to overrun the Marine base there.

By the second week in February, Westmoreland had committed six battalions to cutting off Huê. The reinforced 3d Brigade, 1st Cavalry Division attacked from the west and north, and two battalions of the 101st Airborne Division attacked from the south. The Marines also continued to feed forces into the fight. By the time the south bank of the city was cleared on 10 February, elements of the 1st Battalion, 1st Marines, and 1st and 2d Battalions, 5th Marines were in the fight.

Late on 11 February, the 1st Battalion, 5th Marines crossed the river and joined the fight for the Citadel. ARVN forces, which now had close to eleven battalions in the city, had cleared about three quarters of the Citadel, but the enemy stubbornly held the southernmost section against the river. For two more weeks, bitter house-to-house fighting continued. In one of the few such instances in the Vietnam War, both sides used CS (tear) gas.

On 21 February, the 1st Cavalry Division finally closed off the last Communist supply route into the city. Three days later, the ARVN 2d Battalion, 3d Regiment overran the defenders on the south wall of the Citadel. On 25 February, ARVN troops swept into the Imperial Palace to find that Communist troops there had slipped away during the night. The battle for Huê was over.

On 26 February, the Allies unearthed the first of the mass graves containing civilian victims of the Communist occupation. This systematic slaughter, apparently carried out by local VC cadres rather than PAVN regular troops, had started as soon as the Communists moved into Huê. Foreigners, intellectuals, religious and political leaders, and other "cruel tyrants and reactionary elements" were purged. Searchers eventually found 2,810 bodies; thousands more remained missing. Vietnamese scholar Douglas Pike has estimated that the Communists may have assassinated as many as 5,700 people.

Huê was a costly battle. The U.S. Army suffered 74 dead and 507 wounded; the U.S. Marines lost 142 dead and 857 wounded; and ARVN losses totaled 384 dead and 1,830 wounded. PAVN and VC losses exceeded 5,000 dead, 89 captured, and countless more wounded. In addition to civilians executed by the Communists, many others died or were hurt in the crossfire. Fifty percent of the city was destroyed, leaving 116,000 civilians homeless—of a population of approximately 140,000. The experience produced a sharp change in the attitude of the population there against the Communists, even among Communist sympathizers.

—David T. Zabecki

References: Braestrup, Peter. *Big Story* (1977); Hoàng Ngoc Lung. *General Offensives of 1968–69* (1981); Oberdorfer, Don. *Tet!* (1971); Palmer, Dave. *Summons of the Trumpet* (1978); Pearson, Willard. *The War in the Northern Provinces 1966–1968* (1975); Pike, Douglas. *The Viet-Cong Strategy of Terror* (1971); Stanton, Shelby. *The Rise and Fall of an American Army: U.S. Ground Forces in Vietnam 1965–1973* (1985).

See also: Airmobility; Huê and Đà Nang, Battles of; Ngô Quang Truong; Têt Offensive: Overall Strategy; Têt Offensive: The Sài Gòn Circle; United States: Army; United States: Marine Corps; Vietnam, Democratic Republic of: Army (People's Army of Vietnam [PAVN]); Vietnam, Republic of: Army (ARVN); Westmoreland, William Childs.

Huê and Đà Nang, Battles of (1975)

The fall of Huê and Đà Nang to the Communists compounded the disaster created by the Republic of Vietnam (RVN) withdrawal from the Central Highlands. Not directly assaulted, Huê was threatened in early March by attacks on all sides. On 19 March, to prevent the orderly withdrawal of Army of the Republic of Vietnam (ARVN) forces from Huê to Đà Nang, Communist forces attacked aggressively, particularly in Quang Tri Province, prompting a massive refugee exodus. In Huê, memories of Communist massacres during the 1968 Têt Offensive heightened civilian fears, and residents joined the refugee throng moving south toward Đà Nang.

President Nguyên Van Thiêu's withdrawal of the airborne division to bolster the defenses of Sài Gòn further complicated a rapidly deteriorating situation, leaving I Corps Commander Gen. Ngô Quang Truong with insufficient troops to defend both Huê and Đà Nang. Although Thiêu had told Truong to defend Huê, he changed his mind when Truong protested that he needed the 1st Division there to defend Đà Nang. Thiêu then led Truong to believe that he was to defend Huê only as long as he could still withdraw the unit, but in a taped televised address Thiêu also publicly committed himself to the city's defense.

As Communist units moved on Huê, the level of anxiety in the demoralized city increased. Troops in Huê began to desert, and by 23 March, the situation was too chaotic for a defense or an orderly withdrawal. Unopposed, Communist troops occupied Huê on 24 March.

As the pressure on Huê increased, Communist units also encircled Đà Nang, cutting Route 1 south of that city on 21 March, taking Tam Ky on 24 March and occupying Quang Ngãi the following day. The Đà Nang airport became a scene of constant activity as the government and the U.S. embassy in Sài Gòn increased flights out of the city. Initially, the airlift proceeded in an orderly fashion, but after 25 March, as Communist forces pressed toward the city from all sides, the situation became chaotic. By 27 March, desperate crowds at the airport rushed planes, and more than one plane took off with people clinging to its landing gear. At the deepwater pier, people crowded onto tugs and barges, and ships arriving offshore were quickly surrounded by small craft filled with refugees.

The situation deteriorated as the city, airport, and docks came under Communist fire. Looting soldiers and civilians rampaged through the streets while the Communist troops held back their advance, allowing panic to destroy any semblance of order among the city's defenders. The Communists occupied Đà Nang on 29 March.

In less than a month, the Communist offensive had destroyed virtually all ARVN forces in I Corps. Combined with the disaster in the Highlands, the losses were significant: 150,000 regulars and militia, and roughly $1 billion of equipment, including approximately half of the Sài Gòn government's planes and helicopters. Despite predictions in some quarters of a bloodbath, in the days following the Communist victory only a few hundred people were killed.

—John M. Gates

References: Dougan, Clark, David Fulghum, and the editors of Boston Publishing Company. *The Fall of the South* (1985); Hosmer, Stephen T., Konrad Kellen, and Brian M. Jenkins. *The Fall of South Vietnam: Statements by Vietnamese Military and Civilian Leaders* (1980); Isaacs, Arnold R. *Without Honor: Defeat in Vietnam and Cambodia* (1983); Le Gro, William E. *Vietnam from Cease-Fire to Capitulation* (1981); Van Tiên Dung. *Our Great Spring Victory* (1977). **See also:** Ban Mê Thuột, Battle of; Hồ Chí Minh Campaign; Huê, Battle of (1968 Tết Offensive); Ngô Quang Truong; Nguyên Van Thiêu.

Humphrey, Hubert H. (1911–1978)

U.S. senator, vice-president, and Democratic Party candidate for president in 1968. One of many ironies of 1968 was the New Left's repudiation of Humphrey until the closing days of the presidential campaign. Throughout his public life, Humphrey was a chief voice of the liberal wing of the Democratic Party.

After becoming vice-president in 1964, Humphrey irritated Presdient Johnson by arguing against expansion of the Vietnam War. In 1966, however, Humphrey returned from an Asian fact-finding trip full of praise for administration policies, angering many liberals and intellectuals.

The Vietnam War undid Humphrey. After Johnson announced his withdrawal from the 1968 presidential campaign, Humphrey entered the race. Johnson endeavored to keep Humphrey on a short leash, but Humphrey's dilemma was his need to distance himself from the president's unpopular Vietnam policies while maintaining the support of the party apparatus. The June assassination of Robert Kennedy ensured Humphrey of the Democratic Party's nomination, although the Democratic convention was divisive, bitter, and bloody.

The public associated Humphrey with this chaos and vented on him its dissatisfaction with the war. Some of Humphrey's advisors urged him to break completely from Johnson, but he refused. During the campaign, Humphrey was constantly heckled by antiwar protesters, who left Republican candidate Richard Nixon largely alone. At Salt Lake City on 30 September, Humphrey finally distanced himself a bit from Johnson, announcing that as president, he would stop the bombing of the North. Energized, Humphrey began picking up support as the "peace" candidate. He attacked Nixon's refusal to debate and tore into American Independence candidate George Wallace for his appeals to racism and intolerance.

On 31 October, Johnson announced a halt in the bombing of North Vietnam. Undoubtedly the bombing halt helped Humphrey, but it came too late. Nixon's victory margin was 43.3 percent to 42.7 percent for Humphrey and 13.5 percent for Wallace. Nixon's Electoral College margin was much larger, however (302, 191, and 5 votes, respectively).

In 1970 Humphrey returned to the Senate, winning the seat vacated by Eugene McCarthy. Looking back on the Vietnam War in 1974, Humphrey said, "Like many things in our national life, we miscalculated. We overestimated our ability to control events, which is one of the great dangers of a great power. Power tends to be a substitute for judgment and wisdom."

—Spencer C. Tucker

References: Eisle, Albert. *Almost to the Presidency: A Biography of Two American Politicians* (1972); Humphrey, Hubert H. *Beyond Civil Rights: A New Day of Equality* (1968); —. *The Education of a Public Man: My Life and Politics* (1976); Solberg, Carl. *Hubert Humphrey: A Biography* (1984). **See also:** Democratic Party National Convention, 1968; Elections, U.S.: 1968; Johnson, Lyndon Baines; Kennedy, Robert Francis; McCarthy, Eugene Joseph; Nixon, Richard Milhous; Read, Benjamin Huger; Wallace, George Corley, Jr.

Hun Sen (1951–)

Cambodian military commander, party leader, and cabinet minister. During fighting against the Lon Nol regime (1970–1975), Hun Sen was wounded five times. He remained with the Khmer Rouge after their capture of Phnom Penh on 17 April 1975, until he defected to Vietnam in June 1977.

In June 1977, with relations between Democratic Kampuchea and Vietnam deteriorating, Hun Sen and 200 of his men in the Eastern Zone defected after being ordered to attack Vietnamese villagers. When the Vietnamese invaded Cambodia and expelled the Khmer Rouge from Phnom Penh in January 1979, Hun Sen became foreign minister of the new pro-Vietnamese regime, the People's Republic of Kampuchea (PRK). He became a member of the governing Kampuchean People's Revolutionary Party (KPRP) at an unknown date and in January 1985 became prime minister. He continued war against the Khmer Rouge, holed up in western Cambodia on the border with Thailand, and their non-Communist allies led by Prince Sihanouk and Son Sann.

As a consequence of international peace negotiations, the PRK changed its name to the State of Cambodia (SOC). At a plenum in Phnom Penh on 19 October 1991, four days before the Paris Peace Agreement was signed ending the Cambodian fighting, Hun Sen became vice-chairman of the KPRP, which was renamed the Cambodian People's Party at the same plenum. The new party platform endorsed a multi-party political system, free enterprise, and freedom of religion, with Buddhism as the state religion.

A United Nations peacekeeping force entered Cambodia to supervise implementation of the Paris Peace Agreement. From 23 to 28 May 1993, elections were held throughout Cambodia for a Constituent Assembly. Hun Sen's Cambodian People's Party won 51 seats, compared with the royalist United Front for an Independent, Neutral, Peaceful and Cooperative Cambodia (FUNCINPEC, from its French initials) party's 58 seats. In an arrangement brokered by Prince Sihanouk (who then took the position of king), Hun Sen and Prince Norodom Ranariddh (Sihanouk's son) agreed to form a coalition government and became co–prime ministers of the new Kingdom of Cambodia. Hun Sen as second prime minister wielded more effective power, however, since the SOC had controlled the administrative machinery and armed forces over most of the country, compared with FUNCINPEC's control of relatively small areas and limited armed forces.

Relations between Hun Sen and Ranariddh gradually deteriorated, and the rivalry between the two men finally came to a head over the opening of negotiations in late summer 1996 with Khmer Rouge remnants on the Thailand border for their reintegration into Cambodia's political life. Efforts by Cambodian political figures to form third parties also contributed to the rising tension, with grenade-throwing incidents in Phnom Penh.

On 5 and 6 July 1997, forces loyal to Hun Sen moved against Ranariddh, who was forced to leave the country. Hun Sen had the Constituent Assembly vote into office a replacement who was much more amenable to the Cambodian People's Party's manipulation. Some 40 of Ranariddh's close lieutenants were reportedly killed in this action, which some (although not the U.S. Department of State) called a coup d'état.

—Arthur J. Dommen and Stephen Denney

Reference: Human Rights Watch/Asia. *Cambodia: Aftermath of the Coup* (1997).
See also: Heng Samrin; Pol Pot.

Huston Plan

Nixon administration plan to coordinate intelligence-gathering agencies to control "subversive elements" within the United States during the Vietnam War. Formally known as "Domestic Intelligence Gathering Plan: Analysis and Strategy," the Huston Plan (named for one of its sponsors, administration staffer Tom Huston) was developed in June 1970 in response to the antiwar demonstrations. The plan called for the formation of a permanent interagency intelligence committee to coordinate domestic intelligence gathering by elements of the Central Intelligence Agency (CIA), Federal Bureau of Investigation (FBI), National Security Agency, and the Defense Intelligence Agency.

Unrestricted domestic surveillance was to be carried out using wiretaps, infiltration of subversive groups, mail opening, electronic surveillance, and break-ins to gather information on individuals and groups believed to be an internal threat. Although the plan was highly illegal, Nixon initially approved it on 14 July. After FBI Director J. Edgar Hoover and Attorney General John Mitchell voiced their opposition, Nixon withdrew his approval. Although the Huston Plan was never implemented, a new Intelligence Evaluation Committee and the CIA's Operation CHAOS were later established to gather internal intelligence.

The Huston Plan offered a preview of things to come. Illegal efforts to stamp out criticism of Nixon's Vietnam policy and plug information leaks resulted in the Watergate scandal and Nixon's downfall.

—Cynthia Northrup

References: Genovese, Michael A. *The Nixon Presidency: Power and Politics in Turbulent Times* (1990); Haldeman, H. R. *The Haldeman Diaries: Inside the Nixon White House* (1994).
See also: Antiwar Movement, United States; Central Intelligence Agency (CIA); Federal Bureau of Investigation (FBI); Hoover, J. Edgar; Mitchell, John Newton; United States: Department of Justice; Watergate.

Huynh Phú Sô (1919–ca. 1947)

Also known as Huynh Giáo Chu; founder of Hòa Hao Buddhism, one of the most important religious sects in South Vietnam. Sô's first converts were modern and traditional doctors, intellectuals, and peasants. His followers grew rapidly to two million people, and his popularity attracted French concern. The French placed Sô under house arrest at Nghi, then under administrative surveillance first at Cho Quán (mental) Hospital and then in the town of Bac Liêu.

After the Japanese surrender, Sô called on political and religious leaders to set up a National Unified Front (NUF). The NUF was later integrated into the Viêt Minh Front, with Sô as the representative of South Vietnam. Following the signing of the 6 March 1946 Hô-Sainteny Agreement, Sô joined other nationalist leaders to create the Front for National Union and became Commissioner of the Administrative Committee of South Vietnam. In September 1946, he founded the Dân Xã Đang (Social Democratic Party). The threat posed by Huynh Phú Sô led to a 1947 Communist ambush at Dôc Vang in which Sô disappeared and was probably killed.

—Pham Cao Duong

References: Hoa Hao Buddhism. *Bibliography and Teaching of Prophet Huynh-Phu-So* (1983); Nguyên Long Thanh Nam. *Phât Giáo Hòa Hao Trong Dòng Lich Su Dân Tôc* (1991).
See also: Buddhists; Hòa Hao; Hô-Sainteny Agreement.

Huynh Tân Phát (1913–)

Southern Vietnamese revolutionary, secretary general of the National Front for the Liberation of South Vietnam (NFLSV) (1964–1969), and president of the Provisional Revolutionary Government. During the Indo-China War, Huynh Tân Phát led the Information Service of the Southern Revolutionary Region and served as a member of the Administrative and

Resistance Committee of the Sài Gòn–Gia Đinh area. In 1960 he was a founding member of the NFLSV and in 1964 assumed its top leadership post. In 1969 he became president of the Provisional Revolutionary Government of South Vietnam. After the Vietnam War, Phát was one of the few southern Communists who maintained a key political position, serving as a vice-minister to the central government.

—Robert K. Brigham

References: *Personalities of the South Vietnam Liberation Movement* (1965); Thayer, Carlyle A. *War by Other Means: National Liberation and Revolution in Viet-Nam, 1954–60* (1989); Truong Nhu Tang. *A Viet Cong Memoir: An Inside Account of the Vietnam War and Its Aftermath* (1985).

See also: National Front for the Liberation of South Vietnam (NFLSV); Provisional Revolutionary Government of South Vietnam (PRG).

Huynh Van Cao (1927–)

Army of the Republic of Vietnam (ARVN) general and commander of the IV Corps during the disastrous battle of Ấp Bac in the Mekong Delta. Cao's devotion to Republic of Vietnam (RVN) President Ngô Đình Diêm led the latter to promote him over more competent officers.

In December 1962, intelligence reported three Việt Công (VC) companies in the neighborhood of Ấp Bac. This was the situation that U.S. Military Advisor Lt. Col. John Paul Vann had been waiting for, in which the VC would be forced to stand and fight. The battle of Ấp Bac opened when the Việt Công defeated two prongs of an ARVN attack. Vann advised Cao to send paratroopers to block the VC avenue of retreat, but Cao did not want to commit more troops. He finally sent them, but to the west, where they would be practically useless. The troops arrived at twilight, when they could not distinguish friend from foe. The confusion resulted in skirmishes between ARVN units, while the VC slipped away.

In planning the Diêm coup in 1963, the plotters felt that the weakest link to their plans was dealing with Cao's troops in the Mekong Delta. They devised a strategy in which Col. Nguyên Huu Có would take charge of the nearest division to Cao at My Tho and move these soldiers to block his forces from moving into Sài Gòn. This maneuver proved successful.

—Michael R. Nichols

References: Fishel, Wesley R., ed. *Vietnam: Anatomy of a Conflict* (1968); Karnow, Stanley. *Vietnam: A History* (1991); Smith, R. B. *An International History of the Vietnam War* (1985).

See also: Ấp Bac, Battle of; Cân Lao Nhân Vi Cách Mang Đang (Revolutionary Personalist Labor Party); Ngô Đình Diêm; Ngô Đình Diêm, Overthrow of; Ngô Đình Nhu; Nguyên Huu Có; Vann, John Paul.

I

Ia Drang, Battle of (19 October–26 November 1965)
Battle between U.S. and People's Army of Vietnam (PAVN) forces, significant because it prevented the PAVN from seizing control of the Central Highlands and cutting South Vietnam in two. It also demonstrated the effectiveness of airmobility against regular army units.

On 19 October 1965 PAVN troops attacked the Plei Me Special Forces camp southwest of Pleiku. Initially the 1st Cavalry helped Army of the Republic of Vietnam (ARVN) troops relieve Plei Me. On 27 October Military Assistance Command, Vietnam (MACV) Commander Gen. William Westmoreland ordered the 1st Cavalry to seek and destroy the 32d, 33d, and 66th PAVN regiments commanded by Brig. Gen. Chu Huy Mân. Gen. Mân also sought battle to learn how to fight the 1st Cavalry, whose base at An Khê blocked his route of advance to the coast.

The location of PAVN units was unclear until 1 November, when the 1st Squadron of the 9th Cavalry (1/9th), commanded by Lt. Col. John B. Stockton, captured a hospital area five miles west of Plei Me, killing or capturing 135 PAVN troops. Further reconnaissance indicated a PAVN presence in the Ia Drang Valley and on the Chu Pong Massif. The 1/9th Cavalry sprang a night ambush and developed contacts that were turned over to the infantry.

The heaviest contact developed on 14 November as Lt. Col. Harold G. Moore's 1st Battalion, 7th Cavalry (1/7th) assaulted landing zone (LZ) X-Ray on Chu Pong. Vegetation and tall anthills obstructed fields of fire. Moore made heavy contact before his whole understrength battalion could be landed. PAVN Lt. Col. La Ngoc Châu's 66th Regiment, under intense artillery fire and bombardment by the U.S. Air Force, tried to outflank LZ X-Ray to the south, but Moore got his companies in line just in time. One of Moore's platoons advanced too far and was cut off and almost destroyed, but it delayed Châu in locating the main U.S. line. His line fully extended to the south, Moore called for help and received Company B of the 2d Battalion, 7th Cavalry.

At first light on 15 November, Châu resumed the attack, and Lt. Col. Robert Tully's 2d Battalion, 5th Cavalry (2/5th) marched in to give much-needed support. Châu's vicious attacks were repulsed. The lost platoon's survivors were pulled to safety, and B-52s began six days of strikes on Chu Pong. Two more batteries of artillery arrived at LZ Columbus to provide a total of 24 pieces in support. During the night the 66th PAVN regiment withdrew.

Early on 16 November Châu launched a last attack, which was easily repulsed. By body count, PAVN losses were 634, but U.S. estimates placed the number at 1,215 killed, more than ten times the 1st Cavalry's losses. Moore's battalion was lifted to Camp Holloway at Pleiku, but Tully's 2/5th Cavalry and McDade's 2/7th Cavalry remained to secure LZ X-Ray.

On 17 November, continued B-52 raids on Chu Pong forced Tully and McDade to move from X-Ray and seek PAVN forces elsewhere. McDade's 2/7th Cavalry, with

Company A of the 1/7th Cavalry attached, was ordered to march toward LZ Albany to try to resume contact with PAVN units. Tully's unit was ordered to march to the fire base at LZ Columbus.

Having little combat experience and not yet working as a cohesive unit, McDade's men blundered into a PAVN ambush, and a savage battle ensued. The head of the column had just reached LZ Albany when McDade halted it and assembled his company commanders for a council. At the same time, Châu, who was on his way to attack the artillery fire base, used one battalion of his 66th Regiment and one battalion of the 33d to ambush McDade.

Bunched up at rest, McDade's men were easy targets for PAVN mortars and grenades. All unit cohesion was lost as the commanders were separated from their companies and the battle devolved into individual combats. PAVN troops moved about, killing the wounded. No artillery fire or air support was possible until McDade's men could mark their positions. After two hours of close combat, the survivors threw smoke grenades, and artillery fire and napalm rained down on the 66th and 33d.

By late afternoon, Company B of the 1st Battalion, 5th Cavalry (1/5th) was ordered to help McDade's men. It fought its way into LZ Albany and collected the wounded for helicopter evacuation. At dusk, Company B of the 2/7th Cavalry also reinforced McDade. Châu withdrew his men during the predawn of 18 November. His losses were unknown; McDade's unit lost 151 men killed.

When the Ia Drang campaign ended on 26 November, the 1st Cavalry Division had successfully spoiled the PAVN attack along Route 19 to the sea. It also demonstrated the effectiveness of airmobility warfare. In the entire campaign, U.S. losses were 305 killed; PAVN killed were estimated at 3,561.

—John L. Bell

References: Kinnard, Harry W. O. "A Victory in the Ia Drang: The Triumph of a Concept" (1967); Moore, Harold G., and Joseph Galloway. *We Were Soldiers Once . . . and Young: Ia Drang, The Battle That Changed the War in Vietnam* (1992); Stanton, Shelby. *The Anatomy of a Division: 1st Cav in Vietnam* (1987); Tolson, John J. *Airmobility, 1961–1971* (1973).
See also: Airmobility; Central Highlands; United States: Army: Vietnam, Democratic Republic of: Army (People's Army of Vietnam [PAVN]).

IGLOO WHITE, Project. *See* McNamara Line.

India

Asian nation and member of the International Commission for Supervision and Control (ICSC). From the beginning of war in Vietnam, official Indian policy and public opinion generally favored Hô Chí Minh's government against the French and, later, the Việt Cộng against the Republic of Vietnam (RVN) and the United States. The 1962 Sino-Indian War and continuing tension with China to some extent lessened India's sympathy for the Democratic Republic of Vietnam (DRV), an ally of China. Even so, the Indian government resisted appeals from successive U.S. administrations to take a more favorable view of U.S. policies in Vietnam.

After the 1954 Geneva Conference, India was one of the three neutral nations (with Poland and Canada) that formed the ICSC, which was to oversee the cease-fire, elections, and reunification of Vietnam envisaged in the Geneva Accords. Over time the ICSC became badly fractured, as India and Poland tended to support North Vietnamese positions, while Canada took a more pro-U.S. position. The Indian stance contributed to continuing tension with the United States. From 1965 onward, Indian criticism of U.S. policies led the United States to restrict food shipments to India, further exacerbating a difficult relationship. India withdrew from the ICSC in 1973.

In 1965 the Indian Ministry of External Affairs issued a report calling for an end to U.S. bombing of North Vietnam and the convening of an international conference to reach a solution of the Vietnam imbroglio based on withdrawal of all troops from South Vietnam and reunification of Vietnam. The report largely rejected the prospect of a military solution of the war. In 1970 Indian Foreign Minister Swaran Singh called for withdrawal of U.S. forces from Vietnam, and in 1972 the Indian consulate in Hà Nôi was upgraded to an embassy, whereas the consulate in Sài Gòn remained as such. Upon the fall of Sài Gòn in 1975, India promptly recognized the Provisional Revolutionary Government of Vietnam.

—Priscilla Roberts

References: Brands, H. W. *India and the United States: The Cold Peace* (1990); Chary, M. Srinivas. *The Eagle and the Peacock: U.S. Foreign Policy Toward India Since Independence* (1995); Kux, Dennis. *Estranged Democracies, 1941–1991: India and the United States* (1994); McMahon, Robert J. *Cold War on the Periphery: The United States, India, and Pakistan* (1994); SarDesai, D. R. *Indian Foreign Policy in Cambodia, Laos, and Vietnam 1947–1964* (1968); Sridharan, Kripa. *The ASEAN Region in India's Foreign Policy* (1996); Thakur, Ramesh. *Peacekeeping in Vietnam: Canada, India, Poland, and the International Commission* (1984).

See also: Canada; Geneva Conference and Geneva Accords; International Commission for Supervision and Control (ICSC); Poland.

Indo-China War (1946–1954)

Although there were other explosions of nationalist sentiment in the French Empire after World War II, that in Indo-China was by far the most damaging. Hô Chí Minh predicted how the war would be fought: It would be, he said, the war of the tiger and the elephant. The tiger could not meet the elephant in an equal contest, so he would lay in wait for it, drop on his back from the jungle, and rip its flesh with his claws. Eventually the elephant would bleed to death. The war played out very much along those lines.

Initially it did not appear that way. Gen. Jacques-Philippe Leclerc used his small yet mobile force of about 40,000 men to dash through the country and secure the South and Cambodia. The Viêt Minh were quickly forced out into the countryside and life returned to nearly normal. Some dreaded the Viêt Minh's retreat into the jungle. Leclerc was one, convinced that the Viêt Minh was a nationalist movement that France could not subdue militarily. Unlike most of his compatriots, he was aware of the difficulties of jungle warfare and favored negotiations. In a secret report to Paris, Leclerc said there would be no solution through force in Indo-China.

Although the French Socialist Party showed interest in ending the war through peace talks, the steady drift of the coalition government to the right and increasing bloodshed prevented this. French High Commissioner to Indo-China Admiral Georges Thierry d'Argenlieu and other French colonial administrators opposed meaningful concessions to the nationalists, and in summer 1946 Leclerc departed Indo-China in frustration. Leclerc was followed by Generals Jean-Etienne Valluy, Roger Blaizot, Marcel Carpentier, Jean de Lattre de Tassigny, Raoul Salan, Henri Navarre, and Paul Henri Romuald Ely. This frequent change in commanders undoubtedly affected the overall efficiency and morale of the Expeditionary Force.

Most French leaders assumed the conflict would be little more than a classic colonial reconquest, securing the population centers and then expanding outward in the classic "oil slick" (*tache d'huile*) method they had practiced so effectively in Morocco and Algeria. Meanwhile, the Viêt Minh, led by Gen. Vô Nguyên Giáp, steadily grew in strength and controlled more and more territory.

In May 1947 the French made a stab at settling the war peacefully when Paul Mus traveled from Hà Nôi to meet with Hô Chí Minh in the latter's jungle headquarters. Mus was an Asian scholar sympathetic to the Vietnamese nationalist point of view and a personal advisor to Emile Bollaert, who had replaced d'Argenlieu as high commissioner. Mus told Hô that France would agree to a cease-fire on condition that the Viêt Minh lay down some arms, permit French troops freedom of movement in their zones, and turn over some deserters from the French Foreign Legion. Hô rejected this offer, and in May Bollaert declared, "France will remain in Indo-China."

The French fought the Indo-China War less for economic reasons (by 1950 French military expenditures surpassed the total value of all French investments there) than for political and psychological reasons. Colonial advocates argued that if France were to let go of Indo-China, the rest of its overseas possessions would soon follow. This idea bore some similarity to the domino theory that was widely believed in the United States during the Vietnam War.

Altough determined to hold Indo-China, the French never made the necessary commitment in manpower. The war was essentially fought by the professional soldiers, officers and noncommissioned officers who led the French Expeditionary Corps. The French government never sent draftees to Indo-China. The small number of effectives available to French commanders left them few strategic options. Shortages of noncommissioned officers, a lack of trained intelligence officers and interpreters, and little interest in or knowledge of the mechanics of pacification hampered the French military effort.

The French held much of Cochin China largely because the powerful religious sects and Buddhists there opposed the Viêt Minh. The French also controlled the Red River Delta in the north, along with the capital, Hà Nôi. But the Viêt Minh controlled much of the countryside, and the area they dominated grew in time. Initially the Viêt Minh largely withdrew into the jungle to indoctrinate and train their troops. The French invested little attention and few resources to pacification efforts, and their heavy-handedness alienated many Vietnamese. The French scenario had the Viêt Minh eventually tiring of their cause and giving up. It never played out that way.

Paris sought to provide at least the facade of an indigenous Vietnamese regime as a competitor to the Viêt Minh. After several years of negotiations, in March 1949 the French government concluded the Elysée Agreements with former Emperor Bao Đai. These created the State of Vietnam, and Paris made a key concession that Vietnam was in fact one country. The State of Vietnam allowed the French government to portray the war as a conflict between a free Vietnam and the Communists—and thus not a colonial war at all. Washington, which supported France in Indo-China because it needed French military support in Europe, claimed to be convinced.

The problem for Vietnamese nationalists was that the State of Vietnam never truly became established. The French continued to control all of its institutions, and its promised army never really materialized. France simply added the recruited soldiers to its own Expeditionary Corps, in which they were commanded by French officers. In effect, there were only two choices for the Vietnamese: the Viêt Minh or the French. The French, therefore, pushed Vietnamese nationalists into the Viêt Minh camp.

In October 1947 the French mounted Operation LEA. Involving 15,000 men and conducted over three weeks, it was devoted almost exclusively to the capture of Hô Chí Minh and the Viêt Minh leadership and the destruction of their main battle units. LEA involved 17 French battalions, and while it succeeded in taking Thái Nguyên and other Viêt Minh–controlled cities, it failed both to capture the Viêt Minh leadership and to destroy the main Communist units. It also showed the paucity of French resources in Indo-China. The troops in LEA were badly needed elsewhere, and their employment in the operation opened up much of the countryside to Viêt Minh penetration. The military situation continued to deteriorate for the French, even though by the end of 1949 Paris had spent $1.5 billion on the war.

The Indo-China War changed dramatically in fall 1949, when the Communists came to power in China. That event and the recognition of the Democratic Republic of Vietnam (DRV) by the People's Republic of China (PRC) helped change Washington's attitude toward the war. In effect, the war was lost for the French then and there. The long China-Vietnam border allowed the Chinese to supply arms and equipment to the Viêt Minh and provided Chinese sanctuaries in which the Viêt Minh could train and replenish their troops. Plenty of arms were available from the substantial stocks of weapons that the United States had supplied to the Chinese Nationalists.

The Korean War, which began in June 1950, also profoundly affected the U.S. attitude toward the war in Indo-China. Korea and Vietnam came to be viewed as mutually dependent theaters in a common Western struggle against communism. Washington recognized the State of Vietnam and changed its policy of providing only indirect aid to the French effort in Indo-China. In June 1950 President Truman announced that the United States would provide direct military aid to French forces in Indo-China and establish a military assistance and advisory group there. By the end of the Indo-China War in 1954, the United States had provided $2.5 billion in military aid to the French.

The French insisted that all U.S. military assistance be given directly to them rather than channeled through the State of Vietnam. Although a Vietnamese National Army was established in 1951, it remained effectively under French control, and France continued to dominate the State of Vietnam down to the 1954 Geneva Conference. Regardless, the Truman and Eisenhower administrations assured the American people that real authority in Vietnam had been handed over to the Vietnamese. With Paris refusing to concede real authority to the State of Vietnam, Vietnamese nationalists had no other recourse but the Viêt Minh. In the end, Vietnamese nationalism was completely usurped by communism.

The Indo-China War became an endless quagmire, costing France between 40 and 45 percent of its entire military budget and more than 10 percent of the national budget by 1950. That same year, Giáp and the Viêt Minh won control of Colonial Highway (RC 4) in the far north, paralleling the Chinese frontier and running from the Gulf of Tonkin to Cao Bang. With the loss of this critical frontier section, for all practical purposes the war was over for France. The Viêt Minh now had ready access to China. That the war was allowed to drag on past this point is proof of the dearth of political leadership in Paris.

In 1951 Giáp, who believed the circumstances were ripe for conventional large-unit warfare, went on the offensive in Operations HOÀNG HOA THÁM and HÀ NAM NINH. His divisions were stopped cold by French forces led by Gen. Jean de Lattre de Tassigny, probably the most capable French commander in the war. After these rebuffs, Giáp simply shifted back to his strategy of engaging the French in circumstances of his own choosing.

In November 1951 de Lattre initiated a battle outside the important Red River Delta area. What became the Battle of Hòa Bình was a meat-grinder battle as de Lattre envisioned, but for both sides. By the end of the battle in February 1952, the Viêt Minh had paid a heavy price, but they had learned how to deal with French tactics and weapons, and they had penetrated the French defensive ring as never before.

Giáp now undertook the conquest of the Thai Highlands in northwestern Vietnam. By the end of November, Viêt Minh units had penetrated to the Lao border. New French commander Gen. Raoul Salan tried to halt this offensive by striking at Viêt Minh supply lines, but Giáp refused to take the bait, and Operation LORRAINE was soon in reverse. By December Viêt Minh units were still at the Lao border, and the French were back within their heavily fortified "de Lattre" defensive line of the Red River Delta.

The Viêt Minh also made significant gains in central Vietnam. French control in the plateau area of the Central Highlands was narrowed to a few beachheads around Huê, Đà Nang, and Nha Trang. The only areas where the French enjoyed real success were in Cochin China and neighboring Cambodia.

In spring 1953 Giáp assembled a powerful force to invade Laos, which had an army of only 10,000 men supported by 3,000 French regulars. Giáp employed four divisions totaling 40,000 men and had the assistance of 4,000 Communist Pathet Lao troops. Once more the French were compelled to disperse their slender resources. They were, however, successful in preventing the Communists from overrunning the Plaine des Jarres, and in late April the French halted the Viêt Minh and inflicted heavy casualties on them. The onset of the rainy season forced the Viêt Minh to fall back on their bases, and Laos was saved for another summer.

In July 1953 a new French commander, Gen. Henri Navarre, arrived in Indo-China. Buoyed by promises of increased U.S. military aid, Navarre attempted a "general counteroffensive." The press in France and the United States gave much attention to the so-called Navarre Plan. Unknown to the public, however, was Navarre's secret pessimistic assessment to his government that the war could not be won militarily and the best that could be hoped for was a draw.

Using his increased resources (French forces now numbered about 517,000 men; the Viêt Minh had perhaps 120,000), Navarre vowed to go over to the offensive. He ordered the evacuation of a series of small posts, and this was accomplished successfully. The State of Vietnam's army was given more responsibility, a case of too little, too late.

At the same time, Giáp was gathering additional resources for a larger invasion of Laos. With five divisions, he hoped to overrun all of Laos and perhaps Cambodia, then join up with Viêt Minh units in the south for an assault on Sài Gòn. In the meantime, 60,000 guerrillas and five regular regiments would tie down the French in the North. In December 1953 and January 1954 the Viêt Minh overran much of southern and central Laos.

Navarre's response was the establishment of an airhead in far northwestern Vietnam astride the main Viêt Minh invasion route into Laos. Navarre envisioned this either as a blocking position or as bait to draw enemy forces into a setpiece conventional battle, in which they would be destroyed by French artillery and air power. Navarre selected the village of Điên Biên Phu, in a large valley, and conceded the high ground around it to the Viêt Minh. When asked later how he got into this position, Navarre said that at the time the French arrived, the Viêt Minh did not have artillery and so there was no danger from the heights. It was an astonishing statement. Điên Biên Phu was 200 miles by air from Hà Nôi, and the French had only a limited transport airlift capability (approximately 100 aircraft).

Giáp took the bait, but he sent four divisions, rather than the one that Navarre had envisioned, to engage the French at Điên Biên Phu. The siege of the French fortress lasted from 13 March to 7 May 1954. The battle's outcome was largely decided by two key factors: the Viêt Minh's ability to bring Chinese-supplied artillery to the heights by an extensive supply network of coolies (the "People's Porters," Giáp called them) and the inadequacy of French air support. On 7 May the French garrison surrendered. Despite debate in Washington over possible U.S. military intervention (Operation VULTURE), President Eisenhower rejected it because the British would not go along.

The French defeat at Điên Biên Phu allowed political leaders in Paris to shift the blame to the generals and at last bring the war to an end. Attention turned to a conference previously scheduled in Geneva to deal with a variety of Asian problems. New French Premier Pierre Mendès-France imposed a 60-day timetable for an agreement, threatening to resign if one was not reached; the Geneva Accords were signed on the last day of the deadline.

The Vietnamese were pressured by China and the Soviet Union into an agreement that gave them less than they had won on the battlefield. Cambodia and Laos were declared independent, but the key provision was recognition of the unity of Vietnam. Pending unification there was to be an armistice and a *temporary* dividing line at the 17th parallel. The agreements also provided for compulsory regroupment of troops and, if they desired, civilians. Nationwide elections were to be held in two years. Ultimately a new government in South Vietnam headed by Ngô Đình Diêm refused to permit the elections, and the United States supported Diêm in his stand. This led to a renewal of the war in an American phase.

In this "first" Indo-China War, the French and their allies sustained 94,581 dead or missing and 78,127 wounded, broken down as 140,992 French Union casualties (75,867 dead or missing and 65,125 wounded) with allied Indo-China states losing 31,716 (18,714 dead or missing and 13,002 wounded). Viêt Minh losses were perhaps three times those of the French and their allies. Some 25,000 Vietnamese civilians died.

For France the struggle had been a distant one. Paris had not dared send draftees to Indo-China, and the conflict had been fought largely by the professionals. Paris almost immediately transferred these men to Algeria, where another insurrection had broken out. The soldiers pledged that this time there would be no such betrayal.

—Spencer C. Tucker

References: Duiker, William J. *The Communist Road to Power in Vietnam* (1981); Dunn, Peter M. *The First Vietnam War* (1985); Fall, Bernard B. *Hell in a Very Small Place, The Siege of Dienbienphu* (1966); —. *Street Without Joy* (1961); —. *The Two Vietnams* (1964); Gras, Général Yves. *Histoire de La Guerre d'Indochine* (1992); Hammer, Ellen J. *The Struggle for Indochina* (1954); Kelly, George A. *Lost Soldiers: The French Army and Empire in Crisis, 1947–1962* (1965); Maneli, Mieczyslaw. *The War of the Vanquished* (1969);

Porch, Douglas. *The French Foreign Legion: A Complete History of the Legendary Fighting Force* (1991).

See also: Bao Đại; CASTOR, Operation; Casualties; de Lattre de Tassigny, Jean Joseph Marie Gabriel; Điên Biên Phu, Battle of; Eisenhower, Dwight David; Elysée Agreement; Geneva Conference and Geneva Accords; Hai Phòng, Shelling of; Hô Chí Minh; Hòa-Bình, Battle of; HOÀNG HOA THÁM, Operations; L HÔNG PHONG II, Operation; LEA, Operation; Leclerc, Jacques-Philippe; LORRAINE, Operation; Mendès-France, Pierre; Na San, Battle of; Navarre, Henri Eugène; Ngô Đình Diêm; *Tache d'huile*; Truman, Harry S; Vô Nguyên Giáp; VULTURE, Operation.

Indo-Chinese Communist Party. *See* Lao Đông Party.

Indonesia

Asian nation and member of the International Commission for Control and Supervision (ICCS). As a former colonial possession, the Republic of Indonesia (previously the Dutch East Indies) was necessarily interested in the events of South Asia.

On 17 August 1945, Sukarno and other Indonesian nationalists declared independence. Sukarno became president of the new Republic of Indonesia, although the Dutch did not formally surrender their rule until December 1949. Indonesia joined the United Nations the following year, but withdrew in 1965. Under Sukarno the Indonesian government was critical of U.S. policy in Vietnam, in part because much of its national debt was owed to Communist states.

In a bloody 1966 coup Gen. Suharto seized power. He helped stabilize the economy and moved the country closer to the West, and in September 1966 Indonesia rejoined the United Nations. The government even attempted without success to play a peacemaking role in Vietnam. Later, Indonesia replaced India as a member of the ICCS, a revamped version of the International Commission for Supervision and Control (ICSC) that was mandated in the 1973 Paris Peace Accords.

—Leslie-Rahye Strickland

References: Crouch, Harold. *The Army and Politics in Indonesia* (1988); Osborne, Milton. *Southeast Asia: An Illustrated History* (1990); Sievers, Allen M. *The Mystical World of Indochina: Culture and Economic Development in Conflict* (1974).

See also: Paris Peace Accords.

International Commission for Supervision and Control (ICSC)

Watchdog body established by the 1954 Geneva Conference to oversee implementation of the armistice agreements in Vietnam, Cambodia, and Laos; frequently referred to as the International Control Commission (ICC). Although having largely the same mandate and rules of procedure in the three countries, the ICSC operated independently in each. The ICSC was made up of India as chairman and Canada and Poland as members. It had no enforcement powers other than sending reports on armistice violations to the United Kingdom and the Soviet Union, cochairs of the 1954 Geneva Conference.

In Laos, the ICSC played a useful role in encouraging the Royal Lao Government and the rebel Pathet Lao to open negotiations for reintegration of the latter. The 1957 agreement for a coalition government and full restoration of royal authority in Sam Neua and Phong Saly Provinces was due largely to the ICSC's facilitating role. After Prince Souvanna Phouma declared that the May 1958 elections had fulfilled the obligations assumed by the royal government at Geneva, the ICSC adjourned *sine die* on 20 July 1958.

The peaceful respite was to be brief. When large-scale fighting resumed in spring 1961, the ICSC was reactivated at the suggestion of Indian Prime Minister Nehru. ICSC delegates were present at truce talks among the three Laotian factions at Ban Namone and remained in Laos in accordance with new provisions in the 1962 Geneva Protocol on the Neutrality of Laos. After 1964, however, when it had to remove its field teams from the embattled Plain of Jars, the ICSC played a declining role in the escalating war and finally left Laos following the 1975 Communist takeover.

In Vietnam the ICSC operated under close surveillance of the rival Sài Gòn and Hà Nôi governments. It was so unpopular that demonstrators ransacked its hotel in Sài Gòn, some said at the instigation of the government. The major question with which the ICSC grappled was to what extent the escalating guerrilla war in South Vietnam was the result of North Vietnam's intervention. The ICSC's most decisive answer was a special report, issued over Polish objections in June 1962, accusing the Hà Nôi government of violating the 1954 agreement with respect to its actions in the South.

In 1963, Polish delegate Mieczyslaw Maneli was active in a diplomatic move never envisioned in the ICSC mandate. ICSC delegates traveled periodically between Sài Gòn and Hà Nôi by way of Vientiane—the only diplomats to have such freedom. The Polish delegate acted as an intermediary between Presidents Ngô Đình Diêm and Hô Chí Minh when the former wished to sound out the latter about restoring peace. Nothing came of these soundings, however, before Diêm was killed in a November 1963 coup. The ICSC remained in Vietnam until the war escalated beyond retrieval except by negotiations involving the United States, which in 1964 unsuccessfully attempted to use Canadian delegate J. Blair Seaborn as a channel to open talks with Hà Nôi.

In Cambodia the ICSC presence was always at the pleasure of Prince Norodom Sihanouk, who fitted it into his policy of maintaining neutrality between more powerful neighbors. The ICSC was revived from a largely inactive role by Sihanouk's insistence that it investigate and condemn bombings of Cambodian border villages by South Vietnamese and U.S. aircraft. However, ICSC investigations in the eastern border regions of Cambodia carried the risk of stumbling upon North Vietnamese and Viêt Công military installations, and some believe it was mainly for this reason that Sihanouk demanded the ICSC withdraw from Cambodia at the end of 1969.

Although an integral part of the 1954 Geneva settlement, the overall role of the ICSC in the Vietnam War can be characterized as marginal.

—Arthur J. Dommen

Reference: Randle, Robert F. *Geneva 1954: The Settlement of the Indochinese War* (1969).
See also: Cambodia; Canada; Geneva Conference and Geneva Accords; India; Laos; Poland; Sihanouk, Norodom; Souvanna Phouma; Vietnam, Democratic Republic of: 1954–1975; Vietnam, Republic of: 1954–1975.

International Control Commission (ICC).
See International Commission for Supervision and Control (ICSC)

International Rescue Committee
Primary humanitarian organization concerned with resettlement of Vietnamese refugees during and after the Vietnam War. The International Rescue Committee (IRC) was organized during World War II, and although its primary focus had been Europe, its board of directors recognized the need for humanitarian assistance in Vietnam after division of the country in 1954 resulted in 40,000 to 50,000 civilians per day fleeing to the South. The IRC was the first organization to assist these refugees, rushing food, clothing, and medical supplies to refugee camps. After the initial crisis, the IRC focused on education, rural self-help programs, orphanages, public sanitation, establishment of medical facilities, and coordination of volunteer medical teams. Following the fall of Sài Gòn, the IRC began locating sponsors and finding employment for 150,000 Vietnamese refugees, resulting in their relocation within a few months. The organization continues to assist refugees worldwide.

—Cynthia Northrup

References: Buttinger, Joseph. *Vietnam, A Dragon Embattled* (1967); —. *Vietnam, A Political History* (1968).
See also: Refugees and Boat People.

International War Crimes Tribunal
Antiwar organization sponsored by the Bertrand Russell Peace Foundation. The International War Crimes Tribunal, also known as the Russell Tribunal, met in Stockhlom in May 1967 and in Copenhagen in November 1967. The tribunal indicted the United States for "genocide" and violations of various international treaties, including the 1907 Hague Convention, the 1928 Kellogg Briand Pact, the 1949 Geneva Convention, and the United Nations Charter. The rulings received scant attention and had minimal impact on U.S. foreign policy.

—Lacie Ballinger

References: Kutler, Stanley I., ed. *Encyclopedia of the Vietnam War* (1996); Zaroulis, Nancy, and Gerald Sullivan. *Who Spoke Up? American Protest Against the War in Vietnam, 1963–1975* (1984).
See also: Antiwar Movement, United States; Defoliation; Herbicides; Napalm.

Iron Triangle
Việt Công (VC) base area and sanctuary 15 miles north of Sài Gòn. In January 1967 Operation CEDAR FALLS was launched to eliminate the Iron Triangle as a VC base area. Native residents were evacuated, villages were razed, hun-

dreds of acres of jungle were cut back by Rome plows, and the tunnels lying underneath were destroyed. The Iron Triangle became a wasteland under the surveillance of U.S. bombers and artillery, but this did not keep the Communists from returning. By 1995 the Iron Triangle area was resettled, the village of Bên Súc was again a thriving fishing and agricultural area, and jungle reclaimed the wasteland.

—John F. Votaw

Reference: Summers, Harry G., Jr. *Vietnam War Almanac* (1985).
See also: Bên Súc; CEDAR FALLS, Operation; Geography of Indo-China and Vietnam; National Front for the Liberation of South Vietnam (NFLSV).

IRVING, Operation (1–24 October 1966)
Military operation between U.S. Army and Army of the Republic of Vietnam (ARVN) forces and the People's Army of Vietnam (PAVN) in southeastern Bình Định Province. Technically an extension of Operation THAYER I, IRVING developed as units of the U.S. 1st Cavalry Division (Airmobile) forced the 18th Regiment of the 3d PAVN Division to retreat from the Kim Son Valley east to the coastal plain. As elements of the Republic of Korea Capital Division and 22d ARVN Division moved into blocking positions from the south, a reconnaissance team of the 1st Squadron, 9th Cavalry (1/9th) discovered an unknown number of entrenched PAVN forces.

Supported by artillery, helicopter gunships, and naval gunfire, five battalions of the 1st Cavalry's 1st and 3d Brigades were inserted by air from the west and north. They immediately were engaged in pitched battles with heavily armed soldiers of the 18th PAVN Regiment and a local Việt Công force. The heaviest fighting occurred when Lt. Col. James T. Root, Jr.'s 1st Battalion, 12th Infantry (1/12th) entrapped several companies of the 7th and 8th Battalions of the 18th PAVN Regiment at Hòa Hôi. As the 1st Cavalry Division's 1st Battalion, 5th Cavalry (1/5th) was inserted to complete the encirclement, hundreds of civilians exited the village safely.

IRVING produced 681 known Communist casualties and more than 1,000 prisoners identified as PAVN regulars or members of the Việt Công infrastructure. Remarkably, 1st Cavalry forces suffered fewer than 40 killed or wounded. An intensive psychological warfare effort by civic action teams generated more than 10,000 refugees, while only ten civilians died.

IRVING was recognized as a brilliant display of airmobility and, to that date, the most successful combined operation for the 1st Cavalry working with Allied forces. Nevertheless, the remaining units of the 18th PAVN Regiment were able to exfiltrate back to the Kim Son and Suôi Cá areas.

—John D. Root

References: Marshall, S. L. A. *The Fields of Bamboo* (1967); Stanton, Shelby L. *Anatomy of a Division: The 1st Cav in Vietnam* (1987); Tolson, John J. *Airmobility, 1961–1971* (1973).
See also: Airmobility; Korea, Republic of; MASHER/WHITE WING, Operation; PERSHING, Operation; Psychological Warfare Operations (PSYOP); Vietnam, Republic of: Army (ARVN).

J

Jackson State College

Site of a major protest that resulted in the deaths of two students. On 14 May 1970, ten days after the Kent State University killings, a similar incident took place at Jackson State College, a predominantly African American institution in Mississippi. After two nights of campus demonstrations, a violent confrontation ended as police and state highway patrolmen fired into a dormitory, killing two students and wounding twelve. Law enforcement officials claimed that they fired in response to an alleged sniper, but a thorough investigation by the Commission on Campus Unrest found no evidence of student sniping. The Jackson State incident evoked little national attention, unlike Kent State, leading many to believe that the killing of black students was not taken as seriously as that of whites.

—J. Nathan Campbell

References: *Report of the President's Commission on Campus Unrest* (1970); Spofford, Tim. *Lynch Street: The May 1970 Slayings at Jackson State College* (1988).
See also: Antiwar Movement, United States; Kent State University.

Jacobson, George D. (ca. 1913–1989)

U.S. Army officer; U.S. Agency for International Development (USAID) and Civilian Operations and Revolutionary Development Support (CORDS) official. Jacobson arrived in Vietnam in 1954 and by 1962 headed MAAG's Organization and Training Division. He retired from the Army in 1964 and in 1965 arranged to work for USAID on pacification. At the time of the 1968 Têt Offensive, he was coordinator of the Mission Council. After Têt he held a key position in the pacification program as assistant chief of staff for CORDS under William Colby and succeeded Colby as head of CORDS in 1971. After the 1973 Paris Peace Accords, Jacobson served as special assistant to the ambassador for Field Operations, the successor to CORDS. He was among the last Americans to leave Sài Gòn in April 1975.

—Richard A. Hunt

References: Hunt, Richard A. *Pacification: The American Struggle for Vietnam's Hearts and Minds* (1995); Oberdorfer, Don. *Tet: The Turning Point in the Vietnam War* (1984); Sheehan, Neil. *A Bright Shining Lie* (1988).
See also: Civilian Operations and Revolutionary Development Support (CORDS); Colby, William Egan; Military Assistance and Advisory Group (MAAG), Vietnam; O'Daniel, John W.; Pacification; Têt Offensive: Overall Strategy; Têt Offensive: the Sài Gòn Circle; U.S. Agency for International Development (USAID).

James, Daniel "Chappie," Jr. (1920–1978)

U.S. Air Force combat pilot in Korea and Vietnam; first U.S. African American four-star general. In 1967 James, as wing vice-commander of the 8th Fighter Tactical Wing in Thailand, flew 78 combat missions over North Vietnam. He returned to the United States briefly in 1969, but in August became commander of Wheelus Air Force Base in Libya. In March 1970 James, by then a brigadier general, was stationed at the Pentagon as deputy assistant secretary of defense for public affairs, a job that required him to talk to college students during the height of the Vietnam War protests. His rhetoric and booming voice made him an eloquent spokesman. In 1975 James received promotion to four-star general and was assigned as commander in chief of the North American Air Defense Command (NORAD).

—Laura Matysek Wood

Reference: Phelps, J. Alfred. *Chappie. America's First Black Four Star General. The Life and Times of Daniel James, Jr* (1991).
See also: African American Personnel in U.S. Forces in Vietnam.

Japan

Japan had a considerable impact on the Vietnam conflict before and during U.S. involvement. The Japanese victory in the Russo-Japanese War (1904–1905) forever demolished the image of European military invincibility and inspired Asian nationalists everywhere, including those in Vietnam.

The Viêt Minh formed as a nationalistic front in the wake of Japan's seizure of Southeast Asia in 1940. Although many Vietnamese nationalists welcomed the Japanese as liberators, Hồ Chí Minh and the Vietnamese communists were as wary of Japanese imperialism as they were of French colonialism. The Viêt Minh deliberately masked its Communist roots and as a result established itself as the principal organ of Vietnamese resistance and nationalism during World War II and after.

After World War II, Japan became the most important Asian ally of the United States, providing a major rationale for U.S. intervention. U.S. anti-Soviet containment policy predicted that Southeast Asian states would fall like dominoes if only one went the way of China and North Korea. U.S. leaders argued that intervention was necessary to protect Japan and maintain access to neighboring resources and markets.

Japan served as a vital staging area for U.S. forces in Vietnam, providing ports, repair facilities, supply dumps, airports, and hospitals critical to the U.S. military effort. Despite a growing Japanese protest movement, the United States used the bases provided by the 1960 Japanese-American Security Treaty to dispatch troops and supplies to the war zone, interpreting the terms of the treaty as broadly as possible to support almost unrestricted operations out of its 88 bases in Japan. Although Article IX of the Japanese Constitution prohibited direct Japanese involvement in the Vietnam War, Tokyo tolerated Washington's approach because Japanese businesses reaped huge profits by supplying U.S. forces with a broad range of supplies, weapon components, and ammunition.

—Noel D. Fulton

References: Blaker, Michael, ed. *Development Assistance to Southeast Asia: The U.S. and Japanese Approaches* (1984); Havens, Thomas R. *Fire Across the Sea: The Vietnam War and Japan 1965–1975* (1987).
See also: Domino Theory; Korea, Republic of; Southeast Asia Treaty Organization (SEATO); United States: Involvement in Indo-China

through 1954; United States: Involvement in Vietnam, 1954–1965; United States: Involvement in Vietnam, 1965–1968; United States: Involvement in Vietnam, 1969–1973; United States: Involvement in Vietnam, 1973–1975; United States: Involvement in Vietnam, 1975 to the Present; Việt Minh (Việt Nam Độc Lập Đồng Minh Hội [Vietnam Independence League]).

"Jaunissement, Le" (Yellowing)

Term used to describe the "Vietnamization" of the Indo-China War. The 8 March 1949 Elysée Agreements had called for the creation of a Vietnamese National Army. Paris lauded this as proof that Vietnam was "independent," and the agreement helped convince Washington that the war in Indo-China had been transformed into a civil war rather than a colonial conflict. Proof that the new State of Vietnam was not independent is evident in the fact that the Vietnamese National Army was completely controlled and officered by the French. The French also insisted that all U.S. military support be channeled only to the French.

Carpentier's successor, Gen. Jean de Lattre de Tassigny, pushed *"le jaunissement,"* creating wholly Vietnamese units commanded by Vietnamese officers. However, he was adamant that France retain overall authority and that the United States channel all aid through French authorities in Indo-China. Perhaps it was already too late; hopes of the French attracting nationalists to their cause had already been lost as most Vietnamese nationalists rallied to the Việt Minh.

—Spencer C. Tucker

References: Hammer, Ellen J. *The Struggle for Indochina* (1954); Spector, Ronald H. *Advice and Support: The Early Years, 1941–1960. The U.S. Army in Vietnam* (1983).

See also: Carpentier, Marcel; de Lattre de Tassigny, Jean Joseph Marie Gabriel; France: Army; French Indo-China.

Javits, Jacob Koppel (1904–1986)

U.S. Senator and sponsor of the War Powers Act that restricted presidential war-making authority. Javits was the leading Senate Republican critic of the Vietnam War. He voted for the Cooper-Church Amendment and the Hatfield-McGovern Amendment.

In 1970, following the Allied incursion into Cambodia, Javits sponsored legislation to restrict presidential war-making authority. What became known as the War Powers Act, passed on 7 November 1973 over President Nixon's veto, requires that the president consult with Congress before sending military forces into combat abroad, or into areas where hostilities are likely, and to report in writing within 48 hours after troops are deployed. The president must then terminate the use of military force within 60 to 90 days. Deployment can continue for another 60 days, and for 30 days beyond that, if the president certifies to Congress in writing that the safety of the force so requires. Unless Congress authorizes a continuation, through a declaration of war, a concurrent resolution, or other appropriate legislation, the deployment cannot be continued beyond 90 days. Javits explained the reasons behind the act in his 1973 book, *Who Makes War: The President versus Congress.*

—Spencer C. Tucker

References: Fisher, Louis. *Presidential War Power* (1995); Javits, Jacob K., with Donald Kellerman. *Who Makes War: The President versus Congress* (1970); Javits, Jacob K., with Rafael Steinberg. *Javits: The Autobiography of a Public Man* (1981); Stern, Gary M., and Morton Halperin, ed. *The U.S. Constitution and the Power to Go to War: Historical and Current Perspectives* (1994).

See also: Church, Frank Forrester; Cooper, John Sherman; Cooper-Church Amendment; Fulbright, J. William; Hatfield, Mark Odum; Hatfield-McGovern Amendment; Kennedy, Edward Moore; Mansfield, Michael Joseph; McGovern, George S.; Morse, Wayne Lyman.

JEFFERSON GLENN, Operation
(September 1970-October 1971)

Last major U.S. ground combat operation of the war. Following the failure of LAM SON 719, the U.S. 101st Airborne Division (Airmobile) gradually disengaged from aggressive field operations in accordance with the decreasing combat role of U.S. ground forces. On 5 September 1970, however, three battalions from the 101st Airborne inaugurated Operation JEFFERSON GLENN, establishing fire support bases in the coastal lowlands of Thua Thiên Province. Their objective was to shield Thua Thiên and Quang Tri Provinces by patrolling Communist "rocket belts" that threatened critical installations. As JEFFERSON GLENN continued, the 101st gradually disengaged and turned the fighting over to Army of the Republic of Vietnam (ARVN) troops. The 101st and the ARVN 1st Infantry Division claimed a total of 2,026 casualties inflicted on People's Army of Vietnam and Việt Công forces before JEFFERSON GLENN was terminated on 8 October 1971.

—Edward C. Page

References: Fulghum, David, and Terrence Maitland. *South Vietnam on Trial, Mid 1970 to 1972* (1984); Stanton, Shelby, *The Rise and Fall of an American Army: U.S. Ground Forces in Vietnam 1965–1973* (1985).

See also: Airborne Operations; Airmobility; LAM SON 719, Operation; Vietnamization.

Jiang Jieshi (Chiang Kai-shek) (1887–1975)

Chinese general and political leader. Jiang Jieshi became one of China's most important military and political leaders, heading the Nationalist government in China and then the Nationalist opposition government on the island of Taiwan.

Although Jiang did not play a direct political or military role in the Vietnam War, Taiwan became an important Pacific base for U.S. missiles. Taiwanese industry proved to be a valuable economic asset by providing essential goods and services to the U.S. military. Taiwan was a popular rest-and-relaxation destination for GIs on leave from Vietnam. U.S.-Taiwanese diplomatic relations changed dramatically in 1972, however, when the United States opened talks with the People's Republic of China. In 1979 President Carter terminated U.S. recognition of the Taiwanese government.

—Bruce Elleman

References: Chiang Kai-shek. *Soviet Russia in China* (1957); Crozier, Brian. *The Man Who Lost China, The First Full Biography of*

Chiang Kai-shek (1976); Hu Pu-yu. *The Military Exploits and Deeds of President Chiang Kai-shek* (1971); Loh, Pichon. *The Early Chiang Kai-shek* (1971).

See also: Carter, Jimmy; China, People's Republic of (PRC); China, Republic of (ROC; Taiwan); Chinese in Vietnam; Domino Theory; Mao Zedong (Mao Tse-tung).

Johnson, Harold K. (1912–1983)

U.S. Army chief of staff, 1964–1968. Johnson was selected from far down the list of lieutenant generals for promotion to four stars and assignment as Army Chief of Staff at a most critical point—when U.S. involvement in Vietnam started to accelerate.

It fell to Johnson to manage a huge and rapid expansion of the Army for the war without resorting to reserve forces, a daunting task that he handled with characteristic energy and conscientiousness. Publicly, Johnson supported Gen. William Westmoreland's tactics and requests for additional troops, but negative findings in a study Johnson ordered in spring 1965—Program for the Pacification and Long-Term Development of South Vietnam—reinforced his misgivings about how the war was being conducted. He worked behind the scenes to get the tactics changed, the commander replaced, or both. When Gen. Creighton Abrams took over the top post in Vietnam, he essentially put into effect the study's findings, with results that vindicated Johnson's judgment.

Widely admired for his dedication and ethical standards, Johnson retired from military service in 1968.

—Lewis Sorley

Reference: Johnson, Harold K. *Challenge: Compendium of Army Accomplishment: A Report by the Chief of Staff: July 1964–April 1968* (1968).

See also: Abrams, Creighton; United States: Involvement in Vietnam, 1965–1968; Westmoreland, William Childs.

Johnson, Lyndon Baines (1908–1973)

Congressman; vice-president; president of the United States, 1963–1968. Johnson took the oath of office following President Kennedy's assassination on 22 November 1963. As president, he tried to establish "the Great Society," an ambitious program of civil rights and social legislation, but he was less deft and less successful in foreign relations. The war in Vietnam consumed Johnson's energy and his presidency. Johnson, who believed in containment and the domino theory, saw Vietnam as a test of national resolve. His foreign policy advisors, many retained from the Kennedy administration, shared his views. Johnson had been in Congress when China became Communist, and he vividly recalled the domestic political turmoil that followed as Republicans attacked Democrats for "losing" China. He would not, he said, "be the president who saw Southeast Asia go the way China went."

Soon after taking office, Johnson began escalation of the war. In February 1964 he authorized Operation Plan (OPLAN) 34A to provide U.S. support for South Vietnamese raids against North Vietnam. In April he appointed Gen. William C. Westmoreland as U.S. commander in Vietnam. In June he replaced Ambassador Henry Cabot Lodge with Gen. Maxwell Taylor. Westmoreland and Taylor favored increased troop levels in Vietnam.

The 1964 Tonkin Gulf crisis was a crucial event in the war's escalation. In retaliation for reported attacks on U.S. destroyers, Johnson ordered bombing of North Vietnamese naval bases and oil depots and asked Congress to pass the Tonkin Gulf Resolution, authorizing him to take "all necessary measures to repel any armed attacks against the forces of the United States and to prevent further aggression." The measure passed the House by a vote of 416–0 and the Senate by 88–2, with dissenting votes by Democratic senators Ernest Gruening and Wayne Morse.

In the years that followed, the Tonkin Resolution was used to justify presidential war-making in Vietnam. In February 1965 Johnson ordered retaliatory bombing of North Vietnam after Communist forces attacked U.S. military posts at Pleiku and Qui Nhon. When McGeorge Bundy, after a visit to Vietnam, warned Johnson that without increased U.S. action, defeat appeared inevitable "within the next year or so," Johnson commenced Operation ROLLING THUNDER, and with intensified bombing came increased troop commitments. In April 1965 Johnson approved Westmoreland's request to use U.S. forces for offensive operations anywhere in South Vietnam. In July 1965, Johnson announced that U.S. forces there would be increased from 75,000 to 125,000 men, with additional troops to be provided as Westmoreland requested them. The war became increasingly Americanized. Before the close of Johnson's presidency in January 1969, there were more than 500,000 U.S. troops in Vietnam.

Johnson frequently expressed a desire for peace. On 10 May 1965, he called the first of several bombing halts, but when Hà Nôi did not respond, air strikes resumed. Speaking in San Antonio on 29 September 1967, Johnson offered to stop air and naval attacks on the DRV in exchange for a promise not to take advantage of the halt to infiltrate men and supplies into South Vietnam. Hà Nôi refused, insisting that discussions could not take place until the U.S. stopped bombing without conditions.

The war devastated Johnson's Great Society as costs forced cutbacks in programs and fostered inflation. Johnson agreed to a $6 billion budget reduction in nondefense spending in 1967 and in 1968 imposed a 10 percent tax surcharge. The federal deficit grew from $8.7 billion in 1967 to $25.2 billion in 1968. By 1968 the Johnson administration suffered from a "credibility gap" resulting from public disillusion produced by falsely optimistic statements about the war. Opposition to the Vietnam War developed at home. Democratic Senator J. William Fulbright, chairman of the Senate Foreign Relations Committee, began hearings on the war in 1966. George F. Kennan, the father of the containment doctrine, was among those who appeared before the committee to criticize the war. In October 1967, 100,000 war protestors gathered in Washington, D.C.

Debate also swirled within the administration. Undersecretary of State George W. Ball opposed the war early on and continued to argue against escalation until he resigned in 1966. Presidential advisor Clark Clifford on 17 May 1965 cautioned Johnson to keep ground forces in Vietnam to a minimum and warned that U.S. presence there could turn into a "quagmire." By spring 1967 Secretary of Defense Robert McNamara, once a proponent of escalation, recommended restricting bombing and limiting troop levels. These critics were opposed by Westmoreland and the Joint Chiefs of Staff, who continued to press for a more intensive ground war, additional troops, and increased bombing. In November 1967, Johnson requested that Clifford arrange a meeting of a group of elder statesmen headed by Dean Acheson, subsequently dubbed the "Wise Men," to advise him on Vietnam policy. In their meeting with the president on 21 November, they offered divided opinions that bolstered Johnson's determination to continue the war.

The January 1968 Tết Offensive caused Johnson to reevaluate the war. When Westmoreland requested another 205,000 troops after Tết, the president asked Clifford—who had just replaced McNamara as secretary of defense—to head a task force examining the request. The task force offered a dramatic reassessment of Vietnam, recommending only a 20,000-man increase and urging increased responsibility for the war effort by the government and army of the Republic of Vietnam. Johnson's acceptance of the task force's recommendations marked the first change in policy since escalation began in 1964.

Preliminaries to the 1968 presidential election demonstrated the political costs of the Vietnam War. In the 13 March 1968 New Hampshire primary election, Senator Eugene McCarthy, running on an antiwar platform, won 42 percent of the Democratic vote, which was regarded as a defeat for the president (who was not officially entered in the primary). Soon afterward, Robert F. Kennedy entered the nomination race as an antiwar candidate.

In a television address to the nation on 31 March, Johnson announced a halt to naval and air attacks on North Vietnam except in the area just north of the Demilitarized Zone. At the end of his speech he made the stunning announcement that he would neither seek nor accept the Democratic nomination for president.

The DRV expressed willingness to enter peace talks, which began in May 1968 in Paris, with the United States represented by W. Averell Harriman. On 31 October Johnson ordered a complete cessation of air and naval attacks on North Vietnam. The Paris talks, bogged down in disagreements about the shape of the negotiating tables, proved inconclusive through the end of Johnson's presidency. In the November presidential election Richard Nixon defeated Vice-President Hubert Humphrey in a decision that was seen as a referendum on "Johnson's War."

Johnson retired to his Texas ranch following Nixon's inauguration. Vietnam continued to trouble him. He told biographer Doris Kearns Goodwin, "I knew from the start that I was bound to be crucified either way I moved. If I left the woman I really loved—the Great Society—in order to get involved in that bitch of a war on the other side of the world, then I would lose everything at home.... But if I left that war and let the Communists take over South Vietnam, then I would be seen as a coward and my nation would be seen as an appeaser and we would both find it impossible to accomplish anything for anybody anywhere on the entire globe."

—Kenneth R. Stevens

References: Barrett, David M. *Uncertain Warriors: Lyndon Johnson and His Vietnam Advisors* (1993); Berman, Larry. *Lyndon Johnson's War: The Road to Stalemate in Vietnam* (1989); —. *Planning a Tragedy: The Americanization of the War in Vietnam* (1982); Goldman, Eric F. *The Tragedy of Lyndon Johnson* (1969); Goodwin, Doris Kearns. *Lyndon Johnson and the American Dream* (1976); Herring, George C. *LBJ and Vietnam: A Different Kind of War* (1994); Johnson, Lyndon B. *The Vantage Point: Perspectives on the Presidency, 1963–1969* (1971); Schandler, Herbert Y. *The Unmaking of a President: Lyndon Johnson and Vietnam* (1977); VanDeMark, Brian. *Into the Quagmire: Lyndon Johnson and the Escalation of the Vietnam War* (1991).

See also: Acheson, Dean G.; Ball, George W.; Bundy, McGeorge; Clifford, Clark M.; Containment Policy; Domino Theory; Federal Bureau of Investigation (FBI); Fortas, Abe; Fulbright, J. William; Goldwater, Barry Morris; Gruening, Ernest Henry; Humphrey, Hubert H.; Joint Chiefs of Staff; Kennan, George Frost; Kennedy, John Fitzgerald; Kennedy, Robert Francis; Kosygin, Aleksei Nikolayevich; Lodge, Henry Cabot, Jr.; Manila Conference; MARIGOLD, Operation; McCarthy, Eugene Joseph; McCone, John Alex; McNamara, Robert S.; Morse, Wayne Lyman; Nixon, Richard Milhous; Pearson, Lester Bowles; Project 100,000; ROLLING THUNDER, Operation; Roosevelt, Franklin Delano; San Antonio Formula; Stevenson, Adlai E.; Taylor, Maxwell Davenport; Tết Offensive: Overall Strategy; Tết Offensive: the Sài Gòn Circle; Tonkin Gulf Incidents; Tonkin Gulf Resolution; United States: Department of Justice; United Nations and the Vietnam War; Vietnam Information Group (VIG); Westmoreland, William Childs; "Wise Men."

Johnson, U. Alexis (1908–)

U.S. career diplomat and State Department official. His 1964 appointment as deputy ambassador to the Republic of Vietnam (RVN) under Gen. Maxwell D. Taylor was intended to underscore the importance of the Sài Gòn embassy. In 1965 the two men initially opposed the commitment of U.S. ground troops to Vietnam, but once made, they believed that the United States should not retreat from it. Johnson opposed any bombing halt or attempt to open negotiations with the Democratic Republic of Vietnam (DRV).

As undersecretary of state for political affairs (1969–1973), Johnson, like other State Department officials, was largely excluded from major decisions on Vietnam. Johnson believed that Vietnamization of the war was too hastily implemented to be successful and that the United States should have been more generous in supplying the RVN with military advisors and equipment. He retired from the State Department in 1977.

—Priscilla Roberts

References: Gibbons, William Conrad. *The U.S. Government and the Vietnam War* (1986, 1989); Johnson, U. Alexis, with Jef Olivarius McAllister. *The Right Hand of Power* (1984).

See also: Rogers, William Pierce; Taylor, Maxwell Davenport;

United States: Involvement in Vietnam, 1954–1965; United States: Involvement in Vietnam, 1965–1968; United States: Involvement in Vietnam, 1969–1973; Vietnamization; Washington Special Actions Group (WSAG).

Joint Chiefs of Staff

U.S. military body established early in 1942 as a counterpart to the British Chiefs of Staff Committee. The arrangement was formalized and codified by the 1947 National Security Act that created the Department of Defense out of the former War and Navy Departments.

The Joint Chiefs of Staff (JCS) is a corporate body consisting of the chiefs of staff of the Army and Air Force, the chief of naval operations, and the commandant of the Marine Corps. It is headed by the chairman of the Joint Chiefs of Staff (CJCS). As required by the 1947 National Security Act, as amended, the corporate body of the JCS has the responsibility and duty to advise the U.S. National Command Authorities (NCA) (the president and the secretary of defense) and National Security Council (NSC) and give strategic guidance to joint commanders in war. Because each member, excluding the CJCS, is the chief of his particular service, service interests and interservice competition for scarce resources can influence each chief's recommendations. In addition, the personality and style of every president and secretary of defense affects the level of impact the advice of the JCS provides.

Early in U.S. involvement in Vietnam, the Joint Chiefs of Staff, fearing the French would draw the United States into deeper involvement, recommended that the military not assume the mission to train the Vietnamese Army until a stable Vietnamese government formally requested that help. On the other hand, the State Department argued that one way to strengthen and stabilize that government would be to reorganize and train its army. President Eisenhower agreed with the State Department and approved U.S. assistance in creating indigenous military forces for internal security in Vietnam.

President Kennedy partially dismantled the formal NSC organization in favor of a more ad hoc, collegial style of decision-making that diminished access to the president by the JCS in national security decisions. Despite his failure to consult with the JCS until after the decision to launch the disastrous Bay of Pigs invasion of Cuba, Kennedy blamed them for poor military advice. Until he could maneuver the current chiefs and chairman out of office and replace them with men of his own choosing, Kennedy appointed retired Gen. Maxwell D. Taylor to the concocted position of military representative to the president.

Taylor was eventually recalled and appointed CJCS; his overwhelming influence on the NCA made any opposition to his views by the other chiefs futile. Taylor's belief in reduced reliance on massive nuclear retaliation in favor of a stronger conventional response influenced Kennedy and McNamara to put their faith in the concept of flexible response, particularly in combating Soviet-supported wars of national liberation. Vietnam became the Kennedy administration's test case for limited war concepts under flexible response. By summer

1963, Kennedy had replaced the CJCS, the Army chief of staff, and the chief of naval operations with younger men more amenable to his style and outlook. Although old and new members did not see eye-to-eye over the concept of fighting limited wars, they were united in their opposition to a coup against Republic of Vietnam (RVN) President Ngô Đình Diêm as disruptive to the U.S. effort in Vietnam.

Kennedy's death bequeathed to Lyndon Johnson an advisory circle that effectively excluded the advice of the JCS. The JCS did not agree with the administration's proposed strategy of measured, graduated pressure against North Vietnam, preferring a hard, decisive blow to the North and "hot pursuit" of the enemy into neutral sanctuaries. The chiefs did not have direct access to the president, nor were their views ever conveyed to the president by McNamara or Taylor.

Stymied in their attempts to establish a strategic alternative to graduated pressure, the JCS began to focus on ways the war could be prosecuted. Its members became accomplices in the failure to establish a clear objective in Vietnam, hoping that escalation by degrees would eventually lead to achieving maximum force and a decisive blow. Rather than resign in protest over what they believed to be a failing policy, they stayed on in mistaken loyalty to their commander-in-chief and the belief that they were needed to protect the interests of their individual services.

—Arthur T. Frame

References: Davidson, Phillip B. *Vietnam at War: The History, 1946–1975* (1988); Herring, George C. *LBJ and Vietnam: A Different Kind of War* (1994); Kinnard, Douglas. *The War Managers* (1985); McMaster, H. R. *Dereliction of Duty: Lyndon Johnson, Robert McNamara, The Joint Chiefs of Staff, and the Lies That Led to Vietnam* (1997).

See also: Bundy, McGeorge; Collins, Joseph Lawton; Counterinsurgency Warfare; Eisenhower, Dwight David; Flexible Response; Greene, Wallace M.; Hilsman, Roger; HOT PURSUIT Policy; Johnson, Harold K.; Joint General Staff; Kennedy, John Fitzgerald; LeMay, Curtis Emerson; Lemnitzer, Lyman; McNamara, Robert S.; Military Assistance and Advisory Group (MAAG), Vietnam; Military Assistance Command, Vietnam (MACV); Radford, Arthur W.; Ridgway, Matthew B.; Shoup, David M.; Taylor, Maxwell Davenport; Taylor-McNamara Report; Tonkin Gulf Resolution; United States: Involvement in Indo-China through 1954; United States: Involvement in Vietnam, 1954–1965; United States: Involvement in Vietnam, 1965–1968; Wheeler, Earle G.

Joint General Staff

Senior military body of the Republic of Vietnam Armed Forces (RVNAF). The Joint General Staff (JGS) was subordinate to civilian control, answering to the minister of defense, and exercised operational control over the RVNAF. From its Sài Gòn headquarters it controlled JGS reserve forces—the Airborne and Marine Divisions—and directed the war effort through the Army, Air Force, and Navy chiefs of staff and the four Army of the Republic of Vietnam (ARVN) corps commanders.

The Vietnamese National Armed Forces (VNNAF) were officially created on 11 May 1950. The Ministry of Defense, although authorized by treaty, initially assumed the duties of the General Staff when it began functioning in May 1951. The Joint General Staff was created a year later in May 1952.

On 26 October 1955, the VNNAF became the RVNAF. Under this structure, the president of the republic was also minister of defense, assisted by a secretary of state for defense. Therefore the chief of the General Staff and the corps and division commanders were required to report directly to the president for important matters or at his summons. The president also made all promotion decisions within the armed forces. The U.S. Military Assistance and Advisory Group (MAAG), Vietnam, recommended a different command structure, but President Diêm rejected it.

After Diêm's assassination in 1963, the JGS ostensibly remained in existence, but control of the RVNAF and the war effort fell under authority of the Military Revolutionary Council, composed of the ruling military junta. In mid-1965, political power was turned over to ten young generals who formed the National Leadership Committee (NLC), with Lt. Gen. Nguyên Van Thiêu, as chairman, becoming chief of state and Air Marshal Nguyên Cao Ky, as deputy chairman, becoming prime minister. Other members of the NLC filled roles as minister of defense and chief of the Joint General Staff.

During the rule of the NLC, and later under the Thiêu presidency, the JGS again played the role for which it was created, and the U.S. Military Assistance Command, Vietnam (MACV) worked closely with the JGS on overall military plans and operations. The JGS rejected a combined MACV/RVNAF command and staff arrangement because of political sensitivities. Instead, a Free World Military Assistance Council—composed of the chief of the JGS, the senior Korean officer in Vietnam, and the MACV commander—provided operational guidance to, but not control of, Free World Forces.

—Arthur T. Frame

References: Cao Van Viên. "Leadership" (1981); Clarke, Jeffrey J. *Advice and Support: The Final Years, 1965–1973* (1988); Palmer, Bruce, Jr. *The 25-Year War: America's Military Role in Vietnam* (1985); Summers, Harry G. *Vietnam War Almanac* (1985).

See also: Bao Đai; Cao Van Viên; Elections (National), Republic of Vietnam: 1955, 1967, 1971; Free World Assistance Program; High National Council (HNC); Joint Chiefs of Staff; Military Assistance and Advisory Group (MAAG), Vietnam; Military Assistance Command, Vietnam (MACV); Military Revolutionary Council; National Leadership Council; Ngô Đình Diêm; Nguyên Cao Ky; Nguyên Khánh; Nguyên Van Thiêu; Vietnam, Republic of: 1954–1975.

Joint U.S. Public Affairs Office (JUSPAO)

Office handling media relations and psychological warfare operations. The Joint U.S. Public Affairs Office (JUSPAO), created in 1965 under the direction of Barry Zorthian, coordinated a huge propaganda campaign but is best remembered as a quasi-military/civilian ministry of information. Daily briefings by information officers of the Military Assistance Command, Vietnam (MACV) at JUSPAO's Sài Gòn head-

quarters—known as the "Five O'clock Follies" because of reliance on fragmentary, inaccurate field reports—became the main source of hard news about U.S. military activities. Each Thursday, JUSPAO released "body counts," which the media routinely passed on without comment. Before the 1968 Têt Offensive, the press usually took claims of impending victory at face value, but reporters coming from the action would sometimes rise to tell "what really happened." JUSPAO's more than 600 employees provided abundant services to reporters. Peter Braestrup recalled, "by late 1967, JUSPAO was an extremely helpful, even luxurious, logistics center for newsmen."

The confusion of Têt negated an extensive campaign to counteract negative reporting, and JUSPAO made major public relations errors. Optimistic early descriptions of the combat situation in Sài Gòn and Huê and soaring Communist casualty statistics contradicted realities observed by reporters. Fragmentary communiqués were inadequate for providing overviews of countrywide trends or the performance of the Army of the Republic of Vietnam—conspicuously excluded from MACV reports. Efforts by JUSPAO to inculcate a sense of the importance of public relations among leaders of the Republic of Vietnam and its armed forces were largely unsuccessful.

—John D. Root

References: Braestrup, Peter. *Big Story* (1978); Hallin, Daniel C. *The "Uncensored War": The Media and Vietnam* (1986); Hammond, William M. *Public Affairs: The Military and the Media, 1962–1968* (1988).

See also: Body Count; "Five O'Clock Follies;" Media and the War; Military Assistance Command, Vietnam (MACV); Têt Offensive: Overall Strategy; Têt Offensive: the Sài Gòn Circle; Zorthian, Barry.

Jones, David C. (1921–)

Deputy commander for operations and vice-commander of the U.S. Seventh Air Force in Vietnam in 1969. As deputy commander of operations and vice-commander of the Seventh Air Force, Jones coordinated mission planning and operations, including air missions over North Vietnam and Cambodia. Jones was promoted to full general in 1971 and in 1978 was appointed chairman of the Joint Chiefs of Staff. He retired from the Air Force in 1982.

—Cynthia Northrup

Reference: Cole, Robert H., Lorna S. Jaffe, Walter S. Poole, and Willard J. Webb. *The Chairmanship of the Joint Chiefs of Staff* (1995).
See also: Air Power, Role in War; United States: Air Force.

JUNCTION CITY, Operation (22 February–14 May 1967)

Second corps-sized operation of the war; one of the largest offensive operations conducted by Allied forces. JUNCTION CITY involved four Army of the Republic of Vietnam (ARVN) and 22 U.S. battalions, including elements of the U.S. 1st, 4th, 9th, and 25th Infantry Divisions, the 11th Armored Cavalry Regiment, and the 196th Infantry and 173d Airborne Brigades.

JUNCTION CITY followed by one month Operation CEDAR FALLS. Its launch had been delayed a month to allow planners to correct some operational problems that surfaced during CEDAR FALLS. JUNCTION CITY's primary objective was elimination of the Viêt Công (VC) 9th Division in War Zone C, a Communist-controlled sanctuary from which the VC had long operated freely. War Zone C was a 50- by 30-mile marshy area along the Cambodian border, northwest of Sài Gòn, dominated by Núi Bà Đen (Black Woman Mountain), a 3,235-foot-high land mass honeycombed with caves and suspected as the forward headquarters of the Central Office for South Vietnam (COSVN).

The JUNCTION CITY plan called for the 3d Brigade, 4th Infantry Division and the 196th Infantry Brigade to take up a western blocking position along the Cambodian border. The 1st Infantry Division would block the east, along Highway 4. The 173d Airborne Brigade and the 1st Brigade, 1st Infantry Division would seal off the northern section. The 11th Armored Cavalry Regiment (on the right) and the 2d Brigade, 25th Infantry Division (on the left) would then sweep into this giant inverted horseshoe from the south. On 2 February the 25th Infantry Division launched Operation GADSDEN, and twelve days later the 1st Infantry Division launched Operation TUCSON. The objective of both operations was to position the western and eastern flank forces.

JUNCTION CITY commenced on 22 February with the north envelopment. The 173d Airborne Brigade's 2d Battalion, 503d Infantry parachuted unopposed into drop zones near Cà Tum, seven miles from Cambodia, the only major U.S. "combat" jump of the war. Simultaneously, 249 helicopters inserted eight infantry battalions into the north side in one of the largest mass helicopter lifts of the war. The following day, the southern forces positioned along Highway 247 started sweeping north into the horseshoe.

On 28 February, units of the 173d Airborne Brigade discovered the Viêt Công's Central Information Office. That same day, near the eastern tip of the horseshoe, the 1st Division's 1st Battalion, 16th Infantry engaged the 2d Battalion, 101st People's Army of Vietnam (PAVN) Regiment at Prek Klok. On 10 March, the 272d VC Regiment attacked the 168th Engineer Battalion, which was building a Special Forces base camp at Prek Klok. The engineers were defended by the mechanized 2d Battalion, 2d Infantry, and the 2d Battalion, 33d Artillery firing howitzers point blank into the attackers.

On 18 March JUNCTION CITY entered Phase II, which focused on clearing the eastern sector of War Zone C. The 173d Airborne Brigade pulled out of the operation and was replaced by the 1st Brigade, 9th Infantry Division. Over the course of the next two weeks, the three major engagements of Operation JUNCTION CITY followed in rapid succession. During the night of 19 March, the 273d VC Regiment attacked and almost overran the 9th Infantry Division's Troop A, 3d Squadron, 5th Cavalry in their defensive perimeter at Âp Bàu Bàng. While Troop A continued to hold on, the 3/5th Cavalry's Troops B and C fought their way into the beleaguered perimeter. Throughout the night the Air Force conducted 87 close air support runs under flare illumination.

In the early morning of 21 March, the 273d VC Regiment attacked the 4th Infantry Division's 3d Battalion, 22d Infantry and 2d Battalion, 77th Artillery at Fire Support Base (FSB) Gold near Suôi Tre. As that battle wore on, a relief force from the 2d Battalion, 12th Infantry fought its way into FSB Gold, where fighting continued into the daylight hours. FSB Gold was finally relieved by elements of the 2d Battalion, 34th Armor.

The last big fight of JUNCTION CITY took place near Âp Gù, at Landing Zone (LZ) George. The 1st Battalion, 26th Infantry, commanded by Lt. Col. Alexander M. Haig, had occupied LZ George on 26 March. Five days later the battalion was moving east from LZ George when Company B came under heavy fire. Haig had to commit his Company A to break Company B free. Near day's end, both companies were able to withdraw to the defensive perimeter near the LZ, which had been reinforced by elements of the 1st Battalion, 16th Infantry. In the early morning of 1 April, the 271st VC Regiment and the 1st Battalion, 70th VC Guards Regiment attacked in force. A combination of artillery fire, helicopter gunships, and tactical air support finally drove them off.

Although Operation JUNCTION CITY was originally planned to have only two phases, Phase III kicked off on 15 April. A "floating brigade" of one mechanized battalion from the 25th Infantry Division and an ARVN battalion made constant sweeps through War Zone C while the 196th Infantry Brigade was sent north to the I Corps tactical zone. Phase III sweeps turned up mostly empty countryside.

On the tactical level, Operation JUNCTION CITY was a success. Although Communist propaganda organs claimed huge U.S. and ARVN losses, actual tallies were 282 killed and 1,576 wounded. Communist forces lost 2,728 killed and an undetermined number of wounded. However, JUNCTION CITY, as with so many other U.S. efforts, failed to yield long-term strategic leverage. Although the three regiments of the VC 9th Division were temporarily shattered, they would be back in force less than a year later for the 1968 Têt Offensive.

War Zone C was far from neutralized, but JUNCTION CITY made Gen. Vô Nguyên Giáp painfully aware that VC bases in the South were vulnerable to U.S. mobility and firepower. As a result, the Communists moved their headquarters into Cambodia, where North Vietnamese regular forces were already based. With the United States unwilling to expand large-scale offensive operations into Cambodia, U.S. military planners were left with little option but to pursue a defensive campaign with the objective of wearing down the VC and PAVN through attrition.

—David T. Zabecki

References: Rogers, Bernard W. *Cedar Falls–Junction City: A Turning Point* (1974); Stanton, Shelby L. *The Rise and Fall of an American Army: U.S. Ground Forces in Vietnam, 1965–1973* (1985). **See also:** CEDAR FALLS, Operation; COSVN (Central Office for South Vietnam or Trung Uong Cuc Miên Nam); DePuy, William E.; Haig, Alexander Meigs, Jr.; Iron Triangle; Vô Nguyên Giáp; War Zone C and War Zone D; Westmoreland, William Childs.

K

Kampuchea. *See* Cambodia.

Kampuchean National Front

Socialist Republic of Vietnam (SRV)–sponsored organization formed in 1978 to combat the Khmer Rouge regime in Kampuchea.

The Khmer Rouge was hostile to Vietnam as a result of what it perceived as an earlier lack of support for its cause by the Democratic Republic of Vietnam (DRV), disputes over borders and the sovereignty of some small islands in the Gulf of Thailand, and the position of Khmer peoples living in southern Vietnam. These clashes soon escalated into open conflict. In September 1977 the SRV claimed that four Kampuchean divisions had invaded Tây Ninh Province, and in September and December Vietnam retaliated. In December, 60,000 troops, supported by tanks and artillery, struck as far as the outskirts of Svay Rieng and Kompong Cham. After the Vietnamese withdrew from Kampuchea in early January 1978, the Khmer Rouge carried out a purge in which up to 100,000 Cambodians were executed. Many Khmer Rouge fled into Vietnam and later formed the backbone of the Vietnamese-sponsored anti–Khmer Rouge resistance.

In December 1978, the Vietnamese government assisted in the formation of the Kampuchean National Front from several Kampuchean dissident groups opposed to the Pol Pot regime. Led by Heng Samrin, a Khmer Rouge defector, their forces numbered about 20,000 men, mostly former Khmer Rouge. On 25 December 1978, twelve regular Vietnamese infantry divisions invaded Kampuchea on a wide front. The Khmer Rouge withdrew into the country's western hinterlands.

Heng Samrin's small army walked into Phnom Penh unopposed on 7 January 1979. A pro-Vietnamese government, the People's Republic of Kampuchea, with Heng Samrin as president, was then installed. Fighting in Kampuchea continued, however, even after the September 1989 withdrawal of the SRV.

—Edward C. Page

References: Becker, Elizabeth. *When the War Was Over* (1986); Chanda, Nayan. *Brother Enemy* (1986); Etcheson, Craig. *The Rise and Fall of Democratic Kampuchea* (1984); Hardy, Gordon, Arnold R. Isaacs, and MacAlister Brown. *Pawns of War: Cambodia and Laos* (1987); Isaacs, Arnold R. *Without Honor: Defeat in Vietnam and Cambodia* (1983); O'Ballance, Edgar. *The Wars in Vietnam, 1954–1980* (1981).

See also: Cambodia; Heng Samrin; Khmer Rouge; Lon Nol; Pol Pot; Sihanouk, Norodom; Vietnam, Socialist Republic of: 1975 to the Present.

Kattenburg, Paul (1922–)

U.S. State Department desk officer on Vietnam, 1963–1964. As an Indo-China research analyst from 1952 to 1956, Kattenburg opposed Dean Rusk and others in the State Department who pushed for U.S. assistance to the French in Indo-China. He frequently visited South Vietnam and came to believe that the Ngô Đình Diêm government could not survive and that the Viêt Công would ultimately win the conflict. In the early 1960s he was one of a group of Vietnam skeptics, centering on W. Averell Harriman, in the State Department.

At a 31 August 1963 meeting of the National Security Council, Kattenburg, then head of the Interdepartmental Working Group on Vietnam, expressed doubts about U.S. involvement in Vietnam and recommended withdrawal, the first time a U.S. government official had done so. In 1964 Kattenburg was transferred to the less sensitive position of director of regional planning, concentrating on peace negotiation scenarios, and was deliberately excluded from all Vietnam-related issues until his 1972 retirement from government.

—Priscilla Roberts

References: Kattenburg, Paul. *The Vietnam Trauma in American Foreign Policy, 1945–75* (1980).

See also: Harriman, W. Averell; McNamara, Robert S.; Ngô Đình Diêm; Rusk, Dean; United States: Involvement in Vietnam, 1954–1965.

Katzenbach, Nicholas (1922–)

U.S. Attorney General, 1965–1966; under secretary of state, 1966–1969. In 1964 Katzenbach succeeded Robert F. Kennedy as attorney general upon the latter's resignation.

In June 1965 President Johnson and his close advisors sought Katzenbach's professional opinion on the legality of committing U.S. military forces in Vietnam under the Tonkin Gulf Resolution. Then, and in later congressional hearings, Katzenbach stated that the resolution was sufficiently broad to encompass such action and that the president need seek no further authority from Congress to increase U.S. troops in Vietnam to 95,000 men. He also warned that, should Johnson consult Congress again on this issue, it might attach conditions to any troop commitment.

Despite his lack of training or expertise in foreign affairs, Katzenbach in September 1966 was appointed under secretary of state, succeeding George Ball, an outspoken opponent of U.S. involvement in Vietnam. Katzenbach's legal background initially led him to perceive his role as that of an advocate and representative of his client rather than that of an active shaper of alternatives. Before congressional committees, he continued to justify the government's 1965 troop commitment. Privately, he came to feel that the war was unwinnable. By May 1967 he joined those in the administration, notably Secretary of Defense Robert McNamara, who favored negotiating a compromise peace plan and U.S. withdrawal.

In November 1967, Katzenbach and McNamara argued that the government should resist further increases in U.S. troop levels and move toward stabilizing the existing government of South Vietnam and a U.S. withdrawal, advice that

Dean Rusk and Walt Rostow rejected. As acting secretary of state, Katzenbach attended the crucial meetings of the president's senior advisors in late March 1968 that concluded that the United States should withdraw from Vietnam, a decision that contributed to Johnson's decision not to seek reelection. Katzenbach then helped to develop potential U.S. negotiating positions for use in anticipated peace talks with the Democratic Republic of Vietnam.

—Priscilla Roberts

References: Berman, Larry. *Lyndon Johnson's War* (1989); Gibbons, William Conrad. *The U.S. Government and the Vietnam War* (1989); Halberstam, David. *The Best and the Brightest* (1973).

See also: Clark, William Ramsey; Johnson, Lyndon Baines; Kennedy, John Fitzgerald; Kennedy, Robert Francis; McNamara, Robert S.; Rostow, Walt Whitman; Rusk, Dean; Tonkin Gulf Resolution; United States: Department of Justice; United States: Involvement in Vietnam, 1965–1968.

Kelly, Charles L. (1925–1964)

The Vietnam War's foremost exponent of aeromedical evacuation (medevac). On 11 January 1964, Maj. Kelly assumed command of the 57th Medical Detachment (Helicopter Ambulance) and quickly instilled his pilots with his own philosophy of putting the patient—American, South Vietnamese, and even Việt Công—before all else.

Kelly aggressively pushed his pilots and pioneered new techniques in dangerous night evacuations. He also fought a running bureaucratic battle with the Army Surgeon General's Office in Washington and with Sài Gòn-based U.S. Army Support Command chief Brig. Gen. Joseph W. Stilwell, who believed valuable helicopters should be used for general duties and fitted with removable red crosses only when they were actually needed for medevac missions. Kelly fought hard to keep his five Hueys dedicated to his unit's primary mission.

Kelly led by example and flew as many missions as his pilots. On 1 July 1964 near Sóc Trang in the Mekong Delta, Kelly was taking on wounded from a supposedly secure area when he came under fire and was killed. He was awarded a posthumous Distinguished Service Cross.

As other medevac units arrived in Vietnam, they adopted Kelly's philosophy, although few ever reached the standards of the 57th. According to Patrick Brady, one of Kelly's pilots, all medevac units also eventually adopted the 57th's radio call sign; 30 years later, "dustoff" still means aeromedical evacuation in the U.S. Army.

—David T. Zabecki

References: Brady, Patrick H. "When I Have Your Wounded" (1989); Dorland, Peter, and James Nanney. *Dust Off: Army Aeromedical Evacuation in Vietnam* (1982).

See also: Helicopters, Allied and Democratic Republic of Vietnam; Helicopters, Employment of, in Vietnam; Medevac; Medicine, Military.

Kennan, George Frost (1904–)

U.S. career diplomat and historian, articulator of the policy of containment, and realist critic of U.S. foreign policy. Kennan achieved a notable record as a scholar of foreign policy, and

his reputation as a diplomat and scholar made his views on the Vietnam War important.

Kennan believed the war was based on a flawed understanding of his containment doctrine, overemphasis on the domino theory, and an unrealistic assessment of U.S. interests. In February 1965 he testified before the Senate Foreign Relations Committee that a Communist Vietnam posed no probable threat to U.S. security and would likely adopt a foreign policy independent of Moscow or Beijing. The Unites States should not precipitately leave Vietnam, he asserted, but should gradually withdraw, leaving the effort to the South Vietnamese. He denied that withdrawal would weaken U.S. credibility.

In 1968 Kennan supported Eugene McCarthy as Democratic candidate for the upcoming election, although he remained a social conservative who criticized the behavior of the student antiwar movement.

—Kenneth R. Stevens

References: Hixson, Walter L. *George F. Kennan: Cold War Iconoclast* (1990); Kennan, George F. *American Diplomacy, 1900–1950* (1951); —. *Memoirs, 1925–1950* (1967); —. *Memoirs, 1950–1963* (1983); —. "The Sources of Soviet Conduct" (1947); Mayers, David. *George Kennan and the Dilemmas of US Foreign Policy* (1988); Miscamble, Wilson D. *George F. Kennan and the Making of American Foreign Policy, 1947–1950* (1992); Stephanson, Anders. *George Kennan and the Art of Foreign Policy* (1989).

See also: Acheson, Dean G.; Containment Policy; Domino Theory; Kennedy, John Fitzgerald; McCarthy, Eugene Joseph.

Kennedy, Edward Moore (1932–)

U.S. senator from Massachusetts who vocally opposed the war in Vietnam. In 1962 Edward won his brother John's abandoned Senate seat and in 1964 won election to his first full Senate term, the youngest senator ever elected.

Although initially supportive of U.S. involvement in Southeast Asia, Kennedy turned against the war as U.S. participation escalated and casualties increased. He began to speak out against the war with his brother Robert, who was assassinated in 1968. Edward, devastated by this event, vowed to help end the war in Vietnam. He introduced a four-point plan that included an unconditional halt of the bombing of North Vietnam and a unilateral reduction of U.S. forces. He spoke out across the country, supported resolutions against the war, condemned President Nixon's Vietnamization policy, and used Senate hearings to focus on the plight of Vietnamese refugees.

Kennedy has retained his Senate seat into the 1990s and continues to speak frankly as a pragmatic liberal.

—Laura Matysek Wood

References: Burner, David. *The Torch is Passed* (1984); Sherrill, Robert. *The Last Kennedy* (1976).

See also: Kennedy, John Fitzgerald; Kennedy, Robert Francis; Nixon, Richard Milhous; Vietnamization.

Kennedy, John Fitzgerald (1917–1963)

President of the United States, 1960–1963. Kennedy's policies in Vietnam led to a neutralization of Laos, a dramatic increase in U.S. military assistance and advisors in South Vietnam, and complicity in the overthrow of the Ngô Đình Diêm government.

Vietnam was a nemesis with which Kennedy struggled until his assassination on 22 November 1963. Following the Bay of Pigs fiasco and Soviet leader Nikita Khrushchev's laying down the gauntlet at the Vienna summit and in Berlin, Kennedy felt compelled to take a stand in Vietnam against Communist "wars of national liberation." In 1961, increasing infiltration of men and arms from the Democratic Republic of Vietnam (DRV) into the Republic of Vietnam (RVN) led Kennedy to approve sending 400 U.S. Special Forces personnel to Vietnam, using roadside defoliants and crop herbicides (Operation RANCH HAND), and undertaking covert operations against the DRV. Kennedy agreed to provide funding to equip 30,000 new troops in the Army of the Republic of Vietnam (ARVN) (rather than the 100,000 President Diêm requested) and to increase the U.S.-funded and advised Meo army in Laos from 9,000 to 11,000 men. U.S. advisors were placed at every level of the RVN government and military.

Although his government accepted military reform and adopted the Strategic Hamlets Program, Diêm became increasingly less willing to accept U.S. advice on political reform. Thus the Kennedy administration focused on increasing efficiency in the war effort, providing helicopters and establishing a command-level headquarters, the Military Assistance Command, Vietnam (MACV), in 1962.

Continuing Pathet Lao offensives in Laos and North Vietnamese exploitation of the Hô Chí Minh Trail led the Kennedy administration to attempt to renegotiate the neutrality of Laos. The Kremlin, which had supplied arms to the Communist Pathet Lao in Laos since 1960, assured Assistant Secretary of State for East Asian Affairs W. Averell Harriman that they would cooperate in keeping the DRV from using Laos as a corridor into South Vietnam. Kennedy sent U.S. Marines to the Thai-Lao border, sent the Seventh Fleet to the region, and obtained the neutralization of Laos at Geneva in July 1962. But the DRV did not withdraw its troops or cease exploitation of the Trail. The United States accepted a false neutrality in southern Laos in return for preservation of a shaky neutrality in northern Laos, but conceded the Lao corridor to the Communists and severely limited U.S. strategic options.

As a result, Kennedy was more determined to prevail in Vietnam, but Diêm lost some confidence in U.S. resolve and became more resistant to U.S.-advocated reform, which he charged would only make his country a protectorate. In the Buddhist crisis that began in May 1963, the Kennedy administration and U.S. reporters saw religious persecution and repression that drove seven Buddhist bonzes to self-immolation. On 21 August 1963, Diêm's brother Ngô Đình Nhu orchestrated raids on pagodas in Huê, Sài Gòn, and other cities, arresting many Buddhists. The raids strained U.S. patience and seemed to endanger the war effort.

Three days after the pagoda raids, a cable from acting Secretary of State George Ball—the real authors of which were Harriman and Roger Hilsman at the State Department

and Michael Forrestal at the White House—instructed the new U.S. Ambassador to Sài Gòn, Henry Cabot Lodge, to provide direct support to "appropriate military commanders … urgently examine all possible alternate leadership and make detailed plans how we might bring about Diêm's replacement if this should become necessary." The administration was divided as never before on this issue, but adopted a policy of "not thwarting" a coup. A military assessment by Gen. Maxwell Taylor and Secretary of Defense Robert McNamara indicated the war effort had not been hurt by the crisis, but this impression was not correct, because the Vietnamese had greatly exaggerated their success. Although they did not see a coup as imminent, they warned that Diêm and Nhu could be assassinated. Kennedy was sufficiently concerned to send Congressman Torbert MacDonald to warn Diêm and urge him to drop brother Nhu. Diêm remained adamant despite the cut in aid to his government that Lodge ordered as a signal to the generals who were plotting the removal of the Ngô brothers.

Kennedy tried to halt the coup after learning that the generals might have insufficient strength to prevail. The generals struck on 1 November and Diêm and Nhu surrendered the next day, only to be executed. The news shook Kennedy, who had little time to act before falling to an assassin's bullets three weeks later.

—Claude R. Sasso

References: Hammer, Ellen, J. *A Death in November: America in Vietnam, 1963* (1987); Hannah, Norman. *The Key to Failure: Laos and the Vietnam War* (1988); Reeves, Richard. *President Kennedy: Profile of Power* (1993); Thompson, Kenneth, ed. *The Kennedy Presidency: Seventeen Intimate Perspectives of John F. Kennedy* (1985).

See also: Ball, George W.; Buddhists; Flexible Response; Forrestal, Michael V.; Geneva Accords; Harriman, W. Averell; Hilsman, Roger; Johnson, Lyndon Baines; Kennedy, Robert Francis; Lodge, Henry Cabot, Jr.; McCone, John Alex; McNamara, Robert S.; Ngô Đình Diêm; Ngô Đình Nhu; Nolting, Frederick, Jr.; RAND Corporation; Stevenson, Adlai E.; Taylor, Maxwell Davenport; Taylor-McNamara Report.

Kennedy, Robert Francis (1925–1968)

U.S. attorney general, 1961–1964; U.S. senator, 1965–1968; presidential candidate, 1968. In 1960 Robert Kennedy managed his brother's successful campaign for the presidency and thereafter became attorney general. As one of his brother's chief advisors, he became increasingly involved in foreign policy and national security issues and supported U.S. initiatives in Southeast Asia.

Following his brother's assassination, Robert Kennedy stayed on as attorney general under Lyndon Johnson but in 1964 resigned to run for the Senate from New York. In the Senate, Kennedy initially supported U.S. efforts in Vietnam. He did lament the toll the war took upon his brother's Alliance for Progress and Johnson's Great Society programs, and he criticized the 1965 U.S. intervention in the Dominican Republic. Despite his growing apprehension toward the war, especially the massive bombing of North Vietnam, he refrained from openly opposing administration policy. He was also acutely aware of the appearance of opportunism and the public perception of his political motives. But as racial strife and urban violence intensified along with mounting antiwar sentiment, Kennedy found it increasingly difficult to avoid the fray.

After Senator Eugene McCarthy's unexpectedly strong performance in the 1968 New Hampshire primary, Kennedy entered the race and quickly emerged as a serious contender for the presidency. On 4 June 1968 he won the all-important California primary, thereby becoming his party's front runner. That night, after addressing his supporters at the Ambassador Hotel in Los Angeles, he was shot by Sirhan Sirhan and died the following day. Kennedy's assassination, only weeks after that of Martin Luther King, Jr., devastated the nation.

—David Coffey

References: *Dictionary of American Biography* (1988); Schlesinger, Arthur M., Jr. *Robert Kennedy and His Times* (1978).
See also: Antiwar Movement, United States; Democratic Party National Convention, 1968; Humphrey, Hubert H.; Johnson, Lyndon Baines; Kennedy, Edward Moore; Kennedy, John Fitzgerald; King, Martin Luther, Jr.; McCarthy, Eugene Joseph; McCarthy, Joseph Raymond; Nixon, Richard Milhous; Schlesinger, Arthur M., Jr.

Kent State University (4 May 1970)

Site of an incident involving members of the Ohio National Guard and student demonstrators that left four students dead and nine wounded. The protests at Kent State were part of a widespread, spontaneous reaction to the announcement by President Nixon of an "incursion" into Cambodia. Other universities voted at the time to strike in protest against the war, and by 4 May nearly 100 campuses were on strike or planning to strike.

At Kent State demonstrations began on 1 May. Property was damaged, and the mayor of Kent called for the National Guard. On 2 May a large rally took place on campus, after which the Reserve Officers' Training Corps (ROTC) building was burned. The following day, the National Guard took up positions on campus. That evening, students who gathered on the Commons were tear-gassed and dispersed.

On 4 May the Guard, after unsuccessfully attempting to disperse a crowd of perhaps 2,000 people, suddenly began firing at students gathered in a parking lot. The firing began at 12:25 P.M. and lasted for 13 seconds. Approximately 61 rounds were fired, killing Allison Krause, Jeffrey Miller, Sandra Scheuer, and William Schroeder. Only Krause and Miller had been active participants in the rally. The university was closed by court order later that day, but the Guard remained on duty until 8 May.

The President's Commission on Campus Unrest (the Scranton Commission) issued a report in September criticizing violent protest, but condemning the Guard's actions as "unnecessary, unwarranted, and inexcusable."

—Michael Richards

References: Anderson, Maggie, and Alex Gildzen, eds. *A Gathering of Poets* (1992); Bills, Scott L., ed. *Kent State/May 4: Echoes Through a Decade* (1982); Gordon, William A. *The Fourth of May: Killings and Coverups at Kent State* (1990); Morgan, Edward P. *The 60s Experience: Hard Lessons about Modern America* (1991); Zaroulis, Nancy, and Gerald Sullivan. *Who Spoke Up? American Protest against the War in Vietnam, 1963–1975* (19840.
See also: Antiwar Movement, United States; Cambodia; Cambodian Incursion; Jackson State College; Media and the War; Nixon, Richard Milhous; Television and the Vietnam Experience.

Kerry, John Forbes (1943–)

Vietnam veteran, war hero, and U.S. senator. After enlisting in the Navy and serving on a destroyer off the coast of Vietnam, Kerry volunteered to return in command of a "swift boat." Stationed first at Cam Ranh Bay and then on Phú Quôc Island, he was awarded the Silver Star, the Bronze Star, and three Purple Hearts.

Proud of his service and his men but "furious" about the goals and definition of the mission, Kerry made a moral commitment to oppose the war. He took part in the 1969 Moratorium to End the War in Vietnam demonstrations and later served as national coordinator for Vietnam Veterans Against the War (VVAW). He participated in the Winter Soldier Investigation in Detroit in 1971, during which more than 100 veterans testified about crimes they had participated in or witnessed. He testified before the U.S. Senate Foreign Relations Committee, posing the question "How do you ask a man to be the last man to die for a mistake?"

Kerry won election to the U.S. Senate from Massachusetts in 1984, one of the first Vietnam veterans elected to national office. He chaired the Senate Select Committee on POW/MIA Affairs from its creation in 1991 through its final, unanimous, highly charged 1993 report, which found "no compelling evidence that proves that any American remains alive in captivity in Southeast Asia."

—Paul S. Daum, with Joseph Ratner

References: *Congressional Quarterly Almanac.* 102d Congress. 2d Session (1993); Kimery, Anthony. "John Kerry: The Senate's Rising Voice for Veterans" (1990); Moritz, Charles, ed. *Current Biography Yearbook 1988;* Weiss, Stephen, Clark Dougan, David Fulghum, Denis Kennedy. *Vietnam Experience: A War Remembered* (1986).
See also: Antiwar Movement, United States; HOMECOMING, Operation; Missing in Action, Allied; Moratorium to End the War in Vietnam; Prisoners of War, Allied; Quach Tom; Riverine Warfare; Vietnam, Republic of: Commandos; Vietnam Veterans Against the War (VVAW).

Key West Agreement (March 1948)

Agreement made by the Joint Chiefs of Staff and Secretary of Defense James Forrestal during a meeting at the Key West Naval Base 11–14 March 1948. Forrestal called the meeting after confusion over roles and missions arose because the National Security Act of 1947 failed to specify the contingencies in which one service might operate in another's primary area of responsibility.

The Key West agreement specified that the Navy would retain its aviation but would not develop a strategic air arm; naval aviation should be used over land for interdiction and close air support, but only with Air Force concurrence; the Marine Corps would be limited in size to four divisions and one field corps; and the Air Force and Army would divide responsibility for air defense of land.

The Key West Agreement gave the Air Force control of all land-based armed aircraft, but it allowed the Army to keep its small aircraft and helicopters for artillery spotting and a few other missions. In the 1950s the Army expanded this aviation charter to include transportation of troops into battle and supplying them inside the combat zone. The Army also armed its helicopters for defense. The Key West Agreement was the charter that ultimately made possible U.S. Army air-mobility in Vietnam.

—John L. Bell

References: Condit, Kenneth W. *The History of the Joint Chiefs of Staff: The Joint Chiefs of Staff and National Policy* (1979); Wolf, Richard I., ed. *The United States Air Force Basic Documents on Roles and Missions* (1987).

See also: Helicopters, Allied and Democratic Republic of Vietnam; Helicopters, Employment of, in Vietnam; United States: Air Force; United States: Army; United States: Marine Corps; United States: Navy.

Khâm Đuc, Fall of (11–12 May 1968)

Khâm Đuc Special Forces Camp was located in northwestern Quang Tín Province, ten miles from the Laotian border and 90 miles southwest of Đà Nang. The base was a launch site for cross-border Military Assistance Command, Vietnam (MACV) Studies and Observation Group (SOG) reconnaissance teams engaged in special operations along the Hô Chí Minh Trail. The garrison included U.S. and Republic of Vietnam Special Forces, Civilian Irregular Defense Group (CIDG) soldiers, and U.S. Army engineers. A satellite camp at Ngoc Tavak was three miles closer to the Laotian border.

Khâm Đuc became the only remaining Special Forces camp along the Laotian border in I Corps after the fall of Làng Vei during the 1968 Tết Offensive. Throughout April 1968, Communist units concentrated near Khâm Đuc. Because of the growing threat to the camp, 632 troops, primarily from the Americal Division, were flown in on 10 and 11 May, nearly doubling the size of the defending force. Early on the morning of 10 May, Ngoc Tavak was assaulted by two People's Army of Vietnam (PAVN) regiments. After fierce resistance, the camp was abandoned later that day.

Subsequent B-52 strikes apparently had little effect on PAVN forces, and encircling Communist forces pounded Khâm Đuc during 10 and 11 May. On 11 May, Gen. Westmoreland ordered the camp evacuated, and that night, all seven Allied hilltop outposts overlooking Khâm Đuc were overrun. During the morning of 12 May, massive ground assaults were launched against the camp perimeter.

At 0605 the commander of the Seventh Air Force was notified of the decision to evacuate the camp. All in-country and out-country Air Force units were ordered to make a maximum effort to support the evacuation. The first helicopter to land was hit by Communist fire and exploded, temporarily blocking the runway. After the runway was cleared, a C-130 was crippled by gunfire while landing but subsequent-

ly managed to take off. Meanwhile, Marine Corps and Army helicopters brought in ammunition and carried out wounded. At 1646, the evacuation of nearly 1,500 personnel was complete. Two days later, a helicopter rescued three U.S. Army soldiers who had escaped from an outpost overrun on the night of the 11th.

—Glenn E. Helm

References: Gropman, Alan L. *Airpower and the Airlift Evacuation of Kham Duc* (1979); Singlaub, John K., with Malcolm McConnell. *Hazardous Duty: An American Soldier in the Twentieth Century* (1991); Spector, Ronald H. *After Tet: The Bloodiest Year in Vietnam* (1993).

See also: Air Power, Role in War; Civilian Irregular Defense Group (CIDG); United States: Special Forces; Vietnam, Democratic Republic of: Army (People's Army of Vietnam [PAVN]); Vietnam, Republic of, Special Forces (Luc Luong Đac Biêt [LLDB]).

Khe Sanh, Battles of

(April–October 1967; January–March 1968)
The 1967 first Battle of Khe Sanh evolved from U.S.–Communist engagements in northern South Vietnam. As part of his overall strategy, Gen. William Westmoreland ordered the construction of interconnected bases along the Demilitarized Zone (DMZ) to act as an infiltration barrier, later using sensors and motion detectors to alert each base to enemy movements. The outposts were not to stop infiltration, but to funnel it to areas where bombers could strike Communist troop concentrations.

One outpost was Khe Sanh, a base camp on high ground surrounded by heights up to 3,000 feet, six miles from Laos and 14 miles from the DMZ. These Allied defenses, roughly connecting a series of valleys, were designed to prevent enemy forces from cutting South Vietnam in half. The village of Khe Sanh, inhabited by Vietnamese and Montagnards, was surrounded by smaller villages and French coffee plantations. Westmoreland hoped that Khe Sanh could serve as a patrol base for blocking enemy infiltration from Laos, a base for long-range patrol operations in Laos, a Western anchor for defense south of the DMZ, an airstrip for reconnaissance planes surveying the Ho Chi Minh Trail, and an eventual jump-off point for ground operations to cut the Trail.

In August 1962, U.S. Military Assistance Command, Vietnam (MACV) officials ordered U.S. Special Operations Forces (SOF) and Allied troops to establish a camp for surveillance operations near the village of Khe Sanh. SOF units, called Study and Observation Groups (SOGs), used it to launch extended long-range reconnaissance operations into Laos to observe enemy infiltration. If they found a large enemy concentration, they called in air strikes.

In April 1966, a single Marine battalion temporarily occupied the base. Six months later, Gen. Westmoreland directed U.S. Marines, over their objections, to build a single-battalion base immediately above the SOG base. In October one battalion of Marines occupied the base. By spring 1967 they had been reinforced to regimental strength by the III Marine Amphibious Force (MAF).

Soon afterward, SOGs observed marked increases in traffic on the Hô Chí Minh Trail, as did observation posts along the DMZ. Westmoreland believed the Communists were planning a siege at Khe Sanh, and in September he directed Seabees to upgrade the Khe Sanh landing strip to accommodate C-130s. Twenty-mile-range 175-mm guns were placed at Camp Carroll, 12 miles away in a secure area. Marine forces occupied these defenses.

In April 1967, a Marine patrol was ambushed west of Khe Sanh. A large rescue patrol suffered heavy casualties when many of their M16 rifles jammed, an incident leading to Congressional hearings and Army reforms that produced more reliability in the M16.

From 24 April to 12 May 1967, the 3d Marines initiated several major assaults on three Communist-occupied hills surrounding Khe Sanh. Fierce hand-to-hand fighting left 160 Marines dead and 700 wounded, but the Americans destroyed one entire People's Army of Vietnam (PAVN) regiment and a large artillery emplacement in progress. At the end of this period, the 3d Marines were replaced by the 26th Marines. These operations were part of Operations CROCKETT (April–July 1967) and ARDMORE (July–October 1967). Both were supported by a massive bombing campaign (SLAM) planned by U.S. Air Force Gen. William Momyer.

These 1967 engagements convinced Westmoreland that with adequate bombing and aerial resupply, U.S. outposts could survive even when outnumbered—a notion he sold to the Johnson administration. Thus, U.S. military planning called for maintaining and enlarging DMZ outposts, leading to the 1968 Battle of Khe Sanh.

Between October and December 1967, the Communists greatly built up their forces near Khe Sanh. U.S. Marines, reluctant to garrison the base in the first place, were ordered to fortify their defensive positions. At 2030 on 2 January 1968, a Marine reconnaissance patrol spotted six figures on a slope near the base's outer defenses and opened fire, killing five PAVN officers. The incident convinced Gen. Westmoreland that several thousand enemy soldiers were near Khe Sanh. Westmoreland, who was clearly using the Marines as bait to draw out the PAVN units, saw this as an opportunity for a decisive engagement.

Indeed, two regiments of the PAVN 325C division that had fought at Điên Biên Phu had crossed into South Vietnam from Laos and gathered northwest of Khe Sanh. Two regiments of the 320th Division had crossed the DMZ and were 20 miles northeast. They were supported by an armored regiment, two artillery regiments, and the 304th Division in Laos. PAVN forces totaled 20,000 to 30,000 men, many of whom were actually support or reserve forces.

Route 9, the only road to Khe Sanh, had been cut by the Communists months earlier, so Westmoreland poured in supplies and reinforcements via air. On the flights were numerous reporters anxious for a big story. By mid-January 6,000 Marines defended the main plateau and four surrounding hills named for their height—950, 881, 861, and 558. Approximately 3,000 Marines defended the Khe Sanh base itself, with 3,000 more split among the hill positions. Infantry at each garrison were supported by 105-mm howitzers and mortars.

At 0530 on 20 January, Capt. William Dabney and 185 men of Company I launched a patrol from Hill 881 South to Hill 881 North. Dabney sensed he would make contact that day and requested additional support. Col. David Lownds, commander of the 26th Marines, deployed 200 additional men to support the patrol. Dabney divided his group, sending one platoon up one ridge and another two platoons up the other. As they ascended, the Marines were preceded by a rolling artillery barrage. Dabney hoped the Communist troops would respond and give away their positions. Instead the PAVN veterans waited until a platoon led by Lt. Thomas Brindley came within close range and opened up with automatic rifles, machine guns, and rocket-propelled grenades. The point man was killed immediately and several other platoon members were hit.

Dabney sent a second platoon to flank the enemy position while Brindley called in artillery directly on his position. The second unit was hit as it advanced, and a massive firefight followed. Brindley ordered his men to make a dash for the enemy position. Although Brindley was killed and dozens of his men were wounded, with the support of fighter-bombers dropping napalm, the Marines took the position.

Lownds concluded early the same morning that a larger attack would ensue, and he ordered Dabney to withdraw. By nightfall Dabney's men were back on Hill 881S and the Khe Sanh combat base was on maximum alert. That night the Marines received information from an apparent Communist deserter that a major attack was planned on 881S and 861 at 0030 on the 21st. The Marines brought up several special weapons, including two Ontos assault vehicles capable of firing flechette rounds, each with 10,000 steel darts, and set out several layers of razor-sharp concertina wire, hundreds of claymore mines, and trip-flares.

PAVN forces attacked 861 on schedule, using bangalore torpedoes to break through Marine defenses. The Marines' initial position was overrun, but at 0500, supported by mortars, they counterattacked with success. At 0530 the PAVN began an intense rocket and artillery attack against Khe Sanh proper and hit the main ammunition dump, leaving the defenders with barely enough ordnance to return fire. Despite heavy damage to the landing strip, that afternoon six C-130 planes arrived. Their 24 tons of cargo was mostly artillery shells, but Col. Lownds estimated he would need 160 tons of supplies per day to hold out.

At 0630 the PAVN attacked the village of Khe Sanh. Allied troops utilized air and artillery support to repel the attack. Thousands of villagers fled to seek refuge with the Marines, who did not allow them into their lines for fear of sabotage. Nearly 3,000 tried to escape down Route 9 to Đông Hà but only 1,432 arrived. Despite setbacks, Marine defenses remained strong.

The ammunition dump explosion produced headlines that fed public concerns about U.S. involvement in Vietnam. President Johnson became so concerned that he had hourly reports sent to him and a map room set up in the White House basement with a large board replica of Khe Sanh.

Westmoreland controlled air operations, personally picking targets based on advice from Gen. Momyer. For several days after the first attacks, B-52s bombed targets every three hours, dropping between 60,000 to 75,000 tons of bombs by March 31. U.S. fighter-bombers flew an average of 300 sorties daily, and B-52s struck PAVN command center caves in Laos. At times they dropped bombs within 1,000 yards of the Khe Sanh perimeter. Still, regular PAVN rocket attacks continued, making life on the plateau both difficult and dangerous. Sniper duels were commonplace and became macabre games of life and death. Despite these tensions, morale at Khe Sanh remained high throughout the siege.

Between 21 January and 5 February, the enemy mounted several small attacks against new Marine positions on Hill 861A. On 5 February PAVN troops overran a portion of Hill 861, killing seven Marines. The Marines retook the position using tear gas and air and artillery support. Mortar crews on 881S fired 1,100 rounds into PAVN positions. The fighting ended in hand-to-hand combat. In mid-February the defenders were completely overrun. Twenty-one Marines were killed and 26 injured. Dead Marines lay on the field unburied for a month until the siege ended.

On 6 March Communist forces began their withdrawal. By the 9th only a few thousand rear guard units remained. Operation SCOTLAND, the final part of the siege at Khe Sanh, ended on 1 April, officially terminating the battle. The same day Allied units began Operation PEGASUS to reopen Route 9. On the 8th they linked up with Khe Sanh. The next day was the first since 21 January that no enemy shells struck the Marine base. Two months later, on 26 June 1968, U.S. forces abandoned Khe Sanh base.

The official casualty count for the Second Battle of Khe Sanh was 205 Marines killed in action and more than 1,600 wounded. Base Chaplain Ray W. Stubbe placed the death toll closer to 475. This does not include Americans killed in collateral actions, Army of the Republic of Vietnam (ARVN) Ranger casualties on the southwest perimeter, 1,000 to 1,500 Montagnards who died during the fighting, or the 97 U.S. and 33 ARVN troops killed in relief efforts. MACV estimated PAVN losses at 10,000 to 15,000 men, mostly the result of U.S. B-52 ARC LIGHT bombing raids and other aerial and artillery support. The official body count was 1,602.

The siege of Khe Sanh in particular and the Tết Offensive in general disheartened the American public, who began to question the cost and worth of Vietnam to America. Khe Sanh and Tết marked the beginning of the end for U.S. involvement in Southeast Asia.

Who won the second Battle of Khe Sanh? Marine historian Jack Shulimson observed, "Controversy still surrounds the battle. It is not known if the North Vietnamese really intended to take Khe Sanh or if the attack was merely a feint to lure U.S. forces away from the cities." Gen. Giáp claimed victory for the PAVN, claiming the Communists never intended to overrun the Marine base. If the siege of Khe Sanh was meant to be only a Communist ruse, then it was a successful one. Significant U.S. military assets were diverted to this isolated area of South Vietnam, permitting Communist forces to attack many key cities of South Vietnam during the Tết Offensive.

For the U.S., Khe Sanh was meant to be the best opportunity to implement the strategy of attrition, to destroy Communist military forces at a rate above which they could be replaced. In the battle, U.S. forces achieved one of their most satisfying victories. Col. Lownds was convinced that they destroyed two entire PAVN divisions. Thus, if Khe Sanh was intended as another Điên Biên Phu, it failed.

—William Head and Peter Brush

References: Head, William, and Lawrence Grinter, eds. *Looking Back on the Vietnam War: A 1990s Perspective on the Decisions, Combat, and Legacies* (1993); Momyer, William. *Air Power in Three Wars* (1978); Nalty, Bernard C. *Air Power and the Fight for Khe Sanh* (1973); Pisor, Robert. *The End of the Line: The Siege of Khe Sanh* (1982); Prados, John, and Ray W. Stubbe. *Valley of Decision* (1991); Shulimson, Jack. *U.S. Marines in Vietnam, 1966* (1982).
See also: ARC LIGHT (B-52 Raids); Demilitarized Zone (DMZ); Hồ Chí Minh Trail; Johnson, Lyndon Baines; Momyer, William W.; PEGASUS–LAM SON 207A, Operation; SCOTLAND, Operation; Tết Offensive: Overall Strategy; Tết Offensive: the Sài Gòn Circle; United States: Marine Corps; United States: Special Forces; Võ Nguyên Giáp; Westmoreland, William Childs.

Khieu Samphan (1931–)

A top Khmer Rouge leader. As a student in France, Khieu Samphan already showed left-wing tendencies, and on returning to Phnom Penh in 1959, he started the biweekly French newspaper *L'Observateur*, which mixed praise of Cuba, China, and the Soviet Union with articles on Cambodia. By 1962 he had joined Sihanouk's Sangkum and been elected to the National Assembly. Reelected to the National Assembly in 1966, he fled to the countryside the following year when the Samlaut uprising provoked Sihanouk to denounce the Khmer Rouge.

After Sihanouk's deposition, Khieu Samphan reappeared as deputy prime minister and defense minister in Sihanouk's resistance government, then as commander in chief of the resistance forces. He also became a member of the Central Committee of the Communist Party of Kampuchea. After 1976 he was the chairman of the State Presidium, the head of state of Democratic Kampuchea. Following the Vietnamese invasion, he returned to the jungle, where his forces continued to be supplied arms by China.

Under the 1991 peace agreement, Khieu Samphan was the senior Khmer Rouge member of the Supreme National Council, composed of two representatives of each faction under the chairmanship of Sihanouk. His return to Phnom Penh was marked by a violent demonstration, thought to have been organized by the security services of the Phnom Penh government faction, which forced him to flee temporarily to Bangkok. The Khmer Rouge having withdrawn from the peace agreement, Khieu Samphan resurfaced in 1994 as prime minister and minister of the national army of the clandestine Provisional Government of National Union and National Salvation opposed to the Phnom Penh coalition government.

—Arthur J. Dommen

References: Carney, Timothy Michael. *Communist Party Power in Kampuchea (Cambodia)* (1977); Khieu Samphan. *Cambodia's Economy and Industrial Development* (1979).
See also: Cambodia; Khmer Rouge; Sihanouk, Norodom.

Khmer. *See* Cambodia.

Khmer Kampuchea Krom (KKK)

Anti-Communist faction, loosely allied with the Khmer Serai, that sought autonomy for Khmer Krom people living in the Mekong River Delta of South Vietnam in return for their military services. During the 1960s numerous ethnic regular and irregular force battalions within the Army of the Republic of Vietnam (ARVN) were composed of Khmer Krom soldiers.

A Khmer Krom battalion from the ARVN 25th Division participated in Cambodian Gen. Lon Nol's 17 March 1970 coup against Prince Norodom Sihanouk. Afterward, Sài Gòn sent further Khmer Krom forces from the Republic of Vietnam (RVN) to Phnom Penh to strengthen the newly organized Forces Armées Nationale Khmer (FANK).

Traditionally aggressive, Khmer Krom soldiers were highly experienced from years of fighting in South Vietnam. By February 1972 they made up a high percentage of the FANK's effective military strength, serving in 13 infantry brigades and the Khmer Special Forces. However, extensive casualties in largely unsuccessful operations, as well as increasing disaffection among some units kept in Cambodia past their promised return dates, led to an increase of nonethnic replacements and a dilution of the best Khmer Krom formations. By March 1972 only the Khmer Krom 7th, 44th, and 51st Brigades were still highly regarded. Six months later, a mutiny in a Khmer Krom battalion caused recruiting in South Vietnam to dry up, and the reputation of Khmer Krom military prowess came to an ignominious end.

—Edward C. Page

References: Caldwell, Malcolm, and Lek Tan, *Cambodia in the Southeast Asian War* (1973); Conboy, Kenneth, and Kenneth Bowra, *The War in Cambodia 1970–75* (1989).

See also: Cambodia; FANK (Forces Armées Nationale Khmer); Khmer Serai (Free Khmer); Lon Nol; Sihanouk, Norodom.

Khmer Rouge

The name most commonly used for the most extreme and violent faction of Cambodian Communists. In power between 1975 and 1979, the Khmer Rouge herded millions of Cambodians into slave labor camps, executed hundreds of thousands, and were responsible for many more deaths from starvation, exhaustion, and disease. After being driven out of Phnom Penh by Vietnamese forces in early 1979, the Khmer Rouge waged a guerrilla resistance that was still active in large areas of the country more than 15 years later, despite a United Nations–sponsored agreement that was supposed to bring peace to Cambodia.

The origins of the Khmer Rouge date to the early 1960s, when a small group of revolutionaries launched a rebellion against Cambodian ruler Prince Norodom Sihanouk. Among the leaders was Saloth Sar, a French-educated Communist who later adopted the pseudonym Pol Pot as leader of the Khmer Rouge.

The uprising remained small during the 1960s, while the war in neighboring Vietnam exploded. Khmer insurgents received no help from the Vietnamese Communists, who had reached an accommodation with Sihanouk that allowed them to resupply and rest their troops on Cambodian territory, and who refrained, in return, from aiding Sihanouk's enemies.

To Saloth Sar and his colleagues, this branded the Vietnamese as enemies of their own struggle, even though both groups were Communist. Making a virtue of their isolation, they nurtured an increasingly extreme and violent vision of a "pure" revolution, which would succeed through sheer ideological zeal and an utter indifference to sacrifice or suffering.

After Sihanouk's overthrow in March 1970, the Khmer Rouge and Vietnamese Communists became mistrustful partners, both allied with Sihanouk, whose injured pride and thirst for revenge led him to join forces with his former enemies. Besides the Khmer Rouge, there appeared a Vietnamese-sponsored Cambodian resistance force led mainly by a cadre of Cambodians who had fought with the Viêt Minh against the French and had lived in Vietnam since the 1950s. Old antagonisms were submerged for several years, but around the beginning of 1973 the Khmer Rouge moved to seize full control of the revolution. Hundreds of Vietnamese-trained cadres were secretly executed, as were resistance leaders associated with Sihanouk, even while the prince himself, living in China, remained the figurehead leader of the revolutionaries' exile government.

Throughout the war, almost nothing was known of the Khmer Rouge outside Cambodia. The very name of the Communist Party of Kampuchea was kept secret, remaining so for two years after the war—history's only case of a Communist party remaining clandestine even after winning power. The insurgents were hardly less shadowy to the Cambodians themselves, who commonly referred to them only as the *peap prey* ("forest army"). But behind their curtain of secrecy, as they consolidated their power and pressed ever more heavily against Lon Nol's increasingly decrepit regime, the revolutionaries nursed their hatred of the Vietnamese and their fantasies of a revolution so sweeping that it would obliterate every trace of Cambodia's past.

17 April 1975, when Lon Nol's hapless army surrendered and the victorious guerrillas marched into Phnom Penh, was for the Khmer Rouge the first day of "Year Zero," the beginning of the total transformation of Cambodian society. Within hours the new rulers ordered the entire population of Phnom Penh to be expelled to the countryside, at once and with no exceptions.

Teen-aged revolutionary soldiers, remembered by one witness as "grim, robotlike, brutal," herded dazed civilians out of the capital. Sick and wounded hospital patients were turned out of their beds and forced to join the exodus. About half of the country's entire population was marched to the countryside. Former city-dwellers were put to work in slave labor camps, while the new regime, identifying itself only as *Angka Loeu* ("Organization on High"), embarked on a murderous purge of its former enemies and everyone else considered to represent the old society. Soldiers and civil servants of the former government were slaughtered, as were teachers, Buddhist priests and monks, intellectuals, and professionals. The party's frenzied search for enemies led inexorably to fantasies of traitors in its own ranks. In waves of purges, high-ranking leaders and their followers were killed, usually after gruesome torture. Approximately 20,000 executions were documented at Tuol Sleng, a Phnom Penh school converted into an interrogation center.

Meanwhile, the Khmer Rouge engaged in increasingly violent clashes with the Vietnamese. On 25 December 1978, 100,000 Vietnamese troops invaded, capturing Phnom Penh two weeks later. The city was still virtually empty, although after the Khmer Rouge fled, residents began trickling back.

The Vietnamese installed a new government headed by former Khmer Rouge commander Heng Samrin, but they were unable to quell continued resistance from Khmer Rouge soldiers who had regrouped in the countryside. Vietnamese forces withdrew in 1989 after a ten-year occupation. Two years later the Khmer Rouge and two smaller rebel factions signed a peace agreement with the Phnom Penh regime, now led by Hun Sen, but the Khmer Rouge never disarmed, nor did they take part in the May 1993 election for a new government. For several years Khmer Rouge guerrillas harassed government forces in widespread areas of the country. Beginning in 1996, however, the movement began to splinter. In August 1996 Ieng Sary, Pol Pot's ex–brother-in-law and one of his closest collaborators while the Khmer Rouge were in power, came over to the government side, bringing with him about 4,000 guerrillas who had been operating in western Cambodia. In return, Sary requested a royal amnesty, although he had been under a death sentence since 1979 for the bloodshed committed by the Khmer Rouge regime. King Sihanouk reluctantly granted his request.

The following spring, while increasingly violent conflict between the rival co–prime ministers Hun Sen and Prince Norodom Ranariddh all but paralyzed the Phnom Penh government, a new split opened up among Khmer Rouge leaders in their remaining stronghold in northern Cambodia. Dissident Khmer Rouge officials led by Khieu Samphan, the nominal "prime minister," held meetings with negotiators representing Prince Ranariddh to discuss terms for a ceasefire and the eventual reintegration of Khmer Rouge troops and territory under the national government. As part of the deal, the Khmer Rouge would overthrow Pol Pot, symbolically shedding their bloody past, and join Ranariddh's National United Front, a multiparty alliance organized to oppose Hun Sen's Cambodian People's Party. Their guerrillas would not be disarmed or disbanded and would remain in control of the territory they occupied.

The talks led to a last spasm of bloodletting within the Khmer Rouge in June 1997, as Pol Pot and his supporters sought to block an agreement. On Pol Pot's orders, longtime Khmer Rouge defense minister Son Sen was executed, along with family members. Shortly afterward, Pol Pot's group seized Khieu Samphan and the other senior members of the Khmer Rouge negotiating team. By this point, however, nearly all of Pol Pot's comrades, including his old colleague Ta

Mok, the Khmer Rouge military commander, had turned against him. Replenishing their supplies with weapons and ammunition flown in on government helicopters, anti–Pol Pot forces pursued their former "Brother No. 1" through the jungles near the Khmer Rouge base at Anlong Veng. On June 19 the 72-year-old leader, sick and exhausted and being carried on a stretcher, was captured.

With Pol Pot's arrest, the bloody history of the Khmer Rouge should have reached its final page. But the bargaining between his former comrades and Prince Ranariddh's negotiators had not just divided the Khmer Rouge. It also fatally split the unstable coalition in Phnom Penh. On 6 July, a day before an agreement with the new Khmer Rouge leaders was to be announced, Hun Sen seized power, forestalling the alliance between the Khmer Rouge and Ranariddh's forces. The prince fled the country and the Khmer Rouge melted back into their forest camps.

Several weeks later, the Khmer Rouge staged an extraordinary show trial to condemn Pol Pot—not for the hundreds of thousands of murders carried out under his rule in the 1970s, but for plotting against his fellow-executioners Son Sen and Ta Mok during the final breakup of the movement. After the charges against him were read out, the tribunal announced a sentence of life imprisonment.

Instead of being peacefully reabsorbed into Cambodian life, however, the Khmer Rouge and its new leaders were again engaged—in alliance with military units that had remained loyal to Prince Ranariddh—in armed resistance against the pursuing government army. Ieng Sary, Khieu Samphan, Ta Mok, and others with a good deal of blood on their own hands continued to play their part in a sorrowful cycle of vengeance and violence that had already lasted more than 30 years.

—Arnold R. Isaacs

References: Becker, Elizabeth. *When the War Was Over* (1986); Chanda, Nayan. *Brother Enemy* (1986); Ponchaud, François. *Cambodia Year Zero* (1978).

See also: Cambodia; Heng Samrin; Hun Sen; Lon Nol; Parrot's Beak; Pol Pot; Sihanouk, Norodom; Vietnam, Socialist Republic of: 1975 to the Present.

Khmer Serai (Free Khmer)

Anti-Communist Cambodian resistance group led by nationalist Son Ngoc Thanh. Throughout the 1960s the Khmer Serai waged an intermittent struggle against the Communists and the Cambodian government of Prince Norodom Sihanouk. Loosely allied with the Khmer Kampuchea Krom, the Khmer Serai could not always depend on assistance from the Republic of Vietnam, although many Khmer Serai members served in unconventional warfare units organized and run by U.S. Army Special Forces.

The Khmer Serai operated from two main base areas. One was in Cambodia's Dongrek Mountains along the Thailand border. Dongrek Serai soldiers wore yellow or blue scarves and regular Army of the Republic of Vietnam (ARVN) field uniforms and were armed with AK47 rifles to enable them to use captured Communist ammunition. The other Khmer Serai base area was in the Mekong River Delta within the ARVN IV Corps operational area. These soldiers wore red scarves and South Vietnamese Police field uniforms and were armed with U.S. weapons to prevent their being mistaken for Communist insurgents.

On 17 March 1970, Khmer Serai rebel forces participated in Gen. Lon Nol's ouster of Prince Sihanouk. Dongrek Serai troops, after retraining in Thailand, then formed the core of the Siem Reap Special Brigade, which later became the highly regarded 9th Brigade Group of the Forces Armées Nationale Khmer (FANK).

—Edward C. Page

References: Caldwell, Malcolm, and Lek Tan. *Cambodia in the Southeast Asian War* (1973); Conboy, Kenneth, and Kenneth Bowra. *The War in Cambodia 1970–75* (1989).
See also: FANK (Forces Armées Nationale Khmer); Khmer Kampuchea Krom (KKK); Lon Nol; Sihanouk, Norodom; United States: Special Forces; Vietnam, Republic of: Army (ARVN).

Khrushchev, Nikita Sergeyevich (1894–1971)

Soviet politician/leader. Khrushchev succeeded Joseph Stalin as the party first secretary in 1953, then won a series of power struggles against other Soviet leaders to become the Soviet Union's supreme leader.

Although he never visited Vietnam, Khrushchev was the first Soviet leader to show sustained interest in Southeast Asia. Soviet influence with the Democratic Republic of Vietnam (DRV) declined in the early 1960s as Hà Nôi increasingly sided with the People's Republic of China in the rivalry between the two Communist giants.

Khrushchev's reasoning regarding Vietnam was twofold. On one hand, the growing prospects of war between the United States and the DRV presented the Soviet Union with great opportunities. A U.S. failure could reduce the West's influence in Asia and improve the Soviet bargaining position vis-à-vis the United States. Soviet assistance to the DRV would project a vitalized image of Soviet-style communism to counter the growing appeal of Maoism within the Third World. On the other hand, Vietnam offered danger of a possible military confrontation with the United States. Following the 1962 Cuban missile crisis, Khrushchev sought better relations with the United States and would tread very carefully in Vietnam.

As time passed, Khrushchev became disillusioned with the idea that Vietnam presented great opportunities. U.S. intelligence agents believed that Khrushchev favored only minimal involvement in the region. His perceived weak response following the Gulf of Tonkin incidents made him appear indecisive and fatally weakened his political base. DRV leaders despised Khrushchev and understood that he was willing to sacrifice Vietnam for the sake of peaceful coexistence with the West.

Khrushchev's efforts to decentralize the Soviet economy alienated the entrenched bureaucracy, which in October 1964 removed him from power. Khrushchev essentially became a nonperson, remaining in obscure retirement until his death.

—Michael Share

References: Cohen, Steven, ed. *The Soviet Union Since Stalin* (1980); Khrushchev, Nikita S. *Khrushchev Remembers* (1971); Medvedev, R. A., and A. A. Medvedev. *Khrushchev* (1978).
See also: Brezhnev, Leonid Ilyich; Union of Soviet Socialist Republics (USSR; Soviet Union); United Nations and the Vietnam War; Vietnam, Democratic Republic of: 1954–1975.

King, Martin Luther, Jr. (1929–1968)

U.S. civil rights leader and critic of involvement in Southeast Asia. A strong advocate of nonviolent protest, King followed the example of India's Mahatma Gandhi by urging civil disobedience to effect change.

King had been a solid supporter of President Johnson, who had produced a sweeping domestic agenda and landmark civil rights legislation. But King grew concerned over U.S. involvement in Vietnam and, as his concerns became increasingly public, his relationship with the Johnson administration deteriorated.

King viewed U.S. intervention in Southeast Asia as little more than U.S. imperialism carried out under the banner of fighting communism. He lamented that a disproportionate share of draftees were African Americans and that, as the conflict escalated, they made up a disproportionate share of battle casualties. But chief among King's concerns was his belief that growing U.S. commitment to Vietnam seriously threatened hard-won civil rights and social gains in the United States.

In 1967 King began called for a cessation of bombing in North Vietnam and for meaningful negotiations, offering himself as a moderator. King's antiwar stance drew widespread criticism. Civil rights advocates implored him not to endanger the movement by linking it with the controversial antiwar struggle. To King the two issues were inseparable, and he resolved to make them major issues in the 1968 presidential election. By this time, King and his followers were subjected to FBI surveillance and government smear tactics. In the midst of his most ambitious campaign to date, King was assassinated on 4 April 1968 in Memphis, Tennessee.

—David Coffey

References: Dougan, Clark, Stephen Weiss, et al., eds. *A Nation Divided* (1984); Oates, Stephen B. *Let The Trumpet Sound: The Life of Martin Luther King, Jr* (1982).
See also: African-American Personnel in U.S. Forces in Vietnam; Antiwar Movement, United States; Federal Bureau of Investigation (FBI); Great Society Program; Hoover, J. Edgar; Johnson, Lyndon Baines; Kennedy, Robert Francis; Project 100,000.

KINGFISHER, Operation (16 July–31 October 1967)

Military operation conducted in the Demilitarized Zone (DMZ) area by the 3d Marine Division. Its mission was to stop entry of the People's Army of Vietnam (PAVN) into Quang Tri Province. The five battalions that made up the 3d and the 9th Marines initiated the early stages of the operation.

The operation began on 16 July. Through 28 July there was minimal contact with the PAVN. On 28 July the 2d Battalion, 9th Marines (2/9), reinforced with tanks, went into the DMZ along Route 606. On the morning of 29 July the battalion began its withdrawal south of the DMZ when it came under fire from PAVN units in prepared positions along Route 606. Air strikes were then ordered to provide support for the Marines. Company M of the 3d Battalion, 4th Marines (3/4), which had been ordered to move up from Côn Thiên, assisted the command group in breaking through PAVN lines and setting up a defensive position. The number of casualties in the other companies of the 2d Battalion prevented further movement south until perimeter defenses were strengthened and medevac helicopters could evacuate wounded personnel.

Prior to 2/9's movement into the DMZ, an apparently minor incident occurred that later had significant tactical impact in northern I Corps. Marines uncovered a PAVN base camp, ambush sites, and antipersonnel mines along Route 9, a discovery that led to the end of vehicle convoys into Khe Sanh. Until Operation PEGASUS (1–15 April 1968), the Khe Sanh base relied on air resupply.

With elections in the Republic of Vietnam (RVN) scheduled for 3 September 1967, the Communists were determined to achieve victory at Côn Thiên. The most effective enemy attack took place on election day, destroying the ammunition storage area and bulk fuel farm at Đông Hà. Côn Thiên became the primary PAVN target; their forces fired 200 rounds almost daily on Marine positions there.

On 10 September, the 3d Battalion, 26th Marines (3/26) engaged a major element of the 812th PAVN Regiment around Côn Thiên and suffered more than 200 casualties. Following this attack, 3/26 moved back near Phú Bài to refit and was replaced by Lt. Col. James Hammonds, Jr.'s, 2d Battalion, 4th Marines. On 21 September, 2/4 started a search-and-destroy operation east of Côn Thiên, and by day's end, elements of the battalion were locked in a fierce firefight with part of the 90th PAVN Regiment. At dusk the battalion was forced to pull back inside its main perimeter.

Before the end of September, the PAVN mounted and failed in three attacks from three directions on Côn Thiên. More than 3,000 mortar, artillery, and rocket rounds were fired on Côn Thiên during 19–27 September. The Americans retaliated by massing one of the greatest concentrations of firepower in support of a single division in the Vietnam War. Nonetheless, by early October 2/4 had been reduced from 952 to 462 men.

On the early morning of 14 October, while defending a bridge south of Côn Thiên, 2/4 was taken under attack by a large PAVN force. By late morning it had pushed the attackers back. The PAVN had been attempting to destroy the only supply line to Côn Thiên. Again 2/4 sustained heavy casualties.

The last major action of Operation KINGFISHER took place between 25 and 28 October. During this period the 2/9's battalion strength dropped to fewer than 300 men. On 28 October 2/4 moved back to Đông Hà and assumed the role of regimental reserve. The Marines reported that Operation KINGFISHER resulted in 1,117 PAVN deaths; 340 Marines were killed in action, and 1,461 were wounded. A message from Gen. Cushman to 2/4 summed up the opinion of all concerning the heroic fighting around Côn

Thiên, reading, "2/4 has met and beaten the best the enemy had to offer. Well done."

—W. E. Fahey, Jr.

References: Command After Action Report, "Kingfisher" (1967); Tefler, Gary L., Lane Rogers, and V. Keith Fleming, Jr. *U.S. Marines in Vietnam: Fighting the North Vietnamese* (1984).

See also: Côn Thiên; Demilitarized Zone (DMZ); Khe Sanh, Battles of; United States: Marine Corps; Vietnam, Democratic Republic of: Army (People's Army of Vietnam [PAVN]).

Kinnard, Harry William Osborn (1915–)

U.S. Army general and first commander of an airmobile division in Vietnam. In 1965 Maj. Gen. Kinnard took the 1st Cavalry Division (Airmobile) to Vietnam after lobbying unsuccessfully to locate it in Thailand. The 1st instead was located at An Khê in the Central Highlands. Its mission was to seek and destroy People's Army of Vietnam (PAVN) units that might cut South Vietnam in half along Route 19.

Kinnard's hard-fought, successful Ia Drang campaign in 1965 demonstrated the effectiveness of airmobility in crippling PAVN forces in their secure areas. Kinnard wanted to pursue fleeing PAVN troops into Cambodia, but the White House would not allow it, leading him to believe that the U.S. would not win the war. Early in 1966 the 1st Cavalry moved to the coast to seek out Viêt Công and PAVN units and deny them access to the rice harvest. More hard fighting proved the division's abilities in pursuit.

Kinnard departed the 1st Cavalry in May 1966 and retired from the Army in 1969. His achievement was to demonstrate the effectiveness of airmobility.

—John L. Bell

References: Kinnard, Harry W. O. "A Victory in the Ia Drang: The Triumph of a Concept" (1967); Stanton, Shelby. *Anatomy of a Division: 1st Cav in Vietnam* (1987).

See also: Airmobility; Ia Drang, Battle of; United States: Army.

Kissinger, Henry Alfred (1923–)

Academic, foreign policy consultant, national security advisor to President Nixon (1969–1973), and secretary of state (1973–1977).

When Richard Nixon was elected president in 1968, he named Kissinger his national security advisor. The two shared a suspicion of traditional, bureaucratic State Department diplomacy, which they considered uncreative and slow moving. Nixon intended to keep control of foreign relations in the White House, with Kissinger as a more important advisor than Secretary of State William P. Rogers. They agreed that foreign policy should be based on realism rather than wishful idealism or moralism. Self-interest required that foreign policy rely on strength and the willingness to use force, and that other nations understood this.

In developing their realist policy, Kissinger and Nixon perceived a shift from the bipolar balance of power between the United States and the Soviet Union to a triangular order that also included the People's Republic of China. Working together—though often not harmoniously—Nixon and Kissinger eventually brought an end to U.S. participation in the Vietnam War, reached a détente with the Soviet Union that culminated in the Strategic Arms Limitation Talks (SALT) agreement, established diplomatic relations with the People's Republic of China, and helped achieve peace in the Middle East following the 1973 Yom Kippur War.

The war in Vietnam was the most difficult issue Kissinger faced. His concern about the conflict predated his service in the Nixon administration. Kissinger visited Vietnam in October 1965 and July 1966 as a government consultant. He concluded that U.S. military victory was unlikely, and in 1967, using French contacts, he acted as an intermediary between the Democratic Republic of Vietnam (DRV) and the Johnson administration in a fruitless effort to start negotiations. In a critique of the Vietnam War, written before he became national security advisor but published in the January 1969 issue of *Foreign Affairs*, Kissinger argued that the United States could not win the war "within a period or with force levels politically acceptable to the American people," but could not precipitately withdraw without damaging its credibility.

Soon after taking office, Kissinger ordered a study of the Vietnam problem from the RAND Corporation. The resulting National Security Study Memorandum 1 (NSSM-1), headed by Daniel Ellsberg, collected responses from government departments and agencies to 78 queries about the war. The responses demonstrated the differences that had developed within the government over the prospect of a satisfactory end to the war, with the Central Intelligence Agency (CIA) and the State Department generally more pessimistic than the military.

Peace talks between the United States and the DRV, initiated on 31 March 1968, had stalled by the time Nixon took office. Before his inauguration Nixon, with Kissinger's encouragement, sent a message to the DRV indicating the new administration's desire for serious discussions. The North Vietnamese reply of 31 December 1968 insisted on two points: unilateral withdrawal of U.S. forces and removal of the government of the Republic of Vietnam (RVN). These demands, which Nixon and Kissinger found unacceptable, were repeated in the first substantive private meeting between U.S. and DRV officials on 22 March 1969 and remained constant until nearly the end of negotiations in 1973.

Negotiations were further hindered by events in Cambodia. In March 1969 Nixon ordered the secret bombing of Cambodia (Operation MENU), which continued until May 1970. When news of this was leaked to the *New York Times* in May 1969, Nixon—with Kissinger's knowledge—initiated wiretaps on government officials and reporters.

In a 14 May 1969 press conference, Nixon unveiled his Vietnam policy, proposing simultaneous mutual withdrawal of U.S. and North Vietnamese forces, supervised free elections in South Vietnam with participation by the National Liberation Front, and a cease-fire. On 8 June, during a meeting with South Vietnamese president Nguyên Van Thiêu at Midway Island, Nixon announced U.S. troop withdrawals. Kissinger questioned this policy of "Vietnamization" in a memorandum to the president, arguing that unilateral troop withdrawals would encourage DRV intransigence in negotiations, demoralize troops remaining in Vietnam, and result in further demands for troop reductions in the United States.

Kissinger began intermittent secret peace talks with North Vietnamese representatives in Paris in August 1969. The negotiations deadlocked on DRV insistence that the United States unilaterally withdraw its forces and that the Thiêu government in Sài Gòn be removed.

On 1 May 1970, 31,000 U.S. and 43,000 South Vietnamese troops invaded Cambodia, and antiwar demonstrations erupted in the United States. Several of Kissinger's longtime aides resigned over Cambodia. In the aftermath of the Cambodian invasion, Nixon and Kissinger developed a proposal to restart negotiations. On 31 May 1971, Kissinger spelled out the offer in detail, agreeing to unilateral withdrawal of U.S. troops according to a timetable, with an understanding that there would be no further infiltration of "outside forces" into Vietnam. There would be a cease-fire-in-place throughout Indo-China, guarantees for the neutrality and territorial integrity of Laos and Cambodia, release of prisoners of war, and an agreement to leave the political future of South Vietnam up to its people. Although these provisions signaled significant concessions from the United States, the DRV rejected them, probably because it felt it could win greater concessions regarding the political settlement in South Vietnam.

The Nixon administration's overtures to China and the Soviet Union may have had some impact on the Vietnam negotiations. In July 1971, Kissinger secretly traveled to Beijing, where he and Chinese leader Zhou Enlai arranged for an official presidential visit to China. The historic summit in February 1972 reversed a policy of nearly 25 years during which the United States denied the legitimacy of the People's Republic of China. Following Nixon's trip, China moderated its protests against U.S. action in Vietnam. In August 1972, following Nixon's May summit meeting with Soviet premier Leonid Brezhnev in Moscow, the Hà Nôi politburo authorized a negotiated settlement with the United States.

In a meeting with Kissinger on 8 October, DRV representative Lê Ðuc Tho proposed an accord settling military questions—a cease-fire, withdrawal of U.S. forces, acceptance of continuing U.S. aid to the RVN, and return of prisoners of war—while leaving political matters—namely the future of the South Vietnamese government—to an "Administration of National Concord" representing the Sài Gòn government and South Vietnamese Communists. These terms were agreed to on 11 October, with details to be worked out later. On his return to the United States, Kissinger announced on 26 October "We believe that peace is at hand." On 7 November, Richard Nixon easily won reelection as president over George McGovern.

Peace was not at hand, however. President Thiêu refused to accede to the terms. Discussions with the DRV bogged down in disagreements about changes demanded by Thiêu, details of prisoner exchanges, withdrawals, and other matters. Talks broke off on 13 December.

This interruption led to one of the most controversial acts of Nixon's presidency. On 18 December the United States began the so-called Christmas bombing of North Vietnam (Operation LINEBACKER II), for the first time using B-52s over Hà Nôi and Hai Phòng. The raids proved costly for the United States and the DRV. Nixon halted the raids on 30 December after Hà Nôi indicated its willingness to return to negotiations. The bombing met with outrage in the United States and throughout the world.

Kissinger and Lê Đuc Tho reached a final agreement on 9 January 1973. The terms were substantially the same as those reached the previous October and close to those discussed in 1969, except for provisions regarding the continuance of the South Vietnamese government. Nixon announced the agreement on inauguration day, 20 January 1973.

Ending U.S. involvement in the war in Vietnam was the capstone of Kissinger's diplomacy and earned him wide acclaim. In December 1972, *Time* magazine named Nixon and Kissinger "Men of the Year," and a 1973 Gallup poll rated Kissinger first in a list of most admired Americans. In September 1973 Kissinger replaced William P. Rogers as secretary of state, a position he retained through the end of the Ford administration. In October Kissinger and Lê Đuc Tho were jointly awarded the Nobel Peace Prize for their Vietnam settlement. The DRV representative rejected the prize; Kissinger accepted but donated the prize money to a scholarship fund for children of military personnel killed in Vietnam.

Kissinger had achieved only what became known as a "decent interval" between removal of U.S. forces and a Communist takeover. Within a few months of the peace accord, the Watergate scandal began to unravel Nixon's presidency, and the Vietnam peace accords came apart. Sài Gòn fell to the Communists on 30 April 1975.

—Kenneth R. Stevens

References: Herring, George, ed. *The Secret Diplomacy of the Vietnam War: The Negotiating Volumes of the Pentagon Papers* (1983); Hersh, Seymour. *The Price of Power: Kissinger in the Nixon White House* (1983); Isaacson, Walter. *Kissinger: A Biography* (1992); Kalb, Marvin, and Bernard Kalb. *Kissinger* (1974); Kissinger, Henry. *White House Years* (1979); —. *Years of Upheaval* (1982); Morris, Roger. *Uncertain Greatness: Henry Kissinger and American Foreign Policy* (1977); Schulzinger, Robert. *Henry Kissinger: Doctor of Diplomacy* (1989); Stoessinger, John. *Henry Kissinger: The Anguish of Power* (1976).

See also: Elections, U.S.: 1968; Elections, U.S.: 1972; Ellsberg, Daniel; Johnson, Lyndon Baines; Kent State University; Lake, William Anthony Kirsopp; Lê Đuc Tho; LINEBACKER II, Operation; Madman Strategy; McGovern, George S.; Midway Island Conference; Nguyên Van Thiêu; Nixon, Richard Milhous; Paris Negotiations; Paris Peace Accords; Perot, H. Ross; Rogers, William Pierce; San Antonio Formula; Vietnamization; Washington Special Actions Group (WSAG).

Kit Carson Scouts

Former Vietnamese Communists, both military and political, who defected and then agreed to serve in combat units with U.S., Australian, and Thai military forces, primarily as scouts but also as soldiers, interpreters, and intelligence agents. The idea of using former Communists to aid U.S. military efforts began in May 1966 when a group of Viêt Công (VC) soldiers surrendered to units of the 9th Marines in the I Corps tactical zone, asking for asylum. The Communists immediately started a rumor among peasants that the Marines had tortured and killed Ngô Van Bay, one of the defectors. In response the Marine regimental commander asked Bay and two fellow defectors to return to the village, talk to the peasants, and put the rumor to rest. They did so and had such a positive effect on the local population that it was decided that other VC defectors brought under control of the Republic of Vietnam (RVN) through the Chiêu Hôi program could be used to aid U.S. military and pacification efforts. Eventually all Marine commands in tactical areas began using small numbers of rallied VC for a variety of combat and pacification tasks.

The Kit Carson Scout program was officially established in October 1966. The scout units proved so effective in their work for the Marine Corps that Gen. William Westmoreland soon encouraged all U.S. units to create similar units. By mid-1968 more than 700 former VC were serving with U.S. forces in South Vietnam. Many served with or supplemented U.S. Army Special Forces long-range reconnaissance patrols; others led U.S. units to VC and People's Army of Vietnam (PAVN) caches, camps, and trails during search-and-destroy operations. Kit Carson Scouts repeatedly proved themselves a valuable propaganda tool when working with villagers who were far more willing to listen to, and cooperate with, fellow peasants who had defected from the Communists than they were representatives of the RVN government.

When U.S. combat units withdrew from South Vietnam, most of the scouts volunteered to serve in ARVN units. After April 1975 most were sentenced to prison.

—Clayton D. Laurie

References: Shulimson, Jack. *The U.S. Marines in Vietnam: An Expanding War, 1966* (1982); Westmoreland, William C. "Report on Operations in South Vietnam, January 1964–June 1968" (1969).

See also: Chiêu Hôi (Open Arms) Program; Long-Range Reconnaissance Patrols (LRRPs); Pacification; United States: Marine Corps; United States: Special Forces.

Knowland, William F. (1908–1974)

Republican U.S. senator from California. Knowland was an ardent anti-Communist and leader of the right wing of the Republican Party. He gained notoriety as leader of the so-called China Lobby during the Truman and Eisenhower administrations. The China Lobby was a group of congressmen who staunchly defended Nationalist China, vehemently opposed admission of Communist China to the United Nations, and urged increased U.S. intervention to stop the spread of Communism in Korea, Vietnam, and China.

Knowland was an especially vocal supporter of Republic of Vietnam leader Ngô Đình Diêm. His influence affected the 1954 Geneva Conference. The senator and his supporters believed that any negotiations with the Communist Chinese would amount to U.S. recognition of the Communist regime, and they pressured Secretary of State John Foster Dulles into refusing to recognize Chinese Foreign Minister Zhou Enlai (Chou En-lai) in Geneva. Knowland, a member of the Senate Foreign Relations Committee, also prevailed on Dulles to downgrade the U.S. delegation to "observer" status, and Undersecretary of State Walter B. Smith took no part in negotiations. Despite these successes, Knowland considered Geneva a "Communist victory."

—John M. Barcus

References: Randle, Robert F. *Geneva 1954: The Settlement of the Indochinese War* (1969); Schoenebaum, Eleanora W., ed. *Political Profiles: The Eisenhower Years* (1980).

See also: Dulles, John Foster; Geneva Conference and Geneva Accords; McCarthy, Joseph Raymond; Ngô Đình Diêm; Smith, Walter Bedell; Zhou Enlai (Chou En-lai).

Komer, Robert W. (1922–)

Deputy to the Commander, U.S. Military Assistance Command, Vietnam (MACV), for Civil Operations and Revolutionary Development Support, 1967–1968. As a deputy special assistant to the president for national security affairs (1965–1966), and later as special assistant (1966–1967), Komer became increasingly involved with the pacification program in Vietnam. In February 1966 President Johnson appointed him Washington coordinator for pacification activities.

Komer's office became useful to young Army officers trying to overcome institutional resistance to results of the PROVN study, which concluded that the attrition strategy and search-and-destroy tactics being employed by Gen. William Westmoreland were not working and could not work. According to the study, the key to success was to concentrate on population security and pacification. Komer was sympathetic to that viewpoint and helped advance such ideas. Reporting on a June 1966 trip to Vietnam, Komer told Johnson, "Until we can get rolling on pacification in its widest sense—securing the villages, flushing out the local VC (not just the main force) and giving the peasant both security and hope for a better future, we cannot assure a victory."

Soon Komer drafted a proposal that responsibility for support of pacification be assigned to the U.S. military establishment in the Republic of Vietnam (RVN), with a civilian deputy running it. He had in effect written his own job description, although it took Secretary of Defense Robert McNamara's backing for the idea to gain acceptance. In March 1967 the decision was announced to put the Civil Operations and Revolutionary Development Support (CORDS) program under Westmoreland with Komer as his deputy. In May 1967 Komer, given the personal rank of ambassador, headed for Vietnam to undertake his new duties.

Ambassador Ellsworth Bunker recalled in his oral history that Komer was both "very able" and "very abrasive." Once on the job, Komer was given a free hand by Gen. Westmoreland who, according to William Colby in *Lost Victory*, did so "with some relief that he could let Komer do it while he continued to conduct the military war that he saw as his primary responsibility." Colby credited Komer with an overdue effort to build up the territorial forces and with pulling together disparate elements of the U.S. advisory effort at the province level.

Komer's overall influence on the pacification program remains uncertain. McNamara accords him a single sentence in his memoirs—hardly an indication of substantial impact. The record shows that only after Gen. Creighton Abrams assumed command of MACV, William Colby took over as deputy for CORDS, and President Nguyên Van Thiêu personally launched and pushed the Accelerated Pacification Campaign in November 1968 did pacification really began to show results.

—Lewis Sorley

References: Clarke, Jeffrey J. *Advice and Support: The Final Years, 1965–1973* (1988); Komer, Robert W. *Bureaucracy at War: U.S. Performance in the Vietnam Conflict* (1986); Scoville, Thomas W. *Reorganizing for Pacification Support* (1982).

See also: Abrams, Creighton; Bunker, Ellsworth; Civilian Operations and Revolutionary Development Support (CORDS); Colby, William Egan; McNamara, Robert S.; Nguyên Van Thiêu; Pacification; Westmoreland, William Childs.

Kong Le (1934–)

Laotian army officer. As a captain he led his paratroop battalion in the August 1960 coup d'état that overthrew the pro-Western government in Vientiane, hoping to put an end to the civil war in Laos.

Driven out of Vientiane by Phoumi Nosavan's troops in December 1960, Kong Le captured the Plain of Jars from Phoumi's troops in January 1961 with North Vietnamese help. A neutralist at heart, Kong Le grew disillusioned with the North Vietnamese intervention in Laos and by summer 1963 was again on the side of Phoumi Nosavan in supporting Prince Souvanna Phouma's efforts to neutralize Laos with international backing. Promoted to general, he fought the Pathet Lao and North Vietnamese as commander of the Neutralist army.

As a result of intrigues within the neutralist and rightist armies, Kong Le was discredited and, fearing for his life, he took refuge in the Indonesian embassy in Vientiane in 1966. A fierce opponent of Vietnamese communism, Kong Le visited China during the Vietnam-China war in 1979 in an attempt to gain Chinese support for liberating Laos from the Pathet Lao regime.

—Arthur J. Dommen

Reference: Dommen, Arthur J. *Conflict in Laos; the Politics of Neutralization* (1971).

See also: Laos; Phoumi Nosavan; Souvanna Phouma.

Korea, Democratic People's Republic of

North Korea. Established on 9 September 1948, the Democratic People's Republic of Korea (DPRK) formally recognized the Democratic Republic of Vietnam (DRV) as the legitimate government of all Vietnam in January 1950. North Korean Premier Kim Il Sung and his government in Pyongyang were well established allies of North Vietnam by 1965. Kim Il Sung believed that unity between all

Communist nations in Asia was vital to expelling the United States from the region, as evidenced by North Korean participation in the Asian Communist Summit of October 1959.

North Korean aid to Communist forces in Vietnam was mostly indirect, being largely technical and financial. Numerous agreements promised assistance and provided terms for reciprocal trade between the two countries, but the exact nature and extent of this is somewhat ambiguous. North Korea sent technicians to North Vietnam as early as 1960 and undoubtedly continued the practice throughout the war. Events such as the arrival of the North Korean defense minister in Hà Nôi on 18 December 1964 pointed strongly to military aid from Pyongyang.

North Korea never did provide large-scale direct military aid to the DRV. Kim Il Sung advocated direct aid, spurred by deployment of Republic of Korea (ROK) Army units to South Vietnam in October 1965. Pyongyang pledged to Hà Nôi that it would match South Korea's troop contribution to South Vietnam, but the DRV rejected the offer, preferring aid agreements of a more ambiguous nature. North Korea did supply minor direct military aid, however. In September 1965 the U.S. State Department confirmed the presence of 25 to 50 North Korean pilots in North Vietnam who served as trainers and participated in combat missions.

North Korea provided indirect assistance to the DRV with its attack on the spy ship U.S.S. *Pueblo* on 23 January 1968, although this was motivated by other reasons than the war in Vietnam. This action by Pyongyang did, however, force the redeployment of some U.S. military assets.

Although North Korea did not achieve the level of participation Kim Il Sung desired, the DPRK was by no means a passive observer.

—Eric W. Osborne

References: Fishel, Wesley R. *Vietnam: Anatomy of a Conflict* (1968); Koh, Byung Chul. *The Foreign Policy of North Korea* (1969); Smith, R. B. *An International History of the Vietnam War* (1983); Wintle, Justin. *The Vietnam Wars* (1991).

See also: Korea, Republic of; *Pueblo* Incident; United States: Air National Guard (ANG).

Korea, Republic of

The United States often defended its commitment in Vietnam because of obligations incurred under the 1954 Southeast Asia Treaty Organization (SEATO) pact, although two major signatories of that treaty, France and Great Britain, felt no such obligation after 1954 and the nations of Southeast Asia were forbidden to enter into any such arrangement by the Geneva Accords. Ironically, the country that contributed the most troops to Vietnam after the United States, the Republic of Korea (ROK), was not a member of SEATO.

The United States eagerly sought participation of the ROK Army, noted for its fighting ability. As early as 1953 ROK President Syngman Rhee suggested to the United States that he would furnish troops to aid the French in Vietnam. The Eisenhower administration carefully studied the offer but took no action. In 1953 the American people were unlikely to accept the use of ROK troops in Vietnam while U.S. troops were still in Korea. In addition, U.S. policymakers reacted negatively to Rhee's demand for a significant increase in U.S. aid to Korea. In June 1954, with events going poorly at Geneva, the idea resurfaced. Although Rhee's offer was more favorably considered on that occasion, the French rejected it.

Throughout the remainder of the 1950s the United States was engaged in the difficult task of establishing a democratic, non-Communist government in South Vietnam. For leadership, the United States turned to Ngô Đình Diêm. By early fall 1963, however, the experiment in nation-building was foundering. Diêm's stubborn refusal to heed U.S. advice to institute reforms, and his unpopular campaign against Vietnamese Buddhists, led to his November 1963 overthrow and subsequent assassination. The virtual anarchy that followed Diêm's fall led in 1964 to renewed calls for the introduction of third-country troops.

The Johnson administration was obsessed with the need to widen participation from other countries to support the unstable Sài Gòn government. The ensuing attempt to attract other nations was called the Many Flags program. Armies from the Republic of Korea provided the largest contingent to that program.

ROK troops began to arrive in Vietnam on February 26, 1965. In March the U.S. Joint Chiefs of Staff recommended deployment of two U.S. divisions and one ROK division to South Vietnam for ground combat operations, the first such recommendation for an open-ended commitment to combat. Gen. William Westmoreland decided that ROK troops would be deployed in the II Corps sector on Vietnam's east coast, scattered between Nha Trang north to an area just below Đà Nang.

Gen. Westmoreland wanted troops from each third country to operate under their own command. He hoped with this administrative structure to avoid any resemblance to French colonialism and, at the same time, eliminate the complications inherent in a multinational operation. He assumed, however, that these forces would follow orders from the United States. The assumption proved correct for most of the third countries involved, but not for the ROK, whose commanders operated as if on the same level as Westmoreland.

In October 1965 the pride of the ROK army, the Capital Division, arrived in South Vietnam. By March 1966 there were 23,000 third-country troops involved, most of them South Korean. At the close of 1969 there were 47,872 ROK troops in Vietnam, the most deployed at any one time. However, the Many Flags program included only four other nations (Australia, New Zealand, the Philippines, and Thailand), and all but Australia and New Zealand demanded and received remuneration for their service. None, however, demanded as much or received more than did the Republic of Korea.

In addition to funds designed to upgrade the ROK army in Korea, the United States paid Korean officers and enlisted men more for their services in Vietnam than the ROK government paid their counterparts at home. Between 1966 and 1970, Washington doled out more than $900 million to the Seoul government, and the figure grew as the Nixon administration added additional millions to persuade the ROK to leave two divisions in place until 1973. In that regard, forces from the Republic of Korea were mercenaries, not allies, and there is serious doubt that the United States received adequate dividends for such an enormous investment.

Although the ROK army was certainly a capable, well-trained fighting force, its soldiers were under orders from Seoul to take as few casualties as possible and were hesitant to move without significant support from U.S. air and ground forces. Also, reports of atrocities committed by ROK troops against Vietnamese civilians are far too numerous to overlook. In the final analysis, Col. Bruce Palmer was correct when he stated that "we never did get our full 'money's worth' from the ROKs."

—Francis H. Thompson

References: Kahin, George McT. *Intervention: How America Became Involved in Vietnam* (1987); Palmer, Bruce, Jr. *The 25-Year War: America's Military Role in Vietnam* (1984); Palmer, Dave R. *Summons of the Trumpet: U.S.-Vietnam in Perspective* (1995); Sheehan, Neil. *A Bright Shining Lie: John Paul Vann and America in Vietnam* (1988).

See also: Australia; IRVING, Operation; Korea, Democratic People's Republic of; New Zealand; Ngô Đình Diêm; Order of Battle; Philippines; Southeast Asia Treaty Organization (SEATO); Thailand; Westmoreland, William Childs.

Korean War (1950–1953)

In a 15-year span, the United States fought two wars on the Asian mainland: one in Korea and the other in Vietnam. Both were unpopular and at the time little understood by the American public.

On 25 June 1950, North Korea invaded South Korea. Five days later President Truman committed U.S. ground forces as part of a United Nations force to help defend South Korea. The North Koreans were halted at the so-called Pusan Perimeter and, after a successful amphibious operation at Inchon, United Nations (UN) forces crossed the 38th parallel and headed for the Yalu River. In November, forces of the People's Republic of China (PRC) entered the war in support of the North Koreans. After offensives on both sides, the war became one of attrition and stalemate roughly along the 38th parallel, where it had begun.

Many Americans regarded Korea as an Asian "domino," believing that if communism was not stopped there, other Asian countries would fall. Paris and Washington made the same case, and French officials were angry when the United States, fearing availability of additional Chinese resources for Korea, prevented a more favorable settlement with the Việt Minh than the one Paris secured in 1954. Washington's July 1953 cease-fire in Korea constituted at least a breach of faith with Paris and also enabled the PRC to concentrate its resources on one front, in Vietnam.

The Korean experience influenced military tactics in the Vietnam War. In Korea the U.S. Army fought a conventional war with obvious phase lines and military boundaries. Based on that experience, the Army also insisted that the South Vietnamese build a conventional military establishment. This turned out to be a serious error; unlike the military

approach of the North Koreans, the Democratic Republic of Vietnam (DRV) under the leadership of Gen. Võ Nguyên Giáp depended largely on guerilla warfare.

Many U.S. military personnel who fought in Korea also served in Vietnam. In Vietnam, as had been the case in Korea, U.S. military personnel confronted the lack of domestic support for a limited war, and political decisions profoundly affected military strategy in both wars. Perhaps in part influenced by Truman's firing of Gen. Douglas MacArthur from his command in Korea for publicly arguing for a widening of the war, Gen. William C. Westmoreland and the Joint Chiefs of Staff were reluctant to challenge President Johnson directly regarding his Vietnam policy.

The Korean War haunted U.S. policymakers during the Vietnam War. Although the Chinese Army had been poorly led and suffered massive casualties in Korea, China was considered an omnipresent threat. The possibility of a Chinese military intervention remained a major consideration for Washington, and thus an invasion of North Vietnam was never considered viable.

On 27 July 1953, an armistice was signed that halted the fighting in Korea. As of 1999, no peace treaty has yet been signed. U.S. government figures claim 33,651 Americans killed and 103,284 wounded, with war costs in the billions of dollars. The Republic of Korea later sent 50,000 troops to aid the U.S. in South Vietnam.

—Susan Goodier Kalaf and Spencer C. Tucker

References: Donovan, Robert J. *Nemesis: Truman and Johnson in the Coils of War in Asia* (1984); Kaufman, Burton I. *The Korean War: Challenges in Crisis, Credibility, and Command* (1986).

See also: China, People's Republic of (PRC); Containment Policy; Domino Theory; Eisenhower, Dwight David; Johnson, Lyndon Baines; Korea, Republic of; Korea, Democratic People's Republic of; MacArthur, Douglas; Rusk, Dean; Truman, Harry S; Westmoreland, William Childs.

Kosygin, Aleksei Nikolayevich (1904–1980)

Soviet premier. In *Vietnam and the Soviet Union*, Douglas Pike described Kosygin as a "careful cadre and true Soviet man."

In November 1964 Kosygin sent a message of support to the National Liberation Front of South Vietnam, the first by a Soviet leader, and in February 1965 was the first Soviet premier to visit the Democratic Republic of Vietnam (DRV). Seeking to restore Soviet influence in Hà Nôi, he promised financial aid and signed a defense pact, the latter the start of a long military alliance between the two states.

Although Soviet funding made possible a full-scale conflict in the region, it is difficult to assess Kosygin's attitude toward escalation of the war. China accused him of being too moderate, and yet it was after Kosygin's trip to the DRV that the war escalated with major southern offensives and direct attacks on U.S. military personnel. Possibly these were unilateral decisions by DRV leadership to thwart any attempt by Kosygin to force negotiations.

In his speeches Kosygin consistently urged Communist unity against U.S. actions in Vietnam. In June 1967 he met President Johnson at Glassboro, New Jersey, and urged that the United States stop its bombing of North Vietnam. In September 1969 he headed the Soviet delegation at Hồ Chí Minh's funeral in Hà Nội. When President Nixon went to Moscow in May 1972, he met Kosygin, who bluntly told Nixon that the Americans were trying to solve the Vietnamese question solely on a military basis. Kosygin was a signatory to the Soviet-Vietnam Treaty of Friendship and Cooperation signed in Moscow in November 1978, which renewed close military and economic links between the two countries.

As a reward for his support, the DRV presented Kosygin its Order of the Golden Star, the country's highest decoration. Kosygin resigned all his government and party posts in 1980.

—Michael Share

References: Edmunds, Robin. *Soviet Foreign Policy: The Brezhnev Years* (1983); Longmire, R. A. *Soviet Relations with South-East Asia: An Historical Survey* (1989); Pike, Douglas. *Vietnam and the Soviet Union: Anatomy of an Alliance* (1987).

See also: Brezhnev, Leonid Ilyich; Bruce, David K. E.; Hồ Chí Minh; Johnson, Lyndon Baines; Khrushchev, Nikita Sergeyevitch; Nixon, Richard Milhous; Union of Soviet Socialist Republics (USSR; Soviet Union); Vietnam, Democratic Republic of: 1954–1975; Vietnam, Socialist Republic of: 1975 to the Present.

Krulak, Victor H. (1913–)

U.S. Marine Corps general and commanding general, Fleet Marine Force, Pacific, from March 1964 to May 1968. In February 1962 Krulak became special assistant for counterinsurgency and activities of the Joint Chiefs of Staff, and over the next two years spent much of his time gathering information on the developing conflict in South Vietnam. After a "fact-finding" mission to Vietnam, Krulak held that the war was winnable if the Kennedy administration firmly supported the Ngô Đình Diêm government. His findings contradicted those of State Department official Joseph Mendenhall, who accompanied Krulak to Vietnam.

In March 1964 Lt. Gen. Krulak assumed command of Fleet Marine Force (FMF), Pacific, and served in that post until he retired from active duty in May 1968. While commander of FMF, Pacific, Krulak disagreed with Gen. William Westmoreland on several key points. He was strongly opposed to Westmoreland's "search-and-destroy" strategy and believed that attrition of forces favored the enemy. He saw search and destroy as a waste of time and effort that reduced the effectiveness of air and artillery support and believed that guerrillas constituted the main threat. His "three-cornered strategy" included protecting the South Vietnamese people from guerrillas; concentrating air power on rail lines, power, fuel, and heavy industry in the Democratic Republic of Vietnam (DRV); and placing maximum effort in pacification. Krulak believed that the Vietnamese people were the key to victory, and if the Communists could be denied access to them, the war could be won. Thus the first order of business had to be to protect the civilian population. Krulak constantly pointed out to his superiors that the manpower necessary to protect the villages was sapped by the requirements of a war of attrition.

—W. E. Fahey Jr.

References: Krulak, Victor H. *First to Fight* (1984); Zaffiri, Samuel. *Westmoreland: A Biography of General William C. Westmoreland* (1994).

See also: Attrition; Mendenhall, Joseph A.; Pacification; Search and Destroy; Taylor-McNamara Report; United States: Involvement in Vietnam, 1954–1965; United States: Involvement in Vietnam, 1965–1968; United States: Marine Corps; Westmoreland, William Childs.

L

Laird, Melvin R. (1922–)

U.S. secretary of defense, 1969–1973. As President Nixon's first secretary of defense, Laird faced difficult problems in formulating policy, budgets, and force structure during a period of declining resources and shrinking manpower committed to defense. He gave the service secretaries and the Joint Chiefs of Staff more of a role in these matters than had his predecessor, a welcome development from their standpoint. He also proved effective in dealing with Congress.

Sensitive to declining Congressional support for the war in Vietnam, Laird pushed hard for rapid withdrawal of U.S. ground forces, putting him frequently at odds with National Security Advisor Henry Kissinger on such issues as the 1970 cross-border operation into Cambodia. A later analysis found that Laird had been bypassed on the planning for that incursion. Richard Nixon noted in his memoirs that "it was largely on the basis of Laird's enthusiastic advocacy that we undertook the policy of Vietnamization." Laird was committed to making it work, so much so that in *Lost Victory* William Colby, who headed U.S. support for pacification in South Vietnam, called Laird "the unsung hero of the whole war effort." Laird was also supportive of Gen. Creighton Abrams as the U.S. field commander, admiring his stoicism in fighting on while his forces were progressively being taken from him and insisting that Abrams be named Army Chief of Staff when he returned from Vietnam. Then the two men devised and promulgated a "total force" policy that sought to ensure that reserve forces would be utilized in any future conflicts.

In his final report as secretary of defense, Laird stated, "as a consequence of the success of the military aspects of Vietnamization, the South Vietnamese people today … are fully capable of providing for their own in-country security against the North Vietnamese." However dubious that view was at the time, Laird had accomplished his major objective of getting U.S. forces out of Vietnam.

—Lewis Sorley

References: Kissinger, Henry. *White House Years* (1979); Nixon, Richard M. *RN: The Memoirs of Richard Nixon* (1978).
See also: Abrams, Creighton; Cambodian Incursion; Kissinger, Henry Alfred; Nixon, Richard Milhous; Palmer, Bruce, Jr.; United States: Involvement in Vietnam, 1969–1973; United States: Involvement in Vietnam, 1973–1975.

Lake, William Anthony Kirsopp (1939–)

Special assistant to National Security Advisor Henry Kissinger, 1969–1970. Lake joined the Foreign Service in 1962 and was assigned in 1963 to South Vietnam as staff assistant to Ambassador Henry Cabot Lodge, Jr. He then became vice-consul in Huê (1964–1965), where he became dismayed by the incongruity he observed in the optimistic military briefings and the more realistic field reporting by journalists.

Lake returned to the United States, served as a staff assistant in the Far Eastern bureau of the State Department from 1965 to 1967, then took a two-year leave of absence to earn an M.A. in public affairs from Princeton. He became convinced that the Vietnam War not only was wrong, but was being lost by the United States.

Hoping to convince President Nixon to remove the United States from the war in Vietnam, Lake in 1969 accepted the job as special assistant to National Security Advisor Henry Kissinger and accompanied Kissinger to secret negotiations with North Vietnamese representatives in Paris. When U.S. forces invaded Cambodia in April 1970, Lake resigned in protest.

—Laura Matysek Wood

References: Lake, Anthony, I. M. Destler, and Leslie H. Gelb. *Our Own Worst Enemy: The Unmaking of American Foreign Policy* (1984); Lake, Anthony, ed. *The Vietnam Legacy: The War, American Society and the Future of American Foreign Policy* (1976).
See also: Cambodian Incursion; Clinton, William Jefferson; Kissinger, Henry Alfred; Lodge, Henry Cabot, Jr.; Nixon Richard Milhous.

LAM SON 719, Operation (8 February–24 March 1971)

Army of the Republic of Vietnam (ARVN) campaign to curtail southbound supply shipments on the Hô Chí Minh Trail. In 1971, with Vietnamization under way and the withdrawal of U.S. forces proceeding, troops and supplies continued to flow down the Hô Chí Minh Trail and into South Vietnam, U.S. Air Force claims of having destroyed legions of trucks in its COMMANDO HUNT campaigns notwithstanding.

Operation LAM SON 719 had two objectives. The first was to capture Tchépone in Laos, a key transshipment point on Route 9, 25 miles west of Khe Sanh. As part of this effort, the ARVN was to destroy supplies in nearby Base Area 604 and in Base Area 611 south, adjacent to the border of South Vietnam. The second, and more optimistic, objective was to sever the Hô Chí Minh Trail, a logistical network that was vital to North Vietnam's ongoing war inside South Vietnam.

Although the Cooper-Church Amendment forbade use of U.S. ground forces in Laos, U.S. forces played a key part in LAM SON 719. U.S. helicopters ferried ARVN troops into Laos, and U.S. fighter-bombers and B-52s provided air cover. On the ground in South Vietnam, the 1st Brigade of the 5th Infantry Division led the way back into Khe Sanh as a part of Operation DEWEY CANYON II. From Khe Sanh, and from surrounding fire support bases (FSBs) inside South Vietnam, 9,000 U.S. troops gave logistical support to the ARVN and provided artillery fire into Laos.

On 8 February 1971, a task force of 15,000 ARVN troops invaded Laos. The main thrust was along Route 9. At first the troops moved easily through low hills that, within miles, turned more rugged and then changed to jungle as the road wound toward Tchépone. In imitation of the Americans, the ARVN built FSBs to serve as base camps and placed 105-mm and 155-mm howitzers in them to provide artillery support. The camps were also supposed to serve as bases from which patrols and raids could be mounted into the surrounding countryside.

LAM SON 719 was a major test of Vietnamization. Because of the Cooper-Church Amendment, the ARVN was on its own, with no U.S. advisors and no U.S. forward air guides. The ARVN had few English-speaking soldiers who could serve as forward air guides.

Intelligence estimates indicated that 11,000 to 12,000 People's Army of Vietnam (PAVN) troops would be present. About half of those were thought to be workers assigned to routine daily activities along the Trail. The other half were security forces used to patrol the Trail and to man the 1,400 to 2,000 heavy machine guns and antiaircraft artillery (AAA) in the area. In one of the greatest intelligence miscalculations of the war, it was thought that it would take up to a month for the PAVN to move one division from the panhandle of North Vietnam into the LAM SON 719 area of operations. In fact, within two weeks as many as five PAVN divisions, including the fabled 304th, 308th, and 320th Divisions, were engaging the ARVN.

By the third week of LAM SON 719, the ARVN advance had stalled at A Luoi, a fire support base 12 miles inside Laos. ARVN armor was bottled up along Route 9, and other ARVN units had holed up inside A Luoi and other fire support bases in the area. PAVN forces attacked these FSBs, first pounding them with Soviet-built 122-mm and 130-mm guns. After the artillery had softened the ARVN positions, North Vietnamese infantry supported by PT-76 light tanks and, for the first time, heavier T-34 and T-54 tanks, attacked the FSBs. One after another the FSBs fell to the counterattacking PAVN.

Conventional wisdom held that U.S. air power would be the pivotal, if not the deciding, factor. This was another miscalculation. As the PAVN counterattack commenced, low clouds prevented use of U.S. jet fighter-bombers. B-52s could bomb through the cloud cover and were useful against large-area targets, but PAVN leaders knew that the B-52s would not be used on targets closer than three kilometers from friendly forces, except in the most dire circumstances. Accordingly, the PAVN stayed close to the ARVN, negating the effective use of B-52s.

When the weather cleared, there was North Vietnamese antiaircraft fire with which to contend. As they did in the North, the PAVN relied on AAA and heavy machine guns to deny the Americans effective use of the air. Heavy machine guns, supplemented by 23-mm and 37-mm AAA guns, covered virtually every potential helicopter landing zone. The 23-mm and 37-mm guns blanketed the area, and SA-2 surface-to-air missile (SAM) sites were placed in Ban Raving Pass, threatening B-52s bombing within 17 miles of the pass and fighter-bombers flying above 1,500 feet in the same area. During LAM SON 719, the U.S. Air Force directed 1,285 sorties against AAA guns, reportedly destroying 70 of them. In support of LAM SON 719, B-52s flew 1,358 sorties and dropped 32,000 tons of bombs, with most missions directed against suspected supply dumps in Base Area 604, well away from Ban Raving Pass.

Despite increasingly heavy opposition from the PAVN, President Nguyên Van Thiêu ordered the commander of Operation LAM SON 719, Gen. Hoàng Xuân Lãm, to launch an airborne assault on Tchépone. By 1 March Tchépone had been abandoned by the PAVN and had little military value, but its psychological and political value seemed significant to Thiêu. On 6 March, 120 U.S. Army UH-1 Huey helicopters, protected by AH-1G Cobra helicopter gunships and U.S. Air Force fighter-bombers, lifted two battalions from the U.S. Marine base at Khe Sanh into Tchépone. Only one helicopter was lost to AAA en route. Two days later another two ARVN battalions reached Tchépone on foot. The South Vietnamese troops spent the next two weeks ferreting out PAVN supply caches around the village.

The capture of Tchépone achieved one of LAM SON 719's primary objectives. Thiêu then ordered Gen. Lãm to begin withdrawing the ARVN from Laos. However, the ARVN units were not well enough trained, led, or disciplined to conduct an orderly retreat, and the PAVN intensified its attacks on the withdrawing ARVN. Poor weather again hampered effective air operations, but when it cleared, devastating AAA fire and the inability of Air Force pilots to coordinate their attacks with ground units diminished the effectiveness of air power. The retreat turned into a rout.

Meanwhile, nearly 40,000 PAVN troops, including at least two armored regiments, hammered home attacks on a massively outnumbered and increasingly demoralized South Vietnamese force. In large part due to the selflessness and bravery of U.S. Army helicopter pilots, about half of the original ARVN force of 15,000 made its way to safety. At least 5,000 South Vietnamese troops were killed or wounded, and more than 2,500 were unaccounted for and listed as missing. Additionally, 253 Americans were killed and another 1,149 wounded during LAM SON 719. Although no Americans fought on the ground inside Laos, many were killed or wounded when the PAVN counterattack spilled into South Vietnam and when Khe Sanh came under artillery attack on 15 March.

In operations over Laos, at least 108 U.S. Army helicopters were destroyed and another 618 were damaged, many so badly that they were scrapped. Seven Air Force fixed-wing aircraft were shot down.

Despite the outcome and the losses, the Allies declared victory. President Nixon, in a televised address to the nation on 7 April 1971 stated, "Tonight I can report Vietnamization has succeeded." In North Vietnam, Radio Hà Nôi proclaimed "The Route 9–Southern Laos Victory [as they called it] the heaviest defeat ever for Nixon and Company."

—Earl H. Tilford, Jr.

References: Fulghum, David, and Terrence Maitland. *South Vietnam on Trial: Mid 1970 to 1972* (1984); Nolan, Keith William. *Into Laos: The Story of Dewey Canyon II/Lam Son 719* (1986); Palmer, Dave Richard. *The Summons of the Trumpet: U.S.-Vietnam in Perspective* (1977).

See also: Air Power, Role in War; Cao Van Viên; COMMANDO HUNT, Operation; Cooper-Church Amendment; DEWEY CANYON II, Operation; Hô Chí Minh Trail; Laos; Nguyên Van Thiêu; Nixon, Richard Milhous; Vietnam, Democratic Republic of: Army (People's Army of Vietnam [PAVN]); Vietnam, Republic of: Army (ARVN); Vietnamization.

Land Reform

Confiscation of land from wealthy landlords for distribution to poor peasants. Its impact would be greatest in the Mekong Delta, where most of the land was owned by large landlords and worked by tenant farmers. Tenancy was much less prevalent in central and northern Vietnam

During most of the First Indo-China War, the Viêt Minh compromised its doctrines of class struggle somewhat to gain greater support against the French. Land reform, however, was the most important way Communist principles of class struggle could be applied to Vietnam. Initially the Viêt Minh confiscated land from landlords who supported the French; those who supported the Viêt Minh had only to reduce rents.

In 1953 this compromise was rejected, and a radical campaign of land reform was initiated. Beginning in a pilot phase in Thái Nguyên Province north of the Red River, it was more brutal in Thanh Hóa and Ninh Bình provinces. It led thousands of non-Communist cadres in North Vietnam to defect from the Viêt Minh. The campaign paused after the 1954 Geneva Accords but was restored in mid-1955 to September 1956 on a larger scale and spread through all ethnically Vietnamese areas of the Democratic Republic of Vietnam (DRV). It became more radical as it spread, both economically—with far more people being classified as "landlords" than actually met the official definition of the term—and politically, with an increasingly frenzied search for landlords and landlord agents within the Viêt Minh village leadership. On average, two landlords or "reactionaries" from each village were executed.

As the campaign was carried out in 3,653 villages, probably fewer than 8,000 landlords and would-be opponents of the regime were put to death, but many others were sent to reeducation camps.

In mid-1956 the DRV leadership realized how disastrously they were attacking their own political base. On 31 October 1956 they initiated a correction in which Viêt Minh village leaders who had been falsely accused of being enemy agents were rehabilitated and people who had been wrongly classified as landlords had part of their confiscated land returned to them. The need to repair the damage that land reform had done to Communist political power in the DRV was one reason that there was so little DRV pressure on Ngô Đình Diêm's Republic of Vietnam (RVN) government in the South from 1956 to 1958.

Hô Chí Minh admitted no responsibility. Deputy Minister for Land Reform Hô Viêt Thang was sent to a reeducation camp for a long term, and Truong Chinh resigned as party general secretary to become chairman of the parliament. In June 1958 the party affirmed that the purpose of the campaign was not only to confiscate land for the poor but also "*phát dông quân chúng*" (to motivate the masses). According to Communist ideology the landlord class was a threat, and through 1997 children and grandchildren of landlords were considered untrustworthy of party membership until proven otherwise by investigation. Certainly the Land Reform campaign was among the greatest events in the history of the DRV, second only to the Vietnam War.

Diêm, meanwhile, was making the RVN an ally of the landlord class. In the Mekong Delta, where most landlords were closely associated with the French, the Viêt Minh had redistributed large amounts of land even before 1953. The RVN nullified this redistribution and assisted former landlords in resuming rent collection, averaging probably between one-quarter and one-third of crops. At U.S. urging Diêm passed a land reform law of his own, Ordinance 57 of 22 October 1956, but his program was much less generous to the peasants than that of the Communists in three ways: it asked tenants to pay for land they received; it did not promise a thorough resolution of the tenancy problem (landlords were entitled to retain much of their land); and corruption and apathy on the part of officials kept it from being thoroughly implemented. The law specified accurate land surveys and ownership certificates, thus creating vast amounts of paperwork. The amount of land actually distributed to the peasants was far less even than the limited amount that under law was supposed to be distributed.

The result was that when the Vietnam War began the RVN was still basically allied with absentee landlords. The National Liberation Front (NLF) land reform program, which dramatically reduced rent levels or simply gave land to tenant farmers, was an important part of its political appeal, especially in the Mekong Delta.

Only late in the war did the RVN become truly serious about bidding against the Communists for the allegiance of tenant farmers. The land reform law signed by President Nguyên Van Thiêu on 26 March 1970 was far more radical than that of Ngô Đình Diêm. It redistributed almost all landlord land to tenants and did not ask that the tenants pay for it. Furthermore, Thiêu's land reform law was actually carried out in a reasonably thorough fashion. Land reforms of the Viêt Minh and the NLF had considerably reduced tenancy in South Vietnam; Thiêu's abolished almost all of what remained.

—Edwin E. Moise

References: Callison, Charles S. *Land-to-the-Tiller in the Mekong Delta: Economic, Social and Political Effects of Land Reform in Four Villages of South Vietnam* (1983); Hoàng Van Chí. *From Colonialism to Communism* (1966); Moise, Edwin E. *Land Reform in China and North Vietnam* (1983); Sansom, Robert L. *The Economics of Insurgency in the Mekong Delta* (1970).

See also: Agricultural Reform Tribunals; Mekong Delta; National Front for the Liberation of South Vietnam (NFLSV); Ngô Đình Diêm; Nguyên Van Thiêu; Viêt Minh (Viêt Nam Đôc Lâp Đông Minh Hôi [Vietnam Independence League]); Vietnam, Democratic Republic of: 1945–1954.

Laniel, Joseph (1889–1975)

French politician and premier during the 1954 Battle of Điên Biên Phu. Laniel was regarded as lacking imagination in foreign affairs. He was premier when the 1954 Geneva Conference opened, but its apparent lack of progress haunted his government. Not kept informed by Gen. Henri Navarre of military plans, he was forced to share blame for the debacle of

Điên Biên Phu. Laniel's government failed to secure last-ditch U.S. military aid and, dressed in black, Laniel announced the fall of the fortress to the National Assembly. His government fell three days later, on 12 June 1954. Laniel was followed as premier by Pierre Mendès-France.

Laniel's defenders have pointed out that his government was close to a breakthrough in talks with the Viêt Minh and that his resignation helped preserve the peace process. Jules Roy wrote of him, "An honest weaver and a man who stood loyally by his friends. Never understood anything about politics, Indochina, and Dienbienphu, and went bravely to the slaughterhouse...."

—Spencer C. Tucker

References: *Biographical Dictionary of French Political Leaders Since 1870* (1990); Laniel, Joseph. *Jours de Gloire et Jours Cruels (1908–1958)* (1971); —. *Le Drame Indochinois, de Dien Bien Phu au pari de Genève* (1957); Roy, Jules. *The Battle of Dienbienphu* (1965).
See also: Điên Biên Phu, Battle of; Geneva Conference and Geneva Accords; Indo-China War; Mendès-France, Pierre.

Lansdale, Edward Geary (1908–1987)

Father of modern U.S. counterinsurgency doctrine. Lansdale is known for his successful labors resisting "People's Wars" in the Philippines and in Vietnam and for his ideas on nation building. His career was extolled (or lambasted) in two major novels: Eugene Burdick and William Lederer's *The Ugly American* (1958) and Graham Greene's *The Quiet American* (1955).

Under CIA authority, Lt. Col. Lansdale went to newly divided Vietnam in June 1954. As chief of the covert-action Saigon Military Mission (SMM), his task was to weaken Hô Chí Minh's Democratic Republic of Vietnam (DRV) through any means available while helping to strengthen Bao Đai's southern State of Vietnam as a separate and non-Communist nation. Within weeks Lansdale became a principal advisor to Ngô Đình Diêm, who was simultaneously premier, defense minister, and commander of the military. Diêm accepted many of Lansdale's ideas, including urging northerners to move south (ultimately, 1.25 million did so); bribing sect leaders to merge their private armies into Diêm's or face battle with him; instituting service organizations and a government bureaucracy; planning reforms; and, in October 1955, offering himself and a new constitution as an alternative to the tired administration of Bao Đai. A lopsided and manipulated vote for Diêm ensued. While Lansdale worked with Diêm in the South, part of his SMM team labored in the Democratic Republic of Vietnam (DRV), with mixed and largely insignificant results, to carry out sabotage and to effect a psychological warfare campaign against the Communist government there.

Lansdale was a close personal friend of Diêm, one of the few men outside of his own family to whom Diêm listened. Diêm had great respect for Lansdale's ideas and enthusiasm. Their unofficial relationship bypassed normal channels of diplomatic relations, causing many in the U.S. government to view Lansdale with distrust. Yet Lansdale's record of success in the Philippines, his early accomplishments in

Vietnam, and his network of friends and contacts in high places prevented his enemies from dismissing either the man or his ideas.

His influence lessened by Diêm's growing reliance on his brother, Ngô Đình Nhu, Lansdale returned to the United States in early 1957 and served the Eisenhower and Kennedy administrations as deputy director of the Office of Special Operations, Office of the Secretary of Defense. He also sat as a member of the U.S. Intelligence Board (USIB) and formulated national covert intelligence policy. Kennedy briefly considered naming Lansdale as ambassador to Vietnam, but Secretary of State Dean Rusk and Secretary of Defense Robert McNamara vetoed the idea. He retired from the Air Force in October 1963 as a major general.

President Johnson recalled Lansdale to government service between 1965 and 1968, sending him to Vietnam with the rank of minister to work on pacification problems. His influence was less than in previous years, and his authority not clearly defined. He accomplished little, and those years were for Lansdale a time of great frustration.

—Cecil B. Currey

References: Currey, Cecil B. *Edward Lansdale: The Unquiet American* (1988); Lansdale, Edward G. *In the Midst of Wars: An American's Mission to Southeast Asia* (1972).
See also: Central Intelligence Agency (CIA); Eisenhower, Dwight David; Greene, Graham; Johnson, Lyndon Baines; Kennedy, John Fitzgerald; McNamara, Robert S.; Ngô Đình Diêm; Ngô Đình Nhu; Office of Strategic Services (OSS); Pacification; Rusk, Dean.

Lao Đông Party

Ruling party formed in 1951 in the Democratic Republic of Vietnam and in existence until 1986. Its formal name was Dang Lao Đông Viet Nam. The Lao Đông Party was in fact synonymous with the Indo-Chinese Communist Party, which underwent a number of twentieth-century metamorphoses.

The failure of moderate nationalism in Vietnam in the 1920s provided an opportunity for the more radical Communists. By 1930 there were three Communist parties within Vietnam, and on 3 February they agreed to merge into one party and to form common institutions, including labor unions and youth, women's, and peasants' organizations. In October 1930, at the first plenum of the new Central Committee, the party took the name of Đang Công San Đuong (Indo-Chinese Communist Party, or ICP). Trân Phú was named its first general secretary. The party adopted two basic goals: national independence by expelling the French and "to struggle against feudalism, and give the land to the tillers."

In November 1945 Hô Chí Minh nominally dissolved the ICP in a bid to enlarge his support within Vietnam, win Chinese departure from North Vietnam, and secure support from the United States and other Western nations.

In February 1951 Hô changed the name of the ICP to the Đang Lao Đông Viêt Nam (Vietnamese Workers' Party), popularly known as the Lao Đông (or Workers' Party). Again, the intention was to play down communism and widen nationalist support throughout Vietnam. Pressure from the People's Republic of China may also have played a part. At the same time, separate national parties were founded for Laos and Cambodia.

It was through the Lao Đông Party that Hô carried out his policies. The most controversial of these was land reform that lasted into fall 1956, leading to the execution of at least 15,000 "landlords" and open revolt by some peasants that required intervention by the People's Army of Vietnam (PAVN). Truong Chinh was made the scapegoat and Lê Duân replaced him as head of the party, a position he continued to hold until his death in 1986.

In December 1976 at the Fourth National Congress, the Lao Đông renamed itself the Đang Công San Viêt Nam (Vietnamese Communist Party, or VCP).

The Socialist Republic of Vietnam (SRV) remains very much a one-party state today, with the 1.5 million–member Vietnamese Communist Party dominating the political life of the SRV.

—Spencer C. Tucker

References: *An Outline History of the Vietnam Workers' Party, 1930–1975* (1978); Nguyen Khac Vien. *Vietnam: A Long History* (1987); Patti, Archimedes L. A. *Why Viet Nam? Prelude to America's Albatross* (1980); Pike, Douglas. *A History of Vietnamese Communism, 1923–1978* (1978).
See also: Agricultural Reform Tribunals; An Nam; Cochin China; Lê Duân; Tonkin; Truong Chinh (Đang Xuân Khu); Vietnam, Democratic Republic of: 1954–1975; Vietnam, Socialist Republic of, 1975 to the Present; Vietnamese Communist Party (VCP); Women in the War, Vietnamese.

Laos

Nation on the mainland of Southeast Asia, surrounded by China, Vietnam, Cambodia, Thailand, and Myanmar (Burma). Laos is inhabited by lowland rice cultivators, mostly Lao, and by highlanders from dozens of tribes who grow rice in forest clearings, raise a variety of other crops, and tend animals. Although the Lao are Theravada Buddhists, the highlanders are mainly animists. In the towns are minority Chinese, Vietnamese, and Indian populations, mainly traders and shopkeepers. Total population is estimated at 4.7 million people, of whom 85 percent live in rural areas.

When the French signed a protectorate agreement in 1884 with the Vietnamese court at Huê, which had been worried about Siamese expansion, they saw themselves as entitled to establish a presence on the left bank of the Mekong in the name of the Vietnamese emperor by right of historic claims and proceeded to expel the Siamese garrisons. However, instead of claiming the left bank, the French established direct rule over southern Laos and signed a protectorate treaty with the king of Luang Prabang. French rule in Laos was consolidated by the treaty of 3 October 1893, signed with the king of Siam. The French ruled Laos with a generally light hand and established hospitals, schools, and a unified civil service.

Laos was hardly affected by World War II until 9 March 1945, when the Japanese suddenly ousted the French administration and made a brief but brutal appearance. In the wake of the Japanese surrender, a group of nationalist-minded Laotians led by Prince Phetsarath, the viceroy of the kingdom of Luang Prabang, took the opportunity to seize power and form an independent government, ignoring the king's proclamation that the French protectorate had been restored.

Advocates of independence, known as the Lao Issara, received support from the Viêt Minh in neighboring Vietnam and prepared to oppose return of the French. The French received significant support, however, from some highlanders, particularly the Hmong, and with the approval of the king and Prince Boun Oum na Champassak, the most influential figure in the south, succeeded in reimposing their presence in Laos by mid-1946. The Lao Issara fled to Thailand, where they continued to agitate for opposition to France.

The French progressively granted the attributes of independence to the royal government in Vientiane and in 1947 unified the country under the rule of the king of Luang Prabang, who became the king of Laos. Elections were held, a constitution promulgated, and political parties flourished. Complete independence, including foreign affairs and defense, was granted by France in October 1953. Laos also took part in the 1954 Geneva Conference that ended the Indo-China War.

The major problem facing the royal government was the reintegration of the Pathet Lao rebels, some of them ex–Lao Issara, who had fought alongside the Viêt Minh during the war. The Pathet Lao had been awarded two northern provinces by the terms of the cease-fire agreement in which to regroup while the Viêt Minh regular units withdrew from Laos into North Vietnam. Difficulties soon arose in the operations of the joint armistice commission and the International Commission for Supervision and Control (ICSC or ICC) that consisted of representatives from India, Canada, and Poland. Higher-level negotiations between the royal government and the Pathet Lao led to the formation of a coalition government in 1957, a move supported by the powers who had been represented at Geneva. The United States, however, was deeply suspicious of the Pathet Lao's Communist ties and worried that Congress would cut off aid to Laos for having Communists in its government. It maneuvered behind the scenes to bring down the coalition in 1958, when partial elections revealed the popular strength of the party formed by the Pathet Lao, the Neo Lao Hak Sat (NLHS).

The Pathet Lao, for their part, had not given up their arms, and now, having rejected integration into the royal army on their own terms, resumed military action against the U.S.-backed royal army in the two northern provinces. A series of attacks against royal army outposts in Sam Neua in 1959 produced an international crisis in which the royal government charged that the Democratic Republic of Vietnam (DRV) was aiding the insurgents and appealed for help to the United Nations. The NLHS deputies to the National Assembly in Vientiane were imprisoned on charges of sedition but were never tried.

The United States stepped up aid to the royal army, which was channeled through a clandestine military aid mission, the Programs Evaluation Office (PEO). Following the establishment of a rightist government that excluded the NLHS, and the escape from prison of the NLHS deputies, on 9 August 1960 a young army captain, Kong Le, staged a coup d'état in Vientiane and demanded the resignation of the government and an end to the civil war.

A new government was formed that vowed to end the fighting and renew negotiations for a peaceful settlement with the Pathet Lao. This initiative met with overt hostility from Thailand, which instituted a blockade of Vientiane, and more camouflaged opposition from the United States, which maintained its aid to the Laotian army outside Vientiane in view of the threat posed by the Pathet Lao.

Attempts to find grounds for compromise proved unavailing, and even the king, Savang Vatthana, was totally ineffectual in steering the country away from disaster. Rightist forces under Gen. Phoumi Nosavan, with U.S. arms, attacked Vientiane in mid-December 1960 and after three days of artillery and tank shelling drove Kong Le's paratroop battalion out. However, Kong Le had received arms and ammunition flown into Vientiane by Soviet aircraft from Hà Nôi, and as his troops retreated northward along the road toward Luang Prabang, Soviet aircraft continued to drop supplies. After the leftist troops captured the Plain of Jars on 1 January 1961, they were supplied by Soviet aircraft flying into the airfield there. The entry of the Soviet Union into the Laos crisis led to U.S. protests to Moscow. Furthermore, North Vietnamese troops were now openly involved as "volunteers" fighting on the side of the Pathet Lao–Kong Le alliance.

Prime minister Prince Souvanna Phouma, who had fled to Phnom Penh before the battle, proclaimed the continued legitimacy of his government and began a campaign to drum up international support for a neutral Laos. The new Kennedy administration had decided not to intervene with U.S. troops and was not averse to any plan to neutralize Laos, a solution propounded in January by the U.S. ambassador in Vientiane, Winthrop Brown. Kennedy asked roving ambassador W. Averell Harriman to meet with Souvanna Phouma in New Delhi and see whether a non-Communist outcome to the crisis could be salvaged. From that point on, the Kennedy administration worked for a new international conference on Laos of the Geneva type, a plan already suggested by Prince Norodom Sihanouk of Cambodia. After much diplomatic activity on all sides, a 14-nation conference convened in Geneva in June 1961, and over the next year worked on a solution by coalition government.

Several factors favored the tripartite coalition that emerged in June 1962. One was the growing disinterest of Soviet premier Nikita S. Khrushchev in the Laos affair. His actions had been dictated by Moscow's rivalry with Beijing, but by 1962 the Sino-Soviet split had grown so wide he no longer had any leverage to compete with Beijing's radical line. He admitted as much in his June 1961 meeting with Kennedy in Vienna, where the two leaders agreed a neutral Laos without involvement of either power was in their mutual interest. The North Vietnamese, while receiving pledges of militant solidarity from Beijing, were finding their campaign to seize

South Vietnam much more difficult than they had expected, and their interest in the revolution in Laos had accordingly diminished, at least temporarily. The DRV did not, however, withdraw its troops from Laos as outlined under the 1962 Geneva Agreement, leaving them instead to revive the effort at a later date.

After 1963 the second coalition existed in name only. Ignoring the cease-fire, both sides resumed military operations. The North Vietnamese and Pathet Lao subverted a section of Kong Le's army, compelling Kong Le to withdraw from the Plain of Jars and ally himself with the rightists once again. The irregular Meo (Hmong) troops of Gen. Vang Pao became among the most effective forces against the renewed North Vietnamese-Pathet Lao offensive, staying in the field thanks to a large-scale resupply effort mounted by the U.S. Central Intelligence Agency (CIA). Another important factor in keeping the Communists at bay was bombing by the U.S. Air Force and Navy from 1964 to 1973. The war seesawed back and forth, with the Hmong capturing the Plain of Jars only to have to abandon it again.

By 1973 Laos was in effect divided, with the Communists holding the entire east from China to the Cambodian border. This was the area through which the Hô Chí Minh Trail passed. It was defended by regular People's Army of Vietnam (PAVN) units in complete mockery of Lao sovereignty and the royal government, with which Hà Nôi nevertheless maintained diplomatic relations. The lowlands along the Mekong, on the other hand, were held by the royal government. The mountainous area between Vientiane and the Plain of Jars was held by the Hmong.

Under an agreement signed in Vientiane on 21 February 1973, a new cease-fire was declared to take effect on the following day giving the Pathet Lao equal status with the royal government for the first time. The U.S. bombing, which had dropped almost 2.1 million tons of ordnance on Laos (more than the total tonnage dropped by the U.S. in the European and Pacific theaters in World War II), halted at noon on 22 February. The new coalition government took office on 5 April 1974, and each ministry had a minister from one side and a vice-minister from the opposite side. Although the 1973 cease-fire left 300 U.S. personnel unaccounted for in Laos, no U.S. prisoners were returned by the Pathet Lao other than eight who had been held in North Vietnam and were released in Hà Nôi.

On 27 April 1975, North Vietnamese–Pathet Lao forces launched a strong attack against Gen. Vang Pao's Hmong, at the strategic road junction of Sala Phou Khoun, and drove southward toward Vientiane. Wishing to avoid a resumption of the war, Souvanna Phouma ordered Vang Pao to defend himself as best he could, but without the benefit of air strikes by the small Royal Laotian Air Force. Feeling himself abandoned, Vang Pao had a last stormy meeting in Vientiane with the prime minister and then appealed to the CIA for evacuation of his troops and their families to safe haven in Thailand. On 10 May, Vang Pao and 12 Hmong leaders signed a treaty reminding the United States of past pledges and agreeing to leave Laos and never return. The CIA refused an airlift, the only possible exit by that stage, although it did evacuate Vang Pao and his wives on 14 May as the North Vietnamese Pathet Lao closed in on his base at Long Chieng, which was captured without a fight.

Meanwhile, a campaign of intimidation against the non–Pathet Lao members of the coalition government gathered momentum in Vientiane. Key ministers, including the defense minister, fled across the Mekong. Demonstrators occupied the U.S. aid mission compound, forcing termination of the large aid program and the evacuation of its U.S. employees. The takeover of government offices and orchestrated demonstrations led to the entry of the Pathet Lao into the other major towns of Laos without their being damaged by fighting. The Pathet Lao seizure of power was completed on 23 August. Military units belonging to the royal army were said to have requested Pathet Lao "advisors," thereby facilitating the integration of the army. Officers and high-ranking government officials who remained in Vientiane, hoping for the best, were sent to attend "seminars" at camps in Sam Neua, where many of them died.

At the beginning of December 1975 the Pathet Lao did away with the last facade of the coalition government, abolishing the 600-year-old monarchy, and proclaimed the Lao People's Democratic Republic (LPDR). Political parties were prohibited. King Savang Vatthana was named an advisor to the new president, but in fact played no role after his abdication. He died in a seminar camp in 1978, along with the queen and their eldest son.

The December 1975 events also saw the emergence of the Lao People's Revolutionary Party (LPRP), the Communist party behind the Pathet Lao front. The LPRP acknowledged its lineage from the Indo-Chinese Communist Party (ICP) and declared itself a Marxist-Leninist party. As the sole ruling party in the LPDR, it began elaborating policies.

For the first decade, LPRP policies were centered on state control of every aspect of life, although efforts to collectivize agriculture amounted to little more than rhetoric. A constitution was not elaborated until 1991. Meanwhile, the party's propaganda organs extolled the heroic deeds of the victorious "people's army" against the superior forces of the United States. Surprisingly, the U.S. embassy in Vientiane, manned by a skeleton staff since the departure of the last ambassador to the royal government in May 1975, was untouched, and the United States maintained diplomatic relations with the LPDR.

The LPRP counted 60,000 members by March 1996, when the party held its Sixth Congress. Party leadership continued to be dominated by the veteran leaders of the 30-year struggle against the French and the Americans. Eight of the nine Politburo members named in 1996 were military officers. The 49-member Central Committee, however, included several younger figures, more in keeping with economic reforms enacted between 1986 and 1996. Overall, the degree of stability of leadership the party has exercised during its two decades as the only legal political party in the country has been remarkable.

The lingering effect of the war also manifested itself in two major issues between the LPDR and the United States:

the prisoners of war/missing in action issue, and the LPDR's demand for U.S. humanitarian aid to help cope with the unexploded bombs left scattered about the countryside, which continued to take a toll on civilians, particularly in the north, more than two decades after the end of hostilities.

Faced with the problems of economic opening coupled with political repression, lack of government funding for development projects, and leftovers from the war, it will be some time before Laos frees itself from the ranks of the least developed nations and catches up with the other, non-Communist, Southeast Asian countries.

—Arthur J. Dommen

References: Cordell, Helen, compiler. *Laos* (1991); Lewis, Judy, ed. *Minority Cultures of Laos: Kammu, Lua', Lahu, Hmong, and Iu-Mien* (1992); Savada, Andrea Matles, ed. *Laos: A Country Study* (1995); Stuart-Fox, Martin, and Mary Kooyman. *Historical Dictionary of Laos* (1992); Zasloff, Joseph J., and Leonard Unger, eds. *Laos: Beyond the Revolution* (1991).

See also: Harriman, W. Averell; Hmong; International Commission for Supervision and Control (ICSC); Kennedy, John Fitzgerald; Khrushchev, Nikita Sergeyevitch; Kong Le; Pathet Lao; Phoumi Nosavan; Plain of Jars; Souphanouvong; Souvanna Phouma; Vang Pao; Vientiane Agreement; Vientiane Protocol.

Lavelle, John D. (1916–1979)

U.S. Air Force general and commander, Seventh Air Force, 1971–1972. In July 1971 Lavelle was promoted to four-star general and given command of the Seventh Air Force in Southeast Asia.

Lavelle soon became concerned for the safety of his pilots. Forced to operate under complex and strict rules of engagement during missions over North Vietnam, they were permitted to strike targets only in cases where "protective reaction" could be claimed. What came to be known as "the Lavelle case" stemmed from charges that on occasion Gen. Lavelle directed strikes against certain targets, a violation of those rules of engagement. Furthermore, returning air crews were found to fabricate enemy actions in an effort to justify these strikes.

Lavelle's rationale was that a Democratic Republic of Vietnam wide-area radar network, used to alert target acquisition radars and missile sites, gave air crews little or no warning or reaction time and greatly increased their risk, and thus constituted hostile action.

Lavelle was subsequently determined to have acted improperly. He was relieved of command and retired as a major general, a rank two grades below that which he had held.

—Lewis Sorley

References: Ginsburg, Gordon A. *The Lavelle Case: Crisis in Integrity* (1974); Sorley, Lewis. *Thunderbolt: General Creighton Abrams and the Army of His Times* (1992).

See also: Air Power, Role in War; Hersh, Seymour Myron; United States: Air Force.

Lê Duân (1907–1986)

Secretary general of the Communist Party of Vietnam and de facto leader of the Democratic Republic of Vietnam (DRV) following the 1969 death of Hô Chí Minh.

An ardent opponent of French rule, Lê Duân was twice imprisoned (1931–1936 and 1940–1945) on charges of political subversion. Following World War II, he emerged as a trusted lieutenant of Hô Chí Minh and a key figure in the Viêt Minh challenge to continued French rule. A capable strategist and tactician, Lê Duân directed Viêt Minh efforts in the Mekong Delta and in 1952 became commander of Viêt Minh military headquarters in South Vietnam. The 1954 brokered agreement at the Geneva Conference left Vietnam divided, and Lê Duân, who clung to the nationalist ideal of a united and independent Vietnam, openly opposed the agreement. He nonetheless worked with Hô Chí Minh to secure Communist control in the North.

Lê Duân's long service resulted in his continued upward advance within the party. A member of the Lao Ðông Politburo and the Central Committee and Secretariat, he moved to the top echelon of the DRV power structure and remained one of the North's most influential military planners.

In 1959 Lê Duân secretly visited the South and returned with recommendations for a dramatic escalation. Hà Nôi-supported Viêt Công (VC) guerrillas operating against the U.S.-backed government of Ngô Dình Diêm faced total destruction, he warned, unless the effort was prosecuted vigorously. Over the next three years, largely under Lê Duân's direction, the VC launched a sweeping program of assassination and urban terrorism while stepping up more conventional forms of military confrontation.

Lê Duân continued to play an important role in Hà Nôi's prosecution of the conflict. A consistent advocate of the offensive, he supported the infusion of People's Army of Vietnam (PAVN) forces to the South as well as stronger support for the Viêt Công. In 1965, as U.S. involvement increased, he advocated the move to conventional warfare, joining other Northern leaders in shunning Chinese advice to de-escalate. With Hô Chí Minh's death in September 1969, Lê Duân assumed direction of the Lao Ðông Party, and as such became the effective leader of the DRV. He held a hard line during cease-fire negotiations with the United States: Continued division of Vietnam was unacceptable, and the conflict would be pressed until the invaders withdrew and unity was achieved. Under the concerted leadership of Lê Duân, Vô Nguyên Giáp, and Pham Van Ðông, Communist forces cemented their victory over the Republic of Vietnam (RVN) with the capture of Sài Gòn in 1975.

As the leader of a united Vietnam, Lê Duân faced the mammoth task of rebuilding a war-ravaged country. Reconciling opposing ideologies, restoring the economy, and feeding the people all posed obstacles with which he dealt with varying degrees of success. A devoted Marxist, he maintained close ties with the Soviet Union, a relationship he solidified with the signing of the Friendship Treaty in 1978.

—David Coffey

References: Burgess, Patricia, ed. *The Annual Obituary 1986* (1989); Karnow, Stanley. *Vietnam: A History* (1983); *Who's Who in the World 1984–1985* (1989).

See also: Ðiên Biên Phu, Battle of; Geneva Conference and Geneva Accords; Hô Chí Minh; Lao Ðông Party; Pham Van Ðông; United Front; Viêt Minh (Viêt Nam Ðôc Lâp Ðông Minh Hôi [Vietnam Independence League]); Vietnam, Democratic Republic of: 1945–1954; Vietnam, Democratic Republic of: 1954–1975; Vietnam, Socialist Republic of: 1975 to the Present; Vô Nguyên Giáp.

Lê Ðuc Anh (1920–)

Vietnamese Communist Party (VCP) official, People's Army of Vietnam (PAVN) general, and, since 1992, president of the Socialist Republic of Vietnam (SRV). Anh was a deputy to the Sixth (1976) and Eighth (1987) National Assemblies. During the Ninth National Assembly in September 1992 he was elected president of the Socialist Republic of Vietnam. Anh has gained the reputation as party troubleshooter. He has been credited with the 1989 Vietnamese withdrawal from Cambodia and with resolving vexing issues with the United States regarding soldiers missing in action (MIAs).

—Ngô Ngoc Trung

References: Biographical Files, Indo-China Archives, University of California at Berkeley.

See also: Hô Chí Minh Campaign; Lao Ðông Party; Vietnam, Democratic Republic of: Army (People's Army of Vietnam [PAVN]); Vietnam, Socialist Republic of: 1975 to the Present.

Lê Ðuc Tho (1910–1990)

Vietnamese revolutionary and influential member of the Lao Ðông (or Communist) Party Political Bureau and Secretariat; also Democratic Republic of Vietnam's (DRV's) chief negotiator at the Paris peace talks.

Lê Ðuc Tho was a founder of the Indo-Chinese Communist Party and spent much of the 1930s in the French island prison of Poulo Condore. During most of the war with France he served as the Party's Chief Commissar for the Nam Bô (southern) region of Vietnam. In the 1950s Tho gained the reputation of a skilled theoretician and was often called upon to guide Party directives. From the late 1950s until the beginning of the peace talks in Paris, he played a major role in directing the war in South Vietnam. Vietnamese author Vu Thu Hiê contends that on occasion Tho's views overrode those of Hô Chí Minh.

When the Paris peace talks opened on 13 May 1968, Tho was the principal DRV negotiator. The Central Committee of the Lao Ðông Party gave Tho considerable latitude for discussion but insisted that no serious negotiations could take place unless the United States stopped bombing the North unconditionally and accepted a coalition government in the South, in accordance with the National Front for the Liberation of South Vietnam's platform. Furthermore, they demanded that any settlement address the political and military struggles together, beginning with the dismantling of Nguyên Van Thiêu's Sài Gòn regime. Henry Kissinger balked at these demands. Beginning 21 February 1970, Kissinger and Tho met secretly in Paris to discuss a way out of the stalemate. The talks produced few substantive results, however; and in spring 1972 President Nixon renewed bombing of the North.

By early summer 1972, Kissinger and Tho had made substantial compromises. The United States now suggested that North Vietnamese troops could remain in the south after a cease-fire and supported a tripartite electoral commission in the South that represented a major step away from its absolute support of the Sài Gòn regime. Tho dropped his insistence on Thiêu's ouster, accepting a cease-fire that would leave Thiêu in partial control. These compromises angered Southern allies of both the United States and the DRV. The Sài Gòn regime called the compromise a sell-out; the Provisional Revolutionary Government (PRG) questioned the wisdom of leaving Thiêu in control. In addition the PRG worried that the freedom of southern political prisoners was no longer linked with the release of U.S. prisoners of war. In October 1972, Tho and Kissinger appeared to have settled the major issues, but for weeks they debated the subtleties of the settlement. Finally, Nixon ordered air strikes over the North to force an agreement. The air attacks, now known as the "Christmas bombings," lasted for 12 days during which the United States dropped more than 36,000 tons of bombs, representing the most intensive and devastating attacks of the war. The attacks did little to change the scope and nature of the final accord, however, and Nixon's approval rating plummeted to 39 percent.

Negotiations between Kissinger and Tho resumed on 8 January 1973, and a final agreement was signed on 27 January. Differing little from the October draft, the final peace accord left Thiêu in power temporarily and allowed North Vietnamese troops to remain in the South. The PRG was accorded meaningful status and the possibility of obtaining broader political power. Ironically, the major question over which the war had been fought—the political future of the South—was left undecided. Both sides claimed victory, and both violated the spirit and nature of the agreement, causing the war to drag on for two more years until the Communists forced Sài Gòn's collapse.

Late in 1973 the Nobel Peace Committee awarded Kissinger and Tho its peace prize, but Tho refused to accept the award because the war continued. In 1975 Tho returned to the South to oversee the final stages of the Communist offensive against Sài Gòn (the Hô Chí Minh Campaign). Between 1975 and 1986 he remained an active member of the Vietnamese Communist Party Central Committee and helped direct the Vietnamese invasion of Cambodia. During this time he was also the director of the powerful Party Organization Department, the bureau that oversaw the assignment of cadres in both party and state organs. Tho's power diminished in the mid-1980s, however. After the sweeping economic reforms introduced at the 1986 Sixth Party Congress, he resigned his post and retired from public life.

—Robert K. Brigham

References: Boudarel, Georges, ed. *La bureaucratic au Vietnam* (1983); Herring, George C. *America's Longest War: The United States in Vietnam, 1950–1975* (1986); —, ed. *The Secret Diplomacy of the Vietnam War: The Negotiating Volumes of the Pentagon Papers* (1983); Kalb, Marvin, and Bernard Kalb. *Kissinger* (1974); Karnow, Stanley. *Vietnam: A History* (1983); Porter, Gareth. *A Peace Denied: The United States, Vietnam, and the Paris Agreement* (1975); Turley, William S. *The Second Indochina War: A Short Political and Military*

History, 1954–1975 (1986); Vu Thu Hiên. *Đêm Giua Ban Ngày* (1997); Young, Marilyn B. *The Vietnam Wars, 1945–1990* (1991).

See also: Hô Chí Minh Campaign; Kissinger, Henry Alfred; Lao Đông Party; Missing in Action and Prisoners of War, Viêt Công and People's Army of Vietnam; Nguyên Van Thiêu; Nixon, Richard Milhous; Paris Negotiations; Paris Peace Accords; Poulo Condore (Côn Son); Prisoners of War, Allied; Provisional Revolutionary Government of South Vietnam (PRG); Vietnamese Invasion and Occupation of Cambodia.

Lê Dynasty (1428–1788)

Longest dynasty in Vietnamese history. The Lê dynasty (in Vietnamese, Nhà Lê, or Nhà Hâu Lê) ruled Vietnam from 1428 when Lê Loi, its founder, drove the Minhs out of the country, until 1788, when it was ended by the Tây Son revolt. This long era was divided into two periods: the direct and unified Lê government period (1428–1527) and the North-South period (1527–1788), during which the Trinh Lords controlled the North and the Nguyên Lords controlled the South, both in the name of the Lê kings. Lê Thánh Tông (1460–1497) promulgated the Luât Hông Đuc (Hông Đuc Code), one of the most important law codes in Vietnamese history.

—Pham Cao Duong

References: Lê Kim Ngân. *Tô Chuc Chính Quyên Trung Uong Duoi Triêu Lê Thánh Tông, 1460–1497* (1963); Le Thanh Khoi. *Le Viet Nam: Histoire et Civilisation* (1955); Trân Trong Kim. *Viêt Nam Su Luoc* (1971). Uy Ban Khoa Hoc Xa Hôi Viêt Nam. *Lich Su Viêt Nam, tâp I* (1971).

See also: Lê Loi (Lê Thái Tô); Lê Thánh Tông; Nguyên Dynasty; Trinh Lords; Vietnam: from 938 through the French Conquest.

L HÔNG PHONG II, Operation
(September–October 1950)

Viêt Minh campaign along Route Coloniale (RC) 4 that in effect ended the Indo-China War for the French, although the conflict dragged on for four more years.

In early 1950 Viêt Minh forces penetrated deeply into the French-controlled Red River Delta defensive belt, and in Operation L HÔNG PHONG I they took the key frontier post of Lào Cai. By the end of the offensive, the Viêt Minh controlled virtually the entire northeastern corner of Tonkin. His army well trained and equipped by the Chinese, Viêt Minh commander Gen. Vô Nguyên Giáp was ready for a major offensive against French forts along the China border. In late May 1950 the Viêt Minh, supplied by the People's Republic of China with U.S. howitzers captured from the Nationalists, took the key outpost of Đông Khê. Although the French retook it a few days later by airborne assault, the supply run to Cao Bang from Lang Son got no farther than Thât Khê, and after January 1950 Cao Bang and Đông Khê had to be resupplied by air.

On 16 September 1950 Giáp launched L HÔNG PHONG II, ordering 15 of his battalions supported by an artillery regiment to take Đông Khê, which was held by two Foreign Legion companies. Despite French air strikes, Đông Khê fell two days later, cutting communications with Cao Bang and French garrisons to the northwest.

On 24 September, with much time already lost, Gen. Carpentier ordered the evacuation of Cao Bang. His decision to order the garrison to retreat on RC 4 rather than RC 3 led to a disaster. Although RC 3 was a longer route to the French main defensive line, it was safer. RC 4 ran close to the Chinese border and was marked by difficult terrain. In any case, no one in the high command seems to have anticipated a Viêt Minh reaction, and no intervention force had been organized. As it worked out, the Viêt Minh were far more numerous than the French forces. Remnants of the two French forces met in the hills around Đông Khê, only to be wiped out on 7 October 1950. Only 12 officers and 475 men reached Thât Khê.

The French High Command now panicked. On 17 October it ordered the evacuation of Lang Son, which had not been under attack and whose good airfield and excellent fields of fire would have allowed a protracted defense. Most of its 1,300 tons of supplies fell into Viêt Minh hands. By the end of October 1950, most of northeastern Vietnam was a Viêt Minh stronghold with the French largely forced back into their Red River Delta bastion. Except for a brief paratroop raid on Lang Son in July 1953, the French did not penetrate this area again. The debacle from Cao Bang cost the French at least 5,000 killed and missing, and at Lang Son alone the French lost 10,000 weapons—enough to supply an entire Viêt Minh division.

—Spencer C. Tucker

References: Fall, Bernard. *Street Without Joy* (1961); —. *The Two Viet Nams* (1964); Gras, Général Yvres. *Histoire de La Guerre d'Indochine* (1992); Porch, Douglas. *The French Foreign Legion: A Complete History of the Legendary Fighting Force* (1991).
See also: Điên Biên Phu, Battle of; France: Air Force; France: Army; Indo-China War; Viêt Minh (Viêt Nam Đôc Lâp Đông Minh Hôi [Vietnam Independence League]); Vô Nguyên Giáp.

Lê Kha Phiêu (1931–)
Prominent People's Army of Vietnam (PAVN) general and Vietnamese Communist Party (VCP) official.

In December 1997 Phiêu replaced Đô Muoi as general secretary of the VCP. Although the PAVN is widely seen as being overwhelmingly loyal to the ruling VCP, Phiêu is a younger-generation general who seems to adapt more easily to the changing situation in Vietnam than the aging core of veteran guerrilla fighters. His public pronouncements reveal a concern that free markets and outside influences might undermine party rule.

—Ngô Ngoc Trung

References: Biographical Files, Indo-China Archives, University of California at Berkeley.
See also: Lao Đông Party; Vietnam, Socialist Republic of: 1975 to the Present; Vietnamese Invasion and Occupation of Cambodia.

Lê Loi (Lê Thái Tô) (1385–1433)
Founder of the later Lê dynasty (1428–1788) and exemplar of Vietnamese resistance to foreign domination. Angered at the willingness of his fellow officials to accept and participate in the imposition of Chinese rule in 1407, Lê Loi raised the standard of revolt that attracted the support of Vietnam's preeminent scholar-poet and military strategist, Nguyên Trãi. The harshness of the Chinese occupation and his own populist sympathies led Lê Loi to mount a prolonged guerrilla campaign, during which he pursued Nguyên Trãi's dictum that "it is better to win hearts than conquer citadels." His protracted war strategy laid the foundation for more conventional operations that ultimately forced a withdrawal of the exhausted Minh forces in 1428.

Lê Loi won the peace as well as the war. His attempt to discourage further Chinese intervention by offering Peking (Beijing) the traditional vassal-state tribute—while proclaiming the complete independence of Vietnam on the home front—was pragmatic and effective and led to more than 300 years of Sino-Vietnamese amity. He addressed the ever-vexing problem of landlessness by resuming the early Lê Dynasty's "equal field" system and introduced a nationwide sliding-scale land redistribution program, albeit one that acknowledged the claims of age, rank, and wealth. Lê Loi's patriotism, his "hearts and minds" approach to war and politics, and his pragmatic military and diplomatic strategies served as models for modern Vietnamese revolutionary nationalists.

—Marc Jason Gilbert

References: Buttinger, Joseph. *The Smaller Dragon: A Political History of Vietnam* (1958); Nguyen Khac Vien. *Vietnam: A Long History* (1987); Whitfield, Danny J. *Historical and Cultural Dictionary of Vietnam* (1976).
See also: Lê Dynasty; Nguyên Dynasty; Trinh Lords; Vietnam: from 938 through the French Conquest.

Le Myre de Vilers, Charles Marie (1833–1918)
French colonial administrator. Appointed governor of Cochin China in 1879, he generally favored a policy of peaceful integration. It is therefore ironic that he gave Captain Henri Rivière his orders to attack Tonkin in 1883, setting off the chain of events connected to French-Chinese rivalry for hegemony over Vietnam that culminated in the signing of the 1885 Treaty of Tientsin between France and China. Following his retirement he was elected a deputy to the National Assembly from Cochin China in 1889 and was reelected in 1893 and 1898.

—Arthur J. Dommen

Reference: McAleavy, Henry. *Black Flags in Vietnam: The Story of a Chinese Intervention* (1968).
See also: Black Flag Pirates; French Indo-China.

Lê Nguyên Khang (? –1996)
Army of the Republic of Vietnam (ARVN) general instrumental in developing the Republic of Vietnam (RVN) Marine brigade. A favorite of President Ngô Đình Diêm, he did not participate in the November 1963 coup. Following Gen. Nguyên Khánh's assumption of power in February 1964, Khang returned to his former duties. In 1968, in addition to his marine duties, he became commander of the Capital Military District, military governor of Sài Gòn, commander of III Corps Tactical Area, governor-delegate for the III Corps

Tactical Zone, and a member of the National Leadership Committee. Following the fall of Sài Gòn in April 1975, Khang settled in the United States.

—Robert G. Mangrum

References: Kutler, Stanley I., ed. *Encyclopedia of the Vietnam War* (1996); Palmer, Bruce. *The Twenty-five Year War: America's Military Role in Vietnam* (1984).

See also: Ngô Đình Diêm; Ngô Đình Diêm, Overthrow of; Nguyên Khánh; Nguyên Van Thiêu.

Lê Nguyên Vy (1933–1975)

Army of the Republic of Vietnam (ARVN) brigadier general. Vy served with a battalion in the Mekong Delta and after 1960 was in the 5th Infantry Division. He was its deputy commander during the bloody Battle of An Lôc in summer 1972. After a year as deputy commander of the 21st Infantry Division, Vy returned to the 5th Division in 1973 as its commander. In spring 1975 he was with the 5th Division at Lai Khê. Upon receiving an order to surrender, Gen. Vy shot himself to death.

—Nguyên Công Luân (Lu Tuàn)

Reference: Hà Mai Viêt. "Famous Generals of the Republic of Viêt Nam Armed Forces" (n.p.)

See also: Vietnam, Republic of: Army (ARVN).

Lê Phuoc Tho (aka Sau Hau) (?–?)

Prominent Vietnamese Communist Party (VCP) official. Little information is available about Tho's activities during the Indo-China and Vietnam Wars except that he was a southerner who took part in revolutionary activity in the Mekong Delta. In 1986 Tho became a member of the Secretariat of the VCP Central Committee and was named head of the Central Committee Agriculture Department. In 1991 he was promoted to the Politburo and was assigned as head of the Central Committee Organization Department, one of the most important bodies in the party apparatus in charge of personnel. In June 1996 Tho retired from the Politburo.

—Ngô Ngoc Trung

References: Biographical Files, Indo-China Archives, University of California at Berkeley.

See also: Lao Đông Party; Vietnam, Socialist Republic of: 1975 to the Present.

Lê Quang Tung (ca. 1923–1963)

Army of the Republic of Vietnam (ARVN) colonel. Lê Quang Tung came to the head of the Republic of Vietnam's Special Forces (Luc Luong Đac Biêt, or LLDB) under Republic of Vietnam (RVN) President Ngô Đình Diêm. Tung had charge of the program secretly run by the CIA in which ARVN volunteers set up espionage networks and sabotaged Communist activities. The program was a total failure, and Tung's forces were later criticized, even in the United States, as having been Ngô Đình Nhu's tool for repressing Buddhist dissidents.

Tung was amomg the most dangerous enemies of the coup plotters against Diêm. His Special Forces could be counted on to defend the Ngô brothers, leading the conspirators to decide early in the planning that Tung would have to be eliminated. In September 1963 coup planners convinced Washington to approve a sanction that deprived Tung's forces of U.S. funding unless they were deployed outside Sài Gòn. Unfortunately for the Ngô brothers, Nhu relied heavily on Tung's forces in the planning of Operations BRAVO I and II, the Ngô pseudo-coup. BRAVO I called for a fake revolt in Sài Gòn led by soldiers and police disguised as insurgents. BRAVO II was to have Tung's Special Forces enter the city to quell the "disturbance." The plan was flawed because it relied heavily on Gen. Tôn Thât Đính, one of the coup leaders. On 29 October 1963, however, Đính ordered Tung's troops from Sài Gòn.

On 1 November a group of generals and senior officers, including Tung, met at the officers' club inside staff headquarters near Tân Son Nhut airport. At 1330 Gen. Trân Van Đôn announced that a military revolutionary council was taking power. All but Col. Tung stood up to applaud. Capt. Nguyên Van Nhung then took Tung to another room in the building. As he was being led away, Tung shouted, "Remember who gave you your stars!" Later that same day, Nhung supervised the execution of Tung and his brother, Maj. Lê Quang Triêu.

—Michael R. Nichols

References: Karnow, Stanley. *Vietnam: A History* (1991); Smith, R. B. *An International History of the Vietnam War* (1985).

See also: BRAVO I and BRAVO II, Operations; Buddhists; Kennedy, John Fitzgerald; Ngô Đình Diêm; Ngô Đình Diêm, Overthrow of; Ngô Đình Nhu; Tôn Thât Đính; Trân Van Đôn; Viêt Minh (Viêt Nam Đôc Lâp Đông Minh Hôi [Vietnam Independence League]); Vietnam, Republic of: Special Forces (Luc Luong Đac Biêt [LLDB]).

Lê Thanh Nghi (real name, Nguyên Khac Xung) (1911–1989)

Prominent leader in the Vietnamese Communist Party (VCP), the Democratic Republic of Vietnam (DRV), and the Socialist Republic of Vietnam (SRV). During the Indo-China War, Nghi was a key leader of the III Military Zone, and he held a number of important party and governmental posts. In 1951 the Indo-China Communist Party split into national branches and the Vietnamese party was renamed the Lao Đông (Workers') Party. At the 1951 Second Party Congress, Nghi was elected a member of its Executive Committee. In October 1956 he was elected to the Politburo. Nghi coordinated all foreign assistance to the DRV during the Vietnam War and later, until his death, to the SRV. Shortly after having been named the SRV's economic czar, Nghi died in Hà Nôi.

—Ngô Ngoc Trung

References: Biographical Files, Indo-China Archives, University of California at Berkeley.

See also: Lao Đông Party; Vietnam, Democratic Republic of: 1954–1975; Vietnam, Socialist Republic of: 1975 to the Present.

Lê Thánh Tông (1442–1497)

Prominent Vietnamese emperor. Lê Thánh Tông's key reform was to restructure the administration along Confucian lines.

This system continued until the French conquest 400 years later. The emperor also built up a standing army of almost 200,000 men. Lê Thánh Tông's most important contribution was a comprehensive legal code, the Hông Đuc Code. Unusually liberal for its day, it allowed women to own property brought into the wedding. If divorced without children, such women might reclaim their property. If the couple had children, common property passed to the possession of the children after the divorce. Severe punishments, such as banishment and strangulation, were retained for crimes threatening stability and order.

—Michael R. Nichols

References: Karnow, Stanley. *Vietnam: A History* (1991); Nguyên Huyên Anh. *Viêt Nâm: Danh Nhân Tù Điên* (1990); Nguyên Khac Viên. *Vietnam: A Long History* (1993).

See also: Lê Dynasty; Vietnam: from 938 through the French Conquest.

Lê Trong Tân (1914–1986)

Full general in the People's Army of Vietnam (PAVN). In December 1945 Tân became a member of the Indo-Chinese Communist Party. During the Indo-China War, he held various important positions and worked to build up and train the armed forces.

During the Vietnam War, Tân was one of the Democratic Republic of Vietnam's (DRV) generals in direct command on battlefields in the South. He became deputy general commander of the Liberation Armed Forces of South Vietnam, general commander of the Route 9 and Southern Laos Campaign in 1971, commander of Tri-Thiên Province Campaign in 1972, general commander of the Campaign to Liberate Huê and Đà Nang, and deputy general commander of the 1975 Hô Chí Minh Campaign.

Tân was also named Special Envoy of the Joint Staff of the People's Army of Vietnam (PAVN) to the Laos Liberation People's Army and participated in the Plain of Jars campaigns in northern Laos during the 1970s. In 1979 Tân participated in the invasion of Cambodia. He was promoted to full general in December 1984.

—Ngô Ngoc Trung

References: Biographical Files, Indo-China Archives, University of California at Berkeley.

See also: Hô Chí Minh Campaign; Huê and Đà Nang, Battles of; Indo-China War; Vietnam, Democratic Republic of: Army (People's Army of Vietnam [PAVN]); Vietnam, Socialist Republic of: 1975 to the Present.

Lê Va Ty (? –1964)

Army of the Republic of Vietnam (ARVN) general and chief of Republic of Vietnam (RVN) Joint General Staff from 1955 to 1963. RVN Premier Ngô Đình Diêm promoted Lê Va Ty to brigadier general and later made him chief of the joint general staff, the top RVN military post. President Diêm and the military respected Ty; he was affectionately known as "Bon Papa." Cancer forced Lê Va Ty to leave the military in 1963.

—Nguyên Công Luân (Lu Tuân)

See also: Ngô Đình Diêm; Vietnam, Republic of: Army (ARVN).

Lê Van "Bay" Viên (?–?)

Leader of the bandit Bình Xuyên in South Vietnam. Before World War II, Lê Van Viên escaped from Poulo Condore (Côn Son), the French prison island in the Gulf of Siam, and made his way to the Mekong Delta area, where he joined a band of river pirates calling themselves the Bình Xuyên, after a tiny village that for a time served as their base of operations. By the end of World War II, this illiterate man had become the Bình Xuyên's chief, and under his tutelage, the Bình Xuyên expanded their scope of operations.

In the chaotic days that marked the close of the war, Bay moved his headquarters to the Cho Lon district of Sài Gòn, raised a private army, and, for a time, collaborated with the Viêt Minh in their efforts to establish themselves as the legitimate government of all Vietnam. Appreciative Viêt Minh officials named him deputy commander of their military forces in Cochin China. In one instance Bay ordered the slaying of 150 French civilians, including women and children. By 1947, however, with Viêt Minh prospects in the South very dim, Bay opened negotiations with the French and agreed to shift his allegiance when they offered to recognize the Bình Xuyên gang as a "sect." Now holding a commission as a colonel in the Vietnamese National Army, Bay launched his own soldiers in attacks against his former Viêt Minh allies.

Soon Bay Vien was a very rich man in control of all vice activities in and around Cho Lon. The huge gambling complex in Cho Lon, Le Grande Monde, many riverboat gambling dens, and the Hall of Mirrors (the largest brothel in Asia) belonged to him. He owned or controlled most of the opium trade in southern Indo-China and ran his own factory to supply his outlets. Such enterprises led Bay Viên into gold smuggling, currency manipulation, and other enterprises. He was now a vice lord with whom to be reckoned, but it was all still illegal, and so Viên diversified, buying up some of Sài Gòn's best department stores and real estate.

In an effort to find funds necessary to sustain his foundering State of Vietnam, Bao Đai promoted Bay to general and sold him control of the national police. Thus, he received complete and official control over all racketeering in the South. He shared a portion of his profits with Bao Đai. To protect his lucrative tourist business in Vung Tàu, Viên deployed his Công An Xung Phong (Assault Police) to ensure the security of the highway from Sài Gòn to Vung Tàu.

After becoming prime minister in the South in 1954, Ngô Đình Diêm recognized Lê Van Viên as the most immediate threat to his authority. By then Viên had an army of more than 40,000 men. Diêm instigated a showdown on 27 April 1955 when he ordered Viên to remove his troops from Sài Gòn. Viên refused, and Diêm's soldiers attacked. A battle raged inside the city, killing more than 500 people and leaving 25,000 homeless. Both the French and Bao Đai tried to assist Viên, but Diêm prevailed. By the end of May, the National Army pushed the Bình Xuyên forces out of Sài Gòn and into the swamps of the Mekong Delta. Many later joined the Viêt Công. Lê Van Viên escaped with much of his fortune to France, never to return to Vietnam.

—Cecil B. Currey

References: Currey, Cecil B. *Edward Lansdale: The Unquiet American* (1988); Fall, Bernard. "The Political-Religious Sects of Viêt-Nam" (1955); Lansdale, Edward, Joseph Baker, Lucien Conein, and Rufus Philipps. Interviews with the author.
See also: Bao Dai; Bình Xuyên; Ngô Đình Diêm; Viêt Minh (Viêt Nam Độc Lâp Đông Minh Hôi [Vietnam Independence League]); Vietnam, Republic of: 1954–1975.

Lê Van Hung (1933–1975)

Army of the Republic of Vietnam (ARVN) brigadier general. Hung proved to be a talented and brave infantry commander in the bloody battle of An Lôc in summer 1972. His men held the city despite fierce enemy attacks over a two-month period. When Communist forces captured Sài Gòn on 30 April 1975, Hung's troops still held the city of Cân Thu. A delegation of citizens convinced him that his forces should not prolong the fight because that would lead to a bloodbath and destruction of the city. Gen. Hung and his commander, Gen. Nguyên Khoa Nam, then decided not to fight to the end, as had been their intention. Hung bid farewell to his men, his wife, and children, and committed suicide by shooting himself with a pistol.

—Nguyên Công Luân (Lu Tuân)

Reference: Hà Mai Viêt. "Famous Generals of the Republic of Viêt Nam Armed Forces" (n.p.).
See also: An Lôc, Battle of.

Lê Van Kim (1918–)

Army of the Republic of Vietnam (ARVN) general and leading figure in the November 1963 coup against Republic of Vietnam (RVN) President Ngô Đình Diêm. In November 1960 the Viêt Nam Quôc Dân Đang (VNQDD, Vietnam National Party) prepared to replace Diêm with Kim. This mutiny of military officers collapsed as a result of indecision and internal problems, however. After the failed coup, Kim held various unimportant jobs until November 1963.

In 1963 Kim became involved, with his brother-in-law Gen. Trân Van Đôn, in another coup attempt against Diêm. Together they recruited other discontented military officers. After the 1 November 1963 coup, Kim, Đôn, and Gen. Duong Van Minh held power. On 30 January 1964, Gen. Nguyên Khánh seized control of Sài Gòn and placed the three generals under arrest. He then accused Đôn and Kim of conspiring with the French to neutralize the RVN. In the court-martial that followed, Khánh was not able to produce any evidence against the two, making him look foolish, and he tried to repair the damage by appointing both generals to advisory positions. Kim retired from the ARVN in 1965 to enter business in Sài Gòn.

—Michael R. Nichols

References: Bain, Chester A. *Vietnam: The Roots of Conflict* (1967); Duncanson, Dennis J. *Government and Revolution in Vietnam* (1968); Karnow, Stanley. *Vietnam: A History* (1983); Smith, R. B. *An International History of the Vietnam War.* Vol. 2, *The Struggle for South-East Asia, 1961–65* (1985).
See also: Duong Van Minh; Ngô Đình Diêm; Ngô Đình Diêm, Overthrow of; Nguyên Khánh; Trân Van Don; Viêt Nam Quôc Dân Đang (Vietnam National Party).

LEA, Operation (October 1947)

Indo-China War French military operation, mounted over three weeks beginning in October 1947. Devoted almost exclusively to the capture of Hô Chí Minh and the Viêt Minh leadership and the destruction of main Viêt Minh battle units, LEA involved 17 French battalions, including three armor and three airborne. The operation succeeded in taking Thái Nguyên and other Viêt Minh–controlled cities, but it failed to capture the Viêt Minh leadership or destroy main Viêt Minh units. Hô Chí Minh escaped in disguise, but the French shot to death a well-known scholar, Nguyên Va Tô, whose white beard made him resemble Hô.

The operation revealed the difficulty of the French position in Indo-China, especially the paucity of resources. Troops involved in LEA were badly needed elsewhere, and their employment in the operation opened up much of the countryside of Vietnam to Viêt Minh penetration.

—Spencer C. Tucker

References: Fall, Bernard. *Hell in a Very Small Place: The Siege of Dien Bien Phu* (1967); —. *The Two Viet Nams* (1964).
See also: France: Army; Hô Chí Minh; Indo-China War.

Leclerc, Jacques-Philippe (1902–1947)

General and commander of French Far Eastern forces, 1945–1946. In June 1945, de Gaulle appointed Leclerc to command the French Expeditionary Corps to restore French sovereignty in Indo-China. Leclerc was unenthusiastic.

On 5 October 1945 Leclerc arrived in Sài Gòn. He achieved an agreement with the British that preserved France's position in southern Vietnam, and on 25 October he began the reconquest of Indo-China for France, predicting it would take about a month for "mopping-up operations" to conclude. Leclerc's highly mobile mechanized forces quickly established French authority over southern Vietnam and Cambodia but, as they numbered only 40,000 men, they controlled little beyond the cities and main routes.

Leclerc became convinced that the Viêt Minh was a nationalist movement that France could not subdue militarily, and he supported the talks that resulted in the March 1946 Hô-Sainteny Agreement with the Democratic Republic of Vietnam (DRV). Unlike most of his compatriots, Leclerc was aware of the great difficulties of jungle warfare, and he favored a course of negotiations that would mean abandoning the attempt to create an independent Cochin China. In a secret report to Paris on 27 March, he said there would be no solution through force in Indo-China.

The return of Admiral Georges Thierry d'Argenlieu, French High Commissioner to Indo-China, to assume political control relegated Leclerc to military functions. d'Argenlieu and other French colonial administrators opposed meaningful concessions to the nationalists, and Leclerc departed Indo-China in frustration at his own request.

—Spencer C. Tucker

References: Clayton, Anthony. *Three Marshals Who Saved France: Leadership after Trauma* (1992); de Gaulle, Charles. *The War Memoirs of Charles de Gaulle.* Vol. 3, *Salvation, 1944–1946* (1960); Hammer, Ellen J. *The Struggle for Indochina* (1954).

See also: d'Argenlieu, Georges Thierry; de Gaulle, Charles André Marie Joseph; French Indo-China; Hô-Sainteny Agreement; Indo-China War.

Lefèbvre, Dominique (?–?)

Nineteenth-century Catholic priest and missionary to Vietnam who set in motion a chain of events that brought French military intervention in Vietnam. Lefèbvre arrived in Vietnam in 1835. He began converting Vietnamese to Catholicism and, with other French missionaries, began intriguing on behalf of the Lê pretender to the throne. In 1845 he was arrested and sentenced to death. From his prison at Huê he smuggled a message to the captain of the U.S. frigate *Constitution*, anchored at Tourane (present-day Đá Nang). Admiral Cécille learned of Lefèbvre's situation and immediately dispatched the French warship *Alcmène* to Tourane, and Emperor Thiêu Tri released Lefèbvre. His intention was not to persecute foreign missionaries, but to see them and French warships gone from Vietnam.

The matter did not end there, for once again Lefèbvre provided an excuse for French armed intervention in Vietnam. In May 1846 Lefèbvre and another priest tried to reenter Vietnam by bribing border guards. Promptly apprehended, Lefèbvre was again sentenced to death. Cécille now sent two warships, the *Gloire* and the *Victorieuse*, to Tourane to demand not only the priests' release, but freedom of worship for Catholics in Vietnam. The two French Navy commanders arrived at Tourane in early spring 1847. As a precaution, the French captains demanded that Vietnamese vessels at Tourane be stripped of their sails. After several weeks of waiting for a reply to their demands, the French became impatient. On 15 April 1847, four Vietnamese vessels approached the French warships, shots were fired, and within 70 minutes three of the Vietnamese ships were sunk. The French warships then sailed away without ever finding out what had become of Lefèbvre. When he returned to France from the Far East in 1847, Admiral Cécille called for France to talk to Vietnam in the future "only with guns."

According to most books on the period, Lefèbvre was expelled from Vietnam for a second time some weeks before the arrival of the French. He later returned there to continue missionary activities.

—Spencer C. Tucker

References: Buttinger, Joseph. *The Smaller Dragon: A Political History of Vietnam* (1968); Cady, John F. *The Roots of French Imperialism in Eastern Asia* (1954); Karnow, Stanley. *Vietnam: A History* (1983).
See also: Guizot, François; Rigault de Genouilly, Charles; Vietnam: from 938 through the French Conquest.

LeMay, Curtis Emerson (1906–1990)

U.S. Air Force general and candidate for vice-president of the United States. In 1961 President Kennedy appointed LeMay chief of staff of the Air Force, a position he held until retiring on 31 January 1965.

LeMay was at odds with the Kennedy and Johnson administrations on a variety of issues, including the switch from massive retaliation to flexible response as the focus of U.S. defense policy, whether or not to develop the XB-70 experimental aircraft, and conduct of the Vietnam War. Of the latter LeMay said, "Instead of swatting flies we should be going after the manure pile." The general's background and experience led him to believe the concept of limited war was an oxymoron. To attain victory, LeMay believed, "We must return to the strategic bombing doctrine that was tried and proved in World War II."

In 1968, as vice-presidential candidate on George Wallace's American Independent Party ticket, LeMay stated that in Vietnam, "I would use any weapon in the arsenal that is necessary." The press and the opposing candidates depicted Wallace and LeMay as reckless and unstable, and Wallace responded by sending LeMay on a fact-finding trip to Vietnam, keeping the general out of the country until after the election.

—Earl H. Tilford, Jr.

References: Clodfelter, Mark. *The Limits of Air Power: The American Bombing of North Vietnam* (1989); Coffee, Thomas M. *Iron Eagle: The Turbulent Life of General Curtis E. LeMay* (1986); LeMay, Curtis E. *America Is in Danger* (1968); LeMay, Curtis E., with MacKinlay Kantor. *Mission with LeMay: My Story* (1965).
See also: Air Power, Role in War; Elections, U.S.: 1968; Johnson, Lyndon Baines; Kennedy, John Fitzgerald; RAND Corporation; United States: Air Force; Wallace, George Corley, Jr.

Lemnitzer, Lyman L. (1899–1988)

U.S. Army general and chairman of the Joint Chiefs of Staff (JCS), 1960–1962. Lemnitzer pressed President Kennedy to increase U.S. military strength in South Vietnam in the belief that if the Communists were successful there, it would encourage similar insurgencies elsewhere. Lemnitzer believed that the major military threat to South Vietnam was not guerrillas, but rather an invasion by conventional forces across the Demilitarized Zone. After a trip to Vietnam in spring 1961, he stated that too much emphasis on counterinsurgency measures would impair the ability of the Army of the Republic of Vietnam to defeat a conventional-style attack from the North.

Lemnitzer believed the American public would not support guerrilla war, and in early 1961, when Kennedy was considering intervention in Laos, he and the other members of the JCS warned the president not to do so with anything less than a substantial military force. His views clearly clashed with Kennedy's support for counterinsurgency as opposed to conventional war. In November 1962 Kennedy appointed Lemnitzer commander of U.S. Forces in Europe.

—Spencer C. Tucker

References: Dupuy, Trevor N., Curt Johnson, and David L. Bongard. *The Harper Encyclopedia of Military Biography* (1992); Hilsman, Roger. *To Move a Nation: The Politics of Foreign Policy in the Administration of John F. Kennedy* (1967); Kellner, Kathleen. "Broker of Power: General Lyman L. Lemnitzer" (1987); Korb, Lawrence J. *The Joint Chiefs of Staff: The First Twenty-Five Years* (1976); Walton, Richard J. *Cold War and Counter-Revolution: The Foreign Policy of John F. Kennedy* (1972).
See also: Kennedy, John Fitzgerald; Laos; Military Assistance and Advisory Group (MAAG), Vietnam; Taylor, Maxwell Davenport.

Levie, Howard S. (1907–)

U.S. Army officer; law professor; scholar. During the Vietnam War, Levie wrote thoughtfully on a variety of war-related subjects, including prisoner-of-war issues, chemical weapons, and defoliants. In 1971 and 1972 Levie held the Stockton Chair of International Law at the U.S. Naval War College. He was then on the law faculty at Washington University of St. Louis, where he received emeritus status in 1977. A scholar of international law, Levie's writings include *Prisoners of War in International Armed Conflict* (awarded the 1983 Ciardi Prize), *The Status of Gibraltar and The Code of International Armed Conflict,* and *Terrorism in War: The Law of War Crimes* (1993). In 1994 the Naval War College named the Military Chair of Operational Law in Levie's honor for his contributions in the area of the law of armed conflict.

—Robert G. Mangrum

References: Levie, Howard S. "Maltreatment of Prisoners of War in Vietnam" (1968); —. "Weapons of Warfare" (1975); Lewy, Guenter. *America in Vietnam* (1978).

Levy, Howard B. (1937–)

U.S. Army officer tried in one of the first antiwar courts-martial of the Vietnam War era. Levy accepted a commission in the Army Medical Corps and was posted to Fort Jackson, South Carolina, where he was to provide dermatological training for Special Forces personnel about to leave for Vietnam. After several months he refused to participate further, despite a direct order from his commanding officer, Col. Henry F. Fancy.

Long before this incident, Levy had been placed under surveillance because of off-duty activities that included operating a free clinic and promoting black voter registration. Levy later claimed that he was prosecuted in order to punish him for his civil rights activities. Indeed, a secret intelligence dossier described him as appearing "to think more of the Negroid race than of the White race." Col. Fancy decided against an administrative reprimand and formally charged Levy with willful disobedience and "intent to create disloyalty and disaffection among enlisted men."

The general court-martial, convened in May 1967, attracted widespread attention when Levy invoked the so-called Nuremberg defense, justifying his refusal to instruct Green Berets on the grounds that they would use the training for criminal purposes. In a precedent-setting decision, Col. Earl Brown, the Army's chief law officer, ruled that the Nuremberg principles could be a standard and allowed Levy's civilian attorney, Charles Morgan, Jr. (provided by the American Civil Liberties Union), to offer evidence of criminal actions by Special Forces personnel in Vietnam. But Morgan was unable to satisfy Brown that there was proof of a "criminal command practice." According to Telford Taylor, the defense's argument was fraught with difficulties, since nothing decided at Nuremberg suggested that "a soldier is entitled to disobey an intrinsically legal order … because other soldiers, halfway around the world, are given illegal orders."

Levy also argued that training the Green Berets compelled him to violate canons of medical ethics. Being soldiers first and aidmen second, the Green Berets' provision of medical treatment (other than first aid) to civilians in order to make friends was illegitimate, for it could be taken away as easily as given. The court was not persuaded.

Although the prosecution tried but failed to prove that a single person was made "disloyal or disaffected" by Levy's words or actions, the ten-officer jury found him guilty on all charges and sentenced him to three years at hard labor and dismissal from the service.

Viewed by many as a martyr, Levy became a widely admired figure in the GI antiwar movement. His experience left him a committed radical who became active in the "GI coffeehouse protests" in Army towns around the country.

Morgan appealed Levy's case on constitutional grounds for several years and also accused the Army of suppressing most of Levy's secret intelligence dossier. In 1973 a U.S. Court of Appeals ruled that Levy had been wrongfully convicted on two of the charges, but in 1974 the Supreme Court upheld the convictions.

—John D. Root

References: Di Mona, Joseph. *Great Court-Martial Cases* (1972); Hayes, James R. "The War Within: Dissent in the Military with an Emphasis on Vietnam" (1975); Strassfeld, Robert. "The Vietnam War on Trial: The Court-Martial of Dr. Howard B. Levy" (1994); Taylor, Telford. *Nuremberg and Vietnam: An American Tragedy* (1970).

See also: Antiwar Movement, United States.

LEXINGTON III, Operation (17 April–9 June 1966)

U.S. Army 1st Infantry Division operation in Rung Sát Special Zone. On 17 April 1966, a battalion from the U.S. Army's 1st Infantry Division ("Big Red One") was ordered into the Rung Sát Special Zone, a thick mangrove swamp south of Sài Gòn. Long considered impenetrable by the Army of the Republic of Vietnam (ARVN) command, it was a haven for main force Việt Công (VC) and People's Army of Vietnam (PAVN) units operating in the Capital Military District that posed a direct threat to Sài Gòn.

The 1st Battalion, 18th Infantry (1/18th), detached from the 1st Division, conducted operations with the objective of finding and engaging sizable Communist forces. Assuming that no major action occurred, the 1/18th was to conduct search-and-clear operations within the zone. The soldiers often had to wade in hip-deep mud. The battalion's rifle companies were rotated every 48 hours to minimize trench foot and other ailments and to allow troops to rest and replenish their supplies.

LEXINGTON III produced no major fighting. There were, however, numerous small-unit actions along the Rung Sát's waterways as U.S. ambush patrols engaged VC sampans and small boats. On 9 June the 1/18th was ordered to rejoin the division near Lộc Ninh, where 1st Division commander Maj. Gen. William DuPuy was planning division-sized operations (EL PASO I and EL PASO II) against known concentrations of PAVN forces.

—J. A. Menzoff

Reference: Stanton, Shelby. *The Rise and Fall of an American Army: U.S. Ground Forces in Vietnam 1965–1973* (1985).

See also: EL PASO, Operation; United States: Army; United States: Involvement in Vietnam, 1965–1968; Vietnam, Democratic Republic of: Army (People's Army of Vietnam [PAVN]).

Lifton, Robert Jay (1926–)

Psychiatrist and psychohistorian known for his work on post-traumatic stress disorder (PTSD) in the 1970s. Lifton's study of prisoners of war who had been subjected to "brainwashing" during the Korean conflict led to his first book, *Thought Reform and the Psychology of Totalism: A Study of "Brainwashing" in China* (1961). During the Vietnam War, he participated in antiwar activities, including the 1970 Winter Soldier Investigation and the 1971 Operation DEWEY CANYON III. In December 1970 Lifton began a series of group therapy ("rap") sessions with members of the New York chapter of Vietnam Veterans against the War (VVAW). From these sessions grew most of the subsequent definitions and treatment methods for PTSD, including the Vet Centers established in 1979 as part of the Veterans Administration system.

In 1972, with the National Council of Churches, Lifton sponsored the "First National Conference on the Emotional Needs of Vietnam-Era Veterans," attended by national VA officials. In 1973 he published his landmark book on the subject, *Home from the War*, based on his work with the New York groups, a book that is frequently cited in professional literature and the popular media. In 1976 Lifton headed the American Psychiatric Association's task force to develop a description of PTSD for the *Diagnostic and Statistical Manual*. The task force's work, also based on Lifton's work with the New York groups, was published in 1980.

—Phoebe S. Spinrad

References: Kimnel, Michael S. "Prophet of Survival" (1988); Lifton, Robert J. *Death in Life: Survivors of Hiroshima* (1968); —. *Home from the War: Vietnam Veterans, Neither Victims Nor Executioners* (1973); —. *Thought Reform and the Psychology of Totalism: A Study of "Brainwashing" in China* (1961).

See also: Antiwar Movement, United States; Post-Traumatic Stress Disorder (PTSD); Vietnam Veterans Against the War (VVAW).

Lima Site 85 (Phou Pha Thi)

A distinctive mountain in Sam Neua Province, Laos, prized during the Vietnam War as a stronghold near the border of North Vietnam. The mountain, named Phou Pha Thi in Laotian, has almost sheer cliffs on three sides and a flat summit. It was used as a landing site for helicopters during the war and was code-named Lima Site 85. Its principal importance was as the location of a tactical air control and navigation (TACAN) beacon that guided U.S. jet aircraft to targets in the Red River Delta of North Vietnam. Using the beacon, jets were able to fly into the areas of Hà Nội and Hai Phòng in all weather and deliver their bomb loads with accuracy. In March 1968, in the course of a combined military action involving North Vietnamese and Pathet Lao forces, the TACAN station was overrun by a North Vietnamese sapper squad, and several Americans on station there were killed. The TACAN equipment was put permanently out of action,

and the mountain and its commanding terrain were lost to the United States and its allies.

—Arthur J. Dommen

See also: Air Power, Role in War; Laos; Pathet Lao.

LINEBACKER I, Operation (10 May–23 October 1972)

U.S. air power response to the Democratic Republic of Vietnam's (DRV's) 1972 Spring Offensive. Operation LINEBACKER I remains a classic aerial interdiction operation. It was arguably the most effective use of air power in the Vietnam War, and it was the first modern air campaign in which precision guided munitions—laser-guided bombs (LGBs) and electro-optically guided bombs (EOGBs)—played a key role.

What made LINEBACKER I effective was the use of conventional air power against the DRV to stop a conventional invasion by 14 divisions of People's Army of Vietnam (PAVN) troops. By spring 1972 the war involved two modern, relatively well-equipped armies, the PAVN and the Army of the Republic of Vietnam (ARVN). U.S. air power provided close air support for the ARVN while simultaneously attacking the transportation system, military installations, and other vital military targets inside the DRV.

LINEBACKER I had three operational objectives: to destroy military supplies inside North Vietnam; to isolate the DRV from outside sources of supply; and to interdict the flow of supplies and troops to the battlefields of South Vietnam. The targets were basically the same as those attacked during Operation ROLLING THUNDER—highways, railroads, bridges, warehouses, petroleum storage facilities, barracks, and power generating plants. Operationally, two things were different. First, military commanders were given more latitude to select targets and to determine the best combination of tactics and weapons. Second, technological advances such as LGBs, EOGBs, and the introduction of the long-range electronic navigation (LORAN) bombing system made it possible to attack a greater variety of targets with the kind of precision that minimized collateral damage and civilian casualties.

LINEBACKER I commenced on 10 May 1972 when 32 U.S. Air Force F-4 Phantoms successfully attacked Long Biên Bridge and the Yên Viên railroad yard in Hà Nội. Two days earlier, U.S. Navy A-6 and A-7 fighter-bombers had sown 2,000-pound mines at the entrance to Hai Phòng Harbor, initiating the isolation of the DRV from outside sources of supply. During the next few days, LGBs and EOGBs were used to destroy bridges and tunnels along the highways and railroads leading from Hà Nội to the Chinese border. The bridges spanned gorges in the rugged Annamite Mountains and were not easily repaired. By the end of June more than 400 bridges and tunnels had been destroyed, including the infamous Thanh Hóa and Long Biên Bridges.

Once the bridges were down and the railroads and highways had been interdicted, LINEBACKER focused on petroleum storage facilities, power generating plants, military barracks, training camps, and air defense facilities. Again, precision guided munitions made it possible to attack targets proscribed during ROLLING THUNDER because of their prox imity to civilian structures. On 26 May a flight of four F-4s used LGBs to destroy the three main buildings of the Son Tây warehouse complex in the middle of a residential area. All bombs hit their targets without damaging the surrounding dwellings.

By September it was evident that LINEBACKER I was having an effect. Imports into the DRV dropped to half what they had been in May. The PAVN offensive inside South Vietnam stalled, and the ARVN regained much of the territory lost in the initial onslaughts of April and May. U.S. air power continued to pummel PAVN units inside South Vietnam while LINEBACKER missions pounded the North.

Although LINEBACKER I was a classic interdiction campaign, it was one with a strategic effect. There were two strategic objectives: to prevent North Vietnam from using military force to win the war, and to force the DRV to negotiate seriously. Peace talks, which had been suspended on 2 May 1972, resumed ten days later, just as the first LINEBACKER strikes hit North Vietnam. But the North Vietnamese did not negotiate seriously until September, when 27,500 tons of bombs fell on their country. Between 8 and 23 October a peace agreement acceptable to Washington and Hà Nôi took shape. On 23 October 1972 President Nixon ordered a halt to bombing north of 20 degrees latitude, but Sài Gòn balked at the peace terms.

Still, LINEBACKER I had achieved its stated objectives and succeeded where ROLLING THUNDER had failed. There were four reasons for its success. First, Nixon used air power more decisively than Johnson, who had worried about Chinese or Soviet intervention and was constantly searching for political consensus among his advisors. By 1972 Henry Kissinger's diplomacy had exploited the Sino-Soviet split, and intervention was no longer a major concern. Furthermore, Nixon's primary political concern was with the Republican right, which trusted him and wanted an end to the war. He was comparatively unconcerned with the political left. Second, the nature of the war had changed. The 14 PAVN divisions attacking South Vietnam required about 1,000 tons of supplies a day to sustain its offensive. Third, Nixon provided the military more latitude in deciding what targets should be struck and when. Finally, the employment of LGBs, EOGBs, and LORAN bombing techniques made precision strikes possible and helped limit collateral damage. These factors combined to make LINEBACKER I the most effective use of air power in the Vietnam War. It remains the classic air interdiction campaign.

—Earl H. Tilford, Jr.

References: Clodfelter, Mark. *The Limits of Air Power: The American Bombing of North Vietnam* (1989); Momyer, Gen. William W. *Airpower in Three Wars* (1978); Morrocco, John. *Rain of Fire: Air War, 1969–1973* (1986); Sharp, U.S. Grant, *Strategy for Defeat: Vietnam in Retrospect* (1978); Tilford, Earl H., Jr. *Crosswinds: The Air Force's Setup in Vietnam* (1993).
See also: Air Power, Role in War; Airplanes, Allied and Democratic Republic of Vietnam; Bombs, Smart (PGMs); Johnson, Lyndon Baines; Kissinger, Henry Alfred; LINEBACKER II, Operation; Nixon, Richard Milhous; ROLLING THUNDER, Operation.

LINEBACKER II, Operation (18–29 December 1972) U.S. bombing campaign over North Vietnam. On 13 December 1972 the Paris negotiations broke down and President Nixon issued an ultimatum to the Democratic Republic of Vietnam (DRV) to return to the conference table within 72 hours "or else," which Hà Nôi rejected. Nixon turned to air power to enforce his ultimatum.

Plans already existed for a winter phase of the original LINEBACKER campaign. Winter weather precluded operations focused on the use of laser-guided bombs (LGBs) or electro-optically guided bombs (EOGBs). The only planes in the U.S. military inventory capable of all-weather bombing operations were the Air Force's B-52s and F-111 fighter-bombers and the Navy's A-6 Intruders. However, there were not enough F-111s and A-6s to allow continued bombing of North Vietnam at the desired intensity. Targets suitable for B-52 attacks were airfields, petroleum storage facilities, warehouse complexes, and railroad marshaling yards.

On 14 December, Nixon ordered mines resown in Hai Phòng Harbor. Meanwhile, the evacuation of Hà Nôi and Hai Phòng proceeded in anticipation of what was to come. On 18 December LINEBACKER II, originally conceived as a three-day, maximum effort strategic bombing campaign, commenced. By that time over half of the Strategic Air Command (SAC) B-52 force was in the theater with 150 bombers at Andersen Air Force Base, Guam, and 60 B-52s based at U-Tapao Royal Thai Air Force Base, Thailand.

Flying in three-ship cells, each designated by a different color, the B-52s carried the brunt of the "Christmas Bombing." Just after dark on 18 December, the first wave of 48 B-52s struck the Kinh No storage complex, Yên Viên rail yard, and three airfields around Hà Nôi. An SA-2 surface-to-air missile (SAM) claimed one B-52 over Yên Viên. At midnight thirty Guam-based B-52s bombed additional targets around Hà Nôi. A second B-52 was severely damaged by a SAM but limped back to Thailand before crashing. The third wave struck just before dawn, and a third B-52 went down. The 3 percent loss rate, while regrettable, was also predictable and acceptable.

The second night was a rerun of the first. Ninety-three B-52s struck the Thái Nguyên thermal power plant and the Yên Viên rail yard. Although SAMs damaged two bombers, there were no losses. On the night of 21 December the same basic attack plan was used when three waves of 33 B-52s each returned to the Yên Viên rail yard and Thái Nguyên thermal power plant while oil storage areas at Kinh No and other storage facilities around Hà Nôi were also struck. Six B-52s were lost and a seventh was heavily damaged.

A 6-percent loss could not be sustained for long given the relatively small number of B-52s in the SAC inventory. The fault lay squarely with the Air Force and the Strategic Air Command. Years of "jungle-bashing" missions in the relatively safe skies over South Vietnam, Laos, and Cambodia had lulled SAC planners into a false sense of security. Furthermore, whereas LINEBACKER I had been a truly modern air campaign, LINEBACKER II was a throwback to World War II. The B-52 bomber streams during the first three nights were up to 70 miles long with three-plane cells lumbering toward their targets at essentially the same altitude, speed, and heading. Turn points were uniform and predictable, and losses were inevitable.

The Strategic Air Command was forced to make a switch in force packaging and strategy. Over the next two nights, the number of bombers scheduled dropped from 100-plus to 33. On the night of 21 December, the air defense support system took top priority as B-52s bombed SAM storage facilities, but two more B-52s were lost, and missions in the immediate vicinity of Hà Nôi were curtailed. On the following night B-52s pounded petroleum storage areas and rail yards around the Hai Phòng port. There were no losses. One B-52 was shot down over each of the next two nights before bombing was suspended for a 36-hour period to mark Christmas. At that point eleven B-52s had been shot down. By Christmas, most legitimate targets in North Vietnam had been reduced to rubble.

The differences between LINEBACKER I and II were in their objectives and in their intensity. LINEBACKER I was an interdiction campaign that had the strategic effect of compelling the DRV to negotiate seriously for the first time in the war. LINEBACKER II was a strategic bombing campaign aimed at the will of the North Vietnamese leadership. Its sole objective was to force the Hà Nôi government to come to quick agreement on a cease-fire. Parts of the transportation system were targeted simply because they, along with airfields and storage complexes, were suitable for area bombing. Other than the Thái Nguyên steel works, the DRV had no war industries. Most destruction wreaked on North Vietnam during LINEBACKER I had been inflicted by fighter-bombers. The bombing, although substantial, had taken place over several months, and the DRV had time to adjust to the bombing. LINEBACKER II was much more focused and intensive, with more bombs falling on North Vietnam in a shorter period. The B-52 attacks were therefore psychologically more devastating. Nevertheless, by Christmas the Hà Nôi leadership had given no indication that it was ready to negotiate seriously.

The bombing resumed at dawn on 26 December. The objective was to make the Politburo feel desperate by rendering North Vietnam defenseless. At dawn on 26 December "Ironhand" F-105 and F-4 fighter bombers, planes specially modified to attack SAM sites and their guidance radars, pummeled North Vietnam's air defense system. Sixteen USAF F-4 Phantoms used the LORAN bombing technique to blast the main SAM assembly area in Hà Nôi. Once the remaining operational SAM sites fired the missiles on hand, there would be no resupply. At dusk Air Force F-111 swingwing fighter-bombers cratered the runways at major airfields so that MiG interceptors could not take off. By dark North Vietnam lay almost defenseless before the most concerted B-52 attack in history.

That night's B-52 assault was awesome. Instead of bombing throughout the night, 120 B-52s struck ten different targets in a 15-minute period. Surviving SAM sites still had missiles, and two B-52s were lost. But the 1.66-percent loss rate was acceptable, especially since those seasoned in the art of aerial warfare knew that the end game was at hand.

The 26 December bombing got the Politburo's attention. Hà Nôi cabled Washington asking if 8 January 1973 would be an acceptable date to reopen negotiations. Nixon replied that negotiations must begin on 2 January, and that there would a time limit for reaching an acceptable agreement. Until Hà Nôi acknowledged and accepted these terms, bombing would continue.

On 27 December, B-52s struck airfields and warehouses around Hà Nôi and Vinh and the Lang Dang rail yard. SAMs knocked down two more B-52s, but returning pilots noted that missile firings were more random and that the entire DRV defense effort seemed uncoordinated and sporadic. No more B-52s were lost during LINEBACKER II. Sixty B-52 sorties were flown during each of the next two nights. Virtually no SAM firings were recorded, and B-52 crews were confident that they could fly over North Vietnam with impunity. On 28 December, Hà Nôi agreed to all of Nixon's provisions for reopening negotiations. The next day Nixon limited the bombing to targets south of the 20th parallel and LINEBACKER II came to an end.

Although LINEBACKER II ended, the bombing did not. B-52s and fighter-bombers continued to pound North Vietnamese troops, supply lines, roads, bridges, and other military facilities in North Vietnam's southern panhandle. People's Army of Vietnam (PAVN) troops inside South Vietnam were bombed up until the cease-fire agreement was signed. This continued bombing was meant to encourage the North Vietnamese to negotiate quickly, seriously, and in good faith.

For airmen, the "Eleven-Day War" took on special meaning. Air power enthusiasts claimed that, if given the opportunity, bombing on the scale of LINEBACKER II could have ended the war just as quickly at any time. Antiwar activists held that the raids constituted "another Dresden." Both interpretations, although overly simplistic, took on mythological proportions among their proponents, and both were wrong.

During LINEBACKER II, 739 B-52 sorties struck North Vietnam, dropping 15,237 tons of bombs. Air Force and Navy fighter-bombers added another 5,000 tons. The North Vietnamese launched virtually every SAM in their inventory to shoot down 15 B-52s, 9 fighter-bombers, a Navy R-5A reconnaissance plane, and an Air Force Jolly Green Giant rescue helicopter.

Damage inflicted on North Vietnamese targets was significant, but the country was far from devastated. Neighborhoods in Hà Nôi, Hai Phòng, Vinh, and elsewhere, were left largely unscathed. According to Hà Nôi's own figures, 1,312 people perished in the capital and 300 more were killed in Hai Phòng. What LINEBACKER II did was to have a psychological effect on Hà Nôi's leaders. With their air defense in shambles and virtually all the military targets left in rubble, they could not risk the neighborhoods and dike system being next. Accordingly, peace talks moved ahead expeditiously. On 23 January 1973, the United States, the DRV, the Republic of Vietnam, and the Viêt Công signed a cease-fire agreement that took effect five days later.

—Earl H. Tilford, Jr.

References: Clodfelter, Mark. *The Limits of Air Power: The American Bombing of North Vietnam* (1989); Eschmann, Karl J. *Linebacker: The Untold Story of the Air Raids Over North Vietnam* (1989); Momyer, William W. *Airpower in Three Wars* (1978); Morrocco, John. *Rain of Fire: Air War, 1969–1973* (1985); Tilford, Earl H., Jr. *Crosswinds: The Air Force's Setup in Vietnam* (1993).

See also: Air Defense, Democratic Republic of Vietnam; Air Power, Role in War; Airplanes, Allied and Democratic Republic of Vietnam; LINEBACKER I, Operation; LORAN; Nixon, Richard Milhous; Paris Negotiations; Surface-to-Air Missiles (SAMs).

Lippmann, Walter (1889–1974)

Respected journalist and political philosopher who openly opposed U.S. policy in Vietnam. Considered one of America's greatest journalists, Lippmann wrote a widely read syndicated column through which he influenced public opinion with his literary style and ability to grasp the essence of a situation. Vietnam proved his toughest topic. Lippmann first viewed the conflict as a colonial struggle, then as an example of great power maneuvering, and finally as a struggle against the white man's world. He never saw Vietnam as vital to U.S. interests, and he believed the costs to the United States of staying there were too high. Lippmann stated that a reunited, independent, and neutral Vietnam would not fall under the control of China. He cautioned President Johnson in 1964 that the Democratic Republic of Vietnam would not be pummeled into submission by U.S. firepower and urged Johnson to outline a reasonable settlement. Dismayed by Johnson's escalation of the war in 1965, Lippmann openly criticized the president in his columns, for which he was attacked by the administration. He retired in 1967 but continued to speak out against the war in Vietnam.

—Laura Matysek Wood

References: Adams, Larry. *Walter Lippmann* (1977); Luskin, John. *Lippmann, Liberty, and the Press* (1972); Steel, Ronald. *Walter Lippmann and the American Century* (1980).

See also: Johnson, Lyndon Baines; Media and the War.

Lôc Ninh, Military Operations near (1967–1968)

Lôc Ninh was a village about 80 miles north of Sài Gòn, at the northern limit of National Route 13 near the Cambodian border. It was the focal point of major People's Army of Vietnam (PAVN) infiltrations into present-day Sông Bé and Tây Ninh Provinces. During the April 1972 Easter Offensive, PAVN forces overran Lôc Ninh as part of their unsuccessful attempt to seize the provincial capital at An Lôc, occupied it, and designated it the capital of the Provisional Revolutionary Government of South Vietnam (PRG). During the 1975 Spring Offensive, the PAVN launched a major attack from Lôc Ninh, funneling armored columns south.

In 1967 and 1968 Lôc Ninh was the site of many serious clashes. In October 1967 the 1st Brigade of the U.S. 1st Infantry ("Big Red One") Division, participating in Operation SHENANDOAH II, fought a major engagement at

Lôc Ninh. In the early morning of 29 October, U.S. Special Forces and Civilian Irregular Defense Group (CIDG) camps were hit by heavy Communist mortar fire. Within three hours the first assault had been repulsed, but a Communist attack at 0515 succeeded in breaching the perimeter defenses. Army of the Republic of Vietnam (ARVN) Recondo troops with U.S. Special Forces advisors arrived at the Lôc Ninh airfield shortly thereafter and were joined by Company C of the 2d Battalion, 28th Infantry (2/28th) of the Big Red One, which had set up a fire support base (FSB) with an artillery battery at the south end of the runway. The Allied counterattack ejected the Communists from their positions after a fierce firefight.

The commander of the Big Red One, Maj. Gen. John H. Hay, Jr., posted four night defensive positions (NDPs) in the jungle behind the attacking Communist units to intercept their return to Cambodian sanctuaries. In November the Communists attacked these battalion NDPs arrayed around Lôc Ninh, each time with disastrous results. In the fighting around Lôc Ninh, five PAVN regiments were engaged. The 271st and 273d were rendered combat ineffective with nearly 1,000 soldiers killed. Operation SHENANDOAH II concluded on 19 November 1967.

In fall 1968, Lôc Ninh was the scene of more fierce combat between the 1st Infantry Division and the PAVN. In October the 2d Battalion (mechanized) of the 2d Brigade, 1st Infantry Division, and an infantry battalion of the 5th ARVN Division were under operational control of the 1st Cavalry ("The First Team") Division near Lôc Ninh. There had been two previous battles around the town in August and September, and the air cavalrymen were brought in to increase efforts to interdict the flow of Communist troops from Cambodia. On 28 November, Company C, 2d Battalion, 2d Infantry (2/2d), was responding to mortar fire received on their NDP just north of the junction of National Highways 13 and 14a when it was attacked by fire from a line of PAVN bunkers. At the end of the action, Company C had lost one APC but had killed 70 PAVN soldiers. The next day, joined by Company A, mechanized infantry swept through the previous day's battle area and again contacted a PAVN battalion falling back on its bunkers. Following air strikes and intense artillery fire on the bunker complex, the infantry swept through the area against light resistance. PAVN losses over two days totalled 148; the two U.S. companies lost seven killed in action.

The superior mobility of U.S. infantry and artillery units was a major innovation of the battles for Lôc Ninh.

—John F. Votaw

References: Haldane, Robert, ed. *The First Infantry Division in Vietnam, 1965–1970* (1993); Hay, John H., Jr. *Tactical And Materiel Innovations* (1974); Palmer, Bruce, Jr. *The 25-Year War: America's Military Role in Vietnam* (1984); Summers, Harry G., Jr. *Vietnam War Almanac* (1985).

See also: Civilian Irregular Defense Group (CIDG); Sông Bé, Battle of; United States: Army; United States: Involvement in Vietnam, 1965–1968; United States: Special Forces; Vietnam, Democratic Republic of: Army (People's Army of Vietnam [PAVN]).

Lodge, Henry Cabot, Jr. (1902–1985)

U.S. ambassador to the Republic of Vietnam, 1963–1964 and 1965–1967. President Kennedy appointed Lodge ambassador to the Republic of Vietnam (RVN) following the 1963 recall of Frederick Nolting, Jr. A firm believer in the domino theory regarding Southeast Asia, Lodge thought Vietnam could be kept free of Communist control with sufficient time purchased by the presence of U.S. troops. He became convinced that the United States could not win with President Ngô Đình Diêm as an ally and acted to undermine that regime. Opposition South Vietnamese generals were contacted through Lucien Conein, a Central Intelligence Agency operative. Lodge circumvented the pro-Diêm Gen. Paul Harkins, head of the U.S. Military Assistance Command, Vietnam (MACV), by withholding State Department communications from his purview and undercutting his upbeat assessments.

In late August 1963, the State Department instructed Lodge to give Diêm an opportunity to oust Ngô Đình Nhu, his controversial brother. If Diêm proved unwilling, Lodge was directed to tell the dissident generals that the Kennedy administration was ready to desert Diêm and back a successor regime. Fearing the Ngô family's repressive rule might affect the military situation in the countryside, Lodge wanted to temporarily withhold economic and military assistance, hoping to exert leverage and force a policy change. Such actions would also demonstrate support for the conspiring officers. By 5 October President Kennedy endorsed Lodge's proposals.

After a number of confrontations with Diêm, Lodge advocated a coup and gave tacit support to the generals' planned overthrow of the Ngôs. Operation BRAVO II, the coup against Diêm, started at 1330 on 1 November 1963. Three hours later, Diêm phoned Lodge from the besieged Gia Long Palace and inquired about the U.S. attitude about the uprising. Lodge, feigning ignorance, pretended to be alarmed for the safety of Diêm and Nhu and offered both safe conduct out of the country or sanctuary in the embassy. Diêm, determined to restore order and stay in power, refused. Diêm and his brother were later apprehended and murdered by the putschists.

Lodge soon lost confidence in the languid military leadership of Gen. Duong Van Minh, one of the anti-Diêm coup leaders. By early 1964 he supported Minh's overthrow by Lt. Gen. Nguyên Khánh. That summer Lodge resigned as ambassador and was replaced by Gen. Maxwell Taylor. Ostensibly, Lodge returned to the United States to run against Senator Barry Goldwater for the Republican presidential nomination. In reality, he was weary and disappointed with Sài Gòn politics, had no fresh thoughts on policy, and was ready to advise an air campaign against the Democratic Republic of Vietnam.

Lodge succeeded Gen. Taylor for a second tour as ambassador to the RVN in 1965. He expressed qualms about holding free elections that might result in a neutral regime. When Buddhists launched the "Struggle Movement" against the Sài Gòn government of Nguyên Cao Ky and Nguyên Van Thiêu

in 1966, Lodge championed the regime in overcoming the dissidents and their ally Gen. Nguyên Chánh Thi, who was discharged from command of I Corps. Before leaving his post, the ambassador drafted a pacification scheme he labeled Hop Tác (Cooperation), which emphasized subduing the areas around Sài Gòn.

Lodge served as one of the Johnson administration's "Wise Men" in 1968 and advocated the termination of search-and-destroy missions. In early 1969 President Nixon assigned him as a negotiator to the Paris Peace Talks, but he resigned because of a lack of progress.

—Rodney J. Ross

References: Blair, Anne E. *Lodge in Vietnam: A Patriot Abroad* (1995); Halberstam, David. *The Best and the Brightest* (1973); Hammer, Ellen J. *A Death in November: America In Vietnam, 1963* (1987); Herring, George C. *America's Longest War: The United States and Vietnam, 1950–1975* (1986).

See also: BRAVO I and BRAVO II, Operations; Conein, Lucien Emile; Domino Theory; Duong Van Minh; Goldwater, Barry Morris; Harkins, Paul D.; HOP TAC; Kennedy, John Fitzgerald; Lake, William Anthony Kirsopp; Lê Quang Tung; Ngô Đình Diêm; Ngô Đình Diêm, Overthrow of; Ngô Đình Nhu; Nguyên Cao Ky; Nguyên Chánh Thi; Nguyên Khánh; Nguyên Van Thiêu; Nixon, Richard Milhous; Nolting, Frederick, Jr.; Paris Negotiations; Richardson, John H.; Sheehan, Cornelius Mahoney (Neil); Taylor, Maxwell Davenport; Taylor-McNamara Report; United States: Involvement in Vietnam, 1954–1965.

Logistics, Allied and People's Army of Vietnam/Viêt Công

The equipping, supplying, quartering, and transporting of troops. Logistics ultimately played a crucial role in deciding the outcomes of both phases of the war in Vietnam: the Indo-China War (1946–1954) and the Vietnam War (1961–1975).

During the Indo-China War French forces, with massive assistance from the United States, generally were well supplied and equipped but were never strong enough logistically to win. Although possessing the supplies and much of the equipment necessary for victory, the French lacked the logistical means to deliver them or to sustain them during battle, where and when they were most needed.

In contrast, during the Vietnam War the United States possessed the equipment and the means to employ it effectively. Despite their logistical strength, the Americans played into their enemy's hands by utilizing tactics designed for a long war without the necessary domestic support for such a protracted strategy. The Viêt Minh and their successors—the Viêt Công (VC) and People's Army of Vietnam (PAVN, the DRV military)—were able to dictate the pace of the conflict, successfully tailoring operations to their own inferior resources and often crude, although not ineffective, logistical abilities.

The most important physical characteristics of Vietnam from a logistical standpoint are its subtropical climate, vast forests, and rugged mountainous areas. Two monsoon seasons each year hampered military operations. The southwest monsoon starts in mid May and ends in mid-October; the northeast monsoon lasts from mid-September to the end of December. Whereas the latter affects only areas along the central coast, the southwest monsoon brings rain, drizzle, and fog to the entire country, having by far the greater impact on military operations. Most military operations in both phases of the war took place during the dry season, between early January and mid-May.

The triple-canopy jungle covering much of Vietnam provided cover for troop movements, concealment for supply lines and depots, and excellent defensive positions that the Việt Minh, VC, and PAVN used to great advantage. Even in more open areas, vegetation and marshy ground restricted modern, motorized forces to the underdeveloped road system. Wet weather turned Vietnam's roads into quagmires, flooding low-lying areas and making cross-country movement impossible by wheeled transport and precarious even for tracked vehicles. Demolished bridges, ambushes, and landslides exacerbated the situation. Dry weather brought clouds of dust that clogged engine intakes and damaged machinery and equipment. Vietnam's only railway line, running from Sài Gòn through Hà Nội and into China, was vulnerable to sabotage.

Most Vietnam ports were underdeveloped and unprotected from the elements. Typhoons endangered berthed vessels, snapped lines, and halted unloading. Vietnam's most important port complexes, Hai Phòng in the North and Sài Gòn in the South, played vital roles in both phases of the conflict. During the Vietnam War the United States developed other installations at great effort and expense.

Strategically, the proximity of Laos, Cambodia, and China to Vietnam offered the Vietnamese Communists invaluable logistical advantages over their French and American adversaries. The inability of Cambodia and Laos to deny the use of their territory permitted construction of two main lines of communication that carried huge quantities of personnel, war materials, and supplies throughout the conflict. The first and best-known route, the Hồ Chí Minh Trail, ran south down the eastern side of Laos into northern Cambodia. The second, the Sihanouk Trail, began at Sihanoukville in Cambodia, where neutral ships unloaded supplies in safety, and ran via Phnom Penh to extensive base sanctuaries just across the border from the Republic of Vietnam.

North Vietnam's most important geographic feature became its border with China. The 1949 Communist victory in China enabled the People's Republic of China (PRC) to provide logistical assistance to the Việt Minh. Although China and Vietnam were traditional rivals, the PRC's opposition to the West, and particularly to the United States, prompted it to supply first the Việt Minh and later the North Vietnamese with war materials. The USSR, motivated in part by the desire to offset Chinese influence, followed suit.

French soldiers were well trained, experienced, and led by battle-seasoned veterans. The condition of their equipment, however, was parlous at best. U.S. observers were especially critical of French aircraft technicians for habitually ignoring safety precautions, failing to undertake preventive maintenance, and drinking on the job. The French logistics system

was similarly chaotic, with no effective stock control system. Since most deliveries in Vietnam were made by armed convoy, stocks tended to accumulate in forward areas in compensation for the hazardous and intermittent resupply cycle. Under such conditions, MAAG concluded in 1951 that no amount of U.S. logistical support would greatly reduce the difficulties experienced by the French in maintaining their forces at high operational levels.

Also contributing to French logistical problems was the enormously long line of communications from Hai Phòng and Sài Gòn to the United States. To help alleviate the delays that such lengthy transport entailed, MAAG advisors suggested that the French manufacture simple articles in Vietnam using native workers. The French, however, rejected the idea of a local military equipment industry. They feared it would forfeit their control over the distribution of military materials, permit at least some to fall into enemy hands, and weaken the dependence of the indigenous population on France.

Between October 1951 and February 1952, the United States delivered more than 130,000 tons of military equipment to French forces in Indo-China. By early 1953, 137,000 more tons of U.S. military equipment reached the French, and the French Air Force also took delivery of 160 F-6F and F-8F fighters, 41 B-26 light bombers, and 28 C-47 Dakota transport planes. The latter increased the all-important French air transport fleet available to support the 1954 defense of Điên Biên Phu to a maximum of 75 to 100 aircraft, of which only an estimated 56 to 75 were serviceable at any one time. Events proved these air assets totally inadequate. The French Air Force was able to deliver no more than 120 tons on average of the calculated 200 tons of supplies needed per day by the doomed garrison at Điên Biên Phu. In the end, logistics decided the battle.

At the start of their conflict against the French, Việt Minh units possessed a hodgepodge of captured French or Japanese equipment, supplemented by U.S. supplies parachuted in with the Office of Strategic Services (OSS) during World War II. The Việt Minh, short of all classes of supplies, had only a handful of trucks and no means to maintain them. Unlike the French, the Việt Minh at once set up "cottage industry" factories, hand-producing rifle ammunition, mines, grenades, light machine guns, and, eventually, 120-mm mortars. Heavy equipment remained beyond their capabilities. From late 1949 the PRC supplied most of the Việt Minh's equipment and ammunition, but only as far as the border. Distribution farther south was up to the Vietnamese.

Although the Việt Minh later had a number of trucks, porters still contributed greatly to the defeat of the French, especially in the Battle of Điên Biên Phu. Porters carried their own rations—on long trips, as much as 90 percent of their load. Approximately 40,000 porters were required to supply a 10,000-man Việt Minh division in the field. It took about a month to stock the logistic base for one attacking Việt Minh division. A time-consuming process that could not respond to unexpected changes at short notice, this supply cycle was responsible for the typical attack-lull-attack-lull pattern of

Việt Minh and later VC/PAVN attacks. Nevertheless, the porter system worked to an extent never fully understood by the French and Americans.

One commodity absolutely indispensable to the Việt Minh was rice. The main food staple of their soldiers and porters, it was also the currency in which they were paid. Goods and services provided by local communities were also reimbursed in rice. It was also the Việt Minh's Achilles' heel. The French occupation and near-pacification of the Tonkin Delta in late 1949 and early 1950 denied the Việt Minh reinforcements, taxes, and, most importantly, rice. As a result, Việt Minh supplies were halved, their forces dwindled, and some units faced virtual starvation. But by the end of 1950 the French had lost or abandoned all their posts separating Vietnam's northern border from the PRC, opening the way for Chinese assistance and yielding to their enemy an invaluable logistical prize. The Việt Minh gained food, clothing, medical supplies, and ammunition, and enough equipment to outfit a complete division.

The Chinese connection provided other items that proved essential to eventual Việt Minh victory: large amounts of artillery, heavy mortars, antiaircraft guns, and 600 trucks, most with Chinese drivers. Reequipped and resupplied, Việt Minh Main Force units grew to the offensive equivalent of eight or nine divisions. In addition, irregular forces tied down about 100,000 of the 175,000 French troops in Indo-China, leaving them with the equivalent of only three divisions for mobile operations.

The Việt Minh also greatly enhanced their logistical capabilities during this period, improving roads from their main base areas and expanding their porter force to hundreds of thousands of people. By early 1953, although it lacked the flexibility conferred by air power, the Việt Minh logistics system had become more flexible and better suited to the terrain than that of the French. Whereas French logistics were largely road- or river-bound and thus highly vulnerable to attack, the Việt Minh porter system could operate unimpeded and largely undetected.

The Việt Minh supply system at Điên Biên Phu comprised about 1,000 trucks and 260,000 porters. The porters mostly carried rice. The line of communication to Điên Biên Phu, which crossed nearly 100 streams and negotiated numerous steep gradients, ran from crossing points on the Vietnamese-Chinese border to the forward base at Tuân Giao. To support trucks, the route needed to be completely rebuilt. Once completed, it supplied a force of 49,000 combat troops and 40,000 to 50,000 logistical troops deployed along the route. In the end, the Việt Minh emerged victorious at Điên Biên Phu because they were able to supply their forces, whereas the French were not.

In the 11 years following the 1954 Geneva Conference, the DRV undertook a complete restructuring of its logistical system, replacing their army's mixture of French, Japanese, Chinese, and U.S. weapons and equipment with more standardized types, simplifying the supply of spares and ammunition. They increased their numbers of trucks and native drivers, and they rebuilt and improved their roads, railways,

and ports—chiefly Hai Phòng, Hòn Gai, and Bên Thuy. They were not as successful, however, in restructuring their battlefield support system. The great mobility and air power of the United States precluded a conventional logistics system. Moving stockpiled supplies forward from protected areas quickly enough and in amounts sufficient to support major battles without disruption from the air remained beyond their ability. The same problem impaired attempts to rapidly regroup or switch directions of emphasis. Therefore, attacks were followed by pauses while stocks were redirected or rebuilt. This logistical weakness largely accounted for the spasmodic pattern of VC and PAVN offensives that prevailed until the final stages of the war.

In the South the new Republic of Vietnam attempted to equip and train the ARVN. This task, initially envisioned as a joint French-U.S. venture, ran into immediate difficulty. French bitterness prompted a conflict over the disposition of military equipment previously supplied to the French Army. Although the terms of the contract stipulated that all equipment would revert to U.S. control, the French instead took much of it. From the moment of its formation, the rudimentary ARVN logistical system was overwhelmed with inferior and unserviceable equipment. The ARVN was thus poorly equipped to meet the growing attacks on its country by the VC. By early 1961, with the prospect of an imminent South Vietnamese collapse and the loss of an estimated $500 million investment, President Kennedy committed U.S. helicopter units in support of the faltering ARVN.

Initially, the introduction of helicopters befuddled the VC, who had little experience with them. Although their use reflected the most primitive of airmobile operations—employed only as "battle taxis" with no heavy lift or offensive capacities—helicopters contributed to a resurgence of ARVN fortunes. The VC soon learned that helicopters were highly vulnerable to ground fire, adjusted their tactics accordingly, and reversed the trend. By mid-June 1965 the VC appeared once again on the verge of victory.

With American prestige again at stake, U.S. ground troops were introduced. By the end of 1965 there were 184,300 U.S. soldiers in South Vietnam, the first wave of a commitment that would ultimately reach more than 500,000 men. Even the traditionally lavish U.S. logistic system was swamped by such a huge and sudden upsurge in manpower. Vietnam presented the United States with logistics contingencies drastically different from those of previous wars. With the conventional differentiation between combat and communication zones being nonexistent, no secure areas existed for the establishment of logistical installations. With few fixed-terrain objectives and most operations mounted from isolated base camps, there were no linear axes along which supplies could flow.

The troop buildup was also unbalanced, with the initial proportions of combat troops to logistics personnel abnormally high. Consequently, transport, storage, and distribution arrangements were overwhelmed. Supplies streamed into Vietnam faster than they could be inventoried or stored, often in greater quantity than needed. In September 1968 the surplus was estimated at more than two million tons. Consequently, huge backlog snarls—the most infamous being the so-called Sài Gòn fish market—accumulated across the country. At the height of the buildup, deep-draught ships waited 20 days for a berth to unload at any of the ten ports used by U.S. forces in Vietnam.

There are no recorded instances of U.S. operations being constrained by insufficient logistical support. Indeed, supplies were lavish. Soldiers at some fire support bases routinely enjoyed fresh roast beef, ice cream, and eggs to order, made possible by the lift ability of the helicopter and tactical transport aircraft, most notably the Army C-7A Caribou and the Air Force C-123 and C-130. By 1966 scarcely a site existed that was not within 25 miles of an airstrip capable of handling C-130s. Operations once logistically impossible for the French became almost commonplace for the Americans.

Roads and railroads also played vital logistical roles. In 1968 road transport delivered nearly ten times the supply tonnage as helicopters. The heavily damaged Vietnamese railway system was repaired enough to enable the movement of rock and gravel to construction and improvement sites.

U.S. logistics were not without problems. From April to July 1965, ammunition delivery methods created a troublesome situation. Ammunition was supplied in "push packages" containing mixed ammunition types based on predetermined expenditure rates that often proved inappropriate in Vietnam. Shortages arose as expenditure exceeded supply of the most used types, while sites were inundated with huge quantities of less crucial items. Stocks also accumulated when anticipated consumers were diverted from predesignated disembarkation points. Only with the establishment of Headquarters, U.S. Army Vietnam in July 1965 did order finally take root.

An impressive example of U.S. logistical resource application came in the 1968 siege of Khe Sanh. Whereas the French failed under similar circumstances at Điên Biên Phu, U.S. forces at Khe Sanh were never seriously endangered, thanks to enhanced air resupply. In addition to normal supply by parachute, fixed-wing transports, and helicopters, supplies were delivered by the Low-Altitude Parachute Extraction System (LAPES) and the Ground Proximity Extraction System (GPES). In LAPES runs, a C-130 flew with its tailgate down only five feet above the runway. A drogue parachute extracted roller-mounted cargo pallets from the aircraft, allowing them to skid to a stop on the runway. In GPES runs, a long hook attached to the cargo caught an arrester wire, similar to that on aircraft carriers, on the runway.

Helicopters delivered supplies directly to hill outposts around Khe Sanh using a close-cooperation air technique, the Super-Gaggle. A typical mission involved 12 CH-46 helicopters, each underslung with 2 tons of supplies, 12 A-4 Skyhawk ground attack jets for flak suppression, four UH-1E helicopter gunships flying "shotgun" behind the CH-46s, and one TA-4 for overhead coordination. Super-Gaggle missions were so successful that, despite their colorful description as "flying madhouses," only two CH-46 helicopters were shot down during the siege.

The Vietnamization program encountered immediate logistic difficulties. The Vietnamese possessed neither sufficient training to use U.S. military equipment nor the expertise to store, maintain, or repair it. Complex equipment required a sophisticated logistical system, but ARVN training standards never evolved substantially from mid-1950s levels. ARVN armored forces, supplied by the United States with the most advanced equipment, were typical. Lack of fuel and spare parts, and a minimal forward-repair capability, seriously impaired fighting effectiveness. Serviceable vehicles were used to tow damaged pieces out of action, reducing the number available for fighting and often damaging the towing vehicle.

Having followed the U.S. example of lavish consumption, the ARVN faced enormous problems following deep cutbacks in U.S. military assistance. Its training was reduced to practically nothing, its use of helicopters and transport aircraft was cut by up to 70 percent, and its vehicles were cannibalized for parts. Depleted fuel stocks could not be replenished. Ammunition, clothing, and medical supplies ran short. The effect of these logistical shortfalls on ARVN morale was devastating. When inflation destroyed military pay, desertions grew to 15,000 to 20,000 per month. Some soldiers sold their equipment, turned to graft, or avoided their duties to "moonlight."

Meanwhile, supplied with massive quantities of Russian-built equipment, the PAVN underwent a much more successful transition. Units were recalled from the South, reequipped, retrained, and returned to their former positions. By spring 1972 the PAVN was able to deploy a conventional army of 120,000 men in 14 divisions and 26 independent regiments—a force equivalent of 20 divisions, with masses of tanks and artillery. PAVN logistical systems, however, remained inflexible and incapable of supporting an attack by the whole of their forces on a single front, especially in the face of U.S. air power. Consequently, despite substantial territorial gains, the objectives of their 1972 Easter Offensive were not achieved.

In 1973 and 1974 the PAVN leaders took steps to improve their logistical system to support a large, mobile conventional army. The Hồ Chí Minh Trail was widened and surfaced, and a new all-weather road was constructed down the east side of the Annamite Mountains from Khe Sanh to Lôc Ninh. An oil pipeline also ran down the trail. PAVN crews built 12,000 miles of new roads in areas they controlled in the South, a fuel pipeline from North Vietnam to Lôc Ninh, a military telephone system, and huge supply depots with hospitals, training centers, repair facilities, and airfields.

On 26 December 1974 PAVN forces mounted their final offensive against South Vietnam. With a force equal to 18 fully equipped divisions organized into five army corps, supported by engineers, artillery, tanks, flak units, and even a new, rudimentary tactical air force, they swept all opposition before them and took Sài Gòn on 30 April 1975. In the end, the PAVN logistic system, laboriously built and adapted over years, proved the key to their success.

—Edward C. Page

References: Fall, Bernard. *Street without Joy* (1964); Heiser, Joseph M., Jr. *A Soldier Supporting Soldiers* (1991); Karnow, Stanley.

Vietnam: A History (1984); Kinnard, Douglas. *The War Managers* (1985); Thompson, Julian. *The Lifeblood of War: Logistics in Armed Conflict* (1991).

See also: Air Power, Role in War; France: Air Force; France: Army; Geography of Indo-China and Vietnam; Hô Chí Minh Trail; Indo-China War; Transportation Group 559; United States: Army; Viêt Minh (Viêt Nam Độc Lâp Đông Minh Hôi [Vietnam Independence League]); Vietnam, Democratic Republic of: Army (People's Army of Vietnam [PAVN]); Vietnam, Republic of: Army (ARVN).

Lon Nol (1913–1985)

Cambodian army officer; prime minister at the time of the overthrow of Norodom Sihanouk; president of the short-lived Khmer Republic, 1972–1975. Lon Nol was sufficiently popular with the Cambodian elite that at a National Congress convoked by Sihanouk in August 1969, he received the highest number of votes (115) among ten possible candidates to head a "national salvation" government to deal with mounting economic and foreign problems. Prince Sisowath Sirik Matak received the second highest vote (99). These two men emerged within months as Cambodia's leaders, albeit extraordinarily reluctant ones. Both declined the Congress's offer to form the new government. Only on Sihanouk's virtual order did Lon Nol finally agree to become prime minister.

Lon Nol has often been accused of plotting Sihanouk's overthrow, but during most of the crucial period preceding the National Assembly's vote of no confidence in Sihanouk, he was in France undergoing medical treatment, having left Sirik Matak in charge in Phnom Penh. Whatever ambitions Lon Nol might have harbored, his actions were hardly those of a coup plotter.

Lon Nol met with Sihanouk in Europe at the beginning of January and reportedly persuaded the prince to sanction tougher measures against the North Vietnamese and Viêt Cộng (VC) in their operations inside Cambodia—notably their requisitioning of rice and other supplies and the use of base camps opposite the South Vietnam border to support offensives against the Sài Gòn government. In February, the small Cambodian army began artillery bombardments against People's Army of Vietnam (PAVN) and VC positions on Cambodian soil. Lon Nol called in all outstanding 500-riel notes, thereby creating chaos with the Communist Vietnamese rice purchasing operations.

On 8 March 1970, the first of a series of anti-Vietnamese demonstrations occurred in Svay Rieng, a province containing large North Vietnamese base areas. Four days later Lon Nol sent Sihanouk a telegram through the Cambodian Embassy in Paris demanding that Cambodia's military forces be increased to 100,000 men. Sihanouk was outraged by publication of the message and threatened execution of his ministers, so frightening Lon Nol that he decided to join with Sirik Matak in ousting Sihanouk. However, the night before the decisive vote in the National Assembly, Lon Nol reportedly had to be persuaded at gunpoint by Sirik Matak to sign a document authorizing the ouster. On 18 March, after a debate in which his conduct was criticized by all speakers, Sihanouk was voted out. Cheng Heng, chairman of the National

Assembly, became head of state pending election of a new head of state under the constitution. Lon Nol and Sirik Matak remained as prime minister and deputy prime minister, respectively.

Faced with the determination of the North Vietnamese and VC forces to retain their Cambodian sanctuaries and sources of supply, and the growing threat posed by an indigenous Khmer Communist movement headed by Pol Pot, the Phnom Penh government blundered from one failure to another. Its rapid loss of control of most of the provinces was not helped by massive military maneuvers along the main roads, and Phnom Penh became a beleaguered city crowded with refugees. The country's strained economy collapsed; the Chinese merchant class fled. A pogrom against Vietnamese residents resulted in thousands of civilian deaths.

In this crisis, Lon Nol showed a surprising lack of leadership. He relied increasingly on mystical solutions and consulted with astrologers. Always a superstitious man, he called the Vietnamese *thmil*, a Khmer word for evil forest spirits. Resisting suggestions that he step down to pave the way for a negotiated armistice with Sihanouk in Beijing, he stayed on doggedly. But Lon Nol faced real health problems, and a few weeks before the Khmer Rouge entered Phnom Penh, he departed for Hawaii to receive medical treatment. He then moved to California.

—Arthur J. Dommen

References: Chandler, David P. *The Tragedy of Cambodian History: Politics, War and Revolution since 1945* (1991); Hamel, Bernard. *Sihanouk et le Drame Cambodgien* (1993); Kirk, Donald. *Wider War: The Struggle for Cambodia, Thailand and Laos* (1971).

See also: Cambodia; Khmer Rouge; Pol Pot; Sihanouk, Norodom.

Long Bình

Principal U.S. Army base in the Republic of Vietnam (RVN), established in 1967, 20 miles north of Sài Gòn near Biên Hòa air base. It eventually covered more than 25 square miles and housed 50,000 soldiers. With paved roads and a rail line, Long Bình became the center for command, administration, logistics, and medical support for troops operating in the RVN's southern provinces. The II Field Force and Army of the Republic of Vietnam (ARVN) III Corps had their headquarters there. By the end of the war, Long Bình contained major surgical hospitals, restaurants, movie theaters, and other facilities. Post exchanges offered amenities enjoyed in the United States.

The 18th Engineer Brigade constructed six cargo barge unloading points on the Sài Gòn River near the Long Bình Depot, and vast amounts of war supplies flowed through the redistribution facilities at Long Bình. The base also served as a replacement depot and transit base for personnel entering or leaving Vietnam. Long Bình also contained the U.S. Army prison for Vietnam. Known by troops as LBJ (Long Bình Jail), it had a reputation for uncompromising discipline and harsh living conditions. On 29 August 1968, military police ruthlessly crushed a priosners' riot there.

Long Bình epitomized the dichotomy of the war in Vietnam. Support troops lounged in air-conditioned barracks while combat troops fought in the steamy jungles and rice paddies. However, the Việt Cộng targeted Long Bình for rocket and mortar attacks, as they did all U.S. bases. As part of the Communist 1968 Tết Offensive, a Việt Cộng regiment attacked the base but was repelled with heavy losses by the 199th Light Infantry Brigade. In 1975 People's Army of Vietnam forces destroyed the base during the Hồ Chí Minh Campaign.

—Stanley S. McGowen

References: Clarke, Jeffrey J. *The United States Army in Vietnam: Advice and Support: The Final Years, 1965–1973* (1988); Dunn, Carroll H. *Vietnam Studies: Base Development in South Vietnam, 1965–1970* (1972); Olson, James S., ed. *Dictionary of the Vietnam War* (1988); Sheehan, Neil. *A Bright Shining Lie: John Paul Vann and America in Vietnam* (1988); Stanton, Shelby L. *The Rise and Fall of an American Army: U. S. Ground Forces in Vietnam, 1965–1973* (1985); Westmoreland, William C. *A Soldier Reports* (1989).

See also: U.S. Army Vietnam Installation Stockade (USARVIS).

Long Chieng

Main military base of the Hmong irregular forces in Laos, located in a valley in the southwestern corner of Xieng Khouang Province. Long Chieng was off limits to the press because of sensitivity on the part of the U.S. embassy in Vientiane to the presence of Americans on the ground supporting the Hmong troops and their T-28 aircraft, as well as others flying in light aircraft as forward air controllers. Late in the Vietnam War, however, journalists visited Long Chieng, incurring the wrath of Gen. Vang Pao.

—Arthur J. Dommen

See also: Laos; Vang Pao.

Long-Range Reconnaissance Patrols (LRRPs)

Tactical innovation developed by U.S. forces and their allies in reaction to a war in which front lines were nonexistent, enemy locations were unknown, and rugged terrain concealed staging and base areas and supply routes.

The first LRRP teams consisted of special reconnaissance units organized by the U.S. Army Special Forces as part of Project LEAPING LENA. Detachment B-52 was organized under this program in May 1964 and eventually grew to include 93 Special Forces soldiers and more than 1,200 Vietnamese and ethnic personnel. Detachment B-52 was initially responsible for training Republic of Vietnam (RVN) Special Forces and South Vietnamese belonging to the Civilian Irregular Defense Group (CIDG) in long-range reconnaissance patrolling and intelligence gathering.

In June 1964 Project LEAPING LENA was transferred to U.S. Military Assistance Command, Vietnam (MACV) and became Project DELTA with its own LRRP and intelligence gathering mission. Organized into a reconnaissance component, a reaction force, and a command section, Project DELTA consisted of 600 personnel. The typical reconnaissance element contained eight patrol teams of four Vietnamese or ethnic members, and 16 reconnaissance teams of two Special Forces soldiers and four indigenous personnel. The reaction force usually was a battalion equivalent, organized into 12 reconnaissance teams whose mission was to collect intelligence on Communist troop movements, assess bomb damage, coordinate artillery and air strikes, and conduct special operations. Project DELTA also had 12 "Roadrunner" teams that conducted reconnaissance along trail networks. Based at Nha Trang, Project DELTA was under the control of MACV and was used throughout South Vietnam. In September 1966 it received the additional duty of training LRRP teams being organized by other U.S. Army units.

In August 1966 an additional Special Forces LRRP unit, Detachment B-50 (Project OMEGA), was formed at Ban Mê Thuột in II Corps tactical zone consisting of 127 Special Forces members and 894 ethnic troops. Similar in organization to Project DELTA, it was placed under the control of I Field Force Vietnam. At the same time a third unit, Detachment B-56 (Project SIGMA), was formed at Hô Ngoc Nau under the control of II Field Force Vietnam. In November 1967 OMEGA and SIGMA were taken over by the MACV Special Operations Group.

Special Forces had other highly classified intelligence collection units, such as Detachment B-57 (Project GAMMA), which conducted LRRP missions into Cambodia. Another highly classified unit was MACV's Studies and Observation Group, which included U.S. Army Special Forces, U.S. Navy SEALs, and U.S. Marine Corps reconnaissance personnel who conducted cross-border patrols and other tasks.

The early success of the LRRP concept prompted MACV Commander Gen. William Westmoreland in 1966 to order all divisions and separate brigades to form their own LRRP units on a priority basis, even while formal approval was pending. The shortage of trained soldiers, however, prevented the order from being immediately carried out.

LRRPs raised outside the Special Forces generally consisted of a platoon organized by a division's cavalry squadron, which had always had reconnaissance and intelligence-gathering missions. Beginning in 1967 several separate LRRP companies were organized, including the only U.S. Army National Guard rifle company to serve in Vietnam, Indiana's Company D, 151st Infantry. Later converted to Companies C through I and K through P, 75th Infantry (Ranger), these soldiers were assigned to U.S. Army divisions and separate infantry brigades as LRRPs.

Allied contingents created their own LRRP units. The Australians, for example, deployed a Special Air Service squadron to the RVN in April 1966 to perform LRRP functions in Phuoc Tuy Province in the III Corps Tactical Zone.

—Clayton D. Laurie

References: Keely, Francis J. *U.S. Army Special Forces, 1961–1971* (1973); Stantob, Shelby L. *Rangers at War: Combat Recon in Vietnam* (1992).

See also: Australia; Civilian Irregular Defense Group (CIDG); DELTA, Project; Military Assistance Command, Vietnam (MACV); Montagnards; OMEGA, Project; SIGMA, Project; Studies and Observation Group (SOG); United States: Special Forces; Westmoreland, William Childs.

LORAN

Acronym for long-range electronic navigation. This system uses two or more pairs of ground-based transmitting stations to allow the crew of an aircraft or ship to find their position. The master unit of each pair transmits a series of pulses, each repeated by the slave station located several hundred miles away. Since the period between the signals of the two stations is fixed and known, the length of time between the reception of each signal can be used to determine how much closer the aircraft is to one station than to the other. This time difference is determined either by computer or by plotting the signal on an oscilloscope. A second pair of stations allows the crew to triangulate to derive its position. The system operates at ranges up to several thousand miles, but accuracy deteriorates at longer distances. Under ideal conditions LORAN systems can be accurate to within one hundred yards.

The Vietnam War was the first conflict in which fighter-bomber aircraft attempted to strike with precision under adverse weather conditions and at night. Electronic navigation aids like LORAN and TACAN (tactical air control and navigation) systems made these attempts possible. LORAN was the more useful system because its signals were impossible to corrupt and, unlike TACAN, it allowed the aircraft to remain electronically "quiet." This radio silence made incoming aircraft more difficult to track and defend against, improving survivability. LORAN-guided strikes were less accurate than visual navigation and bombing, however. Employed extensively during Operation LINEBACKER II against storage facilities and power transformers, such strikes proved only marginally effective.

—Matthew A. Crump

References: Crump, Herschel W. Interview with the author (1997); Glister, Herman L. *The Air War in Southeast Asia: Case Studies of Selected Campaigns* (1993); Pierce, J. A., et al., eds. *LORAN: Long Range Navigation* (1948); Williams, J. E. D. *From Sails to Satellites: The Origin and Development of Navigational Science* (1992).

See also: Air Power, Role in War; ELINT (Electronic Intelligence); LINEBACKER II, Operation.

LORRAINE, Operation (October–November 1952)

French military operation mounted in haste against Viêt Minh base areas in order to compel Viêt Minh commander Gen. Vô Nguyên Giáp to return divisions to their defense and abandon his campaign to conquer the Thai (T'ai) Highlands. Giáp, having seen the limitations of French heavy equipment in earlier battles, decided to attack across the top of the Indo-Chinese peninsula, forcing the French to fight at long range in difficult terrain. He reasoned that the French would find it difficult or impossible to bring heavy equipment to bear against his forces there.

LORRAINE, begun on 29 October 1952, started well but bogged down on its long and precarious supply lines. On 14 November the French began their withdrawal. Now fully alerted, the Viêt Minh attacked retreating French units. By 1 December the French had returned to their defensive positions along the so-called De Lattre Line, and Giáp's forces were still on the Laos border. Operation LORRAINE failed because Giáp refused to abandon his strategy of leaving small units to fend for themselves, even if it meant sacrificing his 36th and 176th infantry regiments. He was certain that such French operations would eventually come to an end. In fact, the larger the operation, the more likely it would be of short duration, for its component units, drafted just for the operation at hand, would soon be required elsewhere.

—Spencer C. Tucker

References: Fall, Bernard. *Hell in a Very Small Place: The Siege of Dien Bien Phu* (1967); —. *Street Without Joy* (1961); —. *The Two Viet Nams* (1964); Simpson, Howard R. *Dien Bien Phu: The Epic Battle America Forgot* (1994).

See also: CASTOR, Operation; Điên Biên Phu, Battle of; Dinassauts; Salan, Raoul Albin Louis; Vô Nguyên Giáp.

Lowenstein, Allard K. (1929–1980)

Liberal activist and U.S. congressman best known for leading the challenge to Lyndon Johnson's renomination in 1968. Convinced that Johnson would not de-escalate in Vietnam, Lowenstein and Curtis Gans organized what some called the "Dump Johnson" movement. They enticed Senator Eugene McCarthy to run and helped mobilize younger campaign workers, who propelled McCarthy to a shocking near-defeat of Johnson in the New Hampshire primary. This showing convinced Senator Robert Kennedy to enter the Democratic race and helped persuade Johnson to withdraw.

—Mitchell K. Hall

References: Chafe, William H. *Never Stop Running: Allard Lowenstein and the Struggle to Save American Liberalism* (1993); Cummings, Richard. *The Pied Piper: Allard K. Lowenstein and the Liberal Dream* (1985); Harris, David. *Dreams Die Hard* (1982).

See also: Antiwar Movement, United States; Elections, U.S.: 1968; Johnson, Lyndon Baines; Kennedy, Robert Francis; McCarthy, Eugene Joseph.

Lu Hán (?–?)

General commanding Chinese troops that in 1945 occupied northern Vietnam. Hán arrived in Hà Nôi on 14 September 1945 and, at a news conference the next day at Đôn Thuy, announced that China was sending 200,000 men to Vietnam to be stationed throughout the region north of the 16th parallel. Hán said the Chinese mission was to disarm the Japanese and not to interfere in the internal affairs of Vietnam. However, the Chinese brought with them Nguyên Hai Thân, an exiled leader of the Vietnam National Party (Viêt Nam Quôc Dân Đang), with the plan of installing a government led by Thân to replace that of Hô Chí Minh.

Lu Hán left Hà Nôi in 1946 and surrendered to the Chinese Communist Forces in 1949.

—Ngô Ngoc Trung

References: Biographical Files, Indo-China Archives, University of California at Berkeley.

See also: China, People's Republic of (PRC); Vietnam, Democratic Republic of: 1945–1954.

Luce, Henry R. (1898–1967)

News mogul and advocate of a U.S. role in world affairs. Luce's missionary zeal culminated in "The American Century," an essay published in the 17 February 1941 issue of *Life*, in which he proclaimed that the world was the United States' frontier and hungered for American know-how. Virulently anti-isolationist, Luce's essay stirred interventionists and formed the background for much of U.S. foreign policy well into the 1960s. Opponents criticized "The American Century" as rehashed imperialism, although Luce insisted he was merely defining America's mission in world history.

Luce died in Pheonix, Arizona, on 28 February 1967.

—Brenda J. Taylor

References: Herzstein, Robert E. *Henry R. Luce: A Political Portrait of the Man Who Created the American Century* (1994); Jessup, John K., ed. *The Ideas of Henry Luce* (1969).

See also: Roosevelt, Franklin Delano; Truman, Harry S.

Luong Ngoc Quyên (aka Luong Lâp Nhâm) (1890–1917)

Prominent Vietnamese nationalist and leader of an uprising against the French in 1917. In December 1915 British police in Hong Kong arrested Quyên and handed him over to French authorities. Returned to Hà Nôi, he was given a life sentence and held in Thái Nguyên Prison, where he was brutally tortured. His patriotism helped him recruit numerous Vietnamese soldiers in the French colonial administration, including Trinh Van Cân (Đôi Cân). On 31 August 1917, an uprising occurred in Thái Nguyên Province led by Đôi Cân. Quyên was released and became advisor and deputy commander. The rebels controlled the province for one week until French reinforcements arrived from Hà Nôi and forced them to retreat into the jungle. Handicapped as the result of torture during his imprisonment, Quyên committed suicide to make it easier for revolutionary troops to retreat.

—Ngô Ngoc Trung

References: Biographical Files, Indo-China Archives, University of California at Berkeley.

See also: French Indo-China; Phan Bôi Châu.

Ly Bôn (?–548)

Founder of the early Ly Dynasty. Ly Bôn left government service to prepare for an uprising that forced the Chinese governor out of Vietnam. Bôn took Thang Long (Hà Nôi) and built a new independent state named Van Xuân (Ten Thousand Years of Spring). Following his death, his resistance movement continued under the leadership of Triêu Quang Phuc. Although Ly Bôn had freed Vietnam for only a brief time, his revolt marked the beginning of a resistance movement that lasted until 939, with the establishment of an independent state under the leadership of King Ngô Quyên.

—Ngô Ngoc Trung

References: Biographical Files, Indo-China Archives, University of California at Berkeley.

See also: Ngô Quyên; Vietnam: Prehistory to 938.

Lynd, Staughton (1929–)

Radical Quaker pacifist and New Left intellectual who operated at the center of antiwar activism throughout most of the Vietnam era. An early participant in the Vietnam antiwar movement, Lynd chaired the April 1965 Students for a Democratic Society (SDS) march in Washington and spoke at that spring's Berkeley teach-in. His greatest notoriety came when he traveled to the Democratic Republic of Vietnam (DRV) in December 1965 with Tom Hayden and Herbert Aptheker to hear North Vietnamese terms for peace and to encourage a negotiated settlement of the war. The trip violated federal law and temporarily resulted in the cancellation of Lynd's passport, although the courts restored it on appeal.

Lynd preferred attacking the system from without rather than through electoral politics, which he believed diverted the movement away from fundamental change. His continued antiwar protests included partial income tax refusal, vigorous support for draft resistance, and sponsorship of the 1967 Spring Mobilization. Disillusioned with the militant drift of the younger New Left, by 1971 Lynd became increasingly involved with economic issues .

—Mitchell K. Hall

References: Finn, James. *Protest: Pacifism and Politics* (1967); Hayden, Tom. *Reunion: A Memoir* (1988); Lyttle, Bradford. *The Chicago Anti-Vietnam War Movement* (1988); Moritz, Charles, ed. *Current Biography Yearbook* (1983); Zaroulis, Nancy, and Gerald Sullivan. *Who Spoke Up? American Protest Against the War in Vietnam, 1963–1975* (1984).

See also: Antiwar Movement, United States; Draft; Hayden, Thomas E.; National Coordinating Committee to End the War in Vietnam (NCC); Spring Mobilization to End the War in Vietnam.

M

MacArthur, Douglas (1880–1964)

U.S. Army general. After the 25 June 1950 North Korean invasion of South Korea, MacArthur became supreme commander of United Nations forces in Korea. Believing there was "no substitute for victory," MacArthur clashed with the concept of limited war advocated by President Truman and the Joint Chiefs of Staff. In April 1951, after MacArthur communicated critical views regarding conduct of the war directly to members of Congress, Truman dismissed him. MacArthur returned to a hero's welcome and then retired.

MacArthur reportedly told President Kennedy that there was no end of Asian manpower and that solving U.S. domestic problems should have a higher priority than the war in Vietnam. Shortly before his death, MacArthur also warned President Johnson not to commit U.S. ground forces to Vietnam, nor anywhere else on the Asian mainland. It is thus indeed ironic that MacArthur was regarded as a prophet by those who argued for an unremitting anti-Communist Asian crusade.

—Spencer C. Tucker

References: James, D. Clayton. *The Years of MacArthur*. Vol. 3. *Triumph and Disaster, 1945–1964* (1985); Manchester, William. *American Caesar: Douglas MacArthur, 1880–1964* (1978).

See also: Johnson, Lyndon Baines; Kennedy, John Fitzgerald; Korean War; Truman, Harry S.

MACARTHUR, Operation

(13 October 1967–31 January 1969)

Military operation in the western Central Highlands. In its 1967 phase, it became more commonly known as the Battle of Đak Tô.

When Operation GREELEY ended on 12 October 1967, only a single 4th Division battalion remained in Kontum Province until a reinforced People's Army of Vietnam (PAVN) division again threatened the Đak Tô Special Forces camp. Acting Military Assistance Command, Vietnam (MACV) commander Gen. Creighton Abrams countered by deploying 16 maneuver battalions.

Undetected, PAVN forces had spent months establishing well-fortified positions on the peaks and ridge-lines overlooking Đak Tô. On 3–4 November, companies of the 4th Division's 3d Battalion, 12th Infantry (3/12th) and 3d Battalion, 8th Infantry (3/8th) successfully cleared out PAVN positions on hills south and southwest of Đak Tô, but on 6 November, Task Force Black of the 173d Airborne's 4/503d Infantry took heavy casualties while attempting to establish a firebase on Hill 823 south of Ban Het. Though reinforced by companies of the 4/503d and the 1/503d, U.S. paratroopers were caught in a deadly U-shaped ambush on 11 November by the 66th PAVN Regiment. The jungle canopy made artillery and tactical air support ineffective.

Beginning on 14 November, five ARVN battalions fought the 24th PAVN Regiment at Hill 1416 northeast of Đak Tô for four days before taking the hill. On 15 November, PAVN mortar fire hit the Đak Tô airfield, touching off the ammunition dump and destroying two C-130 cargo planes, but causing only light casualties. As more Allied troops poured in, the 32d and 66th PAVN Regiments withdrew to entrenched positions to the southwest. The 3/12th Infantry engaged the 32d Regiment on Hill 1338 for two days, taking the summit after furious fighting. Meanwhile, the PAVN 174th Regiment occupied Hill 875, 16 kilometers west of Đak Tô near the Cambodian border.

On 19 November, 173d Airborne commander Brig. Gen. Leo H. Schweiter ordered the 2/503d Infantry to assault Hill 875. This would be the climax of the Battle for Đak Tô. Following artillery and air strikes, Companies C and D started up the northern slope but were stopped by fire from an intact system of interconnected bunkers. Waves of PAVN soldiers counterattacked and enveloped the Americans, virtually annihilating two platoons. In reserve 200 meters back, Company A was decimated by fire from the rear. The shattered battalion established an emergency perimeter. PAVN gunners shot down six helicopters, but one managed to drop pallets of ammunition inside the shrinking perimeter. Still, the battalion was left without food or water for 50 hours. Compounding the tragedy, an errant U.S. bomb fell inside the perimeter, killing 42 men and horribly wounding 45 more. On 20 November, companies of the 4/503d moved up the hill but did not reach the survivors' perimeter until evening. At daybreak, they cut a landing zone from the jungle, and helicopters extracted the wounded. On 22 November, helicopters brought in food and removed the dead and, following a seven-hour air and artillery barrage, the 4/503d resumed the attack up Hill 875. The advance reduced to a crawl, but despite dozens of casualties, the battalion captured two trench lines before digging in 250 feet from the crest. More air strikes turned the top of Hill 875 into a wasteland, and on 23 November, the 1st Cavalry's 1/12th Infantry joined the remaining troops of the 4/503d for a final attack. These reached the summit by noon, but the battered PAVN regiments already had decamped, leaving behind their dead and weapons, to descend the western slope into their Cambodian sanctuary.

Throughout November, U.S. forces fired more than 170,000 artillery rounds into the mountains surrounding Đak Tô and flew more than 2,000 tactical air strikes and 300 B-52 sorties. At least 40 U.S. helicopters were lost. The Army reported PAVN losses as 1,644 dead, their costliest battle since the Ia Drang Valley campaign.

Debate over the worth of the fight for Hill 875 continues. The cost of the Battle of Đak Tô was staggering—at least 73 ARVN lives in addition to the official count of 376 Americans killed and 1,441 wounded. Actual U.S. battle deaths probably exceeded 700, but this number was reported only in the context of the larger Operation MACARTHUR. The 173d Airborne Brigade received a Presidential Unit Citation but was so decimated that it was never again deployed as a complete combat unit.

Though shocked by the extent of U.S. casualties, Gen. Westmoreland proclaimed that the Battle of Đak Tô signaled "the beginning of a great defeat for the enemy." Gen. Võ Nguyên Giáp probably thought otherwise. U.S. forces, especially on Hill 875, were completely outmaneuvered by PAVN troops, who chose the time and place for the "decisive" engagement. Although only the 24th PAVN Regiment would take part in the coming 1968 Têt Offensive, the other three PAVN regiments were not, as MACV claimed, "virtually destroyed."

The 4th Division and assorted South Vietnamese units continued to pursue the elusive Communist troops in Kontum and Pleiku, but there were no memorable battles throughout 1968. MACARTHUR became an undefined border-watch operation to inhibit PAVN infiltration. At the formal end of Operation MACARTHUR, MACV claimed a total of 5,731 enemy casualties.

—John D. Root

References: Maitland, Terrence, Peter McInerney, and the editors of Boston Publishing Company. *A Contagion of War* (1983); Murphy, Edward F. *Dak Tô: The 173rd Airborne Brigade in South Vietnam's Central Highlands, June–November 1967* (1993); Stanton, Shelby L. *The Rise and Fall of the American Army: U.S. Ground Forces in Vietnam, 1965–1973* (1985).

See also: Abrams, Creighton; Body Count; Casualties; Đak Tô, Battle of; Friendly Fire; GREELEY, Operation; Military Assistance Command, Vietnam (MACV); United States: Army; United States: Involvement in Vietnam, 1965–1968; Vietnam, Democratic Republic of: Army (People's Army of Vietnam [PAVN]); Westmoreland, William Childs.

Machine Guns, Allied and People's Army of Vietnam

Almost all machine guns used during the Vietnam War were of U.S. or Soviet design. Although the Viêt Công (VC) and People's Army of Vietnam (PAVN) used any weapons available, most of their machine guns were either Soviet-made or Chinese-manufactured from Soviet designs. Two of the most widely used Soviet designs were the 7.62-mm Goryunov SG-43 and the heavy 12.7-mm Degtyarev DShK. With the proper mount, the DShK was an effective antiaircraft gun, especially against helicopters. The Communists also used weapons captured from the French during the first Indo-China War and U.S. weapons taken from the Army of the Republic of Vietnam (ARVN) or from the Americans.

Early in the war, ARVN units were equipped with older, but still highly effective, U.S. machine guns. Their primary vehicle-mounted machine gun was the Browning M1919A4, an American mainstay in World War II. The Browning M1919A6 was the infantry version of the same gun, equipped with a bipod on the front of the barrel and a shoulder stock that permitted the gun to be fired from the prone position. Both weapons fired the .30–06 bullet, the same round fired by the M1 rifle, which was issued to the ARVN in large numbers.

In U.S. service, the M1919A4 and M1919A6 were replaced during the early 1960s by the M60 machine gun, a truly outstanding weapon modeled closely after the World War II German MG-42 machine gun. Instead of the traditional U.S. .30–06 round, the M60 fired the 7.62-mm North Atlantic Treaty Organization (NATO) standard round. The M14 rifle also fired the 7.62-mm NATO standard, but most U.S. troops in Vietnam carried the M16 rifle, which fired the much smaller 5.56-mm round. Thus, for the first time in the twentieth century, U.S. units did not have rifles and machine guns that fired the same ammunition.

The M60 was used in every conceivable role for a machine gun, mounted on trucks, jeeps, armored personnel carriers (APCs), and other vehicles; on tripods inside fortifications; and on aircraft and boats. A version designated the M60D was fitted with a rear trigger mechanism and handles (called spade grips) for use by helicopter door gunners.

The M60 saw its widest use by far on the ground with the infantry. An infantry machine gun section officially consisted of three soldiers: the gunner, the assistant gunner, and the ammunition carrier. In practice, all members of a patrol carried extra machine-gun ammunition, which was passed up to the gun crew when needed. This accounts for the ubiquitous photographs of U.S. infantrymen with belts of machine gun ammunition draped around their bodies. That was the easiest way to carry the heavy load, and it left the soldier's hands free to use his own weapon.

The standard U.S. heavy machine gun was also among the oldest weapons in the inventory. The basic Browning .50-caliber M2 was introduced in 1921 and slightly modified in 1933. It remains the best heavy machine gun ever designed. In Vietnam the heavy-barrel version, the M2(HB), was mounted on larger vehicles and occasionally on tripods on the ground. The gun delivered a massive half-inch-diameter bullet. The M2 was highly prized by the VC, who thought nothing of sacrificing many of their own troops in an attempt to capture one. It took a well-trained gunner to operate the sometimes temperamental M2 effectively, and M2 gunners tended to specialize in their job. The troops loved the guns, which they called the "Mod Deuce" or "Ma Deuce." Both the M60 and the M2 are expected to remain in the U.S. military inventory well into the twenty-first century.

During the Vietnam War, modern technology resurrected the multibarrelled Gatling gun, obsolete for almost 100 years. Instead of a hand crank, the drive mechanism was operated by an electric motor. Modern Gatling guns had tremendous rates of fire but were too large and bulky for general infantry use. They did, however, make ideal aircraft-mounted weapons.

The M61 Vulcan fired a massive 20-mm round at the cyclic rate of 6,600 rounds per minute. Vulcans initially were designed for Air Force fighter aircraft. In the mid-1960s they were mounted on old World War II–era C-47 transports and rigged to fire sideways, out the cargo door. The result was the AC-47, known as "Puff the Magic Dragon." The M134 minigun was a scaled-down version of the Vulcan, firing as many as 6,000 7.62-mm rounds per minute. The much lighter minigun was designed for helicopters and became one of the primary weapons of the helicopter gunship. The Vulcan-firing AC-47 and the minigun-firing Cobra helicopter were feared and respected by VC and PAVN troops.

—David T. Zabecki

References: Hobart, F. W. A. *Pictorial History of the Machinegun* (1972); Hogg, Ian V. *The Complete Machinegun: 1885 to the Present* (1979); Smith, W. H. B. *Small Arms of the World* (1973).

See also: Airplanes, Allied and Democratic Republic of Vietnam; Armored Personnel Carriers (APCs); Helicopters, Allied and Democratic Republic of Vietnam; Rifles.

Madman Strategy

President Nixon's plan to bluff Hà Nôi into ending the Vietnam War. Nixon sought to use the same tactic that Eisenhower had used shortly after becoming president in 1953, when he let it be known that if the Korean stalemate continued, he would seek to win the war militarily, even with nuclear weapons. An armistice was concluded three months later. Nixon called this the "Madman Theory." According to Harry Haldeman in *The Ends of Power,* Nixon told his aide Bob Haldeman, "We'll just slip [North Vietnam] the word to them that, 'for God's sake, you know Nixon is obsessed about Communism. We can't restrain him when he's angry—and he has his hand on the nuclear button'—and Ho Chi Minh himself will be in Paris in two days begging for peace." This did not work with Hà Nôi, and ultimately Nixon fell back on, and intensified, the same failed Johnson policies, especially the use of air power.

—Spencer C. Tucker

References: Haldeman, Harry R., with Joseph DiMina, *The Ends of Power* (1978); Kissinger, Henry. *White House Years* (1979).

See also: Eisenhower, Dwight David; Kissinger, Henry Alfred; Nixon, Richard Milhous.

Mailer, Norman (1923–)

American author and novelist. A cofounder of *The Village Voice,* Mailer became increasingly radicalized against totalitarianism and America's technocratic society. Invited by Jerry Rubin to the Vietnam Day Protest in Berkeley, California, on 2 May 1965, Mailer spoke against President Johnson's policies. Mailer developed his antiwar ideas in two novels. *Why Are We in Vietnam?* (1967) allegorically insinuates, through a hipster narrator, that America's use of technology is cowardly. *The Armies of the Night* (1968) recounts Mailer's personal experiences at the antiwar march against the Pentagon in October 1967. Employing the methods of the New Journalism, Mailer demonstrated the power of subjective histories in understanding wartime experiences.

—Charles J. Gaspar

References: Louvre, Alf. "The Reluctant Historians: Sontag, Mailer, and American Culture Critics in the 1960s" (1986); Wenke, Joseph. *Mailer's America* (1987).

See also: Antiwar Movement, United States; Central Intelligence Agency (CIA); Fiction, U.S., and the Vietnam Experience; Greene, Graham; Prose Narrative and the Vietnam Experience; Rubin, Jerry.

Malaysia

Independent Asian federation of former British possessions, formed in 1963. Malaysia's significance to the Vietnam War lies both in its role as a model of a successful counterinsurgency and in its later aid to the Republic of Vietnam (RVN) government. In 1946, while the area was still a British protectorate, the large ethnic Chinese minority played a major role in a Communist uprising. The British sent 40,000 troops to control the situation and received military equipment and economic support from the United States. The British and the Malaysian government largely subdued the rebels by 1963, using direct military measures and social programs such as the establishment of new, fortified villages for the Chinese peasants. The latter program formed the model for the unsuccessful RVN Strategic Hamlet program.

The British experience in Malaysia seemed to prove that counterinsurgency operations were winnable. Those who used this argument in defense of intervention in Vietnam frequently overlooked vital differences in the two countries, including the relative populations and level of outside support for the Communists.

Malaysia also contributed to the anti-Communist effort in Vietnam, training more than 3,000 South Vietnamese military and police officers between 1961 and 1966 and providing materiel support. In 1966 Malaysian Deputy Premier Tun Razak offered to send combat troops, but this was not accepted. In 1967 Malaysia sent a team of experts to Vietnam to confer on matters of village pacification and psychological warfare, but the RVN government largely disregarded its advice.

—Matthew A. Crump

References: Gould, James W. *The United States and Malaysia* (1969); Larsen, Stanley Robert, and James Lawton Collins, Jr. *Allied Participation in Vietnam* (1975); Smith, R. B. *An International History of the Vietnam War,* Vol. III. *The Making of a Limited War, 1965–66* (1991).

See also: Strategic Hamlet Program; Thompson, Robert Grainger Ker.

MALHEUR I and II, Operations (May–August 1967)

A series of search-and-destroy operations conducted by the U.S. Army during a three-month period in the Đuc Phô District of Quang Ngãi Province. In spring 1967, increased Communist activity in the five northernmost provinces of the Republic of Vietnam (RVN) prompted the U.S. Military Assistance Command, Vietnam (MACV) to shift north two U.S. Army units to assist U.S. Marine Corps and Army of the Republic of Vietnam (ARVN) forces already in the area. These reinforcements consisted of 3,000 men of the 2d Brigade, 1st Cavalry Division, who started moving north into Quang Ngãi Province from neighboring Bình Đinh Province on 8 April, and 4,500 troops of the 196th Light Infantry Brigade that was moved from its Tây Ninh Province base north of Sài Gòn to Chu Lai in Quang Tín Province.

On 22 April 1967, MACV announced creation of the 15,000-man Task Force Oregon in the five-province area. Gen. Westmoreland's Chief of Staff, Maj. Gen. William B. Rosson, commanded the task force, which was ordered to provide security along the coast, to open Highway 1, and to relieve Communist pressure in northern Bình Đinh, Quang Ngãi, and southern Quang Tín Provinces. As Task Force Oregon deployed, it permitted the Marines to move units north to the Demilitarized Zone (DMZ) and eased the efforts of the 1st Cavalry Division in its ongoing operations in Bình Định Province.

On 11 May, five U.S. Army battalions of Task Force Oregon began Operation MALHEUR I near Đuc Phô, south of Quang Ngãi City. Many hamlets in this area were heavily fortified with bunkers, air-raid tunnels, communications trenches, booby traps, and punji pits. Physical destruction was enormous in this densely populated coastal region, and Communist forces would often allow patrolling U.S. troops to enter a village before opening fire. In the ensuing firefights, U.S. forces would call in massive naval gunfire, artillery, and tactical air support, often destroying houses next to the spider holes and fortified bunkers they were seeking to reduce. By the end of May, significant sections of Highway 1 were cleared from northern Quang Ngãi Province to southern Quang Nam Province. Light fighting, consisting of ambushes and intense patrolling, continued through July 1967.

Operation MALHEUR II immediately followed the close of MALHEUR I, and the troops of Task Force Oregon again experienced almost daily contact. Under continued heavy pressure from U.S. mechanized and helicopter units, and from naval gunfire and B-52 bomber strikes, Việt Công (VC) and People's Army of Vietnam (PAVN) troops in Quang Ngãi Province were forced to disperse into the jungle-covered mountains further inland. Both MALHEUR operations concentrated first upon eliminating regular Communist formations to reduce pressure on the local populace. Once this was accomplished, the emphasis shifted to eliminating VC infrastructure. During the operations, the Communists found it increasingly difficult to operate among the people in the countryside.

Task Force Oregon distributed more than 23 million leaflets to the population of the Đuc Phô District, which, like the rest of the province, had been under Communist domination for decades. Such appeals had little effect, however, because many villagers were Việt Công members. Since Allied forces were not numerous enough to leave detachments in the villages they searched, the VC often returned hours after the Americans had departed.

At the end of the MALHEUR operations, Task Force Oregon reported 869 VC and PAVN soldiers killed at a cost of 81 American dead. The force also reported the evacuation of 8,885 villagers and the burning of their houses to deny the use of these facilities to VC troops in the area and to discourage the peasants from returning. The extensive use of artillery and air strikes with high explosives and napalm helped keep down U.S. casualties, but it also resulted in large-scale destruction and the deaths of villagers and refugees. According to the U.S. Agency for International Development, more than 6,400 civilian casualties were admitted to Quang Ngãi hospitals in 1967, half of them women and children.

The operations of Task Force Oregon in Quang Ngãi Province destroyed or drove away Communist main force units, but in the process U.S. forces contributed materially to the depopulation and destruction of large portions of the province. The operations concluded without having fully eradicated the 2d VC Regiment or the 2d PAVN Division, both known to be operating in the area. According to U.S. intelligence reports, the Việt Công were soon moving freely again, in broad daylight, disrupting travel on Highway 1 and still ready to fight.

—Clayton D. Laurie

References: Shulimson, Jack. *The U.S. Marines in Vietnam: Fighting the North Vietnamese, 1967* (1984); Stanton, Shelby L. *The Rise and Fall of an American Army: U.S. Ground Forces in Vietnam, 1965–1973* (1985); Westmoreland, William C. *Report on the War in Vietnam*, Section II: *Report on Operations in South Vietnam, January 1964–June 1968* (1969).

See also: Airmobility; Booby Traps; Search and Destroy; United States: Army; United States: Involvement in Vietnam, 1965–1968; United States: Marine Corps; U.S. Agency for International Development (USAID); Vietnam, Democratic Republic of: Army (People's Army of Vietnam [PAVN]); Vietnam, Republic of: Army (ARVN).

Manila Conference (24–25 October, 1966)

Conference concerning the Vietnam War attended by representatives of the Republic of Vietnam (RVN), the United States, Australia, New Zealand, Thailand, the Republic of Korea (ROK), and the Philippines. The conference, which took place in the Philippine capital, has been viewed as a response to several international efforts by the United Nations (UN) as well as by Communist and nonaligned nations over the previous two years to gain a settlement of the growing conflict in Southeast Asia. The Johnson administration was also involved in secret talks to de-escalate the conflict.

The Manila Conference was one of several attempts to offer publicly a program for a negotiated settlement of the war in terms impossible for the DRV to accept. Following that line of reasoning, the entire affair was staged largely for U.S. and South Vietnamese public and political consumption.

—Paul R. Camacho

References: Frankel, Max. "Ky Tells 6 Allies at Manila Talks Civil Rule Is Near" (1966); —. "Manila Talks End" (1966); Kahin, George McTurnan, and John W. Lewis. *The United States in Vietnam* (1966); Kraslow, David, and S. H. Loory. *The Secret Search for Peace in Vietnam* (1966); Schurmann, Franz, P. D. Scott, and R. Zelnik. *The Politics of Escalation in Vietnam* (1966).

See also: Johnson, Lyndon Baines; Nguyễn Cao Ky; U Thant; Westmoreland, William Childs.

Mansfield, Michael Joseph (1903–)

U.S. senator, 1952–1977. Although initially supportive of President Johnson's Vietnam policies, Mansfield became disillusioned and counseled against deployment of ground troops in 1965. In 1966 he went to South Vietnam on a fact-finding mission and, upon his return, privately tried to persuade Johnson that a military solution was impossible. Rebuffed by Johnson, he openly criticized the war.

This criticism continued during President Nixon's first term, when Mansfield supported the Cooper-Church and Hatfield-McGovern Amendments. In 1971 he introduced his own "end-the-war" amendment, which called for the withdrawal of all U.S. military forces within nine months, subject to the release of all prisoners of war. Although it passed the Senate, the amendment was defeated by the House.

—Robert G. Mangrum

References: Herring, George C. *America's Longest War: The U.S. and Vietnam, 1950–1975* (1986); Karnow, Stanley. *Vietnam: A History* (1984); Lewy, Guenter. *America in Vietnam* (1980); Olson, James S., ed. *Dictionary of the Vietnam War* (1988); Summers, Harry G. *Vietnam War Almanac* (1985).

See also: Church, Frank Forrester; Cooper, John Sherman; Cooper-Church Amendment; Hatfield, Mark Odum; Hatfield-McGovern Amendment; Johnson, Lyndon Baines; McGovern, George S.; Nixon, Richard Milhous.

Mao Zedong (Mao Tse-tung) (1893–1976)

Chinese political leader/dictator. With Karl Marx and Vladimir Lenin, Mao was considered one of the three main theorists of Marxism. Mao's most important contribution was in explaining how to tap the discontented peasant masses in China to bring about a Communist revolution there. His philosophy was in sharp contrast to that of Marx and Lenin, who had emphasized the primary role of the industrial working classes in bringing about such a revolution.

Mao Zedong's greatest revolutionary contribution was to synthesize a Communist-led guerrilla force with agrarian revolution. Mao Zedong became famous, along with Gen. Zhu De, for successfully leading the Communists' guerrilla army against much larger and better-armed opponents. Mao's strategic principles were largely based on China's traditional military texts, such as Sun Tzu's *Art of War*, and were codified during 1944 in the following sayings: "Enemy advances, we retreat; enemy halts, we harass; enemy tires, we attack; enemy retreats, we pursue." Mao's guerrilla tactics were ultimately responsible for bringing the Chinese Communist Party to power throughout mainland China and became the model for other Asian revolutionaries such as those in Vietnam.

Although the United States had backed the Nationalists during the Civil War in China, Mao made attempts to sponsor friendly relations with the United States during the late 1940s. When these failed, he allied China more closely with the USSR. According to a 1994 account by Mao's private physician, Mao upon hearing in August 1964 that the United States intended to send additional troops to South Vietnam, secretly ordered Chinese troops to wear Vietnamese uniforms and fight alongside the Việt Công. China also provided arms, money, and technical support to the DRV.

However, soon after the PRC engaged in a series of bitter border disputes with the USSR during 1969, Mao turned to the United States as a means of balancing Beijing's worsening relations with Moscow. In February 1972, Mao met with President Nixon, and the two nations signed the Shanghai Communiqué, a document that opened diplomatic relations between China and the United States and also helped lead to the end of U.S. involvement in the Vietnam War.

—Bruce Elleman

References: Harrison, James Pinckney. *The Long March to Power* (1972); Li Zhisui, Dr. *The Private Life of Chairman Mao* (1994),

Meisner, Maurice. *Mao's China: A History of the People's Republic* (1977); Selden, Mark. *The Yenan Way in Revolutionary China* (1971); Terrill, Ross. *Mao: A Biography* (1980).

See also: China, People's Republic of (PRC); Union of Soviet Socialist Republics (USSR; Soviet Union); Vietnam, Democratic Republic of: 1945–1954; Vietnam, Democratic Republic of: 1954–1975; Zhou Enlai (Chou En-lai).

March on the Pentagon (21 October 1967)

Among the most significant national antiwar demonstrations. The March on the Pentagon represented for many a shift from protest to resistance. The Student Mobilization and National Mobilization Committees cosponsored the demonstration in Washington, D.C., and project director Jerry Rubin focused on the Pentagon as a symbol of American militarism. Federal officials attacked the event with misleading accusations of Communist domination, and the government mobilized thousands of troops for protection.

The event began with a rally at the Lincoln Memorial that drew perhaps 100,000 people, followed by a march to the Pentagon by about 35,000. Though most participants acted peacefully and legally, several hundred sat down near the Pentagon and awaited arrest, often appealing to the troops to join them. As the crowd dwindled over the next 24 hours, taunts by radicals and clubbings by federal marshals punctuated the confrontation. Officials made 647 arrests and hospitals treated 47 injured.

Government and media reactions were overwhelmingly unsympathetic. The apparent ineffectiveness of peaceful and legal protests made civil disobedience and more confrontational tactics increasingly attractive options within the antiwar movement.

—Mitchell K. Hall

References: Halstead, Fred. *Out Now! A Participant's Account of the American Movement against the Vietnam War* (1978); Mailer, Norman. *The Armies of the Night* (1968); Wells, Tom. *The War Within: America's Battle over Vietnam* (1994).

See also: Antiwar Movement, United States; Rubin, Jerry.

MARIGOLD, Operation (June–December 1966)

Code name for peace initiative centered around U.S. Ambassador Henry Cabot Lodge, Jr. and Polish representative on the International Control Commission Janusz Lewandowski, with Italian Ambassador to the RVN Giovanni D'Orlandi acting as go-between. Lewandowski's claim to have a "very specific peace offer" from Hà Nội led to secret talks and a proposed U.S.-DRV December 1966 meeting in Warsaw.

Historian George Herring notes that, with MARIGOLD, Moscow made its first effort in the "diplomacy of peacemaking." But the Soviet and Polish roles were unclear, and Lewandowski's unorthodox diplomatic approach led to misunderstanding. The U.S. government thought Lewandowski's draft of U.S. views misrepresented its de-escalation bargaining position. In the final analysis, Lewandowski's inept diplomacy and U.S. skepticism thwarted the possibility of substantial results.

—Paul S. Daum, with Joseph Ratner

References: Cooper, Chester L. *The Lost Crusade: America in Vietnam* (1970); Herring, George C. *LBJ and Vietnam: A Different Kind of War* (1994); —, ed. *The Secret Diplomacy of the Vietnam War: The Negotiating Volumes of the Pentagon Papers* (1983); Kraslow, David, and Stuart H. Loory. *The Secret Search for Peace in Vietnam* (1968); Radvanyi, Janos. *Delusion and Reality: Gambits, Hoaxes, and Diplomatic One-Upmanship in Vietnam* (1978).
See also: International Commission for Supervision and Control (ICSC); Lodge, Henry Cabot, Jr.; Paris Negotiations; Poland; Read, Benjamin Huger; Union of Soviet Socialist Republics (USSR; Soviet Union); United States: Marine Corps; Vietnam, Republic of: Marine Corps (VNMC).

Marine Combined Action Platoons (CAPs)

U.S. Marine Corps pacification initiative. The tactical area of responsibility (TAOR) assigned to U.S. Marines in Vietnam lay in the northernmost portion of the Republic of Vietnam (RVN), designated as I Corps. The Marines took countryside pacification seriously, and Marine officers realized that they had to gain the confidence of villagers if they were to deny the Viêt Công (VC) local support and bases of operations.

Called at various times by such names as Internal Defense and Development, Rural Reconstruction, Stability Operations, Revolutionary Development, Internal Security, Nation Building, and Neutralization Operations, pacification was not "the other war," as Gen. William Westmoreland and many others thought of it. It was the supporter of military combat operations and was at least as important. Based on earlier experiences in the Caribbean and in Central America, III Marine Amphibious Force (MAF) formed combined action platoons in fall 1965 to support the RVN's Revolutionary Development Program.

Administered by the G-5 Civil Affairs section based in Đà Nang, III MAF fielded four battalions of CAPs between October 1967 and July 1970. Each consisted of one Marine rifle squad and one Navy corpsman plus one platoon of Regional Force/Popular Force (RF/PF) soldiers of the RVN. These men were assigned to a particular village, often one that was home to the RF/PF members of the unit, and made it their base of operations for extended periods. Marines got to know villagers as individuals, helped in civic and health projects, and taught locals the arts of booby-trapping, entrapment, ambush, and self-defense.

As noted by Jean Sauvageot, an Army officer who spent several years in Vietnamese pacification projects: "There was absolutely no comparison between CAP and what most Army units were doing. For example, if CAP killed fifteen enemy soldiers, they usually had fifteen weapons to show for it. At the same time, Army units were killing fifteen or five or fifty enemies and might not have a single weapon to show when the firing stopped ... they were killing noncombatants and claiming them as dead enemy soldiers." In 1970 the program changed to "combined action groups," using a Marine company and an RF/PF battalion. The last such unit was withdrawn in spring 1971.

—Cecil B. Currey

References: Cincinnatus [Cecil B. Currey]. *Self-Destruction: The Disintegration and Decay of the United States Army during the Vietnam Era* (1981); Corson, William. *The Betrayal* (1968); Sauvageot, Lt. Col. Jean. Interview with the author (1977).
See also: Civilian Operations and Revolutionary Development Support (CORDS); Pacification; Territorial Forces; United States: Marine Corps.

MARKET TIME, Operation (1965–1972)

Allied naval operation to conduct surveillance of the 1,200-mile South Vietnamese coastline and halt seaborne infiltration of supplies to Communist troops. Initially the Seventh Fleet commanded the U.S. operation, which was designated the Vietnam Patrol Force, or Task Force 71. Weeks later, naval leaders code-named the operation MARKET TIME. On 31 July 1965, operational command transferred from the Seventh Fleet to Naval Advisory Group (NAG), and the Vietnam Patrol Force became the Coastal Surveillance Force, or Task Force 115. On 1 April 1966, the newly created NAVFORV (Naval Forces Vietnam) assumed command of Operation MARKET TIME.

NAVFORV created a three-pronged patrol system consisting of outer and inner ship barriers and an air barrier, which comprised the farthest outer barrier. Using Dixie Station (in the South China Sea, southeast of Cam Ranh Bay), propeller-driven A-1 Skyraiders operated for a short time in 1965 but soon were replaced by P-3 Orions. Other aircraft of Operation MARKET TIME included P-2 Neptunes and P-5 Marlins. The P-2s and P-3s operated from several bases, including Cam Ranh Bay, Tân Son Nhut, U-Tapao in Thailand, and Sangley Point in the Philippines. The P-5s, before their withdrawal in 1967, operated out of Sangley Point and had seaplane tenders at Cam Ranh Bay, Poulo Condore, and the Cham Islands. Air surveillance duties included identifying suspicious vessels, photographing them, then reporting them to one of five Coastal Surveillance Centers along the South Vietnamese coastline to disseminate to other aircraft and surface ships for further investigation.

The outer ship barrier operated within 40 miles of the South Vietnamese coast, stretching from the 17th parallel to the Cambodian border in the Gulf of Thailand. Ships included high-endurance Coast Guard cutters, destroyer escorts, radar picket escort ships, ocean and coastal minesweepers, and patrol gunboats. Their mission was the interdiction of seaborne supplies carried by trawler-type vessels. MARKET TIME forces neutralized more 50 infiltrating vessels.

The inner ship barrier operated in the shallow waters along the South Vietnamese coastline, where Communists, using wooden junks to transport men and supplies, could easily intermingle with thousands of innocent junks and sampans. Thus the South Vietnamese government authorized U.S. MARKET TIME forces to stop, search, and seize any vessel involved in fishing or trade within a 12-mile limit. U.S. naval leaders realized that the South Vietnamese Junk Force needed to be phased into the Republic of Vietnam Navy (VNN) in order to investigate junk traffic sailing close to shore. In July 1965, the Junk Force integrated into the VNN. To augment the junks, the U.S. Navy adopted the fast patrol craft, or Swift boats, originally used by oil companies in the Gulf of Mexico to transport crews to offshore rigs.

Additional duties of MARKET TIME forces included fire support for ground troops. And in 1968, elements of Task Force 115 became MARKET TIME Raiders, which operated with the newly created SEALORDS forces to conduct river raiding operations. As U.S. withdrawal began, under Vietnamization MARKET TIME forces slowly shifted materiel to the VNN, while U.S. sailors transferred to other duties.

—R. Blake Dunnavent

References: Cutler, Thomas J. *Brown Water, Black Berets: Coastal and Riverline Warfare in Vietnam* (1988); Marolda, Edward J. *By Sea, Air, and Land: An Illustrated History of the U.S. Navy and the War in Southeast Asia* (1994); Schreadley, R. L. *From the Rivers to the Sea: The United States Navy in Vietnam* (1992); Wunderlin, Clarence E., Jr. "Paradox of Power: Infiltration, Coastal Surveillance, and the United States Navy in Vietnam, 1965–1968" (1989).

See also: Airplanes, Allied and Democratic Republic of Vietnam; Riverine Craft; Riverine Warfare; SEALORDS (South East Asia Lake Ocean River Delta Strategy); Sea Power in the Vietnam War; United States: Coast Guard; United States: Navy; Vietnam, Republic of: Navy (VNN).

Marshall, Samuel Lyman Atwood (1900–1977)

One of the most influential military historians of the twentieth century. For the 60 years, S. L. A. Marshall (known universally as "Slam") pursued parallel careers as a reserve officer and as a journalist and writer, covering most of the world's major wars during that period.

Marshall emphasized direct interviews with participants of combat actions as soon as possible after the event. As a result of these interviews, Marshall in 1947 wrote *Men against Fire*, a penetrating analysis of the U.S. infantryman and small unit cohesion and effectiveness. He pointed out many problems with U.S. combat performance and offered recommendations to correct them. The Army later adopted many of his recommendations.

During the Vietnam War, as a retired brigadier general, Marshall made several tours to the war zone under U.S. Army sponsorship. With Col. David H. Hackworth, he wrote *Vietnam Primer*, which the Army published as *DA Pamphlet 525–2*. More than two million copies of the lessons-learned manual were printed.

Some historians have criticized Marshall's work by exposing flaws and inconsistencies in his data. A disillusioned Hackworth referred to him as "the Army's top apologist." Marshall, nonetheless, had a profound impact on the U.S. Army. Many veterans of infantry combat continue to agree that, regardless of the flaws in Marshall's data or collection methods, his conclusions in *Men against Fire* were correct.

—David T. Zabecki

References: Marshall, S. L. A. *Battles in the Monsoon* (1967); —. *Bird*; —. *Bringing Up the Rear: A Memoir* (1979); —. *Men against Fire* (1947); —. *Vietnam: Three Battles* (1982); Williams, Frederick D. *SLAM: The Influence of S. L. A. Marshall on the United States Army* (1990).

See also: Hackworth, David H.; Media and the War; Prose Narrative and the Vietnam Experience.

Martin, Graham A. (1912–1990)

U.S. ambassador to the Republic of Vietnam (RVN), 1973–1975. In 1963 Martin was named ambassador to Thailand, where he fostered strong military ties and served as a U.S. representative to the Southeast Asia Treaty Organization (SEATO). A staunch anti-Communist, Martin was selected in 1973 to replace Ellsworth Bunker as ambassador to the RVN.

Martin was ill suited for the tenuous situation he inherited. His no-nonsense personality rendered problematic his relationship with RVN President Nguyên Van Thiêu, who required constant nurturing. Martin also drastically underestimated the seriousness of the situation in Vietnam and ignored the rampant corruption within Thiêu's government and the Army of the Republic of Vietnam (ARVN) that eroded local support.

Martin believed until the end that Sài Gòn would be held. He was so confident that Sài Gòn could withstand the spring 1975 People's Army of Vietnam (PAVN)/Viêt Công offensive that he refused to order rescue operations until it was almost too late. Finally, as Communist forces prepared to overrun Sài Gòn, Martin ordered an emergency evacuation. On 29 April 1975, Option IV (Operation FREQUENT WIND), the largest helicopter extraction in history, went into effect. Martin, carrying the embassy flag, led his wife to the embassy's roof, where they boarded a Marine helicopter, leaving behind his personal belongings that he had refused to remove earlier.

—David Coffey

References: *Facts on File 1991* (1991); Findling, John E. *Dictionary of American Diplomatic History* (1980); Karnow, Stanley. *Vietnam: A History* (1983).

See also: Bunker, Ellsworth; EAGLE PULL, Operation; FREQUENT WIND, Operation; Harriman, W. Averell; Kissinger, Henry Alfred; Nguyên Van Thiêu.

MASHER/WHITE WING, Operation

(24 January–6 March 1966)

The first major search-and-destroy operation of the Vietnam War. Operation MASHER/WHITE WING, also known as the Bông Son Campaign, entailed a 42-day sweep over 2,000 square miles of forested mountains and rugged valleys in northern Bình Đinh Province in II Corps Tactical Zone. The operation was conducted by the U.S. 1st Cavalry Division, the Army of Republic of Vietnam (ARVN) 22d Division and Airborne Brigade, and the 1st Regiment of the Republic of Korea (ROK) Capitol Division. The operation was renamed WHITE WING on 4 February because of President Johnson's concern over public reaction to the name MASHER.

This operation was the first major campaign to cross corps boundaries. During the same period, the 3d Marine Division conducted Operation DOUBLE EAGLE in I Corps Tactical Zone (CTZ) and entered Bình Đinh Province to join the 1st Cavalry. The U.S. sweeps were supported by two ARVN operations, THÂN PHONG II and LI N K T-22.

Operation MASHER/WHITE WING opened when four battalions of the 3d Brigade, 1st Cavalry, began helicopter assaults eight miles north of Bông Son against 8,000

Communists of the 1st and 2d Viêt Công (VC) Regiments and 18th and 98th People's Army of Vietnam (PAVN) Regiments. Contact was established early and major firefights occurred on 28 and 29 January at Phung Du and An Thoi. Using massive air support, the Americans forced the Communists to retreat north into the ARVN Airborne Brigade.

After being reinforced by the 2d Brigade, on 6 February the 3d Brigade moved into the An Lão Valley to destroy any remaining Communist forces and to link up with the Marines. The 1st Brigade, meanwhile, conducted a series of actions south of Bông Son on Highway 1, while the 2d Brigade drove a Communist battalion from the Cay Giep Mountains into a blocking force of the 22d ARVN Division. Most of the VC/PAVN units had already fled the area, however, having been severely mauled in the actions on the coast. The operation ended on 6 March 1966 as the 1st Cavalry completed its full circle of air mobile assaults around Bông Son to arrive back in the Cay Giep Mountains.

Officially, the operation was said to have returned 140,000 people to government control and to have ended the threat to Bông Son, Quang Ngãi, and Qui Nhon. Yet critics charged that the lavish use of firepower caused a major increase of refugees, without providing additional security. Only limited pacification efforts were undertaken, and, because the Communists soon returned, the 1st Cavalry had to launch Operation THAYER/IRVING in the same area later in the year.

—Clayton D. Laurie

References: Hymoff, Edward. *The First Air Cavalry Division: Vietnam* (1967); Westmoreland, William C. *Report on the War in Vietnam.* Section II: *Report on Operations in South Vietnam, January 1964–June 1968* (1969).

See also: Airmobility; DOUBLE EAGLE, Operation; IRVING, Operation; Search and Destroy; United States: Army; United States: Marine Corps; Vietnam, Democratic Republic of: Army (People's Army of Vietnam [PAVN]); Vietnam, Republic of: Army.

MASSACHUSETTS STRIKER, Operation
(1 March–8 May 1969)
101st Airborne Division (Airmobile) assault into the A Shau Valley. On 1 March 1969, the U.S. 101st Airborne Division (Airmobile) began operations in response to Military Assistance Command, Vietnam (MACV) intelligence reports of increased People's Army of Vietnam (PAVN) logistical activity in the A Shau Valley. The division's first objective was to build two fire support bases (FSBs) at the southern edge of the valley. This was soon accomplished, but bad weather prevented aviation and infantry units from conducting airmobile operations until later that day.

On their initial sweep, soldiers of a rifle company of 1st Battalion, 502d Infantry (1/502d) encountered immediate resistance. Anticipating a major engagement, the 101st's 2nd Brigade immediately airlifted an additional four infantry battalions into the area. Although there was little contact with Viêt Công (VC) or PAVN forces because they immediately broke contact, the "Screaming Eagles" began to uncover massive amounts of supplies. Throughout April 1969, the units of the 101st destroyed numerous caches of weapons, ammuni-

tion, equipment, and food. On 1 May, the 1/502d discovered a major PAVN supply base that contained a complete field hospital and a heavy machine repair facility.

MASSACHUSETTS STRIKER did not produce any major battles, but it did disrupt the Communist logistics system. In response to the PAVN buildup, MACV launched a more ambitious operation in the A Shau, named APACHE SNOW.

—J. A. Menzoff

Reference: Stanton, Shelby. *The Rise and Fall of an American Army: U.S. Ground Forces in Vietnam 1965–1973* (1985).

See also: Airmobility; APACHE SNOW, Operation; Logistics, Allied and People's Army of Vietnam/Viêt Công.

May Day Tribe
Anti-Vietnam War protesters. Led by Rennie Davis, this group staged an attempted shutdown of Washington, D.C., for three days beginning 3 May 1971. Davis, one of the Chicago Eight, proposed the idea of a massive, nonviolent act of civil disobedience at a National Student Association (NSA) conference. Though his proposal was not endorsed by the NSA, Davis gathered supporters on college campuses.

Davis and his group, which came to be known as the May Day Tribe, with support from the People's Coalition for Peace and Justice, gave the government an ultimatum: Adopt the People's Peace Treaty, or the Tribe would try to immobilize the capital. The protests, though unsuccessful in their aim of shutting down the city, led to more than 12,000 arrests, the largest number from any demonstration in U.S. history. Those arrested were detained in Robert F. Kennedy Stadium for up to 48 hours. On 5 May, the remaining demonstrators heard speeches from congressional members opposed to the war, including New York representatives Bella Abzug and Charles Rangel. This gathering resulted in more arrests, effectively ending the May Day protests.

—John M. Barcus

References: De Benedetti, Charles. *An American Ordeal: The Antiwar Movement of the Vietnam Era* (1990); Wells, Tom. *The War Within: America's Battle over Vietnam* (1994); Zaroulis, Nancy, and Gerald Sullivan. *Who Spoke Up? Protest against the War in Vietnam, 1963–1975* (1984).

See also: Antiwar Movement, United States; Chicago Eight; Students for a Democratic Society (SDS).

Mayaguez Incident (12–14 May 1975)
Two weeks after the abandonment of the U.S. embassy in Sài Gòn, the Cambodian Khmer Rouge fired upon the U.S. merchant ship *Mayaguez* in the Gulf of Siam. Arguing that the ship had entered Cambodian territorial waters, the Khmer Rouge boarded it and took the crew prisoner. Intelligence sources reported to President Ford that the ship was being taken to Kompong Som on the Cambodian mainland; the crew's whereabouts were unclear. Negotiating with the Khmer Rouge was never seriously considered. Ford refused to accede to another hostage situation like the 1968 seizure of the *Pueblo* and decided to use force to retrieve the crew.

Late in the afternoon of 12 May, the *Mayaguez* weighed anchor and appeared to be headed for Kompong Som.

Unsure whether the crew was still aboard, Ford nevertheless ordered Thai-based F-4 fighters to intercept the ship and fire across its bow. The vessel then altered its course to Koh Tang Island, off the Cambodian shore. Even after the ship halted, intelligence reports could not confirm whether the crew of the *Mayaguez* had been transferred to Koh Tang. Early on 13 May, Ford ordered that any ship leaving Koh Tang be stopped to prevent the crew from being taken to the mainland. Late that evening, the Cambodians tried to break away from the island, but were stopped by U.S. fire.

The attempted Cambodian escape from Koh Tang Island apparently convinced Ford that the crew was being held there. At 1040 on 13 May, Ford ordered the armed forces to develop a three-pronged plan of action: a helicopter assault on the *Mayaguez* to retrieve control of the ship, an amphibious invasion of Koh Tang Island to retrieve the crew, and a series of air strikes on Kompong Som so that Koh Tang Island could not be reinforced.

Throughout 14 May, U.S. troops began to move into position—the main assault force numbered 175 Marines. At 1909, U.S. Marines landed on Koh Tang Island. Informed by intelligence reports that they would encounter no more than 20 Cambodians and their families, the Marines were surprised to find 150 to 200 dug-in Khmer Rouge troops. Cambodian resistance continued for almost an hour before the U.S. command—still not in possession of the crew of the *Mayaguez*—declared the mission a "success." At approximately 2100 hours, the first air strike was conducted against Kompong Som; ten minutes later, the destroyer *Holt* pulled alongside the *Mayaguez*, but the American crew was not aboard.

With the mission in danger of failure, press secretary Ron Nessen read a statement indicating that the United States would cease its military operation if and when the crew was completely and unconditionally released. One hour later, a Navy reconnaissance pilot saw the crew of the *Mayaguez* waving from the bow of a fishing boat. They were quickly retrieved by the destroyer *Wilson*. The bombing of Kompong Som continued until midnight but would have gone on longer had a fourth strike, ordered by Ford, not been countermanded. (According to Ford in his memoirs, Secretary of Defense James Schlesinger, who was opposed to using force to retrieve the *Mayaguez*, countermanded the order.) The crew of the *Mayaguez* had been retrieved, at a total cost of 40 U.S. dead and 50 wounded.

—John Robert Greene

References: Greene, John Robert. *The Presidency of Gerald R. Ford* (1995); Guilmartin, John F. *A Very Short War: The Mayaguez and the Battle of Koh Tang* (1995); Lamb, Christopher Jon. *Belief Systems and Decision Making in the Mayaguez Crisis* (1988).
See also: Cambodia; Ford, Gerald R.; Khmer Rouge; Schlesinger, James R.

MAYFLOWER, Operation (12–18 May 1965)

The first of several diplomatic initiatives to end the war in Vietnam via bombing halts. Operation MAYFLOWER was the first deliberate bombing pause by the United States since the start of Operation ROLLING THUNDER. As with most diplomatic efforts toward peace in Vietnam War, it ended in failure.

In the months before Operation MAYFLOWER, the Johnson administration was under increasing pressure from domestic and international critics to halt the bombing campaign. The White House developed a peace initiative centered on a limited bombing pause with the hope that the pause would defuse criticism, expose the fallacy of DRV posturing, and set the stage for resumption of even larger air strikes.

Operation MAYFLOWER proceeded in secrecy. U.S. Ambassador to the Soviet Union Foy Kohler tried to deliver a communiqué to the DRV ambassador in Moscow announcing that the United States would suspend air attacks against North Vietnam starting on 12 May. The DRV ambassador and Soviet foreign minister rebuffed Kohler, and the document delivered to the Vietnamese embassy was returned, apparently unopened. After additional attempts to deliver the Washington communiqué through other channels met with failure, President Johnson ordered a resumption of bombing missions on 18 May. Although the DRV then responded through the French, this initiative also faltered.

Despite the actual and perceived failure of Operation MAYFLOWER, it ultimately allowed the Johnson administration temporarily to deflect criticism of its policies in Vietnam by pointing out the DRV's refusal to negotiate. It also served as a cover and a justification for the subsequent escalation of ROLLING THUNDER.

—John G. Terino, Jr.

References: Goodman, Allan E. *The Search for a Negotiated Settlement of the Vietnam War* (1986); Herring, George C. *LBJ and Vietnam: A Different Kind of War* (1994); Herring, George C., ed. *The Secret Diplomacy of the Vietnam War: The Negotiating Volumes of the Pentagon Papers* (1983); Karnow, Stanley. *Vietnam: A History* (1991).
See also: Air Power, Role in War; Johnson, Lyndon Baines; ROLLING THUNDER, Operation.

McCain, John S., III (1936–)

Navy pilot and prisoner of war (POW) during the Vietnam War; later, United States senator and advocate of normalized U.S. relations with Vietnam.

McCain graduated fifth from the bottom of his U.S. Naval Academy class, but his devil-may-care attitude and leadership skills made him a highly effective pilot. On 26 October 1967, McCain was shot down while piloting an A4 Skyhawk. McCain was probably the most seriously injured pilot to enter the Hoa Lò Prison (Hà Nôi Hilton). He was a tough and highly respected POW, who, despite his serious condition, refused the opportunity to be sent home in June 1968.

Released at the end of the war, McCain retired from the Navy to enter politics. In 1982 he was elected to the U.S. House of Representatives, and in 1986 he became a U.S. Senator (R-Arizona). An influential figure in the Senate, McCain came to be a strong supporter for ending economic sanctions against the Socialist Republic of Vietnam (SRV).

—Joe P. Dunn

References: Howes, Craig. *Voices of the Vietnam POWs: Witnesses to*

Their Fight (1993); Hubbell, John G., et al. *P.O.W.: A Definitive History of the American Prisoner of War Experience in Vietnam, 1964–1973* (1976); Rowan, Stephan A. *They Wouldn't Let Us Die: The Prisoners of War Tell Their Story* (1973); Tinberg, Robert. *The Nightingale's Song* (1995).

See also: Hà Nội Hilton (Hoa Lò Prison); McCain, John Sidney, Jr.; Prisoners of War, Allied; United States: Navy; Vietnam, Socialist Republic of: 1975 to the Present.

McCain, John Sidney, Jr. (1911–1981)

U.S. Navy admiral and commander in chief, Pacific Command (CINCPAC), July 1968–September 1972. As CINC-PAC, Admiral McCain officially commanded all U.S. forces in the Pacific, including those in Vietnam. He believed that the Vietnamese conflict was a prologue to further Communist expansion in Asia, that China was the major long-term threat, and that Vietnam was only one piece of the puzzle. McCain was a vigorous supporter of President Nixon's Vietnamization program and a vocal advocate of renewed bombardment in 1972.

McCain's strong anticommunism complicated command and control of U.S. forces in Vietnam. As overall commander of U.S. forces in the Pacific, McCain had an impact on the disposition of local units, and his office acted as a superfluous command layer between commander of the Military Assistance Command, Vietnam (MACV) Gen. Creighton Abrams and Washington. McCain saw this as necessary, but Army and Air Force commanders accused the Navy (and Air Force) of "fighting its own war," such as conducting air strikes independent of the war effort in the South.

McCain was neither directly responsible for making policy, nor always for implementing it; yet he exercised a measure of control and influence that affected the outcome of the war. This was particularly true in 1972 when he successfully advocated the mining of Democratic Republic of Vietnam (DRV) ports and the resumption of strategic air attacks to bring Hà Nội back to the negotiating table.

McCain retired from service in 1972 and became president of the U.S. Strategic Institute.

—Joel E. Higley

References: *A Study of Strategic Lessons Learned in Vietnam,* Vol. VI: *The Conduct of the War* (1980); Momyer, William W. *Air Power in Three Wars* (1978); Olson, James S., and Randy Roberts. *Where the Domino Fell: America and Vietnam, 1945–1990* (1991); Sorley, Lewis. *Thunderbolt: From the Battle of the Bulge and Beyond, General Creighton Abrams and the Army of His Times* (1992).

See also: Abrams, Creighton; McCain, John S., III; Military Assistance Command, Vietnam (MACV); United States: Navy.

McCarthy, Eugene Joseph (1916–)

U.S. senator, Democratic candidate for president in 1968, and leading critic of U.S. involvement in Vietnam. McCarthy attempted to merge the antiwar movement with politics, and his early success helped bring down a sitting president. A member of the Senate Foreign Relations Committee, McCarthy voted for the 1964 Tonkin Gulf Resolution but considered it a vote for a holding action rather than a vote for

war. In McCarthy's view, the war escalated in 1966 into a war of conquest. His opposition began to be evident in that year.

On 30 November 1967, McCarthy announced his bid for the 1968 presidential nomination as a candidate committed to bringing about a negotiated settlement of the war. Large numbers of idealistic antiwar students flocked to his campaign. McCarthy's surprisingly strong showing in the New Hampshire primary, although later shown to be primarily an anti-Johnson vote rather than a vote for McCarthy, prompted Senator Robert F. Kennedy to join the presidential race. Within a few weeks, Johnson announced that he would not seek reelection. Kennedy's campaign soon eclipsed McCarthy's, although McCarthy remained in the race. Kennedy's assassination again changed the dynamics of the race. At the violence-marred August 1968 Democratic Party National Convention in Chicago, Vice-President Hubert Humphrey received the nomination, ending McCarthy's idealistic antiwar political crusade.

In 1969 McCarthy resigned from the Foreign Relations Committee, and he left the Senate on completion of his second term in 1970.

—James E. Southerland

References: Eisele, Albert. *Almost to the Presidency: A Biography of Two American Politicians* (1972); Herzog, Arthur. *McCarthy for President* (1969); McCarthy, Eugene. *The Year of the People* (1969); White, Theodore. *The Making of the President 1968* (1969).

See also: Antiwar Movement, United States; Democratic Party National Convention, 1968; Elections, U.S.: 1968; Harriman, W. Averell; Humphrey, Hubert H.; Johnson, Lyndon Baines; Kennedy, Robert Francis; Knowland, William F.; Tonkin Gulf Resolution.

McCarthy, Joseph Raymond (1908–1957)

U.S. senator, leader of the political Right, and anti-Communist crusader. His methods of character assassination gave rise to a new word, "McCarthyism," and finally resulted in his censure by the Senate in 1954. During his career, and even after his death, McCarthy affected the Vietnam policy of four U.S. presidents.

The 1949 Communist victory in China, coupled with McCarthy's attacks on the State Department for harboring Communists, resulted in the purge of the "China Hands" (Asia experts) from the State Department, producing an anti-Communist conformity that precluded the department from offering alternatives to America's active intervention in Vietnam.

President Truman, attacked by McCarthy as "soft on communism" and faced with the "Who-Lost-China?" witch-hunt as well as the outbreak of the Korean War, portrayed the French struggle in Indo-China as a contest between the Free World and communism and offered military aid to the French. The Eisenhower administration also feared the "loss" of Indo-China. By the end of the Indo-China War in 1954, the U.S. government had paid 80 percent of the cost of the French military effort and even considered direct military intervention. As a senator in the 1950s, President Kennedy had advocated independence for the State of Vietnam and reportedly feared that, if the United States withdrew entirely from

Vietnam, the country would undergo another McCarthyesque Red Scare. President Johnson similarly feared that defeat of the Republic of Vietnam (RVN) would lead to a repetition of the nightmare experienced by Truman over China at the hands of McCarthy and other right-wing adversaries.

—Paul S. Daum, with Trevor Curran

References: Cooper, Chester L. *The Lost Crusade: America in Vietnam* (1970); FitzGerald, Frances. *Fire in the Lake: The Vietnamese and the Americans in Vietnam* (1972); Fried, Richard M. *Nightmare in Red: The McCarthy Era in Perspective* (1990); Karnow, Stanley. *Vietnam: A History* (1983); Kearns, Doris. *Lyndon Johnson and the American Dream* (1976).
See also: Eisenhower, Dwight David; Johnson, Lyndon Baines; Kennedy, John Fitzgerald; Truman, Harry S; United States: Involvement in Vietnam, 1954–1965.

McCloy, John Jay (1895–)

Lawyer, diplomat, banker, and advisor to U.S. presidents. With his Ivy League education and years of government service, McCloy typified the Washington Establishment figure. Johnson used McCloy's talents in March 1968 as a member of the Senior Advisory Group on Vietnam—the "Wise Men"—convened to counsel the president on further troop commitments in Vietnam. McCloy, although dissatisfied with existing policy, remained reluctant to recommend drastic changes and argued in favor of sending an additional 200,000 men to the conflict. His view was a minority position, and on 31 May 1968, Johnson announced his decision to reduce the U.S. presence in Southeast Asia. McCloy later served as chairman of the Council on Foreign Relations and remained a valuable advisor to presidents Nixon, Carter, and Reagan.

—Mark Barringer

References: Bird, Kai. *The Chairman: John J. McCloy and the Making of the American Establishment* (1992); Isaacson, Walter. *The Wise Men: Six Friends and the World They Made* (1988); McCloy, John J. *The Challenge to American Foreign Policy* (1953).
See also: Eisenhower, Dwight David; Johnson, Lyndon Baines; Kennedy, John Fitzgerald; "Wise Men."

McCone, John Alex (1902–1991)

Director of the Central Intelligence Agency (CIA), 1961–1965. On 27 September 1961, several months after the abortive Bay of Pigs invasion, President Kennedy appointed McCone, a conservative Republican, to head the CIA, succeeding Allen Dulles. McCone, who had virtually no intelligence experience, inherited an agency in turmoil.

McCone immediately convened a study group to identify the duties of the director and submit suggestions about reorganization of the agency, an association of three directorates desperately in need of centralized planning and organization to achieve unity. The endeavor under McCone took two years to complete and substantially improved scientific and technological research and development capabilities, added a cost analysis system, and created a position of comptroller. In addition, Kennedy publicly strengthened

the agency by announcing that the director would be charged with developing policies and coordinating procedures at all levels across the intelligence community. The announcement came less than a month after the President's Foreign Intelligence Advisory Board recommended dismantling the CIA. Kennedy's stance strengthened McCone's immediate position but fueled resentment among other agencies and White House and cabinet figures such as Robert McNamara. McCone's aggressive and confident style irked many of his peers.

Although McCone was considered a hard-line massive retaliation advocate who could help the president deflect pressure from the political Right, he apparently was not one to take political and military risks lightly. He argued against the coup to oust Republic of Vietnam President Ngô Đình Diêm in 1963.

In spite of opposition, McCone remained CIA director after Kennedy's assassination but may have initiated his own demise under President Johnson by criticizing escalation in Vietnam. In 1965 he left the CIA, apparently convinced that Johnson did not hold the agency in the same esteem as did his predecessor.

—Paul R. Camacho

References: Halberstam, David. *The Best and the Brightest* (1972); Hersh, Burton. *The Old Boys: The American Elite and the Origins of the CIA* (1992); Kirkpatrick, Lyman D, Jr. *The Real CIA* (1968); Powers, Thomas. *The Man Who Kept the Secrets: Richard Helms and the CIA* (1979).
See also: Central Intelligence Agency (CIA); Dulles, Allen Welsh; Johnson, Lyndon Baines; Kennedy, John Fitzgerald; McNamara, Robert S.; Ngô Đình Diêm, Overthrow of; ROLLING THUNDER, Operation.

McConnell, John Paul (1908–1986)

U.S. Air Force general; Air Force chief of staff, 1965–1969. In 1964 McConnell was made vice–chief of staff of the Air Force. The next year he succeeded Gen. Curtis LeMay as Air Force chief of staff, a position he held until his retirement in 1969. As chief of staff during the Vietnam War, McConnell urged full-scale bombing of North Vietnam. He believed in the ability of the Air Force to destroy through strategic bombing the willingness and capability of the Democratic Republic of Vietnam (DRV) to continue the war. He failed to grasp the political strategy or limitations of strategic bombing in Vietnam.

—Laura Matysek Wood

References: Clodfelter, Mark. *The Limits of Air Power: The American Bombing of North Vietnam* (1989); Dupuy, Trevor N., Curt Johnson, and David L. Bongard. *The Harper Encyclopedia of Military Biography* (19920.
See also: United States: Air Force.

McGee, Gale William (1915–1992)

U.S. senator, 1958–1977. Long before U.S. involvement in Southeast Asia was a matter of public debate, McGee established himself as a firm devotee to the domino theory. He viewed a U.S. stand in Vietnam as essential to the promotion of democracy worldwide, and as congressional and public criticism mounted, he continued to back military approaches to the Vietnam conflict. Although something of an independent, McGee was one of President Johnson's chief congressional allies, remaining loyal despite major defections by many previous Johnson supporters.

—David Coffey

References: Dallek, Robert. *Lone Star Rising: Lyndon Johnson and His Times, 1908–1960* (1991); Karnow, Stanley. *Vietnam: A History* (1983).

See also: Domino Theory; Goldwater, Barry Morris; Johnson, Lyndon Baines; McCarthy, Eugene Joseph; Mansfield, Michael Joseph; Stennis, John Cornelius.

McGovern, George S. (1922–)

U.S. senator, 1963–1981; Democratic Party presidential candidate, 1972. In the Senate, McGovern backed the Nuclear Test Ban Treaty and called for reductions in military spending. He long criticized Cold War policies and anti-Communist obsessions and warned against U.S. involvement in Southeast Asia.

Although McGovern supported President Johnson's call for military force to protect South Vietnamese independence and the Tonkin Gulf Resolution, he soon became a leader of the congressional opposition to U.S. involvement in Southeast Asia. After a 1965 visit to South Vietnam, he pressed for a political rather than military approach to a situation that he viewed as civil war. He maintained that U.S. anti-Communist fervor resulted in support for corrupt and ineffective dictatorships. He called for improved relations with the People's Republic of China and staunchly opposed offensive operations against North Vietnam.

Briefly a candidate for the Democratic presidential nomination in 1968, McGovern continued to oppose the war effort during Richard Nixon's presidency. In 1970 McGovern introduced with Senator Mark Hatfield the Hatfield-McGovern Amendment, which called for the removal of U.S. forces from Southeast Asia by the end of 1971 and the stoppage of all funding for the war.

In 1972 McGovern secured the Democratic Party presidential nomination on the strength of his antiwar position. Nixon capitalized on this to cast McGovern as a radical and draw moderate Democrats to his camp. McGovern's criticism of Nixon's prosecution of the war and the emerging Watergate scandal largely was ignored. His campaign was further damaged by running mate Thomas Eagleton's admission that he had been treated for mental illness. His second choice, Sargent Shriver, brought little to the ticket. McGovern's platform, including amnesty for draft resistors and drastic cuts in defense spending, proved too liberal for many Democrats. Nixon won the November election by one of the largest margins in U.S. history.

—David Coffey

References: Anson, Robert S. *McGovern: A Biography* (1972); Moritz, Charles, ed. *Current Biography Yearbook, 1967* (1967); *Who's Who in American Politics, 1995–1996* (1995).

See also: Antiwar Movement, United States; Church, Frank Forrester; Elections, U.S.: 1968; Elections, U.S.: 1972; Hatfield-McGovern Amendment; Hatfield, Mark Odum; Humphrey, Hubert H.; Johnson, Lyndon Baines; Kennedy, Edward Moore; Kennedy, John Fitzgerald; Nixon, Richard Milhous; Watergate.

McNamara, Robert S. (1916–)

Secretary of defense, 1961–1968. McNamara came to the job determined to take control of the Pentagon bureaucracy. Among his early initiatives were the installation of a programming-planning-budgeting system, the introduction of systems analysis into the department's decision-making process, and the revitalization of conventional forces, neglected under the prior administration's defense policy based on "massive retaliation." The Kennedy administration's new approach became known as "flexible response." McNamara also evinced a continuing concern for the control of nuclear weapons, a subject that continued high on his personal agenda even after he had left his Pentagon post.

McNamara soon went on record as supporting Maxwell Taylor's and Walt Rostow's recommendations that the United States commit itself to preventing the fall of South Vietnam to communism. During successive levels of increasing U.S. commitment, including the deployment of increasingly more ground combat forces to Vietnam, McNamara supported meeting the field commander's requirements, at the same time insisting on a "graduated response" to North Vietnamese "aggression," particularly with regard to the air war against the North. By the end of 1965, though, McNamara had begun to doubt the possibility of achieving a military solution in Vietnam, a view he expressed to President Johnson. A month later, however, McNamara recommended adding 200,000 men to forces in Vietnam and expanding air operations. At the same time, he suggested that the odds were even that the result would be "a military standoff at a much higher level."

By May 1967 McNamara had advised Johnson in writing that it was time "to change our objectives in Vietnam and the means by which we sought to achieve them," refusing to support Gen. William Westmoreland's most recent request for 200,000 more troops and arguing instead that his approach "could lead to a major national disaster." But then in July 1967, back from a trip to Vietnam, McNamara told the president that there was not a stalemate in the war and indeed, according to Tom Johnson's notes of the meeting, "he felt that if we follow the same program we will win the war and end the fighting." Faced with McNamara's pervasive inconsistency, Johnson soon decided to replace him. Later McNamara admitted that he "misunderstood the nature of the conflict."

In their book *The Economics of Defense in the Nuclear Age*, Charles J. Hitch (McNamara's comptroller in the Defense Department) and Roland N. McKean observed that "there are excellent reasons for making most decisions at lower levels. Officials on the spot have far better technical information; they can act more quickly; giving them authority will utilize and develop the reservoir of ingenuity and initiative in the whole organization." McNamara, meanwhile, brought an unprecedented degree of centralization to the management of the Defense Department, even though Hitch and McKean also observed that "if large numbers of detailed decisions are attempted at a high level ... the higher levels will become swamped in detail, decisions will be delayed, the organization will become muscle-bound, and the higher levels will have neither time nor energy for their essential functions of policymaking." The accuracy of this analysis became clear when McNamara, in his book *In Retrospect*, observed that he was just too busy to deal with the Vietnam War—that "an orderly, rational approach was precluded by the 'crowding out' which resulted from the fact that Vietnam was but one of a multitude of problems we confronted."

Under McNamara, there were huge gaps between rhetoric and reality. As late as 1971, more than three years after McNamara had left the Pentagon, Alain Enthoven and K. Wayne Smith argued in *How Much Is Enough?* that one strength of McNamara's regime was his insistence on "integrating and balancing the nation's foreign policy, military strategy, force requirements, and defense budget." Instead, he had so ineptly managed the war in Vietnam and competing commitments elsewhere that the U.S. Army in Europe was virtually destroyed to make up for Vietnam shortfalls, while reserve forces were similarly ravaged. By the time McNamara was through, wrote Gen. Bruce Palmer, Jr. in *The 25-Year War*, the Seventh Army "ceased to be a field army and became a large training and replacement depot for Vietnam." As a result, it "became singularly unready, incapable of fulfilling its NATO mission."

McNamara left office at the end of February 1968, in the midst of the debate over Vietnam policy precipitated by the Têt Offensive. His 1995 book, *In Retrospect: The Tragedy and Lessons of Vietnam*, reignited Vietnam passions, but did little to rebuild his reputation.

—Lewis Sorley

References: Enthoven, Alain C., and K. Wayne Smith. *How Much Is Enough? Shaping the Defense Program, 1961–69* (1971); Hitch, Charles J. *Decision Making for Defense* (1965); McNamara, Robert S., with Brian VanDeMark. *In Retrospect: The Tragedy and Lessons of Vietnam* (1995); Palmer, Gregory. *The McNamara Strategy and the Vietnam War: Program Budgeting in the Pentagon, 1960–1968* (1978); Shapley, Deborah. *Promise and Power: The Life and Times of Robert McNamara* (1993).

See also: Bundy, McGeorge; Bundy, William P.; Clifford, Clark M.; Gelb, Leslie H.; Johnson, Lyndon Baines; Joint Chiefs of Staff; Kennedy, John Fitzgerald; McNamara Line; Project 100,000; RAND Corporation; Read, Benjamin Huger; Rostow, Walt Whitman; San Antonio Formula; Taylor, Maxwell Davenport; Taylor-McNamara Report; United States: Involvement in Vietnam, 1965–1968; Westmoreland, William Childs; "Wise Men."

McNamara Line

On 7 September 1967, Secretary of Defense Robert McNamara announced plans for the construction of an electronic anti-infiltration barrier below the Demilitarized Zone (DMZ) in Vietnam. The principal purpose of the "McNamara Line" was to alert U.S. forces when People's Army of Vietnam (PAVN) forces crossed the barrier. Allied air and artillery strikes would then be brought to bear to curb infiltration from the North.

In 1966 Harvard professor Roger Fisher formulated a proposal that would block infiltration down the Hô Chí Minh Trail in Laos and across the DMZ with a high-technology barrier. In April 1966, McNamara turned the Fisher proposal over to the Jason Division, a group of scientists formed in 1959 by the Institute for Defense Analyses. The Jasons' task was to develop a plan for a barrier laden with state-of-the-art electronic devices. The Jasons proposed an infiltration barrier of two components: an antipersonnel barrier, staffed by troops across the southern side of the DMZ from the South China Sea to Laos; and an antivehicular barrier, primarily an aerial operation, emplaced in and over the Laotian panhandle to interdict traffic on the Hô Chí Minh Trail. Certain features were common to both barriers, including use of new technology such as remote sensors (tiny mines that made noise when stepped on, alerting acoustic sensors) and Gravel mines (small, cloth-covered squares designed to wound legs and feet when stepped on). The purpose of these sensors was to facilitate target acquisition for U.S. aircraft. The sensors would be monitored by aircraft that would relay data to a central computer site in Thailand, which would then guide attack aircraft to their targets.

The Barrier in Vietnam The U.S. Military Assistance Command, Vietnam (MACV) modified the original Jason proposal, calling for a linear barrier consisting of a 600- to 1,000-meter-wide stretch of cleared ground containing barbed wire, minefields, sensors, and watchtowers backed by a series of manned strongpoints. Behind these points would be a series of artillery bases to provide an interlocking pattern of artillery fire. This part of the system would begin at the coast of South Vietnam below the DMZ and continue westward for 30 kilometers, beyond which the barrier would be less comprehensive. Construction began in summer 1967. The McNamara Line, originally code-named Project PRACTICE NINE, later was renamed DYE MARKER.

Marines and Navy Seabees quickly ran into difficulty in their efforts to construct DYE MARKER. In September 1967, the PAVN launched Phase I of their General Offensive, General Uprising. In I Corps, Phase I began with heavy attacks on Marine positions along the DMZ. Phase II of the offensive took place during Têt in 1968. By January, when the McNamara Line should have been operational, it was clear that the North Vietnamese were massing around the Marine base at Khe Sanh, leading Gen. William Westmoreland to give top priority to Khe Sanh. Sensors and related equipment slated to be installed along the DMZ were instead given to the defenders of Khe Sanh. Aircraft dropped seismic and acoustic sensors on likely approaches. Almost immediately the sensors began indicating PAVN activity.

The siege at Khe Sanh ended in April, and sensors that had been deployed in its defense were highly praised, but the fighting at Khe Sanh effectively stopped further construction on the McNamara Line. The defenders at Khe Sanh did not face their enemy across a broad front; rather, they were almost surrounded by them. The fighting there showed that sensor technology worked in 360-degree applications. There was no compelling evidence that the barrier technique would work in a linear application as envisioned by the McNamara plan. Commanders familiar with the success of sensor technology at Khe Sanh desired to implement the concept in a variety of operations throughout South Vietnam.

The Antivehicular Barrier in Laos To destroy trucks on the Hô Chí Minh Trail, the United States deployed aircraft gunships equipped with night-viewing devices. Another sensor contained a cathode ray tube that reacted to ignition systems found in vehicles. Targets acquired by these devices would be destroyed by aerial cannon capable of firing up to 6,000 rounds per minute. Other improvements in the methods of weapons delivery included automation of the release process. Computers could carry out calculations to direct the aircraft's approach run and the automatic release of munitions at the appropriate time. Munitions were modified to increase accuracy. Laser-guided bombs were conventional bombs fitted with a laser guidance unit. The target was illuminated by shining a laser beam on it, allowing the bomb to follow the beam to its target.

Ground sensors also were developed and deployed on the Trail. Dropped from aircraft, they landed on the ground or hung from foliage. Battery-operated sensors located and tampered with would self-destruct. Sensors detected motion or sound or were sensitive to metallic objects or to chemicals emanating from the bodies of mammals. Data produced by these sensors were transmitted via radio to receivers located at ground stations or aboard orbiting aircraft. From these stations, the data was relayed to a central processing site base in Thailand.

The Infiltration Surveillance Center (ISC) was the heart of this antivehicular system, which was code-named IGLOO WHITE. After the data was sorted by computer, it was passed to analysts who would send their assessments to the strike aircraft and direct them to their targets. ISC computers contained extensive mapping of the Hô Chí Minh Trail. They were used to predict the expected path and speed of truck convoys by sensor readout. Aircraft were guided to a particular point and munitions automatically released at a time that would coincide with the arrival of the truck convoy in the kill zone. This interdiction system had all-weather capability and required no ground forces.

Project IGLOO WHITE was in operation until the end of 1972. U.S. Air Force figures claimed that the bombing campaign destroyed a great number of trucks, but such figures were invariably greater than Central Intelligence Agency (CIA) figures for all of North Vietnam and Laos. Still, the U.S. Air Force estimated that in 1971 only 20 percent of the supplies entering the Trail system made it to their destination. IGLOO WHITE operations began shutting down in December 1972. The last U.S. bombing raid on the Hô Chí Minh Trail was a B-52 strike in April 1973.

The antipersonnel barrier across the DMZ was never constructed as planned. Much of the proposed barrier was within range of PAVN artillery situated just north of the DMZ, and the entire area was the object of frequent PAVN probes. U.S. military forces were never of sufficient strength to construct and run the barrier adequately while fighting at the same time.

Had an effective barrier been constructed, the PAVN would undoubtedly have chosen to go around it. PAVN units needed in Military Regions II, III, and IV clearly would have had an easier time outflanking the barrier via the Hô Chí Minh Trail than fighting their way through hundreds of thousands of U.S. and ARVN soldiers located in I Corps. Such fighting as did occur in I Corps was usually initiated by the enemy for the purpose of tying up U.S. and South Vietnamese military assets.

Unlike the antipersonnel barrier, the antivehicular barrier across the Laotian panhandle was a thorough implementation of the Jason plan. It was successful in destroying a great quantity of military supplies. Undoubtedly many PAVN soldiers were killed as well, but the Trail network was too extensive to be shut down by any amount of bombing. The PAVN was largely successful in controlling the level of fighting during the war. When supplies were inadequate to support military activity at high levels, Hà Nôi reduced operations until sufficient materiel became available.

—Peter W. Brush

References: Dickson, Paul. *The Electronic Battlefield* (1976); Littauer, Raphael, and Norman Uphoff, ed. *The Air War in Indochina* (1971); Prados, John, and Ray W. Stubbe. *Valley of Decision: The Siege of Khe Sanh* (1991).

See also: Air Power, Role in War; Bombs, Smart (PGMs); COMMANDO HUNT, Operation; Demilitarized Zone (DMZ); Hô Chí Minh Trail; McNamara, Robert S.; Mines, Antipersonnel and Antitank; ROLLING THUNDER, Operation.

McNaughton, John T. (1921–1967)

U.S. deputy assistant secretary of defense for international security affairs, 1961–1962; general counsel to the Department of Defense, 1962–1964; assistant secretary of defense for international security affairs, 1964–1967. McNaughton's approach to war as a logical business between rational adversaries was reflected in memoranda that he drafted for his superior, Secretary of Defense Robert McNamara.

To liberal friends and colleagues, McNaughton often presented himself as a closet dove who personally sympathized with their opposition to U.S. actions in Vietnam. Yet after the passage of the 1964 Tonkin Gulf Resolution, he was a strong supporter of forceful U.S. action against the Democratic Republic of Vietnam (DRV). In 1964 and 1965 he drafted many of the memoranda, later presented to President Johnson by McNamara, that argued most strongly in favor of committing substantial U.S. forces to the Republic of Vietnam (RVN). He was a major architect of the strategy of limited air war, which resulted in the 1965 ROLLING THUNDER bombings, and recommended commitment of combat units and the construction of air bases in South Vietnam.

McNaughton's memoranda at this time made it clear that he viewed the situation in Vietnam as a test of U.S. international credibility and felt little concern for the welfare or security of the Vietnamese per se. Even in July 1965, he was skeptical whether the United States could win the war in the sense of preserving the RVN as an independent country, and he made these doubts plain to McNamara; however, they were not aired elsewhere. In 1966 McNaughton privately suggested to McNamara that the United States should extricate itself from the war and negotiate a compromise peace, perhaps facilitating this by bombing dikes in North Vietnam and so starving the population. In summer 1966, McNaughton helped draft the Jason Study, which argued that U.S. intervention and air raids had inflicted little damage on the DRV economy, but had reinforced nationalistic determination and encouraged increased infiltration into the South.

By 1967 McNaughton and his staff in the International Security Affairs section of the Pentagon were among the strongest advocates of a U.S. withdrawal. Alarmed by growing public sentiment against the war, McNaughton, in conversations with McNamara that summer, warned that Vietnam "could cause the worst split in our people in more than a century." Publicly, both men still supported administration policy and claimed that the war could be won, but ultimately McNaughton's arguments seem to have influenced McNamara, who by 1967 also privately urged that the U.S. government had made a mistake and should change course.

—Priscilla Roberts

References: Berman, Larry. *Planning a Tragedy: The Americanization of the War in Vietnam* (1982); Gibbons, William Conrad. *The U.S. Government and the Vietnam War* (1989); Halberstam, David. *The Best and the Brightest* (1973); McKahin, George McT. *Intervention: How America Became Involved in Vietnam* (1986).
See also: Clifford, Clark M.; Johnson, Lyndon Baines; McNamara, Robert S.; McPherson, Harry Cummings; RAND Corporation; ROLLING THUNDER, Operation; Warnke, Paul C.

McPherson, Harry Cummings (1929–)
Deputy secretary of the Army (1963), assistant secretary of state (1964), special assistant to the president (1965–1969). As a White House aide and speech writer, McPherson witnessed many decisions concerning Vietnam. The 1968 Têt Offensive convinced McPherson that the war was futile. Working with Secretary of State Clark Clifford, he attempted to change Johnson's mind concerning de-escalation. He later related that the president was greatly shaken by the media reports, although the official intelligence reports offered by Walt Rostow directly refuted the media. At the end of March 1968, Johnson told McPherson and others that he wanted a speech that made a peace pronouncement. McPherson was the first of Johnson's aides to realize that the president intended to announce at the end of that speech that he would not seek reelection in 1968.

—Robert G. Mangrum

References: Davidson, Phillip B. *Vietnam at War: The History 1946–1975* (1988); Herring, George C. *America's Longest War: The U.S. and Vietnam, 1950–1975* (1986); Karnow, Stanley. *Vietnam: A History* (1984); *Who's Who in America, 1980–1981.*
See also: Clifford, Clark M.; Johnson, Lyndon Baines; McNamara Robert S.; McNaughton, John T.; Media and the War; Rostow, Walt Whitman.

Meaney, George (1894–1980)
Labor leader, political activist, and ardent anti-Communist. With the concurrence of the Johnson administration, Meaney sent labor consultants to Vietnam, where they established the Confederation of Vietnamese Trade Unions. When the war became unpopular and threatened economic and social destabilization, Meaney continued to support Johnson, despite criticism from other labor leaders. Meaney disapproved of Richard M. Nixon but defended his administration's efforts in Southeast Asia. Meaney also publicly supported the invasion of Cambodia, explaining that Nixon, as commander in chief, had a responsibility to pursue any means necessary to end the war. During the Watergate scandal, however, he advocated Nixon's impeachment.

—Dean Brumley

References: Goulden, Joseph C. *Meaney* (1972); Halberstam, David. *The Best and the Brightest* (1986); Johnson, Lyndon Baines. *The Vantage Point: Perspectives of the Presidency, 1963–1969* (1971); Karnow, Stanley. *Vietnam: A History* (1984).
See also: Johnson, Lyndon Baines; Nixon, Richard Milhous; Watergate.

Medevac
Movement of casualties from the battlefield to more secure locations for immediate medical attention; an acronym combining the words "medical" and "evacuation." The frontless nature of the guerrilla war in Vietnam called for exploitation of a Korean War innovation—casualty evacuation via helicopter.

The U.S. Army had experimented with aeromedical evacuation from the introduction of crewed flight, but it did not come into its own until the Korean War, when that country's rugged mountainous terrain and poor road network made overland movement difficult. By war's end, medevac helicopters had evacuated 17,700 casualties, and nonmedical helicopters supplemented that number with many more. Although Korea made the potential of helicopter medical evacuation obvious, Vietnam proved its worth.

Vietnam added dense jungle, tropical heat, and a frontless battlefield to the problems medical evacuation faced in Korea. General-use helicopters provided aeromedical evacuation before U.S. Army Medical Department air ambulance units were introduced into Vietnam in April 1962. Expanding with the surge of U.S. ground troops, they remained in Vietnam until total U.S. troop withdrawal in 1973. Nicknamed "dustoff" missions, air ambulances evacuations lifted between 850,000 and 900,000 Allied military and Vietnamese civilian casualties during their period of service. With their crews landing virtually almost anywhere without consideration of the dangers, medevacs provided rapid response and reduced time from injury to treatment; this helped reduce the "deaths as a percentage of hits" rate from 29.3 percent in World War II and 26.3 percent in Korea, to 19 percent in Vietnam.

—Arthur T. Frame

References: Dorland, Peter, and James Nanney. *Dustoff: Army Aeromedical Evacuation in Vietnam* (1982); Neel, Spurgeon. *Medical*

Support of the U.S. Army in Vietnam, 1965–1972 (1973); Office of Information Management and Statistics. *Data on Vietnam Era Veterans* (1983).

See also: Attrition; Casualties; Helicopters, Employment of, in Vietnam; Kelly, Charles L.; Medicine, Military; Medics and Corpsmen.

Media and the War

For some veterans of the Vietnam War, the word "media" was a pejorative term that even today evokes feelings of anger and hostility. For those military people, the print and broadcast journalists were as much the "enemy" as the Communist forces. In *Paper Soldiers*, Clarence R. Wyatt has written that the U.S. government successfully manipulated the media to its own ends during the war, concluding that "The press was more a paper soldier than an antiwar, antigovernment crusader."

As with most strongly held views, the truth lies somewhere between the stereotypical extremes. On one hand, the patriotism of most U.S. journalists covering the Vietnam War was every bit as intense as that of their predecessors; on the other hand, some viewed their constituency as international, not parochially national. Accountability was to the parent news agency, not necessarily a national government. For example, in *Live from the Battlefield*, Peter Arnett related a story about newsmen being "pushed around" by U.S. military policemen in 1966. Reporters trying to cover the Buddhist demonstrations were ordered off the street by the military police. Arnett identified himself as a New Zealander and another reporter, Eddie Adams said, "You have no right to order American newsmen off the streets, you have no jurisdiction over us." Adams was technically correct, but the implication of not being accountable to government authority in a war zone was present in his assertion as well, and that was a new twist.

For many military professionals, who had been taught not to reveal intentions to the enemy by careless statements to the press, journalists were to be tolerated, not embraced. They were an obstacle to smooth military operations, not an adjunct. They were independent of military jurisdiction, but depended on military transport to the sites of their stories. However, those military commanders who made the effort to gain the confidence of journalists usually received an important payoff in terms of reciprocated trust. Journalists who looked exclusively for the story that featured only mistakes, casualties, and the aura of disaster often missed the human drama that was played out by ordinary soldiers, sailors, Marines, and airmen. Genuinely important news stories from the battlefield received the most accurate reporting when journalists and military commanders cooperated, even when the story was not completely favorable to the military.

Press coverage of the Vietnam War was carried out within an often fragile alliance between military establishment and journalists. Some components of the alliance worked more smoothly than others. "Court journalism" was produced by the *Stars and Stripes*, Armed Forces Radio and Television Network, and a host of military unit publications designed mostly to inform troops and to bolster morale, although the soldiers who worked in those ranks would claim that their freedom of expression was not constrained.

In juxtaposition to those producing official news were the television and radio network reporters and the newspaper and news magazine specialists sent to the war zone to get the story before the competition. These on-the-scene journalists often had superior modes of communication with their offices in the United States and around the world, so that a remote combat action in the morning could be on the evening news that night in the United States. Vietnam was America's "living room war," as one writer aptly put it. The downside of this instant reporting was that the thoughtful, deliberate process of review and editing that used to take place in newspaper offices prior to publication often took place in minutes or hours in the television newsroom so that the story did not lose its freshness or urgency.

Television and news magazine journalism was a competitive business, and as a result, viewers sitting down to dinner often saw young soldiers lying in a pools of blood on distant battlefields. Local rules imposed by Military Assistance Command, Vietnam (MACV) discouraged close-ups of wounded or dead soldiers and interviews with wounded troops without the attending medical officer's permission. There were few violations, according to Barry Zorthian, U.S. Mission spokesman in Vietnam, and journalists who violated the rules quickly lost their credentials.

Maj. Gen. William E. DePuy wrote in *Changing an Army* that journalists "who worked with the combat troops were fine. I liked them, and I thought they were fair enough, and very brave, and as good as combat reporters have ever been." If there was a problem in interpreting the news, he said, it lay with "the editors back in the United States," who seemed to have a social agenda that romanticized the Vietnamese freedom fighters. In *Vietnam War Almanac*, Col. Harry Summers agrees that the correspondents in Vietnam "by and large, accurately reported what they saw" but the "editors and producers ... were not always able to keep their own political agendas and their awareness of shifts in American public opinion out of the editing process." Censorship of the media was considered and discussed by government officials in 1965, but it was never imposed in Vietnam, probably because of the enormous impracticalities.

Peter Arnett captured the essence of the journalist at war in his book *Live from the Battlefield*. Commenting on the booklet he was given by Malcolm Browne, the bureau chief, upon arrival at the Sài Gòn bureau in 1962, Arnett read the advice, which stated in part, "Figures on casualties and reports of military engagements are especially subject to distortion. In covering a military engagement you must make every effort to count the bodies yourself before accepting any tabulation of results." The guide also named "certain officials ... and their relative credibility indices" as sources not to be accepted at face value.

Journalists in Vietnam were managed, not controlled, by public affairs officers (PAOs) at Headquarters MACV and major combat units. The job of the PAO was to respond to the journalists' requests for information and facilitate movement of journalists to the sites of stories they wanted to cover. At peak strength, there were 500 accredited news people in the war zone, representing more than 130 organizations. About one-third worked as reporters; the remainder were hangers-on or support personnel.

The process of covering the war was understood differently by the military command and the major media organizations. Westmoreland explained in an interview in December 1994, "Information officers naturally wanted to influence the news product in a positive way ... favorable to the Allied war effort. Unfortunately, hyperbole and unrestrained optimism during information briefings at MACV headquarters early in the war tended to jaundice even the most receptive journalist. There was an abundance of information available to the reporters that seemed to be in direct contradiction to what they were hearing in their official briefings.... As the war progressed, information officers found themselves caught between the president's efforts to bolster support and their own judgment that the military should remain above politics."

Other players in the information sweepstakes were the members of the U.S. Embassy in Sài Gòn, members of other U.S. agencies—such as the U.S. Agency for International Development (USAID)—and representatives of other foreign governments, including the Republic of Vietnam government.

News coverage of the Vietnam War was a collision of technology and ethics on the modern battlefield. Competitive reporters—young novices and old hands alike—knew that "getting there first with the most" was an essential element of success.

Whether operational security of the armed forces engaged in combat was ever compromised by the lack of censorship and control of the media remains an open question deserving of further study. Some of that thoughtful examination has begun because of the different approaches taken to military-media relations in the post–Vietnam era.

—John F. Votaw

References: Arnett, Peter. *Live from the Battlefield* (1994); Braestrup, Peter. *Big Story: How the American Press and Television Reported and Interpreted the Crisis of Tet 1968 in Vietnam and Washington* (1977); Hammond, William M. *Public Affairs: The Military and the Media, 1962–1968* (1988); —. *Public Affairs: The Military and the Media, 1968–1973* (1996); Moeller, Susan D. *Shooting War: Photography and the American Experience of Combat* (1989) Summers, Harry G., Jr. *Vietnam War Almanac* (1985); Trotta, Liz. *Fighting for Air: In the Trenches with Television News* (1991); Wyatt, Clarence R. *Paper Soldiers: The American Press and the Vietnam War* (1993).
See also: Arnett, Peter; Art and the Vietnam War; Association of Foreign Correspondents in Vietnam (AFCV); Burchett, Wilfred; Cronkite, Walter Leland; "Five O'Clock Follies"; Halberstam, David; Joint U.S. Public Affairs Office (JUSPAO); Luce, Henry R.; Military Assistance Command, Vietnam (MACV); Moyers, Bill; Order of Battle Dispute; Vietnam Information Group (VIG); Westmoreland, William Childs.

Medicine, Military

Medical advances during the Vietnam conflict were the culmination of a century of progress in treating trauma and controlling infectious diseases. The nature of the conflict engendered a unique spectrum of psychiatric, medical, and traumatic problems. Helicopter evacuation, more rapid resuscitation, and readily available specialty surgery characterized military medicine in Vietnam.

In 1965 the U.S. Army had a single 100-bed hospital at Nha Trang. At the war's peak in 1968, the U.S. Department of Defense operated 5,283 beds at 19 fixed sites and MUSTs (medical unit self-contained, transportable). With no clearly defined front, medical facilities were geographically dispersed throughout Vietnam and tended to remain in the same locations rather than follow troop movements, as in previous wars. By June 1969, the Army Medical Corps in Vietnam comprised 16,000 physicians, 15,000 nurses, and 19,000 other officers.

The military medical system was divided into five echelons. The first echelon began with the aid man, who initiated emergency care and evacuation from the battlefield. He was responsible for arresting hemorrhage, securing an airway, dressing wounds, splinting fractures, relieving pain, and positioning the patient safely for transport. The physician at the battlefield aid station began more definitive resuscitation, including starting an intravenous line, doing thoracentesis or tracheostomy, beginning positive pressure ventilation, ligating small bleeding vessels, and starting either salt solutions, plasma expanders, or uncrossmatched whole blood.

The second echelon was the division clearing station, which had a larger staff of physicians, a better supply of whole blood, and oxygen. Antibiotics were begun, and tetanus antitoxin was given at this level.

The third echelon was the mobile surgical or evacuation hospital. Here major hemorrhage could be controlled and patency of difficult airways ensured. Whole blood and bicarbonate to correct acid-base imbalance were used. A major difference in resuscitative practices between Vietnam and earlier wars was the more liberal use of either uncrossmatched or type-specific whole blood.

The fourth echelon was the general hospitals in Okinawa and Japan, which had facilities for specialty medical and surgical services and psychiatric treatment. Okinawa was 1,800 miles from Vietnam, and the first fully equipped hospital was 2,700 miles away in Japan. Soldiers expected to return to duty in Southeast Asia were treated at one of these facilities or in the Philippines.

The fifth echelon comprised military and Veterans Administration hospitals in the United States. The nearest of these was at Travis Air Force Base, California, although a significant number of casualties went on to Andrews Air Force Base near Washington, D.C. Soldiers not expected to return to duty in Vietnam were transferred to these facilities. Besides active duty facilities, the Veterans Administration (VA) hospitals were a major resource for reconstructive and rehabilitative services. Between 1965 and 1969, 11,584 patients were transferred into the VA system.

Vietnam's climate favored development of tropical diseases, and the 12-month rotation schedule ensured a constant supply of nonimmune military targets for these diseases. Military physicians instituted preventive measures (vaccination and prophylaxis) from the beginning of the war; consequently, whereas disease had accounted for 90 percent of hospitalizations in the China-Burma-India theater in World War II, it accounted for only approximately 70 percent of hospitalizations of active duty personnel in Vietnam. The disease-to-injury admission rate for Vietnam was 4:1, 25 percent lower than in Korea.

Major disease problems were malaria, viral hepatitis, infectious diarrhea, fungal and other skin diseases, and venereal disease (usually gonorrhea or other urethritis). Less common problems included melioidosis, dengue, scrub typhus, murine typhus, and leptospirosis. Although plague and rabies were endemic to Vietnam, they never appeared in U.S. military personnel. Because of its severity and high incidence of resistance to standard drug therapy, falciparum malaria—the most common type in Vietnam—was a major medical problem compounded by the soldiers' reluctance to take necessary prophylactic medications. Drug-resistant gonococcus received publicity out of proportion to its clinical import. Parasitic disease as a cause of discharge from military service was five times as common in the Pacific Theater in World War II as in Vietnam. In fact, cancer was almost twice as common a cause of medical discharge as infectious disease in the latter conflict.

The psychiatric casualty rate was only 1 percent in Vietnam. In World War II, 33.1 percent of discharges were for psychiatric reasons, in Korea this dropped to 23.9 percent, and in Vietnam it was 13.7 percent. This surprisingly low rate was initially attributed to modern methods of combat psychiatry, but in retrospect may have been factitious since a number of veterans developed incapacitating psychiatric illnesses after discharge from the service. Although only 70,000 workdays were lost to psychiatric illness in 1965, that number rose to 175,510 by 1970, making this the second worst disease in terms of lost work. Post-traumatic stress disorder, characterized by nightmares, flashbacks, excessive startle response, hyperalertness, sleep disorders, and detachment from one's surroundings, stayed with the patient long after return to civilian life.

Drug abuse in Vietnam was widespread. In one study, 23 percent of soldiers interviewed had used marijuana, 10 percent used amphetamine, 7 percent used LSD, and 1.6 percent used heroin.

Most deaths in the Vietnam War were battle-related. The ratio of wounded to killed in action rose from 3.1:1 in World War II to 4:1 in Korea to 5.6:1 in Vietnam. Although some of this might be due to a change in types of weapons, much of the improvement can be credited to better battlefield medicine and surgery. Partial support for this statement can be found in the fact that mortality after arrival at a hospital was 4.5 percent in World War II and 2.5 percent in Vietnam.

Improved evacuation of the wounded was a hallmark of military medicine in Vietnam. Lack of roads, jungle terrain (some helicopters were equipped with spring-loaded penetrators to make holes in the forest canopy), and the strategic situation made helicopter evacuation uniquely suited to Southeast Asian warfare. At its height of activity, the Army

Medical Corps operated 116 air ambulances, each capable of carrying six to nine litters. In World War II, the average time to treatment had been 10.5 hours, in Korea it was 6.3 hours, and in Vietnam it was 2.8 hours, with many patients being hospitalized within 20 minutes of injury. During the 1968 Tết Offensive, helicopter ambulances evacuated an average of 8,000 casualties a month.

A second hallmark of Vietnam military medicine was an abundance of well-trained surgical specialists. U.S. residency programs were producing large numbers of surgeons capable of complex procedures that had not been available in previous wars. Vascular surgery typifies this improvement. In World War II, only 81 attempts were made to repair major vessels. That number rose to 300 in Korea, but the procedure became standard in Vietnam, where several thousand such repairs were done. Survival in patients burned over less than 60 percent of their bodies improved dramatically. The number of amputations in Vietnam was less than half that of World War II or Korea.

Part of the improved surgical results in Vietnam can be attributed to a difference in ordnance in that war compared with ordnance in previous conflicts. Unsophisticated weapons and the more common use of mines resulted in more extremity wounds than in previous wars, and the environment made the wounds more likely to be contaminated. The type of wound changed as the war evolved. Whereas 42.7 percent of wounds were from small arms in 1966, that number had decreased to 17 percent by 1970. In 1966, 42.6 percent of the wounds were from mines and booby traps, a number that increased to 80 percent by 1970. Artillery and mortar injuries—which accounted for 75 percent of casualties in World War II and Korea—were never that common in Vietnam. Injuries from purposely contaminated punji sticks were unique to the Southeast Asian war.

Medical and surgical improvements also decreased morbidity in Vietnam. Average duration of treatment in World War II was 129 days, in Korea 93 days, and in Vietnam 65 days. Of the 194,716 wounded in Vietnam, 31 percent (61,269) were treated and released. Of those hospitalized for injury, 75.3 percent returned to duty in some capacity, though only 42 percent returned to duty in Vietnam. Only 3.3 percent of those injured in battle died. Of non–battle-related hospitalizations, 77.8 percent returned to duty and only 0.3 percent died.

In all, improvements in evacuation and medical, perioperative, and intraoperative care led to fewer and shorter hospitalizations and improved survival in Vietnam soldiers as compared with survival of soldiers of earlier conflicts.

—Jack McCallum

References: Drapanas, Theodore, and Martin Litwin. "Trauma: Management of the Acutely Injured Patient" (19733); Government Printing Office. *The Vietnam Veteran in Contemporary Society: Collected Materials Pertaining to Young Veterans* (1972); Heaton, Leonard, Carl Hughes, Harold Rosegay, George Fisher, and Robert E. Feighny. "Military Surgical Practices of the United States Army in Viet Nam" (1966); Mullins, William S., ed. *A Decade of Progress: The United States Army Medical Department: 1959–1969* (1971); Neel,

Spurgeon. *Medical Support of the U.S. Army in Vietnam: 1965–1970* (1973); Sonnenberg, Stephen, and Arthur Blank. *The Trauma of War: Stress and Recovery in Viet Nam Veterans* (1985).

See also: Casualties; Booby Traps; Drugs and Drug Use; Helicopters, Employment of, in Vietnam; Medevac; Medics and Corpsmen.

Medics and Corpsmen

Medics and corpsmen have been designated as noncombatants by the military and by the rules of war in international law; in the Vietnam War, however, medics frequently carried weapons to protect their wounded and themselves, which invalidated their noncombatant status and Geneva Convention protection. In many cases, conscientious objectors (COs) lost their status when they chose to carry a gun.

By 1969, 90 percent of U.S. Army medics serving in Vietnam were draftees. Medics and corpsmen had to meet standards on tests given during basic training. Some recruits requested and received a medical military occupational specialty (MOS), but most were handed their medical MOS according to Army or Navy needs. Medics and corpsmen usually had some college background and were considered to be highly motivated.

Army medics were trained at Fort Sam Houston, Texas, in a ten-week, 480-hour course, and those receiving orders for Vietnam were given 14 hours of battle preparedness training outside the classroom. Basic naval medical training classes were at Hospital Corps Schools at San Diego, California, and Great Lakes Naval Training Station, Illinois. The Navy's basic medical course lasted four months, comprising human biology, pharmacology, and basic patient care, with practical experience in hospital wards. At the end of the basic course, some students took specialized training work. Marines received four to five weeks of battlefield training at either Camp Lejeune, North Carolina, or Camp Pendleton, California, and received additional training in managing battlefield casualties, triage, and direct patient care.

Combat medics and corpsmen, once in Vietnam, were normally assigned to infantry units. Under ideal conditions, each line platoon had two medics or corpsmen assigned to them, but heavy casualty rate among medics and corpsmen caused most units to be understaffed. U.S. search-and-destroy tactics in Vietnam normally were platoon-sized operations, and line medics and corpsmen accompanied these missions. While on patrol, medics and corpsmen carried out many of the same responsibilities as the infantry. Their basic responsibility was to care for the wounded; however, medics also stood perimeter guard and participated in firefights.

Medics and corpsmen contributed to the fact that the mortality rate for wounded—between 1 to 2.5 percent—was less than in any prior American war. When a man was injured, medics evaluated the wound and began treatment. If there were multiple casualties, corpsmen had to triage their patients. They also arranged for evacuation and determined who should be evacuated first. Medics provided psychological, emotional, and medical support and were widely respected by the troops.

The Army assigned combat medics to seven-month rotations with the remainder of their tour in rear areas and non-combat assignments, a policy based on studies of the psychological effect of combat on the medics. Time between patrols was normally spent at a base camp. Corpsmen performed sick call or were involved with the Medical Civic Action Program (MEDCAP), providing medical care to the rural population. Medics and corpsmen also managed base sanitation and water purification.

During the Vietnam War, medics were a vital part of the military structure. Of 238 Medals of Honor awarded in the war, 12 went to Army medics and 4 to Navy corpsmen. An estimated 1,300 medics and 690 corpsmen died in the war.

—Pia C. Heyn

Reference: Heyn, Pia Christine. "The Role of Army Combat Medics in the Viet Nam War, 1965–1971" (1994).

See also: Casualties; Conscientious Objectors (COs); Helicopters, Employment of, in Vietnam; Medicine, Military; Medevac.

Medina, Ernest L. (1936–)

U.S. Army captain and principal in the My Lai 4 atrocity. In 1966 Medina was promoted to captain and given command of Company C, 1st Battalion, 20th Regiment, 11th Brigade, 23d Infantry (American) Division, which in December 1967 was sent to Vietnam.

Medina won the Bronze and Silver Stars for valor while serving in Vietnam. He commanded Charlie Company during the 16 March 1968 action, later known as the My Lai 4 massacre. Subsequently Medina was court-martialed, charged with murder, manslaughter, and assault. On 22 September 1971, Medina was acquitted, the result of flawed instructions by the military judge to the court-martial. The prosecution originally wanted to charge Medina with commanding a homicide; but, uncertain of evidence on this charge, it went instead to involuntary manslaughter, the failure to exercise sufficient control over men engaged in a homicide. The military judge instructed the jury that to convict Medina on this charge, they would have to be convinced that he had actual knowledge as well as a wrongful refusal to act, and the jury believed this was not sufficiently proven. Had the jury been instructed instead on the general guidelines of proper command responsibility, it might have convicted him.

Medina was also acquitted on the charge of aggravated assault stemming from his interrogation of a suspected Việt Cộng. Although Medina admitted hitting the prisoner and firing pistol shots into a tree about eight inches from the suspect's head to get him to talk, the jury found that there was no explicit written prohibition of such interrogation methods.

On 15 October 1971, Medina resigned his Army commission, explaining: "I cannot wear the uniform with the same pride I had before."

—Charlotte A. Power

References: Bilton, Michael, and Kevin Sim. *Four Hours in My Lai* (1991); Goldstein, Joseph, Burke Marshall, and Jack Schwartz. *The My Lai Massacre and Its Cover-Up: Beyond the Reach of the Law?* (1976); Hersh, Seymour M. *My Lai 4: A Report on the Massacre and Its Aftermath* (1970); Lewy, Gunter. *America in Vietnam* (1978).

See also: Atrocities during the Vietnam War; Calley, William Laws, Jr.; My Lai Massacre; Peers Inquiry.

Mekong Delta

The Mekong River flows through Laos and Cambodia into Vietnam, forming the Mekong Delta south of Hô Chí Minh City (formerly Sài Gòn). The Mekong Delta was of great strategic importance during both French and U.S. involvement in Vietnam, and it saw some of the heaviest fighting of those wars. From 1962 to 1966, the Viêt Công controlled most of the northern half of the Delta. Pacification efforts after the 1968 Têt Offensive widened the area of Republic of Vietnam (RVN) control, although the Viêt Công remained a strong presence. Many urban targets of the 1968 Têt Offensive were in the Delta. By 1974 the Viêt Công controlled about 500 of the strategic hamlets in the Delta, and the region fell into chaos during the final 1975 Hô Chí Minh Offensive.

—Justin Marks

References: FitzGerald, Frances. *Fire in the Lake: The Vietnamese and Americans in Vietnam* (1972); Jamieson, Neil R. *Understanding Vietnam* (1993).

See also: Vietnam, Climate of; Easter Offensive (Nguyên Huê Campaign); Geography of Indo-China and Vietnam; Hô Chí Minh Campaign; Têt Offensive: Overall Strategy; Têt Offensive: the Sài Gòn Circle.

Mekong River Project

Project initiated in 1957 by the United Nations Economic Commission for Asia and the Ear East (ECAFE) to develop the irrigation, navigational, and hydroelectric potentials of the Mekong River. Based on the successful Tennessee Valley Authority in the United States and the Snowy River Project in Australia, the Mekong River Project was larger in its scope and was expected to take 20 years to complete.

In 1957 ECAFE issued a report, "Development of Water Resources in the Lower Mekong Basin," centered around the potential benefits to the then 17 million people living along the Mekong River. In response to this report, four of the six nations included in the Mekong Basin area—Cambodia, Laos, Thailand, and the Republic of Vietnam (RVN)—formed a committee to coordinate investigations of the lower Mekong Basin. Burma and the Democratic Republic of Vietnam (DRV) rejected participation in the project.

No manmade structure crossed the river in its 2,625-mile length. Basic hydrological information, vital to dam building, was virtually nonexistent. The RVN in particular was concerned that excessive damming, irrigation, and flood control might reduce the river level to the point where the sea would flow into the river mouth and contaminate the rich agricultural lands in the Delta. Most of these concerns were put to rest.

By 1970, 26 nations outside the Mekong Basin area, and some United Nations agencies and private organizations (such as the World Bank and Ford Foundation), had supplied funds or technical assistance for the project. After the Vietnam War the project continued, with virtually the same participating countries, and three multipurpose dams have been built. The Mekong Basin could furnish more than 40 billion kilowatts/hour of electricity.

—George J. Gabera

References: Ortiz, Elizabeth. "The Mekong Project of Vietnam" (1958); Whitfield, Danny J. *Historical and Cultural Dictionary of Vietnam* (1976).

See also: Geography of Indo-China and Vietnam; Mekong Delta.

Mendenhall, Joseph A. (1920–)

U.S. State Department official, director of the U.S. Agency for International Development's Laos Mission. In 1963 President Kennedy dispatched Mendenhall and Gen. Victor Krulak on a fact-finding mission to Vietnam. Arriving in Sài Gòn on 8 September, the two officials, who wanted little to do with each other, separated immediately to conduct individual appraisals. Mendenhall concentrated on urban areas, where he interviewed South Vietnamese and American civilians. Mendenhall and Krulak spoke little on their return trip and apparently kept their individual findings to themselves.

On 10 September the two men presented their findings at the White House. Addressing the president and his national security advisors, Krulak reported that the war against the Viêt Công was being waged effectively and maintained that the war would be won if U.S. military and sociological programs were continued. Mendenhall presented a starkly contrasting view, suggesting that the Ngô Đình Diêm regime was dangerously close to collapse and that an important segment of the population seemed more interested in ousting Diêm than in defeating the Viêt Công. He also pointed out the possibility of a major religious war between the Catholics and Buddhists. Mendenhall concluded that the war could not be won under the present circumstances. At the very least, Diêm's unpopular brother Nhu and his even more unpopular wife had to be removed from influence before real progress was possible. Krulak's and Mendenhall's reports differed to such an extent that Kennedy reportedly asked the two men if they had visited the same country.

In January 1964, Mendenhall became director of the State Department's Vietnam Working Group and, in July, director of the Office of Far Eastern Regional Affairs. In 1965 he was named director of the U.S. Agency for International Development (AID) Mission in Laos, then the second largest in the world. In 1968 he returned to Washington as deputy director, and later head, of the AID Vietnam Bureau.

—David Coffey

References: Mendenhall, Joseph A. Letter and documents to the author (1995); Newman, John M. *JFK and Vietnam: Deception, Intrigue, and the Struggle for Power* (1992); Rust, William J., et al. *Kennedy in Vietnam: American Vietnam Policy, 1960–1963* (1985).

See also: Kennedy, John Fitzgerald; Krulak, Victor H.; Ngô Đình Diêm; Ngô Đình Nhu; Ngô Đình Nhu, Madame (Trân Lê Xuân); Taylor-McNamara Report; U.S. Agency for International Development (USAID).

Mendès-France, Pierre (1907–1982)

French politician and premier, 1954–1955. After the May 1954 Battle of Điên Biên Phu, the government headed by Joseph Laniel fell. Mendès-France assumed the premiership on 17 June. His goal was to reinvigorate and modernize the

French economy, but he was forced to spend most of his premiership concentrating on foreign affairs.

On 20 June, Mendès-France electrified the National Assembly with a startling proposal to end the war in Indo-China within 30 days or resign as premier. The Geneva Conference was already in session, but he won his gamble on the last day of the deadline (but only because the clocks had been stopped on 20 July; the agreement was actually signed on 21 July). With the war terminated, Mendès-France set in motion events that led in 1956 to independence for Morocco and Tunisia. Hated by many as "the gravedigger of the French Empire," Mendès-France was overthrown by the Chamber on 5 February 1955. After his fall, the Radical Party split and Mendès-France lost his post of party leader. Although brief, the Mendès-France premiership was among the notable episodes in the history of the Fourth Republic. Its failure disillusioned many young reformers and helped pave the way for the 1958 return to power of Charles de Gaulle.

—Spencer C. Tucker

References: Fauvet, Jacques. *La Quatrième République* (1959); Lacouture, Jean. *Pierre Mendès-France* (1984); Matthews, Ronald. *The Death of the Fourth Republic* (1954); Mendès-France, Pierre, and Gabriel Ardant. *Economics and Action* (1955); Werth, Alexander. *The Strange History of Mendès-France and the Great Struggle over French North Africa* (1957).

See also: de Gaulle, Charles André Marie Joseph; Ðiên Biên Phu, Battle of; European Defense Community (EDC); Faure, Edgar; Geneva Conference and Geneva Accords; Indo-China War; Laniel, Joseph.

MENU, Operation (18 March 1969–26 May 1970)

Code name for the secret bombing of Cambodia. Operation MENU had three objectives. Tactically, its first objective was the destruction of supplies and the disruption of People's Army of Vietnam (PAVN) and Viêt Công (VC) base camps in the border area between Cambodia and South Vietnam. A commonly held belief in the U.S. intelligence community was that the Central Office for South Vietnam (COSVN), thought to be a massive Communist headquarters, was located in that region. Its destruction was the second objective. At the strategic level, President Nixon's plan for disengagement would have been imperiled had the Communists launched another attack on the scale of the 1968 Têt Offensive before Vietnamization and the withdrawal of U.S. troops was complete—or nearly so. The third objective was to prevent such an attack..

The first B-52 missions into Cambodia were flown on 18 March 1969. The target was Base Area 353, a network of supply caches and staging points just west of the border. The Pentagon assigned the code name BREAKFAST to this mission. Additional missions to other base areas were codenamed SUPPER, LUNCH, DESSERT, and SNACK. The series was dubbed the MENU Bombing.

The president, White House Chief of Staff Gen. Alexander Haig, National Security Advisor Henry A. Kissinger, key members of Congress, and a select few military and civilian defense officials were among the few who knew that the targets were actually in Cambodia. Secretary of the Air Force Dr. Robert Seamans, Air Force Chief of Staff Gen. John D. Ryan, and the pilots flying the B-52s were not advised.

Air Force Col. Ray B. Sitton, who had a background in the Strategic Air Command, worked out a system that used ARC LIGHT (B-52) strikes in South Vietnam as a cover for the secret bombing. Radar bomb navigators in the B-52s controlled the heading input for the plane in the final moments before the bombs were dropped. The pilot, whether actually flying the plane or on automatic pilot, would be unaware of the change in heading. Since the actual targets in Cambodia were, at most, only a few kilometers from the targets originally briefed to the aircrews, pilots would not know the difference. After the routine mission briefings, radar navigators were told that, when they neared their drop points, new sets of coordinates would be secretly forwarded to them by Air Force radar operators inside South Vietnam. The bombs would be dropped on the new coordinates rather than the designated targets. Poststrike reports would indicate that the original targets had been struck. A top-secret "back channel" communications network would then transmit the actual target information to the handful of civilian and military officials cleared for MENU Bombing intelligence.

The secrecy began unraveling just before the bombing came to an end. On 2 May 1970 *The New York Times* ran a brief article on the bombing. By that time, 3,630 B-52 sorties had dropped close to 100,000 tons of bombs inside Cambodia.

The need for secrecy passed after Gen. Lon Nol deposed Prince Norodom Sihanouk on 18 March 1970. Two days later, a Cambodian commander asked South Vietnamese spotter planes and artillery to help repulse a VC attack on his outpost. Army of the Republic of Vietnam (ARVN) operations inside Cambodia began in earnest a week later. On 29 April, U.S. planes supported 6,000 ARVN troops when they launched an attack into the Parrot's Beak area of Cambodia.

Covert MENU Bombing continued until 26 May 1970. After that, until a congressionally mandated end to all U.S. air strikes took effect on 15 August 1973, bombing in Cambodia, although still classified, was no longer covert. Even after May, missions into the base areas struck during the secret bombing were still referred to as "MENU Bombing" by the Strategic Air Command, but the veil of self-deception was lifted. The covert passing of coordinates to radar bomb navigators stopped, as did the double reporting.

The extent of the secret bombing of Cambodia was revealed by retired Air Force Maj. Hal Knight, Jr., a former "Combat Skyspot" radar site operator, in a January 1973 letter to Senator William Proxmire. As a result of this letter, in July and August 1973, the Senate Armed Services Committee held hearings on the MENU Bombing. By exposing the extent of the secrecy, the hearings further damaged the credibility of the Nixon administration, already under increasing pressure from unfolding revelations that became the Watergate scandal.

The extent to which the bombing disrupted Communist military operations can only be speculated. Undoubtedly, supply caches were hit and some base camps were destroyed. Since the end of the Vietnam War, it has been learned that COSVN was hardly a Communist "Pentagon." Rather it consisted of a radio transmitter and a dozen or so individuals who moved around constantly. On the other hand, Vietnamization continued and the withdrawal of U.S. ground forces was nearly complete before the DRV launched its Easter Offensive on 31 March 1972.

—Earl H. Tilford, Jr.

References: Berger, Carl, ed. *The United States Air Force in Southeast Asia: 1961–1973, An Illustrated Account* (1984); Littauer, Raphael, and Norman Uphoff. *The Air War in Indochina.* Cornell Air War Study Group (1971); Shawcross, William. *Sideshow: Kissinger, Nixon and the Destruction of Cambodia* (1979).

See also: Air Power, Role in War; ARC LIGHT (B-52 Raids); Cambodia; COSVN (Central Office for South Vietnam or Trung Uong Cuc Miên Nam); Easter Offensive (Nguyên Huê Campaign); Fishhook; Haig, Alexander Meigs, Jr.; Kissinger, Henry Alfred; Nixon, Richard Milhous; Proxmire, William.

Meo. *See* Hmong.

Michigan State University (MSU) Advisory Group

Team of U.S. public administration experts, sociologists, and other academics who, under U.S. government sponsorship, went to South Vietnam in 1955 to help organize President Ngô Đình Diêm's newly installed government.

Led by Professor Wesley Fishel, the Michigan State University (MSU) Advisory Group guided the Republic of Vietnam (RVN) in developing prototypes for the Popular Forces, which were to challenge the Viêt Công in the countryside, and the 50,000-man Civil Guard, which would perform provincial defense. However, Diêm, with the support of the U.S. Military Assistance and Advisory Group (MAAG), resisted the MSU Advisory Group's suggestion for a lightly armed Civil Guard to defend the countryside, preferring a force trained for small-scale military operations rather than police duties. Ultimately, Diêm rejected the MSU plan and used the Civil Guard as a dumping ground for incompetent military officers. The result was a regional defense force assigned the impossible task of defending the countryside against heavily armed Viêt Công guerrillas. Meanwhile, public administration experts from the MSU group had similar difficulties in developing an honest and efficient civil service in the RVN.

Although Dr. Fishel defended Diêm's authoritarian rule as necessary, given Vietnam's lack of experience with democratic government, other members of the group became increasingly critical of the RVN leader. When members of the group published articles critical of Diêm and his brother Ngô Đình Nhu in 1962, Diêm annulled the contract between the RVN government and the MSU advisors.

In providing academic and administrative assistance to Ngô Đình Diêm's government, the U.S. government and the MSU group hoped to stabilize South Vietnam politically. They did not succeed. Diêm's regime remained corrupt, inefficient, and unable to support itself. Ultimately, the MSU Advisory Group failed in its efforts to build a self-sustaining Republic of Vietnam.

—John E. Grenier

References: FitzGerald, Frances. *Fire in the Lake: The Vietnamese and the Americans in Vietnam* (1972); Herring, George C. *America's Longest War: The United States and Vietnam 1950–1975* (1986).

See also: American Friends of Vietnam; Fishel, Wesley Robert; Military Assistance and Advisory Group (MAAG), Vietnam; Ngô Đình Diêm; Ngô Đình Nhu; Territorial Forces; United States: Involvement in Vietnam, 1954–1965.

Midway Island Conference (June 1969)

First meeeting between Republic of Vietnamese (RVN) President Nguyên Van Thiêu and U.S. President Richard Nixon. Thiêu believed that the historically anti-Communist Nixon would never abandon the South Vietnamese, and he had thrown his support behind him in the 1968 U.S. presidential election.

Thiêu requested that the meeting take place in Honolulu, but Nixon, wishing to avoid antiwar riots, instead chose Midway Island, a refueling stop in the middle of the Pacific. Arrangements for the meeting hit several snags. Nixon wanted Thiêu to arrive first, but Thiêu refused, believing that, as host, Nixon should be at Midway awaiting him. In the meeting room, Thiêu was angered to discover that the chair reserved for Nixon was a taller, higher-backed one. Thiêu had hoped to meet with Nixon alone, but the U.S. president insisted on having National Security Advisor Henry Kissinger remain with him, so Thiêu kept his Special Assistant for Foreign Affairs Nguyên Phú Đuc in the room also.

Anticipating that Nixon would propose beginning U.S. withdrawals, Thiêu preempted him by suggesting a redeployment of U.S. and South Vietnamese forces. Nixon agreed but stated that he needed time to develop his strategy. Thiêu sought to buy time and avoid agreeing to a total U.S. withdrawal; he apparently hoped for a Korean-type solution in Vietnam, with a demilitarized zone occupied by U.S. troops separating North and South Vietnam.

Nixon wanted Thiêu's acquiescence to begin secret talks with Hà Nôi concerning U.S. and North Vietnamese troop withdrawals. He suggested private talks at the presidential level with North Vietnam, and Thiêu agreed, but with the provision that he be kept informed of political decisions. He apparently believed that these talks were to set the stage for a North-South conference. Nixon wanted Thiêu's approval to act on behalf of the RVN government in negotiations with the North.

Nixon believed the meeting had been a success. He was elated that U.S. troops would immediately begin withdrawing from Vietnam and hoped that this would gain him favor with antiwar protesters at home and provide time to negotiate a complete withdrawal on U.S. terms. Thiêu, on the other hand, believed he had been promised continued U.S. support and that he would have a staunch anti-Communist ally. He liked Nixon and believed him to be forthright. Although angered and annoyed by what he saw as slights perpetrated against him at the conference, Thiêu attributed these to

Kissinger rather than the president. Although he feared U.S. betrayal and a unilateral withdrawal of troops, Thiêu remained confident in his ally. Nixon and Kissinger, however, had already decided that the U.S. would withdraw from Vietnam, with or without South Vietnamese consent.

—Laura Matysek Wood

Reference: Nguyên Tiên Hang and Jerrold L. Schechter. *The Palace File* (1986).

See also: Kissinger, Henry Alfred; Nixon, Richard Milhous; Nguyên Van Thiêu.

Military Airlift Command (MAC)

U.S. Air Force agency conducting tactical and strategic air movements. The Military Airlift Command (MAC) was established in 1966; it combined the assets from the existing Military Air Transport Service (MATS) and incorporated the airlift components then assigned to Strategic Air Command (SAC) and Tactical Air Command (TAC). MAC was given the mission of operating the entire spectrum of airlift and airdrop missions, deployment and redeployment operations, operation of a single passenger and reservation system for intercontinental travel, and aerial port management. Additional MAC tasks included air weather operations, aeromedical evacuation, and aerospace search and rescue (SAR). The secretary of the Air Force and the MAC commander would be responsible for interfacing with all government agencies on matters pertaining to airlift. MAC's charter implied a combat role with the inclusion of search and rescue and all-inclusive airlift missions. Prior to 1966, SAR and tactical airlift missions were assigned to the Tactical Air Command.

During the initial buildup in the Republic of Vietnam (RVN), MATS was the primary air movement agency. It committed virtually all of its aircraft and crews to the Southeast Asian deployment. The RVN mission forced MATS to supplement regular Air Force squadrons with selected Air Force Reserve (AFR) and Air National Guard (ANG) units. In addition, AFR and ANG units undertook missions previously flown by regular Air Force units so that these additional squadrons would be available for the Southeast Asia buildup. Since President Johnson had not declared a national emergency, federal law prohibited the activation of the Civil Reserve Air Fleet.

MATS also contracted with several commercial airlines for passenger service to the RVN, most notably PAN AM and World Airways. These civilian flight crews faced the same risks as their military counterparts in traveling to airports in the major cities of the RVN.

With MAC's establishment in 1966, the new command acquired additional aircraft, thereby expanding the airlift mission to the RVN. In 1965 the average monthly traffic was approximately 34,000 passengers and 10,000 tons of cargo. In 1967 the average monthly traffic increased to 66,000 passengers and 43,000 tons of cargo. MAC operated all aerial ports, established forward weather stations, and supervised all tactical airlift missions within the RVN, including search-and-rescue operations throughout the Southeast Asian theater of operations. As the U.S. presence expanded to countries such as Thailand, MAC elements colocated with its TAC and SAC counterparts. Additionally, MAC flew all aeromedical evacuations out of the RVN to hospitals in Japan, the Philippines, and the continental United States.

MAC also participated in several strategic combat deployments of entire troop units from the U.S. directly to RVN. Between 23 December 1965 and 23 January 1966, MATS/MAC ferried the entire 3d Brigade, 25th Infantry Division from its home station in Hawaii to Pleiku, RVN. Operation BLUE LIGHT included approximately 90 aircraft transporting 3,000 soldiers and 5,000 tons of cargo. In November 1967, during Operation EAGLE THRUST, MAC airlifted almost the entire 101st Airborne Division from Fort Campbell, Kentucky, directly to Biên Hòa, RVN.

In the arena of tactical airlifts, MAC flew virtually all intratheater missions. These ranged from airborne operations involving U.S. and Army of the Republic of Vietnam (ARVN) forces to regularly scheduled cargo and resupply operations throughout the RVN. During Operation JUNCTION CITY, MAC pilots flew all transport aircraft involved in the only major U.S. airborne operation of the Vietnam War, dropping a battalion of the Army's 173d Airborne Brigade. MAC was the controlling air agency during the Khe Sanh airlift, as well as the major command that directed all search-and-rescue operations throughout Southeast Asia. MAC HH-3E helicopters, specially modified to a gunship configuration, transported Army Special Forces troops on the abortive Son Tây Raid in the DRV.

MAC flew a variety of aircraft. From 1963 to 1964, the primary aircraft assigned to MATS/MAC for strategic lift were the C-124 Globemaster, C-133 Cargomaster (military version of the Boeing 707), and C-135 Stratolifter. During 1964–1965, the Air Force acquired the jet-powered C-141 Starlifter, significantly increasing MAC's ability to conduct long-distance airlifts in reduced time. The C-141 served as the backbone of MAC's intertheater forces throughout the remainder of the conflict. In 1969 the giant C-5A entered service and the next year made its maiden flight to the RVN. The C-5A increased average cargo capacity by 600 percent and could withstand the rigors of service in Southeast Asia. This aircraft provided most of the tonnage delivered during Operation ENHANCE PLUS.

The aircraft assigned the missions of tactical airlift were the C-123 Provider, C-47 Gooney Bird (modified into a gunship dubbed "Puff the Magic Dragon"), C-7 Caribou, and the workhorse of the conflict—the C-130 Hercules. MAC preferred helicopters for search-and-rescue missions, with the ability to land in small spaces or hover while downed pilots were extracted from jungle locations using cables and winches. The UH-1 Iroquois (Huey), HH-43 Masher, and HH-3E "Jolly Green Giant" were the most common types of aircraft employed. Aeromedical evacuations required specially configured C-133 aircraft. MAC refueled strike aircraft during operations and transports during long-distance flights. The KC-135 and KC-130 were tanker versions of the cargo aircraft.

The Vietnam War revolutionized the doctrine of airlift. The principal emphasis in airlift doctrine changed from a purely logistical role to an all-inclusive combat support function. MAC's intertheater lift changed from propeller-driven aircraft to jets, allowing the United States rapidly to project power throughout the world. MAC also gave a theater commander the means to sustain ground forces engaged in prolonged combat. In the post-Vietnam War era, MAC became a specified command directly under the Joint Chiefs of Staff and the sole proponent of airlift operations within the U.S. military.

—J. A. Menzoff

Reference: Smith, Jay H. *Anything, Anywhere, Anytime: An Illustrated History of the Military Airlift Command, 1941–1991* (1991).

See also: Airborne Operations; Airplanes, Allied and Democratic Republic of Vietnam; BLUE LIGHT, Operation; ENHANCE PLUS, Operation; Helicopters, Allied and Democratic Republic of Vietnam; Helicopters, Employment of, in Vietnam; JUNCTION CITY, Operation; Medevac; Search-and-Rescue (SAR) Operations; Son Tây Raid.

Military Assistance and Advisory Group (MAAG), Vietnam

Organization to channel U.S. military assistance against the Communists in Indo-China. The U.S. Military Assistance and Advisory Group (MAAG), Vietnam, was established in September 1950 as MAAG, Indo-China. In March 1950, President Truman approved National Security Council (NSC) memorandum 64, which proclaimed French Indo-China a key area of Southeast Asia and suggested that its fall to the Communists would put the rest of the region in serious jeopardy. Although NSC 64 argued for U.S. support against Communist aggression, it did not specify to whom the support should go—the French or their Vietnamese subjects/allies. Hesitant to appear to support colonialism, the U.S. favored providing aid directly to the Vietnamese chief of state, former emperor Bao Đai. The French threatened to reject any direct aid to Vietnam and initially opposed even the presence of a U.S. advisory group.

In July 1950 a joint Defense Department–State Department survey team was dispatched to Sài Gòn to determine the long-term nature and objectives of the aid program and the best organization for implementing it. Military members of the team recommended establishment of a U.S. military assistance advisory group. The French initially balked, but the U.S. argued that the military advisory group would be necessary to ensure proper requisitioning, procurement, and receipt of supplies and equipment. Based on that recommendation, MAAG, Indo-China, was established in September. It consisted of inspection teams with the mission to observe the distribution and use, by the French and Vietnamese, of U.S.-supplied equipment, but had no training or advisory role.

From the arrival of MAAG, Indo-China, the United States encouraged creation of an independent, indigenous Vietnamese army with a U.S. role in its development and training. The French parried U.S. pressure by developing indigenous Vietnamese units commanded and led by French officers and sergeants, but they steadfastly rejected any U.S. role in training the Vietnamese National Army (VNA) until spring 1954, when their military position became more precarious. As the fall of Điên Biên Phu approached, the French agreed to let Americans participate in training and advising Vietnamese units. At the beginning of June 1954, they formally requested that the United States join France in organizing and training the VNA.

Concerned that the French now intended to draw the United States into the war, the U.S. Joint Chiefs of Staff (JCS) recommended that the United States not train the VNA until a stable Vietnamese government formally requested that help. On the other hand, the State Department reasoned that one way to strengthen and stabilize that government would be to reorganize and train its army. The NSC and President Eisenhower agreed with the State Department, and on 12 August 1954, NSC 5429/1 was approved, providing U.S. assistance in creating indigenous military forces for internal security in Vietnam. However, NSC 5429/1 said nothing about training the VNA, and on 22 October 1954, the State Department, with JCS acquiescence, directed the U.S. mission in Sài Gòn to develop and implement a military training program. By June 1955, with the withdrawal of French forces, creating and training a South Vietnamese army became an entirely American task.

Under the direction and tutelage of the American MAAG, the new 150,000-man Army of the Republic of Vietnam (ARVN) gradually took shape. However, U.S. officials misread guerilla activity, believing it to be a diversion for a conventional attack across the Demilitarized Zone (DMZ). Thus the new army's mission and training centered on repelling a Korean War–style invasion from North Vietnam.

Before 1960, U.S. advisors were involved primarily in training and high-level staff work. In 1960 they began advising ground combat units at regimental level in the field. In 1961 advisors were at the battalion level, and by 1964 they were with the paramilitary forces. Gradually, U.S. advisors became involved in combat, but by then MAAG, Vietnam, had been replaced by Military Assistance Command, Vietnam (MACV).

—Arthur T. Frame

References: Cao Van Vien, et al. *The U.S. Advisor* (1980); Collins, James Lawton, Jr. *The Development and Training of the South Vietnamese Army, 1950–1972* (1975); Eckhardt, George S. *Command and Control, 1950–1969* (1974); Herring, George C. *America's Longest War: The United States and Vietnam, 1950–1975* (1986); Spector, Ronald H. *Advice and Support: The Early Years, 1941–1960* (1983).

See also: Eisenhower, Dwight David; Military Assistance Command, Vietnam (MACV); O'Daniel, John W.; Truman, Harry S; Vietnam, Republic of: Army (ARVN); Vietnamese National Army (VNA); Williams, Samuel T.

Military Assistance Command, Vietnam (MACV)

U.S. joint service headquarters that coordinated all U.S. military activities in the Republic of Vietnam (RVN). The

Military Assistance Command, Vietnam (MACV) was technically subordinate to the United States Pacific Command (USPACOM) in Hawaii, but the MACV commander worked closely with the U.S. ambassador to the RVN and the U.S. Joint Chiefs of Staff (JCS) in the Pentagon. The MACV area of responsibility (AOR) was limited to operations within the territory of the RVN, while the USPACOM commander controlled sea operations beyond the territorial waters and air operations against North Vietnam.

Between 1960 and 1964, the size of the Republic of Vietnam Armed Forces (RVNAF) grew from 150,000 to 250,000 men in an effort to counter the Viêt Công insurgency. U.S. support also grew during this period from just over 500 advisors in 1960 to more than 23,000 in 1964. This consisted not only of advisors but units providing aviation, signal, medical, engineer, and intelligence support.

MACV was established on 6 February 1962 to control all U.S. Army support units in Vietnam in addition to the Military Assistance and Advisory Group (MAAG) advisory program. In May 1964, MAAG missions and functions were integrated into those of the MACV staff, the MAAG was disestablished, and the advisory effort ceased to have a separate command and support organization.

MACV also worked closely with the RVN government and RVNAF Joint General Staff (JGS) on overall military plans and operations. Although a combined command and staff arrangement was suggested to the Vietnamese JGS, the South Vietnamese rejected it because of their political sensitivity to the charge advanced by Communist propaganda that they were puppets of the United States. Instead, a Free World Military Assistance Council, composed of the Chief of the Vietnamese JGS, the senior Korean officer in Vietnam, and the commander, MACV provided operational guidance to, not control of, Free World Forces through the annual Combined Campaign Plan. First published at the end of 1965, the Combined Campaign Plan was not a true operational plan; rather it broke the operational effort down geographically and assigned no tasks or goals.

Coordination of combat operations without the benefit of an integrated command at the top was provided through joint agreements between local Free World commanders and Army of the Republic of Vietnam (ARVN) ground commanders. While ARVN corps commanders retained overall responsibility for military actions in each Corps Tactical Zone (CTZ) (also known as Military Regions), U.S. and other Free World force commanders accepted responsibility for tactical areas of responsibility (TAORs), arbitrary geographical areas in which U.S. and Free World units conducted combat operations.

In addition to U.S. Army, Vietnam (USARV), which was primarily an administrative and logistics headquarters, Naval Forces, Vietnam, and the Seventh Air Force, operational ground commands subordinate to MACV included the 5th Special Forces Group, the III Marine Amphibious Force (MAF), I Field Force, II Field Force, and IV Corps Advisory Group. The latter four controlled U.S. combat units and field advisory teams within their areas of responsibility that coincided with the ARVN CTZs (actually no U.S. combat units operated in the IV Corps area, only advisory teams). The commanders of these four U.S. operational commands, as with their MACV superior, were the senior advisors to the respective ARVN CTZ commander.

Each of the four MACV commanders, Gen. Paul D. Harkins (February 1962–June 1964), Gen. William Westmoreland (June 1964–June 1968), Gen. Creighton W. Abrams, Jr. (June 1968–June 1972), and Gen. Frederick C. Weyand (June 1972–March 1973), in addition to commanding all U.S. forces in South Vietnam, was also senior advisor to the RVNAF JGS. He also commanded the MACV army component, USARV.

As MACV commander, between 1965 and 1968 Westmoreland oversaw the buildup of U.S. forces to over 550,000 men. Likewise, it was Gen. Abrams as commander, MACV, who was the primary overseer of Vietnamization between 1969 and 1972. The bulk of U.S. combat operations took place under the command of these two men.

—Arthur T. Frame

References: Clarke, Jeffrey J. *Advice and Support: The Final Years, 1965–1973* (1988); Eckhardt, George S. *Command and Control, 1950–1969* (1974); Herring, George C. *America's Longest War: The United States and Vietnam, 1950–1975* (1986); Karnow, Stanley *Vietnam: A History* (1983); Stanton, Shelby L. *The Rise and Fall of an American Army: U.S. Ground Forces in Vietnam, 1965–1973* (1985).
See also: Abrams, Creighton; Free World Assistance Program; Harkins, Paul D.; Military Assistance and Advisory Group (MAAG), Vietnam; Military Regions (MR); Westmoreland, William Childs; Weyand, Frederick C.

Military Regions (MR)

Name given by the U.S. military to geographical and operational divisions of the Republic of Vietnam (RVN) that coincided exactly with the four Republic of Vietnam Armed Forces (RVNAF) Corps Tactical Zones (CTZ). Before 1954 the State of Vietnam was divided into four Military Regions: MR I, former Cochin China; MR II, Central Vietnam; MR III, former Tonkin; and MR IV, Central Highlands. In 1961 each RVN Army Corps took responsibility for a former Military Region, numbered I to IV: CTZ I, five provinces from Quang Tri to Quang Ngãi; CTZ II, the Central Highlands and five provinces south of Quang Ngãi; CTZ III, north of the Mekong; and CTZ IV, the remainder of the Mekong Delta. Each infantry division took charge of an area within a CTZ, known as a Division Tactical Area (DTA). Each DTA had several sectors and the provincial military headquarters. In the U.S. phase of the war, DTAs were done away with, and CTZs became Military Regions until the Communist victory of April 1975.

No single combined headquarters provided for unified operations within the four regions. Despite U.S. suggestions, the Vietnamese Joint General Staff rejected a combined command and staff arrangement for political reasons. Instead, operational guidance was provided through an annual Combined Campaign Plan, produced by the Free World Military Assistance Council comprising the chief of the Vietnamese Joint General Staff, the senior Republic of Korea officer in Vietnam, and the commander, Military Assistance Command, Vietnam (MACV). The Combined Campaign Plan was not a true operational plan. It assigned no tasks or goals; rather, it broke the operational effort down geographically.

Coordination of combat operations without the benefit of an integrated command at the top was provided through joint agreements between local Free World Military Force commanders and Army of the Republic of Vietnam (ARVN) ground commanders. While ARVN corps commanders retained overall responsibility for military actions in each CTZ, U.S. and other Free World force commanders accepted responsibility for tactical areas of responsibility (TAORs). These TAORs, like the larger MRs/CTZs, were arbitrary geographical areas in which U.S. and Free World units conducted combat operations.

U.S. operational ground force commands subordinate to MACV that controlled U.S. combat units and field advisory teams within each MR (actually no U.S. combat units operated in the IV MR/CTZ area, only advisory teams and special forces units) included, from north to south, respectively, the III Marine Amphibious Force (MAF), I Field Force, II Field Force, and IV Corps Advisory Group. All corps operated with equivalent command levels with lieutenant generals commanding.

As with their MACV superior, commanders of these four operational U.S. commands were the senior advisors to the respective RVNAF CTZ commander.

—Arthur T. Frame

References: Clarke, Jeffrey J. *Advice and Support: The Final Years, 1965–1973* (1988); Eckhardt, George S. *Command and Control, 1950–1969* (1974); Herring, George C. *America's Longest War: The United States and Vietnam, 1950–1975* (1986); Larsen, Stanley R., and James L. Collins, Jr. *Allied Participation in Vietnam* (1975); Stanton, Shelby L. *The Rise and Fall of an American Army: U.S. Ground Forces in Vietnam, 1965–1973* (1985).

See also: Free World Assistance Program; Military Assistance Command, Vietnam (MACV).

Military Revolutionary Council

Group of senior generals who dominated political affairs in the Republic of Vietnam (RVN) behind the scenes from early November 1963 to mid-December 1964. After the overthrow of Ngô Đình Diêm in November 1963, a 12-member military junta, the Military Revolutionary Council, took power, with Gen. Duong Van Minh as chief of state. The new regime was no more responsive to the people of South Vietnam than Diêm had been and had the added disadvantage of political instability. Members of the Military Revolutionary Council soon fell to quarreling among themselves. Minh had boasted that the collective leadership would ensure that no one else would have Diêm's power, but Minh showed no inclination to govern.

On 30 January 1964, Maj. Gen. Nguyên Khánh led a coup against Minh. Surprised U.S. officials hailed Khánh, who promised to rule with a strong hand. Although shrewd and

energetic, Khánh showed no more aptitude for governing than had Minh, and his history of changing sides hardly engendered trust. Khánh purged some generals but allowed Minh to remain on as titular head of state.

Khánh persuaded Đai Viêt leader and Catholic physician Dr. Nguyên Tôn Hoàn to return from exile in Paris and serve as premier. When it was clear that the Đai Viêt was hopelessly splintered, Khánh named himself premier, with Hòan as his deputy. Hòan then began to conspire with Buddhists and other opposition groups against Khánh. RVN political instability was now rampant, and in 1964 there were seven changes of government. In serious difficulty, Khánh announced a national emergency, imposed censorship and other controls, and hastily assembled a new constitution, promoting himself to the presidency and dismissing Minh. In August, students and then Buddhists took to the Sài Gòn streets. U.S. Ambassador Maxwell Taylor urged Khánh not to yield to minority pressure. On 25 August Khánh quit, and the Military Revolutionary Council met to choose a new head of state.

After lengthy political maneuvering, a triumvirate emerged of Generals Khánh, Minh, and Trân Thiên Khiêm. Khánh retained the premiership but left the capital. Khánh, meanwhile, named economist Nguyên Xuân Oánh prime minister in his absence. Turbulence continued, with threats from dissident army units in the Mekong Delta and militant Buddhists from Huê. In November, new riots in Sài Gòn protested Khánh's rule, and Taylor urged him to leave the country. By this time the "Young Turks," a faction of younger military officers, had come to the fore. Headed by Nguyên Cao Ky, one of the younger officers in the coup against Diêm, the group also included army Maj. Gen. Nguyên Van Thiêu. Disillusioned by the ineffective national government, in mid-December 1964 the Young Turks overthrew the Military Revolutionary Council.

—Spencer C. Tucker

References: Karnow, Stanley. *Vietnam: A History* (1983); Nguyên Cao Ky. *Twenty Years and Twenty Days* (1976).

See also: Duong Van Minh; Ngô Đình Diêm, Overthrow of; Nguyên Cao Ky; Nguyên Khánh; Nguyên Van Thiêu; Taylor, Maxwell Davenport; Trân Thiên Khiêm; Vietnam, Republic of: 1954–1975.

Military Sealift Command

U.S. Navy command responsible for logistical support to the U.S. military effort in Vietnam. The U.S. Navy's Military Sealift Command (MSC, designated in September 1970), and its predecessor, the Military Sea Transportation Service (MSTS), supported U.S. forces throughout the conflict in Southeast Asia. From August 1954 to May 1955, MSTS transports carried many of the 293,000 Vietnamese who emigrated by sea from North to South Vietnam.

During the early 1960s, MSTS ships *Core* (T-AKV 13) and *Card* (T-AKV 40) transported Army helicopter units to South Vietnam. From 1965 to 1973, MSTS maintained the massive military buildup in Indo-China. At the height of the war, MSTS operated a fleet of 527 reactivated World War II ships and chartered vessels, managed by offices in the United States, Japan, and South Vietnam. Many types of vessels sailed in the MSTS fleet, including aircraft ferries, a helicopter repair ship, standard cargo hulls, roll-on/roll-off ships, tankers, troop transports, tank landing ships, tugs, and barges. The Navy's sealift effort ensured that the U.S. contingent in the Republic of Vietnam (RVN) was well supplied.

In March and April 1975, when the Democratic Republic of Vietnam (DRV) launched its major conventional offensive against the Republic of Vietnam (RVN), the Navy called on MSC to evacuate friendly Vietnamese troops and civilians from the northern and central regions of the country. On 27 March, MSC began rescuing an increasingly desperate horde of soldiers and civilians from Đà Nang and other ports to the south. Crowding, insufficient food, and displeasure with the choice of isolated Phú Quôc Island as the disembarkation point led armed passengers to threaten the U.S. crews. As a result, the Navy deployed 50-man U.S. Marine security detachments to the ships. By 10 April, MSC had transported to Phú Quôc 130,000 U.S. and Vietnamese refugees.

At the end of April, with the defeat of the RVN virtually certain, President Ford ordered Operation FREQUENT WIND, the final evacuation of Sài Gòn. Anticipating such an order, the MSC had filled its ships with food, water, and medicine and stationed Marine security detachments on board. In concert with the U.S. Seventh Fleet, which began lifting refugees by helicopter from Sài Gòn to the offshore flotilla, MSC took on board a growing flood of refugees. Between 29 April and 2 May, when the operation ceased, MSC ships had embarked more than 50,000 evacuees. The MSC ships, the Seventh Fleet contingent, and a flotilla of 26 Vietnam Navy ships, after embarking an additional 30,000 evacuees and their families, set sail for the Philippines.

—Edward J. Marolda

References: Marolda, Edward J. *By Sea, Air, and Land: An Illustrated History of the U.S. Navy and the War in Southeast Asia* (1994); Schreadley, Richard L. *From the Rivers to the Sea: The U.S. Navy in Vietnam* (1992).

See also: Ford, Gerald R.; FREQUENT WIND, Operation; PASSAGE TO FREEDOM, Operation; United States: Navy.

Mine Warfare, Water

The Việt Công (VC) and People's Army of Vietnam (PAVN) employed thousands of mines against U.S. and Allied naval forces throughout the Vietnam conflict, much as they had against the French during the Indo-China War. Between 1959 and 1964, VC mines, often homemade devices, took an increasing toll of naval and civilian craft on South Vietnamese rivers and canals, ending commercial traffic on some primary waterways.

The danger was especially acute on waterways near Sài Gòn, the Republic of Vietam's (RVN's) most important port. VC closure of the Lòng Tào River would have put an enormous strain on Allied logistic resources in the southern regions of South Vietnam. As a result, on 20 May 1966, the U.S. Navy established Mine Squadron 11, Detachment Alpha (Mine Division 112 after May 1968) at Nhà Bè. The minesweeping detachment operated 12 or 13 fiberglass-hulled minesweeping boats (MSBs). The MSBs fought with

machine guns and grenade launchers and carried surface radars and minesweeping gear for clearing explosives from the rivers. The Navy also set up three-boat sections at Đà Nang and Cam Ranh Bay. Detachment Alpha's strength increased in July 1967, when the first of six mechanized landing craft, minesweeping (LCM(M)), reached Nhà Bè.

Despite the presence of Mine Squadron 11 and other river warfare forces, in the second half of 1966 and early 1967 the enemy mounted a serious effort to interdict the waterway. The Việt Công employed mines, 122-mm rockets, rocket-propelled grenades, recoilless rifles, machine guns, and small arms against U.S. and RVN naval forces and merchant ships. In August 1966, VC mines severely damaged the SS *Baton Rouge Victory*, a Vietnamese Navy vessel, and *MSB 54*. That November, the VC sank *MSB 54*. In February 1967, Communist direct-fire weapons and mines destroyed *MSB 45* and heavily damaged *MSB 49*.

By spring 1967, Allied naval units moved in force into the Rung Sát area, refined their mine countermeasures tactics, and brought better weapons and equipment into play against the VC sappers. Vietnamese Regional Forces, U.S. Army 9th Division troops, and Navy SEAL (Sea Air Land) commandos, working with helicopter, river patrol boat, MSB, and LCM(M) units, scoured the shorelines. During the next year, Communist guerrillas periodically ambushed ships on the Lòng Tào, but the fast and devastating reaction by Allied forces kept casualties and damage to vessels relatively light. Often, the minesweeping force swept up mines before they could do damage, while river patrol boat and SEAL patrols disrupted enemy attack plans. Consequently, Việt Công were unable to cut or seriously slow logistic traffic on the Lòng Tào, even when their comrades were fighting for their lives in Sài Gòn during the 1968 Têt Offensive.

During 1968 and 1969, the Navy deployed strong mine countermeasures forces to the Cua Việt River, just south of the Demilitarized Zone (DMZ), and defeated the PAVN's attempt to cut that vital waterway.

—Edward J. Marolda

References: Marolda, Edward J. *By Sea, Air, and Land: An Illustrated History of the U.S. Navy and the War in Southeast Asia* (1994); Schreadley, Richard L. *From the Rivers to the Sea: The U.S. Navy in Vietnam* (1992).

See also: Mining and Mine Clearance in North Vietnam; Riverine Craft; Riverine Warfare; SEAL (Sea, Air, Land) Teams; United States: Navy.

Mines, Antipersonnel and Antitank

The art of mining was deftly practiced by Việt Công (VC) and People's Army of Vietnam (PAVN) forces. Mines, rockets, and mortars substituted for the Communists' lack of artillery resources and were well integrated into basic tactical perspectives. Trip-wired/pressure contact and command-detonated mines in unison provided the basis of devastating ambushes unmatched by U.S. artillery barrages. U.S. mining centered on "area denial"—dropping tens of millions of antipersonnel mines (XM48 "button bomblets," BLU43 "Short Dragontooth," BLU44 "Long Dragontooth," and

XM41E1 "Gravel mines") from aircraft deep behind Communist lines.

Communist forces effectively employed mines against military personnel and armored vehicles. Antipersonnel mines were made from such items as pipe, cement, artillery and mortar shells, and cartridge cases. Whereas ground-placed mines were predominately used by the VC, the U.S. claymore (M18 series) was standard issue to U.S. and Army of the Republic Vietnam forces. This mine sprayed steel fragments in a fan-shaped pattern 2 meters in height and 50 meters in width (with a 95 percent casualty probability) and was both command and trip-wire detonated.

U.S. casualties resulting from antipersonnel mines were significant. Reportedly 22.8 percent of Marines wounded in action from July 1965 through December 1966 were wounded by mines and booby traps. The lethality of these devices were low, however, because of their makeshift nature and the emphasis placed on using larger mines in an antitank role.

Antitank and anti–armored personnel carrier (anti-APC) mines represented a considerable danger in Vietnam. Because they were more lightly armored, APCs were vulnerable to large mines constructed from such items as TNT demolition blocks, explosive-filled five-gallon cans, and modified large-caliber mortar shells, as well as conventional Soviet and Chinese antitank mines deployed in far smaller numbers.

Antitank mines were sometimes placed in random patterns as nuisances, or placed where armored vehicles would be channeled onto road networks because of vegetation and wet terrain. Favorite VC tactics were to place mines in the seemingly safe road tracks of an armored fighting vehicle (AFV) that had passed by earlier and in likely night laager positions. These tactics were effective; an estimated 70 percent of U.S. armor losses in Vietnam were attributed to mines. Comparable French losses were calculated at 85 percent.

Another form of mining, antihelicopter mining, had its origins in this war. The Communists mined likely landing zones in Operation JUNCTION CITY with an assortment of command-detonated artillery rounds, TNT, and directional DH10 devices (much like claymore mines).

—Robert J. Bunker

References: Doleman, Edgar D. *The Vietnam Experience: Tools of War* (1984); Smith, Herbert L. *Landmine and Countermine Warfare: Vietnam, 1964–1969* (1972); Stolfi, Russel H. *Mine and Countermine Warfare in Recent History* (1972); U.S. Marine Corps Base Quantico. *Vietcong Mine Warfare* (1966).

See also: Armor Warfare; Armored Personnel Carriers (APCs); Booby Traps; JUNCTION CITY, Operation; Mine Warfare, Water.

Minh Mang (1791–1841)

Second emperor of the Nguyên Dynasty (1820–1841); real name Nguyên Phuoc Đom or Đam. Under Minh Mang the Vietnamese Empire was greatly enlarged to cover most of the territories of Cambodia and Laos. Minh Mang's concern for moral and cultural protection of Vietnamese society led to the prohibition and persecution of Christianity. He rejected all French proposals for permanent diplomatic relations, but was receptive to commerce as regulated by Vietnamese laws. He was also receptive to, if not admiring of, Western technology. President Andrew Jackson sent Edmund Roberts as his envoy to the Minh Mang court as early as 1832. Irreconcilable differences in diplomatic customs led Roberts to leave Vietnam without seeing the emperor at his court, however. During Minh Mang's reign, the forces of Western imperialism became stronger; this pressure increased under his son and successor, Thiêu Tri.

—Pham Cao Duong

References: Lê Huu Muc. *Huân Dich Thập Điêu: Thánh Du Cua Vua Thánh Tô, Diên Nghia Cua Vua Duc Tông* (1971); Le Thanh Khoi. *Le Viet-Nam: Histoire et Civilisation* (1955); Nguyên Huyên Anh. *Viêt Nam Danh Nhân Tu Điên* (1990); Quôc Su Quán. *Quôc Triêu Chánh Biên Toát Yêu* (1971); Trân Trong Kim. *Viêt Nam Su Luoc* (1971); Woodside, Alexander B. *Vietnam and the Chinese Model: A Comparative Study of Nguyen and Ch'ing Government in the First Half of the Nineteenth Century* (1971).

See also: Nguyên Phúc Ánh (Gia Long); Thiêu Tri; Vietnam: from 938 through the French Conquest.

Mining and Mine Clearance in North Vietnam

During the ROLLING THUNDER bombing campaign, the U.S. Navy's carrier air squadrons released thousands of mines along the key Communist supply routes in the panhandle area of North Vietnam. The object was to make difficult, if not prohibitive, movement around ferry crossings, bridges, storage areas, truck parks, and fuel dumps. Carrier attack aircraft also "seeded" inland waterways and roads used by the People's Army of Vietnam (PAVN) to transport munitions into Laos and South Vietnam with Mark 36 Destructors, which contained 500 pounds of explosives and detonated when trucks or other metal objects disturbed their magnetic fields. Neither the Navy's mining effort nor the overall bombing campaign stopped the flow of munitions to the fighting front, but they forced the Communists to devote scarce resources to the defense of their supply line.

Another mining operation carried out by the Navy during 1972 and early 1973 had a greater impact on the war. Early on 8 May 1972, naval aircraft laid strings of 36 1,000-pound Mark 52 mines in the water approaches to Hai Phòng, through which most of the Democratic Republic of Vietnam's (DRV's) imported war material and all of its fuel supply passed. During succeeding months, thousands more mines and 500-pound Mark 36 Destructors were dropped in the seaways of the DRV's secondary ports and reseeded in the Hai Phòng approaches.

For the remainder of 1972, 27 Sino-Soviet merchant ships remained immobile in Hai Phòng rather than risk transit of the mined waters. The mining campaign, along with U.S. air attacks on DRV supply lines ashore, helped shorten the PAVN Easter Offensive in South Vietnam. Eventually, the mining operation and the LINEBACKER bombing campaign induced the North Vietnamese to negotiate an end to the war.

On 27 January 1973, U.S. and DRV officials signed a protocol to the Paris agreement that called for the United States to neutralize the Navy mines. On 28 January, following months of preparation, Rear Adm. Brian McCauley's Mine Countermeasures Force (Task Force 78), of the Seventh Fleet, deployed from the Philippines to Hai Phòng. To coordinate actions, on 5 February the commander of Task Force 78 met in the city with his North Vietnamese counterpart, Col. Hoàng Huu Thái. Operation END SWEEP began the next day. On board the newly arriving ships were 31 CH-53 Sea Stallion helicopters from the Navy's Helicopter Mine Countermeasures Squadron 12 and from Marine helicopter squadrons HMM-165 and HMH-463, which towed minesweeping sleds and other devices. The helicopters swept the main shipping channel to Hai Phòng on 27 February and the ports of Hòn Gai and Câm Pha on 17 March. In early April, Task Force 78 deployed to the formerly mined waters MSS 2, a decommissioned LST filled with buffer material and crewed by volunteers, which carried out eight passages of the Hai Phòng channel to ensure no mines remained active in the vital waterway. Elsewhere in North Vietnam, U.S. Navy technical personnel prepared 50 North Vietnamese sailors to conduct their own minesweeping operations. While this was taking place, U.S. C-130 transport aircraft delivered minesweeping gear to Cát Bi airfield outside the city. Until 17 April, the Navy task force continued its mission. Then, because Washington believed that Hà Nôi had failed to carry out its obligations under the Paris agreement, it ordered a suspension of minesweeping operations.

END SWEEP resumed on 18 June, after U.S. leaders were persuaded that the North Vietnamese would once again act in good faith. Shortly afterward, Admiral McCauley notified the North Vietnamese that the ports of Hai Phòng, Hòn Gai, and Câm Pha were free from the threat of U.S.-laid mines. Next, Task Force 78 concentrated on the coastal areas off Vinh. Finally, on 18 July 1973, McCauley led his flotilla out to sea, officially ending Operation END SWEEP.

—Edward J. Marolda

References: Marolda, Edward J. *By Sea, Air, and Land: An Illustrated History of the U.S. Navy and the War in Southeast Asia* (1994); Marolda, Edward J., ed. *Operation End Sweep: A History of Minesweeping Operations in North Vietnam* (1993); Schreadley, Richard L. *From the Rivers to the Sea: The U.S. Navy in Vietnam* (1992).

See also: Aircraft Carriers; Mine Warfare, Water; United States: Navy.

Missing in Action, Allied

Military personnel whose fate remains unclear. The term *missing in action* (MIA) is normally applied to approximately 2,500 missing Americans, the exact number and fate of whom has long been a source of political disputes. There are no reliable figures of how many Army of the Republic of Vietnam (ARVN) soldiers are MIA—some estimates are as high as 330,000 for both North and South—nor is there evidence of other Allied missing.

Under the Paris peace accords of January 1973, the Democratic Republic of Vietnam (DRV) and National Liberation Front (NLF) agreed to return all U.S. prisoners of war (POWs) and to make every effort to provide information on the fate of MIAs. Following the agreement, the North

Vietnamese returned 591 Americans POWs, and President Nixon announced on 29 March 1973 that "all our American POWs are on their way home." Questions were immediately raised about the low number of POWs, but various executive and Congressional studies concluded that there was no credible evidence that any U.S. MIAs were still alive. In 1977, under President Carter, the Pentagon reclassified more than 1,000 POW/MIAs to "killed in action/body not recovered" (KIA/BNR)—that is, definitely dead—while the rest would be presumed dead. Only Air Force Col. Charles Shelton was then listed, apparently simply to keep the issue active, as a possible POW.

Under pressure from the National League of Families of American Prisoners and Missing in Southeast Asia and others, in 1979 Congress changed the status of soldiers considered KIA/BNR back to POW/MIA. This action restored higher benefits to family members (some of whom offered to return the money so as not to cloud the issue) and kept the hopes of loved ones alive. After 1982 President Reagan repeatedly stated his belief that some Americans might still be held against their will in Indo-China. Under his direction, a POW/MIA flag designed by the National League has flown at the White House one day per year, and by 1990 all 50 states had an officially recognized "National POW/MIA Recognition Day." Similarly, in the 1992 presidential campaign, candidate Ross Perot stated his belief that Americans were still alive and made clear that he had funded previous efforts to retrieve them. Yet another congressional committee was then founded under the direction of Vietnam veteran Senator John Kerry of Massachusetts, and the U.S. Postal Service issued a POW/MIA stamp. Meanwhile, a number of popular movies showed live Americans being rescued.

The belief that there were live U.S. POWs was partly fueled by Bobby Garwood, a U.S. Marine POW and alleged Communist collaborator who claimed to have seen up to 70 Americans held against their will. Additional evidence included reports by thousands of Vietnamese of "live sightings," photos or military identification tags of alleged POWs, and allegedly genuine documents from the former Soviet Union suggesting that U.S. airmen had been sent to the USSR. Behind such evidence lay deep suspicions of the credibility of the U.S. and Indo-China governments. Nixon's inquiry about the fate of certain "discrepancy cases" (Americans known to have been captured alive but not returned), while stating publicly that all U.S. POWs were returning home, suggested that he had not been completely candid. Subsequent anger over the insensitive handling of this issue added to the problem.

Those who believed that the POW/MIA issue was not being properly handled were further angered that hard-liners within the Vietnamese government had initially linked the fulfillment of their obligations under Article 8a of the Paris Peace Treaty to the U.S. promise (under Article 25) to provide reconstruction aid. Even after the Vietnamese government recognized that the POW/MIA issue was a humanitarian rather than political one and agreed in 1987 to let a U.S. mission headed by retired U.S. Gen. John Vessey work in Vietnam on the issue, the Vietnamese tendency to produce information they once claimed not to have fueled the worst suspicions of its critics.

In Cambodia, neither the Khmer Rouge regime, still in effective control of parts of the country, nor its generally ineffective successors were much help. Similarly, neither the Laotian nor Vietnamese governments have been willing to pursue the fate of the relatively large number of Americans lost in Laos. Compounding the problem is the assumption made by many that the locations where some Americans were lost might have been altered because they were on illegal missions.

Countering all this were the arguments of those who believe that, at least in recent years, both governments have done all that they could to resolve an inherently tragic issue. Supporters of this position point out that roughly 80,000 U.S. citizens are still listed as missing from World War II and about 8,000 are still unaccounted for from the Korean War. They point to the continued fighting and grave difficulties that the North Vietnamese and National Liberation Front had after 1973 and conclude that it was extremely difficult for the Vietnamese to tackle the MIA question during the initial years, when bodies might most likely have been recovered, and they see no reason why Vietnam should want to hold Americans captive for so long.

Some critics charge that many Southeast Asians report sightings and manufacture photos or dog tags to make money, and that many POW/MIA advocates are motivated by anger at having lost the war, the wish to avoid paying reconstruction costs, or the desire to advance their own fortunes. In their view, an alliance of the noble, the gullible, and the unsavory has for too long kept alive the sad hopes of the families of MIAs.

By 1995 President Clinton felt that enough progress had been made, particularly on the 100 to 300 discrepancy cases, to justify the recognition of Vietnam. Yet the sad search continued, as did the mistrust by conservatives of the U.S. and Vietnamese governments. In September 1996, U.S. officials listed 2,143 Americans still missing in action in Southeast Asia, more than 1,600 of them in Vietnam.

—Peter K. Frost

References: Groom, Winston, and Duncan Spencer. *Conversations with the Enemy* (1983); Jensen-Stevenson, Monika, and William Stevenson. *Kiss the Boys Goodbye: How the United States Betrayed Its Own POWs in Vietnam* (1991); Keating, Susan Katz. *Prisoners of Hope: Exploiting the POW/MIA Myth in America* (1994); McConnell, Malcolm. *Inside Hanoi's Secret Archives* (1995); U.S. Senate. *Report of the Select Committee on POW/MIA Affairs* (1993).

See also: Clinton, William Jefferson; Garwood, Robert "Bobby" Russell; Nixon, Richard Milhous; Paris Peace Accords; Prisoners of War, Allied; Vessey, John W.

Missing in Action and Prisoners of War, Viêt Công and People's Army of Vietnam

After the Vietnam War, America's attention centered on its own military personnel missing in action (MIA). Most Americans were not interested in or aware of the much larger number of Communist MIA in the war. Many Vietnamese families had only red-bordered Socialist Republic of Vietnam (SRV) government certificates that proclaimed their loved one as a "Vietnamese martyr in the struggle against America."

According to the SRV government, more than 300,000 Vietnamese are missing and presumed dead from the Vietnam War. More than three-quarters of these are from the central or north-central provinces of Vietnam. The figure includes Viêt Công (VC) and People's Army of Vietnam (PAVN) presumed dead as well as Vietnamese who served in the Army of the Republic of Vietnam (ARVN). In talks to normalize relations between the SRV and the United States, Hà Nôi officials never made a major issue of Vietnamese MIAs but did point out in subtle ways that at least 150 times as many Vietnamese are missing as Americans. Few Northerners killed in the South have been returned to the North for reburial.

In a country in which ancestor worship dominates spiritual life, many believe it essential that remains be located and properly buried. Vietnamese endeavoring to locate remains of their loved ones have virtually no leads. Government announcements of deaths in the war provided no information on where a body might be buried, and often years passed before a surviving relative was notified. Soldiers killed in battle usually were hastily buried in unmarked graves, and no identifiable remains exist of many who died in B-52 strikes. Identification of recovered bodies is daunting because the SRV does not have the technological means to identify them. Dental records, a key in identifying Americans who died in the war, usually are not available for Vietnamese.

Vietnam's military cemeteries contain many empty graves with markers that include no death date. Vietnamese attempting to locate MIAs do so without government assistance. Some U.S. help has come forward. In September 1996, representatives of the American Vietnam Veterans' Association gave Hà Nôi information on mass graves in which 600 Vietnamese servicemen were believed buried. Previously the association had provided information on the burial sites of an estimated 6,000 Vietnamese.

Prisoners of war (POWs) were another matter. After 1954, captured VC soldiers were considered Communist rebels and were incarcerated in prisons known as "Communist rebel camps" under the control of the ARVN and run by the Military Police. VC political operatives were kept in regular prisons controlled by the Ministry of the Interior. From 1961, the Communist rebel camps were renamed "prisoners of war" camps. There were four such camps, one in each Military Region—Phú Quôc Island (the largest), Tân Hiêp, Cân Tho, and Đà Nang. After initial interrogation, all Communist POWs came under RVN rather than U.S. jurisdiction. Just before the 1973 Paris agreement, more than 40,000 Communist prisoners were being held.

In 1960 there were about 126 prison camps of all kinds. The most famous was the notorious French-built correctional center at Côn Son (Poulo Condore Island), which detained thousands of Vietnamese political prisoners. Before 1975,

Communists who were not members of the VC Armed Forces, and thus not protected by the Geneva Convention, were sent to Côn Son after sentencing, as were non-Communist opponents of the RVN government. Except for some POWs guilty of murder in POW camps, no PAVN POWs were held at Côn Son. Conditions in most civilian prisons were harsh. In the early 1970s, Côn Son became notorious for its "tiger cages," where prisoners who violated regulations were held incommunicado.

—Gary Kerley, Nguyên Công Luân, and Spencer Tucker

References: Gerassi, John. *North Vietnam: A Documentary* (1968); Vu Thu Hiên. *Đêm Giua Ban Ngày* (1997).

See also: Casualties; Missing in Action, Allied; Poulo Condore (Côn Son); Prisoners of War, Allied; Tiger Cages; Vietnam, Socialist Republic of: 1975 to the Present.

Mitchell, John Newton (1913–1988)

U.S. attorney general, 1969–1972. In 1968 Mitchell managed Richard Nixon's successful presidential campaign, and in 1969 the president appointed Mitchell attorney general. Controversy filled Mitchell's tenure as attorney general. He advocated prosecution of antiwar demonstrators and labeled them Communists. Fearing further erosion of support for the Vietnam War, Mitchell unsuccessfully sought to stop *The New York Times* from publishing the Pentagon Papers, first with a simple request and then with a restraining order. He also approved the conspiracy indictment of Daniel Ellsberg, who had revealed the existence of the documents. On 1 March 1974, Mitchell faced indictment—and eventual conviction—for his role in the Watergate cover-up. He spent 19 months in jail, the first U.S. attorney general to serve a prison term.

—Dean Brumley

References: Haldeman, H. R. *The Haldeman Diaries: Inside the Nixon White House* (1994); Harris, Richard. *Justice: The Crisis of Law, Order, and Freedom in America* (1970); Karnow, Stanley. *Vietnam: A History* (1984); Schoenebraun, Eleanor W., ed. *Political Profiles: The Nixon/Ford Years* (1979); Sheehan, Neil, Hedrick Smith, E. W. Kenworthy, and Fox Butterfield. *The Pentagon Papers* (1971).

See also: Ellsberg, Daniel; Huston Plan; Nixon, Richard Milhous; United States: Department of Justice; Watergate

Mobile Guerrilla Forces (MGF)

Republic of Vietnam (RVN) counterinsurgency force. In fall 1966, Special Forces commanders began experimenting with deploying indigenous troops on extended offensive combat operations. The result was the Mobile Guerrilla Forces (MGFs), company-sized units trained and led by a Special Forces detachment.

Envisioned by Col. Francis J. Kelly, these units were to deploy on intensive combat operations for up to 60 days. Following approximately five weeks of training in offensive tactics and surveillance, Vietnamese volunteers were normally deployed by helicopter to attack remote Viêt Công (VC) outposts and supply routes, missions normally labeled Operation BLACKJACK. First deployed in November 1966 as Task Force 777, Mobile Guerrilla Forces immediately proved to be an excellent counterinsurgency asset. By January 1967,

these operations were experiencing tactical successes and becoming more widespread throughout South Vietnam.

Despite their success, Mobile Guerrilla Force units faced many problems. They were not true guerrilla forces. The soldiers were seldom natives of the region where they operated, and lack of firsthand intelligence hampered effectiveness. Resupply of the forces was such a problem that deployments seldom lasted longer than two weeks. Training was rudimentary, and MGFs lacked the tactical proficiency and unit cohesion needed for extended field operations.

Nevertheless, Mobile Guerrilla Forces were a successful experiment for the Special Forces. These units greatly aided intelligence gathering and proved adept at search-and-destroy and other offensive operations in remote sections of South Vietnam. In May 1968, the Mobile Guerrilla Forces were merged with the Mobile Strike Force to form Mobile Strike Force Commands. The decision to form these new units was based, to some degree, on the tactical success of the Mobile Guerrilla Forces.

—Richard D. Starnes

References: Kelly, Francis J. *U.S. Army Special Forces, 1961–1971* (1985); Krepinevich, Andrew F. *The Army and Vietnam* (1986); Stanton, Shelby L. *Green Berets at War: U.S. Army Special Forces in Southeast Asia, 1956–1975* (1985).

See also: ATTLEBORO, Operation; Civilian Irregular Defense Group (CIDG); Mobile Strike Force Commands; Search and Destroy; United States: Special Forces.

Mobile Riverine Force (1966–1969)

U.S. joint Army-Navy force created in mid-1966 for search-and-destroy operations in the Mekong Delta. In early 1967, this operation was designated Task Force 117, or the Mekong Delta Mobile Riverine Force. The Mobile Riverine Force (MRF) concept developed from a study of the French experiences with Dinassauts, integrated French tactical units comprising naval and army forces for riverine warfare during the Indo-China War. Like the French operation, the MRF required a ground element to deploy from the naval component. Since Gen. William Westmoreland had deployed the U.S. Marines to I Corps Tactical Zone (I CTZ) in 1965, the MRF relied on a specially trained Army force consisting of the 2d Brigade, 9th Division.

The MRF's naval arm, River Assault Flotilla 1, consisted of troop-carrying and support boats divided into four river squadrons. The key boats were 26 armored troop carriers (ATCs), or converted mechanized landing craft (LCM-6s), which had a variety of armament and could carry 40 combat troops. Specially converted ATCs served as the Brown Water (Riverine) Fleet's refuelers, landing pads for helicopters, and medical aid stations.

The River Assault Squadrons' flagships were two command-and-control boats (CCBs), also converted LCM-6s, which served as headquarters for the ground and naval force commanders. A spoon-bowed LCM-6 conversion, the monitor, became the battleship of the Brown Water Fleet. A modified monitor, dubbed a "Zippo," mounted two flamethrowers forward. All of these boats were equipped with a wide assortment of weapons, and all carried upgraded armor and stand-off armor to predetonate incoming rockets. The destroyer/minesweeper of the fleet was the assault support patrol boat (ASPB). Each squadron had 16 of these boats, which were mission-designed and built for the MRF.

From its inception, the MRF had bases ashore and afloat. The MRF's principal land base was Đồng Tâm, located northwest of My Tho. The afloat element consisted of the mobile riverine base (MRB), which could move anywhere on large waterways throughout the Delta. The MRB included one barracks barge (APL), two barracks ships (APBs), two tugs (YTBs), one landing craft repair ship (ARL), two landing ship tanks (LSTs), and one salvage craft (LLC). A different type of base, the mobile support base (MSB), built on four pontoons, included a helicopter landing pad, crews quarters, and mess area.

When Commander Naval Forces, Vietnam (COMNAVFORV) launched South East Asia Lake Ocean River Delta Strategy (SEALORDS) in 1968, elements of the MRF contributed to the campaign. Also in 1968, Vietnamization began, and by August 1969, Task Force 117 was disestablished.

—R. Blake Dunnavent

References: Cutler, Thomas J. *Brown Water, Black Berets: Coastal and Riverine Warfare in Vietnam* (1988); Marolda, Edward J. *By Sea, Air, and Land: An Illustrated History of the U.S. Navy and the War in Southeast Asia* (1994); Schreadley, R. L. *From the Rivers to the Sea: The United States Navy in Vietnam* (1992).

See also: Dinassauts; Mekong Delta; Riverine Craft; Riverine Warfare; SEALORDS (South East Asia Lake Ocean River Delta Strategy); United States: Navy; Westmoreland, William Childs.

Mobile Strike Force Commands (1964–1970)

Vietnamese forces involved in counterinsurgency operations. From the beginning of U.S. involvement in Vietnam, indigenous forces played a role in attempts to defeat Communist insurgents. Organized, trained, and usually led by U.S. Army Special Forces advisors, native irregulars began as village defenders tasked with local security missions. As time passed, the Special Forces organized indigenous battalions capable of projecting combat power throughout Vietnam. To understand the significance of the Mobile Strike Force Commands, the evolution of indigenous forces must first be considered.

Success with strike forces in the Civilian Irregular Defense Group (CIDG) program led Special Forces advisors to use highly trained native troops in offensive operations. In October 1964, the "Eagle Flight" platoon was formed at Pleiku, and by June 1965 its success led U.S. Military Assistance Command, Vietnam (MACV) to authorize the creation of similar units in each Corps Tactical Zone. Known as Mobile Strike Forces, these company-sized units were used for reconnaissance and camp defense missions and had success against Việt Công and People's Army of Vietnam (PAVN) forces. They received the appellation "Mike Forces" because the letter "M" (for Mobile) is expressed as "Mike" in the military phonetic alphabet. Mobile Guerrilla Forces, another stage in this evolutionary process, originated as Operation BLACKJACK, company-size units that were inserted into Việt

Công areas for combat operations. This successful offensive use of indigenous forces led to the 26 May 1968 merger of Mike Forces and Mobile Guerrilla Forces into new units called Mobile Strike Force Commands.

With the creation of the Mobile Strike Force Commands, the use of U.S.-led indigenous troops reached its most significant level. The Mobile Strike Force Commands were of brigade strength and were often deployed in joint offensive operations with regular U.S. and Army of the Republic of Vietnam forces. The new formations gave Special Forces advisors the capability to attack Việt Công strongholds without relying on support from sometimes reluctant U.S. commanders. Disbanded on 31 December 1970, these effective forces played an important role in subsequent combat operations within the Republic of Vietnam.

—Richard D. Starnes

References: Kelly, Francis, J. *U.S. Army Special Forces, 1961–1971* (1985); Krepinevich, Andrew F. *The Army and Vietnam* (1986); Stanton, Shelby L. *Green Berets at War: U. S. Army Special Forces in Southeast Asia, 1956–1975* (1985).

See also: ATTLEBORO, Operation; Civilian Irregular Defense Group (CIDG); Military Assistance Command, Vietnam (MACV); Mobile Guerrilla Forces (MGF); United States: Special Forces.

Molotov (born Scriabin), Vyacheslav Mikhailovich (1890–1986)

Foreign Minister of the USSR, 1939–1948 and 1953–1956. Although the Soviet Union paid scant attention to Indo-China before 1950, Molotov played a central role in the 1954 Geneva Conference. Having initiated the conference with his offer to broker a cease-fire in February 1954, Molotov served as cochair, with Britain's Anthony Eden. Molotov engineered several key compromises that found their way into the final agreement. Under Soviet influence, the Democratic Republic of Vietnam (DRV) agreed to exclude the Cambodian and Laotian resistance movements from the conference, while the French accepted a two-year delay in holding elections in Vietnam. The tactic of pressing concessions on DRV representatives at Geneva, however, led to accusations that Molotov had deceived the Việt Minh and made a personal deal with French Premier Mendès-France to keep France from joining the European Defense Community. There is little indication that the Soviets took seriously the concessions made at Geneva; Molotov privately told Western diplomats that there would never be free elections in Vietnam.

—Timothy C. Dowling

References: Bromage, Bernard. *Molotov: The Story of an Era* (1961); Chuev, Feliks. *Molotov Remembers* (1980); Fishel, Wesley R., ed. *Vietnam: Anatomy of a Conflict* (1968).

See also: Eden, Anthony; Geneva Conference and Geneva Accords; Mendès-France, Pierre; Union of Soviet Socialist Republics (USSR; Soviet Union).

Momyer, William W. (1916–)

U.S. Air Force general. Advanced to four-star rank in December 1967, "Spike" Momyer became commander, Seventh Air Force and deputy commander for Air

Operations, Military Assistance Command, Vietnam (MACV). As such, he was responsible for Operation ROLLING THUNDER, the prolonged bombing of North Vietnam, and the massive air effort in South Vietnam. Momyer believed that air power could have done more if restraints had been lifted but also maintained that the USAF did all that it was asked to do.

In 1968 Gen. Momyer became Commander, Tactical Air Command, a position he held until his retirement in 1973. Throughout his career, he was known as a no-nonsense commander and an ardent advocate of air power. His book, *Airpower in Three Wars* (1978), provides a detailed description of the application of tactical and strategic air power in World War II, Korea, and Vietnam.

—Earl H. Tilford, Jr.

References: Clodfelter, Mark. *The Limits of Air Power: The American Bombing of North Vietnam* (1989); Momyer, William W. *Airpower in Three Wars: World War II, Korea, and Vietnam* (1978); Schlight, John. *The War in South Vietnam: The Years of the Offensive, 1965–1968* (1988); Tilford, Earl H., Jr. *Crosswinds: The Air Force's Setup in Vietnam* (1993).

See also: Air Power, Role in War; ROLLING THUNDER, Operation; United States: Air Force.

Montagnards

Indigenous peoples of the Vietnamese Central Highlands. Known to the French and Americans as *Montagnards* (mountain people or mountaineers), these peoples have referred to themselves in recent years as *Dega* (from the Rhadé) or *Ana Chu* (from the Jarai). According to Gerald C. Hickey, their principal ethnographer, both terms mean "Sons of the Mountains." The Montagnards were often referred to as "moï" or "savages" by the Vietnamese but officially became "highland compatriots," "Đông Bào Thuong" or "Sac Tôc Thiêu Sô to the South Vietnamese, and "Dân Tôc It Nguoi" to the North Vietnamese—all in attempts to win their allegiance.

The Montagnard population numbered perhaps one million people just prior to the 1968 Têt Offensive. Their traditional subsistence base is dry rice farming in swidden plots (slash-burn agriculture), but in some areas, wet rice or paddy cultivation is practiced. Hunting and gathering supplement the diet. Villages vary from 5 to perhaps 100 longhouses that usually are shared by extended families organized along kinship lines with unilineal (patrilineal and matrilineal) and bilateral descent patterns. The men's house, with a high and steeply sloped roof and decorated with symbolic carvings, is a prominent feature in the village center. Animistic spirits reflect the Montagnards' intense attachment to the land.

The Montagnards have lived in the Central Highlands as a distinct cultural grouping at least since the Kingdom of Champa. Their physical separation from the Vietnamese, who settled primarily in the coastal lowlands and river valleys, enabled the Montagnards to retain their distinct cultural identity. Until the more recent events of the colonial era, the Montagnards existed in relative independence.

Development of a common ethnic identity among the 30-odd tribal groups was spurred by French land appropria-

tions, labor corvées, and head taxes. On 27 May 1946, in return for Montagnard support in the struggle against the Viêt Minh, French Indo-China High Commissioner Admiral Thierry d'Argenlieu issued an ordinance declaring that the highland provinces of Darlac, Haut Donnai, Lang Bian, Pleiku, and Kontum would be formed into a Special Administrative Circumscription with its administrative center at Ban Mê Thuôt. On 1 June 1946, d'Argenlieu proclaimed the area the Autonomous Republic of Cochinchina. By 25 July 1950, a Special Administrative Division, referred to as the Crown Domain of the Southern Highlander Country, was created under direct authority of Emperor Bao Đai. In 1954 the Geneva Agreements, the departure of the French, and the division of Vietnam brought the Montagnards under authority of the government of the Republic of Vietnam (RVN), which classified them as "ethnic minorities." Thus the Montagnards saw their dreams of a homeland shattered at a conference where they had no representation.

RVN President Ngô Đình Diêm's Land Development Program resulted in the forced resettlement of Montagnard villages and confiscation of tribal lands. In opposition to these policies, the highlanders in 1955 formed Le Front pour la Libération des Montagnards, which evolved into Bajaraka (a consolidation of Bahnar, Jarai, Rhadé, and Koho) in 1958. It made a formal request to the Vietnamese government for highland autonomy. By 1964 Bajaraka had evolved into FULRO, or Le Front Unifié de Lutte des Races Opprimées (United Struggle Front for Oppressed Races), the ethnonationalistic movement of Montagnard, Khmer Krom, and Cham. With uprisings at Special Forces camps around Ban Mê Thuôt during September 1964, FULRO attempted to reclaim Montagnard lands taken by the Vietnamese. In response, the Sài Gòn government created the Ministry for Development of Ethnic Minorities to implement social and economic programs and improve Montagnard conditions. With the 1972 Easter Offensive by the Communists, programs collapsed and the Montagnards could only struggle to survive on their own.

During the war, Montagnards were recruited by both sides but became known to Americans primarily through the Civilian Irregular Defense Group (CIDG) that operated out of Special Forces camps. Working with the Rhadé in the Ban Mê Thuôt area, David Nuttle became concerned about their protection from the Viêt Công. Nuttle's idea of a village defense program was developed by Gilbert Layton of the Central Intelligence Agency (CIA) into a project combining self-defense capabilities with social and economic programs to gain the allegiance of the highland peoples. The Special Forces would implement the project.

In February 1962 the village of Buon Enao, five miles east of Ban Mê Thuôt, was the first to be fortified in the village defense program under a Special Forces detachment. Within 18 months, 27 CIDG camps with 40,000 militia and 11,000 strike force troops operated across the Central Highlands. The Montagnards saw this service as an opportunity to arm themselves in defense of their mountain homelands against Vietnamese encroachment. Vietnamese Special Forces teams (Luc Luong Đac Biêt, or LLĐB) were also assigned to the camps.

The Vietnamese became alarmed at the Montagnard military capacity. FULRO uprisings during 1964–1965 exacerbated the tensions and resulted in the elimination of the village defense program. The CIDG strike force, now under the military chain of command in lieu of CIA control, was concentrated in 25 camps along the Laotian and Cambodian borders, where the mission was to seal the border and infiltrate the Hô Chí Minh Trail. From CIDG camps, Montagnard strikers, with their U.S. counterparts and the LLĐB, operated on familiar terrain, patrolling the border area and into Cambodia and Laos. With Vietnamization during the latter years of U.S. involvement, however, the U.S. Fifth Special Forces Group relinquished operations to the LLĐB, and the CIDG units were integrated into South Vietnamese Ranger battalions or disbanded.

The impact of the war proved catastrophic to the Montagnards. The high casualty rates among Montagnard strikers were devastating, and modern technological warfare killed thousands of villagers. The creation of free-fire zones destroyed the fabric of Montagnard culture by forcing resettlement of traditional villages. Gerald C. Hickey estimated that by the end of the Vietnam War, approximately one-third of the one million Montagnards were casualties of war and 85 percent of their villages were forcibly evacuated or abandoned. More than 200,000 Montagnards had died. The Montagnards charge that the expropriation of traditional Montagnard lands to resettle Vietnamese in new highland economic zones and the resettlement of Montagnard villagers to integrate them into the government is but a continuation of the policies begun before the war by Ngô Đình Diêm and continued after the war by the Communist government.

Even after the fall of Sài Gòn in 1975, the Montagnards continued to resist Vietnamese domination. The Dega Highlands Provisional Government, with its military arm, the Dega Highlands Liberation Front, held out against superior Vietnamese forces for ten years before ending their struggle in 1984. Many of the fighters returned to the highlands, but the leaders of the movement, 200 men who formed the core of resistance against the Vietnamese, fled to the refugee camps on the Thai-Cambodian border in 1985. There they were found in Site 2 South by three Americans, Don Scott, Pappy Hicks, and Jim Morris, who arranged for their passage to the United States. Armed resistance against the Vietnamese in the highlands continued at least through 1993, when 400 Montagnards were found in Cambodia and demobilized prior to resettlement in the United States. Under the leadership of Ksor Kok, executive director of the Montagnard Foundation, they continue to represent the Montagnard peoples in their struggle for cultural survival.

—David M. Berman

References: Condominas, George. *We Have Eaten the Forest: The Story of a Montagnard Village in the Central Highlands of Vietnam* (1977); Hickey, Gerald Cannon. *Free in the Forest: Ethnohistory of the Vietnamese Central Highlands, 1954–1976* (1982); —. *Shattered World: Adaptation and Survival among Vietnam's Highland Peoples during the Vietnam War* (1993); —. *Sons of the Mountains: Ethnohistory of the Vietnamese Central Highlands to 1954* (1982); Lebar, Frank C., Gerald C. Hickey, and John Musgrave. *Ethnic Groups of Mainland Southeast Asia* (1964); Rubin, Jonathan. *The Barking Deer* (1974); Wiesner, Louis A. *Victims and Survivors: Displaced Persons and Other Victims in Viet-Nam, 1954–1975* (1988).

See also: Ban Mê Thuôt, Battle of; Bao Đai; Central Highlands; Central Intelligence Agency (CIA); Civilian Irregular Defense Group (CIDG); Cochin China; d'Argenlieu, Georges Thierry; Enoul, Y Bham; FULRO (Le Front Unifié de Lutte des Races Opprimées); Hickey, Gerald Cannon; Mobile Strike Force Commands; Ngô Đình Diêm; United States: Special Forces; Vietnam, Republic of: Special Forces (Luc Luong Đac Biêt [LLDB]).

Moore, Robert Brevard (1909–)

U.S. Navy rear admiral, commanding naval units during the Tonkin Gulf incidents. In June 1963, Moore assumed command of Carrier Division Five, then deployed in the western Pacific with his flag in the *Constellation*. Following the Tonkin Gulf incidents, Moore directed retaliatory air strikes on 5 August 1965 against the Democratic Republic of Vietnam from the *Constellation* and *Ticonderoga* in Operation PIERCE ARROW. Two months later, Moore assumed command of naval air operations at San Diego. He retired from the Navy in March 1967.

—Spencer C. Tucker

Reference: Naval History Division, U.S. Navy Department, Washington, DC.

See also: DeSoto Missions; Operation Plan 34A (OPLAN 34A); PIERCE ARROW, Operation; Tonkin Gulf Incidents.

Moorer, Thomas H. (1912–)

U.S. Navy admiral who commanded or directed U.S. military forces during much of the Vietnam War. Moorer, a gruff, straight-talking, combat veteran of World War II, first exerted influence on U.S. actions in Southeast Asia from October 1962 to March 1965 as Commander, Seventh Fleet and then Commander in Chief, U.S. Pacific Fleet.

Moorer strongly advocated using naval and air power to dissuade the Democratic Republic of Vietnam (DRV) from its support of insurgents in South Vietnam and Laos. He also called for extension of the DeSoto Patrol maritime reconnaissance program to include the Gulf of Tonkin off North Vietnam and the use of the resulting intelligence in support of Washington's covert Operation Plan 34A. On 2 August 1964, when North Vietnamese torpedo boats unsuccessfully attacked USS *Maddox,* Moorer responded by immediately ordering *Maddox* and another destroyer, *Turner Joy,* to resume the operation along North Vietnam's coastline. Convinced that Communist naval vessels carried out a second attack on the night of 4 August, Moorer helped persuade Washington to launch retaliatory air strikes against the DRV the following day.

Before departing the theater for another command in March 1965, Moorer strongly endorsed the use of U.S. warships to stop Communist seaborne infiltration, the deployment of U.S. Marines to Đà Nang, and the start of systematic bombing operations in Laos and North Vietnam. He was an early critic of Secretary of Defense Robert MacNamara's efforts to micromanage the Navy–Air Force bombing campaign from Washington.

In 1967 Moorer again assumed a leading role in the Vietnam War when President Johnson appointed him chief of naval operations. Between July 1970 and July 1974, Moorer assumed even greater responsibility as chairman of the Joint Chiefs of Staff. Although unable to persuade President Nixon to slow the pace of the U.S. military withdrawal from Southeast Asia, he did convince him to resume the bombing of the DRV and to mine the ports of North Vietnam in spring 1972. Moorer retired in 1974, but remained critical of U.S. conduct of the Vietnam War, stating his belief that the United States should have invaded North Vietnam.

—Edward J. Marolda

References: Marolda, Edward J. *By Sea, Air, and Land: An Illustrated History of the U.S. Navy and the War in Southeast Asia* (1994); Marolda, Edward J., and Oscar P. Fitzgerald. *From Military Assistance to Combat, 1959–1965.* Vol. II. In *The United States Navy and the Vietnam Conflict* (1986); Schreadley, Richard L. *From the Rivers to the Sea: The U.S. Navy in Vietnam* (1992).
See also: DeSoto Missions; LINEBACKER II, Operation; McNamara, Robert S.; Mining and Mine Clearance in North Vietnam; Nixon, Richard Milhous; Operation Plan 34A (OPLAN 34A); Tonkin Gulf Incidents; United States: Navy.

Moratorium to End the War in Vietnam
(15 October 1969)

Largest nationwide protest against U.S. involvement in the Vietnam War. The Moratorium originated as a call by Jerome Grossman, at a meeting of MassPax on 20 April 1969, for a nationwide general strike in October if the war had not ended by then. Grossman found only limited interest in something as radical as a general strike.

David Hawk and Sam Brown, veterans of Eugene McCarthy's presidential campaign, liked Grossman's idea, but suggested changing "strike" to "moratorium." MassPax put $25,000 behind the idea, and on 30 June, Hawk and Brown opened a Moratorium office in Washington, D.C. Set for 15 October, the Moratorium was to express a broad, moderate, majority position against the war. The Moratorium originally aimed at organizing campuses, but the idea soon spread beyond universities, in part because of the efforts of the New Mobilization Committee to End the War in Vietnam. Word was also spread by an editorial in *The New Republic*.

The day was an overwhelming success, and many participated who had not protested before. The largest turnout was in Boston, where 100,000 gathered to hear Senator McGovern. Millions participated, with very little violence, but millions of others considered the participants to be traitors.

In November, a followup to the Vietnam Moratorium was organized by the New Mobilization Committee to End the War in Vietnam. The Moratorium group hesitated to associate itself with the plans until President Nixon's "Silent Majority" speech on 3 November 1969. The Moratorium group was also led to participate by plans for the March against Death on 13 November 1969. The March involved 45,000 participants, each with a placard bearing the name of a soldier who had died in Vietnam, marching past the White House and calling out the names of the dead for two nights and into Saturday morning, 15 November 1969.

On 15 November, up to 750,000 people converged on the Washington Monument for an antiwar rally. Although the speeches were not memorable, Pete Seeger; Arlo Guthrie; Peter, Paul, and Mary; and touring casts of the musical "Hair" kept the rally going. A rally in San Francisco that same day drew up to 250,000 people.

The events of October and November were a high point for the antiwar movement, but it was not possible to sustain the momentum.

—Michael Richards

References: Halstead, Fred. *Out Now! A Participant's Account of the American Movement against the Vietnam War* (1978); Morgan, Edward P. *The 60s Experience: Hard Lessons about Modern America* (1991); Zaroulis, Nancy, and Gerald Sullivan. *Who Spoke Up? American Protest against the War in Vietnam, 1963–1975* (1984).
See also: Antiwar Movement, United States; Brown, Samuel Winfred, Jr.; Kent State University; McGovern, George S.

Mordant, Eugène (1885–?)

French Army general and commander of French forces in Indo-China, 1940–1944. In spring 1944, Charles de Gaulle called on Mordant to organize a Free French movement in Indo-China and that August appointed Mordant as delegate general of the French government for Indo-China and vice-president of the secret Indo-Chinese Council. In effect, Mordant became de facto head of the French government in Indo-China. On 9 March 1945, Japanese forces under Yuitsu Tsuchihashi carried out a coup in which they captured most of the French military and administration in Indo-China. The Japanese imprisoned Mordant in Hà Nôi; he was released from there by the Chinese at the end of the war.

—Spencer C. Tucker

References: Marr, David G. *Vietnam 1945: The Quest for Power* (1996); Mordant, Eugène. *Au Service de la France en Indochine, 1941–1945* (1950); Patti, Archimedes L. A. *Why Viet Nam? Prelude to America's Albatross* (1980).
See also: de Gaulle, Charles André Marie Joseph; Decoux, Jean; Sabattier, Gabriel; Tsuchihashi, Yuitsu.

Morse, Wayne Lyman (1900–1974)

U.S. senator, 1943–1969; one of the earliest opponents of U.S. military involvement in Vietnam. In August 1964, Morse and Senator Ernest Gruening cast the only two votes against the Tonkin Gulf Resolution. Morse denounced the launching of air strikes against North Vietnam and the deployment of U.S. ground troops to South Vietnam. He believed the conflict in Vietnam was a civil war that did not warrant U.S. involvement, especially since the Sài Gòn regime was despotic. In February 1966, he condemned the Johnson administration for pursuing an illegal war, as Congress had not formally declared war. In March 1966, the Senate defeated his proposal to repeal the Tonkin Gulf Resolution.

—Robert G. Mangrum

References: Austin, Anthony. *The President's War: The Story of the Tonkin Gulf Resolution and How the Nation Was Trapped in Vietnam* (1971); Olson, James S., ed. *Dictionary of the Vietnam War* (1988); Summers, Harry G. *Vietnam War Almanac* (1985).

See also: Gruening, Ernest Henry; Johnson, Lyndon Baines; Tonkin Gulf Resolution.

Mortars, Allied and Democratic Republic of Vietnam

Portable, muzzle-loaded, smooth- or rifle-bored infantry weapons used to fire shells at low velocities, short ranges, and high-angle trajectories. Mortars consist primarily of a tube or barrel, baseplate, supporting bipod, and sight. They are smaller, lighter, and easier to move than artillery.

Mortars used by Allied troops in Vietnam varied from 4.2-inch (which had a maximum range of 5,650 meters and was usually mounted on vehicles or emplaced at firebases) to the smaller, troop-carried 81-mm and 60-mm at the battalion and company levels, respectively. Commonly used mortar ammunition included high explosive (impact or proximity fused) for use against troops and light material; white phosphorus ("willy pete") for screening, signaling, and incendiary action; illumination; and tactical gas rounds.

Viêt Công and People's Army of Vietnam forces used primarily Soviet- and Chinese-supplied mortars. The most commonly used mortar in Communist service was the 82-mm, which was lighter than the 122-mm, would also fire U.S.-made 81-mm rounds, and had an effective range of approximately 3,000 meters. Communist operators were able to place accurate fire and displace quickly before effective counterbattery fire could be brought to bear. They did this by "hanging" several rounds in the air toward a target, then quickly disassembling and moving the mortars before Allied radar could spot their mortar positions by tracking the trajectory of the projectiles. Communist forces often used mortars in place of artillery, almost always preceding any ground attack with a mortar barrage.

—James H. Willbanks

Reference: Doleman, Edgar C., Jr. *The Vietnam Experience: Tools of War* (1984).

See also: Artillery, Allied and People's Army of Vietnam; Grenades, Hand, Allied and Democratic Republic of Vietnam; Grenades, Launched, Allied and Democratic Republic of Vietnam; Rockets.

Moyers, Bill (1934–)

Advisor, White House chief of staff, and press secretary to President Johnson. Moyers became White House chief of staff in October 1964 and encouraged Johnson to seek peaceful solutions in Southeast Asia. Moyers managed the president's 1964 television advertising campaign and, upon becoming press secretary in July 1965, worked to mend Johnson's relations with the press corps. He hoped to influence Johnson's foreign policy by becoming national security advisor, but was denied the post. Believing that Johnson had become too engrossed with the Vietnam War and was turning away from domestic reforms, Moyers resigned in December 1966. As editor of *Newsday*, Moyers defended the peace marches and antiwar demonstrations of the late 1960s.

—Laura Matysek Wood

Reference: Moyers, Bill D. *Listening to America: A Traveller Rediscovers His Country* (1971).

See also: Johnson, Lyndon Baines; Kennedy, John Fitzgerald; Media and the War.

Munich Analogy

An analogy that compared attitudes toward the expansion of communism to the 1930s policy of appeasement championed by the British toward the expansion of Nazi Germany. The Munich analogy dominated the thinking of U.S. policymakers on Vietnam, who remembered events preceding World War II and resolved not to repeat those mistakes in Indo-China. They believed that Communist North Vietnam, if given the opportunity to take over the South, would continue to widen its influence throughout Indo-China, leading to the mistaken conclusion that Hô Chí Minh was a bully who would back down if confronted with military force. The combination of this analogy, the principle of containment, and the domino theory formed the foundation of U.S. policy toward Vietnam and served as a justification to commit U.S. soldiers to South Vietnam in 1965.

—Eric W. Osborne

References: Karnow, Stanley. *Vietnam: A History* (1991); Olson, James, and Randy Roberts. *Where the Domino Fell: America and Vietnam, 1945–1990* (1991); Young, Marilyn B. *The Vietnam Wars, 1945–1990* (1991).

See also: Containment Policy; Domino Theory.

Murphy, Robert D. (1894–1978)

Undersecretary of state for political affairs, 1953–1959; member of the "Wise Men." Murphy fully supported the U.S. decisions of the mid-1950s to resist the spread of communism in Indo-China by supporting non-Communist regimes in South Vietnam, Cambodia, and Laos. Murphy was one of the "Wise Men," the group of senior advisors President Johnson consulted on Vietnam. In early 1968, after the Tết Offensive, Johnson requested that the Wise Men undertake a major reassessment of U.S. policy toward Vietnam. The group as a whole argued that the war could not be won and recommended that the United States seek a negotiated peace, advice that Johnson accepted, but Murphy strongly dissented, arguing that the United States should press the war to a successful conclusion whatever the cost.

—Priscilla Roberts

References: Berman, Larry. *Lyndon Johnson's War: The Road to Stalemate in Vietnam* (1989); Brands, H. W. *Cold Warriors: Eisenhower's Generation and American Foreign Policy* (1988); Murphy, Robert D. *Diplomat among Warriors* (1964); Schandler, Herbert Y. *The Unmaking of a President: Lyndon Johnson and Vietnam* (1977).

See also: Dulles, John Foster; Eisenhower, Dwight David; "Wise Men."

Music and the Vietnam War

Rock music permeated the American experience in Vietnam. Many GIs imported their tastes in music into the war zone, and rock music was the most popular genre. Among the military branches, there was not much deviation in musical preference. There was a great rift between officers and enlisted men, however. According to an interview in *Rolling Stone,* most enlisted men preferred hard rock or psychedelic music; 30 percent enjoyed rhythm and blues; 10 percent, country; 5 percent, classical; and 10 percent, folk. The men often complained that Armed Forces Vietnam Radio broadcasts were geared to officers, with light classical music scattered among what the soldiers called "bubble-gum" music.

Some constraints on the type of music allowed on the airwaves came from the Republic of Vietnam (RVN) government, which prohibited, among other songs, the Animals' "We Gotta Get outa This Place." Most radio programs were prerecorded in Los Angeles and included top 40 hits. Because radio did not reflect the preferences of most soldiers, cassette tapes were the most popular medium for music in Vietnam. Battery-operated portable tape players were easily carried into the field.

Rock music mirrored the confusion of war and firefights and helped define the Vietnam War. Snatches from lyrics of popular songs were used in the context of the war. "Rock-and-roll" substituted for "lock and load," referring to the procedure for readying the M-16 for firing or for switching the weapon from semiautomatic to automatic fire. Songs were written alluding to Vietnam, or those connections were assumed. "Purple Haze," by Jimi Hendrix, a former Screaming Eagles paratrooper, had references to the purple smoke used at landing zones. Phrases from the Beatles' "Magical Mystery Tour," such as "Coming to take you away, dying to take you away," had special meaning for Marines at Khe Sanh.

Popular among the enlisted men were Asian bands that could imitate British and American rock groups and their hits with uncanny accuracy, even though band members could not speak English. These groups played in enlisted men's clubs and civilian bars in Vietnam. The sixties generation's catchphrase, "sex, drugs, and rock-and-roll," was also nurtured in Vietnam, partly because of the black market and prostitution that inevitably spring up on the outskirts of war. Psychedelic rock music praised the virtues of being stoned.

In previous wars, the music had always been supportive. Vietnam was the first war in which the GIs listened to antiwar and protest songs while fighting.

—Charles N. Fasanaro

Reference: Herr, Michael. *Dispatches* (1978).
See also: Baez, Joan Chandos; Draft; Drugs and Drug Use; Dylan, Bob; Media and the War.

Muste, Abraham J. (1885–1967)

U.S. antiwar activist and key figure in organizing and maintaining the unity of early antiwar coalitions. In his late 70s, this influential proponent of nonviolent civil disobedience was among the first to publicly criticize U.S. Vietnam policy.

An active participant in numerous demonstrations, Muste was a significant presence in the most visible local antiwar organization, New York's Fifth Avenue Peace Parade Committee. In 1966 he was selected to chair the Spring Mobilization to End the War in Vietnam, a national coalition planning demonstrations for April 1967. Muste's diverse background earned respect among people from a broad range of political ideologies, enabling him to mediate between competing factions within the antiwar movement. He visited Sài Gòn in April 1966 and Hà Nôi in January 1967, shortly before he died of a heart attack.

—Mitchell K. Hall

References: Hentoff, Nat. *Peace Agitator: The Story of A. J. Muste* (1963); —. *The Essays of A. J. Muste* (1967); Robinson, Jo Ann Ooiman. *Abraham Went Out: A Biography of A. J. Muste* (1981).
See also: Antiwar Movement, United States; Spring Mobilization to End the War in Vietnam.

My Lai Massacre (16 March 1968)

Most notorious U.S. military atrocity of the Vietnam War. On 16 March 1968, 200 to 500 Vietnamese civilians were massacred by U.S. soldiers of Company C, 1st Battalion, 20th Infantry, 11th Infantry Brigade (Light) of the 23d (American) Division. Equally infamous was the cover-up of the incident perpetrated by the brigade and division staffs.

The broad range in numbers of civilian deaths was the result of varying reports provided to the panel of inquiry through the testimony of participants and observers. Some reports included an alleged related massacre in the nearby hamlet of My Khê 4 by Company B, 4th Battalion, 3d Infantry. False reporting and the subsequent cover-up make actual casualty figures difficult to substantiate.

The Americal Division's primary operation was WHEEL-ER/WALLOWA, but numerous side operations were also conducted. The operation in the hamlets of Son My village, nicknamed "Pinkville" by the division's soldiers because of the concentration of Communist sympathizers and Viêt Công (VC) activity in the area, was one such operation. It was to be a classic search-and-destroy sweep intended to snare some of the estimated 250 VC operating in the area as part of the 48th VC Local Force Battalion. Such sweeps were characterized by only lightly scattered direct VC contact, but a high rate of friendly losses to snipers, mines, and booby-traps. The My Lai operation was no different.

Charlie Company, 1st Battalion, 20th Infantry, was organized as part of an ad hoc battalion known as Task Force Barker, named after its commander, Lt. Col. Frank A. Barker, Jr., reinforcing the 11th Infantry Brigade. The 23d (American) Division was itself an ad hoc organization of separate infantry brigades put together during the U.S. military buildup and, by many accounts, suffered from weak leadership that originated with division commander Maj. Gen. Samuel H. Koster. Some elements of the 11th Brigade, commanded at the time by Col. Oran K. Henderson, have been described as little more than "organized bands of thugs" and had been ordained the "Butcher Brigade" by its soldiers in the field.

The airmobile assault into My Lai was timed to arrive shortly after the local women had departed for market. The soldiers had been briefed to expect to engage elements of the 48th VC Local Force Battalion, one of the most successful units in the area, but instead found only women, children, and mostly old men still cooking breakfast. The soldiers of Charlie Company, commanded by Capt. Ernest Medina, ran wild, particularly the men of 1st Platoon, commanded by 1st Lt. William Laws Calley, Jr. They indiscriminately shot people and then systematically rounded up survivors, allegedly led them to a nearby ditch, and executed them. More villagers were killed as huts and bunkers were destroyed by fire and explosives. The killing reportedly was halted some time later when WO Hugh Thompson, an aero-scout pilot supporting the operation, landed his helicopter between the Americans and fleeing Vietnamese and confronted the soldiers. The museum at My Lai claims that 504 Vietnamese perished that day.

The incident, uncovered a year later, was investigated by the Army Criminal Investigation Division and an Army board of inquiry headed by Lt. Gen. William Peers. Although the findings and recommendations of the board of inquiry did not attempt to ascribe causes for the massacre, many have cited the frustrations of soldiers too long faced with losses of comrades to snipers, mines, and booby traps; the lack of experience of junior leaders and poor leadership, from the division commander on down the ranks; and the confusion of the war's measurement of success by the statistical yardstick of body count, which became objectives in place of occupation of enemy terrain.

The Peers report produced a list of 30 persons, mostly officers (including the division commander), who knew of the atrocities; however, only 14 were charged with crimes. All eventually had their charges dismissed or were acquitted by courts-martial except the most junior officer, Lt. Calley, whose platoon allegedly killed 200 civilians. Calley was found guilty of murdering 22 civilians and sentenced to life imprisonment. The sentence was reduced to 20 years by the Court of Military Appeals and then later reduced to ten years by the Secretary of the Army. Proclaimed by much of the public as a "scapegoat," Calley was paroled by President Nixon in November 1974.

On 6 March 1998, the Army recognized Hugh Thompson, his former gunner Lawrence Colburn, and his crew chief Glenn Andreatta (who was killed in April 1968) with the Soldier's Medal for gallantry.

—Arthur T. Frame

References: Goldstein, Joseph, et al. *The My Lai Massacre and Its Cover-up: Beyond the Reach of Law?* (1976); Hersh, Seymour M. *Cover-Up: The Army's Secret Investigation of the Massacre at My Lai 4* (1972); —. *My Lai 4: A Report on the Massacre and Its Aftermath* (1970); Peers, W. R. *The My Lai Inquiry* (1979).

See also: Atrocities; Barker, Frank A., Jr.; Body Count; Calley, William Laws, Jr.; COWIN Report; Hersh, Seymour Myron; Medina, Ernest L.; Nixon, Richard Milhous; Peers Inquiry; WHEELER/WAL-LOWA, Operation.

Na San, Battle of (November–December 1952)

French military operation in late 1952 that foreshadowed the Battle of Điên Biên Phu. Commander of French forces in Indo-China Gen. Raoul Salan believed that Viêt Minh commander Vô Nguyên Giáp intended to resume the offensive in the mountains of northwest Vietnam in August 1952. Hoping to forestall that, Salan established a base deep inside Viêt Minh–held territory, in the Na San Valley, as the meeting point for garrisons from scattered French border posts and as a base to protect Laos and the Thai (T'ai) Highlands. Salan hoped to tempt Giáp into frontal assaults at the base, which he planned to smash with artillery and air power. The first phase of the operation went well, with most of the scattered French garrisons extracted to Na San and the airfield and base fortifications constructed in record time.

On 30 November and 1 December 1952, the 308th and 312th Viêt Minh Divisions attacked the French garrison but were repulsed. On 2 December, the Viêt Minh withdrew after suffering 500 to 1,000 dead. The battle seemed a great success for the French. Little noticed at the time was the loss to the Viêt Minh on 30 November of the small French post and airfield at Điên Biên Phu, then held by a Laotian infantry unit.

After putting a deception plan into effect, the French evacuated Na San by air without incident on 11 August 1953, removing about 1,500 Thai peasants and local officials who had cooperated with them.

The Na San operation should have demonstrated convincingly to French commanders the great difficulty of supplying a distant garrison with an inadequate airlift capacity. French occupation of Na San was little obstacle to Viêt Minh military operations in the area, which simply flowed through the jungle around the French base. Giáp later remarked that the Battle of Na San taught him that a fortified enemy camp supplied by air could be taken only by bringing the landing strip under heavy artillery fire.

—Spencer C. Tucker

References: Fall, Bernard. *Street without Joy* (1961); Roy, Jules. *The Battle of Dienbienphu* (1965); Simpson, Howard R. *Dien Bien Phu: The Epic Battle America Forgot* (1994).

See also: Điên Biên Phu, Battle of; LORRAINE, Operation; Salan, Raoul; Vô Nguyên Giáp.

Nam Đông, Battle of (6 July 1964)

Battle at the Nam Đông Special Forces camp near the Republic of Vietnam (RVN) borders with Laos and North Vietnam. The 12 Americans, 1 Australian, and 311 Vietnamese soldiers who defended the camp were there to provide security and improve living conditions for about 5,000 Vietnamese civilians. Capt. Roger Donlon commanded a U.S. Special Forces "A" Detachment that advised RVN Special Forces and Civilian Irregular Defense Group (CIDG) companies in the camp.

At 0226 on 6 July 1964, the camp was subjected to an intense mortar barrage followed by a ground attack by 800 to 900 Viêt Công (VC) soldiers. All camp buildings were soon destroyed. The defenders were able to send a message that they were under attack, but air support did not reach them until 0400. By dawn the fighting was over. On 5 December 1964, for his actions in the Nam Đông battle, Captain Donlon was awarded the first Medal of Honor since the Korean conflict.

—Richard L. Kiper

Reference: Donlon, Roger H. C., and Warren Rogers. *Outpost of Freedom* (1965).

See also: Civilian Irregular Defense Group (CIDG); United States: Special Forces; Vietnam, Republic of: Special Forces (Luc Luong Đac Biêt [LLDB]).

NANTUCKET BEACH, Operation. *See* BOLD MARINER, Operation.

Napalm

Gasoline thickened to a gel, one of the U.S. military's primary incendiary weapons in Vietnam; its use attracted public protest as a weapon of terror. Harvard Professor Louis Fieser directed the research that developed napalm (named for its original thickening agents, aluminum naphthenate and aluminum palmitate, though the ingredients changed over time), applying for a patent on 1 November 1943. Its advantages over unthickened fuel included longer burning time and more effective spreading, which increased the probability of igniting targeted materials. The U.S. military first used napalm toward the end of World War II in bombs and flamethrowers. Napalm bombs required igniting, generally by a high-explosive rod such as TNT, surrounded by white phosphorus.

Napalm-B, used during the Vietnam War, was composed of 50 percent polystyrene thickener, 25 percent benzene, and 25 percent gasoline. The thick, sticky liquid was developed at Eglin Air Force Base, Florida, by the Dow Chemical Company. Napalm-B burns hotter (about 850 degrees centigrade) and longer (up to 15 minutes) than ordinary napalm. It also doubled the coverage area, making possible much greater destruction to targets. During the Vietnam War, napalm bombs constituted roughly 10 percent of all fighter-bomber munitions.

Humans caught in the open by napalm attacks have little defense. The jellied mixture sticks to virtually everything it touches and is almost impossible to remove. Death occurs by burning and carbon monoxide asphyxiation. Only those on the perimeter of the strike zone usually survive, although many suffer severe burns.

The brutal effects of napalm led antiwar activists to protest its use in Vietnam. Dow Chemical Company, the major napalm manufacturer during the war years, faced a boycott of its consumer products, an organized effort to persuade shareholders to sell their stock, and demonstrations at Dow offices and against campus recruiters. The protests affected Dow's image and profits and in 1969, whether deliberately or not, Dow lost the government contract for napalm to another company. The production and use of napalm, however, continued for the war's duration.

—Mitchell K. Hall

References: Dreyfus, Gilbert. "Napalm and Its Effects on Human Beings" (1968); Stockholm International Peace Research Institute. *Incendiary Weapons* (1975); United Nations. *Napalm and Other Incendiary Weapons and All Aspects of Their Possible Use: Report of the Secretary-General* (1973).

See also: Air Power, Role in War; Antiwar Movement, United States; Bombs, Dumb; International War Crimes Tribunal.

Napoleon III (1808–1873)

Emperor of France, 1852–1870. As early as 1853, the French Foreign Office had urged the acquisition of a port in Indo-China, and in 1857 Napoleon III ordered the French China squadron to intervene there in hopes of obtaining a Vietnamese port in the fashion of Hong Kong and establishing a protectorate over Cochin China.

On 31 August 1857, French Adm. Rigault de Genouilly's squadron appeared off Tourane (now Đà Nang), inaugurating the first phase of the French conquest of Indo-China. Within a few months, the French were forced from Tourane, and de Genouilly shifted operations southward to the fishing village of Sài Gòn, which fell to the French on 17 February 1859. In 1861 Tu Đuc agreed to cede to France three of the eastern provinces of Cochin China, allow the free practice of Catholic worship in the dominions, and accept a protectorate. The remainder of Cochin China was taken from An Nam between 1866 and 1867.

—Michael R. Nichols

References: Bury, J. P. T. *Napoleon III and the Second Empire* (1964); MacMillan, James F. *Napoleon III* (1991); Smith, W. H. C. *Napoleon III* (1972).

See also: An Nam; Cochin China; French Indo-China; Rigault de Genouilly, Charles; Tu Đuc; Vietnam: from 938 through the French Conquest.

National Assembly Law 10/59

Repressive legislation aimed at the Communists and enacted by the Republic of Vietnam (RVN) government in October 1959 in response to Hà Nôi's March 1959 decision to increase support for the insurgency in the South.

The RVN National Assembly passed Law 10/59 on 6 May 1959, legalizing courts-martial and executions of individuals convicted of working with the Viêt Công, the name arbitrarily given to anyone who opposed the regime. Special courts were run by military personnel only. Proceedings could take place without any preliminary inquiry, and a summons was served 24 hours before the court sat. The courts preferred a straight-out denunciation, quick verdict, and immediate execution. There were only two types of punishment: death or life imprisonment. In theory, there was an appeal to President Diêm against the death sentence, but there was none against life imprisonment. About half of those condemned to death were actually executed, many on the spot by mobile guillotines.

The U.S. government provided specialized help by training Diêm police agents in the United States and sending a special mission to Sài Gòn to reorganize police methods and improve the system of dossiers and control lists. Diêm ultimately closed this down after some specialists returned to the United States and wrote anti-Diêm articles.

In October 1959, the Assembly passed another law ordering Viêt Công, former Viêt Minh, their friends, relatives, and associates to be executed. Both laws reflected the determination of Diêm and his brother Ngô Đình Nhu to handle the Communist threat forcefully. The National Assembly itself was not a decision-making legislative body, but was rather a rubber stamp for the Diêm regime. These repressive measures helped provoke popular uprisings in Quang Ngãi Province in August 1959 and in Ban Tre in January 1960. Although Army of the Republic of Vietnam troops suppressed these, loyalty to the Sài Gòn government was never successfully restored in the countryside.

Although Law 10/59 imposed brutal measures, it must be understood against the background of brutal and rampant Communist terrorist activities in the remote areas between 1957 and 1959. At the time, there was no effective legislation to cope with this situation. After Diêm's assassination, Law 10/59 was quietly dropped.

—Zsolt J. Varga

References: Burchett, Wilfred G. *The Furtive War: The United States in Vietnam and Laos* (1963); Karnow, Stanley. *Vietnam: A History* (1983); Moss, George Donelson. *Vietnam: An American Ordeal* (1990); Scigliano, Robert. *South Vietnam: Nation under Stress* (1963); Wintle, Justin. *The Vietnam Wars* (1991).

See also: Ngô Đình Diêm; Ngô Đình Nhu; Vietnam, Republic of: 1954–1975.

National Bank of Vietnam

State banks of the Democratic Republic of Vietnam (DRV) and Republic of Vietnam (RVN). After the 1954 division of Vietnam, the National Bank became the official state bank of the DRV. After 1960, all foreign currency and business profits were deposited in the National Bank, and within five years, 95 percent of North Vietnam's economy was state owned.

In South Vietnam in 1955, President Ngô Đình Diêm created another National Bank of Vietnam and named his brother Ngô Đình Nhu as chairman. To receive U.S. imports, local merchants contributed national currency called piasters into the bank's "counterpart fund." Under the Commercial Import Program, $1.9 billion in economic aid was directed to South Vietnam by 1964, but the imports were largely luxury goods for the Sài Gòn upper class and did little to assist the South Vietnamese economy as a whole.

In 1975, after the fall of Sài Gòn, the North Vietnamese bank assumed control of South Vietnam's economy by requiring residents to exchange their piasters for dông at a 500:1 exchange rate. In an attempt to squelch the capitalists, every household was given a form to declare the amount of old money in its possession. Despite garnering money for the government treasury and creating some socioeconomic leveling, the currency exchange scheme affected most of the population in the South by causing distrust and loss of confidence in the central government, its banking system, and the value of its currency. Partly as a result of this distrust, the new currency steadily lost value and was reluctantly floated by the National Bank of Vietnam in 1989. By destroying the economic power of the moneyed class, Vietnam left no avenue for the huge amounts of government-issued money to make its way back to the central banks, which added to the already spiraling inflation.

—J. Nathan Campbell

References: Dacy, Douglas C. *The Fiscal System of Wartime Vietnam* (1969); Davies, S. Gethyn. *Central Banking in South and East Asia* (1960); Emery, Robert F. *The Financial Institutions of Southeast Asia* (1970); Honey, P. J. *Communism in North Vietnam* (1962); Lansdale, Edward Geary. *In the Midst of Wars* (1972); Ngô Vinh Hai. "Postwar Vietnam: Political Economy" (1991); Taylor, Milton C. "South Vietnam: Lavish Aid, Limited Progress" (1961).
See also: Vietnam, Republic of: 1954–1975.

National Coordinating Committee to End the War in Vietnam (NCC)

First effort to build a national coalition of antiwar organizations during the Vietnam War. The original purpose of the National Coordinating Committee to End the War in Vietnam (NCC) was to help coordinate the 15–16 October International Days of Protest announced by Berkeley's Vietnam Day Committee. The NCC lacked any decision-making authority for its 33 affiliated organizations, but provided a central location for receiving and distributing information about antiwar activities. Initiative for the demonstrations remained primarily with local groups. The NCC generated broad support, though liberal groups such as SANE opposed close cooperation with radicals and rejected formal affiliation. The October protests attracted roughly 100,000 participants in 80 cities and several nations.

The first NCC convention, held 25–29 November 1965 in Washington, failed to develop an ongoing antiwar program as the meeting degenerated into factional disputes, largely between the Communist Party and the Socialist Workers Party (SWP). The conference's only accomplishment was to set a date for demonstrations in the spring.

An NCC standing committee meeting on 8–9 January 1966 brought no resolution. The organization continued as a clearinghouse and formally sponsored the Second International Days of Protest (25–26 March 1966), but local groups again carried the burden of planning and conducting antiwar demonstrations. The results exceeded the previous effort, attracting more than 100,000 demonstrators in perhaps 100 cities and several foreign countries.

NCC leadership resisted planning summer demonstrations, and activists dissatisfied with this hesitation bypassed the NCC staff. A series of antiwar conferences in Cleveland during 1966 produced a temporary coalition to organize protests, the 5–8 November Mobilization Committee, which was in turn succeeded by the Spring Mobilization Committee. The NCC continued to operate, but declined as a national body and instead functioned as a local Wisconsin organization within the larger coalition.

—Mitchell K. Hall

References: DeBenedetti, Charles, and Charles Chatfield. *An American Ordeal: The Antiwar Movement of the Vietnam Era* (1990); Halstead, Fred. *Out Now! A Participant's Account of the American Movement against the Vietnam War* (1978); Wells, Tom. *The War Within: America's Battle over Vietnam* (1994).
See also: Antiwar Movement, United States; Spring Mobilization to End the War in Vietnam.

National Council of National Reconciliation and Concord (NCNRC)

Organization established to implement political provisions of the 1973 Paris Peace Agreement within the Republic of Vietnam. The South Vietnamese people were to decide their future through "genuinely free and democratic elections under international supervision." Organization of the elections was to be in the hands of the National Council of National Reconciliation and Concord (NCNRC), composed of representatives of the government of the Republic of Vietnam (RVN), the Provisional Revolutionary Government (PRG), and the neutralists. It was to work on the basis of unanimity, which in effect gave each party a veto. The NCNRC was to promote observance of the agreement and the democratic liberties it guaranteed as well as national reconciliation and concord. The country was to be reunified step by step by mutual agreement, and relations between North and South Vietnam were to be normalized.

President Nguyên Van Thiêu had proclaimed before the Paris Peace Agreement a national policy known as the "Four Nos": no negotiating, no Communist activity in the South, no coalition, and no surrender of territory. Thiêu objected to the tripartite NCNRC structure, seeeing the neutralists as favoring the Communists and the NCNRC as a stalking horse for a coalition government, and he believed that he would be maneuvered into a position in which the RVN would be seen as blocking a peaceful solution. In fact, little came of the NCNRC, as Thiêu and the Communists opted to renew the war.

Leftist opposition circles continued to demand adoption of the NCNRC until the Thiêu government collapsed in April 1975, but the Vietnam War was decided on the battlefield.

—Ho Diêu Anh and Spencer C. Tucker

References: Isaacs, Arnold R. *Without Honor: Defeat in Vietnam and Cambodia* (1983); Le Gro, William E. *Vietnam from Ceasefire to Capitulation* (1981); Porter, D. Gareth. *A Peace Denied: The United States, Vietnam, and the Paris Agreement* (1975).
See also: Nguyên Van Thiêu; Paris Peace Accords.

National Front for the Liberation of South Vietnam (NFLSV)

The National Front for the Liberation of South Vietnam (NFLSV), usually known as the National Liberation Front (NLF), was formed on 20 December 1960 in Tây Ninh Province, South Vietnam, after the Communists concluded that a new revolutionary strategy was needed to overthrow the U.S.-backed Sài Gòn regime. After six years of trying to unify the country through political means, the Lao Đông Party (the name then used by the Communist Party) accepted the recommendations of Central Committee member Lê Duân and approved the use of armed violence. The NFLSV-led insurgency against the Republic of Vietnam (RVN) government of President Ngô Đình Diêm caused great concern in Sài Gòn and Washington.

From the birth of NFLSV in 1960, Washington policymakers claimed that Hà Nôi alone directed the armed struggle in South Vietnam. Key members of the Kennedy and Johnson administrations argued that the flow of troops and supplies from North to South kept the revolution alive. This remained the underpinning of the official explanation for U.S. involvement in the Vietnam War and provided its justification. Stop this externally supported insurgency, U.S. officials believed, and South Vietnam could be stabilized. Those who opposed U.S. intervention claimed that the insurgency was essentially a civil war, suggesting that the NFLSV was a Southern organization that had risen at Southern initiative in response to Southern demands.

The NFLSV, known as the Viêt Công by its enemies, was a classic Communist front organization comprising Communists and non-Communists, organized with the purpose of mobilizing the anti-Diêm forces in Southern society. As with its predecessors, the Viêt Minh and Liên Viêt fronts, the NFLSV made temporary alliances with all elements of Southern society who opposed U.S. intervention and the Sài Gòn regime. Nguyên Huu Tho, supposedly a non-Communist, presided over the NFLSV. But it clearly was dominated by Communist Party members.

The NFLSV's military arm was the People's Liberation Armed Forces (PLAF). PLAF attacks against U.S. Army installations at Pleiku and Quy Nhon in February 1965 convinced the Johnson administration that something had to be done to stop the infiltration of soldiers and supplies. It was impossible, the president concluded, to build a stable government in Sài Gòn while the Democratic Republic of Vietnam (DRV) and its Communist supporters waged a war of aggression. Johnson therefore ordered retaliatory attacks on North Vietnamese targets that paved the way for Operation ROLLING THUNDER, the sustained bombing policy that many of his advisors had long advocated. Punishing the DRV for NFLSV military action in the South became standard U.S. policy. PLAF attacks also changed the scope of U.S. military requirements on the ground. In late February 1965, Military Assistance Command, Vietnam (MACV) commander Gen. William Westmoreland requested two U.S. Marine battalions to protect the air base at Đà Nang from NFLSV reprisal attacks. Johnson approved Westmoreland's request, and the first U.S. ground troops came ashore in Vietnam in March 1965.

Over time, U.S. troops missions changed from protection of air bases to interdiction and combat against combined PLAF and People's Army of Vietnam (PAVN) forces. The U.S. strategy was based on attrition—Westmoreland hoping he could inflict more casualties among the PLAF and PAVN than either could replace. Theoretically, the end result would be a diminished Communist will and a negotiated settlement.

The NFLSV reached its zenith during the 1968 Têt Offensive, when the Communists launched a coordinated attack against key urban centers throughout the South. Although it suffered tremendous military losses, the NFLSV gained a tremendous psychological victory over the Americans and their Sài Gòn allies. The Front had demonstrated its ability to attack heavily guarded cities, long thought of as the base of support for the Sài Gòn regime. In addition, the PLAF attack on the U.S. embassy in Sài Gòn produced political upheaval in Washington and caused many long-time supporters of the war to question the Johnson administration's optimistic predictions. Shortly after the Têt Offensive, peace talks opened in Paris and the NFLSV sent its representatives, Nguyên Thi Bình and Trân Buu Kiêm, to the conference.

In 1969, the NFLSV oversaw the creation of a government-in-waiting, the Provisional Revolutionary Government (PRG). The PRG hoped to come to full power in the South after the political and military struggles were concluded. As the war dragged on, PAVN conventional forces played a more active role in the Southern strategy. Eventually, this created a great deal of tension between the NFLSV and Northern Party leaders in Hà Nôi. After the fall of Sài Gòn, only a handful of NFLSV officials were incorporated into the new national government.

—Robert K. Brigham

References: Duncanson, Dennis. *Government and Revolution in Vietnam* (1968); Fall, Bernard. *Viet-Nam Witness, 1953–1966* (1966); Kahin, George McT., and John Lewis. *The United States in Vietnam* (1967); Nguyen Thi Dinh. *No Other Road to Take: Memoir of Mrs. Nguyen Thi Dinh* (1976); Pike, Douglas. *Viet Cong: The Organization and Techniques of the National Liberation Front of South Vietnam* (1966); Race, Jeffrey. *War Comes to Long An: Revolutionary Conflict in a Vietnamese Province* (1972); Thayer, Carlyle A. *War by Other Means: National Liberation and Revolution in Viet-Nam, 1954–1960* (1989); Truong Nhu Tang. *A Viet Cong Memoir: An Inside Account of the Vietnam War and Its Aftermath* (1985).

See also: Đâu Tranh; Duong Quynh Hoa; Lê Duân; Ngô Đình Diêm; Ngô Đình Nhu; Nguyên Cao Ky; Nguyên Huu Tho; Nguyên Khánh; Nguyên Thi Bình; Nguyên Van Thiêu; Paris Negotiations; Paris Peace Accords; Provisional Revolutionary Government of South Vietnam (PRG); ROLLING THUNDER, Operation; Têt Offensive: Overall Strategy; Têt Offensive: the Sài Gòn Circle; Trân Buu Kiêm; United Front; Westmoreland, William Childs.

National Leadership Council (1965–1967)

Governing political body in the Republic of Vietnam (RVN), established in June 1965. On 17 February 1965, a new civilian government was installed in Sài Gòn with Phan Huy Quát as premier, but military was still strongly represented, with three generals holding ministerial positions. The civilian government maintained an uneasy relationship with younger Army generals, known as the "Young Turks," and a series of threatened or attempted coups imperiled political stability.

On 9 June, Quát turned to the Armed Forces Council to settle a dispute with Head of State Phan Khac Suu and was told to resign. After Quát resigned, on 12 June a triumvirate of

Young Turks—Generals Nguyên Cao Ky, Nguyên Van Thiêu, and Nguyên Huu Có—announced the formation of a National Leadership Committee to rule the RVN. The youngest and least experienced government to date, it was subsequently expanded to include ten members. This body was in effect an inner circle of the 50-member Armed Forces Council, which, much to U.S. Ambassador Maxwell Taylor's chagrin, then elected Ky as chairman of the Central Executive Committee, or premier, charged with conducting the day-to-day government operations. Nguyên Van Thiêu occupied the relatively powerless position chairman of the National Leadership Committee (chief of state). Ky recalled in his memoirs that Thiêu, who was senior to him and the Army chief of staff, at that time declined the top post. Nonetheless, the two men were soon locked in a bitter rivalry for power.

The ninth RVN government in less than two years, it proved to be the most durable since that of Diêm. In September 1966, South Vietnam elected a Constituent Assembly, which was to draft a new constitution. This document came into effect in April 1967. On 3 September, presidential and senatorial elections were held under the auspices of the new constitution. Thiêu and Ky were nominated by the Armed Forces Council to run for the presidency on the same slate, with Ky forced to yield the top spot to Thiêu on the grounds of military seniority. This slate won only 34.8 percent of the votes, but it was sufficient for victory, as the remainder of the vote was split among ten other slates. The new government, still military dominated, then assumed power.

—Ho Diêu Anh and Spencer C. Tucker

References: FitzGerald, Frances. *Fire in the Lake: The Vietnamese and the Americans in Vietnam* (1972); Nguyên Cao Ky. *Twenty Years and Twenty Days* (1976).

See also: Elections (National), Republic of Vietnam: 1955, 1967, 1971; Ngô Đình Diêm; Nguyên Cao Ky; Nguyên Van Thiêu; Phan Huy Quát; Taylor, Maxwell Davenport.

Naval Bombardment (1965–1972)

Naval bombardment during the Vietnam conflict can be divided between the SEA DRAGON interdiction and harassment operations directed against the Democratic Republic of Vietnam (DRV) from 1966 to 1968 and gunnery support for friendly troops in South Vietnam. In the latter role, U.S. warships fired their first missions in 1965 and would continue to do so until the end of active U.S. naval operations in 1972. With its 1,200-mile coastline, the Republic of Vietnam (RVN) offered the U.S. Navy an ideal theater for its gunships. Cruisers, frigates, and destroyers could cover one-third of the land area of I Corps and large portions of II and III Corps.

Planning for naval gunfire support began at a joint Navy–Air Force conference in Sài Gòn on 3–5 May 1965. The Seventh Fleet tasked its gunfire support ships with delivering two types of artillery fire: unobserved saturation bombardment of preselected areas and call fire controlled by ground or aerial spotters. Targets included Communist forces opposing amphibious landings and People's Army of Vietnam (PAVN) artillery batteries that fired across the Demilitarized Zone (DMZ).

The first U.S. naval bombardment occurred in mid-May 1965, when the 8-inch gun cruiser *Canberra* and five destroyers fired at Việt Công assembly areas, caches, and troops on the move. Operation STARLITE in August 1965 clearly demonstrated the effectiveness of naval gunfire support. By spring 1966, escorts, rocket landing ships, and the inshore fire support ship *Carronade* had joined the effort and were joined in 1968 by the battleship *New Jersey* for one tour. In 1967 the ships fired a half million projectiles. During the 1968 Têt Offensive, twenty-two gunships were in action at once, providing key support in the defeat of Communist forces at Huê.

On occasion, the gunships came to close quarters with the Communists. For example, the destroyer *Ozbourn* was damaged by mortar fire when steaming only two miles offshore. The large number of gunfire support missions wore on equipment, necessitating regunning, which was usually done at Subic Bay in the Philippines. Some newer pieces of ordnance malfunctioned, with the first such instance occurring in May 1965 with an in-bore 5-inch gun explosion on the destroyer *Somers*. By 1969 seven additional ships suffered such accidents, some of which killed crewmen.

From its high point in spring 1968, the gunfire support mission decreased as the war wound down. By 1971 an average of only three ships patrolled the gunline. A last surge of activity came during the PAVN Easter Offensive, when as many as 20 ships fired against PAVN forces in Quang Tri and Thua Thiên Provinces and were a key force in staving off attacks on Huê.

—Malcolm Muir, Jr.

References: Marolda, Edward J. *By Sea, Air, and Land: An Illustrated History of the U.S. Navy and the War in Southeast Asia* (1994); Muir, Malcolm, Jr. *Black Shoes and Blue Water: Surface Warfare in the United States Navy, 1945–1975* (1996); Shumlimson, Jack. *U.S. Marines in Vietnam: An Expanding War, 1966* (1982).

See also: *New Jersey* (BB-62); SEA DRAGON, Operation; STARLITE, Operation; United States: Navy; Warships, Allied and Democratic Republic of Vietnam.

Navarre, Henri Eugène (1898–1983)

French Army general and commander of French forces in Indo-China (1953–1954), chiefly remembered as the architect of the Điên Biên Phu debacle. On 8 May 1953, the René Mayer government named Navarre to replace Gen. Raoul Salan as commander of French Union forces in Indo-China with the task of finding an honorable way out of the war. Navarre, who made his decisions in isolation, soon changed the French tactics from largely static defense to fluid offensive operations. Determined to take the war to the Việt Minh, he ended up hastening the French military defeat. Navarre withdrew forces from various defensive positions to create a large mobile strike force.

In July he flew to Paris to present French leaders with his plans to step up the war, including negotiations with the Indo-Chinese states that would grant them greater independence but secure their support for a wider war. He also proposed deployment of an additional 20,000 French troops and 108 native Indo-Chinese battalions. Navarre later claimed that he never thought he could win the war and only hoped to restore the military situation in a *coup nul* (draw).

Navarre's decision to send significant military resources to occupy the remote outpost of Điên Biên Phu, as the key element of Operation CASTOR, was prompted by his desire to secure a blocking position on the main Viêt Minh invasion route into Laos. He also hoped to draw limited Viêt Minh resources into a pitched battle, where they might be destroyed. His plan rested on the assumption that the French would enjoy absolute superiority in air power and artillery, but Điên Biên Phu was too far removed from French air bases in Hà Nôi and Hai Phòng, and French air assets were insufficient. Navarre seriously underestimated his enemy. Gen. Vô Nguyên Giáp committed all available resources in hope of administering a resounding defeat. Điên Biên Phu's valley location left its French defenders vulnerable to heavy artillery, which Viêt Minh porters dragged over the mountains to the battlefield, something Navarre had thought impossible.

An embittered Navarre retired from the army in 1956 to run a brick factory and write his memoirs (*Agonie de Indochine*) free from military censorship. Although Navarre took responsibility for Điên Biên Phu, he blamed the politicians, who "entangled France in the Geneva Conference," for the ultimate French defeat in Indo-China.

—Spencer C. Tucker

References: Fall, Bernard. *Hell in a Very Small Place: The Siege of Dien Bien Phu* (1967); Navarre, Gén. Henri. *Agonie de Indochine* (1956); —. *Le Temps des Vérités* (1979); Roy, Jules. *The Battle of Dienbienphu* (1965).
See also: CASTOR, Operation; Điên Biên Phu, Battle of; Indo-China War; Navarre Plan; Salan, Raoul Albin Louis; Vô Nguyên Giáp.

Navarre Plan

Plan developed by French commander in Indo-China Lt. Gen. Henri Navarre to find an honorable way for France out of the Indo-China War. The Navarre Plan included negotiations with the Indo-China states that would grant them greater independence in exchange for their support for a wider war. He also proposed deploying an additional 20,000 French troops and raising 108 native Indo-Chinese battalions. The U.S. government supported the Navarre Plan in 1953 with nearly $400 million in assistance. Secretary of State John Foster Dulles described the plan to a Senate committee as designed to "break the organized body of Communist aggression by the end of the 1955 fighting season."

—Spencer C. Tucker

References: Fall, Bernard. *Hell in a Very Small Place: The Siege of Dien Bien Phu* (1967); Navarre, Gén. Henri. *Agonie de Indochine* (1956.); Roy, Jules. *The Battle of Dienbienphu* (1965); Simpson, Howard R. *Dien Bien Phu: The Epic Battle America Forgot* (1994).
See also: CASTOR, Operation; Điên Biên Phu, Battle of; Dulles, John Foster; Indo-China War; Navarre, Henri Eugène.

Neutrality

Under international law, regimes declaring themselves neutral in wartime are required to live up to that pledge. In the Vietnam War, the neutral status of Laos and Cambodia was compromised beginning in 1959 as the Democratic Republic of Vietnam (DRV) began covertly using their territories for supply routes into South Vietnam. By the early 1960s, Viêt Công and People's Army of Vietnam (PAVN) troops were using Laotian and Cambodian territories as rest, resupply, and retraining sanctuaries, and as early as 1964, the North Vietnamese headquarters directing operations in South Vietnam (the Central Office for South Vietnam [COSVN]) was located in Cambodia. The fragile governments of Laos and Cambodia were unable to prevent these violations of their neutrality.

Covert responses by the U.S. military began with the introduction in 1959 of Special Forces teams who trained Hmong to attack Vietnamese moving along the Ho Chi Minh Trail, but political sensitivities over the neutral status of Laos led to their withdrawal in 1962. Thereafter, unannounced U.S. bombing and artillery attacks began targeting Laotian portions of the Trail in 1963 and Cambodian positions by 1966.

The watershed of this activity came on 28 April 1970, when U.S. and Army of the Republic of Vietnam (ARVN) troops invaded Cambodia. The political fallout of this operation was immediate and substantial. When President Nixon revealed the "Cambodian incursion" to the nation in a televised address on 30 April 1970, domestic opposition to the war exploded over this invasion of a "neutral" country.

Ironically, Laotian and Cambodian neutrality had long been a myth. However, the public reaction to the Cambodian invasion dramatically increased pressures within the Nixon administration to find a negotiated peace in Vietnam and fostered congressional attempts to legislate an end to U.S. military involvement in Southeast Asia by prohibiting the expenditure of public funds for such purposes. The violation of Cambodia's "neutrality" helped speed the termination of the American phase of the war.

—Ralph G. Carter

References: Ambrose, Stephen E. *Rise to Globalism: American Foreign Policy Since 1938* (1991); Karnow, Stanley. *Vietnam: A History* (1991); Lomperis, Timothy J. *The War Everyone Lost—and Won: America's Intervention in Viet Nam's Twin Struggles* (1993); Spanier, John and Steven W. Hook. *American Foreign Policy Since World War II* (1995); Summers, Harry G., Jr. *On Strategy: A Critical Analysis of the Vietnam War* (1982).
See also: Antiwar Movement, United States; Cambodia; Cambodian Incursion; COSVN (Central Office for South Vietnam or Trung Uong Cuc Miên Nam); Hô Chí Minh Trail; Kent State University; Laos; Nixon, Richard Milhous.

NEVADA EAGLE, Operation (May 1968–February 1969)

Military operation involving the U.S. 101st Airborne (Airmobile) Division conducted during the 1968 Têt Counteroffensive. On 17 May 1968, the 101st launched NEVADA EAGLE as part of the overall Allied post-Têt Counteroffensive. The operation was one of many battalion-sized forays designed to smash Viêt Công (VC) and People's Army of Vietnam (PAVN) forces throughout South Vietnam. Except for some sharp engagements during airmobile sweeps in the mountains of Thua Thiên Province, NEVADA EAGLE made little contact with Communist units in the field.

The 101st's main mission became keeping open major road networks that protected the South Vietnamese rice harvest. The division aggressively engaged in combat and ambush patrols, road clearing sweeps, and small operations to try to bring VC/PAVN units into open battle. The Communists refused to be drawn into a major conflict and used mines and booby traps to inflict U.S. casualties.

NEVADA EAGLE revealed the North Vietnamese ability to entice U.S. helicopters pilots into ambushes. The North Vietnamese used small groups of personnel to present an obvious target, then, as the helicopters came in to engage, opened fire with carefully concealed machine guns. U.S. forces responded with increased use of artillery fire in support of their aviation assets.

The one major engagement of Operation NEVADA EAGLE occurred on 21 May 1968. While most of the 101st's combat elements were dispersed on sweeps, a PAVN battalion struck the division base camp near Huê. The North Vietnamese broke through the outer perimeter, pushing the defending 1st Brigade back to its final defensive bunkers. Helicopter gunships and artillery, used in the direct fire mode, used "beehive" rounds to break up the attack. By dawn on 22 May, what remained of the PAVN battalion broke contact and retreated.

—J. A. Menzoff

References: Olson, James, ed. *Dictionary of the Vietnam War* (1988); Stanton, Shelby. *The Rise and Fall of an American Army: U.S. Ground Forces in Vietnam 1965–1973* (1985).
See also: Airmobility; Artillery, Allied and People's Army of Vietnam; Helicopters, Employment of, in Vietnam; Search and Destroy; United States: Army.

New Jersey (BB-62)

The only U.S. battleship to serve in the Vietnam conflict; recommissioned to supplement the few cruisers operating in Southeast Asian waters. A Pacific Fleet gunfire support review in May 1967 concluded that certain key North Vietnamese targets, such as the Thanh Hóa Bridge and the Song Giang–Kiên Giang logistic bottleneck, would be vulnerable to the battleship's nine 16-inch guns, which fired shells over 22 miles. The principal objections to returning the *New Jersey* to service were the costs of supporting a "one-of-a-kind" ship.

At the direction of Secretary of Defense Robert S. McNamara, the *New Jersey*, originally completed in 1943, underwent an "austere" modernization costing $21.5 million. Arriving in Vietnamese waters on 29 September 1968, the battleship found many of the most lucrative targets in North Vietnam removed from its reach by President Johnson's order forbidding SEA DRAGON operations above the 19th parallel. After 1 November, when SEA DRAGON was scrapped altogether, the *New Jersey* engaged in gunfire support missions south of the Demilitarized Zone, where her performance earned accolades from hard-pressed troops ashore and won for the ship the Navy Unit Commendation "for exceptionally meritorious service."

Leaving the gunline on 31 March 1969, the battleship returned to the United States for upkeep and was mothballed when the Nixon administration scaled down U.S. participation in the war.

—Malcolm Muir, Jr.

References: Muir, Malcolm, Jr. *The Iowa Class Battleships: Iowa, New Jersey, Missouri, & Wisconsin* (1987); Stillwell, Paul. *Battleship New Jersey: An Illustrated History* (1986); Sumrall, Robert F. *Iowa Class Battleships: Their Design, Weapons & Equipment* (1988).
See also: McNamara, Robert S.; Naval Bombardment; SEA DRAGON, Operation; United States: Navy; Warships, Allied and Democratic Republic of Vietnam.

New Zealand

New Zealand sent military and nonmilitary assistance to South Vietnam based upon the rationale that the decline of British power made New Zealand's security dependent upon the United States and that communism in Southeast Asia threatened New Zealand's vital interests.

New Zealanders in Vietnam served with Australian forces. A New Zealand civic action contingent arrived in 1964 and was replaced with an artillery battery the following year that supported the Australian task force in Phuoc Tuy Province. In May 1967, a New Zealand rifle company was transferred from Malaysia to Vietnam. Later that year, additional infantry, reconnaissance, and engineer troops were dispatched and integrated with the Australians to form an Australian/New Zealand (ANZAC) battalion. New Zealand troop strength was 517 men, and its financial aid to the Republic of Vietnam was $350,000 annually. Nonmilitary assistance included health teams to support refugee camps, vocational experts, surgical personnel, and funding for universities in Huê and Sài Gòn.

Domestic opposition grew to the war in Vietnam, and in 1970, concomitant with the U.S. policy of Vietnamization, New Zealand proposed replacing one rifle company with a 25-man army training team. New Zealand Prime Minister Keith Holyoake, in tandem with the Australian government, announced that his nation's combat troops would be withdrawn from Vietnam by the end of 1971.

—Peter W. Brush

Reference: Larsen, Stanley R., and James L. Collins, Jr. *Allied Participation in Vietnam* (1975).
See also: Australia; Civic Action; Free World Assistance Program; Order of Battle; Southeast Asia Treaty Organization (SEATO).

Ngô Đình Cân (?–1963)

Younger brother of RVN President Ngô Đình Diêm and pro consul of northern South Vietnam. Trusted by his brother, Cân came to be, in effect, the warlord of central Vietnam from Phan Thiêt Province north to the 17th parallel. He held no official position within the RVN government but had almost untrammeled power, ruling his area as if it were a feudal satrapy. Cân's personal army and secret police fought the Viêt Công, terrified opponents, and enforced his will. Cân became rich, seeking out lucrative U.S. aid contracts and allegedly heading a smuggling ring that shipped rice to Hà Nôi and distributed opium across Asia. Undeterred by such corruption, Diêm referred to him in matters relating to Cân's area of control. Sometimes at odds with Diêm's policies, Cân nevertheless was a staunch supporter of the Ngô regime. Following the 1963 assassination of his brothers Diêm and Nhu, Cân was tried and executed by the new administration.

—Cecil B. Currey

References: Baker, Joseph. Interview with author; Baritz, Loren. *Backfire: A History of How American Culture Led Us into Vietnam and Made Us Fight the Way We Did* (1985); Conein, Lucien. Interview with author; Karnow, Stanley. *Vietnam: A History* (1984); Lansdale, Edward. Interview with author.

See also: Ngô Đình Diêm; Ngô Đình Khôi; Ngô Đình Luyên; Ngô Đình Nhu; Ngô Đình Nhu, Madame (Trân Lê Xuân); Ngô Đình Thuc.

Ngô Đình Diêm (1901–1963)

President of the Republic of Vietnam (RVN), June 1954–November 1963.

In 1933 Emperor Bao Đai, upon French advice, appointed Diêm interior minister and chief of the newly formed Commission for Administrative Reforms, positions Diêm soon discovered were powerless. After three months he resigned, and French authorities stripped him of his decorations and rank and threatened to arrest him. For the next ten years, Diêm lived in seclusion in Huê with his mother and younger brother, Ngô Đình Cân. He met regularly with nationalist comrades even though the French closely watched him and dismissed his older brother, Ngô Đình Khoi, as governor of Quang Nam Province. In early 1942, after the Japanese took over in Vietnam, Diêm tried to persuade them to grant independence. Instead, they operated through the Vichy French colonial bureaucracy.

With the Japanese surrender in September 1945, and fearing that Bao Đai's puppet government might side with the powerful Viêt Minh forces of Hô Chí Minh and Võ Nguyên Giáp, Diêm set out for Hà Nôi to convince the emperor otherwise. On the way, he was kidnapped by Viêt Minh agents and taken to a remote village near the Chinese border, where he contracted malaria. After six months, Diêm was taken to Hà Nôi, where he met Hô Chí Minh, who asked him to join the Communists. Diêm refused, although he expected this would cost him his life. Instead Hô released him. Later, Communist leaders realized this had been a mistake and sentenced Diêm to death in absentia. Over the next four years, Diêm traveled over Vietnam trying to gain political support. An attempt on his life in 1950 convinced him to leave the country.

In 1951 Diêm went to the United States, where he met Justice William O. Douglas, Senator John F. Kennedy, and other prominent individuals. Diêm effectively argued that he opposed both the French and the Communists and represented the only real nationalist course. A devout Catholic, Diêm became a close friend of Cardinal Spellman, and Spellman became Diêm's greatest U.S. promoter. In May 1953, frustrated by the Eisenhower administration's support of the French, Diêm went to a Benedictine monastery in Belgium from which he regularly traveled to Paris. There he met with the large community of Vietnamese exiles, including his youngest brother, Ngô Đình Luyên, a prominent engineer through whom Diêm finally began to gain supporters and real political power.

In 1954, delegates at the Geneva Conference restored Indo-China as three nations—Cambodia, Laos, and Vietnam. Vietnam was temporarily divided at the 17th parallel with national elections set for 1956. At this time, Bao Đai was in Cannes, fearful that his future as emperor was in jeopardy. Diêm needed Bao Đai to legitimate his rise to power, and Bao Đai needed the support of Diêm's powerful allies, including his brother Ngô Đình Nhu, who had set up the influential Front for National Salvation in Sài Gòn as an alternative to Hô Chí Minh. Because of Diêm's meetings with U.S. leaders, Bao Đai believed that the U.S. government backed Diêm. On 18 June 1954, Bao Đai summoned Diêm to his chateau in Cannes and appointed him prime minister. With growing U.S. support, Diêm returned to Sài Gòn on 26 June and on 7 July officially formed his new government, technically for all of Vietnam.

Fearing that the Communists would overrun this fledgling Asian "domino," President Eisenhower and Secretary of State John Foster Dulles began sending aid to the new regime. Unfortunately, Diêm's power base was limited to minority Catholics, rich and powerful Vietnamese, and foreigners. But his earlier trip to the United States meant that Diêm was the only non-Communist Vietnamese that U.S. officials knew. Washington dispatched Col. Edward Lansdale, the successful architect of Philippine anti-Communist counterinsurgency, to counsel Diêm.

In early 1955, Diêm moved to consolidate his power. Employing five loyal army battalions, Diêm moved against his opponents, culminating the action on 6 May 1955, when his forces defeated those of the Bình Xuyên in Sài Gòn. He also moved against the political cadres of the Viêt Minh, allowed in the South by the Geneva Convention. In 1955 Diêm ignored an effort by Bao Đai (then in France) to remove him from office; instead, Diêm called an October election for the people to choose between them. Clearly he would have won any honest election, but Diêm ignored appeals of U.S. officials for this and managed the results so that the announced vote in his favor was 98.2 percent. On 26 October 1955, using the referendum as justification, Diêm proclaimed the Republic of Vietnam with himself as president. Washington, prompted by Lansdale, officially recognized him in this position and withdrew its support of Bao Đai.

During Eisenhower's last six years as president, material aid from Washington to the RVN totaled $1.8 billion. In an effort to bolster Diêm's image, Eisenhower arranged state visits to the RVN by Dulles in 1955 and Vice-President Nixon in 1956. In 1957 Diêm addressed a joint session of the U.S. Congress.

By 1960 the situation in South Vietnam was poor. The Viêt Minh had resumed guerrilla activities and, in spite of massive U.S. aid to fight communism, Diêm used eight of every ten aid dollars for internal security. He estranged himself from the peasants, doing little to carry out land reform, and by 1961, 75 percent of the land in the South was owned by 15 percent of the population.

When John F. Kennedy became president, he reexamined U.S. policy in Vietnam and demanded that Diêm institute domestic reforms. But, seeing no alternative to Diêm, Kennedy also sent 400 Special Operations military advisors to Vietnam and dispatched Vice-President Johnson on a fact-finding mission. Despite reservations, Johnson publicly called Diêm the "Winston Churchill of Southeast Asia." Less than a week after Johnson returned, Kennedy agreed to increase the size of the Army of the Republic of Vietnam (ARVN) from 170,000 to 270,000 men. ARVN forces, as a rule, did not perform well, and by October 1963, U.S. forces in Vietnam had increased to 16,732 men.

Concurrently, Diêm's oppression of the Buddhist majority and his political opponents grew. To U.S. officials, it seemed that internal opposition to Ngô Đình Diêm rivaled opposition to the Communists. Diêm threw political adversaries, real or imagined, into hellish prison camps, and hundreds were tortured and assassinated. His family and friends, mostly Catholics, held all senior government positions. Most influential were his brother Nhu and his wife Madame Nhu. Diêm himself was celibate. His oldest brother, Archbishop Thuc, controlled Catholic property in the South that included 370,000 acres of nontaxable farmland exempt from redistribution.

Nhu was particularly embarrassing. He set up the Personalist Labor Party, which used totalitarian techniques such as "self-criticism" sessions, storm troops, and mass rallies. He was also the leading advocate of the Agroville and Strategic Hamlet programs that forcibly resettled whole villages into armed compounds to protect them from the Việt Công. Rampant corruption in the program soon alienated most peasants from the regime.

Madame Nhu used her position as state host to enrich herself and influence her brother-in-law to violent acts against the Buddhist majority. She undertook morality campaigns, persuading Diêm to outlaw divorce, dancing, beauty contests, gambling, fortune-telling, boxing, kung fu, cockfighting, prostitution, contraception, and adultery. The harsh punishments that accompanied these excessive rules eventually antagonized large sections of the Southern population.

In summer 1963, Buddhist protests and rallies became more frequent and intense. On 11 June, elderly Buddhist monk Thích Quang Đuc publicly burned himself alive. By November, six more monks had followed suit. Madame Nhu exacerbated the situation by referring to them as "barbecues."

On 24 August Henry Cabot Lodge, who had replaced Frederick Nolting as U.S. ambassador, reported to Washington that an influential faction of South Vietnamese generals wanted to overthrow Diêm. With the president and most senior officials out of Washington, Acting Secretary of State George Ball, Acting Secretary of Defense Roswell Gilpatrick, and Gen. Maxwell Taylor formulated a reply. After a phone consultation with Kennedy and Secretary of State Dean Rusk, they cabled Lodge that, while they wanted to afford Diêm a reasonable time to remove the Nhus, the United States was "prepared to accept the obvious implications that we can no longer support

Diêm … [and] to tell the appropriate military commanders we will give them direct support in any interim period of breakdown of the central government mechanism."

Lodge immediately met with senior U.S. officials in Vietnam and then cabled Washington that Diêm would never replace Nhu and that to ask him to do so would only alert Nhu and lead to a bloodbath, since Nhu had loyal troops in Sài Gòn. Lodge recommended going straight to the generals, bypassing Diêm, and leaving it up to them if they wanted to keep Diêm. Ball and Roger Hilsman agreed, and Kennedy later affirmed their instructions. Lodge decided to distance the United States from the proposed coup and expressed support for the generals through lower-ranking Central Intelligence Agency (CIA) officers, specifically Lt. Col. Lucien Conein, who had a long-standing friendship with many of the conspiring generals.

By September, most U.S. administration officials began to have second thoughts, especially Gen. Taylor. At his urging, Kennedy called a meeting of the National Security Council. It was hopelessly divided, with the State Department favoring the coup and Taylor, Secretary of Defense Robert McNamara, and especially Johnson vehemently opposed. Kennedy, although coy about the matter, never acted to prevent the coup or to restrain Lodge.

On 2 October, Kennedy suspended economic subsidies for South Vietnamese commercial imports, froze loans for Sài Gòn water works and electrical power plant projects, and cut off financial support of Nhu's Vietnamese Special Forces units. Just over an hour after midnight on 1 November 1963, the generals, led by Maj. Generals Duong Van "Big" Minh, Military Governor of Sài Gòn Tôn Thât Đính, and Trân Van Đôn, began their coup.

Upon learning of the coup, Diêm phoned Lodge to inquire about the U.S. attitude. Lodge feigned ignorance but assured Diêm that he would do anything possible to guarantee Diêm's personal safety. Diêm and Nhu fled the presidential palace through a tunnel and took refuge in Cho Lon, the Chinese section of Sài Gòn. About 0600 the next morning, the two men agreed to surrender. The generals leading the coup guaranteed them safe passage out of the country. While negotiations for their flight dragged on, they were discovered by troops commanded by a long-time foe and subsequently shot to death. Madame Nhu was in Los Angeles at the time.

Washington never found a viable alternative to Ngô Đình Diêm. Certainly no subsequent leader of the Republic of Vietnam had his air of legitimacy. As a result, U.S. leaders, who had seen Diêm as an alternative to Hô Chí Minh and an agent to stop the spread of communism, soon found themselves taking direct control of the war in Vietnam.

—William Head

References: Karnow, Stanley. *Vietnam: A History* (1983); Warner, Denis. *The Last Confucian* (1964); U.S. Senate Committee on Foreign Relations. *U.S. Involvement in the Overthrow of Diem, 1963* (1972).

Kennedy, John Fitzgerald; Lansdale, Edward Geary; National Assembly Law 10/59; National Bank of Vietnam; Ngô Đình Cẩn; Ngô Đình Diêm, Overthrow of; Ngô Đình Khôi; Ngô Đình Luyên; Ngô Đình Nhu; Ngô Đình Nhu, Madame (Trân Lê Xuân); Ngô Đình Thuc; Richardson, John H.; Spellman, Francis Joseph; Taylor, Maxwell Davenport; Taylor-McNamara Report; Tôn Thât Đính; Trân Van Đôn; Vietnam, Republic of: National Police.

Ngô Đình Diêm, Overthrow of (November 1963)

The Ngô Đình Diêm government tended to favor Roman Catholics over the predominately Buddhist population of South Vietnam. Catholics received lands, business favors, military and government jobs, and rewards. Over the years, Diêm's predilection toward Catholic citizens increased.

On 8 May 1963, when Buddhists gathered in Huê to honor the 2,527th birthday of Buddha, the Catholic deputy province chief prohibited the Buddhists from displaying their flag, in accordance with a Diêm decree that flags of religions, associations, and other countries be displayed outside only with the national flag. When the protesters gathered at the radio station, a concussion hand grenade thrown by a Regional Force soldier to break up the crowd killed several people and wounded others. Diêm blamed the situation, as he often did, on the Communists.

The Buddhists speedily coordinated strikes and protests and kept the U.S. news media fully informed of developments. They met with U.S. officials and urged them to get rid of Diêm or at least force reforms from him. Ambassador Frederick Nolting urged Diêm to act more responsibly, but the president refused to modify his stance. Then on 11 June 1963, Thích Quang Đuc, a Buddhist monk, committed self-immolation in a busy Sài Gòn' intersections to protest Diêm and his policies. Other Buddhist self-immolations followed and unrest grew. In August, Nolting was replaced by Henry Cabot Lodge.

Now members of Diêm's own military—Generals Trân Van Đôn, Lê Van Kim, Duong Van Minh, and others—began questioning whether he should continue in office and began secretly meeting with Central Intelligence Agent (CIA) agent Lucien Conein, supposedly serving as an advisor to the RVN's ministry of interior but in reality the conduit between the generals and Ambassador Lodge. The generals wanted assurance that U.S. aid would continue if Diêm fell.

On 21 August, the Diêm government mounted another raid on the Buddhists, this time in Sài Gòn, arresting hundreds and beating and clubbing others. Voices in the Kennedy administration began calling for Diêm's replacement; others, just as strident, claimed that would only help the Communists. Lodge supported a coup. Gen. Paul Harkins, head of the U.S. Military Assistance and Advisory Group (USMAAG) in Vietnam, demurred and informed Gen. Trân Van Đôn that any coup would be a grave mistake. Đôn then told Conein that he was postponing the coup despite Conein's insistence that the USMAAG chief did not speak for the U.S. government. President Kennedy waffled. Ngô Đình Nhu, aware of the plotting, considered an accommodation with Hà Nôi as a means of blackmailing U.S. support for his brother's government.

Kennedy sent Robert McNamara and Gen. Maxwell Taylor to Sài Gòn on a fact-finding mission. Their report did little to ease the president's mind. CIA station chief in Sài Gòn John Richardson told Lodge that he doubted Gen. Minh could conduct a successful coup. Lodge then dismissed Richardson and informed Kennedy that the plotters were ready to act. Conein told Gen. Trân Van Đôn that the United States would not stand in the way. On 29 October, during a meeting of the National Security Council, Taylor spoke out strongly on behalf of Diêm. At the last minute, Kennedy cabled Lodge to order the generals to postpone any action. Lodge never delivered the message, and the coup went ahead as scheduled, culminating on 1 November when rebels seized the radio station and police headquarters and besieged the presidential palace. Diêm telephoned Lodge for help; it was not forthcoming. Diêm and Nhu secretly left the palace early in the evening and sought refuge in Cho Lon at St. Francis Xavier Church.

Early the next morning, Diêm telephoned Gen. Duong Van Minh, asking to negotiate. The plotters had already told Lodge that Diêm's life would be spared if he and Nhu agreed to go into exile. Although Nhu would never be allowed to return, Diêm might be invited back one day to serve in a figurehead capacity. By now Minh had changed his mind and so rejected Diêm's telephoned plea. Diêm then called Gen. Trân Van Đôn, offered to surrender, and revealed his hiding place. The two brothers were arrested by Gen. Mai Huu Xuân, who arrived at the church with an M-113 armored personnel carrier (APC) and four jeeploads of soldiers. Among his entourage, were Maj. Duong Hiêu Nghia and Capt. Nguyên Van Nhung, Gen. Minh's bodyguard. Nghia and Nhung drove them away in the APC. On the road back to Sài Gòn, they stopped and murdered their prisoners, spraying them with bullets and stabbing them. The Diêm regime had ended.

—Cecil B. Currey

References: Conein, Lucien, and Edward Lansdale. Interviews with author; Karnow, Stanley. *Vietnam: A History* (1983).

See also: Conein, Lucien Emile; Duong Van Minh; Harkins, Paul D.; Lodge, Henry Cabot, Jr.; McCone, John Alex; Military Revolutionary Council; Ngô Đình Diêm; Ngô Đình Nhu; Nolting, Frederick, Jr.; Richardson; John H.; Trân Van Đôn.

Ngô Đình Khôi (?–1945)

Eldest brother of Republic of Vietnam President Ngô Đình Diêm and prominent figure in the government of An Nam. Khôi's advance was rapid, and by 1933 he was governor in charge of the provinces south of central Vietnam. During the early 1940s, Khôi reportedly had personal disagreements with Pham Quynh, a famous scholar and high mandarin, and retired from the administration in 1943. In August 1945, the Communists killed Khôi as part of their plan to remove all potential rivals for power. His death was a principal factor in Ngô Đình Diêm's rejectection of Hô Chí Minh's offer of a Democratic Republic of Vietnam cabinet post in 1945.

—Ngô N. Trung

References: Biographical Files, Indo-China Archives, University of California at Berkeley.

See also: French Indo-China; Ngô Đình Cẩn; Ngô Đình Diêm; Ngô Đình Luyên; Ngô Đình Nhu; Ngô Đình Thuc.

Ngô Đình Luyên (1914–1990)

Youngest brother of President Ngô Đình Diêm and prominent political figure in the Republic of Vietnam (RVN). After his brother Diêm became president of the RVN, Luyên held the important post of RVN ambassador to the United Kingdom (1955–1963). Luyên was said to be the most liberal person in Diêm's immediate family. During the early days of his administration, Diêm considered Luyên his most trusted advisor, but Luyên was supplanted by his very conservative brother, Ngô Đình Nhu. Luyên visited the United States a few times after 1975 and met with Vietnamese emigré friends.

—Ngô N. Trung

References: Biographical Files, Indo-China Archives, University of California at Berkeley.

See also: Ngô Đình Diêm; Ngô Đình Nhu; Ngô Đình Thuc; Vietnam, Republic of: 1954–1975.

Ngô Đình Nhu (1910–1963)

Younger brother of Republic of Vietnam President Ngô Đình Diêm. A capable organizer, Nhu organized the Cân Lao Nhân Vi Cách Mang Đang, or Revolutionary Personalist Labor Party, a party based on the obscure French philosophy of "personalism" conceived in the 1930s by Emmanuel Mounier. Copying Communist organizations and using the Cân Lao Party as a basis, Nhu organized a system of covert political, security, and labor groups structured in five-man cells that reported on opponents of the regime and allowed the Diêm brothers to maintain their power rather than establish democracy or build national unity. The party never held a convention and never voiced a public stand on any issue, and its controlling body never met as a group.

Nhu appeared on the Vietnamese nationalist political scene in September 1953 at Sài Gòn, when he organized demonstrations against the French and Communists and masterminded the beginning phases of the revolution in the South against Emperor Bao Đai. Aiming to support a new government headed by his brother Diêm, Nhu formed the National Union for Independence and Peace and enlisted the support of the leadership of the Cao Đài, the Hòa Hao, and the Bình Xuyên. This too-open effort to oust Bao Đai came before the time was judicious and was a failure.

The French defeat in the 1954 Battle of Điên Biên Phu made the anti–Viêt Minh nationalists, and even Bao Đai, realize that their future depended upon a break with the French and the formation of a new government not subject to French control. In Sài Gòn, Nhu formed another coalition called the Front for National Salvation comprising the political-religious sects, the organized Catholics, the Đai Viêt, and other nationalist groups. These "Front" groups, some of which Nhu and his brother would soon move to destroy, called for Diêm to head a new regime to fight communism. Many did so believing that the task would destroy anyone who tried—a fate that they wished on Diêm. Consequently, on 16 June 1954, Bao Đai invited Diêm, the most prominent nationalist to oppose the French "Bao Đai experiment," to form a new government as prime minister.

For the new government to survive, it had to gain control of the army, take control of the police from the Bình Xuyên, and consolidate areas controlled by the Cao Đài and Hòa Hao sects into the national administration. With the assistance of the United States, the army was brought into line in late 1954. However, in spring 1955, when the Bình Xuyên and the sects refused to cooperate, it became necessary to destroy them. Diêm, with Nhu's able assistance, maneuvered to divide the sects from the Bình Xuyên and then from each other, and then use the army to crush each separately.

In the midst of this struggle to consolidate power, Nhu allegedly hatched the final scheme to oust Bao Đai. On 30 April 1955, a group of 200 people calling itself the General Assembly of Democratic and Revolutionary Forces of the Nation, and representing 18 political "parties," gathered at the Sài Gòn town hall and called for the emperor's abdication and the formation of a new government under Ngô Đình Diêm. On 7 July 1955, Diêm announced that a national referendum would be held on 23 October to decide the future form of Vietnam's government. Nhu used his secret police to control the election, and on 26 October 1955, Diêm was declared president of the new Republic of Vietnam.

Throughout his brother's reign, Nhu used his Cân Lao party and secret service apparatus to keep the family in power. As head of the secret police, he created 13 intelligence units and even commanded the Vietnamese Special Forces, his own personal army. Nhu helped administer the Khu Trù Mât farm communities known as Agrovilles and recommended and administered the later Strategic Hamlet program, both designed to isolate the rural population from the Communists. Both were poorly administered, hampered by corruption, and easily subverted by the Viêt Công.

Nhu thwarted several attempts to depose his brother. However, the intrigue, corruption, and brutality of the regime caught up with Nhu in 1963, when he used his forces to suppress Buddhist demonstrations against the Diêm government. Because of the brutal nature of the suppression and inflammatory statements by him and his wife, Madame Nhu, the United States demanded Nhu's removal. When Diêm refused, U.S. officials notified plotting Vietnamese generals that Washington would not oppose a coup. The coup began on 1 November 1963, and the next day Nhu and Diêm were assassinated.

—Arthur T. Frame

References: Boetcher, Thomas D. *Vietnam: The Valor and the Sorrow* (1985); Buttinger, Joseph. *Vietnam: A Political History* (1968); Collins, J. Lawton. *Lightning Joe: An Autobiography* (1979); Karnow, Stanley. *Vietnam: A History* (1984).

See also: Cân Lao Nhân Vi Cách Mang Đang; Cao Đài; Collins, Joseph Lawton; Conein, Lucien Emile; Duong Van Minh; Elections (National), Republic of Vietnam: 1955, 1967, 1971; Geneva Conference and Geneva Accords; Lodge, Henry Cabot, Jr.; National Assembly Law 10/59; National Bank of Vietnam; Ngô Đình Diêm; Ngô Đình Diêm, Overthrow of; Ngô Đình Nhu, Madame (Trân Lê Xuân); Richardson, John H.; Sheehan, Cornelius Mahoney (Neil); Taylor-McNamara Report; Thích Quang Đuc; United States: Involvement in Vietnam, 1954–1965; Vietnam, Republic of: National Police.

Ngô Đình Nhu, Madame (Trân Lê Xuân) (1924–)
Wife of Ngô Đình Nhu, born Trân Lê Xuân. Although Vietnamese, her family was thoroughly Gallicized and amassed a fortune while in service to the French colonial administration. A mediocre student, she was fluent in French, but never learned to write her native Vietnamese. Lê Xuân married Nhu in 1943. Upon her brother-in-law Diêm's ascendancy to the presidency in 1955, the Nhus moved into the presidential palace in Sài Gòn. Because Diêm never married, Madame Nhu acted as official host and became, in effect, the Republic of Vietnam's First Lady and an outspoken and powerful force in her own right. Madame Nhu's father was appointed ambassador to the United States, her mother became an observer at the United Nations, and two of her uncles were cabinet ministers.

Madame Nhu's imperious manner and insensitivity toward anyone or anything outside the ruling family clique earned her the sobriquet "Dragon Lady." Shortly into the Diêm regime, U.S. Ambassador Gen. J. Lawton Collins encouraged Diêm to get rid of her, but Diêm opted to keep the family together. This attempt caused Madame Nhu to heap reproach upon the United States and claim that Americans were aiding Vietnamese factions attempting to topple the Diêm regime. Impervious to the suffering of the Vietnamese people, Madame Nhu issued decrees backed by the force of law. Her edicts banned divorce, contraceptives, dancing, beauty contests, fortune-telling, and boxing matches. Fancying herself a feminist, she lectured on women's issues and formed her own paramilitary force, the Women's Solidarity Movement. She often embarrassed her brother-in-law with provocative remarks, but he tolerated her out of family fidelity.

Madame Nhu contributed to Diêm regime's decay with her vitriolic remarks. After she referred to several Buddhist self-immolations as "barbecues," her husband followed suit, declaring "if the Buddhists want to have another barbecue, I will be glad to supply the gasoline." Such statements helped to turn public opinion and the Kennedy administration against the Diêm regime, and even Madame Nhu's parents resigned their posts in response. Diêm's refusal to get rid of the Nhus paved the way for the November 1963 coup that cost Diêm and Nhu their lives.

In Los Angeles when her husband and Diêm were assassinated, Madame Nhu later withdrew into exile in Rome.

—Arthur T. Frame

References: Boetcher, Thomas D. *Vietnam: The Valor and the Sorrow* (1985); Buttinger, Joseph. *Vietnam: A Political History* (1968); Karnow, Stanley. *Vietnam: A History* (1984).

See also: Collins, Joseph Lawton; Conein, Lucien Emile; Duong Van Minh; Elections (National), Republic of Vietnam: 1955, 1967, 1971; Lodge, Henry Cabot, Jr.; Ngô Đình Diêm; Ngô Đình Diêm, Overthrow of ; Ngô Đình Nhu; Thích Quang Đuc; United States: Involvement in Vietnam, 1954–1965; Women in the War: Vietnamese.

Ngô Đình Thuc (1897–1984)
Roman Catholic archbishop; older brother of Republic of Vietnam (RVN) President Ngô Đình Diêm. Thuc, who want-

ed a truly independent Vietnamese state, was an important bridge between Diêm and the U.S. political circle that supported him. In 1950 Thuc met Cardinal Francis Spellman and in June applied for a visa to stop in the United States. Traveling with Thuc were his younger brother, Ngô Đình Diêm, and Nguyên Viêt Canh. In August, Thuc and Diêm met Prince Cuong Đê in Tokyo to discuss the establishment of an anti-Communist Vietnamese government. Thuc and Diêm arrived in the United States in September and met with Spellman and William S. B. Lacy, head of Philippines and Southeast Asia Affairs in the Department of State. Thuc raised the issue of building a Vietnam centered on Catholics, an idea later supported by the U.S. Department of State.

During the first years of Diêm's government, Thuc's diocese became a training base for the cadre of the Cân Lao Nhân Vi Cách Mang Đang (Revolutionary Personalist Labor Party) headed by Ngô Đình Nhu, a younger brother of Thuc. In 1961 Thuc became archbishop of Huê, where in 1963 he intervened to forbid display of the Buddhist flag during celebration of Buddha's birthday. This incident began a chain of events leading to the 1 November 1963 coup that overthrew Diêm. Thuc was in Rome and so survived the coup, but was later excommunicated for investing priests without permission from Rome.

—Ngô N. Trung

References: Biographical Files, Indo-China Archives, University of California at Berkeley.
See also: Bao Đai; Buddhists; Kennedy, John Fitzgerald; Mansfield, Michael Joseph; Ngô Đình Diêm; Ngô Đình Nhu; Spellman, Francis Joseph.

Ngô Quang Truong (1929–)
Army of the Republic of Vietnam (ARVN) general who commanded, successively, 1st ARVN Division, IV Corps, and I Corps. In June 1966 he took command of the ARVN 1st Division. His U.S. advisor wrote to Gen. Harold K. Johnson that Truong was "dedicated, humble, imaginative and tactically sound," an assessment validated when Truong and his division played a key role in the fight for Huê, the most difficult and protracted fighting of the 1968 Têt Offensive.

Early in 1971, Truong took command of IV Corps in the Mekong Delta, where he was so successful that he voluntarily offered up forces for redeployment to other more threatened regions of the country. When the People's Army of Vietnam (PAVN) 1972 Easter Offensive erupted and initially made serious inroads in I Corps, Truong was brought up to assume command. With characteristic directness he began by issuing an order, broadcast throughout the region, that military deserters who had not returned to their units within 24 hours would be shot on sight. Truong then went on television and promised that he would hold Huê and repulse the Communist thrust. Truong organized and fought a stubborn defense, halting further PAVN advances, then successfully counterattacked with three divisions against six PAVN divisions to retake Quang Tri City.

Truong distinguished himself during the 1975 all-out Communist offensive. Following the final collapse of the

Republic of Vietnam, Gen. Truong made his way to the United States, where he has lived since 1975.

—Lewis Sorley

References: Hoang Ngoc Lung, Col. *The General Offensives of 1968–69* (1981); Jones, James. *Viet Journal* (1973); Warner, Denis. *Certain Victory* (1978).

See also: Easter Offensive (Nguyên Huê Campaign); Hô Chí Minh Campaign; Huê, Battle of; Vietnam, Republic of: Army (ARVN).

Ngô Quyên (898–944)

Vietnamese national hero whose victory over the Southern Han on the Bach Đang River marked the end of 1,000 years of Chinese domination. In 938, on the Bach Đang River, using iron-tipped poles planted underwater, Ngô Quyên won a victory that ended Chinese rule and opened a new era in Vietnamese history. After the victory, Ngô Quyên declared himself king and moved the capital to Cô Loa, the ancient capital of the Thuc, a Vietnamese independent dynasty that ruled the country long before the Chinese invasion. Cô Loa was selected to show Ngô Quyên's willingness to build a new nation completely independent from China.

—Pham Cao Duong

References: Lê Thành Khôi. *Histoire du Viet-Nam des origines à 1858* (1981); Pham Cao Duong. *Lich Su Dân Tôc Viêt Nam, Quyên I: Thoi Ky Lâp Quôc* (1987); Phan Huy Lê, Trân Quôc Vuong, Hà Van Tân, Luong Minh. *Lich Su Viêt Nam* (1991); Taylor, Keith W. *The Birth of Vietnam* (1983).

See also: Vietnam: from 938 through the French Conquest.

Nguyên Bình (1906–1951)

Viêt Minh lieutenant general. In October 1945, Hô Chí Minh named Bình a member of the Southern Region Military Committee and commander of the Southern front. Bình apparently contributed to the unification of factions in the South against the French, and in November 1947 he was promoted to lieutenant general. He was best known for his commando attack on the French ammunition depot at Thi Nghè, Sài Gòn. Tradition holds that he warned the French beforehand. On 29 September 1951, Bình was ambushed and killed by the French on his way to the North to attend a conference. There is some suggestion that this was not without the assistance of the Communist leadership.

—Ngô N. Trung

References: Biographical Files, Indo-China Archives, University of California at Berkeley.

See also: Hô Chí Minh; Indo-China War; Viêt Minh (Viêt Nam Đôc Lâp Đông Minh Hôi [Vietnam Independence League]).

Nguyên Cao Ky (1930–)

Republic of Vietnam Air Force (RVANF) air vice-marshal; premier, 1965–1967; vice-president, 1967–1971. After training in Morocco and France, in 1954 Ky graduated as a fully qualified pilot and returned to Vietnam, by which time the Indo-China War was over. In 1959 he took command of the RVNAF 43d Air Transport group. In 1960 he assumed command at Tân Son Nhut Air Base and began working with William Colby, Central Intelligence Agency (CIA) station

chief in Sài Gòn, flying agents into North Vietnam, an operation that Ky publicly disclosed to worldwide attention in July 1964. In the November 1963 coup that overthrew President Ngô Đình Diêm, Ky played the key role in securing RVNAF support and in return was immediately promoted to full colonel. Ten days after the coup, new chief of state Gen. Duong Van Minh promoted Ky to brigadier general and named him commander of the RVNAF, a post he held until June 1965.

In January 1964, Ky supported Maj. Gen. Nguyên Khánh in a coup against Minh. That year saw seven changes of government. Khánh promoted Ky to major general and then named him air vice-marshal. By this time, Ky was the leader of a faction of officers known as the "Young Turks" that included Army Maj. Gen. Nguyên Van Thiêu. Disillusioned by the ineffective national government, in mid-December 1964 they overthrew the Military Revolutionary Council of older officers. In late January 1965, the new Armed Forces Council decided that Premier Trân Van Huong would have to be replaced. Khánh, who replaced him as premier, was in turn ousted in February in a coup led by Gen. Lâm Van Phát. Ky was not involved in this coup, but his threat to bomb headquarters toppled Phát. Phan Huy Quát then became premier with Phan Khac Suu as chief of state.

In June 1965, the new Republic of Vietnam (RVN) government collapsed, and on 12 June a triumvirate of Generals Nguyên Cao Ky, Nguyên Van Thiêu, and Nguyên Huu Có announced formation of a National Leadership Committee to rule the RVN. Subsequently expanded to include ten members, this body was an inner circle of the 50-member Armed Forces Council, which then elected Ky as chief executive of the council, or premier, charged with conducting the day-to-day government operations. Nguyên Van Thiêu occupied the relatively powerless position of chief of state. It was the ninth government in less than two years.

When U.S. Ambassador Henry Cabot Lodge asked him about his program, Ky replied with the words "social justice." He took steps to strengthen the armed forces but also launched a campaign to remove corrupt officials and instituted needed land reforms, programs for the construction of schools and hospitals, and price controls. But Ky also instituted unpopular repressive actions against civilians, including a newspapers ban.

The new government was soon embroiled in controversy with the Buddhists. The issue was over Army of the Republic of Vietnam (ARVN) I Corps commander Gen. Nguyên Chánh Thi. Ky and others in the government believed that Thi was too powerful and posed a threat to the government. In early March 1966, they secured his agreement to resign and go into exile in the United States. Buddhist leaders seized on this, and on 14 March Đà Nang workers began a two-day general strike that seriously affected U.S. activities. Buddhist students in Huê also protested. Thi took advantage of this, refusing to relinquish command and attending rallies in Huê and Đà Nang to address supporters. Thi's removal was soon no longer the central issue as Buddhist leaders sought a complete change of government. The Buddhists took control of radio stations in Huê and Đà Nang, and it was evident that there was growing sympathy for the movement among the civil service and many ARVN units. On 3 April, Ky announced "Đà Nang is in communist hands," but it is by no means clear what role, if any, the Communists played.

Ky tried to control the situation by appointing Gen. Tôn Thât Đính as the new commander of I Corps on 10 April, but Đính could not assert his authority with Thi still in Huê. After a significant military operation to suppress the Buddhists and rebel ARVN units, Thi accepted his dismissal on 24 May and, following a "reconciliation" with Ky, went into exile in the United States. In June, supported by U.S. forces, Ky's troops crushed opposition in Huê.

Ky's popularity and political clout were enhanced following a February 1966 conference with President Johnson in Hawaii, where they agreed on social and economic reforms and the need for national elections. In May 1966, a government decree set up a committee to draft election laws and procedures. In October, 117 delegates met in Sài Gòn to draft a constitution, which was completed in March 1967. It provided for a president with wide powers and a premier and cabinet responsible to a two-chamber house. Local elections were held in May 1967, and elections for the lower House in October.

Tensions were high between Ky and Thiêu, both of whom openly vied for control of the government. In his memoir, Ky was sharply critical of Thiêu, who "wanted power and glory but... did not want to have to do the dirty work." He also accused Thiêu of corruption and involvement in heroin traffic. Although Thiêu had stepped aside in 1965 to allow Ky to take the premier's post, his determination to challenge Ky for the highest office in the 3 September 1967 elections led the Armed Forces Council to force Ky and Thiêu onto a joint ticket, giving the presidential nomination to Thiêu and the vice-presidential nomination to Ky, simply on the basis of seniority. The Thiêu-Ky ticket won the election with 34.8 percent of the vote against ten other slates.

After the election, Ky's influence was gradually eclipsed by Thiêu's consolidation of power, though Ky tried to suppress Thiêu's followers in the military. In 1971 Thiêu engineered an election law to disqualify his major opponents, Ky and Duong Van Minh. Although the Supreme Court said that Ky could run, he chose not to. Thiêu's election made one-person rule a reality and did serious injury to the RVN government's image.

Ky was sharply critical of Thiêu's handling of the 1975 Communist Hô Chí Minh Offensive and his abandonment of the Central Highlands, claiming "Thiêu's strategic error turned a tactical withdrawal into a rout and the eventual disintegration of our entire armed forces." In early April 1975, Ky led a well-publicized demonstration at the U.S. embassy in Sài Gòn, during which he and several hundred other officers promised never to leave Vietnam. On April 29, however, Ky commandeered a helicopter and flew it to the USS *Midway*.

Ky went to the United States, where he opened a liquor store in Los Angeles. In 1985 he filed for bankruptcy.

—Spencer C. Tucker

References: Nguyên Cao Ky. *Twenty Years and Twenty Days* (1976); Olson, James S., ed. *Dictionary of the Vietnam War* (1988).

See also: Đà Nang; Duong Van Minh; Elections (National), Republic of Vietnam: 1955, 1967, 1971; FLAMING DART, Operation; Honolulu Conference; Johnson, Lyndon Baines; Lodge, Henry Cabot, Jr.; Manila Conference; Military Revolutionary Council; Ngô Đình Diêm, Overthrow of; Nguyên Khánh; Nguyên Van Thiêu; Vietnam, Republic of: 1954–1975; Trân Van Huong.

Nguyên Chánh Thi (1923–)

Army of the Republic of Vietnam (ARVN) general and commander of I Corps, whose removal sparked countrywide Buddhist protests. A devout Buddhist who resented Diêm's favoritism toward the Catholics, Thi participated in the November 1960 coup attempt against the Republic of Vietnam (RVN) president. The coup failed, and Thi fled to Cambodia. He returned to the RVN following Diêm's November 1963 assassination and received command of I Corps, which included Huê and Đà Nang. As corps commander he exercised significant control over the region. Premier Nguyên Cao Ky and others in the government believed that Thi was too powerful and posed a threat to the government. On 4 March 1966, Ky convinced the National Leadership Committee in Sài Gòn to dismiss Thi from I Corps command.

At first Thi appeared to accept the decision, but on 14 March workers in Đà Nang went on a two-day general strike that affected U.S. activities. Thi sought to use the situation to his advantage, refusing to relinquish command. Buddhist leaders seized control of radio stations in Huê and Đà Nang, and on 3 April, Ky announced "Đà Nang is in Communist hands." Although the Communist role in events is unclear, the Communists took advantage of the situation by trying to turn public opinion against the Americans.

On 10 April, Ky appointed Gen. Tôn Thât Đính as commander of I Corps, but Đính was unable to take command with Thi still in Huê. After a government-mounted operation to suppress the Buddhists and the rebel ARVN units, Thi agreed to step down on 24 May. Following a "reconciliation" with Ky at Chu-Lai on 27 May, Thi left for exile in the United States.

—Michael R. Nichols

References: Bain, Chester A. *Vietnam: The Roots of Conflict* (1967); Duncanson, Dennis J. *Government and Revolution in Vietnam* (1968.); FitzGerald, Frances. *Fire in the Lake: The Vietnamese and the Americans in Vietnam* (1972); Harrison, James P. *The Endless War: Vietnam's Struggle for Independence* (1989); Smith, R. B. *An International History of the Vietnam War* (1991).

See also: Buddhists; Ngô Đình Diêm; Nguyên Cao Ky; Thích Trí Quang; Tôn Thât Đính.

Nguyên Chí Thanh (1914–1967)

Senior general in the People's Army of Vietnam (PAVN); director of the Central Office for South Vietnam (COSVN), 1965–1967. Thanh spent much time traveling in the Communist world, one of the few PAVN leaders to do so. He possessed considerable political and diplomatic talents but was a warrior first and a politician second. During the Vietnam War, he advocated a battlefield victory at all costs.

When some in Hà Nôi suggested Thanh adopt a pragmatic approach more in line with Moscow's thinking in the early 1960s, he openly rebelled. Once a close colleague of Vietnamese Communist Party Secretary Gen. Lê Duân, Thanh became a maverick in his strong opposition to the protracted war strategy adopted by the Central Committee in December 1965. His leadership of COSVN was highly controversial, and many scholars have suggested that Thanh's view of military matters made him a candidate for conflict with Gen. Vô Nguyên Giáp. Thanh's official obituary says that he died in Hà Nôi of a heart attack, but many officers who served with him in the southern theater say he died during a U.S. bombing raid.

—Robert K. Brigham

References: Duiker, William J. "Waging Revolutionary War: The Evolution of Hanoi's Strategy in the South, 1959–1965" (1993); Herring, George C. *America's Longest War: The United States and Vietnam, 1950–1975* (1986); Lockhart, Greg. *Nation in Arms: The Origins of the People's Army of Vietnam* (1989); Pike, Douglas. *PAVN: People's Army of Vietnam* (1986); Theis, Wallace J. *When Governments Collide: Coercion and Diplomacy in the Vietnam Conflict, 1964–1968* (1980).

See also: COSVN (Central Office for South Vietnam or Trung Uong Cuc Miên Nam); Lê Duân; National Front for the Liberation of South Vietnam (NFLSV); Vietnam, Democratic Republic of: Army (People's Army of Vietnam [PAVN]); Vô Nguyên Giáp.

Nguyên Co Thach (1932–)

Vietnamese revolutionary; Democratic Republic of Vietnam (DRV) ambassador to India, 1956–1960; head of the DRV delegation to the 1962 Geneva Conference; minister for foreign affairs for the Socialist Republic of Vietnam (SRV), 1975–1991. Thach played a role in the "Ronning Missions," 1966 secret peace initiatives spearheaded by retired Canadian diplomat Chester A. Ronning. In March 1966, Ronning met in Hà Nôi with Thach, Nguyên Duy Trinh, and Pham Van Đông and was assured by Phaam Van Đông that, if the United States stopped the bombings, the DRV was prepared to enter into talks. The Johnson administration flatly rejected this proposal, instead calling for a reciprocal de-escalation in return for a bombing halt. Thach and Ronning met again in June 1966, with few results.

In 1975 Thach became minister of foreign affairs. In 1976 he became a member of the Vietnamese Communist Party's Central Committee and was elected as an alternative member to the Political Bureau in 1981. During the 1986 Sixth Party Congress, Thach was instrumental in moving the party toward economic reform (*dôi moi*), advocating a more international outlook. Working closely with U.S. presidential emissary John W. Vessey, Jr., he also supervised the return of the remains of U.S. servicemen killed in action. In 1991, during a period of backlash against *dôi moi*, Thach was removed from the Political Bureau and the Foreign Ministry.

—Robert K. Brigham

References: Herring, George C., ed. *The Secret Diplomacy of the Vietnam War: The Negotiating Volumes of the Pentagon Papers* (1983); Marr, David G., and Christine White, eds. *Postwar Vietnam: Dilemmas in Socialist Development* (1988); Nguyen Van Canh. *Vietnam under Communism, 1975–1982* (1983); Porter, Gareth.

Vietnam: The Politics of Bureaucratic Socialism (1993); Thayer, Carlyle A. "Political Reform in Viet Nam: Doi Moi and the Emergence of Civil Society" (1992).

See also: Đôi Moi; Missing in Action, Allied; Paris Negotiations; Vietnam, Socialist Republic of: 1975 to the Present.

Nguyên Duy Trinh (1910–1988)

Member of the Lao Đông (Communist Party of Vietnam) Central Committee and foreign minister of the Democratic Republic of Vietnam (DRV), 1965–1975. In 1960 Trinh became the deputy prime minister of the DRV, a post he held until the end of the Vietnam War. From 1965 to 1975, Trinh gained international recognition as the DRV's minister of foreign affairs. He participated in the DRV's secret contacts with the United States through third parties before the Paris peace talks and played a key role in the ASPEN and PENN-SYLVANIA peace initiatives. He also supervised the first secret contact in Paris between DRV delegate Mai Van Bô and American Edmund Gullion, known in the west as XYZ. Trinh is best known for his 29 December 1967 declaration that serious peace talks "will" (rather than "could") begin when the United States stopped bombing the North unconditionally. The statement represented a dramatic shift in Hà Nôi's negotiating stance, and some suggested that this compromise would lead to a quick settlement. However, little came of Trinh's comment. As the war continued, Trinh's role in the peace talks diminished.

—Robert K. Brigham

References: Herring, George. C., ed. *The Secret Diplomacy of the Vietnam War: The Negotiating Volumes of the Pentagon Papers* (1983); Huynh Kim Khanh. *Vietnamese Communism, 1925–1945* (1982); Porter, Gareth. *Vietnam: The Politics of Bureaucratic Socialism* (1993); Thies, Wallace J. *When Governments Collide: Coercion and Diplomacy in the Vietnam Conflict, 1964–1968* (1980).

See also: Lao Đông Party; Nguyên Co Thach; Paris Negotiations; Paris Peace Accords.

Nguyên Dynasty (1802–1945)

Ruling family in Vietnam, 1802–1945. In the seventeenth century, Vietnam was divided in two. The Trinh lords ruled the North, while the Nguyên lords came to control then-Southern Vietnam. Each family hated the other and ruled in the name of the powerless Lê kings at Thang Long (present-day Hà Nôi).

In 1776 the Tây Son attacked the Nguyên stronghold in Gia Đinh Province and took Sài Côn (later Sài Gòn and present-day Hô Chí Minh City). Only one Nguyên prince, Nguyên Phúc Ánh, escaped; he and some supporters fled into the swamps of the western Mekong Delta. Nguyên Ánh eventually befriended French missionary Pigneau de Béhaine, who supported his cause and secured military assistance in the form of French mercenary troops from India. With Western advisors and weaponry, Nguyên Ánh launched a military campaign to establish his rule over all Vietnam, something he accomplished in 1802. Nguyên Ánh then founded the Nguyên Dynasty. He took the dynastic name Gia Long (Gia from the customary name for Sài Gòn, *Gia Đinh*; and Long from *Thang Long*.)

Gia Long moved the capital from Hà Nôi in the North to Huê in the central part of the country. He died in 1820 and was followed by Minh Mang (1820–1841), Thiêu Tri (1841–1847), Tu Đuc (1847–1883), Duc Đuc (July 1883), Hiêp Hòa (August–November 1883), Kiên Phúc (1883–1884), Hàm Nghi (1884–1888), Đông Khánh (1885–1888), Thành Thái (1889–1907), Duy Tân (1907–1916), Khai Đinh (1916–1925), and Bao Đai (1925–1945).

Gia Long's successors lacked his understanding of Western strengths and weaknesses. Perhaps they would have been unable to resist Western military technology in any case, but it was under them that the French conquered the country and established their authority. The Nguyên Dynasty lasted in Vietnam until the 1945 abdication of Bao Đai.

—Spencer C. Tucker

References: Lê Thành Khôi. *Histoire de Viêt Nam des Origines à 1858* (1981); Nguyên Khac Viên. *Vietnam: A Long History* (1987).
See also: Bao Đai; Duy Tân; Hàm Nghi; Minh Mang; Nguyên Huê (Quang Trung); Nguyê Phúc Ánh (Gia Long); Tây Son Uprising; Thiêu Tri; Tu Đuc.

Nguyên Hà Phan (1933–)

Leader in the Vietnamese Communist Party (VCP) and the Socialist Republic of Vietnam (SRV). Elevated to full member at the Seventh Party Congress, Phan became head of the Department of Economics. In June 1991, he became secretary of the VCP Central Committee's Secretariat and in January 1994 was promoted to the political bureau of the VCP Central Committee. Phan was also active in the government. After the division of Hâu Giang Province into two provinces, he was elected as a deputy to the National Assembly from Cân Tho Province, and in July 1992 became deputy chairman of the National Assembly. Regarded as one of the likely candidates to replace Võ Van Kiêt as premier, Phan in April 1996 was suddenly removed from the Politburo and the National Assembly, apparently over his opposition to a more open economy. He was the highest-level party official expelled in more than a decade.

—Ngô N. Trung

References: Biographical Files, Indo-China Archives, University of California at Berkeley.
See also: Vietnam, Socialist Republic of: 1975 to the Present.

Nguyên Hai Thân (1869–1951)

Nationalist Vietnamese leader who opposed Hô Chí Minh. In 1942 Nguyên Hai Thân helped found the Viêt Nam Cách Mang Đông Minh Hôi (VNCMDMH) with help from Chinese Gen. Chang Fa Kwei. When the latter imprisoned Hô Chí Minh, Vietnamese nationalist leaders in South China (who thought of Hô as a compatriot rather than a Communist) urged Thân to intercede with Jiang Jieshi for Hô's freedom. He did, obtaining Hô's release. Hô then joined the VNCMDMH, of which Thân was chairman. Hô's (new) Viêt Nam Đôc Lâp Đông Minh Hôi (VNDLDMH, or Viêt Minh) Party joined the umbrella VNCMDMH organization.

Within the VNCMDMH, Hô was assigned to observe the situation in Vietnam and determine the right time for the

league to attempt a general uprising in which all member parties were to participate, but in August 1945, Hô's Viêt Minh seized power. Although the other league-affiliated nationalist parties, especially the Viêt Nam Quôc Dân Đang (VNQDĐ), were more powerful than the Viêt Minh, they were not prepared for the imminent defeat of the Japanese.

Aware of the Viêt Minh betrayal, the nationalist parties held an emergency meeting on 18 August 1945 in Hà Nôi to decide whether they should try to drive the Viêt Minh from power. The majority concluded that, since the Viêt Minh were fighting for independence, a civil war should be avoided.

Too late, Thân returned to Hà Nôi. Although supported by Jiang Jieshi, Thân did not get full assistance from commander of Chinese forces in northern Vietnam Gen. Lu Hán. Meanwhile Hô maneuvered skillfully to marginalize Thân and minimize nationalist influence, essential because the nationalist forces were more powerful than the Viêt Minh. Hô practiced every stratagem to fool Thân and finally went to see him at VNCMDMH headquarters. They spent a day in discussions, with Hô warning Thân that, if he refused a coalition and civil war were to break out, the Vietnamese people and history would condemn him. That was what Thân most feared, and he agreed to accept the vice-presidency and place his supporters in cabinet posts, including foreign affairs, treasury, public health, and agriculture. Hô also offered 70 seats of 350 seats of the Parliament to parties allied with Nguyên. Of this number, the VNQDĐ received 50 seats, and the others shared the remaining 20. This meant that the two sides agreed to rig the 6 January 1946 elections.

After the preliminary agreement with the French on 6 March 1946, the nationalist forces were routed by an all-out surprise Viêt Minh offensive (ironically during the Great Solidarity Campaign). In many places in North Vietnam, French forces also attacked nationalist strongholds.

Thân soon left Vietnam for China. Subsequently he was blamed for the failure to overthrow the Viêt Minh when it was still possible. Although Thân was a virtuous leader of unquestioned morality, he was not a talented politician, especially when faced with the likes of Hô Chí Minh.

—Nguyên Công Luân (Lu Tuân)

Reference: Hoàng Van Đào. *Viêt Nam Quôc Dân Đang* (1970).
See also: August Revolution (1945); French Indo-China to 1946; Hô Chí Minh; Hô-Sainteny Agreement; Jiang Jieshi (Chiang Kai-shek).

Nguyên Huê (Quang Trung) (1752–1792)

Most important military strategist and national hero in Vietnamese history; also known as Vua Quang Trung (King Quang Trung) or Quang Trung Hoàng Đê (Emperor Quang Trung). With 100,000 men he successfully defeated a Chinese army of 200,000 in January 1789. Nguyên Huê's victory at Đông Đa on the fifth day of Têt Ky Dâu became a national holiday in the official calendar of South Vietnam before 1975 and is now celebrated by Vietnamese throughout the world.

Quang Trung did much domestically for Vietnam and worked with capable individuals regardless of their past loyalties, which helped attract the best men to his service. He reorganized the army, carried out fiscal reforms, and redistributed unused lands, mainly to the peasants. He promoted the crafts and trade and pushed for reforms in education. He wanted to open trade with the countries of the West, and Western missionaries in Vietnam at the time noted the safe conditions in which they were able to carry out their religious activities. Quang Trung was the first Vietnamese leader to stress the importance of science, insisting it be added to requirements for the Mandarinate examinations. He also introduced a Vietnamese currency and insisted that Chu Nôm, the demotic writing system combining Chinese characters with Vietnamese, be used rather than Chinese in court documents.

Quang Trung died of an unknown illness in 1792. Many Vietnamese believe that had he lived a decade longer, their history would have developed quite differently.

—Pham Cao Duong and Spencer C. Tucker

References: Hoa Bang. *Quang Trung Nguyên Huê: Anh Hùng Dân Tôc (1788–1792)* (1950); Le Thanh Khoi. *Le Viet-Nam, Histoire et Civilisation* (1955); Nguyên Huyên Anh. *Viêt Nam Danh Nhân Tu Điên* (1990); Trân Trong Kim. *Viêt Nam Su Luoc* (1971).

See also: Hà Nôi (Đông Đa), Battle of; Nguyên Phúc Ánh (Gia Long); Nguyên Dynasty; Vietnam: from 938 through the French Conquest.

Nguyên Huu Có (1923–?)

Army of the Republic of Vietnam (ARVN) general and Republic of Vietnam (RVN) defense minister in 1966. Có's first public appearance came during the coup that overthrew Ngô Đình Diêm. As one of Gen. Tôn Thât Đính's deputies, Có, then a colonel, was in charge of preventing Diêm loyalists in the Mekong Delta from coming to Sài Gòn to rescue the Ngô brothers, a task he successfully fulfilled. In 1965 he became chief of ARVN Joint General Staff and in 1966 became deputy prime minister and minister of defense. In this turbulent period in RVN politics, there was little Có could do in his position, and reportedly he was more interested in real estate speculation than in national affairs. After the 1975 Communist victory, Có was sent to a prison camp along with other ARVN officers. He was released in 1990.

—Ho Diêu Anh

References: Stanley, Karnow. *Vietnam: A History* (1983); *Who's Who in Vietnam* (1974).

See also: Ngô Đình Diêm, Overthrow of ; Tôn Thât Đính; Vietnam, Republic of: 1954–1975.

Nguyên Huu Tho (1910–1994)

Southern Vietnamese revolutionary; first president of the National Front for the Liberation of South Vietnam (NFLSV). In 1949 Tho helped organize a successful anti-French protest in Sài Gòn, and in 1950 the French deported him to Lai Châu, where he remained until the signing of the Geneva Accords in 1954. Tho returned to Sài Gòn in 1954 and resumed his resistance activities, founding the Sài Gòn–Cho Lon Peace Movement in 1955. Although Tho never joined the Communist Party officially, Ngô Đình Diêm claimed that Tho was a party member and had him arrested. Tho served several years in southern jails before Diêm put him under

house arrest in Phú Yên. A commando raid by Southern revolutionaries liberated Tho and brought him to NFLSV headquarters in Tây Ninh Province.

At the 20 December 1960 organizational meeting of the NFLSV, Tho was the delegates' choice as its first president. From 1961 through 1968, Tho served as the president of the Presidium of the NFLSV's Central Committee. He insisted that the NFLSV was independent and autonomous from the Communists in Hà Nôi and that the Front had come into being in response to Southern demands. From 1962 to 1968, he was the international spokesperson for the NFLSV. In 1969 Huynh Tân Phát replaced Tho as the newly formed Provisional Revolutionary Government's president. Tho continued as chairman of the NFLSV's Central Committee and in 1976 was named to the purely ceremonial position of acting vice-president of the Socialist Republic of Vietnam (SRV). Tho's powerlessness after the fall of Sài Gòn became symbolic of the difficulties and tensions between Northern and Southern Communists after the war.

—Robert K. Brigham

References: Kahin, George McT., and John Lewis. *The United States in Vietnam: An Analysis in Depth of the History of America's Involvement in Vietnam* (1967); *Personalities of the South Vietnam Liberation Movement* (1965); Porter, Gareth. *Vietnam: The Politics of Bureaucratic Socialism* (1993); Truong Nhu Tang. *A Viet Cong Memoir: An Inside Account of the Vietnam War and Its Aftermath* (1985).

See also: Huynh Tân Phát; National Front for the Liberation of South Vietnam (NFLSV); Ngô Đình Diêm; Nguyên Thi Bình; Provisional Revolutionary Government of South Vietnam (PRG); Trân Buu Kiêm; Truong Nhu Tang; Vietnam, Republic of 1954–1975.

Nguyên Huu Tri (ca. 1903–1954)

Leader of the Đai Viêt Quôc Dân Đang (National Party of Greater Vietnam); nationalist governor of northern Vietnam for the State of Vietnam during much of the Indo-China War. Initially, Tri presided only over the municipalities, since the countryside was controlled by the Viêt Minh. The nationalist cause was hurt when in 1951 French Gen. Jean de Lattre de Tassigny ordered Tri removed from office.

Subsequently reappointed governor, Tri was considered by the American Special and Economic Technical Mission (Mutual Security Agency) in North Vietnam as the most competent of the Vietnamese administrators. He pressed the French for real independence, organized the Đông Quan pacification project south of Hà Nôi, and worked closely with the Americans and the French to create other pacification centers to protect the population from Viêt Minh infiltration in the Red River Delta. The pacification centers that Tri organized with U.S. funding became mostly refugee centers to accommodate the tens of thousands of Vietnamese fleeing Viêt Minh–controlled areas. He was called to Sài Gòn by the government in mid-1954 and died there under mysterious circumstances.

—Claude R. Sasso

References: Buttinger, Joseph. *Vietnam: A Dragon Embattled* (1967); Hendrick, James P. *Papers.* Harry S Truman Library.

See also: Đai Viêt Quôc Dân Đang (National Party of Greater Vietnam); de Lattre de Tassigny, Jean Joseph Marie Gabriel; Đông Quan Pacification Project; United States: Involvement in Indo-China through 1954; Vietnam, Democratic Republic of: 1945–1954.

Nguyên Khánh (1927–)

Army of the Republic of Vietnam (ARVN) general whose political ambitions led him through two coups eventually to become premier of the Republic of Vietnam (RVN). Khánh supported President Ngô Đình Diêm in 1954 and successfully defended the presidential palace during the attempted coup of November 1960. But as the commander of II Corps, Khánh was vital in the November 1963 coup against Diêm. In a move essential to the coup's success, principal plotters Generals Trân Van Đôn, Duong Van Minh, and Lê Van Kim, secured the support of Khánh and I Corps commander Gen. Đô Cao Trí.

In the months following the coup, the new government leaders failed to capitalize on their initial popularity by not asserting the leadership that the nation and the situation demanded. Before Gen. Minh could begin a reform program, Generals Khánh, Đô Mâu, and Trân Thiên Khiêm carried out a bloodless coup on 31 January 1965 on the pretext that others in the new government were preparing to institute a neutralist program. Khánh asked Minh to remain as chief of state while he became premier and chairman of the Military Revolutionary Council (MRC).

The Americans were impressed with Khánh's promises of urban and rural development, renewal of the Strategic Hamlet program (under the name New Rural Life Hamlets), and institution of a civilian government with a constitution. The South Vietnamese were less impressed, resentful that Khánh had ousted the popular Gen. Minh. Many were demoralized by the purge he instituted and the rapid turnover of chiefs at provincial and district levels.

Khánh, himself a Buddhist, tried to appease the United Buddhist Association by recognizing it and donating land for a national pagoda. Although he removed favored legal status for Catholics and endorsed the use of a Buddhist chaplain corps for the armed forces, Buddhists still complained of repression, and many military commanders were not happy with the new chaplains.

Thinking this an opportune moment to begin a dictatorship, Khánh declared a national emergency and instituted a new constitution, the Vung Tau Charter, giving the president nearly absolute powers. The MRC then elected Khánh president. Protests broke out in Sài Gòn, Đà Nang, and Huê as Communists infiltrated many demonstrations to aggravate the religious tension. Khánh then withdrew the charter and resigned. The MRC elected a triumvirate of Khánh, Minh, and Khiêm as an interim government to restore order. Khánh remained commander in chief of the new government, but was ousted in February 1965 by Generals Nguyên Cao Ky and Nguyên Van Thiêu.

—Michael R. Nichols

References: Bain, Chester A. *Vietnam: The Roots of Conflict* (1967); Davidson, Phillip B. *Vietnam at War, the History: 1946–1975* (1988); Duncanson, Dennis J. *Government and Revolution in Vietnam*

(1968); Fishel, Wesley R., ed. *Vietnam: Anatomy of a Conflict* (1968); Karnow, Stanley. *Vietnam: A History* (1991); Olson, James, ed. *Dictionary of the Vietnam War* (1987); Smith, R. B. *An International History of the Vietnam War* (1991).

See also: Buddhists; Đô Cao Trí; Duong Van Minh; Lê Van Kim; Military Revolutionary Council; National Front for the Liberation of South Vietnam (NFLSV); Ngô Đình Diêm; Ngô Đình Diêm, Overthrow of; Nguyên Cao Ky; Nguyên Van Thiêu; Trân Thiên Khiêm; Trân Van Đôn; Viêt Minh (Viêt Nam Đôc Lâp Đông Minh Hôi [Vietnam Independence League]); Vietnamese National Army (VNA).

Nguyên Khoa Nam (1927–1975)

Army of the Republic of Vietnam (ARVN) major general. Nam took command of the 5th Airborne Battalion in 1965 and the 3d Airborne Brigade in 1968. In September 1969, he was promoted to brigadier general and command of the 7th Infantry Division. Nam was promoted to major general in November 1972, and after November 1974 he had command of IV Corps. After Sài Gòn fell, Nam committed suicide.

—Nguyên Công Luân (Lu Tuân)

Reference: Hà Mai Viêt. "Famous Generals of the Republic of Viêt Nam Armed Forces" (n.p.).

See also: Lê Van Hung.

Nguyên Luong Bang (1904–1979)

Prominent leader in the Indo-Chinese Communist Party (ICP), Democratic Republic of Vietnam (DRV), and Socialist Republic of Vietnam (SRV). In 1941 Bang was president of the Viêt Minh and head of the Financial Department of the Viêt Minh. In October 1943 he became an alternate member of the Vietnamese Communist Party Central Committee in charge of financial affairs and military recruiting. In 1945 Bang was elected a full member of the ICP Central Committee. After the 1945 August Revolution, he held important party and state posts, was a member of the ICP Central Committee and vice-president of the DRV (1969). In 1976 he became vice-president of the Socialist Republic of Vietnam, a post he held until his death.

—Ngô N. Trung

References: Biographical Files, Indo-China Archives, University of California at Berkeley.

See also: Hô Chí Minh; Lao Đông Party; Viêt Minh (Viêt Nam Đôc Lâp Đông Minh Hôi [Vietnam Independence League]); Vietnam, Democratic Republic of: 1954–1975; Vietnam, Socialist Republic of: 1975 to the Present.

Nguyên Manh Câm (1929–)

Leader in the Vietnamese Communist Party (VCP); minister of foreign affairs of the Socialist Republic of Vietnam (SRV). Câm joined the Democratic Republic of Vietnam (DRV) ministry of foreign affairs in 1952 and was assigned to various departments of the ministry. A Soviet specialist who studied Russian in China and the USSR, Câm was in the USSR as a junior embassy official from 1952 to 1956 and as embassy first secretary from 1962 to 1966. He served as DRV ambassador to Hungary, Austria, and Iran concurrently (1973–1977) and in 1977 was appointed ambassador concurrently to the Federal Republic of Germany, Switzerland, and Iran. Câm became minister of foreign affairs in August 1991, a post he apparently accepted with reluctance. In January 1994 he was rewarded with a Politburo post. A career diplomat with a reputation for integrity, Câm is credited with normalizing relations with the United States in July 1995.

—Ngô N. Trung

References: Biographical Files, Indo-China Archives, University of California at Berkeley.

See also: Lao Đông Party; Vietnam, Socialist Republic of, 1975 to the Present.

Nguyên Ngoc Loan (?–?)

Republic of Vietnam Air Force (VNAF) brigadier general; director of National Police, 1966–1968. Loan is best known for his cold-blooded execution of a Viêt Công (VC) suspect, photographed during the 1968 Têt Offensive.

In June 1967 Nguyên Cao Ky, lacking a political base, money, and connections to build an effective government, chose Loan as his power broker. In this, Ky was given wholehearted support by the United States, which was pleased to see this strong man take control of the police and intelligence services. A U.S. embassy official favorably reported that from October 1966 to January 1968, not a single terrorist incident nor a National Liberation Front (NLF) meeting was recorded in districts 7, 8, or 9 of Sài Gòn, where previously the NLF had held daytime meetings and there had been more than 40 terrorist incidents a month. Loan and his men engaged in systematic, large-scale corruption to finance the war against urban guerrillas. Opium traffic, which he oversaw, was an important source of cash for rewards to paid agents who delivered information about NLF activities.

Loan was known for his unique problem-solving methods and ability to deal by extralegal means with political rivals. He once marched with armed guards into the National Assembly to force its members to break a legislative logjam. He achieved international attention during the Têt Offensive on 3 February 1968, when he shot a VC suspect (reportedly a member of a death squad) through the head with a revolver on a Sài Gòn street. Associated Press photographer Eddie Adams recorded the event. The photograph undermined Loan's career and displayed a shocking image of the RVN government. The execution drew immediate rebukes from U.S. officials.

Severely wounded on 5 May 1968 while leading his men against the VC in a Sài Gòn suburb, Loan was forced to resign his position. Loan soon disappeared from the political arena.

—Ho Diêu Anh

References: McCoy, Alfred. *The Politics of Heroin* (1991); Oberdorfer, Don. *Tet!* (1971); Westmoreland, William C. *A Soldier Reports* (1976); Wirtz, James. *The Tet Offensive: Intelligence Failure in War* (1991).

See also: Media and the War; Nguyên Cao Ky; Têt Offensive: Overall Strategy; Têt Offensive: the Sài Gòn Circle.

Nguyên Phúc Ánh (Gia Long) (1761–1820)

Vietnamese emperor, 1802–1820. Nguyên Ánh, pretender to the throne, was one of the few surviving members of the Nguyên family, which had ruled in the South since the sixteenth century. He was forced to flee into the Mekong Delta when Gia Đinh (Sài Gòn), the only important territory left under the Nguyên lords, fell to the Tây Son in 1778. Nguyên Ánh was determined to prevail over the Tây Son Dynasty, but the outlook was bleak until he met French missionary Pierre Pigneau de Béhaine, who strongly supported Nguyên Ánh's cause. He arranged for Nguyên Ánh's son, Nguyên Canh, to visit France in 1787 to seek help from the government. In return for financial support and the use of French naval craft and troops to defeat his rivals, the Nguyêns established the Treaty of Versailles with Louis XVI, granting France commercial and missionary rights, the city of Đà Nang (renamed Tourane by the French), and the island of Côn Son, which the French later turned into a prison colony for Vietnamese political activists.

The promised French governmental help failed to materialize, but Pigneau de Béhaine raised the armed forces necessary for Nguyên Ánh to overcome his enemies. Nguyên Ánh then launched a campaign against those who resisted his rule. By 1802 the Tây Son were either dead or in exile, and Nguyên Ánh founded the Nguyên Dynasty, which lasted until the abdication of Bao Đai in 1945. Nguyên Ánh took the dynastic name Gia Long and, after an official investiture by China, declared himself emperor, thus uniting the land for the first time in centuries.

Gia Long changed his capital from Hà Nôi to Huê and the name of his nation from Đai Viêt to Vietnam. Enamored of his giant neighbor to the north, the new emperor promulgated his Gia Long Penal Code, based on the one used by the Chinese Ch'ing Dynasty. This new system of law took less note of local and village customs and strengthened the hand of the emperor. He replaced *Chu Nôm*, the written form of Vietnamese then in use, with Chinese as the official written language. He ordered the construction of public granaries, developed an effective postal service, gathered in Cambodia (Kampuchea) as a client state, and repaired the Old Mandarin Road. Gia Long tolerated French missionary activity to some extent but resisted any increase in French commercial growth. He was succeeded by his son, Chí Đam, who assumed the dynastic name of Minh Mang.

—Cecil B. Currey

References: Buttinger, Joseph. *The Smaller Dragon: A Political History of Vietnam* (1968); Duiker, William J., ed. *Historical Dictionary of Vietnam* (1989); Olson, James, ed. *Dictionary of the Vietnam War* (1988).

See also: Minh Mang; Nguyên Dynasty; Nguyên Huê (Quang Trung); Pigneau de Béhaine, Pierre; Vietnam: from 938 through the French Conquest.

Nguyên Thái Hoc (1902–1930)

Leader of the Viêt Nam Quôc Dân Đang (VNQDĐ). Established on 25 December 1927, the VNQDĐ was the first well-organized Vietnamese revolutionary party to advocate armed revolt to achieve independence. Drawing the bulk of its members from the middle class, it was also the largest such party. Hoc was elected chairman in late 1927, and Phan Bôi Châu became VNQDĐ honorary chairman.

The French soon launched a large-scale campaign to eradicate the VNQDĐ, and the party leadership approved Hoc's call for an uprising. From 10 to 15 February 1930, the VNQDĐ struck major French military bases around Hà Nôi, although communication failures prevented these from being simultaneous. Collectively these are known in Vietnamese history as the Yên Báy (or Yên Bái) Uprising. The French soon put down the uprising. Hundreds of VNQDĐ members were killed or subsequently executed, and thousands more were imprisoned. Hoc was arrested on 20 February 1930. On 23 March 1930, Hoc and 82 party members the French thought the most dangerous were tried in a special court. The next morning, Hoc and 38 comrades were sentenced to death; the others received prison terms. In early June 1930, the president of France approved 27 death sentences, including that of Hoc. Early on 17 June 1930, Hoc and 18 comrades were guillotined at Yên Bái. Reportedly all met their deaths bravely. Hoc was the last to die. Nguyên Thi Giang was among those watching the executions. Hoc was romantically linked with Giang, who had assisted him as a liaison officer and was one of the first female members of the VNQDĐ. That afternoon she visited Hoc's mother, then committed suicide with a pistol.

Although Hoc and his comrades had not won the decisive victory they sought for their country and people, their revolutionary activity and uprising boosted Vietnamese nationalism.

—Nguyên Công Luân (Lu Tuân)

References: Cao Thê Dung. *Viêt Nam Huyêt Lê Su* (1996); Hoàng Van Đào. *Viêt Nam Quôc Dân Đang* (1970); Pham Kim Vinh. *The Vietnamese Culture* (1995).

See also: Viêt Nam Quôc Dân Đang (Vietnam National Party).

Nguyên Thi Bình (1927–)

Southern Vietnamese revolutionary who served as a diplomat for the National Front for the Liberation of South Vietnam (NFLSV) and as the Provisional Revolutionary Government's (PRG) Foreign Minister. From 1962 until 1969 Bình served in the Front's diplomatic corps and toured the world, offering interviews to hundreds of reporters. For many in the West, Madame Bình became the symbol of the NFLSV and its most important spokesperson.

Once the Paris peace talks opened in 1968, Bình assumed the role of chief negotiator for the NFLSV, although official recognition of the Front was a major stumbling block to successful talks. In 1969 the Provisional Revolutionary Government appointed her as its foreign minister, sending her to Paris as its official representative. As a negotiator, Bình was determined to exact a settlement that diminished Nguyên Van Thiêu's monopoly on political power in the South and that coupled the freedom of southern political prisoners with the release of U.S. prisoners of war. During the fall 1972 negotiations she criticized the Tho-Kissinger accord because it did not deal adequately with the prisoner-of-war issue. Eventually she signed the final accord on behalf of the

PRG. Bình later served in various government positions in Hà Nôi, and in the early 1990s she assumed the vice-presidency of the Socialist Republic of Vietnam.

—Robert K. Brigham

References: *Personalities of the South Vietnam Liberation Movement* (1965); Pike, Douglas. *Viet Cong: The Organization and Techniques of the National Liberation Front of South Vietnam* (1966); Porter, Gareth. *A Peace Denied: The United States, Vietnam, and the Paris Agreement* (1975); Trân Van Giâu, and Lê Van Chât. *The South Vietnam Liberation National Front* (1962).

See also: National Front for the Liberation of South Vietnam (NFLSV); Ngô Đình Diêm; Ngô Đình Nhu; Nguyên Cao Ky; Nguyên Huu Tho; Nguyên Van Thiêu; Paris Peace Accords; Paris Negotiations; Provisional Revolutionary Government of South Vietnam (PRG); Trân Buu Kiêm.

Nguyên Thi Đinh (1920–)

Military leader of the Armed Forces for the Liberation of the South and leader of the National Liberation Front Women's Union during the Vietnam War. Đinh joined the Viêt Minh movement in 1944 and participated in the 1945 Bên Tre uprising. In 1946 she was elected to the Executive Committee of the Bên Tre Women's Union and was sent in a delegation of southern revolutionaries to visit Hô Chí Minh and request assistance in waging war against the French in the south.

Đinh was in charge of the first shipload of weapons and financial assistance sent to the south in November 1946. She continued Viêt Minh activities, was charged with mobilization, and after the 1954 Geneva Accords chose to stay in the South. After 1954 she took charge of rebuilding the revolutionary movement and coordinating Viêt Minh cadres remaining in Bên Tre. Later she had charge of disrupting and troubling the Diêm government's Agroville program in Châu Thành and Mo Cày.

In early 1960, Đinh was appointed a member of the Bên Tre Central Committee. She was also a member of the Central Committee for Đông Khoi, a popular uprising in late January 1960 to seize power from Diêm administration officials in villages in Bên Tre. During Đông Khoi, she was the founder of the Long-Haired Army (Đôi Quân Toc Dài), an organization of revolution sympathizers, largely women, established to plan protest demonstrations against the Diêm government and to persuade Army of the Republic of Vietnam soldiers to desert. This was considered the political struggle that went along with military activities. Đinh became one of the founders of the National Liberation Front and helped build its armed forces. When the People's Revolutionary Party, the southern branch of the Lao Đông Party, was formed in 1962, she became a member of its Central Committee.

After 1975 Đinh continued as a member of the Central Committee of the Vietnamese Communist Party, but she was active only in the women's movement, holding the post of vice-chair of the Women's Union of the Socialist Republic of Vietnam. From May 1982, she was its chair. In 1991 she was elected vice-chair of the Socialist Republic of Vietnam State Council.

—Ho Diêu Anh

References: Eisen, Arlene. *Woman and Revolution in Vietnam*

(1984); Nguyên Thi Đinh. Trân Huong Nam, ed. *Không Còn Con Đuong Nào Khác* (1968).

See also: Agroville Campaign; Lao Đông Party; National Front for the Liberation of South Vietnam (NFLSV); Vietnam, Socialist Republic of: 1975 to the Present; Vietnamese Communist Party (VCP); Women in the War: Vietnamese.

Nguyên Tuong Tam, or Nhât Linh (1906–1963)

Leader of the Viêt Nam Quôc Dân Đang (VNQDĐ) and highly respected writer. In the mid-1930s, Tam founded the Tu Luc Van Đoàn (Self-Reliance Literary Group) of a dozen modern writers. They advocated cultural reforms, focusing primarily on a literary movement to promote a new style of writing, as well as social reforms, including new housing in slum areas. The Tu Luc Van Đoàn published the *Phong Hóa Weekly* and *Ngày Nay Weekly* and a series of novels. Using humorous stories, caricatures, and theme novels, the group radically changed Vietnamese literature. Their novels were best sellers at the time. Indirectly the group promoted patriotism among Vietnamese youth, although some critics saw this as a kind of romanticism.

In the early 1940s, Nhât Linh participated in revolutionary activities, such as organizing the Đai Viêt Dân Chính, then then fled to China, where he was arrested. Returning to Viêt Nam in 1945, Nhât Linh became minister of foreign affairs in the first coalition government of the Democratic Republic of Vietnam (DRV). He led the DRV delegation that negotiated with the French at Đà Lat in April 1946. He was to have been chief negotiator in talks with the French in Paris, but he left Vietnam before his scheduled departure for France, reportedly to avoid imminent danger from Viêt Minh groups. In 1950 he returned to Viêt Nam and in 1958 tried unsuccessfully to revive his literary movement.

The Diêm government accused Nhât Linh of involvement in the 1960 attempted coup. Nhât Linh committed suicide before his trial began. Though unsuccessful in politics, Nhât Linh was the greatest writer of modern Vietnam.

—Nguyên Công Luân (Lu Tuân)

References: Cao Thê Dung. *Viêt Nam Huyêt Lê Su* (1996); Hoàng Van Đào. *Viêt Nam Quôc Dân Đang* (1970); Pham Kim Vinh. *The Vietnamese Culture* (1995).

See also: Hô-Sainteny Agreement; Viêt Nam Quôc Dân Đang (Vietnam National Party); Vietnamese culture.

Nguyên Van Cu (1934–)

Republic of Vietnam Air Force (VNAF) pilot who bombed the presidential palace on 27 February 1962. Cu was the second son of Nguyên Van Luc, a leader of the Viêt Nam Quôc Dân Đang (VNQDĐ) nationalist party and opponent of Republic of Vietnam (RVN) President Ngô Đình Diêm. Cu's father's revolutionary council wanted to assassinate Diêm. They planned for Cu and Pham Phú Quôc, another pilot recruited by Cu from his squadron, to attack the Đôc Lâp (Independence) Palace on the morning of 27 February 1962.

Clouds forced the pilots to bring their AD-6 Skyraiders below the safe altitude to drop bombs. They strafed the palace with rockets, and one 500-pound bomb penetrated a room in which Diêm was located. The bomb failed to detonate, and the only casualty was a Nhu family servant, who was wounded. Pham Phú Quôc's plane was damaged, and he was forced to land in Nhà Bè near Sài Gòn. He was arrested and imprisoned, but released after Diêm's death the next year. Cu's plane was also damaged, but he was able to fly it to Phnom Penh, where he worked as a language teacher until his return to Vietnam after Diêm's overthrow. In June 1975, Cu was arrested and sent to a reeducation camp. Released in 1985, he immigrated to the United States in 1991.

—Nguyên Công Luân (Lu Tuân)

References: Nguyên Va Cu and Chu Tu Ky. Interviews with the author.

See also: Ngô Đình Diêm.

Nguyên Van Bình (1910–1991)

Catholic archbishop of Sài Gòn from 24 November 1960 until 1991. Despite the aggressive role played by Catholics in the earlier period of the Vietnam War, Nguyên Van Bình was considered a moderate religious leader. After 1975 his moderate stance helped keep the Catholic Church at relative peace with the new government. Following his death in Sài Gòn, the government permitted the Catholic Church in Vietnam to hold memorial services for the archbishop that lasted several days.

—Ho Diêu Anh

Reference: *Who's Who in Vietnam* (1974).

See also: Roman Catholicism in Vietnam; Vietnam, Republic of: 1954–1975; Vietnam, Socialist Republic of: 1975 to the Present.

Nguyên Van Cao. *See* Van Cao.

Nguyên Van Hiêu (?–1975)

Army of the Republic of Vietnam (ARVN) major general. Hiêu rose through the ranks to chief of staff, II Corps/Tactical Zone 2 (1964); commander of the 22d Infantry Division (1964 and 1966); and commander of the 5th Infantry Division (1970). Hiêu was regarded as one of the most incorruptible ARVN generals. That reputation brought him the post of inspector general of the army under Vice-President Trân Van Huong, who promoted an anticorruption program, which failed despite their enthusiastic efforts. In 1974 Hiêu became deputy commander of III Corps/Military Region III at Biên Hòa. Hiêu died of a pistol shot; official reports held that he died while cleaning his pistol, but there were rumors that he had been murdered.

—Nguyên Công Luân (Lu Tuân)

Reference: Hà Mai Viêt. "Famous Generals of the Republic of Vietnam Armed Forces" (n.p.).

See also: Trân Van Huong.

Nguyên Van Hinh (1915–)

General in the State of Vietnam, Republic of Vietnam (RVN), and French Air Force. In 1949, following the Elysée Agreements, Hinh volunteered and became the first air force officer of the State of Vietnam's Armed Forces. In 1952 he was promoted to major general, and that March he became chief of staff of the State of Vietnam's Armed Forces. In 1954, during the confrontation between Premier Ngô Đình Diêm and the southern religious sects, Hinh at first opposed Diêm. Later he asked Emperor Bao Đai to reconcile with Diêm, but Bao Đai refused. On 26 October 1954, Hinh attempted a coup d'état against Premier Diêm. The U.S. government warned Hinh that it would halt military assistance, and the coup collapsed. On 20 November 1954, Hinh left Vietnam for France to be replaced as chief of the general staff by Gen. Nguyên Van Vy. Hinh's subsequent effort to return to power failed.

After 1954 Hinh rejoined the French Air Force and was made a general, eventually becoming its deputy commander. He retired in 1969 and started a small air cargo company in which Bao Đai also invested.

—Ngô N. Trung

References: Biographical Files, Indo-China Archives, University of California at Berkeley.

See also: Bao Dai; Elysée Agreement; Ngô Đình Diêm.

Nguyên Van Linh (Nguyên Van Cúc) (1915–)

Prominent leader in the Indo-Chinese Communist Party (ICP). During the Vietnam War, Linh was in charge of mass mobilizations in the Sài Gòn–Gia Đinh Special Zone. He was secretary of the Sài Gòn City Party Committee (1972–1973 and 1975) and in December 1976 was elected to the Politburo of the Vietnamese Communist Party Central Committee and served as secretary of the Secretariat. Six years later, he was dropped from the Politburo and returned to Sài Gòn as secretary of the Party City Committee. In June 1985 he was again elected to the Politburo and in December 1986 was named general secretary of the Vietnamese Communist Party (VCP). Linh initiated the Party-led renovation in Vietnam beginning in 1986. However, as the Communist bloc collapsed, Linh was hesitant to push for more reforms. At the 1991 Seventh Party Congress, he retired on grounds of poor health, but remained an advisor to the VCP.

—Ngô N. Trung

References: Biographical Files, Indo-China Archives, University of California at Berkeley.

See also: COSVN (Central Office for South Vietnam or Trung Uong Cuc Miên Nam); Lao Đông Party; Vietnam, Socialist Republic of: 1975 to the Present.

Nguyên Van Thiêu (1923–)

Army of the Republic of Vietnam (ARVN) general; president of the Republic of Vietnam (1967–1975). Thiêu joined the Viêt Minh in 1945 but became disillusioned with their ruthless disregard for life. He then fought on the State of Vietnam side with the French. He graduated from the National Military Academy in 1949 and also attended infantry school in France and the staff college in Hà Nôi. As a battalion commander in 1954, he drove the Viêt Minh out of his native village. In 1955 Thiêu commanded the Republic of Vietnam (RVN) Military Academy in Đà Lat.

In 1957 Col. Thiêu graduated from the Command and General Staff College at Ft. Leavenworth, Kansas. In 1962 he joined the secret Cân Lao Party organized by Ngô Đình Nhu. After commanding the ARVN's 1st Infantry Division for two years, Thiêu assumed command of the 5th Infantry Division in 1963, leading one of his regiments against the presidential bodyguard in the coup that brought down Diêm. Promoted to brigadier general, he commanded IV Corps.

While serving on the Armed Forces Council in 1964, he cooperated with the coup by Air Vice-Marshal Nguyên Cao Ky, who led a faction of generals against Gen. Nguyên Khánh. Thiêu served as deputy premier in the short-lived government of Dr. Phan Huy Quát until 12 June 1965, when he became chief of state in Prime Minister Ky's new government. Together, in 1966 they made plans to strengthen the armed forces, met with President Johnson in Honolulu and Manila, successfully quashed a coup by Gen. Nguyên Chánh Thi, gained Buddhist support, and promised a constitution. Despite temporary cooperation, the two leaders were political rivals. Thiêu's determination to challenge Ky for the highest office in the 1967 elections led the Armed Forces Council to force Ky and Thiêu onto a joint ticket, giving the presidential nomination to Thiêu and the vice-presidential nomination to Ky on the basis of seniority. The Thiêu-Ky ticket won the election with 34.8 percent of the vote against ten other tickets.

During the 1968 Têt Offensive, with Thiêu away, Ky handled the counterattack in the capital. As a result, the U.S. pressed Thiêu to give more responsibility to Ky, leading to renewed bickering. Thiêu took advantage of the Têt Offensive to push through a general mobilization and doubled the size of the armed forces. Fighting charges of widespread official corruption, he launched an anticorruption campaign, but the prospect of negotiations with the Democratic Republic of Vietnam (DRV) in Paris made him more reluctant to broaden the base of his government. His initial refusal to attend the Paris peace talks was an attempt to ensure direct negotiations between the DRV and RVN and also an effort to help Richard Nixon in his presidential race against Hubert Humphrey, who had threatened Thiêu with an aid cutoff if he did not effect significant reform.

Thiêu distributed land to 50,000 families and by 1968 had gotten laws passed that froze rents and forbade landlords from evicting tenants. He also began the restoration of elected village chiefs so that, by 1969, 95 percent of villages under RVN control had elected chiefs and councils. Chiefs were given a role in national defense and control over Popular Forces (PFs) and police; they also received government financial support.

After the United States began Vietnamization, coupled with gradual withdrawal of its forces beginning in 1969, Thiêu was faced with the challenge of replacing U.S. units. In 1970 he mobilized high school and colleges students for the war effort, resulting in considerable opposition that in turn led to arrests and trials. Increased draft calls and payroll taxes produced a surge of support for the National Front for the Liberation of South Vietnam (NLF).

On 26 March 1971, Thiêu presented land to 20,000 people in an impressive ceremony following the passage of the Land-to-Tiller Act, which reduced tenancy to only 7 percent. With the U.S. Congress considering measures to end U.S.

involvement in Vietnam, in 1971 Thiêu engineered an election law to disqualify his major opponents, Air Vice-Marshall Ky and Gen. Duong Van Minh. Although the Supreme Court said Ky, who had charged Thiêu's government with corruption, could run, he chose not to. Thiêu's election made one-person rule a reality and did serious damage to his government's image.

During Operation LAM SON 719, Thiêu disappointed U.S. Military Assistance Command, Vietnam Commander Gen. Creighton Abrams by withdrawing his forces prematurely. However, PAVN units suffered heavy losses to U.S. airpower in Laos and in the 1972 Easter invasion.

As a result of the Paris peace talks, Henry Kissinger brought a draft agreement to President Thiêu, who insisted on 26 changes and accused the United States of betraying the RVN. His chief objection was that PAVN forces did not have to withdraw from the South but merely promise not to reinforce. Kissinger was furious with Thiêu for torpedoing the agreement, but following LINEBACKER II, Kissinger secured a new agreement with the DRV (the Paris accords of 23 January 1973) which, however, left approximately 145,000 PAVN troops in the South. Thiêu, who was the beneficiary of a massive last-minute airlift of military supplies (Operation ENHANCE PLUS), was threatened with a total cutoff of U.S. aid and acquiesced to heavy U.S. pressure to sign.

Gen. Trân Van Trà, a key PAVN commander in the South, wrote that it was ironic that after the cease-fire there was "not a day on which the guns fell silent" on South Vietnamese battlefields, and yet he conceded that "the puppet administration" had become "stronger politically, militarily and economically." He also pointed out that PAVN and NLF units were in disarray from their 1972 Easter Offensive as well as from fighting in Laos and Cambodia. This permitted Thiêu's forces to recapture some areas, abolish hamlet and village elections in an effort to keep them in government hands, and bar neutralist protest activities against the government. The latter was a violation of Article 11 of the Paris accords, but the Communists were violating Article 20 with regard to the neutrality of Laos and Cambodia and had sent 30,000 cadres and 70,000 troops from the DRV to build new base areas from Quang Tri Province south to the Central Highlands. To no one's surprise the "Third Indo-China War" was under way as soon as the dry season came in 1974 and Thiêu's forces drove the PAVN back in Quang Tri Province and other southern positions, even pursuing them into the Parrot's Beak region of Cambodia. This proved to be the last ARVN offensive. By the summer, the ARVN was sustaining losses of 500 men per week to reequipped PAVN and NLF forces and had to impose rigid supply controls because of severe shortages.

Thiêu was shocked when Nixon resigned in August 1974. This called into question the written and verbal promises that the U.S. would respond militarily if the RVN were threatened. Nixon had gotten Congress to set a $1 billion ceiling on military aid to the RVN, but the Senate appropriated $700 million, and only about $280 million was actually received because of shipping and other expenses. Ammunition was now rationed, 224 aircraft and 21 riverine units were placed

in storage, and only 55 percent of available transport could be fueled. Sài Gòn was in turmoil, and a People's Anti-Corruption Movement led by a Catholic priest developed into a massive antigovernment crusade. Thiêu tried to sidestep the problem and place all blame on the Communists. When the PAVN unleashed their offensive in the Central Highlands, and the Ford administration did not respond in accord with the terms of the Paris accords, Thiêu made the fateful decision to abandon the northern half of the country. To make matters worse, the government made no public announcement and had no plan for its execution. Government supporters in Military Regions I and II felt that they had been abandoned, first by the Americans and then by their own government and army. Although the ARVN put up a good fight at Xuân Lôc, it lost the battle, and four PAVN corps continued toward the capital.

On 21 April 1975, President Thiêu resigned in a tearful address to the nation. Five days later, he left Vietnam.

—Claude R. Sasso

References: Bùi Diêm, with David Chanoff. *In the Jaws of History* (1987); Pike, Douglas, ed. *The Bunker Papers: Reports to the President from Vietnam, 1967–1973* (1990). Westmoreland, William C. *A Soldier Reports* (1976).

See also: Cân Lao Nhân Vi Cách Mang Đang (Revolutionary Personalist Labor Party); Easter Offensive (Nguyên Huê Campaign); ENHANCE PLUS, Operation; Ford, Gerald R.; Humphrey, Hubert H.; Joint General Staff; Kissinger, Henry Alfred; LAM SON 719, Operation; Military Revolutionary Council; Nixon, Richard Milhous; Ngô Đình Diêm; Ngô Đình Diêm, Overthrow of; Nguyên Cao Ky; Paris Negotiations; Paris Peace Accords; Vietnam, Republic of: 1954–1975; Vietnam, Republic of: Army (PAVN).

Nguyên Van Toàn (1932–)

General in the Army of the Republic of Vietnam (ARVN) and one of its most competent commanders. Toàn participated in the November 1963 military coup that overthrow President Ngô Đình Diêm. In November 1964, he became commander of the 4th Armor Squadron, a post he held until May 1966. In June 1966 he commanded the ARVN 1st Infantry Division. From January 1967 to May 1972, he commanded the 2d Infantry Division. Toàn was promoted to major general in July 1971.

In May 1972, Toàn became commander of Military Region II. He was forced to give up this post in 1974 because of rumors relating to an inappropriate exploitation of cinnamon in Quang Ngãi Province. In March 1975 he was named commander of Military Region III, but this came too late to save the situation there. In mid-April 1975, he succeeded in stopping the Communist advance in Long Khánh Province, in what was the last significant battle of the Vietnam War. It only gained additional time for evacuation efforts. After the April 1975 Communist victory, Toàn left Vietnam.

—Ngô N. Trung

References: Biographical Files, Indo-China Archives, University of California at Berkeley.

See also: Hô Chí Minh Campaign; Ngô Đình Diêm; Ngô Đình Diêm, Overthrow of; Vietnam, Republic of: Army (ARVN).

Nguyên Van Xuân (1892–?)

General and leading figure of the State of Vietnam. An advocate of an autonomous, separate republic in the South, Xuân was named vice-premier of the Republic of Cochin China by the French on 1 June 1946. In December 1946 he left Vietnam for France, but returned to Sài Gòn in September 1947 to announce the establishment of a provisional government for a separate republic in the South and replaced Lê Van Hoach as premier. On 23 May 1948, Xuân became premier of the Provisional Government of Vietnam and also kept the post of minister of defense. In those capacities, on 5 June 1948 Xuân signed the Ha Long Bay Agreement that mandated an independent State of Vietnam and the return of Bao Đai. On 20 June 1949, Xuân's government collapsed, but he was promoted to lieutenant general and served as vice-premier and minister of defense in the next government until January 1950. On 17 September 1954, Xuân was again named vice-premier, but he resigned a week later.

—Ngô N. Trung

References: Biographical Files, Indo-China Archives, University of California at Berkeley.

See also: Bao Đai; Bollaert, Emile; France: Army.

Nguyên Viêt Thanh (?–1971)

Army of the Republic of Vietnam (ARVN) lieutenant general. Thanh was a devout Buddhist and one of the most incorruptible ARVN generals. He was killed in 1971 when the helicopter in which he was supervising a battle accidentally collided with another craft. Thanh was quite popular with the people in Military Region IV, and in the early 1980s there were reports of his apparition and sanctification. Many people secretly bought small portraits of the general to worship on their family altars.

—Nguyên Công Luân (Lu Tuân)

Reference: Hà Mai Viêt. "Famous Generals of the Republic of Vietnam Armed Forces" (n.p.).

NIAGARA, Operation (January–March 1968)

Massive U.S. air power and artillery effort directed at People's Army of Vietnam (PAVN) concentrations in Khe Sanh. By late January 1968, U.S. intelligence detected the presence of 20,000 or more PAVN soldiers in the vicinity of Khe Sanh. U.S. tactics were to allow PAVN units to surround the Marines there in order to produce the most spectacular targets of the war for U.S. firepower. NIAGARA I was an intelligence-gathering effort to pinpoint targets; NIAGARA II was the destruction of these by aircraft and artillery.

Intelligence concerning target selection was generated by remote sensors, ground and aerial observers, photo reconnaissance, crater analyses, infrared imagery, analysis of intercepted communications, and other means. U.S. Marine and Army Special Forces reconnaissance patrols, Central Intelligence Agency personnel, and the MACV Studies and Observation Group all provided input.

During the night of 3–4 February 1968, sensor arrays indicated up to 2,000 PAVN troops in the vicinity of Marine hill outposts near Khe Sanh. This information was used to plot and execute artillery fire against PAVN troop concentrations. PAVN units were devastated, and the intended attack was broken up in one of the earliest examples of a ground attack thwarted on the basis of sensor data.

Khe Sanh had top-priority claim on all U.S. air assets in Southeast Asia. Gen. Westmoreland personally planned B-52 strikes launched from Guam, Thailand, and Okinawa. Meanwhile, the Marines and U.S. Air Force provided fighter-bombers from bases within South Vietnam, and U.S. Navy aviators flew sorties from aircraft carriers in the South China Sea. South Vietnamese and U.S. Army aviation also provided aerial support. Usually there were fighter-bombers overhead at Khe Sanh around the clock. Such aircraft flew 16,769 sorties and delivered 31,238 tons of ordnance in defense of Khe Sanh. B-52s in ARC LIGHT strikes attacked troop concentrations, supply areas, and bunker complexes. To catch PAVN survivors above ground, artillerymen at Khe Sanh often placed artillery fire into the ARC LIGHT target area a few minutes after the departure of the heavy bombers. ARC LIGHT attacks delivered a total of 59,542 tons of munitions during the siege. Westmoreland maintained that ordnance delivered by the B-52s is what defeated the PAVN at Khe Sanh.

U.S. forces expended nearly 100,000 tons of munitions at a cost of $1 billion. Photo reconnaissance and direct observation credited NIAGARA with having caused 4,705 secondary explosions, 1,288 PAVN deaths, destruction of 1,061 structures, and damage to 158; 891 bunkers were claimed destroyed, with another 99 damaged. Total PAVN casualties were estimated at 10,000.

—Peter W. Brush

Reference: Nalty, Bernard C. *Air Power and the Fight for Khe Sanh* (1973).

See also: Air Power, Role in War; ARC LIGHT (B-52 Raids); Artillery Fire Doctrine; Khe Sanh, Battles of; Military Assistance Command, Vietnam (MACV); Studies and Observation Group (SOG); Westmoreland, William Childs; Vietnam, Democratic Republic of: Army (People's Army of Vietnam [PAVN]).

Nitze, Paul Henry (1907–)

U.S. assistant secretary of defense, 1961–1963; secretary of the Navy; 1963–1967; deputy secretary of defense, 1967–1969. In April 1967, Nitze and Secretary of Defense Robert McNamara proposed that the United States cease bombing above the 20th parallel in order to begin negotiations, but President Johnson rejected this. In June 1967, Nitze was appointed deputy secretary of defense and two months later joined McNamara in formulating the so-called San Antonio formula, a conciliatory proposal modifying the Johnson administration's previous demand for the People's Army of Vietnam (PAVN) de-escalation before peace negotiations could begin, which was rejected by Hà Nôi in October.

Nitze was a member of an ad hoc study group formed to review the request for an additional 200,000 troops following Têt 1968. He warned that any increase in U.S. troops could lead to a direct confrontation with China and could jeopardize U.S. commitments worldwide. He recommended instead a strengthening of the Army of the Republic of Vietnam

(ARVN) while withdrawing U.S. forces. Although the study group rejected his warning, on 31 March Johnson announced de-escalation. Nitze resigned from the Defense Department in January 1969.

—Robert G. Mangrum

References: Davidson, Phillip B. *Vietnam at War: The History 1946–1975* (1988); Herring, George C. *America's Longest War: The U.S. and Vietnam 1950–1975* (1986); *International Who's Who, 1984–85.*

See also: Acheson, Dean G.; Containment Policy; Johnson, Lyndon Baines; Kennedy, John Fitzgerald; McNamara, Robert S.

Nixon, Richard Milhous (1913–1994)

U.S. congressman, 1947–1951; U.S. senator, 1951–1953; vice-president, 1953–1961; president of the United States, 1969–1974. In October 1953, Nixon visited French Indo-China as part of his first overseas trip as vice-president. He came away convinced that France's troubles in the region stemmed from their failure to win the hearts and minds of the Indo-Chinese peoples. Privately concerned that the Eisenhower administration was not doing enough to prevent the spread of communism in Southeast Asia, Nixon was among the earliest supporters of a Southeast Asia Treaty Organization (SEATO), with the United States at its head.

Nixon vociferously argued for U.S. military intervention in April 1954, when the French were trapped at Điên Biên Phu. At a National Security Council (NSC) meeting, Nixon spoke in favor of a proposal put forth by Adm. Arthur Radford, chairman of the Joint Chiefs of Staff, to bomb and destroy Viêt Minh positions with three small tactical atomic bombs. Code-named Operation VULTURE, the plan was rejected by Eisenhower. Nixon then suggested that the United States send more technicians and supplies to Vietnam, but despite Nixon's vigor, Eisenhower refused to intervene. The situation cemented in Nixon's mind the need to halt what he viewed as Communist aggression in the region. Nixon came away from a June 1956 meeting with Republic of Vietnam (RVN) President Ngô Đình Diêm feeling that, despite Diêm's excesses, the South Vietnamese leader was capable of establishing order in his nation.

After his devastating loss to John F. Kennedy in the 1960 presidential election and subsequent failure in California's 1962 gubernatorial race, Nixon emerged in 1968 as the unlikely Republican candidate for president. The war in Vietnam was potentially the major issue in the 1968 campaign. Nixon had nothing to gain from meeting the issue head-on, and he refused to do so. Concentrating his efforts on denouncing President Johnson's record on law and order, Nixon would only promise that he had a "secret plan" to end the war—a plan that he later admitted to an interviewer never existed. The tactic worked; even Johnson's decision to stop the bombing of the North less than a week before the election could not turn the tide against Nixon.

The Nixon presidency must be seen through the prism of Vietnam. On many occasions, Nixon wrote or stated that ending the Vietnam War was his "first priority"; détente with the People's Republic of China and the Soviet Union would

follow. Yet he did not seriously entertain an escalation of the conventional war in 1969. Indeed, Nixon was convinced that Hô Chí Minh could achieve his objective of a unified Vietnam under Communist rule if the United States continued to prosecute the war as it had under Johnson. As a result, Nixon drastically changed U.S. military strategy in Vietnam. Refusing for the moment to order the reinstatement of the bombing of the North, Nixon instead looked to withdraw U.S. troops from combat and protect that withdrawal by widening the war into Cambodia and Laos. Nixon hoped this strategy would force the North Vietnamese to entertain serious negotiations.

Nixon's plan was immediately put to the test in February 1969 when Hà Nôi launched its spring offensive. Gen. Creighton Abrams asked Nixon, as he had asked Johnson many times before, to bomb North Vietnamese supply lines in Cambodia. Unlike Johnson, Nixon supported the plan from the start. Nixon viewed Southeast Asia not as four separate countries, but as one theater of war. He had come to believe that the key to winning the war was in the destruction of supply lines in Laos and Cambodia. He gave the approval for Operation MENU, a wide plan for bombing suspected Communist sanctuaries in Cambodia. Nixon ordered that the bombings be kept secret to skirt what would be certain worldwide condemnation for bombing a technically neutral nation. Operation MENU succeeded only in driving the North Vietnamese deeper into Cambodia. It also began the chain of abuses of power known collectively as Watergate, as Secretary of State Henry Kissinger ordered phone taps of several White House aides in an effort to find out who leaked the story about the bombing to *The New York Times.*

Nixon combined the secret bombings with attempts to show the world that U.S. commitment to the war was winding down. In June he ordered an immediate withdrawal of 25,000 troops from Vietnam. In July he articulated what became known as the Nixon Doctrine: Unless directly attacked, the United States should not commit its troops to the defense of a third-world country. Hoping that these moves would show his good faith, Nixon secretly gave the North Vietnamese a 1 November deadline to show significant steps toward peace. However, Nixon's moves did not satisfy the antiwar movement at home, whose 15 October and 15 November Moratoria against the War were huge successes. As a result, Nixon was forced to let his deadline go by unchallenged. In an effort to regain the initiative, on 2 November Nixon spoke directly to his middle-class supporters—those whom he dubbed the "great, silent majority"—and begged them to help him control dissent in the nation. By the end of 1969, Nixon had promised a further withdrawal of 50,000 troops by 15 April 1970.

However, Nixon's response to events threatened to widen the scope of the war just as withdrawals were becoming significant. Nixon argued that the advent of the Democratic Republic of Vietnam (DRV) attack on Cambodia, begun in the wake of the overthrow of the Sihanouk government on 11 March 1970, convinced him to take further military action there. Other observers note the failure of the MENU bomb ings as the cause. Either way, the 26 March decision to send U.S. troops into Cambodia to search out and destroy Communist sanctuaries along the border was consistent with Nixon's desire to support his withdrawals by cutting off North Vietnam's western supply route. This decision was the most fateful of Nixon's presidency. He tried to soften the blow by announcing on 20 April the withdrawal of 150,000 more U.S. troops before the end of 1971. However, his 30 April announcement of what had become known as the Cambodian incursion led to a firestorm of protest on college campuses, culminating in the deaths of student protesters at Kent State University and Jackson State University.

The Cambodian incursion proved little, except that the Army of the Republic of Vietnam (ARVN) was not ready to fight on its own. In an attempt to rectify that situation and take one more step toward cutting supply lines, Nixon sanctioned an offensive into Laos (LAM SON 719) using only ARVN troops in January 1971. The initiative began on 8 February, but within six weeks ARVN troops were forced to withdraw, leaving the Hô Chí Minh Trail virtually intact. The Laotian disaster stiffened Nixon's resolve and may have contributed to the harshness of his response to the 13 June 1971 release of the Pentagon Papers in *The New York Times*. Yet despite the criticism that followed in the press, Nixon would not be rushed. Convinced that his February 1972 rapprochement with the People's Republic of China would scare their DRV clients back to the peace table, Nixon continued to withdraw troops and wait.

However, for the fourth straight year, Hà Nôi did not bow to Nixon's tactics. The DRV spurned Nixon's request for further talks and, on 30 March 1972, launched the largest offensive of the war to that point. Furious, Nixon on 1 April authorized Operation LINEBACKER, bombing within 25 miles of the Demilitarized Zone. Two weeks later, he expanded the bombing zone up to the 20th parallel. On 8 May, he ordered the mining of Hai Phòng Harbor, certain that only a massive show of force would convince the North to negotiate. Kissinger and Lê Đuc Tho resumed their peace talks within a month of the start of LINEBACKER. By late fall, the talks were in earnest.

It was soon clear that RVN President Nguyên Van Thiêu was the only party who could not agree to a truce. In an effort to gain his support, Nixon secretly promised Thiêu that if the North Vietnamese broke the truce, the United States would recommit troops to South Vietnam. But when the North balked at changes in a document already agreed to, Nixon finally had enough. At Camp David, he told Chairman of the Joint Chiefs of Staff Adm. Thomas Moorer, "This is your chance to use military power effectively to win the war, and if you don't, I'll consider you responsible." On 17 December, Nixon ordered LINEBACKER II. Also known as the "Christmas Bombing," it dropped 36,000 tons of bombs in 11 days. On 26 December, Hà Nôi signaled it wanted to resume negotiations; on 9 January 1973 in Paris, Secretary of State William Rogers initialed the truce.

Nixon understood that the truce was a particularly weak one, writing later that the only way he had been able to get the North to buy into the deal was to allow them to keep a military presence in the South. As a result, Nixon never believed that the truce meant that the United States was to stop sending monies and supplies to the RVN, which he continued to do until the 30 June 1973 Cooper-Church Amendment precluded him from doing so. Nevertheless, Nixon's memoranda make it clear that he fully expected to uphold his secret pledge to Thiêu and to push the Congress to recommit troops when the DRV violated the peace. However, the 7 November passage of the War Powers Act would have precluded Nixon from making such a move. His 9 August 1974 resignation in the wake of the Watergate investigation left such a decision to his successor, Gerald R. Ford.

Nixon believed that his policies had won what could have been a lasting peace had Congress not weakened his hand or that of his successor in terms of enforcing that settlement. In a 1985 defense of his Vietnam policies entitled *No More Vietnams*, Nixon argued that "In the end, Vietnam was lost on the political front in the United States, not on the battlefront in Southeast Asia." Nixon was also convinced that his numerous escalations of the war, far from being a useless waste of life, shortened that conflict. He later told a British audience that his only regret about expanding the war into Cambodia was not having done it sooner.

Despite his concentration on the war and other foreign policy initiatives, Nixon and his staff developed innovative proposals for welfare reform and for new financial relationships between state and local government. However, these initiatives were defeated by a Congress had become increasingly alienated from Nixon's administration because of his heavy-handed conduct of the war. Nixon made his mark largely in foreign affairs. The success of his overtures to the PRC and the USSR was based largely upon his success in playing these nations against the other, as well as against the North Vietnamese. Nixon called this "linkage diplomacy." As a condition of doing business, Nixon required that the PRC and USSR lessen their overt commitment to North Vietnam. Although both states continued publicly to support Hô Chí Minh, the amount of military and financial aid they gave to North Vietnam decreased dramatically after 1972.

Following his resignation, Nixon played the role of elder statesman, writing eight books between 1978 and 1994. His *No More Vietnams* (1985) was a thoughtful defense of his administration's policies, as well as an acerbic critique of Congress's refusal to fund the requests of the Ford administration for further aid to South Vietnam in 1975. His successors in the White House kept Nixon informed on major foreign policy initiatives; Ronald Reagan and George Bush even solicited his advice several issues.

—John Robert Greene

References: Ambrose, Stephen E. *Nixon* (1987); Greene, John Robert. *The Limits of Power: The Nixon and Ford Administrations* (1992); Litwak, Robert S. *Détente and the Nixon Doctrine: American Foreign Policy and the Pursuit of Stability, 1969–1976* (1984); Nixon, Richard. *No More Vietnams* (1985).

See also: Abrams, Creighton; Amnesty; Antiwar Movement, United States; Cambodian Incursion; Cooper-Church Amendment;

Eisenhower, Dwight David; Federal Bureau of Investigation (FBI); Fishhook; Ford, Gerald R.; Kent State University; Kissinger, Henry Alfred; LAM SON 719, Operation; LINEBACKER I, Operation; LINEBACKER II, Operation; Madman Strategy; MENU, Operation; Midway Island Conference; Mitchell, John Newton; Moorer, Thomas H.; Moratorium to End the War in Vietnam; Nguyên Van Thiêu; Nixon Doctrine; Paris Negotiations; Paris Peace Accords; Parrot's Beak; Pentagon Papers and Trial; Radford, Arthur W.; Rogers, William Pierce; United States: Department of Justice; Vietnamization; VULTURE, Operation; War Powers Act; Washington Special Actions Group (WSAG); Watergate.

Nixon Doctrine (July 1969)

Foreign policy statement by President Nixon. In July 1969, Nixon began his first foreign trip as president with a stop at the Guam Naval Air Station, where he promised "we will keep our treaty commitments" to Asian nations, but cautioned that "as far as the problems of internal security [and] military defense, except for the threat of a major power involving nuclear weapons, the United States … has a right to expect that this problem will be increasingly handled by … the Asian nations themselves." Many interpreted the statement, which the press quickly dubbed the "Nixon Doctrine," as meaning that Nixon planned to abandon Vietnam once U.S. troops had withdrawn. Nixon later argued in his *Memoirs* that such interpretations were false and that the doctrine was meant to be a platform that would allow the United States to "play a responsible role" in helping non-Communist nations win and defend their independence.

—John Robert Greene

References: Greene, John Robert. *The Limits of Power: The Nixon and Ford Administrations* (1992); Nixon, Richard M. *Memoirs* (1978).
See also: Nixon, Richard Milhous; Nguyên Van Thiêu; United States: Involvement in Vietnam, 1969–1973; Vietnamization.

Nolting, Frederick, Jr. (1911–1989)

U.S. ambassador to the Republic of Vietnam (RVN), 1961–1963. Nolting had no knowledge of or firsthand experience with Asia. His appointment by President Kennedy to succeed Elbridge Durbrow in Sài Gòn signaled a tactical shift in policy. Dealings with President Ngô Đình Diêm changed from candid exchanges to cordial relations. Backed by Gen. Paul D. Harkins, commander of the Military Assistance Command, Vietnam (MACV), the gracious Nolting, who disliked controversy, supported the regime completely. He applauded the Strategic Hamlet program and upheld the RVN's account of the battle of Âp Bac (1963) in a bitter clash with resident correspondents.

Nolting identified with the South Vietnamese upper class and believed that political reforms were less significant than effective operations. Consequently, he criticized the country's dissenters for their unwillingness to make common cause with the regime. Opposed to an enlarged U.S. military involvement, he perceived the central issue facing U.S. policymakers as political in nature. Instead of coercion, he advocated placing faith in Diêm's ability to secure the nation against the Viêt Công.

In 1963 the State Department ordered Nolting to press President Diêm to reconcile with Buddhist dissidents. He declined and departed for a European vacation in the midst of a developing crisis. In his absence, William Truehart, an embassy representative, subverted Nolting's conciliatory approach and cautioned Diêm that he risked forfeiting U.S. assistance if he continued to suppress the Buddhists. In a series of heated White House meetings, Kennedy reproved Nolting for his absence and chastised him for faulty intelligence. He then dispatched the ambassador back to his post with instructions to win Diêm's cooperation. Still, Nolting remained hesitant to pressure Diêm, and the crisis intensified.

The Kennedy administration, by now dissatisfied with Nolting's performance and reporting, replaced him with Henry Cabot Lodge, Jr. Nolting, preoccupied with family concerns and a desire to enter international banking, was ready to resign and return to the United States by summer 1963. His 1988 memoir is highly critical of the Kennedy administration while praising Diêm.

—Rodney J. Ross

References: Halberstam, David. *The Best and the Brightest* (1973); Hammer, Ellen J. *A Death in November: America in Vietnam, 1963* (1987); Karnow, Stanley. *Vietnam: A History* (1983); Nolting, Frederick. *From Trust to Tragedy: The Political Memoirs of Frederick Nolting, Kennedy's Ambassador to Diem's Vietnam* (1988).
See also: Âp Bac, Battle of; Durbrow, Elbridge; Harkins, Paul D.; Kennedy, John Fitzgerald; Lodge, Henry Cabot, Jr.; Ngô Đình Diêm; United States: Involvement in Vietnam, 1954–1965.

Nông Đuc Manh (1940–)

Leader in the Vietnamese Communist Party (VCP) and the Socialist Republic of Vietnam (SRV). In June 1991, during the Seventh Party Congress, Manh was appointed to the Political Bureau. In July 1992, he was elected deputy to the Ninth National Assembly, and that September he was elected chairman of the National Assembly. Manh is a protegé of former VCP Gen. Secretary Nguyên Van Linh; he has never denied rumors that he is a son of Hô Chí Minh.

—Ngô N. Trung

References: Biographical Files, Indo-China Archives, University of California at Berkeley.
See also: Hô Chí Minh; Lao Đông Party; Nguyên Van Linh (Nguyên Van Cúc); Vietnam, Socialist Republic of: 1975 to the Present.

North Vietnam. *See* Vietnam, Democratic Republic of: 1945–1954; Vietnam, Democratic Republic of: 1954–1975.

North Vietnamese Army (NVA). *See* Vietnam, Democratic Republic of, Army (People's Army of Vietnam [PAVN]).

Nùng. *See* Montagnards.

Nurses. *See* United States: Nurses.

O

O'Daniel, John W. (1894–1975)

U.S. Army general and commander of the Military Assistance and Advisory Group (MAAG), Indo-China (March 1954–October 1955). O'Daniel's involvement with Vietnam began as commanding general of the U.S. Army in the Pacific. In June 1953, the Joint Chiefs of Staff (JCS) sent him to Vietnam to assess French requirements for military aid. O'Daniel returned with an optimistic report and support for the Navarre Plan.

During his second visit in November 1953, O'Daniel convinced French Gen. Henri Navarre to accept four U.S. officers on his staff and permit a small increase in the size of the MAAG, then under the command of Maj. Gen. Thomas Trapnell. O'Daniel reported "real military progress" to the JCS. Army Chief of Staff Gen. Matthew B. Ridgeway, however, thought O'Daniel's report overly optimistic.

In February 1954 O'Daniel visited the French position at Điên Biên Phu. Several aspects of the French position disturbed him. French bunkers did not appear strong, and he was bothered that the French had failed to secure the surrounding high ground. The French initially objected to O'Daniel being named to replace Trapnell as MAAG chief and insisted he be demoted to major general so he would not be equal in rank to Navarre. O'Daniel was willing to accept a temporary reduction, but Ridgeway objected strongly. O'Daniel finally assumed command of the MAAG on 31 March, weeks before Điên Biên Phu fell.

When O'Daniel assumed command of the MAAG, its primary mission was to provide equipment support. O'Daniel pushed for authority to reorganize and train the Vietnamese Army. He believed that a loose interpretation of the MAAG's responsibility to perform "end use checks of American equipment" could be stretched to cover training. Ridgeway, however, gave strict instructions to "make no commitments whatsoever in regard to training."

In August 1954 the South Vietnamese government requested U.S. assistance in evacuating from the North those Vietnamese who did not wish to remain under Communist control. O'Daniel established the Evacuation Staff Group, headquartered in Sài Gòn. On 16 August, U.S. Navy Task Force 90 began evacuating French and Vietnamese from Hai Phòng.

In November 1954 the internal political situation in Sài Gòn became unstable. Rumors were rife that South Vietnamese Chief of Staff Gen. Nguyên Van Hinh was about to stage a coup against the government of Ngô Đình Diêm. Because of the delicacy of the situation, U.S. Ambassador Donald Heath ordered all U.S. personnel to avoid contact with Hinh. However, on 12 November O'Daniel, convinced that Hinh was only hours away from launching the coup, visited Hinh and impressed upon him the negative U.S. reaction such a course of action would trigger. O'Daniel left the meeting convinced that he had derailed the coup, but Heath was furious because his orders had been disobeyed.

On 12 February 1955, O'Daniel finally received authority to reorganize and train the South Vietnamese Army. Under the terms of the Collins-Ely Agreement, all U.S. and French advisory training personnel were to come under O'Daniel's command by March. O'Daniel tried to convince President Diêm to allow a sizable French combat force to remain in South Vietnam, but Diêm believed that the French could not be relied upon and should leave as soon as possible.

O'Daniel's advisory effort focused on preparing the South Vietnamese to resist a conventional attack from North Vietnam. He believed that an army so equipped and organized would also be capable of performing internal security. After he retired from the Army in 1955, O'Daniel founded the American Friends of Vietnam, a group that lobbied effectively for U.S. support of the Diêm government.

—David T. Zabecki

Reference: Spector, Ronald H. *Advice and Support: The Early Years, 1941–1960* (1983).

See also: American Friends of Vietnam; Điên Biên Phu, Battle of; Navarre, Henri Eugène; Navarre Plan; Ngô Đình Diêm; Nguyên Van Hinh; Ridgeway, Matthew B.

Office of Strategic Services (OSS)

Predecessor to the Central Intelligence Agency (CIA); it assisted the Vietnamese in their fight against the Japanese in World War II. In August 1941, President Franklin D. Roosevelt created the Office of the Coordinator of Information, headed by 58-year-old William Joseph "Wild Bill" Donovan. In May 1942, Donovan's group was renamed the Office of Strategic Services (OSS).

As was their practice worldwide during World War II, OSS operatives in Indo-China sought contact with any group fighting the Axis. Their earliest contact in Vietnam was Cal-Texaco executive Lawrence Gordon. Throughout 1941 and 1942, Gordon traveled across Vietnam, pretending to be a free-lance oil agent, and set up a vast network of spies, most of them Vietnamese and former Cal-Texaco workers.

In 1942 Gordon was joined by two Americans—former Cal-Texaco employee Harry V. Bernard and Chinese American Frank "Frankie" Tan. By 1943 the group had established radio-listening posts all over Indo-China and was providing vital information to, among others, Gen. Claire Chennault's 14th Air Force in China. Concurrently, the OSS sought to undermine the Japanese by supporting nationalist guerrillas in Indo-China. In Vietnam it soon established ties with Viêt Minh forces led by Hô Chí Minh and Vô Nguyên Giáp. Throughout the war and immediately afterward, OSS agents advocated U.S. support for Vietnamese independence from France. Although many high administration officials saw these reports, and Donovan leaned in this direction, it is not clear what President Roosevelt intended. President Truman was clearly less sympathetic.

In March 1945, the previously docile French in Vietnam, led by Gen. Marcel Alessandri, planned a revolt against Japanese occupation. The Japanese struck first and arrested most of the French. This Japanese victory greatly harmed OSS efforts and left the Viêt Minh as the only viable anti-Japanese force in Indo-China. Hô, accompanied by OSS agents, entered Hà Nôi on 19 August 1945. When puppet emperor Bao Đai abdicated on 25 August, Hô's "pro-U.S." forces seemed to have won an important victory.

At the Potsdam Conference, however, Allied leaders thwarted Viêt Minh hopes by deciding that the Nationalist Chinese would occupy northern Vietnam while the British would occupy the South. During this occupation, the Chinese tolerated Hô's government in the North, but the British soon returned control of the South to the French. The cordial OSS–Viêt Minh relationship continued, but the accidental Viêt Minh killing of Lt. Col. Dewey in Sài Gòn on 26 September 1945 foretold the tragic future of U.S.-Vietnamese relations. Hô was "shaken" by the death of an American at Viêt Minh hands while he was seeking U.S. support. In effect, Dewey became the first U.S. serviceman to die at the hands of Hô's soldiers.

On 1 October 1945, President Truman disbanded Donovan's 12,600-member organization, replacing it in early 1946 with the Central Intelligence Group, and in 1947, with the CIA.

—William Head

References: Boettcher, Thomas. *Vietnam: The Valor and the Sorrow* (1985); Karnow, Stanley. *Vietnam: A History* (1983); Smith, Ralph Harris. *OSS: The Secret History of America's First Central Intelligence Agency* (1972).
See also: Dewey, Albert Peter; Central Intelligence Agency (CIA); Donovan, William Joseph; Hô Chí Minh; Patti, Archimedes L. A.; Roosevelt, Franklin Delano; Truman, Harry S; United States: Involvement in Indo-China through 1954; Viêt Minh (Viêt Nam Đôc Lâp Đông Minh Hôi [Vietnam Independence League]); Vô Nguyên Giáp.

Olds, Robin (1922–)

U.S. Air Force fighter pilot and commander of the 8th Tactical Fighter Wing (1966–1967). He became a career Air Force officer and a triple ace, having shot down 17 enemy aircraft during World War II and the Vietnam War combined. During the Vietnam War, he flew a F-4 Phantom II and, using air-to-air missiles, shot down two MiG-17 and two MiG-21 aircraft over North Vietnam. As commander of the U.S. 8th Tactical Fighter Wing at Ubon Royal Thai Air Force Base, Thailand, from September 1966 until December 1967, Col. Olds devised and led Operation BOLO, in which U.S. Air Force jets downed seven MiG-21's over North Vietnam on 2 January 1967. Promoted brigadier general in June 1968, Olds served as commandant of cadets at the U.S. Air Force Academy before retiring from the Air Force in June 1973.

—James H. Willbanks

References: Berger, Carl, ed. *The United States Air Force in Southeast Asia, 1961–1973* (1977); Hanak, Walter, ed. *The United States Air Force in Southeast Asia—Aces and Aerial Victories, 1965–1973* (1976).
See also: Airplanes, Allied and Democratic Republic of Vietnam; Air Power, Role in War; BOLO, Operation; United States: Air Force.

OMEGA, Project (August 1966–1 November 1967)

Designation for U.S. Special Forces (SF) operation headquartered at Ban Mê Thuôt to fill a growing need for military intelligence. Established in August 1966, comprising personnel from the 5th Special Forces Group, and controlled by Detachment B-50 on orders from I Field Force, the OMEGA unit was committed to combat on 11 September and created to supplement Project DELTA. OMEGA supplied corps-level special reconnaissance and long-range patrol capabilities, mainly in the Central Highlands of II Corps Tactical Zone (II CTZ).

OMEGA operated within the framework of the Civilian Irregular Defense Group (CIDG) program. Assuming that well-trained, dependable, ethnic minorities would be most successful in this type of mission, it recruited indigenous troops from the Montagnards and Chinese Nùngs.

Organizationally a smaller version of DELTA, OMEGA consisted of a reconnaissance element and a reaction force (a combined total of about 600 men). A modified B Team served as an advisory command. Reconnaissance responsibilities were divided. Eight reconnaissance teams with six members each (two SF and four indigenous personnel) carried out patrols in specified reconnaissance zones to gather intelligence and conduct terrain analysis. Four roadrunner teams of four scouts each (all indigenous personnel)—dressed in Communist uniforms and equipped with appropriate weapons and documents—operated for extended periods in Communist-controlled territory.

The reaction force provided a reinforcing component of a battalion of three Mobile Strike Force Command ("Mike Force") companies, each with 25 SF members and 150 highly trained, airborne-qualified CIDG soldiers. Only later did Republic of Vietnam Special Forces participate. These units gathered information, helped extract compromised teams, and called in air strikes.

One of the most important contributions of the SF to the war effort, OMEGA yielded valuable intelligence and negatively affected its enemy's morale. On 1 November 1967, the assets of Detachment B-50 were transferred to Military Assistance Command, Vietnam's Studies and Observation Group (MACV-SOG).

—Paul S. Daum, with Trevor Curran

References: Kelly, Francis J. *U.S. Army Special Forces, 1961–1971* (1973); Simpson, Charles M., III. *Inside the Green Berets: The First Thirty Years, a History of the U.S. Army Special Forces* (1983); Stanton, Shelby L. *Green Berets at War: U.S. Army Special Forces in Southeast Asia, 1956–1975* (1985); —. *Special Forces at War: An Illustrated History, Southeast Asia 1957–1975* (1990).
See also: Civilian Irregular Defense Group (CIDG); DELTA, Project; Mobile Strike Force Commands; Montagnards; SIGMA, Project; United States: Special Forces.

Operation Plan 34A (OPLAN 34A)

U.S.–backed covert harassment and intelligence-gathering efforts conducted along the Democratic Republic of Vietnam (DRV) coastline. In November 1963 President Kennedy approved a new covert action program in Vietnam, called Operation Plan 34A (OPLAN 34A), that would include minor raids by mercenaries and South Vietnamese commandos along the northern coastline of the DRV. The commandos penetrated Communist territory, usually at night, and blew up defensive positions and supply dumps, attacked coastal radar transmitters, and kidnapped individuals marked by intelligence as worthy of interrogation in the South.

Covert U.S. naval operations mounted by the Navy and Marines, known as DeSoto missions, had been conducted since the 1950s against the Soviet Union, North Korea, and the People's Republic of China. OPLAN 34A were covert intelligence missions. Electronic intelligence (ELINT) vessels surveyed northern coastal radar and other electronic installations above the 17th parallel, monitored transmissions, determined radio and radar frequencies used, and pinpointed locations of transmission units.

The first DeSoto mission against the DRV came in 1962. In 1964 the destroyer *Maddox* began conducting electronic surveillance along the northern coast. Additionally, DeSoto missions were to search for ships bringing supplies south to Viêt Công units, counter seaborne resupply efforts by the DRV's Group 759, and record navigational information for use by OPLAN 34A commando teams landing along the DRV coastline. Those teams regularly traveled to the North from their base at Đà Nang using U.S.-built boats, called "Swifts," sometimes captained by Norwegian skippers. These boats were found to be too slow and so were phased out and replaced with Norwegian-built craft, called "Nasties," captained by Americans. These craft were armed with twin .50-caliber machine guns on the deckhouse and a combined .50-caliber and 81-mm mortar aft. The crew consisted of an officer and five enlisted men. Occasionally U.S. patrol torpedo (PT) boats were also used.

During the night of 30–31 July 1964, an OPLAN 34A group conducted raids against two small islands, Hòn Ngu and Hòn Mc. The strike force was unable to land any commandos, but did fire on island installations before returning to base. The *Maddox*, 120 miles away, monitored resulting radar and radio transmissions.

On 2 August the *Maddox* moved to no closer than five miles of Hòn Me when the small North Vietnamese Navy reacted with a PT boat attack against her. On 4 August came a possible second strike against the *Maddox* and a sister ship, the destroyer *C. Turner Joy*. In both cases, the destroyers were supported by planes from the carrier *Ticonderoga*. These incidents, growing out of OPLAN 34A and DeSoto missions, gave rise to the Tonkin Gulf incidents and the Tonkin Gulf Resolution of 10 August, the functional equivalent of a declaration of war.

—Cecil B. Currey

References: Marolda, Edward J., and G. Wesley Pryce III. *A Short History of the United States and the Southeast Asian Conflict, 1950–1975* (1984); Preston, Anthony. "The Naval War in Vietnam" (1985).

See also: DeSoto Missions; ELINT (Electronic Intelligence); Kennedy, John Fitzgerald; Morse, Wayne Lyman; Quach Tom; Tonkin Gulf Incidents; Tonkin Gulf Resolution; Vietnam, Republic of: Commandos; Vietnam, Republic of: Navy (VNN).

Order of Battle Dispute (1967)

In 1965 the United States sent ground troops into Vietnam without having adequate intelligence on the forces U.S. troops were to fight. When Military Assistance Command, Vietnam (MACV) began to issue monthly reports on Communist organization and strength in South Vietnam— order of battle—the figures were at first incomplete.

As intelligence improved during 1966, the figures for Communist regular combat units came to be reasonably accurate. Order of battle reports, however, contained figures for three other types of Communist personnel: (1) "combat support" or "administrative services": those people handling supply, transport, medical care, and other support functions; (2) "Political cadres" or "political infrastructure": local administrators, tax collectors, police, and other political operatives in the areas of South Vietnam that were partially or wholly under Communist control; (3) "irregulars": a variety of guerrilla and militia organizations, of which the two having the least capability for conventional military combat would eventually become the subject of particular controversy—the "self-defense" militia in Communist-controlled villages and the "secret self-defense" militia in government-controlled villages.

Most Communist personnel in South Vietnam fell in these three categories, but no serious study of their numbers was made before 1966. For lack of anything better, officers responsible for the order of battle reports repeated each month the previous month's unfounded estimate.

By early 1967, U.S. intelligence officers (mostly in military intelligence in Vietnam, but also at Central Intelligence Agency [CIA] headquarters in the United States) had compiled enough information to make realistic estimates for all categories. This created a major problem. The new estimates, especially for administrative services and irregulars, were far higher than the old ones. Public support for the war was already shaky in the United States, and a dramatic increase in the official estimate of total Communist personnel in South Vietnam could have serious repercussions.

There followed a series of acrimonious conferences at which the CIA argued for comparatively high estimates, and MACV intelligence argued for much lower estimates. In September 1967, an agreement was worked out under which the definitions used in compiling the estimates were drastically changed. U.S. intelligence simply stopped estimating the number of people in the self-defense and secret self-defense militia. Estimates for the "infrastructure" continued to be compiled but were no longer treated as part of the military order of battle. Having dropped these categories, MACV accepted higher estimates of some others (though not as high as CIA estimates) without any increase in the overall total.

The 1968 Tết Offensive came a few months later. Debate continues between those who say the course of combat during Tết proved that MACV estimates had been valid and those who say that Tết proved that MACV had been grossly underestimating Communist strength.

Samuel Adams, a CIA analyst of order of battle issues, was one of the CIA negotiators at the 1967 conferences. He believed that the estimates agreed upon at the September conference had been incomplete and inaccurate to an extent that caused dangerous complacency as Têt approached. After retiring from the CIA, Adams made his view public in a May 1975 *Harper's Magazine* article. The story aired on a 23 January 1982 CBS documentary, "The Uncounted Enemy: A Vietnam Deception." It argued that the intelligence figures had been deliberately falsified and that Gen. William Westmoreland bore part of the blame.

Westmoreland filed a libel suit for $120 million against CBS, several CBS employees, and Adams. CBS presented considerable evidence for the central thesis of its program: that military intelligence officers under Westmoreland's command had reported fewer Communist personnel of all types than were actually present in South Vietnam. Several such officers testified as witnesses for CBS. Col. Gains Hawkins, who was immediately responsible for MACV's overall estimates, testified that under pressure from his superiors he had ordered his subordinates to lower their estimates in mid-1967. He was not aware of any evidence justifying lower estimates; he said that the evidence suggested that the estimates were already too low. On the witness stand, he described the estimates that MACV had presented to other intelligence agencies in August 1967 as "crap."

For the most part, Gen. Westmoreland had not been directly involved. His immediate subordinates had passed down the chain of command what they believed to be his wishes, without necessarily consulting him in detail. CBS was able to present two witnesses, however—Gen. Joseph McChristian and Col. Hawkins—who in May 1967 had presented directly to Westmoreland more accurate figures that they wanted to substitute for the underestimates in the order of battle.

On 18 February 1985, Westmoreland withdrew his suit in return for a carefully worded statement in which CBS did not retract or apologize for anything in the broadcast, but said that it "never intended to assert, and does not believe, that Gen. Westmoreland was unpatriotic or disloyal in performing his duties as he saw them."

—Edwin E. Moise

References: Adams, Sam. *War of Numbers: An Intelligence Memoir* (1994); Brewin, Bob, and Sydney Shaw. *Vietnam on Trial: Westmoreland vs. CBS* (1987); Moise, Edwin. "Why Westmoreland Gave Up" (1985).

See also: Adams, Samuel A.; Central Intelligence Agency (CIA); Davidson, Phillip Buford, Jr.; Media and the War; Military Assistance Command, Vietnam (MACV); Westmoreland, William Childs.

P

Pacification

Array of programs that sought to bring security, economic development, and local self-government to rural South Vietnam. Pacification played an essential role in the conduct of the Vietnam War. Following the 1954 Geneva Accords, Republic of Vietnam (RVN) leaders relied on various pacification plans to extend rule into the countryside, gain political loyalty, and defeat a Communist insurgency. The management and focus of pacification changed throughout the war, but the underlying philosophy and purpose remained constant.

Security was a prerequisite of pacification. To provide local security, the government raised the paramilitary Civil Guard and Self Defense Corps, which in 1964 became the Regional Forces and Popular Forces (RF/PF). The militia, the People's Self-Defense Force, and police forces also had a security role. Revolutionary Development (RD) cadre teams lived in the villages, trained local citizens, and worked on self-help projects. The goal was to make the villages secure, but sometimes nearby fighting or operational requirements forced peasants from their homes into camps in secure areas. After 1960, to counter the political propaganda and terrorism of the Việt Công infrastructure (VCI), the Sài Gòn government under the Phoenix program used its police forces to identify and arrest VCI members. Under the Chiêu Hôi (Open Arms) program, the government used psychological and economic inducements to encourage the Việt Công (VC) to defect.

Pacification also sought to improve the lives of the people in the countryside. Sài Gòn instituted land reform, provided assistance to refugees and attempted to resettle them, sent out cadres to teach and organize villagers, set up schools and infirmaries, organized local elections, and provided funds for local development projects.

Although pacification programs were conducted by the South Vietnamese government, Americans played an indispensable role as financiers and advisors at all levels of government. Much of the history of pacification concerns U.S. efforts to push the RVN to carry out mutually agreed-upon plans. U.S. attempts to influence the Vietnamese produced frustrating results; frequent disappointments offset the occasional successes.

Measuring meaningful change or progress in the countryside was difficult. The Americans devised several nationwide statistical indices, based on standardized questions, to track such things as the expenditure of funds and the distribution of weapons. But in a war for political support and popular loyalty, tools such as the Hamlet Evaluation System proved more useful for managing programs and resources than for assessing change or gauging popular loyalty in a convincing way.

President Ngô Đình Diêm instituted limited land reform in 1956, but his harsh tactics in suppressing his opposition alienated many South Vietnamese. To many, Diêm's policies seemed designed to benefit wealthy landowners, and this gave the Communists an issue to gain popular support. In 1959 the Politburo in Hà Nôi decided to take active steps to topple Diêm. In 1960 the National Liberation Front (NLF) was created to merge the efforts of Diêm's Communist and non-Communist opponents inside the RVN and to win political support overseas. The NLF recruited and operated within South Vietnam, but direction and leadership came largely from Hà Nôi. The NLF, or Việt Công (VC), was a revolutionary organization that combined political indoctrination with military action, tight organization, and coercion to build their movement. Their strategy skillfully blended intimidation and reform and used political and military means to gain control.

Under Mao Zedong's theory of revolutionary warfare, the VC sought to destroy the government's presence in the countryside, isolating the cities from the people. Without a base of popular support, the government would eventually fall. Primary VC targets were local officials, political leaders, and teachers—Sài Gòn's links with the villages. Assassination, kidnapping, or intimidation effectively ended government presence in many areas. Diêm mounted several projects to counter this threat. The most ambitious, the Strategic Hamlet program (1962), sought to put villagers in fortified hamlets and protect them from VC raids and political organizers. However, the government built too many hamlets too quickly, uprooted villagers from their ancestral homes, and herded them into inadequate hamlets that offered few amenities and no real protection. Relocating people instead of bringing security to their native villages proved a major defect.

Dissatisfied with Diêm's leadership and worried about his prosecution of the war, the RVN's armed forces, with U.S. acquiescence, overthrew him in November 1963, only worsening matters. Ongoing pacification programs, including the Strategic Hamlets, essentially stopped. Efforts that began after Diêm's overthrow—Chiên Thang or Hop Tác—proved ineffective. The coup produced political instability in Sài Gòn and turmoil in the provinces. Officials carrying out pacification plans were replaced when the government in Sài Gòn changed, which it frequently did. In the absence of political stability, and emboldened by signs of Sài Gòn's collapse, Hà Nôi began to send conventional army units into South Vietnam in late 1964 to administer the coup de grace.

In February 1965, Gen. William Westmoreland and Gen. William DePuy, Westmoreland's operations officer, concluded that pacification was irrelevant at that point. Attrition became the strategy in Vietnam. To accomplish it, Westmoreland wanted more troops. Johnson agreed to send the requested soldiers, but at the same time he realized that pacification could not be long ignored and pondered how to revive it. Prompted by National Security advisor McGeorge Bundy and his assistant, Chester Cooper, Johnson first tried to improve U.S. management of pacification by empowering two successive ambassadors, Maxwell Taylor and Henry Cabot Lodge, to act as "proconsuls." As head of the country team, the ambassador was expected to unify and integrate the various programs run by separate U.S. agencies—the Central Intelligence Agency (CIA), U.S. Agency for International Development (USAID), State Department, U.S. Information Agency (USIA), and U.S. Armed Forces—that supported Vietnamese pacification efforts. Throughout 1965 the president resisted suggestions that he appoint a "czar" to manage pacification from Washington.

That reluctance began to soften early in February 1966, after Johnson conferred in Honolulu with South Vietnamese leaders Nguyên Van Thiêu and Nguyên Cao Ky. This conference spotlighted pacification. The president sought to energize officials in Washington and Sài Gòn, as well as the RVN leadership, and to make clear that pacification was equal in importance to the war being fought by the military. The pacification program showed new life under the dynamic but temperamental Gen. Nguyên Đuc Thang, Minister of Revolutionary Development, and the return of political stability in Sài Gòn in 1966 under Thiêu and Ky.

After the conference, Johnson chose Ambassador William Porter, Lodge's deputy, to pull together the U.S. effort in Sài Gòn to support pacification. To improve military cooperation, Porter was later given a military assistant, Brig. Gen. Willis Crittenberger. To enhance management and improve support for pacification in Washington, Johnson appointed Robert Komer as his special presidential assistant for pacification. Johnson granted Komer authority to deal directly with the secretaries of state and defense, the director of the CIA, the administrator of AID, and most significantly, the president himself.

Porter's and Komer's efforts were a study in contrasts. Porter became bogged down with administrative chores that Lodge insisted he perform. Lodge was reluctant to let Porter take steps that would centralize U.S. management of pacification support or diminish the autonomy of separate U.S. agencies and their programs. Komer, armed with Johnson's mandate, ran roughshod over Washington bureaucrats, earning the nickname "Blowtorch" for his efforts. By summer 1966, Komer was convinced that a single manager was needed to run the array of U.S. pacification programs in Vietnam and that the military needed to be involved in pacification support, perhaps even in charge. Komer bluntly told Porter, who adamantly opposed military control, that compared to military operations, the civil side was "still farcical."

Unwilling in fall 1966 to strip responsibility for pacification support from the embassy, Johnson gave Porter and Lodge a last chance to manage pacification support and show results. The agency that emerged, the Office of Civilian Operations, was hampered by Lodge's continued insistence that Porter devote his time to running the embassy, in spite of Johnson's admonitions. Convinced that the military would have to be involved, Komer lobbied for the unification of civilian and military support of pacification under Westmoreland. In May 1967 Johnson finally agreed, appointing Komer as Westmoreland's deputy for pacification, with the rank of ambassador.

Komer established a new organization, Civilian Operations and Revolutionary (later changed to Rural) Development Support (CORDS), to put under a single manager most U.S.

civilian and military programs that supported pacification. CORDS was a unique amalgamation of military and civilian personnel. It assumed control of some CIA and USAID programs and appointed military advisors to districts and provinces, which gave the new organization access to military support. CORDS was designed to prevent military domination of pacification, a sensitive point for U.S. civilian agencies. Komer regularly met with the U.S. ambassador, RVN leaders and cabinet officials, and Westmoreland and his military staff principals and unit commanders. As a staff principal in Westmoreland's headquarters, Komer could raise issues with the U.S. commander and had access to military logistics, supplies, manpower, and engineering support.

Komer took immediate steps to unify pacification. He greatly increased the number of U.S. advisors to the RVN Regional Forces (RF) and Popular Forces (PF) and sought better training and equipment for them. He believed the neglected paramilitary forces offered the best opportunity to achieve sustained local security, a key factor absent from earlier pacification efforts. He gained Westmoreland's approval for Phoenix, a new program to attack the VCI. Over the U.S. military's objections, Westmoreland gave CORDS responsibility for gathering intelligence on the VCI. Phoenix attempted to mesh the collection efforts of RVN and U.S. civilian and military intelligence agencies. The goal was to make timely, accurate information from all sources available to regular and special police so they could arrest VCI members in a timely manner. Getting the South Vietnamese to agree to this program, enact it into law, and initiate it took many frustrating months. Westmoreland approved the concept in July 1967; it became operational a year later.

For the first six months of its existence, CORDS worked to unify existing programs, add staff, bring on board additional advisors, and get new efforts such as Phoenix in gear. The 1968 Têt Offensive occurred before CORDS had demonstrated any visible results. At the same time, it proved difficult to get the ministries of newly elected President Thiêu's government to act decisively. Without doubt, Têt set back pacification, but it also energized it. The first comprehensive, integrated pacification plan, the Accelerated Pacification Campaign (APC), from 1 November 1968 to 31 January 1969, materialized from apparent defeat.

The Têt Offensive evoked wildly disparate assessments in Sài Gòn and Washington. In Sài Gòn, U.S. and South Vietnamese officials viewed the Communist military effort as a failure; Washington viewed the offensive as a political and psychological defeat. To Komer, the spent offensive offered an opportunity to demonstrate that pacification could indeed make the visible gains that had eluded earlier plans. He overcame significant resistance from CORDS and the U.S. command to his ambitious plan to improve security in 1,000 contested and Communist-controlled hamlets within 90 days. Gen. Creighton Abrams, who had replaced Westmoreland as the U.S. commander, agreed that the VC would be unable to resist, and in September 1968 he approved the concept of a special pacification offensive. Only a concerted effort by Ambassador Ellsworth Bunker, Komer, and his deputy,

William Colby persuaded President Thiêu and his generals that they had ample Revolutionary Development cadre teams and RF/PF units to carry out the APC offensive. APC set targets for all major pacification programs and committed the RVN's ministries and armed forces to carry them out. Critical to the APC was Abrams's commitment of U.S. military support. During the campaign, nearly half of all U.S. ground operations were launched in support of the APC.

The APC enjoyed mixed success. Most statistical goals were reached or exceeded, and the VC offered little overt armed resistance to the expansion. But Komer's overriding purpose for the APC was not achieved. The offensive failed to persuade the U.S. press or government that the war was being won and that pacification had made real, lasting progress. After the APC, civilian agencies in Washington argued that the recent gains in pacification were fragile and reversible, should the Communists choose to contest them more vigorously.

The APC initiated a period of gains and improvements in pacification that lasted until the 1972 Easter Offensive. The population living in government-controlled hamlets rose from 42 percent in 1967 to 80 percent in 1972, according to Hamlet Evaluation Survey data. Regional Forces and Popular Forces grew from 300,000 in 1967 to 520,000 at the end of 1972 and were better armed and trained. The RVN police grew from 74,000 to 121,000 over the same period. The VC lost strength and prominence. The VCI shrank from an estimated 85,000 in August 1967 to 56,000 in February 1972. The ranks of VC guerrilla units dropped from 77,000 in January 1968 to 25,000 in May 1972. To replenish these losses, Hà Nôi filled many guerrilla units with soldiers from its army, outsiders in South Vietnam's villages. Many key VC leaders and cadre, largely native Southerners, had been killed or captured or had defected, and their replacements were generally of lower caliber. The APC brought unprecedented success to the pacification program and gave the government the chance, beginning at the end of 1968, to consolidate control over the countryside and build a national political community.

In November 1968 Colby took over CORDS after Komer was named ambassador to Turkey. He assumed control of an established, functioning organization. Colby could be less concerned with local security than his predecessor. Although the RF/PF, police, and Chiêu Hôi and Phoenix programs remained as high priorities, Colby oriented CORDS toward rural economic development and political programs, taking advantage of improved security. In his view, the RVN needed to develop the political and social resources to sustain itself over the long term, a position that accorded well with President Nixon's Vietnamization policy. The "three selfs" summarized his approach to pacification: self-defense, self-government, and self-development.

Colby also benefited from extensive military support for pacification under Abrams. The APC had established a precedent for meshing pacification plans and military operations, and Abrams preached the importance of pacification over attrition to his commanders. Results were mixed. Operations such as WASHINGTON GREEN in Bình Đinh Province (1968, 1969) were models of cooperation between U.S. and ARVN units and between U.S. pacification advisors and local governmental officials. Others, such as RUSSELL BEACH (1969), proved as inimical to provincial pacification plans as Operation CEDAR FALLS had in 1966. Both operations forced villagers from their homes into hastily prepared and inadequate refugee camps, and both caused emotional and physical harm to the persons displaced. Neither resulted in long-term improvement of security.

A basic problem for pacification was assessing "progress" in a political war without front lines. The Hamlet Evaluation Survey attempted to measure the percentage of people living in areas under government control, clearly a different yardstick than persons committed to the government. By its nature, pacification had few objective measures, and some that seemed objective, such as the numbers of RF/PF and militia under arms, were not as critical as the subjective evaluations of their combat ability and willingness to fight. U.S. advisors were frequently frustrated both by the performance of Vietnamese forces in fighting the VC and by government officials in carrying out pacification programs honestly and effectively.

There were doubts about Communist losses. Clearly, the VC and the VCI were weaker in 1972 than in 1967, and programs such as Phoenix and Chiêu Hôi definitely weakened the insurgency. But Phoenix proved so controversial that it is moot whether its overall impact was positive or negative. The Communist leadership's commitment to replace losses and continue the war was unshaken.

Historians and participants disagree over the accomplishments of pacification. The evidence is inconclusive. The war ended with a conventional military offensive, an indication to some that pacification had succeeded and forced the Communists to take up a "big-unit" war in 1972 and 1975. Yet the VC, though weakened, remained formidable in difficult provinces like Hâu Nghia and Bình Đinh and were found throughout South Vietnam. Pacification was hard to judge in isolation, because its gains depended to a significant extent on Allied military support and they occurred after the VC suffered heavy losses in Têt 1968. It cannot be determined in retrospect to what degree pacification would have flourished against a stronger foe. The program did not realize its potential until after the Têt Offensive, too late to affect the growing perception in America that the war was stalemated.

The critical element in pacification was the Vietnamese parties. The Communists were determined to conquer South Vietnam and unify the country, and they adjusted their strategy and tactics several times during the war to attain that end. Some have argued that the war could have been won if a substantial and coordinated civil military pacification program had been launched in 1965. That interpretation fails to acknowledge how moribund pacification then was and also underestimates the enormously difficult task of transforming the RVN into a viable nation-state, an outcome that would have taken so long it would probably have exhausted U.S. support.

—Richard A. Hunt

References: Hunt, Richard. *Pacification: The American Struggle for Vietnam's Hearts and Minds* (1995); Thayer, Thomas. *How to Analyze a War without Fronts* (1985).

See also: Abrams, Creighton; Bundy, McGeorge; Bunker, Ellsworth; Chiêu Hôi (Open Arms) Program; Civilian Operations and Revolutionary Development Support (CORDS); Colby, William Egan; Hamlet Evaluation System (HES); Honolulu Conference; Johnson, Lyndon Baines; Komer, Robert W.; Lodge, Henry Cabot, Jr.; Mao Zedong (Mao Tse-tung); Ngô Đình Diêm; Nguyên Cao Ky; Nguyên Van Thiêu; Nixon, Richard Milhous; Phoenix Program; Porter, William James; Refugees and Boat People; Strategic Hamlet Program; Taylor, Maxwell Davenport; Territorial Forces; U.S. Agency for International Development (USAID); Vietnamization.

Palme, Olaf J. (1927–1986)

Swedish premier; peace and disarmament advocate and critic of U.S. involvement in Vietnam. Palme angered Americans in 1968 when he joined the North Vietnamese ambassador to the Soviet Union in a Stockholm demonstration against U.S. Vietnam policy and when he compared Richard Nixon and the Hà Nôi bombings to the actions of Hitler.

—Clayton D. Laurie

References: Freeman, Ruth. *Death of a Statesman: The Solution to the Murder of Olaf Palme* (1989); Mosey, Chris. *Cruel Awakening: Sweden and the Killing of Olaf Palme* (1991).
See also: Nixon, Richard Milhous.

Palmer, Bruce, Jr. (1913–)

U.S. Army general and Vietnam War author. From March to July 1967 Palmer commanded II Field Force, the largest U.S. Army combat command in Vietnam. During his tenure as commander, II Field Force executed Operations JUNCTION CITY and MANHATTAN, the two largest operations of the war to that time. From July 1967 to June 1968, Palmer was the deputy commander of U.S. Army, Vietnam (USARV). Although the commander of Military Assistance Command, Vietnam (MACV), Gen. Westmoreland, was also "dual hatted" as USARV commander, the USARV deputy commander actually ran USARV's daily operations.

Promoted to full general, Palmer was vice chief of staff of the Army from August 1968 to June 1972. When Gen. Creighton Abrams was selected to succeed Westmoreland as chief of staff, his confirmation was delayed by Senate hearings investigating allegations that U.S. commanders in Vietnam had exceeded their authority by conducting unauthorized air strikes in North Vietnam. During that interim period until October 1972 Palmer served as the acting chief of staff. He retired from the Army in September 1974.

Palmer wrote one of the most important books about Vietnam, *The 25-Year War: America's Military Role in Vietnam* (1984), a penetrating analysis of the U.S. military decision-making process during the formative years of the war. He also provides a thorough critique of the disjointed operational chain of command for the war: Although the MACV commander controlled military operations within South Vietnam, the commander in chief, U.S. Pacific Command controlled the offensive air war over the North, while B-52 strikes remained under the control of the Strategic Air Command.

Palmer reveals a major flaw of U.S. strategy: placing too

much faith in the air war. Although the air interdiction program was the most effective element of that aspect of the war, it too was weakened by the lack of supporting ground operations. In assessing what military strategy might have worked, Palmer suggests that defeating the insurgent threat in South Vietnam should have been the primary responsibility of the South Vietnamese. According to Palmer, U.S. ground forces should have prevented People's Army of Vietnam regular forces and supplies from moving into South Vietnam by massing in the northern part of the country and cutting lines of communications within Laos. In an August 1995 interview in *The Wall Street Journal*, Bùi Tín, a former colonel on the PAVN general staff, agreed that those very actions would have cost the Communists the war.

In discussing the larger lessons of the war, Palmer emphasizes that the employment of military force is an art, not an exact science. He concludes, "Vietnam demonstrated how the lack of such understanding [of the capabilities and limitations of military power] can lead to disastrous failure." Palmer does not imply that all the fault for the failure in Vietnam lay with the nation's political leadership. He also states, "I feel that our top-level military leaders must share the onus of failure."

—David T. Zabecki

References: Bell, William G. *Commanding Generals and Chiefs of Staff: 1775–1983* (1983); Palmer, Bruce, Jr. *The 25-Year War: America's Military Role in Vietnam* (1984); Young, Stephen. "How North Vietnam Won the War" (1995).
See also: Abrams, Creighton; JUNCTION CITY, Operation; Military Assistance Command, Vietnam (MACV); United States: Army; Westmoreland, William Childs.

Paracel and Spratly Islands

Two island groups in the South China Sea; their Vietnamese names are Quân Đao Hoàng Sa (Paracel Islands) and Quân Đao Truong Sa (Spratly Islands). The Paracels comprise about 15 to 30 islands, depending on how they are counted. The Spratlys are made up of about a hundred large and small islands. Several nations dispute the sovereignty of these islands. After two decades of occupation by the Army of the Republic of Vietnam, in 1974 the Paracels were seized by force by People's Republic of China troops. The Spratlys have been claimed by Vietnam, the People's Republic of China, Taiwan, the Philippines, Malaysia, and Brunei. China claims the rights of discovery, while Vietnam emphasizes its continuous occupation since the seventeenth century. The Philippines and Malaysia emphasize the Spratlys' proximity to their territory.

Disputes over these islands have been triggered by their strategic positions and the possibility of nearby off-shore oil deposits. From the Paracels a naval power could control navigation in the northern part of the South China Sea, and from the Spratlys it could follow all ship traffic within Southeast Asia between the Pacific and the Indian Oceans.

—Pham Cao Duong

References: Chi-kin Lo. *China's Policy toward Territorial Disputes* (1989); Lafont, Pierre-Bernard. "Les Frontières en Mer de Chine

Meridionale" (1989); Vo Long Te. *Les Archipels de Hoang-Sa et de Truong-Sa Selon Les Anciens ouvrages de l'Histoire et de Geographie* (1974).

See also: China, People's Republic of (PRC); China, Republic of (ROC; Taiwan); Philippines.

Paris Negotiations (1968–1973)

On 31 March 1968 President Johnson announced that the United States would stop bombing north of the 20th parallel in the Democratic Republic of Vietnam (DRV) and seek to open negotiations. Four days later Hà Nôi agreed to send a representative to meet with U.S. officials to discuss an "unconditional" halt to the rest of the bombing. Both sides agreed to meet in Paris.

U.S. and DRV negotiators faced each other for the first time on 10 May; three days later the talks formally opened. Averell Harriman headed the U.S. delegation; veteran diplomat Xuân Thuy represented the DRV. During the next five months the DRV insisted that nothing else could be negotiated until all air strikes on its territory had stopped. Johnson hesitated but finally, on 31 October 1968, announced the halt. U.S. negotiators refused to call it unconditional, as the DRV demanded.

The next hurdle was the refusal of the DRV and its ally, the National Liberation Front (NLF), to accept the Sài Gòn government as a legitimate participant. Just as adamantly, the Republic of Vietnam (RVN) refused to recognize the NLF. To skirt the impasse, Harriman and his deputy Cyrus Vance proposed that instead of officially identifying the four parties, negotiators simply refer to "our side" and "your side." This diplomatic fiction allowed the NLF representatives to join the DRV team without acknowledgement by Sài Gòn's delegates. Similarly, RVN negotiators could sit with their U.S. allies without acknowledgement by the DRV-NLF. Hà Nôi agreed, but South Vietnam's President Nguyên Van Thiêu balked, delaying the first session until 16 January 1969, four days before Richard Nixon's inauguration.

Nixon named Henry Cabot Lodge to replace Harriman as the chief U.S. negotiator. Lodge resigned in November and was replaced in 1970 by David K. E. Bruce. Meanwhile, in June 1969 the NLF proclaimed the establishment of a new Provisional Revolutionary Government of South Vietnam, giving its delegation the same governmental status as the other three participants. After a flurry of hope that the war might be settled quickly, the talks failed to come close to an agreement. The Nixon administration, meanwhile, shifted its negotiating effort from the official talks into a new, secret channel. On 4 August 1969 Henry Kissinger, Nixon's national security advisor, held the first secret meeting with Xuân Thuy in Paris. Lê Đuc Tho, one of Hà Nôi's senior leaders, took over as the DRV negotiator in subsequent sessions.

For more than three years, the DRV insisted in both official and secret talks that the only way to end the war was for the U.S. to dissolve the Sài Gòn government, disband its army, and install a new coalition that would negotiate for a truce. Its position began to soften in summer 1972, in the aftermath of that year's Easter Offensive. On 8 October 1972, Tho agreed for the first time that the Thiêu regime could remain in exis-

tence and negotiate with the PRG, after a cease-fire, for a permanent political settlement. Over the next ten days, Kissinger and Tho reached agreement on a final draft, but Thiêu balked, objecting that the draft treaty did not require North Vietnamese troops to leave the South. Thiêu also objected to the proposed National Council of National Reconciliation and Concord, which was to oversee political negotiations and elections for a new South Vietnamese government.

Talks resumed in November, then broke off in mid-December. Kissinger and Tho returned to Paris in early 1973 and on 23 January initialed a treaty that was essentially the same as their October draft. The formal signing was set for 27 January, bringing the negotiations to a conclusion.

—Arnold R. Isaacs

References: Goodman, Allan E. *The Lost Peace: America's Search for a Negotiated Settlement of the Vietnam War* (1978); Kissinger, Henry A. *White House Years* (1979).

See also: Bruce, David K. E.; Harriman, W. Averell; Johnson, Lyndon Baines; Kissinger, Henry Alfred; Lê Đuc Tho; Nguyên Van Thiêu; Nixon, Richard Milhous; Paris Peace Accords; Xuân Thuy.

Paris Peace Accords (January 1973)

The "Agreement on Ending the War and Restoring Peace in Vietnam," signed in Paris on 27 January 1973, ended direct U.S. military involvement in the conflict but failed to end the war itself. The signing ceremony revealed the hostility that remained between the warring sides. The foreign ministers of the two South Vietnamese opponents, the Republic of Vietnam (RVN) and the Provisional Revolutionary Government (PRG), would not sign the same copy of the document, but signed on separate pages, while representatives of the United States and the Democratic Republic of Vietnam (DRV) signed yet a third copy.

The agreement opened by declaring that "the United States and all other countries respect the independence, sovereignty, unity and territorial integrity of Vietnam as recognized by the 1954 Geneva Agreements on Vietnam." This reflected the position the Communist side had argued for years: that Vietnam was one country, not two, and thus their revolution was not "foreign aggression," as Sài Gòn and the United States maintained, but a legitimate struggle to regain national independence and unity.

The agreement's other provisions called for:

- A cease-fire, to take effect 27 January at midnight, Greenwich Mean Time (0800 the next day, Sài Gòn time), following which the Vietnamese forces would remain in place; resupply of weapons, munitions, and war materiel would be permitted but only to replace items destroyed or used up during the truce.
- Withdrawal of all U.S. and other foreign troops within 60 days, with the release of all U.S. war prisoners "carried out simultaneously" with the troop withdrawal. The signers also promised to assist in accounting for missing personnel and to help find, identify, and repatriate the remains of those who had died.
- Negotiations between South Vietnamese parties for a settlement that would "end hatred and enmity" and

allow the South Vietnamese people to freely decide their political future. A National Council of National Reconciliation and Concord, with members representing both South Vietnamese sides and a neutral "third force," would oversee the negotiations and organize elections for a new government. Following a settlement in South Vietnam, reunification of the two Vietnams was to be "carried out step by step through peaceful means."

Other clauses covered such matters as establishing an international observer force and respect for the neutrality of Laos and Cambodia.

Withdrawal of U.S. forces was completed as promised during the 60 days following the truce. On the final day, the U.S. command issued its last general order: "Headquarters Military Assistance Command Vietnam is inactivated this date and its mission and functions reassigned." At 1800 the last troops boarded a U.S. Air Force transport out of the country. Only truce observers, Marine embassy guards, a team of missing in action (MIA) negotiators, and 50 military personnel assigned to the Defense Attaché Office remained in the RVN. The DRV released 591 U.S. prisoners of war (POWs). Although the POW issue remained contentious for many years afterward, Hà Nôi never wavered from its insistence that it had turned over all POWs in its hands at the time of the agreement.

Although it ended U.S. military involvement, the agreement achieved none of its other objectives. No political settlement was reached, no national reconciliation council was created, and no election was held. The fighting did not stop, or even slow down. Only the United States observed the cease-fire. For the Vietnamese, the war continued as before. The failure of the truce was ordained even before it was supposed to take effect. The agreement called for a "cease-fire in place" but did not establish where each side's forces belonged. Consequently, both sides tried to seize territory in the final hours. The Communist side struck more aggressively in the 36 hours before the cease-fire was to begin, penetrating more than 400 towns and villages and cutting every major highway in the country. Although not technically violating the agreement, the attacks drastically altered the true battle lines the truce was intended to preserve. Had the RVN frozen in place at the cease-fire hour, its enemy would have been left occupying hundreds of positions normally under Sài Gòn's control. President Thiêu and his generals did not accept that situation. Thiêu ordered his forces to keep fighting, even if offensive operations continued after the cease-fire hour.

In about two weeks RVN troops recaptured most of the territory seized in the pre–cease-fire fighting. Had they paused at that point, the cease-fire might have taken hold, but they remained on the offensive. Both sides took the position that attacks anywhere in the enemy's zone were justified by the other side's prior cease-fire violations. With no way to restore the lines that were supposed to have been frozen by the truce, there was only an endless chain of retaliations, with 51,000 South Vietnamese soldiers killed in 1973 and 1974—the highest two-year toll of the entire war. Two years after it was signed, the agreement was all but forgotten.

—Arnold R. Isaacs

References: Isaacs, Arnold R. *Without Honor: Defeat in Vietnam and Cambodia* (1983); Le Gro, William E. *Vietnam from Ceasefire to Capitulation* (1981); Porter, D. Gareth. *A Peace Denied: The United States, Vietnam, and the Paris Agreement* (1975).
See also: National Council of National Reconciliation and Concord (NCNRC); Nguyên Van Thiêu; Paris Negotiations.

Parrot's Beak

Fertile, densely populated area of Cambodia that projects into South Vietnam above the Mekong Delta. Communist forces maintained semipermanent installations in the Parrot's Beak from which they infiltrated into southern III Corps and northern IV Corps. Though Army of the Republic of Vietnam (ARVN) forces frequently pursued Communists into sanctuaries in Cambodia, U.S. forces were not permitted to do so. Beginning in March 1969, however, President Nixon authorized secret B-52 bombing missions (Operation MENU) to deter Communist infiltration.

Communist Base Areas 367 and 706, in the Parrot's Beak, became the primary objectives of the third phase of the so-called Cambodian Incursion, ordered by Nixon to begin on 1 May 1970. This phase was conducted entirely by ARVN III and IV Corps ground forces; the U.S. 9th Infantry Division provided only artillery and logistical support. Not bound by the 30-mile penetration limit imposed on U.S. forces, ARVN units moved deep inside Cambodia, uncovering large caches of weapons and ammunition. ARVN forces successfully engaged People's Army of Vietnam (PAVN) and Khmer Rouge forces up to positions north and south of Phnom Penh.

ARVN penetration of the Parrot's Beak was the first real test of Nixon's Vietnamization policy and was termed a great success. But the operation was complicated because ARVN forces, while engaging PAVN forces, also found themselves protecting and evacuating indigenous Vietnamese who were being massacred by Gen. Lon Nol's Cambodian forces. ARVN forces remained in Cambodia for a time, and acquitted themselves well, but were powerless to impede reoccupation by Communist military units. By the end of 1971, despite daily B-52 bombings, Communist bases were again fully operational. They served as the springboard for massive infiltrations during the 1972 Easter Offensive.

—John D. Root

References: Coleman, J. D. *Incursion* (1991); Stanton, Shelby L. *The Rise and Fall of an American Army: U.S. Ground Forces in Vietnam: 1965–1973* (1985).
See also: Cambodia; Cambodian Incursion; Fishhook; Khmer Rouge; Nixon, Richard Milhous.

PASSAGE TO FREEDOM, Operation (1954)

Operation transferring nearly one million Vietnamese refugees south of the 17th parallel after the 1954 Geneva Accords. Most were Catholics who, prompted to flee by U.S. and French propaganda, could solidify a constituency for South Vietnamese Catholic leader Ngô Đình Diêm. A dramatic U.S. rescue operation (code-named PASSAGE TO FREEDOM by the Navy and Operation EXODUS by Diêm), in cooperation with French forces and voluntary agencies, evacuated

768,672 refugees from the North in U.S., French, and British ships and aircraft. The U.S. provided emergency food, medical care, clothing, and shelter at reception centers in Vung Tàu and Sài Gòn, at a cost of $93 million. By December, U.S. government and nongovernment agencies had allocated millions of additional dollars to resettle these refugees, deepening America's commitment to nation-building in South Vietnam.

—Delia Pergande

References: Hooper, Edwin, Dean Allard, and Oscar Fitzgerald. *The United States Navy and the Vietnam Conflict.* Vol. 1 (1976); Kahin, George McT. *Intervention: How America Became Involved in Vietnam* (1986); Wiesner, Louis. *Victims and Survivors: Displaced Persons and Other War Victims in Viet-Nam, 1954–1975* (1988).
See also: Geneva Conference and Geneva Accords; Ngô Đình Diêm; United States: Involvement in Vietnam, 1954–1965.

Pathet Lao

Front group for Communist forces in Laos. The name (meaning "Land of the Lao") was first applied to the clandestine resistance government formed by Prince Souphanouvong in August 1950 to fight the French. The Pathet Lao's early history generally paralleled that of the Viêt Minh, which also was controlled by a small core of Communist leaders. The Pathet Lao front was formed at a meeting inside the border in the Democratic Republic of Vietnam (DRV). Although its program was designed to appeal to non-Communist nationalists with its slogan, "Peace, independence, neutrality and prosperity," the Pathet Lao never achieved the same degree of popularity among the Laotians as the Viêt Minh did in Vietnam, probably because they were so evidently dependent on the Vietnamese Communists.

—Arthur J. Dommen

Reference: Zasloff, Joseph J., and MacAlister Brown. *Apprentice Revolutionaries: The Communist Movement in Laos, 1930–1985* (1986).
See also: Laos; Souphanouvong; United Front; Viêt Minh.

Patti, Archimedes L. A. (1913–)

U.S. Army officer serving in the Office of Strategic Services (OSS) who formed a friendship with Hô Chí Minh in 1945 and witnessed the assumption of power by the Viêt Minh in Hà Nôi. Captain Patti's Indo-China experience began with his arrival on 13 April 1945 at OSS headquarters at Kunming, China. Patti was ordered to investigate the establishment in Indo-China of a network using independence-minded Vietnamese to provide intelligence on Japanese troop strengths and movements. This assignment led to his acquaintance with Hô Chí Minh, who offered the services of the Viêt Minh in return for arms and funds from the OSS.

After the Japanese surrender, Patti headed a group of OSS officers who flew into Hà Nôi on 22 August, ostensibly to locate and arrange for repatriation of Allied prisoners of war. Patti remained in Hà Nôi, freuqently seeing Hô and his lieutenant Vô Nguyên Giáp, until 1 October. In his memoirs, Patti emphasized Hô's aspirations for independence and played down his Communist background.

—Arthur J. Dommen

References: Charlton, Michael, and Anthony Moncrieff. *Many Reasons Why: The American Involvement in Vietnam* (1978); Patti, Archimedes L.A. *Why Vietnam? Prelude to America's Albatross* (1980).
See also: Dewey, Albert Peter; Hô Chí Minh; Office of Strategic Services (OSS); Viêt Minh; Vô Nguyên Giâp.

PAUL REVERE I–IV, Operations (May–December 1966)

Allied screening operations along the Cambodian border in Pleiku Province. No single Allied force operated primarily in Pleiku Province in 1966, but special task forces were formed. Gen. William Westmoreland favored making the western Central Highlands an area of U.S. concentration, hoping for more main force battles with the People's Army of Vietnam (PAVN) to develop. In March and April the 2d Brigade of the 1st Cavalry joined the newly arrived 3d Brigade of the 25th Infantry Division to conduct two operations in the Chu Pong area that killed more than 500 PAVN soldiers.

The mission of PAUL REVERE I/THÂN PHONG (10 May–30 July), led by Brig. Gen. Glenn Walker of the 25th Division, was to counter a possible offensive of the PAVN "Yellow Star" Division against the Special Forces border camps. Joining the task force were a battalion of the 2d Brigade and Troop B, 1st Squadron, 9th Cavalry from the 1st Cavalry Division, two Army of the Republic of Vietnam (ARVN) and Republic of Korea (ROK) battalions, and six artillery batteries. The relatively small task force sparred with PAVN units over a large area from the Chu Pong Massif to Đuc Co, and from the Cambodian border to Plei Me. U.S. forces engaged in heavy fighting at Chu Pong, killing more than 200 PAVN soldiers while taking only light casualties.

PAUL REVERE II (1–25 August) was a larger operation in the Chu Pong War Zone. When patrolling units of the 3d Brigade of the 25th Division began to take casualties, the 2d and 3d Brigades of the 1st Cavalry were airlifted from An Khê in just 12 hours, followed by the insertion of two ARVN and ROK battalions. For nearly three weeks the 1st Cavalry's Maj. Gen. John Norton led 14 battalions against two PAVN regiments in a battle that resulted in 861 PAVN soldiers killed.

PAUL REVERE III (September) was uneventful, but Paul Revere IV (18 October–30 December) was a major search-and-destroy operation along the Cambodian border conducted primarily by the newly arrived 4th Infantry Division, augmented by elements of the 25th Division and by the 2d Brigade of the 1st Cavalry. The operation centered on the Chu Pong–Ia Drang area. Although U.S. forces suffered heavy casualties in ambushes, a regiment of the PAVN 10th Division left 977 known dead on the battlefield.

—John D. Root

References: Hymoff, Edward. *The First Air Cavalry Division, Vietnam* (1967); Marshall, S. L. A. *Battles in the Monsoon: Campaigning in the Central Highlands Vietnam, Summer 1966* (1967); Westmoreland, William C. *Report on Operations in SVN, January 1964–June 1968* (1968).
See also: Airmobility; Free World Assistance Program; Ia Drang, Battle of; IRVING, Operation; Military Assistance Command, Vietnam (MACV); Search and Destroy; United States: Army; Westmoreland, William Childs.

Pearson, Lester Bowles (1897–1972)

Canadian prime minister, 1963–1968. Pearson's tenure as prime minister coincided with U.S. escalation in Vietnam. His relationship with President Johnson was negatively altered following an April 1965 convocation address at Temple University in which Pearson suggested that the United States should cease its bombing of North Vietnam. The remark incensed Johnson and, despite Pearson's subsequent apology, created a permanent rift between the two. U.S. Secretary of State Dean Rusk characterized Canadian-U.S. relations in 1967 as "deteriorated."

—Wes Watters

References: Bothwell, Robert, Ian Drummond, and John English. *Canada Since 1945: Power, Politics, and Provincialism* (1981); English, John. *The Worldly Years: The Life of Lester Pearson* (1992); Pearson, Lester B. *Mike: The Memoirs of the Right Honourable Lester B. Pearson* (1972).

See also: Canada; Johnson, Lyndon Baines; Rusk, Dean.

Peers, William R. (1914–1984)

U.S. Army general and chairman of the 1969–1970 commission appointed to investigate the cover-up of the My Lai massacre. Peers set about the task with uncompromising intensity, eventually putting together an exhaustive account that fixed responsibility at several levels.

Gen. Peers served a final tour of duty as deputy commanding general of the Eighth Army in Korea before retiring in 1973. Dissatisfied with the Army's failure to call to account those who had been responsible for My Lai and the cover-up, he wrote a hard-hitting book, *The My Lai Inquiry*, in which he stated those concerns explicitly: "The failure to bring to justice those who participated in the tragedy or were negligent in following it up … casts grave doubts upon the efficacy of American justice—military and civilian alike."

—Lewis Sorley

References: Hilsman, Roger. *American Guerrilla* (1990); Peers, William R. *The My Lai Inquiry* (1979); Peers, William R., and Dean Brelis. *Behind the Burma Road: The Story of America's Most Successful Guerrilla Force* (1963); U.S. Department of the Army. *The My Lai Massacre and Its Cover-Up: Beyond the Reach of Law? The Peers Commission Report* (1976).

See also: Atrocities during the Vietnam War; My Lai Massacre; Peers Inquiry.

Peers Inquiry

Commission of inquiry appointed to investigate the My Lai massacre of 16 March 1968. Lt. Gen. William R. Peers headed the investigation. Eventually several officers and men were charged with murder and other crimes, and more than a dozen officers were charged with suppression of information relating to the incident. Of those brought to trial by court-martial, only Lt. William L. Calley, Jr. was convicted. Found guilty of murder, he was sentenced to life imprisonment. Because of subsequent actions ordered by President Nixon, Calley served less than five years, much of it in what amounted to house arrest.

Maj. Gen. Samuel W. Koster was demoted one grade and relieved of his assignment as superintendent of the U.S. Military Academy at West Point. All others charged were acquitted or absolved administratively. Lt. Gen. Jonathan O. Seaman made a determination that there was insufficient evidence to bring to trial any of the senior officers except Col. Oran K. Henderson, who was court-martialed and acquitted. Thus, virtually all of those who perpetrated the atrocity and its cover-up escaped serious punishment. "I found the dismissal of charges, particularly those without benefit of an Article 32 investigation, most difficult to understand," Peers later wrote.

Nixon's involvement in the aftermath of My Lai was pervasive and malignant. Peers wrote that Westmoreland had revealed to him that, in contemplating an investigation of My Lai, "he had encountered considerable resistance from within the Department of Defense, which he strongly suspected had originated in the White House." Westmoreland met with Gen. Alexander Haig, then assigned to the White House staff, and told him that if the obstruction did not cease, he would go directly to the president.

The Peers Inquiry uncovered devastating and conclusive evidence of what had taken place, going beyond the individuals involved with My Lai and its cover-up to indict the state of leadership within the Army. "The principal breakdown was in leadership," wrote Peers. "Failures occurred at every level within the chain of command. It was an illegal operation in violation of military regulations and of human rights…." In transmitting the report, Peers added a cover letter that led Westmoreland to institute a study on military professionalism. Conducted at the Army War College, the 1970 study documented beyond question the validity of Peers's wider concerns about the health of Army leadership.

—Lewis Sorley

References: Peers, William R. *The My Lai Inquiry* (1979); U.S. Department of the Army. *The My Lai Massacre and Its Cover-Up: Beyond the Reach of Law? The Peers Commission Report* (1976).

See also: Atrocities during the Vietnam War; Calley, William Laws, Jr.; My Lai Massacre; Peers, William R.; Westmoreland, William Childs.

PEGASUS–LAM SON 207A, Operation

(1–15 April 1968)

Joint military operation to lift the People's Army of Vietnam (PAVN) siege of Khe Sanh Base. In January 1968 at least two PAVN divisions surrounded the 26th Marine Regiment and an Army of the Republic of Vietnam (ARVN) Ranger battalion at Khe Sanh. It was feared that Khe Sanh might become another Điên Biên Phu.

Maj. Gen. John J. Tolson's U.S. 1st Cavalry Division redeployed northward from II to I Corps in January, and Tolson was ordered on 10 March to prepare plans to relieve Khe Sanh. Code-named PEGASUS–LAM SON 207A, the operation was to start on 1 April. In addition to the 1st Cavalry, Tolson had two battalions of the 1st Marines, an ARVN airborne task force, an ARVN Ranger battalion at Khe Sanh, and operational control of the 26th Marine Regiment in Khe Sanh. Tolson commanded about 30,000 troops.

The operation required construction of a forward base just north of Cà Lu near Route 9, which a joint force of Army and Marine engineers and Navy Seabees completed in 11 days. Called landing zone (LZ) Stud, it included a 450-meter landing strip, ammunition bunkers, refueling points, and a communications and operations center.

Lacking intelligence on PAVN forces, Tolson sent Lt. Col. Richard W. Diller's 1st Squadron, 9th Cavalry (1/9th) to find PAVN strong points, destroy antiaircraft guns, and locate landing zones. Under cover of U.S. Air Force and Marine fighters, Diller conducted reconnaissance by fire for six days before the attack. The resulting air bombardment of PAVN positions was so effective that no aircraft were lost to antiaircraft or artillery fire.

On 31 March, Marines attacked north toward the Demilitarized Zone (DMZ) to confuse PAVN forces. On 1 April Col. Stanley S. Hughes's 1st Marines attacked westward afoot on Route 9, with the 11th Marine Engineers improving the road as they advanced. This was the beginning of PEGASUS–LAM SON 207A. That afternoon Col. Hubert S. Campbell's 3d Brigade of the 1st Cavalry Division air assaulted to LZs halfway to Khe Sanh. Quickly converting the LZs to fire bases, the 3d Brigade cleared parts of Route 9 ahead of the Marines.

On 2 April the 3d Brigade air assaulted a battalion farther west and two 1st Marine companies air assaulted westward to keep up the momentum of attack. The next day Col. Joseph C. McDonough's 2d Brigade of the 1st Cavalry air assaulted into LZs southeast of Khe Sanh, leapfrogging the 3d Brigade. On 4 April Col. David E. Lownds's 26th Marines at Khe Sanh took Hill 471, overlooking the base, while the 2d Brigade attacked an old French fort south of Khe Sanh. Both efforts met heavy PAVN resistance.

On 5 April Col. John E. Stannard's 1st Brigade air assaulted south of Khe Sanh, repulsing a sharp PAVN attack. The next day the 3d Brigade met stubborn resistance as it advanced westward along the highway. The ARVN airborne task force assaulted to an LZ north and east of Khe Sanh to block escape routes to Laos; fighting was sporadic. On 8 April the 1st Cavalry linked up with Khe Sanh and on 11 April the 1st Marines opened Route 9. Tolson planned other attacks in the area, but on April 10 was ordered to disengage to attack into the A Shau Valley.

Gen. Tolson had conducted an aggressive, fast-moving operation that demoralized PAVN troops and relieved Khe Sanh. It was the first full-division air cavalry raid in history.

—John L. Bell

References: Prados, John, and Ray W. Stubble. *Valley of Decision: The Siege of Khe Sanh* (1991); Stanton, Shelby. *Anatomy of a Division: 1st Cav in Vietnam* (1987); Tolson, John J. *Airmobility, 1961–1971* (1973).

See also: Airmobility; Khe Sanh, Battles of; United States: Army; United States: Marine Corps; Vietnam, Democratic Republic of: Army (People's Army of Vietnam [PAVN]); Vietnam, Republic of: Army (ARVN).

PENNSYLVANIA, Operation (June–October 1967)

Diplomatic attempt to end the Vietnam War. In June 1967 Henry Kissinger met Raymond Aubrac (a World Health Organization official and Socialist who knew Hô Chí Minh) and Herbert Marcovich (a French biologist) in Paris. Aubrac and Marcovich wanted to travel to the Democratic Republic of Vietnam (DRV), appeal to Hô for an end to the war, and explore conditions for peace. Although Secretary of State Dean Rusk and President Johnson were skeptical, they let Kissinger set up the unofficial visit, code-named Operation PENNSYLVANIA.

On July 21 1967 Aubrac and Marcovich arrived in Hà Nôi. Kissinger stayed in Paris as intermediary between them and Johnson. Following a courtesy visit with an ill Hô, Aubrac and Marcovich had substantive discussions with Premier Pham Van Đông, who insisted on an unconditional halt in U.S. bombing of the North as a prelude to official negotiations. He said that the air offensive could end without public announcement because the DRV did not desire to publicly humiliate the United States. Đông appeared willing to keep this channel open through DRV Consul Gen. Mai Van Bô in Paris. Aubrac and Marcovich left Hà Nôi on 26 July and met with Kissinger in Paris.

On 8 August Robert McNamara obtained approval from Johnson and Rusk of Đông's terms with the conditions that any bombing halt lead directly to negotiations and that the DRV not take advantage of the situation to strengthen its forces in the South. On 19 August Johnson agreed to halt the bombing within a ten-mile radius of Hà Nôi from 24 August to 4 September. Unfortunately, bad weather beforehand had led to an increased target list, and when the weather cleared on 20 August, the U.S. flew more sorties than on any previous day of the war.

On 21 August Hà Nôi canceled Aubrac's and Marcovich's visa applications, claiming it was unsafe for them to visit the DRV capital. As McNamara noted, "Once again, we had failed miserably to coordinate our diplomatic and military actions." On 20 October the DRV broke off the Aubrac and Marcovich channel.

—Kevin Arceneaux and Spencer C. Tucker

References: Kissinger, Henry. *Diplomacy* (1994); Karnow, Stanley. *Vietnam: A History* (1983); McNamara, Robert S., with Brian VanDeMark. *In Retrospect, the Tragedy and Lessons of Vietnam* (1995).

See also: Bundy, McGeorge; Hô Chí Minh; Johnson, Lyndon Baines; Kissinger, Henry Alfred; Lodge, Henry Cabot, Jr.; McNamara, Robert S.; Pham Van Đông; ROLLING THUNDER, Operation.

Pentagon Papers and Trial (1971)

U.S. Defense Department study of the course of American Vietnam policy and the trial resulting from publication of the study. In 1967 Secretary of Defense Robert McNamara, questioning the course of the war, created a task force within the Defense Department to investigate the history of U.S. policy in Vietnam. It conducted no interviews; its work was based on written materials, mostly files from the Departments of Defense and State, the Central Intelligence Agency (CIA), and to some extent the White House. The end product was a history accompanied by many of the documents on which it had been based. Formally titled *United States–Vietnam Relations,*

1945–1967, but commonly referred to as the Pentagon Papers, it totaled more than 7,000 pages in 47 volumes. There were only 15 copies—seven for distribution within the Department of Defense (DOD) and eight elsewhere.

Dr. Daniel Ellsberg, a researcher with the RAND Corporation (which had been given two copies), was one of the study's authors. Ellsberg already doubted U.S. Vietnam policy, and reading the Pentagon Papers convinced him that U.S. involvement there had been fundamentally immoral and should be ended immediately. Believing that the evidence should be available to Congress and the public, in 1969 he began photocopying sections of the papers. In March 1971, after failing to persuade several senators to make the material public, he delivered it to Neil Sheehan of *The New York Times*.

Sheehan and others at the *Times*, working in extreme secrecy, produced a series of articles intended for publication on ten consecutive days. Each daily installment included a long article plus major supporting documents. The articles were written by *New York Time* reporters using information from the narrative documents in the Defense Department version. The first installment was published on 13 June 1971.

On 14 June Attorney General John Mitchell informed the *Times* that "publication of this information is directly prohibited by the provisions of the Espionage Law." He asked the newspaper to cease publication immediately and return the documents to the DOD. The *Times* refused, amd on 15 June the Justice Department sought an injunction forbidding publication of further installments. Judge Murray I. Gurfein, Southern District of New York, issued a restraining order preventing publication for four days to allow time for the case to be argued. This was the first occasion on which a U.S. court restrained a newspaper, in advance, from publishing a specific article. Ellsberg immediately gave a substantial portion of the papers to the *Washington Post*, which began publishing articles based on this material on 18 June. The Justice Department filed suit against the *Post* the same day.

The Justice Department had obtained the initial restraining order without first proving to Judge Gurfein's satisfaction that such restraint was necessary or legal. All courts that became involved in the case agreed that such an order could not remain in effect for the period usually required for the U.S. court system to decide a matter of such importance. District courts in New York and Washington took only a few days to hand down decisions favoring the newspapers, citing freedom of the press and a lack of evidence that publication of the papers posed a serious danger to the nation.

The government appealed, and both cases reached the Supreme Court on 24 June. Four justices voted to reject the government's appeal without a hearing and to allow the newspapers to proceed with publication forthwith. The majority, however, voted to combine the two cases and hear them on 26 June.

The two newspapers had refused, as a matter of principle, to reveal what information they intended to publish, or even what portions of the papers Ellsberg had given them. Four volumes dealing with efforts made through various interme-

diaries to negotiate an end to the war—disclosure of which, the government warned, might impede future negotiations—were not given to either newspaper because Ellsberg shared the government's view of that risk. Of the material that Ellsberg furnished, the *Times* exercised some restraint in its disclosure, avoiding publication of information about which there might be legitimate national security concerns. The *Post* exercised greater restraint, avoiding publication of texts from the source documents. Had the newspapers been less secretive, court proceedings might have centered on the articles scheduled for publication, rather than on the whole text of the Pentagon Papers, and the argument that publication would imperil national security might have been strengthened.

The Supreme Court heard arguments on 26 June, by which time the Justice Department had shifted the legal basis of its case from the Espionage Act to the inherent powers of the presidency. Solicitor General Erwin Griswold argued that the president's responsibility for the conduct of foreign policy and his role as commander in chief of the armed forces required that he have the ability to forbid the publication of military secrets. On 30 June, the Court found for the newspapers, 6 to 3. Justices Black, Brennan, Douglas, Marshall, Stewart, and White agreed on a short statement that, given the constitutional protection of freedom of the press, a request by the government for prior restraint of publication "carries a heavy burden of showing justification," and the government had not met that burden. Each, however, wrote a separate concurring opinion. No common thread unites all six. Important elements found in various aspects of them included assertions that (1) Congress had passed no law, and indeed had repeatedly rejected proposed laws, under which the government could enjoin publication of government secrets by the press; (2) the government had failed to prove that publication of the Pentagon Papers would cause such dire harm as to justify making an exception to the general principles of the First Amendment; and (3) the government's claims for the inherent powers of the presidency could not be accepted.

The dissenters—Chief Justice Burger and Justices Blackmun and Harlan—were more nearly in agreement with one another. In the realm of foreign affairs, they were willing to grant the executive branch almost unfettered authority to decide which government secrets the press should be forbidden to publish. They did not claim that the government had proved that publication of the Pentagon Papers would cause such dire harm to the nation as would justify an exception to the First Amendment; they did not feel that the government should have been required to provide such proof. They argued that only the executive branch was qualified to decide whether publication threatened the national security and that the courts should enforce the judgment of the executive branch on the press without asking for any detailed explanation of the basis for that judgment.

The Supreme Court rejected prior restraint of publication in this case. The key to the outcome had rested with Stewart and White, the two justices who had not been willing to find for the newspapers on 25 June without a hearing, but who did find for them on 30 June. They suggested that the government protect its secrets through the deterrent effect of criminal prosecution, rather than prior restraint of publication. The Justice Department did not attempt criminal action against the newspapers, but indicted Ellsberg for conspiracy, theft of government property, and violation of the Espionage Act.

The trial of Ellsberg and an alleged coconspirator, Anthony Russo, began 3 January 1973. Its verdict might have clarified some issues left unresolved by the 1971 decision, but on 11 May the judge dismissed the charges, citing a pattern of government misconduct, including the White House's burglary of the office of Ellsberg's psychiatrist.

Before the end of 1971, two much more comprehensive selections from the Pentagon Papers appeared in book form, one published by the U.S. Government Printing Office after formal declassification and the other released by Senator Mike Gravel and published by Beacon Press. Between them, these contained essentially all of the narrative history other than sections dealing with negotiations to end the war; those were published only in 1983. Many source documents were included in versions published in 1971, but many others remained unreleased.

—Edwin E. Moise

References: Herring, George C., ed. *The Secret Diplomacy of the Vietnam War: The Negotiating Volumes of the Pentagon Papers* (1983); Schrag, Peter. *Test of Loyalty: Daniel Ellsberg and the Rituals of Secret Government* (1974); *The Pentagon Papers, as Published by The New York Times* (1971); *The Pentagon Papers: The Defense Department History of United States Decisionmaking on Vietnam.* (1971–1972); Ungar, Sanford J. *The Papers & The Papers: An Account of the Legal and Political Battle over the Pentagon Papers* (1972); *United States–Vietnam Relations, 1945–1967: Study Prepared by the Department of Defense* (1971).

See also: Ellsberg, Daniel; Gelb, Leslie H.; Gravel, Maurice Robert (Mike); McNamara, Robert S.; Media and the War; Nixon, Richard Milhous; Russo, Anthony J., Jr.; Sheehan, Cornelius Mahoney (Neil); Watergate.

People's Army of Vietnam (PAVN)
See Vietnam, Democratic Republic of: Army (People's Army of Vietnam [PAVN]).

People's Liberation Armed Forces (PLAF). *See* National Front for the Liberation of South Vietnam (NFLSV).

People's Republic of China. *See* China, People's Republic of (PRC).

People's Self-Defense Forces
Officially created by the Republic of Vietnam in the General Mobilization Law of June 1968, the result of the Têt Offensive. All male citizens ages 16 to 17 and 39 to 50 were required to participate in the People's Self-Defense Forces (PSDF) program, except those who volunteered to serve in the military and those age 18 to 38 who were exempted from service for reasons other than poor health. Those over 50, disabled veterans, women, and teenagers under 16 were encouraged to

volunteer for the PSDF in a supporting role. Combat Youth, Rural Combatants, Civil Defense, and similar organizations were disbanded and their membership shifted to the PSDF.

The PSDF existed at every level of national undertaking except the military. PSDF committees were chaired, in descending order, by the premier, city mayors or province chiefs, district, village, and hamlet chiefs, or their urban counterparts. The PSDF had combat and support components. The foundation of the combat PSDF was the 11-man team, three of which formed a section under a section leader and a deputy. Two or three sections could be joined in a group—the largest combat unit—under a group leader and a deputy. All team, section, and group leaders and deputies were elected by PSDF members based on leadership qualifications. All-volunteer support elements also were organized into teams, sections, and groups but were separated into different categories—elders, women, and teenagers—as dictated by traditional Vietnamese culture.

A four-week formal training course was conducted at national training centers for team and section leaders. The PSDF employed guerrilla tactics, eschewing fixed defense positions but moving to alert positions at night in three-man cells. PSDF members rarely confronted their enemy directly and when confronted by superior force were to hide their weapons and act as ordinary civilians.

By 1972 the PSDF combat component had more than one million members, about half of them armed with individual weapons. Most had received some combat training. The PSDF support component was even larger, with 2.5 million members. PSDF achievements varied from one locality to another, but in general, local security improved noticeably where the program was well executed.

—George J. Gabera

References: Guenter, Lewy. *America in Vietnam* (1978); Ngô Quang Truong. *Territorial Forces* (1981).

See also: Territorial Forces; Vietnam, Republic of: 1954–1975.

Perot, H. Ross (1930–)
U.S. businessman and politician. In 1969 National Security Advisor Henry Kissinger sought Perot's assistance in getting the North Vietnamese to improve conditions for U.S. prisoners of war (POWs). In response Perot formed United We Stand to collect money and buy newspaper advertisements to pressure North Vietnam into improving conditions for the POWs. In December 1969 Perot announced that United We Stand would deliver Christmas dinner to the POWs, but DRV authorities refused to cooperate. Perot, however, remained much committed to the POW issue. In 1992 and 1996 he made unsuccessful runs for the U.S. presidency as a third-party candidate.

—Michael R. Nichols

References: Mason, Todd. *Perot: An Unauthorized Biography* (1990); Posner, Gerald. *Citizen Perot: His Life and Times* (1996).

See also: Kissinger, Henry Alfred; Prisoners of War, Allied.

PERSHING, Operation (February 1967–February 1968)
U.S. 1st Cavalry Division operation in Bình Định Province; largest continuous operation of the 1st Cavalry Division

(Airmobile) since arriving in Vietnam. Following inconclusive operations in the longtime Communist stronghold of Bình Định throughout 1966, the 1st Cavalry became the exclusive U.S. presence there.

Under the command of Maj. Gen. John Tolson, PERSHING's primary mission was to conduct cordon-and-search operations with Army of the Republic of Vietnam (ARVN) forces to rout the entrenched Việt Công (VC) infrastructure and help establish Republic of Vietnam (RVN) government control. Tolson concluded that the more than 900 cordon-and-search operations conducted by the division rendered 50 percent of VC cadre ineffective.

Throughout PERSHING, the 1st Cavalry's three brigades continuously swept the coastal areas and reconnoitered the valleys in pursuit of VC regulars and the 3d People's Army of Vietnam (PAVN) "Yellow Star" Division. The 1st Cavalry's complement of 450 helicopters brought a new dimension to airmobility, as armed reconnaissance troops of the 1st Squadron, 9th Cavalry, would spot and engage Communist forces, followed by the rapid insertion of infantry battalions. When Communist forces retreated from remote areas, 1st Cavalry units forcibly removed the inhabitants, turning over nearly 100,000 refugees to RVN authorities by August. U.S. Air Force planes then smothered the depopulated areas with crop-destroying Agent Orange, ruining their usefulness as havens for Việt Công labor and recruits. March saw victories over large PAVN forces north of Bông Son at Tam Quan, and at Đầm Tra-O Lake to the south.

Until September, the entire division operated throughout Bình Định, except for a brief foray in April by the 2d Brigade into southern Quang Ngãi Province, and a June airlift of two battalions of the 3d Brigade to support U.S. forces engaged at Đak Tô. However, By December PERSHING had become a holding operation, with only one full brigade remaining in Bình Định.

When the 22d PAVN Regiment established entrenched positions near Tam Quan, the last major battle of PERSHING occurred. From 6 to 20 December, the 1st Brigade and the 1st Battalion, 50th Infantry (Mechanized) and 22d ARVN units killed 650 PAVN troops. According to Tolson, the battle's significance was that the Bông Son Plain "was the least affected of any part of South Vietnam during Tết."

Before rejoining the division in I Corps in late February, the 1st Brigade inflicted 614 more PAVN/VC casualties in Operation PERSHING II. Military Assistance Command, Vietnam (MACV) proclaimed Bình Định province to be "relatively secure," but the 3d PAVN Division would return in force.

—John D. Root

References: Stanton, Shelby L. *Anatomy of a Division: The First Cav in Vietnam* (1987); Tolson, Gen. John. *Airmobility, 1961–1971* (1973). **See also:** Airmobility; Đak Tô, Battle of; IRVING, Operation; MASHER/WHITE WING, Operation; United States: Army; Westmoreland, William Childs.

Peterson, Douglas "Pete" (1935–)

First U.S. ambassador to the Socialist Republic of Vietnam (SRV). In 1990 Peterson was elected to the House of Representatives from Florida and served three terms. Following normalization of relations between the United States and the SRV, President Clinton nominated Peterson to be the first U.S. ambassador to the SRV. On 10 April the Senate confirmed Peterson, who had announced during the hearings that his top priority as ambassador would be efforts to account for American's missing in action. SRV Premier Vô Van Kiệt said that Peterson's arrival in Hà Nội in May 1997 affirmed that both countries were interested in closing the past in order to look to the future. Among Peterson's chief tasks was to work toward a trade pact and most-favored nation status for the SRV.

—Spencer C. Tucker

References: Duncan, Philip, and Christine Lawrence. *Congressional Quarterly's Politics in America 1996: The 104th Congress* (1997); *The 1995–1996 Official Congressional Directory, 104th Congress* (1997). **See also:** Bush, George Herbert Walker; Clinton, William Jefferson; United States: Involvement in Vietnam, 1975 to the Present.

Phạm Công Tac (1890–1959)

Leader of the Cao Đài religious sect. As a 17-year-old student, Tac took part, with Phan Bôi Châu and Phan Chu Trinh, in a movement to gain independence for Vietnam. In 1941 the French deported Tac to Madagascar. During his absence, Cao Đài leader Trân Quang Vinh cooperated with the Japanese and formed a Cao Đàist army to resist the French. During the Indo-China War the Cao Đàist forces joined in a loose alliance with the French against the Việt Minh. In 1946 Tac returned from exile. He was not successful in his efforts to organize a general election to reunify the country, and in 1956 he took refuge in Cambodia, where he died.

—Bùi Đac Hùm

References: Hôi Thánh Cao Đài. *Tiêu Su Đuc Hô Pháp Phạm Công Tac.* (1992). **See also:** Cao Đài; Phan Bôi Châu.

Phạm Duy (1921–)

Musician whose songs are closely associated with the Indo-China and Vietnam wars. Phạm Duy's patriotic songs enjoyed great success in North Vietnam and were important in the fight against the French. In 1950, however, the Lao Đông Party instituted a new cultural policy and instructed Phạm Duy to publicly renounce his most beloved songs and follow the "socialist" cultural style. That led him in 1951 to move with his family to Sài Gòn, where he published his songs (popularized by his sister Thái Thanh, an important Vietnamese vocalist) and hosted several radio programs. Because of Phạm Duy's anti-Communist stance, the Socialist Republic of Vietnam continues to ban his songs.

—Nguyên Công Luân (Lu Tuân)

References: Phạm Duy. *Hôi Ký (Memoirs)* (1991); Phạm Duy. Interview with the author (1998). **See also:** Vietnamese Culture.

Phạm Hùng (1912–1988)

Official of the Vietnamese Communist Party (VCP), Democratic Republic of Vietnam (DRV), and Socialist

Republic of Vietnam (SRV). During the Vietnam War Hùng was head of the Central Office for South Vietnam (COSVN) and political commissar for Communist forces in the South. During the 1975 Hồ Chí Minh Campaign, Hùng was political commissar of the campaign headquarters. From 1956 to 1988 Hùng was a member of the VCP Central Committee and the Politburo. Within the SRV government, Hùng held several important posts, including minister of interior and vice chairman of the Council of Ministers. In 1987 he became chairman of the Council of Ministers (premier). Hùng was the most powerful leader sent from the North to direct the war in the South, but he helped forge the orthodox policies later blamed for economic ruin.

—Ngô Ngoc Trung

References: Biographical Files, Indo-China Archives, University of California at Berkeley.
See also: COSVN (Central Office for South Vietnam or Trung Uong Cuc Miên Nam); Hồ Chí Minh Campaign; Lao Đông Party; Vietnam, Socialist Republic of: 1975 to the Present.

Pham Ngoc Thao (1922–ca. 1965)

Viêt Công (VC) agent within the Republic of Vietnam (RVN) military. Thao duped the Central Intelligence Agency, U.S. military personnel, and even journalists such as Stanley Karnow into believing that he was loyal to the government. By 1963 he had been promoted to colonel and was in charge of the Strategic Hamlet program. Thao's mission as a VC operative seems to have been to create division within the Army of the Republic of Vietnam, thereby weakening the government and crippling RVN military effectiveness. His role was not discovered until after the war.

Thao's forces played a key role in seizing strategic installations during the November 1963 coup against Ngô Đình Diêm. In 1964 he succeeded Gen. Nguyên Khánh as press attaché to RVN Ambassador to the United States Trân Thiên Khiêm. He resurfaced in South Vietnam in 1965 when he was involved in an unsuccessful coup attempt against Khánh. Thao escaped in the confusion, then disappeared in mid-1965. Most political observers assumed that Gen. Nguyên Van Thiêu secured his death. Another scenario, circulated in Vietnam after 1975, holds that Thao rallied to the RVN side and helped its counterintelligence services hunt down high-ranking cadres and leaders of the Central Office for South Vietnam.

The RVN promoted Thao posthumously to the rank of one-star general and awarded him the title of Liêt Si (heroic war dead). There were other cases where Communist defectors faithfully served the RVN and were killed after the April 1975 Communist victory. As a counterpropaganda measure, the SRV awarded them the same title and paid pensions to their wives.

—Charlotte A. Power and Nguyên Công Luân (Lu Tuân)

References: Fitzgerald, Francis. *Fire in the Lake: The Vietnamese and the Americans in Vietnam* (1972); Karnow, Stanley. *Vietnam: A History* (1972); Post, Ken. *Revolution, Socialism, and Nationalism in Vietnam.* Vol. 4, *The Failure of Counter-Insurgency in the South* (1990).
See also: Ngô Đình Diêm; Nguyên Khánh; Nguyên Van Thiêu; Strategic Hamlet Program.

Pham Thê Duyêt (?–)

Vietnamese Communist Party (VCP) and Socialist Republic of Vietnam government official. Little is known about Duyêt's activities during the Indo-China and Vietnam Wars. He was first identified as a prominent national leader in 1982, when he was an alternate member of the VCP Central Committee and vice-chairman of the Vietnam Confederation of Trade Unions. In late 1988 he was promoted to the powerful post of Secretary of the VCP Committee of Hà Nôi City. Duyêt is credited with opening up the Hà Nôi administration to more liberal, dynamic, and younger leaders, which has led to a surge of development in the capital.

—Ngô Ngoc Trung

References: Biographical Files, Indo-China Archives, University of California at Berkeley.
See also: Lao Đông Party; Vietnam, Socialist Republic of: 1975 to the Present.

Pham Van Đông (1906–)

One of the three most influential leaders of the Democratic Republic of Vietnam (DRV) and its most public figure. After the French government outlawed the Communist Party on 26 September 1939, its Central Committee ordered Đông and Võ Nguyên Giáp to China to be trained in guerilla warfare. In June 1940 they met Hồ Chí Minh, who instructed them to go to Yenan and learn military techniques and politics. This was soon interrupted by the defeat of the French by Germany, whereupon Hồ instructed Đông, Giáp, and other Vietnamese Communists in China to return to Vietnam and set up an organization to fight for independence. They formed the Viêt Minh and organized camps in the mountains along the Vietnamese-Chinese border from which they engaged in propaganda, minor ambushes, and assassinations. The French and Japanese saw them as a minor annoyance.

Đông played a leading role in the Viêt Minh during the fight against the Japanese and the French. He headed the Viêt Minh delegation to the 1954 Geneva Conference and initially demanded that the Vietnamese be allowed to settle their own differences. The French rejected this demand, the conference ground to a halt, and Zhou Enlai, Vyacheslav Molotov, and Pierre Mendès-France took over negotiations. Đông's role was reduced to accepting or rejecting proposals. Đông wanted a six-month cease-fire and a demarcation line drawn at the 13th parallel. He left the conference—which moved the division to the 17th parallel and set the cease-fire at two years—believing that Zhou had sold out the Viêt Minh.

From 1950 to 1975 Đông served as the DRV's premier. Throughout U.S. involvement in Vietnam, he consistently refused any discussions until U.S. bombing of the DRV ended. He also required that any settlement include the creation of a neutral coalition government in Sài Gòn with Viêt Công representatives. Đông's negative attitude toward negotiations with the Americans stemmed from his experience with the French and the failure of the Geneva Accords.

After Hồ's death on 2 September 1969, Đông became the most public figure in the DRV. He skillfully used the U.S. press to encourage American antiwar protestors by stating that the

Vietnamese appreciated their support. Many of Đông's speeches carried humorous elements. When a reporter asked how he could refer to RVN leaders as "puppets" when they acted so consistently against U.S. policy, Đông replied that they were just "bad puppets."

Đông played a key role in the secret 1970 Paris peace negotiations between Henry Kissinger and Lê Đuc Tho. His influence was evident in Tho's initial demands for nothing less than a simultaneous armistice and coalition government to include the removal of President Nguyên Van Thiêu. Negotiations were deadlocked until August 1972, when Đông came to believe that temporary compromise on the matter of Thiêu would allow for a settlement. On 1 August Tho no longer demanded that military and political issues be resolved at one time. He also hinted that the DRV would no longer require Thiêu's withdrawal. The final resolution was delayed when, in an 18 October interview with Arnaud de Borchgrave, Đông referred to the National Council of National Reconciliation and Concord as a "coalition of transition." This again raised the specter of coalition government and temporarily halted the agreement. The final agreement was signed on 27 January 1973.

Đông continued in office after the capitulation of the Republic of Vietnam on 30 April 1975. He remained as chairman of the Council of Ministers of the Socialist Republic of Vietnam until a series of economic setbacks forced his resignation in December 1986. He then became advisor for the Central Committee of the VCP, although without actual power. Many North Vietnamese regarded Đông as one of their few incorruptible leaders though never, despite his many years as prime minister, a skillful administrator.

—Michael R. Nichols

References: Bain, Chester A. *Vietnam: The Roots of Conflict* (1967); Davidson, Phillip B. *Vietnam at War, the History: 1946–1975* (1988); Duncanson, Dennis J. *Government and Revolution in Vietnam* (1968); Fishel, Wesley R. *Vietnam: Anatomy of a Conflict* (1968); Karnow, Stanley. *Vietnam: A History* (1991); Olson, James S., ed. *Dictionary of the Vietnam War* (1987).
See also: Geneva Conference and Geneva Accords; Hô Chí Minh; Kissinger, Henry Alfred; Lê Đuc Tho; Mendès-France, Pierre; Molotov (born Scriabin), Vyacheslav Mikhailovich; Ngô Đình Diêm; Nguyên Van Thiêu; Nixon, Richard Milhous; Paris Negotiations; Paris Peace Accords; Viêt Minh; Vô Nguyên Giáp; Zhou Enlai (Chou En-lai).

Pham Van Phú (1928–1975)

Army of the Republic of Vietnam (ARVN) major general and corps commander. In 1954 Phú was a company officer in the 5th Parachutist Battalion of the Army of the State of Vietnam, fighting alongside the French at Điên Biên Phu. In the ARVN Phú commanded the Republic of Vietnam (RVN) Special Forces, then the 2d Infantry Division, the Quang Trung Training Center, and then II Corps/Military Region 2 in Pleiku. His troops suffered heavy losses in the withdrawal to the coast ordered by President Thiêu in March 1975, and Phú committed suicide in Sài Gòn the following month.

—Nguyên Công Luân (Lu Tuân)

Reference: Hà Mai Viêt, "Famous Generals of the Republic of Viêt Nam Armed Forces" (unpublished).

Phan Bôi Châu (1867–1940)

Vietnamese scholar and gentry activist. Phan initially advocated a reformed Vietnamese monarchy modeled along Meiji lines. When the Chinese Revolution of 1911 occurred, Phan hastened to Canton and, under the spell of Sun Yat-sen's Guomindang (Kuomintang), discarded the idea of a reformed monarchy. He created the Viêt Nam Quang Phuc Hôi (Vietnam Restoration Society) with the goal of creating a Vietnamese democratic republic. Forming an exile regime, he installed Cuong Đê as chief executive and himself as vice-president.

Phan's exiled underground inspired resistance in Vietnam between 1907 and 1918. In 1925, however, the French captured Phan in Shanghai, tried him, and sentenced him to life in prison. Reports circulated among Vietnamese nationalists that Hô Chí Minh and his associate Lâm Đuc Thu had sold information on Phan's whereabouts to the French secret service. In late 1945 Lâm publicly disclosed this and was subsequently shot to death in front of his home by the Viêt Minh. Prince Cuong Đê, however, confirmed the account.

Eventually paroled, Phan lived in restrictive retirement until his death at Huê.

—Rodney J. Ross

References: Buttinger, Joseph. *Vietnam: A Political History* (1968); Duiker, William J. *The Rise of Nationalism in Vietnam, 1900–1941* (1976); Hoàng Van Chí. *From Colonialism to Communism* (1964); Marr, David G. *Vietnamese Anticolonialism, 1885–1925* (1971).
See also: Cuong Đê; French Indo-China; Phan Chu Trinh.

Phan Chu Trinh (1872–1926)

Vietnamese scholar and gentry reformer. Phan helped to establish the Đông Kinh Nghia Thuc (Free School of the Eastern City [Hà Nôi]) to encourage progressive change and prevent bloody revolution in Vietnam. In 1908 he instigated disorders during the tax uprising in An Nam. Arrested and sentenced to death, he was confined to Côn Son island. Once pardoned and freed, Phan traveled to France and publicly reproached the colonial regime. He and Hô Chí Minh composed a draft of eight points for Vietnam's liberation that was submitted to the 1919 Paris peace conference. Phan returned to Vietnam in 1925 and published two speeches, one censuring the monarchy and the other considering the possible Vietnamese assimilation of European values. Following his death in Sài Gòn, mourners turned out for a seven-day funeral that became a national event.

—Rodney J. Ross

References: Buttinger, Joseph. *Vietnam: A Political History* (1968); Duiker, William J. *The Rise of Nationalism in Vietnam, 1900–1941* (1976); Marr, David G. *Vietnamese Anticolonialism, 1885–1925* (1971).
See also: Beau, Jean-Baptiste-Paul; French Indo-China; Hô Chí Minh; Phan Bôi Châu.

Phan Đình Phùng (1847–1895)

Most prominent Confucian scholar of the anti–French royalist movement in the late nineteenth century. In 1885, after Huê fell to the French, Phan Đình Phùng raised an army with the support of people from his native village and chose as his headquarters Mount Vu Quang, a strategic point on the road linking Vietnam with Laos and Thailand. From Vu Quang, Phan Đình Phùng's army could operate in Hà Tinh Quang Bình, Thanh Hóa, and Nghê An provinces. His army was well trained and organized, and one of his lieutenants, Cao Thang, was able to produce 300 rifles patterned after the French model of 1874. Phan Đình Phùng caused serious problems for the French for ten years. To force him to surrender, the French excavated his ancestors' tombs, arrested his family members, and in 1895 launched several successful attacks against his base. The rebels then abandoned Vu Quang, and Phan Đình Phùng died shortly thereafter of dysentery.

—Pham Cao Duong

References: Đào Trinh Nhât. *Phan Đình Phùng* (1950); Lê Thành Khôi. *Le Viet-Nam: Histoire et Civilisation* (1955); Nguyên Huyên Anh. *Viêt Nam Danh Nhân Tu Điên* (1990); Nguyên Thê Anh. *Viêt Nam Duoi Thoi Pháp Đô Hô* (1970).

See also: French Indo-China; Tôn Thât Thuyêt; Tu Đuc.

Phan Huy Quát (1909–1979)

Republic of Vietnam (RVN) politician, foreign minister, and premier. During the early 1940s Quát founded the Tân Việt Nam (New Vietnam) Party. From 1950 to 1954 Quát was minister of defense in the consecutive governments of Premiers Nguyên Phan Long, Nguyên Van Tâm, and Buu Lôc. Despite the recommendation of U.S. Ambassador Donald Heath, the next premier, Ngô Đình Diêm, refused in 1954 to give Quát a ministerial post. Quát then joined the so-called Caravelle Group, eighteen prominent South Vietnamese politicians who on 26 April 1960 signed a petition calling on Diêm to carry out political reforms.

Quát was imprisoned after the abortive 11 November 1960 coup. Released in July 1963 after acquittal by a military court, he returned to politics in 1964 as minister of foreign affairs in Premier Gen. Nguyên Khánh's government. In February 1965 the Armed Forces Council named him premier, but within a few months Quát had a falling out with Chief of State Phan Khac Suu. Under Catholic pressure, Quát resigned the premiership in June 1965. He was the last civilian RVN premier.

Quát continued to appear in the international arena and was president of the Asian Section of the World Anti-Communist Alliance until the Communist victory of April 1975. He died in the Sài Gòn central prison.

—Ngô Ngoc Trung

References: Biographical Files, Indo-China Archives, University of California at Berkeley.

See also: Ngô Đình Diêm; Nguyên Khánh; Phan Khac Suu; Vietnam, Republic of: 1954–1975.

Phan Khac Suu (1905–ca. 1972)

Republic of Vietnam politician and president, 1964–1965. On 1 July 1949 Suu became minister of agriculture, welfare, and labor in the Bao Đai government. He saw this as an opportunity to negotiate with the French for the return of power to the Vietnamese but, disappointed with the French colonial administration, held the post for only two months. On the return of Ngô Đình Diêm to Vietnam in 1954, Suu became his minister of agriculture but soon resigned after Diêm ignored his advice and oppressed the Cao Đài and Hòa Hao religious sects. In 1959 Suu was elected to the National Assembly but was arrested after the abortive 11 November 1960 coup. Condemned to eight years of solitary confinement in July 1963, he was freed after the 1 November 1963 overthrow of Diêm.

In September 1964 Suu was named chairman of the High National Council, the consulting and legislative body set up by the new Armed Forces Council headed by Gen. Nguyên Khánh. On 13 June 1965 the Armed Forces Council decided to abolish the High National Council to form a new War Government headed by President Nguyên Van Thiêu and Premier Nguyên Cao Ky, and Suu was dismissed. In 1966 he was elected to the Constituent Assembly and served as its chairman until the next election in 1967. He ran for the presidency in 1967, finished third behind Thiêu and Truong Đình Dzu, and retired from politics.

—Ngô Ngoc Trung

References: Biographical Files, Indo-China Archives, University of California at Berkeley.

See also: Cao Đài; Hòa Hao; Ngô Đình Diêm; Nguyên Cao Ky; Nguyên Khánh; Nguyên Van Thiêu; Phan Huy Quát; Truong Đình Dzu.

Phan Quang Đán (1918–)

Staunch Vietnamese anti-Communist and anticolonialist. In 1950 Phan formed his Vietnamese Republican Party and arranged an unsuccessful international forum to engage the Communists in negotiations following the 1954 Geneva Agreement. Under the Ngô Đình Diêm regime, Phan was arrested and tortured many times, in particular following the 11 November 1960 coup attempt. He was released after the overthrow of Diêm in November 1963. An elected deputy in the 1966 Constituent Assembly, Phan was unsuccessful in the presidential election of 3 September 1967. He then joined the Republic of Vietnam (RVN) government as foreign affairs minister (1969) and later served as a deputy prime minister for social welfare and refugees. His most prominent role in the Vietnam War was his effort to resettle thousands of war victims and refugees. After the defeat of the RVN in May 1975, Phan resettled in the United States, where he devotes himself to the struggle for freedom and democracy in Vietnam.

—Long Bá Nguyên

References: Fontaine, Ray. *The Dawn of Free Vietnam* (1992); Phan Quang Đán. "From the Homeland to Overseas" (1994).

See also: Bao Đai; Ngô Đình Diêm; Phan Khac Suu; Vietnam, Republic of: 1954–1975.

Phan Van Khai (1933–)

Leader in the Vietnamese Communist Party (VCP) and the Socialist Republic of Vietnam (SRV); premier of the SRV from September 1997. Foreign observers credit the Russian-trained Khai with the success of the SRV's economic renovation program. An economist by profession, Khai was considered a technocrat rather than a dynamic leader. Although Khai was perceived as lacking a political base and ambition, the VCP Central Committee on 19 September 1997 selected him to be chairman of the Councils of Ministers, or premier, replacing Võ Vân Kiêt. As a formality, the rubber-stamp parliament then elected Khai to the post on 25 September.

—Ngô Ngoc Trung

References: Biographical Files, Indo-China Archives, University of California at Berkeley.

See also: Vietnam, Socialist Republic of: 1975 to the Present.

Philastre, Paul-Louis-Félix (1837–1902)

French administrator and diplomat. Philastre arrived in Cochin China in 1861, was named to the post of inspector of indigenous affairs at My Tho in 1863, and was appointed chief of native law in 1868. After commanding an artillery regiment in the Franco-Prussian War, in 1873 he returned to Sài Gòn. Under pressure from Paris to resolve the Garnier-Dupuis affair in Tonkin, Admiral Dupré commissioned Philastre his ambassador to the court at Huê. In concert with Emperor Tu Ðuc, Philastre disavowed Francis Garnier's actions in Tonkin and ordered evacuation of all French garrisons there. He made the preliminary arrangements for the treaty of protectorate (sometimes referred to as the Philastre Treaty) signed at Huê on 15 March 1874. Philastre's French translation of the Vietnamese legal code and its commentaries was published as *Le Code Annamite* ("The Annamite Code") in Paris in 1876. After a year's service in Cambodia, Philastre returned to Huê and served as French chargé d'affaires from 1877 to 1879.

—Arthur J. Dommen

References: Buttinger, Joseph. *The Smaller Dragon: A Political History of Vietnam* (1958); Whitfield, Danny J. *Historical and Cultural Dictionary of Vietnam* (1976).

See also: Dupuis, Jean; French Indo-China; Garnier, Francis; Tu Ðuc.

Philippines

The Philippines assisted the United States in the Vietnam War. After the 1949 Communist victory in China, U.S. strategists feared the loss of Southeast Asia to communism, and the Philippine archipelago seemed especially vulnerable if dominoes began to fall.

U.S. officials perceived the Philippine experience as a prototype for Vietnam policy. Through 1953 and 1954 U.S. operatives in Manila supported Ramón Magsaysay for secretary of defense and later assisted his successful campaign for the presidency while aiding his efforts to suppress a strong Communist-directed, peasant-rooted rebellion, the Hukbalahap. Believing comparable outcomes attainable in Indo-China, Washington sent Col. Edward G. Lansdale, who had assisted Magsaysay, to Vietnam in 1954 to implement the psychological warfare techniques he had sharpened in the Philippines. Lansdale promoted Ngô Ðình Diêm as the Vietnamese Magsaysay.

Filipino foreign policy followed that of Washington. The U.S. call for united action envisioned Philippine cooperation, and Manila hosted the conference creating the Southeast Asia Treaty Organization (SEATO). The Philippines became a member and by 1955 extended diplomatic recognition to the Republic of Vietnam (RVN).

After the 1954 Geneva Accords, Manila dispatched assistance to the Sài Gòn regime. Operation Brotherhood assigned Filipino medical personnel to the South Vietnamese countryside and obtained nearly all funding from nonpublic Philippine associations. The Freedom Company of the Philippines, established in 1955 and controlled by the U.S. Central Intelligence Agency (CIA), used Filipino military veterans to execute covert missions in Indo-China. It carried out a range of activities, encompassing unconventional military actions north of the Demilitarized Zone (DMZ), authorship of the RVN constitution, and training for President Ngô Ðình Diêm's executive guard. Operation Brotherhood was phased out early in the 1960s, but the Freedom Company operated through the 1960s. It became known as the Eastern Construction Company once the CIA withdrew its backing.

In 1964 the Philippine government joined the Free World Assistance Program ("Many Flags") and, with South Korea, Australia, New Zealand, Thailand, and Taiwan, pledged assistance to the RVN. Intended to create the impression that the war was an allied effort, the program initially sought noncombat assistance but soon sought the use of Free World soldiers in a military role. A dispute between the Philippines and the United States soon resulted over the nature of Filipino aid. Manila offered nonmilitary engineers and medical units; Washington preferred military teams. In 1965, as the military situation deteriorated, the United States urged President Diosdado Macapagal to win approval for assistance from the Philippine Congress. Despite opposition, the Filipino legislature authorized the Philippine Contingent (PHILCON I) of two military surgical groups and a psychological warfare team, but stipulated that the amount of assistance depended on the extent of Washington's economic support for the Philippines.

After much wrangling over funding, newly elected President Ferdinand Marcos endorsed deployment of the Philippine Civil Action group (PHILCAG), a 2,300-man engineering group, financed mainly by the U.S. Agency for International Development. Himself opposed to the employment of combat troops, Marcos won the Philippine Congress' sanction to fund PHILCAG for 12 months, and by September 1966 the unit began debarking in Vietnam. Secret economic concessions by President Johnson smoothed the procurement of PHILCAG. Yet, by 1967, antipathy to PHILCAG in the Philippines caused the unit's reduction in size. Nine Filipinos in PHILCAG died in action.

—Rodney J. Ross

References: Blackburn, Robert M. *Mercenaries and Lyndon Johnson's "More Flags"* (1994); Kahin, George McT. *Intervention: How America Became Involved in Vietnam* (1986); Karnow, Stanley. *In Our Image: America's Empire in the Philippines* (1989).

See also: Free World Assistance Program; Lansdale, Edward Geary; Order of Battle; Southeast Asia Treaty Organization (SEATO); U.S. Agency for International Development (USAID); VULTURE, Operation.

Phoenix Program

Program to identify and eliminate the Viêt Công Infrastructure (VCI) in South Vietnam. The VCI represented the political and administrative arm of the insurgency in South Vietnam and logistically supported Viêt Công (VC) operations, recruited new members, and directed terrorist activities against Allied forces.

Initially, the South Vietnamese intelligence apparatus and elimination forces proved inadequate at gathering intelligence. Hence, in May 1967 Robert Komer arrived in Vietnam to head U.S. Civilian Operations and Revolutionary Development Support (CORDS). This organization combined U.S. and Vietnamese civilian and military intelligence and pacification programs and was placed within the Military Assistance Command, Vietnam (MACV) chain of command. Supervised by CORDS, and financially supported and directed by the Central Intelligence Agency (CIA), a new Intelligence Coordination and Exploitation (ICEX) program began building district intelligence and operations coordinating centers (DIOCCs) to collect, disseminate, and forward information to field units. Additional centers were built at the province level.

In early 1968, questions were raised regarding whether the CIA had violated the sovereignty of the Republic of Vietnam (RVN). To justify the legality of ICEX, William Colby, chief of the CIA's Far East Division, obtained a decree signed by President Nguyên Van Thiêu formally establishing an organization named Phuong Hoàng (Phoenix) to assume ICEX operations. It became the deadliest weapon against the VCI. With renewed fervor, U.S. and RVN personnel began collecting and analyzing data while arresting and neutralizing targeted individuals.

The DIOCCs circulated blacklists of known VCI operatives consisting of rankings from A (most wanted) to D to Phoenix field forces, who then apprehended or "neutralized" (killed) the individuals. These forces included Vietnamese units such as the National Police, the National Police Field Force, Provincial Reconnaissance Units, as well as U.S. Navy Sea Air Land teams. If not killed, the targeted individual was transported to a provincial interrogation center (PIC). PIC personnel—CIA advisors and their Vietnamese counterparts—then sent the information obtained up the chain of command for analysis by DIOCC and CORDS officials.

With the advent of Vietnamization and the withdrawal of U.S. personnel, the Phoenix program suffered. Public pressure, generated by news reports that Phoenix was an assassination program, caused Phoenix to come under congressional investigation. In 1971 Colby appeared before a House Committee to explain it. Another factor in the program's demise was the 1972 Easter Offensive, which forced the RVN to focus its military strength against conventional rather than unconventional forces. In spring 1972 the National Police assumed responsibility for Phoenix, and by December 1972 the U.S. had ended its role in the program.

Despite negative media reports, top-ranking CIA officials as well as VC and Democratic Republic of Vietnam leaders agreed that the Phoenix program was a success. Available sources cite approximately 34,000 captured VCI operatives from 1968 to 1972. Proof of Phuong Hoàng's success could be seen in Quang Tri province during the 1972 Easter Offensive. For the first time there were front lines behind which civilians and troops could move freely at night. When Communist forces took northern Quang Tri, they were unable to find trustworthy sympathizers at the village level.

—R. Blake Dunnavent

References: Andrade, Dale. *Ashes to Ashes: The Phoenix Program and the Vietnam War* (1990); Colby, William. *Lost Victory: A Firsthand Account of America's Sixteen-Year Involvement in Vietnam* (1989); DeForest, Orrin, and David Chanoff. *Slow Burn: The Rise and Fall of American Intelligence in Vietnam* (1990); Herrington, Stuart A. *Silence Was a Weapon: The Vietnam War in the Villages* (1982).

See also: Central Intelligence Agency (CIA); Civilian Operations and Revolutionary Development Support (CORDS); Colby, William Egan; Counterinsurgency Warfare; Komer, Robert W.; Pacification; Psychological Warfare Operations (PSYOP); Territorial Forces; Vietnam, Republic of: Special Forces (Luc Luong Ðac Biêt [LLDB]).

Phoumi Nosavan (1920–1985)

Laotian general and political leader. Nosavan was involved in the unsuccessful effort to remove Phoui Sananikone from power in December 1959. In the succeeding government he was made defense minister and organized his own political party, the Paxa Sangkhom. After the fraudulent elections of 25 April 1960, he was once again defense minister in the government of Tiao Somsanith.

When Captain Kong Le overthrew the government in a coup d'état on 9 August 1960, Phoumi appealed to Marshal Sarit to help him restore the pro-Western Somsanith government. Phoumi was backed by the Central Intelligence Agency (CIA) and the U.S. Defense Department, which ordered that aid be furnished to him at his base at Savannakhet. Unable to patch things up with Prince Souvanna Phouma, the new prime minister, Phoumi formed a Counter-Coup d'Etat Committee (later renamed Revolutionary Committee) under the nominal leadership of Prince Boun Oum. With U.S. and Thai backing (clandestine, because the United States still recognized the legal government in Vientiane), Phoumi attacked and captured Vientiane in December, forcing Prince Souvanna to flee to Cambodia.

U.S. hopes that Phoumi could defeat the Communists in Laos were soon dashed. It became apparent that his troops controlled little of Laos outside the major towns. Eventually, Phoumi and Prince Boun Oum became leaders of the rightist faction in a tripartite agreement brokered with international help for a coalition government with the Neutralists and Pathet Lao. Phoumi became deputy premier in this government, which took office in June 1962. Caught in a Februaruy 1965 rightist coup plot, apparently of others' making, he fled to Thailand. He was convicted in absentia by a commission of the National Assembly of numerous crimes, including corruption. Despite attempts to restore his reputation and personal appeals to Prince Souvanna,

Phoumi never returned to Laos. He died in comfortable exile in Thailand.

—Arthur J. Dommen

Reference: Dommen, Arthur J. *Conflict in Laos; the Politics of Neutralization* (1971).
See also: Kong Le; Laos; Souvanna Phouma.

PIERCE ARROW, Operation (August 1964)

Air strikes launched against the Democratic Republic of Vietnam (DRV) as a result of the Tonkin Gulf incidents. When it was reported that DRV torpedo boats had attacked two U.S. destroyers in the Gulf of Tonkin on 4 August 1964, President Johnson quickly ordered retaliatory air strikes, code-named PIERCE ARROW. The targets were DRV naval vessels along the North Vietnamese coast and a petroleum storage facility at Vinh. Sixty-four sorties were flown from the aircraft carriers *Ticonderoga* and *Constellation*.

U.S. military planners preferred a dawn attack, and Johnson was determined that it be made early enough that he could announce it before much of the American public had gone to bed, but there were long delays. The *Ticonderoga* was short of strike aircraft and more were flying in from the Philippines; the *Constellation*, coming from Hong Kong at top speed, was not yet in position. Johnson went on the air to announce the strikes at 2337 Washington time (1037 in North Vietnam). Only four of the *Ticonderoga*'s aircraft, and none of the *Constellation*'s, were in the air. No bombs fell for another 90 minutes.

The Vinh petroleum storage facility, the priority target, was destroyed. Most naval vessels attacked were Swatow boats, coastal patrol vessels. The U.S. sank at least one, but probably not more than three. A few torpedo boats and one submarine chaser were damaged but not sunk. Two U.S. aircraft were shot down, both from the *Constellation*. Each side claimed victory, exaggerating its success in the action. The American public approved of the air strikes overwhelmingly, so much so that public opinion polls showed a dramatic improvement in ratings of the president's overall handling of the situation in Southeast Asia.

—Edwin E. Moise

Reference: Moise, Edwin E. *Tonkin Gulf and the Escalation of the Vietnam War* (1996).
See also: Aircraft Carriers; Alvarez, Everett, Jr.; DeSoto Missions; Johnson, Lyndon Baines; Operation Plan 34A (OPLAN 34A); Tonkin Gulf Incidents.

Pigneau de Béhaine, Pierre (1741–1799)

French Catholic bishop and advisor to Emperor Gia Long who probably did as much as any Frenchman to involve France in Vietnam. Pigneau devoted his life to the restoration of the Nguyêns to power in Vietnam. Partly through Pigneau's tireless lobbying on behalf of Nguyên Phúc Ánh and his raising of troops from among French navy deserters, this aim was finally accomplished in 1802, two years after his death.

—Arthur J. Dommen

References: Buttinger, Joseph. *The Smaller Dragon: A Political History of Vietnam* (1958); Whitfield, Danny J. *Historical and Cultural Dictionary of Vietnam* (1976).
See also: Nguyên Phúc Ánh (Gia Long); Vietnam: from 938 through French Conquest.

Pignon, Léon (1908–1976)

French high commissioner in Indo-China, 1948–1950. A strong proponent of the French Empire, Pignon refused to negotiate with the Viêt Minh but did work with Bao Đai to enhance the facade of Vietnamese independence. The Elysée Agreement, containing an outline for a unified Vietnam but one in which France maintained control of its defense, diplomacy, and finance, was completed in March 1949. Pignon's short tenure as high commissioner ended the following year.

—David Coffey

References: Karnow, Stanley. *Vietnam: A History* (1983); *International Who's Who 1976–1977* (1977).
See also: Bao Đai; Bollaert, Emile; d'Argenlieu, Georges Thierry; Elysée Agreement.

PIRANHA, Operation (September 1965)

Allied military operation, begun on 7 September 1965 and running for three weeks, on the Batangan Peninsula along the coast of southern Quang Ngãi Province. PIRANHA followed the conclusion of Operation STARLITE, the first major U.S. ground operation in the Vietnam War. It targeted a Viet Con (VC) buildup, possibly by remnants of their battered 1st Regiment, on the Batangan Peninsula, which was reported to be a place of entry for seaborne infiltration of enemy supplies. PIRANHA differed significantly from STARLITE in that a relatively small number of Marines coordinated with several battalions of the Army of the Republic of Vietnam (ARVN) 2d Division and a battalion of Vietnamese Marines. Although PIRANHA lasted two weeks longer than STARLITE, its results were less spectacular. U.S. Marine forces counted 183 VC killed in action, 66 of them in a cave blown up by Marine engineers. South Vietnamese forces claimed an additional 66 VC killed. Marine casualties in PIRANHA were extremely light. Both STARLITE and PIRANHA may have disabused the VC of any illusion that they could defeat U.S. Marines in a stand-up battle, but Quang Ngãi Province remained a Communist sanctuary well into 1968.

—John D. Root

References: Simmons, Edwin H. "Marine Corps Operations in Vietnam, 1965–1966" (1985); Stanton, Shelby L. *The Rise and Fall of an American Army: U.S. Ground Forces in Vietnam, 1965–1973* (1985).
See also: STARLITE, Operation; United States: Marine Corps.

PIRAZ Warships (1965–1973)

U.S. destroyers, frigates, and cruisers operating in the Gulf of Tonkin to provide support for Allied war planes. To warn of air attack, U.S. Navy surface combatants first took up station in April 1965 between the Democratic Republic of Vietnam (DRV) and aircraft carriers on Yankee Station. The surface warships soon assumed other duties. In the first successful performance of that mission, the destroyer *Joseph Strauss* in June 1965 controlled two F-4 Phantoms to an interception of two MiG-17s, contributing to the initial U.S. aerial victories of the conflict.

Formalized in July 1966, the patrols were dubbed PIRAZ for "Positive Identification Radar Advisory Zone." In addition to early warning and fighter control duties, PIRAZ ships were to provide a precise navigational reference point for U.S. aircraft, track all planes flying over the Gulf of Tonkin and eastern areas of North Vietnam, keep U.S. aircraft from crossing into People's Republic of China airspace, and direct search-and-rescue helicopters to downed aircrews. These multiple missions frequently involved tracking hundreds of aircraft simultaneously; the nuclear-powered cruiser *Long Beach*, for example, tracked about 30,000 U.S. aircraft sorties during a four-month tour in 1967. Thus vessels assigned to PIRAZ were the most modern surface warships, especially those equipped with the computerized Naval Tactical Data System and antiaircraft missile batteries for self-defense.

PIRAZ missiles downed North Vietnamese aircraft on several occasions, but PIRAZ warships enjoyed even greater successes by controlling U.S. interception of DRV planes. The top-scoring ship in this field was the cruiser *Chicago*, whose radarman Master Chief Larry Nowell won the Navy's Distinguished Service Medal in August 1972 for vectoring Navy and Air Force fighters to 12 successful interceptions.

PIRAZ warships made their greatest contribution in the performance of more mundane duties and also validated the Navy's newest electronic and missile systems. In so doing, they helped demonstrate the capabilities of the surface warship in a navy dominated by carrier aviation.

—Malcolm Muir, Jr.

References: Marolda, Edward J. *By Sea, Air, and Land: An Illustrated History of the U.S. Navy and the War in Southeast Asia* (1994); Muir, Malcolm, Jr. *Black Shoes and Blue Water: Surface Warfare in the United States Navy, 1945–1975* (1996).

See also: Airplanes, Allied and Democratic Republic of Vietnam; United States: Navy; Warships, Allied and Democratic Republic of Vietnam.

Pistols

During the Indo-China War, French forces used domestic and foreign pistols. Based primarily on a Browning design, the French M1935A and M1935S pistols are chambered for the 7.65-mm "long" cartridge. Both pistols are recoil-operated, semiautomatic weapons fed by eight-round detachable box magazines. French forces also used German 9-mm P38s and P08 Lugers and American .45-caliber 1911 and 1911A1 Colts. Experience with those weapons spurred designers at the Saint Etienne Arsenal to develop a new French service pistol. The resulting 9-mm M1950 is essentially a modification of the U.S. .45-caliber Colt 1911A1 chambered for the German 9-mm parabellum cartridge and utilizing a nine-round detachable box magazine.

During the Vietnam War the standard sidearm issued to U.S. forces was the .45-caliber Model 1911A1, designed by John Browning and originally designated 1911 after its year of adoption. Various manufacturers produced more than 2.4 million .45-caliber 1911 and 1911A1s for the U.S. government. It is a recoil-operated semiautomatic utilizing a .45-caliber rimless cartridge and features a seven-round, detachable box magazine.

The government also purchased commercial pistols for special-purpose use, and individuals at times carried privately purchased or captured sidearms. Secondary military-issued pistols included the Colt .32- and .380-caliber semiautomatic pistol, the .38-caliber Colt Detective Special Revolver, Colt Police Positive Revolver, Colt Special Official Police, Colt Combat Masterpiece, Smith & Wesson Model 10, and Smith & Wesson Military and Police Revolvers.

During the Indo-China and Vietnam Wars, Viêt Minh, People's Army of Vietnam (PAVN), and Viêt Công (VC) forces used sidearms ranging from primitive, homemade "zip-guns" to captured World War II Japanese and well-made French and American pistols. Large numbers of weapons were also imported from Communist countries. Produced by the Soviet Union and the People's Republic of China, the most commonly used sidearm was the Soviet-designed Tokarev TT Model 1933 semiautomatic pistol (designated Type 51 in Chinese nomenclature). Modified at the Tula arsenal by Fedor V. Tokarev from a Colt-Browning design, the TT Model 1933/Type 51 is chambered for a bottlenecked 7.62-mm cartridge and fed by an eight-round, in-line detachable box magazine.

—Jeff Kinard

References: Chant, Christopher, ed. *How Weapons Work* (1976); Rosa, Joseph G., and Robin May. *An Illustrated History of Guns and Small Arms* (1984); Smith, W. H. B., revised by Joseph E. Smith. *Small Arms of the World*, 9th ed. (1969).

See also: Grenades, Hand, Allied and Democratic Republic of Vietnam; Grenades, Launched, Allied and Democratic Republic of Vietnam; Machine Guns, Allied and People's Army of Vietnam; Rifles; Rockets.

Plain of Jars

Rolling plain in Xieng Khouang Province of northern Laos near the border of Vietnam named for a large number of stone urns or jars of unknown origin. The plain was heavily bombed by U.S. planes, and unexploded ordnance continues to kill people in the area. An ordnance defusing team has worked to correct the situation, supported by international aid from foreign governments, including the United States, and nongovernmental organizations.

—Arthur J. Dommen

See also: Air Power, Role in War; Geography of Indo-China and Vietnam; Laos.

Plain of Reeds

Location, primarily in Kiên Phong and Kiên Tuong Provinces west of Sài Gòn, that was a stronghold for Communist guerrilla operations throughout the war. Formed by a depression in the Mekong River Delta, the plain consists largely of harsh, sparsely populated marshland. Viêt Minh manipulated the local population against the French; similarly, the Viêt Công controlled the population against U.S. and South Vietnamese forces. Although no large American units were deployed against the small-scale guerrilla maneuvers, two significant battles took place there on 1–8 January 1966 and 29 July 1969. In 1969 the U.S. Navy conducted Operation BARRIER REEF, successfully inhibiting the Communists' ability to traverse the plain to heavily populated areas farther south. The plain was a staging area for the 1970 incursions into Cambodia against guerrilla sanctuaries and resupply routes. The final battles in the area occurred in 1972 during the Easter Offensive.

—Charles J. Gaspar

References: Andrade, Dale. *Trial by Fire: The 1972 Easter Offensive* (1995); Coleman, J. D. *Incursion* (1991); Schreadley, R. L. *From the Rivers to the Sea* (1992).

See also: Cambodian Incursion; Easter Offensive (Nguyên Huê Campaign); Mekong Delta.

Poetry and the Vietnam Experience

Poetry that documents the attitudes toward the Vietnam War—as well as the origins, development, and conduct of the war—is pervasive and significant.

Few French poems reflect that country's involvement, but the Vietnamese tradition of poetic expression produced a large body of work, both personal and political, by soldiers and civilians of the Democratic Republic of Vietnam (DRV) and the Republic of Vietnam (RVN). Unfortunately, except for the efforts of American poets John Balaban, Yusef Komunyakka, Kevin Bowen, and Bruce Weigl, most of these poems are not available in translation. Only the Vietnamese expatriate Thích Nhât Hanh published a significant collection in English. His *The Cry of Vietnam* (1968) contains fifteen poems about the devastation of war and the horrors inflicted by all sides. Poems by Vietnamese, Cambodian, and Lao refugee poets appeared in the numerous volumes of the Viêt Nam Forum Series and the Lac-Viêt Series published after 1983 by the Council on Southeast Asia Studies at Yale University. In Viêt Nam Forum 14 (1994), for instance, Viêt Thanh Nguyên wrote in a moving poem about a burning ash heap that he was "yearning to find a clue/ in the ash to my people,/ severed from me with the finality of a butcher's cleaver."

American poets—veterans and nonveterans—best chronicled the changing, often conflicting, attitudes and experiences of those fighting in Southeast Asia. Their poetry ranges from bawdy ballads sung by U.S. fighter pilots, collected in Joseph F. Tuso's *Singing the Vietnam Blues* (1990), and short, sometimes humorous verses in publications such as the satiric *Grunt* magazine or the *Pacific Stars and Stripes*, to immensely ambitious and moving works that rank with the best poetry of the age.

Poetry about Vietnam falls into three general categories: political protest poems, usually written by established poets who had not been to Vietnam; verse novels, in which chronologically linked poems depict one person's experiences at war; and the hundreds of usually short, personal lyrics that present individual scenes, character sketches, or events.

The first significant protest volume was *A Poetry Reading Against the Vietnam War* (1966), edited by Robert Bly and David Ray. In 1967 Walter Lowenfels edited the anthology *Where is Vietnam?*, with 87 contributing poets including James Dickey, Lawrence Ferlinghetti, and Denise Levertov. *Out of the Shadow of War* (1968) and *Poetry Against the War* (1972) followed. Although a few poems are set in Southeast Asia, most works presented in these anthologies reflect the writers' attitudes toward U.S. involvement in Vietnam by references to the political scene, the war as reported by various media, and antiwar themes in general. These anthologies, and numerous individual poems, served to define and sustain the general intellectual opposition to the war.

Of the verse novels, three stand out: *Vietnam Simply* (1967) by Dick Shea; *How Audie Murphy Died in Vietnam* (1972) by McAvoy Layne; and *Interrogations* (1990) by Leroy Quintana. In discursive, often sardonic selections, Shea presents the observations of a Navy lieutenant about the entrance of U.S. Marines into the war and other scenes and events in 1965 Vietnam. In short, staccato verses, Layne's book traces a Marine recruit (who bears the name of the legendary American war hero) through basic training and combat, then becomes allegorically fanciful as Audie is captured by the Viêt Công and holds telephone conversations from Hà Nôi with the president of the United States while humming "The/Theme/From/Marlboro/Country." Quintana, the only Hispanic veteran to publish a major collection of poetry, shows how a young army draftee experiences training, combat, and the aftermath of the war.

The movement from innocence to experience was perhaps the most universal theme explored by American poets, most of whom served in Vietnam, either in the military or as conscientious objectors. Before the 1975 fall of Sài Gòn, many poet-veterans joined protest organizations, using their poems to substantiate their opposition not only to war in general but to the Vietnam War in particular.

What characterizes most of the individual poems is their specificity. Brutally frank, many of these poems are filled with the soldiers' jargon and profanity, often requiring the use of a glossary because of the many references to historical events as well as specific people and place names. The themes are both universal and particularly modern. Many show the horrors of war, the deaths of innocent civilians, the tragic ending of youthful lives, and the general sundering of moral and ethical values. Reflecting the consciousness of the 1960s and 1970s, however, many poems mirror the feelings of all participants as America's longest war began to seem unwinnable: the sense of loss of individuality; the feeling of guilt at having participated; the impossibility of anyone's understanding the totality of the experience; the realization of having been betrayed by higher authority; and most often, the anger and bitterness at feeling like what Larry Heinemann called "a slab of meat on the table." Many poems contain racial and ethnic themes, using both black versus white and white versus Asian conflicts.

Few war veteran poets achieved literary prominence. Army veteran Yusef Komunyakaa won the 1994 Pulitzer Prize for his *Neon Vernacular: New and Selected Poems* (1993). The selections in one of his earlier books, *Dien Cai Dau* (1988), are about the war and present not only richly metaphoric poems about Hà Nôi Hannah, Bob Hope, and night patrols, but also offer the acute vision of a black soldier. Another major prizewinning poet is former Marine W. D. Ehrhart, whose numerous collections of poetry, four nonfiction books, and many edited anthologies made him one of the most prolific and widely known Vietnam War writers. In *A Generation of Peace* (1977), his poem "A Relative Thing," which details the feelings of many returned veterans, reminds America that "We are your sons," and that "When you awake,/we will still be here."

The oldest of the major poets was Walter McDonald, a career officer teaching at the Air Force Academy when he was assigned to Vietnam in 1969. An editor and fiction writer, McDonald was best known for his many volumes of poems such as *After the Noise of Saigon* (1988), in which the subject of war is balanced by poems about flying and scenes in West Texas. Another professor was Bruce Weigl, whose Army service in Vietnam sparked several collections, such as *Song of Napalm* (1988), in which most of his war poems appear. The title poem is a haunting testament to his wife as he confesses his inability to forget aspects of the war. Yet another college instructor, John Balaban, spent three years in Vietnam, the first two as a conscientious objector. He published fiction and numerous translations of Vietnamese poetry. His collections *After Our War* (1974), nominated for a National Book Award, and *Blue Mountain* (1982) contain memorable poems such as "April 30, 1975," written about the last day of the war.

Among other poets and their major books are Michael Casey, *Obscenities* (1972); David Huddle, *Stopping by Home* (1988); Kevin Bowen, *Playing Basketball with the Viet Cong* (1994); D. F. Brown, *Returning Fire* (1984); Horace Coleman, *Between a Rock and a Hard Place*, in *Four Black Poets* (1977); Gerald McCarthy, *War Story* (1977); Bill Shields, *Nam Poems* (1987); Steve Mason, *Warrior for Peace*, with an introduction by Oliver Stone (1988); Bryan Alec Floyd, *The Long War Dead* (1976); Perry Oldham, *Vinh Long* (1976); and D. C. Berry, *Saigon Cemetery* (1972).

Individual works by these and other poets can be found in the anthologies *Winning Hearts and Minds*, edited by Larry Rottman, Jan Barry, and Basil T. Paquet (1972); *Listen: The War*, edited by Fred Kiley and Tony Dater (1973); *Demilitarized Zones*, edited by Jan Barry and W. D. Ehrhart (1976); *Carrying the Darkness*, edited by W. D. Ehrhart (1985, 1989); *Shallow Graves: Two Women in Vietnam*, by Wendy Wilder Larsen and Trân Thi Nga (1986); and *Unaccustomed Mercy*, edited by W. D. Ehrhart (1989).

Coincident with the dedication of the Vietnam Veterans Memorial in Washington, D.C., the first major public readings by Vietnam War creative writers was held in New York City on 23 March 1984. There, Ehrhart defined what became apparent in most of the poetry that had been and was to be published. Although most veteran-poets wrote about many other subjects, the war consumed them in their art and inspired their best poems because, according to Ehrhart, that experience was "the single most important experience of [one's] life." Accordingly, the poetry of the Vietnam War provides a historical, intellectual, and emotional chronology of people at war that is indeed unique.

—John Clark Pratt

References: Beidler, Philip D. *American Literature and The Experience of Vietnam* (1982); Beidler, Philip D. *Re-Writing America: Vietnam Authors in Their Generation* (1991); Gotera, Vince. *Radical Visions: Poetry by Vietnam Veterans* (1994); Lomperis, Timothy J., and John Clark Pratt. *Reading The Wind: The Literature of the Vietnam War* (1987); Newman, John. *Vietnam War Literature* (1996).
See also: Art and the Vietnam War; Drama and the Vietnam Experience; Fiction, U.S., and the Vietnam Experience; Film and the Vietnam Experience; Prose Narrative and the Vietnam Experience; Vietnam Veterans Against the War (VVAW).

Pol Pot (1928–1998)

Cambodian Communist revolutionary leader infamous as the architect of a genocidal policy. In 1953 Pol Pot joined the anti-French, Vietnamese-dominated underground movement and the Communist Party and emerged as a well-known left-wing journalist. In 1960 Cambodia's secret Communist Party elected him to its Central Committee and named him secretary-general in 1963. Distrusting Prince Norodom Sihanouk's 1963 invitation to join in forming a new government, Pol Pot—now a full time militant known as Brother Secretary or Brother Number One—fled into the jungles and organized the Khmer Rouge, a Communist guerilla army.

In March 1970 Gen. Lon Nol seized power in Cambodia. After visiting the Democratic Republic of Vietnam (DRV) and the People's Republic of China in 1969 and 1970, Pol Pot became military commander of the Cambodian Communist component of the National Front, the Sihanouk-led government in exile that sought to overthrow Lon Nol's pro-U.S. regime. The ensuing five-year civil war gave Pol Pot an opportunity to increase his military power and devote attention to political matters and organizational development. These contributed greatly to the Khmer Rouge seizure of Phnom Penh on 16 April 1975.

As prime minister of Democratic Kampuchea (1976–1978), Pol Pot envisioned an agricultural utopia populated by the new Cambodian collectivist man. Declaring the "Year Zero," he emptied Phnom Penh and turned the country into a vast concentration camp, with the population as rural forced labor. Khmer Rouge actions obliterated the middle class, and up to two million Cambodians died, some 25 percent of the population.

In December 1978 the Socialist Republic of Vietnam (SRV) invaded Cambodia and created the People's Republic of Kampuchea. In 1979 Pol Pot received sanctuary in Thailand, and the Khmer Rouge used that country as the base for its insurgency, first against the Vietnamese-installed Phnom Penh government and later to attempt to sabotage a United Nations–brokered peace plan and election.

Pol Pot's power stemmed partly from the mystery surrounding him. He gave his last public interview in 1980. In September 1985 the Khmer Rouge faction of the Kampuchean coalition government announced that Pol Pot was relinquishing command of the rebel army that had battled the Vietnamese since 1978. This had long been sought by Western nations supporting the rebel alliance and by the SRV as a first step toward ending the six-year civil war, but it left unclear Pol Pot's real status.

After 1985 Pol Pot's status was the stuff of much speculation in the West. Then in late July 1997 Pol Pot surfaced, the centerpiece in a show trial in western Cambodia by the Khmer Rouge leadership. Found guilty, he was sentenced to life under house arrest. His trial was probably the result of the June 1997 killing of Khmer Rouge leader Son Sen and his family on Pol Pot's orders. Pol Pot spent his last months in a shack in the Dangrek Mountains. He died on 15 April 1998, reportedly of a heart attack. No autopsy was conducted, and there were suspicions he might have been murdered by some of his lieutenants who feared increasing pressure on the part of Washington for his trial and their possible implication in his misdeeds.

—Paul S. Daum, with Joseph Ratner

References: Becker, Elizabeth. *When the War Was Over: Cambodia's Revolution and the Voices of Its People* (1986.); Chandler, David P. *Brother Number One: A Political Biography of Pol Pot* (1992); Moritz, Charles, ed. *Current Biography 1980* (1980); Shawcross, William. *Sideshow: Kissinger, Nixon, and the Destruction of Cambodia* (1979).
See also: Cambodia; Heng Samrin; Hun Sen; Khmer Rouge; Lon Nol; Sihanouk, Norodom; Vietnamese Invasion and Occupation of Cambodia.

Poland

Polish People's Republic; member, with Canada and India, of the International Commission for Supervision and Control (ICSC) established in the 1954 Geneva Accords. A socialist state, Poland joined other Warsaw Pact members in support of the Democratic Republic of Vietnam (DRV) during the Vietnam conflict. Polish diplomat Janusz Lewandowski secured an opening for negotiations between the United States and the DRV (Operation MARIGOLD) in June 1966, which was torpedoed by U.S. bombings near Hà Nôi. A second attempt to host negotiations in November 1966 also failed due to U.S. refusal to halt its bombings of the North.

—Robert G. Mangrum

References: Davidson, Phillip B. *Vietnam at War* (1988); Karnow, Stanley. *Vietnam: A History* (1984); Summers, Harry G. *Vietnam War Almanac* (1985).
See also: International Commission for Supervision and Control (ICSC); MARIGOLD, Operation.

Popular Forces. *See* Territorial Forces.

Porter, William James (1914–1988)

U.S. diplomat; chief negotiator for the U.S. delegation to the Paris peace talks, 1971–1973. In 1965, at the request of Ambassador Henry Cabot Lodge, Porter became deputy ambassador to the Republic of Vietnam (RVN). Lodge relieved Porter of routine duties and gave him full charge of the pacification program designed to win the loyalty of the South Vietnamese people. Porter had charge of all nonmili-

tary aspects of the U.S. effort in the RVN. Despite reservations about his role and lack of full support by Lodge, Porter pulled together several overlapping agencies that had duplicated functions. His Office of Civilian Operations (OCO) trained and installed agricultural and educational workers and community organizers. Such efforts at pacification and rural development won Henry Kissinger's praise and convinced President Johnson that the government was on the right course. However, after 18 months under Porter's control, the program fell short of Washington's expectations and was reassigned to military control.

Porter's most significant role in the Vietnam War came with his September 1971 appointment by President Nixon to replace David K. E. Burns as chief U.S. delegate at the Paris peace talks. His dynamic, unconventional style bolstered the 19-member U.S. delegation and moved the talks forward. Porter took the offensive and unnerved the other side by adopting their own tactics. He postponed meetings, lectured opposing delegates, and refused to let the other side use the negotiations as a stage for propaganda. Complementing Kissinger's efforts with Democratic Republic of Vietnam delegate Lê Đuc Tho, Porter is credited with breaking the deadlocked negotiations, thus opening the way for U.S. troop withdrawal, a cease-fire, and the return of U.S. prisoners of war.

—Gary Kerley

References: *Current Biography Yearbook 1974* (1975); Herring, George C. *LBJ and Vietnam: A Different Kind of War* (1994); Olson, James S., ed. *Dictionary of the Vietnam War* (1988); *The Pentagon Papers: The Defense Department History of United States Decisionmaking on Vietnam*, vol. 2. (1971).
See also: Johnson, Lyndon Baines; Kissinger, Henry Alfred; Lodge, Henry Cabot, Jr.; Nixon, Richard Milhous; Pacification; Paris Negotiations.

Post-Traumatic Stress Disorder (PTSD)

Term developed to describe and treat stress reactions in Vietnam War veterans. It has since been used for diagnosis and treatment of sufferers of other traumas such as natural disaster, hostage and prisoner-of-war (POW) experiences, and violent crime. As defined in the American Psychiatric Association's *Diagnostic and Statistical Manual*, 4th edition (DSM-IV), five conditions are necessary for the diagnosis of post-traumatic stress disorder (PTSD):

1. The existence of a traumatic experience "outside the normal range of human experience." This experience may have come in undergoing or witnessing imminent threat of death, violent physical injury, or systematic physical abuse, and must have resulted at the time in intense fear, helplessness, or horror.

2. Persistent reexperiencing of the stressor event. The individual is subject to vivid and uncontrollable memories and/or recurrent dreams of the event and may lose track of his or her current surroundings entirely, in what has come to be called a "flashback." There may be intense psychological or physiological reactions to external or internal cues that remind the individual of the event.

3. Persistent avoidance of thoughts, people, places, and

other aspects associated with the traumatic event, along with a numbing of emotional responses and/or feelings of detachment from other people. There may also be partial amnesia about the past event and/or an inability to project a normal life for the future. Three indicators in this category are required.

4. Increased arousal, including at least two of the following: sleep problems, outbursts of anger, difficulty in concentrating, hypervigilance, and an exaggerated startle response.

5. A duration of the condition for at least one month.

The condition may occur immediately after the traumatic event, or, in the case of "delayed stress," may manifest itself months or years after the event.

The National Vietnam Veterans Readjustment Study (NVVRS), commissioned by Congress in 1983 and published in 1990, claims that approximately 15.2 percent of Vietnam-theater veterans suffer from PTSD. This figure generally agrees with previous studies conducted by the Department of Veterans Affairs and the Centers for Disease Control. Although lower than figures gathered in other wars—World War II estimates, for example, exceed 30 percent—accurate comparisons are difficult, since the definition of the disorder has changed since previous wars.

Some psychologists and psychiatrists began using the term "Vietnam War Syndrome" in 1969. In December 1970 psychiatrist Robert Jay Lifton, who was active in the anti-war movement, began a series of experimental "rap groups" with members of the New York chapter of Vietnam Veterans Against the War (VVAW). These were a form of group therapy in which veterans talked through their experiences during and after the war. In 1973 Lifton described the rap groups and his conclusions drawn from them in his influential book *Home from the War*, which became the basis for diagnosis and treatment of PTSD. However, Lifton acknowledged he had used a nonrepresentative sample (disaffected veterans in an activist organization) and that his goal was primarily to train a group of vocal advocates against the war.

In 1972 Lifton and his colleague Chaim Shatan, with help from the National Council of Churches, sponsored the First National Conference on the Emotional Needs of Vietnam-Era Veterans, in St. Louis. There Veterans Administration (VA) officials were introduced to Lifton's recommendations for the counseling systems that would later be used by the VA. Congress approved funding for such systems in 1979. An important part of the counseling system was the establishment of Veteran Outreach Centers (Vet Centers) outside normal VA facilities where veterans could talk in an informal atmosphere and receive job training, benefits counseling, and psychological counseling.

There was still no officially recognized definition of the disorders being treated, however. In 1976, Lifton and his colleagues, as part of a task force for the American Psychiatric Association, had begun work on such a definition, which in 1980 was published in DSM-III. Although slightly modified and clarified in two subsequent editions, the definition today remains essentially unchanged.

A disturbing number of reported PTSD cases have been found to be based on erroneous reporting of the supposed traumatic event or reported symptoms. Assumptions originally made about Vietnam veterans have had to be modified. It is possible that the developmental history of PTSD definitions and treatment has led to these discrepancies. The diagnostic and treatment research was originally done with a nonrepresentative sample and a presupposed outcome; furthermore, statistical data on recovery rates and numbers of cases were not collected until the definitions had been established, five years after the end of the war. Meanwhile, cases that might have been reported have been diagnosed under other categories of disorder and treated accordingly.

—Phoebe S. Spinrad

References: American Psychiatric Association. *Diagnostic and Statistical Manual of Mental Disorders*. 4th ed. (1994); Brende, Joel Osler, and Erwin Randolph Parson. *Vietnam Veterans: The Road to Recovery* (1985); Figley, Charles R., and Seymour Leventman, eds. *Strangers at Home: Vietnam Veterans since the War* (1980); Hendin, Herbert, and Ann Pollinger Haas. *Wounds of War: The Psychological Aftermath of Combat in Vietnam* (1984); Kulka, Richard A., et al., eds. *National Vietnam Veterans Readjustment Study: Tables of Findings and Technical Appendices* (1990); Kulka, Richard A., et al., eds. *Trauma and the Vietnam War Generation: Report of Findings of the National Vietnam Veterans Readjustment Study* (1990); Lifton, Robert Jay. *Home from the War: Vietnam Veterans, Neither Victims nor Executioners* (1973); Scott, Wilbur J. *The Politics of Readjustment: Vietnam Veterans since the War* (1993); Sonnenberg, Stephen M., Arthur S. Blank, Jr., and John A. Talbott, eds. *The Trauma of War: Stress and Recovery in Vietnam Veterans* (1985).
See also: Fiction, U.S., and the Vietnam Experience; Film and the Vietnam Experience; Lifton, Robert Jay; Vietnam Veterans Against the War (VVAW).

Potsdam Conference (16 July–1 August 1945)

Final meeting of Allied leaders—Winston Churchill, Joseph Stalin, and Harry S Truman—in World War II. Several aspects of the conference affected French Indo-China. First, the United States denied the French representation at Potsdam. Second, a minor item of the agenda involved procedures for the Japanese surrender in Vietnam. The British were to receive the surrender south of the sixteenth parallel; the Chinese Nationalists would take the Japanese surrender in the North. This scheme proved to be a disaster. In the South, British commander Gen. Douglas Gracey, a highly paternalistic colonial officer, violated Lord Mountbatten's orders to avoid Vietnam's internal problems by affirming that "civil and military control by the French is only a question of weeks." In the North, while Chinese forces plundered and pillaged, Hô Chí Minh was nonetheless able to proclaim the independence of the Democratic Republic of Vietnam (DRV).

—Brenda J. Taylor

Reference: Gormly, James L. *From Potsdam to the Cold War* (1990).
See also: French Indo-China; Gracey, Douglas D.; Jiang Jieshi (Chiang Kai-shek); Truman, Harry S; Vietnam, Democratic Republic of: 1945–1954.

Poulo Condore (Côn Son)

One of 14 islands in the Côn Son Island group in the South China Sea. The French converted the island into a prison where they incarcerated Vietnamese who opposed French colonial administration. A principal feature was its "tiger cages," cells approximately five feet square and nine feet high, roofed with metal bars that served as overhead walkways for guards. Three or more prisoners were shackled to the floor and fed little more than rice and water. This means of confinement often hardened the spirit of defiance among prisoners who survived it, among whom were some leading lights of the Vietnamese revolution: Phan Chu Trinh, Lê Duân, Lê Đuc Tho, and Pham Van Đông.

After expulsion of the French, the Republic of Vietnam (RVN) used the renamed Côn Son Correctional Facility to house Communists who were not members of the Viêt Công Armed Forces as well as non-Communist opponents of the RVN government. Except for some prisoners of war (POWs) guilty of murder in POW camps, no PAVN POWs were held at Côn Son. The Red Cross ultimately documented ill treatment there and judged it to be in violation of the Geneva Convention.

Vietnamese and U.S. leaders continually denied the existence of any "relics" of French penal administration and maintained that nothing done on Côn Son Island deprived prisoners of "physical necessities and human dignity." These officials thereby constructed a public relations time bomb that exploded with devastating effect in spring 1970 when a Congressional team dispatched to the RVN by President Nixon visited Vietnamese prisons. Upon hearing from Câu Loi Nguyên, a student recently released from Côn Son, that many student leaders were in the island's tiger cages, congressional aide Tom Harkin, Don Luce of the World Council of Churches, and Congressmen Augustus Hawkins and William Anderson visited the island. They returned with evidence of political repression so embarrassing that it ultimately helped convince Congress to begin to curtail further assistance to the RVN.

The site of the prison complex has been preserved as a monument to the Vietnamese independence movement. A full-scale replica of a tiger cage is on display at the War Crimes Museum in Hô Chí Minh City.

—Marc Jason Gilbert

References: Buttinger, Joseph. *The Smaller Dragon: A Political History of Vietnam* (1958); Brown, Holmes, and Don Luce. *Hostages of War: Saigon's Political Prisoners* (1973); Ciabatari, Jane. "Senator Harkin Returns to the Tiger Cages of Con Son" (1995); Leslie, Jacques. *The Mark: A War Correspondent's Memoir of Vietnam and Cambodia* (1995).
See also: Hayden, Thomas E.; Lê Duân; Lê Đuc Tho; Missing in Action and Prisoners of War, Viêt Công and People's Army of Vietnam; Nguyên Phúc Ánh (Gia Long); Pham Van Đông; Phan Chu Trinh.

Powell, Colin L. (1937–)

U.S. Army general; first African American to serve as chairman of the Joint Chiefs of Staff. Powell was profoundly influenced in his military thinking by his Vietnam experiences.

During Powell's second Vietnam tour, he served as an assistant operations officer in the 23d ("Americal") Division and became involved with the My Lai massacre investigation. Assigned responsibility of drafting the 23d Division's first official response to rumors concerning My Lai, Powell reported that the rumors were unfounded. Investigators came to consider Powell's report as part of the cover-up, but he staunchly maintained he knew nothing about the massacre until word of it became public in November 1969.

—David T. Zabecki

References: Barry, John. "The Very Model of a Political General: On Duty with Powell, from Vietnam to the Gulf" (1995); Powell, Colin. *My American Journey: An Autobiography* (1995); Roth, David. *Sacred Honor: A Biography of Colin Powell* (1993).
See also: My Lai Massacre; Schwartzkopf, H. Norman, Jr.

PRACTICE NINE, Project. *See* McNamara Line.

PRAIRIE, Operation (3 August 1966–18 March 1967)

Code name for the combat operations of the U.S. 3d Marine Division in the Côn Thiên and Gio Linh regions of I Corps. The Marine assignment was to stop the People's Army of Vietnam (PAVN) 324B Division from crossing the Demilitarized Zone (DMZ) and invading Quang Tri Province. Operation PRAIRIE consisted of two stages. During both stages of the operation, the 3d Marine Division claimed more than 2,000 PAVN soldiers killed. In driving the North Vietnamese back across the Bên Hai River, the Marines also succeeded in preventing the PAVN from establishing a major operating base in northern Quang Tri Province. However, the Marines sustained casualties of 200 dead and well over 1,000 wounded. PAVN units regrouped and later in 1967 crossed back into South Vietnam.

—James H. Willbanks

References: Pearson, Willard. *The War in the Northern Provinces, 1966–1968* (1975); Shulimson, Jack. *U.S. Marines in Vietnam: An Expanding War 1966* (1982); Stanton, Shelby L. *Vietnam Order of Battle* (1986); Telfer, Gary L., Lane Rogers, and Keith Fleming. *U.S. Marines in Vietnam: Fighting the North Vietnamese, 1967* (1984).
See also: HASTINGS, Operation; United States: Marine Corps; Vietnam, Democratic Republic of: Army (People's Army of Vietnam [PAVN]).

Prisoners of War, Allied (1964–1973)

In February and March 1973, 565 U.S. military and 26 civilian prisoners of war (POWs) were released by the Democratic Republic of Vietnam (DRV). Two military persons and two civilians held in the People's Republic of China were released at the same time. Civilians included contract pilots; Central Intelligence Agency (CIA), State Department, and Voice of America personnel; agricultural specialists; missionaries; and other nonmilitary personnel. Six foreign nationals—two Canadians, two South Koreans, and two Filipinos—also departed. A few civilians and accused defector Bobby Garwood came home after the 1973 release.

During the war, Hà Nôi had turned over 12 POWs to visiting "peace delegations," and early in the war the Viêt Công

(VC) released a few prisoners. A few Americans escaped from the VC or from Communist forces in Laos. Although many pilots shot down over hostile territory evaded capture until being rescued, no one actually brought into the prison system successfully escaped from North Vietnam.

Estimates of POW deaths in captivity vary. The North Vietnamese listed 55 deaths. One U.S. source cited 54 military and at least 13 American and foreign civilians; another gives the number as 72. Returned POWs cited eight known deaths of military personnel in the Hà Nội system—two considered outright murder, three from a combination of brutality and neglect, and three from substandard medical care. Most deaths of military personnel and civilians occurred in the jungle camps in the South.

POWs, who attempted to register every individual in the North Vietnamese system, recorded at least 766 verified captives at one point or another, but accountability for those outside the system was less certain. Of the hundreds who disappeared in Laos, only ten came home in 1973, and no one knows the fate of the many captives of local VC units. At the time of release, more than 2,500 men were listed as missing in action. Some who were known to be alive on the ground and even in the prison system mysteriously disappeared.

All but 71 of the military personnel who returned in early 1973 were officers, primarily Air Force or Navy aviators shot down during combat missions. Other than a handful of Air Force personnel, the enlisted men consisted of Army and Marine personnel captured in the South. The fliers had received survival and captivity training; most of those captured in the South had not. The first pilot captured by the North Vietnamese was Navy Lt. (jg) Everett Alvarez, shot down on 5 August 1964. The longest-held POW was Army Special Forces Capt. Floyd James Thompson, whose light reconnaissance plane was shot down on 26 March 1964.

One commentator surveying the 356 aviators held in 1970 recorded that the average flier was approximately 32 years old, an Air Force captain or Navy lieutenant, and married with two children. They were for the most part career-minded officers, skilled pilots of high-performance aircraft, highly disciplined, intensely competitive, college graduates.

American POWs were held in eleven prisons in North Vietnam, four in Hà Nội, six others within 50 miles of the city, and one on the Chinese border. The most famous was Hoa Lò Prison in downtown Hà Nội, which POWs dubbed the "Hanoi Hilton." They gave the other prisons names as well—Briarpatch, Faith, Hope (Son Tây), Skidrow, D-1, Rockpile, Plantation, the Zoo, Alcatraz, and Dogpatch.

A test of wills existed between the Hà Nội Camp Authority and U.S. military personnel over the Code of Conduct, which had been promulgated in 1955 in response to the allegedly disgraceful performance of U.S. POWs during the Korean Conflict. The Vietnam POWs were determined to maintain a record of honor that would reflect well upon themselves, the U.S. military, and the nation. The Camp Authority employed every means at its disposal, including isolation, torture, and psychological abuse, to break POW discipline. Senior commanders such as Air Force Lt. Col.

Robinson Risner, Navy Comdr. James Stockdale, and Navy Lt. Comdr. Jeremiah Denton emerged as the leaders in the POW resistance campaign.

From 1965 through 1969, prisoners were isolated, kept in stocks, bounced from one camp to another, malnourished, and brutally tortured. After the death of Hồ Chí Minh in September 1969, the torture ended and conditions improved in the camps. Following the Son Tây Raid in November 1970, the North Vietnamese closed the outlying camps and consolidated all the POWs in Hà Nội. Compound living began in what the prisoners called Camp Unity. In February 1971, Air Force Col. John Flynn, the highest-ranking POW, who had spent most of his captivity isolated from the others, assumed command and organized the military community into the 4th Allied POW Wing. A few Thais and South Vietnamese POWs, who had distinguished themselves in working with the Americans, were included in the Wing. From this point, the greatest attention was given to how the POWs would return home. Amnesty was tendered to those who had cooperated with the enemy if they would now adhere to the Code of Conduct. All but a few accepted the offer. During the final two years, the collective POW story was collected, shaped, and honed.

With the end of the war, POWs returned in Operation HOMECOMING to great fanfare as the only heroes of a frustrating war. Much to the dismay of senior POW officers, the Defense Department decided that POWs who had collaborated would not be prosecuted. Only Robert Garwood, who returned to the United States in 1979, faced court-martial. Although many divorces resulted during their captivity, the Vietnam POWs adjusted relatively well. Ten years later, only about 30 had been treated for psychological or mental problems, although two had committed suicide. Almost half were still in the military.

—Joe P. Dunn

References: Doyle, Robert C. *Voices from Captivity: Interpreting the American POW Narrative* (1994); Dunn, Joe P. "The Vietnam War and the POWs/MIAs" (1990); Howes, Craig. *Voices of the Vietnam POWs: Witnesses to Their Fight* (1993); Hubbell, John G., et al. *P.O.W.: A Definitive History of the American Prisoner of War Experience in Vietnam, 1964–1973* (1976); Rowan, Stephan A. *They Wouldn't Let Us Die: The Prisoners of War Tell Their Story* (1973).

See also: Alvarez, Everett, Jr.; Denton, Jeremiah A. Jr.; Garwood, Robert "Bobby" Russell; Hà Nội Hilton (Hoa Lò Prison); HOMECOMING, Operation; LINEBACKER I, Operation; LINEBACKER II, Operation; McCain, John S., III; ROLLING THUNDER, Operation; Stockdale, James B.

Prisoners of War, Việt Công and People's Army of Vietnam. *See* Missing in Action and Prisoners of War, Việt Công and People's Army of Vietnam.

Project 100,000

Great Society program designed to extend the social and economic benefits of military service to disadvantaged or underqualified Americans. Johnson administration officials hoped that by easing military admission standards, underprivileged young men could gain valuable skills, discipline, and useful benefits that would enhance employment opportunities and help stabilize families.

Announced in August 1966, Project 100,000's goal was to bring 100,000 previously ineligible men into the Army and Marines each year by relaxing entrance requirements. Between 1966 and 1972, the U.S. military accepted 350,000 men under Project 100,000. A high percentage came from broken homes or low-income families; most were high school dropouts; many had low IQs or read at a grade-school level; 41 percent were black; and the majority, black and white, were from the South.

Project 100,000 had practical as well as political implications for the U.S. effort in Vietnam by adding badly needed bodies to the manpower pool. More than half of the Project 100,000 men went to Vietnam, and most received combat-related assignments. One report indicates that Project 100,000 men died at almost twice the rate of nonproject combat troops, although this is disputed. The expanded manpower pool helped Johnson to avoid calling up the Reserves as the demand for troops intensified. Critics cited increased disciplinary problems and poor military performance among relaxed-standards inductees, but many special-standards inductees performed well, and some combat commanders preferred them to more educated troops in the field.

As a social engineering program, Project 100,000 largely failed. Few of the men received training or developed skills that would benefit them in civilian life. Many, especially those with less-than-honorable discharges, came away from the experience worse off than before. With decreased force demands after 1969, Project 100,000 quotas dropped accordingly. The project was terminated in 1972 with the advent of an all-volunteer military.

—Paul R. Camacho and David Coffey

References: Baskir, Lawrence M., and William A. Strauss. *Chance and Circumstance: The Draft, The War, and The Vietnam Generation* (1978); Dougan, Clark, Samuel Lipsman, et al. *A Nation Divided* (1984); Hsiao, Lisa, "Project 100,000: The Great Society's Answer to Military Manpower Needs in Vietnam" (1989); Moynihan, Daniel P. *Maximum Feasible Misunderstanding: Community Action in the War on Poverty* (1970); Rainwater, Lee, and W. L. Yancey. *The Moynihan Report and the Politics of Controversy* (1967); Starr, Paul. *The Discarded Army: Veterans after Vietnam* (1973).

See also: African American Personnel in U.S. Forces in Vietnam; Conscientious Objectors (COs); Draft; Johnson, Lyndon Baines; King, Martin Luther, Jr.; McNamara, Robert S.

Prose Narrative and the Vietnam Experience

Nonfiction prose narrative dealing with the American involvement in Vietnam includes biography, memoir, combat narrative, oral history collections, and journalistic reporting. Sometimes the categories blur, not only among themselves, but between fiction and nonfiction, memoir and formal history.

The most prevalent type of prose narrative is the combat narrative, usually written by a former combatant and often indistinguishable from memoir. In most such narratives, a new recruit arrives in-country, usually with high ideals.

Immediately faced with physical hardships and combat conditions, he may either become disillusioned or grow to admire the fortitude of the other troops. The pattern is essentially the traditional one of a "coming of age." The focus is normally on the narrator's own development; others presented in the narrative tend to be "types" and remain background for the narrator's own development or sounding boards for his opinions. Vietnamese are also normally portrayed as background figures.

The chief events in these narratives are military engagements in which the narrator's views are solidified. In some, the culminating event is not a battle, but an atrocity. This is particularly true of Philip Caputo's *A Rumor of War* (1977), among the most famous books of its kind. Caputo, a Marine who was charged with ordering the killing of two Vietnamese civilians (the charges were subsequently dropped), shapes his narrative around the attitudes and events leading up to the event in an attempt to explain how such things happen, implying that they happened with great frequency. The narrator of such books emerges from the experience with an understanding of the destructive influence of war, and especially of the Vietnam conflict, on combatant and noncombatant alike.

Even the nondisillusioned narratives of this type may include an atrocity. In David Christian's *Victor Six* (1991)—actually a celebration of a particular unit's prowess in combat—members of the unit at one point desecrate the body of a dead enemy. This event is held up as an evil omen for the unit, and surely enough, shortly afterward the unit meets its first defeat. The heroes have ceased to be heroic, and so must be defeated. In Craig Roberts and Charles W. Sass's *The Walking Dead* (1989), also a fairly positive memoir, there is another variation on this theme. One member of a unit who has killed a suspected Việt Cộng collaborator in anger later talks another man out of doing the same thing, telling him that the deed will haunt him afterward.

Other motifs are the loss of a best friend in combat and the first encounter with the gruesome carnage of war. In the "disillusioned" narrative, such scenes often become almost inverted conversion experiences, causing a loss rather than a gaining of faith. *A Rumor of War* contains a typical scene of this sort, as does Lynda Van Devanter's *Home Before Morning* (1983), one of the few such narratives by a woman. Van Devanter's repeated question, "Why, why, why?" about the maimed and dying soldiers she has seen as a combat nurse remains unanswered, implying that the war itself has no purpose.

Among other "disillusioned" memoirs and combat narratives are W. D. Ehrhart's *Vietnam-Perkasie* (1983); Tim O'Brien's *If I Die in a Combat Zone* (1973); and Ron Kovic's *Born on the Fourth of July* (1976). Later made into a film, Kovic's book follows a paralyzed veteran home and through the peace movement, and has sometimes been said to overlap into the fiction category. Combat narratives focusing on the positive development of the individual and the unit mission include Michael Lee Lanning's *The Only War We Had: A Platoon Leader's Journal of Vietnam* (1987) and its sequel, *Vietnam, 1969–1970: A Company Commander's Journal* (1988); Larry Chambers's *Recondo: LRRPs in the*

101st Airborne (1992); Lynn Hampton's *The Fighting Strength: Memoirs of a Combat Nurse in Vietnam* (1990), an interesting counterview to Van Devanter's more jaundiced one; Eric Bergerud's *Red Thunder, Tropic Lightning* (1993); and Otto J. Lehrack's *No Shining Armor: The Marines at War in Vietnam* (1992).

Oral histories are particularly pervasive forms of narrative emerging from the Vietnam conflict. The most widely read of these are Mark Baker's *Nam* (1981), marred by its failure to document the speakers' identities and units of service, so that the accuracy of the accounts cannot be verified; and Al Santoli's *Everything We Had* (1981), which is more extensively documented but includes at least one questionable narrative. Women's experiences have been assembled in Catherine Marshall's *In the Combat Zone* (1987) and Keith Walker's *A Piece of My Heart* (1985). The African American experience has been documented in Wallace Terry's *Bloods* (1982). Al Santoli's *To Bear Any Burden* (1985) adds more oral histories to his earlier collection and also presents numerous accounts of Southeast Asian experiences during and after the war. The fall of Sài Gòn and the flight of the refugees from South Vietnam is presented in oral histories collected by Larry Engelmann in *Tears Before the Rain: An Oral History of the Fall of South Vietnam* (1990). Bob Greene's *Homecoming* (1989) addresses the experiences of troops returning from the war in a collection of letters written by veterans in response to questions he posed in his newspaper column.

Michael Herr's *Dispatches* (1977) is difficult to categorize. An account of his experience as a journalist in the field and in his bureau's Sài Gòn headquarters, it originally was written as a series of travel pieces for *Esquire*. Revised for book publication, this narrative describes the journalists' milieu as strongly as it does that of the soldier in the field. The accuracy of some episodes has been questioned, particularly where the book differs from the magazine. But on the whole, Herr presents a view of U.S. involvement that has become pervasive in all the literature: Vietnam as metaphor as much as event, the shaping influence of post-1965 American society, and at the same time a reflection of what it shaped. His closing statement is one of the most often quoted in all of Vietnam literature: "Vietnam, Vietnam, Vietnam, we've all been there."

—Phoebe S. Spinrad

References: Beidler, Philip. *American Literature and the Experience of Vietnam* (1982); Butler, Deborah A. *American Women Writers on Vietnam: Unheard Voices, a Selected Annotated Bibliography* (1990); Jason, Philip K., ed. *Fourteen Landing Zones: Approaches to Vietnam War Literature* (1991); Lewis, Lloyd B. *The Tainted War: Culture and Identity in Vietnam War Narratives* (1985); Pratt, John Clark. *Vietnam Voices* (1984); Searle, William, ed. *Search and Clear: Critical Responses to Selected Literature and Films of the Vietnam War* (1988); Wilson, James C. *Vietnam in Prose and Film* (1982); Wittman, Sandra M. *Writing About Vietnam: A Bibliography of the Vietnam Conflict* (1989).
See also: Art and the Vietnam War; Drama and the Vietnam Experience; Fiction, U.S., and the Vietnam Experience; Film and the Vietnam Experience; Media and the War; Poetry and the Vietnam Experience.

Protective Reaction Strikes

Designation for 1970 air strikes conducted to suppress North Vietnamese air defenses that targeted U.S. reconnaissance flights. Although all U.S. "offensive" bombing operations against North Vietnam were informally suspended by 31 October 1968, there was an understanding between the United States and the Democratic Republic of Vietnam (DRV) that U.S. reconnaissance flights would continue. When these were fired on, Washington authorized U.S. Seventh Air Force commander Gen. John D. Lavelle to retaliate against DRV air defense installations south of the 19th parallel.

The rules of engagement stipulated that, as soon as DRV radar guidance systems locked on U.S. aircraft, escorts would attack the sites. In April 1970 Protective Reaction Strikes expanded to target surface-to-air missile (SAM) and antiaircraft installations protecting the Hô Chí Minh Trail south of the 20th parallel as well as Communist infiltration across the Demilitarized Zone (DMZ). Over 1,100 Protective Reaction Strike sorties were flown in 1970.

In fall 1972 Gen. Lavelle was called before the House and Senate Armed Forces Committee to answer charges that, between November 1971 and March 1972, he had launched 28 Protective Reaction Strike missions involving 147 sorties in violation of existing guidelines. Lavelle defended his actions by intimating that he had been "encouraged" by higher authorities to do so. He was relieved of his command, reduced in rank, and retired.

—Edward C. Page

References: Lewy, Guenter. *America in Vietnam* (1978); Morrocco, John. *Rain of Fire: Air War, 1969–1973* (1984).
See also: Air Defense, Democratic Republic of Vietnam; Lavelle, John D.

Provincial Reconnaissance Units (PRUs) (Đon Vi Thám Sát Tinh)

Republic of Vietnam (RVN) special paramilitary force created in April 1969 as an addition to the National Police forces. Provincial Reconnaissance Units (PRUs) were detached in platoon-sized units and assigned to provincial headquarters to carry out special missions. They were part of the Phoenix program, which targeted Viêt Công (VC) infrastructure in the South. The special missions included killing or capturing VC political cadre, tax collectors, intelligence agents, administrators, and propagandists; destabilizing VC influence among the peasant population; and encouraging support for the RVN government.

Although under the authority of the RVN National Police, PRUs were directed, armed, and trained by the U.S. Central Intelligence Agency (CIA). As part of the police forces, they were not subject to the control and discipline of the RVN armed forces. The U.S. Military Assistance Command, Vietnam (MACV) provided approximately 100 U.S. advisors to these units, which were commanded by Army of the Republic of Vietnam (ARVN) officers. Gen. Creighton Abrams recognized the units' political nature and reluctantly bowed to CIA pressure to commit military resources to the program. His chief frustration was that

MACV had no operational control over the PRUs.

Many PRU members were criminals or VC or People's Army of Vietnam defectors with grudges against the Communists. At times they tortured captives and behaved in a way that alienated the peasant population. Critics of U.S. involvement often accused U.S. advisory personnel of participating in PRU actions or training PRUs in torture techniques. In reality, U.S. advisors had little control over the PRUs. As part of the Phoenix program, PRUs freely operated against the VC infrastructure as well as political enemies of the RVN government.

PRUs engaged in clandestine operations and were armed with a variety of weapons. The CIA reportedly supplied the PRUs with Russian and Chinese weapons. They wore a mixture of uniforms, the most common being the black "pajamas"—common peasant garb throughout Vietnam—or tiger-stripe camouflage uniforms.

In 1970 Abrams directed MACV to withdraw its support from the PRUs and ordered PRU advisors not to participate in field operations or sanction torture. During this period, MACV began to streamline and consolidate the RVN military establishment and attempted to eliminate the private armies within the system. The PRUs, like other RVN territorial forces, were not reorganized, as they were not part of the military establishment. They continued to operate under the auspices of the RVN government until the end of hostilities in 1975.

—J. A. Menzoff

References: Clarke, Jeffery J. *Advice and Support: The Final Years 1965–1973* (1988); Spector, Ronald H. *After Tet: The Bloodiest Year in Vietnam* (1993).

See also: Abrams, Creighton; Central Intelligence Agency (CIA); Phoenix Program; Vietnam, Republic of: National Police.

Provisional Revolutionary Government of South Vietnam (PRG)

Communist alternative or rival to the government of the Republic of Vietnam, established in 1969 by representatives of the Alliance of National, Democratic, and Peace Forces (ANDPF) and the National Liberation Front (NLF). The first president of the Provisional Revolutionary Government of South Vietnam (PRG) was Huynh Tân Phát; he and other PRG leaders had been active in the National Front for the Liberation of South Vietnam (NFLSV).

The PRG's major responsibilities included foreign policy. Its best-known spokesperson was Madame Nguyên Thi Bình, foreign minister and earlier head of the NLF delegation at the Paris peace talks. In 1969 the PRG received diplomatic recognition from Communist states in eastern and central Europe, Cambodia, China, Cuba, Mongolia, North Korea, North Vietnam, Syria, and the Soviet Union.

Gen. Trân Van Trà headed the PRG delegation on the Four-Power Joint Military Commission responsible for supervision of the 1973 cease-fire and implementation of prisoner exchanges. He was the major PRG representative present at Đôc Lâp Palace when Sài Gòn fell on 30 April 1975. Although it aspired to play a role in a reunited Vietnam, the PRG was quickly integrated into the Socialist Republic of

Vietnam. Madame Nguyên Thi Bình became minister of education for the Socialist Republic, one of only a few PRG leaders to receive an important position in the SRV.

—Ernest C. Bolt, Jr.

References: Nguyên Khac Viên. *Vietnam, A Long History* (1993); Trân Van Trà. *Vietnam: History of the Bulwark B2 Theatre*. vol. 5, *Concluding the 30-Years War* (1983); Truong Nhu Tang, with David Chanoff and Doan Van Toai. *A Vietcong Memoir: An Inside Account of the Vietnam War and Its Aftermath* (1986).

See also: Huynh Tân Phát; National Front for the Liberation of South Vietnam (NFLSV); Nguyên Thi Bình; Trân Van Trà; Truong Nhu Tang.

Proxmire, William (1915–)

U.S. senator, 1957–1988. Proxmire, a liberal Democrat, won election to fill Joseph McCarthy's vacant seat in 1957 and made an instant impression in the Senate, most of it negative. He butted heads with Senators Lyndon Johnson and John Kennedy and opposed excessive military spending and the growing military-industrial complex that, he maintained, threatened social, educational, and civil rights programs. Still, he supported U.S. intervention in Southeast Asia and remained hawkish well into the Johnson administration. After the 1968 Têt Offensive he joined increasingly persistent legislative efforts to end the Vietnam War and signed the Hatfield-McGovern Amendment. Later he opposed the B-1 bomber and the C-5A jumbo cargo plane.

—David Coffey

References: *Current Biography Yearbook, 1978* (1978.); *Who's Who in American Politics, 1996* (1995).

See also: Church, Frank Forrester; Hatfield, Mark Odum; Hatfield-McGovern Amendment; Humphrey, Hubert H.; Johnson, Lyndon Baines; Kennedy, John Fitzgerald; Mansfield, Michael Joseph; McCarthy, Joseph Raymond; McGee, Gale William; McGovern, George S.

Psychological Warfare Operations (PSYOP)

The U.S. Military Assistance Command, Vietnam (MACV) was well aware of the importance of psychological operations (PSYOP) in Vietnam. Throughout the war the Joint U.S. Public Affairs Organization (JUSPAO) was responsible for supervising, coordinating, and evaluating all U.S. PSYOP in North and South Vietnam, Laos, and Cambodia, and for providing PSYOP support to Republic of Vietnam (RVN) programs. MACV commander Gen. William Westmoreland and his successor Gen. Creighton Abrams strongly supported PSYOP, as did many of their staff.

JUSPAO's mixture of military and civilian personnel was well suited to the dual nature of this war and demonstrated the U.S. military's early awareness that "winning the hearts and minds of the people" was fully as important as the armed conflict. JUSPAO's stated first mission priority was to bolster the image of the RVN government. Its second priority was the Chiêu Hôi (Open Arms) defector program.

In addition to its combat PSYOP, the U.S. effort enlightened civilians about RVN government programs and provided information services that would normally come under the heading of "nation building," and was, in turn, supported by JUSPAO and other military and civilian agencies in-country. In dealing with the VC in areas they dominated, JUSPAO PSYOP often became something closer to civil affairs (CA) than in any previous U.S. conflict.

There were basically four military PSYOP targets: the VC guerillas in the South, People's Army of Vietnam (PAVN) regulars, the civilian population of South Vietnam, and civilians of North Vietnam. Psychological operations directed toward each target had to be quite distinct.

On 1 December 1967 the 4th Psychological Operations Group (POG) was activated, headquartered in Sài Gòn but with its four battalions (the 6th, 7th, 8th, and 10th) operating in direct support of U.S. and Allied forces in each of the four Corps Tactical Zones (CTZs). In the field, PSYOP was initially conducted by four psychological operations companies, one in each of the major CTZs. Finally, 13 HA (command and control), 13 HB (loudspeaker) and 33 HE (audio-visual) three-man teams were deployed by the 4th POG's battalions to units and areas in the field. The HA teams provided command and control to the HB and HE teams and supported pacification and stability operations as well. The HE teams were ideal for "one-on-one" PSYOP; they gave medical civilian assistance (MEDCAP), distributed leaflets and posters, showed movies, conducted public opinion polls, and gathered information on Communist weapons and food caches and intelligence on the local VC infrastructure.

This insurgency conflict saw considerable overlapping of missions, but also an intelligent sharing of resources. For example, JUSPAO would receive prisoners of war who had defected as a result of MACV operations and use them for their own PSYOP. A useful means of improving PSYOP coordination between the U.S. Army and the ARVN was the Combined PSYOP Center (CPOC), established at each CTZ in 1969. The CPOCs pooled, collated, evaluated, and distributed PSYOP intelligence and planned combined operations. Each CPOC differed in its functions and team composition, but each was headed by a Vietnamese with an American as his deputy.

Civilian PSYOP operations could often be mounted on a quick, ad hoc basis. When a local defense guard was injured by a booby trap, the PSYOP liaison team attached to the 1st Armored Cavalry Division quickly made a tape informing the local people of the man's injuries and pointing out that the victim could just as easily have been an innocent villager or a child.

The most intensive civilian PSYOP of the war was that conducted by U.S. Army Special Forces among the indigenous Montagnard tribes of the Central Highlands. Special Forces worked through the Civilian Irregular Defense Group (CIDG), originally established by the Central Intelligence Agency, and welded them into an effective field force that both protected the villages and engaged in offensive operations.

Army PSYOP in Vietnam utilized most of the themes of previous U.S. psywars, including the surrender pass, "Happy POW," "Allied Might," nostalgia, good soldier–bad leaders, and other reliable methods. The 1st Infantry Division's G-5

broadcast a "family appeal" designed to make insurgents think of home and family. A typical leaflet, addressed to the VC, depicted a lissome Vietnamese beauty and carried the plaintive message from her husband, "Take a husband, my love.... with my life's blood I write this last plea...."

A new theme was the offer of money for defectors or weapons. One such leaflet promised the equivalent of $20,000 U.S. for any Communist infantry company that defected with its commander, political officer, platoon leader, and at least 80 percent of its men. Another listed a price scale for weapons turned in by defectors. Some leaflets simply showed a plentifully stocked marketplace in an RVN city. JUSPAO also dropped leaflets from B-52s on troops in the field.

JUSPAO personnel undoubtedly enjoyed composing the "disillusioning" leaflet carrying photos of Communist China's Mao Zedong and Zhou Enlai (Chou En-lai) meeting with President Nixon. The reaction to the widely disseminated spectacle of this "Mad Bomber" cordially conferring with the "Elder Brothers" must have indeed been sobering.

U.S. loudspeaker operators had to adopt new approaches to deal with a situation in which civilians and insurgents were seemingly inextricably intertwined. The new messages often concentrated upon the burdens heaped by the VC on the people. Loudspeaker teams brought their messages close-in, but they also suffered the only PSYOP battlefield fatalities of the war, with 11 killed in action.

The 4th POG disseminated several apparently effective news journals for both civilians and Communist troops, including a daily two-page news summary *Tin Chiên Truong* ("News From the Front"), and *Canh Hoa*, a single-page news update distributed during field operations. With lightweight presses, copiers, and Polaroid cameras, PSYOP troopers often could produce almost complete PSYOP in the field. Creative psywarriors could copy captured VC self-criticism diaries, with their depressing sentiments in the subject's verifiable handwriting, and print copies to drop over the diarist's comrades within hours. The U.S. Air Force developed improved, side-mounted speakers on its PSYWAR-converted C-47 transport aircraft, and the helicopter made accurate leaflet dissemination possible. By all accounts, most of the contested areas of South Vietnam had been well "papered" long before the end of hostilities.

Tactical radio also came into its own in this war. The 4th POG operated a 50,000-watt radio station at Pleiku in II Corps area, targeting Communist troops within a 200-mile radius. Allied PSYOP also used television for the first time in the field, beginning in 1966. The novel medium attracted large crowds, sometimes including VC who occasionally shot the sets.

U.S. PSYOP in Vietnam had its deficiencies. Soldiers served their one-year tour of duty in Vietnam and then rotated back to the States just as they were beginning to understand how things worked "in-country." Fewer than 40 percent of PSYOP personnel were PSYOP or Army school trained. Conventional tactical unit commanders often remained unaware of the mission or value of PSYOP.

The nature of psychological operations complicates any evaluation of its success. A study circa late 1968 of 337 Hồi Chánhs throughout CTZ I claimed that no less than 90 percent were "influenced by what [they] read"; 96 percent said they had seen PSYOP leaflets; 91 percent said they had heard broadcasts. The U.S. PSYOP effort in Vietnam can be termed a substantial, albeit temporary, success.

—Stanley Sandler

References: Chandler, Robert W. *War of Ideas: U.S. Propaganda Campaign in Vietnam* (1981); Sandler, Stanley. *"Cease Resistance: It's Good For You," A History of U.S. Army Combat Psychological Operations* (n.d.).

See also: Abrams, Creighton; Chiêu Hồi (Open Arms) Program; Civic Action; Civilian Irregular Defense Group (CIDG); Civilian Operations and Revolutionary Development Support (CORDS); Kit Carson Scouts; Montagnards; Pacification; Westmoreland, William Childs.

Pueblo Incident (1968)

Incident involving a U.S. Navy vessel captured by the Democratic People's Republic of Korea (North Korea). Originally a light cargo vessel, the *Pueblo* was refitted as a spy ship, equipped with electronic and cryptographic gear and manned—in addition to its regular crew—by communications technicians specially trained in electronic intelligence operations. The lightly armed *Pueblo* carried only two .50-caliber machine guns.

On 23 January 1968 the *Pueblo*, captained by Comdr. Lloyd Bucher, was attacked by North Korean forces off Wonsan, North Korea. One seaman was killed and several crew members wounded. The crew were held prisoner in North Korea, tortured, and forced to sign confessions. On 22 December 1968 they were released at Panmunjon Bridge.

A Navy court of inquiry recommended the court-martial of Bucher and the officer in charge of intelligence operations on the *Pueblo*. Navy Secretary John Chafee overruled the recommendation, stating that the men had "suffered enough." The episode was a blow to U.S. prestige and a severe indictment of the Navy command structure, which had sent an inadequately armed vessel on a dangerous mission without adequate support.

—Kenneth R. Stevens

References: Brandt, Ed. *The Last Voyage of USS Pueblo* (1969); Bucher, Lloyd M., with Mark Rascovich. *Bucher: My Story* (1970); Schumacher, F. Carl, Jr., and George C. Wilson. *Bridge of No Return: The Ordeal of the U.S.S. Pueblo* (1971).

See also: ELINT (Electronic Intelligence); Korea, Democratic People's Republic of; United States: Navy.

Puller, Lewis B., Jr. (ca. 1945–1994)

Vietnam War hero and prize-winning biographer; son of Marine Corps Gen. Lewis B. ("Chesty") Puller, the most decorated Marine. In 1968 Marine 2d Lt. Puller was horribly wounded by a booby-trapped howitzer shell, losing both legs just below his hips and most of both hands. He was awarded the Silver Star and two Purple Hearts. Puller willed himself to live, although he said "the psychological and emotional wounds never healed." In 1971 he turned against the war, although he could not bring himself to return his medals: "They had cost me too dearly," he wrote, "and although I now saw clearly that the war in which they had been earned was a wasted cause, the medals still represented the dignity and caliber of my service and of those with whom I had served." Puller died at his home in 1994 of a self-inflicted gunshot wound.

—Spencer C. Tucker

Reference: Puller, Lewis B. *Fortunate Son: The Autobiography of Lewis B. Puller, Jr.* (1991).

See also: Prose Narrative and the Vietnam Experience.

Quach Tom (1932–1997)
Vietnamese commando who parachuted into North Vietnam in a Central Intelligence Agency–sponsored operation. Democratic Republic of Vietnam authorities were informed in advance of the parachute drop, and Quach was the only member of his unit not immediately captured. He avoided capture for nearly three months, longer than any other commando sent into the North by U.S. authorities.

In 1996 declassified documents revealed that the U.S. government had lied to the "widows" of commandos sent into the North by declaring all of them dead. Quach's wife was so notified and was paid a $50 gratuity. Sedgwick Tourison, a former Defense Intelligence Agency analyst, has identified 360 surviving commandos. Quach survived almost 19 years of harsh imprisonment and arrived in the United States in 1996. His lawyer, John C. Mattes, sued in Federal court on behalf of the commandos and has lobbied both Congress and President Clinton for compensatory legislation. Legislation introduced by Senators John Kerry and Bob Kerrey to provide $20 million to the commandos (about $40,000 each) came too late for Quach, who died on 26 August 1997.

—Spencer C. Tucker

Reference: Tourison, Sedgwick D. *Project Alpha: Washington's Secret Military Operations in North Vietnam* (1997).
See also: Central Intelligence Agency (CIA); Hmong; Kerry, John Forbes; Operation Plan 34A (OPLAN 34A); Vietnam, Republic of: Commandos.

Quadrillage/Ratissage

Key elements in the "oil slick" (*tache d'huile*) pacification method pursued by the French in Vietnam during the Indo-China War. The technique split the territory to be pacified into grids or squares. Once this gridding (*quadrillage*) was accomplished, each square was then "raked" (*ratissage*) by pacification forces familiar with the area. Carried out on a regular basis by a sufficient number of troops, it could be successful, but French forces in Indo-China never had the numbers of men necessary.

—Spencer C. Tucker

Reference: Fall, Bernard. *The Two Viet Nams* (1964).
See also: *Tache d'huile*.

Quang Tri, Battle of (1972)

One of the opening battles of the three-pronged 1972 People's Army of Vietnam (PAVN) Easter Offensive. In preparation for the battle, Hà Nôi had moved long-range 130-mm field guns and 152-mm howitzers to positions just north of the Demilitarized Zone (DMZ). On 30 March 1972, under supporting fire from heavy artillery, the PAVN launched a coordinated ground attack spearheaded by T-54 and PT-76 tanks south across the DMZ and from the west through Khe Sanh. Four PAVN divisions moved into Quang Tri Province in Military Region I. The newly formed Army of the Republic of Vietnam (ARVN) 3d Division, charged with defending Quang Tri, was overwhelmed by the PAVN onslaught, and many units fled in panic. The situation for the ARVN was exacerbated by friction between its troops and Republic of Vietnam (RVN) Marines also operating in the area. Thus, the continuity of the RVN defensive effort in Quang Tri Province was fatally weakened from the beginning.

Cloud cover during the first two weeks of April inhibited U.S. close air support, but when the weather cleared in mid-April, B-52 strikes were heavy. Undaunted, PAVN forces crossed the Cam Lô–Cua Viêt River barrier and attacked Quang Tri City from three directions, while heavy artillery struck hard at ARVN forces south of the city. On 27 April cloud cover returned and the PAVN 304th Division increased the intensity of its attack. Thousands of South Vietnamese refugees flooded Highway 1. The PAVN targeted the road, killing so many civilians that a 0.3-mile stretch at Truong Phuoc Bridge was known to most Vietnamese as "*Đoan Đuong Kinh Hoàng*" (Road of Horrors). Đông Hà fell on 28 April. On 1 May, PAVN forces took Quang Tri City, and the rest of the province fell under its control two days later.

The offensive then stalled and degenerated into a stalemate. Toward the end of the summer RVN forces, buoyed by massive B-52 air support and somewhat rejuvenated by new senior leadership, launched a counteroffensive. After weeks of intense house-to-house fighting, on 15 September ARVN forces recaptured Quang Tri City. The fighting and bombing had nearly obliterated the city, and RVN forces had suffered more than 5,000 casualties, but the North Vietnamese attackers had been stopped and pushed back. This action and the ARVN victories at Kontum and An Lôc effectively foiled the North Vietnamese Easter Offensive of 1972.

—James H. Willbanks

References: Clarke, Jeffrey J. *Advice and Support: The Final Years* (1988); Ngo Quang Truong. *The Easter Offensive of 1972* (1980); Turley, G. H. *The Easter Offensive* (1985).
See also: An Lôc, Battle of; Easter Offensive (Nguyên Huê Campaign); Vietnam, Democratic Republic of: Army (People's Army of Vietnam [PAVN]); Vietnam, Republic of: Army (ARVN); Vietnamization; Vô Nguyên Giáp.

Quôc Ngu

Literally translated as "national language," a writing system for Vietnamese based on the Roman alphabet. *Quôc ngu* was created in the seventeenth century by Catholic missionaries from Portugal, Spain, Italy, and France. At the beginning of the twentieth century, Confucian scholars in the Đông Kinh Nghia Thuc school used *quôc ngu* as an instrument to spread new ideas and knowledge of Western science among the population. However, only when the traditional examinations were abolished between 1915 and 1918 did *quôc ngu* become established as the national writing system for the Vietnamese language, replacing Chinese characters.

—Pham Cao Duong

References: Nguyên Dình Hòa. *Language in Vietnamese Society: Some Articles by Nguyen Dinh Hoa* (1980); Nguyên Khac Kham. "Vietnamese National Language and Modern Vietnamese Literature" (1976).

See also: de Rhodes, Alexandre; French Indo-China.

R

Radford, Arthur W. (1896–1973)

Chairman, U.S. Joint Chiefs of Staff, 1953–1957. Predicting ominous results if France was defeated in Indo-China, Radford urged U.S. air strikes in support of the French at Điên Biên Phu in 1954. In March 1954 Radford favored implementing Operation VULTURE, a proposed U.S. bombing mission. Despite Radford's enthusiasm, President Eisenhower refused to contemplate bombing in the absence of endorsements from Congress and the Allies.

During discussions about possible U.S. involvement in Indo-China, Radford advanced some unique notions, recommending employment of tactical nuclear arms at Điên Biên Phu and suggesting that the United States assist in forming an international volunteer air corps. Ely rejected Radford's idea to increase the number of U.S. advisors available to train Vietnamese forces and showed only slight concern when Radford urged the use of psychological and unconventional methods.

Two years later, Radford argued to the National Security Council that the United States should contain the Democratic Republic of Vietnam with air power. The U.S. Army would play only a restricted role; South Vietnamese ground forces would bear primary responsibility for stopping the invader. Army strategists expressed dissatisfaction with Radford's concepts, and he retired from the Navy in 1957.

—Rodney J. Ross

References: Arnold, James R. *The First Domino: Eisenhower, the Military, and America's Intervention in Vietnam* (1991); Short, Anthony. *The Origins of the Vietnam War* (1989); Spector, Ronald H. *Advice and Support: The Early Years, 1941–1960* (1983).

See also: Điên Biên Phu, Battle of; Eisenhower, Dwight David; Ely, Paul Henri Romuald; Twining, Nathan Farragut; VULTURE, Operation.

Radio Direction Finding

The study of radio signal origins, targets, frequency of communications, and extent of command nets. Radio direction finding (RDF) and associated signals intelligence activities were used by the major antagonists in Indo-China, at least as early as the beginning of World War II.

RDF provides essential information about command structure and unit deployment. Two of the most important signals intelligence activities are to locate enemy headquarters and track troop movements. During the Indo-China War, Viêt Minh communications, including RDF data gathered by an American facility in Manila, were exchanged for signals intelligence from French intercept stations in Vietnam and Laos. During the Vietnam War, the Army Security Agency, the Air Force Security Service, and the Naval Security Group were deployed in the Indo-China region under the operational control of the National Security Agency (NSA), which was responsible for the centralized coordination, direction, and performance of American signals intelligence.

Ground installations included Phú Bài, Đà Nang, Pleiku, Tân Sơn Nhut, Côn Son Island, and Cam Ranh Bay in South Vietnam; Nakhon Phanom and Udorn in Thailand; bases in the Philippines; and the cooperating British facility at Little Sai Wan in Hong Kong. Phú Bài, equipped and technically assisted by Taiwan, had previously been the only similar installation within the Republic of Vietnam. Mobile capabilities included U.S. Navy ships and aircraft; U.S. Army aircraft, as well as teams at division and separate brigade level; U.S. Marine Corps elements; and U.S. Air Force aircraft such as the EC-47, EC-121, and EC-130.

Allied RDF depended on obtaining two or more readings, from different locations, of the direction of a Communist transmitter. A line of position (LOP) would be plotted for each reading. After obtaining several LOPs on a transmitter, the lines would converge on a common point, or fix—the physical location of the transmitter. Techniques used by the Communists to thwart RDF included using mobile transmitters, transmitting in extremely short bursts, repeatedly changing frequency and power output, and ceasing transmission upon the approach of Allied aircraft.

The limitations of RDF were demonstrated when U.S. intelligence analysts were misled into thinking that a Communist division was deployed along the Cambodian border, when in fact it had approached Biên Hòa to participate in the Têt Offensive. To deceive Allied intelligence, the division's transmitters had been left at a border site.

Throughout the Vietnam War, swift reaction to RDF information enabled ground forces, artillery, tactical aircraft, and B-52 bombers to attack Communist forces, often precluding or disrupting operations. Eventually, airborne RDF, by which a single aircraft could rapidly obtain a fix on a transmitter, became the most important single source of intelligence for Allied ground commanders in Indo-China. Notable RDF successes include the 1967 Battle of Dak Tô and the 1968 Battle of Khe Sanh. With RDF assistance, every company and battalion of the two North Vietnamese divisions besieging Khe Sanh was located. During the Têt Offensive, RDF was particularly useful at Ban Mê Thuột and Nha Trang. In the Mekong Delta, as other sources of information dried up during Têt, the Mobile Riverine Force became almost completely dependent on RDF for intelligence.

—Glenn E. Helm

References: Bergen, John D. *Military Communications: A Test for Technology* (1986); Fulghum, David, Terrence Maitland, and the editors of Boston Publishing Company. *South Vietnam on Trial: Mid-1970 to 1972* (1984); LeGro, William E. "The Enemy's Jungle Cover Was No Match for the Finding Capabilities of the Army's Radio Research Units" (1990); "U.S. Electronic Espionage: A Memoir" (1972).

See also: Dak Tô, Battle of; Khe Sanh, Battles of; Têt Offensive: Overall Strategy; Têt Offensive: the Sài Gòn Circle.

RANCH HAND, Operation (1961–1971)

Code name for missions involving the aerial spraying of herbicides. RANCH HAND operations' primary objectives were to deny Communist forces the use of jungle cover through defoliation and to deny them access to food crops in South Vietnam. In 1961 a joint U.S.-RVN counterinsurgency center was established. Its principal task was to evaluate the use of herbicides against guerrilla food sources and foliage that shielded Việt Công (VC) activities. Dr. James Brown, deputy chief of the Army's Chemical Warfare Center, supervised the tests. Little was known about South Vietnamese vegetation, and the only airplane available for testing was the old C-47, although other delivery systems, such as the H-34 helicopter and a ground-based turbine sprayer, were tested. However, the success of these tests led Brown to recommend, through Gen. Maxwell Taylor and Walt W. Rostow, that the Special Aerial Spray Flight (SASF) from Langley Air Force Base, Virginia, be deployed to Vietnam. Expecting President Kennedy's approval (which indeed came on 30 November), on 28 November 1961, six C-123s under the FARM GATE Program—with newly installed MC-1 1,000-gallon spray tanks—departed on the first leg of a deployment to South Vietnam.

After a month's delay in the Philippines, on 7 January 1962 three C-123s arrived at Tân Sơn Nhứt Airport; their crews expected to remain there on temporary duty (TDY) for less than 90 days. They began operational missions on 12 January. Initially their assignment was to clear foliage along a major roadway north of Sài Gòn; later, mangrove forests near the coast and rice-growing areas in the Mekong Delta were added as approved targets.

Although the aircrews were using Agents Purple and Blue (military code names for specific herbicides), the results were less successful than expected. Following further testing, the number of nozzles on each wing boom was decreased from 42 to 35 to increase the droplet size to 300–350 micrometers, which was expected to minimize drift.

Another concern was the dangerous mission profile. Aircrews needed to fly low, about 150 feet above the ground, in a straight, level flight path at a relatively slow airspeed of about 130 miles per hour. This left the aircraft vulnerable to ground fire. Although tactics changed somewhat throughout the war, the basic herbicide delivery parameters kept the crews constantly at risk. The difficulty of the aerial tactics increased as operations were expanded from relatively flat areas in the South to rugged mountain passes in the more northern provinces.

In October 1964, following the Tonkin Gulf incidents, tactics were further complicated. Previously, crop destruction missions were flown by South Vietnamese helicopter pilots. On 3 October RANCH HAND aircrews, initially with South Vietnamese observers, flew against crop targets in War Zone D north of Sài Gòn. Because crops were planted in tightly defined areas, delivery tactics necessitated use of more dangerous maneuvering and even dive-bombing approaches to the target box. With this range of tactics and the addition of a fourth aircraft in December 1964, the unit had established its value in the war effort.

In 1965, to meet the need for more experienced aircrews, TDY personnel were replaced with aircrews assigned for a full year's rotation. In November three additional aircraft (by

then known as the UC-123B) were added to the inventory. While Agent Blue continued to be used against crops, the cheaper and more effective Agent Orange was added for jungle defoliation missions. That year also saw a detachment of aircraft deployed to Đà Nang Air Base for operations against the Hồ Chí Minh Trail.

This pattern of exponential growth continued. In 1966 the unit had 14 authorized aircraft; in 1969, 33 of the improved C-123K aircraft were authorized. In October 1966 the name was changed from the 309th Spray Flight to the 12th Air Commando Squadron; nearly concurrently, the unit moved to Biên Hòa Air Base to increase the logistical efficiency of the operations. With expansion to squadron status, RANCH HAND aircrews assumed collateral duties, flying airlift missions during the 1968 Tết Offensive and flying classified missions in Laos and Thailand. In 1968, the squadron's busiest year, 5,745 herbicide sorties were flown in addition to 4,000 collateral sorties.

RANCH HAND operations contracted quickly. In 1969 a National Cancer Institute study reached the Department of Defense linking possible serious health problems to herbicide exposure. Public disapproval erupted when the Cambodian government made an unsubstantiated claim that 170,000 acres of its land had been intentionally sprayed. These concerns, along with a drastic decrease in funding from a requested $27 million to $3 million under Vietnamization, caused a rapid decline in the number of operational sorties flown.

In mid-1970 the unit was reduced to eight aircraft, reassigned to Phan Rang Air Base as a Flight, and restricted from using Agent Orange, replacing that herbicide with the less effective Agent White. On 7 January 1971, after nine years of operations, RANCH HAND aircrews flew the last three herbicide missions of the war.

—Charles J. Gaspar

References: Buckingham, William. "Operation Ranch Hand" (1983); Cecil, Paul. *Herbicidal Warfare: The Ranch Hand Project in Vietnam* (1986); Wolfe, William. "Health Status of Air Force Veterans Occupationally Exposed to Herbicides in Vietnam" (1990).
See also: Airplanes, Allied and Democratic Republic of Vietnam; Defoliation; FARM GATE, Operation; Herbicides.

RAND Corporation

U.S. government–funded "think tank" that contemplated various scenarios for nuclear war and for the limited war in Vietnam. RAND began as an outgrowth of British and U.S. operational research groups in World War II. In March 1946, Theodore Von Karman, head of the Army Air Force Scientific Advisory Board, officially started Air Force Project RAND (Research and Development). Gen. Curtis LeMay, deputy chief of air staff for research and development, had charge of oversight and guidance for the program. A nonprofit organization, the RAND Corporation comprised physicists, political strategists, economists, and mathematicians. In the 1960s, RAND devotees moved into positions of considerable influence with the inauguration of John F. Kennedy and appointment of Secretary of State Robert S. McNamara.

Many RAND ideas became national policy during the Vietnam War. McNamara's approach to U.S. involvement in Vietnam in early 1965 stemmed from RAND strategist William Kaufmann's concepts of "limited war." Kaufmann advocated not victory but stalemate, in which no larger power would be drawn into the war and the United States could convince the Democratic Republic of Vietnam (DRV) that the costs of fighting were higher for the Vietnamese than for the Americans. He called for "discreet" methods of destruction rather than the use of nuclear weapons. Assistant Secretary of Defense John McNaughton, a student of RAND policymaker Thomas Schilling, advocated a gradual increase of troop strengths.

The Vietnam conflict disillusioned many within RAND, especially Bernard Brodie, one of its founders. Brodie—who came to realize that Communist leaders were not irrational barbarians but shared many of the same concerns over nuclear weapons as U.S. leaders—moved away from the idea of providing options for the use of nuclear weapons. The war also disillusioned Dr. Daniel Ellsberg, a RAND researcher and one of the authors of *United States–Vietnam Relations, 1945–1967*, commonly referred to as the Pentagon Papers. Ellsberg leaked copies of portions of the secret study to the press.

Still, throughout the 1970s and 1980s, RAND continued to author strategies for nuclear war, and RAND alumni such as James Schlesinger remained key figures in the government.

—Michael R. Nichols

References: FitzGerald, Frances. *Fire in the Lake: The Vietnamese and the Americans in Vietnam* (1972); Kaplan, Fred. "Scientists at War: The Birth of the RAND Corporation" (1983); —. *The Wizards of Armageddon* (1983).
See also: Ellsberg, Daniel; Kennedy, John Fitzgerald; LeMay, Curtis Emerson; McNamara, Robert S.; McNaughton, John T.; Pentagon Papers and Trial; ROLLING THUNDER, Operation; Schlesinger, James R.; Vietnam, Democratic Republic of: 1954–1975.

Raven Forward Air Controllers (FACs)

Individuals controlling air strikes in Laos. The Raven Forward Air Controller program began during the winter of 1965–1966 with the assignment of U.S. Air Force enlisted personnel who had been trained as forward air guides by the Air Commandos. Using the radio call sign of "Butterfly," these men directed attacks by the Royal Lao Air Force and the U.S. Air Force in northern Laos while riding aboard aircraft from Air America and Continental Air Services.

In October 1966, Gen. William E. Momyer, commander of the Seventh Air Force, inaugurated the Steve Canyon program to replace enlisted forward air guides. Under this program, officers who had spent six months in South Vietnam as forward air controllers were eligible to volunteer for a six-month tour in Laos. Assigned to the U.S. embassy in Vientiane and wearing civilian clothes, they would use the radio call sign "Raven" to direct airstrikes in support of Central Intelligence Agency (CIA)–led guerrilla forces in northern Laos, or Military Region II. In the later 1960s, they would perform the same task in southern Laos.

The Ravens, free from usual military restraints, sometimes irritated their more traditional superiors. Although frequently accused of immature personal behavior, no one doubted their skill or courage. Flying at low levels over the battlefields of Laos, they played a vital role in bringing airpower to bear against the Communist Pathet Lao and their North Vietnamese allies. Between 1966 and 1973, more than 30 Ravens lost their lives in the little-noticed but frequently vicious sideshow to the main conflict in Vietnam.

—William M. Leary

Reference: Robbins, Christopher. *The Ravens* (1987).
See also: Air America; Central Intelligence Agency (CIA); Continental Air Services; Laos; Momyer, William W.; Pathet Lao.

Read, Benjamin Huger (1925–1993)

U.S. State Department official, 1963–1965. In 1963 Read became executive secretary to U.S. Secretary of State Dean Rusk. As a result of his association with Rusk, Read had access to the top foreign policy group around President Johnson. He worked diligently to keep Rusk, who had virtually no personal staff, apprised of continuing developments in the State Department regarding Vietnam. To ensure secrecy, Read at one point reduced access to the file code-named MARIGOLD to only six people. Read worked with Vice President Hubert Humphrey in the 1968 presidential campaign, then left the State Department in 1969.

—Wes Watters

References: Cooper, Chester L. *The Lost Crusade: America in Vietnam* (1970); Herring, George C. *LBJ and Vietnam: A Different Kind of War* (1994); Herring, George C., ed. *The Secret Diplomacy of the Vietnam War: The Negotiating Volumes of the Pentagon Papers* (1983); Schoenbaum, Thomas J. *Waging Peace and War* (1988).
See also: Bundy, McGeorge; Humphrey, Hubert H.; Johnson, Lyndon Baines; MARIGOLD, Operation; McNamara, Robert S.; Rusk, Dean.

Reagan, Ronald (1911–)

Actor; governor of California, 1967–1975; president of the United States, 1981–1989. A staunch anti-Communist, Reagan strongly supported U.S. intervention in Vietnam. During his 1966 California gubernatorial campaign, he propelled himself into office by assailing student antiwar protesters on the campuses of the University of California. In his gubernatorial and presidential campaigns between 1966 and 1980, Reagan reaffirmed his continuing suspicion of the Soviet Union and his belief that U.S. intervention in Vietnam was morally and strategically justified. As president, he continued the policy of nonrecognition of the Socialist Republic of Vietnam. Ironically, Reagan was extremely cautious in committing U.S. military forces in action abroad. His concern with avoiding long and politically damaging foreign military entanglements was symptomatic of the continuing legacy of Vietnam for U.S. politicians.

—Priscilla Roberts

References: Cannon, Lou. *President Reagan: The Role of a Lifetime* (1991); Dallek, Robert. *Ronald Reagan: The Politics of Symbolism* (1984); Johnson, Haynes. *Sleepwalking through History: America in* *the Reagan Years* (1991); Reagan, Ronald. *Ronald Reagan: An American Life* (1990).

See also: Antiwar Movement, United States; Bush, George Herbert Walker; Carter, Jimmy; Vietnam, Socialist Republic of: 1975 to the Present.

Red Cross Recreation Workers. *See* United States: Red Cross Recreation Workers ("Donut Dollies").

Red River Delta

Geographical heartland of Vietnam; an alluvial accumulation at the mouth of the Red River in northern Vietnam. By 1968, two large overhead dikes had been erected that funneled the Red River down the Delta and regulated its raging waters. Spreading over 15,000 miles, the entire system aided transportation with a line of roadways atop the dikes. Despite the dikes' vulnerability to air attack, the U.S. Joint Chiefs of Staff did not officially recommend their targeting except for the destruction of levees around Nam Định in 1972.

—Rodney J. Ross

References: Buttinger, Joseph. *Vietnam: A Political History* (1968); Fisher, Charles A. *Southeast Asia: A Social, Economic and Political Geography* (1966).

See also: Dikes; Geography of Indo-China and Vietnam; Mekong Delta; Tonkin.

Reeducation Camps

Camps established in Vietnam, Cambodia, and Laos following the victories of Communist forces there. They were based on the dozen "Production Camps" established in North Vietnam after 1947. More were added after 1954, and all were renamed "Reeducation Camps." The most notorious of these were Ly Bá Su, named for its camp chief, and Công Troi (Gate to Heaven).

After the Communist victory in April 1975, many more such camps were built in South Vietnam, a number of them at former U.S./Republic of Vietnam (RVN) military bases. These camps held officials of the defeated RVN government, Army of the Republic of Vietnam (ARVN) soldiers, teachers, and employees of the U.S. military. Although figures vary, Ginette Sagan and Stephen Denney estimated that more than one million Vietnamese were kept in more than 150 camps, subcamps, and prisons. They claimed that 500,000 prisoners were released within the first three months and that in 1983 60,000 remained. These figures coincide closely with those released in 1980 by the government of the Socialist Republic of Vietnam (SRV), which informed Amnesty International that one million Vietnamese were held for "short reeducation courses," and about 40,000 were detained longer.

Reeducation camps also kept common lawbreakers. These individuals had been sentenced by courts or incarcerated without trial by decision of district Public Security Chiefs under authority of Resolution 49 to three-year terms, which could be renewed without limit.

Conditions in the camps varied widely. Systematic brutality was not the pattern in Vietnam, but there were occasional beatings, torture, and executions. Medical care varied widely, and hard physical labor was interposed with politi-

cal study sessions. Each camp had an incommunicado ward of dark cells where inmates violating camp regulations were put in stocks for weeks or months. Beatings and torture were more freely meted out to prisoners incarcerated for criminal offenses.

The SRV freed many inmates in the 1970s and 1980s. Beginning in 1982 the SRV on several occasions publicly offered to permit camp inmates to depart from the country. In September 1987 Hà Nôi announced that it was releasing 6,685 prisoners, among them several hundred military and civilian personnel of the former RVN government. In June 1989 Foreign Minister Nguyên Cò Thach claimed that only about 120 people remained interned. In 1990 the U.S. State Department arranged to bring some 2,000 Vietnamese who had been in the camps to the United States. Early that year a U.S. government spokesman said that about 100,000 former camp inmates were among the 600,000 Vietnamese who had applied to emigrate to the United States.

The situation was far worse in Laos, where tens of thousands may have perished. Among those executed in "seminar camps," as the Laotian reeducation camps were known, were members of the Lao royal family, including King Savang Vatthana, the queen, and their eldest son. Gen. Vang Pao put the toll at more than 46,000 people.

—Spencer C. Tucker and Nguyên Công Luân

References: Đoàn Van Toai. *The Vietnam Gulag* (1986); Nguyên Long. *After Saigon Fell* (1981); Sagan, Ginette, and Stephen Denney. *Violations of Human Rights in the Socialist Republic of Vietnam* (1983); Vang Pao, Maj. Gen. Speech delivered at the Vietnam Seminar (18 April 1996).

See also: Laos; Refugees and Boat People; Vietnam, Socialist Republic of: 1975 to the Present.

Refugees and Boat People

Vietnamese refugees who fled on fishing boats, makeshift vessels, and unseaworthy craft. In spring 1975, more than 60,000 people took to the South China Sea during the death throes of the Republic of Vietnam (RVN) in desperate efforts to reach ships of the U.S. Seventh Fleet. This first wave of boat people, rescued under U.S. Operation FREQUENT WIND, included prominent political and military figures, those whose U.S. or Sài Gòn connections marked them for Communist retribution, and various professionals.

After the April 1975 exodus, only 377 boat people made their way during the next eight months to first-asylum countries such as Malaysia, Indonesia, Singapore, the Philippines, and Hong Kong. These were intended as only temporary sanctuaries but in some cases became permanent homes. The number of refugees jumped dramatically in 1976, when an estimated 5,619 people departed Vietnam. In 1977 the total number of boat people rose to 21,276, despite official estimates that one-third of refugees died at sea.

In June 1977 the Vietnamese Communist Party Central Committee announced the complete transformation of the South to socialism. Confiscation of private businesses and properties, freezing of assets, currency changes, collectivization of farmland, and forced removals to New Economic

Zones (NEZ) took a heavy toll on many ethnic Chinese (or Hoa, as the Vietnamese called them). Another change after the reunification of Vietnam was the process of indoctrination and reeducation in labor camps. Many Hoa, who for generations prospered in commerce and dominated the private business sector in banking and trading in the South, now opted to leave. They were encouraged to do so by the Public Security Bureau after paying bribes and a departure fee of five taels ($1,500) per adult. From 1977 to 1979, trafficking in refugees was a thriving enterprise for the Hà Nôi government.

Vietnam's war with China in 1979 also sparked a major migration of ethnic Chinese in northern Vietnam to China and a mass exodus of Hoa from Sài Gòn. Of 1.7 million Hoa in Vietnam, the majority of the 1.4 million who lived in the South left, creating a huge vacuum in Vietnam's already weakened economy. Ethnic Vietnamese who were caught or suspected of trying to escape were severely punished.

Not until 1979, when the exodus reached alarming proportions, did the world community became interested in their plight. An international crisis was precipitated when Thailand, Malaysia, Singapore, Indonesia, the Philippines, and Hong Kong announced they would no longer accept refugees. The estimated number of boat people in 1979 stood roughly at 100,000 with some 10,000 to 15,000 arriving each month. In July 1979 UN Secretary General Kurt Waldheim convened a conference in Geneva to address the problem. This meeting resulted in monetary aid to the UN High Commissioner for Refugees (UNHCR) and pledges for the resettlement of 260,000 refugees, including a U.S. pledge to double its admission rate from 7,000 to 14,000 Indo-Chinese per month. The UNHCR also exacted a promise from Hà Nôi to stem the flow of illegal departures and to establish a program of orderly departure. In 1980 and 1981 the flow of refugees leaving Vietnam fell drastically, temporarily alleviating the crisis.

In 1979 another refugee problem took on urgency when border disputes between Vietnam and Cambodia led 150,000 Cambodian Khmer to cross the Thai border into UNHCR camps. By early 1980 an additional 500,000 to 700,000 refugees were on the border.

Even in 1995, after resettlement of nearly 480,000 Vietnamese in the United States and 210,000 in other countries since 1975, the boat people constituted the bulk of refugees in Southeast Asia. Southeast Asian governments, with UNHCR cooperation, announced their intentions to close the camps, which safeguarded over 840,000 Vietnamese who fled their homeland after 1975. A lucky few would receive offers to resettle in the West; most would be compelled to return to Vietnam. The possibility of violence over forced repatriation of the remaining refugees was a source of concern for UNHCR. In many of the camps, stranded boat people said they would rather die than return to Vietnam.

In January 1996 the UNHCR said that 39,000 Vietnamese remained in the camps. The UN announced that it would stop paying for the refugee camps and would close them by July, a sign of its determination to end a lingering problem.

—Thomas T. Phu

References: Dalglish, Carol. *Refugees from Vietnam* (1989); Dougan, Clark, and David Fulghum. *The Fall of the South* (1985); Shenon, Philip. "Boat People Prefer Death To Homeland"(1995); United Nations High Commissioner for Refugees. *Resettlement Section: Statistics Concerning Indochinese in East and South East Asia* (1995); U.S. Department of State, Bureau of Public Affairs. *Indochinese Refugees* (1981).

See also: Chinese in Vietnam; FREQUENT WIND, Operation; International Rescue Committee; Sino-Vietnamese War; United Nations and the Vietnam War; Vietnamese Invasion and Occupation of Cambodia.

Regional Forces. *See* Territorial Forces.

Reinhardt, George Frederick (1911–1971)

U.S. diplomat; ambassador to the Republic of Vietnam (RVN), 1955–1957. Reinhardt's chief objective as ambassador to the RVN, despite strong misgivings voiced by his predecessor, J. Lawton Collins, was to solidify the relationship between the United States and Prime Minister Ngô Đình Diêm. Although he was the top U.S. official in Vietnam, Reinhardt exercised little personal control over the U.S. mission. Still, by the end of his tenure in 1957, Reinhardt had fulfilled his government's wishes—the United States was firmly committed to the RVN.

—David Coffey

References: Findling, John E. *Dictionary of American Diplomatic History* (1989); Spector, Ronald H. *Advice and Support: The Early Years of the U.S. Army in Vietnam, 1941–1960* (1983).

See also: Collins, Joseph Lawton; Eisenhower, Dwight David; Geneva Conference and Geneva Accords.

Republic of Vietnam. *See* Vietnam, Republic of: 1945–1954; Vietnam, Republic of: 1954–1975.

Research and Development (R&D) Field Units

U.S.-sponsored research and development initiatives in Southeast Asia. In 1961 the U.S. Defense Department Advanced Research Projects Agency established two research and development (R&D) field units in Southeast Asia: the Combat Operations Research Center (CORC) in Sài Gòn and the Combat Development and Test Center (CDTC) in Bangkok, Thailand. Both were joint and combined operations including personnel from all U.S. forces, as well as all forces from the host country, and British and Australian military personnel.

CORC was located at Military Assistance Command, Vietnam (MACV) Headquarters. CDTC was housed at the Thai Ministry of Defense. The primary mission of each unit was to conduct counterinsurgency-related R&D for U.S. forces. In addition, each was to conduct R&D to enhance the capabilities of the host nation's forces, the results of which did not have to be suitable for U.S. use. Although the bulk of the work of both units consisted of testing equipment developed in R&D laboratories in the U.S., both also initiated projects of their own.

CORC was intended primarily to conduct testing that required a combat environment. Early projects included the first in-country tests of the Colt AR-15 rifle, an evaluation of personnel-detection radar, and tests of the Canadian-built Caribou cargo aircraft.

CDTC's primary purpose was to conduct testing that required the Southeast Asia environment but that did not require, or could not be conducted in, a combat environment. Early projects included measurement of radio propagation characteristics at the geomagnetic latitude of Thailand and Vietnam; tests of personnel detection devices, such as the AN/GSS-9 break-wire detector and a seismic intrusion detector; tests of a portable loudspeaker unit for propaganda purposes; and tests of U.S. military vehicles in paddy fields and rain forests. Not all CDTC activities involved hardware testing. One project involved an anthropological study of northeast Thailand near Laos to evaluate the potential for growth of an insurgency in that area.

Locally initiated projects at CDTC included development for the Thai Army of a water buffalo–drawn sled to provide troop mobility in mud flats and a magnetic detector for rapidly inspecting sampans for concealed weapons as they floated along a canal.

Since the initial focus of the R&D field units was counterinsurgency, they became less relevant to U.S. forces as the war escalated to conventional levels; they continued to operate until 1971, however. CDTC in particular added to the military capabilities of the host nation.

—Joseph P. Martino

See also: Counterinsurgency Warfare; Thailand.

Reserve Forces

President Johnson's July 1965 decision not to call up reserve forces for service in Vietnam was one of the most important and unfortunate decisions of the war. His decision forced the U.S. armed services, and particularly the Army, to support rapid and massive expansion without recourse to the assets in manpower, knowledge, experience, and leadership represented by the National Guard and the Army Reserve. It rendered the reserve forces havens for draft evaders, resulting in humiliation and frustration among professionals within those forces. Reserve force units were stripped of essential equipment to support new formations being organized to go to Vietnam in their place, so that when some reserve force units were called up much later, they were less ready and did not represent themselves as well as they could have at the outset.

The military establishment expected Johnson to approve the use of reserves. Secretary of Defense Robert McNamara had recommended it. Among senior military leaders only Gen. William Westmoreland was opposed. All contingency plans for operations as extensive as the deployments then being ordered for Vietnam were based on the availability of reserve forces.

Then, at the last moment, President Johnson drew back. Large formations were being sent to Vietnam, he told the American people, but reserve forces would take no part. Instead, draft calls would be increased to provide the needed additional manpower. For the Army, this meant growing from about 965,000 in early 1965 to more than 1,527,000 by mid-1968. The increases, as Gen. Creighton Abrams later ruefully observed, consisted "entirely of privates and second lieutenants."

As the war went on and the Army grew ever larger, levels of experience and maturity in the force continued to drop, particularly among junior officers and noncommissioned officers. Further dilution resulted from the prospect of repetitive tours in Vietnam for those in the regular Army. Many, again especially among the junior leadership, came under heavy family pressure and resigned rather than go through yet another separation at risk. At the same time, there were increasing problems of poor discipline, racial strife, and drug abuse in the armed forces.

The Joint Chiefs of Staff repeatedly appealed to Johnson and McNamara to call up reserve forces. Each time they were rebuffed. Not until early 1968, following the Tết Offensive in Vietnam, would a small number of units from the reserve forces be brought to active duty. In May 1968 a few additional units were called up, and some were eventually dispatched to Vietnam, usually after extended periods of postmobilization training. Deployments were in some cases delayed by individual and class-action lawsuits challenging the legality of the call-ups. Eventually the Supreme Court ruled that the mobilization was legal. All those mobilized had been returned to inactive status by December 1969.

A subsequent assessment by the Army War College's Strategic Studies Institute concluded that, insofar as the Army was concerned, "mobilization for the Vietnam War occurred far too late to be of any political significance, and was far too small to be of any military significance."

—Lewis Sorley

References: National Guard Association of the United States. *The Abrams Doctrine: Then, Now and in the Future: A National Guard Association Symposium: Report and Transcript* (1994); Sorley, Lewis. "Creighton Abrams and Active-Reserve Integration in Wartime" (1991); Stuckey, Col. John D., and Col. Joseph H. Pistorius. *Mobilization of the Army National Guard and Army Reserve: Historical Perspective and the Vietnam War* (1984).

See also: Johnson, Lyndon Baines; McNamara, Robert S.; *Pueblo* Incident; Tết Offensive: Overall Strategy; Tết Offensive: the Sài Gòn Circle; United States: Army.

Revers Report (1949)

Secret French report on policy and military strategy in Indo-China that became famous when its contents were leaked. The report was the work of French chief of staff Gen. Georges Revers, who headed a fact-finding mission to Indo-China in May 1949.

The Revers Report recommended consolidating French military resources, including the evacuation of Cao Bang, and concentrating on defense of the vital Red River Delta area. Revers sharply criticized the Bao Đai government for its corruption and other deficiencies. He recommended strictly respecting the agreements with Bao Đai that created a Vietnamese national army, and doing away with a large number of civil servants. These criticisms were seen as an attack on high commissioner Léon Pignon in Sài Gòn.

Viêt Minh radio began broadcasting extracts of the leaked report in August. Investigation revealed that Revers had given a copy of his report to a fellow officer, Gen. Mast, whom some suspected of being his candidate to replace Pignon. Mast had passed along sections of the report to various Vietnamese, whence it had been conveyed to the Viêt Minh. The scandal and its political ramifications rocked French politics for months afterward.

—Arthur J. Dommen

References: Dalloz, Jacques. *The War in Indo-China, 1945–54* (1990); Gras, Général Yves. *Histoire de la Guerre d'Indochine* (1992); Hammer, Ellen J. *The Struggle for Indochina* (1954).

See also: Blaizot, Roger; Indo-China War; Pignon, Léon.

Rheault, Robert B. (1925–)

U.S. Army officer and commander of 5th Special Forces Group, 1969. Shortly after Col. Rheault's assignment to Vietnam in the summer of 1969, Thái Khac Chuyên, a Vietnamese employed to gather cross-border intelligence, came under suspicion as a double agent. With Rheault's knowledge and approval, members of his command murdered Chuyên. A sergeant who was involved talked about the matter with the Central Intelligence Agency, and Gen. Creighton Abrams summoned Rheault to Sài Gòn. Rheault maintained there was no truth to rumors that Chuyên had been killed, but when officers of his command confessed the murder to Army criminal investigators, Rheault was exposed as a liar. Abrams relieved him of command, and court-martial charges were brought against Rheault and others.

The defendants generated enough political pressure to cause President Nixon to have the charges against them dismissed. Col. Rheault was then offered another assignment, but he elected to retire. He continued to argue that what he had done was proper and appropriate.

—Lewis Sorley

References: Simpson, Col. Charles M., III. *Inside the Green Berets* (1984); Sorley, Lewis. *Thunderbolt: General Creighton Abrams and the Army of His Times* (1992).

See also: Abrams, Creighton; Atrocities during the Vietnam War; Nixon, Richard Milhous; United States: Special Forces.

Richardson, John H. (1913–)

U.S. Central Intelligence Agency (CIA) station chief in Sài Gòn, 1962–1963. Richardson developed a close relationship with Republic of Vietnam President Ngô Đình Diêm and his brother Ngô Đình Nhu. Nevertheless, Richardson and William Colby laid the groundwork for the coup against Diêm during the summer of 1963.

Because of his close ties to Nhu, Richardson was mistrusted by the generals conspiring against Diêm, so Lucien Conein acted as the go-between. In August Richardson reported that the Ngô family was determined to hold out but that the conspiracy would succeed. But experiencing second thoughts about the coup, Richardson changed his instructions to Conein. When Ambassador Henry Cabot Lodge discovered this, he ordered Conein to report directly to him about discussions with the conspirators. Richardson's chang-

ing position, and his still-close ties with the Diêm regime, led Lodge to request Richardson's recall. Richardson left Sài Gòn on October 5, 1963.

—Robert G. Mangrum

References: Hammer, Ellen J. *A Death in November: America in Vietnam 1963* (1987); Karnow, Stanley. *Vietnam: A History* (1983); Rust, William J. *Kennedy in Vietnam* (1985).

See also: Conein, Lucien Emile; Lodge, Henry Cabot, Jr.; Ngô Đình Diêm; Ngô Đình Nhu.

Ridgway, Matthew B. (1895–1993)

U.S. Army general and chief of staff, 1953–1955. Ridgway opposed U.S. involvement in France's colonial war in Indo-China. When Secretary of State John Foster Dulles and Chairman of the Joint Chiefs of Staff Admiral Arthur Radford urged intervention during the Điên Biên Phu crisis, Ridgway advised against rashness. Remembering the protracted Korean conflict, Ridgway criticized Operation VULTURE's proposed U.S. air strikes against Viêt Minh positions, since he believed ground operations would inevitably follow. The political nature of the war, Ridgway said, would mean an extended commitment. His arguments influenced President Eisenhower's decision against intervention in 1954.

Ridgway recognized the problems inherent in the defense doctrine of "massive retaliation" and was a chief spokesman for the concept of "flexible response." He remained skeptical of U.S. Vietnam policy and served as one of President Johnson's senior advisors known as the "Wise Men."

—Rodney J. Ross and Spencer C. Tucker

References: Dupuy, Trevor N., Curt Johnson, and David L. Bongard. *The Harper Encyclopedia of Military Biography* (1992); Halberstam, David. *The Best and the Brightest* (1973); Ridgway, Matthew. *Soldier: The Memoirs of Matthew B. Ridgway* (1956); Spector, Ronald H. *Advice and Support: The Early Years, 1941–1960* (1983).

See also: Eisenhower, Dwight David; Johnson, Lyndon Baines; MacArthur, Douglas; Radford, Arthur W.; Truman, Harry S; VULTURE, Operation; "Wise Men."

Rifles

During the Indo-China War, French forces used various rifles, including the German 8-mm 98K and the U.S.-made .30-caliber M1 Garands, and M1 and M2 carbines. During the latter part of France's involvement in Indo-China, the standard rifle was the 7.5-mm rifle M1949 (MAS) (designation for St. Etienne Arsenal). Well-made and reliable, the M1949 is a gas-operated semiautomatic weapon chambered for the French 7.5-mm M1929 cartridge and fed by a ten-round detachable box magazine. Not issued with a bayonet, it features an integral grenade launcher and mounting grooves for detachable telescopic sights.

Combat experiences in Vietnam spurred a rapid evolution in U.S. infantry rifles. Early military advisors in Southeast Asia were issued various World War II and Korean War vintage weapons, including the .30-caliber M1 and M2 carbines and the .45-caliber M1A1 Thompson and M3A1 submachine guns. As U.S. involvement in Vietnam escalated, the American military adopted the 7.62-mm M14 rifle as its standard rifle. Based on the .30-caliber M1 Garand action, the M14 features several improvements. Chambered for the 7.62-mm North Atlantic Treaty Organization cartridge, the M14 is capable of semiautomatic and automatic fire. Although retaining the Garand's basic action, the M14 features an improved gas system and a detachable 20-round magazine, increasing both rate of fire and accuracy. A total of 1,381,581 M14s were produced by Harrington and Richardson Arms Company, Thompson Products, Winchester-Western Arms Division of Olin Mathieson Corporation, and the Springfield Armory. Replaced in the Air Force and Army with the M16 and M16A1, the M14 continued service with a number of Marine Corps units.

In the late 1950s Eugene Stoner and the Armalite Corporation developed the AR-15 rifle. After obtaining manufacturing rights from Armalite, Colt's Patent Fire Arms Manufacturing Co. began producing it for the U.S. government in the early 1960s. Adopted as the 5.56-mm rifle M16, the new weapon exhibited some advanced innovations, including an improved gas system and reduced weight and caliber. The M16 and M16A1 select-fire weapons introduced the smaller 5.56-mm (.223-caliber) cartridge.

The M16 originally was developed for air base security, not as an infantry weapon. Consequently, when introduced into field service in Vietnam, it evidenced some shortcomings. Its susceptibility to jamming earned the M16 the mistrust of troops in the field. Modifications to the cartridge and to the weapon itself greatly improved the rifle, which was redesignated the M16A1. Advantages of the M16A1 include its light weight and the reduced cartridge size, permitting more ammunition to be carried in the field.

The Viêt Minh used rifles of varying origin, including World War II and older weapons. In late 1945, the Viêt Minh acquired more than 30,000 Japanese 6.5-mm and 7.7-mm small arms. They also purchased U.S.-manufactured small arms from the Chinese Nationalists.

During the Vietnam War, Viêt Công and People's Army of Vietnam arms ranged from modern Soviet and Chinese assault rifles to crudely fashioned single-shot weapons. As during the war with France, Communist forces in Vietnam used any weapons available, including French Model 49 and Chinese Type 50 submachine guns, World War II vintage German 98Ks, Soviet Model 44s, and captured U.S. weapons.

Two weapons most associated with Communist forces in Vietnam are the Simonov SKS carbine and the Kalashnikov AK47 assault rifle. Both are Soviet designs and were produced by Soviet bloc countries and the People's Republic of China. Simple and robust, they are ideal for issue to poorly trained troops in adverse conditions. The semiautomatic Simonov SKS carbine is equipped with a folding bayonet, is chambered for the 7.62-mm M1943 cartridge, and is fed by a ten-round nondetachable box magazine.

The selective-fire 7.62-mm Automat Kalashnikov assault rifle was issued in a number of variations. The original AK design, commonly known as the AK47, is composed predominantly of milled steel components and was issued with either wooden or folding metal stocks. The later AKM is a

modification of the AK47, differing mainly in the extensive use of stamped metal in its construction. Both weapons utilize a 30-round detachable box magazine. The construction changes, however, reduced the AK47's 10.58-pound weight to the AKM's 8.87 pounds.

—Jeff Kinard

References: Chant, Christopher, ed. *How Weapons Work* (1976); Rosa, Joseph G., and Robin May. *An Illustrated History of Guns and Small Arms* (1984); Smith, W. H. B., revised by Joseph E. Smith. *Small Arms of the World*. 9th ed. (1969).
See also: Grenades, Hand, Allied and Democratic Republic of Vietnam; Grenades, Launched, Allied and Democratic Republic of Vietnam; Machine Guns, Allied and People's Army of Vietnam; Pistols.

Rigault de Genouilly, Charles (1807–1873)

French admiral who in 1857 carried out the first major European military incursion into Vietnam. Both Spain and France sought redress from Vietnam for the execution of missionaries, and Emperor Napoleon III hoped to secure a port there in the fashion of Hong Kong. The French chose to penetrate southern Vietnam first because it was the newest part of the country and its inhabitants were not as wedded to Vietnamese institutions. Indeed, the French conquest proved more difficult the farther it moved north.

In January 1858 Rigault de Genouilly received instructions that operations in Indo-China were to be only an appendix, and entirely subordinate, to those in China. Paris instructed him to halt persecution and ensure toleration of Catholics in Indo-China. Paris thought this could best be achieved by occupying Tourane, mistakenly considered the key to the entire kingdom. On 31 August 1858, Rigault de Genouilly's squadron anchored off Tourane, and on 1 September he landed his troops, including 300 Filipino troops sent by Spain. These took the Tourane forts and the port, inaugurating the first phase of the French conquest of Indo-China.

Within months, heat, disease, and a lack of supplies forced the French from Tourane. Rigault de Genouilly then shifted his attack southward to the fishing village of Sài Gòn, selected because of its proximity and the importance of the rice trade. It fell to the French after a brief fight on 17 February 1859. This attack was subsequently criticized in Paris, and in November 1859 Rigault de Genouilly was replaced by Admiral Page, who was instructed by Paris not to seek territorial concessions but to sign a treaty with the Vietnamese that would guarantee religious liberties and French consuls in the major Vietnamese ports.

—Spencer C. Tucker

References: Jenkins, E. H. *A History of the French Navy* (1973); Thompson, Virginia. *French Indo-China* (1968).
See also: French Indo-China; Lefèbvre, Dominique; Napoleon III.

Riverine Craft

During the Vietnam War, the Republic of Vietnam (RVN) and U.S. navies used naval craft to conduct riverine ("brownwater") operations along the inland waterways of Vietnam. All riverine craft involved had a shallow draft, without which no boat could navigate rivers and canals during the dry season.

To implement Operation GAME WARDEN and SEALORDS (South East Asia Lake Ocean River Delta Strategy) the U.S. Navy's riverine force, the Mobile Riverine Force (MRF), required small, heavily armed shallow-draft boats. The river patrol boat (PBR) fit these requirements and became the workhorse of the River Patrol Force. The PBR was adapted from a 1965 design by the founder of the Hatteras Yacht Company, Willis Slane. It appeared in two versions: the MK-I and the MK-II. Built by United Boatbuilders, the MK-I used two diesel-powered water jets instead of propellers. When operating at high speeds up to 30 knots or on "the step" (when planing), the PBR had only a 9-inch draft. About 160 MK-Is were built in 1966.

The MK-II, built in 1967, was slightly longer, wider, and heavier than the MK-I, which had minimal effect on the boat's speed and draft. Both versions of the PBR contained the same weaponry. The main armament consisted of twin .50-caliber machine guns mounted in a turret forward and a single .50-caliber machine gun aft. In addition, several starboard and port mounts existed for M60 machine guns; a 40-mm automatic grenade launcher was also on board. Although naval designers placed ceramic armor at weapons stations and the coxswain's "flat," firepower and speed were this small boat's advantages.

The fast patrol craft (PCF), although not initially selected for riverine operations, proved valuable along the larger rivers during SEALORDS, enabling the shallower-draft PBRs to move onto smaller waterways. The Navy adapted the PCF, or Swift boat, from the Sewart Seacraft Company vessel used by oil companies to transport offshore oil rig crews. From 1965 to 1967 the Navy had two versions constructed, the MK-I and MK-II. The MK-I was a diesel-powered, dual-propeller–driven boat that could make 25 knots. About 104 MK-Is were built between 1965 and 1966. The MK-II, of which only eight were constructed, was slightly longer, wider, and heavier. The armament consisted of a .50-caliber machine gun mounted atop an 81-mm mortar aft and twin .50-caliber machine guns mounted in a turret on top of the pilot house.

The only craft designed keel-up for use in Vietnam was the assault patrol boat (ASPB), the MRF's destroyer and minesweeper. Equipped with diesel engines, the ASPB could make 15 knots. More than 30 of these boats were shipped to Vietnam by late 1967. Its armament included a 20-mm cannon mounted in a turret forward, an 81-mm mortar aft, one .50-caliber machine gun amidships, and one aft.

Most of the MRF's brown-water fleet were conversions of the World War II LCM-6, or mechanized landing craft. The three predominant versions of the LCM-6 included the monitor, the ATC (armored troop carrier), and the CCB (command-and-communications boat). All had two propellers powered by diesel engines that gave them a top speed of 6 knots, and all drew 36 to 41 inches of water. The monitor had an 81-mm mortar in a pit amidships and aft two .50-caliber and M60 machine guns along with one 20-mm cannon. A turret forward housed a 40-mm cannon and a .50-caliber machine gun. A modified monitor, dubbed a "Zippo," mounted two flame throwers forward. The ATCs could carry 40 troops. Armament included one 20-mm cannon, two .50-caliber machine guns, and either four .30-caliber or four M60 machine guns. The CCBs maintained the same specifications of the monitor except for the mortar pit amidships. Instead the CCBs had radar and radio equipment. Other LCM-6 conversions included helipad craft and tankers for the brown-water fleet. All conversions had stand-off armor to predetonate incoming rockets.

The patrol air cushion vehicle (PACV), an experimental craft adopted for naval purposes, resembled hover ferries used to cross the English Channel. When airborne, it had a hull-borne clearance of 4 feet. With a gas turbine engine that operated the air screw and lift fan, the PACV could easily reach 70 knots. The PACV had two .50-caliber machine guns above the pilot house.

Until Vietnamization, the most common boats in the Vietnamese Navy's (VNN's) river fleet, or River Assault Groups (RAGs), were STCAN/FOMs (Services Techniques des Construction et Armes Navales/France Outre Mere), LCVPs (personnel landing craft vehicles), LCM-6s or LCM-8 conversions, and RPCs (river patrol craft). Following French withdrawal, the FOMs became part of the VNN. FOM armament included one .50-caliber machine gun forward and three .30-caliber machine guns dispersed amidships and aft. The converted LCVP could make 9 knots and drew only 3 feet 5 inches of water. Each LCVP had a variety of weapons such as .30-caliber and .50-caliber machine guns. In an attempt to replace the FOMs, 34 RPCs were built in 1965. The RPC's two diesel-driven propellers enabled the boat to navigate at 14 knots while drawing only 3 feet 6 inches of water. Each RPC had either one set of twin .30-caliber and a set of .50-caliber machine guns or two sets of twin .30-caliber machine guns.

Although both navies used and experimented with other craft, these represent the primary craft used by the American and Vietnamese navies.

—R. Blake Dunnavent

References: Cutler, Thomas J. *Brown Water, Black Berets: Coastal and Riverine Warfare in Vietnam* (1988); Marolda, Edward J. *By Sea, Air, and Land: An Illustrated History of the U.S. Navy and the War in Southeast Asia* (1994); Schreadley, R. L. *From the Rivers to the Sea: The United States Navy in Vietnam* (1992); U.S. Naval History Division. *Riverine Warfare: Vietnam* (1972).

See also: GAME WARDEN, Operation; MARKET TIME, Operation; Mekong Delta; Mobile Riverine Force; Riverine Warfare; SEALORDS (South East Asia Lake Ocean River Delta Strategy); United States: Navy; Vietnam, Republic of: Navy (VNN).

Riverine Warfare

The contest for control of South Vietnam's waterways. The Mekong Delta, an alluvial plain created by the Mekong River and its many tributaries, was the geo-strategic center of the Republic of Vietnam (RVN). It constituted almost one-fourth of the country's territory, held about half of its population, and was the agricultural production center of the entire region. Only one hard-surfaced road, Highway 4, traversed the Delta south of Sài Gòn. However, the region had 2,400 kilometers of navigable natural waterways, interconnected by 4,000 kilometers of manmade canals. It was a perfect area for river-borne operations.

Although virtually no People's Army of Vietnam (PAVN) units operated in the Mekong Delta, it was a major Việt Cộng (VC) stronghold and home of the VC 9th Division. In mid-1966 it held an estimated 28 VC battalions and 69 separate companies, totaling 82,500 troops. Almost one-third of all VC actions against the RVN took place in the Delta, and the VC controlled an estimated 24.6 percent of the region's population. As part of their overall strategy, the VC attempted to cut off the flow of rice from the Delta.

The Delta constituted the Army of the Republic of Vietnam's (ARVN's) IV Corps Tactical Zone. Three ARVN divisions—the 7th, 9th, and 21st—were stationed there. The RVN Navy (VNN) also operated six river assault groups and 11 coastal groups patterned directly after the Dinassauts, operated by the French in the Indo-China War.

The U.S. military first entered the Delta in 1957 when U.S. Navy advisors replaced their French counterparts. By 1966 no U.S. ground units were yet in the Delta, but the U.S. Army's 13th Combat Aviation Brigade provided support to the ARVN. The U.S. Navy had two task forces operating in Delta waters. Task Force (TF) 115, under Operation MARKET TIME, patrolled the coastal areas to prevent VC infiltration and resupply from the sea. In Operation GAME WARDEN, TF 116, also known as the River Patrol Force, worked the rivers. Operating with a Navy helicopter attack squadron, SEAL teams, and a minesweeping division, the River Patrol Force conducted reconnaissance patrols, salvage operations, day and night ambushes, and hit-and-run raids.

The concept of a joint Army-Navy riverine force for the Delta emerged from a March 1966 study by the Military Assistance Command, Vietnam (MACV), *Delta Mobile Afloat Force Concept and Requirements*. Its missions were to secure U.S. base areas and lines of communication; conduct offensive operations against VC forces in the area; isolate the most heavily populated and key food-producing areas from the VC; interdict VC supply routes; and provide reserve and reaction forces for ARVN units operating in the IV Corps Tactical Zone.

A principal reason behind the concept of the Mobile Riverine Force (MRF), as it came to be designated, was the lack of a suitable land base area for a large U.S. ground force in the densely populated Delta. The MACV plan called for establishment of a relatively small land base, created by dredging, to house units of the force's support structure and equipment the force would not need while afloat. In June 1966 Gen. William Westmoreland selected a site near My Tho for the new base, Đông Tâm.

The planners felt that at least a brigade-sized unit was needed in the Delta. The original concept called for a force consisting of two river assault groups (later called river assault squadrons) supported by five self-propelled barracks ships. The plan was approved by the Department of Defense on 5 July 1966; but at the same time, Secretary of Defense Robert McNamara decided to cut the number of barracks

ships from five to two. Consequently, the authorized force had afloat berthing space for only one of a brigade's three maneuver battalions. The Navy created berthing space for another battalion by providing a towed barracks barge. The force, however, could still maintain only two battalions afloat, so the brigade habitually operated with only two battalions, while the third secured the land base at Đông Tâm.

The Army element of the MRF was the 2d Brigade of the 9th Infantry Division. Under its first commander, Col. William B. Fulton, the 2d Brigade consisted of the 3d and 4th Battalions, 47th Infantry Regiment; the 3d Battalion, 60th Infantry; and the 3d Battalion, 39th Artillery—a towed 105-mm unit. The 9th Infantry Division was activated specifically for the Vietnam War, and its lead elements arrived in Vietnam on 16 December 1966. Initially the division's 1st and 3d Brigades operated from Bearcat, just south of Sài Gòn and north of the Mekong Delta, in the III Corps Tactical Zone. The 2d Brigade operated from Đông Tâm.

The Navy component of the MRF was River Assault Flotilla 1, also known as the Riverine Assault Force and Task Force 117. Under the initial command of Capt. Wade C. Wells, TF 117 consisted of the 9th and 11th River Assault Squadrons, which were further organized into river assault divisions. A river assault squadron could carry a battalion and a river assault division could carry a company. By the time the MRF was disbanded, TF 117 had grown to four river assault squadrons, with the addition of the 13th and the 15th.

A 400-man river assault squadron was a powerful flotilla consisting of up to three command-and-communications boats (CCBs), five monitors, 26 armored troop carriers (ATCs), 16 assault support patrol boats (ASPBs), and one refueler, plus a supporting underwater demolition team (UDT), an explosive ordnance detachment (EOD), and a riverine survey team.

Local innovations led to improvements in MRF equipment and operating procedures. Most important was the mounting of artillery on barges, which greatly increased the mobility—and therefore the operational range—of the brigade's artillery battalion. Each barge carried two 105-mm howitzers. Field artillery requires stationary firing platforms and fixed aiming points, so the barges had to be beached along a river or canal bank to fire effectively. This did, however, allow for direct support fire to ground units once they were landed. Other important innovations included the building of helicopter landing platforms on the ATCs and the use of helicopter landing barges.

The MRF was not a true joint task force with a single commander. According to *MACV Planning Directive 12–66* of 10 December 1966, MRF Army units came under the commanding general of II Field Force, who exercised operational control through the designated subordinated headquarters, in this case the 9th Infantry Division. MRF Navy units came directly under the operational control of the commander, U.S. Naval Forces in Vietnam. The document further stipulated that the relationship between Army and Navy units would be one of coordination, with the Navy providing close support to the Army. Although in U.S. practice the doctrinal concept of close support implies that the supported force directs operations, the determination of mission and area of operation of the MRF was a constant source of friction between the Army and Navy component commanders.

In practice, the target and area of operations usually was selected by the commander of the 2d Brigade or a higher-echelon Army commander. The 2d Brigade and TF 117 commanders then agreed on the general timing and task organization of the mission. A joint planning staff then developed the scheme of maneuver in the target area. From there they worked backwards, determining details of the assault or landing, the water movement, and the loading phases. The final operations plan was briefed to the two commanders, usually aboard the MRF's flagship, the landing ship *Benewah*.

MRF operations consisted of coordinated airmobile, ground, and waterborne attacks, supported by air and naval forces. Once the force made contact with the VC, commanders cut off possible escape routes by moving units into blocking positions on the VC flanks and rear. After directing artillery fire, helicopter gunship fire, and tactical air strikes into the VC positions, ground troops swept the area. During the MRF's first year of operations, these tactics proved effective. The VC often were disoriented and caught by surprise, since they had anticipated attacks primarily coming from the land and air. Their defenses, therefore, almost always faced away from the water.

Over time the VC learned to deal with the new situation. While under way, the principal security threats to the MRF came from command-detonated mines in the waterway and ambushes along the shore, with heavy fire from recoilless rifles and B-40 rockets. While anchored, the most critical threats were from floating mines, swimmer saboteurs, and suicide attack boats. The MRF developed security measures to deal with all of these.

During operations all troop movements were controlled and coordinated from the joint tactical operations center on the flagship. The Army element of the staff normally was supervised by the brigade executive officer. The brigade commander operated with his forward command group from a fire base. During daylight hours, they were usually aloft in a command-and-control helicopter. Battalion command posts were divided into forward and rear tactical operations centers. The battalion commander operated from the forward command post aboard the command ship of the river assault squadron. The battalion rear command posts were controlled by the executive officers and located aboard ship at the mobile riverine floating base.

Operating in a riverine environment presented special challenges. Salt water caused maintenance problems, often corroding weapons. Operations were constrained by tides, water depth, obstructions, bridge clearances, and the suitability of river and canal banks for landing sites. Wet, marshy terrain also caused immersion foot, dermatophytosis, and other foot problems that increased whenever the troops operated on land for more than two consecutive days.

The main body of the 2d Brigade arrived in Vietnam on 31 January 1967. On 15 February the VC attacked an ocean-going freighter on the Lòng Tào, the main shipping channel between Vung Tàu on the coast and Sài Gòn. In reaction, the 3d Battalion, 47th Infantry was ordered to conduct operations in the Rung Sát Special Zone, a mangrove swamp in the northeastern Delta. The resulting operation, RIVER RAIDER I, was the first joint operation between the U.S. Army and Navy units that would later form the MRF. The operation lasted from 16 February to 20 March, with Army units supported by River Assault Division 91 of River Assault Squadron 9.

The 2d Brigade's headquarters became operational at Đông Tâm on 10 March. A month later, the first of the river assault divisions moved to Đông Tâm and began operations with the 3d Battalion, 47th Infantry. The Mobile Riverine Force became fully operational on 1 June 1967. Between then and March 1968, the MRF conducted a series of wide-ranging riverine and combined airmobile and riverine operations designated CORONADO I through XI.

The Navy component of the MRF continued to grow. By the fall of 1968 it reached its full strength of four river assault squadrons, including 184 river assault craft, four barracks ships, two barracks barges, three repair ships, two support ships, and two resupply ships, and various other craft. About the same time, the MRF was reorganized into two Mobile Riverine Groups. Group Alpha had five river assault divisions and Group Bravo had three.

In mid-1968 the 9th Infantry Division underwent a major change in its mission. On 25 July the division headquarters relocated from Bearcat to Đông Tâm and the other two brigades also moved into the Delta. For the first time, an entire U.S. infantry division was in the Mekong Delta. As part of this shift, the 2d Brigade's mission changed to an almost exclusive focus on the pacification of Kiên Hòa Province. The 2d Brigade finally received its third maneuver battalion afloat, but the newly restricted area of operations greatly reduced the mobility advantages demonstrated during the wider-ranging operations of the MRF's first year. Mobile Riverine Group Alpha continued to support the 2d Brigade in Kiên Hòa Province, while Mobile Riverine Group Bravo carried out operations in the southern Delta with units of the 2d, 3d, and 4th Battalions of the Republic of Vietnam Marine Corps.

In November 1968 Mobile Riverine Group Bravo initiated the first of the SEALORDS (South East Asia Lake Ocean River Delta Strategy) operations, designed to keep Communist forces away from the rivers and canals in western Long An and Kiên Tuong Provinces. On 1 February 1969, the 25 river assault craft of River Assault Division 91 were turned over to the RVN Navy. The 9th Infantry Division, meanwhile, was informed that it was to be the first division withdrawn from Vietnam, with the 2d Brigade to be first unit deactivated. As part of the Vietnamization process, TF 117 started turning over the rest of its boats to the RVN Navy. On 25 August 1969 the MRF, and with it River Flotilla 1 and the 2d Brigade, 9th Division, were deactivated.

On tactical and operational levels, the MRF was successful. The MRF effectively wrested control of the northern Delta from the VC and opened Highway 4 for the first time since

1965, which in turn freed the flow of agricultural products from the Delta for both export and domestic use.

One intriguing question remains about the composition of the MRF. By doctrine, the U.S. Marine Corps is organized and trained for amphibious warfare missions. It seems odd then that U.S. Marine units in Vietnam were deployed in the mountainous north of the country and that a brigade of a newly raised Army division was assigned the amphibious mission that is supposed to be the Marine Corps's raison d'être.

—David T. Zabecki

References: Croizat, Victor. *The Brown Water Navy: The River and Coastal War in Indochina and Vietnam, 1940–1972* (1984); Cutler, Thomas J. *Brown Water, Black Berets: Coastal and Riverine Operations in Vietnam* (1988); Fulton, William B. *Riverine Operations, 1966–1969* (1985); Sheppard, Don. *"Riverine": A Brown Water Sailor in the Delta, 1967* (1992).
See also: Dinassauts; GAME WARDEN, Operation; MARKET TIME, Operation; McNamara, Robert S.; Mobile Riverine Force; Riverine Craft; SEAL (Sea, Air, Land) Teams; SEALORDS (South East Asia Lake Ocean River Delta Strategy).

Rivers, L. Mendel (1905–1970)

U.S. congressman, 1941–1970. Rivers was one of the staunchest advocates of the U.S. military establishment and of escalating military procurements. As chairman of the House Armed Services Committee, he had significant influence on military legislation and appropriations. In return for his unswerving support, various administrations rewarded him with an enormous number of military installations for his district. Rivers's only serious criticism of the Vietnam War was that it had not been fought vigorously enough. After the 1968 Tết Offensive, he recommended the use of nuclear weapons against the Democratic Republic of Vietnam. Rivers also supported the military in opposing the civilian systems analysts often favored by the Department of Defense. He conducted hearings in support of an ultimately unsuccessful proposal to abolish the Office of Systems Analysis, a creation of Secretary of Defense Robert McNamara.

—Eric Jarvis

References: Baritz, Loren. *Backfire* (1985); Gibbons, William Conrad. *The U.S. Government and the Vietnam War, Parts 1–3* (1986); Hopkins, George W. "From Naval Pauper to Naval Power: The Development of Charleston's Metropolitan-Military Complex" (1984).
See also: Goldwater, Barry Morris; McGee, Gale William; McNamara, Robert S.; Stennis, John Cornelius; Tết Offensive: Overall Strategy; Tết Offensive: the Sài Gòn Circle.

Road Watch Teams (RWTs)

U.S. Central Intelligence Agency (CIA)–sponsored teams monitoring North Vietnamese traffic down the Hồ Chí Minh Trail in Laos. Road Watch Teams (RWTs) originated in mid-1966 and were eventually controlled jointly by the CIA in Laos and the Military Assistance Command, Vietnam (MACV), Studies and Observations Group (SOG) in Sài Gòn.

Because U.S. military personnel were prohibited from conducting ground combat operations in central and northern Laos, participants in the RWT program were indigenous Laotians. Teams were composed of six to 12 men each. Individual teams were sometimes inserted overland, but the usual procedure was by helicopter. Each team was assigned a Royal Laotian officer or sergeant to identify team members. The teams were not to engage in combat and had as their primary mission surveillance of the Hồ Chí Minh Trail. Their operational area ran from the southern boundary of the People's Republic of China to the northern Cambodian border.

U.S.-led reconnaissance teams from SOG's Operation 35 (Ground Studies Group) were the exception to the ban on U.S. combat forces in Laos. By presidential order they were authorized to reconnoiter in Laos up to 20 kilometers from the Republic of Vietnam border. Operation 35's zone of operations (code-named PRAIRIE FIRE) ran from the Demilitarized Zone south to the northern Cambodian border. RWTs and Operation 35 teams were purposely kept separated. RWTs operated deeper, beyond limitations set for Operation 35 in Laos. RWT members reported enemy activity via short-burst, coded radio transmissions to U.S. aircraft flying around-the-clock designated orbits over Laos. The U.S. Air Force utilized this information to conduct bombing missions against enemy truck convoys. RWTs also assessed damage from these strikes, and they aided propaganda leaflet drops over Laos. The RWT project was a model of cooperation between the U.S. Air Force, U.S. Special Forces, and the CIA.

—Harve Saal and Spencer C. Tucker

References: Saal, Harve. *MACV-Studies and Observation Group (SOG)* (1990); Secord, Richard, with Jay Wurts. *Honored and Betrayed. Irangate, Covert Affairs, and the Secret War in Laos* (1992).
See also: Central Intelligence Agency (CIA); Laos; STEEL TIGER, Operation; TIGER HOUND, Operation; United States: Special Forces.

Rockefeller, Nelson A. (1908–1979)

Governor of New York, 1959–1973; vice-president of the United States, 1974–1977. A firm anti-Communist and believer in the prevailing Cold War orthodoxy, Rockefeller was originally a strong supporter of the U.S. commitment to Vietnam. In the 1964 election campaign he attacked Lyndon Johnson's Vietnam policies as insufficiently firm and assertive. Rockefeller was fully supportive of the military escalation from 1965 to 1967. During the 1968 presidential campaign, he advanced a program for peace, an impractical proposal that envisaged the supervision of Vietnam by a neutral international peacekeeping force, and free elections to decide whether or not North and South Vietnam should be reunited.

At the 1968 Republican convention both Rockefeller and Richard Nixon supported and won a platform plank favoring peace negotiations over the opposition of Ronald Reagan's followers, who urged a more aggressive prosecution of the war. After Nixon's election, Rockefeller loyally supported his policies toward Vietnam. In the turmoil that followed Nixon's resignation, President Gerald Ford selected Rockefeller as his vice-president, a move that angered the conservative wing of the Republican Party.

—Priscilla Roberts

References: Dietz, Terry. *Republicans and Vietnam, 1961–1968* (1986); Persico, Joseph. *The Imperial Rockefeller* (1982).
See also: Elections, U.S.: 1968; Ford, Gerald R.; Goldwater, Barry Morris; Johnson, Lyndon Baines; Nixon, Richard Milhous; Reagan, Ronald.

Rockets

Rockets were used extensively in the Vietnam War by Allied and Communist military forces, principally in antiarmor/antibunker, artillery, and aerial ground support roles. The United States employed M20 and M72 antiarmor weapons that fired high-explosive antitank (HEAT) rockets. The M20, a 3.5-inch rocket launcher known as the "super bazooka," replaced the earlier M9A1 2.36-inch bazooka of World War II fame. The M20 was in turn replaced by the M72 light antitank weapon (LAW), a one-man, single-shot 66-mm rocket launcher. The rockets these launchers fired were used primarily in antibunker roles.

Communist forces used the Chinese Type 51 rocket launcher modeled on the American M20 super bazooka. The 90-mm HEAT rocket this launcher fired was used in its traditional role against tanks and armored personnel carriers. Viêt Công (VC) and People's Army of Vietnam (PAVN) units used artillery rockets principally because of their deficiency in field artillery early in the war. This deficiency was alleviated by the extensive employment of mortars and mines in coordination with these rockets. The components were portable and, because of their low trajectory, they often escaped detection by U.S. AN/MPQ-4 (Q-4) countermortar radar.

The Communists relied on three principal types of artillery rockets: the BM 14–16 and BM 21 from the USSR and the Type 63 from China. The BM 14–16 was an early 1950s 16-round 140-mm multiple-rocket system. The BM 21 was a 40-round 122-mm multiple-rocket system. Both systems were initially truck mounted. The Type 63 was a 12-round 107-mm multiple-rocket system that could be truck or towed-carriage mounted.

In guerrilla warfare, single rocket tubes, wooden stakes, and sandbags were frequently used to fire these rockets. The DKZ-B antibuilding and antipersonnel launcher, for instance, was a tripod-mounted tube from a BM 21. The Type 63 was also often fired from a single-round launcher. It was favored because three could be transported as easily as one 122-mm rocket. Such rockets were primarily area-fire weapons that were launched against towns, fire bases, and air fields. Often overcaliber rockets were created by attaching larger warheads to the original assemblies. However, if properly employed, the circular error probability of the Soviet rockets allowed them to function almost as point-attack weapons.

Aerial rockets were used exclusively by Free World forces. Between 1965 and 1973 U.S. procurement of 2.75-inch rockets reached almost 16 million units. Warhead variants included fragmentation, phosphorus, flechette, and armor piercing. Aerial Rocket Artillery battalions were created by

the U.S. Army to provide firepower support for ground operations. These battalions were originally composed of UH-1B/C helicopters, each equipped with 48 2.75-inch rockets. The AH-1G Huey Cobra, introduced in 1968, carried 76 rockets that contained either high-explosive or flechette (beehive) antipersonnel warheads. The early WDU-4/A warhead carried 6,000 flechettes and was later superseded by the WDU-4A/A model, which carried 2,200 heavier flechettes with better penetrative power. In 1970 these battalions were given the new designation Aerial Field Artillery.

The U.S. Navy also deployed artillery rockets aboard LSMRs (landing ships medium, rocket) and IFSs (in-shore fire support ships) in support of amphibious operations.

—Robert J. Bunker

References: Doleman, Edgar D. *Tools of War* (1984); Ott, David Ewing. *Field Artillery, 1954–1973* (1975); Robinson, Anthony, Anthony Preston, and Ian V. Hogg. *Weapons of the Vietnam War* (1983); Rosser-Owen, David. *Vietnam Weapons Handbook* (1986). Stockholm International Peace Research Institute. *Anti-personnel Weapons* (1978).
See also: Armor Warfare; Artillery, Allied and People's Army of Vietnam; Bombs, Dumb; Bombs, Smart (PGMs); Grenades, Hand, Allied and Democratic Republic of Vietnam; Grenades, Launched, Allied and Democratic Republic of Vietnam; Helicopters, Employment of, in Vietnam; Mortars, Allied and Democratic Republic of Vietnam.

Rogers, William Pierce (1913–)

U.S. secretary of state, 1969–1973. Rogers had no background in foreign policy, and his appointment as secretary of state reflected Richard Nixon's desire to keep control of foreign policy in his own hands. Rogers was no match for National Security Advisor Henry Kissinger, under whose direction the National Security Council within a few weeks wrested from the State Department the crucial power to set the agenda for U.S. foreign policy discussions. As secretary of state, Rogers remained a marginal figure, overshadowed by the flamboyant, publicity-hungry Kissinger. Nixon and Kissinger often kept Rogers ignorant of major foreign policy initiatives, including arms control, secret negotiations to end the Vietnam War, and the opening of China.

On Vietnam and Indo-China, Rogers normally favored caution, conciliation, and negotiation over the generally more militant instincts of Nixon and Kissinger. In February 1969 he and Secretary of Defense Melvin Laird persuaded Nixon to temporarily defer resumption of U.S. bombing of North Vietnam, although in March, over Rogers's objections, the president finally authorized this course. In April 1970 he opposed the U.S. invasion of Cambodia, preferring to continue the existing policy of minor cross-border raids by Army of the Republic of Vietnam (ARVN) forces. He also spoke against the February 1971 ARVN attack on the Hô Chí Minh Trail, an operation that ended in an inglorious military rout.

In an unusual twist, Kissinger briefed Rogers in full on the final version of the Paris Peace Accords, which were signed in January 1973, and of which Rogers became a strong supporter. Kissinger stayed home, out of the lime-light, while Rogers went to Paris to sign the Accords. In September 1973 Nixon asked for Rogers's resignation and replaced him with Kissinger.

—Priscilla Roberts

References: Ambrose, Stephen E. *Nixon: The Triumph of a Politician 1961–1972* (1989); Ambrose, Stephen. *Nixon: Ruin and Recovery 1973–1990* (1991); Isaacson, Walter. *Kissinger: A Biography* (1992).
See also: Kissinger, Henry Alfred; Laird, Melvin R.; Nixon, Richard Milhous; Paris Peace Accords.

ROLLING THUNDER, Operation
(2 March 1965–31 October 1968)

Prolonged U.S. bombing campaign against North Vietnam. ROLLING THUNDER was the longest bombing campaign ever conducted by the U.S. Air Force. The bombing cost the Democratic Republic of Vietnam (DRV) more than half its bridges, virtually all its large petroleum storage facilities, nearly two-thirds of its power generating plants, and an estimated 52,000 citizens. DRV air defenses cost the United States nearly 1,000 aircraft, hundreds of prisoners of war, and hundreds of airmen killed or missing in action. Although the Air Force, Navy, and Marines flew almost a million sorties (one plane, one mission) to drop nearly three-quarters of a million tons of bombs, ROLLING THUNDER failed to achieve its major political and military objectives. ROLLING THUNDER stands as the classic example of air-power failure.

Preparations for an extended bombing campaign against North Vietnam began in early 1964. Over the course of the year competing plans emerged. The U.S. Air Force (USAF), led by chief of staff Gen. Curtis E. LeMay, advocated an "all-out" assault wrapped around 94 targets. The USAF's air campaign was designed to bomb the DRV "back to the Stone Age" by destroying its industrial base and war-making capability. The State Department advocated an escalating campaign that would increase in intensity with the number of targets, expanding over time until the Hà Nôi regime stopped supporting the Viêt Công (VC) and agreed to allow the Republic of Vietnam (RVN) to develop as an independent, non-Communist state. The Navy, because its planes did not have the range to strike targets deep inside North Vietnam, proposed an interdiction campaign south of 20 degrees north latitude, concentrating on roads, bridges, and railroads in the southern panhandle.

President Johnson and his advisors turned to air power in 1965 out of frustration. The war was going poorly in South Vietnam. The RVN political situation remained unstable and Viêt Công guerrillas, with growing support from the DRV, seemed close to achieving victory. Based on their perceptions of the accomplishments of air power in World War II and in Korea, Air Force and Navy air power advocates promised quick victory at an acceptable cost by striking at an enemy's vital centers. They argued that by "holding hostage" the small industrial base of North Vietnam, Hà Nôi would be faced with the choice of either abandoning its efforts inside South Vietnam or risking economic ruin.

The war in Vietnam was not World War II nor Korea, a fact that seemingly escaped air power leaders. Furthermore, President Johnson's objectives were both limited and negative. The limited objective was to secure the right of the RVN to exist as a free and independent state. The DRV did not have to be destroyed to achieve this objective. It had only to be persuaded to desist from supporting the insurgents. The negative objective was to avoid military action that might risk Chinese or Soviet intervention. Such limited and negative objectives were not readily amenable to what air power—at least theoretically—can deliver: decisive victory through vigorous offensive action. The U.S. Air Force was structured and equipped to deliver that kind of victory in total, nuclear war with the Soviets. The Air Force, and to a lesser extent the Navy, was not structured, equipped, or doctrinally inclined to engage in limited warfare.

On 2 March 1965 the first ROLLING THUNDER mission took place when 100 U.S. Air Force and Republic of Vietnam Air Force (VNAF) sorties struck the Xóm Bang ammunition depot 35 miles north of the Demilitarized Zone (DMZ). Twelve days later, USAF and Navy planes struck an ammunition dump 100 miles southeast of Hà Nôi. ROLLING THUNDER was under way.

The first objective was strategic persuasion. Emanating from deterrence theory, the concept behind strategic persuasion was to employ air power in ever-intensifying degrees in an effort to persuade the DRV to stop supporting the Viêt Công and enter negotiations to end the war. Military planners and civilian officials alike seemed convinced that when faced with vigorous demonstrations of American power, Hà Nôi would demur.

By July no one in Hà Nôi had blinked. But in Sài Gòn Gen. William Westmoreland, commander of Military Assistance Command, Vietnam (MACV), asked Secretary of Defense Robert McNamara to pass along his request for 44 combat maneuver battalions to take the war to the Viêt Công. This was the beginning of a massive ground-force buildup, and ROLLING THUNDER switched from strategic persuasion to interdiction. Another objective was to boost the morale of RVN political and military elites by demonstrating U.S. resolve.

Targets in ROLLING THUNDER included ammunition depots and storage areas; highways and railroads; bridges and marshaling yards; warehouses; petroleum, oil, and lubricant (POL) storage facilities; airfields; army barracks; and power generating plants. North Vietnam possessed three major factories—the Thái Nguyên Steel Works, an ammunition plant, and a cement factory—and all were eventually destroyed. The target list grew from the original 94 devised by the Joint Chiefs of Staff (JCS) in 1964 to nearly 400 targets by late 1967.

ROLLING THUNDER went through five phases. In phase one (March—June 1965), various targets, including ammunition depots, radar sites, and barracks, were struck as Washington tried to convince the DRV of the seriousness of its intentions. Hà Nôi responded by increasing its support for the VC, who had started attacking American air bases in the south. When U.S. troops began arriving in substantial numbers to protect those bases, the focus of ROLLING THUNDER switched from strategic persuasion to interdiction. Although the bombing retained the objective of persuading the DRV to withdraw its support from the VC and negotiate an end to the conflict, after July 1965 ROLLING THUNDER remained basically an interdiction campaign.

During phase two (July 1965–June 1966), despite several bombing halts to accommodate bad weather and to allow for diplomatic efforts, the bombing focused on roads, bridges, and railroads. There were two kinds of targets: numbered and unnumbered. The former included such targets as the Hàm Rông (Dragon Jaw) Bridge in Thanh Hóa Province and the Thái Nguyên Steel Works. Those targets were difficult to strike, not only because they were well defended but also because the targeting process for attacking a numbered target was cumbersome and time consuming. Clearance procedures that extended from Sài Gòn through Honolulu to the Pentagon, the State Department, and into the White House were not unusual. More than 75 percent of the interdiction effort in 1965 and 1966 concentrated on trucks, railroad rolling stock, locomotives, and boats moving along the rivers and down the coast of North Vietnam.

The attacks were costly. In the first 20 months of ROLLING THUNDER, more than 300 planes were shot down, and the General Accounting Office estimated that it cost the United States $6.60 to inflict $1.00 worth of damage in North Vietnam. The price for bombing the DRV was going to go up. Meanwhile, between 150,000 and 200,000 North Vietnamese were pressed into various forms of active and passive antiaircraft defenses, while 500,000 more repaired roads, railroad beds, and bridges. Accordingly, the flow of troops and supplies moving from north to south doubled during the first year of ROLLING THUNDER. In January 1966, U.S. Commander in Chief, Pacific, Admiral Ulysses S. Grant Sharp, told the JCS that the destruction of North Vietnam's POL storage facilities would make it difficult for them to support the war in the South.

At the end of June 1966, phase three of ROLLING THUNDER got under way. The concerted attack on the DRV's POL facilities lasted into early autumn. In that time, estimates were that 70 percent of North Vietnam's POL storage capacity had been destroyed. The remaining 30 percent had been dispersed into 55-gallon drums and placed in areas that U.S. bombers were not likely to strike.

Phase four began in October 1966 with a shift to industrial targets and electric power generating capabilities. Targets in and around Hà Nôi, previously off limits for fear of inflicting collateral damage on nonmilitary structures and causing civilian casualties, were struck. The Thái Nguyên Steel Works, North Vietnam's only cement plant, power generating plants, and transformers were bombed. After May 1967 sporadic attacks on what remained of the industrial infrastructure, the transportation system, and the "fleeting" targets continued. But it was increasingly evident that the bombing was not having the desired effect.

The 1968 Têt Offensive ushered in the final phase of ROLLING THUNDER. On 31 March President Johnson, in an effort to get peace negotiations started, limited the bombing of North Vietnam to areas in the southern panhandle below 19 degrees north latitude. Seven months later, on 31 October 1968, to boost the prospects for the Democratic Party's nominee for the presidency in the November elections, Johnson ended ROLLING THUNDER.

For the most part, ROLLING THUNDER was over. Escorted reconnaissance flights were flown and, from time to time, attacks on North Vietnam were undertaken. Officially these were called ROLLING THUNDER missions, but they were rare, sometimes covert, and always militarily inconsequential.

During ROLLING THUNDER, more than 643,000 tons of bombs fell on North Vietnam. The bombing destroyed 65 percent of North Vietnam's POL storage capacity and an estimated 60 percent of its power generating capability. At one time or another, half of its major bridges were down. Nearly 10,000 trucks, 2,000 railroad cars, and 20 locomotives were destroyed. Of the 990 Air Force, Navy, and Marine aircraft lost over North Vietnam during the war, most were shot down flying ROLLING THUNDER missions. By 1967 it was costing the United States $9.60 to inflict $1.00 worth of damage on its enemy. Air Force pilots flying the F-105 Thunderchiefs, the primary fighter-bombers involved in ROLLING THUNDER, stood a 50 percent chance of surviving a one-year tour. In some squadrons, attrition rates reached 75 percent.

Although the bombing intensified in 1967, its effect was not apparent on South Vietnam battlefields. According to MACV's own estimates, the flow of troops and supplies moving from North Vietnam into South Vietnam doubled each year of ROLLING THUNDER. The North responded to the bombing by building redundancy into its transportation system so that by 1968 it was capable of handling three times as much traffic through the panhandle as it could in 1965.

Other than perhaps boosting the morale of a few ARVN generals and RVN politicians, ROLLING THUNDER failed to achieve its objectives. Its primary failure was one of strategy. Conventional air power used on North Vietnam had little impact on the unconventional war in South Vietnam. Air power leaders, especially Air Force generals, blinded by their perceptions of air power gained in World War II and Korea, were unable to devise a strategy appropriate to the war at hand.

There are three more specific reasons for the failure of ROLLING THUNDER. First, the DRV was a preindustrial, agricultural country and not vulnerable to the kind of bombing that played a role in defeating industrial powers such as Nazi Germany and Imperial Japan. North Vietnam had no war-making industries. Its primitive economy could not be held hostage to an emerging industrial base. Besides, its leadership held that reunification was more important than industrialization. Second, the potential effectiveness of the bombing was hampered by politically conceived constraints. President Johnson exercised far more control than was prudent or necessary, partly out of fear of prompting Chinese or Soviet intervention and partly out of his inherent distrust of generals. Third, the North Vietnamese were a very determined foe. Hà Nôi remained constant in its war aims, which were both total and limited. Against South Vietnam, Hà Nôi had the total war aim of overthrowing the RVN government and reunifying the country under a single, Communist system. Against the United States, war aims of the DRV were limited. Hà Nôi had only to compel the United States to withdraw both its troops from South Vietnam and its support for the RVN. To accomplish this, they had to make the war more costly for the Americans than it was worth. The defeat inflicted on the air forces of the United States during ROLLING THUNDER helped realize that objective.

—Earl H. Tilford, Jr.

References: Cable, Larry. *Unholy Grail: The U.S. and the Wars in Vietnam, 1965–68* (1991); Clausewitz, Carl von. *On War* (1976); Clodfelter, Mark. *The Limits of Air Power: The American Bombing of North Vietnam* (1989); Littauer, Raphael, and Norman Uphoff, eds. Air War Study Group, Cornell University. *The Air War in Indochina* (1971); Thompson, James Clay. *Rolling Thunder: Understanding Policy and Program Failure* (1979); Tilford, Earl H., Jr. *Crosswinds: The Air Force's Setup in Vietnam* (1993).

See also: Air Defense, Democratic Republic of Vietnam; Air Power, Role in War; Antiaircraft Artillery, Allied and Democratic Republic of Vietnam; Bombs, Dumb; Bombs, Smart (PGMs); Johnson, Lyndon Baines; LeMay, Curtis Emerson; LINEBACKER I, Operation; LINEBACKER II, Operation; McCone, John Alex; McNamara, Robert S.; Momyer, William W.; Ngô Đình Diêm, Overthrow of; RAND Corporation; Sharp, Ulysses Simpson Grant, Jr.; Vietnam, Republic of: Air Force (VNAF); Yankee Station.

Roman Catholicism in Vietnam

The Roman Catholic Church left a significant mark on Vietnam. The first Catholic missionaries arrived in Vietnam in the fifteenth century, but Catholic proselytizing made its greatest inroads two centuries later. By 1700 hundreds of thousands of Vietnamese had embraced Catholicism, but Vietnamese government attitudes toward Catholics vacillated. Vietnamese Catholics' divided loyalties and adherence to Vatican decrees made them a potentially subversive force; the emperors correctly assumed that most Catholic missionaries were allied with European advocates of imperial conquest. Consequently, Vietnamese governments, to varying degrees, limited Catholic activities, jailed priests, deported missionaries, and persecuted converts. In the nineteenth century, France used Vietnam's increasing hostility toward Catholicism as a pretext for military intervention and colonial domination. Although Vietnamese Catholics often refused to support French forces, the dying mandarinal regime executed an estimated 20,000 of them for allegedly cooperating with France.

Vietnamese Catholics both supported and resisted the return of French colonial forces after World War II. Still, the Viêt Minh accused all Catholics of collaboration, attacked their villages and, after the 1954 Geneva Accords, confiscated church property and arrested priests. With help from the U.S. and South Vietnamese governments, the Church launched a propaganda campaign to entice an estimated 800,000 Catholics to flee the Communist-controlled North.

Life for the approximately 600,000 Catholics who stayed in the Democratic Republic of Vietnam (DRV) was not easy. The Liaison Committee of Patriotic and Peace Loving Catholics encouraged them to "reintegrate" into society. Although the church supposedly retained links to the Vatican, most of its foreign priests fled to the South or were expelled, and the church lost control of its property. Although officially free to worship, Catholics were forbidden to question collective socialism.

A devout Cathlic, Republic of Vietnam (RVN) President Ngô Đình Diêm welcomed the Catholics who moved South after 1954. He and U.S. officials viewed these refugees as a critical part of his regime's anti-Communist constituency and allocated millions of dollars to resettle them. Worldwide Catholic support for Diêm contributed to the misconception that the RVN was a predominantly Catholic nation. Under Diêm, Catholics enjoyed advantages in commerce, education, and the professions; occupied positions of power at all government levels; and helped polarize South Vietnamese society and politics. They strongly rejected accommodation with the Communists, the democratic left, or southern insurgents. Diêm's brother Ngô Đình Thuc, as archbishop of Huê, exercised great influence within the government and among Vietnamese Catholics. Such patronage and intransigence precipitated a political crisis that eventually toppled Diêm.

Catholics were among its first targets of the National Liberation Front (NLF). NLF leaders pushed rural anti-Communists, especially Catholics, out of land development centers and villages, increasing the RVN's refugee burden. Southern Catholics became a wandering underclass, and thousands fled the country in anticipation of the 1975 Communist takeover.

An estimated 2.9 million Catholics remained in Vietnam after April 1975. The new regime promised to rebuild churches, but the government still viewed Catholicism as a reactionary force and urged church members to join a Communist Party–controlled "renovation and reconciliation" movement. When Catholics continued to oppose Communist authority, the state created various organizations to recruit recalcitrant elements of the Catholic community and unite them behind socialism. An estimated 4 to 6 million Catholics continue to practice in Vietnam, but surveillance of Catholic activities by the Religious Affairs Committee persists.

—Delia Pergande

References: Buttinger, Joseph. *Vietnam: A Political History* (1968); Cima, Ronald, ed. *Vietnam: A Country Study* (1989); Karnow, Stanley. *Vietnam: A History*. Rev. Ed. (1991); Wiesner, Louis. *Victims and Survivors: Displaced Persons and Other War Victims in Vietnam, 1954–1975* (1988).

See also: Buddhists; Confucianism; de Rhodes, Alexandre; Lefèbvre, Dominique; Ngô Đình Diêm; Ngô Đình Thuc.

Romney, George W. (1907–1995)

Presidential candidate for the Republican nomination in 1967; cabinet member under President Nixon. A liberal Republican, Romney opposed the war in Vietnam. In 1967 he was the first to announce his candidacy for the Republican presidential nomination. Initially the front-runner in early campaigning in New Hampshire, Romney in the following weeks was ridiculed for a statement in which he said that he had originally supported the Vietnam War because he had been "brainwashed" by generals and diplomats during a 1965 visit there. Appointed housing secretary by Nixon, Romney found himself increasingly frustrated because he remained outside the president's inner circle. He resigned in 1972 after Nixon's reelection and retired from public life.

—Michael R. Nichols

See also: Nixon, Richard Milhous.

Roosevelt, Franklin Delano (1882–1945)

President of the United States, 1933–1945. As early as November 1941 Roosevelt made public pronouncements concerning the territorial integrity of Indo-China and proposed a multilateral nonaggression pact with Japan concerning the Pacific region. The Japanese attack on Pearl Harbor on 7 December nullified Roosevelt's overtures.

As the World War II progressed, questions concerning the resolution of French Indo-China persisted. In a January 1944 memo to Secretary of State Cordell Hull, the president proposed the establishment of a trusteeship whereby developed nations would prepare native elites for eventual self-government. Although a compromise to Roosevelt's goal of colonial independence, the trusteeship seemed to offer the best hope for the stability of indigenous societies while they moved toward independence. Roosevelt especially condemned the French administration of Indo-China, stating that "the people are worse off than they were at the beginning."

In February 1945 Roosevelt declared that Jiang Jieshi (Chiang Kai-shek) and Joseph Stalin supported his plans for an Indo-Chinese trusteeship. Within months, however, Roosevelt reversed his stance, promising to not interfere with colonial rule. British Prime Minister Winston Churchill and Free French leader Charles de Gaulle had clearly stated their opposition to tampering with European colonial possessions. The Roosevelt administration recognized that insistence on colonial self-rule could create excessive strains between the Allies and imperil cooperation in Western Europe, the most vital arena of U.S. foreign policy. Additionally, defense planners argued that postwar national security would require the United States to maintain control over several former Japanese-controlled islands. Imposition of trusteeships could easily be applied to the United States as well as to the European colonial powers. Roosevelt, although still favoring independence, reluctantly acceded to the return of Indo-China to France.

—Brenda J. Taylor

References: Anderson, David L., ed. *Shadow on the White House: Presidents and the Vietnam War, 1945–1975* (1993); Dallek, Robert. *F.D.R. and American Diplomacy* (1979); Williams, William Appleman, ed. *America in Vietnam: A Documentary History* (1985). See also: de Gaulle, Charles André Marie Joseph; Jiang Jieshi (Chiang Kai-shek); Potsdam Conference; Truman, Harry S; United States: Involvement in Indo-China through 1954.

Rostow, Eugene Victor (1913–)

U.S. under secretary of state for political affairs, 1966–1969. Rostow saw the United States as maintaining a policy of containing communism while simultaneously avoiding armed confrontation. This, he believed, was the primary U.S. role in Vietnam.

Rostow believed that President Johnson was obligated to fulfill U.S. responsibilities in Vietnam, as established by the Southeast Asia Treaty Organization (SEATO) treaty, the United Nations charter, and the policies of former presidents backed by several Congresses. He strongly supported Johnson's Vietnam policies and believed that Johnson's position of restraint in the use of force, coupled with maximum diplomatic effort, represented the best approach in dealing with the Vietnam situation. He maintained that the Gulf of Tonkin Resolution was a constitutional mandate similar to a declaration of war. With its passage, there was little doubt in his mind that Johnson had the full weight of the nation behind his policies.

Rostow admitted that the U.S. made mistakes in Vietnam that negatively affected foreign policy decisions for many years after the war. Errors notwithstanding, he remains convinced that the United States helped establish a strong economic infrastructure in Southeast Asia.

—Dean Brumley

References: Goulden, Steven L. *Political Profiles: The Johnson Years* (1976); Halberstam, David. *The Best and the Brightest* (1983); Johnson, Lyndon Baines. *The Vantage Point: Perspectives of the Presidency, 1963–1969* (1971); Rostow, Eugene V. *Law, Power, and the Pursuit of Peace* (1968); —. *Toward Managed Peace: The National Security Interests of the United States, 1759 to the Present* (1993). See also: Johnson, Lyndon Baines; Tonkin Gulf Resolution.

Rostow, Walt Whitman (1916–)

Chairman, State Department Policy Planning Council, 1961–1966; special assistant to the president for national security affairs, 1966–1969. During the election campaign of 1960, Rostow was an informal advisor to Democratic presidential candidate Senator John F. Kennedy, with whom he had been close since 1958. Initially he was appointed deputy to the Special Assistant to the President for National Security Affairs McGeorge Bundy.

In early February 1961 he passed on to Kennedy, and enthusiastically endorsed, Brig. Gen. Edward G. Lansdale's report suggesting that a serious crisis was impending in South Vietnam and recommending a major expansion of U.S. programs there. Rostow's argument that bombing North Vietnam or occupying its southern regions should be considered made him one of the strongest hawks in the administration, a stance he retained throughout the Vietnam War era.

In October 1961 Rostow and Gen. Maxwell D. Taylor visited Vietnam to assess the situation and the merits of potential U.S. courses of action. They recommended that the United States change its existing advisory role to one of "limited partnership" with the Republic of Vietnam (RVN) and advocated increased U.S. economic aid and military advisory support. A secret annex suggested that 8,000 American combat troops be deployed there. All but the last of these recommendations were implemented.

In late 1961 Rostow was appointed a State Department counselor and chairman of the department's Policy Planning Council. By late 1964 he believed that escalating U.S. military measures, including commitment of U.S. ground forces, a naval blockade, and bombing of North Vietnam, would convince Hà Nôi that victory over the RVN was impossible. When these measures were implemented in 1965, Rostow urged their expansion, as he continued to do after his March 1966 appointment as special assistant to the president for national security affairs. In late 1967, however, he endorsed Secretary of Defense Robert McNamara's proposals to try to reduce U.S. casualties and shift the burden of fighting to the South Vietnamese. Remaining a committed hawk, Rostow opposed the March 1968 decision to open negotiations with the DRV. He resigned in January 1969.

In his voluminous writings, Rostow has argued that U.S. involvement in the war gave other Southeast Asian nations the breathing space they required to develop strong economies and become staunch regional anti-Communist bastions.

—Priscilla Roberts

References: Berman, Larry. *Planning a Tragedy: The Americanization of the War in Vietnam* (1982); Gibbons, William Conrad. *The U.S. Government and the Vietnam War*, parts 2 and 3 (1986, 1989); Halberstam, David. *The Best and the Brightest* (1973); Rostow, Walt W. *The Diffusion of Power, 1957–1972: An Essay in Recent History* (1972).
See also: Bundy, McGeorge; Bundy, William P.; Clifford, Clark M.; Johnson, Lyndon Baines; Kennedy, John Fitzgerald; McNamara, Robert S.; Rusk, Dean; Taylor, Maxwell Davenport.

Route Coloniale (RC) 4, Battles for. *See* L HONG PHONG II, Operation.

Rowe, James N. (1938–1989)

U.S. Army officer; captive of the Viêt Công (VC). On 29 October 1963, Rowe was captured by the VC while on patrol with South Vietnamese irregular forces in the Mekong Delta. Knowing that Communist forces summarily executed captured Special Forces soldiers, Rowe hid his identity and attempted to escape at least three times. As a prisoner of war (POW), Rowe spent most of his time in a cramped bamboo cage. The VC eventually learned Rowe's true identity. On 31 December 1968, as he was being led to his execution, Rowe struck his guard and made a break for a clearing, where he was picked up by a U.S. helicopter crew.

Rowe was a first lieutenant when he was captured, but over the five-years he was imprisoned he was routinely promoted to captain and then to major. He also received the Silver Star for his actions while a POW. After returning from Vietnam, he wrote a book about his experiences. In 1981 Rowe established the Army's Survival, Evasion, Resistance, and Escape training program to teach soldiers how to avoid

and deal with capture. He was killed in an ambush in the Philippines in 1989.

—David T. Zabecki

References: Miles, Donna. "A Real Hero: Col. Nick Rowe Assassinated in the Philippines" (1989); Rowe, James N. *Five Years to Freedom* (1971).
See also: Prisoners of War, Allied; United States: Special Forces.

Rubin, Jerry (1938–1994)

Leading antiwar activist. As a leader of the Vietnam Day Committee, Rubin was recognized as a skilled organizer with a flair for gaining media attention. In August 1965 the committee staged well-publicized attempts to stop troop trains in the San Francisco area.

Rubin believed that the antiwar movement was a generational conflict and advised followers "not to trust anyone over thirty." In 1967 he moved to New York City, where he met Abbie Hoffman and organized an October march on the Pentagon. In January 1968, Rubin, Hoffman, and Paul Krassner formed the Youth International Party (Yippies), which staged demonstrations in Chicago at the August 1968 Democratic National Convention. Rubin was one of the "Chicago Eight" tried in 1969 on charges of conspiracy and intent to riot.

—Clayton D. Laurie

References: Rubin, Jerry. *Do It! Scenarios of the Revolution* (1970); —. *Growing (Up) at 37* (1976).
See also: Antiwar Movement, United States; Chicago Eight; Democratic Party National Convention, 1968; Hayden, Thomas E.; Hoffman, Abbie; March on the Pentagon; Youth International Party ("Yippies").

Rules of Engagement (ROE)

According to the Department of Defense Dictionary, Joint Publication 1–02, "directives issued by competent military authority which delineate the circumstances and limitations under which United States forces will initiate and/or continue combat engagement with other forces encountered." Rules of engagement (ROE) often have two primary purposes: to limit the destruction of property and the injury and death of noncombatants, and—particularly important in a conflict like the Vietnam War, without front lines or often a clearly identifiable enemy—to prevent casualties from friendly fire.

For the ground and air war in South Vietnam, the competent military authority was the Commander, Military Assistance Command, Vietnam (COMUSMACV), with supplementation by the U.S. Joint Chiefs of Staff (JCS). But for the air war in North Vietnam it was ultimately the president of the United States and his secretary of defense through the JCS.

In a conventional conflict, with lines of contact between enemy and friendly forces generally well defined, property destruction is considered a necessary evil of war, and injury inflicted on noncombatants is difficult to control or prevent. In a conflict like the war in Vietnam involving insurgency and counterinsurgency—with no clearly defined front lines and the resulting prosecution of the war among the civilian population, whose support is actively sought by the insurgents—

rules of engagement were necessary to prevent losses and retain the support of the populace.

The rules of engagement imposed by the JCS in South Vietnam were designed primarily to keep the war limited and to prevent international incidents in border areas and in the Demilitarized Zone. The JCS also prescribed rules for B-52 strikes in the South, for example, requiring that targets for such strikes must be at least one kilometer from any area inhabited by noncombatants. The problem was the difficulty in distinguishing noncombatants from guerrillas.

The air war over North Vietnam was completely controlled from Washington by the White House and the Pentagon. Washington dictated not only the strategy of the air war, but the tactics as well. Most missions were directed at roads, bridges, and railroads; nonmilitary facilities generally were not targeted, except for power plants and other installations that indirectly affected North Vietnam's ability to support the war. However, the extended bombing campaign caused considerable damage to civilian structures and the deaths of many noncombatants, both because of proximity to military targets and because pilots flying through intense antiaircraft fire could not always bomb with precision.

In South Vietnam, three types of operations were employed in the conduct of the war: search and destroy, clearing, and securing. Search and destroy was the primary tactic of U.S. forces. It meant taking the war to the Communists by searching them out and then bringing massive firepower to bear. The objective of clearing operations, usually done by regular forces of the Army of the Republic of Vietnam (ARVN), was to drive large enemy forces out of populated areas so that pacification could take place. Securing operations were conducted primarily by ARVN Regional and Popular Forces or police to protect pacification teams and eliminate local guerrilla units.

To protect the South Vietnamese civilian population and their property, the COMUSMACV issued more than 40 directives on ROE containing explicit guidance on the proper treatment of civilians and their property and the discriminating use of firepower. ARVN forces, however, were not specifically bound to comply with these ROE directives, although U.S. advisors at every level made efforts to gain their compliance.

Search-and-destroy tactics meant the substitution of firepower for maneuver to minimize friendly casualties. Although the Military Assistance Command, Vietnam (MACV) maintained that its forces closely followed very restrictive ROE, massive firepower employed on a relatively random basis often alienated the civilian population and provided the Communists with an excellent source of propaganda. With emphasis on achieving "body counts" associated with the strategy of attrition, there was strong incentive for commanders to circumvent the ROE. In addition, ROE were often misunderstood or received "creative application" while sanctions against violators were virtually nonexistent, which created an environment in which allegations of war crimes may have been well founded, as in the case of the 1968 My Lai massacre.

Two uses of firepower—harassment and interdiction

(H&I) fires and free fire zones—received considerable criticism in relation to ROE. H&I fires were unobserved fires placed on likely Communist positions or routes of movement, usually selected by map or aerial reconnaissance. A large quantity of firepower was expended on these types of missions, and the likelihood of injuring or killing unsuspecting noncombatants was just as high as for Communist forces. Free fire zones were established only in uninhabited areas or areas totally under Communist control, and permission had to be obtained from Vietnamese province and district chiefs before an area could be designated a free fire zone. Although these areas were generally free of noncombatants and their property, noncombatants could inadvertently wander into designated free fire zones and become subject to attack. This so-called unrestrictive fire control measure may have on occasion increased the likelihood of two uncoordinated friendly elements placing one another under fire, believing that the other was an enemy force.

—Arthur T. Frame

References: Kinnard, Douglas. *The War Managers* (1985); Krepinevich, Andrew F., Jr. *The Army and Vietnam* (1986); Ott, David E. *Field Artillery, 1954–1973* (1975); Palmer, Bruce, Jr. *The 25-Year War: America's Military Role in Vietnam* (1984); Westmoreland, William C. *A Soldier Reports* (1989).

See also: Air Power, Role in War; Artillery, Allied and People's Army of Vietnam; Artillery Fire Doctrine; Atrocities during the Vietnam War; Attrition; Body Count; Free Fire Zones; Friendly Fire; Harassment and Interdiction (H&I) Fires; My Lai Massacre.

Rusk, Dean (1909–1994)

U.S. secretary of state, 1961–1969. Upon assuming office, Rusk immediately confronted myriad international problems, the most serious being Communist threats in Berlin, Cuba, and Southeast Asia. A staunch anti-Communist, Rusk worked largely behind the scenes in the Kennedy administration. He had little faith in Ngô Đình Diệm and urged a stronger U.S. commitment in South Vietnam. Along with Secretary of Defense Robert McNamara, Rusk usually deferred to the Pentagon position on Southeast Asia.

When Lyndon Johnson assumed the presidency, Rusk continued as secretary of state. He took a much more active role and quickly became one of Johnson's most trusted advisors. As antiwar sentiment intensified, Rusk steadfastly supported Johnson's position and backed Pentagon calls for larger troop commitments and the bombing of North Vietnam. Rusk did not, as is often suggested, oppose negotiations with Hà Nôi; in 1967 he suggested that Johnson pursue negotiations. Rusk left office in 1969.

Other than Johnson, no other political figure became more closely associated with U.S. failure in Vietnam than Rusk. He was an outsider who never fell in with Johnson's "Wise Men." Shunned by more prestigious academic institutions, he eventually accepted a position at the University of Georgia. His memoir, *As I Saw It*, was published in 1990 to much less hoopla than Robert McNamara's subsequent effort.

—David Coffey

References: *Current Biography Yearbook, 1961* (1961); *Current Biography Yearbook, 1995* (1995); Halberstam, David. *The Best and* *the Brightest* (1972); Isaacson, Walter, and Evan Thomas. *The Wise Men: Six Friends and the World They Made* (1986); Karnow, Stanley. *Vietnam: A History* (1983).

See also: Bowles, Chester B.; Bundy, McGeorge; Bundy, William P.; Clifford, Clark M.; Containment Policy; Halberstam, David; Johnson, Lyndon Baines; Kennedy, John Fitzgerald; MacArthur, Douglas; McNamara, Robert S.; Ngô Đình Diêm; Pearson, Lester Bowles; Read, Benjamin Huger; Stevenson, Adlai E.; Truman, Harry S; "Wise Men."

Russell, Richard B., Jr. (1897–1971)

One of the most powerful members of the U.S. Senate during the years of the Vietnam War. As chairman of the Senate Armed Services Committee from 1951 to 1969, he was highly influential during the Vietnam War era. Russell believed that U.S. involvement in the war had been a mistake from the beginning and that Southeast Asia offered no security threat to the United States. However, mindful of the need to be supportive of the president and the soldiers in the field, Russell never joined the growing antiwar faction in the Senate. Indeed, he was openly critical of the peace movement and its public protests. This paradoxical stance caused him much frustration, exacerbated by White House failure to heed his opinions about the war. In spite of grave misgivings, Russell supported the government's war policies to the end of his life.

—Eric Jarvis

References: Fite, Gilbert C. *Richard B. Russell Jr., Senator From Georgia* (1991); Gibbons, William Conrad. *The U.S. Government and the Vietnam War, parts 1–3* (1986); Halberstam, David. *The Best and the Brightest* (1969).

See also: Fulbright, J. William; Humphrey, Hubert H.; Johnson, Lyndon Baines; McGee, Gale William; Proxmire, William; Stennis, John Cornelius.

Russo, Anthony J., Jr. (1936–)

Indicted codefendant in the Pentagon Papers trial (1972–1973). Russo joined the RAND Corporation in 1964 and worked in Vietnam (February 1966–January 1968) analyzing crop destruction programs and interviewing Việt Công prisoners for the RAND-conducted study "Việt Công Morale and Motivation." During this period he became high-

ly disillusioned with U.S. policy in Southeast Asia. Terminated by RAND in July 1968, Russo was allowed a six-month grace period to complete his work. By this time he was a devoted antiwar crusader and a fledgling member of the counterculture.

Russo met Daniel Ellsberg in Vietnam, but the two did not become close friends until 1968. When Ellsberg decided to copy the sensitive documents that came to be known as the Pentagon Papers, Russo secured the use of a Xerox machine and assisted in photocopying. Shortly after the first installments of the papers appeared in *The New York Times* in June 1971, the FBI questioned Russo, who refused to cooperate. On 23 June he was subpoenaed by a federal grand jury in Los Angeles. Declining to testify on the grounds that he might incriminate himself, he was granted full immunity but again refused to cooperate. Cited for contempt, Russo was jailed on 16 August. He later claimed that during his 47-day imprisonment he was chained, tortured, and held in solitary confinement.

On 1 October a federal judge ordered Russo's release and ruled that he be given a transcript of any grand jury testimony he provided. Pending appeal, Assistant U.S. Attorney David Nissen would not supply a copy of confidential testimony, and Russo again refused to testify. On 29 December 1971 the grand jury returned a new 15-count criminal indictment, charging Ellsberg and Russo with conspiracy, theft and misuse of government property, and espionage. The Pentagon Papers trial began in Los Angeles on 10 July 1972.

The unfolding Watergate drama brought new revelations into play. On 11 May 1973, citing governmental misconduct, Federal Judge William Matthew Byrne declared a mistrial and dismissed all charges against Ellsberg and Russo. Russo remained a staunch antiwar campaigner and worked zealously for the impeachment of Richard Nixon.

—David Coffey

References: Schrag, Peter. *Test of Loyalty: Daniel Ellsberg and the Rituals of Secret Government* (1974); Ungar, Sanford J. *The Papers & The Papers: An Account of the Legal and Political Battle over the Pentagon Papers* (1972).

See also: Ellsberg, Daniel; Pentagon Papers and Trial; Watergate.

S

Sabattier, Gabriel (1892–1966)

French Army lieutenant general, commander of French forces in Tonkin in 1945, and delegate-general of Indo-China. In 1944 Sabattier became commander of the Tonkin Division. He sought permission from the French Army commander in Indo-China, Lt. Gen. Eugène Mordant, to begin preparations to wage guerrilla warfare in the event of a Japanese attack. Mordant refused, fearful of provoking the Japanese. Alarmed by reports that the Japanese might be intending something, Sabattier on the morning of 8 March 1945 ordered his troops placed on "armed exercise" status. Later that day the Japanese carried out their well-planned coup.

The Japanese failed on the 9th to attack Sabattier's two forces positioned just to the west and northwest of Hà Nôi, enabling some 6,000 men to evacuate their camps. In their retreat westward the French hoped for assistance from the U.S. Air Force, but President Roosevelt opposed it, despite pleas from Paris.

Maj. Gen. Marcel Alessandri commanded the Second Tonkin Brigade. On 11 March 1945 he decided to disarm his Indo-Chinese riflemen and leave them behind to fend for themselves. Most were staunchly loyal to the French and the action wounded them deeply; later the Viêt Minh used it as an example of French perfidy. Sabattier and Alessandri hoped the Japanese would be content to control the populous delta regions, allowing French forces that escaped the initial coup to remain in the Tonkin highlands until the end of the war.

In late March Paris granted Sabattier full civil and military powers as delegate-general. Sabattier busied himself with political activities, turning over military matters to Alessandri. But the Japanese were determined to get rid of the French altogether. Their military actions against the French made retreat to Yunnan the only viable course of action. The French had to destroy their artillery and vehicles at river crossings because of lack of adequate ferries and rafts, and the Japanese blocked the two most important border exits at Lào Cai and Hà Giang.

In all some 5,000 French troops made the 600-mile-long anabasis to southern China, where they were accorded a chilly reception. Sabattier continued as the senior French military representative there for three months. But on 15 August 1945, Charles de Gaulle replaced Sabattier, naming Admiral Georges Thierry d'Argenlieu as high commissioner for Indo-China and instructing him "to restore French sovereignty in the Indo-China Union."

—Spencer C. Tucker

References: Dalloz, Jacques. *The War in Indo-China, 1945–1954* (1990); Marr, David G. *Vietnam 1945: The Quest for Power* (1996); Patti, Archimedes L. A. *Why Viet Nam? Prelude to America's Albatross* (1980); Sabattier, Gabriel. *Le Destin de l'Indochine: Souvenirs et documents, 1941–1951* (1952).

See also: Alessandri, Marcel; d'Argenlieu, Georges Thierry; Franco-Thai War; Mordant, Eugène; Roosevelt, Franklin Delano.

Sài Gòn Military Mission

Effort by Allen Dulles of the Central Intelligence Agency (CIA) and Secretary of State John Foster Dulles to accomplish two tasks simultaneously: weaken the government of the Democratic Republic of Vietnam (DRV) and support and strengthen former emperor Bao Đai's State of Vietnam non-Communist government south of the 17th parallel. Organized in summer 1954, the Sài Gòn Military Mission (SMM) was headed by Air Force Col. Edward Lansdale, who for some time had been on loan to the CIA. His orders called for him to serve in Sài Gòn as assistant air attaché on embassy duty, but his real mission was to assist in the birth of a southern government capable of successfully competing with and opposing Hô Chí Minh's DRV. Lansdale had an unlimited budget and complete operational freedom. He was authorized to put together a small team to help him. He selected many CIA operatives, some on loan from active or reserve military units and some career agents.

Lansdale was in place, although without his team members, before Ngô Đình Diêm, Bao Đai's newly appointed prime minister, arrived in Sài Gòn on 26 June 1954. The two met at Independence (Đôc Lâp) Palace and within three weeks were fast friends, largely due to Lansdale's sympathetic and receptive manner, behind which he couched his advice. He urged Diêm to become more a "man of the people," create a loyal bureaucracy, and implement social, economic, and political reforms to suggest to rural inhabitants the benefits that might be theirs if they supported the Sài Gòn government. Lansdale also counseled Diêm to establish service clubs after the model of Rotary International, and he helped Filipinos set up Operation BROTHERHOOD and the Freedom Company in Vietnam. He also persuaded Diêm to take advantage of the provision of the Geneva Accords that, during the first 300 days, allowed civilians living in either zone to remove to the other. Aided by the Seventh Fleet and Civil Air Transport (a CIA front organization), some 1.5 million people ultimately came South in the Great Migration while perhaps 90,000 resettled in the North. It was a coup for Diêm and for Lansdale.

Using the Great Migration as a cover, Lansdale sent part of his team, under Lucien Conein's leadership, into the North to carry out acts of sabotage. Conein and the northern team recruited and trained two groups of Vietnamese, the Hòa and Bình teams, who would serve as "stay-behind" agents. Conein and the others buried caches of weapons and attempted unsuccessfully to close the Hai Phòng port, contaminate northern petroleum supplies, and sabotage rail and bus transportation. Most of their efforts were ultimately futile. Northern officials quickly rolled up the Hòa and Bình teams and located the caches.

The SMM had better luck in the south. It foiled an attempted assassination of Diêm by his army chief of staff, set up a Palace Guard under the leadership of Filipino Napoleon Valeriano, and bribed leaders of the Hòa Hao and Cao Đài sect armies to give up their independence for commissions in the Army of the Republic of Vietnam (ARVN). SMM members recall such men carrying suitcases crammed with CIA-supplied bribe money. Many sect generals and their men became part of the ARVN, strengthening the hand of Diêm. Cao Đài Gen. Nguyên Thành Phuong demanded and received $3.6 million for his loyalty, besides monthly payments for his troops. Gen. Trân Van Soái, a Hòa Hao warlord, cost $3 million.

This additional manpower gave Diêm the courage to stand up to the Bình Xuyên sect in fighting that began 26 April 1955. By 9 May, Bình Xuyên troops had been driven from Sài Gòn into southern swamps. Yet perhaps the most successful action of the SMM was its support of Diêm when he called for a nationwide election in 1955 to determine whether the country should remain under the leadership of Bao Đai or become an independent republic with him as its president. Lansdale told Diêm there should be no stuffing of ballot boxes and that voting should be fair; Diêm ignored the advice. The polls opened on 23 October 1955. Diêm won the election, receiving 98 percent of the overall vote and in Sài Gòn receiving one-third more votes than the total number of registered voters there. Lansdale left Vietnam soon afterward; the work of the SMM had ended.

—Cecil B. Currey

Reference: Currey, Cecil B. *Edward Lansdale: The Unquiet American* (1988).

See also: Bao Đai; Bình Xuyên; Cao Đài; Conein, Lucien Emile; Dulles, Allen Welsh; Dulles, John Foster; Hòa Hao; Lansdale, Edward Geary; Ngô Đình Diêm; United States: Involvement in Vietnam, 1954–1965; Vietnam, Republic of: 1954–1975.

Sainteny, Jean (1907–1978)

Key French diplomat in negotiations with Hô Chí Minh and the Viêt Minh at the end of World War II. Sainteny and Hô Chí Minh negotiated what became known as the Hô-Sainteny Agreements of 3 March 1946. These provided for French recognition of the independence of the Democratic Republic of Vietnam (DRV) within the Indo-China federation and the French Union, the return of 15,000 French troops into northern Vietnam (but with a phased five-year withdrawal), and a plebiscite for southern Vietnam to determine if it wished to join the DRV.

In June 1946 Sainteny returned to France with Hô Chí Minh to take part in negotiations at the Fontainebleau Conference, which were torpedoed while he was away by the actions of the French proconsul in Indo-China, Admiral Thierry d'Argenlieu. From 1954 to 1958 Sainteny was the senior French representative ("delegate") to the DRV. He left the DRV in 1957 "on temporary leave," his mission of protecting French property a failure.

Sainteny made several trips to the DRV during the Vietnam War, providing useful information on DRV policies. His memoir, *Histoire d'une Paix Manquée: Indochine 1945–1947* (1953), leaves no doubt that a policy of open negotiation with the Viêt Minh would have prevented the unhappy events that followed.

—Spencer C. Tucker

References: Fall, Bernard. *The Two Viet Nams.* (1964); Fourcade, Marie-Madeleine. *Noah's Ark: A Memoir of Struggle and Resistance* (1974); Sainteny, Jean. *Histoire d'une Paix Manquée: Indochine, 1945–1947* (1953).

See also: d'Argenlieu, Georges Thierry; de Gaulle, Charles André Marie Joseph; Fontainebleau Conference; Hô Chí Minh; Hô-Sainteny Agreement; Indo-China War.

Salan, Raoul Albin Louis (1899–1984)

French Army general; commander of French forces in Indo-China (1952–1953). At the end of World War II, Salan took part in peace negotiations that secured the Chinese withdrawal from northern Vietnam. As commander of French troops in Tonkin, in April 1946 he signed the accords establishing the size and location of French and Vietnamese garrisons within the Democratic Republic of Vietnam (DRV). In 1948 Salan commanded all French troops in the Far East.

Salan succeeded de Lattre as commander in chief on the latter's death in January 1952. As military commander, Salan followed largely defensive tactics against the Viêt Minh. The inability of French forces to halt a Viêt Minh invasion of Laos in April 1953—a seemingly easy task—led to Salan's replacement by Gen. Henri Navarre. Following the Battle of Điên Biên Phu, Salan returned to Indo-China with Gen. Paul Ely on a fact-finding mission that recommended evacuation of all French troops from North Vietnam and French concentration on the area south of the 16th parallel.

—Spencer C. Tucker

References: Salan, Raoul. *Indochine Rouge: le Message d'Ho Chi Minh* (1975); —. *Le Sens d'un Engagement, 1899–1946* (1970); —. *Mémoires: Fin d'un Empire, "Le Viet-Minh Mon Adversaire" October 1946–October 1954* (1954); *The International Who's Who, 1983–1984* (1983).

See also: de Lattre de Tassigny, Jean Joseph Marie Gabriel; France: Army; LORRAINE, Operation; Na San, Battle of; Navarre, Henri Eugène.

Salisbury, Harrison E. (1908–1993)

New York Times editor and correspondent, 1949–1973. Salisbury played a controversial role in the reporting of the Vietnam War. In December 1966 he was the first American newsman to be admitted to the Democratic Republic of Vietnam (DRV). For several weeks he sent back controversial dispatches asserting that the heavy U.S. bombing campaign was not having the anticipated incapacitating effects upon the DRV's economy but was killing thousands of innocent civilians. He also emphasized that North Vietnamese morale remained high.

President Johnson, Pentagon officials, and some journalists strongly criticized Salisbury for, among other things, lending aid and comfort to the enemy. But others applauded his reporting for presenting unpalatable but necessary facts to the American public. As a result, well-established newspapers showed greater willingness to challenge official administration accounts of the war. Salisbury's articles failed, however, to win Pulitzer recognition despite substantial support from editors and correspondents.

—Priscilla Roberts

References: Karnow, Stanley. *Vietnam: A History* (1983); Salisbury, Harrison. *A Journey for Our Times: A Memoir* (1983); —. *A Time of Change: A Reporter's Tale of Our Time* (1988); —. *Behind the Lines: Hanoi, December 23, 1966–January 7, 1967* (1967).
See also: Burchett, Wilfred; Fall, Bernard B.; Johnson, Lyndon Baines; Media and the War.

San Antonio Formula (29 September 1967)

President Johnson's proposed formula for peace talks between the Democratic Republic of Vietnam (DRV) and the United States. On 29 September 1967 President Johnson delivered a speech in San Antonio, Texas, in which he publicly offered to stop "all aerial and naval bombardment" of North Vietnam if DRV leader Hô Chí Minh would agree immediately to enter productive peace negotiations. Johnson also demanded that while discussions proceeded, the DRV not take advantage of a bombing cessation or limitation to infiltrate men or supplies into the South.

Johnson's offer stemmed from the so-called Pennsylvania Channel, the private diplomatic initiative of two French intermediaries, Herbert Marcovich and Raymond Aubrac. Henry Kissinger, then a private citizen, traveled to Hà Nôi to present Johnson's proposal, which later became known as the San Antonio Formula. The DRV leadership rejected the offer. Johnson renewed the offer on 31 March 1968. Although Hà Nôi never responded positively to it, the San Antonio Formula served as the basis for future negotiations.

—Mary L. Kelley

References: Clifford, Clark. *Counsel to the President: A Memoir* (1991); Cooper, Chester L. *The Lost Crusade* (1970); McNamara, Robert S. *In Retrospect: The Tragedy and Lessons of Vietnam* (1995).
See also: Hô Chí Minh; Johnson, Lyndon Baines, Kissinger, Henry Alfred; McNamara, Robert S.

Sanctuaries

Places of refuge or protection. In the Vietnam War context, they were places where the Viêt Công (VC) and People's Army of Vietnam (PAVN) soldiers could retreat and be safe from attack. Although places like the U Minh Forest and the Iron Triangle were sometimes referred to as sanctuaries, Communist forces there were not safe from attack, and thus they were not true sanctuaries.

In theory, Cambodia and Laos became sanctuaries during the war because their so-called neutrality was used by VC and PAVN forces to gain protection from attack throughout the war. Eventually, what had begun as sanctuaries, because of violations of neutrality, became extensions of the battlefield.

—Arthur T. Frame

References: Herring, George C. *America's Longest War: The United States and Vietnam, 1950–1975.* 2d ed.(1986); Karnow, Stanley. *Vietnam: A History* (1984); Lewy, Gunther. *America in Vietnam* (1978).
See also: BARREL ROLL, Operation; Cambodia; Hô Chí Minh Trail; Iron Triangle; LAM SON 719, Operation; Laos; MENU, Operation; Sihanouk, Norodom; STEEL TIGER, Operation; TIGER HOUND, Operation; White Star.

Sarraut, Albert (1872–1962)

French politician, premier, and governor-general of Indo-China (1911–1914 and 1917–1919). As governor-general he represented the best in French liberal republican ideals and helped shift French policy from assimilation to association.

Sarraut carried out judicial reform and worked to revise legal codes to ensure justice for the natives and to end torture and corporal punishment. He worked to improve medicine and promoted the building of hospitals and clinics. Sarraut also worked to raise the standard of living through attention to public works and by improving education. He opened more secondary schools to natives and discouraged sending Vietnamese to study in France. Virginia Thompson, in *French Indo-China*, called him the first governor-general "to win native devotion" and "the most popular man France ever sent to the colony."

—Spencer C. Tucker

References: Hammer, Ellen J. *The Struggle for Indochina* (1954); Hutton, Patrick H., ed. *Historical Dictionary of the Third French Republic, 1870–1940.* Vol. 2. (1986); Thompson, Virginia. *French Indo-China* (1968).
See also: French Indo-China.

Schlesinger, Arthur M., Jr. (1917–)

Prominent American scholar; special assistant to the president (1961–1964). In 1961 Schlesinger joined President Kennedy's circle of advisors as a special assistant. In 1966 he joined the faculty of the City University of New York and began to examine the Vietnam conflict.

At first Schlesinger opposed an American withdrawal from Vietnam for fear of Chinese encroachment but, dismayed by the increasing American involvement, he gradually pushed for de-escalation and negotiation. Schlesinger refused to blame the problems in Vietnam on any specific U.S. policy or individual. He lambasted revisionist policy analysts who blamed a deliberately aggressive U.S. foreign policy. He believed that in foreign policy, moral considerations should not exceed national interests.

Alarmed by the growing power of the presidency, Schlesinger wrote *The Imperial Presidency*, which studied the gradual assumption of power by the executive branch, mainly through the conduct of an independent foreign policy and war making.

—Laura Matysek Wood

References: Anderson, Patrick. *The President's Men* (1968); Depoe, Stephen. *Arthur M. Schlesinger, Jr. and the Ideological History of American Liberalism* (1994).
See also: Fall, Bernard B.; Kennedy, John Fitzgerald; Salisbury, Harrison E.

Schlesinger, James R. (1929–)

Director, Central Intelligence Agency, January–June 1973; secretary of defense, June 1973–November 1975. Schlesinger served in several positions during the Nixon administration, including brief stints as director of central intelligence and as Nixon's last secretary of defense. Nixon largely ignored him in making Vietnam policy.

President Ford disliked the often imperious Schlesinger but retained him in his cabinet to appease conservative Republicans. On Vietnam, Schlesinger one of the more moderate voices among Ford's national security advisors. He argued in favor of Ford's plan to grant limited amnesty to Vietnam-era draft offenders, and he was one of the first cabinet members (as early as September 1974) to push for a swift withdrawal of U.S. embassy personnel from Sài Gòn. Ford ultimately ignored Schlesinger's counsel on Vietnam, widening the rift between the two men. Suspecting that Schlesinger had defied a presidential order during the *Mayaguez* crisis and had refused to order a fourth air strike on the Cambodian mainland, Ford on 2 November 1975 replaced Schlesinger with former White House Chief of Staff Donald Rumsfeld.

—John Robert Greene

Reference: Greene, John Robert. *The Presidency of Gerald R. Ford* (1995).
See also: Central Intelligence Agency (CIA); Ford, Gerald R.; *Mayaguez* Incident; Nixon, Richard Milhous; RAND Corporation.

Schwarzkopf, H. Norman, Jr. (1934–)

U.S. Army general. Following graduation from West Point, Schwarzkopf held normal career assignments before serving two tours in Vietnam. His first tour was as an advisor to Army of the Republic of Vietnam (ARVN) airborne troops. During his second tour, as an infantry battalion commander, he received his third Silver Star and a second Purple Heart.

As commander of Central Command, Schwarzkopf was charged with ousting Iraqi forces from Kuwait during Operation DESERT STORM in 1991. Remembering Vietnam and the gradual escalation strategy, he insisted that a maximum build-up of forces be undertaken before any military action was taken against the Iraqis. Schwarzkopf believed that the Gulf War may finally have brought the American people to terms with Vietnam.

—Robert G. Mangrum

References: Birnbaum, Jesse. "Stormin' Norman on Top" (1991); Schwarzkopf, H. Norman. *It Doesn't Take A Hero* (1992).
See also: Powell, Colin L.

SCOTLAND, Operation (1 November 1967—March 1968)

U.S. Marine Corps operation in Quang Tri Province. Succeeding Operation ARDMORE, Operation SCOTLAND began in western Quang Tri Province. Initially, the 3d Battalion, 26th Marines (3/26th) encamped at the Khe Sanh Combat Base, with the 1st Battalion, 26th Marines (1/26th) positioned on strategic hills west and north. In January 1968, the 2d Battalion, 26th Marines (2/26th) reinforced Khe Sanh, as it appeared that three People's Army of Vietnam (PAVN) divisions were massing in the area. After several quiet weeks, on 20 January a company of the 1/26th, joined by a reaction force from the 3/26th, engaged a PAVN battalion entrenched between Hills 881 South and 881 North, killing 103, while losing seven dead and 35 wounded. The Second Battle of Khe Sanh had begun.

On 21 January, PAVN forces failed to take Hill 861 but overran Khe Sanh and showered artillery shells and rockets

on the area, blowing up a large ammunition dump. The previous day's action had deterred a simultaneous attack on Hill 881S. The Marines had thwarted a PAVN plan to use both hills as fire bases. The Army of the Republic of Vietnam (ARVN) 37th Ranger Battalion then joined the five Marine battalions in and around Khe Sanh, now supported by 46 artillery pieces, five 90-mm tank guns, and ninety-two 106-mm recoilless rifles. Khe Sanh Combat Base itself never was seriously threatened by ground forces. Less well known, but perhaps more significant militarily, is the valor displayed by the Marines on the outlying hills and listening posts. Two companies occupied Hill 881S, perhaps the most isolated Marine fire base in Vietnam, while three companies and a reinforced platoon occupied Hills 861, 861A, 558, and 950. From these outposts overlooking the Khe Sanh plateau, the Marines directed artillery and air strikes on moving PAVN units. PAVN forces held Hill 881N, from which they launched 122-mm rockets at Khe Sanh. From 881S, Marines could observe these launches and alert the base; thus they became a target themselves and were shelled heavily, losing 40 killed and 150 wounded.

The night of 5 February, a battalion of the PAVN 325C Division assaulted a Marine company on the west slope of Hill 861A, breaching the perimeter but leaving 109 dead after hand-to-hand fighting. Marine casualties were seven killed and 35 wounded. The next day, a regiment of the PAVN 304th Division overran Làng Vei Special Forces camp southwest of Khe Sanh. But the worst day for the 26th Marines was 25 February, when a PAVN company ambushed the 3d Platoon, Company B, 1/26th, patrolling south of the base, and also decimated a relief platoon. Company B lost almost two-thirds of its men, including every soldier in the so-called Doomed Patrol, whose bodies were not recovered until two weeks later. By mid-March, PAVN units began their exit from the Khe Sanh area, although the shelling continued. On 24 March, a patrol from Company A, 1st Battalion, 9th Marines (1/9th), killed 31 PAVN soldiers in fighting northwest of the base. In the last encounter, on 30 March, Company B, 1/26th Marines, attacked an entrenched PAVN battalion south of the base, killing 34 while losing five.

Operation SCOTLAND officially ended on that day, with the 26th Marines counting more than 1,600 PAVN dead (excluding thousands killed by bombing). Their own casualties officially numbered 205 killed and 1,668 wounded. John Prados and Ray Stubbe, however, have identified by name 353 Marines killed between 20 January and 31 March alone. Operation PEGASUS (1–15 April), a combined Army, Marine, and ARVN force, effected the relief of Khe Sanh as the PAVN withdrawal continued. It accounted for 1,304 PAVN dead, while U.S. forces sustained 92 killed (51 Marines) and 667 wounded; the ARVN lost 33 men and 206 wounded. Meanwhile, Marines from the 3/26th moved from Hill 881S to attack PAVN forces still entrenched around Hill 881N, killing more than 200, while losing six men.

The day PEGASUS ended, the Marines launched Operation SCOTLAND II, which lasted until 28 February 1969. Initially, the 3/26th Marines swept the valley floor west from Khe Sanh toward Hill 881S and found themselves stepping over hundreds of skeletal remains. The 1/9th Marines endured intense fighting against PAVN bunker complexes near Hill 689, losing nine dead, 53 wounded, and 32 missing in action. Ironically, the 3/26th Marines took more casualties leaving Khe Sanh than during the siege itself, with 301 killed and more than 1,500 wounded by 11 July. The Khe Sanh base was abandoned by 27 June, even though at least ten PAVN battalions remained in western Quang Tri. Now employing mobile tactics, by the end of SCOTLAND II, Marines had killed more than 3,000 and captured 64 PAVN soldiers while suffering 435 dead and 2,395 wounded.

—John D. Root

References: Prados, John, and Ray W. Stubbe. *Valley of Decision: The Siege of Khe Sanh* (1991); Shore, Moyers S., II. *The Battle for Khe Sanh (1969)* (1977).

See also: Khe Sanh, Battles of; PEGASUS–LAM SON 207A, Operation; United States: Marine Corps; Vietnam, Democratic Republic of: Army (People's Army of Vietnam [PAVN]).

SEA DRAGON, Operation (October 1966–October 1968)

U.S. Navy campaign designed to cut the southward flow of munitions and to bombard positions of military significance in the Democratic Republic of Vietnam (DRV). Designated Operation SEA DRAGON, the first U.S. surface ship foray into waters north of the Demilitarized Zone (DMZ) occurred on 25 October 1966 when the destroyers *Mansfield* and *Hanson* commenced patrols to counter Communist waterborne logistics movements from North Vietnam into Quang Tri Province. Although this initial sweep was unproductive, by February 1967 SEA DRAGON ships had extended their raids 230 miles above the DMZ to the 20th parallel.

The vessels involved were usually older gunships of the Seventh Fleet. At the height of the campaign, in May 1967, two cruisers and 12 destroyers were assigned to SEA DRAGON missions. Normal tactics called for surface action groups to make high-speed dashes from 20 miles offshore to logistics choke points such as the mouths of the Sông Giang and Kiên Giang Rivers. Targeted were radar stations, coastal guns, and supply craft. Truck columns, boat repair facilities, bridges, and surface-to-air missile sites were occasional victims. U.S. ships also detected and analyzed Communist radar transmissions.

Results were frequently gratifying. After one year of this effort, Seventh Fleet headquarters calculated that SEA DRAGON warships had sunk or damaged 2,000 logistics craft and drastically stemmed the flow of supplies from the DRV to the south.

The U.S. effort did not go unchallenged, and the North Vietnamese increased their shore batteries in numbers and caliber. Mobile and difficult to locate, these guns often subjected SEA DRAGON ships to heavy fire. During summer 1967, DRV batteries engaged U.S. warships 10 to 15 times monthly. Overall, 29 SEA DRAGON ships were damaged, five sailors were killed, and 26 wounded.

With President Johnson's bombing halt of April 1968, U.S. forces were restricted to waters from the DMZ 150 miles north to the 19th parallel, a one-third reduction in the operating area. The SEA DRAGON campaign ended on 31 October 1968, when U.S. units withdrew south of the DMZ, but Seventh Fleet cruisers, frigates, and destroyers ranged north one last time from April to September 1972 to fire more than 110,000 rounds in retaliation for the Easter Offensive.

—Malcolm Muir, Jr.

References: Marolda, Edward J. *By Sea, Air, and Land: An Illustrated History of the U.S. Navy and the War in Southeast Asia* (1994); Muir, Malcolm, Jr. *Black Shoes and Blue Water: Surface Warfare in the United States Navy, 1945–1975* (1996); Uhlig, Frank, Jr., ed. *Vietnam: The Naval Story* (1986).

See also: Artillery, Allied and People's Army of Vietnam; Australia; Naval Bombardment; Sea Power in the Vietnam War; United States: Navy; Warships, Allied and Democratic Republic of Vietnam.

Sea Power in the Vietnam War

Bernard Brodie, writing in the 1960s, dissected the advantages to be derived from a state of naval dominance: (1) sea power protects the movement over water of one's own military forces and their supplies; (2) it guards friendly shipping from enemy attacks; (3) it prevents an enemy from using the sea to transport their own forces; (4) it exerts military and economic pressure on an enemy by preventing them from maintaining trade; and (5) it bombards land targets. During the conflict in Southeast Asia, the United States held every one of these advantages, yet could not achieve its desired results.

The United States and its allies enjoyed from the beginning of the Vietnam War unquestioned, and essentially unchallenged, supremacy on the oceans. Nevertheless, this supremacy did not garner the expected fruits, an anomaly due partly to the nature of the struggle and partly to the unreadiness of the United States to exploit its advantages at sea.

U.S. sea power, configured during the 1950s for nuclear war, was unready to rapidly move U.S. military forces and supplies 7,000 miles to the theater of action. Lacking adequate sealift in 1965, the United States was forced to charter foreign merchantmen to transport equipment and supplies badly needed in South Vietnam.

Better executed was the U.S. task of protecting shipping from enemy attacks. Whereas the Democratic Republic of Vietnam (DRV) had only a small navy composed of coastal craft, U.S. Navy vessels were at hazard only in port or in rivers, where individual ships might be struck by Communist saboteurs or mines. Following widely publicized Việt Công successes early in the war, the U.S. Navy instituted Operation STABLE DOOR, an effective long-term venture to secure South Vietnamese ports.

The Navy was also largely able to prevent the North Vietnamese from transporting their military forces and supplies southward by sea. Beginning in March 1965, the Navy's MARKET TIME patrols of airplanes, destroyers, and small craft augmented by Coast Guard cutters were so effective at reducing the flow of Communist supplies down the coast that the North Vietnamese were forced to rely heavily on the Hô Chí Minh Trail and to open the Sihanouk Trail to the Mekong Delta.

U.S. seapower was less successful in preventing North Vietnam from maintaining trade with its Communist-bloc supporters. The Johnson administration, wary of intervention by the People's Republic of China or the USSR, made no effort to close the principal North Vietnamese port, Hai Phòng. When the Nixon administration finally ordered the mining of Hai Phòng harbor in retaliation for the 1972 Easter Offensive, the move proved one of the most effective ploys of the war. No vessels entered the port for more than 300 days, thus slashing North Vietnam's imports, especially of critical munitions, by 85 percent.

The U.S. Navy made ample use of its ability to bombard shore targets. With a 1,500-mile coastline and averaging only 80 miles in width, Vietnam was especially suited for such operations. Operating off South Vietnam, Allied warships lent direct fire support to friendly troops. From 1966 to 1968, and again in 1972, U.S. gunships in Operation SEA DRAGON shelled targets above the DMZ. Naval aircraft flying from carriers on station in the Gulf of Tonkin also delivered a great weight of explosives against North Vietnamese targets. Political limitations hobbled these air and surface strikes, making them far less militarily effective than they might have been.

Sea power also exerted pressure by force projection through amphibious assaults and riverine operations, although here, too, the potential advantages were neglected or exploited halfheartedly. Landings by U.S. and South Korean Marines failed, usually because of security leaks, to achieve important results. Operation BOLD MARINER (January 1969), the largest amphibious action of the war, resulted in the capture of only one Viêt Công sapper company.

In the Mekong Delta, the U.S. Navy conducted riverine ("brown-water") patrols, code-named Operation GAME WARDEN, beginning in March 1966. However, the hastily improvised river patrol boats were too few in number. Their Jacuzzi waterjet pumps were prone to fouling, while their truck engines made such noise as to render surprise almost impossible. Moreover, top Navy officers, such as the aviator chiefs of naval operations (CNOs), were most interested in the carrier war. Only after the 1968 Têt Offensive did the patrol craft reach the minimum number (250 boats) deemed necessary for successful large-scale operations. By that point the tide of the war had turned. In somewhat similar fashion, the Mobile Riverine Force, designed to carry specially trained soldiers to attack Viêt Công bastions in the Mekong Delta, was handicapped by a lack of speedy troop carriers and the substitution of the Army's 9th Division for Marines (assigned to I Corps in the north).

With the collapse of South Vietnam in 1975, Allied sea power was harnessed to rescue friendly military personnel and civilians fleeing the final Communist offensive. In Operation FREQUENT WIND in April, U.S. Marines and soldiers evacuated thousands of U.S. and Allied civilian and military personnel from Sài Gòn. Over the next several months Seventh Fleet warships plucked tens of thousands of refugees from the South China Sea.

The war in Southeast Asia demonstrated both the capabilities and inherent limitations of sea power in such a conflict. Sea power in the end could not bring decisive weight to bear, but it helped for a decade to stymie the DRV effort to conquer South Vietnam.

—Malcolm Muir, Jr.

References: Cutler, Thomas J. *Brown Water, Black Berets: Coastal and Riverine Warfare in Vietnam* (1988); Hagan, Kenneth J. *This People's Navy: The Making of American Sea Power* (1991); Hooper, Edwin B. *United States Naval Power in a Changing World* (1988); Uhlig, Frank, Jr. *Vietnam: The Naval Story* (1986).

See also: BOLD MARINER, Operation; FREQUENT WIND, Operation; GAME WARDEN, Operation; MARKET TIME, Operation; Riverine Craft; Riverine Warfare; SEA DRAGON, Operation; United States: Navy; Warships, Allied and Democratic Republic of Vietnam.

Seabees. *See* United States: Seabees.

SEAL (Sea, Air, Land) Teams

U.S. Navy special operations force, evolved from the underwater demolition teams (UDTs), or "frogmen," used in World War II and the Korean War. They were trained to operate underwater and on land and were parachute qualified, hence the acronym SEAL (sea, air, land). Their missions consisted of intelligence gathering, raids, ambushes, prisoner captures, and disruption of enemy rear-area operations. They also projected U.S. military power by training forces friendly to the United States in a fashion similar to that of the Army's Special Forces. Each of the two SEAL teams—one permanently stationed on the East Coast and the other on the West Coast of the United States—consisted of approximately 200 officers and men.

The training program was grueling; candidates had to complete the 25-week Basic Underwater Demolition/SEAL (BUD/S) course and the Army's 3-week Airborne School. SEALs received training in small arms use, hand-to-hand combat, patrolling, land and water navigation, and other specialized skills.

SEALs conducted missions up to 20 miles inland. They could infiltrate hostile shores by disembarking from submerged submarines and swimming to the beach or using small boats. These included river patrol boats (PBRs), fast patrol craft (PCF), mechanized landing craft (LCM), light SEAL support craft (LSSC), SEAL team assault boats (STABs), and medium SEAL support craft (MSSC). These vessels provided a wide variety of mobility and fire support for assault and reconnaissance missions.

Three submarines—*Grayback*, *Perch*, and *Tunny*—were reconfigured to carry UDT/SEAL teams on covert missions and remained dedicated to support naval unconventional warfare operations. In the Vietnam War, SEALs were allotted one squadron of UH-1 Iroquois helicopter gunships and one squadron of OV-10 Broncos. The OV-10, a dual-propeller light aircraft that carried a wide array of ordnance, could respond quickly to calls for assistance and could loiter over target areas for long periods. These two squadrons operated primarily in the Mekong River Delta.

From 1962 until 1964, SEALs trained Republic of Vietnam (RVN) Biêt Hai naval commandos (the RVN's unconventional force that conducted patrol and other operations using armed and upgraded civilian junks) and the regular naval UDTs, the Liên Đôi Nguoi Nhái (LĐNN). U.S. UDT personnel also conducted hydrographic surveys along the RVN coast and made covert incursions into the Democratic Republic of Vietnam (DRV) to collect intelligence and carry out coastal mapping. In 1963 SEALs supported numerous raids into the DRV by LĐNN forces to destroy coastal rail lines, power plants, and harbor facilities. Personnel assigned to SEAL Team 1 or 2 regularly saw service in the RVN as part of fleet deployment rotations. Neither team was permanently stationed in the RVN but regularly assigned personnel for tours of duty there. Twenty separate SEAL detachments of varying strengths were established in the RVN under the Commander of Naval Forces, Vietnam (COMNAVFORV).

In early 1964 several SEAL detachments were assigned to the U.S. Military Assistance Command, Vietnam's Studies and Observations Group (MACV-SOG). MACV-SOG was responsible for all covert operations conducted in the RVN and included all branches of the U.S. military, the Central Intelligence Agency (CIA), and the RVN's special warfare forces. Operations into the DRV continued, as did numerous missions throughout the Mekong Delta to capture Viêt Công (VC) and People's Army of Vietnam (PAVN) personnel, weapons, and documents.

In 1965 MACV, acting jointly with COMNAVFORV, ordered the SEALs into the Rung Sát Special Zone (RSSZ), a thick mangrove swamp seven miles south of Sài Gòn. It was one of the most difficult areas in Vietnam in which to conduct military operations. This area was a VC stronghold and presented a direct threat to Sài Gòn. SEAL operations in the RSSZ consisted of hunter-killer teams of three to seven men each that targeted VC land concentrations and small boat traffic. SEALs patrolled in small boats or swam and waded through thick mud to establish ambushes. SEALs assaulted VC-controlled villages and other substantial targets using small craft that carried machine guns and mortars and provided increased firepower. They also targeted the Communist infrastructure by killing or capturing VC leaders whenever possible. By mid-1966, SEAL operations were so effective that the RSSZ was no longer a VC safe haven.

In 1967 MACV-SOG ordered an increase in SEAL operations throughout the Mekong Delta. SEALs also provided intelligence to, and scouted for, the combined U.S. Army-Navy Mobile Riverine Force (MRF). The MRF consisted of the U.S. Army's 9th Division backed by U.S. Navy small boats: armored fire-support ships (dubbed "monitors" because of their resemblance to Civil War ironclads), landing craft, supply, and fire support barges.

From 1968 to 1970, SEAL and UDT personnel engaged in covert operations along the entire RVN coast as well as conventional operations within their designated operational areas. UDT personnel kept shipping channels clear of mines and explosives and facilitated navigation by removing wrecked ships or deepening the waterways by clearing natural obstacles. SEALs in advisory duty, working with Army Special Forces, assisted and trained the ARVN's Provincial Reconnaissance Units (PRUs). The PRUs recruited personnel from Vietnamese Chiêu Hôi centers, and from prisons, to perform counterterrorist missions within the RVN. The U.S. advisors tried to exert great control and discipline over these rather unsavory characters to ensure they functioned as soldiers and not bandits. Despite the 1970 announcement of "Vietnamization," the pace of SEAL/UDT operations continued unabated.

SEALs played a key role in Operation BRIGHTLIGHT (1970–1972), the attempted rescue of prisoners of war (POWs) held by the VC in the Mekong Delta. Despite success, including the recovery of numerous ARVN POWs, not one U.S. POW was found during BRIGHTLIGHT. The Allied raiders often found empty camps—termed "empty holes"—or large caches of weapons and equipment, but raid after raid demonstrated the Allied command's failure to use intelligence in a timely manner, despite possessing special operations forces capable of rapid response.

The years 1970–1972 saw SEAL and UDTs advising and training the LĐNN and accompanying them on forays into the DRV. Covert coastal mapping and hydrographic surveys also continued. The last SEAL platoons were withdrawn from the RVN in 1972.

From their inception and deployment to the RVN, U.S. Navy SEALs established an enviable combat record. Their unique personnel selection and unsparing training program produced successful combat results with very low casualties. During the Vietnam War, 49 naval special warfare personnel died in action; none were captured. In 1973 the UDTs were disbanded and their missions absorbed by SEAL teams.

—J. A. Menzoff

References: Bosiljevac, T. L. *SEALs: UDT/SEAL Operations in Vietnam* (1990); Marolda, Edward J., and Oscar P. Fitzgerald. *The United States Navy in the Vietnam Conflict: From Military Assistance to Combat* (1986); Thompson, Leroy. *U.S. Elite Forces–Vietnam* (1985).

See also: Mobile Riverine Force; Riverine Craft; Riverine Warfare; United States: Navy; United States: Special Forces; Vietnam, Republic of: Navy (VNN); Vietnam, Republic of: Special Forces (Luc Luong Đac Biêt [LLDB]).

Seale, Bobby (1936–)

Political activist and cofounder of the Black Panther Party for Self-Defense (BPP), which advocated black power and black opposition to the Vietnam War. Seale's ten-point party platform demanded political freedom, exemption from military service, black control of black communities, full employment, better housing, education, community health, and an end to police brutality.

Clad in black leather jackets and berets and carrying weapons, Black Panthers became the most visible of black radical groups. This visibility attracted the attention of the Federal Bureau of Investigation, which launched a domestic counterintelligence program (COINTELPRO) to create dissension and undermine the BPP. Seale was arrested and tried as one of the Chicago Eight for his part in protest activities at the 1968 Democratic Party National Convention. The case attracted nationwide attention when Judge Julius Hoffman ordered Seale, who attempted to act in his own defense, bound and gagged in the courtroom. His case was separated from the other defendants, and Seale was sentenced to 48 months in prison for 16 acts of contempt. He was then charged with killing a BPP informant in Connecticut. The contempt charges were dismissed, the murder trial ended with a hung jury. Internal dissension led to the demise of the BPP by the early 1970s.

—Laura Matysek Wood

References: O'Reilly, Kenneth. *"Racial Matters." The FBI's Secret File on Black America 1960–1972* (1989); Seale, Bobby. *A Lonely Rage: The Autobiography of Bobby Seale* (1968); Seale, Bobby. *Seize the Time: The Story of the Black Panther Party and Huey P. Newton* (1970).

See also: Antiwar Movement, United States.

SEALORDS (Southeast Asia Lake Ocean River Delta Strategy) (1968–1971)

U.S. combined-force interdiction, harassment, and pacification effort in the Mekong Delta of South Vietnam. In October 1968, Commander Naval Forces, Vietnam Vice-Adm. Elmo R. Zumwalt, Jr. established SEALORDS (Task Force 194) to operate along the Mekong Delta waterways to interdict Việt Công infiltration routes from Cambodia, harass Communist forces, and (with assistance from ground and air forces) pacify the Delta. This idea emerged when Zumwalt realized that water barriers or blockades could be placed in and around the Delta and along the Cambodian border. Zumwalt combined all Naval Forces, Vietnam (NAVFORV) assets: Task Force 115, The Coastal Surveillance Force; Task Force 116, The River Patrol Force; and Task Force 117, the Mobile Riverine Force. He believed that these forces together could project an offensive deep into the Mekong Delta and along less-traveled but still vital waterways of IV Corps Tactical Zone (CTZ).

In early October, before the inception of SEALORDS, the Coastal Surveillance Force expanded its mission to include river incursions into the III and IV CTZs. These initial forays into territory previously dominated by the Việt Công destroyed numerous structures, sampans, and tax collection stations. Such operations proved the practicality of transiting the waterways and caught the insurgents off guard. Thus on 18 October 1968, when SEALORDS became official, the tempo of these transits increased.

Zumwalt wanted to establish a patrol barrier on the Vinh Té Canal bordering Cambodia, but first he had to test the validity of his barrier concept. He suggested that Capt. Robert S. Salzer establish a blockade along the canal in the center of the western part of the Delta. If this worked, it would be feasible to move the barrier up to the Vinh Té Canal. Salzer immediately drew up the plan for the operation, subsequently code-named SEARCH TURN.

After approval by Military Assistance Command, Vietnam (MACV) head Gen. Creighton W. Abrams, the initial assault began on 1 November 1968. Four days later NAVFORV established an interdiction barrier consisting of a 24-hour river boat patrol. SEARCH TURN's area of operations (AO) encompassed the Rach Giá–Long Xuyên Canal from the Bassac River to the Rach Soi Canal and then southwest on the latter canal to the Gulf of Thailand. The success of Operation SEARCH TURN, combined with transits of the Rach Gang Thân River and the Vinh Té Canal, contributed to the establishment of Operation TRÂN HUNG ĐẠO along the Cambodian border on 21 November 1968.

On 6 December SEALORDS expanded with a new barrier, GIANT SLINGSHOT. This operation was so named because the AO encompassed the east and west branches of the Vàm Co River that flowed along converging routes on either side of the Parrot's Beak and joined near the town of Bên Luc, forming what looked like a giant slingshot. The Parrot's Beak extended Cambodian territory southeastward to within a few miles of Sài Gòn, and from their base camps there, the Communists had but a short trip to the capital. Hence, the largest amounts of infiltration had occurred here. Before GIANT SLINGSHOT, friendly movement on these rivers did not exist, thus Admiral Zumwalt sought to stop infiltration and make these rivers accessible to the local inhabitants.

In late 1968, an idea emerged for a fourth barrier. The concept was to connect Trân Hung Đao in the west to GIANT SLINGSHOT in the east. This new operation, BARRIER REEF, or the Border Interdiction Campaign, began on 2 January 1969. The AO was located in the Plain of Reeds, a vast open area that during the rainy months became a huge shallow lake. The AO extended from the GIANT SLINGSHOT on the Vàm Co Tây along the Lagrange Canal from Tuyên Nhon to Âp Bac and westward along the Ông Lon Canal to the upper Mekong River at An Long. The Lagrange–Ông Lon Canal bisected many secondary canals leading from the Cambodian border toward the populous portion of the Delta east-southeast of the Plain of Reeds, including the city of My Tho.

Besides these operations, Zumwalt on 27 June 1969 established Sea Float, a mobile advance tactical support base (MATSB) composed of 11 ammi pontoons heavily laden with mortars, rockets, and machine guns and capable of operating a wide range of river craft and providing living quarters for boat crews while floating in midstream on the Cua Lon River in An Xuyên Province. Then in September 1969 Zumwalt activated Breezy Cove, an advance tactical support base (ATSB) containing similar defensive measures and also located in An Xuyên on the riverbank of the Ông Đôc.

Despite the offensive nature of SEALORDS, Zumwalt had created the barrier plans with one overarching goal: to enable the Republic of Vietnam Navy to take over as U.S. forces withdrew. ACTOV (Accelerated Turnover to Vietnamese), the Navy's Vietnamization program, began in fall 1968. By April 1971 all SEALORDS operations had been turned over to the RVN Navy.

—R. Blake Dunnavent

References: Cutler, Thomas J. *Brown Water, Black Berets: Coastal and Riverine Warfare in Vietnam* (1988); Marolda, Edward J. *By Sea,*

Air, and Land: An Illustrated History of the U.S. Navy and the War in Southeast Asia (1994); Schreadley, R. L. *From the Rivers to the Sea: The United States Navy in Vietnam* (1992).

See also: GAME WARDEN, Operation; Geography of Indo-China and Vietnam; MARKET TIME, Operation; Mekong Delta; Mobile Riverine Force; Riverine Craft; Riverine Warfare; United States: Navy; Vietnam, Republic of: Navy (VNN); Zumwalt, Elmo R., Jr.

Search and Destroy

U.S. military tactic of attrition used in Vietnam, 1965–1968. Developed by Gen. William Westmoreland and his deputy, Brig. Gen. William DePuy, search and destroy was an ad hoc approach that grew out of discussions between the two men.

Although Westmoreland later denied that search and destroy was even a specific tactic, it certainly was the dominant approach followed by U.S. fighting units in Vietnam. Search and destroy relied on the assumption that U.S. firepower and technology were so superior and could cause such severe casualties that neither the Viêt Công (VC) nor the People's Army of Vietnam (PAVN) would be able to withstand the punishment the U.S. could visit upon them. Search and destroy was to be an aggressive military tool. Ground forces, transported by Army aviation helicopter units and supported by artillery, would locate and destroy enemy forces and, occasionally, their base areas. It emphasized attacking Communist forces, not acquiring territory. Troopers struck into areas of supposed Communist strength to "find, fix, and finish" their enemy. Mission accomplished, they withdrew to their home base until ordered out on the next such operation.

Not everyone agreed with this approach. Air Force Chief of Staff Gen. John P. McConnell and Marine Corps Commandant Gen. David M. Greene opposed it. Army Gen. James Gavin called for U.S. military aid to Vietnam to be restricted to sending forces to certain enclaves, providing those locations with protection, and freeing troops of the Army of the Republic of Vietnam (ARVN) to carry the brunt of the fight. Gen. Edward Lansdale argued that the main U.S. commitment should be directed toward countrywide pacification and counterinsurgency rather than employing combat maneuver battalions.

Westmoreland wanted no static defensive posture, was unwilling to confine his command to a defensive role, and repudiated the enclave strategy. An early indication of his desire to expand in-country operations came in summer 1965 when he ordered the 173d Airborne, which had arrived in Vietnam on 7 May, deployed to the Central Highlands. On 26 June the Pentagon gave Westmoreland authority to assign U.S. troops to field action. Two days later, 3,000 soldiers of the 173d moved into War Zone D, twenty miles northwest of Sài Gòn. Perhaps Westmoreland felt he had no choice. Previous military preparation had equipped and prepared the Army only to fight in Europe. Suddenly faced with Vietnam, planners sent military forces intact to Southeast Asia.

Westmoreland has been soundly criticized for adopting this tactic of attrition. It grew from his erroneous assumption that U.S. soldiers and firepower could inflict devastating losses on Communist forces in Vietnam while keeping U.S. casualties to an acceptable level. His hopes were doomed by wartime reality. The level of attrition he was able to bring to bear on the Communists was neutralized by more than 200,000 North Vietnamese males who reached draft age every year. Westmoreland's army never came close to inflicting that many casualties in any 12-month period. A bigger problem with Westmoreland's tactics was that the Communists, rather than U.S. forces, generally initiated hostilities, choosing favorable battle locations and often ending combat when they saw fit, leaving the site of an attack along safe avenues of retreat.

Dave Richard Palmer roundly criticized Westmoreland's war of attrition as an indication of his failure to conceive of an alternative, as irrefutable proof of the absence of any strategy, and as an approach demonstrating that the U.S. Army was strategically bankrupt in Vietnam. Others also criticized the strategy, but Westmoreland stubbornly relied on search and destroy throughout his tenure as commander of U.S. Military Assistance Command, Vietnam (MACV). Following the 1968 Têt Offensive, however, MACV public affairs officers did not often use the term search and destroy, replacing it with the phrase "reconnaissance in force." An observer would have been hard pressed, however, to note any actual change in American approaches to locating Communist forces.

—Cecil B. Currey

References: Palmer, Dave Richard. *Readings in Current Military History* (1969); Shaplen, Robert. *The Road From War: Vietnam, 1965–1970* (1970).

See also: Attrition; Bên Súc; Casualties; Clear and Hold; DePuy, William E.; Gavin, James M.; Military Assistance Command, Vietnam (MACV); United States: Army; Westmoreland, William Childs.

Search-and-Rescue (SAR) Operations

Location and rescue of downed aircrewmen. In all, 8,588 U.S. Air Force, Army, Navy and Marine fixed-wing and rotary-wing aircraft were lost in the Vietnam War. Thousands of aircrewmen were killed, reported missing in action, or taken prisoner. The U.S. Air Force's Aerospace Rescue and Recovery Service (ARRS) played a key role in minimizing these losses.

On 1 April 1962 Detachment 3, Pacific Air Rescue Center (Det 3, PARC) was established at Tân Son Nhut Air Base in Sài Gòn. This detachment possessed no rescue aircraft and was only able to coordinate operations that relied on Army, Marine, and Vietnamese Air Force helicopters and search aircraft.

The first Air Force search-and-rescue (SAR) helicopters, Kaman HH-43Bs, arrived at Nakhon Phanom Royal Thai Air Force Base (RTAFB), Thailand, in June 1964. With a combat radius of less than 100 miles, these choppers were virtually useless for aircrew recovery. Real rescue capability did not exist until 1965, when the first modified Sikorsky CH-3C/Es arrived at Udorn RTAFB, Thailand. These were soon replaced with air-refuelable HH-3Es that could reach any point in North Vietnam. The even larger Sikorsky HH-53s, introduced in late 1967, gave rescue forces a formidable aircrew recovery capability.

The introduction of helicopters with more powerful engines and better hovering characteristics, armor, and the jungle penetrator survivor extraction system allowed rescue forces to use the inhospitable jungle, karst formations, and mountains to their advantage. When a fighter-bomber received battle damage over North Vietnam, the pilot tried to keep his crippled aircraft aloft until it reached either the Gulf of Tonkin or, if traveling west, one of several designated jungle regions called SAFE (Selected Area for Evasion) areas.

Democratic Republic of Vietnam (DRV) air defenses remained troublesome throughout the war. From 1965 to 1972 the DRV claimed 35 rescue aircraft; 10 other rescue aircraft suffered noncombat operational losses, and 71 rescuemen perished. Tactics and improved equipment helped to overcome expanding DRV defenses. The greatest innovation was the search-and-rescue task force (SARTAF) that included a control aircraft, two to four fighter-bomber escorts, and at least two rescue helicopters. The types of aircraft in the SARTAF changed as better airframes became available. Tactics evolved, with flexibility as the primary principle.

The airborne mission control airplane was the SARTAF nerve center. Originally Grumman HU-16 amphibians performed this role. In 1965 these were replaced by four-engine Douglas HC-54s, which, the following year, were replaced by Lockheed HC-130P Hercules four-engine turboprops with the call sign "Crown" and later "King." Douglas A-1 Skyraiders, propeller-driven attack aircraft designed in World War II for the Navy, excelled in the rescue escort (RESCORT) mission. In 1972, when all Air Force and Navy A-1s were turned over to the South Vietnamese Air Force, Vought A-7 single-engine jets proved to be a poor replacement.

The helicopters evolved from HH-43s to the HH-3s to the HH-53s, some of which, by 1971, had a limited nighttime recovery capability. The HH-43s were designed to suppress aircraft fires and pick up crews near bases, but the HH-43Fs were modified to perform limited long-range aircrew recovery. The HH-3 and HH-53 "Jolly Green Giants" could, with refueling from Crown/King HC-130Ps, remain aloft up to 18 hours. These choppers almost always flew in pairs, with the "low bird" making the actual pickup, while the "high bird" was available as a backup should the low bird be shot down.

Aircrew recovery was a bright spot in the long air war, with 3,883 lives credited to the ARRS. Rescue forces also saved 555 Allied military men, 476 civilians, and 45 other people.

—Earl H. Tilford, Jr.

References: Berger, Carl, ed. *The United States Air Force in Southeast Asia: An Illustrated Account* (1984); Tilford, Earl H., Jr. *A History of U.S. Search and Rescue Operations in Southeast Asia, 1961–75* (1980).

See also: Airborne Operations; Airplanes, Allied and Democratic Republic of Vietnam; EAGLE PULL, Operation; Helicopters, Allied and Democratic Republic of Vietnam; Helicopters, Employment of, in Vietnam; Medevac; Son Tây Raid.

Sharp, Ulysses Simpson Grant, Jr. (1906–)

U.S. Navy admiral and commander in chief, U.S. Pacific Command, 1964–1968. In June 1964 Sharp became commander in chief of the Pacific Command (CINCPAC), the largest U.S. unified command. As CINCPAC, Sharp was responsible for the defense of an area of 85 million square miles, extending across the Pacific to the Indian Ocean, and from the Aleutian Islands to the Antarctic.

Sharp oversaw air strikes against North Vietnamese torpedo boat bases following the August 1964 Gulf of Tonkin incident. Subsequently, the Joint Chiefs of Staff (JCS) gave him overall supervision of military actions in Vietnam. Sharp had overall military responsibility for the air operations of ROLLING THUNDER, the bombing of North Vietnam that began in early 1965, although ultimate authority lay with President Johnson. His view of operational objectives often differed sharply from those of Secretary of Defense Robert McNamara and the JCS, especially Chief of Naval Operations Admiral Thomas H. Moorer.

McNamara and Johnson believed that limited bombing could force a diplomatic solution. Sharp, Moorer, and most service leaders balked at such an idea. Sharp was as convinced as the Air Force generals that strategic bombing against the Democratic Republic of Vietnam would have been successful. He chafed under what he saw as "absurd" restrictions on strategic air power.

In August 1968 Sharp retired as CINCPAC and from active duty. In 1978 Sharp wrote *Strategy for Defeat: Vietnam in Retrospect*. In it, Sharp declared that if the United States had undertaken massive and constant B-52 LINEBACKER-style raids against North Vietnam beginning in 1965, it could have won the war without fear of Soviet or Chinese intervention.

—William Head

References: Momyer, William. *Air Power in Three Wars* (1978); Sharp, U. S. G. *Strategy for Defeat: Vietnam in Retrospect* (1986); Tilford, Earl H., Jr. *Crosswinds: The Air Force Setup in Vietnam* (1993); Westmoreland, William C., and U. S. G. Sharp. *Report on the War in Vietnam* (30 June 1968).

See also: Johnson, Lyndon Baines; McNamara, Robert S.; Moorer, Thomas H.; ROLLING THUNDER, Operation.

Sheehan, Cornelius Mahoney (Neil) (1936–)

Among the first and finest correspondents of the Vietnam War. Sent to Sài Gòn in April 1962, Sheehan did not question the righteousness of the Vietnam conflict or U.S. involvement but soon learned to suspect the false optimism of senior military officials such as Gen. Paul Harkins, and to listen to field advisors such as Lt. Col. John Paul Vann, who admitted mistakes.

Sheehan first angered U.S. officials with his reporting of the January 1963 Battle of Ấp Bac, in which an Army of the Republic of Vietnam (ARVN) division experienced a stunning defeat. Vann called Ấp Bac "a miserable damn performance"; Harkins proclaimed it a victory, announcing 101 VC killed, although only three bodies were found. Washington accepted Harkins's characterization of the battle and assailed the press, and especially Sheehan, for misrepresenting it.

The Republic of Vietnam (RVN) government began to harass U.S. correspondents after they reported that the May 1963 Buddhist crisis might bring down the government. When Ngô Đình Nhu's security troops raided Buddhist pagodas in August, Sheehan had to smuggle the true story out while the U.S. Embassy endorsed Nhu's version of events. That September he and David Halberstam revealed that the CIA was backing dissident generals in a planned coup against Ngô Đình Diệm. Sheehan's editors killed his story and recalled him to Tokyo, causing him to miss the story of the coup and assassinations of Diệm and Nhu. In January 1964 Sheehan rebutted Ambassador Henry Cabot Lodge's report of significant progress in the Mekong Delta, concluding that the war there was "a long way toward being lost." Sheehan then left Vietnam to join the staff of *The New York Times*.

Returning to Vietnam in 1965, Sheehan was among the first to dispatch first-hand accounts of the bloody fighting in the Ia Drang Valley. When he left again in 1966, still neither dove nor hawk, Sheehan had concluded that not only would Gen. Westmoreland's strategy of attrition not destroy the enemy's will to fight, but that it was certain to cost thousands of civilian and American lives.

Sheehan continued to cover the war from Washington but would not return to Vietnam until 1972. His notoriety increased with a lengthy March 1971 article in *The New York Times Book Review* that questioned whether U.S. leaders had committed war crimes in Vietnam. But his biggest story came when he led a team in editing the Pentagon Papers, excerpts of which appeared in June 1968 issues of *The New York Times* and *The Washington Post*.

In 1972 Sheehan took a leave from *The New York Times* to write one of the most ambitious books about the war, *A Bright Shining Lie: John Paul Vann and America in Vietnam* (1988). Vann served in Vietnam as a high-ranking civilian advisor until his death in 1972. At Vann's funeral Sheehan recognized that "We were burying the whole era of … boundless self-confidence that led us to Vietnam," and that Vann's career could serve as a metaphor for America's involvement. Even Vann had lost the sense of reality because he could not admit defeat. More than a biography, Sheehan's book is a virtual history of the American phase of the Vietnam War, a penetrating analysis of how intelligent men had behaved stupidly and brought upon the United States and the people of Southeast Asia an enormous tragedy. The book earned Sheehan a Pulitzer Prize and a National Book Award.

Sheehan's three post-1975 visits to Vietnam are recounted in *After the War Was Over* (1995).

—John D. Root

References: Prochnau, William. *Once Upon a Distant War: David Halberstam, Neil Sheehan, Peter Arnett—Young War Correspondents and Their Early Vietnam Battles* (1995); Sheehan, Neil. *A Bright Shining Lie: John Paul Vann and America in Vietnam* (1988); Wyatt, Clarence R. *Paper Soldiers: The American Press and the Vietnam War* (1993).
See also: Ấp Bắc, Battle of; Ellsberg, Daniel; Halberstam, David; Harkins, Paul D.; Lodge, Henry Cabot, Jr.; McNamara, Robert S.; Ngô Đình Nhu; Pentagon Papers and Trial; Vann, John Paul; Westmoreland, William Childs.

SHINING BRASS, Operation (October 1965)

U.S. Special Forces cross-border operations into Laos to locate and disrupt North Vietnamese infiltration along the Hồ Chí Minh Trail into South Vietnam. Operation SHINING BRASS was carried out by 12-man teams that normally included three Americans and nine Montagnard civilians under control of the Military Assistance Command, Vietnam Studies and Observation Group (MACV-SOG). The command and control center was in Đà Nang at Marble Mountain; forward operating bases were usually located in Special Forces Civilian Irregular Defense Group (CIDG) camps along the border with Laos. Initially, its primary mission was the location of targets for aerial bombing, but at times the teams had to fight. Later operations were expanded to include emplacing antipersonnel devices, engaging People's Army of Vietnam (PAVN) or Pathet Lao personnel in open combat, assessing bomb damage, and controlling air strikes. Eventually, three battalions of American-led Vietnamese were used as a reaction force to carry out larger missions in Laos. The authorized areas for operations were specified strips of Laos along the border that stretched 20 kilometers into the country.

Initially SOG commanders were not allowed to lift reconnaissance teams in by helicopter, although they were authorized to extricate them by air if necessary. However, daily movements of reconnaissance teams were severely limited by the rugged terrain, so helicopter infiltration ultimately was authorized and became the norm. Reconnaissance teams directed air strikes on known targets through an elaborate procedure that included securing permission on a target-by-target basis from the U.S. ambassador to Laos.

SHINING BRASS became one of the largest and most important Special Forces strategic reconnaissance and interdiction campaigns in Southeast Asia. SHINING BRASS was renamed PRAIRIE FIRE in 1968, and finally PHU DUNG in April 1971.

—James H. Willbanks

References: Kelly, Francis J. *U.S. Army Special Forces, 1961–1971* (1973); Simpson, Charles M. *Inside the Green Berets.* (1983); Stanton, Shelby L. *The Green Berets at War* (1985).
See also: Civilian Irregular Defense Group (CIDG); Hồ Chí Minh Trail; Laos; Montagnards; Studies and Observation Group (SOG); United States: Special Forces.

Shoup, David M. (1904–1983)

Commandant, U.S. Marine Corps, 1960–1963. Gen. Shoup believed strongly that the military should serve the national interest as defined by its civilian leaders. He refused to participate in what he referred to as the "hate-the-Communists" movement, saying he would fight the Communists if required by circumstances, but that he did not find it necessary to hate them. He was opposed to the massive military buildup in Southeast Asia and, after his retirement, he continued his crusade against the Vietnam War. In the April 1969 edition of *Atlantic Monthly*, Shoup collaborated with Col. James Donovan, USMC (Ret.), on a widely reviewed article that held that anticommunism provided the perfect climate and foundation to nurture a "new American militarism" in the defense establishment.

—W. E. Fahey, Jr.

Reference: Shoup, David M. "The New American Militarism" (1969).
See also: United States: Involvement in Vietnam, 1954–1965; United States: Marine Corps.

SIGMA, Project (1966–1967)

U.S. military long-range reconnaissance initiative. Encouraged by the success of Project DELTA, in August 1966 Westmoreland organized Projects OMEGA (Detachment B-50) and SIGMA (Detachment B-56). OMEGA and SIGMA were created to give the commanders of I and II Field Forces, Vietnam, a long-range reconnaissance capability to use in remote areas of their corps tactical zones (CTZs).

OMEGA and SIGMA were similarly organized. Each consisted of approximately 900 Civilian Irregular Defense Group (CIDG) troops and 125 U.S. Special Forces (SF) personnel. Each included a reconnaissance element, a reaction force, and an advisory command element, organized as a modified B detachment.

The reconnaissance element was composed of eight "Roadrunner" teams and eight reconnaissance teams. The "Roadrunner" teams, made up of four indigenous personnel each, conducted long-distance reconnaissance over trail networks by infiltrating Việt Công–held territory, using members dressed in regional People's Army of Vietnam (PAVN)/VC uniforms, armed with appropriate weapons, and carrying proper paperwork.

The reconnaissance teams, composed of two U.S. Special Forces personnel and four indigenous members, conducted saturation patrols throughout specified reconnaissance zones, gathering detailed intelligence on PAVN/VC movements, routes, and installations, and generated detailed terrain analysis.

Backing up the reconnaissance elements were three Mobile Strike Force Command ("Mike Force") reaction companies, each consisting of 150 airborne qualified CIDG personnel, led by 25 SF officers and men. Mike Force companies were employed to exploit small contacts, to aid in the extraction of compromised teams, and to perform reconnaissance-in-force missions.

Project SIGMA forces also participated in raids on prisoner-of-war camps in conjunction with mobile strike forces, but none of these missions was successful in recovering any American or allied prisoners of war.

Project SIGMA was located at Camp Hô Ngoc Tao near Thu Đuc, along Highway 1 between Sài Gòn and Long Bình. SIGMA forces were first sent into combat during Operation GOLF on 11 September 1966. Project SIGMA performed 15 operations in War Zones C and D before its assets were transferred to MACV's Studies and Observation Group (SOG) on 1 November 1967.

—James H. Willbanks

References: Kelly, Francis J. *U.S. Army Special Forces, 1961–1971* (1985); Simpson, Charles M. *Inside the Green Berets: The First Thirty Years* (1983); Stanton, Shelby L. *Green Berets at War* (1985); —. *Vietnam Order of Battle* (1986).
See also: Civilian Irregular Defense Group (CIDG); DELTA, Project; Mobile Guerrilla Forces; Mobile Strike Force Commands; OMEGA, Project; Studies and Observation Group (SOG); United States: Special Forces.

SIGMA I and II

U.S. military assessment operations; "war games." In 1963 the U.S. Joint Chiefs of Staff staged a war game code-named SIGMA I. The outcome confirmed fears that a military victory over the Việt Công in South Vietnam would require more than 500,000 U.S. combat troops. In September 1964 the Joint Chiefs of Staff conducted another war game, code-named SIGMA II, to assess the potential impact of a major air offensive against North Vietnam. The results of this game were no more encouraging. The war game report concluded that industrial and military bombing of North Vietnam "would not quickly cause cessation of the insurgency in South Vietnam." Indeed, the results of SIGMA II seemed to indicate that the United States had little chance of stopping a Việt Công victory. Despite these findings, political and diplomatic events during the next eight months pushed the United States closer to large-scale military intervention.

—James H. Willbanks

References: Karnow, Stanley. *Vietnam: A History* (1983); McNamara, Robert S. *In Retrospect: The Tragedy and Lessons of Vietnam* (1995).
See also: Bundy, McGeorge; LeMay, Curtis Emerson; McNaughton, John T.; United States: Involvement in Vietnam, 1954–1965; Wheeler, Earl G..

Sihanouk, Norodom (1922–)

Leading figure of modern Cambodia; at various times prince, king (1941–1955; 1993–1997), prime minister (1955–1960), head of state (1960–1993), palace prisoner, and guerrilla figurehead. Sihanouk tried in vain to keep his country out of the Vietnam War.

In the first of many displays of his independent will, Sihanouk expressed support for the Japanese when they temporarily interned the French administration in Indo-China on 9 March 1945 and proclaimed the end of the French protectorate. Within five years, motivated by an unshakable belief that he knew what was best for Cambodia, he managed to secure a firm grip on Cambodia's political evolution that he was not to give up until 1970. In 1953 Sihanouk embarked upon what he called a "royal crusade for independence" involving exchanges with Paris, travels abroad (in the United States, he was unimpressed by his reception by the Eisenhower administration), and even a well-publicized period of "exile."

The instrument of Sihanouk's political power in Cambodia was the Sangkum Reastr Niyum (People's Socialist Community), which he founded a month after his dramatic announcement of 2 March 1955 that he was abdicating the throne. Persuading his father to succeed him, Sihanouk took the title *Samdech Upayuvareach* (the Prince who has been King).

Sihanouk's efforts to keep Cambodia at peace proved only temporarily successful. First, he experienced increasing difficulties with two powerful neighbors, Thailand and the Republic of Vietnam. Their pro-Western regimes gave sanctuary to armed dissidents, which under the name of Khmer Serei broadcast anti-Sihanouk propaganda to Cambodia. A more serious threat to Sihanouk's control, however, was the growing use of Cambodia's eastern border provinces by Viêt Công and North Vietnamese forces fighting the Sài Gòn government. Such use of Cambodian territory was carefully camouflaged by Hà Nôi and the South Vietnamese National Liberation Front, which went to great lengths to maintain correct relations with Sihanouk's government.

When his father died in 1960, Sihanouk chose to leave the throne vacant and took the title head of state to let people know who was in charge. By the mid-1960s he was again having difficulties controlling Cambodia's destiny. On the border, there were repeated bombings of Cambodian villages by South Vietnamese and U.S. planes. In late 1963 Sihanouk ended the small U.S. economic and military aid programs in Cambodia; in April 1965 he severed diplomatic relations entirely. Trying to counterbalance the influence of Hà Nôi, whose demands on Cambodia now included the furnishing of rice and other goods for its soldiers, Sihanouk steered ever closer to China. But here, too, there was no salvation in sight; the Cultural Revolution absorbed China's attention, and his old friend Zhou Enlai had little influence. Moreover, Sihanouk suspected China of being involved in the only insurgency within Cambodia's borders, an agrarian-based movement that instigated a popular uprising against the army in the western region of Samlaut in 1967 and whose leaders Sihanouk habitually derided as "Khmer Rouge."

In 1969 Sihanouk renewed diplomatic relations with the United States and named a "national salvation government" headed by Gen. Lon Nol to deal with mounting insecurity in the countryside and to reverse his previous socialist economic policies, which were unpopular with the emerging middle class. The situation continued to deteriorate, and in early March 1970 demonstrations took place in Phnom Penh against the Viêt Công and North Vietnamese presence in Cambodia. On 18 March, while Sihanouk was abroad, the National Assembly unanimously voted to depose him as head of state.

Sihanouk arrived in Beijing hours later and issued a call for armed resistance to the leaders in Phnom Penh. It was the decisive moment in his career. Assured of China's and North Vietnam's backing, he refused to accept the Phnom Penh decision and proceeded to establish a broad political front and a military command, even though this meant accepting the preponderant influence of the Khmer Rouge, the only Cambodian group with the organization and the means to wage a guerrilla war against the Phnom Penh government and its U.S. backers. Sihanouk remained in Beijing, except for one hurried 1973 visit to Cambodian guerrilla bases, until after the Khmer Rouge capture of Phnom Penh in April 1975.

Sihanouk was returned to the royal palace in Phnom Penh by the Khmer Rouge as their virtual prisoner. They had no use for someone who represented in their eyes both the feudalism and the nexus of connections to Western democracies of the past. They used him only as a tool to preserve their seat at the United Nations (UN). Sihanouk wrote movingly of his detestation for the Khmer Rouge. Khmer Rouge xenophobia extended to the newly reunified Vietnam, and Sihanouk's cozy relations with Hà Nôi became a thing of the past.

A Chinese plane spirited Sihanouk to safety just before invading Vietnamese troops entered Phnom Penh in 1978. Once again he assumed the role of figurehead leader of a resistance movement, this time a coalition of two small non-Communist groups and the Khmer Rouge, who were still supported by China. This situation lasted for a decade, until the withdrawal of Vietnamese troops from Cambodia and an internationally brokered peace agreement under UN peacekeeping safeguards allowed Sihanouk to return in triumph to the refurbished royal palace in Phnom Penh in November 1991.

Expressing annoyance at UN interference in Cambodia's affairs, Sihanouk immediately declared that the policies of Hun Sen's government had been correct and likened them to those of the Sangkum instead of presiding impartially over a four-sided Supreme National Council as called for in the peace plan. In an astute move, he adopted the title *Samdech Euv* (Father Prince) and embraced Hun Sen as his adopted son. Elections to the National Assembly in May 1993 gave his followers, who had capitalized on his popularity in the countryside, a majority; however, they were forced to share power with the former Phnom Penh government in a two-sided arrangement in which his son, Prince Norodom Ranariddh, became first prime minister.

Sihanouk, never forgiving those who had deposed him, declared himself to have been retroactively head of state since 18 March 1970. No one in Phnom Penh dared contest his right to be head of state. A new constitution tailored to the requirements of the situation made him king once more, although Sihanouk himself modestly proclaimed he would reign but not rule in a parliamentary democracy in which he would remain above politics. The only factors that detracted from his triumph were his health and the Khmer Rouge. Cancer of the bone marrow forced him to spend months at a time in Beijing undergoing radiation treatment. Meanwhile the Khmer Rouge, having boycotted the elections, renewed insurgency while avoiding criticizing Sihanouk.

On 5 July 1997 Second Premier Hun Sen seized power in Cambodia and ousted Ranariddh, who fled abroad. After trying without success to mediate a solution, in October 1997 Sihanouk left Cambodia.

—Arthur J. Dommen

References: Chandler, David P. *The Tragedy of Cambodian History: Politics, War and Revolution since 1945* (1991); Hamel, Bernard. *Sihanouk et le Drame Cambodgien* (1993); Osborne, Milton. *Sihanouk: Prince of Light, Prince of Darkness* (1994).

See also: Cambodia; China, People's Republic of (PRC); Heng Samrin; Hun Sen; Khieu Samphan; Khmer Rouge; Lon Nol; Pol Pot; Vietnamese Invasion and Occupation of Cambodia; Zhou Enlai (Chou En-lai).

Simons, Arthur D. (1918–1979)

U.S. Army officer and strike force commander of 1970 Son Tây raid. On the night of 20 November 1970 Col. Simons led a 56-man strike team into Son Tây Prison, 23 miles from Hà Nôi, only to discover that the U.S. prisoners of war (POWs) had been moved weeks earlier. Simons's team, nonetheless, got in and out without sustaining a single casualty and inflicted many enemy casualties in the process.

Although some considered the Son Tây raid a dismal failure, for American POWs it was a much-needed psychological boost—proof that they had not been abandoned by their country. The North Vietnamese reacted by consolidating the widely scattered POWs, many of whom had been held in virtual solitary confinement for more than five years. Subsequently, they were together and could give each other support.

Simons received the Distinguished Service Cross from President Nixon. In 1971 he retired from the Army after being passed over for promotion to brigadier general.

—David T. Zabecki

References: Schemmer, Benjamin F. "Requiem for a Warrior: Col. Arthur D. 'Bull' Simons" (1979); —. *The Raid* (1976).

See also: Laird, Melvin R.; Nixon, Richard Milhous; Prisoners of War, Allied; Son Tây Raid; United States: Special Forces; Westmoreland, William Childs.

Sino-Vietnamese War (17 February–5 March 1979)

Eighteen-day war between the People's Republic of China (PRC) and Socialist Republic of Vietnam (SRV); sometimes referred to as the Third Vietnam War. The causes of the war were border disputes between the two states, the SRV's treatment of its Chinese minority, the PRC's determination to punish Vietnam for its invasion of Cambodia, and China's desire to weaken ties between Vietnam and the Soviet Union.

Although the actual territory in dispute was quite small, beginning in 1974 border incidents multiplied. Negotiations over the disputed territory, begun in 1977, broke off in 1978. More important economically were quarrels between the two states over the Paracel and Spratly Islands in the South China Sea and territorial waters in the Gulf of Tonkin, spurred on by the possibility of oil deposits.

The second major cause of the war was Vietnam's treatment of its Chinese minority, the Hoa. In the late 1970s, 1.5 million Hoa lived in Vietnam; many had been there for generations. Many Hoa, who were an important economic element of the country, refused to become Vietnamese citizens. In March 1978 the government abolished private trading and ordered removal of those in private enterprise into the countryside for agricultural work. Faced with this prospect, 170,000 Chinese fled overland into China, and many more attempted to escape by sea.

The flow of refugees reached crisis proportions as Southeast Asian countries refused to take in the large numbers arriving on their shores. The PRC protested, canceled aid to Vietnam, and withdrew technical advisors, accusing Hà Nôi of deliberately expelling its Chinese minority. The exodus slackened after July 1979 when Hà Nôi announced it

would take steps to prevent illegal departures, but it was nonetheless a serious cause of friction between the PRC and the SRV.

The third major cause of the war was disagreement over the 1978 Vietnamese invasion of Cambodia. Beijing regarded Kampuchea as being within its sphere of influence, and in early February 1979 PRC Vice Premier and Chief of Staff of the People's Liberation Army Teng Hsiao-ping said, "Vietnam must be punished severely, and China is considering taking appropriate counteraction." Chinese leaders also hoped that military action by the PRC against the SRV would relieve pressure on the Khmer Rouge, which it was supporting militarily.

A fourth cause of the conflict has been suggested by historian Bruce Elleman. He believes that the Chinese leadership used the brief war as a means to expose as a fraud Soviet assurances of military support for Vietnam.

The PRC appeared to enjoy tremendous advantages over its opponent, with its population of nearly a billion people and regular army of 3.6 million. But the 1979 war revealed Chinese weakness rather than military prowess. Other than a month-long clash with India in 1962, the People's Liberation Army (PLA) had not fought a major war since the Korean conflict. It was basically an infantry army, sadly deficient in many respects, and commanded by old men.

The PRC massed 18 divisions totaling 180,000 men; eight divisions made up the initial invading force. Eventually the Chinese had 600,000 men available for deployment. The entire Vietnamese military establishment was approximately 615,000 men. It was a modern army, relatively well equipped, well disciplined, and hardened in war. Unfortunately it was also widely dispersed, with only five divisions in Vietnam, four of which protected Hà Nôi. Guarding the China border were 70,000 well-armed members of the Border Security Force and some lightly armed militia units. The Vietnamese emplaced obstacles and minefields along the border and covered possible invasion approaches by artillery and mortars.

On 17 February 1979 Chinese forces led by Gen. Hsu Shih-yu attacked simultaneously at 43 points along the border to spread the Vietnamese defenders and probe for weak spots. The main attacks were along the half-dozen traditional invasion routes to Hà Nôi. The Chinese hoped to secure the key mountain passes as quickly as possible. Meeting intense Vietnamese opposition, the Chinese nonetheless accomplished this within several days. Soon there were some 200,000 Chinese troops inside Vietnam.

Cao Bang and Hà Giang fell on 22 February; by that date the Chinese controlled all the frontier passes. The Chinese resumed their advance a day later, while the Vietnamese made two small counterattacks into Chinese territory, both of which had only limited success.

The Chinese hoped to force SRV Defense Minister Vô Nguyên Giáp into redeploying units from Kampuchea and Laos, but Giáp chose to wait and see where the major Chinese thrust would develop. As Vietnamese frontier towns continued to fall, Giáp was forced to act. On 3 March he committed the 308th Division to the battle for the key railhead city of Lang Son. He also moved a second division north from Đà

Nang to support Vietnamese forces fighting around Móng Cái on the coast, and he ordered one division from Kampuchea, although it did not arrive in Tonkin before the end of the war. Had the war lasted longer, Giáp would have been forced to shift other divisions from Kampuchea. Not until 5 March, however, did Giáp order a general mobilization.

By early March the Chinese advance had bogged down. On average the Chinese had advanced about 20 miles into Vietnam. Then on 5 March Beijing abruptly announced that it had accomplished its ends and was withdrawing its forces. The Chinese carried out scorched earth policies, destroying what they could not carry away. The Vietnamese simply watched the Chinese depart. By 15 March the Chinese had withdrawn from Vietnam. The war exposed many Chinese weaknesses, especially in communications (largely bugles and whistles), transport, and weaponry. Remarkably, neither side committed its air forces.

Beginning on 22 February the Soviet Union initiated an airlift of supplies to Vietnam and over the next year doubled its military advisors and increased naval units in Vietnamese waters. In May 1979 the first Soviet submarines arrived at Cam Ranh Bay, where the Russians had been given naval facilities. Despite these Soviet moves, the war exposed the weakness of Soviet-Vietnam ties, effectively ending the SRV-USSR military pact.

—Spencer C. Tucker

References: Elleman, Bruce. "Sino-Soviet Relations and the February 1979 Sino-Vietnamese Conflict" (1996); O'Ballance, Edgar. *The Wars in Vietnam, 1954–1980.* Rev. ed. (1981); Young, Marilyn B. *The Vietnam Wars, 1945–1990* (1991).

See also: Cambodia; China, People's Republic of (PRC); Paracel and Spratly Islands; Refugees and Boat People; Union of Soviet Socialist Republics (USSR; Soviet Union); Vietnam, Socialist Republic of: 1975 to the Present; Vietnamese Invasion and Occupation of Cambodia.

SLAM

Military acronym for Seek, Locate, Annihilate, and Monitor. In September 1967, stung by media's portrayal of the siege of Côn Thiên as another Điên Biên Phu, Gen. William Westmoreland introduced the SLAM concept to Operation NEUTRALIZE. Devised by Gen. William M. Momyer, commander of the U.S. Seventh Air Force, it involved close coordination of the entire spectrum of Allied fire support to break the siege. Naval gunfire, tactical air support, B-52 bomber strikes, artillery, and other ground weapons were combined in a devastating concentration of firepower.

Beginning 11 September, SLAM elements pounded known and suspected Communist positions for 49 days. Momyer coordinated the strikes from a combined intelligence center in Sài Gòn. More than 3,100 Air Force, Navy, and Marine air sorties delivered almost 40,000 tons of bombs on targets around Côn Thiên, turning the area into a cratered moonscape. By early October the siege of Côn Thiên was lifted.

SLAM's success convinced Westmoreland that massed firepower alone could thwart future sieges of isolated posts. After Côn Thiên, Westmoreland criticized the media for its

pessimism as well as Vô Nguyên Giáp for foolishly providing such a target-rich environment. "If comparable in any way to Dien Bien Phu," Westmoreland concluded, "it was a Dien Bien Phu in reverse."

—Edward C. Page

References: Maitland, Terrence, and Peter McInerney. *A Contagion of War* (1983); Morrocco, John, et al., eds. *Thunder From Above: Air War 1941–1968* (1984); Westmoreland, William C. *A Soldier Reports* (1976).

See also: Côn Thiên; Khe Sanh, Battles of; Momyer, William W.; Westmoreland, William Childs.

Smith, Walter Bedell (1895–1961)

U.S. Army officer and diplomat. In February 1952 President Eisenhower appointed Smith under secretary of state. Many of Smith's efforts at the State Department were devoted to resolving problems in Indo-China. At a National Security Council meeting in January 1954, Smith argued for U.S. intervention to relieve the French garrison at Điên Biên Phu. In May he was unsuccessful in convincing the British to join the United States in an intervention for the same purpose.

Smith led the U.S. delegation to the 1954 Geneva Conference, where he played an important role in ending the first Indo-China War. He presented a plan to Soviet Foreign Minister Vyacheslav Molotov for an immediate armistice followed by a plebiscite, and he articulated U.S. resolve to support any anti-Communist government in South Vietnam. At the end of the negotiations, Secretary of State John Foster Dulles instructed Smith not to sign the Geneva Accords. Ironically, Smith's ideas served as a framework for the final settlement. In addition, Smith declared U.S. support for the security of the government of South Vietnam.

—Richard D. Starnes

References: Billings-Yun, Melanie. *Decision Against War: Eisenhower and Dien Bien Phu, 1954* (1988); Cable, James. *The Geneva Conference of 1954 on Indochina* (1986); Crosswell, D. K. R. *The Chief of Staff: The Military Career of General Walter Bedell Smith* (1991).

See also: Dulles, John Foster; Eden, Anthony; Eisenhower, Dwight David; Geneva Conference and Geneva Accords; Knowland, William F.; Molotov (born Scriabin), Vyacheslav Mikhailovich; Truman, Harry S.

SOMERSET PLAIN/LAM SON 246, Operation
(August 1968)

Joint U.S./Army of the Republic of Vietnam (ARVN) military operation in the A Shau Valley. SOMERSET PLAIN/LAM SON 246 occurred after the successful Operation DELAWARE, in which U.S. and South Vietnamese forces captured large amounts of war material and supplies in the A Shau Valley. The U.S. Military Assistance Command, Vietnam (MACV) then planned a follow-on operation to destroy the Communist forces and gain control of the valley, a Communist stronghold. While the 1st Cavalry continued its operations, the 101st Airborne Division (Airmobile) would move into the A Shau and block retreating People's Army of Vietnam (PAVN) forces. Combined U.S. and ARVN forces would then force the North Vietnamese into a decisive engagement.

SOMERSET PLAIN began in early August 1968 as the 1st Cavalry's 1st Squadron, 9th Cavalry guided in the initial assault elements from the 101st. Allied airmobile forces faced intense antiaircraft fire; one U.S. Air Force F-4 fighter-bomber was brought down, and seventeen helicopters were lost or damaged. Once the 101st had secured their landing zones, they linked up with ARVN and 1st Cavalry units. PAVN forces broke contact, refusing to commit to a major action against the Allies, and the operation became a series of patrols with minimal fighting. The major combat units of the 101st withdrew from the A Shau while their reconnaissance teams emplaced mines and booby-traps and set out sensors.

On 19 August helicopters lifted out the remaining 101st personnel as SOMERSET PLAIN terminated. For insignificant PAVN losses, the 101st had sustained significant losses in aviation assets.

—J. A. Menzoff

References: Olson, James S., ed. *Dictionary of the Vietnam War* (1988); Stanton, Shelby. *The Rise and Fall of an American Army: U.S. Ground Troops in Vietnam, 1965–1973* (1985).

See also: Airmobility; DELAWARE–LAM SON 216, Operation; Helicopters, Employment of, in Vietnam; United States: Army; Vietnam, Democratic Republic of: Army (People's Army of Vietnam [PAVN]); Vietnam, Republic of: Army (ARVN).

Son Tây Raid (20–21 November 1970)

Raid against a Democratic Republic of Vietnam (DRV) prison camp believed to hold U.S. prisoners of war (POWs). Planning for the Son Tây raid began on 5 June 1970 when U.S. Air Force (USAF) Brig. Gen. Donald D. Blackburn undertook a study to determine the feasibility of rescuing up to 50 POWs from Son Tây Prison, north of Hà Nôi. Meanwhile, a heavy rainy season fouled the well at the prison, and on 14 July the Son Tây POWs were moved to another compound. DRV military personnel remained at the prison, however.

On 8 August, Blackburn formed a task group to plan and carry out the raid. Brig. Gen. Leroy J. Manor and Army Col. Arthur "Bull" Simons had charge of the raid, and over the next three weeks they assembled a planning team to work out details of "Operation IVORY COAST." Training for the raid began on 20 August.

The plan called for Army Rangers to be flown to Son Tây by one HH-3 and four HH-53 Aerospace Rescue and Recovery Service (ARRS) helicopters supported by five Special Operations Force A-1E Skyraiders and two SOF "Combat Talon" C-130Es. The HH-3 was to crash-land inside the compound. Rangers would pour out of that helicopter to "neutralize" any opposition while other Rangers, landed outside the walls, would break in to complete the rescue operation.

Training was completed by mid-November, and the force assembled at Takhli Royal Thai Air Force Base (RTAFB), Thailand. With a typhoon developing over the Gulf of Tonkin, Gen. Manor decided to launch on 20 November 1970. At 1600 the raiders learned of their destination; by 2330 the task force was airborne and headed for the DRV. Meanwhile, an Air

Force and Navy air armada descended on North Vietnam. North Vietnamese defenses were completely befuddled, with one radar operator even announcing that an atomic bomb had been dropped on Hà Nôi.

Over Son Tây the two C-130s dropped napalm as reference points. In a moment of confusion, three rescue helicopters attacked a North Vietnamese sapper school near the Son Tây prison. One landed about 50 Rangers led by Col. Simons, who burst into the school, where a firefight erupted. The Rangers, who took no casualties, left scores of People's Army of Vietnam (PAVN) troops dead, or so confused they could not interfere with nearby operations. Within six minutes of hitting the ground at the wrong compound, the Rangers were back on the ground and battering their way into Son Tây prison.

Meanwhile, the HH-3E had crash-landed inside the walls at Son Tây, and Army Rangers were already killing the guards, but no prisoners were found. Twenty-seven minutes after the raid began the helicopters headed back to Thailand. The only U.S. casualty was an Air Force flight mechanic who broke his ankle. One USAF F-105F Wild Weasel was shot down, but its two-man crew was rescued.

The raid succeeded tactically; had American POWs been present they would have been rescued. On another level, Hà Nôi was sent the message that the United States was far from beaten. A substantial force, inserted a few miles from their capital, had wreaked considerable havoc before successfully withdrawing. To make any further such efforts more difficult, Hà Nôi ordered all POWs moved to several central prison complexes. This afforded the prisoners more contact with each other, which boosted morale.

—Earl H. Tilford, Jr.

References: David, Heather. *Operation Rescue* (1970); Schemmer, Benjamin F. *The Raid* (1976); Tilford, Earl H., Jr. *A History of United States Air Force Search and Rescue Operations in Southeast Asia, 1961–1975* (1980).

See also: Helicopters, Allied and Democratic Republic of Vietnam; Helicopters, Employment of, in Vietnam; Prisoners of War, Allied; Search-and-Rescue (SAR) Operations; Simons, Arthur D.

Sông Bé, Battle of (27 October 1967)

People's Army of Vietnam (PAVN) attack on the Army of the Republic of Vietnam (ARVN) base at Sông Bé. The area around the village of Sông Bé was one of five Allied-controlled enclaves in Communist-dominated Phuóc Long Province, near the Cambodian border. The province was a major route of passage for Communist troops and supplies moving from Cambodian sanctuaries to War Zone D, a Communist base area centered to the southeast of the province. During fall 1967 PAVN and Viêt Công (VC) forces initiated a series of battles to draw Allied forces to the peripheries of South Vietnam and practice mass assaults prior to the 1968 Têt Offensive.

Just after midnight on 27 October, the 88th PAVN Regiment attacked headquarters of the 3d Battalion, 9th ARVN Infantry Regiment, 2.5 miles south of Sông Bé. The assault opened with mortar and recoilless rifle fire striking the small ARVN installation, defended by 200 men. PAVN troops from at least two battalions of the 88th Regiment then attacked with 4-to-1 superiority in three waves, each of which reached the outpost perimeter before being driven off. As the PAVN attacks finally ceased at dawn, 50 ARVN soldiers aggressively pursued withdrawing Communist troops.

—Glenn E. Helm

References: Davidson, Philip B. *Vietnam at War* (1988); Westmoreland, William C. *A Soldier Reports* (1976); Wirtz, James J. *The Tet Offensive: Intelligence Failure in War* (1991).

See also: Côn Thiên; Đak Tô, Battle of; Lôc Ninh, Military Operations near; Têt Offensive: Overall Strategy; Têt Offensive: the Sài Gòn Circle; Vietnam, Democratic Republic of: Army (People's Army of Vietnam [PAVN]); Vietnam, Republic of: Army (ARVN); War Zone C and War Zone D.

Souphanouvong (1909–1995)

Laotian prince and Communist leader, the first president of the Lao People's Democratic Republic (1975–1991). When the Communists dissolved the third coalition government and seized power in December 1975, Souphanouvong was elected by a people's congress to be the president of the Lao People's Democratic Republic. In 1986, after suffering a stroke, he was forced to hand over effective power to an acting president and retired to his home, where he received visiting delegations from other socialist nations but played no other role in the conduct of state affairs. He was replaced as president in 1991 by Kaysone Phomvihan.

—Arthur J. Dommen

Reference: Zasloff, Joseph J., and MacAlister Brown. *Apprentice Revolutionaries: The Communist Movement in Laos, 1930–1985* (1986).

See also: Geneva Conference and Geneva Accords; Laos; Pathet Lao; Souvanna Phouma; Vientiane Agreement.

Southeast Asia Treaty Organization (SEATO)

U.S.-sponsored collective security arrangement for Southeast Asia. Instigated by President Eisenhower and forged by Secretary of State John Foster Dulles. The Southeast Asia Treaty Organization (SEATO) was created by the Pact of Manila of 8 September 1954. Eisenhower and the National Security Council agreed an alliance was essential to bind the imperiled countries of Southeast Asia, and Eisenhower directed Dulles to negotiate an accord to contain any Communist aggression against the free territories of Vietnam, Laos, and Cambodia, or Southeast Asia in general.

SEATO contained a protocol that thwarted the Geneva Accord's provisions designed to neutralize the new Indo-China states by naming Laos, Cambodia, and southern Vietnam as lands that, if endangered, could menace the tranquility and safety of the treaty's signers. Dulles insisted that the attached clause was necessary, despite its questionable legality, so that a blanket of security could be thrown around the region. Although France opposed full membership by its former colonies, Paris and Sài Gòn approved of the protocol's safeguard for a limited time over the military regroupment zone below the 17th parallel. Cambodia's Norodom Sihanouk

rejected the provision, and international accords affecting Laos in 1962 excluded it.

Ratified by the U.S. Senate in 1955, SEATO differed from the North Atlantic Treaty Organization (NATO) by failing to establish an effective multilateral defense system. Without permanent armed forces, members were to confer in case of aggression against a signatory or protocol state. SEATO fell short of gaining general support throughout the area because so few regional nations became members. The Eisenhower administration relied on SEATO, regardless of its shortcomings, to discourage potential Communist aggressors and to provide a diplomatic facade behind which the Republic of Vietnam emerged with a recognizable political boundary south of the 17th parallel.

SEATO proved its usefulness in the next decade. The protocol cover for Indo-Chinese countries provided legitimacy for U.S. involvement in South Vietnam in order to restrain the North Vietnamese. SEATO expired on 30 June 1977.

—Rodney J. Ross

References: Arnold, James R. *The First Domino: Eisenhower, the Military and America's Intervention in Vietnam* (1991); Hess, Gary R. *Vietnam and the United States* (1990); Moss, George Donelson. *Vietnam: An American Ordeal* (1994).

See also: Dulles, John Foster; Eisenhower, Dwight David; Geneva Conference and Geneva Accords; United States: Involvement in Vietnam, 1954–1965.

Souvanna Phouma (1901–1984)

Laotian prince, parliamentarian, and statesman, who played a major role in his country's independence movement and became the leader of the Neutralist faction in three successive coalition governments.

Souvanna Phouma first became prime minister on 21 November 1951. His government, having presided over Laos's participation in the 1954 Geneva Conference, lasted until 20 October 1954.

Souvanna Phouma became prime minister again on 21 March 1956, on a platform of reintegrating the pro-Communist Pathet Lao rebel faction. Although the Pathet Lao were under the titular leadership of Prince Souphanouvong, negotiations between the government and the Pathet Lao were a long process that brought Souvanna Phouma into conflict with U.S. opposition to a prospective coalition with the Pathet Lao. Souvanna Phouma persisted, claiming that Souphanouvong was not a Communist and that a neutral Laos had the support of neighboring China, with which he was on good terms—although China was not represented in Vientiane. His relations with the Democratic Republic of Vietnam (DRV) remained tense because of the Hà Nôi government's continued armed support of the Pathet Lao.

In November 1957, agreements were signed under which the Pathet Lao restored to the authority of the royal government the provinces of Sam Neua and Phong Saly and promised to integrate its soldiers into the royal army and to participate in elections as a legalized political party. A coalition government with Souvanna Phouma as prime minister was constituted. But after the Pathet Lao's political party, the

Neo Lao Hak Sat, won an electoral victory in partial elections to the National Assembly in May 1958, Souvanna Phouma faced a cabinet crisis and was compelled to resign on 23 July 1958. He then went to France as ambassador.

Returning to Laos, Souvanna Phouma was reelected to the National Assembly in 1960, and was subsequently elected its chairman. Kong Le, the royal army captain who staged a coup in August of that year, turned to Souvanna Phouma to form a government in the wake of the previous cabinet's resignation, and the prince became prime minister once more on 16 August. Souvanna Phouma resigned at the end of August, then was called upon by the king to form a new cabinet to include certain rightist ministers. The deal fell through and the rightists rebelled against him, with covert U.S. support, from their base at Savannakhet.

In December 1960 rightists attacked Kong Le's troops, and Souvanna Phouma fled to Phnom Penh, where he continued to maintain he was the legal prime minister. His government was no longer recognized by the United States and its allies. He set up his headquarters at Khang Khay on the Plain of Jars. After sporadic heavy fighting between the rightist army (supported by U.S. advisors) and Kong Le's neutralist army (allied with the Pathet Lao and the DRV, and supplied by a Soviet airlift), a cease-fire was negotiated on 3 May 1961. A 14-nation conference, convened in Geneva in June to deal with the Laos crisis, gave support to a coalition government with Souvanna Phouma as prime minister. The second coalition soon fell apart, but Souvanna Phouma remained in office throughout the war years, recognized by all foreign powers and eventually reconciled with the United States.

A fresh round of negotiations resulted in a new agreement, signed on 21 February 1973, and a bilateral coalition, the third. The Pathet Lao and North Vietnamese maintained pressure, and on 2 December 1975 proclaimed the dissolution of the coalition and the advent of a people's republic in which the hitherto clandestine Laotian Communist party, the Lao People's Revolutionary Party, held exclusive power. Souvanna Phouma resigned and was named advisor to the government of the Lao People's Democratic Republic, an honorary post he held until his death.

—Arthur J. Dommen

References: Dommen, Arthur J. *Conflict in Laos; The Politics of Neutralization* (1971); Stuart-Fox, Martin, and Mary Kooyman. *Historical Dictionary of Laos* (1992).

See also: Geneva Conference and Geneva Accords; Kong Le; Laos; Pathet Lao; Phoumi Nosavan; Plain of Jars; Souphanouvong.

Special Forces. *See* United States: Special Forces; Vietnam, Republic of: Special Forces (Luc Luong Đac Biêt, LLĐB).

Special Services. *See* United States: Special Services.

Spellman, Francis Joseph (1889–1967)

American Roman Catholic cardinal and strong supporter of U.S. involvement in Vietnam. One of the most politically influential religious leaders after World War II, Spellman obdurately supported U.S. intervention in Vietnam. After France's defeat in 1954, he rallied U.S. support for Ngô Đình Diêm and helped organize a pro-Diêm lobby in Washington. Although distancing himself from Diêm before the 1963 coup, Spellman hawkishly supported military escalation and served as vicar of the U.S. Armed Forces. Some antiwar protesters called the conflict "Spellman's war." As Pope Paul VI promoted a negotiated peace, Spellman argued that the Vietnam conflict was a "holy war" against communism that required total American victory. This break with the Vatican, and the American public's increasing polarization over Vietnam, diminished the cardinal's influence by the time of his death.

—Delia Pergande

References: Buttinger, Joseph. *Vietnam: A Dragon Embattled* (1967); Cooney, John. *The American Pope: The Life and Times of Francis Cardinal Spellman* (1984).

See also: American Friends of Vietnam; Antiwar Movement, United States; Ngô Đình Diêm; Roman Catholicism in Vietnam.

Spock, Benjamin M. (1903–1998)

Noted writer and antiwar activist. Between 1944 and 1946 Lt. Comdr. Spock practiced psychiatry in the U.S. Naval Reserve and wrote *The Common Sense Book of Baby and Child Care*, which would become the world's second-best selling book after the Bible. In 1960 he campaigned for John F. Kennedy, and he supported Lyndon Johnson's 1964 candidacy, accepting his campaign promises for peace. Frustrated by Johnson's failure to act, Spock began to speak against the war and to urge draft resistance. On 5 January 1968 he was indicted with four others for conspiring to counsel, aid, and abet violations of the Selective Service law and hinder administration of the draft. All but one of the "Boston Five" were found guilty, fined, and sentenced to two years' imprisonment. The U.S. First Circuit Court of Appeals reversed the convictions of Spock and one other defendant, declaring that "vigorous criticism of the draft and of the Vietnam war is free speech protected by the First Amendment."

—Brenda J. Taylor

Reference: Mitford, Jessica. *The Trial of Dr. Spock* (1969).

See also: Antiwar Movement, United States; Draft; Spring Mobilization to End the War in Vietnam; United States: Department of Justice.

Spratly Islands. *See* Paracel and Spratly Islands.

Spring Mobilization to End the War in Vietnam (15 April 1967)

First of the mass demonstrations in the United States against the war sponsored by national coalitions. The Spring Mobilization Committee to End the War in Vietnam set 15 April 1967 as the date to hold major demonstrations in New York and San Francisco. Organizers hoped that by focusing on only two sites, they could draw impressive crowds that would pressure the Johnson administration to alter its policy. The "Spring Mobe" leadership, which included veteran activists A. J. Muste, Dave Dellinger, and Robert Greenblatt, brought in James Bevel of the Southern Christian Leadership

Conference to direct the planning. The coalition invited cooperation regardless of political ideology, a stance that led some conservative groups to withhold formal endorsement. Still, the Spring Mobilization received broad support and revealed the breadth of antiwar sentiment.

On 15 April the New York crowd reached perhaps 200,000 people. Martin Luther King, Jr., served as keynote speaker, and Benjamin Spock, Pete Seeger, and Stokely Carmichael also spoke. The demonstration attracted a diverse crowd, including many first-time protesters. Preceding the New York march, nearly 150 people held a collective draft card burning in Central Park. In San Francisco, 50,000 people rallied in Kezar Stadium to hear Coretta Scott King, Julian Bond, Robert Scheer, and other speakers. The turnout was the city's most impressive to date.

The Spring Mobilization revealed that the antiwar movement was representative of the American mainstream. This challenge drew more attacks from the White House and Congress, whose members inaccurately criticized antiwar forces as Communist dominated and accused the protesters of providing encouragement to the enemy. Undaunted, the movement continued to grow.

—Mitchell K. Hall

References: DeBenedetti, Charles, and Charles Chatfield. *An American Ordeal: The Antiwar Movement of the Vietnam Era* (1990); Halstead, Fred. *Out Now! A Participant's Account of the American Movement against the Vietnam War* (1978); Wells, Tom. *The War Within: America's Battle Over Vietnam* (1994).

See also: Antiwar Movement, United States; Dellinger, David; King, Martin Luther, Jr.; Muste, Abraham J.; Spock, Benjamin M.

Staley, Eugene (1906–1989)

International economist who led a fact-finding mission to South Vietnam. Reporting to President Kennedy in August, Staley stressed the need for a self-sustaining Vietnamese economy and for meaningful and continued social and political reform. But his most lasting recommendation centered on protection of the civilian population. To this end he advocated major increases in Army of the Republic of Vietnam forces, the Civil Guard, and local militias. He also called for issue of better arms and equipment at the local level. Finally, he called for construction of a network of strategic hamlets. Although this plan appeared conceptually sound, it was poorly suited for South Vietnam. Begun with high expectations in 1962, the program was fraught with corruption from the start, and the United States abandoned the effort within a year.

—David Coffey

References: Asprey, Robert B. *War in the Shadows: The Guerrilla in History* (1994); Fall, Bernard B. *The Two Viet-Nams: A Political and Military Analysis* (1963).

See also: Agroville Campaign; Ngô Đình Diêm; Strategic Hamlet Program; Thompson, Robert Grainger Ker.

STARLITE, Operation (18–24 August 1965)

U.S. Marine Corps operation aimed at eliminating the 1st Viêt Công (VC) Regiment. Operation STARLITE began near the Van Tuong Peninsula in Quang Tri Province.

Marine planners designed a three-pronged attack. It called for elements of the 7th Marines at Chu Lai to move south and block any VC escape north while units of the 4th Marines were helicoptered to three landing zones, named Red, White, and Blue, west and southwest of the hamlets Nam Yên and An Cuong. These Marines would then drive the VC northeastward toward the sea. Finally, elements of the 3d Marines would land on the beach due east of these hamlets, with amphibian and armored support, and drive west and north. Despite stiff resistance from VC forces, STARLITE succeeded in pushing the insurgents to the coast. Close air support, tanks, and naval gunfire were critical to the operation's outcome. STARLITE terminated on 24 August.

—R. Blake Dunnavent

References: Shulimson, Jack, and Charles M. Johnson. *U.S. Marines in Vietnam: The Landing and the Buildup, 1965* (1978); Stanton, Shelby L. *The Rise and Fall of an American Army: U.S. Ground Forces in Vietnam, 1965–1973* (1985).

See also: Airmobility; Amphibious Warfare; Armor Warfare; Naval Bombardment; PIRANHA, Operation; Tanks, Allied and Democratic Republic of Vietnam; United States: Marine Corps.

STEEL TIGER, Operation (April 1965–December 1968)

U.S. air interdiction campaign over the Hô Chí Minh Trail, particularly in the northern panhandle of Laos. Operation STEEL TIGER represented an unsuccessful use of limited air power in the Vietnam War. Although air planners hoped STEEL TIGER would complement the larger ROLLING THUNDER campaign, the political dangers of bombing Laos haunted the Johnson administration. Concern over possible Chinese or Soviet intervention, coupled with the potential wrath of the world community, drove Washington to restrict Navy and Air Force target lists. Civilians in Washington selected the targets, whch were then sent to air planners in Sài Gòn for implementation.

As with most limited uses of air power, STEEL TIGER did not stop the flow of North Vietnamese men and materials to the South. Visibility from the air was poor, and damage assessments were largely inaccurate. If U.S. airmen bombed a critical choke point, the North Vietnamese repaired it quickly or transferred supplies to bicycles. During the monsoon season most of the traffic was by foot, complicating air operations even further.

The development of target lists in Washington caused the command and control of air operations over Laos to become hopelessly muddled. Navy and Air Force planners were loath to compromise their autonomy by fully cooperating with each other. A simple cost-benefit analysis showed that the insurgents in the South were still getting enough supplies to prosecute the war. Hitting one North Vietnamese truck on the Hô Chí Minh trail cost the United States thousands of dollars.

In 1968 STEEL TIGER merged with Operation TIGER HOUND, which had focused on interdicting Communist supply routes in the southern Laotian panhandle. The newly christened Operation COMMANDO HUNT was to interdict supplies from the Democratic Republic of Vietnam all along the Hô Chí Minh trail.

—Lincoln Hill

References: Berent, Mark. *Steel Tiger* (1990); Berger, Carl, ed. *The United States Air Force in South East Asia 1961–1973* (1984); Gurney, Gene. *Vietnam: The War in the Air* (1985).

See also: Air Power, Role in War; BARREL ROLL, Operation; COMMANDO HUNT, Operation; ROLLING THUNDER, Operation; TIGER HOUND, Operation.

Stennis, John Cornelius (1901–1995)

U.S. senator, 1947–1989; conservative Democrat who opposed social welfare programs and supported military appropriations. Although wary of American entanglements overseas and skeptical about South Vietnam, Stennis believed that once committed, the U.S. could not retreat. A member of the powerful Senate Armed Services Committee, he favored maximum use of American air power against the Democratic Republic of Vietnam and Viêt Công positions in the South. Increasingly concerned that the war was draining stockpiles of weapons and supplies, he began to express a fear that the war might establish a precedent for U.S. entry into future wars without congressional approval. Although he supported President Nixon's Southeast Asia policies, Stennis worked to limit presidential war-making power. In 1971 he and Senator Jacob Javits cosponsored the War Powers Act.

—Robert G. Mangrum

References: Congressional Quarterly. *Congress and the Nation*. Vol. 7, *1985–1988* (1990); Davidson, Phillip B. *Vietnam At War: The History, 1946–1975* (1988); Karnow, Stanley. *Vietnam: A History* (1984); Olson, James S., ed. *Dictionary of the Vietnam War* (1988); Summers, Harry G. *Vietnam War Almanac* (1985); *Who's Who in America, 1984–1985* (1984).

See also: Fulbright, J. William; Humphrey, Hubert H.; Javits, Jacob Koppel; Johnson, Lyndon Baines; McGee, Gale William; Proxmire, William.

Stevenson, Adlai E. (1900–1965)

U.S. presidential candidate; U.S. ambassador to the United Nations, 1961–1965. A Cold War liberal, Stevenson favored anticommunism, internationalism, and containment. Visiting Vietnam in April 1953, Stevenson observed strong support among the people for insurgent leader Hô Chí Minh but never grasped the reasons. To counter Hô, he advocated land reform, national independence, and free elections. His belief in the domino theory shaped his later responses.

If Stevenson had private misgivings about military escalation, he kept them to himself. After Lyndon Johnson's 1964 election, Stevenson went on record in favor of restricting Chinese Communist expansion in Vietnam by political and economic means. He hoped to enlist Japanese and Indian assistance in the endeavor. In fall 1964, when UN Secretary General U Thant pressed for face-to-face negotiations between North Vietnam and the United States, Stevenson supported the idea but elicited no enthusiasm from Rusk or Johnson.

A controversy developed over Stevenson's real views soon after his death. In November 1965 CBS newsman Eric

Severeid reported his impression that Stevenson was ready to resign in a protest over Vietnam. During a previous encounter in June 1965 with the writer Paul Goodman, an antiwar advocate, Stevenson denied any intention of leaving the Johnson administration. Later he composed, but never sent, a letter to Goodman, couched in standard Cold War rhetoric, in which he endorsed the Johnson policy of containing Chinese Communist aggression by standing strong in South Vietnam. Subsequently he remained outwardly a Cold War warrior.

—Mark T. Gilderhus

References: Broadwater, Jeff. *Adlai Stevenson and American Politics, The Odyssey of a Cold War Liberal* (1994); Martin, John Bartlow. *Adlai Stevenson of Illinois* (1977); —. *Adlai Stevenson and the World* (1978); Walton, Richard J. *The Remnants of Power: The Last Tragic Years of Adlai Stevenson* (1968).

See also: Containment Policy; Domino Theory; Goldwater, Barry Morris; Johnson, Lyndon Baines; Kennedy, John Fitzgerald; Rusk, Dean; U Thant.

Stilwell, Richard G. (1917–1991)

U.S. Army general; chief of staff, Military Assistance Command, Vietnam (MACV), 1963–1965. In the first of two tours in Vietnam, Stilwell served as chief of operations (1961–1963) and later chief of staff (1963–1965), MACV. In 1965 he became chief of the Joint U.S. Military Advisory Group, Thailand, but in 1967 he returned to the United States to command the 1st Cavalry Division at Fort Hood, Texas. In 1968 Stilwell began a second tour of duty in Southeast Asia as commander of XXIV Corps. In 1972 he assumed command of the Sixth Army at San Francisco, California. The following year he was promoted to full (four-star) general and was given overall command of United Nations forces in South Korea. He retired from the Army in 1976.

—David Coffey

Reference: *Who Was Who in America with World Notables, 1989–1993* (1993).

See also: Military Assistance Command, Vietnam; United States: Army.

Stockdale, James B. (1923–)

Highest ranking U.S. Navy prisoner of war (POW) in Vietnam. Commander Stockdale was carrier air-group (CAG) commander on the U.S.S. *Oriskany* when he was shot down over North Vietnam on 9 September 1965. Stockdale was the leader of the Alcatraz Gang, the POW's Hall of Fame for hard-line resisters, and he authored the standard orders on adhering to the Code of Conduct. While Stockdale acted as the intellectual and political leader of the POWs, his wife Sybil founded the National League of Families of American Prisoners and Missing in Southeast Asia. Following his return from Vietnam in 1973, Stockdale was named president of the Naval War College and was awarded the Medal of Honor in 1976.

—Joe P. Dunn

References: Howes, Craig. *Voices of the Vietnam POWs: Witnesses to Their Fight* (1993); Stockdale, James B. *A Vietnam Experience: Ten*

Years of Reflection (1984); Stockdale, Jim and Sybil. *In Love and War: The Story of a Family's Ordeal and Sacrifice During the Vietnam Years* (1984).

See also: Hà Nôi Hilton (Hoa Lò Prison); McCain, John S., III; Prisoners of War, Allied; Tonkin Gulf Incidents.

Strategic Hamlet Program

Effort by Republic of Vietnam (RVN) President Ngô Đình Diêm to pacify the countryside and neutralize the Viêt Công (VC) insurgents. The Strategic Hamlet program was to provide security and a better life for the rural populace by settling them in protected hamlets, where government cadres could carry out economic and political programs. Based on the earlier Agroville campaign, the Strategic Hamlet program was inaugurated in 1961 and derived from British counterinsurgency expert Sir Robert Thompson's experiences in quashing the 1950s Malayan emergency. The situation in Vietnam was more complex than in Malaya, however. Well established and of the same ethnicity as the villagers, the VC were not easily identified and segregated.

Roger Hilsman and Walt Rostow in the State Department and embassy personnel in Sài Gòn favored the Strategic Hamelt program, but U.S. military leaders criticized the concept, believing that it tied military forces into a defensive posture. Lt. Gen. Lionel McGarr, head of the U.S. Military Assistance and Advisory Group (MAAG), felt this role was more appropriate for police than regular forces and instead urged military clearing operations.

Diêm, who undertook the Strategic Hamlet program without first informing the U.S., saw it as a way to get U.S. assistance while managing the program himself. Afraid of being perceived by the Vietnamese as an American puppet, he wanted control of the program to fend off critics, retain independence, and resist Washington's pressure for political reforms. Diêm and his brother Ngô Đình Nhu, who carried out the program, significantly changed Thompson's concept. Thompson proposed surrounding existing hamlets with security forces; Diêm and Nhu instead embarked on an ambitious plan to build fortified hamlets and relocate villagers. Nhu established three goals: the government would link the people in fortified hamlets in a communications network, allowing them to summon local forces in an emergency; the program would unite the people and bind them to the government; and the government would work to improve living standards.

Nhu wanted half of South Vietnam's 14,000 hamlets completed by early 1963 and exerted severe pressure on province chiefs, despite their lack of authority over local officials. The plans led to overexpansion, creating far more hamlets than Sài Gòn's forces could protect or its cadres could administer. Province officials often appeased Nhu with meaningless data. In 1962 the government designated 2,600 settlements in I, II, and III Corps as "completed," but U.S. officials concluded the quality of defenses and percentage of the population under government control varied greatly from hamlet to hamlet. Unrealistic goals encouraged a focus on superficial aspects of the program, such as erecting fences,

which often sufficed to officially reclassify an existing settlement as a strategic hamlet. The program imposed burdens on the people, controlling their movement and demanding guard duty.

In May 1963 Gen. Paul Harkins criticized the program's execution as superficial, because it left Communist-controlled hamlets and salients in government areas. He urged Diêm to expand the program more logically to consolidate his hold on the countryside.

The Communists initially limited their opposition, disseminating propaganda that compared strategic hamlets to prisons and inserting agents to collect taxes, recruit, and stir up resentment. By summer 1963, however, they were directly attacking the poorly built and weakly defended hamlets, severing links between them and nearby reaction forces. By July 1964, only 30 of the 219 strategic hamlets in Long An Province remained under government control.

After the Strategic Hamlet program ended, Thompson criticized its implementation on three grounds: Nhu attempted to control the program from the top down instead of winning political and popular support at the bottom; he created divisions between the youth and the village elders, the traditional leaders; and he underestimated the extent of VC penetration and was unprepared to take the measures necessary to eliminate it within the hamlets.

Faulty execution compromised a promising pacification program. The corruption-plagued Strategic Hamlet program failed to halt the insurgency, and it manifested the arbitrary and repressive aspect of Diêm's rule. However, the program's failure had a larger significance—pacification would be supplanted as a strategy for fighting the war. Two later pacification efforts, *Chiên Thang* and *Hop Tác*, were also poorly executed and failed to reverse Sài Gòn's declining fortunes in the countryside. In late 1964 the emboldened Communists began to infiltrate conventional People's Army of Vietnam units into South Vietnam to administer the coup de grace, a situation beyond the scope of pacification to remedy. Washington was forced to intervene with a bombing campaign and ground troops.

—Richard A. Hunt

References: Colby, William E. *Lost Victory: A Firsthand Account of America's Sixteen-Year Involvement in Vietnam* (1989); Hunt, Richard. *Pacification: The American Struggle for Vietnam's Hearts and Minds* (1995); Osborne, Milton. *Strategic Hamlets in Vietnam* (1965); Thompson, Sir Robert. *Defeating Communist Insurgency* (1966).

See also: Agroville Campaign; Harkins, Paul D.; Hilsman, Roger; Malaysia; Military Assistance and Advisory Group (MAAG), Vietnam; Ngô Đình Diêm; Ngô Đình Nhu; Pacification; Rostow, Walt Whitman; Staley, Eugene; Thompson, Robert Grainger Ker.

Students for a Democratic Society (SDS)

Leading campus-based antiwar organization. The Students for a Democratic Society (SDS) was organized in January 1960 to support civil rights and politically organize the urban poor. Tom Hayden, a University of Michigan student, was the organization's first secretary. In mid-1962 the SDS issued the

Port Huron Statement, calling for "true democracy" in the United States and an end to the arms race. It energized student activists to increase their involvement with the liberal wing of the Democratic Party, but SDS involvement with traditional politics was short-lived.

Hayden and his colleagues became increasingly radicalized, and following the Gulf of Tonkin incidents the SDS began to organize campus demonstrations and teach-ins to protest the Vietnam War. SDS members developed a sophisticated draft resistance program. In 1965–1966 the number of SDS chapters at U.S. colleges and universities doubled from 124 to 250, with membership of 31,000. At its peak, SDS had approximately 400 chapters.

In the later 1960s dissension overtook the organization, and antiwar demonstrations became more unruly. During the "Stop the Draft" week of October 1967, SDS leader Carl Davidson demanded that protesters burn government draft centers. Still worse was the 1968 Chicago Democratic National Convention, where SDS members and sympathizers fought with, and were battered by, riot police in the streets.

Vietnamization, a growing revulsion with violence, and the fragmentation of the New Left led to the SDS's demise. The organization's impact was significant, however. Although it did not change U.S. foreign policy, it did help block or scale back the military options Presidents Johnson and Nixon were initially prepared to use.

—Tracy R. Szczepaniak

References: Gitlin, Todd. *The Sixties: Years of Hope, Days of Rage* (1987); Miller, James. *Democracy Is in the Streets: From Port Huron to The Siege of Chicago* (1987); O'Neill, William L. *Coming Apart: An Informal History of America in the 1960s* (1971); Viorst, Milton. *Fire in the Streets: America in the 1960s* (1979).

See also: Antiwar Movement, United States; Democratic Party National Convention, 1968; Hayden, Thomas E.; Johnson, Lyndon Baines; May Day Tribe; Nixon, Richard Milhous; Teach-Ins, Sit-Ins; Weathermen.

Studies and Observation Group (SOG)

U.S. Military Assistance Command, Vietnam (MACV) subordinate command primarily concerned with covert operations and intelligence gathering. In 1964 the MACV organized the Studies and Observation Group (MACV-SOG), supposedly to evaluate the success of the military advisor program. Actually, this mission was a cover for highly classified clandestine operations throughout Southeast Asia. MACV-SOG was activated in January 1964 as a MACV subordinate command (not a Special Forces unit) under the direction of the special assistant for counterinsurgency and special activities (SACSA) in the Joint Chiefs of Staff at the Pentagon. SOG was a joint-service (Army, Air Force, Navy, Marines) command that by 1966 included more than 2,000 U.S. personnel, most of whom were Army Special Forces; and 8,000 indigenous personnel, including South Vietnamese and Montagnard troops. U.S. forces assigned to MACV-SOG also included personnel from the Air Force 90th Special Operations Wing, Navy SEALs, and Marine Force Recon. MACV-SOG's area of responsibility included Burma,

Cambodia, Laos, the Democratic Republic of Vietnam (DRV), and the Republic of Vietnam (RVN), as well as the Chinese provinces of Yunnan, Kwangsi, Kwangtung, and Hainan Island.

SOG was divided into several groups. The Psychological Studies Group, operating out of Huê and Tây Ninh, made false radio broadcasts. The Air Studies Group specialized in dropping and recovering special intelligence groups into Laos, Cambodia, and North Vietnam. The Maritime Studies Group concentrated its efforts on commando raids along the DRV coast and the Mekong Delta. The Ground Studies Group carried out the most missions, including ambushes and raids, monitoring the location of U.S. prisoners of war, assassinations, kidnapping, rescuing airmen downed in Communist-controlled territory, long-range reconnaissance patrols, training and dispatching agents into North Vietnam to run resistant movements, and booby-trapping infiltration routes and ammunition supply facilities.

In 1967 SOG reorganized its ground strike elements into three field commands: Command and Control Central (CCC) in Kontum, responsible for classified unconventional warfare operations throughout the triborder region of Laos, Cambodia, and Vietnam; Command and Control North (CCN) in Đà Nang, responsible for special unconventional warfare missions into Laos and North Vietnam; and Command and Control South (CCS) in Ban Mê Thuôt, responsible for clandestine unconventional warfare operations inside Viêt Công–dominated areas of South Vietnam and throughout Cambodia. These organizations included Spike Recon Teams, each composed of three U.S. Special Forces and eight indigenous personnel; Hatchet Forces, composed of five U.S. Special Forces and 30 indigenous personnel; and SLAM (seek, locate, annihalate, monitor) companies.

In March 1971 MACV-SOG's CCN, CCC, and CCS were redesignated as Task Force Advisory Elements 1, 2, and 3, respectively, and were charged with advising the RVN Strategic Technical Directorate Liaison Service, but this change had little impact on the actual activities of the former SOG commands. MACV-SOG was deactivated on 30 April 1972.

—James H. Willbanks

References: Simpson, Charles M. *Inside the Green Berets: The First Thirty Years* (1983); Stanton, Shelby L. *Green Berets at War* (1985); Stanton, Shelby L. *Vietnam Order of Battle* (1986).

See also: Civilian Irregular Defense Group (CIDG); DELTA, Project; Montagnards; OMEGA, Project; SIGMA I and II; SEAL (Sea, Air, Land) Teams; United States: Special Forces.

Sullivan, William Healy (1922–)

American diplomat; ambassador to Laos, 1964–1969. In 1961 Sullivan came to the attention of W. Averell Harriman, who had been charged by President Kennedy with negotiating an end to the Laos crisis.

Over the objections of more senior foreign service officers, Harriman designated the junior Sullivan as deputy U.S. representative to the Geneva Conference. Harriman and Sullivan successfully concluded the Declaration on the

Neutrality of Laos, signed on 23 July 1962. The relationship continued after the Geneva Conference, with Sullivan serving as special assistant to Under Secretary of State Harriman.

In December 1964, Sullivan arrived in Laos as U.S. ambassador and over the next four years was responsible for the conduct of military operations. Sullivan insisted on an efficient, closely controlled country team and imposed two conditions on his subordinates. First, the thin fiction of the Geneva Accords had to be maintained to avoid possible embarrassment to the Lao and Soviet governments; thus, military operations had to be carried out in relative secrecy, largely by Central Intelligence Agency (CIA)–led Hmong tribesmen. Second, no regular U.S. ground troops were to become involved, although U.S. airpower would be necessary. In general, Sullivan successfully carried out this policy. Sullivan occasionally clashed with U.S. military authorities in South Vietnam. He usually won these bureaucratic battles, as he had the confidence of President Johnson.

Sullivan left Laos in March 1969. As deputy assistant secretary of state for East Asian and Pacific affairs, he helped to formulate the proposals that the United States would put forward at the Paris peace talks on Vietnam. Sullivan then acted as chief deputy to national security advisor Henry Kissinger in Paris and played an important role in negotiating the agreement signed on 27 January 1973.

—William M. Leary

References: Castle, Timothy N. *At War in the Shadow of Vietnam. U.S. Military Aid to the Royal Lao Government, 1955–1975* (1993); Stevenson, Charles A. *The End of Nowhere: American Policy Towards Laos Since 1954* (1972); Sullivan, William H. *Obbligato, 1939–1979: Notes on a Foreign Service Career* (1984).

See also: Carter, Jimmy; Harriman, W. Averell; Johnson, Lyndon Baines; Kennedy, John Fitzgerald; Kissinger, Henry Alfred; Laos; Paris Negotiations; Paris Peace Accords; Rostow, Walt Whitman; Taylor-McNamara Report.

Summers, Harry G., Jr. (1932–)

U.S. Army officer and analyst of U.S. Vietnam policy. Summers served in Vietnam from February 1966 to June 1967, then attended the U.S. Army Command and General Staff College. He returned to Vietnam in July 1974 as chief of the Negotiations Division of the Four Party Joint Military Commission. In that capacity, he flew to Hà Nôi to negotiate with members of the North Vietnamese General Staff. When People's Army of Vietnam forces overran Sài Gòn, Summers was on the last helicopter to leave the American Embassy on 30 April 1975.

In 1979 Summers joined the faculty of the U.S. Army War College Strategic Studies Institute, where he wrote *On Strategy*, perhaps the most influential analysis of America's failure in Vietnam. After retiring from the Army, Summers became a widely noted military commentator and writer and the editor of *Vietnam* magazine. His writings have had a profound impact on American military thinking. In the continuing debate over the U.S. performance in Southeast Asia, Summers is a leading voice on the side that maintains that

U.S. forces never lost a battle. Tactical performance, however, is only a peripheral piece of Summers's broader, more significant argument.

On Strategy focuses primarily on the strategic level. Summers points out that the United States had no clearly defined goal and no strategic objective in Vietnam. He also shows that the lack of internal political support for the war violated Clausewitz's concept of the "Remarkable Trinity," which requires a unity of purpose among the government, the military, and the people before any nation's war effort can succeed. Summers's arguments underlie many important statements of U.S. national policy, most significantly the 1984 "Weinburger Doctrine." Many ideas in the U.S. Army's 1993 capstone manual of warfighting doctrine, *FM 100–5 Operations*, are paraphrased directly from *On Strategy*.

—David T. Zabecki

References: Bassford, Christopher. *Clausewitz in English: The Reception of Clausewitz in Britain and America 1815–1945* (1994); Summers, Harry G. *On Strategy: A Critical Analysis of the Vietnam War* (1984).

See also: Four-Party Joint Military Commission (FPJMC); Hackworth, David H.; Powell, Colin L.

SUNFLOWER, Operation (5 January–15 February 1967)

Peace initiative following the failure of Operation MARIGOLD. Operation SUNFLOWER consisted of a direct U.S. approach to Hà Nôi through the Democratic Republic of Vietnam (DRV) embassy in Moscow and a parallel attempt in London by British Prime Minister Harold Wilson, working with Soviet Premier Aleksei Kosygin. Lingering questions about MARIGOLD probably motivated both the United States and the DRV. These included whether the North Vietnamese had been serious about negotiating and whether the United States had been willing to use Janusz Lewandowski's Ten Points as the basis for a settlement.

In Moscow, the U.S. and DRV representatives essentially restated previous positions. Washington insisted on mutual de-escalation, while Hà Nôi demanded an unconditional halt to U.S. acts of war on the North as a precondition for talks. This impasse killed the Moscow channel; on 15 February the DRV terminated contact.

While Wilson pursued his peace overture with Kosygin, the U.S. position on the sequence of de-escalatory moves hardened. This was complicated by a letter from President Johnson to Hô Chí Minh. Although Wilson's impropriety in presenting a U.S. offer without permission contributed to the problems, U.S. bungling doomed this channel, strained American-British relations, and confused the Soviet Union and the DRV.

SUNFLOWER, during which the DRV and United States perceived each other becoming more rigid in its negotiating stance, stands as a diplomatic debacle.

—Paul S. Daum with assistance from B. J. Rogers

References: Cooper, Chester L. *The Lost Crusade: America in Vietnam* (1970); Herring, George C. *LBJ and Vietnam: A Different Kind of War* (1994); Herring, George C., ed. *The Secret Diplomacy of*

the Vietnam War: The Negotiating Volumes of the Pentagon Papers (1983); Kraslow, David, and Stuart H. Loory. *The Secret Search for Peace in Vietnam* (1968); Radvanyi, Janos. *Delusion and Reality: Gambits, Hoaxes, & Diplomatic One-Upmanship in Vietnam* (1978).
See also: Kosygin, Aleksei Nikolayevich; MARIGOLD, Operation.

SUNRISE, Operation (March 1962–August 1963)

Early pacification effort. Operation SUNRISE was a pilot project in the Strategic Hamlet program. The plan called for Army of the Republic of Vietnam (ARVN) troops to establish hamlets in one of the least secure areas in South Vietnam, an inhospitable area north of Sài Gòn in War Zone D.

In November 1962 correspondent Peter Arnett reported that only four of the planned fourteen hamlets had been constructed; that Bên Tuong, the main hamlet, "was falling apart"; and that hamlets had become "expensive internment camps." Gen. William Westmoreland noted in August 1963 Ben Tuong was overrun by the Viet Công but was nonetheless "a mecca for visiting congressmen and journalists, proof that American money was being spent wisely and well." Operation SUNRISE failed in its attempt at forced relocation of the peasants into strategic hamlets, and the National Liberation Front once again took control of the area. The operation ended in August 1963.

—Paul S. Daum, with B. J. Rogers

References: Arnett, Peter. *Live from the Battle Field: From Vietnam to Baghdad: 35 Years in the World's War Zones* (1994); Karnow, Stanley. *Vietnam: A History* (1983); Westmoreland, W. C. "Report on Operations in South Vietnam, January 1964–June 1968" (1968).
See also: Hickey, Gerald Cannon; Ngô Đình Diêm; Ngô Đình Nhu; Strategic Hamlet Program; Westmoreland, William Childs.

Surface-to-Air Missiles (SAMs)

A chief component in the Democratic Republic of Vietnam (DRV) air defense system. On 24 July 1965, a Soviet-built radar-guided surface-to-air missile (SAM) exploded northwest of Hà Nôi amid a flight of U.S. Air Force F-4C aircraft. Code-named the SA-2 "Guideline" by the North Atlantic Treaty Organization (NATO) and known to the Soviets as the S-75, this missile ushered in a new era in air combat. SA-2 missiles carried high-explosive warheads of approximately 300 pounds and could reach speeds up to Mach 3.5, but not until it was well over 25,000 feet in altitude. The SA-2 could compensate for aircraft maneuvers with an electronic guidance system. Its introduction denied U.S. aircraft the ability to operate at medium or high altitudes near SA-2 batteries. New technologies and tactics would be needed before the U.S. could regain these preferred operating altitudes.

The SA-2 and SA-7 were the most potent SAMs in the DRV inventory. The SA-2, although a significant weapon, shot down relatively few aircraft; of approximately 9,000 missiles fired between 1965 and 1972, fewer than 2 percent reached their targets. Nevertheless, the SA-2 triggered the creation of a permanent electronic combat doctrine in U.S. military aviation. Until late 1966, U.S. formations near active SA-2 battalions had to perform evasive maneuvers and sometimes jettison their bombs to escape missile launches. Bombing accuracy was often hindered by SA-2 activity. Without appropriate radar detection equipment, U.S. aviators were rarely aware that an SA-2 had targeted them until it was on the way. They would evade the missile by diving to low altitudes, where the SA-2 was less effective, but this maneuver brought the aircraft into the range of lethal antiaircraft artillery (AAA).

DRV missile sites, usually carved out of the countryside, allowed quick setup of an SA-2's radar vans, service vehicles, and missile launchers. A typical site was set up in a six-pointed star pattern. The lines of the star were roads and pathways for vehicles, with a missile launcher at each of the star's points. Cables were laid out ahead of time to allow for fast connections. Most important, the sites were quickly and expertly hidden. Until the advent of aircraft such as the U.S. Air Force "Wild Weasel," it was virtually impossible to pinpoint an active SA-2 site until its missiles were launched.

Compared to similar Western systems, the SA-2 was durable and required little training to operate. Each operator in the fire control battery had a highly specialized function, and only the battery commander could make decisions for the crew, based on orders from higher authorities. Initially, Soviet technicians manned the sites with North Vietnamese trainees, who assumed more responsibilities as the conflict progressed.

The North Vietnamese quickly proved themselves masters of hit-and-run missile attacks from camouflaged sites. The shuttling of missile battalions between prepared sites amounted to a deadly shell game, especially during Operation ROLLING THUNDER. SA-2 battalions often remained in a dispersed status, hidden in the countryside, until ready to resume firing. The battalions required about three hours to shut down and pack and four to six hours to unpack and begin operations.

After the 1968 bombing halt, SA-2 battalions, heretofore seen only in the DRV, began deploying along the Hồ Chí Minh Trail. SA-2s were also deployed with ground units in the South during the 1972 Easter Offensive, which also saw the first appearance of the hand-held SA-7 "Grail" infrared-guided missile, a "tail chase" weapon. Like the SA-2, the "Grail" could be out-maneuvered by jet fighter aircraft if the latter had enough warning, but this missile proved to be the bane of low-flying aircraft such as Army helicopters and Air Force O-2s, OV-10s, A-1s, and even A-37s. When possible, slow-maneuvering aircraft operated above 10,000 feet to fly above the range of this missile, or used decoy flares.

By 1972 the DRV's SAM system was one of the most sophisticated and formidable in the world. Through 1968 alone, it was partially responsible for downing 922 fixed-wing aircraft over the DRV. The system also forced the United States to respond by developing an equally sophisticated method of aerial attack. This method, which included new aircraft, early precision guided munitions, and substantial improvements in electronic warfare, slowed the rate of U.S. losses, but it never completely overcame the threat posed by DRV SAMs.

—Patrick K. Barker

References: Morocco, John. *Thunder From Above: Air War 1941–1968* (1984); Momyer, William W. *Airpower in Three Wars* (1978); Nordeen, Lon O. Jr. *Air Warfare in the Missile Age* (1985).

See also: Air Defense, Democratic Republic of Vietnam; Antiaircraft Artillery, Allied and Democratic Republic of Vietnam; BARREL ROLL, Operation; LINEBACKER I, Operation; LINEBACKER II, Operation; Rockets; ROLLING THUNDER, Operation.

Tache d'huile

"Oil slick"; French term for the pacification technique of first securing key population centers and then expanding outward from them, much as an oil slick spreads on water. This process, pioneered by Marshal Louis Hubert Gonzalve Lyautey in Morocco, worked well in flat, open areas where there were only a few watering holes, but it was not well suited to Vietnam. Nonetheless, the French attempted to utilize the oil slick method throughout the Indo-China War, first securing the population centers and then attempting to expand their control into the countryside. In Vietnam it never had a chance of success because French forces were insufficient for the task.

—Spencer C. Tucker

Reference: Maurois, André. *Lyautey* (1931).
See also: Quadrillage/Ratissage.

Taiwan. *See* China, Republic of (ROC; Taiwan).

Tân Sơn Nhut

Major Republic of Vietnam Air Force (VNAF) and U.S. Air Force (USAF) base near Sài Gòn; headquarters, U.S. Military Assistance Command, Vietnam (MACV). In October 1961 the first U.S. air control unit was established at Tân Sơn Nhut, and later that month the first USAF tactical reconnaissance missions were flown from there. MACV's Army air operations section was colocated at Tân Sơn Nhut with the joint USAF-VNAF air operations center in August 1964. In 1967 the base became headquarters to MACV. Handling 70,000 sorties per month by 1969, Tân Sơn Nhut became the busiest airfield in the world. Because of its operational and logistical importance, Tân Sơn Nhut was the target of Communist military assaults. The most serious of these occurred during the 1968 Tết Offensive, when an attacking force penetrated 650 yards into the base and wreaked considerable havoc before being repulsed. Tân Sơn Nhut fell to People's Army of Vietnam forces during the 1975 Communist offensive. Rebuilt, it now serves as a major air terminus for the Socialist Republic of Vietnam.

—Timothy G. Grammer

References: Berger, Carl, ed. *The United States Air Force in Southeast Asia, 1961–1973: An Illustrated Account.* Rev. ed. (1989); Cinna, Ronald J., ed. *Vietnam: A Country Study* (1989); Heiser, Joseph M. *Vietnam Studies: Logistic Support* (1974).
See also: Air Power, Role in War; Hồ Chí Minh Campaign; Tết Offensive: Overall Strategy; Tết Offensive: the Sài Gòn Circle; United States: Air Force; Vietnam, Republic of: Air Force (VNAF).

Tanks, Allied and Democratic Republic of Vietnam

Allied forces in Vietnam deployed light tanks, tank-destroyers, and medium tanks, most of U.S. manufacture. Allied light tanks included the M24, M41, and M551.

The lightly armored M24 Chaffee tank, with its 75-mm gun, was a mainstay of French and Army of the Republic of Vietnam (ARVN) armor forces. It served with distinction in the Battle of Điện Biên Phu but had no cross-country ability. Replaced in ARVN units by the M41A3 in 1965, it was largely relegated to static pillbox duty at South Vietnamese installations.

The M41A3 Walker Bulldog mounted a 76-mm gun and used a crew of four men. The M42 Duster variant had twin 40-mm antiaircraft guns mounted on an M41 chassis and was used by U.S. Army forces.

The M551 Sheridan, designated an armored reconnaissance airborne assault vehicle, was deployed in Army armored cavalry squadrons beginning January 1969. With a light aluminum hull, this vehicle had a crew of four and mounted an unusual 152-mm gun capable of firing antitank guided missiles and high-explosive antitank rounds that could be used against vehicular and personnel targets. The Sheridan was unpopular with its crews because of its vulnerability to mines and rocket-propelled grenades and lack of "jungle-busting" ability. Its special cartridge cases could cause a catastrophic secondary explosion if the tank hit a mine.

The M50A1 Ontos was a lightly armored tank-destroyer fielded by U.S. Marine Corps antitank battalions. Its name— meaning "the thing" in Greek—aptly described its appearance, with six 106-mm recoilless rifles jutting from its turret. Its touchy fire-by-wire system resulted in more than one tragedy to friendly forces. Highly vulnerable to mines, it was relegated to static perimeter defense.

The LVTP5Al (land vehicle tracked, personnel) amphibian tractor, commonly referred to as an "amtrac," was used by the Marine Corps in its amphibious tractor battalions. The Marines, lacking armored personnel carriers, initially used the LVTP5A1 in their stead, but its vulnerability to mines led to their abandoning the practice.

The M48A3 Patton was the mainstay of Army and Marine tank battalions in Vietnam. Introduced in 1953, it mounted a 90-mm gun and had a crew of four. Its xenon searchlight provided infrared capability for nighttime engagements. This tank was initially deployed in Vietnam with the first wave of Marines in 1965, and 370 of them were serving in 1969 at the peak of U.S. involvement. A flamethrower variant could spray napalm up to 150 yards. Other variants included a vehicle with an attached 20-ton expendable mine roller and a command tank with a 2-ton dozer kit. ARVN forces were supplied with Pattons beginning in September 1971 as part of Vietnamization.

The M60 main battle tank did not see service in Vietnam. However, two vehicles based on its chassis were present: the M728 combat engineer vehicle (CEV), which carried a 165-mm demolition gun, and the armored vehicle launched bridge (AVLB).

The only non-U.S. tanks used by Allied forces in the Vietnam War were 26 British Centurion 5 tanks deployed there by Australian forces in 1968. The Centurion 5s had 84-mm guns and saw service near Vung Tàu.

Communist forces in Vietnam deployed Soviet and Chinese-variant self-propelled guns, amphibious tanks, and main battle tanks. Elements of the People's Army of Vietnam (PAVN) armored force, officially created in October 1959, appeared in South Vietnam fewer than six times before the end of 1973. As U.S. forces were withdrawn, the use of PAVN armor in the South became more common, and it played a dominant role in the final 1975 offensive.

World War II–vintage Soviet vehicles such as the SU76 and SU122 were used principally as assault guns by PAVN forces. The SU76, based on the obsolete T70 chassis, had a crew of four, mounted a 76-mm gun, and was lightly armored. The more common SU122, based on the T34 chassis, had a crew of five, mounted a 122-mm gun, and was more heavily armored.

The PT76 amphibious tank, first built in 1952 and mounting a 76-mm gun, was popular with the PAVN because of its versatility. The Chinese Type 62 variant mounted an 85-mm gun. About 400 of these vehicles were supplied to the PAVN, but their thin armor made them highly vulnerable to tank guns.

The Soviet T34, a renowned World War II main battle tank, was also supplied to the PAVN. It carried a 76-mm gun and had a crew of four. The T34 and its T34/85 variant that carried an 85-mm gun, while decently armored, were no match for the newer U.S. M48. Thus, they were rarely seen in South Vietnam and were used primarily for training purposes. They were superseded by the Soviet T54 (Chinese T59) and its slightly improved T55 variant. This tank mounted a 100-mm gun and had a crew of four. About 600 of these tanks were used by the PAVN armored force and saw considerable service in South Vietnam later in the war.

—Robert J. Bunker

References: Arnold, James R. *Armor. The Illustrated History of the Vietnam War* (1987); Dunstan, Simon. *Vietnam Tracks: Armor in Battle, 1945–1975* (1982); Pimlott, J. C. "Armour in Vietnam" (1990); Rosser-Owen, David. *Vietnam Weapons Handbook* (1986); Starry, Donn A. *Armored Combat in Vietnam* (1980).
See also: Armor Warfare; Armored Personnel Carriers (APCs); Grenades, Launched, Allied and Democratic Republic of Vietnam; Mines, Antipersonnel and Antitank; Rockets.

Tây Son Uprising (1771–1789)

General uprising led by three brothers from Tây Son (Bình Định Province) that ended in the capture of Gia Định (including present Hô Chí Minh City) and Thang Long (now Hà Nôi) and the weakening of the Nguyên lords in the south and the Trinh lords and the Lê Dynasty in the north. The rebellion began as a peasant protest against the corrupt rule of the Nguyên lords. Victorious over the Chinese, the brothers were propelled to national power and set out on an ambitious course to redistribute land and wealth to the peasants. Unfortunately, all three died in the early 1790s before their program could be completed. Within a decade the surviving Nguyên lord, Nguyên Ánh, came to power and reestablished the dominance of the Nguyên Dynasty under the name Gia Long.

—Robert K. Brigham

References: Lê Thành Khôi. *Histoire du Viet Nam: Des origines à 1858* (1981); Truong Buu Lâm. *Resistance, Rebellion, and Revolution: Popular Movements in Vietnamese History* (1984); Viet Chung. "Recent Findings on the Tay Son Insurgency" (1985); Whitfield, Danny. *Historical and Cultural Dictionary of Vietnam* (1976).
See also: Hà Nôi (Đông Đa), Battle of; Nguyên Phúc Ánh (Gia Long); Lê Dynasty; Nguyên Dynasty; Nguyên Phúc Ánh (Gia Long); Trinh Lords; Vietnam: from 938 through the French Conquest.

Taylor, Maxwell Davenport (1901–1987)

U.S. Army general; military representative of the president, 1961–1962; chairman of the Joint Chiefs of Staff, 1962–1964; ambassador to Vietnam, 1964–1965; presidential consultant on Vietnam, 1965–1968.

In 1960 Taylor wrote *The Uncertain Trumpet*, urging a reappraisal of military policy and advocating a buildup of conventional forces and the doctrine of flexible response. Taylor had long warned that brush-fire wars, not nuclear conflicts, presented the greatest military challenge to the United States. In July 1961 Taylor took on the newly established post of military representative of the president. Serving as Kennedy's chief military advisor, he also apprised the president on the adequacy of U.S. intelligence operations. The position made him the president's senior military representative at home and abroad.

In October 1961 Kennedy sent Taylor and Walt Rostow on a fact-finding mission to Vietnam. Taylor recognized a "double crisis of confidence" there: doubts about U.S. determination to hold Southeast Asia and doubts that Republic of Vietnam (RVN) President Ngô Đình Diêm's methods could defeat the Communists. Taylor advocated sending additional military aid and advisors while urging RVN reforms. Taylor highly recommended the dispatch of 8,000 ground combat troops, under the cover of a "flood control team" to overcome Diêm's sensitivity to foreign combat troops. He also wanted intensive training of local self-defense forces and a large increase in aircraft and support personnel. Kennedy approved the recommendations except for sending ground combat troops. This report, flawed by its deemphasis of political problems and underestimation of the Communists, marked the zenith of Taylor's influence.

In October 1962 Kennedy called on Taylor to serve in the nation's highest military position, chairman of the Joint Chiefs of Staff (JCS). Taylor and Secretary of Defense Robert McNamara were in general agreement on strategy and shared similar management styles that favored clear-cut decisions and emphasis on detail. The two made three trips to Vietnam together; perhaps the most important came in September 1963, when they noted great military progress and expressed confidence that it would continue. Two of their conclusions remain disturbing. The first, that "the security of South Vietnam remains vital to United States security," inhibited discussion of disengagement. The second, advocacy of a training program for the Vietnamese that would allow the

U.S. to withdraw the bulk of its personnel by the end of 1965, showed stunning naiveté about Vietnamese political and military potential.

Taylor was critical of the 1963 coup against Diêm, faulting the State Department and the CIA. In January 1964 he informed McNamara that the JCS favored the elimination of many military restrictions and sought "bolder actions." Taylor advocated an intensified counterinsurgency program and selected air and naval strikes against North Vietnam. He saw bombing as a deterrent to Hà Nôi's "aggression," a morale-booster in the south, and a means to bring the north to the negotiating table.

Taylor undertook his most controversial role in July 1964, when he succeeded Henry Cabot Lodge as U.S. ambassador to the RVN. He and Military Assistance Command, Vietnam (MACV) commander Gen. William Westmoreland began to "Americanize" the war. Taylor had little patience for the political complexities of the RVN, nor could he understand its leaders. By December relations between the ambassador and Prime Minister Nguyên Khánh became so strained that Taylor demanded Khánh resign, while Khánh threatened to ask Washington for Taylor's recall.

In early 1965 Taylor foresaw the probability of U.S. troop commitment, which, according to journalist Stanley Karnow, "rattled him." He now embraced the notion that the United States should avoid Asian land wars and told President Johnson that the Vietnamese lacked motivation rather than manpower. In February Westmoreland requested two Marine battalions to protect the air base at Đà Nang. In March Taylor returned to Washington to voice his objections to what he saw as the beginning of increased U.S. commitment. He believed that such a commitment would take too much of the burden from the Army of the Republic of Vietnam and encourage it to let the United States fight the war.

Taylor did not oppose the introduction of U.S. troops per se, but he did advocate their restrained use. He supported an enclave strategy that would secure major cities, towns, and U.S. military bases, mainly along the coast, by aggressive patrolling, rather than Westmoreland's search-and-destroy strategy. Taylor also opposed the immediate dispatch of additional U.S. troops.

The April 1965 Honolulu Conference saw a major shift in U.S. policy from counterinsurgency to large-scale ground war. It also represented a first step from Taylor's enclave strategy to Westmoreland's big-unit search-and-destroy strategy. Taylor's defeat on this issue ended the fiction of an all-powerful ambassador and was, according to journalist David Halberstam, the last time that Taylor "was a major player, his farewell in fact."

Returning to Washington in July 1965, Taylor was haunted by a sense of failure. Johnson thought that Taylor's intransigence had created unnecessary friction with RVN leaders, some of whom saw him as too outspoken to function as a diplomat. He nonetheless retained an important advisory role and joined Johnson's senior policy consultants, the "Wise Men." As late as 1973 Taylor still hoped for an acceptable outcome to the war.

—Paul S. Daum, with Elizabeth W. Daum

References: Cooper, Chester L. *The Lost Crusade: America in Vietnam* (1970); Halberstam, David. *The Best and the Brightest* (1972); Isaacson, Walter, and Evan Thomas. *The Wise Men: Six Friends and the World That They Made* (1986); Karnow, Stanley. *Vietnam: A History* (1983); Kinnard, Douglas. *The Certain Trumpet: Maxwell Taylor & The American Experience in Vietnam* (1991); Taylor, John M. *General Maxwell Taylor: The Sword and the Pen* (1989); Taylor, Maxwell D. *Responsibility and Response* (1967); —. *Swords and Plowshares* (1972); —. *The Uncertain Trumpet* (1960); Trân Van Đôn. *Our Endless War: Inside Vietnam* (1978); Young, Marilyn R. *The Vietnam Wars, 1945–1990* (1991); Zaffiri, Samuel. *Westmoreland: A Biography of General William C. Westmoreland* (1994).

See also: Central Intelligence Agency (CIA); Eisenhower, Dwight David; Enclave Strategy; Flexible Response; Honolulu Conference; Johnson, Lyndon Baines; Joint Chiefs of Staff; Kennedy, John Fitzgerald; Lodge, Henry Cabot, Jr.; McNamara, Robert S.; Ngô Đình Diêm; Nguyên Khánh; Radford, Arthur W.; Rostow, Walt Whitman; Rusk, Dean; Search and Destroy; Taylor-McNamara Report; Westmoreland, William Childs; "Wise Men."

Taylor-McNamara Report (October 2, 1963)

Report on U.S. government fact-finding mission to South Vietnam in September 1963. Dispatched to Vietnam in late September 1963, the mission was led by Chairman of the Joint Chiefs of Staff Gen. Maxwell Taylor and Defense Secretary Robert S. McNamara. The group included William Bundy of the Defense Department, the CIA's William Colby, White House advisor Michael Forrestal, and diplomat William Sullivan. Their major goals were to evaluate the progress of the war, recommend courses of action, and assess the prospects of a coup d'état. Plans to overthrow Diêm had been in progress since May.

The eight-day visit resulted in different opinions. Taylor was convinced by U.S. Military Assistance Command, Vietnam (MACV) commander Gen. Paul Harkins's optimistic evaluation of the war and thought that 1,000 U.S. advisors might be withdrawn by the end of the year if the war continued to go well. Most civilian members were not as optimistic and agreed with Ambassador Henry Cabot Lodge's warning about Diêm's political fragility. They were even more convinced of this after a meeting with Diem in Sài Gòn, when he rejected McNamara's concerns over South Vietnamese political unrest.

The mission returned to Washington on 2 October. Their subsequent Taylor-McNamara Report reflected mixed opinions. They expressed optimism about the war's progress yet warned that the Ngô brothers' policies could endanger this. The mission believed that there was only a slight chance of a military coup and did not recommend that the United States support such a coup at the time. They also recommended selective economic and psychological measures that would convince Diêm to change his course of policy but would not endanger the war's progress. These measures included a major reduction in U.S. economic and military aid to the RVN and the recall of John Richardson, pro-Diêm chief of the CIA station in Sài Gòn.

In spite of the Kennedy administration's intentions, these

measures did not change President Diêm's domestic policy. They did, however, signal U.S. dissatisfaction with Diêm's regime and helped encourage the 1 November 1963 coup against him.

—Zsolt J. Varga

References: Moss, George Donelson. *Vietnam: An American Ordeal* (1990); Ruskin, Marcus G., and Bernard B. Fall. *The Vietnam Reader: Articles and Documents on American Foreign Policy and the Viet-Nam Crisis* (1965); Rust, William J. *Kennedy in Vietnam* (1985); Young, Marilyn B. *The Vietnam Wars: 1945–1990* (1991).

See also: Âp Bac, Battle of; Bundy, William P.; Colby, William Egan; Forrestal, Michael V.; Harkins, Paul D.; Hilsman, Roger; Kennedy, John Fitzgerald; Krulak, Victor H.; Lodge, Henry Cabot, Jr.; McNamara, Robert S.; Mendenhall, Joseph A.; Ngô Đình Diêm; Ngô Đình Diêm, Overthrow of; Ngô Đình Nhu; Sullivan, William Healey; Taylor, Maxwell Davenport.

Taylor-Rostow Mission (18–25 October 1961)

U.S. fact-finding mission to the Republic of Vietnam. In response to a letter from Republic of Vietnam (RVN) President Ngô Đình Diêm, President Kennedy on 13 October 1961 asked his special military advisor Gen. Maxwell D. Taylor to make a fact-finding trip to Sài Gòn. The mission also included Deputy Special Assistant to the President for National Security Affairs Walt Rostow.

Taylor arrived in Sài Gòn on the day that President Diêm declared a state of emergency following a National Liberation Front (NLF) attack on a provincial capital near Sài Gòn. A flood in the Mekong Delta and increasing NLF violence had also upset the nation. Taylor was dismayed by Diêm's unpopularity, yet he remained convinced that no one was better qualified to run the country. Rostow apparently agreed.

Accordingly, the official Taylor-Rostow report to Kennedy on 3 November 1961 supported claims that the troubles in Vietnam were part of a Communist plan to take over all of Southeast Asia. The situation was considered serious, but the report concluded that the threat of bombing could help keep the Communists at bay. The report recommended that the United States express its willingness to help defend the RVN by upgrading the U.S. Military Assistance and Advisory Group (MAAG) to the U.S. Military Assistance Command, Vietnam (MACV), and by improving various intelligence and aid projects. Its most controversial suggestion was that U.S. military forces be sent to the Mekong Delta to assist in flood control. These units were to fight only if fired upon, but their main purpose was clearly to improve the low morale of South Vietnam's military.

Kennedy did not accept the troop proposal, but he did agree to change MAAG to MACV and to increase economic aid and the number of U.S. military advisors. These measures were largely implemented in December 1961, after a reluctant Diêm signed a letter promising to try and broaden the base of his support.

The Taylor-Rostow Mission marked a significant escalation of U.S. support for South Vietnam. Following closely upon similar recommendations from Vice President Lyndon Johnson, the mission reinforced the domino theory and argued for a far stronger U.S. commitment. After this point, it would be hard for the United States to withdraw aid without a serious loss of prestige.

—Peter K. Frost

References: Herring, George. *America's Longest War.* 2d ed. (1986); Hilsman, Roger. *To Move a Nation* (1967); Taylor, Maxwell D. *Swords and Plowshares* (1972).

See also: Domino Theory; Johnson, Lyndon Baines; Kennedy, John Fitzgerald; Military Assistance and Advisory Group (MAAG), Vietnam; Military Assistance Command, Vietnam (MACV); National Front for the Liberation of South Vietnam (NFLSV); Ngô Đình Diêm; Rostow, Walt Whitman; Taylor, Maxwell Davenport.

Teach-Ins, Sit-Ins

Antiwar protest activities. Teach-ins and sit-ins afforded Americans the opportunity to express their discontent peacefully.

In February 1965, as the United States began Operation ROLLING THUNDER, some University of Michigan faculty members wrote President Johnson to protest escalation of the limited, "brushfire" war. When Johnson subsequently sent 3,000 Marines to Đà Nang, the Michigan group organized a teach-in. On 24 March more than 3,000 students and faculty members participated in the first teach-in, using the forum to question the Vietnam War. Within six weeks of the Michigan forum, virtually all major universities (and several smaller ones) held their own teach-ins. The movement culminated on 15 May 1965 with a National Teach-In.

Sit-ins, used by civil rights advocates in the 1950s to protest segregation, did not gain notoriety until the 1960s, when college administration buildings and Reserve Officers' Training Corps detachments throughout the United States became targets of antiwar sit-ins. The most notorious sit-in occurred during 23–30 April 1968, when 700 to 1,000 students took over five buildings at Columbia University. A key goal was to pressure the school administration to break its ties with the Institute for Defense Analysis, a group of universities (sponsored by the Pentagon) that advised the Johnson administration on military matters.

Teach-ins and sit-ins raised questions and public awareness about the Johnson administration and its policies. They fueled the antiwar movement, put the administration on the defensive, and provided people with a nonviolent way to express their opposition to the war. Neither stopped the war, but their effects were far from negligible. However, as the war escalated, its opponents abandoned teach-ins and sit-ins for more violent forms of protest.

—Tracy R. Szczepaniak

References: Gitlin, Todd. *The Sixties: Years of Hope, Days of Rage* (1987); Miller, James. *Democracy Is in the Streets: From Port Huron to The Siege of Chicago* (1987); O'Neill, William L. *Coming Apart: An Informal History of America in the 1960s* (1971); Viorst, Milton. *Fire in the Streets: America in the 1960s* (1979).

See also: Antiwar Movement, United States; Democratic Party National Convention, 1968; Hayden, Thomas E.; King, Martin Luther, Jr.; ROLLING THUNDER, Operation; Students for a Democratic Society (SDS).

Television and the Vietnam Experience

Known as America's first "television war," Vietnam was the first war for which television was a primary means of providing information to the American public. From 1964 through 1973, reports were broadcast on nightly news telecasts of the three major U.S. television networks. Even the final storming of Sài Gòn and the evacuation of the last Americans from the embassy roof in 1975 was watched by millions of Americans in their living rooms. Viewers were eye-witnesses to the war, and this helped to shape their opinions of the war.

Television coverage of the war has both its critics and its defenders. Critics claim that television producers attempted to make their coverage visually dramatic, using short clips aimed at viewers' emotions rather than intellect, resulting in distorted views of events. More severe critics charge that biased liberal reporters provided distorted, intentionally inaccurate coverage that bordered on propaganda. Extreme views suggest that television helped decide the war's outcome.

Television coverage of the war was limited to available video footage. The U.S. military permitted almost all coverage; press accreditation cards directed "full cooperation and assistance" without censorship from U.S. units. Thus, successes and mistakes were equally available and were aired based on the reporter's or producer's judgment. The Communists, however, controlled access to information and events and limited coverage to footage provided by the state or foreign correspondents deemed acceptable to the state. This footage showed the People's Army of Vietnam (PAVN) and Viêt Công (VC) only in a favorable light.

Defenders of Vietnam War television coverage present it as essentially accurate and even-handed. They agree that it was not perfect, but they argue that the print media was equally prone to mistakes. Supporters claim that sources of inaccuracies were often the military and embassy public affairs officers who conducted daily press briefings, unceremoniously nicknamed the "five o'clock follies." Optimistic, often glowing reports of progress presented at these briefings often did not coincide with information reported from the field.

The 1968 siege at Khe Sanh and the Têt Offensive came to signify the controversy surrounding the media in general and television reporting in particular. Television and print media reporting of the battle at Khe Sanh emphasized parallels with the French defeat at Điên Biên Phu that brought about the French withdrawal from Indo-China. Although there were some similarities, the comparison was inaccurate and obscured the actual events and outcome. Television reporting of the 1968 Têt Offensive has borne the brunt of criticism. Critics claim that coverage focused on the sensational to the point of being inaccurate. Gen. William Westmoreland believed this played a large role in turning the American public against the war, transforming the failed Communist offensive into a "psychological victory." However, in the face of continually optimistic forecasts of victory expressed by the military and the Johnson administration, there is little wonder that televised reporting of the Têt attacks, which fell hard upon American and South Vietnamese strongholds, caused journalists such as Walter Cronkite, and those who trusted his interpretation, to view the war as a no-win situation.

One positive result of television reporting is the extensive video archives amassed primarily by the major networks, which have been helpful in producing documentaries about the war.

—Arthur T. Frame

References: Arlen, Michael. *Living Room War* (1969); Braestrup, Peter. *Big Story* (1983); Herr, Michael. *Dispatches* (1977); Lewinski, Jorge. *The Camera at War* (1978); *Vietnam: A Television History* (1983); *Vietnam: The Ten Thousand Day War* (1987).

See also: Cronkite, Walter Leland; "Five O'Clock Follies;" Johnson, Lyndon Baines; Joint U.S. Public Affairs Office (JUSPAO); Khe Sanh, Battles of; Media and the War; Têt Offensive: Overall Strategy; Têt Offensive: the Sài Gòn Circle; Westmoreland, William Childs.

Territorial Forces

Republic of Vietnam (RVN) military units similar in status to the U.S. National Guard or traditional militia. The Territorial Forces comprised the Regional Forces and the Popular Forces (RF/PF), popularly known as "Ruff-Puffs." Territorial Forces constituted about half of the RVN's military strength during the 1960s and 1970s. Although always poorly supplied and supported, they were the closest thing to a grassroots rural security system ever developed in the RVN.

The Regional Forces traced their roots to the 68,000-man Civil Guard created in April 1955 from the remnants of the Vietnamese National Army, French Union Forces, and other auxiliary units. In 1964 the Civil Guard was renamed the Regional Forces and was integrated into the RVN Armed Forces under control of the Joint General Staff.

The Regional Force's original mission was the manning of 9,000 fixed outposts scattered throughout South Vietnam. After 1955 their duties expanded to include fighting the Viêt Công (VC), providing support to the militia as a provincial quick reaction force, and guarding the nation's infrastructure by protecting communications and transportation systems and government installations.

The basic Regional Forces unit was the rifle company that could be augmented as required by river boat companies, mechanized platoons, heavy-weapons platoons, reconnaissance units, and administration and logistical support companies. Typically, Regional Forces operated in company-sized units, but they were capable of multicompany operations. In 1967 there were 888 RF companies; by 1973 the number increased to 1,810.

The Regional Forces went through several configurations, evolving from separate companies to company groups, battalions, and finally mobile groups. In 1969 the first mobile units were created and grew to 31 mobile battalions and 232 mobile companies by the end of 1970. By late 1974 plans were made to establish 27 Regional Forces mobile groups, but only seven such groups were operational by the fall of South Vietnam in April 1975. At the latest stage of its development, the Regional Forces consisted of 312,000 personnel.

The Popular Forces traced their origins to the 48,000-

man Self-Defense Corps created by the Ministry of the Interior in 1956. They were part-time, volunteer, village militia, whose basic unit of organization was the team. This varied in strength depending on the size and population of the province or district but generally consisted of from four to ten men per 1,000 inhabitants. Popular Forces teams were later increased to 30-man platoons. These teams were essentially infantry units, and their equipment and mode of subsistence were more austere than those of the RF.

Popular Forces teams, whose members held regular jobs in the community, performed security duties and protected their home villages, hamlets, and districts from VC attack. Inherently close to the population, they manned local outposts and watch towers, conducted night patrols and reconnaissance missions, laid ambushes, and searched houses for arms caches.

The Popular Forces were integrated into the South Vietnamese Armed Forces in 1964 and placed under control of the Joint General Staff. Below this level, they were administered by the Central Self-Defense Corps Directorate in Sài Gòn, which controlled offices at the province and district level, and commissioners in the villages. Unlike the Regional Forces, Popular Forces did not have a formal rank structure beyond team and squad leader designations, but all members received a monthly salary. Popular Forces totaled 220,800 members in 8,100 platoons in 1973.

Between 1961 and 1965 the Territorial Forces were under the authority of Army of the Republic of Vietnam (ARVN) corps and division commanders, who often used them as auxiliaries on search-and-destroy operations, for which they were ill suited because of inadequate training and often meager and outdated arms and equipment. This resulted in large losses, depressed morale, and numerous desertions. Although the Territorial Forces could theoretically call on the ARVN in a crisis, the regular military routinely failed to provide the Territorial Forces the necessary level of tactical or logistical support.

The ARVN viewed such groups as second-rate units, and most officers and noncommissioned officers sought to avoid service with them. To many South Vietnamese, however, the Territorial Forces were an alternative to the ARVN, and they often served as a haven for deserters and draft evaders. Recruitment reached record levels after June 1968, when a General Mobilization Law made every male citizen ages 18 to 38 liable for service in either ARVN or the Territorial Forces.

From 1965 to 1969, when the ARVN filled most local security needs with only limited assistance from the Territorial Forces, those forces received scant support from the ARVN and its allies. But Regional and Popular Forces took on a new importance as U.S. forces began to withdraw. As a result, U.S. Military Assistance Command, Vietnam (MACV) sought to improve the Territorial Forces' capabilities. MACV now recognized that the war could not be won without providing security in the hamlets, a role that Regional and Popular Forces could perform if adequately supported.

MACV first pushed to create more Regional and Popular Forces units in 1967 as a cheaper and ultimately more efficient and successful alternative to ARVN divisions. RVN leaders resisted this move, believing that the better-equipped ARVN divisions would be more successful against the VC and the People's Army of Vietnam (PAVN) than the lightly equipped and poorly trained Territorial Forces. Yet, the number of men in Territorial Forces units increased from 300,000 in 1967 to over 530,000 by 1971.

Major improvements were made in training. Starting in 1967 MACV created more than 350 mobile advisory teams (MATs), consisting of U.S. Army personnel, who trained and advised the Territorial Forces on small-unit tactics and pacification techniques while living among them for months at a time. The Americans also built and helped staff 12 provincial training centers throughout South Vietnam that operated until 1972.

Equipping the Territorial Forces was a major undertaking, as most units carried World War II–vintage weapons. After 1969 Territorial Forces received larger quantities of M16 rifles, M60 machine guns, light antitank weapons, M79 grenade launchers, and modern radio sets but remained dependent on the ARVN for their ground and air transport, heavy firepower, and artillery support.

The improved Territorial Forces took on an increased combat role between 1968 and 1972 as U.S. units withdrew. During this period the ARVN lost almost 37,000 soldiers killed in action compared to Regional and Popular Force losses of more than 69,300. The Territorial Forces were often subject to a higher rate of attack by Communist units than regular ARVN formations, and, except for 1968, it was always more dangerous to serve in a Regional or Popular Forces unit than in the ARVN.

Still charged primarily with local defense tasks after U.S. withdrawal, and too lightly armed and equipped to withstand massive and sustained attacks from regular PAVN units, the Territorial Forces were overwhelmed and largely destroyed during the final 1975 Communist offensive.

Overall, Regional and Popular Forces performed well while surmounting many obstacles and handicaps. In most areas in which they operated, they markedly improved rural security efforts. Although they received less than 20 percent of the total South Vietnamese defense budget, they accounted for roughly 30 percent of the Communist combat deaths inflicted by South Vietnamese Armed Forces (depending on the year) and consumed only 2 to 4 percent of the total cost of the war.

—Clayton D. Laurie

References: Donovan, David. *Once a Warrior King* (1985); Krepinevich, Andrew F., Jr. *The Army and Vietnam* (1986); Lewy, Guenther. *America in Vietnam* (1978); Summers, Harry G., Jr. *Vietnam War Almanac* (1985); Trần Đình Thọ. *Pacification* (1980); Ngô Quang Truong. *Territorial Forces* (1981).
See also: Civilian Operations and Revolutionary Development Support (CORDS); Hồ Chí Minh Campaign; Military Assistance Command, Vietnam (MACV); Strategic Hamlet Program; Vietnam, Republic of: Army (ARVN).

Tết Offensive: Overall Strategy (1968)

Decisive turning point of the Vietnam War. On 6 July 1967, the top leadership of the Democratic Republic of Vietnam (DRV) gathered in Hà Nôi for the state funeral of Senior Gen. Nguyên Chí Thanh, after which they met to consider plans to bring the Vietnam War to a speedy and successful conclusion.

Militarily, the war had not been going well for the Việt Công (VC) and People's Army of Vietnam (PAVN), who were unable to compete with U.S. military firepower and mobility. Thanh had favored scaling back operations in South Vietnam and conducting an even more protracted war to wear down the Americans. DRV Defense Minister Gen. Vô Nguyên Giáp, however, favored trying to end the war in one master stroke, like his triumph over the French at Điên Biên Phu. With Thanh dead, there was no major opponent on the Politburo to Giáp's plan. (However, according to Col. Bùi Tín, a former member of the PAVN general staff, the master stroke actually was proposed by Thanh in January 1967.)

Giáp's plan, borrowed from Chinese Communist doctrine, was based on the concept of the "General Offensive." Following the General Offensive would come the "General Uprising," during which the people of South Vietnam would rally to the Communist cause and overthrow the Sài Gòn government. The General Uprising was a distinctly Vietnamese element of revolutionary dogma.

The success of Giáp's plan depended on three key assumptions: The Army of the Republic of Vietnam (ARVN) would not fight but would collapse under the impact of the General Offensive; the people of South Vietnam would follow through with the General Uprising; and American will to continue would crack in the face of the overwhelming shock.

The General Offensive was set for Tết 1968, the beginning of the Lunar New Year and the most important holiday in the Vietnamese year. The exact timing and objectives of the attack were withheld from field commanders until the last possible moment. Giáp's buildup and staging for the Tết Offensive was a masterpiece of deception. Starting in the fall of 1967, VC and PAVN forces staged a series of bloody but seemingly pointless battles in the border regions and the northern part of South Vietnam near the Demilitarized Zone (DMZ).

In November 1967, troops of the 101st Airborne Division captured a Communist document calling for the General Offensive/General Uprising, which U.S. intelligence analysts dismissed as propaganda. Meanwhile, the Communists used the Christmas 1967 cease-fire to move their forces into position while senior commanders gathered reconnaissance on their assigned objectives.

The battles at Lôc Ninh and Đak Tô were part of Giáp's "peripheral campaign" designed to draw U.S. combat units out of the urban areas and toward the borders while giving Communist forces experience in larger-scale conventional attack formations. In January 1968 several PAVN divisions began to converge on the isolated U.S. Marine outpost at Khe Sanh.

Khe Sanh was a classic deception. Giáp depended on the Americans misreading history and seeing another Điên Biên Phu in the making. It worked, with the attention of most of the U.S. military and the national command structure riveted on Khe Sanh. The battle became an obsession for President Johnson, who had a scale model of the Marine base built for the White House situation room.

Lt. Gen. Frederick C. Weyand, commander of U.S. II Field Forces headquartered in Long Bình, was not deceived by the peripheral campaign. He did not like the pattern of increased Communist radio traffic around the capital, combined with a strangely low number of contacts made by his units in the border regions. On 10 January 1968, Weyand convinced Gen. William Westmoreland to let him pull more U.S. combat battalions back in around Sài Gòn. As a result, 27 battalions (instead of the planned 14) were in the Sài Gòn area when the attack came. Weyand's foresight would be critical for the Allies.

The country-wide Communist attacks were set to commence on 31 January, but the secrecy of Giáp's buildup cost him in terms of coordination. At 0015 on 30 January, Đà Nang, Pleiku, Nha Trang, and nine other cities in central South Vietnam came under attack. Commanders in Việt Công Region 5 had started 24 hours too early, apparently because they were following the lunar calendar in effect in South Vietnam rather than a new lunar calendar proclaimed by the DRV leadership for all of Vietnam. As a result of this premature attack, the Tết holiday cease-fire was canceled, ARVN troops were called back to their units, and U.S. forces went on alert and moved to blocking positions in key areas. Giáp had lost the element of surprise.

At 0130 on 31 January, the Presidential Palace in Sài Gòn was attacked. By 0340 the city of Huê was under attack and the Tết Offensive was in full swing. Before the day was over, five of six autonomous cities, 36 of 44 provincial capitals, and 64 of 245 district capitals were under attack. Except for Khe Sanh, Huê, and the area around Sài Gòn, the fighting was over in a few days. Huê was retaken on 25 February, and the Cho Lon area of Sài Gòn was finally cleared on 7 March. By 20 March PAVN units around Khe Sanh began to melt away in the face of overwhelming U.S. firepower.

Militarily, the Tết Offensive was a tactical disaster for the Communists. By the end of March 1968 they had not achieved a single one of their objectives. More than 58,000 VC and PAVN troops died in the offensive; the U.S. suffered 3,895 dead, the ARVN lost 4,954, and non-U.S. Allies lost 214. More than 14,300 South Vietnamese civilians also died.

Giáp had achieved great surprise but was unable to exploit it. By attacking everywhere, he had superior strength nowhere. Across the country the attack had been launched piecemeal, and it was repulsed piecemeal. Giáp also had been wrong in two of his three key assumptions. The people of South Vietnam did not rally to the Communist cause, and the General Uprising never took place—even in Huê, where Communist forces held the city for the longest time. Nor did the ARVN fold. It required significant stiffening in certain areas, but on the whole it fought well.

The biggest loser in the Tết Offensive was the VC. Although a large portion of the PAVN conducted the feint at Khe Sanh, VC guerrilla forces led the major attacks in the South, and they suffered the heaviest casualties. The guerrilla infrastructure developed over so many years was wiped out. After Tết the war was run entirely by the North; the VC were never again a significant force on the battlefield.

Giáp, however, had been absolutely correct on his third major assumption. His primary enemy did not have the will. With one hand the United States delivered the Communists a crushing tactical defeat—and then proceeded to give them a strategic victory with the other. Thus, the Tết Offensive is one of the most paradoxical of history's decisive battles.

The U.S. and the South Vietnamese government and military, although caught by surprise by the timing and the intensity of the Communist offensive, had still won overwhelmingly. As a follow-up, U.S. military planners immediately began to formulate plans to finish off the Communist forces in the South. Westmoreland and Joint Chiefs of Staff chairman Gen. Earle Wheeler were preparing to request an additional 206,000 troops to finish the job when a disgruntled staff member in the Johnson White House leaked the plan to the press. The story broke in *The New York Times* on 10 March 1968. With images of the besieged U.S. embassy in Sài Gòn still fresh in their minds, the press and the public concluded that the extra troops were needed to recover from a massive defeat.

The Tết Offensive was the psychological turning point of the war. U.S. military historian Brig. Gen. S. L. A. Marshall summed up the Tết Offensive as "a potential major victory turned into a disastrous defeat through mistaken estimates, loss of nerve, and a tidal wave of defeatism."

—David T. Zabecki

References: Braestrup, Peter. *Big Story* (1977); Oberdorfer, Don. *Tet!* (1971); Palmer, Bruce, Jr. *The 25-Year War: America's Military Role in Vietnam* (1984); Palmer, Dave. *Summons of the Trumpet* (1978); Summers, Harry G. *On Strategy: The Vietnam War in Context* (1981); Young, Stephen. "How North Vietnam Won the War" (1995); Zabecki, David T., "Battle for Saigon" (1989).

See also: Bùi Tín; Đak Tô, Battle of; Huế, Battle of; Khe Sanh, Battles of; Lộc Ninh, Military Operations near; Nguyên Chí Thanh; Tết Offensive: The Sài Gòn Circle; Võ Nguyên Giáp; Weyand, Frederick C.; Westmoreland, William Childs; Wheeler, Earle G.

Tết Offensive: the Sài Gòn Circle (1968)

The primary Communist objectives during the 1968 Tết Offensive were Sài Gòn and the major U.S. and Army of the Republic of Vietnam (ARVN) bases in nearby Long Bình and Biên Hòa. The vital strategic area was called the "Sài Gòn Circle."

As a gesture of confidence in the ARVN, the U.S. Command on 15 December 1967 turned over sole responsibility for the defense of Sài Gòn to the South Vietnamese military. The main task of securing the capital fell to the ARVN 5th Ranger Group, supported by the 2d Battalion, U.S. 13th Artillery, the only U.S. combat unit remaining inside the city.

Meanwhile, 39 maneuver battalions of the U.S. II Field Forces were earmarked for operations against Việt Công (VC) and People's Army of Vietnam (PAVN) base camps near the Cambodian border. These operations were a direct response to the "peripheral campaign" of PAVN Gen. Võ Nguyên Giáp,

who was attempting to draw U.S. forces away from the major cities prior to launching the Tết Offensive.

Giáp's deception plan almost worked. If the U.S. border campaign had continued on schedule, only 14 U.S. and Free World combat battalions would have been inside the Sài Gòn Circle when the Tết attacks were launched on 31 January 1968. But the commander of II Field Force, Lt. Gen. Frederick C. Weyand, did not like the operational patterns that were emerging, and on 10 January 1968 he took his concerns to Gen. William Westmoreland, who allowed Weyand to pull more of his battalions in toward the capital. When the Communist attacks were finally launched, there were 27 combat battalions back inside the Sài Gòn Circle. Weyand's keen analysis and subsequent action turned the battle before it started.

A primary indicator of the importance the Communists placed on the Sài Gòn Circle objective was reflected in the command structure for the attacks. The entire operation was under the command of Lt. Gen. Trân Van Trà, the second highest-ranking PAVN general. Just prior to Christmas 1967, Trà shifted his headquarters to the outskirts of Sài Gòn, accounting for the increased communications traffic noted by Weyand. Trà's new headquarters was colocated with that of Col. Trân Van Đac, chief VC political officer for the area. They were joined by Maj. Gen. Trân Đô, VC commander for the operation. In all the Communists had a force equivalent of 35 battalions, organized into one PAVN and two VC divisions.

The combined Communist command had eight major objectives for the Sài Gòn Circle, which they believed would cripple the Sài Gòn government and trigger the anticipated "General Uprising." In Sài Gòn itself, VC and PAVN forces were to seize and neutralize all key government command, control, and communications centers; take the artillery and tank depots at Gò Vâp; neutralize Tân Son Nhut Air Base and the U.S. Military Assistance Command, Vietnam (MACV) command center there; seize Cho Lon, the ethnic Chinese district of Sài Gòn; and destroy the Newport Bridge linking Sài Gòn to Long Bình and Biên Hòa on Highway 1. In Long Bình the primary objective was the massive U.S. logistics depot and U.S. II Field Force headquarters. In Biên Hòa the targets were the U.S. Air Base and ARVN III Corps headquarters. Supporting forces on the outer edges of the Circle were to block any attempts by the U.S. 25th Infantry Division to reinforce Sài Gòn from Cu Chi along Highway 1 and prevent the U.S. 1st Infantry Division from reinforcing from Lai Khê along Highway 13.

Because of secrecy in the planning and buildup for the attacks, Communist forces suffered coordination problems. On 30 January, one day before the country-wide attacks were scheduled to start, Việt Công Region 5 commanders launched attacks against Đà Nang and eleven other cities. As a result, the Tết holiday cease-fire was canceled and U.S. and ARVN units were moved into alert positions.

The official start of the Tết Offensive came at 0130 on 31 January, when a 14-man platoon from the Việt Công's C-10 sapper battalion attacked the Sài Gòn Presidential Palace. Forty-five minutes later, a 19-man platoon from the same battalion attacked the U.S. Embassy. Although the attacks spread throughout the city, Gen. Weyand coordinated the U.S. response from his command post at Long Bình. As the morning wore on, his most pressing headache was the most militarily insignificant—the U.S. Embassy. VC sappers never entered the embassy building, but it took until well into the morning to clear them out of the courtyard. The American media, meanwhile, flashed images around the world of the seat of U.S. power in Vietnam under siege. The result was a psychological impact far out of proportion to its actual importance. As the fighting progressed, Weyand sent his deputy commander, Maj. Gen. Keith Ware, into the city to form "Task Force Ware" and assume command of all U.S. forces inside the city proper.

North of the city, another platoon of the C-10 sapper battalion attacked the National Radio Station, accompanied by a PAVN specialist who carried prerecorded tapes announcing the General Offensive and General Uprising. The Communist troops seized the radio station with little difficulty, but they were prevented from making their broadcast when the link to the remote transmission tower was severed on a prearranged signal from the station's technicians.

The ARVN depot complex at Gò Vấp on the northern edge of the city was the objective of the VC 101st Regiment. The Communists succeeded in capturing the depot, only to discover that the tanks had been moved elsewhere the week before. They captured 12 105-mm artillery pieces, but the withdrawing ARVN troops had taken the guns' firing locks with them, rendering the big guns useless. Thus, a key element of the attack on Tân Son Nhut faltered.

During the evening of 30 January a large VC force had infiltrated the Vinatexco textile factory on the west side of Tân Son Nhut. At about 0320 the next day three VC battalions attacked the western end of the air base. In less than an hour, Communist forces were on the runway, and the fighting became hand-to-hand. With its main headquarters under threat, MACV sent a call for help to the 25th Infantry division at Cu Chi. The 3d Squadron, 5th Cavalry was already on alert for a possible relief mission to Tân Son Nhut. Squadron Commander Lt. Col. Glenn K. Otis immediately sent his Troop C down the road but, suspecting VC ambushes, flew ahead of the troop in his command and control helicopter, spotting and attacking the ambush sites from the air, and leading his troops around them. Troop C, vastly outnumbered, crashed into the rear of the Communist attack about 0600. It was mauled in the process, but the momentum of the VC attack was halted temporarily.

Otis flew back to Cu Chi and led his Troop B back down the same road. At Tân Son Nhut, Otis deployed them at a 90-degree angle to Troop C, fixing the VC in an "L." Otis then brought in his air cavalry troop and attack helicopters to finish off the VC. Otis and three of his soldiers were later awarded the Distinguished Service Cross. The 3d Squadron, 4th Cavalry also won a Presidential Unit Citation.

Thirteen miles east of Sài Gòn, the VC 5th Division simultaneously attacked the Long Bình–Biên Hòa complex. They were opposed primarily by the U.S. 9th Infantry Division's 2d Battalion, 47th Infantry, a mechanized unit commanded by Lt. Col. John B. Tower. Company A was sent to relieve the attack on the large prisoner-of-war compound between the two cities, and Company B was sent to reinforce the besieged garrison at Long Bình. As Company B arrived at 0630, VC sappers blew up part of the huge Long Bình ammunition storage dump; miraculously, few Allied casualties resulted.

Meanwhile, Company C was sent into Biên Hòa city to relieve the attack on the ARVN III Corps headquarters compound. At 0545 it plowed into the rear of the VC 238th Battalion inside the city. Dismounting from their armored personnel carriers (APCs), the soldiers engaged in city fighting more typical of World War II than of Vietnam. By that evening the city was secure.

While Company C was fighting to clear the city, Troop A of the 3d Squadron, 5th Cavalry was sent to relieve the attack on Biên Hòa Air Base. It had to fight its way down Highway 1 and through Company C's fight inside the city. Once it reached the air base, Troop A linked up with the 101st Airborne Division's 2d Battalion, 506th Infantry, which had been brought in by helicopter. Together they fought all day to eject Communist forces from the air base. At the end of the day, Troop A's lone tank had taken 19 hits and lost two crews, but it was still in action. Both Troop A and the 2/47th Infantry won Valorous Unit Citations for their actions on 31 January.

Most fighting inside the Sài Gòn Circle was over in days, except in Cho Lon, the teeming ethnic Chinese district of Sài Gòn. Initially, the area was attacked by the VC 5th and 6th Local Force (LF) Battalions; but as the fighting elsewhere petered out, most Communist survivors filtered into Cho Lon. The key to Cho Lon was the Phú Tho Racetrack, the hub of most of the key streets. By holding it the VC could deny its use to the Americans as a helicopter landing zone. The VC 6th LF Battalion took the racetrack, and from there it fanned out to consolidate control of the district. Communist political officers worked the streets to drum up support for the General Uprising, while others served arrest and execution warrants for the district's leaders. A month-long reign of terror in Cho Lon had begun.

Early on 31 January Gen. Weyand ordered units of the 199th Light Infantry Brigade into Cho Lon to reinforce the ARVN Rangers there. Company A, 3d Battalion, 7th Infantry reached Cho Lon about 0800. Six blocks from the racetrack they were ambushed and continued fighting their way house-to-house. After their initial attack on the track was repulsed by a well dug-in VC defense, the Americans tried again at 1630, this time with helicopter gunship support. The racetrack fell, and the Americans consolidated the position and brought in reinforcements by air.

The next day U.S. troops fanned out from the racetrack and started the long and torturous process of retaking Cho Lon. On 5 February the ARVN 5th Ranger Group started a "final push" to clear Cho Lon. For political and prestige reasons the South Vietnamese asked the Americans to pull back and let the ARVN finish the job. Five days later, the South Vietnamese asked the Americans to come back in.

Most of Cho Lon was finally cleared by 7 March, but sporadic fighting continued in Sài Gòn for the rest of the month.

In one of those final aftershocks, on 31 March, Sài Gòn Police Chief Maj. Gen. Nguyên Ngoc Loan was caught on film summarily executing a suspected VC prisoner. The image became one of the most famous of the Vietnam War and produced reactions of horror and outrage throughout the world. It was only one of many such incidents on both sides during the two months of fighting.

A few weeks later, Col. Đac, VC chief political officer for Sài Gòn, defected. The Têt Offensive was over. The VC and PAVN forces had failed to achieve any of their eight principal objectives, and they had suffered heavy casualties in the process.

—David T. Zabecki

References: Braestrup, Peter. *Big Story* (1977); Hoàng Ngoc Lung. *General Offensives of 1968–69* (1981); Oberdorfer, Don. *Tet!* (1971); Palmer, Dave. *Summons of the Trumpet* (1978); Zabecki, David T. "Battle for Saigon" (1989).

See also: Huê, Battle of; Nguyên Ngoc Loan; Têt Offensive: Overall Strategy; Trân Đô; Trân Van Trà; Vô Nguyên Giáp; Ware, Keith L.; Westmoreland, William Childs; Weyand, Frederick C.

TEXAS, Operation (20–24 March 1966)

Combined United States Marine/Army of the Republic of Vietnam (ARVN) reaction force to relieve a besieged Republic of Vietnam (RVN) Regional Forces camp at An Hòa. Operation TEXAS (known to the ARVN as LI N K T 28) resulted from a 19 March 1966 attack by the 1st Viêt Công (VC) Regiment on the An Hòa base, which was garrisoned by a single Regional Forces company. U.S. Marine helicopters flew in ARVN reinforcements and evacuated the wounded, but it appeared that An Hòa could not be held. At dawn on 20 March the 3d Battalion, 7th Marines, and the 5th ARVN Airborne Battalion were flown to within a mile of the fort and immediately went into battle, forcing the Viêt Công to withdraw. The 2d Battalion, 4th Marines, were then helicoptered to a position 4 miles south of An Hòa to intercept the retreating VC regiment. Allied forces successfully trapped and annihilated the VC force during two more days of fierce fighting. The Marines and ARVN claimed a total of 623 dead; Marine and ARVN casualties were termed "light."

—John D. Root

References: Simmons, Edwin H. "Marine Corps Operations in Vietnam, 1965–1966" (1985); Stanton, Shelby L. *The Rise and Fall of an American Army: U.S. Ground Forces in Vietnam, 1965–1973* (1985).

See also: Territorial Forces; United States: Marine Corps; Vietnam, Republic of: Army (ARVN).

TEXAS STAR, Operation (1 April–5 September 1970)

Military operation in I Corps conducted by the U.S. 101st Airborne Division (Airmobile) in cooperation with the Army of the Republic of Vietnam (ARVN) 1st Infantry Division. One brigade of the 101st assumed responsibility for pacification support and development programs. The other two carried out offensive sweeps through the western part of Quang Tri and Thua Thiên provinces. Operation TEXAS STAR clearly reflected U.S. military priorities for 1970: Vietnamization of the war, reduction of U.S. casualties, meeting the timetable

of withdrawal of U.S. forces, and U.S. combat operations only if intended to "stimulate a negotiated settlement."

Operation TEXAS STAR represented an effort to regain the initiative of the 1969 A Shau Valley campaigns lost during RANDOLPH GLEN's pacification efforts. Using a network of fire support bases, active patrolling, and aerial reconnaissance, TEXAS STAR attempted to halt PAVN infiltration. The five-month operation included action at Fire Support Bases (FSBs) Arsenal, Bastogne, Gladiator, Granite, Henderson, Kathryn, Los Banos, Maureen, Mink, O'Reilly, Ripcord, Sarge, and Tomahawk.

At FSB Maureen on the night of 7 May, Pfc. Kenneth M. Kays, a medic with Company D, 1st Battalion, 506th Infantry, earned the Medal of Honor. In the fighting the division's Ranger reconnaissance teams suffered heavy losses, including, on 11 May, an entire six-man team from Lima Company, 75th Infantry (Rangers). The 2d Squadron, 17th Cavalry, within the 101st's tactical area of responsibility, played a major role in supplying aerial reconnaissance and surveillance, but paid a high price in casualties and lost aircraft. On 8 July the largest action of the year saw troopers of the 2/17th engage PAVN forces on the move near Khe Sanh. An intense day-long battle resulted in 139 PAVN killed and four captured.

The battle of FSB Ripcord was the costliest of the year. From 1 to 23 July the firebase came under assault from rockets and 120-mm mortars. Two factors influenced Acting Division Commander Brig. Gen. Sidney Berry to disengage. On 18 July a U.S. Chinook helicopter was shot down and crashed into the main U.S. artillery ammunition dump, destroying the heart of Ripcord's defenses. Two days later Capt. Charles Hawkins, commanding Company A, 2/506th, reported that the opposing PAVN forces were between 9,000 and 11,000 men. On the morning of 23 July, having suffered heavy losses, the 300 remaining defenders of Ripcord executed a fighting withdrawal.

U.S. losses at Ripcord totaled 112 killed, 698 wounded, and 1 missing in action. U.S. Military Assistance Command, Vietnam, claimed for Operation TEXAS STAR 1,782 PAVN casualties. Other sources believe the toll was actually higher.

—Paul S. Daum, with Francis Ryan

References: Hawkins, Capt. Charles. Interviews with the author (1996); Linderer, Gary. "The 101st Airborne Division: The Vietnam Experience" (1995); Kamps, Charles T., Jr. *The History of the Vietnam War* (1987); Sigler, David Burns. *Vietnam Battle Chronology: U.S. Army and Marine Corps Combat Operations, 1965–1973* (1992); Stanton, Shelby L. *The Rise and Fall of an American Army: U.S. Ground Forces in Vietnam, 1965–1973* (1985); —. *Vietnam Order of Battle* (1986).

See also: Airmobility; Khe Sanh, Battles of; Pacification; Têt Offensive: Overall Strategy; United States: Army; Vietnam, Democratic Republic of: Army (People's Army of Vietnam [PAVN]); Vietnamization.

Thailand

Southeast Asian nation and close ally of the United States during the Vietnam War. Thailand provided military bases and combat forces to assist the Republic of Vietnam (RVN).

Although the Thais traditionally maintained a policy of non-intervention in Southeast Asia, they became suspicious of Communist intentions. Wishing to preserve their own independence while taking a more active role in regional defense matters, the Thai government joined 40 other nations in sending forces or other support to the RVN.

In September 1964 a 16-man Royal Thai Air Force contingent arrived in South Vietnam to assist in flying and maintaining cargo aircraft operated by the RVN Air Force. The Royal Thai Military Assistance Group was established in Sài Gòn in February 1966. Later in 1966, when the Thai government announced that it was considering sending combat troops to aid the South Vietnamese, 5,000 men volunteered almost immediately. In January 1967 the Thai government officially announced that it would send a reinforced combat battalion to South Vietnam.

In September 1967 the first elements of the Royal Thai Volunteer Regiment, the "Queen's Cobras," arrived in Vietnam and moved to Bear Cat, near Biên Hòa, where it was colocated with the U.S. 9th Infantry Division. The Queen's Cobras began combat operations almost immediately, launching Operation NARASUAN in October 1967, and quickly proved themselves to be a well-trained and resourceful force. Thai units were also active in civic action projects, building schools and roads and providing medical care to civilians.

Discussions between the Thai government and the U.S. Military Assistance Command, Vietnam (MACV) led Thailand to increase its troop strength in South Vietnam to an entire division. In July 1968 the Queen's Cobras were replaced by the Royal Thai Army Expeditionary Division, the "Black Panthers," which arrived incrementally and eventually included two brigades of infantry, three battalions of 105-mm field artillery, and an armored cavalry unit. The Black Panthers were joined by 48 U.S. Army advisors to assist in their operations. The area of operations (AO) assigned to the Thai force in the III Corps Tactical Zone was characterized by a low level of action because the land was used by the Communist forces as a source of food and clothing; thus, offensive actions were not as significant in the Thai AO as in other areas. Nevertheless, Thai forces fought effectively, primarily conducting search-and-clear operations supported by their own artillery firing from two Thai firebases. They also conducted extensive psychological warfare operations. By 1969 there were nearly 12,000 Thai combat troops in South Vietnam. In August 1970 the Black Panthers Division was redesignated the Royal Thai Army Volunteer Force, a title it retained throughout the rest of its time in South Vietnam.

The Royal Thai Air Force also contributed C-47 and C-123 cargo aircraft to what they called their Victory Flight. In 1971 Thai forces were gradually withdrawn, and the last Thai troops left Vietnam in April 1972. During the course of its commitment to the RVN, Thailand provided more military support than any other country except the United States and South Korea.

Thailand also contributed bases to the U.S. war effort. The U.S. Air Force operated from Thailand with the 8th, 355th, 366th, and 388th Tactical Fighter Wings and the 307th Strategic Wing. Strategic bombing operations over both North and South Vietnam often originated in Thailand. The United States also stationed the 46th Special Forces Company in Thailand, which was tasked with assisting Thai forces in resisting Communist terrorist (CT) guerrilla activity along Thailand's northeastern Laotian border and in the south on the Malay peninsula. Several U.S. servicemen were killed during 1967–1973 in anti-CT campaign. CT forces conducted several raids on U.S. Air Force bases in Thailand, notably at Udorn and U-Tapao, causing U.S. casualties. Other U.S. forces in Thailand included the U.S. Army 9th Logistical Command, 44th Engineer Group, and 40th Military Police (Battle) at Korat, the 29th Signal Group at Bangkok, and the U.S. Marine Corps Marine Air Group 15 at Nam Phong in 1972.

—James H. Willbanks

References: Larsen, Stanley Robert, and James Lawton Collins, Jr. *Allied Participation in Vietnam* (1975); Stanton, Shelby L. *Vietnam Order of Battle* (1986).

See also: Civic Action; Free World Assistance Program; Johnson, Lyndon Baines; Korea, Republic of; Military Assistance Command, Vietnam (MACV); Order of Battle.

Thành Thái (?–1954)

Tenth emperor of the Nguyên Dynasty, 1889–1907. The French placed Thành Thái on the throne after the death of Emperor Đông Khánh in 1889. During his reign, the French forced the Huê Court to eliminate the position of Kinh Luoc Bac Ky (Viceroy of Tonkin) and let its functions be taken over by the French Resident Superior. They also replaced the Co Mât Viên (Secret Council), the highest council of the imperial court, with the Council of Ministers headed by the French Resident in Huê. These events made Thành Thái openly anti-French. On 3 September 1907, the French forced Thành Thái to abdicate and replaced him with his son, Vinh San, who became Emperor Duy Tân.

—Pham Cao Duong

References: Hoàng Trong Thuoc. *Hô So Vua Duy Tân (Thân Thê và Su Nghiêp)* (1993); Lê Thành Khôi. *Le Viet-Nam: Histoire et Civilisation* (1955); Nguyên Huyên Anh. *Viêt Nam Danh Nhân Tu Điên* (1990); Nguyên Thê Anh. *Viêt Nam Duoi Thoi Pháp Đô Hô* (1970).

See also: Duy Tân; French Indo-China; Nguyên Dynasty.

Thích Quang Đuc (1897–1963)

Buddhist monk whose self-immolation in front of invited media protested anti-Buddhist actions carried out by President Ngô Đình Diêm's minority Catholic government in May 1963.

On 11 June 1963 Thích Quang Đuc arrived by automobile at Sài Gòn's intersection of Phan Đình Phùng and Lê Van Duyêt streets. Doused with gasoline by one of his disciples and then ignited, Thích Quang Đuc died without crying out or moving. Thích Quang Đuc's death as a martyr produced worldwide indignation, widespread antigovernment protests within Vietnam, and a growing realization within the Kennedy administration that Diêm was himself part of the Vietnam problem. Although eventually some 30 monks and nuns burned themselves, Thích Quang Đuc's act—as the first—remained the most shocking and served as the catalyst for the impending demise of Diêm and his regime.

—Paul S. Daum, with Trevor Curran

References: Curran, Trevor, and Elizabeth Daum. Interview with Buddhist monks, Thiên Mu Pagoda, Huê (1995); Esper, George, and the Associated Press. *The Eyewitness History of the Vietnam War, 1961–1975* (1983); Halberstam, David. "Diem Asks Peace in Religious Crisis" (1963); Prados, John. "We Are Spiritual in the Material World: The Rise of Buddhist Activism in South Vietnam" (1995).

See also: Buddhists; Media and the War; Ngô Đình Diêm; Ngô Đình Nhu.

Thích Trí Quang (1922–)

Buddhist monk and opponent of the Diêm regime. Buddhist monks such as Thích Trí Quang believed that if the United States left Vietnam and Ngô Đình Diêm's regime was ended, peace talks could be held and the country reunited.

Although the Republic of Vietnam (RVN) officially professed religious freedom, local discrimination and repression created doubts. In 1963, Buddhists in the RVN organized and discussed political action in response to Diêm's repression. On 8 May 1963, a confrontation occurred between Buddhists, who had gathered in Huê to celebrate Buddha's birthday, and Catholics. Thích Trí Quang was scheduled to give a speech but Maj. Đang Si, a Catholic, refused to allow it to be broadcast. Si then ordered his officers to throw a concussion grenade to disperse the crowd, killing a woman and eight children. In the following weeks, Buddhist protests escalated, and the government resorted to brutal means to quell the unrest. Thích Trí Quang and the monks kept up the pressure until Diêm was overthrown.

In 1964 Thích Trí Quang again mobilized Buddhists during the tenuous rule of Gen. Nguyên Khánh. After 1964 the Buddhists were relatively quiet until 1966, when Nguyên Cao Ky fired I Corps commander Gen. Nguyên Chánh Thi, a close friend of Thích Trí Quang. The United States, however, was determined to stand behind Ky, and the power of the Buddhists was broken. Thích Trí Quang was arrested and transferred to a Sài Gòn hospital.

In 1975, when the People's Army of Vietnam took control of the RVN, Thích Trí Quang was placed under house arrest but eventually was released.

—Charlotte A. Power

References: FitzGerald, Francis. *Fire in the Lake: The Vietnamese and the Americans in Vietnam* (1972); Post, Ken. *Revolution, Socialism, and Nationalism in Vietnam.* Vol. 4, *The Failure of Counter-Insurgency in the South* (1990).

See also: Buddhists; Ngô Đình Diêm; Nguyên Cao Ky; Nguyên Chánh Thi; Roman Catholicism in Vietnam.

Thiêu Tri (?–1847)

Third Emperor of the Nguyên Dynasty, 1841–1847; real name Miên Tông. This gentle poet and emperor maintained the works and policies of his father, Emperor Minh Mang, but was less severe toward the Catholics. His short reign was marked by the French bombardment of Đà Nang in 1847 and the Vietnamese abandonment of Trân Tây Thành (Cambodia). Western pressure on Vietnam increased under his successor, Tu Đuc, last emperor of an independent Vietnam.

—Pham Cao Duong

References: Nguyên Huyên Anh. *Viêt Nam Danh Nhân Tu Điên* (1990); Quôc Su Quán. *Quôc Triêu Chánh Biên Toát Yêu* (1971); Trân Trong Kim. *Viêt Nam Su Luoc* (1971).

See also: Minh Mang; Tu Đuc; Vietnam: from 938 through the French Conquest.

Thomas, Allison Kent (1914–)

U.S. Office of Strategic Services (OSS) officer sent to work with the Viêt Minh at the end of World War II. Thomas arrived in Kunming 1 April 1945 and headed a small unit, the "Deer Team," sent into northern Tonkin to train Viêt Minh soldiers. On 16 July 1945 Thomas and his men parachuted from a Dakota cargo plane, landing near the village of Kim Lung (now Tân Trào). In the weeks that followed Thomas worked with Hô Chí Minh, Vô Nguyên Giáp, and other Viêt Minh leaders to carry out his assignment. The evening before his departure, Thomas attended a private dinner with Hô and Giáp and asked Hô if he was a Communist. "Yes," Hô replied, "but we can still be friends, can't we?"

—Cecil B. Currey

See also: Conein, Lucien Emile; Deer Mission; Dewey, Albert Peter; Hô Chí Minh; Office of Strategic Services (OSS); Patti, Archimedes L. A.; Vô Nguyên Giáp.

Thompson, Robert Grainger Ker (1916–1992)

British counterinsurgency expert. Thompson was instrumental in suppressing the Malayan Emergency, a Communist-mounted insurgency. In the 1960s he urged the United States to apply the lessons of Malaya to Vietnam.

At the request of the United States, Thomas went to Vietnam as head of the British Advisory Mission (1961–1965). In this capacity he urged President Ngô Đình Diêm to embark on the Strategic Hamlet program. An opponent of large conventional military operations that often alienated the population and did not deal with the root causes of insurgency, he advocated police and military programs that bolstered the Sài Gòn government's political support in the countryside.

Thompson's Strategic Hamlet concept, derived from his experiences in the Malayan Emergency, was to organize South Vietnamese villagers to provide their own defense. A network of strategic hamlets would, according to Thompson, isolate the insurgents physically and politically from the people and cut them off from their recruiting base.

In Malaya, the failure of the largely Chinese insurgents (who were ethnically different from the Malay villagers) to penetrate the population meant that little more was required to end the insurgency than to organize a local security force supported by local police. The situation in South Vietnam was more complex because the Viêt Công (VC), with its tightly knit political and military organization, was embedded in the structure of many villages and was harder to displace.

The insurgents were of the same ethnicity as the villagers, making them difficult to identify and segregate.

The premise of Thompson's strategic hamlet programs was to bring security to where the people lived. At the start of the program in 1962 Thompson estimated that only 5 percent of the hamlets would have to be moved. But the Republic of Vietnam moved far too many people into hastily built fortified settlements, which failed to segregate them from the insurgents or to improve their lives. The program faltered after a promising start and ended in failure after Diêm's 1963 overthrow.

Thompson exercised less influence after the failure of the Strategic Hamlet program but remained involved in Vietnam, writing influential books (*Peace is Not at Hand* and *Defeating Communist Insurgency*) and advising the U.S. on how to deal with the VC. After the 1968 Têt Offensive, when counterinsurgency or pacification again became a prominent part of the war effort, Thompson's views enjoyed a new appeal. In 1969 he advised President Nixon to enlarge the police and give them a greater role in ending the insurgency.

—Richard A. Hunt

References: Hunt, Richard A. *Pacification: The American Struggle for Vietnam's Hearts and Minds* (1995); Thompson, Robert. *Defeating Communist Insurgency: The Lessons of Malaya and Vietnam* (1966).

See also: Counterinsurgency Warfare; Malaysia; Ngô Đình Diêm; Ngô Đình Nhu; Nixon, Richard Milhous; Pacification; Strategic Hamlet Program.

THUNDERHEAD, Operation (29 May–19 June 1972)

Secret search-and-rescue mission conducted in North Vietnam. U.S. Navy intelligence had received information of a possible escape attempt from a prisoner-of-war (POW) camp near Hà Nôi. As a result, numerous sorties were flown under Lt. Comdr. Edwin Towers's direction to search for the escaped prisoners in enemy territory. Primary surveillance was performed by Navy SEAL teams and HH-3A helicopters at a cost of one man killed. Upon its termination, the mission was labeled a failure because the prisoners had not been extracted.

The fate of the prisoners remained unknown for a year. When released in 1973, they stated that they had planned an escape attempt but called it off because of increased prison security stemming from the breakdown in negotiations between Washington and Hà Nôi.

—Rajesh H. Chauhan

References: Gropman, Alan L. *Air Power and the Airlift Evacuation of Kham Duc* (1985); Lavalle, A. J. C. *Air Power and the 1972 Spring Invasion* (1985); Towers, Edwin L. *Hope for Freedom: Operation Thunderhead* (1981).

See also: Prisoners of War, Allied; SEAL (Sea, Air, Land) Teams.

Tiger Cages

Confinement cells at the Republic of Vietnam (RVN) prison on Côn Son Island that held prisoners of war and political opponents. Built by the French, tiger cages were described as subsurface cement cells of approximately 6 feet by 10 feet,

topped by bars, with ceilings so low that inmates could barely stand. But visiting U.S. officials claimed the cells were entirely above ground in two covered, windowless buildings, with bars forming the ceiling and a catwalk on top, measuring 6 feet 3 inches by 10 feet 6 inches. Such facilities were pictured in a 1970 *Life* magazine article. Sài Gòn claimed that all Côn Son prisoners were humanely treated and confined only temporarily in the tiger cages. But in July 1970 U.S. Congressmen William Anderson and Augustus Hawkins inspected the prison and reported "paralyzed" tiger cage victims who were denied adequate food, water, and exercise. Subsequently, the International Red Cross cited the RVN government for violations of the Geneva Convention.

—Mary L. Kelley

References: Guenter, Lewy. *America in Vietnam* (1978); Nguyên Tiên Hung and Jerrold L. Schecter. *The Palace File* (1986).

See also: Missing in Action and Prisoners of War, Viêt Công and People's Army of Vietnam.

TIGER HOUND, Operation (1965–1973)

Allied air operation in the Laos panhandle designed to reduce Communist infiltration along the Hô Chí Minh Trail. Planned by U.S. Air Force Col. John F. Groom, Operation TIGER HOUND began in December 1965 and focused on infiltration routes in Military Regions (MRs) I and II in the area from Tchépone near the 17th parallel south to Cambodia. It augmented air operations in the northern panhandle designated STEEL TIGER (Mu Già Pass to the 17th parallel), which began in April.

These operations were not constrained by strict rules of engagement (the need to have U.S. embassy or Laotian government permission to attack potential targets). The panhandle was seen as an extension of the South Vietnamese battlefield and was thus under the control of Gen. William Westmoreland.

In TIGER HOUND the Allies employed C-47s and later C-130s as airborne battlefield command and control centers; Air Force O-1s and A-1Es and Laotian T-28s and Army OV-1 Mohawks with side-looking and infrared radar for forward air control; RF-101s and RF-4Cs for target detection; UC-123s to defoliate the jungle; and B-57s, F-100s, F-105s, AC-47 gunships, C-130 flareships, Marine and Navy jets, and Army gunship helicopters as the primary strike aircraft for day and night attacks.

The primary targets in TIGER HOUND were trucks, storage and bivouac areas, bridges, buildings, and antiaircraft artillery (AAA) sites. The secondary mission was to cut roads and create traffic choke areas. TIGER HOUND and STEEL TIGER focused on interdiction of Communist ground forces and support for Army of the Republic of Vietnam (ARVN) and U.S. long-range armed reconnaissance units. In the first half of 1966, TIGER HOUND gained momentum; by May, B-52s had flown more than 400 saturation bombing sorties.

Despite these impressive numbers, infiltration continued and U.S. Air Force commanders decided they needed a long-loitering aircraft. In June, they deployed eight modified World War II A-26s and also used AC-47s, AC-119 "truck killers," and AC-130 gunships with flare capability for night raids. The U.S. also set up in Nakhon Phanom an MSQ-77 Skyport radar with a 200-mile range to improve bombing results. In turn, the Communists increased the number of AAA sites, later including surface-to-air missiles. By summer 1966, 22 TIGER HOUND and STEEL TIGER planes had been shot down. By this time, TIGER HOUND and STEEL TIGER operations had been blended into Seventh Air Force duties and placed under the TIGER HOUND task force. Overall operational responsibility was delegated to the Seventh Air Force commander.

After a summer monsoon lull, full operations resumed between October 1966 and April 1967. U.S. pilots flew more than 2,000 sorties monthly. By the end of 1967, B-52 operations had also increased, and most TIGER HOUND strike aircraft had been equipped with Starlight scopes to increase target detection at night. In 1967 a large number of TIGER HOUND raids were carried out at night, often by B-57 "Canberra" bombers in night camouflage. In November and December 1967 the Allies placed a line of seismic and acoustic sensors along infiltration roads and trails, which transmitted troop and truck movements to high-flying EC-121s.

After President Johnson halted the air war in North Vietnam on 31 March 1968, Operation TIGER HOUND was reduced to a less intense routine. Along with all Allied air operations in Laos, it ended in April 1973. From 1965 to 1972 Allied planes dropped over 1.1 million tons of bombs on the Hô Chí Minh Trail in the southern Laotian panhandle but failed to stop Communist infiltration.

—William Head

References: Berger, Carl, ed. *The United States Air Force in Southeast Asia, 1961–1973: An Illustrated Account* (1984); Momyer, William H. *Airpower in Three Wars* (1978); Morrocco, John. *Rain of Fire: Air War, 1969–1973* (1986); —. *Thunder From Above: Air War, 1941–1968* (1984); Schlight, John. *The Air War in South Vietnam: The Years of the Offensive, 1965–1968* (1988); Tilford, Earl H., Jr. *Crosswinds: The Air Force's Setup in Vietnam* (1994).

See also: Air Power, Role in War; Airplanes, Allied and Democratic Republic of Vietnam; BARREL ROLL, Operation; Hô Chí Minh Trail; Laos; Logistics, Allied and People's Army of Vietnam/Viêt Công; STEEL TIGER, Operation.

Tinker v. Des Moines

U.S. court case relating to the Vietnam War. On 16 and 17 December 1965, John Tinker and several other public school students in Des Moines, Iowa, wore black arm bands to school to mourn the dead in Vietnam and demonstrate support for the Christmas truce there. They were suspended for violating a ban on wearing of arm bands, passed earlier in the week by the Des Moines School Board.

The board upheld the ban on 3 January 1966, by which time the suspended students had returned to school. The Tinker and Eckhardt families, aided by the Iowa Civil Liberties Union, pursued the matter in federal court. On 1 September 1966, District Judge Roy Stephenson ruled in favor of the school district. He acknowledged that the arm bands were indeed a form of speech but did not feel that the

ban deprived the students of their First Amendment rights. The U.S. Court of Appeals for the Eighth Circuit upheld the lower court ruling in November 1967.

The U.S. Supreme Court overturned the lower decisions on 24 February 1969 by 7 to 2, ruling that the wearing of arm bands was a protected act of symbolic speech and espousing the idea that students' rights are not left "at the schoolhouse gate."

—Wes Watters

Reference: Rappaport, Doreen. *Tinker vs. Des Moines: Student Rights on Trial* (1993).

See also: Antiwar Movement, United States.

Tô Huu (1920–)

Prominent Vietnamese Communist Party (VCP) and Socialist Republic of Vietnam (SRV) official. Huu built his career in the party's propaganda apparatus and was notorious for paeans dedicated to the USSR. In December 1976 Huu became an alternate member of the VCP Politburo in charge of cultural affairs and ideology. In September 1985 Huu instigated a currency reform that he had modified on his own initiative and which was a great failure. In June 1986, after the economic collapse of the SRV, Huu was dropped from the post of vice-premier. At the December 1986 party congress he was ousted from the Politburo and disappeared from the Vietnamese political scene.

—Ngô N. Trung

Reference: Biographical Files, Indo-China Archives, University of California at Berkeley.

See also: Vietnam, Socialist Republic of: 1975 to the Present; Vietnamese Communist Party (VCP).

TOÀN THANG (Complete Victory), Operation (8 April–25 May 1968)

First of many Allied military operations with the same code name that took place near Sài Gòn. On 8 April 1968, Allied military forces commenced 11 separate operations in the Republic of Vietnam (RVN) Capital Military District. U.S. Military Assistance Command, Vietnam (MACV) combined these actions into Operation TOÀN THANG, which became the central focus of Allied attentions from 1968 until U.S. armed forces withdrew from South Vietnam. The operation, motivated by the 1968 Têt Offensive, was designed to stop Viêt Công (VC) and People's Army of Vietnam (PAVN) attacks on Sài Gòn. U.S. units committed to the operation included the 3d Brigade, 9th Infantry Division; 1st Infantry Division; 25th Infantry Division; and 199th Infantry Brigade (Separate). Allied units included all ARVN forces assigned to the Capital Military District and the 1st Australian Task Force.

On 3 May 1968 Washington and Hà Nôi announced that peace talks would soon begin, and MACV and ARVN commanders strengthened defenses around Sài Gòn in anticipation of renewed VC/PAVN attacks. Such precautions were warranted. On 4 May the VC launched a major operation against Sài Gòn, known as "Mini-Têt," that lasted through the month. Attacks were concentrated on the Sài Gòn–Biên Hòa highway bridge, but RVN Marines held the bridge. On 6 May the U.S. 25th Infantry Division counterattacked and decisively defeated VC units near Tân Son Nhut Airport.

Despite Allied precautions, the well-equipped VC 267th Local Force Battalion infiltrated Sài Gòn and occupied several key locations. The 38th ARVN Ranger Battalion engaged the intruders and eventually triumphed despite heavy losses. They were then dispatched to the VC-occupied Bình Tiên Bridge and secured the span after two days of grueling combat.

The most serious threat came as two VC battalions captured the Y-Bridge, linking downtown Sài Gòn with the Nhà Bè District, and further fortified several areas around the bridge. The U.S. 2d Battalion, 47th Infantry (Mechanized) and the 5th Battalion, 60th Infantry (Mechanized), 9th Infantry Division were sent to secure this vital artery. It took six days of hard fighting for the Americans to destroy the VC units and retake the bridge and surrounding area, the most costly action fought by U.S. troops during this offensive.

TOÀN THANG's initial phase ended on 25 May 1968. Mini-Têt, however, continued into June as the 5th ARVN Ranger Group worked to clear VC incursions into the Cho Lon section of Sài Gòn.

—J. A. Menzoff

Reference: Stanton, Shelby. *The Rise and Fall of an American Army: U.S. Ground Forces in Vietnam, 1965–1973* (1985).

See also: Khe Sanh, Battles of; National Front for the Liberation of South Vietnam (NFLSV); Têt Offensive: Overall Strategy; Têt Offensive: the Sài Gòn Circle; United States: Army; Vietnam, Republic of: Army (ARVN).

Tôn Đuc Thang (1888–1980)

Prominent Vietnamese Communist Party (VCP), Democratic Republic of Vietnam (DRV), and Socialist Republic of Vietnam (SRV) official. In 1951 Thang was elected to the party Central Committee. He also became chairman of Mat Trân Liên Viêt (Liên Viêt Front) and head of the Standing Committee of the National Assembly. In July 1960 Thang became vice-president of the DRV. He became president after the death of Hô Chí Minh in 1969 and served in that capacity until his death in 1980. Thang is remembered as a veteran of the early days of the VCP and a life-long friend of Hô Chí Minh.

—Ngô N. Trung

Reference: Biographical Files, Indo-China Archives, University of California at Berkeley.

See also: Hô Chí Minh; Lao Đông Party; Vietnam, Democratic Republic of: 1945–1954; Vietnam, Socialist Republic of: 1975 to the Present; Vietnamese Communist Party (VCP).

Tôn Thât Đình (1926–)

Army of the Republic of Vietnam (ARVN) general; key figure in the coup against President Ngô Đình Diêm. His closeness to the Ngô family and the trust that Diêm placed in him led to his appointment in 1961 as the youngest ARVN general.

Eraly in planning the coup against Diêm, Gen. Trân Van Đôn established that Gen. Đình's support was vital because he controlled ARVN forces surrounding Sài Gòn. Đôn convinced Đình to join the coup plotters, but the conspirators did not entirely trust Đình and assigned men to kill him if he changed his mind. Nhu, meanwhile, was convinced of Đình's sincerity and revealed his own plans for a preemptive coup, Operations BRAVO I and BRAVO II. He assigned Đình a pivotal role—to march into Sài Gòn against a staged uprising. Đình immediately revealed Nhu's plans to Đôn and the other generals.

On 29 October, Đình ordered Col. Lê Quang Tung and his special forces out of Sài Gòn in accordance with Nhu's plans. In a key maneuver, Đình also convinced the regime that he could conduct BRAVO II more effectively if he had control over all forces in the region, including troops under the command of Diêm loyalist Gen. Huynh Van Cao. Still believing Đình to be on their side, Diêm and Nhu allowed the general to deploy troops throughout Sài Gòn near key government installations.

When the coup began on the morning of 1 November, Diêm repeatedly attempted to call Đình. In a final test of loyalty for Đình by the conspiring generals, Đình was allowed to speak with Diêm while the plotters listened. Đình won their confidence when he proceeded to shout obscenities at Diêm.

Following the coup, on 4 November Prime Minister Nguyên Ngoc Tho appointed Đình minister of interior. On 29 January 1964, during a coup led by Gen. Nguyên Khánh, Đình was arrested with several other figures for allegedly plotting to negotiate a peace settlement with Hà Nôi.

With the rise of Gen. Nguyên Cao Ky, Đình again took command of an ARVN corps. On 10 April 1966 during the Buddhist uprising, Ky appointed Đình as I Corps commander to replace the rebellious general Nguyên Chánh Thi. Đình, however, lost favor after expressing resentment at Ky's tactics in crushing the Buddhist movement. In the summer of 1966 he lost command of his corps. Đình was elected to the RVN Senate in 1967 and served there until April 1975, when he left Vietnam.

—Michael R. Nichols

References: Duncanson, Dennis J. *Government and Revolution in Vietnam* (1968); Karnow, Stanley. *Vietnam: A History* (1991); Olson, James, ed. *Dictionary of the Vietnam War* (1987); Smith, R. B. *An International History of the Vietnam War* (1988).

See also: BRAVO I and BRAVO II, Operations; Huynh Van Cao; Lê Quang Tung; Ngô Đình Cân; Ngô Đình Diêm; Ngô Đình Diêm, Overthrow of; Ngô Đình Nhu; Nguyên Cao Ky; Nguyên Chánh Thi; Nguyên Huu Có; Nguyên Khánh; Trân Van Đôn.

Tôn Thât Thuyêt (1835–1913)

Influential mandarin, member of the Board of Regents, and leader of the Cân Vuong (Support the King) movement of the mid-1880s. He was responsible for the *binh biên* (military event) of the 13th day of the 5th month of the Ât Dâu Year (1885) at Huê against the French. Tôn Thât Thuyêt appealed to mandarins, scholars, and the people to support the monarch in his fight against the French. The wide response to this was the beginning of the anti-French Support the King Movement.

—Pham Cao Duong

References: Lê Thành Khôi. *Le Viet-Nam: Histoire et Civilisation* (1955); Nguyên Huyên Anh. *Viêt Nam Danh Nhân Tu Điên* (1990); Nguyên Thê Anh. *Viet Nam Duoi Thoi Pháp Đô Hô* (1970).

See also: French Indo-China; Hàm Nghi; Tu Đuc.

Tonkin

Northernmost of the three former French colonies that make up present-day Vietnam. Tonkin is the region surrounding the Red River and bordering China. Vietnamese emperor Lê Loi, who defeated and expelled the Chinese in 1427 after a 20-year occupation, established his imperial capital at the present site of Hà Nôi, which he called "Đông Kinh," from which the name Tonkin was derived.

—Arthur T. Frame

References: Buttinger, Joseph. *Vietnam: A Political History* (1968); Karnow, Stanley *Vietnam: A History* (1984).

See also: An Nam; Cochin China; French Indo-China; Lê Dynasty; Lê Loi (Lê Thái Tô); Minh Mang; Nguyên Phúc Ánh (Gia Long); Vietnam: Prehistory to 938; Vietnam: from 938 through the French Conquest.

Tonkin Gulf Incidents (1964)

Major event that prompted the Tonkin Gulf Resolution. On 31 July 1964 the U.S. Navy destroyer *Maddox* started a reconnaissance cruise off the coast of North Vietnam. It carried extra radio gear and personnel to monitor Democratic Republic of Vietnam (DRV) radio communications but was not a true electronic espionage vessel.

Around the time of the cruise, the United States scheduled an unusually intense string of covert operations (DeSoto Missions) against the North Vietnamese coast. These were carried out by relatively small vessels having Vietnamese crews but operating under U.S. orders. Based near Đà Nang, they were part of Operation Plan 34A (OPLAN 34A). Two islands off the North Vietnamese coast were to be attacked on the night of 30–31 July; two points on the North Vietnamese mainland were to be shelled on the night of 3–4 August; one island was to be shelled, and one fishing boat crew was to be seized for interrogation, on 5 August. One of *Maddox*'s main missions was to learn about North Vietnamese coastal defenses, and it apparently was believed that more would be learned if those defenses were in an aroused state.

On the evening of 1 August the *Maddox* approached within gun range of Hòn Me (one of two islands shelled by OPLAN 34A vessels on 30–31 July), and the coastal defense forces became more aroused than the Americans had planned. On the afternoon of 2 August, three DRV torpedo boats unsuccessfully attacked the destroyer. President Johnson was annoyed that the torpedo boats had not been sunk, but he decided not to order any further retaliation, partly because he had reason to believe that the attack had not been a deliberate decision by the Hà Nôi government.

On 3 August the *Maddox* and another destroyer, the *C. Turner Joy*, resumed the patrol in the Gulf of Tonkin, operating under more cautious orders than those of 31 July. The destroyers were kept farther from the North Vietnamese coast and completely out of the extreme northern section of the Gulf, limitations that seriously reduced the destroyers' ability to collect useful information.

Patrol commander Capt. John Herrick thought that another North Vietnamese attack was likely. For about two hours on the night of 4 August, such an attack seemed to be in progress, but the situation was confused. The *C. Turner Joy* fired at objects on its radar screens that were invisible to the *Maddox*'s radar, while the *Maddox*'s sonar equipment picked up sounds (interpreted as DRV torpedo motors) that could not be heard by the *C. Turner Joy*'s sonar equipment. The overall weight of the evidence is that no attack occurred.

In Washington, after some initial uncertainty, it was decided that there had been a genuine attack. Intercepted North Vietnamese radio messages seemed to provide the clinching evidence, although texts of the messages have never been released. It seems likely that they were descriptions of the combat on 2 August, misinterpreted by the U.S. as references to the more recent event.

President Johnson, believing that an attack had occurred, ordered retaliatory airstrikes (Operation PIERCE ARROW), which were carried out on the afternoon of 5 August. He also asked for and quickly obtained a congressional resolution (the Tonkin Gulf Resolution, passed almost unanimously) authorizing him to do whatever was necessary to deal with Communist aggression in Vietnam. The Tonkin Gulf incidents were politically profitable for Johnson in the short run; polls showed overwhelming approval of his handling of the crisis and a dramatic improvement in ratings of his handling of the Vietnam War as a whole. In the long run, however, the cost to the president's credibility was considerable. It became clear that Congress and the public had been misled about the administration's intentions and about the relationship between the OPLAN 34A raids and the Tonkin Gulf incidents. Eventually, many people came to suspect that the report of the attack had been a deliberate lie rather than the honest mistake it had been.

—Edwin E. Moise

Reference: Moise, Edwin E. *Tonkin Gulf and the Escalation of the Vietnam War* (1996).

See also: DeSoto Missions; ELINT (Electronic Intelligence); Johnson, Lyndon Baines; Operation Plan 34A (OPLAN 34A); PIERCE ARROW, Operation; Stockdale, James B.; Tonkin Gulf Resolution.

Tonkin Gulf Resolution (1964)

Congressional resolution passed in response to the Tonkin Gulf incidents. President Johnson, wary of the prospect of a major war in Vietnam, was especially determined not to get into such a war without prior commitment of congressional support. In May and June 1964, senior administration officials produced drafts of a possible resolution but decided not to present these to Congress. There seemed little chance of such a resolution passing without a politically damaging debate.

In early August, North Vietnamese torpedo boats were reported to have twice attacked U.S. Navy destroyers on the high seas (the Tonkin Gulf Incidents). A revised draft of the resolution was quickly presented to the Congress. Members of Congress were given the impression that the heart of the resolution, the aspect they should consider voting for or against, was a passage about supporting the president in repelling armed attacks on U.S. forces. They were told that they should not worry about the implications of the next paragraph, which authorized the president to do whatever he felt necessary to assist South Vietnam, since the administration had no intention of escalating U.S. involvement in the war. Most accepted these assurances. The resolution passed on 7 August, unanimously in the House of Representatives and with only two dissenting votes, by Ernest Gruening and Wayne Morse, in the Senate.

After Johnson sent U.S. combat forces to Vietnam, citing the Tonkin Gulf Resolution as his authority, some who had voted for the resolution began to investigate the circumstances. They found that the first attack was not so clearly unprovoked as they had been told; that there was reason to doubt the second attack ever happened; and that the administration had been working on preliminary drafts of just such a resolution because it was considering escalation of the war long before the incidents had occurred. By 1968 the resulting disillusionment had become a serious liability for the administration.

When Senator Morse first proposed in 1966 that Congress repeal the Tonkin Gulf Resolution, there was hardly any support. Sentiment gradually shifted, however, and the Resolution was finally repealed in late 1970.

—Edwin E. Moise

Reference: Moise, Edwin E. *Tonkin Gulf and the Escalation of the Vietnam War* (1996).

See also: Gruening, Ernest Henry; Johnson, Lyndon Baines; Morse, Wayne Lyman; Tonkin Gulf Incidents.

Trân Buu Kiêm (1921–)

Southern Vietnamese revolutionary; foreign relations specialist for the National Front for the Liberation of South Vietnam (NFLSV). As the NFLSV's chief diplomat, Kiêm promoted the Front's neutralization plan to nonaligned nations and Western Europe. He called for the creation of a coalition government in South Vietnam with a neutral foreign policy. Kiêm understood that the United States would reject such a plan but realized its propaganda value. Indeed, Washington policymakers quickly condemned the scheme, claiming that it was tantamount to surrender to the Communists. Other world leaders, including President de Gaulle and Prince Sihanouk, urged the Johnson administration to consider neutralization as a possible solution to the Southeast Asian crisis. Kiêm's success hampered U.S. ability to build a coalition of supportive, or at least sympathetic, allies.

When the Paris peace talks opened in 1968, Kiêm joined Madame Nguyên Thi Bình as the NFLSV's representatives. According to some Vietnamese sources, while in Paris Kiêm confronted a senior-level official and was called home to undergo self-criticism. He later returned to Paris under the aegis of the Provisional Revolutionary Government of South Vietnam (PRG), but clearly he had lost considerable power and prestige.

—Robert K. Brigham

References: Herring, George C., ed. *The Secret Diplomacy of the Vietnam War: The Negotiating Volumes of the Pentagon Papers* (1983); *Personalities of the South Vietnam Liberation Movement* (1965); Pike, Douglas. *Viet Cong: The Organization and Techniques of*

the National Liberation Front of South Vietnam (1966); Truong Nhu Tang. *A Viet Cong Memoir: An Inside Account of the Vietnam War and Its Aftermath* (1985).

See also: National Front for the Liberation of South Vietnam (NFLSV); Nguyên Thi Bình; Nguyên Van Thiêu; Paris Negotiations; Paris Peace Accords; Provisional Revolutionary Government of South Vietnam (PRG).

Trân Đô (1923–)

Commander of Viêt Công (VC) forces in South Vietnam and prominent Vietnamese Communist Party (VCP) official. From 1945 to 1955 Đô held high party and military posts in the Viêt Minh. He played an important part in the Battle of Điên Biên Phu.

Đô was sent south at the beginning of the Vietnam War. In 1963 he was identified as head of the Political Department of the Central Office for South Vietnam (COSVN), the office through which Hà Nôi controlled and directed military and political activities under the name of the National Front for the Liberation of South Vietnam (NFLSV) and its military arm, the People's Liberation Armed Forces (PLAF). Đô was one of five deputy commanders of the PLAF during the war.

Đô was believed to be one of the DRV's principal field commanders in the south in charge of political affairs in a triumvirate with Generals Nguyên Chí Thanh and Trân Van Trà. He drafted COSVN directives under the pseudonym of Chín Vinh and lived with his soldiers in jungle camps and underground bunkers, constantly confusing and evading American forces. Đô was a capable leader who prevented factionalism from disrupting the VC war effort.

Đô helped plan and execute the Têt Offensive in January 1968. Although the attacks resulted in thousands of VC and North Vietnamese casualties, he admitted later that the results worked in their favor, stating that "making an impact in the United States…had not been our intention—but it turned out to be a fortunate result." Despite rumors during the Offensive of Đô's death, he was only slightly wounded in a February 1968 B-52 strike.

—Michael R. Nichols and Ngô N. Trung

References: Biographical Files, Indo-China Archives, University of California at Berkeley; Davidson, Phillip B. *Vietnam at War, the History: 1946–1975* (1988); Karnow, Stanley. *Vietnam: A History* (1991); Olson, James S., ed. *Dictionary of the Vietnam War* (1987); Smith, R. B. *An International History of the Vietnam War* (1983).

See also: COSVN (Central Office for South Vietnam or Trung Uong Cuc Miên Nam); Hà Nôi Hilton (Hoa Lò Prison); National Front for the Liberation of South Vietnam (NFLSV); Nguyên Chí Thanh; Nguyên Luong Bang; Têt Offensive: Overall Strategy; Têt Offensive: the Sài Gòn Circle; Trân Van Trà; Vietnam, Socialist Republic of: 1975 to the Present; Vietnamese Communist Party (VCP).

Trân Hung Đao (1228–1300)

Trân Dynasty prince and general, also known as Hung Đao Vuong, Trân Quôc Tuân, or Đuc Thánh Trân. Trân Hung Đao has been considered the most important hero in Vietnamese history. His famous answer to King Trân Nhân Tông is familiar to every Vietnamese. When the king asked whether it would be a good idea to surrender to prevent the people's suffering, Trân Hung Đao replied, "Your Majesty, if you want to surrender, please have my head cut off first." His *Hich Tuong Si* (Proclamation to Generals and Officers) is regarded as a classic work in Vietnamese thirteenth-century literature, as is his *Binh Thu Yêu Luoc* (Essentials of Military Art). Before 1975 the Republic of Vietnam Navy selected him as its patron saint.

—Pham Cao Duong

References: Hà Van Tân and Pham Thi Tâm. *Cuôc Kháng Chiên Chông Xâm Luoc Nguyên Mông Thê Ky XIII* (1972); Lê Thành Khôi. *Histoire du Viet-Nam des Origines à 1858* (1981); Nguyên Huyên Anh. *Viêt Nam Danh Nhân Tu Điên* (1990); Tran Trong Kim. *Viêt Nam Su Luoc* (1971).

See also: Vietnam: from 938 through the French Conquest.

TRÂN HUNG ĐAO I and II, Operations. *See* SEALORDS (South East Asia Lake Ocean River Delta Strategy).

Trân Kim Tuyên (?–1995)

Head of the Republic of Vietnam (RVN) Office of Political and Social Studies; one of many officers to plot against President Ngô Đình Diêm. In the late 1950s Tuyên came to believe that the Diêm government was weak and corrupt. In early 1963, after Lt. Col. Vuong Van Đông's coup attempt failed, Tuyên planned his own coup, quietly consulting with leading military and civilian officials and several senior Army of the Republic of Vietnam (ARVN) officers. Among those he consulted were Nguyên Cao Ky and Col. Pham Ngoc Thao, the latter a clandestine Communist agent. He filled his faction with disgruntled junior officers and dissidents that he had blacklisted.

Hoping to begin their coup before other conspirators could act, Tuyên and Thao planned a quick movement against Diêm. CIA officer Lucien Conein learned of their plans and informed Gen. Trân Thiên Khiêm, ARVN chief of staff, who prevented the coup. Nhu exiled Tuyên to Egypt as consul general, but Tuyên traveled no farther than Hong Kong, where he continued to work against Diêm. He returned to the RVN following Diêm's 1963 assassination but played no important political role. He fled South Vietnam just before the fall of Sài Gòn in April 1975.

—Michael R. Nichols

References: Fishel, Wesley R., ed. *Vietnam: Anatomy of a Conflict* (1968); FitzGerald, Frances. *Fire in the Lake: The Vietnamese and the Americans in Vietnam* (1972); Karnow, Stanley. *Vietnam: A History* (1991); Olson, James S., ed. *Dictionary of the Vietnam War* (1987); Smith, R. B. *An International History of the Vietnam War.* Vol. 2, *The Struggle for South-East Asia, 1961–65* (1985).

See also: Conein, Lucien Emile; Ngô Đình Diêm; Ngô Đình Diêm, Overthrow of; Ngô Đình Nhu; Nguyên Cao Ky; Pham Ngoc Thao; Trân Thiên Khiêm.

Trân Thiên Khiêm (1925–)

Leading Republic of Vietnam (RVN) military and political figure; a leader of the coup against President Ngô Đình Diêm. In late 1963 Khiêm became involved in the coup plot led by Generals Trân Van Đôn, Lê Van Kim, and Duong Van Minh that resulted in the assassination of Diêm. Afterward, Khiêm became military commander of the Sài Gòn region but did not feel properly recompensed. He joined with other disgruntled officers and Gen. Nguyên Khanh in their conspiracy against the military junta. After this coup, of 30 January 1964, Khiêm became minister of defense.

After Khánh's August 1964 resignation, Khiêm sought to head the government. The Armed Forces Council instead created a triumvirate of Khiêm, Khánh, and Minh to rule until a permanent government could be formed, but in October Khánh exiled Minh and Khiêm. Khiêm became ambassador to the United States. From November 1965 to May 1968 he was ambassador to the Republic of China.

Khiêm returned to Sài Gòn in May 1968 as minister of the interior. He served as deputy prime minister for five months in 1969, then became prime minister, a post he held until 1975. In this capacity, Khiêm was involved in narcotics trade and used money from the sale of heroin to fund his political machines. In April 1975, as Communist forces moved into Sài Gòn, he fled South Vietnam.

—Michael R. Nichols

References: Bain, Chester A. *Vietnam: The Roots of Conflict* (1967); Duncanson, Dennis J. *Government and Revolution in Vietnam* (1968); Fishel, Wesley R., ed. *Vietnam: Anatomy of a Conflict* (1968); FitzGerald, Frances. *Fire in the Lake: The Vietnamese and the Americans in Vietnam* (1972); Karnow, Stanley. *Vietnam: A History* (1991); Nguyên Khac Viên. *Vietnam: A Long History* (1993); Olson, James S., ed. *Dictionary of the Vietnam War* (1987); Smith, R. B. *An International History of the Vietnam War.* Vol. 2, *The Struggle for South-East Asia, 1961–65* (1985).

See also: Duong Van Minh; Lê Van Kim; Military Revolutionary Council; Ngô Đình Diêm; Ngô Đình Diêm, Overthrow of; Nguyên Khánh; Pham Ngoc Thao; Trân Kim Tuyên; Trân Van Đôn.

Trân Van Chuong (1898–1986)

Republic of Vietnam (RVN) official; ambassador to the United States, 1954–1963. In July 1954 Chuong became cabinet minister in the first government of Ngô Đình Diêm. He was then ambassador to the United States until he resigned in August 1963 to protest RVN government oppression of the Buddhist movement.

—Ngô N. Trung

Reference: Biographical Files, Indo-China Archives, University of California at Berkeley.

See also: Ngô Đình Diêm; Ngô Đình Nhu; Ngô Đình Nhu, Madame (Trân Lê Xuân).

Trân Van Đô (1904–)

Republic of Vietnam (RVN) political leader; first foreign minister in the Ngô Đình Diêm government. In 1949 Đô founded a newspaper, *Tinh Thân*, to support Diêm. In 1953 Đô joined the Công Nông Chánh Đang (Political Party of Workers and Peasants), predecessor of Cân Lao Nhân Vi Cách Mang Đang (Revolutionary Personalist Labor Party), which included core members of the Esprit Group formed by Ngô Đình Nhu to support his brother, Ngô Đình Diêm. In

July 1954 Đô became minister of foreign affairs in the first Diêm government, in which capacity he was the representative of the State of Vietnam at the 1954 Geneva Conference.

In 1955 Đô was ousted from the Cân Lao Nhân Vi Cách Mang Đang ruling party, accused of supporting the Bình Xuyên. He was one of 18 prominent leaders who held a news conference in Sài Gòn on 26 April 1960, calling on President Diêm to carry out political reforms. Đô served as a vice premier in the 1965 Phan Huy Quát government and as minister of foreign affairs in the cabinet of Premier Nguyên Van Lôc from 1967 to 1968. After the collapse of the RVN in April 1975, Đô took refuge in Paris.

—Ngô N. Trung

Reference: Biographical Files, Indo-China Archives, University of California at Berkeley.

See also: BRAVO I and BRAVO II, Operations; Heath, Donald R.; Ngô Đình Diêm; Ngô Đình Diêm, Overthrow of; Ngô Đình Nhu; Ngô Đình Nhu, Madame (Trân Lê Xuân); Phan Huy Quát.

Trân Van Đôn (1917–)

Army of the Republic of Vietnam (ARVN) general; a key participant in the 1963 overthrow of President Ngô Đình Diêm. Đôn initially supported Diêm, but corruption and other shortcomings in the Diêm government turned him against the regime. In July 1963 Đôn began discussing with other disillusioned army leaders the possibility of a coup. Đôn, the ARVN chief of staff, and his deputy, Gen. Lê Van Kim, met with Central Intelligence Agency (CIA) representatives on 23 August 1963. Đôn and Kim made it clear that Diêm, his brother Nhu, and Nhu's wife should be removed, an act they were prepared to undertake if supported by Washington. This message was passed on to Ambassador Henry Cabot Lodge, who forwarded it to Washington.

Đôn and other generals proposed to Diêm that he declare martial law to strengthen the military in its fight against the Viêt Công, but their real purpose was to strengthen their own position for a coup. After self-immolations by Buddhist monks became a problem in June 1963, Diêm agreed to declare martial law, hoping to crack down on the Buddhists while the army took the blame. This action, however, forced the Kennedy administration to take a stand against Diêm.

After the 1 November 1963 coup, Đôn continued to serve in the army until he was forced to retire in 1965. In 1965 he was elected to the Senate and remained an influential figure in South Vietnam. He arranged to leave for the United States a day before the fall of Sài Gòn in April 1975.

—Charlotte A. Power

References: Olson, James S., ed. *Dictionary of the Vietnam War* (1987); Post, Ken. *Revolution, Socialism, and Nationalism in Vietnam.* Vol. 4, *The Failure of Counter-Insurgency in the South* (1990).

See also: Conein, Lucien Emile; Lê Van Kim; Lodge, Henry Cabot, Jr.; Ngô Đình Diêm; Ngô Đình Diêm, Overthrow of; Ngô Đình Nhu; Ngô Đình Nhu, Madame (Trân Lê Xuân).

Trân Van Giàu (1911–)

Vietnamese Communist intellectual, considered by many the leading Stalinist within the Vietnamese revolutionary move-

ment. Giàu founded several southern front organizations for the Party and oversaw the successful merger between the National United Front and the Viêt Minh in 1945. In 1946 Giàu and other Stalinists were made to go through *kiêm thao* (self-criticism) for their excesses after the August Revolution. Giàu lost much of his political power but became an influential historian of the modern revolution, publishing several important books. He often wrote under the pseudonym Tâm Vu. In his most important essay, "People's War against Special War," he outlined the village- and district-level struggles that undermined the will to fight within the Army of the Republic of Vietnam (ARVN).

—Robert K. Brigham

References: Huynh Kim Khánh. *Vietnamese Communism, 1925–1945* (1982); Marr, David G. *Vietnamese Tradition on Trial, 1920–1945* (1981); Pike, Douglas. *Viet Cong: The Organization and Techniques of the National Liberation Front of South Vietnam* (1966); Tâm Vu (Trân Van Giàu). "People's War Against Special War" (1967).

See also: National Front for the Liberation of South Vietnam (NFLSV); Viêt Minh; Vietnam, Republic of: Army (ARVN).

Trân Van Hai (1925–1975)

Army of the Republic of Vietnam (ARVN) brigadier general. Hai was widely known as incorruptible, outspoken, and a brave officer. During the 1968 Têt Offensive Hai commanded the Ranger Branch Command and supervised the raid to clear the Communist force that had infiltrated into the Cho Lon business district. He was then assigned to the post of national police chief. In 1970 Hai commanded Special Tactical Area 44, then took command of the 7th Infantry Division at Đông Tâm, near My Tho. On 30 April 1975 Hai committed suicide at division headquarters at Đông Tâm.

—Nguyên Công Luân (Lu Tuân)

Reference: Hà Mai Viêt, "Famous Generals of the Republic of Viêt Nam Armed Forces" (unpublished).

Trân Van Huong (1903–mid 1980s)

Republic of Vietnam (RVN) prime minister in a civilian government orchestrated by Gen. Nguyên Khánh. Huong's reputation was based on his opposition to Ngô Đình Diêm. Khánh seems to have chosen him because he was part of the "old guard." During Huong's first three months as prime minister, Buddhists and other political factions staged protest demonstrations. Huong did not rely on either Buddhists or Catholics when making political appointments but drove both into opposition and delivered himself to the military council, the strongest faction that did not want a civilian government.

Younger officers in Army of the Republic of Vietnam (ARVN), the "Young Turks," wanted the old guard forcibly retired. Although Huong was part of this group, he was left alone when on 20 December 1964 the other leaders were rounded up and held at Kontum. He retained his post until 27 January 1965, when the military deposed him and returned Khánh to power.

After the 1968 Têt Offensive, President Nguyên Van Thiêu appointed Huong prime minister, a post he held until 1969. In 1971 Huong became vice president of South Vietnam, remaining in that position until Thiêu resigned on 21 April 1975. He attempted to negotiate a settlement of war, and on April 28 he transferred authority to Gen. Duong Van Minh, on the eve of the North Vietnamese victory. He chose to stay in Vietnam, where he was widely respected. The Communist leadership left him alone, although he adamantly refused to meet with them until the time of his death.

—Charlotte A. Power

References: Karnow, Stanley. *Vietnam: A History* (1983); Moss, George Donelson. *Vietnam: An American Ordeal* (1990); Post, Ken. *Revolution, Socialism, and Nationalism in Vietnam.* Vol. 4, *The Failure of Counter-Insurgency in the South* (1990).

See also: Duong Van Minh; Ngô Đình Diêm; Nguyên Khánh; Nguyên Van Thiêu; Viêt Minh.

Trân Van Lam (1913–)

Republic of Vietnam (RVN) political figure and foreign minister, 1969–1973. He was one of the four signatories of the 1973 Paris peace accords that ended U.S. involvement in the Vietnam War. Reelected to the Senate in 1973, Lam was elected its president until the Communist takeover in April 1975, when he emigrated to Australia. He remains a prominent commentator on Vietnamese affairs.

—Ngô N. Trung

Reference: Biographical Files, Indo-China Archives, University of California at Berkeley.

See also: Paris Peace Accords; Vietnam, Republic of: 1954–1975.

Trân Van Trà (1918–)

People's Army of Vietnam (PAVN) general; chairman, Military Affairs Committee of the Central Office of South Vietnam, 1964–1976; minister of defense, Provisional Revolutionary Government of South Vietnam, 1969–1976. Trà used several aliases, including Tu Chi and Trân Nam Trung ("loyal to the South"). In 1963, under the alias Anh Thu, he took command of a Viêt Công (VC) cadre group in the Mekong Delta.

In 1964 Gen. Trà became chair of the Military Affairs Committee, Central Office of South Vietnam (COSVN), a position he held until 1976. He commanded the VC attack on Sài Gòn during the Têt Offensive in 1968. From 1969 to 1976 he was Minister of Defense for the Provisional Revolutionary Government of South Vietnam. In March 1973 Trà returned to Hà Nôi to plan the final attack on South Vietnam. His task was facilitated by growing economic woes in the South, increasing morale problems among the Army of the Republic of Vietnam (ARVN), and waning U.S. support.

Despite disagreement with Lê Đuc Tho, Lê Duân, Giáp, and other Communist leaders, in October 1974 Trà began the final campaign. Supported by fresh supplies of Soviet weapons, the offensive moved forward successfully through the end of the year. Trà planned the final assault on Sài Gòn led by Gen. Van Tiên Dung and four crack PAVN divisions.

Despite last-minute efforts by President Thiêu to enlist U.S. aid, ARVN forces crumbled in March and were in full retreat by early April. On 7 April 1975 Lê Đuc Tho and Trà arrived at the battlefront to oversee the final phase of the tak-ing of Sài Gòn. On 30 April Gen. Duong Van Minh surrendered. Tho and Trà arrived that afternoon to end the war.

From May 1975 to January 1976, Trà served as head of the Military Occupation Force, Sài Gòn (later Ho Chi Minh City). In 1982 Trà published his controversial five-volume work, *History of the Bulwark B2 Theatre.* In it he criticized wartime policies of the Democratic Republic of Vietnam, especially the 1968 Têt Offensive and the willingness (or, as Trà says, desire) to sacrifice Viêt Công manpower in what he believed was an ill-conceived and needless campaign. Such candor led to his ouster from the Politburo and the banning of the book in Vietnam. Although the Vietnamese government rescinded the ban in the late 1980s and allowed Trà to participate in conferences reappraising the Communist role in the Vietnam War, he lived under something of a house arrest situation. As one of the "grand old men" of the revolution, Trà was allowed to meet visiting dignitaries and veterans groups from the United States, but in controlled settings.

—William Head

Reference: Trân Van Trà. *History of the Bulwark B2 Theatre.* Vol. 5, *Concluding the 30-Year War* (1982).

See also: COSVN (Central Office for South Vietnam or Trung Uong Cuc Miên Nam); Hô Chí Minh Campaign; Lê Duân; Lê Đuc Tho; Têt Offensive: Overall Strategy; Têt Offensive: the Sài Gòn Circle; Vietnamese Communist Party (VCP); Vô Nguyên Giáp.

Transportation Group 559

Organization responsible for opening the supply network through Laos to South Vietnam. In May 1959 Gen. Vô Nguyên Giáp, a reluctant convert to aggressive action in the South, ordered Gen. Vo Bam to begin work on a secret project to move war supplies into South Vietnam through eastern Laos. Bam formed the 559th Transportation Group, and work began in May 1959. Group 759, organized that July, was to arrange resupply by sea. Land resupply, however, was by far the most important means of support for the insurgency in the South. Bam's Group 559 soon opened a "modest track" to the South. Vastly expanded and made more sophisticated over the years, this communications network, which became known as the Hô Chí Minh Trail, was vital to Hà Nôi's military victory. Group 559 also supplied the Pathet Lao, the Communist army in Laos.

—Spencer C. Tucker

Reference: Currey, Cecil B. *Victory at Any Cost. The Genius of Viet Nam's Gen. Vo Nguyen Giap* (1997).

See also: Hô Chí Minh Trail; Logistics, Allied and People's Army of Vietnam/Viêt Công; Order of Battle; Vô Nguyên Giáp.

Triêu Âu (225–248)

Also known as Bà Triêu (Lady Triêu) or Triêu Thi Trinh; leader of the revolt against Chinese rule in 248. Bà Triêu is one of the most important heroines in Vietnamese history. She is famous for her statement that she wanted to "save our people from hell, instead of following the step of common people to bend my back to serve men as their concubines." With her brother Triêu Quôc Đat, she led a revolt in 248 against the Wu. In battle Bà Triêu wore golden armor, sat on the head of an elephant, and fought bravely. After six months her small army was defeated, and Bà Triêu killed herself at age 23.

—Pham Cao Duong

References: Nguyên Huyên Anh. *Viêt Nam Danh Nhân Tu Điên* (1990); Pham Cao Duong. *Lich Su Dân Tôc Viêt Nam. Quyên I: Thoi Ky Lâp Quôc* (1987); Taylor, Keith W. *The Birth of Vietnam* (1983).

See also: Trung Trac and Trung Nhi; Vietnam: Prehistory to 938.

Triêu Đà (258–137 B.C.)

Chao T'o, in Chinese, also known as Triêu Vu Vuong; founder of the Triêu Dynasty (207–111 B.C.) and the Nam Viêt (Nan Yueh, in Chinese) Kingdom that covered the Chinese provinces of Kwang-tung and Kwang-si and the northern part of present Vietnam. To most Vietnamese, Triêu Đà is a Viêt king because he founded a southern kingdom carved within the former territory of the Viêt (Yueh) with the Viêt as the main population, completely separated from the Ch'in in the north. Many consider the two Kwang provinces as Vietnamese territory.

—Pham Cao Duong

References: Lê Thành Khôi. *Histoire du Viet-Nam des Origines à 1858* (1981); Pham Cao Duong. *Lich Su Dân Tôc Viêt Nam, Quyên I: Thoi Ky Lâp Quôc* (1987); Taylor, Keith W. *The Birth of Vietnam* (1983).

See also: Nguyên Phúc Ánh (Gia Long); Vietnam: Prehistory to 938.

Trinh Lords

Rulers of northern Vietnam (Tonkin), 1592–1786. The Trinh succeeded in introducing some administrative and military reforms and in 1711 issued an edict intended to check the greed of provincial mandarins and landlords. The Trinh, however, were unable to halt the continuing efforts of landowners, court notables, and mandarins to seek landed wealth at the expense of the peasantry. As a result, the regime was repeatedly menaced by peasant insurgencies and eventually fell prey to the populist Tây Son Rebellion. Between 1786 and 1789, Tây Son armies defeated the Trinh, their nominal Lê overlords, and even a Chinese army, but their leaders did not govern long enough to eradicate the lust for power and economic self-interest that plagued Vietnam's traditional ruling elites. These traits persisted with fateful results for Vietnam's stability during the dynasty subsequently established by the Trinh's old rivals, the Nguyên, who had managed to survive, if only barely, the challenge of the Tây Son Rebellion.

—Marc Jason Gilbert

References: Buttinger, Joseph. *The Smaller Dragon: A Political History of Vietnam* (1958); Nguyên Khac Viên. *Vietnam: A Long History* (1987); Whitfield, Danny J. *Historical and Cultural Dictionary of Vietnam* (1976).

See also: Lê Dynasty; Nguyên Dynasty; Tây Son Uprising.

Truman, Harry S (1884–1972)

President of the United States, 1945–1952, responsible for initiating U.S. involvement in Vietnam. In July 1945 Truman and Winston Churchill made a far-reaching determination concerning Southeast Asia. The Allied chiefs of staff divided French Indo-China along the 16th parallel for "operational purposes," allowing the Japanese to surrender to the Chinese in the north and to the British in the south. The leaders made no provisions for Indo-Chinese self-determination.

In 1946, reacting to the Communist threat in Greece and Turkey, U.S. policymakers articulated through the Truman and Marshall Plans George F. Kennan's policy of firm containment of Russia. Kennan's policy dominated foreign relations throughout the Cold War and was extended to Southeast Asia. Under Secretary of State Dean Acheson convinced Truman in March 1950 to allocate $15 million to assist the French in defeating the Viêt Minh. On 28 June 1950, eight C-47 cargo aircraft transported to Vietnam the first of this aid, which by 1954 grew to a total of $3 billion.

Truman's decision to assist the French in Indo-China was motivated by the 1949 Russian atomic bomb detonation, the Communist victory in China that same year, and Joseph McCarthy's ensuing attack on the administration for "softness" on communism.

During the Vietnam War, President Johnson visited Truman several times seeking endorsement of his policies, but Truman refused to make a public statement; privately, he was disenchanted with Johnson's leadership.

—Brenda J. Taylor

References: Anderson, David L., ed. *Shadow on the White House: Presidents and the Vietnam War, 1945–1975* (1993); McCullough, David. *Truman* (1992); Williams, William Appleman, ed. *America in Vietnam: A Documentary History* (1985).

See also: Acheson, Dean G.; Containment Policy; Eisenhower, Dwight David; Johnson, Lyndon Baines; Kennan, George Frost; United States: Involvement in Indo-China through 1954.

Trung Trac and Trung Nhi (?–43)

Also known as Hai Bà Trung (The Two Ladies Trung) or Trung Vuong or Trung Nu Vuong (Queens Trung); sisters and Vietnamese heroines, who led the first uprising of Vietnamese against Chinese rule in A.D. 40. Hai Bà Trung are considered by many Vietnamese to be the most important and most revered heroines in Vietnam's history. The anniversary of their deaths has become Vietnamese Women's Day, and ceremonies are organized annually in their honor on the sixth day of the second month of the lunar calendar.

—Pham Cao Duong

References: Bùi Quang Tung. "Cuôc Khoi Nghia Hai Bà Trung Duoi Mat Su Gia" (1959); Nguyên Huyên Anh. *Viêt Nam Danh Nhân Tu Điên* (1990); Pham Cao Duong. *Lich Su Dân Tôc Viêt Nam, Quyên I: Thoi Ky Lâp Quôc* (1987); Taylor, Keith W. *The Birth of Vietnam* (1983).

See also: Triêu Âu; Vietnam: Prehistory through 938; Women in the War, Vietnamese.

Truong Chinh (Đang Xuân Khu) (1907–1988)

General secretary, Indo-Chinese Communist Party (1941–1956); Democratic Republic of Vietnam (DRV) official; general secretary, Vietnamese Communist Party (1986). In 1938 Truong Chinh (as Qua Ninh), in collaboration with Vô Nguyên Giáp (as Vân Đình), published *The Peasant*

Problem, 1937–1938, arguing that a Communist revolution could be both peasant-and proletarian-based. Leftist journalist Wilfred Burchett described the book as forming the basis for the Communist Party and later Viêt Minh policies toward the peasantry.

French authorities banned the Communist Party in 1939, and Truong Chinh fled to China. When Hô Chí Minh in 1941 organized the Viêt Nam Dôc Lâp Dông Minh Hôi, or Viêt Minh (League for the Independence of Vietnam), Truong Chinh became a leading member and successfully helped to portray it as an anti-French and anti-Japanese resistance movement dedicated to the overthrow of foreign dominance in Vietnam. In 1945 he played a leading part in the August Revolution and helped draft the constitution of the Democratic Republic of Vietnam (DRV). He became a member of the DRV's first National Assembly in 1946.

Truong Chinh served as director of Viêt Minh propaganda and oversaw intelligence and counterintelligence activities during the first Indo-China War. By 1953 he was second only to Hô Chí Minh in the northern hierarchy. In the early 1950s, Truong Chinh dictated a strict new party cultural line that imposed severe restrictions on writing, music, and poetry. All had to promote party policies.

A longtime friend and comrade of Vô Nguyên Giáp, Truong Chinh became suspicious of his meteoric rise in the party hierarchy and his control of military forces. After a bitter struggle, Truong Chinh succeeded in having the army placed under the control of political commissars. In 1950 he ordered the execution of Trân Chí Châu, Giáp's chief of logistical services, and accused Giáp of poor judgment in selecting personnel and of stumbling into "useless massacres, which had no other purpose than to promote personal interests." Although they voted together on later issues, the two were never again close.

Hô Chí Minh named Truong Chinh vice-chairman of the Land Reform Committee in 1954, and he implemented a draconian program of agrarian reform that included large-scale dispossession and innumerable executions of "landlords," who were often landless peasants guilty only of being disliked by their neighbors. Truong Chinh demonstrated his zeal for land reform by denouncing his own father. His attempts to impose total collectivization of agriculture based on the Communist pattern greatly diminished production and threatened famine. Hô Chí Minh dismissed Truong Chinh from his positions as land reform vice-chairman and as secretary-general of the Lao Dông Party. Truong Chinh was forced to officially admit "serious mistakes" and "left-wing deviationism" (being more orthodox than the party line required) but retained his number-three position within the Politburo and remained influential within the party leadership. His eclipse did not last long. By 1958 he was one of four vice-premiers of the DRV. In April 1961 he became a member of the Presidium of the Fatherland Front and in August 1964 served as a member of the National Assembly delegation to Indonesia.

His influence waned by 1968, as he urged a "socialist construction" of the North, while Lê Duân and others wanted the DRV to concentrate on winning the war in the South. Lê Duân and his faction won the argument, thus paving the way for the 1968 Têt Offensive. After the 1975 fall of South Vietnam, he again rose in influence. In July 1986 he was again secretary-general of the Vietnamese Communist Party but resigned in December, probably because severe economic problems in the Socialist Republic of Vietnam had eroded his political base.

—Cecil B. Currey

References: Pham Binh, Châu Phong, Lê Mai, Bùi Tín, Trân Công Mân, and Cao Pha, interviews with the author; "Who's Who in North Vietnam" (1972); *Who's Who in the Socialist Countries* (1978).

See also: Burchett, Wilfred; Hô Chí Minh; Lao Dông Party; Lê Duân; Mao Zedong (Mao Tse-tung); Vietnam, Democratic Republic of: 1954–1975; Vietnam, Socialist Republic of: 1975 to the Present; Vietnamese Communist Party (VCP); Vô Nguyên Giáp.

Truong Dình Dzu (1917–mid-1980s)

South Vietnamese politician and unsuccessful candidate for the presidency of the Republic of Vietnam (RVN). In 1961 Dzu declared his intention to run for the RVN presidency against incumbent President Ngô Dình Diêm but he was pressured to withdraw when accused of illegal fund transfers out of the country. In 1967 Dzu again ran for the presidency, calling for negotiations to end the war. Finishing behind the winning ticket of Nguyên Van Thiêu and Nguyên Cao Ky, Dzu—with two other candidates, Phan Khac Suu and Hoàng Co Bình—held a news conference charging fraud on the part of the military ticket to rig the elections. Military leaders then accused Dzu of illegally opening a San Francisco bank account, and in February 1967 Dzu and other leftists were put under police surveillance. Brought before a Special Military Court on 26 July 1968, Dzu was sentenced to five years of hard labor but was released in December thanks to public pressure in the RVN and abroad. After the 1975 Communist victory, Dzu was sentenced to reeducation.

—Ngô N. Trung

Reference: Biographical Files, Indo-China Archives, University of California at Berkeley.

See also: Elections (National), Republic of Vietnam: 1955, 1967, 1971; Ngô Dình Diêm; Nguyên Cao Ky; Nguyên Van Thiêu.

Truong Nhu Tang (1923–)

Southern Vietnamese revolutionary and founding member of the National Front for the Liberation of South Vietnam (NFLSV); minister of justice in the Provisional Revolutionary Government (PRG), 1969–1975. In 1956 Tang joined several prominent individuals in Sài Gòn to oppose the rule of President Ngô Dình Diêm. These contacts led him to the group of revolutionaries who founded the NFLSV on 20 December 1960.

Tang held important positions in Sài Gòn until the early 1960s, when his clandestine revolutionary activities were disclosed. After significant time in a Sài Gòn prison, he traded his professional life for one of a full-time revolutionary in the jungles of Tây Ninh Province. Tang was a dedicated revolutionary, but he became disillusioned after the war as he saw the Southern revolutionaries pushed aside by their Northern compatriots. Although Tang maintained that he was never a Communist, the Lao Đông Party rewarded him with a ministry post after Sài Gòn fell. By 1976, however, he was making plans to cscapc from Victnam.

Tang's highly controversial 1985 book, *A Viet Cong Memoir,* recounts his role in the modern Vietnamese revolution, but there is considerable debate among scholars as to whether Tang is representative of the NFLSV's membership and leadership.

—Robert K. Brigham

References: Dellinger, David. *Vietnam Revisited: Covert Action to Invasion to Reconstruction* (1986); Pike, Douglas. *Viet Cong: The Organization and Techniques of the National Liberation Front of South Vietnam* (1966); Thayer, Carlyle A. *War By Other Means: National Liberation and Revolution in Viet-Nam, 1956–1960* (1989); Truong Nhu Tang. *A Viet Cong Memoir: An Inside Account of the Vietnam War and Its Aftermath* (1985).

See also: National Front for the Liberation of South Vietnam (NFLSV); Nguyên Huu Tho; Nguyên Thi Bình; Provisional Revolutionary Government of South Vietnam (PRG).

Tsuchihashi Yuitsu (ca. 1895–?)

Japanese Army lieutenant general and commander of Japanese forces in Indo-China between December 1944 and September 1945. Tokyo worried that the United States would soon mount an amphibious assault on Vietnam from the Philippines and thought it best to neutralize the French first before having to deal with an American invasion. In March 1945 Tsuchihashi carried out a coup against the French administration and military forces in Indo-China. He surrendered his forces north of the 16th parallel to the Chinese at Hà Nôi on 28 September 1945.

—Spencer C. Tucker

References: Marr, David G. *Vietnam 1945: The Quest for Power* (1996); Patti, Archimedes L. A. *Why Viet Nam? Prelude to America's Albatross* (1980).

See also: French Indo-China; Japan; Mordant, Eugène; Sabattier, Gabriel.

Tu Đuc (1829–1883)

Fourth ruler of the Nguyên Dynasty, second son of Emperor Thiêu Tri and Empress Tu Du, and last emperor of an independent Vietnam; real name Hông Nhâm. Tu Đuc could have been a great emperor but for the French invasion of his country. In the year of his ascension to the throne, French warships shelled Đà Nang. In 1858, using as an excuse the persecution of Catholics, the French and their Spanish allies attacked, seized this citadel, and began their invasion of Vietnam. Biên Hòa, Gia Đinh, and Đinh Tuong were lost to the French in the Treaty of 1862, followed by Vinh Long, An Giang, and Hà Tiên in 1867. At the same time Tu Đuc had to face uprisings in the North, some led by Catholic followers. Tu Đuc died shortly before the Huê Court was to sign the Treaty of Qu″ Mùi (25 August 1883) accepting a French protectorate over the rest of Vietnam.

—Pham Cao Duong

References: Lê Huu Muc. *Huân Dich Thập Điêu: Thánh Du Cua Vua Thánh Tô, Diên Nghia Cua Vua Duc Tông* (1971); Lê Thành Khôi. *Le Viet-Nam: Histoire et Civilisation* (1955); Nguyên Huyên Anh. *Việt Nam Danh Nhân Tu Điên* (1990); Quôc Su Quán. *Quôc Triêu Chánh Biên Toát Yêu* (1971); Trân Trong Kim. *Viêt Nam Su Luoc* (1971).

See also: Hàm Nghi; Minh Mang; Thiêu Tri; Vietnam: from 938 through the French Conquest.

Tu Vê

Self-defense (militia) force made up of young citizens in cities to fight the French at the beginning of the first Indo-China War; also called Tu Vê Thành (city self-defense force) or Tu Vê Chiên Đâu (self-defense combat force). The Tu Vê were neither Communists nor members of the Viêt Minh. The Tu Vê fought bravely in Hà Nôi between 19 December 1946 and 17 February 1947 despite being poorly armed and trained. The 60 days they were able to contain the French in the capital bought the time necessary for the regular military force, the Vê Quôc Đoàn, to withdraw safely to mountainous areas and follow the strategy of "preservation of its main force" (*bao toàn chu luc*). Part of the Hà Nôi Tu Vê force later formed the Trung Đoàn Thu Đô (Regiment of the Capital) and the Trung Đoàn Thang Long (Thang Long Regiment). Both became famous in the history of Vietnamese resistance against the French.

—Pham Cao Duong

References: Ban Nghiên Cuu Lich Su Quân Đôi. *Lich Su Quân Đôi Nhân Dân Viêt Nam, tâp I* (1977); Gras, Général Yves. *Histoire de la Guerre d'Indochine* (1979); Nguyên Khac Viên. *The Long Resistance, 1858–1975* (1975).

See also: Indo-China War; Viêt Minh.

Tunnel Rats

Soldiers who fought the Viêt Công (VC) and People's Army of Vietnam in their underground tunnels and bunkers. Only the U.S. Army 1st and 25th Infantry Divisions maintained formal units of these troops, and the 1st Infantry devoted the most effort to their development and training. The units were small; the 1st Division only had two squads, each led by a lieutenant, and never exceeded 13 men at any time. Lt. Randolph Ellis and Lt. Jerry Sinn formalized the teams and gave them the discipline and procedural guidelines commonly found in elite units. Robert Woods, the first team sergeant, served for three years and contributed as much as anyone to the skills and tactics used by the teams. Each of the 1st Division teams also had a radio telephone operator, a medic, and two former Viêt Công, Hiêp and Tiên, who acted as advisors and translators.

A tunnel rat's basic equipment was a .38-caliber revolver, a flashlight, and a knife. Standard procedure required three men in the tunnels at a time. The tunnel rats' biggest success came between 9 and 11 August 1968, when the team led by Sergeant Woods killed three VC soldiers in an underground firefight and forced 153 more out of a tunnel into captivity.

Outside of the 1st Infantry Division, most tunnel rats were usually ill-trained volunteers. Still, they occasionally scored notable successes. Many of the reports of weapons captured in all of the military regions were the result of explorations by tunnel rats. Although most tunnel rats survived, all 1st Division Tunnel Rats were wounded at least once.

—James T. Gillam

References: Browne, Malcolm. *The New Face of War* (1965); Burchett, Wilfred G. *Vietnam: The Inside Story of the Guerrilla War* (1965); Ebert, James R. *A Life in a Year: The American Infantryman in Vietnam 1965–1972* (1993); Mangold, Thomas, and John Pennycate. *The Tunnels of Cuchi* (1987).
See also: CEDAR FALLS, Operation; Cu Chi, Tunnels of; Iron Triangle; United States: Army.

Twining, Nathan Farragut (1897–1982)

U.S. Air Force general; chairman of the Joint Chiefs of Staff (JCS), 1957–1960. Twining supported President Eisenhower's contention that the threat of massive retaliation would eliminate "brushfire" wars. In 1954 during the Indo-China War, he advocated using atomic weapons at Điên Biên Phu, believing this would lift the siege and strengthen deterrence, but he opposed the use of covert U.S. military advisors. Twining believed that the Viêt Minh's lack of sophisticated air defense capability would make U.S. air power virtually invulnerable over Indo-China. As chief of staff, Twining was an advocate of Air Force expansion, including the B-52 bomber and the ballistic missile program. Twining's hawkish stance led Eisenhower to appoint him chairman of the JCS in 1957. He retired from the military in 1960.

—Stephen R. Maynard

References: Dupuy, Trevor N., Curt Johnson, and David L. Bongard. *The Harper Encyclopedia of Military Biography* (1992); Mrozek, Donald J. "Nathan F. Twining: New Dimensions, a New Look" (1989).
See also: Eisenhower, Dwight David; Radford, Arthur W.; VULTURE, Operation.

U Thant (1909–1974)

United Nations (UN) secretary-general, 1962–1972. Immediately following the August 1964 Tonkin Gulf incidents, Thant spoke directly with President Johnson and offered to arrange a meeting of low-level diplomats from all warring sides. Hô Chí Minh was interested, but Johnson, preoccupied with that fall's presidential election, was not. Howrever, the idea intrigued Adlai Stevenson, U.S. ambassador to the UN, who in January 1965 suggested to Thant that together they make preliminary plans for talks in Burma. Thant quickly agreed to what became known as the "Rangoon initiative," but on 30 January the Johnson administration officially rejected the plan.

Thant then suggested another Geneva peace conference, despite Johnson's July 1964 statement that he would never agree to a second meeting. When Johnson again refused, a furious Thant called a news conference and made public Washington's obstruction of his peace efforts. Caught off guard, the administration denied that such initiatives had been undertaken.

That summer Stevenson and Thant approached Britain and France, hoping those governments would take the lead in the search for a negotiated peace. It was not to be. Stevenson died while on a trip designed to advance these initiatives, and the plan perished with him. Thant retired as secretary-general on 1 January 1972.

—John Robert Greene

References: Kraslow, David, and Stuart H. Loory. *The Secret Search for Peace in Vietnam* (1968); U Thant. *View from the UN: The Memoirs of U Thant* (1978).
See also: Hô Chí Minh; Johnson, Lyndon Baines; Stevenson, Adlai E.; Tonkin Gulf Incidents; United Nations and the Vietnam War.

UNION I and II, Operations (21 April–5 June 1967)

Successive U.S. Marine Corps operations in Quang Nam and Quang Tín Provinces in southern I Corps, Viêt Công (VC) and People's Army of Vietnam (PAVN) strongholds, in which Army of the Republic of Vietnam (ARVN) forces were unable to establish outposts beyond the district capitals. Until 1967, the U.S. Marines lacked assets to control the Phuoc Ha/Quê Son Valley.

On 20 April outside of Thang Bình, a company of the 2d Battalion, 1st Marines, was hit by concentrated automatic weapons and grenade fire from the 3d PAVN Regiment. Operation UNION I began the next morning with the insertion of the 3d Battalion, 5th Marines, and the 1st Battalion, 1st Marines. The 1st ARVN Ranger Group also participated. Heavy fighting in the Phuoc Ha/Quê Son Valley lasted until 25 April, when PAVN forces began to withdraw. As contact diminished, only units of the 5th Marines remained in the area.

On 10 May, these Marines successfully assaulted PAVN mortar emplacements on Hill 110, but Communist forces mauled several Marine companies coming to assist. For the next five days, the 5th Marines continuously assaulted entrenched PAVN positions on thc valley floor. Supported by air strikes and artillery fire, they finally overran the PAVN defenses, and the operation officially ended on 17 May.

Launched nine days later, Operation UNION II was designed to entrap the 3d and 21st PAVN Regiments, spotted in a valley in northern Quang Tín Province. On 26 May, two battalions of the 5th Marines and the 6th ARVN Regiment were inserted. For two days, the 3d Battalion, 5th Marines, battled units of the 3d PAVN Regiment 20 miles northwest of Tam Ky, killing 171. On 2 June, the 1st Battalion, 5th Marines, supported by artillery fire and 138 air strikes, overran entrenched hillside positions of the 21st PAVN Regiment north of Thiên Phuoc in bunker-to-bunker fighting. The operation ended on 5 June.

Operations UNION I and II, although brief, were the bloodiest Marine engagements to date. The two operations produced a total of 1,566 PAVN dead, 196 captured, and 184 weapons seized. Marine losses for both operations totaled 220 killed and 714 wounded. For action in UNION I and II, the 5th Marine Regiment won the Presidential Unit Citation.

—John D. Root

References: Simmons, Edwin H. "Marine Corps Operations in Vietnam, 1967" (1985); Stanton, Shelby L. *The Rise and Fall of an American Army: U.S. Ground Forces in Vietnam, 1965–1973* (1985).
See also: United States: Marine Corps; Vietnam, Democratic Republic of: Army (People's Army of Vietnam [PAVN]); Vietnam, Republic of: Army (ARVN).

Union of Soviet Socialist Republics (USSR) (Soviet Union)

Relations between the Soviet Union and the Democratic Republic of Vietnam (DRV) until well into the 1960s are characterized by Douglas Pike in *Vietnam and the Soviet Union* as "nominal and cursory, having neither much intercourse and emotional attachment for either party." Then during the Vietnam War and until the mid-1980s, relations were close. The Soviet Union fully supported the DRV's war effort militarily, economically, and diplomatically. From 1985 to the mid-1990s, however, relations between the USSR/Russia and the DRV/Socialist Republic of Vietnam (SRV) steadily deteriorated until there was little intercourse between the two on any front.

The Bolshevik Revolution was profoundly meaningful for Vietnamese revolutionaries. Hô Chí Minh attended the fifth Comintern Congress in Moscow in 1924, which denounced Western imperialism and colonialism, including French control of Indo-China. He visited Moscow frequently between 1924 and 1941. Although extensive sentimental and psychological ties existed, there were few specific political and diplomatic connections. Hô considered the Comintern of limited usefulness.

The Stalin years (1929–1953) were ones of complete indifference on the part of the USSR. Joseph Stalin regarded anticolonial activity as sometimes useful but always undependable. Stalin and his government were preoccupied with internal Soviet and European problems, and Vietnam was hardly a concern. During World War II, Hô received no Soviet assistance in his struggle against the Japanese, and Soviet reaction to Hô's August 1945 declaration of independence was guarded. The Soviet Union did not recognize the DRV until January 1950, 13 days after the People's Republic of China (PRC) had done so.

Because the Soviet Union sought good relations with France, political support for the Viêt Minh throughout the Indo-China War was restrained. In addition, Stalin never trusted Hô, regarding him as too independent. Yet behind the scenes, the Soviet Union funneled $1 billion in military aid to the Viêt Minh through the PRC, an important factor in the Viêt Minh's victory against the French.

After Stalin's death, as part of a new foreign policy to relax tensions with the West, Moscow supported the holding of an international peace conference in Geneva in 1954 to settle the Indo-China War. During the conference, the Soviet delegation, led by Foreign Minister V. M. Molotov, forced the Viêt Minh to compromise by accepting terms less favorable than its military achievements might otherwise have dictated. Consequently, relations after the Geneva Conference were cool between the DRV and the Soviet Union.

When Nikita Khrushchev achieved complete power in 1956, DRV leaders held great hopes. Khrushchev shifted Soviet interests to a global scope. He saw potential advantages in Vietnam and stepped up military and economic aid, thus deepening relations and propelling rapid economic development in the DRV. Yet as the war intensified, Khrushchev became more cautious. Originally his goal was to oust the West from Asia, but the increasing Sino-Soviet dispute complicated efforts. Khrushchev feared that a quick and total victory by the Communists in Vietnam would only help China and cause an unnecessary confrontation with the United States. By the end of his rule in 1964, Khrushchev had soured on Vietnam, regarding the war as too risky and the DRV leaders as crafty and manipulative. All that prevented a total Soviet disengagement was the coup that ousted Khrushchev in October 1964.

Soviet Premier Aleksei Kosygin's visit to Hà Nôi in February 1965 initiated full and close relations. Soviet and Vietnamese leaders signed economic and military treaties in which the Soviet Union pledged full support for the DRV's war effort. Soviet and DRV leadership planned military strategy; the USSR would supply the DRV with the necessary war materiel, including air defenses for the North and offensive weapons to be employed in the South.

The Soviet Union also conducted a propaganda war against the United States in the United Nations and other world forums, at times threatening to send Soviet and Eastern European "volunteers" to Vietnam. The Soviet Union hoped to use the war to seek an ideological advantage over China as the dispute between the two Communist powers became increasingly bitter. Yet it became clear that the Soviet Union would not directly intervene in the war, and its policies remained ambiguous and cautious. But as the war intensi-

fied, so did Soviet aid, until it amounted to 80 percent of all supplies reaching the DRV.

After the 1968 Têt Offensive, the Soviets believed for the first time that a total victory was possible. Yet, as the war continued, the Soviet spirit waned, and the Soviets fully endorsed the 1968 Paris peace talks. When the talks deadlocked in 1972, the Soviet Union pressured the DRV to accept a compromise settlement with the Republic of Vietnam (RVN) and the United States in January 1973. The success of the 1975 military offensive came as a great surprise to both the DRV and the Soviet leadership, however.

The Vietnam War served Soviet interests well by keeping the United States fully occupied in an area not of crucial importance to the USSR. Historians are in disagreement, however, regarding Soviet influence over DRV decision making during the war. Economic relations between the two countries were largely a one-way street. The Soviet Union poured billions of rubles into Vietnam, but few rubles returned to the USSR. During 1965–1975 military aid was central, and economic aid was geared entirely to the war effort. By the 1970s Soviet aid amounted to $1 billion or more annually, without which the DRV could not have continued the war.

After 1975, with the near collapse of the Vietnamese economy, the Soviet Union sent the Socialist Republic of Vietnam (SRV) basic food supplies and oil. A more intimate relationship than ever before developed, in part the result of a precipitous decline in relations between China and Vietnam. Wars with China and Cambodia proved costly between 1978 and 1979 and drove Vietnam into near-total dependency on the Soviet Union. In November 1979, the Soviet Union signed a friendship pact with the SRV, in return for which it obtained naval and air bases. Ironically, many were former U.S. bases in South Vietnam. By the mid-1980s, the relationship was so close that Vietnam was considered a Soviet client state.

After Mikhail Gorbachev came to power in 1985, Soviet relations steadily declined. Gorbachev moved away from militarily and ideologically oriented policies to those based on economics and achieved a rapprochement with China. Those changes greatly reduced the value of Vietnam to the Soviet Union. Following the collapse of communism in Eastern Europe and the Soviet Union, Vietnam faded from the attention of Russia's new leaders, who felt no ideological affinity toward the country. Economic and military aid completely stopped. Because of Russia's huge and growing economic crisis, trade itself greatly declined and would be conducted only on a basis of full equality and in hard currency. Relations reached a low ebb with no sign of improvement.

—Michael Share

References: Edmonds, Robin. *Soviet Foreign Policy: The Brezhnev Years* (1983); Gaiduk, Ilya V. *The Soviet Union and the Vietnam War* (1996); Longmire, R. A. *Soviet Relations with South-East Asia* (1989); Pike, Douglas. *Vietnam and the Soviet Union: Anatomy of an Alliance* (1987).

See also: Gorbachev, Mikhail Sergeyevich; Khrushchev, Nikita Sergeyevich; Kosygin, Aleksei Nikolayevich; Paris Peace Negotiations; Paris Peace Accords; Vietnam, Democratic Republic of: 1945–1954; Vietnam, Democratic Republic of: 1954–1975; Vietnam, Socialist Republic of: 1975 to the Present.

UNIONTOWN, Operation (December 1967–March 1968) U.S. Army 199th Infantry Brigade (Light) operation in War Zone D. The 199th combined the 3d Battalion, 7th Infantry and 4th Battalion, 12th Infantry, based at Fort Benning, Georgia, the army's Infantry Center. The light infantry brigade concept called for a rapidly deployable force with minimal heavy equipment and fire support assets. The brigade was to be mixed in task forces with aviation, transportation, logistical, and artillery support from existing forces in Vietnam. U.S. Military Assistance Command, Vietnam (MACV) and, later, U.S. Army, Vietnam (USARV) were designated as the controlling headquarters for the 199th.

Under severe pressure to meet the army's deployment schedule, the 199th arrived at the port of Vung Tàu in early December despite shortages in personnel and equipment. It then moved to its permanent base camp at Long Bình, which would remain home to the brigade for the duration of its Vietnam service.

In December 1967, Operation UNIONTOWN commenced as the 199th, supported by the 11th Armored Cavalry Regiment ("Black Horse"), moved into War Zone C and engaged Viêt Công (VC) and People's Army of Vietnam (PAVN) forces. On 17 December 1967, the brigade's 4th Battalion, 12th Infantry (4/12th) regiment conducted its first airmobile combat assault. The 199th continued to be used as a quick reaction force in the Sài Gòn area during the conflict.

MACV assigned the 199th to cooperate with Army of the Republic of Vietnam (ARVN) forces to provide security for the greater Sài Gòn area. During the 1968 Têt Offensive, the 199th fought insurgents in the capital before being relieved by the 5th ARVN Ranger Group. Other elements of the brigade conducted the defense at Long Bình. As the offensive continued, the brigade moved to positions near Biên Hòa. Meanwhile, the 1st Infantry Division had split War Zones C and D and opened Route 13 between Sài Gòn and Quan Loi, and the "Redcatchers" of the 199th supported 1st Infantry operations in that area. The 199th was later combined with the 196th Light Infantry Brigade (Separate) to form the 23d Infantry Division (Americal). It served through the remainder of the war in Quang Ngãi Province.

—J. A. Menzoff

Reference: Stanton, Shelby. *The Rise and Fall of an American Army: U.S. Ground Forces in Vietnam, 1965–1973* (1985).
See also: Airmobility; Military Assistance Command, Vietnam (MACV); Têt Offensive: Overall Strategy; Têt Offensive: the Sài Gòn Circle; United States: Army; Vietnam, Republic of: Army (ARVN).

United Front

Groups, factions, or organizations united to achieve a political objective; principal organizational strategy used by the Vietnamese Communists to win power. The united front is a powerful weapon in the hands of a small but highly dedicated, disciplined party. It relies on mobilizing sentiment to achieve political aims, sometimes through violence.

The first notable example of the united front in Indo-China was the Viêt Minh, organized by Hô Chí Minh while in China in 1941. The Viêt Minh mobilized Vietnamese nationalists in the war against the French, although its Communist domination became increasingly apparent as the war continued. Similarly, the Communist-dominated National Front for the Liberation of South Vietnam, or National Liberation Front (NLF), established in December 1960, and the Pathet Lao in Laos included among their membership many non-Communist nationalist groups. As Lê Duân, who is generally credited as driving force of the united front strategy following Hô's death, explained in a 1970 newspaper article: "The Front is an organization in which contradictions could be reconciled. The Front includes many different classes that united on the basis of a common and fixed program of action."

—Arthur J. Dommen

Reference: Lê Duân. "Under the Glorious Party Banner, for Independence, Freedom, and Socialism, Let Us Advance and Achieve New Victories" (1970).
See also: Hô Chí Minh; Lê Duân; National Front for the Liberation of South Vietnam (NFLSV); Pathet Lao; Viêt Minh.

United Nations and the Vietnam War

The United Nations' role in the Vietnam War was negligible for several reasons. One resulted from the structure of the organization. Each member of the United Nations (UN) Security Council has the power to veto resolutions. The United States, which supported the Republic of Vietnam (RVN), and the Soviet Union, which supported the Democratic Republic of Vietnam (DRV), used the veto to block resolutions that they perceived to be critical of their Southeast Asian policies.

Another obstacle blocking a meaningful UN role was that neither the DRV nor the RVN were member states. The Soviet Union had proposed admitting both nations in 1957, but the United States rejected the idea and was unwilling to recognize the partition of Vietnam with a Communist regime in the North.

UN Secretary-General U Thant believed the Vietnam problem lay outside the UN mandate, and many UN representatives, including France, agreed. The 1954 Geneva Accords that ended the Indo-China War also weakened the UN's ability to intervene in Vietnam. These agreements called for national elections in Vietnam in 1956 but made no provision for UN participation, rendering unlikely any debate concerning Vietnam in the UN General Assembly.

Despite these obstacles, U Thant attempted in 1964, 1968, and 1970 to negotiate a settlement of the Vietnam War. U Thant used his outstanding credentials as a neutralist and the power of his position to try to broker a peace agreement. His 1964 initiative came closest to success. With President Johnson's tacit approval, U Thant arranged for talks in Rangoon, Burma. The Soviet Union acted as intermediary to transmit the offer to Hà Nôi. The timing coincided with an attempt by Soviet Premier Nikita Khrushchev to get the North Vietnamese to negotiate. DRV leadership listened to Khrushchev's suggestion because the Soviet Union was its major supplier of armaments. However, hopes for a negotiated settlement were soon dashed. Khrushchev's fall from power in October 1964 brought a hardened policy against negotiations and in favor of increased assistance to Hà Nôi. U Thant's two other attempts at negotiation made no headway because of a hardening of positions on both sides resulting from escalation of the war.

Despite its failure to play an active role in the Vietnam War, the UN enjoyed success in issues stemming from the conflict. U Thant made some progress in limiting the use of defoliants. The UN also brokered a ban on biological weapons in April 1972, in part the result of international criticism over their use during the war. The UN accomplished much in easing the suffering of displaced Vietnamese and protected thousands of "boat people" who fled following the 1975 collapse of the RVN. The UN also supervised the emigration of Amerasian children from Vietnam to the United States.

—Eric W. Osborne

References: Boyd, Andrew. *Fifteen Men on a Powder Keg: A History of the U.N. Security Council* (1971); Karnow, Stanley. *Vietnam: A History* (1991); Lewin, Isaac. *War on War* (1969); Olson, James S., and Randy Roberts. *Where the Domino Fell: America and Vietnam, 1945–1990* (1991).

See also: Amerasians; Khrushchev, Nikita Sergeyevich; Johnson, Lyndon Baines; Refugees and Boat People; U Thant.

United States: Air Force

When the United States entered the Vietnam War, the U.S. Air Force (USAF) dominated the defense establishment, with a budget greater than that for the entire U.S. Army. The Air Force won its separate service status in 1947 based on the theory that strategic bombing—the destruction of an enemy's industrial war-making capabilities—was a potentially decisive element in warfare.

In November 1961, President Kennedy ordered the 4400th Combat Crew Training Squadron to the Republic of Vietnam (RVN) under the code name Operation FARM GATE. The air commandos of FARM GATE had three missions: an overt mission to train pilots for the Republic of Vietnam Air Force (RVNAF); a covert mission to fly close air support missions in response to the needs of the Army of the Republic of Vietnam (ARVN); and a hidden agenda to keep the U.S. Army from taking over the close air support with newly developed helicopter gunships.

The air commandos trained several squadrons of RVNAF pilots and performed well in close air support of ARVN and U.S. Army Special Forces units, but the Viêt Công and People's Army of Vietnam (PAVN) troops were gaining the upper hand. By 1964 the situation was grim, and in March, Air Force leaders called for bombing campaigns against North Vietnam. After a series of retaliation raids against North Vietnam beginning with the Gulf of Tonkin incidents in August 1964, President Johnson ordered Operation ROLLING THUNDER, a bombing campaign directed against the Democratic Republic of Vietnam (DRV), which began on 2 March 1964.

ROLLING THUNDER's first objective was strategic persuasion—the use of air power in intensifying degrees to persuade the DRV to stop supporting the Viêt Công and negotiate an end to the war. After massive deployment of U.S. ground forces to South Vietnam began in July 1965, the focus switched to interdiction of roads and railroads, primarily in the North Vietnam panhandle. A continuous but relatively minor objective was to boost the morale of South Vietnamese military and political elites.

ROLLING THUNDER became the longest bombing campaign ever conducted by the U.S. Air Force, lasting from 2 March 1965 to 31 October 1968. During that time, the Air Force flew nearly 500,000 of a total 700,000 sorties over North Vietnam. DRV air defenses claimed over 700 aircraft. In some Air Force F-105 units in 1966 and 1967, attrition rates ran between 50 and 75 percent for a one-year tour. During ROLLING THUNDER, 600,000 tons of bombs fell on North Vietnam.

ROLLING THUNDER's ultimate failure resulted from an inappropriate strategy that dictated a conventional air war on the DRV to affect an unconventional war in the RVN. The bombing failed to accomplish its two primary objectives: strategic persuasion and interdiction. The DRV was a largely agricultural country with virtually no military industries. Destroying its small factories had no impact on the war in South Vietnam or on Hà Nôi's ability to prosecute that war. U.S. Military Assistance Command, Vietnam's (MACV) figures show that the flow of troops and supplies moving into South Vietnam doubled each year of ROLLING THUNDER. Amid growing public dissatisfaction, in March 1968 President Johnson limited ROLLING THUNDER strikes to the southern panhandle of North Vietnam. He ended the campaign a week before the 1968 presidential elections, possibly in an attempt to bolster the prospects of Democratic Party presidential candidate Vice-President Hubert H. Humphrey.

Most USAF air action focused on South Vietnam, where from 1962 until 23 January 1972 some 4 million tons of bombs fell, making it the most bombed country in the history of aerial warfare. Much of this tonnage fell in B-52 ARC LIGHT missions directed against suspected VC and PAVN encampments and troop concentrations. Air power played a key role in keeping four PAVN divisions at bay during the siege of Khe Sanh in 1967 and 1968. Many U.S. and Allied soldiers owe their lives to the USAF's quick response to calls for close air support. Critics, however, ask why air power was not more effective given the scope of the effort.

The bombing did not stop when ROLLING THUNDER ended in October 1968, but shifted to focus on the Hô Chí Minh Trail in Laos. Operation COMMANDO HUNT, a pure interdiction campaign, officially began on 15 November 1968. Before it ended in late April 1972, nearly 3 million tons of bombs fell on Laos, mostly on infiltration corridors, mountain passes, and supply caches along the Trail.

Propeller-driven, side-firing gunships, of which the AC-130 was premier, became the key to the truck war portion of COMMANDO HUNT. At night, gunships blasted trucks on the Hô Chí Minh Trail with computer-aimed 40-mm cannon and, later, 105-mm howitzers. A managerial ethos took control of COMMANDO HUNT operations, with success determined by how many trucks were destroyed or damaged. The total number of trucks estimated destroyed reached a high of 12,368 in 1970, but since CIA figures indicate only 6,000 trucks in North Vietnam and Laos combined, these estimates remain highly suspect.

Undoubtedly COMMANDO HUNT efforts did constrict some supply arteries into South Vietnam, but the extent of damage inflicted is difficult to estimate. During this period, the nature of the war changed from a guerrilla insurgency to a conventional war with some unconventional aspects, meaning that by 1971 it took far more resources to supply PAVN forces fighting in the South than it did to support Viêt Công guerrilla units five years earlier. This changed nature became evident when the DRV launched its massive Easter Offensive on 30 March 1972. Fourteen PAVN divisions poured out of South Vietnam's Central Highlands and Cambodia, while others crossed the demilitarized zone (DMZ). The United States responded with Operation LINE-BACKER (later dubbed LINEBACKER I), a massive air campaign in which the Air Force played a key role.

LINEBACKER I began on 9 May 1972 with the aerial mining of Hai Phòng Harbor. Meanwhile, Air Force, Navy, and Marine squadrons began pounding infiltration routes in the southern panhandle and on the highways and railroads leading from Hà Nôi to the Chinese border. LINEBACKER I was the first air campaign in which precision-guided munitions, laser and electro-optically guided bombs, were used as part of a coherent strategy. By the time LINEBACKER I ended on 23 October 1972, 155,548 tons of bombs had been dropped on North Vietnam, and the PAVN offensive had been halted. LINEBACKER I, the most effective employment of air power during the Vietnam War, succeeded because the nature of the war had changed. This was conventional air power used to stop a conventional invasion. LINEBACKER I is a classic aerial interdiction campaign, but one with a strategic dimension in that it finally compelled Hà Nôi's leaders to negotiate seriously. As a result, the United States and the DRV reached an agreement on terms for a cease-fire in late October.

At this point RVN leadership, who had been excluded from meaningful roles in the peace negotiations, objected. Talks resumed in November but quickly stalemated, and President Nixon ordered LINEBACKER II. Initially intended as a three-day bombing campaign to force the DRV back to the negotiating table, LINEBACKER II began on 18 December 1972. It continued for 11 days, until DRV leadership asked if peace talks could resume. Nixon agreed, but the bombing continued until Hà Nôi and Washington established an agenda for the talks. LINEBACKER II ended on 29 December.

The Air Force's role in the Vietnam War is historically controversial. Air power enthusiasts point to LINEBACKER II as vindication of strategic bombing doctrine. Critics answer that the nature of the war had changed so that in 1972 the DRV was susceptible to that kind of attack, which would not have been the case earlier.

From 1962 though August 1973, when the U.S. Congress mandated an end to the bombing of Cambodia, nearly 8 million tons of bombs fell on Southeast Asia. For its part, the Air Force lost 2,257 aircraft to hostile action or accidents during the Vietnam War. Most were shot down by light antiaircraft fire over South Vietnam. Losses over North Vietnam totalled 990 aircraft, about 700 of which were USAF planes; 2,800 airmen perished.

—Earl H. Tilford, Jr.

References: Berger, Carl, ed. *The United States Air Force in Southeast Asia, 1961–1973: An Illustrated Account* (1984); Clodfelter, Mark. *The Limits of Air Power: The American Bombing of North Vietnam* (1989); Littauer, Raphael, and Norman Uphoff, ed. *The Air War in Indochina.* Rev. ed. (1971); Schlight, John. *The Years of the Offensive: 1965–1968* (1988); Tilford, Earl H., Jr. *Crosswinds: The Air Force's Setup in Vietnam* (1993).

See also: ARC LIGHT (B-52 Raids); Air Defense, Democratic Republic of Vietnam; Air Power, Role in the War; COMMANDO HUNT, Operation; Johnson, Lyndon Baines; LeMay, Curtis Emerson; LINEBACKER I, Operation; LINEBACKER II, Operation; Nixon, Richard Milhous; Order of Battle; ROLLING THUNDER, Operation.

United States: Air National Guard (ANG)

In January 1968, President Johnson ordered 14,000 Air Force and Navy Reservists mobilized in response to North Korea's seizure of the U.S.S. *Pueblo*. The Air National Guard (ANG) subsequently mobilized 9,343 personnel on 25 January 1968. A second mobilization, announced on 11 April 1968 in response to the Têt Offensive, involved 1,333 Air Guardsmen.

On 3 May 1968, the first of four ANG fighter squadrons equipped with F-100s began to arrive in Vietnam and were soon flying combat missions. In addition, 85 percent of one active duty fighter squadron were ANG volunteers. The four ANG fighter units were quickly and effectively integrated into combat operations. In Vietnam they flew 24,124 sorties and amassed 38,614 combat hours (or approximately 30,000 sorties and 50,000 combat hours if the predominantly ANG 355th tactical Fighter Squadron, a regular USAF unit, is included). The ANG squadrons returned to the United States between April and June 1969.

To help stabilize the situation following the seizure of the *Pueblo*, two ANG fighter squadrons were dispatched to the Republic of Korea during summer 1968 to replace Air Force units. They left federal service in May and June 1969.

An ANG tactical reconnaissance wing (TRW) was activated in January 1968 and served as the primary Air Force tactical reconnaissance unit in the continental United States. Elements of its squadrons rotated temporary duty assignments in Asia from July 1968 until April 1969, providing photo reconnaissance support. Its demobilization began in December 1968 and lasted until the following June.

ANG volunteers also supported Air Force operations in Southeast Asia. ANG airlifters were involved there on a significant scale beginning in 1965 and flew regular missions until 1972. In July 1970, two EC-121s from the ANG left the United States for Thailand. During the next six months, about 60 Guardsmen were rotated through the theater on 30- to 60-day tours during Operation COMMANDO BUZZ. Their aircraft served as flying radar stations and airborne control platforms for U.S. tactical air operations over North Vietnam and the Gulf of Tonkin until January 1971.

The 1968 mobilizations demonstrated that the ANG had emerged as a combat reserve force with units capable of rapid global deployment and helped to pave the way for the total force policy in the 1970s. Air Guardsmen demonstrated that well-trained units supplied with modern equipment that were integrated into the Air Force's peacetime operations were capable of performing up to the professional standards of their active force counterparts.

—Charles J. Gross

References: Gross, Charles J. "A Different Breed of Cats: The Air National Guard and the 1968 Reserve Mobilizations" (1983): 94–95; Gross, Charles J. *Prelude to the Total Force: The Air National Guard, 1943–1969* (1985); Gross, Charles J. *Militiaman, Volunteer, and Professional: The Air National Guard and the American Military Tradition* (1996); National Guard Bureau (NGB). *A NGB Activity Input to Project Corona Harvest on Air National Guard Support of U.S. Air Force Operations in Southeast Asia, 1954 to March 31, 1968.* Vol. I. (1970).

See also: Airplanes, Allied and Democratic Republic of Vietnam; Air Power, Role in War; United States: Air Force; United States: Army.

United States: Army

As in all of America's wars, the vast majority of the troops who fought in Vietnam were U.S. Army soldiers. U.S. Army involvement in Vietnam started with the formation of the Military Assistance Advisory Group, Indo-China (MAAG, Indo-China) on 17 September 1950. In 1955, MAAG, Indo-China was redesignated MAAG, Vietnam. The primary MAAG mission was to provide service support, combat arms training, and field advisors to the Republic of Vietnam Armed Forces (RVNAF). Although the MAAG was a joint command, most of its personnel as well as its commander came from the Army.

With the expansion of the U.S. role in Vietnam, the U.S. Military Assistance Command, Vietnam (MACV) was formed on 8 February 1962. MAAG, Vietnam existed for two more years, but MACV eventually took over all advisory functions. As with MAAG, Vietnam, MACV was a joint command, but most of its personnel and its commander were from the Army. MACV became the principal U.S. command in Vietnam. Under it came the U.S. Army Vietnam (USARV), the U.S. Seventh Air Force, the III Marine Amphibious Force, and U.S. Navy units inside Vietnam. Advisors to the Army of the Republic of Vietnam (ARVN) came from the Field Advisory Element of MACV, which at its height in 1968 provided 9,430 advisors.

USARV was established in Vietnam on 20 July 1965. Its primary mission was to control all Army logistical and administrative units in Vietnam. The commanding general of MACV was also the commander of USARV. However, the deputy commander of USARV actually ran day-to-day operations.

Operations of U.S. Army combat units were controlled by corps-level headquarters, commanded by a lieutenant general. Corps are flexible organizations to which divisions and other units can be assigned for specific operations. Many divisions were assigned to more than one corps at different times. Since the ARVN was organized into four corps on a regional basis, the U.S. corps were called "field forces" to avoid confusion. I Field Force controlled operations in the north, while II Field Force controlled operations in the south. In 1968 a third corps was formed and actually called a corps. XXIV Corps, which initially came under the operational control of the III Marine Amphibious Force (MAF), controlled Army units near the Demilitarized Zone (DMZ). In March 1970, the command relationship reversed, with III MAF subordinate to XXIV Corps.

The division, commanded by a major general, is normally the largest tactical unit in the U.S. Army. At the height of the war, seven of the Army's nineteen divisions were in Vietnam. A Vietnam-era division was a fixed unit, normally consisting of ten or eleven infantry battalions, four artillery battalions, an armored cavalry squadron, an aviation battalion, and various support battalions.

Between the division headquarters and the battalions, each division had three brigades, intermediate-level headquarters commanded by a colonel. A brigade controlled three to five maneuver battalions. Brigades were not fixed organizations, and battalions were attached and detached from them as needed for specific operations.

The battalion, commanded by a lieutenant colonel, is the basic tactical unit in the U.S. Army. The structure of the infantry battalions underwent changes several times during the war, and the battalions in Vietnam eventually were organized much differently than similar units in Germany or in the United States. By 1968 the standard light infantry battalion in Vietnam had four rifle companies, a combat support company, and a headquarters and headquarters company. The combat support company provided the battalion reconnaissance section and the heavy (4.2-inch) mortar platoon. The headquarters company provided battalion administration, maintenance, and supply functions. Typical infantry battalion strength was 43 officers, 2 warrant officers, and 875 enlisted soldiers.

Vietnam was a company commander's war—a war of small unit actions. The infantry rifle company, commanded by a captain, consisted of a company headquarters, three rifle platoons, and a mortar platoon. The rifle platoon, led by a lieutenant, had three rifle squads and a weapons squad. The rifle squad was led by a staff sergeant and divided into two fire teams, each led by a sergeant. The weapons squad had two M60 machine guns and one 90-mm recoilless rifle. The mortar platoon had three 81-mm mortars. A rifle squad had 10 soldiers; a rifle platoon had one officer and 41 soldiers; and a rifle company had 6 officers and 158 enlisted soldiers.

The Army also had several separate brigades and regiments that operated independent from the divisions. In some special cases, divisional brigades were detached to operate separately. Separate brigades were augmented with support elements to make them semiself-sufficient. Rather than being commanded by a colonel, these separate brigades often were commanded by a brigadier general. The 11th Armored Cavalry Regiment also was a brigade-sized separate unit that operated directly under the control of a field forces headquarters.

There has been much criticism of the U.S. Army's field performance and poor morale and lack of professionalism among its officer corps. Much of that criticism is accurate and justified, but some is overstated. The mentality of careerism and "ticket-punching" among the officer corps has been well documented in *Crisis in Command* by Richard A. Gabriel and Paul L. Savage. Although the typical infantry, artillery, or armor enlisted man spent his entire 12-month tour of duty assigned to a combat unit, the average officer spent only six months with such a unit. The original purpose of this policy was to give as many officers as possible the opportunity for combat experience. The effect, however, was that the enlisted men came to believe that their officers were not being subjected to the same risks as they were, leading to a loss in confidence in the officer corps.

The careerism and ticket-punching mentality of the Vietnam-era officer corps was adopted from American business and government. Secretary of Defense Robert McNamara himself was a driving force in pushing the military to be more similar to big business. But the "bottom line" in business is measured clearly in dollars and cents; it is impossible to measure military operations in those terms. The businesslike fixation with quantification of results led to ghoulish practices such as "body counts."

The Army's replacement system was another source of severe problems. Soldiers in Vietnam served only 12 months, causing a constant turnover within units that made it impossible for leaders to develop the cohesion, teamwork, and personal bonding so necessary for a unit to survive and succeed in combat. The individual replacement system, made possible by U.S. transportation capabilities, was far easier to manage than rotating entire units in and out of the combat zone. The U.S. Army chose administrative expedience over combat effectiveness; the individual soldiers paid the price.

Vietnam was the only U.S. war in which Army Reserve and National Guard were not mobilized. In all previous wars, a large portion of the force comprised National Guardsmen and Reservists. After the 1968 Têt Offensive, there was a small-scale call-up, and eventually 7,040 Guardsmen and 3,500 Reservists did serve in Vietnam—some 3 percent of the force there. Large-scale reserve involvement resulted from the Johnson administration's reluctance to send too strong a signal to the American people and to the world at large. This lack of a strong signal, however, convinced the American people that involvement in Vietnam was not something that affected the country's vital interests. Gen. Creighton Abrams recognized this, and when he became chief of staff of the Army in 1972, he reconfigured the Army's force structure in such a way that any future large-scale deployments would be impossible without mobilizing its reserve components. This is exactly what happened during the 1991 Persian Gulf War and the 1996 Bosnia peacekeeping mission.

Although the typical soldier on the ground often had no idea why he was in Vietnam, morale was generally good early in the war. This changed when more of the American public began to oppose the war after the 1968 Têt Offensive. Many Americans, particularly in the antiwar movement, focused their anger and frustration on returning soldiers, and as word of this treatment filtered back to the battlefield, morale fell apart, and with it, discipline and combat effectiveness.

Between 1961 and 1975, 30,868 U.S. Army soldiers died in Vietnam as the result of hostile action; 7,193 died from other causes; and 201,536 were wounded in action.

—David T. Zabecki

References: Gabriel, Richard A., and Paul L. Savage. *Crisis in Command: Mismanagement in the Army* (1978); Hackworth, David. *About Face* (1989); Krepinevich, Andrew Jr. *The Army and Vietnam* (1986); Palmer, Bruce. *The 25-Year War: America's Military Role in Vietnam* (1984); Palmer, Dave. *Summons of the Trumpet: U.S.-Vietnam in Perspective* (1978); Stanton, Shelby. *The Rise and Fall of an American Army: U.S. Ground Forces in Vietnam* (1985); —. *Vietnam Order of Battle* (1981).

See also: Abrams, Creighton; African American Personnel in U.S. Forces in Vietnam; Antiwar Movement, United States; Casualties; Draft; Herbert, Anthony; Johnson, Lyndon Baines; McNamara, Robert S.; Military Assistance and Advisory Group (MAAG), Vietnam; Military Assistance Command, Vietnam (MACV); Order of Battle; United States: Air Force; Unites States: Navy; United States: Special Forces; Westmoreland, William Childs.

United States: Coast Guard

On 29 April 1965, President Johnson authorized deployment of U.S. Coast Guard cutters to Vietnam to assist the Navy in preventing arms and supplies from being smuggled to Việt Công guerrillas. Coast Guard Squadron One, with 17 82-foot patrol boats (WPBs) and 250 men, was established on 27 May 1965. The cutters were operated by two officers and nine enlisted men. Each ship was armed with five .50-caliber machine guns and a trigger-fired, flat-trajectory, 81-mm mortar. The twin-screwed cutter, powered by diesel engines, had a speed of 17 knots. The radar-equipped WPBs were shallow-draft (6.5 feet) for working close to shore.

The squadron, divided into two divisions, arrived in Vietnam in July 1965. Division 11, based at Phú Quôc Island in the Gulf of Thailand, patrolled the Cambodian border and Gulf coast of Vietnam. Division 12, based at Đà Nang, patrolled the 17th parallel and the coastline south of the Demilitarized Zone (DMZ). Division 13, a third division of nine cutters sent to Vietnam on 22 February 1966 and stationed at Cát Lo, patrolled the Mekong Delta region south of Sài Gòn.

Cutter crewmen boarded and searched junks and sampans, deterring coastal arms and ammunition smuggling. WPBs were under way on patrol 70 percent of the time, in all weather. Patrol boats supported Special Forces and Marine amphibious operations and routinely provided close-in fire support and illumination with their mortars for outposts under attack and troop operations ashore.

Coast Guard Squadron Three, consisting of five 311-foot Coast Guard high-endurance cutters (WHECs), was commissioned at Pearl Harbor on 24 April 1967. Headquartered at Subic Bay in the Philippines, the squadron kept three cutters on patrol continuously during Operation MARKET TIME.

Cutters interdicted and destroyed DRV supply trawlers, provided naval gunfire support (NGFS), engaged in medical and civil action programs (MEDCAPs), and supported patrol boat operations. When Navy destroyers were withdrawn from MARKET TIME on 30 June 1969, Coast Guard HECs continued to maintain the outer barrier. During Squadron Three's deployments, high-endurance cutters spent 75 percent of their time under way. From April 1967 to January 1972, 4,500 officers and men and 30 ships participated in deployments with Squadron Three. Cutters retained their white paint schemes during deployments.

On 20 February 1966, U.S. Military Assistance Command, Vietnam (MACV) made an urgent request for the assistance of Coast Guard Explosive Loading Detachments (ELDs) in supervising inexperienced Vietnamese stevedores who lacked equipment and skills to safely unload explosives. Two eight-man detachments arrived on 5 June 1966 and were assigned to the Army's 1st Logistical Command (1st Log). By teaching the Vietnamese more efficient procedures and introducing better equipment, operations were made safer and unloading times were halved. During the Vietnam conflict, there was never a major explosive incident due to accident or hostile action at any port where Coast Guard ELDs were assigned.

On 20 July 1966, Gen. William Westmoreland requested the assistance of a Coast Guard Port Security and Waterways Detail (PS&WD), which inspected Army port facilities, trained Army boat crews, and advised 1st Log's commanding general on port security. On 3 December 1966, a Coast Guard marine inspector was assigned to Sài Gòn to assist the Navy's Military Sea Transportation Service (MSTS) in resolving problems aboard the 300 merchant ships supporting U.S. forces. On 1 July 1968, the position was expanded to a Merchant Marine Detail and attached to the U.S. embassy in Sài Gòn. A Coast Guard Aids to Navigation Detail, working out of Sài Gòn, deployed buoy tenders, positioned and maintained buoys, and fixed aids at ports and along the coast to support U.S. military operations.

On 3 April 1968, Coast Guard helicopter pilots began flying rescue missions with the HH-3E and HH-53C helicopters of the Air Force's 37th Aerospace Rescue and Recovery Squadron stationed at Đà Nang. The pilots' mission was to rescue U.S. pilots downed behind enemy lines in North and South Vietnam. The exchange pilot program continued until 1973, and Coast Guard aviators were highly decorated for their daring rescues under fire.

On 14 December 1965, the Defense Department requested that the Coast Guard build an electronic navigation system that would provide precision guidance for Air Force aircraft operating in North and South Vietnam. On 8 August 1966, Operation TIGHT REIGN's LORAN-C chain went on-air as scheduled. To provide better coverage of the Hô Chí Minh Trail, the Coast Guard in 1969 built a second transmitting station in Vietnam at Tân My, 42 miles below the DMZ. After

U.S. forces withdrew in 1973, the Vietnam LORAN stations continued to operate, but with civilian technicians.

Eight thousand Coast Guardsmen served in Vietnam from 1964 to 1973, 3,500 with units in-country. Seven Coast Guardsmen were killed in action.

—Alex Larzelere

References: Kaplan, Hyman R. *Coast Guard in Vietnam* (1971); Larzelere, Alex. *The Coast Guard at War. Vietnam, 1965–1975* (1997); Schreadley, R. L. *From the Rivers to the Sea* (1993); Tulich, Eugene N. *The United States Coast Guard in Southeast Asia during the Vietnam Conflict* (1986).

See also: MARKET TIME, Operation; Military Assistance Command, Vietnam (MACV); Sea Power in the War; Search-and-Rescue (SAR) Operations; United States: Navy; Warships, Allied and Democratic Republic of Vietnam.

United States: Department of Justice

U.S. government executive department, headed by the attorney general of the United States, founded in 1870 to enforce federal law, represent the government in federal cases, determine jurisdiction, and ensure governmental compliance under federal law. Its investigatory branch is the Federal Bureau of Investigation (FBI).

Presidents Johnson and Nixon believed that Communists were responsible for the antiwar movement, that protests threatened domestic order and stability, and that demonstrators were a source of support for the Vietnamese Communists. Both administrations used the Department of Justice and the FBI to infiltrate, subvert, and monitor protest groups.

In 1965 Attorney General Nicholas Katzenbach pledged to initiate a nationwide investigation of antiwar organizations and suggested federal indictments for draft resistance and sedition. FBI Director J. Edgar Hoover ordered his agency to link antiwar leaders to Communists, and the FBI reinitiated counterintelligence programs (COINTELPROs), covert programs directed against dissident domestic groups. Although Katzenbach's successor, Ramsey Clark, refused to support legislation outlawing draft resistance or to cancel large protest marches on Washington, Johnson and the Justice Department increased legal pressure on the antiwar movement. On 5 January 1968, the Justice Department indicted Dr. Benjamin Spock and several prominent antiwar leaders for conspiracy to counsel, aid, and abet young men to violate draft laws. A hesitant Clark prosecuted Spock and four others; all were later acquitted or the charges against them were dropped.

Nixon's Attorney General John Mitchell took a more confrontational approach to the antiwar movement to appease right-wing politicians. In 1969 Mitchell ordered the Justice Department to increase electronic surveillance operations by relaxing restrictions on federal wiretapping. Nixon urged Hoover to wiretap journalists who questioned Vietnam policy. Mitchell tried to justify the wiretapping before the Supreme Court by arguing that the president needed wide latitude in conducting national security, an argument the Court rejected in *U.S. v. U.S. District Court for the Eastern District of Michigan* (1972). The Nixon adminstration's aborted Huston Plan of

1970 proposed far-reaching (and often illegal) activities including wiretaps, burglaries, and infiltration. It called for the creation of an interagency domestic intelligence apparatus under White House control, combining elements of the FBI, the Central Intelligence Agency, and other agencies, which too was illegal. Although Nixon approved the plan, Hoover refused to go along. This willingness on the part of the White House to circumvent or break existing laws foreshadowed the Watergate scandal.

—Mark A. Esposito

References: Elliff, John T. *Crime, Dissent, and the Attorney General: The Justice Department in the 1960s* (1971); Kutler, Stanley. *The Wars of Watergate: The Last Crisis of Richard Nixon* (1990); Wells, Tom. *The War Within: America's Battle over Vietnam* (1994).

See also: Antiwar Movement, United States; Federal Bureau of Investigation (FBI); Huston Plan; Katzenbach, Nicholas; Johnson, Lyndon Baines; Mitchell, John Newton; Nixon, Richard Milhous; Spock, Benjamin M.; Watergate.

United States: Involvement in Indo-China through 1954

Nineteenth- and twentieth-century American missionaries and entrepreneurs saw Asia as fertile ground for trade and for Christianizing and Westernizing the inhabitants of that continent, with each goal complementing the others. The center of Asian activity was mainland China, and the United States was concerned by Russian and Japanese gains there.

Although initial U.S. interest in the region was based on concerns that the French posed a threat to American interests in China, the United States first chose to confront Japan over Vietnam. In July 1941 Japan established bases in South Indo-China. This threat to Siam, Malaya, and the Netherlands East Indies brought a joint U.S., United Kingdom, and Netherlands economic embargo, leading to the Japanese decision to attack Pearl Harbor.

During World War II, the United States provided assistance to the Viêt Minh through the Office of Strategic Services (OSS). The Viêt Minh helped rescue downed American pilots and provided intelligence information on the Japanese. OSS agents asssured the Viêt Minh that the United States would stand on its side against French colonialism. The Atlantic Charter provided encouragement to Hô Chí Minh and Vietnamese nationalists by its support for the right of national self-determination. By 1945, however, growing fear of Russian activity prompted the United States to support French colonialism in Southeast Asia.

In the last months of the war, President Franklin Roosevelt suggested U.S. support for a trusteeship over the region, believing that France had performed poorly as a colonial power. His successor, Harry Truman, more concerned about communism than colonialism, made the initial commitment to the French presence in Vietnam. In August 1945, the Truman administration ordered 12 U.S. merchant ships to transport French combat troops to Sài Gòn. The French government intended to reestablish itself in Indo-China and the U.S. government did not seek to prevent it. U.S. diplomats in Indo-China, however, notified Washington on several occasions of growing nationalism in the area.

A little more than a year after the conclusion of World War II, war erupted in Indo-China. At the center of the conflict was the Communist leader Hô Chí Minh and the Viêt Minh. Although the Viêt Minh had made significant contributions to the Allied cause, the anti-Communist ethos that pervaded the United States made it virtually impossible for leaders to ally themselves too closely with any Communist.

Hô quoted Thomas Jefferson in proclaiming Vietnam's independence on 2 September 1945. Just over one month later, U.S. Secretary of State Dean Acheson publicly noted that the United States would not oppose the reestablishment of French control in Vietnam. Hô made several direct appeals to Washington, praising the United States as champion of the rights of small nations and noting that the Viêt Minh, not the French, contributed to the Allied war effort, but such appeals went unanswered.

Without U.S. or British support, Hô was forced to seek a temporary arrangement with France. Although criticized by his supporters, on 6 March 1946 he concluded an agreement with Jean Sainteny in which the French promised to withdraw all troops by 1952 and recognize the Democratic Republic of Vietnam. The situation was complicated when French High Commissioner for Indo-China Georges Thierry d'Argenlieu arbitrarily created the Republic of Cochin China. Despite such impediments, Hô traveled to France, hoping to finalize the ambiguous arrangement. By August, Hô concluded that the French never intended to allow complete independence. The talks were subsequently canceled, and Hô returned home.

Fighting began in December 1946. In that month, Albert Low Moffat, head of the State Department's division on Southeast Asia, traveled to Hà Nôi to assess the situation. He concluded that Hô was first and foremost a Vietnamese nationalist, determined to win independence for his people, who might be viewed as an Asian Tito. Other officials in Vietnam agreed with Moffat's assessment and argued that the Vietnamese people would reject any other proposed head of state.

Most Washington policymakers believed that the United States must continue to support the French effort in order to gain their crucial backing for U.S. strategy in Europe. From the outset, the U.S. position on Vietnam was hostage to its European policy. France was the major power in Europe to contain a possible Soviet invasion. Before the end of 1946, the United States had sent $160 million to aid the French effort in Vietnam.

Debate continued through 1949 on how the United States should view Hô, especially in comparison to the French puppet Bao Đai. The fall of Nationalist China, combined with Soviet recognition of Hô's regime, solidified Washington's belief that Vietnam was permanently assimilated into the worldwide Communist movement. After 1949, U.S. commitment to France was never in serious doubt. The Korean War that began in 1950 strengthened this.

In 1950 the U.S. government established a Military Assistance and Advisory Group (MAAG) in Vietnam to help train a viable army, to screen French requests for aid, and to make helpful suggestions regarding strategy. The French generally ignored MAAG and seemed insulted that Americans presumed to give them advice. Despite French recalcitrance, Washington continued to pour in aid.

After President Truman left office in 1953, the Vietnam situation grew more complex by the day. President Eisenhower, although unhappy with the French refusal to heed U.S. advice, adopted the previous administration's position with no serious review or reevaluation. The French military effort was going badly, and opposition to the war was growing in France. For that reason, Paris began to talk about a negotiated settlement after the Korean armistice in July 1953. The United States, while still involved in fighting in Korea, had actively opposed negotiations with the Viêt Minh and assured Paris of material aid, short of combat troops or nuclear weapons.

In spring 1954, as the situation at Điên Biên Phu deteriorated, Washington seriously considered military intervention. Among those arguing for such a course was Vice-President Nixon. A plan for U.S. military intervention, codenamed Operation VULTURE, was never implemented, in large part because of British opposition. Congressional leaders informed Eisenhower that they would not support such an operation if the British refused participation.

The May 1954 fall of Điên Biên Phu and the subsequent Geneva Accords marked the beginning of the end of French influence in Vietnamese affairs. Americans would soon replace the French.

—Francis H. Thompson

References: Herring, George C. *America's Longest War: The United States in Vietnam, 1950–1975*, 2d ed. (1986); Kahin, George M. *Intervention: How America Became Involved in Vietnam* (1987); Williams, William A., John McCormick, et al, eds. *America in Vietnam: A Documentary History* (1985); Young, Marilyn. *The Vietnam Wars, 1945–1990* (1991).

See also: Acheson, Dean; Central Intelligence Agency (CIA); Containment Policy; d'Argenlieu, Georges Thierry; Điên Biên Phu, Battle of; Eisenhower, Dwight David; Geneva Conference and Geneva Accords; Hô Chí Minh; Hô-Sainteny Agreement; Military Assistance and Advisory Group (MAAG), Vietnam; Nixon, Richard Milhous; Office of Strategic Services (OSS); Patti, Archimedes L. A.; Roosevelt, Franklin Delano; Sainteny, Jean; Truman, Harry S; Viêt Minh; VULTURE, Operation.

United States: Involvement in Vietnam, 1954–1965

With the French capitulation at Geneva in 1954, the United States, by its own decision, assumed responsibility for South Vietnam. Long frustrated with France's political handling of Indo-China and what was perceived as their weak military performance against the Viêt Minh, the United States sought to play the decisive hand in the future of the area. At first, President Eisenhower attempted to work with the French and other Western allies to contain communism in Southeast Asia. He and Secretary of State John Foster Dulles engineered the Southeast Asia Treaty Organization (SEATO) in September 1954, which under a separate protocol gave Laos, Cambodia, and South Vietnam a special protected status.

Eisenhower sent Gen. J. Lawton Collins to continue a U.S.-French joint effort in the region.

In spring 1955, Eisenhower abandoned the allied approach and moved in a unilateral direction as the United States dedicated itself to building a strong Vietnamese nation in the South under the leadership of the enigmatic Ngô Đình Diêm. Eisenhower tried unsuccessfully to persuade the French to support the Diêm option. In early 1956, the United States took over training of the Vietnamese military establishment, and France was squeezed out within a few months. The United States began to structure the South Vietnamese armed forces as a copy of its own military and prepared the country to fight a mid-intensity conventional war against an invasion from the North. Only slight attention was given to counterinsurgency.

Diêm faced an almost impossible task in "a political jungle of warlords, sects, bandits, partisan troops and secret societies," as one commentator described it. First, he had to deal with the influx of about 900,000 mostly Catholic refugees into the predominantly Buddhist South. The Viêt Minh left cadres behind in the South who would become the vanguard of insurrection. In spring 1955, various contenders for power, including religious sects (the Cao Đài and the Hòa Hao), Sài Gòn gangsters (Bình Xuyên), and several coup factions in the military, challenged Diêm's regime. Washington was ready to cut its ties, but Diêm overcame the challenges and solidified his position in the country, consequently retaining the relationship with his U.S. benefactors.

Seizing on the momentum of his victories, Diêm announced that the Geneva-mandated reunification elections in 1956 would not be held. With the assistance of Central Intelligence Agency (CIA) operative Col. Edward Lansdale, Diêm successfully ousted Emperor Bao Đai, converted the State of Vietnam into the Republic of Vietnam (RVN), and claimed its presidency. Although the RVN was not the citadel of democracy that the United States proclaimed and Diêm not the model leader, the United States had cast its lot with him.

Full-scale insurrection against Diêm resurfaced in 1957. The origins were primarily indigenous, with little direction from the North. However, the U.S. military mission continued to build the Republic of Vietnam Armed Forces (RVNAF) along conventional lines to repel an external aggressor. Diêm, though, focused on the internal threat and employed counterinsurgency military measures. These forces were poorly trained and equipped, and the social-programs component was half-hearted.

U.S. economic assistance was in excess of $250 million per year (80 percent of which went to the military) through the Eisenhower years, resulting in an economically dependent South Vietnamese client state. The first American military casualties occurred in July 1959, when two U.S. advisors were killed in a terrorist attack at Biên Hòa Air Base.

The nature of the U.S. advisory role changed in the early 1960s. In December 1960, Hà Nôi announced the birth of the National Liberation Front (NLF) in South Vietnam, although the organization had already existed for several years.

President Kennedy feared that Indo-China was a prime theater for Soviet-sponsored "wars of national liberation." Influenced by former Army Chief of Staff Gen. Maxwell Taylor's *The Uncertain Trumpet* (1960), Kennedy extended Taylor's proposal for a more "flexible military response" to include low-intensity warfare. He assigned this counterinsurgency role to the U.S. Army Special Forces. The regular military was not enthusiastic about counterinsurgency and did little more than pay it lip service.

The primary area of concern in Indo-China during the first months of the Kennedy administration was Laos, but by spring 1961 the focus began to shift to Vietnam. Kennedy authorized the expansion of the RVNAF from 150,000 to 200,000 men and sent more U.S. advisors—civilian specialists in government, economic affairs, and technical areas as well as military personnel, including Green Berets. With the National Security Council and the Joint Chiefs of Staff considering combat troops, Kennedy dispatched advisors Maxwell Taylor and Walt Rostow to South Vietnam in October 1961 to report on the situation. Their report called for more assistance of all kinds, including combat troops. Diêm, however, did not want U.S. troops. He believed that the presence of U.S. forces would provide the Viêt Công with a significant propaganda issue, and he was concerned about the impact of greater U.S. involvement on his non-Communist opposition in the South. But most importantly, he feared that U.S. troops would lead the the United States to assume control of the war and ultimately the country. Diêm wanted unlimited U.S. aid with no interference in internal politics or the conduct of the war.

Kennedy stepped up assistance but rejected the idea of combat troops. At the same time, he also rejected a negotiated settlement in Vietnam similar to one he was seeking in Laos. Thus Kennedy opted for a midposition between fighting and negotiating, which he recognized from the beginning might prove unsuccessful. But for the most part, Kennedy was optimistic. Like his Secretary of Defense Robert McNamara and other advisors, Kennedy viewed Vietnam predominantly as a military problem to be "managed" successfully. This sanguine approach characterized American policy in 1962.

The upgrading of the Military Advisory and Assistance Group (MAAG) to Military Assistance Command, Vietnam (MACV) in February 1962, was symbolic and substantive. The number of advisors rose from 3,200 in December 1961 to 9,000 by the end of 1962. The increased American presence had a short-term positive impact, but this advantage largely eroded by the end of 1962. American optimism and cultural hubris did not.

Despite talk about winning hearts and minds, U.S. leaders never persuaded Diêm to undertake the reforms needed to win support for his government nor to address seriously the corruption that engulfed the country. The high-profile Strategic Hamlet program ultimately failed; Diêm misused it, primarily to bring the rural countryside under his personal control. Diêm increasingly came to fear the escalating U.S. presence as much as his internal enemies. His concerns were not totally unwarranted.

As American journalists began to attack Diêm and U.S. policy, the buoyancy of 1962 quickly waned. Kennedy was increasingly frustrated by Diêm and his pernicious brother Ngô Đình Nhu. Diêm's inept handling of the 1963 Buddhist uprising weakened American support for his regime. Disenchantment with the ARVN's capacity and willingness to fight grew. With his advisors divided over what to do about Diêm, Kennedy finally tacitly acquiesced to a coup effort by South Vietnamese generals against Diêm in November 1963. However, Kennedy was personally devastated by Diêm's murder during the coup. Following Kennedy's assassination three weeks later, Lyndon Johnson inherited a growing political and military quagmire.

Johnson retained Kennedy's team to run the war and continued the same basic policies. After an extensive policy review in March 1964, Johnson concluded that the only reasonable alternative was "to do more of the same and do it more efficiently." He expanded the number of advisors (from 16,300 when he took office to 23,300 by the end of 1964) and increased assistance by $50 million. Although hoping to keep Vietnam on the back burner through the 1964 presidential election, he authorized secret plans for possible military action against North Vietnam. Through intermediaries, the Johnson administration warned Hà Nôi that the United States was prepared to inflict a heavy punishment on the Democratic Republic of Vietnam (DRV) if it continued to support the insurgency in the South. The DRV responded by mobilizing its own forces for war, expanding the Hô Chí Minh Trail, and preparing to infiltrate regular People's Army of Vietnam (PAVN) units into the South.

Meanwhile, political intrigue and instability dominated the South Vietnamese government and the ARVN. The Viêt Công (VC) controlled more than 40 percent of the territory and more than 50 percent of the population and in many areas was so entrenched that only massive military force would dislodge them.

On 2 August 1964, the budding crises between the United States and North Vietnam intensified with a DRV attack on the U.S.S. *Maddox* in the Gulf of Tonkin off the coast of the DRV. The United States prepared for a possible military retaliation. Two nights later, another attack may have occurred, although Vô Nguyên Giáp told McNamara in November 1995 that it never happened. In any case, the Johnson administration opted for the opportunity to send a message. The United States launched air strikes against the DRV, and Johnson seized the moment to extort from Congress the Southeast Asian Resolution, better known as the Gulf of Tonkin Resolution, which authorized the president to employ military power against the DRV. Senator Ernest Gruening of Alaska, one of only two Senators to vote against the resolution, correctly labeled it a "predated declaration of war."

After the Gulf of Tonkin incident, Johnson reverted to a cautious strategy. Campaigning against Vietnam hawk Barry Goldwater, Johnson emphasized that he did not wish to widen the war or "send American boys to do what Asian boys should do." He did not respond to terrorist attacks that took American lives in South Vietnam in November and

December, but the administration was preparing a retaliatory bombing program against the North to be unleashed at the proper moment.

In early 1965, all the pieces began to fall into place. In response to another provocation, Johnson ordered a retaliatory bombing in early February. Individual reprisal attacks soon transformed into Operation ROLLING THUNDER, a sustained bombing campaign. In reaction to the desperate military situation in the South, U.S. ground troops followed in March. In July, Johnson authorized independent American combat operations and began the massive U.S. troop buildup. The advisory days were over; this was now America's war in Vietnam.

—Joe P. Dunn

References: Anderson, David L. *Trapped by Success: The Eisenhower Administration and Vietnam, 1953–61* (1991); Duiker, William J. *U.S. Containment Policy and the Conflict in Indochina* (1994); Herring, George C. *America's Longest War: The United States and Vietnam, 1950–1975*, 2d ed. (1986); Kahin, George M. *Intervention: How America Became Involved in Vietnam* (1986); Krepinevich, Andrew F., Jr. *The Army and Vietnam* (1986).

See also: Central Intelligence Agency (CIA); Collins, Joseph Lawton; Fishel, Wesley Robert; Gruening, Ernest Henry; Halberstam, David; Johnson, Lyndon Baines; Kennedy, John Fitzgerald; Lansdale, Edward Geary; McNamara, Robert S.; Ngô Đình Diêm; Ngô Đình Diêm, Overthrow of; ROLLING THUNDER, Operation; Rostow, Walt Whitman; Southeast Asia Treaty Organization (SEATO); Taylor, Maxwell Davenport; Tonkin Gulf Incidents; Tonkin Gulf Resolution.

United States: Involvement in Vietnam, 1965–1968

In 1965 the United States committed major ground combat forces to the war in Vietnam, thus deepening an involvement that so far had consisted primarily of logistical, financial, and advisory support to the South Vietnamese. At the end of 1964, about 23,500 Americans were serving in Vietnam; by the end of 1968, that number had grown to 525,000. This buildup was precipitated by February 1965 Viêt Công (VC) attacks on U.S. installations near Pleiku in the Central Highlands. Retaliatory air strikes, deployment into Vietnam of additional air assets, and a consequent need to protect the growing complement of aircraft and their airfields necessitated an increased U.S. troop presence. Thus, in early March 1965 President Johnson authorized deployment of 3,500 U.S. Marines to the Đà Nang area, followed in April by assignment of the Army's 173d Airborne Brigade to Biên Hòa and Vung Tàu.

In early March 1965, Johnson sent U.S. Army Chief of Staff Gen. Harold K. Johnson on a mission to Vietnam. Johnson submitted to the president a report containing 21 recommendations, including an intensified air war against North Vietnam and deployment of many more ground forces to Vietnam. Most of these proposals were approved; in mid-June Secretary of Defense Robert McNamara announced additional deployments to a level of 75,000 men.

In closing his report, Gen. Johnson raised the question of how much more the United States would have to contribute. In the margin, McNamara wrote a blank check: "Anything that will strengthen the position of the GVN [government of Vietnam] will be sent." Meanwhile, Gen. Johnson set in motion within the Army staff a study of how the war was being conducted that would have an enormous, but much delayed, impact on U.S. involvement.

Reports through late spring 1965 indicated that the Army of the Republic of Vietnam (ARVN) could not survive without extensive additional assistance. On 28 July, President Johnson announced that he was sending 50,000 more troops and that draft calls would be increased. Significantly, he did not approve calling up reserve forces. The U.S. command in Vietnam quickly submitted requests for even more forces, and the troop buildup moved into high gear.

Shortly after the series of retaliatory air strikes against targets in North Vietnam in early February 1965, President Johnson authorized a continuing air campaign against the North that became known as Operation ROLLING THUNDER. Commencing in early March 1965, this bombing continued largely unabated until 31 October 1968. The conduct of the air war, however, created the controversy over the administration's "graduated response" approach. The Joint Chiefs of Staff, as well as the field command, sought to apply massive force in the shortest possible time. Instead, frustrating impediments to this strategy were imposed by the civilian hierarchy. The incremental approach to the air war permitted the Communists to make adjustments at successive levels and to put in place a continuously improving air defense system. After leaving office, Johnson reportedly told President Nixon that the bombing pauses had been useless and that he regretted having ordered them. That notwithstanding, in March 1968 Johnson scaled back the bombing of North Vietnam to below the 20th parallel only; in November he terminated it altogether.

In June 1964, Gen. William Westmoreland had taken command of Military Assistance Command, Vietnam (MACV). Westmoreland devised the strategy of attrition and search and destroy tactics that characterized the ground war through the end of his tenure. The measure of merit under this approach became the body count; the defining objective and the so-called crossover point became the point at which enemy soldiers were being killed at a greater rate than they could be replaced by infiltration from North Vietnam or by in-country recruitment in South Vietnam. The strategy marked a subtle change of emphasis, from simply denying the enemy victory and convincing him that he could not win, to defeating the enemy in the South. As noted in the Pentagon Papers, "Written all over the search and destroy strategy was total loss of confidence in the RVNAF [Republic of Vietnam Armed Forces] and a concomitant willingness on the part of the U.S. to take over the war effort."

Seeking to achieve this elusive goal, Westmoreland repeatedly requested additional troops. In February 1966, only months after the first major increases, he asked to raise the troop ceiling to 429,000. In 1967 he was back with further requests for major troop augmentation beyond the 470,000 that by that point had been authorized. Washington approved only a scaled-down addition, to a new total of 525,000. Tolerance for additional commitments was running out.

Westmoreland mounted large multibattalion operations aimed at bringing Communist main force units to battle. The first such engagement took place in the Ia Drang Valley in November 1965, when elements of the newly deployed 1st Cavalry Division (Airmobile) took on People's Army of Vietnam (PAVN) troops from three different regiments. The Americans inflicted an estimated 3,561 deaths on the Communists while losing only 305 of their own, leading Westmoreland to believe that his strategy of attrition could succeed.

The American military establishment in the Republic of Vietnam (RVN) grew larger and more pervasive every year. An elaborate system of base camps was developed, ports and airfields were built or improved, and massive logistical support was provided. Navy and Air Force elements grew proportionately. Meanwhile the essence of Communist control over the populace—the VC infrastructure in the hamlets and villages—continued essentially undisturbed as pacification in the countryside and improvement of South Vietnamese forces were largely ignored. One positive development was that in May 1967 U.S. support for pacification was pulled together under MACV control.

During 1967, Westmoreland made three trips to the United States and addressed various audiences. "I have never been more encouraged," he said in November, only weeks before the 1968 Tết Offensive changed everything.

After the Tết Offensive, Gen. Earle G. Wheeler visited Vietnam and brought back a request for an additional 206,000 U.S. troops. This was yet another bombshell. Westmoreland had described the Tết Offensive as an Allied victory with severe Communists losses. Wheeler's request seemed to undermine the credibility of that claim, just as the Tết Offensive itself had undermined Westmoreland's optimistic forecasts of the preceding year. The request precipitated a comprehensive review of U.S. policy that resulted in a series of dramatic changes. The troop request was denied, the high-water mark of American commitment to the war was passed, and Westmoreland was replaced as U.S. commander in Vietnam.

The Pentagon Papers offered their own summation of the situation: "At this writing, the U.S. has reached the end of the time frame estimated by Gen. Westmoreland in 1965 to be required to defeat the enemy. It has committed 107 battalions of its own forces and a grand total of 525,000 men. The strategy remains search and destroy, but victory is not yet in sight."

On 3 July 1968, Gen. Creighton Abrams formally assumed command of MACV, although Abrams had been de facto commander since shortly after the Tết Offensive. The troop increases requested by Westmoreland had brought the troop ceiling to 549,500 by the time Abrams took command. However, actual deployments never exceeded 543,400, and on Abrams's watch there were no requests for more troops. Abrams understood the war and the dominant influence of the domestic support base, and he understood the need to work within the limits of that fragile and waning support.

After the 1968 Tết Offensive, the Johnson administration changed its policy from seeking military victory brought

about largely by American forces to capping U.S. involvement and shifting the main burden to South Vietnamese forces. In that context, Abrams changed the tactics from scarch and destroy to clear and hold; the measure of merit from body count to population security; and the philosophy to conducting "one war" in which pacification, improvement, and modernization of the RVN armed forces and the conduct of military operations were integrated and of equal importance.

"We need to be more flexible tactically inside South Vietnam," Abrams told Johnson early in 1968, and during the remainder of the year he set about arranging just that. Two early priorities were closing down the static defense of Khe Sanh, getting those forces into a more mobile role; and doing something about protecting Sài Gòn from the frequent rocket and mortar attacks that had plagued it for years.

Soon Abrams had a planning element working on the combined campaign plan for the coming year, one that incorporated the essentials of the study that Gen. Johnson had commissioned in 1965. Known as Program for the Pacification and Long-Term Development of South Vietnam (PROVN), the study maintained that a radical redirection of effort was required to achieve success. Gen. Johnson's study had been rejected by Westmoreland and the MACV staff in March 1966 and had not found many advocates elsewhere. Now it had one very important sponsor, Abrams himself. "The critical actions are those that occur at the village, district, and provincial levels," the study maintained. "This is where the war must be fought; this is where the war and the object which lies beyond it must be won." That object was the security and loyalty of the South Vietnamese people, the single-minded pursuit of which was to be the focus of the final years of U.S. involvement in Vietnam.

—Lewis Sorley

References: Herring, George C. *America's Longest War: The United States and Vietnam, 1950–1975* (1979); Johnson, Lyndon Baines. *The Vantage Point: Perspectives of the Presidency, 1963–1969* (1971); Karnow, Stanley. *Vietnam: A History* (1983); Kinnard, Douglas. *The War Managers* (1977); Lewy, Guenter. *America in Vietnam* (1978); McNamara, Robert S., with Brian VanDeMark. *In Retrospect: The Tragedy and Lessons of Vietnam* (1995); Palmer, Bruce, Jr. *The 25-Year War: America's Military Role in Vietnam* (1984); Westmoreland, William C. *A Soldier Reports* (1976).

See also: Attrition; Body Count; Johnson, Lyndon Baines; McNamara, Robert S.; Military Assistance Command, Vietnam (MACV); Reserve Forces; Search and Destroy; Taylor, Maxwell Davenport; Tết Offensive: Overall Strategy; Tết Offensive: the Sài Gòn Circle; Westmoreland, William Childs; Wheeler, Earle G.

United States: Involvement in Vietnam, 1969–1973

With the advent of a new administration in Washington came formalization of the drastically changed approach to the war in Vietnam initiated following the 1968 Tết Offensive. Vietnamization—the process of progressively turning the primary burden of fighting back over to the South Vietnamese as U.S. forces disengaged—became the dominant theme.

Withdrawal of U.S. ground forces, euphemistically termed "redeployments," began in August 1969, when 25,000 were brought home. Three key criteria were established to guide the pace and magnitude of these withdrawals: improvement of South Vietnam's armed forces; enemy activity; and progress in the Paris peace negotiations. As Henry Kissinger observed, however, the withdrawals took on a life of their own and continued at a steady rate regardless of other developments. "The last elements of flexibility were lost," Kissinger wrote, "when the Defense Department began to plan its budget on the basis of anticipated troop reductions; henceforth to interrupt withdrawals would produce a financial shortfall affecting the procurement of new weapons."

In April 1970, President Nixon announced that 150,000 U.S. troops would be brought out in three increments over the coming year. A year later he announced that an additional 100,000 would come out by the end of November 1971. By the time the Communists launched the 1972 Easter Offensive, U.S. forces stood at 69,000 men, including just one combat brigade. Military Assistance Command, Vietnam (MACV) Commander Gen. Creighton Abrams, by then bereft of Army forces, fought his last battle with air and naval elements.

During these years, a superb team of top leaders was directing U.S. affairs in Vietnam. Ambassador Ellsworth Bunker headed the country team, Abrams led the military establishment, and William Colby (who held ambassadorial rank) directed the American aspects of pacification. Stressing "one war"—the harmonization of all elements of the program—these leaders raced to make the South Vietnamese self-sufficient before U.S. withdrawal was completed. That eventuality became clear in June 1969, when the president enunciated what came to be known as the Nixon Doctrine. Its essence was that henceforth, the United States "would furnish only the materiel and the military and economic assistance to those nations willing to accept the responsibility of supplying the manpower to defend themselves."

The revised tactics specified by Abrams involved U.S. combat units in thousands of small patrols by day and ambushes by night. Early in his tenure, Abrams also issued an order that there would be no bombing or heavy artillery used against inhabited areas without his personal approval. The Program for the Pacification and Long-Term Development of South Vietnam (PROVN) study had pointed out that it made no difference to the peasant whether destruction was caused by enemy or friendly combat actions; it was just as devastating no matter the source. Abrams told his commanders, "We've got to go beyond smashing up the enemy's main-force units. We have to do that selectively, but the way to get off the treadmill is to get after his infrastructure and guerrillas."

Much of that infrastructure was in the villages, where Viêt Công (VC) functionaries collected taxes, distributed propaganda, provided guides for military units, procured food and medicine, and often imposed their will on the populace through terrorism and intimidation. Under Colby, MACV support for pacification (including the Phoenix program, which targeted the VC infrastructure), sought to root out this influence while simultaneously strengthening the mechanisms of the RVN government at every level. Remaining U.S.

units fought to buy time for Vietnamization and pacification to develop and prosper.

Abrams had perceived that the Communists, rather than being served by a logistical "tail" as was common in warfare, were forced to push out in front of planned operations a logistical "nose" of caches, prepared positions, and the like that were essential to battlefield success. Finding and seizing these caches and positions became a primary objective, one that preempted many planned Communist attacks.

But the largest caches were in base areas across the border in Laos and Cambodia. In spring 1970, Nixon authorized U.S. forces to do something about those sanctuaries. Launching attacks coordinated with simultaneous South Vietnamese thrusts, at the end of April U.S. forces drove into Cambodia on a 60-day rampage that captured thousands of tons of weapons, ammunition, supplies, and documents. The latter included bills of lading and other proof that the Communists, contrary to CIA denials, had for years been using the Cambodian port of Sihanoukville to bring in supplies, arms, and munitions. The Cambodian incursion choked off that lifeline, bought up to a year's additional time for Vietnamization to progress, and provided increased security for the dwindling American forces still in the theater. Nixon called it "the most successful military operation of the entire Vietnam War."

In late January 1971, there followed another attempt to sweep enemy sanctuaries and interfere with logistical operations along the Hồ Chí Minh Trail. Known as Operation LAM SON 719, this consisted of a large-scale raid by South Vietnamese forces into southern Laos. U.S. forces had by this time been prohibited by statute from engaging in ground operations in Laos or Cambodia, so they played a supporting, albeit critically important, role in the operation. American engineers upgraded Route 9 to the Laotian border near Khe Sanh, and U.S. artillery fired into Laos from positions near the border. Massive American logistical support was provided to the South Vietnamese, and U.S. aviation of every description supported a multidivision thrust toward Communist base areas around Tchépone.

Again much materiel was captured or destroyed, and the Communists took horrifying casualties, but results were mixed. Because of congressional restrictions, South Vietnamese units operated for the first time without their U.S. advisors, which proved particularly disadvantageous when it came to calling for various kinds of assistance. Meanwhile the Communists, relieved of any necessity to leave forces to defend the North by the perception that U.S. policy foreclosed ground intervention there, concentrated virtually their entire military establishment in the path of the invading forces. An unprecedented density of antiaircraft weaponry proved particularly effective.

The Republic of Vietnam Armed Forces (RVNAF), still inexperienced in multidivision operations, struggled with significant problems of command and control. When token elements reached Tchépone, the operation was terminated earlier than planned. Nevertheless, severe losses were imposed on the Communists, and additional time was gained for Vietnamization to proceed. As the pullout continued, it became clear that LAM SON 719 was the last major action in which U.S. ground elements would take part.

It took the Communists until the spring of 1972 to gear up for another major offensive. When it came, however, it provided a severe test of the expanded and improved South Vietnamese armed forces, now left with only air, naval, and logistical support from the Americans. In what came to be known as the Easter Offensive, at the end of March, People's Army of Vietnam (PAVN) forces struck at three key locations—along the Demilitarized Zone (DMZ), north of Sài Gòn around An Lôc, and in the Central Highlands at Kontum.

These attacks triggered major retaliatory strikes by U.S. air and naval forces, including renewed bombing of Hà Nôi and Hai Phòng in North Vietnam for the first time since November 1968. Large numbers of ships and aircraft were dispatched to the theater of war, and Hai Phòng and other major ports were mined, an action often urged by military leaders but never before authorized by civilian authorities.

The South Vietnamese fought well, having made great progress in integrating air, armor, artillery and infantry. U.S. support had been crucially important, especially at An Lôc, where B-52s saved the day. But Abrams made sure everybody understood that no amount of U.S. support would have mattered had the South Vietnamese not been up to the challenge.

In late June 1972, Abrams departed Vietnam and was succeeded as Commander, U.S. Military Assistance Command, Vietnam (COMUSMACV) by Gen. Fred Weyand, his deputy for the past two years and a man with vast experience in the war. Weyand now inherited the difficult and thankless task of closing down the American expeditionary force.

Apparent progress in the Paris peace talks had hit a snag in late autumn 1972. Ever-narrowing U.S. expectations and aspirations for the war now focused on getting back U.S. prisoners of war. On 18 December, Nixon unleashed the most concentrated bombing campaign of the war on North Vietnam. The onslaught continued until 31 December, when the North Vietnamese agreed to resume peace talks. Agreement was then swiftly reached, and on 23 January 1973, the document was initialed by Henry Kissinger and Lê Đuc Tho.

At that point, the United States was virtually out of the war. Left behind in South Vietnam were a small Defense Attaché Office and the U.S. embassy. The peace agreement, fatally flawed, provided for a cease-fire. The Americans went home, but Communist forces remained largely where they were, in position to fight on.

—Lewis Sorley

References: Clarke, Jeffrey J. *Advice and Support: The Final Years, 1965–1973* (1988); Kissinger, Henry A. *White House Years* (1979); Nixon, Richard M. *RN: The Memoirs of Richard Nixon* (1978); Palmer, Dave R. *Summons of the Trumpet: U.S.-Vietnam in Perspective* (1978); Sorley, Lewis. *Thunderbolt: General Creighton Abrams and the Army of His Times* (1992).

See also: Abrams, Creighton; ARC LIGHT (B-52 Raids); BÌNH TÂY I-IV, Operations; Bunker, Ellsworth; Civilian Operations and Revolutionary Development Support (CORDS); Clear and Hold; Colby, William Egan; Easter Offensive (Nguyên Huê Campaign), Hamburger Hill (Battle of Âp Bia Mountain); Kissinger, Henry Alfred; Laird, Melvin R.; LAM SON 719, Operation; Military Assistance Command, Vietnam (MACV); Nixon, Richard Milhous; Pacification; Paris Peace Accords; Vietnamization; Weyand, Frederick C.

United States: Involvement in Vietnam, 1973–1975

U.S. involvement in Vietnam steadily diminished between the signing of the Paris peace accords in 1973 and the collapse of the Sài Gòn government in 1975. This period is often cynically referred to as the "decent interval," but the greatest significance of U.S. policy during this period may well be the surprisingly small amount of controversy that it generated.

The Paris peace accords, signed on 27 January 1973 by representatives of the United States, the Democratic Republic of Vietnam (DRV), the Republic of Vietnam (RVN), and the Provisional Revolutionary Government (PRG), called for a cease-fire, the withdrawal of all U.S. military forces within 60 days, the return of all captured personnel, efforts to locate missing persons on both sides, and the beginning of talks aimed at achieving "national conciliation and concord."

In March 1973, 591 captured U.S. personnel were returned under Operation HOMECOMING. After stating firmly on 29 March that "all our American POWs are on their way home," President Nixon announced that the last U.S. forces were also returning.

U.S. military involvement in Southeast Asia did not cease, however. Some U.S. bases were signed over to the RVN, enough planes and helicopters were brought in to give the Republic of Vietnam Armed Forces (RVNAF) the fourth largest air force in the world, and at least 9,000 U.S. servicemen hastily resigned their commissions so that they could be legally retained by the Vietnamese as civilians. Nixon ordered occasional reconnaissance flights over North Vietnam so that he could match his previous promises to supply $4.75 billion in reconstruction aid with threats to drop the aid and resume bombing if the cease-fire failed to hold. The U.S. Air Force dropped 250,000 tons of bombs on Cambodia in the first six months of 1973, and heavy bombing also took place in Laos.

Meanwhile, Nixon began to experience political trouble at home on various issues, including the emerging Watergate scandal. The decline in his political power combined with an increasing war weariness among Americans to undercut his military efforts in Southeast Asia. Despite intense Nixon administration lobbying, Congress cut the amount of aid authorized for Vietnam from $2.3 billion in fiscal year 1973 to $1 billion in 1974. Dramatic increases in oil prices following the Arab oil embargo and resulting inflation eroded the buying power of this appropriation. By 1974 the United States was no longer able to replace RVNAF equipment at the level permitted by the Paris peace accords, and RVNAF operations had to be cut by as much as 50 percent.

Deeply upset by the disclosure of illegal bombings in Cambodia, on 10 May 1973 a rebellious Congress cut off all funding for further U.S. air operations in the theater. By late June, Congress went beyond that to pass a law forbidding all further military operations in Southeast Asia. Nixon's angry veto was overridden. On 6 November 1973, Congress overrode another Nixon veto and the War Powers Act became law. This required the president to inform Congress within 48 hours of the dispatch of U.S. troops to another country and specified that the troops must be withdrawn within 60 days unless Congress explicitly authorized their presence.

In August 1974, after the Watergate scandals forced Nixon to resign from office and Gerald Ford assumed the presidency, American interest in Vietnam declined even further. Secretary of State Henry Kissinger still lobbied hard for continued aid, but a generally hostile Congress cut appropriations to only $700 million for fiscal year 1975. Charges that Americans might still be held against their will in Vietnam were largely discounted by a war-weary public. Ambassador Graham Martin and embassy officials in Sài Gòn were thus faced with the difficult task of trying to counter the demoralizing effects of U.S. aid cuts on a government that Americans now regarded as too feeble and corrupt to be worth saving.

The decline in American interest in Vietnam became clear to the North Vietnamese and Provisional Revolutionary Government forces when the United States did not respond to the 7 January 1975 capture of the provincial capital of Phuoc Bình. DRV military leaders now felt that they could push into the Central Highlands. When a disastrous retreat destroyed key elements in the ARVN, DRV forces continued on toward the main Southern cities. The final phase of the war had begun. During this period, the U.S. Congress voted an additional $300 million in humanitarian aid but refused to discuss having U.S. troops reenter the war.

The Sài Gòn government surrendered on 30 April 1975, 55 days after the final Communist offensive began. The speed of that offensive, combined with Martin's determination to keep up morale, meant that many Vietnamese who should have been evacuated by the Americans were left behind. As television screens displayed dramatic images of Americans being evacuated by helicopter from the roof of the embassy in Sài Gòn, Communist forces quickly solidified their power in Cambodia and Laos as well.

Americans did not engage in a great debate over responsibility for the defeat. The sacrifices of the U.S. military, the clear incompetence and corruption of the Sài Gòn forces, and the scope of the effort—not just by the relatively liberal Johnson, but also by the deeply conservative Nixon—combined to give Americans a more realistic sense of their power to implement policy.

—Peter K. Frost

Reference: Isaacs, Arnold R. *Without Honor: Defeat in Vietnam and Cambodia* (1984).
See also: Ford, Gerald R.; FREQUENT WIND, Operation; Hồ Chí Minh Campaign; HOMECOMING, Operation; Nixon, Richard Milhous; Kissinger, Henry Alfred; Martin, Graham A.; Missing in Action, Allied; Paris Peace Accords; Prisoners of War, Allied; Television and the Vietnam Experience; War Powers Act; Watergate.

United States: Involvement in Vietnam, 1975 to the Present

After the fall of the Republic of Vietnam (RVN) in April 1975, the United States conducted a punitive policy toward Vietnam. Washington refused to normalize relations with the newly reunited state and actively sought to isolate Vietnam politically, economically, and diplomatically.

Socialist Republic of Vietnam (SRV) leaders fully believed that the United States would fulfill its part of the 1973 Paris peace accords and supply $3.3 billion dollars in reconstruction aid over five-years. Instead, the trade embargo that had applied to the Democratic Republic of Vietnam under the Trading with the Enemy Act was extended to all of Vietnam, and Japan and other nations were pressured to adhere to the embargo. The United States blocked credits and loans from the World Bank, the International Monetary Fund, and the Asian Development Bank, and $150 million in Vietnamese assets in the United States were frozen. The United States vetoed Vietnam's requests to join the United Nations, which would have given it international legitimacy.

In 1977 the Carter administration cautiously sought to move away from this punitive policy. Washington appeared receptive to establishing diplomatic relations with Vietnam, provided it give a "proper accounting" of the fate of 2,500 Americans missing in action (MIA). Between spring 1977 and fall 1978, preliminary talks came close to a tentative agreement, then fell apart over Vietnamese demands for billions of dollars in war reparations. Washington flatly rejected this, contending that Vietnam violated the Paris accords by invading the RVN in 1975. Carter declared that aid would follow the normalization of relations but could not be linked to normalization or the MIA issue.

In 1978 Vietnam dropped its demands for war reparations as a precondition for recognition, but by then Congress and the American public were decidedly not interested in normalizing relations. The Carter administration became concerned over Vietnamese troop buildups along the Cambodian border, heightened Soviet influence in the region, and a growing exodus of Vietnamese refugees. Most importantly, the Carter administration was moving toward establishing full relations with China. Because of worsening relations between Vietnam and China, the administration believed that normalizing relations with Vietnam could jeopardize good relations with China. Once the United States established full relations with China in 1978, Vietnam was ignored. Then in November 1978, Vietnam signed a treaty of alliance with the Soviet Union, putting it solidly in the Soviet camp when the Cold War heated up again in the late 1970s.

Vietnam's invasion and subsequent occupation of Cambodia, the unresolved issue of MIAs, and other problems led to little progress in normalizing diplomatic relations or in ending the crippling trade embargo. The MIA issue was the most stubborn and sensitive question dividing the two states. American television and cinema conveyed the impression that Americans were still imprisoned in Vietnam, which was bolstered by polls and by congressional sentiment. Although 1,750 Americans were listed as missing in Vietnam (and nearly 2,400 in all of Southeast Asia), the U.S. Department of Defense considered virtually all MIAs legally dead. Despite numerous reports of MIA sightings, none have ever been confirmed. American veterans even conducted forays into Laos searching for MIAs without success. Seeking to break the stalemate in the mid-1980s, Vietnam made concessions. Beginning in July 1985 Vietnam permitted U.S. inspection teams to visit potential MIA burial sites and provided Americans access to war records, archives, and cemeteries. In 1991 the United States opened an office in Hà Nôi to coordinate its MIA search efforts.

Misunderstandings on other issues also divided the two states. First, the United States declared that any negotiations for normalization could not occur until after all Vietnamese troops withdrew from Cambodia. Washington considered Vietnam's occupation as part of a growing Soviet assertiveness in the world. Under strong pressure from Soviet leader Mikhail Gorbachev, who was seeking rapprochement with China and an end to a costly stalemate, Vietnam agreed to withdraw all its forces by September 1989. In return, China and the Association of South East Asian Nations (ASEAN) bloc agreed to cut its support for the Khmer Rouge guerrilla fighters and end Vietnam's international isolation.

Second, the Orderly Departure Program, carried out under the auspices of the UN, was designed to promote an orderly resettlement in the West (mainly the United States) of Vietnamese political refugees who might otherwise try to flee by sea. After years of stalling by Vietnam, the program started functioning properly at the end of the decade. Virtually all of the estimated 35,000 Amerasians and their families were resettled in the United States. In 1990 an agreement was signed that allowed officials and officers of the former RVN government and army to emigrate to the United States. One by one, once-serious problems were resolved to mutual satisfaction.

The Clinton administration moved cautiously, though steadily, toward full normalization of economic and political ties. The American trade embargo was finally lifted in February 1994, allowed U.S. trade and investment. The United States dropped its veto on credits and loans to Vietnam from international lending associations, yet some trade restrictions still impeded U.S. companies from taking a greater role in developing what many consider to be Southeast Asia's "next dragon." Humanitarian aid and cultural and educational exchanges (governmental and private) increased, and American tourism also skyrocketed. In January 1995, U.S. and Vietnamese officials signed an agreement exchanging liaison offices in their respective capitals. Finally, despite opposition from the MIA lobby and Republican conservatives, in July 1995 Clinton extended full diplomatic ties to the SRV. On 6 August 1995, the American flag was raised over the U.S. embassy in Hà Nôi.

In the final step in establishing full diplomatic relations between the United States and the SRV, Clinton nominated Representative Douglas "Pete" Peterson, a former Vietnam POW, as the first U.S. envoy to the SRV. The Senate confirmed Peterson in April 1997, and he took up his duties in Hà Nôi in May. In June, Secretary of State Madeleine Albright visited Hà Nôi to meet with SRV leaders and traveled to Hô Chí Minh City to lay the cornerstone for a new American consulate.

Michael Share

References: Sar Desai, D. R. *Vietnam: The Struggle for National Identity* (1992); Williams, Michael. *Vietnam at the Crossroads* (1992); Young, Marilyn. *The Vietnam Wars, 1945–1990* (1991).
See also: Bush, George Herbert Walker; Carter, Jimmy; Clinton, William Jefferson; Ford, Gerald R.; Khmer Rouge; Missing in Action, Allied; Peterson, Douglas "Pete"; Prisoners of War, Allied; Reagan, Ronald; Vietnam, Socialist Republic of: 1975 to the Present; Vietnamese Invasion and Occupation of Cambodia.

United States: Marine Corps

U.S. Marine Corps involvement in the Vietnam War began in April 1962 when Marine helicopter units deployed to the Mekong Delta to lift Army of the Republic of Vietnam (ARVN) units into battle. On 8 March 1965, two battalions of the 9th Marine Expeditionary Brigade (MEB), the first U.S. ground troops in Vietnam, arrived by sea and air at Đà Nang. As Marine ground and aviation units poured into Vietnam, the 9th MEB became the III Marine Amphibious Force (MAF), and the Marines' mission expanded from defense of the Đà Nang air base to meeting the Communist threat in South Vietnam's five northernmost provinces. In May a Marine base with a jet-capable airstrip was established at Chu Lai.

The Marines emphaszied pacification, which required eradication of the National Liberation Front (NLF) political and military infrastructure in thousands of hamlets and villages. The Marines devised a program of civic action platoons. Each merged a Marine squad with one of Vietnamese militia to provide defense at the hamlet level. Although successful on a limited scale, pacification was never emphasized as much by Military Assistance Command, Vietnam (MACV) as large-unit search-and-destroy operations.

In August 1965, the Marines launched Operation STARLITE, a regimental-sized attack against a large Viêt Công (VC) force south of Chu Lai. Further Marine operations between 1965 and 1966 were predominantly against small VC units in the southern I Corps.

In July MACV obtained evidence that a People's Army of Vietnam (PAVN) division had crossed the Demilitarized Zone (DMZ) and taken up positions in Quang Tri Province. This threat forced the Marines to downplay pacification, deploy northward, and construct a series of combat bases south of the DMZ. The Marines fought a series of bloody battles into 1967 with well-equipped North Vietnamese regulars in such places as the Rockpile, Côn Thiên, Gio Linh, Khe Sanh, and Cam Lô and constructed bases at Phú Bài and Đông Hà to support these operations.

By 1967 the Marines were fighting two wars. In southern I Corps, the 1st Marine Division fought a counterinsurgency war against the VC; to the North the 3d Marine Division waged a more conventional war against the PAVN. Marine bases at Đông Hà, Đà Nang, Chu Lai, and Phú Bài continued to be regular targets for Communist rocket attacks.

In late 1967, Gen. Westmoreland ordered U.S. Army units into southern I Corps, allowing deployment of more Marine units further north. January 1968 saw major PAVN attacks against Marines at Khe Sanh and during the Têt Offensive. As heavy fighting continued into the spring, Westmoreland increased U.S. Army units in what had been a Marine area. After fighting in northern areas tapered off in late 1968, the Marines launched an Accelerated Pacification Plan designed to take back what had been lost in the Tết Offensive. In early 1969, the 3d Marine Division adopted Army-style high mobility operations that deemphasized reliance on fixed positions. Pacification yielded successes.

By mid-1969, Marine positions in northern South Vietnam were the responsibility of the U.S. Army and the ARVN. By October 1969, as a part of Vietnamization, the 3d Marine Division had left Vietnam. In March 1970, the Army XXIV Corps replaced III MAF as the dominant U.S. headquarters in I Corps. The Marine area of responsibility shrank to essentially Quang Nam Province and its capital, Đà Nang. Marine bases were razed or turned over to U.S. Army or ARVN forces. During the 1971 Laos invasion, Marine participation was limited to transportation and engineering support. In April 1971, III MAF headquarters transferred to Okinawa.

During the 1972 Easter Offensive, only a few hundred Marines remained in Vietnam. Marine F-4 Phantom jets provided tactical air support for South Vietnamese armed forces. Other Marines served as air and naval gunfire spotters and advisors to the Vietnamese Marine Corps. No Marine ground combat troops went ashore.

By 1972, 12,926 Marines had been killed in Vietnam and another 88,542 wounded, more casualties than the Marine Corps had suffered in World War II.

—Peter Brush

References: Moskin, Robert J. *The U.S. Marine Corps Story* (1977); Simmons, Edwin H., ed. *The Marines in Vietnam, 1954–1973. An Anthology and Annotated Bibliography*; Simmons, Edwin H., ed. *The United States Marines* (1976).

See also: Amphibious Warfare; Civic Action; Clear and Hold; Đà Nang; Huê, Battle of; Marine Combined Action Platoons (CAPs); Order of Battle; Pacification; STARLITE, Operation; Vietnam, Republic of: Marine Corps (VNMC); Westmoreland, William Childs.

United States: Navy

The U.S. Navy undertook a multitude of missions, many of them novel or unanticipated, throughout the Southeast Asian struggle. The Navy of the early 1960s was not especially well-prepared for a conflict like that in Vietnam, being largely oriented in doctrine and force structure to nuclear war. Naval intelligence focused largely on the support of nuclear operations. Fleet support ships were mostly World War II veterans with outdated equipment and slow transit speeds.

Following the August 1964 Tonkin Gulf incidents and the commitment of the Seventh Fleet to the war, the Navy scrambled to redress these deficiencies. Cruisers and destroyers updated their gunnery skills, and several gun cruisers and the battleship *New Jersey* were returned to service. Attack aircraft were modified to carry conventional munitions, and 250- and 500-pound bombs were produced on an emergency basis. The F-4 Phantom received a pod-mounted 20-mm cannon to give it dogfighting capability. Hurried base expansion at Subic Bay provided essential repair and replenishment support. New planes just entering service, such as the RA-5C and the A-6 Intruder, provided enhanced reconnaissance and strike capabilities. Strike aircraft acquired Shrike missiles to enable them to hit North Vietnamese anti-aircraft radars. The addition of titanium dioxide to ammunition charges significantly extended the service life of shipboard artillery pieces.

Navy missions most in the public eye were the Seventh Fleet carrier operations directed against Communist forces in North and South Vietnam and, occasionally, Laos and Cambodia. Less dramatically, surface warships gave fire support to friendly troops ashore and, in Operation SEA DRAGON, mounted harassment and interdiction raids along the North Vietnamese coastline. Another principal mission was to stop maritime infiltration from the north. Navy MARKET TIME patrols, begun in 1965, established a three-tiered shield of long-range aircraft, medium-sized surface ships, and fast patrol craft ("Swift boats").

Ashore, the Navy's small Sài Gòn advisory group expanded May 1965 with the establishment of Naval Forces, Vietnam command. To carry the war to enemy forces in the Mekong Delta, the Navy improvised a brown-water fleet of patrol boats, shallow-draft landing craft, and fire support monitors. This effort hampered Communist forces all the way to the Cambodian border. SEALs (Sea Air Land teams) and Navy helicopter units searched out opposing troops far from the sea; river convoys resupplied the Army and Marines. The Navy sometimes put Marines ashore in amphibious assaults.

U.S. naval personnel served throughout the war as advisors to their South Vietnamese counterparts, engaged in civic action, and implemented naval aspects of Vietnamization. From 1964 to 1973, 2,636,000 sailors and Marines served in the Southeast Asian operational theater. Fourteen Navy men won the Medal of Honor; 2,551 U.S. naval personnel were killed, excluding Marines.

In the war's last stages, naval forces provided aerial support and naval bombardment to counter the 1972 Easter Offensive and to prosecute the subsequent LINEBACKER campaign. Aerial mining of North Vietnamese harbors was especially effective in forcing the Communists to resume negotiations. The Navy extricated U.S. and friendly personnel following the collapse of South Vietnam in 1975.

These successes aside, the Navy was hurt severely by the Vietnam War. Apart from the decline in popular support and the racial unrest that it shared with the other services, the Navy found it difficult to pay for costly operations in Southeast Asia while defense appropriations declined markedly. As the Soviet Navy grew in size and capability, the U.S. Navy faced the wholesale obsolescence of its many World War II–era ships. To keep its aviation component at strength, the Navy reduced its forces tailored for other missions, yet its aircraft inventory dropped from 10,598 in 1964 to 7,681 in 1973. Especially hurt were the Navy's antisubmarine elements. New construction was deferred, with funding going into other operations.

Certainly the Vietnam War proved the need for a navy with multiple capabilities. Guns, denounced as antediluvian in a missile navy, demonstrated their virtues in reliability, economy, and continuous availability in all types of weather. The aircraft carrier, under severe criticism as outdated or irrelevant with the loss of its nuclear strike mission to submarines, showed its versatility once again.

—Malcolm Muir, Jr.

References: Hooper, Edwin B., Dean C. Allard, and Oscar P. Fitzgerald. *The Setting of the Stage to 1959*. Vol. 1, *The United States Navy and the Vietnam Conflict* (1976); Love, Robert W., Jr. *History of the U.S. Navy.* Vol. 2, *1942–1991* (1992); Marolda, Edward J. *By Sea, Air, and Land: An Illustrated History of the U.S. Navy and the War in Southeast Asia* (1994); Marolda, Edward J., and Oscar P. Fitzgerald. *From Military Assistance to Combat*. Vol. 2, *The United States Navy and the Vietnam Conflict* (1986); Muir, Malcolm, Jr. *Black Shoes and Blue Water: Surface Warfare in the United States Navy, 1945–1975* (1996).

See also: DeSoto Missions; GAME WARDEN, Operation; Gayler, Noel Arthur Meredyth; FREQUENT WIND, Operation; LINEBACKER I, Operation; LINEBACKER II, Operation; MARKET TIME, Operation; Mobile Riverine Force; *New Jersey* (BB-62); Operation Plan 34A (OPLAN 34A); Order of Battle; Riverine Craft; Riverine Warfare; SEA DRAGON, Operation; SEAL (Sea, Air, Land) Teams; Sea Power in the Vietnam War; Tonkin Gulf Incidents; United States: Coast Guard; United States: Marine Corps; United States: Seabees; Warships, Allied and Democratic Republic of Vietnam; Yankee Station.

United States: Nongovernmental Organizations, 1954 to the Present

American nongovernmental organizations (NGOs) provided emergency relief and economic development assistance during the Vietnam War. After the U.S. government severed ties with Vietnam in 1975, NGOs orchestrated refugee evacuations, organized reconciliation movements, and channeled the only American aid available to the Vietnamese.

Although some NGOs provided assistance to refugees during the Indo-China War, more followed with substantial aid programs after the 1954 Geneva Accords. CARE, Catholic Relief Services, International Rescue Committee, Mennonite Central Committee, and Church World Service entered South Vietnam hoping to help people escape political and military upheaval, to save South Vietnam from Communist revolution, and to stabilize a new nation with democratic and capitalist institutions. Encouraged by the State Department's Advisory Committee for Voluntary Foreign Aid, these agencies assisted U.S., French, and South Vietnamese government efforts to evacuate nearly a million mostly Catholic refugees fleeing the Communist-controlled North.

Between 1954 and 1964, American NGOs provided millions of dollars to resettle refugees, helped develop economic projects in villages and cities, and built houses, hospitals, schools, cultural centers, and orphanages in South Vietnam. U.S. and Sài Gòn officials encouraged such projects by granting funds, authorizing programs, advising personnel, and providing transportation and security. Most food distributed by NGOs was made available by the U.S. government through Public Law 480 (the Food for Peace program). As the Communist insurgency intensified, NGOs' connections to and dependence on the U.S. and Republic of

Vietnam (RVN) governments politicized and compromised their humanitarian aims.

NGO activity increased dramatically after 1964, but the war divided NGOs into conflicting camps. Some agencies supported U.S. policy and continued to depend on government funding and security. A few even distributed food aid to Army of the Republic of Vietnam (ARVN) troops and assisted minority populations to provide intelligence information. But other NGOs refused government funds and tried to distance themselves from U.S. actions. The Mennonite Central Committee and American Friends Service Committee offered aid to people on both sides of the conflict and openly criticized U.S. policy. In 1971 International Voluntary Services, a major recipient of government resources, was expelled from the RVN for condemning U.S. military actions.

After the United States withdrew from Vietnam in 1975, most NGOs followed and concentrated their efforts on relocating refugees ("boat people") fleeing the Communist regime. Private agencies that pushed for reconstruction aid and reconciliation found it difficult to circumvent the U.S. government policy of isolating Vietnam by withholding economic aid and humanitarian assistance. Once the political climate improved in 1991, Washington allowed some funds to be channeled through private agencies for disaster relief, agricultural needs, and health programs. NGOs continue to play a pivotal role in promoting improved relations with Vietnam and in encouraging the U.S. government to allow more aid programs to reconstruct and develop the region.

—Delia Pergande

References: Meinertz, Midge Austin, ed. *Witness in Anguish* (1975); Minear, Larry. "Private Aid and Public Policy: A Case Study" (1988); Rawlings, Stuart. *The IVS Experience from Algeria to Vietnam* (1992); Spencer, Dao, ed. *Directory of U.S. NGOs Vietnam Programs* (1992).

See also: American Friends of Vietnam; Refugees and Boat People.

United States: Nurses

U.S. military nurses arrived early in the Vietnam conflict. The first Army nurses arrived at the Eighth Field Hospital, Nha Trang, in March 1962. The first members of the Navy Nurse Corps were stationed in Sài Gòn at the same time, and Air Force nurses soon followed. The number of military nurses serving in Vietnam peaked at 900 in January 1969, coinciding with the largest troop deployment of the war. Nurses served in hospitals throughout Vietnam and on board the hospital ships U.S.S. *Repose* and *Sanctuary*, in addition to serving as flight nurses.

Nurses' work closely paralleled that of physicians and medical corpsmen. Most patients were wounded in battle or sick with infectious diseases. Care of those infected with tropical diseases was primarily supportive, providing liquids, medication, nourishment, and rest. Nurses were often infected themselves and lost days from work.

Men wounded in the field were stabilized by a medic or corpsman and transported, often by helicopter, to one of 19 medical facilities. Although physicians were responsible for the triage of wounded men, nurses often shared this task and were sometimes delegated triage decisions when physicians were needed elsewhere. For the severely wounded, nurses focused on pain relief and psychological support. Some nurses reported that comforting the dying soldier was an essential task, so that the soldier and his family would know he had not died alone.

Most wounded suffered injuries from small arms injuries, mines, or booby traps. Small arms fire typically caused severe tissue damage, interfered with blood supply to the wound, and often resulted in multiple wounds. Explosive devices caused large, contaminated wounds. After surgery was performed, nurses were primarily concerned with infection prevention, pain relief, tissue regeneration, and psychological support.

Nurses served aboard fixed wing evacuation flights transporting patients, most often to Okinawa or Japan, for further treatment or rehabilitation. These nurses were trained in trauma and critical care and worked with significantly more independence than did nurses before the war.

The nurses' role was significantly challenged by the soldiers in Vietnam and conflicts in American culture. Not only was the war unpopular, but alcohol and drug abuse complicated an already complex social milieu, making the traditional role of nurses in providing neutral, unconditional support more difficult. Many nurses encountered the same psychological trauma as the soldiers for whom they cared.

The Vietnam War brought at least three changes in the nursing profession. First, nurses developed practice specialties, much as physicians had. Second, the war afforded nurses opportunities to practice more independently and with greater professional autonomy. Third, in 1966 men were authorized by Congress to join the three nurses' corps and ultimately made up about one-fourth of the nurse corps. Men were a valuable addition to the nurse corps, but many soldiers found female nurses an important factor in morale. This phenomena, reported in other American wars, is probably related to the socialization of women as comforters.

Studies and biographies of nurses who served in Vietnam reveal experiences of a more personal nature. Women there were socially isolated, restricted to the hospital, the barracks, and occasionally the officers' club. Many nurses were frustrated by their inability to see a patient through his recovery. Nurses, like soldiers, experienced difficulty in readjusting to life at home after their Vietnam experience.

One nurse was killed in the Vietnam War: 1st Lt. Sharon Lane was killed by hostile action while on duty at the 312th Evacuation Hospital, Chu Lai, on 8 June 1969. The contribution of nurses to the U.S. military effort was recognized in 1993 with the dedication of a statue near the Vietnam Veterans Memorial.

—Rhonda Keen-Payne

References: Donahue, M. Patricia. *Nursing: The Finest Art* (1985); Kalisch, Phillip A., and Beatrice Kalisch. *The Advance of American Nursing,* 3d ed. (1994); Kalisch, Phillip A., and Beatrice Kalisch. "Nurses under Fire: The World War II Experience of Nurses on Bataan and Corregidor" (1966); Kirkpatrick, Sandra. "Battle Casualty" (1968); Norman, Elizabeth M. "A Study of Female Military Nurses in Vietnam during the War Years 1965–1973" (1986); Smith, Winnie. *American Daughter Gone to War* (1992).

See also: Casualties; Medevac; Medicine, Military; Vietnam Veterans Memorial; Women in the War, U.S.

United States: Red Cross Recreation Workers

The Supplemental Recreation Activities Overseas (SRAO) program, one of five services offered by the American Red Cross in Vietnam, provided recreational activities for U.S. troops. The first SRAO center opened in Đà Nang in October 1965, and 27 other centers eventually were established throughout South Vietnam.

Between 1965 and 1972, 627 female SRAO workers, commonly called "doughnut dollies," served in Vietnam. All were college graduates and volunteers. After a two-week training program in Washington, D.C., they were immediately sent to Vietnam, where they were required to wear the standard blue uniforms. They provided refreshments and recreational activities, visited hospitals, wrote letters for patients, and listened to the men talk about their experiences and feelings. Often the only American civilian females with whom the soldiers came in contact, they frequently took the surrogate roles of mother, sister, and girlfriend.

SRAO women immeasurably boosted the morale of approximately 300,000 American troops each month. Three SRAO women—Hanna E. Crews, Virginia E. Kirsch, and Lucinda J. Richter—were killed in Vietnam. The SRAO program officially ended in May 1972 as the last American combat troops were withdrawn.

—Lori M. Geist

References: Dickerson, Sharon Lewis. "American Red Cross Women in Vietnam" (1993); Marshall, Kathryn. *In the Combat Zone* (1987); Walker, Keith. *A Piece of My Heart* (1985).

See also: Women in the War, U.S..

United States: Seabees

U.S. Navy construction engineers; the name derives from the pronunciation of the initial letters of "construction battalion." Seabee involvement in Vietnam began on 25 January 1963, when two 13-man Seabee Technical Assistance Teams entered the country in support of U.S. Army Special Forces. The Seabees built Special Forces camps, performed civic action tasks, and completed projects in support of the Civilian Irregular Defense Group (CIDG).

The first full Naval Mobile Construction Battalion landed in Vietnam on 7 May 1965 to build an airfield for the Marines at Chu Lai. From 1965 to 1969, the Seabee commitment in South Vietnam rapidly increased, necessitating first the transfer of Atlantic Fleet battalions to the Pacific through a change of home port, then deployment of Atlantic Fleet battalions directly to Vietnam and the reestablishment of nine additional battalions. Finally, in May 1968, two reserve battalions were called to active duty, bringing to 21 the number of battalions rotating to Vietnam at one time or another. In addition, two Amphibious Construction Battalions lent support to the Vietnam effort and two Construction Battalion Maintenance Units were active.

Seabee battalions in Vietnam were under the immediate control of two Naval Construction Regiments. Together they formed the Third Naval Construction Brigade, which provided overall control of Seabee units in Vietnam. Seabees were also assigned to such non-Seabee units as the Naval Support Activities at Đà Nang and Sài Gòn. The Seabee community reached a peak of 26,000 in 1969.

Seabee in Vietnam built critically needed roads, airfields, and other facilities. In addition to the many Seabee teams active at remote locations, construction battalions built large coastal strongholds in I Corps area. Seabees were especially active at Đà Nang, Phú Bài, Chu Lai, and Đông Hà. In 1966 Seabees entered Quang Tri Province and built hilltop concrete bunkers at Làng Vei, overlooking a feeder line of the Hô Chí Minh Trail. In 1967 Seabees built the 2,040-foot "Liberty Bridge" across the Thu Bôn River.

During the Têt Offensive, Seabees built and fought in direct support of the Marine Corps and Army. When sniper fire drove them under cover, they organized their own combat teams and silenced the snipers. In addition to supporting combat forces, Seabees completed innumerable civic action projects while in Vietnam, including the construction of schools, hospitals, housing, and wells.

By the end of 1968, most major base construction was complete and the Seabees began to pull out. The last battalion left Vietnam in November 1971. The three Seabee teams still there finished their tasks and were gone by the end of 1972.

—Vincent A. Transano

References: "Naval Facilities Engineering Command History, 1965–1974." Vol. 2. (n.d.); Naval Facilities Engineering Command Archives, NAVFAC Historical Program Office, Naval Construction Battalion Center, Port Hueneme, CA; Tregaskis, Richard. *Southeast Asia: Building the Bases* (1975).

See also: Civic Action; Civilian Irregular Defense Group (CIDG); Huê, Battle of; Search and Destroy; United States: Army; United States: Marine Corps; United States: Navy.

United States: Special Forces

Elite U.S. Army troops who played a key role in counterinsurgency operations during the Vietnam War. Office of Psychological Warfare (OCPW) chief Brig. Gen. Robert A. McClure suggested the formation of specialized units that were expert in conducting unconventional warfare (UW) operations behind enemy lines. On 20 June 1952 the U.S. Special Forces (USSF), the first permanent UW unit since World War II, was formed at Fort Bragg, North Carolina, using U.S. Army personnel.

Recruiting of Special Forces volunteers began under the "Lodge Bill" (Public Law 597, 30 June 1952). The guidelines specifying requirements for voluntary service were drafted as U.S. Army Special Regulation 600–160–10 for implementation on 25 April 1952. Training stressed infiltration and land navigation techniques and the use of parachutes and small boats. Specialized training followed and included sabotage, intelligence gathering, communications, medicine, and weaponry. Army volunteers who successfully completed the secret training were assigned directly to Special Forces.

Many in the Army's hierarchy were displeased, but by the 1960s President Kennedy and his senior military advisor, Gen. Maxwell D. Taylor, were strong advocates for enhanced Special Forces capability.

Special Forces were the chief instrument of U.S. counterinsurgency policy in Vietnam. The goal was not so much to destroy enemy armed forces as to win the allegiance of the people by inspiring them to defend themselves.

Personnel from the 1st Special Forces Group on Okinawa first entered Vietnam in summer 1957. They trained 58 Vietnamese soldiers in special forces techniques at a training center in Nha Trang, later designated the Military Assistance Command, Vietnam (MACV) Recondo School. These Vietnamese formed the nucleus of the Vietnamese Special Forces (Luc Luong Đac Biêt [LLĐB]).

In 1960 the USSF mission expanded to include training 60 Army of the Republic of Vietnam (ARVN) Ranger companies, and 30 instructors from the 7th Special Forces Group deployed to Vietnam. In early 1961, this arrangement was changed when four men from the 1st Special Forces Group and five other soldiers replaced the 7th SF instructors as a Mobile Training Team (MTT). Such teams rotated from Okinawa for the next two years to train the Rangers. These teams operated under the control of the Central Intelligence Agency's (CIA's) Combined Studies Group (CSG).

In the 11 May 1961 National Security Action Memorandum No. 52, Kennedy directed Secretary of Defense Robert McNamara to examine increasing U.S. counter-guerrilla resources. In his 1961 message to Congress on the defense budget and his State of the Union address, Kennedy announced his intention to expand the military's capability to conduct unconventional warfare. On 21 September 1961, the 5th Special Forces Group (Airborne), 1st Special Forces, was activated at Fort Bragg. Its mission was to train personnel in counterinsurgency methods to be used in Vietnam.

The USSF began training ethnic minorities in Vietnam in 1961, and this became the basis of the Civilian Irregular Defense Group (CIDG). The purpose was to reestablish government control over remote areas and to provide forces capable of combating the Communist insurgents. By August about 10,000 Rhadé had been organized into village defense and mobile strike fiorces, and by 1965 more than 80 fortified CIDG camps had been established. During 1961 the CIA used one SF team to train Vietnamese Special Forces to conduct reconnaissance and harassment operations in North Vietnam. On 1 May 1962, the CSG was attached to MACV headquarters. In addition to training local inhabitants to defend themselves, gather intelligence, and conduct small offensive operations, USSF was deeply involved in civic action programs to encourage civilians to identify more closely with the South Vietnamese government and to improve the living conditions of the people.

In July 1962, Secretary McNamara directed that the CIA's paramilitary operations be transferred to MACV. This was to place SF units under Army control and to emphasize offensive operations rather than pacification. Code-named Operation PARASOL-SWITCHBACK, the transfer was complete by 1 July 1963. SWITCHBACK was completed as scheduled. By that time, the SF had trained 52,636 villagers, 10,904 reaction force soldiers, 515 medical personnel, 3,803 scouts, and 946 trail watchers. and 879 villages had been secured.

USSF were frustrated in their efforts to improve the quality of the LLĐB by incompetent Vietnamese leadership and mistrust of the Sài Gòn government. Part of the concept of the CIDG and border camps was that, once an area was deemed secure, the camps would be turned over to ARVN or LLĐB control, and the defenders would become part of the South Vietnamese Army. Traditional Vietnamese disregard of ethnic minorities, who often composed CIDG forces, and the incompetency of ARVN officers many times led to the abandonment of camps or to the unwillingness of the CIDG to fight for the government. The CIDG often showed themselves more loyal to their USSF advisors than to the Sài Gòn regime.

On 1 November 1963, along with the CIDG program, the CIA relinquished their surveillance responsibilities along the Laotian and Cambodian borders to the USASFV(P) headquarters. By June 1964, 18 border camps had been established. As the SF mission shifted from training indigenous forces to watching infiltration routes into South Vietnam, these camps became increasingly tempting targets for the North Vietnamese. In July 1964, a Việt Công (VC) force attacked the camp at Nam Đông. For this battle, USSF camp commander Capt. Roger Donlon received the first Medal of Honor issued since the Korean War.

Programs to increase the number of indigenous minorities participating in the CIDG effort and to expand CIDG operations, along with greater emphasis on observation along the borders, soon outstripped USSF resources available in Vietnam.

On 1 October 1964, the 5th Special Forces Group officially arrived in Vietnam. Many SF teams were understaffed, replacements often had little or no SF experience, and shortages of personnel with communications and medical skills became critical. Duty tours for USSF teams in Vietnam increased from six months to one year, resulting in troop replacements on an individual rather than team basis, and had a detrimental effect on team operations. USSF reached its highest strength in Vietnam on 30 September 1968 with 3,542 assigned personnel.

From 1964 to 1966, USSF trained and fielded three long-range reconnaissance projects: DELTA, SIGMA, and OMEGA. All had USSF leadership with indigenous battalions as reaction forces. In September 1966, Gen. Westmoreland directed the 5th SF Group to establish the MACV Recondo School to train U.S. and Allied personnel from major combat units in long-range reconnaissance techniques. The USSF was unable to prevent MACV from employing SF and CIDG as regular infantry in offensive operations against the People's Army of Vietnam (PAVN) or VC. Although results of such operations were often disastrous, the CIDG was usually successful in defending camps against Communist attacks. By 1967, increased night operations, extensive training, and missions based on effective intelligence resulted in more effective operations being conducted by SF detachments.

Although USSF composed most of the personnel in MACV-SOG operations, SOG was not subordinate to the 5th Special Forces Group and not answerable to MACV, but uniquely supervised by the president of the United States. Under MACV-SOG direction, combined USSF indigenous mercenary teams conducted operations into North Vietnam, Laos, and Cambodia to gather intelligence about PAVN activities along the Hô Chí Minh Trail. The Provincial Reconnaissance Unit was the armed wing of the PHOENIX program, and MACV-SOG continued to draw off experienced USSF personnel. This only added to the overall shortage of qualified USSF personnel for 5th Special Forces Group missions.

On 27 August 1969, Gen. Creighton Abrams ordered the phase-out of the CIDG program, with the camps and CIDG soldiers to be transferred to ARVN control. A total of 38 light infantry battalions, comprising primarily ethnic minorities, joined the ARVN under this program.

On 1 March 1971, the 5th Special Forces Group ceased all operations in South Vietnam and departed for the United States. Some USSF personnel remained in Vietnam, however, as instructors with the Special Mission Advisory Group (SMAG). These instructors readied Vietnamese soldiers to assume MACV-SOG's unconventional warfare role as the Special Mission Service (SMS). As SMAG was deactivated on 1 April 1972, USSF instructors became advisors to the SMS and the graduated SMAG students. Teams from the 1st Special Forces Group (SFG) continued to train ARVN and Cambodian soldiers until 22 February 1973, when the 1st SFG ceased operations in South Vietnam. The combined USSF-Vietnamese organization, Strategic Technical Directorate (STD), operated under the auspices of the closed MACV-SOG until it was disbanded on 12 May 1973.

—Richard L. Kiper, Harve Saal, and Spencer C. Tucker

References: Donahue, James C. *Mobile Guerrilla Forces with the Special Forces in War Zone D* (1996); Kelly, Francis J. *U.S. Army Special Forces, 1961–1972* (1973); Saal, Harve. *MACV, Studies and Observations Group (SOG). Behind Enemy Lines, A History of the Men and Missions.* 4 vols. (1991); Simpson, Charles M., III. *Inside the Green Berets (The Story of the Special Forces)* (1984); Stanton, Shelby L. *Green Berets at War. U.S. Army Special Forces in Southeast Asia, 1956–1975* (1985); Sutherland, Ian D. W. *1952/1982: Special Forces of the United States Army* (1990).

See also: Abrams, Creighton; Civilian Irregular Defense Group (CIDG); Counterinsurgency Warfare; DELTA, Project; Kennedy, John Fitzgerald; McNamara, Robert S.; Military Assistance Command, Vietnam (MACV); Montagnards; OMEGA, Project; Phoenix Program; Road Watch Teams (RWTs); SEAL (Sea, Air, Land) Teams; SIGMA, Project; Studies and Observation Group (SOG); Taylor, Maxwell Davenport; Vietnam, Republic of: Special Forces (Luc Luong Đac Biêt [LLDB]); Westmoreland, William Childs.

United States: Special Services

Organization providing recreational activities for military personnel. The U.S. Army Special Services program in Vietnam began on 1 July 1966, when responsibility for providing recreational activities for U.S. and Allied military forces was transferred from the U.S. Navy to the U.S. Army, Vietnam (USARV) with operational responsibility assigned to the 1st Logistical Command. Gen. William Westmoreland considered recreational facilities critical for maintaining troop morale and for providing on-base diversions so that U.S. soldiers would not overwhelm the Vietnamese economy.

The Special Services program consisted of arts and crafts, entertainment, library, rest and recuperation (R&R), recreation (sports and motion pictures), and service facilities. Military personnel assumed responsibility for R&R and recreation; civilian volunteers supervised and staffed the remaining branches. Initially USARV supplied only the organizational structure and technical and supervisory administrative personnel, and individual units provided all other administrative and logistical support. In March 1970, Special Services was reorganized and centralized as the USARV Special Services Agency (Provisional). By then, 31 craft shops and photo labs, 6 entertainment offices, 23 service clubs, and 39 libraries were in operation, mostly in permanent structures.

Civilian librarians also administered 250 field library units. Recreation specialists directed leisure activities, coordinated United Service Organizations (USO) tours by commercial entertainers, and created Command Military Touring Shows, sending military personnel to entertain soldiers in areas that commercial shows could not visit for security reasons.

Approximately 200 to 300 civilians, about 75 percent of them women, served with Special Services in Vietnam between 1966 and 1972. Two recreation specialists assigned to service clubs died of nonhostile causes.

—Ann L. Kelsey

References: "General Historical Records" (n.d.); "General Records" (n.d.); Westmoreland, William C. *A Soldier Reports* (1976).

See also: United States: Red Cross Recreation Workers ("Donut Dollies"); Women in the War, U.S.

University of Wisconsin Bombing (24 August 1970)

Bombing by the Weathermen, a radical student group, on the University of Wisconsin campus. Previous Weathermen bombings in Chicago, California, and Long Island, and New York City had not resulted in deaths. That changed in August 1970, when a Weathermen bomb exploded in Sterling Hall at the University of Wisconsin's Madison campus. Known as Army Math, the building was the home of the Army Mathematics Research Center. The purpose of the bombers was to strike a blow at the "government war machine." The bomb caused $6 million in damage, injured three people, and killed Robert Fussnach, a 33-year-old graduate student. His death shocked and angered many radicals.

The bombing was carried out by Madison residents Karl and Dwight Armstrong and University of Wisconsin students David Fine and Leo Burt. The Federal Bureau of Investigation immediately launched an extensive manhunt and between 1972 and 1976 all the bombers except Burt were caught. In 1973 Karl Armstrong was sentenced to 23 years in prison (later reduced to 10 years); Dwight Armstrong and Fine received 7-year sentences. Burt remains at large. Although

terrorist bombings continued for the next several years, the number of Weathermen attacks dropped dramatically after the University of Wisconsin bombing.

—Laura Matysek Wood

References: Dougan, Clark, Samuel Lipsman, and the editors of Boston Publishing Company. *A Nation Divided* (1984); Jacobs, Harold, ed. *Weathermen* (1970); Kutler, Stanley I., ed. *Encyclopedia of the Vietnam War* (1996); Unger, Irwin. *The Movement: A History of the American New Left, 1959–1972* (1974).

See also: Antiwar Movement, United States; Federal Bureau of Investigation (FBI); Weathermen.

U.S. Agency for International Development (USAID)

Agency responsible for administration of the U.S. economic aid program to the Republic of Vietnam (RVN); also known as the Agency for International Development (AID). USAID administered the economic assistance program through the United States Operation Mission (USOM), its field agency in the RVN. USAID provided American economic support to the government of Ngô Đình Diêm and the economic foundation for the survival of the new South Vietnamese government.

Between 1955 and 1960, U.S. economic aid averaged from $220 to $270 million a year, more than 20 percent of the RVN's gross national product. During this period, USAID provided economic assistance through various programs that addressed education, agriculture, public health, public safety projects (including support for the development of a national police force and local security forces), local government, public works, industrial development, land reform, and refugee resettlement. USAID assistance also provided support to cope with resettlement of perhaps one million refugees who fled the North for the South following the 1954 partitioning of Vietnam. In the process, USAID promoted a land reform campaign to gain the refugees' loyalty to the Diêm government. USAID assistance also provided support for the construction of houses, mechanical equipment to farm the land, and daily subsistence needs.

The largest resettlement project involved land reclamation at Cái San in Kiên Giang Province along the Gulf of Thailand extending into An Giang Province. Refugees cleared and drained nearly 200,000 acres of swampland and dug irrigation canals for rice cultivation in what became the showpiece for Diêm's refugee resettlement program. But instead of outright ownership of the land they had reclaimed, the refugees were asked to sign tenancy contracts for lands to be purchased in installments from the government, leading to peasant resentment rather than allegiance to the government. Mismanagement of Cái San showed that projects supported by USAID economic assistance and implemented by the South Vietnamese government were often inconsistent with U.S. political objectives.

USAID monies also provided assistance for the USOM program to resettle refugees in Land Development Centers (LDCs) on supposedly abandoned lands in the Mekong Delta and in undeveloped lands in the Central Highlands, again with the purpose of gaining peasant allegiance to the government. The highlander resettlement program, begun in 1955, resettled Montagnards into defensible areas and made Montagnard lands available to Vietnamese refugees. This in turn alienated many Montagnards and promoted the development of the ethnonationalist Montagnard movement.

Initially, USAID worked primarily through Vietnamese government channels in Sài Gòn to advance economic and political objectives. USAID personnel made inspection trips to rural areas outside Sài Gòn but relied primarily on Vietnamese government officials to implement the projects. Because USAID officials worked and lived primarily in Sài Gòn, they often failed to properly supervise USAID projects in the field. Thus American monies and assistance were often wasted or used for purposes other than those intended, and the economic and political objectives that directed those projects were often subverted by Vietnamese officials and government bureaucracy.

By the early 1960s, USAID had formed the internal Office of Rural Affairs. It began to expand its efforts by sending civilian advisors into rural provinces to take a more active and independent role in economic assistance programs. USAID also continued to fund engineering, industrial, agricultural, public health, and education projects. The intent was to improve the standard of living for the civilian population and thereby attract their support for the Sài Gòn government.

One notable program funded by USAID was the International Volunteer Service (IVS), which served as a model for the Peace Corp. Founded as a private, nonprofit organization in 1953, IVS came to the RVN in 1957. In Vietnam it was funded primarily by USAID, but monies also came from the RVN government during the early years and from private agencies as well. In contrast to most USAID officials, IVS workers received instruction in Vietnamese language and culture. Their two-year tours in Vietnam included assignments at the village level ranging from developing agriculture to teaching English. IVS saw its function as humanitarian and divorced from USAID political objectives. Don Luce, IVS director from 1961 to 1967, resigned to protest U.S. political and military policies that affected his organization's work at the village level. IVS resisted USAID pressure to become more politically involved, and the Sài Gòn government stopped approving its projects in 1971.

By mid-1965, USAID economic support for pacification programs had reached approximately $500 million annually. At the same time, however, long-term development programs often took a back seat to more immediate security concerns and pacification efforts. After 1967, USAID economic assistance was channeled through Civilian Operations and Revolutionary Development Support (CORDS), established under the Military Assistance Command, Vietnam (MACV) to organize all civilian aid programs involved in the pacification effort under the military chain of command.

—David M. Berman

References: Hunt, Richard A. *Pacification: The American Struggle for Vietnam's Hearts and Minds* (1995); Luce, Don, and John Sommer. *Viet Nam: The Unheard Voices* (1969); Sheehan, Neil. *A Bright Shining Lie: John Paul Vann and America in Vietnam* (1988);

Wiesner, Louis A. *Victims and Survivors: Displaced Persons and Other War Victims in Viet-Nam, 1954–1975* (1988).

See also: Civic Action; Civilian Operations and Revolutionary Development Support (CORDS); Land Reform; Marine Combined Action Platoons (CAPs); Michigan State University (MSU) Advisory Group; Military Assistance Command, Vietnam (MACV); Montagnards; Pacification; Strategic Hamlet Program.

U.S. Army, Vietnam, Installation Stockade (USARVIS)

U.S. military correctional facility in Vietnam. Rarely called it by its official name, the U.S. Army, Vietnam, Installation Stockade (USARVIS) was located in a headquarters and logistical complex on the outskirts of Long Bình. Most soldiers knew it as Long Bình Jail, or LBJ. The United States originally established a military prison at a former tennis court at Pershing Field near Sài Gòn. Its move to Long Bình in summer 1966 was necessitated by the huge U.S. troop buildup and the consequent need to house an increasing number of military offenders.

Newly arrived GIs were processed at Long Bình, where they saw firsthand what would happen if they broke the rules. Few officers or senior noncommissioned officers were confined within its perimeter of cyclone fence and concertina wire. Exceptions included Lt. William Calley and Col. Robert Rheault, commander of the U.S. Fifth Special Forces Group, who with six of his officers was charged with premeditated murder of a suspected double agent. LBJ housed those who went absent without official leave (AWOL), those who refused orders, and those convicted of drug abuse, combat refusal, and "fragging." Men convicted of war crimes passed through its gates, as did rapists, thieves, black marketeers, and murderers.

Periods of incarceration at LBJ were "lost time" and did not count toward the fulfillment of one's 365-day tour. Even hardened noncommissioned officers spoke of LBJ in the early days in hushed tones. The simple threat of being sent there was sufficient to keep many GIs obedient to orders.

Initially, the Military Police Corps assigned guards and other personnel to LBJ who had little or no professional training as confinement facility specialists. Size, weight, and toughness were primary qualifications. Guards demanded unthinking obedience at all times and imposed rigid and exacting disciplinary standards. Infractions brought confinement in "the box," a metal container that stood in the open absorbing the blazing rays of the sun. Other punishments included surreptitious beatings and guard-administered midnight baths during which some inmates nearly drowned.

For the first two years of LBJ's existence, official treatment of prisoners regularly exceeded normally allowable limits. Then, on 29 August 1968, rampaging prisoners seized the stockade compound, set fire to the buildings, tore down what would not burn, and beat any guard within reach. Lt. Col. Vern Johnson, commander of LBJ, never recovered from the beating he received and was invalided out of the service. Thereafter, LBJ was reconstructed into a gleaming, modern correctional institute. Guards received appropriate training and became "correctional facility specialists." Social services were upgraded, and punishments became less arbitrary and more rational. LBJ became famous for the quality of its food, attracting officers for meals from units all over Long Bình.

As the U.S. Army's pullout began, LBJ's population dwindled. In 1972 the Army closed the facility, transferring the few remaining prisoners and guards to the original stockade area at Pershing Field. USARVIS' existence terminated on 29 March 1973, as the last combat troops departed from Vietnam.

—Cecil B. Currey

References: Author interviews with more personnel associated with the USARVIS (n.d.).

See also: Atrocities during the Vietnam War; Calley, William Laws, Jr.; Desertion, Allied and Communist; Long Bình.

UTAH, Operation (4–7 March 1966)

Code name (LI N K T 26) for a combined U.S. Marine Corps and Army of the Republic of Vietnam (ARVN) assault northwest of Quang Ngãi City in I Corps against People's Army of Vietnam (PAVN) and Việt Công (VC) main force units. Planning began on 3 March 1966, when Brig. Gen. Jonas Platt, commanding Task Force Delta, learned that the 36th (also called the 21st) PAVN Regiment had taken up a position northwest of the city. He sent Col. Oscar Peatross, who commanded the 7th Marines, to meet with Brig. Gen. Hoàng Xuân Lãm, commanding general of the 2d ARVN Division at Quang Ngãi City. They agreed on a combined operation using one ARVN and one Marine battalion.

On the morning of 4 March, Marine Air Group (MAG) 36, commanded by Col. William Johnson, airlifted the 1st Airborne Battalion of the 2d ARVN Division, followed by Companies F, G, and H of the 2d Battalion, 7th Regiment, U.S. Marines, commanded by Col. Leon Utter, from Chu Lai to southwest of Châu Nhai. Despite heavy PAVN resistance at the landing zones, the landing was completed.

Paddies, hamlets, Hills 97 and 85 to the southwest, and Hill 50 to the northeast stood out as major features. Hill 50 presented the strongest opposition, and extensive fighting occurred at Châu Nhai, southwest of that hill. Artillery saturation of PAVN strongholds produced the largest fire mission to date in the Chu Lai area, 1,900 rounds in two hours. To encircle the PAVN forces, Generals Platt and Lam expanded the operation with additional U.S. Marine units. By midday on 5 March, Company L, 3/1st, with support from the 1st ARVN Airborne Battalion, took Hill 50 after three and one-half hours of combat. Most of the action had ended by early morning of 6 March. Near An Tuyêt, however, Company B, 1/7th (commanded by Capt. Robert Prewitt) came under attack. A dangerous helicopter mission resupplied them with ammunition, and Company B successfully repelled an attack by two PAVN companies. Ordered to relieve the beleaguered command, Company B, 2/4th discovered that the main PAVN force had withdrawn.

Fighting in the northern area of Operation UTAH was unexpectedly light. On 6 March, the 2/7th, 3/1st, and 1/7th Marine battalions discovered abandoned defensive complexes, including caves and tunnels with weapons, supplies, and documents. On 7 March, the operation came to an end when the Marines destroyed PAVN fortifications on Hill 50.

In this short, hard fight, the Marines sustained casualties of 98 dead and 278 wounded; ARVN forces lost 30 killed and 120 wounded. Edward Simmons lists PAVN killed at 586 (Marines claimed 358; ARVN, 228), while Shelby Stanton states there were 632 known enemy casualties.

—Paul S. Daum, with Trevor Curran

References: Shulimson, Jack. *U.S. Marines in Vietnam, 1966: An Expanding War* (1982); Simmons, Edward H. "Marine Corps Operations in Vietnam, 1965–1966" (1985); Stanton, Shelby L. *The Rise and Fall of an American Army: U.S. Ground Forces in Vietnam, 1965–1973* (1985).

See also: United States: Marine Corps; Vietnam, Democratic Republic of: Army (People's Army of Vietnam [PAVN]); Vietnam, Republic of: Army (ARVN).

V

Valluy, Jean-Etienne (1899–1970)

French Army general; commander in chief in Indo-China, late 1946–February 1948. In November 1945, Valluy left for Indo-China as part of Gen. Jacques-Philippe Leclerc's expeditionary corps. He soon found himself at the cutting edge of French efforts first to conciliate the Viêt Minh and then to confront them with a show of force. On Valluy's orders, Col. Pierre-Louis Dèbes gave the ultimatum to the Viêt Minh to evacuate Hai Phòng and then bombarded the town.

On succeeding Leclerc as commander in chief, Valluy demonstrated a high degree of military ability with the forces placed at his disposal. By the end of 1947, the French military position in Tonkin was as favorable as it would ever be during the First Indo-China War. Despite a good grasp of the political nature of the war, Valluy was opposed to Emile Bollaert's offer of negotiations with the Viêt Minh, which he considered premature. Following his return to France in February 1948, Valluy was called upon to participate in several high-level missions to Indo-China.

—Arthur J. Dommen

Reference: Gras, Général Yves. *Histoire de la Guerre d'Indochine* (1992).

See also: Dèbes, Pierre-Louis; Bollaert, Emile; France: Army; Leclerc, Jacques-Philippe; Viêt Minh.

Van Cao (1923–1995)

Vietnamese musician; composer of the national anthem of the Democratic Republic of Vietnam and Socialist Republic of Vietnam. His "Tiên Quân Ca" ("Marching Forward") became the song of the Viêt Minh and was later chosen by Hô Chí Minh as the national anthem. The song's lyrics read in part, "The path to glory passes over the bodies of our foes." In the 1960s Van Cao fell into disgrace after he joined Nhân Van Giai Phâm, an opposition group that included many famous writers and poets and allowed limited freedom of expression. Van Cao stopped composing until late 1975, when he produced his last musical work, "Mùa Xuaân Đâu Tiên" ("The First Spring"). Supposedly praising the Communist April 1975 victory, it was more of a lamentation and was not welcomed by authorities.

In the early 1980s, the Vietnamese Communist Party held a competition for a new national anthem, solely because the party leadership disliked Van Cao. The idea of a new national anthem was dropped after other composers convinced party leaders that none of the entries was comparable to Van Cao's anthem. Van Cao's talents were again recognized during Đôi Moi in the 1990s. At age 70 he was awarded the coveted Medal of Independence.

—Spencer C. Tucker

See also: Hô Chí Minh; Viêt Minh; Vietnam, Democratic Republic of: 1945–1954; Vietnam, Democratic Republic of: 1954–1975; Vietnam, Socialist Republic of: 1975 to the Present.

Van Tiên Dung (1917–)

People's Army of Vietnam (PAVN) general; Army commander in chief, 1974–1980; defense minister, Socialist Republic of Vietnam (SRV), 1980–1986. Throughout the 1960s, Dung remained second in command of the PAVN to Gen. Giáp, who used Dung as an example of true Communist ideals at work: a peasant who had worked hard and risen through the ranks. Dung completely embraced the party line and ideals.

In March 1973, Dung oversaw the infiltration of PAVN troops into the Republic of Vietnam (RVN), which he described as "strong ropes inching gradually, day by day, around the neck, arms, and legs of a demon, awaiting the order to jerk tight and bring the creature's life to an end." He continued the military buildup and conducted small-scale attacks before finally unleashing his force on 1 March 1975 in the Central Highlands. By late March, thousands of refugees were fleeing from Huê into Đà Nang, which fell to Dung's forces on 30 March. Dung then shifted his offensive south to take Sài Gòn before the May rains. The last major military engagement, at Xuân Lôc, 35 miles northeast of Sài Gòn, lasted two weeks. The PAVN rolled into the RVN capital on 29 April.

Dung later led the 1979 invasion of Cambodia and also directed the 1979 Sino-Vietnamese clash. He replaced Giáp as minister of national defense in February 1980 but was dismissed from that position and expelled from the Politburo in 1986. Thereafter he faded into obscurity.

—Charlotte A. Power

References: Karnow, Stanley. *Vietnam: A History* (1983); Post, Ken. *Socialism in Half a Country*. Vol. III, *Revolution, Socialism, and Nationalism in Vietnam* (1989).

See also: Hô Chí Minh Campaign; Lao Đông Party; Sino-Vietnamese War; Vietnam, Democratic Republic of: Army (People's Army of Vietnam [PAVN]); Vietnamese Invasion and Occupation of Cambodia; Vô Nguyên Giáp.

Vance, Cyrus Roberts (1917–)

Department of Defense official; secretary of the Army, 1962–1963; deputy secretary of defense, 1964–1967; negotiator at the 1968 Paris peace talks. As general counsel to the secretary of defense in the Kennedy administration, Vance supervised a reorganization of the Department of Defense that strengthened the authority of the secretary and improved strategic planning and logistics.

In 1962 Vance was appointed secretary of the Army. Supporting new uses of aviation to improve the Army's mobility, Vance helped create the 11th Air Assault Division (Test) that proved the air assault concept. Renamed the 1st Cavalry Division (Airmobile), this unit went to Vietnam in 1965. Vance also organized the Army Concept Team in Vietnam (ACTIV) to experiment with ways to improve counterinsurgency warfare capabilities.

Appointed deputy secretary of defense in 1964, Vance concurred with the decision to bomb North Vietnam after the Gulf of Tonkin incidents and with Operation ROLLING

THUNDER in 1965. After August 1964 he was responsible for approving covert raids against the Democratic Republic of Vietnam (DRV). By 1966, however, Vance came to doubt the effectiveness of the expanded air war, and in 1967 he became disenchanted with the whole war. A back ailment prompted his resignation in 1967. President Johnson recalled Vance in March 1968 as an informal advisor. As one of Johnson's "Wise Men," Vance recommended that the president halt the bombing of the DRV and seek a negotiated settlement to the war.

Vance's most trying assignment was serving with Averell Harriman as deputy negotiator at the Paris Peace Conference in 1968. Harriman and Vance were unable to get substantive talks started while bombing continued. Finally, in November 1968, Johnson declared a bombing halt after the DRV tacitly agreed not to use it to advantage or to block South Vietnamese participation in the conference. The Republic of Vietnam (RVN) then balked at having representatives of the National Liberation Front (NLF) present, and the United States had to pressure South Vietnam not to disrupt the conference. When Vance resigned in early 1969, the conference was on the verge of substantive discussions.

—John L. Bell

References: Johnson, Lyndon B. *The Vantage Point: Perspectives of the President, 1963–1969* (1971); McLellan, David S. *Cyrus Vance* (1985).

See also: ACTIV (Army Concept Team in Vietnam); Carter, Jimmy; Harriman, W. Averell; Johnson, Lyndon Baines; Paris Negotiations; Paris Peace Accords; ROLLING THUNDER, Operation; Tonkin Gulf Incidents; "Wise Men."

Vang Pao (1931–)

Best known military leader of the anti-Communist Hmong. Vang Pao rose through the ranks to general and confounded some of Hà Nôi's best strategists in the war in Laos. When the Vietnam War escalated in January 1961, Vang Pao was a lieutenant colonel. As the senior officer in the region, he made appeals to U.S. and Thai officers for weapons to arm 7,000 of his Hmong followers. An arrangement was worked out to the mutual satisfaction of the two sides. Thereafter, Vang Pao led his well-armed Hmong irregulars, sometimes called the *Armée Clandestine* (Secret Army), in fighting the Pathet Lao and North Vietnamese.

Vang Pao respected the North Vietnamese as soldiers but felt that they lacked his troops' ability to improvise. Observing that North Vietnamese commanders always followed the same routine when they were planning an attack, he found he could throw off their plans by moving his mobile units around immediately beforehand, sometimes inducing his adversaries to call off the attack.

Vang Pao rose to the command of Military Region II and was a major general when the 1973 cease-fire intervened. After the Communist takeover in 1975, he was evacuated to Thailand and eventually settled in the United States, where he became a citizen and remained active in the affairs of the Hmong exile community.

—Arthur J. Dommen

References: Hamilton-Merritt, Jane. *Tragic Mountains: The Hmong, the Americans, and the Secret Wars for Laos, 1942–1992* (1993); Quincy, Keith. *Hmong: History of a People* (1988).

See also: Hmong; Laos; Long Chieng; Pathet Lao; Plain of Jars.

Vann, John Paul (1924–1972)

U.S. Army officer; U.S. Agency for International Development (AID) official; critic of military strategy. During his first tour of duty in Vietnam (March 1962–April 1963), Vann advised a South Vietnamese infantry division in the Mekong Delta. What Vann saw in Vietnam—particularly at the Battle of Âp Bac—made him feel that the war was being lost, despite what the president was being told by his military advisors. He believed that the war could be won if the right tactics and military might were applied. When his reports were ignored, he leaked information to journalists covering the fighting in Vietnam. Reassigned to the Pentagon, where his words still fell on deaf ears, Vann retired on 31 July 1963 and began to speak out publicly on the war.

Vann returned to Vietnam in March 1965 as pacification representative of the Agency for International Development (AID). He was so successful that in 1966 he was made chief of the civilian pacification program for the provinces surrounding Sài Gòn. In 1967 he denounced Gen. Westmoreland's strategy and warned that the Communists were still a threat. The Têt Offensive of 1968 seemed to support his view. Because Vann's critique was aimed at improving the war effort, he was promoted in May 1971 to senior advisor for the Central Highlands and given command over U.S. military forces and the civilians in the pacification program. Although a civilian, he also indirectly commanded the South Vietnamese troops in the area, holding a position equivalent to that of a U.S. Army major general. In effect, he was the third most powerful American in Vietnam. Vann was killed in a helicopter crash in the Central Highlands on 9 July 1972.

Vann seemed to embody the American dilemma in Vietnam. Dedicated to winning the war, he nonetheless openly criticized U.S. strategy. There was much he felt to be wrong about the war in Vietnam, but not about the war itself, and he could not accept an American defeat.

—Laura Matysek Wood

Reference: Sheehan, Neil. *A Bright Shining Lie. John Paul Vann and America in Vietnam* (1988).

See also: Âp Bac, Battle of; Order of Battle; Pacification; Sheehan, Cornelius Mahoney (Neil); U.S. Agency for International Development (USAID).

Vessey, John W. (1922–)

Chairman, U.S. Joint Chiefs of Staff; field artillery battalion commander in Vietnam. In Vietnam Vessey commanded the 25th Infantry Division's 2d Battalion, 77th Field Artillery. On 21 March 1967, during Operation JUNCTION CITY, all three of Vessey's batteries occupied Fire Support Base GOLD when it came under attack from elements of five battalions under the control of the 272d Việt Công Regiment. Vessey's gunners fired more than 1,000 rounds of direct fire in defense of the base, including 30 "beehive" rounds, in the first large-scale combat use of fléchette-firing antipersonnel rounds. Vessey received the Distinguished Service Cross for the action. In August 1974, he assumed command of the 4th Infantry Division.

From 1982 to 1985, Vessey was chairman of the Joint Chiefs of Staff. Following retirement at the rank of full general, Vessey played a prominent role in normalizing relations between the Socialist Republic of Vietnam and the United States when he served as the Bush administration's negotiator with Hà Nôi on prisoner of war and missing in action issues.

—David T. Zabecki

Reference: Webb, Willard J., and Ronald Cole. *The Chairmen of the Joint Chiefs of Staff* (1989).

See also: Artillery, Allied and People's Army of Vietnam; Artillery Fire Doctrine; Bush, George Herbert Walker; JUNCTION CITY, Operation; Missing in Action, Allied; Vietnam, Socialist Republic of: 1975 to the Present.

Vientiane Agreement (21 February 1973)

Cease-fire agreement to end the war in Laos, signed at Vientiane, Laos, on 21 February 1973 by Pheng Phongsavan, representing the Royal Lao government, and Phoumi Vongvichit, representing the Lao Patriotic Forces (Pathet Lao). The agreement, resulting from negotiations that began on 17 October 1972, consisted of 14 articles in five chapters.

The principal provisions included implementation of a cease-fire throughout Laos beginning at noon on 22 February (Article 2); withdrawal of all foreign military personnel and regular and irregular forces from Laos, the dissolution of all foreign military and paramilitary organizations in Laos, the disbanding of all special forces and the dismantling of their bases within 60 days from the establishment of the Provisional Government of National Union (PGNU) and the National Political Consultative Council (NPCC) (Article 4); Reciprocal repatriation of all persons, regardless of nationality, who were captured or detained during the war, within 60 days from the establishment of the NPCC, and responsibility to provide information about those reported missing during the war upon completion of repatriation of captured personnel (Article 5); holding of free and democratic general elections for a national assembly and a permanent coalition government under procedures to be agreed upon by the two sides (Article 6); neutralization of Vientiane and Luang Prabang (Article 9); temporary maintenance of the zones controlled by each side pending establishment of the national assembly and the permanent coalition government (Article 10A); and promotion of normal relations between the zones of temporary control (Article 10B); holding of discussions with the United States regarding the latter's contributing to postwar reconstruction (Article 10C); formation of a joint commission to oversee implementation of the agreement (Article 11); continuation of the work of the International Commission for Supervision and Control (Article 12); and continuation of negotiations between the two sides on protocol to implement the agreement (Article 13).

The protocol mentioned in Article 13 was signed on 14 September 1973. The PGNU and NPCC were finally established on 5 April 1974. Prince Souvanna Phouma was prime minister of the PGNU, and Prince Souphanouvong was chairman of the NPCC.

—Arthur J. Dommen

Reference: Dommen, Arthur J. *Laos: Keystone of Indochina* (1985).

See also: International Commission for Supervision and Control (ICSC); Laos; Missing in Action, Allied; Pathet Lao; Prisoners of War, Allied; Souphanouvong; Souvanna Phouma; Vientiane Protocol.

Vientiane Protocol (14 September 1973)

Protocol giving effect to the Vientiane Agreement of 21 February 1973. The 14 September 1973 Vientiane Protocol, resulting from negotiations between the Royal Lao Government and the Lao Patriotic Forces (Pathet Lao), consisted of 21 articles.

Article 1 provided for establishment of the Provisional Government of National Union (PGNU), to be headed by a prime minister and two deputy prime ministers and consisting of 25 ministers and secretaries of state (deputy ministers). Article 2 allocated the ministerial portfolios in the PGNU. Article 3 committed the PGNU to follow policies of peace, national unity, neutrality, independence, democracy, and prosperity in accordance with the recommendations of the future National Political Consultative Council (NPCC). Article 4 enshrined the principle of unanimity of decision in all important matters, while maintaining the responsibility of each side for its own ministries. Article 5 stipulated the structure of the NPCC to consist of 42 members and various commissions. Article 6 provided for decisions in the NPCC by consensus. Article 9 gave the NPCC a major role in organizing general elections. Article 10 provided for mixed police forces in Vientiane and Luang Prabang to maintain security. Article 12 provided for demarcating the cease-fire lines in places where tension existed between the forces of the two sides. Articles 14–16 dealt with the joint commission's control of troop movements and withdrawal of foreign troops and war materials. Article 17 stipulated the disbanding of the special forces. Article 18 provided for notifying the joint commission of the numbers and nationalities of captured foreign personnel and the names of those reported missing.

The joint commission held meetings to work out procedures for release of prisoners and exchange of information on the missing. But because implementation of such actions had been tied under the Vientiane Agreement into the timetable for formation of the PGNU and NPCC, which was seriously delayed, there was little or no compliance with these provisions before political and military tensions rose once again over such issues as violations of the cease-fire and the king's role in opening the National Assembly that had been carried over from the previous Royal Lao Government.

—Arthur J. Dommen

References: Dommen, Arthur J. *Laos: Keystone of Indochina* (1985).

See also: Laos; Pathet Lao; Vientiane Agreement.

Viêt Minh (Viêt Nam Độc Lập Đông Minh Hôi [Vietnam Independence League])

Communist front organization created to help the Indo-Chinese Communist Party achieve its overall objectives. The

Viêt Nam Đôc Lâp Đông Minh Hôi, commonly known as the Viêt Minh (Vietnam Independence League), was founded at the Eighth Plenum of the Indo-Chinese Communist Party in May 1941. The Viêt Minh served as the organizational nexus for the development of a broad, national program to organize the masses in resistance to French colonial rule and Japanese occupation. Its purpose was tactical, never strategic, and its flexibility allowed the party to alter its course quickly for current conditions. Perhaps most importantly, it downplayed class revolution in favor of national liberation and attempted to involve all elements of society in the national struggle. The Viêt Minh made temporary alliances with its "enemies" to achieve its more immediate objectives.

The Viêt Minh–led August Revolution (1945) is a defining moment of the modern Vietnamese revolution. Shortly after the Japanese invasion of 1940, the Viêt Minh planned for that inevitable moment when the Japanese would turn their guns on the French colonialists. It came on 9 March 1945, when Japanese soldiers carried out a relatively bloodless coup against French colonial forces. After the Japanese surrender five months later left a political void in Indo-China, the Viêt Minh, prepared by their revolutionary training to exploit this situation to its fullest, marched into Hà Nôi to proclaim Vietnamese independence. The Viêt Minh army, headed by Vô Nguyên Giáp, seized power during the August Revolution.

On 2 September 1945 Hô Chí Minh, founder of the Viêt Minh, read aloud in Ba Đình Square an official declaration of an end to French colonialism, Japanese occupation, and the Nguyên Dynasty. Shortly after Hô's declaration of independence, the Indo-Chinese Communist Party announced that it was dissolving, leaving the Viêt Minh front as the only official party apparatus. In 1951 the party resurfaced officially with the formation of the Vietnam Workers Party (Đang Lao Đông Viêt Nam), at which time the Viêt Minh was itself dissolved. According to revolutionary theory, the broad-based front was to be revised whenever historical circumstances changed drastically. The Communists therefore reconstituted the Viêt Minh as the Liên Viêt front during the Indo-China War, and shortly after the Geneva Accords, the Fatherland Front was born.

The actual date of the reconstitution of the Viêt Minh front as the Liên Viêt front (Liên Hiêp Quôc Dân Viêt Nam) is in question. Some scholars have suggested that the Viêt Minh lasted only until the war with France began in 1941. Hoàng Van Đào, in Viêt Nam Quôc Dân Đang, gives April 1946 as the date for the reconstitution of the Liên Viêt front. Others suggest, however, that the Viêt Minh battled the French from 1946 to 1954. In any case, the Viêt Minh has popularly been associated with the army that handed the French their humiliating defeat at the Battle of Điên Biên Phu and that served the Democratic Republic of Vietnam (DRV) so faithfully since its 1945 inception.

—Robert K. Brigham

References: Duiker, William J. The Rise of Nationalism in Vietnam, 1900–1941 (1976); History of the August Revolution (1972); Hoàng Van Đào. Viêt Nam Quôc Dân Đang (1970); Huynh Kim Khanh.

"The Vietnamese August Revolution Reinterpreted" (1971); Marr, David G. Vietnamese Tradition on Trial, 1920–1945 (1981); Woodside, Alexander B. Community and Revolution in Modern Vietnam (1976).
See also: August Revolution; Điên Biên Phu, Battle of; French Indo-China; Geneva Conference and Geneva Accords; Hô Chí Minh; Indo-China War; Japan; Lao Đông Party; Nguyên Dynasty; United Front; Vô Nguyên Giáp; Vietnamese Communist Party (VCP).

Viêt Nam Quôc Dân Đang (Vietnam National Party)

Vietnamese nationalist political party before World War II. The Viêt Nam Quôc Dân Đang, or Vietnam National Party (in Chinese, Viet Nam Guomindang), was established on 27 December 1927 in Hà Nôi by a group of young men led by Nguyên Thái Hoc. This moderate Socialist party, known to most adults in Vietnam as the Viêt Quôc and usually referred to as the VNQDD, was the first revolutionary party in Vietnam, preceding by three years the establishment of the Indo-Chinese Communist Party (ICP).

Although the VNQDD bears the same name as the Nationalist Chinese Party, it was not created by the Chinese. Sun Yat-sen's program may have inspired VNQDD founders to adapt the party name, but it had no direct relation to, nor did it receive any support from, the Chinese Guomindang until after the 1930 Yên Bái uprising. Some assert that, had it received even modest military support from the Chinese Nationalists, Vietnamese history might have developed quite differently.

The VNQDD was organized along clandestine lines and held together with strict discipline. The party's strength grew quickly. Most adherents were teachers, colonial government employees, and army noncommissioned officers (NCOs). Beginning in 1928, the VNQDD attracted considerable Vietnamese support but also the attention of French colonial authorities after a VNQDD death squad killed several French and Vietnamese officials notorious for their cruelty toward the Vietnamese population. With French authorities about to carry out a large-scale crackdown against the VNQDD, its leadership felt it had no choice but to carry out uprisings where possible. After this decision, Nguyên Thái Hoc remarked, "If we fail to succeed we will still build a good cause."

At midnight 10–11 February 1930, VNQDD company-sized forces launched surprise attacks against French colonial army bases northeast of Hà Nôi at Yên Bái, Hung Hoa, Lâm Thao, and Son Tây, as well as grenade attacks in the heart of the capital. On 12 February, VNQDD forces attacked French military camps at Đáp Câu, Pha Lai, east of Hà Nôi. The next day they conducted other attacks at Kiên An and Vinh Bao. The greatest VNQDD success came at Yên Bái, where the rebels killed a dozen French officers and noncommissioned officers and controlled the town for a day before being expelled by French counterattacks. Despite fierce resistance, the French soon reoccupied all of their positions.

The VNQDD relied mostly on homemade cement and black powder grenades, captured rifles, and a few pistols. Although they fought bravely, without effective weapons and communications the VNQDD squads were doomed to defeat. French reprisal raids crushed the VNQDD, and hundreds of its members were executed. Nguyên Thái Hoc and 12 others were guillotined in Yên Bái on 17 June 1930. Their dauntless behavior and the calmness and dignity with which they faced the guillotine made them nationalist heroes in Vietnam. The following months saw several thousand VNQDD members sentenced to prison. Those who escaped arrest fled mainly to China, where they reorganized the party. Along with the VNQDD, many other movements, including the Communists, got limited support from the Chinese government.

In August 1945, the Viêt Minh seized power and set up a provisional government. This violated an agreement between member parties of the Viêt Nam Cách Mang Đông Minh Hôi, which included Hô Chí Minh's Viêt Minh (Viêt Nam Đôc Lâp Đông Minh Hôi), and the VNQDD. After August 1945, hundreds of VNQDD members in exile returned to Vietnam, but many of them were killed by the Viêt Minh when they crossed the border from China. When the main non-Communist parties moved from China back to Vietnam and their local cells revived, the nationalists joined the opposition to the Viêt Minh. Armed clashes between the Viêt Minh and the nationalists occurred regularly in major cities of North Vietnam. After the 6 March 1946 Hô-Sainteny Agreement that allowed French army units to deploy in key cities, the nationalists found themselves under attack from the French as well as the Viêt Minh. At the end of 1946 when the Indo-China War erupted, several thousand VNQDD and other opposition party members were massacred by the Viêt Minh in a bloody purge. The survivors fled to China or to French-controlled areas.

After the 1954 Geneva Accords, many VNQDD members from North Vietnam, including those from Viêt Minh–controlled areas, gathered in South Vietnam. Deeply divided after years of Communist oppression and lack of strong leadership, virtually all of the factions found themselves in opposition to the government of the Republic of Vietnam (RVN). Those VNQDD members who survived the Vietnam War years were again persecuted by the Communist regime after 30 April 1975. Although many former VNQDD members found refuge in the West and have continued to campaign for democracy and human rights in Vietnam, they remain divided politically. The VNQDD still enjoys respect in overseas Vietnamese political communities. Many Vietnamese regard it as the foremost anti-Communist spiritual force.

—Nguyên Công Luân (Lu Tuân)

References: Hoàng Van Đào. *Viêt Nam Quôc Dân Đang* (1970); Karnow, Stanley. *Vietnam: A History* (1988).

See also: French Indo-China; Hô-Sainteny Agreement; Viêt Minh.

Viêt Nam Thanh Niên Cách Mang Đông Chí Hôi (Vietnam Revolutionary Youth Association)

Vietnamese anticolonial organization that represented the beginnings of Vietnamese communism. Known commonly as Thanh Niên (Youth), the Viêt Nam Thanh Niên Cách Mang Đông Chí Hôi was founded by Hô Chí Minh in 1925 as an anticolonial organization that attempted to unite political

and social issues. The Thanh Niên advocated a new Vietnamese society dependent upon national liberation and land reform. To accomplish these goals, the Thanh Niên relied on new revolutionary theory and the blending of Marxist-Leninist teachings with Vietnamese patriotism. The specific revolutionary strategy of the Thanh Niên consisted of three phases: organization, agitation, and insurrection. This reliance on the theoretical perspective distanced the Thanh Niên from other anticolonial organizations and ensured its success during the brutal French purges.

The Thanh Niên's most significant contributions to the resistance movement were its use of the term *cách mang* (revolution) and its acknowledgment of a more stratified anticolonial society. For the Communist leaders, *cách mang* meant the basic transformation of the political structure and the process of rule, not merely the removal of the right to rule. Thus, the revolutionary process was an ongoing dialectic between the people and the party. For years, the party considered all Vietnamese to be anticolonials; only with the development of revolutionary thought within the Thanh Niên did the term "intermediary 'elements" begin to be applied to friends of the most oppressed classes. This thinking helped the Thanh Niên develop the front concept, in which the party could make temporary alliances with non-Communists to achieve the revolution's overall goals.

From 1925 to 1927, the Thanh Niên headquarters in Canton trained more than 300 Vietnamese revolutionaries and published periodicals on various political subjects. Among the most important of these were *Đuong Cách Mang (The Road to Revolution)* and the weekly newspaper *Thanh Niên (Youth)*. By 1927, however, the Thanh Niên had been caught up in revolutionary activities in China and fell victim to Guomindang Communist sweeps. The Thanh Niên activities halted abruptly in 1927, but Vietnamese revolutionaries continued their activities in Vietnam until mid-1929.

The Thanh Niên movement was an important first step in Vietnam's modern revolution. After the Thanh Niên, Vietnam's anticolonialists, led by Hô Chí Minh, embraced a revolutionary movement with a clear ideological base.

—Robert K. Brigham

References: Duiker, William J. *The Communist Road to Power in Vietnam, 1900–1941* (1981); Huynh Kim Khanh. *Vietnamese Communism, 1925–1945* (1982); Marr, David G. *Vietnamese Tradition on Trial, 1925–1945* (1981); Woodside, Alexander B. *Community and Revolution in Modern Vietnam* (1976).

See also: Hô Chí Minh; Jiang Jieshi (Chiang Kai-shek); Lao Đông Party; Trân Van Giàu; Viêt Minh; Vietnamese Communist Party (VCP); Vô Nguyên Giáp.

Vietnam: Prehistory to 938

Legends and Prehistory Vietnamese consider the founder of their nation—then called Van Lang—to be Hùng Vuong, or King Hùng, of the Hông Bàng Dynasty (2879–258 B.C.). The capital was at Phong Châu, in present Vinh Phú Province, and according to legend, this kingdom occupied a great part of southern China, north Vietnam, and part of central Vietnam—approximately, those areas occupied by the Bách

Viêt (One Hundred Yuehs), non-Chinese people living in South China south of the Yangtze River. Hùng Vuong and his 18 successors divided their kingdom into 15 *bô* (districts) and administered them through the *lac hâu* (civil chieftains), *lac tuong* (military chieftains), and the *bô chính* (subaltern officials). The throne was hereditary and so probably were the titles of *lac hâu* and *lac tuong*.

Whether Hùng Vuong, the Hông Bàng Dynasty, and the Van Lang Kingdom really existed is still a controversy of Vietnamese history. Nonetheless, every year Vietnamese throughout the world celebrate the anniversary of King Hùng on the tenth day of the third month of the lunar calendar. Beginning with French discoveries in the 1920s and 1930s of stone age sites in Hòa Bình and Bac Son in North Vietnam and a bronze age site in Đông Son, Thanh Hóa Province, archaeological research has proved that Vietnam has been continuously inhabited since early in its history.

In Vietnam an original civilization different from that of China widely developed. The most important features of this civilization were wet rice cultivation using tidewater movement; a matrilineal organization of society; the worship of ancestors and of the god of the soil; the building of shrines in high places; and a cosmological dualism in which the mountain and the sea are opposed—the winged race and the aquatic race, the men of the heights and those of the coasts. This Austro-Asiatic civilization, as it is known to archaeologists, corresponds to the Dongsonian civilization. To many scholars, it is the Hùng Vuong era.

The Thuc (258–207 B.C.) and the Triêu (207–111 B.C.)
In 258 B.C., Van Lang was invaded by a neighbor king, Thuc Phán, and annexed to his territory. A new kingdom, Âu Lac, was formed, and Thuc Phán became An Duong Vuong. Cô Loa, not far from Hà Nôi, was chosen as the new capital. There a spiral citadel was built that later became the most ancient and important historical vestige of ancient Vietnam.

In 207 B.C., An Duong Vuong was defeated by Triêu Đà (Chao-to), a former general of the Ch'in. Âu Lac was combined with Triêu Đà's territory to make a new kingdom, Nam Viêt (Nan Yueh). Phiên Ngung (Canton) became its capital. Triêu Đà and his successors ruled ancient Vietnam until 111 B.C., when Nam Viêt was invaded by the Han to become a Chinese colony. The country was divided into two *quân* (districts)—Giao Chi and Cuu Chân, each headed by a legate—and enjoyed loose, indirect control from Canton.

Chinese Domination (111 B.C.–A.D. 938)
During the first 100 years of their domination, the Chinese brought almost no change to their southern colony. The two Triêu legates in Giao Chi and Cuu Chân submitted without resistance and were confirmed in office. The *lac hâu* and the *lac tuong* were allowed to keep their territories and lead their own people. No rebellion was recorded. At the beginning of the first century A.D., however, the Chinese governors changed their policies. Through the effort of two governors, Tích Quang (Si Kuang) and Nhâm Diên (Jen Yen), Vietnamese culture was Sinicized and lands were seized for new Chinese immigrants at the expense of local nobles. This new policy reached its climax under Tô Đinh (Su Ting) and led to the uprising of

Trung Trac and her sister Trung Nhi, in A.D. 39 Hai Bà Trung (the Two Ladies Trung) spread their rebellion over 65 fiefs, covering all the territories from Cuu Chân to Hop Phô (Kwang Tung). Tô Đinh fled to Canton.

After two years of careful preparation, a large Chinese army, raised from several provinces in southern China and commanded by Mã Viên (Ma Yuan), moved south to counterattack in 42. The Ladies Trung, defeated at a bloody battle at Lãng Bac in the spring of 43, chose suicide by leaping into the Hát River.

After the failure of Hai Bà Trung, the Han tightened their control over Giao Chi and Cuu Chân. Vietnam became a strictly controlled Chinese province. Rebellions provided Vietnam with a list of national heroes, inluding Bà Triêu (248), Ly Bôn (or Ly Nam Đê) (544–548), Triêu Quang Phuc (or Triêu Viêt Vuong) (549–571), Ly Tu Tiên and Đinh Kiên (687), Mai Thúc Loan (or Mai Hac Đê) (722), Phùng Hung (766–791), and Duong Thanh (819). These rebellions finally ended with Ngô Quyên's victory over the Chinese on the Bach Đang River in 938. The country was again independent after more than a thousand years of Chinese rule.

Ten centuries of Chinese domination greatly affected Vietnam and its people. Under Chinese influence, the country slowly separated from other Southeast Asian nations to become a part of East Asia. A Vietnamese people emerged from ancient local elements and new immigrants from the north. Chinese characters were officially used for writing, and Chinese traditions and customs were widespread. Confucianism, Taoism, and Mahayana Buddhism were introduced and served as a base for Vietnamese intellectual and spiritual life even to the present. The Vietnamese and their culture were not completely Sinicized, however. The combination of local and northern elements was slowly realized throughout ten centuries; what was first foreign took root and became local. Ancient Vietnam was the Southern nation (Nuoc Nam, or Nam Quôc) facing China as the Northern nation (Bac Quôc) in the coming millennium.

—Pham Cao Duong

References: Coedes, Georges. *The Making of South East Asia* (1966); Higham, Charles. *The Archaeology of Mainland Southeast Asia* (1989); Lê Thành Khôi. *Histoire du Viet Nam des Origines à 1858* (1981); Pham Cao Duong. *Lich Su Dân Tôc Viêt Nam, Tâp I: Thoi Ky Lâp Quôc* (1987); Taylor, Keith W. *The Birth of Vietnam* (1983); Trân Trong Kim. *Viêt Nam Su Luoc* (1971); Uy Ban Khoa Hoc Xã Hôi Viêt Nam. *Lich Su Viêt Nam, Tâp I* (1971); Van Tân, Nguyên Linh, Lê Van Lân, Nguyên Đông Chi, Hoàng Hung. *Thoi Đai Hùng Vuong: Lich Su, Kinh Tê, Chính Tri, Van Hóa, Xã Hôi* (1976); Viên Khao Cô Hoc, Uy Ban Khoa Hoc Xã Hôi Viêt Nam. *Nhung Phát Hiên Moi Vê Khao Cô Hoc Nam 1984* (1985).

See also: Ly Bôn; Ngô Quyên; Trung Trac and Trung Nhi.

Vietnam: from 938 through the French Conquest
Ngô Quyên's victory over the Southern Han in 938 marked an end to 1,000 years of Chinese domination (111 B.C.– A.D. 938) and inaugurated the grand period of national independence. From 938 to 1884, the Vietnamese successfully built a new country—to use their own term, a Southern nation (Nam

Quôc, or Nuoc Nam) facing China as a Northern nation (Bac Quôc). Tentative Chinese efforts to regain control of their former colony failed except for a 20 year period (1407–1427) under the Mings. However, the imprint of Chinese civilization on Vietnam proved to be permanent. At the same time, in their Nam Tiên (March to the South), the Vietnamese expanded their territory from south of Đèo Ngang (Ngang Pass) to the point of Cà Mâu at the expense of the Chams and the Khmers. "Resisting the North" (*Bac cu*) and "conquering the South" (*Nam chinh*) became major themes of Vietnamese history, as did the development of an original Vietnamese culture and civilization.

Vietnamese Dynasties In 939 Ngô Quyên declared himself king and chose Cô Loa, ancient capital of the Thuc, for the new capital. This decision was significant, showing Ngô Quyên's determination to put Chinese domination behind and open a new period of independence for his country. Ngô Quyên's dynasty did not last long, however. He died in 944, and his children were unable to maintain order. Ancient Vietnam soon fell into serious troubles. This period, which Vietnamese historians refer to as the Period of the Twelve Lords (Muoi Hai Su Quân), lasted until Đinh Bô Lènh reunified the kingdom in 968.

The Đinh Dynasty gained Chinese recognition. Đinh Tiên Hoàng (who called himself Đinh Tiên Hoàng Đê—First Emperor of the Đinh) named the country Đai Cô Viêt and systematically organized his court and the administration of the country. His dynasty lasted only 12 years, until his assassination in 980. His commanding general, Lê Hoàn, replaced him and founded the Tiên Lê (Early Lê, 980–1009) Dynasty. Lê Hoàn, or Lê Đai Hành, defeated the Sung invasion, preserving national independence, and launched a victorious expedition against Champa in the South in 982.

The Tiên Lê laid a solid foundation for an independent Vietnam that future dynasties would develop to create a great southern nation before it was conquered by the French in the nineteenth century. The following Vietnamese dynasties succeeded the Tiên Lê: the Ly (1010–1225); the Trân (1225–1400); the Hô (1400–1407); the Hâu (Posterior) Trân (1407–1413) and the Ming Domination (1407–1428); the Hâu (Posterior) Lê (1428–1788); the Mac (1527–1592); the Nguyên Tây Son (1788–1802); and the Nguyên (1802–1945).

Preservation of Independence and Cultural Development The Sung invasion of Đai Cô Viêt in 980 was not the only Chinese effort to regain control of their former colony. The Chinese tried several times to reconquer Đai Viêt (the name given to the country by the Ly), and each time they were defeated. Vietnamese efforts to preserve their independence from China added more names to their list of heroes, among them Ly Thuong Kiêt and Tôn Đan (eleventh century); Trân Hung Đao, Trân Quang Khai, Trân Khánh Du, and Pham Ngu Lão (thirteenth century); Lê Loi (or Lê Thái Tô), Nguyên Trãi, and many others (fifteenth century); and Quang Trung (Nguyên Huê) (eighteenth century).

Despite its independent spirit, the Vietnamese monarchy under the Ly, Trân, Lê, and Nguyên retained the methods of government inherited from the Chinese empire. It modeled its institutions after the examples in China, particularly in the use of Confucianism as the major influence in the education of the country's elite and the organization of competitive examinations to recruit mandarins for the state government and administration. The Van Miêu, or Temple of Literature, was built in 1070 in the capital of Thang Long, and the first examination was organized in 1075. Chinese characters were used as the country's official writing system rather than Nôm (the written form of the Vietnamese language, derived from Chinese characters) until the early twentieth century. Buddhism and Taoism had a role equal to Confucianism under the Ly and at the beginning of the Trân, but gradually lost their primary importance in state life, an evolution reflected in Vietnamese poetry and literature.

Nam Tiên, or March to the South Nam Tiên—the effort to expand the national territory further to the south—was accomplished at the expense first of the Chams and later the Khmers. In 1069 after a successful military campaign, Ly Thánh Tông seized the Cham capital and imprisoned the Cham king, who was liberated in exchange for the cession of three Cham districts that later became Quang Bình and Quang Tri Provinces. In the early fourteenth century, two more Cham districts, which later became Thua Thiên Province, were given to Đai Viêt in exchange for Princess Huyên Trân in marriage. In the fifteenth century, the Chams gave up their territory north of the present province of Quang Nam, and in 1471 the Vietnamese took their capital of Vijaya. Once the Vietnamese had secured a permanent foothold south of Hai Vân Pass, the remaining Cham country was quickly subdued. In the seventeenth century, the remnants of this old, Indianized kingdom were definitively absorbed, although a petty Cham king retained nominal independence in the Phan Rang region until 1822.

But southward expansion did not end there. The elimination of Champa brought them into direct contact and conflict with the Khmers in the Mekong River Delta. This part of the lower plain of future Cochin China came under virtual Vietnamese control in the last decades of the eighteenth century.

French Conquest The main reason often cited for French intervention and conquest of Vietnam was to protect Catholic missionaries and their Vietnamese followers. The French action, however, was also undertaken to gain a "balcony" over the Pacific Ocean and was carried out at the same time as the Anglo-French intervention in China to open trading ports.

The French conquest of Vietnam began with an attack on Đà Nang in 1858. Gia Đinh Province fell in 1859, Đinh Tuong in 1861, and Biên Hòa in 1862. These provinces became a French colony following the Treaty of 1862. Three western provinces, Vinh Long, An Giang, and Hà Tiên, were colonized from 1867 to 1875. The rest of the country became a French protectorate in 1884, following two French attacks on North Vietnam in the early 1870s and 1880s and the signing of treaties in 1883 and 1884.

—Pham Cao Duong

References: Chesneaux, Jean. *Contribution à L'Histoire de la Nation Vietnamienne* (1955); Lê Thành Khôi. *Le Viet-Nam: Histoire et*

Civilisation (1955); Nguyên Thê Anh. *Viêt Nam Duoi Thoi Pháp Đô Hô* (1970); Phan Khoang. *Viêt Nam Pháp Thuôc Su: 1862–1945* (1971); Trân Trong Kim. *Viêt Nam Su Luoc* (1971).

See also: Confucianism; French Indo-China; Lê Loi (Lê Thái Tô); Lê Dynasty; Ngô Quyên; Nguyên Huê (Quang Trung); Trinh Lords.

Vietnam, Climate of

Vietnam lies in the tropical belt between the equator and the Tropic of Cancer. The primary seasonal changes are marked variations in rainfall rather than in temperature. The rainy season extends from early May to November in the lowlands below Cape Dinh and in the Central Highlands, with annual rainfall averaging approximately 79 inches in lowland regions. It rains in the coastal area in Central Vietnam above Cape Dinh from November to April. The typhoon season lasts from July through November, with the most severe storms occurring along the central coast. In the North, the rainy season extends from mid-April to mid-October; Hà Nôi has a mean annual rainfall of 69 inches, and annual precipitation in the mountains sometimes exceeds 160 inches. During the Vietnam War, heavy rain and fog during the monsoon season frequently forced curtailments of airborne missions and caused bombing inaccuracies.

Daily temperatures in the North fluctuate considerably in the Red River Delta region and in the dry season may vary by 45 degrees Fahrenheit during one day. The South is more tropical; temperatures in Sài Gòn (Hô Chí Minh City) vary between 64 and 91 degrees throughout the year. Temperatures in the Central Highlands are somewhat cooler, running from a mean of about 63 degrees in winter to 68 degrees in summer.

—Louise Mongelluzzo

Reference: Marshall, S. L. A. *Battles in the Monsoon* (1967).

See also: Geography of Indo-China and Vietnam.

Vietnam, Democratic Republic of: 1945–1954

By May 1945, the Viêt Nam Độc Lâp Đông Minh Hôi, or Viêt Minh (League for the Independence of Vietnam), controlled a free zone in the mountainous region of the North. Under the control of Hô Chí Minh and the Indo-Chinese Communist Party (ICP), it was ready to grab power at the end of World War II. After Japan surrendered, Viêt Minh troops marched into Hà Nôi and occupied key locations, an event that came to be known as the August Revolution. On 2 September 1945, in Ba Đình Square, Hô Chí Minh read his Vietnamese declaration of independence and proclaimed the establishment of the Democratic Republic of Vietnam (DRV), a new government meant to embrace all three regions of the country: Tonkin, Annam, and Cochin China.

Hô's hopes were dashed from the beginning. Under the Potsdam Agreement, British troops under Maj. Gen. Douglas Gracey arrived south of the 16th parallel while Chinese soldiers, loosely commanded by Gen. Lu Hán, moved into the north. Both were charged with disarming and repatriating Japanese forces. Gracey did his best to disrupt Viêt Minh attempts to govern in his domain, while the Chinese soldiery looted the North. Simultaneously, Paris sent agents into the

region to restore French rule. The Viêt Minh faced a prolonged drought followed by flooding in the Red River Delta region and a cholera epidemic.

In the midst of this chaos, Hô tried to establish his government. Hô had little with which to work: no rice stocks, a bankrupt treasury, no bureaucracy, no foreign recognition of his nation, and no one experienced in running a nation. Nor was support for the Viêt Minh solid even among Vietnamese; rival parties struggled for their share of power. To quiet them, on 11 November 1945 Hô dissolved the Indo-Chinese Communist Party (ICP) and on 6 January 1946 held elections for a new National Assembly in which opposition parties were allowed to serve, although without real power. A few months later, with Hô in France, acting president Vô Nguyên Giáp ordered armed units into action. From 11 to 13 July, his units seized property, arrested opponents, and shut down newspapers, while his thugs murdered hundreds who opposed the Communist government.

A new problem then arose. France and China signed an accord whereby China agreed to remove its troops from Indo-China by 31 March 1946. In return, France surrendered its claims to former concessions in China and received Chinese approval to return French troops to Tonkin. Despite opposition from many of his followers, Hô acquiesced in this development. In negotiations with the French, Hô proposed the formation of an independent Vietnam within the French Union. Paris disagreed, insisting that it must retain Cochin China as a colony; however, it would recognize Tonkin and Annam as an autonomous state. Hô then offered to accept recognition of Vietnam as a "free" state and to drop insistence on the word "independent." He also argued that no more than 15,000 French soldiers should return to the North. The French delegation led by Jean Sainteny accepted these stipulations, and the two sides signed an accord on 6 March 1946. They opened a conference at Đà Lat on 18 April 1946 to work out details, but little was accomplished. Newly promoted to the rank of full general, Vô Nguyên Giáp ordered his armed forces to be ready to fight if necessary and began to plan weapons procurement.

Hô left Hà Nôi on 31 May 1946 for a four-month conference at Fontainebleau. During this absence, French High Commissioner for Indo-China Adm. Thierry d'Argenlieu announced recognition of a Republic of Cochin China, further sundering the third of Vietnam's three zones from Hô's influence. During Hô's absence, a series of incidents between Giáp and the French military heightened tensions. French aircraft bombed Viêt Minh positions, and French infantry attacked Viêt Minh roadblocks. d'Argenlieu gave orders to the French army to occupy certain northern provinces and to establish puppet governments in the mountains (the Thái-Ky and Nùng-Thái Republics) to diminish Viêt Minh authority. On 25 June, French soldiers seized the governor-general's mansion in Hà Nôi used by the Viêt Minh. Giáp warned top French commander, Lt. Gen. Jean-Etienne Valluy, to stop these incidents, but they continued.

In October 1946, Hô Chí Minh returned home. His months in France had been futile; its government had refused meaningful concessions. Eager to consolidate power now that Giáp had eliminated so many rivals, Hô directed his National Assembly to approve a new constitution, effective 8 November 1946, that formalized the DRV's status. The assembly then dissolved, not to meet again until 1953 with most nationalist members eliminated.

In the summer of 1946, the French insisted on usurping control of the port of Hai Phòng from the Viêt Minh. The Viêt Minh refused. On 29 August, French troops with tanks and armored vehicles occupied the post office, police station, and customs house and expelled Viêt Minh personnel. Both sides exchanged gunfire. The French did not withdraw for nearly two weeks. On 20 November, the French seized a Chinese junk suspected of carrying arms for the Viêt Minh. In retaliation, the Viêt Minh captured three French soldiers and barricaded themselves with the captives deep within Hai Phòng. Another firefight ensued as the French tried to free their comrades. On 23 November, the French in Hai Phòng issued an ultimatum that the Viêt Minh evacuate Hai Phòng and gave two hours for a response. When the Viêt Minh refused, the French shelled the city, causing extensive civilian casualties. They also insisted that the Viêt Minh surrender control of the Hà Nôi/Hai Phòng road. The Viêt Minh resisted, and Giáp prepared for war.

Hô made a fruitless appeal to Paris as Giáp continued military preparations. On 19 December 1946, Giáp issued a national call to arms, and the next morning Hô broadcast a message asking his people to fight to the end. Giáp needed time to move troops, materiel, and factories back into the northern wilderness, where he felt that the Viêt Minh would be safe from French attack. His soldiers bought him time; the last did not retreat from the fighting in Hà Nôi until 17 February 1947.

The Viêt Minh government had been reduced to one in exile, controlling an area only 50 miles in radius. However, it was largely secure from the French, whose wheel-bound military could get close to, but not into, the area. Gen. Valluy tried, launching Operation LEA—a combined riverine and air assault—on 7 October 1947. His men closed on Hô's headquarters so rapidly that Hô and Giáp saved themselves only by hiding in a hole. Hô escaped safely across French lines, but French soldiers killed the scholar Nguyên Van Tô, whom they mistook for Hô. Valluy's forces made later assaults as well, ultimately claiming to have killed 9,500 Viêt Minh in late 1947. Dissatisfied with these results, Paris replaced Valluy with Lt. Gen. Roger C. Blaizot, who accomplished no more than his predecessor. Giáp knew that he did not have to win many battles to achieve victory in the war. He only had to make the French quit.

A combat lull fell over both sides between 1948 and 1950. The DRV improved its situation in 1949 when Mao Zedong, Communist ruler of the People's Republic of China, gave the DRV legal recognition. During that hiatus, the DRV's army grew to about 300,000. Blaizot was followed by Lt. Gen. Marcel Carpentier, who was replaced by Gen. Jean de Lattre de Tassigny, who was followed by Gen. Raoul Salan and, finally, Gen. Henri Navarre. None were able to stop the Viêt Minh.

In 1950, with Hô's approval, Giáp committed his divisions to battle at Đông Khê and Cao Bang, grinding down the French. In 1951 he suffered savage setbacks at Vinh Yên, Mao Khê, and the Đáy River. Giáp backed away from frontal confrontations for a time and again relied on guerrilla warfare. In late 1952, the French unsuccessfully counterattacked in Operation LORRAINE and other assaults. By 1953 the Viêt Minh controlled most of rural Vietnam and some villages and towns and had extended operations into Laos. Gen. Navarre, commanding 84 battalions and yet unable to smash his enemies, concocted a plan to force a set-piece battle with the Viêt Minh at Điên Biên Phu. After fighting bravely for 55 days against Giáp's besieging soldiers, the French surrendered on 8 May 1954. The DRV had finally defeated the French in the North. The future of Hô's nation would now depend on the great powers at Geneva.

—Cecil B. Currey

References: Davidson, Phillip B. *Vietnam at War: The History, 1946–1975* (1988); Harrison, James Pinckney. *The Endless War: Vietnam's Struggle for Independence* (1982); Vo Nguyen Giap. *Unforgettable Months and Years* (1975); Vô Nguyên Giáp, interviews with the author (1988, 1991).

See also: August Revolution; d'Argenlieu, Georges Thierry; Fontainebleau Conference; Gracey, Douglas D.; Hai Phòng, Shelling of; Hô Chí Minh; Hô-Sainteny Agreement; Lao Dông Party; LEA, Operation; LORRAINE, Operation; Lu Hán; Navarre, Henri Eugène; Sainteny, Jean; Viêt Minh; Vô Nguyên Giáp.

Vietnam, Democratic Republic of: 1954–1975

The leaders of the Democratic Republic of Vietnam (DRV) never deviated from their goal of unifying the whole of Vietnam under Communist rule. The 1954 Geneva Accords provided that Vietnam was one state temporarily divided at the 17th parallel pending national elections. The final declaration, however, was unsigned, and neither the United States nor South Vietnam accepted its operative terms. The Geneva compromise was a great disappointment to DRV leaders, who were induced to accept less, for the time being, by their Soviet and Communist Chinese allies in order to prevent the possibility of U.S. entry into the conflict.

In the mid-1950s, DRV leaders retained two goals: the Marxist consolidation of strength (political and economic) in the North and the struggle for national reunification. In a step toward attaining the first goal and eliminating the dissension and factionalism that characterized Vietnamese culture, DRV leaders sought to obtain the loyalty of the masses by carrying out land reform, although the North, unlike the South, consisted almost entirely of small landholders. In December 1953, the National Assembly of the DRV called for the confiscation of land and property of the entire "landlord" class. The party was not interested in justice as much as it was interested in class warfare. The peasantry was encouraged to denounce and try landholders, with the aim of temporarily redistributing their holdings among landless peasantry, resulting in execution or death by starvation of up to 100,000 "landlords." This so-called land reform was halted in an effort to limit emigration south during the 300-day period of free movement provided by the Geneva Accords across the 17th parallel. The Viêt Minh blocked the emigration of approximately 400,000 people, but more than 928,000 civilians made it to South Vietnam.

When the 300 days ended, people's courts resumed their ideologically driven work. Those who opposed this policy, including party members who refused to participate, were consigned to forced labor camps. Many condemned landholders had only marginal holdings, and unrest led Hô Chí Minh to admit publicly that cadres had committed errors and excesses. There followed a campaign to "rectify errors," which ended the terror and led to the release of thousands of survivors. Some victims were allowed to take revenge on land reform cadres. However, this did not prevent several peasant revolts, the most serious of which occurred in Hô's native province of Nghê An on 2 November 1956. Land reform had succeeded in increasing the number of those dependent on the party's power, but it adversely affected crop production, and famine was averted only through Soviet assistance.

Economic reconstruction of the DRV was essential to continuing the Vietnamese Revolution. Soviet-bloc aid to the DRV was, according to Bernard Fall, comparable to U.S. aid levels for the Republic of Vietnam (RVN). From 1955 to 1961, grants and loans for economic aid exceeded $1 billion. Despite impressive advances in industrial development, agriculture continued to lag behind that of the RVN, which had a smaller population, yet produced more rice. Although many peasants resisted collectivization of the land, the process of forming lower stage agricultural cooperatives was completed by 1962.

The DRV leadership's other preoccupation was reunification. In accordance with the 1954 Geneva Conference agreement, Viêt Minh soldiers were regrouped into the North, but political cadres remained in the South to prepare for the 1956 elections. But the RVN government of Ngô Đình Diêm rebuffed all demands of DRV Premier Pham Van Đông for national elections.

By summer 1956, Diêm's "denunciation of Communists" campaign had allegedly eliminated 90 percent of the party's cells in the South. After the Geneva Accords, the DRV left approximately 3,500 armed guerrillas in South Vietnam, in remote locations such as the U Minh Forest of the Mekong Delta, where they received direction from Politburo member Lê Duân. But the DRV was constrained by the global strategy of the Communist Party of the Soviet Union (CPSU), which at their January 1956 Moscow meeting proclaimed a policy of peaceful coexistence with the West. Resistance to this policy was voiced by Truong Chinh, who had attended the CPSU Congress with Lê Đuc Tho, at the Ninth Plenum of the Central Committee in April 1956. As head of the Regional Committee of the South, Lê Duân proposed before the Plenum the organization of 20 main force battalions and guerrilla units in friendly villages. His work, *The Path of Revolution in the South*, encouraged a more activist approach, with the party leading the masses. This, along with Diêm's campaign in the South, undermined the primacy of political struggle and led the Eleventh Plenum in December 1957 to launch a program of assassination of Diêm govern-

ment supporters, ranging from "wicked landlords" to village officials and teachers. This campaign was officially labeled "extermination of traitors."

Thirty-seven armed companies were organized in the South by October 1957 on orders from Hà Nôi. With the insurgency under way, Diêm rebuffed DRV efforts to arrange trade normalization. Lê Duân was recalled to Hà Nôi as acting first secretary of the party and traveled with Hô to Moscow to seek support for the new approach. In January 1959, the Lao Đông Party's Fifteenth Plenum decided to use armed force to topple the Diêm government. In May 1959, the DRV government authorized the formation of Group 559, which began to enlarge the Hô Chí Minh Trail; meanwhile, Group 779 began seaborne infiltration.

In September 1960, the Third Congress of the Lao Đông Party named Lê Duân as secretary-general. The Congress also made it clear that the Vietnamese revolution retained two strategic tasks: to "carry out the socialist revolution in the North" and to "achieve national reunification." In regard to the first, it is worth noting that in 1960 the DRV obtained a long-term loan from the Soviets for construction of 43 industrial plants, including eight thermal power stations. The People's Republic of China (PRC) provided a similar loan to enlarge 29 existing plants, including the Thái Nguyên steel mill complex and a large fertilizer factory in Bac Giang, which also produced explosives for the PAVN. A First Five Year Plan was initiated in 1961 on the Soviet model, with central planning and priority given to heavy industry. The Soviets also constructed a machine tool plant and a superphosphate factory. The Chinese built roads and plants, Mongolia provided 100,000 breed cattle, and East Germany sent an ocean fishing fleet and supplies to build a hospital. Only about 10 percent of the DRV's trade was with non-Communist nations. Industrial production as a percentage of the gross national product increased from 31.4 percent in 1957 to 53.4 percent by 1964.

To facilitate the second task of the revolution, on 20 December 1960 the party created the National Liberation Front (NLF) and its military branch. This apparently liberal, nationalist front to overthrow the Diêm regime was in fact tightly controlled by the DRV through the newly revived Central Office for South Vietnam (COSVN), but the party's success in concealing this linkage brought the NLF insurgency worldwide sympathy. Military units in the Western Highlands and the Mekong Delta were consolidated into the People's Liberation Armed Forces (PLAF), better known to their enemies as the Viêt Công (VC). The creation of the People's Revolutionary Party in 1962 (in effect, a branch of the Lao Đông Party) was another step toward the takeover of the South.

The DRV accepted the Geneva Accords of 1962 on Laos but failed to live up to its provisions to reduce its advisors with the Pathet Lao and to remove its personnel on way stations along the Hô Chí Minh Trail. When the Ninth Plenum of the Central Committee in December 1963 decided to escalate the war effort in South Vietnam, the Communists received crucial support from the PRC, which provided 90,000 rifles and machine guns to the VC in 1962 alone.

After the August 1964 Tonkin Gulf incidents and the ouster of Soviet Premier Nikita Khrushchev that October, DRV leaders appealed to the Soviets for more aid, at the same time working to preserve their ties with the Chinese. The Chinese agreed in July 1965 to provide the DRV with $200 million in "national defense and economic supplies." An October 1966 Soviet bloc conference in Moscow promised $1 billion in military and financial aid. The DRV decision to move to conventional war could not have been made without these pacts.

In an effort to exploit VC successes, the leadership also decided in 1964 to send regular PAVN troops down the Hô Chí Minh Trail to the South. To this point, most of those sent to the South were native Viêt Minh southern veterans who had been regrouped in the North. By 1964 the Trail, as a result of Soviet and Chinese assistance, could handle trucks and other vehicles. However, the attempt of the PAVN and VC to cut South Vietnam in two from the Central Highlands to the coast was frustrated by the 1965 arrival of U.S. ground troops. The U.S. 1st Cavalry Division (Airmobile) defeated three PAVN regiments in the Ia Drang Valley late that year.

The commitment of 200,000 U.S. troops to the Republic of Vietnam led the Twelfth Plenum of the Central Committee in December 1965 to decide upon protracted war. Big-unit war proved costly in the face of a continuing U.S. troop buildup. By 1967 declining volunteers and heavy casualties forced more PAVN and VC units to seek refuge in sanctuaries in "neutral" Laos and Cambodia. When the Fourteenth Plenum of the Central Committee met in late 1967, it finalized plans for a "general offensive, general uprising" (the Têt Offensive), despite the presence of 500,000 U.S. troops. Reportedly, Giáp opposed risking so much, but he accepted the decision when the party shifted the brunt of the fighting to VC units. Although the party's hopes for a general uprising of the South Vietnamese populace proved illusory, the shock of a countrywide offensive was sufficient to persuade the Johnson administration to seek a negotiated end to the conflict, including a halt to bombing above the 20th parallel. The 1968 Têt Offensive would not have been possible without massive Soviet and Chinese aid.

The Têt Offensive had failed to such an extent that the VC never recovered its former strength, and North Vietnamization of its forces became necessary. Seeking an end to all bombing of the north, the DRV agreed to talks in Paris, but adopted the tactic of "fighting and talking," which was designed to exacerbate differences between the United States and the RVN and to intensify antiwar pressures in the United States. Not surprisingly, these talks achieved little. There was an understanding, however, that, in return for a complete bombing halt over the North, the Communists would refrain from attacks on the cities. When the latter was violated by an offensive in February 1969, the Nixon administration initiated the secret bombing of Communist sanctuaries in Cambodia and announced its Vietnamization policy. The DRV leadership could not protest because it denied having troops in Cambodia, but the bombing of Cambodia prompted them to agree to secret talks in Paris.

Hô's death in September 1969 temporarily resolved the debate in Hà Nôi in favor of those who wanted a guerrilla war. U.S. and Army of the Republic of Vietnam (ARVN) pacification efforts achieved successes between 1970 and 1971, but intensive efforts to rebuild Communist forces were under way. The U.S. incursion into Cambodia to support the forces of Lon Nol in 1970 and the U.S. encouragement of the ARVN effort to destroy Communist bases and cut the Hô Chí Minh Trail in southern Laos (Operation LAM SON 719) probably forced the North Vietnamese to postpone by one year the great offensive approved by the Nineteenth Plenum. By 1971 the USSR had provided the DRV some $3 billion in economic and military assistance, while the PRC had provided an additional $1 billion. Both governments gave additional aid increase for the upcoming offensive.

The Nixon administration had arranged summits with both Beijing and Moscow in 1972 to obtain PRC and USSR cooperation in bringing about a negotiated settlement in Vietnam. Nonetheless, the DRV launched an all-out offensive with 14 PAVN divisions in a conventional attack that employed Soviet-supplied tanks and artillery. The NGUY N HU (Easter Offensive) was timed to impact the U.S. presidential election and was launched when there were only 6,000 U.S. combat troops in Vietnam. But President Nixon's decision to dramatically escalate the air war, resume the bombing of the North, target PAVN forces in the South, and mine Hai Phòng harbor resulted in a crushing PAVN defeat, with losses estimated at 100,000 troops.

Receiving pressure from the Soviets and the Chinese, Hà Nôi sought a settlement through the secret Henry Kissinger–Lê Duc Tho talks in Paris. The breakthrough came on 8 October 1972, with agreement to an immediate cease-fire in place, followed by a completion of U.S. troop withdrawal and a prisoner exchange. But key to the agreement was the concession that North Vietnamese troops did not have to leave territory they occupied inside South Vietnam. This and other substantive problems caused RVN President Nguyên Van Thiêu to balk, delaying the final agreement. Hà Nôi agreed to reopen the negotiations but stalled, hoping the Nixon administration would be compelled to make further concessions based on congressional deadlines or antiwar pressures. When the DRV discontinued the talks on 13 December, Nixon ordered the intense LINEBACKER II bombing, which convinced the DRV to settle, since its air defenses were devastated and its economy was in ruins. Although DRV leaders claimed that the bombing had produced suffering akin to a holocaust, *New York Times* reporter Michael W. Browne observed that "the damage caused by American bombing was grossly overstated by North Vietnamese propaganda."

In return for an end to the bombing, DRV leaders agreed to return to the Kissinger–Lê Duc Tho talks and ultimately agreed to the cease-fire agreement, privately assuring the United States that they would arrange a cease-fire in Laos as well, but claiming that they could not do the same in Cambodia. The DRV was left in control of about 20 percent of the South and redeployed troops in Cambodia to their former jungle sanctuaries on the RVN border.

With the removal of U.S. combat troops and advisors, the DRV concentrated on rebuilding its own forces. Soviet heavy artillery, air defense missiles, and armored vehicles were moved south during the next two years. The Third Indo-China War began almost immediately. The Canadians, representatives on the International Commission of Supervision and Control, withdrew in frustration since they were being arrested and treated as prisoners by the PLAF. They reported that the most serious violations were North Vietnamese disregard for Lao and Cambodian neutrality and continuing infiltration into the RVN.

Secretary of State Kissinger visited Hà Nôi in February 1973 to confront the Communists with a report of more than 200 cease-fire violations, but DRV leaders wanted only to discuss the money promised them for reconstruction. Kissinger assured them that they could not "have their aid and eat Indochina too." Sài Gòn's effort to regain lost territory and the passage of the Case-Church Amendment that ended funding for U.S. forces in Southeast Asia prompted the Twenty-First Plenum of the Central Committee in October 1973 to approve "strategic raids" on isolated ARVN bases to clear their "logistics corridor," cut key communication with Sài Gòn, regain lost territory, and begin preparation for a culminating offensive to win the war. Critical to PAVN's success was the movement of troops and materiel down the Hô Chí Minh Trail, construction of an oil pipeline, and a paved highway from Quang Tri in the north through the Central Highlands to Lôc Ninh in the South. Also important was the aggressive initiative of theater commander Gen. Trân Van Trà, who persuaded Lê Duân to back his plan for attacking Phuoc Long Province, despite concerns over the level of war materiels and the U.S. reaction.

When the United States did not react to the seizing of Phuoc Long Province in December 1974, the DRV, confident that the Ford administration would not send in air power, pushed ahead with an all-out invasion of the south (the Hô Chí Minh Campaign), which they anticipated would take two years to complete. But RVN President Nguyên Van Thiêu's precipitous abandonment of the Central Highlands was the beginning of a rout as PAVN forces, led by Gen. Van Tiên Dung and reequipped with modern Soviet tanks and weapons, completed the conquest of the RVN well ahead of schedule. Sài Gòn fell on 30 April 1975. The DRV also celebrated the victories of its allies in Cambodia and in Laos, where PAVN divisions were instrumental in the Pathet Lao victory.

Chief of the Soviet Armed Forces Gen. Viktor Kulikov had hurried to Hà Nôi after the capture of Phuoc Long Province to offer an estimated 400 percent increase in military aid to complete the destruction of the RVN. The Communist Chinese also provided critical military aid.

During the Second and Third Indo-China Wars, the combined losses of the DRV and the RVN were at least one million troops. The DRV suffered heavy bomb damage in six industrial cities, and 32 towns required major rebuilding. Another challenge facing Vietnam was trying to feed the 49 million people of the reunified country, especially consider-

ing that the Socialist transformation of the South was made a high priority.

—Claude R. Sasso

References: Doyle, Edward, et al., and the editors of Boston Publishing Company. *The North* (1986); Duiker, William, J. *The Communist Road to Power in Vietnam* (1981); Fall, Bernard. *The Two Viet Nams*. Rev. ed. (1964); Kissinger, Henry A. *The White House Years* (1979).

See also: Agricultural Reform Tribunals; Cambodia; China, People's Republic of (PRC); Easter Offensive (Nguyên Huê Campaign); Hô Chí Minh; Hô Chí Minh Campaign; Hô Chí Minh Trail; International Commission for Supervision and Control (ICSC); Kissinger, Henry Alfred; Lao Dông Party; Laos; Lê Duân; Lê Duc Tho; LINEBACKER II, Operation; National Front for the Liberation of South Vietnam (NFLSV); Paris Negotiations; Paris Peace Accords; Union of Soviet Socialist Republics (USSR; Soviet Union); Viêt Minh; Vietnam, Democratic Republic of: 1945–1954; Vietnamese Communist Party (VCP).

Vietnam, Democratic Republic of: Air Force

Before the August 1964 Gulf of Tonkin incident, the Democratic Republic of Vietnam's (DRV) Air Force—30 trainer aircraft, 50 transports, and 4 light helicopters—was obsolete and insignificant. Only two airfields could sustain prolonged jet operations, and only 20 radar sets protected these meager resources from possible attack. However, almost immediately after the confrontation in the Gulf of Tonkin, the People's Republic of China provided a few MiG-15 and MiG-17 jet aircraft, based at Phúc Yên airfield near Hà Nôi, as a precaution against future U.S. air strikes and in the expectation that the DRV was about to embark on a prolonged war. This prodded the Soviet Union to replace the Chinese as the DRV Air Force's main sponsor and supplier.

Between 1965 and 1966, the North Vietnamese and their Soviet sponsors began to build what would become a fearsome air defense system. By the end of 1965, the DRV had 75 MiG fighters and 8 IL-28 light bombers. North Vietnamese pilots spent most of the year training for air defense, which would become their sole mission throughout the war. Ten fighter engagements between U.S. and DRV pilots took place during that year, resulting in the loss of six North Vietnamese and two U.S. aircraft.

The agile MiG-21, which became the primary DRV Air Force interceptor during the war, first arrived in December 1965. By the end of the year, the DRV established the rudiments of a centralized intercept network that could detect approaching U.S. aircraft from multiple directions. Both developments allowed the DRV Air Force to increase its level of activity in 1966. By the end of that year, despite the loss of 29 aircraft in air-to-air combat (U.S. losses were 11 aircraft), 70 MiG fighters remained, including 15 MiG-21s. Clearly, the DRV Air Force was on the brink of a new level of aggressiveness, proficiency, and tactical maturity.

By 1967 the DRV possessed 200 surface-to-air missile (SAM) sites, 7,000 antiaircraft artillery (AAA) guns, and approximately 110 MiGs (including 18 MiG-21s), all working together under a sophisticated ground-control intercept system. The role of the SAMs and MiGs was to destroy enemy aircraft, force them to jettison their bombs prematurely, or compel them to dive into the lethal range of AAA fire. The role of ground fire was to force the attacker back up into the SAM/MiG belt to suffer the same fate. The dense air defense system worked, although MiG operations were not as important as SAM defenses and AAA fire. U.S. losses grew from 171 aircraft in 1965 to 326 in 1967; the cost of causing $1 worth of damage grew from $6.60 to $9.60. U.S. success rate in air combat, based on an average of 20 encounters per month in 1967, was a mere 3:1 (75 DRV versus 25 U.S. aircraft lost). However, the three-to-one ratio included 15 MiGs destroyed on the ground in attacks against DRV's airfields. The attacks disrupted DRV activities to the point that the North Vietnamese moved most of their MiGs to air facilities in southern China. The approximately 50 MiGs remaining in the DRV then individually challenged U.S. aircraft, still operating below the 20th parallel, until the U.S. bombing halt of 31 October 1968.

After the bombing halt, the DRV Air Force operated at a reduced tempo until 1972. At that point, it had an estimated 206 MiGs, including 93 MiG-21s. With the reintroduction of U.S. air strikes above the 20th parallel in LINEBACKER I and II, the North Vietnamese Air Force once again served as a necessary component of the DRV's still-lethal air defense system. U.S. aircraft reached their objectives without significant interference by North Vietnamese fighters, but 23 U.S. airplanes went down between February and October 1972. Thus, the DRV Air Force remained to the end a limited but effective air defense tool designed to harass and disrupt U.S. air attacks against the DRV.

—Peter R. Faber

References: Clodfelter, Mark. *The Limits of Air Power* (1989); Sharp, U. S. G. "Report on Air and Naval Campaigns against North Vietnam and Pacific Command-Wide Support of the War, June 1964–July 1968" (1969).

See also: Air Defense, Democratic Republic of Vietnam; Air Power, Role in War; Antiaircraft Artillery, Allied and Democratic Republic of Vietnam; Order of Battle; ROLLING THUNDER, Operation; Surface-to-Air Missiles (SAMs).

Vietnam, Democratic Republic of: Army (People's Army of Vietnam [PAVN])

Military establishment of the Democratic Republic of Vietnam (DRV), comprising regular and reserve ground forces and small naval and air components. Over 30 years the People's Army of Vietnam (PAVN) evolved from a small insurgent group into one of the world's largest armed forces. The PAVN's roots can be traced to various nationalist military units that battled the French and Japanese during the 1930s and 1940s. The impetus to build an army came with the Viêt Minh resistance during World War II. Originally an umbrella organization that included non-Communist elements, by 1944 the Viêt Minh was dominated by Hô Chí Minh's Communist Party. On 22 December 1944, the party laid the foundation for what would become the PAVN with the establishment of the first Armed Propaganda Team (APT).

Comprising 31 men and 3 women and commanded by Vô Nguyên Giáp, this unit became the party's first full-time formation and served both a political and a military role. Supplied with a few old weapons, including muzzle-loading flintlocks, the APT provided the model for future units.

Under Giáp's leadership, the task of army building went forward. APT, various guerrilla bands, and other independent resistance groups were combined in May 1945 to form the Vietnam Liberation Army with Giáp in overall command. Later that year, this force of only a few thousand spearheaded the August Revolution, after which Hô proclaimed Vietnamese independence and the founding of the Democratic Republic of Vietnam (DRV). Renamed the Vietnam National Defense Army, the force remained largely a guerrilla army, capable of only small-unit operations. But with the DRV's formation came an aggressive drive to expand the army that coincided with the French decision to reassert primacy in Vietnam. The fledgling DRV military force was soon designated the People's Army of Vietnam.

Although the army grew steadily during the war against the French, it initially lacked organization, training, and weapons. Forced to rely on captured French and Japanese equipment, the PAVN fought a largely defensive guerrilla war. Victories along the northern border with China allowed the establishment of staging areas and training bases in that country and opened the door to increased assistance from the People's Republic of China (PRC). The Viêt Minh prosecuted the war in various phases, building to large-scale conventional warfare. The first PAVN infantry division, formed in 1949, went into action in 1951 and was followed by five more, but throughout the war most of the fighting was done by regional or local forces while the regulars were used sparingly and withheld for major actions such as the Battle of Điên Biên Phu. Local units supplied reconnaissance and logistical support and often bolstered combat formations; regional forces carried out much of the everyday fighting. Throughout the Indo-China War, a lack of transport vehicles forced the Viêt Minh to rely almost exclusively on thousands of porters to supply forces in the field. The advent of heavy divisions facilitated the shift to conventional warfare and the 1954 victory at Điên Biên Phu that prompted the French withdrawal from Vietnam. At war's end, the PAVN numbered some 380,000 soldiers, approximately 120,000 of them regulars. The Viêt Minh had been nominally a united front organization, and the PAVN reflected this on a small scale.

With victory over the French came a rapid consolidation by the Communists of political and military organizations. The Communist Party held sway in the DRV as the PAVN's composition boldly illustrated; an overwhelming majority of PAVN officers were party members, and most of soldiers had received political indoctrination. The 1954 Geneva Accords allowed a 300-day regroupment period during which almost one million people fled the North for the South. Some 80,000 Viêt Minh soldiers, mostly regional and local troops who had carried the bulk of the fighting in the South, returned to the North, but 10,000 veterans remained in the South and would form the core of the future People's Liberation Armed Forces (PLAF).

In 1957 PAVN guerrillas attacked Minh Thanh in Thu Dầu Một Province, signaling the beginning of the Vietnam War. DRV leaders now focused on the modernization and professionalization of their army. The government mandated compulsory military service, intensified training for officers and noncommissioned officers (NCOs), instituted uniform regulations, and formalized the command structure. It established formal ranks and insignia for a force that had operated without these mainstays of Western armies. The influx of war materiel from the PRC and the USSR led to formation of artillery and armor units and a small air force. The army still lacked adequate transport and remained heavily infantry oriented.

Unification drove military planning in the late 1950s. The Fifteenth Party Plenum in May 1959 determined that the time was ripe to press the initiative. Acting on Lê Duẩn's recommendations, the party moved to build an army in the South based upon the APT that could evolve into a conventional force. The chief instrument of insurrection in the South became the National Front of the Liberation of South Vietnam, or National Liberation Front (NLF), a nominally indigenous united-front organization that opposed the U.S.-supported Republic of Vietnam (RVN) and its President Ngô Đình Diệm. Despite its denials, the DRV was clearly involved in the Southern insurrection. The NLF's military branch—the PLAF (known to the United States as the Việt Công)—consisted largely of Southern volunteers and carried out most of the fighting against RVN and U.S. forces before 1968. It contained main force and guerrilla components and reached a total strength of almost 400,000 before the 1968 Tết Offensive.

Although Hà Nội insisted that the Southern guerrilla war be self-sufficient, it provided experienced leadership, technical support, and supplies. The DRV directed the Southern effort through its command apparatus, later known as the Central Office for South Vietnam (COSVN). Additionally, PAVN soldiers who had gone north during the regroupment were infiltrated to the South, forming the bulk of PLAF main force units. Still, throughout the Vietnam War, the PAVN and the PLAF viewed themselves as separate entities. After the war, Hà Nội claimed sponsorship of the PLAF, much to the disgust of many PLAF veterans.

The most important aspect of the DRV's early involvement was logistical support. The 1959 commitment to escalate its involvement in the South led to the creation of Group 559 to infiltrate troops and supplies southward on the Hồ Chí Minh Trail. Group 759 was charged with supplying Southern forces by water, while Group 959 was developed to support the Pathet Lao in Laos. These efforts, especially that of Group 559, contributed hugely to the Communist victory.

Until 1965, the PLAF conducted a usually low-level "people's war," employing its guerrilla forces against the Army of the Republic of Vietnam (ARVN) and its Regional and Popular Forces. Political action was equally important to the southern effort, and NLF and Communist Party cadres worked to exploit local dissatisfaction with the Sài Gòn government. But with the commitment of U.S. combat troops, the DRV found it increasingly necessary to augment PLAF formations and finally to commit regular units. The PAVN initially operated in the Central Highlands south of the Demilitarized Zone (DMZ) to keep U.S. and ARVN forces from concentrating on PLAF activities further south. This was especially the case before the 1968 Tết Offensive, as entire PAVN divisions moved below the DMZ in a diversionary effort to draw attention from the targeted areas in the South.

Tết was a military disaster that destroyed the fighting effectiveness of the PLAF, who bore the brunt of the fighting and took devastating losses. Thereafter PAVN regulars assumed the leading combat role and took on an increasingly conventional profile with a large influx of tanks, artillery, and surface-to-air missiles. Regular PAVN divisions, which mainly conducted the 1972 Spring Offensive in the wake of the withdrawal of U.S. ground troops, were beaten back by the ARVN with the aid of substantial U.S. air support. After almost three years of preparation that included massive troop and equipment buildups, the PAVN unleashed its final offensive—the 1975 Hồ Chí Minh Campaign—that overpowered ARVN defenders and culminated in the fall of Sài Gòn.

The PAVN was also responsible for the DRV's defense. PAVN regional and local forces, augmented by as many as two million civilian militia, stood guard against ground attack and staffed coastal defenses. The PAVN, with substantial technical assistance from the PRC and the USSR, operated what became the one of the world's heaviest air defense systems. A small PAVN naval contingent operated a few dozen small craft and devoted itself to coastal defense. Its most notable Vietnam War participation came during the 1964 Tonkin Gulf incidents. The PAVN's air branch grew steadily during the conflict, thanks to the influx of Soviet warplanes, but never assumed more than a limited defensive posture against the U.S. Air Force.

PAVN tactics were dictated by its various stages of engagement and ranged from guerrilla to big-unit conventional warfare. "Death Volunteer" units pressed the close-in battle against French strongpoints, especially at Điện Biên Phu, but against the Americans, all troops pressed in close. Such "hugging tactics" were intended to place PAVN troops too close for U.S. forces to risk using artillery for fear of killing their own personnel. These tactics achieved mixed success against U.S. forces but proved eminently effective against all but the most elite ARVN troops.

Training and combat cohesion were critical elements of PAVN success. Its conscripts were highly motivated and received nearly four months of basic training before reporting to their units for specific training requirements. In contrast to their counterparts in the South, PAVN NCOs and technical personnel received extensive military and political motivational training as well as technical instruction. The result was an army of conscripts led by a technically competent and highly motivated NCO corps. The officers corps received even more intensive training. All social and military activities centered around the unit, resulting in a tightly knit, intensely cohesive force. Additionally, all PAVN units contained military and political leaders of equal stature; military and political objectives were inseparable.

Logistics were key to PAVN success. Its units were weapons-intensive formations with few logistics and support personnel. Supplies were dispersed in hidden caches around likely operating areas and stockpiled near the objective well in advance of an offensive. When necessary, local labor was recruited or conscripted to haul supplies to new locations or units in the field. The deployment of regular forces to South Vietnam was preceded by logistics preparations along the deployment route. Construction of barracks and rest facilities along the Hô Chí Minh Trail began in 1965, and the PAVN ultimately constructed two fuel pipelines along the trail before it dispatched tanks to the South. By 1973 the bulk of PAVN supplies entered South Vietnam via the Hô Chí Minh Trail. Underground storage areas were built within PAVN sanctuaries in Cambodia and South Vietnam's A Shau Valley, from which supplies were then transported to caches deeper in South Vietnam. Sea and river transport was used whenever possible. Communist flag merchant ships also carried supplies to Cambodia's Sihanoukville (Kompong Som) for transport into South Vietnam. This was the most common delivery means for heavier materials before 1970, but Cambodia's entry into the war in 1972 cut this supply route. Supplies were also smuggled through Vietnam's coastal waters until 1975, although U.S. and RVN interdiction efforts proved increasingly successful.

Equipment was initially a PAVN weakness. Originally the small arms were of Japanese origin, but French small arms predominated in the regular infantry until 1960. Artillery and mortars initially came from surrendered French and Japanese stocks, but beginning in the early 1960s, they were gradually replaced by Soviet and Communist Chinese weapons. By 1965 PAVN divisions contained artillery regiments equipped with Soviet 122-mm guns and howitzers and a wide range of mortars (60- to 160-mm) and rocket launcher systems (120- to 130-mm). Small arms were standardized around Communist bloc models as numbers became available. The 7.62-mm SKS carbine and AK-47 assault rifle were the standard infantry weapons; the Soviet RPD light machine gun or its Chinese version provided the squad's automatic fire support element. Every platoon had Soviet-produced rocket propelled grenade launchers (RPG-7s) after 1965. These supplemented the battalion's 57-mm and 75-mm recoilless rifles. Soviet and U.S. heavy machine guns (12.7-mm and .50-caliber, respectively) could also be found in the battalion's heavy weapons company, but mortars were the primary heavy support weapon below division level.

Tanks were introduced in the 1950s. Captured French and Japanese models were discarded after 1954 and were replaced in limited quantities by Chinese and Soviet light and medium tanks. The PT76, the first tank the PAVN deployed southward, was relatively easy to infiltrate into South Vietnam because its light weight and amphibious capabilities enabled it to cross rivers and use all but the most primitive roads. The heavier and more powerful T54 medium tank was not deployed until after the Hô Chí Minh Trail was

improved in 1968. Organized into independent battalions, tanks were deployed against key objectives and astride critical lines of communications. The movement of its armored units signified PAVN intentions after 1970. Since the DRV did not produce its own tanks, these almost irreplaceable weapons were held in reserve for decisive battles. During the 1972 Spring Offensive, the PAVN used T54s for the first time, at Đông Hà, but PAVN commanders seemed not to grasp the importance of combined armor-infantry tactics. Several tanks moved forward to attack without infantry support and were destroyed easily by ARVN M72s. Heavy losses in the failed offensive temporarily halted offensive operations until more tanks could be acquired. The PAVN employed nearly 400 medium tanks in the vanguard of the final offensive that conquered Sài Gòn in 1975, marking the PAVN's successful transition to a highly trained mechanized infantry force.

The PAVN was Gen. Giáp's creation. Its tactics, strategy, and organizational structure all emanated from his genius. His protégés and assistants served him well, if not perfectly. Gen. Nguyên Chí Thanh ably commanded the PLAF and the war effort in the South from 1965 until his death in 1967. But he and Giáp grossly overestimated the South Vietnamese people's desire for "revolution," and his forces suffered accordingly. The 1968 Tết Offensive was a major military disaster, but it paid unexpected political dividends. Giáp and his generals learned from their mistakes and modified their tactics to minimize exposure to U.S. firepower. Few can fault Senior Gen. Van Tiên Dung's 1975 drive on Sài Gòn. More significantly, PAVN military strategy was integrated with that of their political leaders and diplomats. Thus, the DRV's military and diplomatic activities were mutually supporting, something that their opponents never achieved during either the Indo-China or Vietnam War. The PAVN could also rely on the excellent Communist support system that provided food, labor, and military intelligence.

At war's end in 1975, the PAVN numbered nearly a million troops, despite losses of 1.1 million Communist fighters killed between 1954 and 1975—a figure that includes both Viêt Công guerrillas in South Vietnam and PAVN personnel. PLAF formations were either disbanded or absorbed by the PAVN, but the fighting was far from over. In 1978 the PAVN invaded Cambodia, which it occupied until 1989. In response to this, PRC forces attacked into northern Vietnam in early 1979 but withdrew after intense resistance from PAVN regular and regional forces. By the mid-1980s, the PAVN represented the world's third largest standing army, trailing only the PRC and the USSR. Severe economic conditions and the loss of Soviet aid prompted dramatic force reductions, but the PAVN remains a formidable armed force.

—Carl O. Schuster and David Coffey

References: Lanning, Michael L., and Dan Cragg. *Inside the VC and the NVA.* (1992); Miller, David. "Giap's Army" (1976); Pike, Douglas. *The People's Army of Vietnam* (1986); Terzani, Tiziano. *Giai Phong: The Fall and Liberation of Saigon* (1976); Vô Nguyên Giáp. *Big Victory, Great Task* (1968).

See also: Communist Party of Vietnam (CPV); COSVN (Central Office for South Vietnam or Trung Uong Cuc Miên Nam); Đâu

Tranh; Điên Biên Phu, Battle of; Easter Offensive (Nguyên Huê Campaign); Hô Chí Minh Campaign; Hô Chí Minh Trail; Indo-China War; Khe Sanh, Battles of; Lê Duân; Nguyên Chí Thanh; Order of Battle; Sino-Vietnamese War; Têt Offensive: Overall Strategy; Têt Offensive: the Sài Gòn Circle; Tonkin Gulf Incidents; Van Tiên Dung; Vietnamese Invasion and Occupation of Cambodia; Vô Nguyên Giáp.

Vietnam, Republic of: 1954–1975

The 1954 Geneva Conference ending the Indo-China War temporarily divided Vietnam at the 17th parallel. The Viêt Minh regrouped into the North where Hô Chí Minh's Democratic Republic of Vietnam (DRV) held sway. The State of Vietnam, headed by Emperor Bao Đai, dominated the South. A Demilitarized Zone (DMZ) separated the two. National elections to reunify the country were to be held in 1956.

Bao Đai, then living in France, called on nationalist and Catholic leader Ngô Đình Diêm to head a government. Bao Đai needed Diêm's support and that of his brother Ngô Đình Nhu, who had set up the influential Front for National Salvation in Sài Gòn as an alternative to the Viêt Minh. Believing that Washington backed Diêm, Bao Đai on 18 June 1954 appointed him as prime minister. Diêm returned to Sài Gòn on 26 June, and on 7 July officially formed his new government, which technically embraced all Vietnam.

The United States did back Diêm and supplied increasing amounts of aid to his government, the power base of which was quite narrow: Catholics, the landed gentry, and fervent anti-Communist nationalists. Many rich and powerful and Francophiles opposed him, as did most of the nationalist parties and religious sects. Many observers believed that Diêm would not last long in power, but he proved to be an adroit political manipulator. Certainly a key in this was Washington's decision, effective in October 1954, to channel all aid directly to his government, thus undercutting remaining French authority in the South. At the same time, Washington pressured Paris to withdraw its remaining forces, and the last left in April 1956. U.S. officers, meanwhile, arrived to train South Vietnamese armed forces. This angered Army commander Gen. Nguyên Van Hinh, a naturalized Frenchman, and led to a test of wills between him and Diêm that ended when Washington sent Gen. J. Lawton Collins to South Vietnam as special ambassador. He informed Sài Gòn officials that Washington would deal only with Diêm. Hinh went into exile in France.

Internationally the United States supported Diêm by taking the lead in the September 1954 creation of the Southeast Asia Treaty Organization (SEATO), which extended protection to South Vietnam. President Eisenhower sent high-ranking U.S. officals, including Secretary of State John Foster Dulles and Vice-President Richard Nixon, to Vietnam. In May 1957, Diêm addressed a joint session of the U.S. Congress.

Meanwhile Diêm moved quickly to consolidate power in South Vietnam. By this time several opposition groups, including the Cao Đài and Hòa Hao religious sects and the Đai Viêt Party, were carrying out armed resistance to the government. In 1955, Diêm defeated the Bình Xuyên, Sài Gòn–based gangsters who had their own well-organized militia, and moved against the Cao Đài and the Hòa Hao, which also had armed support.

In 1955 Diêm defied an effort by Bao Đai to remove him from office. He turned the tables by calling for a referendum in which the people would choose between them. Diêm would easily have won any honest contest, but he ignored appeals of U.S. officials and falsified the results so that the announced vote was 98.2 percent in his favor. On 26 October 1955, using the results of the referendum as justification, Diêm proclaimed the Republic of Vietnam (RVN) with himself as president. Washington recognized him in this position, and its aid was vital in his growing strength. From 1955 to 1966, Washington provided economic assistance totaling almost $2 billion, not including military equipment. Such aid enabled Diêm to reject talks with Hà Nôi over the elections called for by the Geneva Accords, which the Viêt Minh, confident of electoral victory, so ardently sought.

Diêm put perhaps three-quarters of U.S. assistance into the military budget and the remainder into the bureaucracy and transportation. Only modest amounts were set aside for education, health, housing, and community development. Most nonmilitary aid stayed in the cities, which held only a minority of the population. U.S. financial assistance freed Diêm from implementing economic reforms or income taxes that would have brought real reform and benefits to the impoverished classes. Diêm was out of touch with the peasants in the countryside and did little to carry out much-needed land reform. In 1961, 75 percent of the land was owned by 15 percent of the population; by 1962, less than a quarter of the acreage eligible for expropriation and purchase had been transferred to the peasants. Between 1955 and 1960, less than 2 percent of U.S. aid to Sài Gòn went toward agrarian reform.

In 1956 Diêm launched his Tô Công (denunciation of Communists) campaign to locate arms caches in the South and arrest hundreds of those in Viêt Minh political cadres who had remained in the South to prepare for the planned national elections, a violation of the Geneva Agreements. In part, this campaign was in retaliation for DRV policies regarding landowners and opposition leaders. Diêm imprisoned many non-Communist patriots, and he estranged South Vietnam's ethnic minorities. His effort to impose Vietnamese culture on the Montagnards reversed longstanding French policy. The Montagnards also suffered heavily in Diêm's efforts to relocate rural populations into government-controlled areas in the Strategic Hamlet program, leading dissident Montagnards to form the ethnonationalistic FULRO (Le Front Unifié de Lutte des Races Opprimées, or United Struggle Front for Oppressed Races) movement.

Diêm refused to enter into economic talks with the DRV or to hold the elections called for in the Geneva Accords. He announced that his government was not a party to the agreements and thus was not bound by them, and the U.S. government supported Diêm in that stand. Both Washington and Sài Gòn claimed that no elections could be held until there was a democratic government in Hà Nôi, although this was not a part of the 1954 agreements.

On 4 March 1956, the South Vietnamese elected a 123-member national legislative assembly. A new constitution, heavily weighted toward control by the executive, went into effect on 26 October 1956. The country was divided into 41 provinces, which were subdivided into districts and villages. These apparent reforms were largely a sham, as Diêm increasingly subjected the South to authoritarian rule and completely dominated the National Assembly. The government was also highly centralized. The central administration appointed officials, even at the local level. Diêm oversaw administrative appointees, and most province chiefs were military officers loyal to him. The Catholic Diêm installed Catholics in key positions; other posts went to his supporters and friends. Political loyalty rather than ability was the test for leadership positions, both government and military. Aloof and arrogant, Diêm proved an adroit practitioner of the divide-and-rule concept. He rarely sought advice beyond his immediate family circle; perhaps his closest advisor was his older brother, Bishop Ngô Đình Thuc. Diêm also delegated authority to his brother Ngô Đình Nhu, who controlled the secret police and was the organizer of the Personalist Labor Party (Cân Lao Party).

By 1960, opposition to Diêm was growing within South Vietnam. In April 1960, 18 prominent South Vietnamese issued a manifesto protesting governmental abuses and were promptly arrested. On 11–12 November 1960, there was a near-coup when paratroop units surrounded the presidential palace and demanded that Diêm purge his administration of certain individuals, including Nhu. Diêm outmaneuvered the protesters, but clearly time was running out for his regime. In another coup attempt, on 27 February 1962, two Vietnamese Air Force pilots tried to kill Diêm and Nhu by bombing and strafing the presidential palace. Diêm's political opponents disappeared or languished in prison camps. Then in December 1960, the National Liberation Front for South Vietnam was officially established with Hà Nôi's blessing. It came to be completely dominated by the Lao Đông Party (the renamed Communist Party) Central Committee of the Democratic Republic of Vietnam.

Washington was now having second thoughts about Diêm. When John F. Kennedy took office, he demanded that Diêm institute domestic reforms. But there seemed to be no alternative to Diêm's rule, and Kennedy expanded the U.S. Special Forces presence in that country. In May 1961, Kennedy sent Vice-President Johnson to the RVN on a fact-finding mission. Although Johnson had private reservations concerning Diêm, he publicly hailed him as the "Winston Churchill of Southeast Asia." Less than a week after Johnson's return, Kennedy agreed to increase the size of Army of the Republic of Vietnam (ARVN) from 170,000 to 270,000 men. These troops tended to be poorly trained in guerrilla warfare, indifferently led, and inadequately provided for.

With the ARVN generally performing poorly in the field, in 1962 Washington dramatically increased the U.S. military presence in the RVN. Only belatedly did U.S. officials seek to address problems through a counterinsurgency program. In 1961, with strong U.S. backing, Diêm began the Strategic Hamlet program to forcibly resettle peasants into new fenced and armed compounds. Riddled with corruption, the program was a vast and expensive failure and soon alienated much of the peasantry from the regime.

Madame Ngô Đình Nhu, who acted as the first lady of the state (Diêm was celibate), embarked on her own bizarre puritanical campaign. The harsh punishments for violations of these new rules further antagonized elements of the population.

In January 1963, the ARVN suffered a stinging military defeat in the Battle of Ấp Bac. That summer, Buddhist protests and rallies became more frequent and intense. On 8 May in Huê, where thousands demonstrated against a ban imposed on flying their multicolored flag, riot police killed nine demonstrators, leading to Buddhist demonstrations throughout the country. In June, elderly Buddhist monk Thích Quang Đuc publicly burned himself alive in protest. By November, six more monks had emulated Thích Quang Đuc. Madame Nhu exacerbated the crisis by referring to these self-immolations as "barbecues."

Many Americans came to believe that Diêm should be ousted. Nhu was particularly embarrassing to Washington. In August, Henry Cabot Lodge replaced Frederick Nolting as U.S. ambassador to Sài Gòn. The U.S. Central Intelligence Agency (CIA) had already reported that an influential faction of South Vietnamese generals wanted to overthrow Diêm. Lodge gave this new credence. Washington was initially opposed to a coup, preferring that Diêm purge his entourage, especially the Nhus. But it was clear that to insist on this would alert Nhu and probably result in a bloodbath, since Nhu had troops loyal to him in the capital. At the end of August, Washington assured the generals of its support and President Kennedy publicly criticized Diêm. Following some of the worst government outrages against the Buddhists, on 2 October Washington suspended economic subsidies for RVN commercial imports, froze loans for developmental projects, and cut off financial support of Nhu's 2,000-man Vietnamese Special Forces. This action was a clear signal to the dissidents. Shortly after midnight on 1 November 1963, Major Generals Duong Van Minh, Tôn Thât Đính, and Trân Van Đôn began a takeover of power. In the coup, both Diêm and Nhu, whom Washington assumed would be given safe passage out of the country, were murdered.

Diêm's death began a period of political instability in the RVN government. No subsequent leader of the RVN had his air of legitimacy or as much respect from the general public. U.S. leaders, who had seen in Diêm a nationalist alternative to Hô Chí Minh and means to stop Communist expansion, soon found themselves taking direct control of the war in Vietnam. The United States, which could not win the war with Diêm, also could not win the war without him.

Diêm was followed by a military junta led by Gen. Duong Van Minh as chief of state. No more responsive to the people of South Vietnam, the new regime brought political instability as members of the new 12-member Military Revolutionary Council fell to quarreling among themselves. Minh, the nominal leader, showed no inclination to govern, preferring to pursie his hobbies. On 30 January 1964 came another coup, this time against Minh, led by 37-year-old Maj. Gen. Nguyên Khánh. U.S. officials, caught by surprise, promptly hailed Khánh as the new leader, but Khánh showed no more aptitude for governing than had Minh. Khánh's own history of changing sides hardly engendered trust.

Khánh purged some generals but allowed Minh to remain on as titular head of state. Militant Buddhists, alarmed that Khánh's victory might lead to a return to power of Catholics and those faithful to Diêm, agreed to form a political alliance. Many ARVN officers turned against Khánh for his attempt to try rival Generals Trân Van Đôn and Lê Van Kim on fabricated charges. Khánh sought to resurrect the Đai Viêt Quôc Gia Liên Minh nationalist party and manipulate it to his advantage, but when it was clear that the Đai Viêt was hopelessly splintered, Khánh named himself as premier with Hoàn as his deputy. Hoàn then began to conspire with the Buddhists and other opposition groups against Khánh. Political instability in the RVN was now rampant, with seven changes of government in 1964. As RVN governments rose and fell, Americans became alarmed by the possibility that one of them might enter into accommodation with the Communists.

Hà Nôi, meanwhile, followed the political instability in the South with keen interest. At the end of 1963, the DRV leadership decided that the time was ripe to escalate sharply its support for the war in the South. In a major shift in policy requiring considerable economic sacrifices, the DRV decided to send native Northerners south to fight, to introduce the latest models of Communist small arms, and to authorize direct attacks against Americans in the South.

The war was escalating. In March 1964, Secretary of Defense Robert McNamara visited the RVN and vowed U.S. support for Khánh. On his return to the United States, McNamara publicly pronounced improvement in the RVN, but privately he told President Johnson that conditions had deteriorated since his last visit there and that 40 percent of the countryside was now under Viêt Công (VC) control or influence. Washington agreed to furnish Khánh with additional aid. But although more than $2 million a day was arriving in the country, little of it went to public works projects or reached the peasants. Khánh, despite promises to McNamara to put the country on "a war footing," steadfastly refused to do so, fearful of antagonizing wealthy and middle-class city dwellers whose sons would be inducted into the army.

By summer 1964 Khánh was pleading for major action against the DRV as a distraction from his domestic political difficulties. In August 1964 came the Tonkin Gulf incidents, with the U.S. Congress giving President Johnson special powers to wage war in Southeast Asia. U.S. air strikes following the Tonkin Gulf incidents seem to have energized Khánh. He announced a state of emergency, imposed censorship and other controls, and hastily put together a new constitution for the RVN, promoting himself to the presidency and dismissing Minh. Sài Gòn responded with protests. In August, students took to the streets and were soon joined by Buddhists. Khánh met with Buddhist leaders but revealed his real

strength by telling them that he would discuss their complaints with U.S. Ambassador Maxwell Taylor. Taylor in turn urged Khánh not to yield to minority pressure. On 25 August, when thousands of demonstrators gathered outside his office to demand his resignation, Khánh appeared before them and announced he did not plan to establish a dictatorship. That afternoon, however, he quit, and the Military Revolutionary Council met to choose a new head of state.

After lengthy political maneuvering, a triumvirate emerged of Generals Khánh, Minh, and Trân Thiên Khiêm. Khánh retained the premiership, but flew off to Đà Lat as chaos took over in the capital. Order was restored only after two days of rioting. Turbulence continued as the government was threatened by dissident army units in the Mekong Delta and militant Buddhists from Huê. Buddhist demands had grown to include a veto over government decisions. In November there were new riots in Sài Gòn protesting Khánh's rule, and Taylor urged him to leave the country. By this time, a faction of younger military officers had come to the fore. Known as the "Young Turks," they were headed by Nguyên Cao Ky, one of the younger officers in the coup against Diêm, who had been promoted to major general and given charge of the Republic of Vietnam Air Force (VNAF). The faction also included army Maj. Gen. Nguyên Van Thiêu. Disillusioned by the ineffective national government, in mid-December 1964 the Young Turks overthrew the Military Revolutionary Council of older officers.

In late January 1965, a new Armed Forces Council decided that Premier Trân Van Huong should be ousted. Khánh replaced him as premier, but in February, Gen. Lâm Van Phát ousted Khánh. On 17 February, Dr. Phan Huy Quát became premier with Phan Khac Suu as chief of state. Quát, a physician with considerable governmental experience, appointed a broadly representative cabinet. The Armed Forces Council also announced the formation of a 20-member National Legislative Council. That same month, after Communist attacks that specifically targeted U.S. military personnel, President Johnson authorized retaliatory bombings of the DRV. Operation ROLLING THUNDER, the sustained bombing of North Vietnam, began on 24 February.

On 11 June 1965, the RVN government collapsed and the Armed Forces Council chose a military government with Ky as premier and Nguyên Van Thiêu in the relatively powerless position of chief of state. It was the ninth government in less than two years. Ky took steps to strengthen the armed forces and instituted needed land reforms, school and hospital construction, price controls, and a much-touted campaign to remove corrupt officials. At the same time, however, Ky instituted unpopular repressive actions, including a newspaper ban.

In the meantime, U.S. Marine battalions—the first U.S. combat troops—had arrived in South Vietnam in March 1965 to defend the Đà Nang airfield. U.S. Army divisions soon followed; by the end of 1965, nearly 200,000 U.S. military personnel were in South Vietnam.

The new government was soon embroiled in controversy with the Buddhists and powerful ARVN I Corps commander

Gen. Nguyên Chánh Thi, one of the members of the ten-member National Leadership Committee; the other nine members sought to remove him from his post. In March 1966, workers in Đà Nang began a general strike, and Buddhist students in Huê also began protests. Soon Thi's removal was no longer the central issue as Buddhist leaders pushed for a complete change of government. Growing sympathy for the movement was evident among the civil service and many ARVN units, in early April Ky announced that the Communists had "taken over" in Đà Nang. In fact, it is unclear what role, if any, they played.

On 10 April, Ky appointed Gen. Tôn Thât Đính as the new commander of I Corps, but Đính could not assert his authority with Thi still in Huê. After a significant military operation to suppress the Buddhists and rebel ARVN units, Thi accepted his dismissal on 24 May. Tensions eased with Buddhist leaders when Ky agreed to dissolve the junta and hold elections for an assembly with constituent powers. In June, supported by U.S. forces, Ky's troops ended opposition in Huê.

Ky's popularity and political clout had also been enhanced by a February 1966 meeting with President Johnson in Hawaii. The two delegations agreed on the need for social and economic reforms in the RVN and national elections. In May a government decree set up a committee to draft election laws and procedures. In September 1966, a 117-member constituent assembly was elected to draft a constitution, which was completed in March 1967. The new constitution provided for a president who had wide powers and a premier and cabinet responsible to a bicameral legislature (the new upper house was commonly referred to as the Senate) with strengthened authority. The judiciary was also to be coequal to the executive and legislative branches. The president would serve a four-year term and could stand for reelection once. The president still had command of the armed forces and the ability to promulgate laws and initiate legislation. The two-house legislature was to be chosen by universal suffrage and secret ballot.

Local elections were held in May 1967, with elections for the Lower House in October. The constitution allowed for political parties but specifically forbade those promoting Communism "in any form." The complex electoral law involved the use of ten-member lists, and voters in 1967 had to choose from 48 such slates, a process that favored well-organized voting blocks.

Tensions were high between Ky and Thiêu, who soon openly vied for control of the government. Although the more senior Thiêu had stepped aside in 1965 to allow Ky to take the premier's post, his determination to challenge Ky for the highest office in the 3 September 1967 elections led the Armed Forces Council to force the two men onto a joint ticket, giving the presidential nomination to Thiêu and the vice-presidential nomination to Ky simply on the basis of military seniority. The Thiêu-Ky ticket won the election with only 34.8 percent of the vote; the remaining vote was split among ten other slates.

Thiêu gradually consolidated power and ruled in authoritarian fashion. He was, however, more responsive to the Buddhists, Montagnards, and peasants. He arranged for distribution of land to 50,000 families, and by 1968 he had secured passage of laws that froze rents and forbade landowners from evicting tenants. Thiêu also restored local elections. By 1969, 95 percent of villages under RVN control had elected chiefs and councils. Village chiefs also received control over the local Popular Forces and some central government financial support. On 26 March 1971, Thiêu presented land to 20,000 people in accordance with the Land-to-Tiller Act, which turned over land to those who worked it. This reduced tenancy to only 7 percent. The government took responsibility to compensate former landowners for the confiscated land.

After American forces began to withdraw in 1969, Thiêu was faced with the challenge of replacing U.S. military units. In 1970 he mobilized high school and colleges students for the war effort, bringing considerable opposition that in turn led to arrests and trials. Increased draft calls taxes produced a surge of support for the Communists. In 1971 Thiêu pushed through a new election law that had the practical effect of disqualifying his major opponents, Ky and Minh. It required that candidates obtain the support of at least 40 national assembly members or 100 provincial/municipal councilors. Opposition groups argued that the purpose of the new law was to exclude them from political power. The Senate rejected the law, but it was reinstated by the Lower House, the result of bribery and intimidation. Although the Supreme Court ruled that Ky might run, he chose not to do so; Minh also dropped out. Thiêu's reelection in October 1971 made one-man rule a reality and did serious injury to the RVN government's image abroad.

In October 1972, Thiêu torpedoed the agreement negotiated in Paris by the DRV and the United States. Following massive bombing of the North, in January 1973 Hà Nôi and Washington then concluded a new agreement, which was this time imposed on Sài Gòn. The last U.S. combat troops left South Vietnam at the end of March. Vietnamization imposed severe hardships on the RVN. Although the United States turned over massive amounts of equipment to the RVN, Congress curtailed funding, severely reducing the ability of South Vietnamese forces to fight the high-technology war for which they had been trained.

In January 1974, Thiêu announced the renewal of the war. In August, under increasing pressure over Watergate and his handling of the war, Richard Nixon resigned the presidency and the RVN lost its most ardent supporter. In January 1975, the Communists began a major offensive in the Central Highlands. Thiêu's response to this was at best poor, and his precipitous abandonment of the Central Highlands was a disaster. Ky later charged that Thiêu turned a tactical withdrawal into a rout that led to the eventual disintegration of the entire RVN military. ARVN resistance collapsed, and with Communist forces closing in the capital, on 25 April Thiêu departed the country for Taiwan. Three days later, Vice-President Trân Van Huong transferred authority as chief of state to Gen. Minh. On 30 April, Communist forces captured Sài Gòn. Minh formally surrendered to Col. Bùi

Tín, the highest officer of the Communist forces. The Communists now occupied Độc Lâp Palace, and the Republic of Vietnam came to an end.

—Spencer C. Tucker

References: Herring, George C. *America's Longest War: The United States and Vietnam, 1950–1975.* 2d ed. (1986); Karnow, Stanley. *Vietnam: A History* (1983); Spector, Ronald H. *Advice and Support: The Early Years, 1941–1960. The U.S. Army in Vietnam* (1983).

See also: Bao Đai; Bình Xuyên; Cao Đài; Caravelle Group; Đai Việt Quôc Dân Đang (National Party of Greater Vietnam); Dulles, John Foster; Duong Van Minh; Eisenhower, Dwight David; Elections (National), Republic of Vietnam: 1955, 1967, 1971; FULRO (Le Front Unifié de Lutte des Races Opprimées); Hòa Hao; Honolulu Conference; Johnson, Lyndon Baines; Kennedy, John Fitzgerald; Lodge, Henry Cabot, Jr.; McNamara, Robert S.; Military Revolutionary Council; National Assembly Law 10/59; Ngô Đình Diêm; Ngô Đình Diêm, Overthrow of; Ngô Đình Nhu; Nguyên Chánh Thi; Nguyên Khánh; Nguyên Van Hinh; Nguyên Van Thiêu; Nixon, Richard Milhous; Nolting, Frederick, Jr.; Phan Khac Suu; ROLLING THUNDER, Operation; Strategic Hamlet Program; Taylor, Maxwell Davenport; Territorial Forces; Thích Quang Đuc; Tôn Thât Đính; Tonkin Gulf Incidents; Trân Thiên Khiêm; Trân Van Đôn; Trân Van Huong; United States: Special Forces.

Vietnam, Republic of: Air Force (VNAF)

Despite its own efforts and the support of its sponsors, the Republic of Vietnam Air Force (VNAF) (1955–1975) failed to develop into an independent, war-winning organization.

Before 1964, the VNAF was a small and neglected organization. It received its first consignment of American-built aircraft from France in the summer of 1955, including 28 F-8F fighter-bombers, 35 C-47 transport aircraft, and 60 L-19 reconnaissance aircraft. Three years later, the United States replaced the already obsolescent F-8F with a combat version of the propeller-driven T-28 trainer. The American AD-6 fighter-bomber subsequently complemented the T-28, and by the end of 1962 the VNAF had one squadron each of AD-6s and T-28A/Bs, three L-19 liaison squadrons of 15 aircraft each, and several C-47s. These aircraft performed tactical infantry support missions that included airlift operations, artillery spotting, close air support (CAS), interdiction, medical evacuation, and reconnaissance.

The VNAF performed badly before 1964 for several reasons. First, there were less than a dozen fully qualified flight leaders in the Air Force. Unmotivated and unreliable, they showed an obvious distaste for night combat, all-weather operations, and deployments away from the comforts of home. Second, the Vietnamese had an unresponsive command and control system. Before a pilot could attack a ground target, he had to get permission from the province chief, regional commander, Joint General Staff, and perhaps even President Ngô Đình Diêm himself. The government's fear of civilian casualties made real-time tactical air support against fast-moving guerrilla units almost impossible. Third, ground commanders did not appreciate the value of air power, even in unconventional warfare. They seldom asked the VNAF to protect ground convoys, escort helicopter assault

operations, or fly more CAS and interdiction missions on their behalf. Finally, logistics and maintenance support remained a chronic problem. There were too many missions for the number of aircraft available, and it remained an open question whether the relatively untrained Vietnamese pilots, flying only in daylight and with broken instruments, had any idea of how to combat their foe.

With the upsurge of Viêt Công activity in 1963 and 1964 and the introduction of North Vietnamese regulars into combat in 1965, the VNAF expanded in size and responsibilities. In 1964 it had 8,400 men and 190 aircraft as well as 248 helicopters and 140 aircraft on loan from the United States, although there were restrictions on their use. During the same year, the durable A-1 "Skyhawk" replaced the increasingly ineffectual T-28. By 1965 the South Vietnamese had 150 A-1s, which quickly became the backbone of the VNAF. By 1968 the VNAF had 16,000 men, 398 aircraft (including the A-37 "Dragonfly" and C-130 "Hercules"), and its first squadron of compact F-5 "Freedom Fighter" jets.

With increased size came more responsibilities. Although the United States and Republic of Vietnam first conducted joint air operations in December 1961, they became a formal requirement in Operation ROLLING THUNDER (1965–1968). In February 1965, Washington and Sài Gòn agreed to conduct a limited bombing campaign against the Democratic Republic of Vietnam (DRV), starting with inconsequential targets below the 19th parallel. The Johnson administration hoped that a limited air campaign would convince the DRV to stop aiding and abetting guerrilla campaigns in Laos and the Republic of Vietnam. The campaign began on 2 March 1965 when 104 American aircraft attacked DRV targets while 19 South Vietnamese fighter-bombers struck the naval facilities at Quân Khê. This initial strike began a limited but significant contribution by the VNAF to ROLLING THUNDER. The VNAF provided a minimum of three strike/reconnaissance missions for each of the on again–off again periods of the campaign. The contribution would have been larger if not for the growing number of missions required in the South. By mid-1968 the VNAF was responsible for 25 percent of all combat sorties flown within its borders.

Thus from 1964 to 1968, the role of the VNAF did grow, but the organization still had problems. Although the VNAF had 550 pilots by 1967, finding qualified, English-speaking recruits remained a problem. High accident rates only aggravated existing repair and maintenance problems, particularly because the VNAF relied on the army for most of its supplies. The command and control system had simplified, but now Air Force units responded only to orders from VNAF Headquarters in Sài Gòn. Because U.S. units had their own equipment to replenish, the Vietnamese remained woefully short of new and improved helicopters and aircraft. As a result of these problems, VNAF performance was irregular during the climactic 1968 Têt Offensive.

With Vietnamization came Project ENHANCE, a crash program by the United States to provide the VNAF enough resources to fight by itself. From a numerical standpoint, the results were impressive. By the time of U.S. withdrawal in

1972, the VNAF had a $542.8 million budget, 49,454 personnel, 39 operational squadrons (including 16 fighter/fighter-bomber units), and 27 squadrons either in training or scheduled for activation. Nevertheless, when the final DRV offensive came against the South in 1975, much of the VNAF simply melted away. The reasons for its failure were fourfold. First, even after 20 years, the Air Force's supply system remained chaotic and unreliable. Second, in 1974 and 1975 the U.S. Congress tightened its purse strings, leaving the VNAF to scramble for critical spare parts and fuel. Third, North Vietnamese units introduced hand-held SA-7 surface-to-air missiles in the South, making CAS, airmobile, and interdiction missions more hazardous and significantly less effective. Finally, the United States built up the VNAF only with low-performance, short-range aircraft that had no electronic warfare equipment or sophisticated fire-control systems. These aircraft were ideal for low-intensity warfare, but not for the largely conventional war that they then faced.

—Peter R. Faber

References: Clarke, Jeffrey J. *Advice and Support: The Final Years, 1965–1973* (1988); Futrell, Robert F. *The United States Air Force in Southeast Asia: The Advisory Years to 1965* (1981).

See also: Airplanes, Allied and Democratic Republic of Vietnam; Air Power, Role in War; Hồ Chí Minh Campaign; Ngô Đình Diêm; Order of Battle; ROLLING THUNDER, Operation; Vietnamization.

Vietnam, Republic of: Army (ARVN)

Successor to the French-led Vietnamese National Army (VNA) of the Indo-China War, the Army of the Republic of Vietnam (ARVN) grew from an initial VNA strength of 150,000 in 1950 to nearly one million troops at the time of its collapse in 1975. Suffering from corruption, poor leadership, and low morale throughout its existence, the ARVN never achieved the mobility and combat cohesion required to counter its better-motivated Viêt Công (VC) and People's Army of Vietnam (PAVN) opponents. As a result, it suffered defeats in most of its engagements against the VC and could defeat PAVN units only when supported by massive U.S. firepower. Still, many of its best units were outstanding, proving the military maxim that well-led and well-trained troops will nearly always perform effectively in combat. Unfortunately for the Republic of Vietnam (RVN), its army as a whole enjoyed neither effective leadership nor thorough training.

ARVN traced its roots to November 1949, when the French government and Vietnamese Emperor Bao Đai signed a formal agreement to establish a Vietnamese National Army to resist the Communist-dominated Viêt Minh, who were fighting to drive the French from Indo-China. Recruitment was slow; few Vietnamese recognized Bao Đai's authority, and most were ambivalent about his government, which they believed was controlled by the French. Another inhibiting factor for the Vietnamese was the degree of French control over the VNA; most of its early combat formations were led by French officers and noncommissioned officers (NCOs). Weapons and transportation assets given to the VNA were obsolete and in poor condition, not a policy upon which to build an effective army.

The French had established a training school system, so the initial development of a professional NCO corps and technical services had begun, but the French took the instructors and most of the technicians with them when they left Indo-China. Their departure left the State of Vietnam with an army of four indifferently trained divisions and an inexperienced NCO corps led by a small and generally corrupt cadre of Vietnamese officers. Plans to raise three more divisions by 1958 were scrapped.

The Americans took over upon the French departure. Their combat tactics, doctrine, and philosophy were radically different from those of the French. Whereas the French had preferred to await developments and then maneuver to force their enemy to attack, the Americans preached a more aggressive, firepower-based approach to war, with material superiority and logistics the key. The Americans did not alter the French-based training school system, but worked to model the ARVN after the U.S. Army and in the process generously provided weapons and advisors. The initial training of the troops and NCOs was left as before, and provision of unit transport was considered a Vietnamese government responsibility. The result was an army in which the units had good firepower and were well advised, but lacked the mobility, command, and control to employ their equipment effectively.

The ARVN's most debilitating deficiency, however, was the pervasive corruption—much of it due to the Diêm's government's promotion system—that infected the ARVN leadership and handicapped its logistics structure. Senior leadership positions were awarded on the basis of social position and loyalty to the regime rather than integrity and ability, resulting in a force composed of more than 60 percent Buddhists led by a senior officer corps that was almost entirely Catholic. Corruption's most serious impact was on the logistics and technical services, where senior officers operated their units to their own personal financial benefit. These officers achieved and retained their positions not by providing efficient support to units in the field, but by sharing their "bounty" with superiors and sponsors. Combat leaders also overreported their units' strength and pocketed the surplus pay. ARVN soldiers were poorly paid and had to buy their own rations. Given that a private's pay in 1964 barely bought a month's rice, it is no wonder that pilferage and looting was endemic to the Army. Despite much progress under the Vietnamization program, corruption was never eliminated.

The ARVN's last ten years were marked by an intensive U.S. training program concentrated on junior officers and NCOs. Units that performed well in operations received newer equipment and training. Helicopters were provided to decrease dependence on roads. Logistics and technical service units also received greater training and emphasis. Unfortunately, this had two negative effects: It exacerbated divisions within the officer ranks and caused the ARVN to become dependent upon U.S. support.

At its peak, ARVN numbered nearly one million troops organized into three echelons. The first and best were the 450,000 troops of the regular army, organized in formations of thirteen divisions, seven Ranger groups, and various independent elite battalions and regiments. Nearly 200,000 regulars were also assigned to support units. ARVN's second echelon was its Regional Forces. These were assigned to the Military Region Commanders, of which there were four. The third echelon was made up of the Popular Forces, the ARVN's least trained and equipped units. In rural areas they came under the control of village councils and provided security for particular villages. They also provided security for cities, installations, and key provincial facilities. Regional and Popular Forces (known to American GIs as the "Ruff-Puffs") totaled nearly 525,000 troops. The Civilian Irregular Defense Group (CIDG) rounded out the Vietnamese armed forces. Not part of the ARVN, they were part-time soldiers who defended their villages and towns or augmented the Popular and Regional Forces in doing so.

In 1975 most Vietnamese and senior American leadership took an optimistic view of the ARVN. It had seemingly stood up well against the PAVN 1972 Easter Offensive. The ARVN's almost desperate reliance on American air power in that offensive was overlooked. As PAVN pressure built in the spring of 1975, President Thiêu's intended strategic realignment of his forces seemed a simple expedient to halt what appeared to be a limited PAVN offensive in the Central Highlands. However, following the French tradition in which they had been trained, neither Thiêu nor his staff, corps, and division commanders involved had studied the ground or roads over which the units would move. Thus, as refugees and overloaded military vehicles crammed onto the overloaded road system, units became bunched up. Many officers simply left their units. PAVN forces had only to press their attack and unit cohesion broke down. Only elite Ranger and Airborne units stood their ground, paying a heavy price in the process. Seven regular ARVN divisions melted away. Despite much desperate rallying and troop movements, the situation could not be saved.

The ARVN never had the consistent leadership and direction required in an effective combat force. Regular ARVN units suffered from uneven leadership at the junior officer and NCO level as the best junior NCO and officer leadership was siphoned off into elite units used as "fire brigades" to shore up battered positions or hold key locations and terrain. This was exacerbated by failings in the senior leadership. Generally troops were squandered in wasteful tactics or ineffective deployments. Although the ARVN had an abysmal reputation with its opponents and allies, it would be unfair to characterize it as a uniformly poor army. Its units stood alone for two years against a better-equipped, better-trained, and more highly motivated force. Its better performances and sacrifices are often overlooked in its overall defeat.

—Carl O. Schuster

References: Davidson, Phillip B. *Vietnam at War: The History, 1946–1975* (1988); Momeyer, William W. *Airpower in Three Wars* (1978); Ngo Quang Truong. *The Easter Offensive of 1972* (1980); Pike, Douglas. *PAVN: People's Army of Vietnam* (1986).

See also: Civilian Irregular Defense Group (CIDG); Ngô Đình Diêm; Nguyên Van Thiêu; Order of Battle; Territorial Forces;

Vietnamization; Vietnam, Republic of: Marine Corps (VNMC); Vietnam, Republic of: Special Forces (Luc Luong Đac Biêt [LLDB]).

Vietnam, Republic of: Commandos

South Vietnamese military formations that entered North Vietnam (1961–1968) to gather intelligence, conduct sabotage, and disrupt infiltration into the South. The commando program was run by the U.S. government and Central Intelligence Agency. From 1961 to 1968, more than 50 commando teams were sent into North Vietnam by sea and by air. Democratic Republic of Vietnam (DRV) authorities were routinely notified of these activities and were able to capture most of the commandos immediately. Reportedly every member of these teams was captured or killed, or disappeared. The longest evasion was by Quach Tom, who avoided capture for nearly three months. By the end of the Vietnam War in 1975, more than 300 commandos still languished in DRV prisons.

Documents declassified in 1996 revealed that the U.S. government lied to the families of the commandos by declaring all of them dead and paying their "widows" $50 gratuities. Sedgwick Tourison, a former Defense Intelligence Agency analyst, has identified 360 survivors. Quach Tom's lawyer sued in Federal court on behalf of the commandos and lobbied Congress and President Clinton for legislation to provide compensation. Congressional hearings were held in 1996, and Senators John Kerry and Bob Kerrey introduced legislation to provide $20 million to the former commandos—about $40,000 each.

—Spencer C. Tucker

Reference: Tourison, Sedgwick D. *Project Alpha: Washington's Secret Military Operations in North Vietnam* (1997).

See also: Central Intelligence Agency (CIA); Clinton, William Jefferson; Kerry, John Forbes; Operation Plan 34A (OPLAN 34A); Quach Tom.

Vietnam, Republic of: Đà Lat Military Academy

Republic of Vietnam military academy established in December 1948 as the Officers School of Vietnam at Đâp Đá in Huê. In 1950 the school moved to Đà Lat as the Combined-Arms Military School. After the declaration of the Republic of Vietnam by President Diêm in 1955, the school was reformed with new curriculum. The concept of "combined arms" was to train cadets as platoon leaders but with a general knowledge of all combat arms. In 1960 the school was renamed the Military Academy of Vietnam (VNMA), and a new facility was built near the old installation. Its curriculum and military ceremonies combined those of West Point, St. Cyr, and the traditions of Vietnam. The VNMA provided ARVN units with excellent officers. Up to 30 April 1975, the VNMA graduated 29 classes, totaling more than 6,500 officers. The last classes were still in training when the RVN collapsed.

—Nguyên Công Luân (Lu Tuân)

See also: Vietnam, Republic of: Army (ARVN).

Vietnam, Republic of: Marine Corps (VNMC)

On 13 October 1954, President Ngô Đình Diêm signed a government decree creating within the naval establishment a corps of infantry to be designated the Marine Corps (VNMC). In 1955 the Vietnamese Naval Forces passed from French to Vietnamese command, and all further evolution of the VNMC was in cooperation with the U.S. Marine Corps (USMC). In 1954 U.S. Marine Lt. Col. Victor Croizat became the first senior U.S. advisor to the VNMC. USMC advisory efforts permeated every aspect of VNMC training, force expansion, logistics, and field operations. Under U.S. tutelage the VNMC increased its size to a corps of nine infantry battalions, three artillery battalions, and supporting units.

During the Vietnam War, the VNMC earned a solid reputation as a fighting force. The VNMC, along with Ranger and Airborne units, constituted Sài Gòn's elite national reserve, deployed to exploit battlefield successes and redress emergency situations. The VNMC fought throughout South Vietnam, from anti-infiltration duties in the Mekong Delta to waging conventional war against North Vietnamese forces along the Demilitarized Zone (DMZ). The VNMC participated in the recapture of Huê during the 1968 Tết Offensive and in the 1970 invasion of Cambodia. During the 1972 invasion of Laos, VNMC units took on the difficult task of blunting the People's Army of Vietnam (PAVN) counterattack that had forced regular ARVN units to abandon their firebases on the drive to Tchépone.

During the 1972 Easter Offensive, severely outnumbered Vietnamese Marines and their USMC advisors were instrumental in defeating this major PAVN drive to break the vital Quang Tri defensive line and capture Huê. Reflecting their USMC training, the VNMC staged counterattacks against superior forces and launched their first amphibious assault from U.S. naval vessels. During this fighting, the VNMC units suffered 20 percent combat casualties.

USMC advisors left South Vietnam in 1973. In 1975, with the collapse of the Republic of Vietnam government, the VNMC split into two forces, fighting PAVN forces near Đà Nang and near the presidential palace in Sài Gòn. Fewer than 250 VNMC ultimately escaped to the United States after the fall of Sài Gòn.

—Peter W. Brush

References: Croizat, Victor J. "Vietnamese Naval Forces: Origin of the Species" (1973); Melson, Charles D., and Curtis G. Arnold. *U.S. Marines in Vietnam, 1954–1973. An Anthology and Annotated Bibliography* (1985); Turley, G. H. *The Easter Offensive: Vietnam, 1972* (1985).

See also: Easter Offensive (Nguyên Huê Campaign); Hồ Chì Minh Campaign; Order of Battle; Tết Offensive: Overall Strategy; Tết Offensive: the Sài Gòn Circle; United States: Marine Corps; Vietnam, Republic of: Air Force (VNAF); Vietnam, Republic of: Army (ARVN).

Vietnam, Republic of: National Police

Police force responsible for the preserving social order and apprehending criminals. In 1954 the National Police was totally controlled by the Bình Xuyên gang, headed by Lê Van Viên, but Diêm routed the Bình Xuyên and other warlords in 1955 and gave control of the National Police to his brother Ngô Đình Nhu. Nhu added a secret police to watch dissidents

and ordered them to infiltrate labor unions and social organizations and to build a network of informants to report any potential enemies directly to him. His wife, the flamboyant Madame Nhu, shared with her husband the control of the police forces. The secret police was authorized to arrest and interrogate anyone without warrant. Nhu also increased the size of the police from approximately 20,000 men in 1960 to almost 32,000 in 1963. The Ngô brothers and other wealthy families engaged in graft and other forms of corruption while the police protected many criminal enterprises. The police basically ensured social order and practiced selected suppression of criminal activity within the RVN.

With the renewal of the insurgency in the South, the National Police soon took on more military roles. As the insurgency grew, the Diêm regime used the police and military to combat Buddhists and other dissidents. On 1 November 1963, a coup toppled the Diêm regime. Increasingly the RVN used the National Police as a paramilitary force, although as part of civilian government it was not under control of the RVN military establishment. It conducted special intelligence gathering and counterintelligence, often duplicating the military efforts. It also was responsible for protecting RVN officials and government buildings, again duplicating efforts of the ARVN military police and special forces units.

The National Police Field Force (NPFF) consisted of company-sized units stationed throughout the RVN and was organized and trained as light infantry by the U.S. Military Assistance Command, Vietnam (MACV). These police officers most often engaged in counterinsurgency operations. They were separate from the Regional Forces/Popular Forces, which fell loosely under the control of the ARVN or MACV.

In 1969 as part of a campaign to root out and destroy the Communist infrastructure, Provincial Reconnaissance Units (PRUs) were added to the National Police. The National Police, in conjunction with the U.S. Central Intelligence Agency (CIA), were the controlling forces in the Phoenix program. Police intelligence detachments coordinated with CIA operatives to gather data on known Viêt Công (VC) and also assisted in crime control with U.S. authorities.

The National Police performed an important role for the RVN during the Vietnam conflict. Their duties ranged from political suppression to direct combat with Communist forces. During the 1968 Tết Offensive, they fought with great distinction in Sài Gòn, yet their efforts seemed nullified when Director of National Police General Nguyên Ngoc Loan executed a VC prisoner before an American photographer. The conduct of the PRUs is more suspect, and the National Police, as a whole, must share blame for excesses committed by the PRUs.

—J. A. Menzoff

References: Becker, Harold K. *Police Systems of Europe: A Survey of Selected Police Organizations* (1973); Clarke, Jeffery J. *Advise and Support: The Final Years, 1965-1973* (1988); Karnow, Stanley. *Vietnam: A History* (1991).

See also: Ngô Đình Diêm; Ngô Đình Nhu; Provincial Reconnaissance Units (PRUs) (Đon Vi Thám Sát Tinh).

Vietnam, Republic of: Navy (VNN)

The Vietnam Navy (VNN), with the assistance of U.S. advisors, became one of the world's largest navies, with 42,000 men and women, 672 amphibious ships and craft, 20 mine warfare vessels, 450 patrol craft, 56 service craft, and 242 junks. Organizational changes to the VNN during two decades reflected the evolution of the service's mission and responsibilities. Initially, the chief of the general staff of the Vietnamese armed forces, an Army officer, controlled the Navy staff and its chief. With the encouragement of U.S. Navy advisors, the general staff established the billet of chief of naval operations, which handled the administration, if not the operational control, of the naval service.

In the early years, the Navy's combat forces consisted of the Sea Force (renamed Fleet Command in January 1966), River Force, and Marine Corps (made a separate military service in April 1965). The different missions of the Navy's combat forces determined how they were operationally controlled. The units involved in open sea and coastal patrol missions operated first in five Sea Zones, then in four Naval Zones (after October 1963), and finally in four Coastal Zones (after April 1965). The Coastal Zones, from the 1st in the North to the 4th in the Gulf of Siam, corresponded to the Army's I, II, III, and IV Corps areas. Coastal Force junks patrolled the offshore waters from 28 bases along the coast. Regional operations of the Coastal Force were directed from coastal surveillance centers set up in Đà Nang, Cam Ranh, Vung Tàu, and An Thoi.

The River Force, organized into river assault groups on the French model of the Dinassaut (naval assault divisions), initially served the Army divisions closest to its Mekong Delta naval bases at Sài Gòn, My Tho, Vinh Long, Cân Tho, and Long Xuyên. In the early 1960s, the Navy also formed the River Transport Escort Group, to protect vital foodstuffs being convoyed to Sài Gòn, and the River Transport Group, to move Army forces throughout the Delta. In April 1965, the Joint General Staff established the III and IV Riverine Areas to manage River Force operations. The Navy was given sole responsibility for handling operations in the Rung Sát "Special Zone," a maze of rivers and swamps south of Sài Gòn.

During the 1950s and 1960s, the United States supplemented the modest force of ships and craft turned over to the VNN by the French with hundreds of naval vessels, including escorts (PCE), patrol rescue escorts (PCER), motor gunboats (PGM), large support landing ships (LSSL), large infantry landing ships (LSIL), tank landing ships (LST), medium landing ships (LSM), and minesweeping launches (MLMS). These vessels improved the ability of the oceangoing force to patrol the 1,200-mile coastline, provided gunfire support for troops ashore, and assisted in carrying out amphibious landings and open sea operations.

The River Force received a fleet of smaller vessels, including specially converted mechanized landing craft (LCM), that served as monitors, command boats, troop transports, minesweeping boats, patrol vessels, and fuel barges. The United States also provided the river sailors with 27 U.S.-built river patrol craft (RPC), which proved to be noisy, underarmed, and easily slowed by river vegetation.

The VNN played an increasing role in the fight for South Vietnam. Along with U.S. naval forces, the Fleet Command and the Coastal Force seized or destroyed thousands of craft ferrying munitions and personnel along the coast. The Coastal Force carried out many amphibious raids, patrols of shallow inlets and river mouths, and troop lifts, operations that played an important part in the Allied campaign to deny the Communists easy access to the coastal regions. Fleet Command ships also patrolled the larger Mekong Delta rivers and protected merchant ships moving between the sea and Phnom Penh. The VNN paid a price for its success on the rivers, however. In 1966, river mines sank an LSSL and damaged an LSIL and a utility landing craft (LCU). Mines also sank several minesweeping launches in the Rung Sát during 1966 and 1967.

Serious deficiencies plagued the VNN throughout its existence, but especially during the 1960s. Careerism and political activity on the part of many naval officers weakened the war effort. The 1963 coup against President Diêm and the political troubles of 1965 and 1966, in which the Navy figured prominently, damaged the morale of officers and sailors alike and distracted them from their military mission. Many sailors were unprepared in the technical skills essential for the operation of complex vessels, weapons, and equipment, and training was generally inadequate. Low pay and austere living conditions prompted desertion and frustrated recruitment.

The material condition of the Navy raised even more serious concerns. Hull and equipment deterioration in the World War II–era ships and craft was a serious problem, as was the lack of sufficient spare parts, supplies, and fuel. Repair facilities in South Vietnam were unable to handle the workload generated by the high-intensity operations undertaken from 1967 to 1969. Consequently, the VNN rarely had 50 percent of its ships and craft in operation for ocean, coastal, or river missions.

The VNN's fortunes rose temporarily with the Vietnamization program. The naval part of that process, termed Accelerated Turnover to the Vietnamese (ACTOV), involved the phased transfer to Vietnam of the U.S. Navy's river and coastal combatant fleet. As entire units came under VNN command, control of various combat operations passed to the naval service as well. Hence, the VNN took on sole responsibility for river assault operations when the joint U.S. Army-Navy Mobile Riverine Force transferred 64 riverine assault craft to the VNN in summer 1969.

The VNN performed well during the spring 1970 Allied push into Cambodia. On 9 May, a combined Vietnamese-U.S. naval task force, under Vietnamese command, steamed up the Mekong River and secured control of that key waterway from Communist forces. The combined flotilla stormed Neak Luong, a strategic ferry crossing point on the river, then the Vietnamese contingent pushed on to Phnom Penh.

In July 1970, the U.S. Navy ceased its offensive missions on I Corps's Cua Viêt and Perfume Rivers and by the end of the year closed its other major operations throughout South Vietnam. During that time, U.S. Naval Forces, Vietnam, transferred to the VNN 293 river patrol boats and 224 riverine assault craft. The VNN grouped these fighting vessels into riverine assault interdiction divisions (RAIDs), river interdiction divisions (RIDs), and river patrol groups (RPGs).

The same process worked with the offshore patrol operation in 1970 and 1971. As part of the U.S. Navy's ACTOV program and the U.S. Coast Guard's Small Craft Assets, Training, and Turnover of Resources (SCATTOR) program, the United States transferred to the VNN complete control of the coastal and high seas surface patrol operations. The U.S. naval command transferred four Coast Guard cutters, each equipped with 5-inch guns, radar escort picket ship *Camp* (DER 251), *Garrett County* (LST 786), and various harbor control craft, mine craft, and logistic support vessels. In the midst of this activity, U.S. and Vietnamese naval forces managed to sink or turn back all but one of the 11 DRV ships that attempted to infiltrate contraband into South Vietnam during 1971. In August 1972 the VNN took on responsibility for the entire coastal patrol effort when it took possession of the last of 16 U.S. coastal radar installations.

In addition to ships and craft, the U.S. Navy, under the Accelerated Turnover to the Vietnamese, Logistics (ACTOVLOG) program, transferred its many combat and logistic support bases to the VNN. The first change of command occurred in November 1969 at My Tho; the last, in April 1972. By 1973 the VNN possessed the material resources to carry on the fight alone. The 42,000-sailor naval service marshaled a force of more than 1,400 ships and craft to meet the Communists on the rivers and canals of South Vietnam and in the South China Sea. The still-developing VNN had great potential, but it needed time to mature.

The VNN never got that time. Congress drastically cut financial support for the Vietnamese armed forces during 1973 and 1974, compelling the VNN to reduce its overall operations by 50 percent and its river combat and patrol activities by 70 percent. To conserve scarce ammunition and fuel, Sài Gòn laid up more than 600 river and harbor craft and 22 ships. The Communists did not target the waterways during this period, but the respite was short-lived. During spring 1975, Communist ground forces seized all of northern and central South Vietnam, bypassing any VNN concentrations. VNN ships and sailors soon joined the hurried exodus of troops and civilians from the I and II Corps areas. With the 30 April fall of Sài Gòn, many VNN ships and craft put to sea and gathered off Côn Son Island southwest of Vung Tàu. The flotilla of 26 VNN and other vessels, with 30,000 sailors, their families, and other civilians on board, joined the U.S. Seventh Fleet when it embarked the last of the refugees fleeing South Vietnam and headed for the Philippines.

—Edward J. Marolda

References: Marolda, Edward J., and Oscar P. Fitzgerald. *From Military Assistance to Combat, 1959–1965.* Vol II, *The United States Navy and the Vietnam Conflict* (1986); Schreadley, Richard L. *From the Rivers to the Sea: The U.S. Navy in Vietnam* (1992).

See also: Dinassauts; MARKET TIME, Operation; Mobile Riverine Force; Order of Battle; Riverine Craft; Riverine Warfare; Sea Power in the Vietnam War; United States: Coast Guard; United States: Navy; Warships, Allied and Democratic Republic of Vietnam.

Vietnam, Republic of: Rural Development Cadre Training Center

Republic of Vietnam (RVN) training facility founded in 1966 under the Rural Development Ministry. As most U.S. aid to the RVN went for military assistance, rural development (RD) took second place. RD operations at the hamlet level were conducted by RD teams of more than 50 members each who took charge of their own security. Teams had charge of renovating hamlet and village administrative and security infrastructure, training militia, running political indoctrination, and setting up dispensaries and primary schools. To train these cadres, the RVN established a large facility near Vung Tàu. Supported by direct U.S. assistance and commanded by Col. Nguyên Bé, the center was highly successful. Usually 6,000 to 7,000 students, many of them women, were in training at any one time. Discipline and morale were excellent. In 1970 the facility was renamed the National Cadres Training Center.

—Nguyên Công Luân (Lu Tuân)

See also: Pacification.

Vietnam, Republic of: Special Forces (Luc Luong Đac Biêt [LLDB])

Republic of Vietnam (RVN) elite military units. The Army of the Republic of Vietnam Special Forces (LLDB, or Luc Luong Đac Biêt) came into being at Nha Trang in February 1956 under the designation of First Observation Battalion/Group (FOG). By 1960 most LLDB were involved in counterinsurgency operations within South Vietnam. A smaller number of LLDB personnel were involved in the FOG program. At Long Thanh, they received training in intelligence gathering, sabotage, and psychological operations (PSYOP).

The LLDB's primary duties included recruitment and training of one- to four-member teams sent into North Vietnam on intelligence, sabotage, and psychological warfare missions. Although these teams did foment unrest and create problems by minor sabotage and intelligence gathering, Hà Nôi declared, apparently with justification, that all such agents were captured, interrogated, and executed.

In 1961 the LLDB and Army of the Republic of Vietnam (ARVN) 1st Infantry Division conducted a joint operation against Communist infiltrators in northern Quang Tri Province. That fall, LLDB units began Operation EAGLE at Bình Hung with a night parachute assault.

In September 1962, U.S. Special Forces personnel took over the Central Intelligence Agency's border surveillance and Civilian Irregular Defense Group (CIDG) programs and began working with the LLDB. LLDB organizational structure underwent considerable change in the 1960s, but it continued to expand and that same year was given the additional duty of operating with the CIDG. In 1964 the U.S. Army's 5th Special Forces Group was officially assigned to Vietnam. The LLDB worked closely with this command and, although the U.S. funded the CIDG camps, the LLDB assumed ultimate responsibility for them. These camps were commanded by Vietnamese Special Forces, assisted by U.S. Special Forces advisors. From 24 June to 1 July 1964, under Project DELTA,

LLDB teams made five parachute insertions into Laos to gather intelligence. By 1965 LLDB personnel were working closely with the ARVN in recruiting and training as well as sending teams into Communist sanctuaries to gather information.

In March 1970, with the anticipated withdrawal of U.S. Special Forces personnel from Vietnam and the acknowledged failure of the CIDG program, in part through fraud and corruption, the ARVN and U.S. Military Assistance Command, Vietnam (MACV) agreed to convert CIDG camps into ARVN Ranger camps. No longer needed, the LLDB were disbanded; some former LLDB personnel were formed into a new clandestine unit, the Vietnamese Special Mission Service (SMS). Approximately 5,000 personnel served in the RVN Special Forces during the war. After the April 1975 fall of South Vietnam, some former LLDB personnel escaped to the United States, but others served long years in reeducation camps.

—Harve Saal, Spencer C. Tucker, and Vu Đ Hiêu

References: Kelly, Francis J. *The Green Berets in Vietnam 1961–71* (1991); Saal, Harve. *MACV–Studies and Observations Group (SOG)*. Vol. I, *Historical Evolution*; Vol. IV, *Appendixes* (1990).

See also: Central Intelligence Agency (CIA); Civilian Irregular Defense Group (CIDG); Psychological Warfare Operations (PSYOP); United States: Special Forces; Vietnam, Republic of: Army (ARVN).

Vietnam, Socialist Republic of: 1975 to the Present

On 30 April 1975, Communist forces captured Sài Gòn, capital of the Republic of Vietnam (RVN), officially bringing the Vietnam War to a close. A military administration took charge of the south. In April 1976, general elections were held for a single National Assembly, which convened in June and the next month declared that the reunified country would be known as the Socialist Republic of Vietnam (SRV) with its capital at Hà Nôi. Sài Gòn was renamed Hô Chí Minh City. Tôn Đuc Thang was elected president and Pham Van Đông the premier.

In December 1976, the Lao Đông Party renamed itself the Đang Công San Viêt Nam (Vietnamese Communist Party, VCP). This occurred during the Fourth Party Congress (the fourth since the 1930 founding of the party and first since 1960). These meetings, supposed to be held every five years, were rubber stamp sessions for policies developed by the party Politburo. These policies were then explained by cadres to local units to obtain feedback and create solidarity, and perhaps even slight modification, before the Congresses met.

The Fourth Congress decreed the need to develop socialism throughout the SRV. It stressed the need to speed industrialism, which was seen as the chief means to socialism, and heavy industry received priority. In September 1977, sponsored by a record number of nations, the SRV was admitted to the United Nations. The SRV faced staggering problems, including rebuilding the war-ravaged country, knitting the two halves of the country together after decades of division and war, reconciling very different patterns of economic development, and providing for the needs of a burgeoning population that would double in the next 20 years.

The Communist Party retained its monopoly on power; indeed the constitution guaranteed it as "the only force leading the state and society." Immediately after the war the government conducted a political purge in the south. There were deaths, but nothing like the bloodbath so often predicted by Washington. Thousands of former RVN officials and military officers were sent to reeducation camps to be politically indoctrinated and to undergo varying degrees of physical and mental discomfort, even torture. Efforts were made to force people out of the cities, especially Hô Chí Minh City, and into the "new economic areas" created to develop new land and to get other areas back into cultivation.

Vietnam, even in the best of times, had been been a poor, developing nation. In the immediate aftermath of the war, the Vietnamese set about quite literally picking up the pieces of war—vast amounts of scrap metal and more than $1 billion in unused U.S. military equipment. The broken machines of war fueled the scrap-metal furnaces of the country for years afterward, and the country exported U.S. military hardware. In another move to gain badly needed foreign currency, the government sent 200,000 Vietnamese to work in the USSR and Eastern Europe. These workers, who had to pay the Vietnamese government 40 percent of their salaries, sent home an estimated $150 million a year.

Farm collectivization in South Vietnam, led by Đô Muoi, met silent but determined peasant resistance. New regulations governing business practices led to the collapse of light and medium industry in the south, and the policy was soon abandoned. Economic unrest, however, helped fuel an exodus of refugees from the SRV. Floods in north and central Vietnam in summer 1978 hastened the collapse of agricultural cooperatives. In 1981 the government introduced the new "*khoán san phâm*" system, a contractual arrangement under which local authorities granted each peasant family land to farm. The peasants paid a fixed rent and were able to sell surplus produce on the private market. In September 1982 the government issued a new currency at the rate of one new note for ten of the old. By the end of that year, there was rising criticism of government policy, even within the controlled National Assembly.

Vietnam had no official ties with the United States in these years, although both countries would have benefited economically had they been established early on. In 1977 President Carter prepared to normalize relations. In March, Assistant Secretary of State Richard Holbrooke began talks with Vietnamese officials to explore U.S. recognition, but with Hà Nôi insisting on reparations said to have been promised by the Nixon administration, Washington halted negotiations until summer 1978, when the SRV dropped this demand. Even then, talks did not proceed because of what Washington saw as Hà Nôi's callous disregard for the plight of refugees (the boat people), SRV preparations for an invasion of Cambodia, the SRV's conclusion of a treaty of friendship and cooperation with the USSR that November, and a decision by the Carter administration to make normalization of relations with China a priority over Vietnam.

The December 1978 Vietnamese invasion of Cambodia and subsequent occupation of that country until September 1989 made normalization of relations between the United

States and the SRV impossible. Also troubling from Washington's point of view was Hà Nôi's refusal to cooperate on prisoner of war/missing in action (MIA/POW) matters, a volatile political issue in the United States. (Hà Nôi never made an issue of resolution of its own MIAs, announced in 1995 to total some 330,000 Viêt Công and People's Army of Vietnam (PAVN) personnel.) The Cambodian invasion led the United States to strengthen its 1975 trade embargo of Vietnam by blocking vital loans from multilateral agencies such as the International Monetary Fund, the World Bank, and the Asian Development Bank; forestalling significant international aid; and stifling the SRV's domestic economic development. Carter also committed the United States to aiding Cambodian guerrilla groups that opposed the Vietnamese presence there. The Cambodian incursion made the SRV something of an international pariah.

Throughout the second half of the 1970s, SRV relations with China continued to deteriorate from a variety of reasons, including territorial disputes, the forced exit of many Chinese from the SRV, the Cambodian invasion, and Sino-Soviet tensions in which Vietnam sided with the USSR. The Soviet Union provided important support for the SRV economy, amounting to perhaps $2.25 billion a year (more than half of this in military assistance). Sino-SRV tensions exploded into war when Chinese troops crossed the northern Vietnamese frontier briefly in February 1979. Vietnam decreed a general mobilization. Although Chinese troops soon withdrew from Vietnam and the SRV was not forced to remove its troops from Cambodia, the cost was high for Vietnam; many of its villages in the border area were destroyed.

The SRV continued to maintain a large military establishment. In the mid-1980s, with 1.2 million people armed (not including an estimated 1 million Public Security personnel), it possessed the world's fourth largest armed forces. The military consumed up to a third of the national budget, and a bloated government bureaucracy also consumed revenues. As a result, the economy remained vastly undermechanized. In the mid-1980s there was not a single rice threshing machine in the country. It appeared to many foreign observers that Vietnam worked more effectively at war than at peace, perhaps because the Vietnamese had had little experience with the latter. Vietnam was very much an insular and xenophobic society.

In 1985 famine spread in the SRV, the result of failed farm collectivization and botched currency reform. Inflation ran between 400 and 600 percent per year by 1985. Economic growth of 2 percent per year was outstripped by the 3 percent birthrate, one of the highest in the world. Agricultural production, which had risen after the 1981 reforms, fell again. All of this led to striking policy and leadership changes. At the December 1986 Sixth National Communist Party Congress, the leadership announced changes based on material incentives, decentralized decision making, and limited free enterprise. Party secretary and hard-liner Lê Duân had died in July 1986, and Premier Pham Van Đông, Lê Đuc Tho, and Truong Chinh all retired. In all, six of thirteen Politburo members were dropped. Nguyên Van Linh and Vô Van Kiêt, two leading proponents of change, came to the fore. Linh, who replaced Truong Chinh as party secretary and the most powerful figure in the state, was credited with overseeing the tentative steps toward a free market economy that had helped the south remain more prosperous than the north. Vô Van Kiêt was vice-premier and chairman of the state planning commission.

Linh's reform program, known as *đôi moi* (renovation), introduced profit incentives for farmers, allowing them to market produce privately. Individuals could set up private businesses. Companies producing for export were granted tax concessions, and foreign-owned firms could operate in the country and repatriate their profits (with a guarantee against being nationalized). Linh said there was no need for Vietnam to allow opposition political parties and free elections, but there was some easing of restrictions on the media. Attempts were also made to open Vietnam to the West, including talks in August 1987 on the MIA issue with a U.S. delegation headed by John Vessey, Jr. The regime also sought reconciliation with former South Vietnamese officials and groups once considered its enemies and in September 1987 announced that it was releasing 6,685 military and political prisoners. In 1988, to promote foreign investment, the constitution was amended to remove derogatory references to several Western countries. *Đôi moi* registered successes. Inflation was cut from 300 percent in 1987 to 8.5 percent in 1994. Food production and consumerism increased. But the reform was uneven as party bureaucrats and conservatives inhibited its spread.

In March 1988, Pham Hùng, chairman of the Council of Ministers (premier) since the previous July, died at age 75; Vô Van Kiêt followed him as acting premier, but in June 1988, Đô Muoi, a candidate introduced by the Communist Party Central Committee, was elected premier by the National Assembly. At that time, Muoi was seen as a transitional figure. Economic reforms continued, with uneven results. Most advances came in the cities rather than the countryside, where 80 percent of the population lived. Vietnam remained a poor country with per capita income of less than $200 a year. In 1989 75,000 people fled the country, largely to escape economic poverty.

The leadership came to realize that the SRV had to join the Southeast Asia development race or forever be left behind. Leaving Cambodia would end SRV diplomatic isolation and lead to Western investment. Driven largely by economic reasons, in July 1988 Vietnam began withdrawing its troops from Cambodia, an operation completed in September 1989. The Vietnamese also reduced their troop strength in Laos. Foreign Minister Nguyên Co Thach traveled to Washington for talks, becoming the highest-ranking Hà Nôi official to do so. Not unrelated to this, in 1989 Soviet leader Mikhail Gorbachev embarked on reform programs that resulted in reduced aid to Vietnam. The Soviets also sharply reduced their military presence, especially at Cam Ranh Bay, which had become the largest Soviet military base outside the USSR. Soviet aid ended altogether in 1991, and the USSR announced that henceforward all trade between the two countries would be in dollars at world market prices.

The Soviet cutback was another reason for Vietnam to try to mend its fences with Beijing, and in September 1990, Deputy Prime Minister Vô Nguyên Giáp traveled to China for talks.

At the same time, there were signs of political struggle in Vietnam. Gen. Secretary Linh announced his plan to retire at the next party Congress, and the battle between conservatives and reformers intensified. In 1990, prompted by fears that the upheaval in Eastern Europe might infect Vietnam, the government ordered the arrests of hundreds of people, most of them in the south—some for what the government referred to as too much contact with Westerners. There was also a public campaign against reported efforts of "reactionary forces overseas" to sabotage the state and socialism. SRV leadership was deeply divided. At the Seventh Congress in June 1991, party leaders announced that they would continue economic reforms but stand firm against political changes in the fashion of Eastern Europe. In August 1991 there was a major cabinet shakeup. At the same time, Vietnam announced its intention to patch up relations with China.

Relations with the United States also improved. In February 1991, talks between the Bush administration and the SRV led Hà Nôi to allow Washington to set up a "temporary" office in the Vietnamese capital to coordinate efforts to locate American MIAs. Relations continued to improve as Hà Nôi took steps to account for American MIAs. U.S. businesses that saw themselves losing out as other nations invested in Vietnam also applied pressure, and in September 1993, President Clinton allowed U.S. companies to compete for development projects in the SRV that were to be funded by international lending institutions. Then, on 3 February 1994, Clinton normalized relations with the SRV. In 1997 the two countries exchanged ambassadors. Hà Nôi also agreed to assume debts incurred by the Sài Gòn government before its fall in 1975, and now worth about $140 million, to help pave the way for most-favored nation trading status.

The much-delayed Vietnamese Eighth Communist Party Congress took place at the end of June 1996. The delay reflected concerns in the party about threats from corruption and what it referred to as "peaceful evolution," a perceived Western plot to undermine remaining Communist one-party states. In the weeks leading up to the Congress, the 170-person Central Committee of the 2.2 million-member Communist Party met repeatedly in an effort to resolve some of these issues. The country's ruling septuagenarian leaders—party Gen. Secretary Đô Muoi (age 79), Premier Vô Van Kiêt (73), and President Lê Đuc Anh (75)—were reelected to five-year terms. Apparently there was some discussion that the top leaders might retire, but the leadership believed that this was not the time to change. Rising stars in the new Politburo were Truong Tân Sang, the young and liberal former mayor of Hô Chí Minh City (now secretary of the Hô Chí Minh City Party Committee), and Nông Đuc Manh, chairman of the National Assembly. Other possibilities were two deputy prime ministers, Trân Đuc Luong and Phan Van Khai, and the head of the army's political department, Gen. Lê Kha Phiêu.

In September 1997, the National Assembly elected Phan Van Khai as premier, replacing Vô Van Kiêt. The Russian trained Khai, an economist and technocrat from the south, was perceived as one of the architects of the economic reforms. PAVN influence remained strong. The party Congress increased representation of military and internal security forces on the 19-member Politburo from four to six and gave the military three of five positions on a new standing committee charged with conducting day-to-day affairs. This was seen as an effort by the party leadership to protect the country's political and social structure. From the mid-1980s to 1996, the PAVN shrank by 50 percent. The military budget remains high, however, having risen every year since 1992.

The most contentious issue for the party leadership was the pace of liberalization. Continued rapid economic growth had begun to transform Vietnam in ways that made some party leaders uneasy. Still, the leadership decided to continue its delicate balancing act, attracting increased foreign investment and aiming for an annual growth rate of 10 percent while continuing to accord primacy to less productive state-run economic enterprises. Foreign investors were made nervous, however, when the Congress called for expansion of party cells within business enterprises, including joint ventures with foreign companies. Even the PAVN was involved in these activities, entering into 49 joint ventures with foreign companies. Foreign observers believed that SRV insistence on maintaining centralized control and pouring money into inefficient state-owned enterprises would make it difficult to meet growth targets. The Congress did ease restrictions on "social evils," including foreign advertising.

From 1990, when outside investment in Vietnam was negligible, to 1996, foreign companies committed $20 billion in investments, and thousands of foreign enterprises were registered to do business there. U.S. investment in the SRV rose from $3.3 million in 1993 to $1.2 billion in 1995, although the United States was only the sixth largest investor, trailing Taiwan, Japan, Hong Kong, Singapore, and the Republic of Korea. Since 1992 economic growth has averaged 8 percent per year. With the official currency, the dong, shrinking in value, however, U.S. dollars were the preferred currency. Corruption, red tape, poor infrastructure, and lack of regulations inhibited investment. The main attractions for foreign investment were low wages, untapped natural resources, and the country's great need to modernize.

Although Vietnam with its population of 75 million (ranked thirteenth in the world) aspires to be one of the Asian "tigers," chronic problems remain. Per capita spending is low. SRV per capita income of $250 per year is among the world's lowest. There is also a growing disparity between rich and poor, many of the "new rich" being Communist officials and their associates.

The central issue for an aging SRV leadership remains whether Vietnam can modernize using the Chinese model, successful thus far, without the party relaxing political control. Ironically the party is itself the chief obstacle to reform, as shown by its refusal to privatize state-run industries. The party sees its chief enemies as the multiparty system, the dollar's pervasive influence, the residue of war, corruption, poor management, regional autonomy, Buddhist agitation, growing crime and disrespect for authority, and the menace of China.

Making Vietnam a single entity economically has also yet to be accomplished. The north, with its soil depleted and forests fast disappearing, still trails the south economically. One of the ironies of the Vietnam War may indeed be that the south won after all, at least in the adoption of modified capitalism and in its standard of living. Hô Chí Minh City is the economic engine driving the rest of the country. Northern leaders, however, oppose yielding political power.

—Spencer C. Tucker

Reference: Nguyên Khac Viên. *Vietnam, A Long History* (1987).
See also: Carter, Jimmy; Clinton, William Jefferson; Đô Muoi; Embargo; Lao Đông Party; Lê Đuc Anh; Lê Đuc Tho; Nông Đuc Manh; Nguyên Van Linh (Nguyên Van Cúc); Pham Van Đông; Phan Van Khai; Reeducation Camps; Sino-Vietnamese War; Truong Chinh (Đang Xuân Khu); Vietnamese Invasion and Occupation of Cambodia; Vô Vân Kiêt.

Vietnam Information Group (VIG)

Johnson administration public relations vehicle. Criticized over his Vietnam policies by the news media and Congressional "doves," President Johnson established the Public Affairs Policy Committee for Vietnam in August 1965. This organization, redesignated the Vietnam Information Group (VIG) in 1967, prepared Vietnam-related material from the Johnson administration for public consumption. The VIG released the most optimistic information available concerning U.S. involvement in Vietnam. Its principal task was to discredit Johnson's opponents and win U.S. and foreign favor. Director Harold Kaplan and his staff monitored public reactions to the war and attempted to deal with problems as soon as they appeared.

In an aggressive campaign to mobilize the "silent center" in American politics, Johnson ordered the U.S. embassy and military command in Vietnam to "search urgently for occasions to present sound evidence of progress in Vietnam." The VIG offered reams of favorable statistics as proof of U.S. progress in Vietnam. A loose organization similar to the VIG continued to prepare position papers and press releases during the Nixon administration.

—Stanley S. McGowen

References: Herring, George C. *America's Longest War: The United States and Vietnam, 1950–1975,* 2d ed. (1986); Herring, George C. *LBJ and Vietnam: A Different Kind of War* (1994); Johnson, Lyndon B. *The Vantage Point: Perspectives of the Presidency, 1963–1969* (1971); Small, Melvin. *Johnson, Nixon, and the Doves* (1988).
See also: Johnson, Lyndon Baines; Media and the War.

Vietnam Veterans Against the War (VVAW)

U.S. antiwar organization. Vietnam Veterans Against the War (VVAW) was founded in April 1967 by American veterans who had marched under a banner with that legend in a New York antiwar demonstration. By the time the VVAW was dissolved in 1973, its leaders claimed a membership of several thousand, although it was not clear how many reported members really held active membership, how many were

government infiltrators, and how many had really seen service in Vietnam.

VVAW's initial goal was to add credence to the antiwar movement through veterans who had seen firsthand the events and conditions being protested. Members participated in major demonstrations throughout 1968. In 1969, with the publicizing of the My Lai massacre, their primary focus shifted to atrocities committed by U.S. troops in the war and to the psychologically damaging effects of the war on troops.

In September 1970, VVAW staged Operation RAW (Rapid American Withdrawal), in which 100 participants, not all of them Vietnam veterans, marched from Morristown, New Jersey, to Valley Forge, Pennsylvania dressed in fatigues and carrying combat weapons. Along the way they staged "guerrilla theater" to represent war atrocities. The marchers encountered some hostility along their route but were greeted enthusiastically by a group of 1,500 at Valley Forge, where speeches were delivered by Jane Fonda, Donald Sutherland, attorney Mark Lane, and others.

During 1970 VVAW leaders had been in touch with Robert Jay Lifton, a New York psychiatrist and antiwar activist who had begun speaking in 1969 about the damaging effect of the war on combatants' psyches and on the inevitability of atrocities. In November 1970, VVAW member Jan Crumb approached Lifton about methods of dealing with veterans' psychological problems and of effectively creating public opposition to the war that had caused these problems. In December 1970 Lifton, fellow psychiatrist Chaim Shatan, and members of the New York VVAW chapter began a series of "rap groups," a form of group therapy in which participants explored their "guilt" and then determined to "animate" it by actively exposing the evil of war. Rap groups later became the staple form of Veterans Administration (VA) treatment for war-related stress, particularly in Veterans Outreach Centers.

In February 1971, VVAW members staged the "Winter Soldier Investigation," a media event in Detroit funded mainly by Jane Fonda and Mark Lane. VVAW members and associates testified about "war crimes" they had participated in or witnessed. In his 1978 book, *America in Vietnam*, Guenter Lewy cited evidence in military records indicating that many of the participants had not been present at the scenes they claimed to be describing, and that some had not seen service in Vietnam at all. This remains a hotly debated issue.

Continuing their public antiwar activities in 1971, VVAW members and supporters, led primarily by rap group participants, staged "Dewey Canyon III" (an allusion to DEWEY CANYON I and II, wartime operations in Laos) in Washington, D.C., in April 1971. The main feature of this event was the discarding of medals by an estimated 1,000 veterans on the Capitol steps. A debate arose over whether all the participants were genuine veterans and whether all the medals thrown at the Capitol had been officially awarded to the men discarding them. Some men in uniform, upon being interviewed, acknowledged that they were not veterans, and the count of the most prestigious medals discarded, when correlated with those known to be still in their owners' possession, did not tally with the number issued. Ironically, some genuine veterans may have been deliberately excluded from the demonstration. Lynda Van Devanter, a former Army nurse who served at Pleiku, reported in her memoirs that when she attempted to join the demonstration, she was told not to march with the veterans because she "didn't look like a vet" and might give the impression that ranks were being swelled with nonvets.

VVAW demonstrations continued throughout 1971 and 1972, but public demonstrations were not the only means that the VVAW found to oppose the war publicly. Throughout the 1970s, even after the dissolution of the organization itself, members and former members campaigned relentlessly for treatment of veterans' psychological disabilities and were instrumental in defining post-traumatic stress disorder as a recognized psychological condition, in establishing VA counseling centers, and in staffing the centers as they were developed. VVAW influence proved to be a powerful voice in public perceptions of the veteran and the war, even as far afield as literary studies. The organization's poetry anthology, *Winning Hearts and Minds* (1972), edited by founding members Jan Barry, Larry Rottman, and Basil Paquet, was one of the first collections of poetry written primarily by veterans and became a model for future writing. Former VVAW members went on to found other organizations, the most famous of which is Vietnam Veterans of America, founded by former VVAW member Robert O. Muller.

—Phoebe S. Spinrad

References: Lewy, Guenter. *America in Vietnam* (1978); Lifton, Robert J. *Home from the War: Vietnam Veterans, Neither Victims nor Executioners* (1973); MacPherson, Myra. *Long Time Passing* (1984); Scott, Wilbur J. *The Politics of Readjustment: Vietnam Veterans Since the War* (1993); Van Devanter, Lynda. *Home before Morning* (1984). **See also:** Antiwar Movement, United States; Fonda, Jane Seymour; Kerry, John Forbes; Lifton, Robert Jay; Post-Traumatic Stress Disorder (PTSD); Prose Narrative and the Vietnam Experience.

Vietnam Veterans Memorial

In the late 1970s, sensitivity developed surrounding how to remember those who had perished in the Vietnam War. First, without ceremony, a small, nondescript plaque was added to the Tomb of the Unknown Soldier. Next, Congress became interested in a politically neutral "Vietnam Veterans Week." A more successful idea—the establishment of a memorial in Washington, D.C.—came from outside the bureaucracy. Jan Scruggs, an enlisted man wounded in 1969, became obsessed with constructing "a memorial to all the guys who served in Vietnam." From this humble dream, the Vietnam Veterans Memorial emerged.

The early history of the Memorial was embroiled in controversy. Scruggs, Bob Doubek (a former Air Force officer) and Jack Wheeler (a West Point graduate who had attended Yale Law School) navigated the challenges of the next several years. Incorporated as a nonprofit organization on 27 April 1979, the Vietnam Veterans Memorial Fund fought its first battles in the political arena. With the assistance of Senators Charles Mathias, who had earlier opposed the war, and John

Warner, the bill approving the Memorial passed the Senate on 30 April 1980. The site designated for the Memorial was on the Washington Mall, near the Lincoln Memorial. In signing the bill (PL 96–297) authorizing the Memorial into law on 1 July 1980, President Carter recognized that "We are ready at last to acknowledge ... the debt which we can never fully repay to those who served."

Although Scruggs had expected spontaneous contributions, the Fund had collected only about $250,000 when President Carter signed the authorization bill. In November 1980, Fund leaders learned that the original $2.5 million target was naive; they would need $6 to $10 million to complete the project. A major factor in the turnaround of the fundraising effort came when the release of American hostages held in Iran activated many citizens to demand that more tangible recognition be given to those who had served their country in Vietnam. By the end of 1981 the Fund had more than $8 million dollars. Later, possibly as a result of disagreements over the design of the Memorial, some controversy about the expenditures of these monies surfaced, but a General Accounting Office audit found that all $9.3 million received as of May 1984 had been properly budgeted.

The design competition ran smoothly, partly because billionaire H. Ross Perot donated $160,000 to underwrite it. Scruggs's idea that the Memorial contain the names of all who perished was central; Wheeler suggested that a landscaped, horizontal design be used; Doubek drafted a proposal that the Memorial be apolitical, not addressing the war's causes or conduct. The Fund agreed to an open selection process with eight judges from the disciplines of architecture and landscape art. By the March 1981 deadline, 1,421 entries had been submitted. After a week of deliberations, the judges announced their unanimous decision: Maya Ying Lin's polished, black, V-shaped wall that would contain the names of all who died in Vietnam.

The design was both praised and attacked. Lin, an undergraduate at Yale University, had seen geometric forms used at the war memorial at Thiepval, France, and had attended the memorial ceremony at Yale, when the names of those graduates killed in Vietnam were added to walls listing those who had died in other wars. Despite these impressive models and praise for her design as "reverential" and a "fitting mark of respect," critics saw the wall, which was carved into a gentle embankment, as a "degrading ditch" and a "wailing wall for antiwar demonstrators." Lin, responding to these critics, added short eulogistic words explaining that the list of names memorialized those who made the ultimate sacrifice in Vietnam, but she did not negotiate about keeping the list of names in chronological order, a crucial aspect of the Memorial's powerful effect.

Although this accommodation satisfied most critics, some still wanted a more traditional design. Secretary of the Interior James Watt delayed construction until a compromise could be reached. After much controversy, the Memorial's critics accepted Lin's design if a representational statue and flag could be added later. In March 1982 Watt signed the construction permit.

Black granite from Bangalore, India, was separated into 140 differently sized panels in Vermont and then shipped to Memphis, Tennessee, where the names were cut into the panels. The angles and depth of the letters had been designed to assure that the sun would cast no shadows that might obscure or change the appearance of a name.

Despite the enormity of these tasks, construction proceeded on schedule. The Veterans Day dedication in November 1982 marked a historic turning point in America's search for a healing closure to the divisive war. More than 150,000 people attended. At the National Cathedral, the salute began on 10 November, with a candlelight vigil, a 56-hour nonstop service at which all 58,000 names were read. Emotional reactions outside, when soldiers first encountered the Wall, ran high. One medic felt joy as he found that a buddy he had worked on was not listed; others experienced survivor guilt on seeing the names of dead comrades. After the dedication the crowd dispersed, beginning a practice of leaving flowers, notes, and other memorabilia as tokens of love and loss.

Even after the dedication, controversy raged over the items yet to be added. Frederick Hart, a sculptor who placed third in the overall design competition, was chosen to create the statue. Earlier he had said that Lin's design was "[nihilistic] contemporary art done in a vacuum." For her part, Lin compared the addition of Hart's realistic sculpture to "drawing moustaches on other people's portraits." However, as issues of placement and size were resolved, Lin came to accept both the flag and the statue well before the 1984 rededication of the double memorial.

Experiencing the memorials together one recognizes the powerful artistic qualities supporting the purposes of reflection and healing. At the flag, the standard patriotic feeling is quietly muted by the inscription's reference to the war's trying conditions. The nearby statue of three soldiers emphasizes the melting-pot quality of the war, while its details create a sense of the reality. These soldiers are tired heroes, weary but stoic survivors of a difficult war.

Moving to the Wall itself, the viewer experiences what Robin Wagner-Pacifici and Barry Schwartz called "a kind of *coincidentia oppositorum*—an agency that brings … opposed meanings together without resolving them." Forming a wide "V," the 246-foot-long arms of the Wall embrace the visitor. At the apex, 10 feet below the highest panels, one feels an almost pastoral quiet. The names, listed in chronological order by the soldier's date of death, emphasize both the individual soldier's story and the significance of time, a crucial aspect for soldiers who spent a clearly delimited period of time in the war zone. Facing the Wall, the viewer sees not only the names but also the reflections of trees and clouds and himself or herself and feels drawn in, a part of a war that affected so many Americans. From this position of quiet reflection, one notices that the arms open, signifying the soldier's return to an environment that was still warlike, for the nation was still divided even when the war itself ended. However, looking toward the horizon, the visitor sees along one arm the Washington Monument and along the

other the Lincoln Memorial and begins to sense a placement of this war and suffering in the nation's history.

The strength of that experience has caused countless visitors to make pilgrimages to what has become an almost sacred shrine. Visitors often take a rubbing of an individual soldier's name or leave memorabilia, and this exchange becomes another example of the interactive nature of the Memorial. These items, cataloged and stored at the Museum and Archeological Regional Storage Facility in Glenn Dale, Maryland, form a fast-growing collection that has created its own cultural history and is a powerful testimonial to the effects of the war on the nation's people.

The Vietnam Veterans Memorial has inspired other artifacts to augment the originally intended therapeutic process. Scruggs's coauthored book, *To Heal a Nation* (1985) became a television movie in 1987. Laura Palmer's book *Shrapnel in the Heart* (1987) reproduces several letters left at the Memorial, while Duncan Spencer's and Lloyd Wolf's *Facing the Wall* (1986) evocatively chronicles in text and color photographs one day's events at the Memorial. The Moving Wall, a half-size replica of the Wall, has been shown throughout the United States.

On Veterans Day 1993, near the Wall, the Vietnam Women's Memorial Project dedicated its own statue. Created by sculptor Glenna Goodacre, the 7-foot statue of three women was designed to balance Hart's statue. Because 90 percent of the women who served in Vietnam were nurses, the statue emphasizes the nurse's role by showing three women assisting a fallen soldier. As with the Wall, however, the statue is meant to be inclusive, and it thus memorializes all of the approximately 11,500 American women who served in Vietnam as well as the eight who died there.

Despite its contentious and troubled beginnings, the Vietnam Veterans Memorial has become a powerful cultural memorial for those touched, either directly or indirectly, by America's most divisive twentieth-century war. The most profound effects are felt by those who experience the therapeutic value of its quiet healing touch. The Memorial commemorates the men and women who gave their lives in Vietnam and, by implication, it remembers all Americans whose lives were touched by the war.

—Charles J. Gaspar

References: Allen, Leslie. "The Wall" (1995); Gaspar, Charles J. "The Search for Closure: Vietnam War Literature and the Vietnam Veterans Memorial" (1989); Scruggs, Jan C., and Swerdlow, Joel. *To Heal a Nation* (1985); Sturken, Marita. "The Wall, the Screen, and the Image: The Vietnam Veterans Memorial" (1991); Wagner-Pacifici, Robin, and Barry Schwartz. "The Vietnam Veterans Memorial: Commemorating a Difficult Past" (1991).
See also: Art and the Vietnam War; Casualties; Film and the Vietnam Experience; Lao Đông Party; Prose Narrative and the Vietnam Experience; Women in the War, U.S.

Vietnamese Communist Party (VCP)

Outgrowth of Hô Chí Minh's Viêt Nam Thanh Niên Cách Mang Đông Chí Hôi (Vietnam Revolutionary Youth League) in the late 1920s. Hô's party separated itself from other anticolonial groups in Vietnam during the 1930s by relying on revolutionary theory. The Communist Party developed a plan for the seizure of power based on organization, agitation, and insurrection. During the first two phases in the 1930s, many party members, including Pham Van Đông and Lê Đuc Tho, were arrested and sent to French prisons. These proved to be breeding grounds for young Vietnamese revolutionaries, as many of the party's cadres were politicized there.

Hô's party recruited thousands of new cadres from the lower middle class and peasants. Lacking an industrial proletariat, the Communist Party modified traditional Marxist-Leninist teachings to meet Vietnam's particular needs. It also emphasized the radical nature of its revolution; that is, replacing one existing social system with another. Communist leaders were careful, however, not to deter potential allies. In May 1941, Communist Party leaders founded the Viêt Nam Đôc Lâp Đông Minh Hôi, or Viêt Minh, a national front organization that served as the organizational nexus of the revolution.

The creation of the Viêt Minh allowed the party to mobilize all anticolonial forces in Vietnam under one banner. The Communists' emphasis on national liberation as its primary goal, and its claim that social revolution was an expected outcome in the decades to come, allowed the party to expand its base of support and make temporary alliances with non-Communist Vietnamese to defeat the French. In February 1951, Hô changed the name of the Indo-Chinese Communist Party (ICP) to the Đang Lao Đông Viet Nam (Vietnamese Workers' Party), popularly known as the Lao Đông (or Workers' Party). His intention was to play down communism and widen nationalist support throughout Vietnam.

After the 1954 military victory over the French at Điên Biên Phu, the party turned its attention to reuniting the country under the socialist banner. Under the 1954 Geneva Accords, the party would control Vietnam north of the 17th parallel, with elections in two years to reunify the country. The Geneva Accords, however, were not observed on both Vietnamese sides, and in 1955 non-Communists and the United States established a counterrevolutionary alternative south of the 17th parallel. From 1954 until 1960, the party tried to unify all of Vietnam through political means.

In 1960 the party adopted armed violence in opposition to the U.S.-backed Sài Gòn regime. The party then created the National Front for the Liberation of South Vietnam (NFLSV), another united front, to mobilize disaffected southerners in opposition to the Diêm government. The character and nature of the southern revolution have been the subject of heated debate. The Communist Party denied any relationship with the NFLSV during the war, but Vô Nguyên Giáp and others later admitted the total subordination of the NFLSV. From 1960 to 1975, the party battled the United States and its allies. In April 1975, the party presided over the reunification of the country in the name of socialism, victorious in its efforts begun earlier in the century.

—Robert K. Brigham

References: Duiker, William J. *The Rise of Nationalism in Vietnam, 1900–1941* (1976); Herring, George C. *America's Longest War: The*

United States and Vietnam, 1950–1975, 2d ed. (1986); Huynh Kim Khanh. *Vietnamese Communism, 1925–1945* (1982); Marr, David G. *Vietnamese Tradition on Trial, 1925–1945* (1981); Thayer, Carlyle A. *War by Other Means: National Liberation and Revolution in Viet-Nam, 1954–1960* (1989); Woodside, Alexander B. *Community and Revolution in Modern Vietnam* (1976).

See also: Điên Biên Phu, Battle of; Geneva Conference and Geneva Accords; Hô Chí Minh; Lao Đông Party; Lê Duân; Lê Đuc Tho; National Front for the Liberation of South Vietnam (NFLSV); Ngô Đình Diêm; Pham Van Đông; Viêt Minh; Viêt Nam Thanh Niên Cách Mang Hôi (Vietnam Revolutionary Youth Association).

Vietnamese Culture

Artifacts from ancient sites in Vietnam indicate that early ancestors of today's Vietnamese had a written language and developed culture. Vietnamese archaeologists date the beginning of their civilization to the Phung-Nguyên culture of the late third millennium B.C., which they regard as advanced Neolithic or early Bronze Age culture. This gave way over the next thousands of years to a more hierarchical society centered on small village or family groups, culminating in what Vietnamese archaeologists call the Dong-son civilization (seventh century B.C.–first century A.D.). Burial sites of this period of the legendary Hung kings have yielded considerable bronze artifacts.

Most anthropologists believe that the Viet people lived first in what is today southern China. Pushed out of that area by the Chinese, they moved south and settled in the Red River Delta, mixing there with other Austro-Asian groups, including Malaysians and Indonesians pushing northward. In addition, there were the original aboriginal inhabitants, whom the Vietnamese pushed out of the deltas and into the highlands. The French referred to these people collectively as the Montagnards ("mountain dwellers"). Today there are in Vietnam some 60 different minority ethnic groups with their own languages and cultures.

Early Vietnamese had a self-contained sea-oriented culture. They fished and farmed and lived in a hierarchical society based on a system of hereditary privilege, mutual obligation, and personal loyalty. The people lived in villages or small communities under the rule of the Lac lords. Women have traditionally enjoyed relatively high status in Vietnamese history, and this was true at this time as well. When the Vietnamese rose up against Chinese rule, they were led by women.

Distance and differing climates and living conditions affected dietary habits and outlook, much as Americans of New England and the deep South differ in their culture. Despite this diversity, the population of the country is overwhelmingly Vietnamese, and Vietnam is largely a unified country in terms of language, customs, and traditions.

The Vietnamese language, in the Mon-Khmer group, reflects contributions from many ethnic groups. It is semi-monosyllable with many disyllabic words and even some trisyllables—or to be more accurate, two-word and three-word compounds. Rich in its six tones, Vietnamese is a singing and musical language. During Chinese rule, the Vietnamese adopted many Chinese words, modifying and employing them in Vietnamese patterns. To the end of the nineteenth century, Vietnamese still used Chinese characters for writing, but they pronounced them their own way. They also employed *Chu Nôm,* a transcription of spoken Vietnamese that used Chinese characters with alterations.

In the seventeenth century, Catholic missionaries introduced *quôc ngu* (national language), a romanized transcription of the spoken Vietnamese language. It has been mandatory in Vietnam since the beginning of the twentieth century. *Quôc ngu* was used by colonial administrations to eliminate the political and cultural influence of Vietnamese Confucian scholars, but it also greatly facilitated popular education and the training of skilled workers. This was a two-edged sword for the French, for it also brought cultural and education concepts that helped undermine their position in Vietnam.

Despite their adoption of Chinese cultural patterns, the Vietnamese retained a sense of nationalism and cultural identity. The Vietnamese slightly modified Chinese culture and philosophy for their own use and preserved their identity, language, and traditions. Thus Vietnamese women have traditionally enjoyed higher social status than women in many Asian countries, and there are significant differences in the ways that Vietnamese celebrate the Chinese Lunar New Year (Têt). The Vietnamese effort to maintain a distinct cultural identity, especially regarding China, has been a constant element in their history.

The Vietnamese adopted Confucianism and Taoism, but in moderate and more tolerant forms. Buddhism reached full development in Vietnam during the Ly Dynasty (1010–1225). French and Portuguese priests brought Catholicism in the sixteenth century, and Protestantism arrived in the early twentieth century. The Communists opposed both Catholicism, mainly because of its Western orientation and value systems, and Buddhism, because of its spirit of nonviolence and philosophy of "cause and effect."

Most Vietnamese practice veneration of their ancestors and believe that souls lives on. Dead and living coexist in the world and remain in communication with each other. Many believe that, because the souls of the dead can affect the living, descendants must provide for them and remember them on the anniversaries of their birthdays and marriages as well as holy days. Such days serve to cement family ties. Ancestral tombs must be properly maintained, and houses contain altars honoring the ancestors. Failure to venerate the departed will cause their souls to wander aimlessly and carry out destructive acts. Vietnamese consider it their duty to provide for the aged. Older people are held in high esteem, and even verbal criticism of them or the departed is not tolerated.

Vietnamese families are patriarchal, and Vietnamese highly regard filial loyalty. Such strong family ties have often led to nepotism, however. For men, the societal ideal is *quân tu* ("kiun tseu" in Chinese), a preference for honesty and honor over material possessions. Polygamy was legal in Vietnam during the French period, but marriage to concubine(s) had to be approved by the first wife. A new Family Law, introduced by Madame Nhu and passed by the Republic of Vietnam Congress in 1959, ended the practice. However, polygamy still exists, particularly in northern Vietnam and in part because of the impact of warfare in decimating so many males.

Vietnam has a rich literature, especially poetry, both in Chinese characters and in *Chu Nôm.* In the twentieth century, all forms of literature prospered, including novels and poetry in *quôc ngu.* In the late 1930s, a new literary movement, known as the Tu Luc Van Đoàn (Self-Reliance Literary Group), sought to revolutionize literature and promote positive change in Vietnamese society. The leader of this movement, Nguyên Tuong Tam (pen name Nhât Linh), later became a leader of the Quôc Dân Đang and, in 1946, foreign minister of the Democratic Republic of Vietnam (DRV). He is still regarded as Vietnam's greatest modern writer.

Music, mostly songs, is the principal form of entertainment in Vietnam. Traditional Vietnamese music on a pentatonic scale is rich in folk songs and musical dramas such as *chè cô* (old musical plays), traditional in North Vietnam for thousands of years. *Cai luong* (modern musical drama) dates from the early twentieth century and is popular throughout Vietnam, particularly in the South. Some instruments come from China; some were invented and are played by Vietnamese only, such as the *dàn bâu,* or mono-string.

Western scale diatonic music arrived in Vietnam with the French. At first, Western music drew the interest of only those who were close to the French or had attained a Western education. Songs composed by Vietnamese began appearing in the 1930s. This "new music," as it was called, developed quickly and came to be regarded as a weapon in the fight for national independence as these songs changed from romantic songs and those praising nature to heroic and patriotic themes. After the proclamation of the Democratic Republic of Vietnam (DRV) and with the war against the French, the DRV government aggressively promoted nationalist and anti-French music. "Field cultural shows" with songs, poems, and plays helped instill high morale in Viêt Minh troops before they went into battle against the French. Among the most influential musicians in this period were Van Cao, Pham Duy, and Luu Huu Phuoc.

During the Vietnam War, the DRV government promoted anti-American songs, although in the north there was always a clandestine interest in South Vietnamese and Western music, carried by radio broadcasts from South Vietnam, Australia, the Voice of America (VOA), and the British Broadcasting Corporation (BBC). The VOA, BBC, and Radio France International still broadcast South Vietnamese pre-1975 music.

There was little interest during the period of the State of Vietnam in promoting anti-Communist songs. This came in South Vietnam only after 1955. However, South Vietnamese were not interested in music composed on government order, and the only songs that were popular were those by free-lance composers, which included those praising Army of the Republic of Vietnam (ARVN) soldiers, and in any case tended to be of higher artistic value. Most music in the south consisted of love songs. Although the Republic of Vietnam (RVN) government employed entertainment groups to serve its combat troops, these groups presented love songs more than heroic and patriotic songs. After the 1975 Communist victory, books and music from South Vietnam flooded North Vietnam. Há Nôi then permitted songs from the pre-1975 South Vietnam, except for those critical of communism and all songs by Pham Duy.

Other fine arts are not as popular. Painting, wood-block printing, carving, and sculpture draw on ancient China and the modern West. Although some Vietnamese kings left behind famous structures, these are not as imposing as those of China. Vietnamese have chosen to regard this as a sign that their rulers were not as tyrannical as those in other countries. A dozen temples, relics of the Cham Kingdom built many hundreds of years before the Vietnamese invasions, draw many foreign tourists. The film industry, still in its infancy, has yet to attract a foreign audience. Nearly all Western sports are played in Vietnam, but the national favorite is soccer. Before 1975 the Republic of Vietnam won several Asian Games gold medals in soccer, tennis, and table tennis. Education is highly prized in Vietnam.

Rice is the staple diet in Vietnam. Vietnamese also consume a lot of pork fat. Most Vietnamese season their food with fish sauce (*nuoc mam*), which has a 16–18 percent protein content. Probably the two greatest Vietnamese delicacies for Americans are *pho* (noodle soup) and *cha giç* (meat roll).

Traditionally, peasants dress in a pajama-like garment, black in the south and deep brown in the north. City dwellers dress in Western-style clothing. Vietnamese women alone wear the *áo dài* (long dress).

After the division of the country following the 1954 Geneva Accords, South Vietnam adopted the worldwide standard 12-grade general education system. The curriculum somewhat overworked students of average ability and below but produced a large number of professionals. Artists, poets, and composers had complete creative license, providing they did not propagandize for the Communists. Leftist opinions and antiwar music were not banned. Freedom of press was limited, but much less strictly than in many countries at war. Many South Vietnamese easily assimilated Western ways during the Vietnam War.

In North Vietnam, education and culture were tightly controlled and subordinated to Communist Party goals. Romantic poetry and music not conforming to Communist teachings were strictly forbidden. Until the break with Beijing in 1975, most official Vietnamese songs of the DRV, and later the Socialist Republic of Vietnam (SRV), conformed closely to those of the People's Republic of China. Education in the north was in a 10-grade system in which students had to attend political indoctrination lessons four hours per week. Children of Communist cadres received preferential treatment. Many customs and traditions were banned, including saying "thank you," labeled as against the "new way of life." Many believed that the Vietnamese language in the north deteriorated from improper usage and the influence of Chinese Communist political literature.

The land reform campaign in the north had as one of its principal aims the eradication of traditional social and cultural structures in the countryside. Between 1956 and 1957, the Nhân Van Giai Phâm (Humanist Masterpieces) movement arose in opposition to this and included many well-known writers, artists, composers, and poets who had been members of the Viêt Minh. It and other dissident movements were crushed on Hô Chí Minh's order.

Since the 1980s, the SRV government has restored many institutions and regulations of the former RVN. The south was defeated militarily and politically, but it triumphed culturally. The SRV has surrendered unconditionally to South Vietnamese culture, especially in music and mores. Most Vietnamese living in the West are proud of their culture and have made great efforts to preserve and promote it.

—Nguyên Công Luân (Lu Tuân)

References: Pham Duy. *Hôi K"* (1991); Pham Kim Vinh. *The Vietnamese Culture* (1994); Pham Van Son. *Viêt Su Toàn Thu* (1960); Vu K". *Luân Cuong Vê Van Hóa Viêt Nam* (1995).
See also: Buddhists; Quôc Ngu.

Vietnamese Invasion and Occupation of Cambodia
(25 December 1978–26 September 1985)

The Vietnamese invasion and occupation of Cambodia isolated the Socialist Republic of Vietnam (SRV) from much of the international community, exacerbated troubled relations with the People's Republic of China (PRC), led to a brief war in 1979 between the PRC and the SRV, proved a serious drain on the Vietnamese economy, and delayed normalization of relations between Vietnam and the United States. It also drove the Khmer Rouge from power.

The background of the conflict lay not in ideology but in traditional animosity between Vietnam and Cambodia. Khmer Rouge leaders were also bitter that in the 1960s the Vietnamese Communists, anxious to keep their own useful accommodation with Prince Norodom Sihanouk's government intact, had given the Khmer Rouge no support. This permanently embittered Khmer Rouge leaders, who were instinctively anti-Vietnamese. After entering into an uneasy alliance with the Vietnamese Communists after Sihanouk's fall, Khmer Rouge leaders believed they had been betrayed a second time after the Vietnamese Communists signed the 1973 Paris peace accords. Khmer Rouge leaders ordered the Vietnamese to leave Cambodian territory and even launched a purge to eliminate pro-Vietnamese elements within the Khmer Rouge, killing nearly all the "Khmer Viêt Minh," Cambodians who had fought against the French and had lived in the Democratic Republic of Vietnam (DRV) until 1970, when the government there ordered them south to help lead the Cambodian resistance.

From the spring of 1973, the Vietnamese Communists no longer played any role in the Khmer Rouge fight against the Lon Nol government. They remained in their Cambodian sanctuaries, however, and occasionally engaged in armed clashes with the Khmer Rouge.

In April 1975, the Khmer Rouge defeated the Lon Nol government. They then ordered the people out of Phnom Penh and larger towns and put them to work in agricultural labor camps in the countryside. Private property was abolished, and paper money was replaced by ration tickets earned by productive labor. Schools were closed and Buddhist temples destroyed. Thousands died, including many ethnic Vietnamese; 200,000 Vietnamese were expelled from the country.

In January 1976, the Khmer Rouge promulgated a new constitution and changed the name of the country to the Democratic Republic of Kampuchea. In April Prince Sihanouk resigned as head of state. Khieu Samphan took his place, but Pol Pot, another Khmer Rouge leader, was the dominant figure in the cabinet. Meanwhile, the government announced that 800,000 people (roughly 10 percent of the population) had died in the war that brought the Khmer Rouge to power.

By 1977 border disputes between Vietnam and Cambodia led to serious fighting. In September, Vietnam claimed that four Kampuchean divisions had invaded its Tây Ninh Province. In September and December, Vietnam retaliated. The December incursion saw 60,000 troops, supported by tanks and artillery, striking as far as the outskirts of Svay Rieng and Kompong Cham. On 31 December 1977, an angry radio broadcast from Phnom Penh denounced the Vietnamese. A week later the Vietnamese withdrew, probably on their own accord, but the Khmer Rouge declared a "historic victory" and rejected calls for negotiations. The Khmer Rouge also carried out a violent purge centered on its armed forces in the eastern part of the country that were supposed to defend the regime from the Vietnamese, executing up to 100,000 Cambodians. Many Khmer Rouge fled into Vietnam and later formed the backbone of the Vietnamese-sponsored anti–Khmer Rouge resistance.

Kampuchea also laid claim to much of Cochin China (southernmost Vietnam), with its large Khmer minority, and to small islands in the Gulf of Thailand. A major clash between the two states in May 1975 over these islands was almost certainly prompted by the belief that there was oil in the area.

As the border conflicts escalated, Hà Nôi supported an anti–Khmer Rouge resistance. Eastern Cambodia had been an important part of the People's Army of Vietnam (PAVN) and Viêt Công logistics system during the Vietnam War, and ties between the people there and Vietnam were strong. This was strengthened by the fact that many of those opposed to the Khmer Rouge fled to the border area. Hà Nôi now organized those who had fled to Vietnam, including many ex–Khmer Rouge fighters, into anti–Khmer Rouge units to fight alongside the Vietnamese Army against Kampuchean forces. Much of this fighting occurred in the Parrot's Beak area. From June 1978 both sides used aircraft, with Chinese pilots flying on the Kampuchean side. Hà Nôi's offers to negotiate were rebuffed by the Khmer Rouge.

In October 1978, Hà Nôi claimed that the Khmer Rouge had killed two million Kampucheans. At the time, this was thought to be propaganda, but clearly something was happening. Kampuchea, regarded as a rice bowl in Southeast Asia, was close to starvation.

Tensions between Vietnam and Kampuchea were abetted by the fact that the two states became proxies in the developing Sino-Soviet rivalry. Kampuchea was a client state of China; Vietnam, of the Soviet Union. Loyalties of the Communist world divided accordingly. Most of the Warsaw Pact nations and Cuba, then relying heavily on financial assistance from the Soviet Union, supported Vietnam; North Korea supported Kampuchea.

At the beginning of December 1978, several anti–Khmer Rouge factions came together to form the Kampuchean National Front led by Khmer Rouge defector Heng Samrin, former deputy commander in eastern Cambodia. Hà Nôi gave the Front full support, including military assistance, and it soon fielded an army of 20,000.

Finally, on 25 December 1978, the Vietnamese Army invaded Cambodia on a broad front. Initially the SRV committed 12 divisions, or half of its army, to the operation. Ultimately there were 200,000 Vietnamese troops in Cambodia, along with Heng Samrin's army. Pol Pot's army numbered only approximately 60,000 in four divisions and three independent regiments and was armed with a mix of weapons. Heavily outnumbered and outgunned, the Khmer Rouge retreated into the countryside and waged guerrilla warfare. Heng Samrin and his forces took Phnom Penh unopposed and soon had all principal Kampuchean cities under their control. Heng Samrin became president of the country, but only the presence of several Vietnamese divisions enabled him to remain in power. The Soviet Union, Laos, the SRV, and most other Communist states recognized the new government. In January 1979, the USSR used its veto in the United Nations Security Council to kill a resolution demanding the withdrawal of all foreign troops from Kampuchea. Heng Samrin, meanwhile, entered into treaties with the SRV and Laos.

With his forces down to only about 25,000 troops, Pol Pot continued to conduct guerrilla warfare, concentrating what remained of his army in the thick jungles of northeastern Kampuchea near the Thai border. China, meanwhile, aided the Khmer Rouge, funneling this assistance through Thailand. Thai generals profited handsomely from the misery, allowing the transit of military assistance to the Khmer Rouge and securing gems and timber from their area of control.

In yet another ironic legacy of the Vietnam War, the United States also aided the Khmer Rouge. Supposedly, Washington sent military assistance only to the non–Khmer Rouge resistance groups, but it was an open secret that much of this aid was in fact used by the Khmer Rouge. Only the Vietnamese occupation prevented the Khmer Rouge from returning to power and continuing their genocidal policies. Indeed, it was only because of the Vietnamese invasion that the mass killings of Cambodians by the Khmer Rouge were confirmed.

China, meanwhile, threatened the SRV with force to punish Hà Nôi for the invasion of Kampuchea, and divisions of the PRC's People's Liberation Army actually invaded Vietnam in a brief war in February and March 1979. The Chinese invasion did not drive the Vietnamese from Cambodia. That came about from the sheer expense of the operation and resultant drain on the Vietnamese economy, and the SRV's attendant isolation in the international community at a time when the leadership recognized the need to revitalize the national economy and secure foreign investment.

Finally, in May 1988 Hà Nôi announced that it would withdraw 50,000 troops, about half of its forces, from Cambodia by the end of the year. In July the Phnom Penh government and rebel coalition met for the first time face-to-face in inconclusive peace talks in Indonesia. On 5 April 1989, Hà Nôi and Phnom Penh announced jointly that all Vietnamese troops would leave Cambodia by the end of September, even if no settlement was found. On 26 September 1989, Vietnam announced that all its troops had withdrawn from Cambodia. Some 25,000 Vietnamese troops had died there.

In late 1990, after prolonged negotiations, rival Cambodian factions, including the Vietnamese-installed regime—then headed by Hun Sen—and the Khmer Rouge agreed to a supreme national council headed by Prince Sihanouk. The United Nations also mounted a vast peace-keeping operation and supervised elections. The Khmer Rouge—into 1996 at least—had not returned to power.

—Spencer C. Tucker

References: Becker, Elizabeth. *When the War Was Over* (1986); Chanda, Nayan. *Brother Enemy* (1986); Chen, King C. *China's War with Vietnam, 1979: Issues, Decisions, and Implications* (1987); Etcheson, Craig. *The Rise and Fall of Democratic Kampuchea* (1984); Hardy, Gordon, Arnold R. Isaacs, and MacAlister Brown. *Pawns of War* (1987); Isaacs, Arnold R. *Without Honor: Defeat in Vietnam and Cambodia* (1983); O'Ballance, Edgar. *The Wars in Vietnam, 1954–1980.* Rev. ed. (1981).

See also: Cambodia; China, People's Republic of (PRC); Heng Samrin; Kampuchean National Front; Khmer Rouge; Lon Nol; Pol Pot; Sihanouk, Norodom; Vietnam, Socialist Republic of: 1975 to the Present; Union of Soviet Socialist Republics (USSR; Soviet Union).

Vietnamese National Army (VNA)

Indigenous Vietnamese force created by the French to fight the Viêt Minh. The 8 March 1949 Elysée Agreement recognized the Associated State of Vietnam within the French Union, complete with its own military, the Vietnamese National Army (VNA), to operate in conjunction with French forces against the Viêt Minh. Although Chief of State Bao Đai was the nominal supreme commander of the VNA from 1949 to 1955, in effect it remained under control of the French High Command.

French commanders for the most part persisted in recruiting Vietnamese for their own forces, making VNA recruitment more difficult. Marcel Carpentier, French military commander in Indo-China (1949–1950), welcomed the expanded military support promised by the VNA, but wanted it firmly in French hands. He steadfastly refused to allow U.S. military aid to be channeled directly to the Vietnamese.

Jean de Lattre de Tassigny, commanding general and French high commissioner in Indo-China (1950–1951) felt differently. One of his chief policies was *le jaunissement* (yellowing), the building up and training of wholly Vietnamese

units. de Lattre launched a program to increase the number of NVA battalions; added armored squadrons, artillery batteries, and support units; and saw to it that some of his best officers and men volunteered to serve as cadres. But this effort came too late, and de Lattre left Indo-China in December 1951.

In May 1951 the VNA had less than 40,000 troops. In July 1951, the Trân Van Huu government decreed a "general mobilization" to conscript 60,000 men for two months' training. The small number of officer candidates (1,000) and specialists (600) attracted under this plan were less than a quarter the number actually needed, but even this modest plan soon encountered difficulties. Fewer than half the officer candidates reported for duty, and the government called up only half the planned conscripts. These did not receive full training, and less than 10 percent of them joined the VNA. VNA recruiting lagged, and in January 1952 the Bao Đai government cut the training period for officer candidates from 12 months to 8. Of 1,000 officer candidates projected as required in the mobilization plan, only 690 were in training. The VNA also suffered from a severe lack of trained senior officers; it had no general staff, chief of staff, or minister of defense.

The VNA suffered chiefly from conflict between the French and the Bao Đai government and a lack of financial support. Yet until the VNA was genuinely independent of French control, it was unlikely to attract many recruits. In May 1953, the Viêt Minh showed the VNA's true situation when, for the second time in less than two years, three companies attacked the training school at Nam Đinh and captured much of its 600-member student body and all school weapons without incurring any casualties.

Gen. Henri Navarre also wanted to increase the size of the VNA, form progressively larger units, and give it operational autonomy and more responsibility. He succeeded in creating 107 new battalions of 95,000 troops, although the VNA was never well trained and led. In 1955 the Ngô Đình Diêm government took over the VNA, which became the nucleus of the Army of the Republic of Vietnam (ARVN).

—Gary Kerley and Spencer C. Tucker

References: Clayton, Anthony. *Three Marshals of France: Leadership after Trauma* (1992); Đông Van Khuyên. *The RVNAF* (1980); Duicker, William J. *Historical Dictionary of Vietnam* (1989); Fall, Bernard B. *The Two Viet-Nams: A Political and Military Analysis.* Rev. ed. (1967); Herring, George C. *America's Longest War: The United States and Vietnam, 1950–1975.* Rev. ed. (1986); Spector, Ronald H. *Advice and Support: The Early Years, 1941–1960. The U.S. Army in Vietnam* (1983).

See also: Bao Đai; Carpentier, Marcel; de Lattre de Tassigny, Jean Joseph Marie Gabriel; Ngô Đình Diêm; Vietnam, Republic of: Army (ARVN); Viêt Minh.

Vietnamization

American term for the process of progressively turning primary responsibility for conduct of the Vietnam War back over to the South Vietnamese. Secretary of Defense Melvin Laird is often credited with coining the term in the spring 1969, although Gen. Creighton Abrams had almost a year earlier told a White House meeting that he was training the South Vietnamese army for the purpose of "Vietnamizing" the war.

Many elements were essential if Vietnamization were to succeed: improving and modernizing the armed forces, providing pacification of rural areas, strengthening the political apparatus, delivering essential services to the populace, nurturing a viable economy, and most important, ensuring security for the people. From these goals derived a host of subsidiary tasks, including expanding and improving the police and territorial forces, implementing land reform, controlling inflation, holding hamlet and village elections, rooting out the Viêt Công (VC) infrastructure, and increasing the rice harvest. Ambassador Ellsworth Bunker stated that South Vietnam's plan for community defense and local development had "three overall objectives: self-defense, self-government, and self-development, which explains why the Vietnamese refer to 'Vietnamization' as 'the three selfs.'"

Without security, nothing else could proceed. Perhaps even more important than the regular armed forces, therefore, were the territorial forces and the People's Self-Defense Force. The latter, sponsored by President Nguyên Van Thiêu when all his advisors were cautioning against it, resulted in half a million weapons being issued to ordinary citizens. Neutralizing the VC infrastructure was a crucially important task. The enemy needed guerrilla forces and the cadre in the South Vietnamese hamlets and villages, Gen. Abrams stressed. Dealing with the VC infrastructure was, in Abrams's view, the way to get off the treadmill that U.S. forces had been on in Vietnam.

Richard Nixon recalled of Vietnamization that "our principal objectives shifted to protecting the South Vietnamese at the village level, reestablishing the local political process, and winning the loyalty of the peasants by involving them in the government and providing them with economic opportunity. Gen. Creighton Abrams had initiated this shift in strategy when he took command of our forces in Vietnam in 1968."

The Americans could only help so much; the rest was up to the Vietnamese. Ambassador Bunker admired what the Vietnamese were able to achieve in the midst of so much conflict. "Considering that the country was at war," Bunker stated, "I think it was quite remarkable how well the government functioned." Among the many indicators of effective government functioning were skillful handling of refugees, progress in land reform, and resurgence of the agricultural sector.

Soon the last American forces had been withdrawn, and the South Vietnamese were left to cope with the continued war as best they might, eventually without major financial or material assistance from their former American allies, much less the swift retribution that had been promised in the event the DRV violated the agreement. Thus the accomplishments of Vietnamization were squandered.

—Lewis Sorley

References: Bunker, Ellsworth. *The Bunker Papers: Reports to the President from Vietnam, 1967–1973,* edited by Douglas Pike (1990); Clarke, Jeffrey J. *Advice and Support: The Final Years, 1965–1973* (1988); Colby, William, with James McCargar. *Lost Victory* (1989); Nguyên Duy Hinh. *Vietnamization and the Cease-Fire* (1980); Thompson, Robert. *No Exit from Vietnam* (1969).

See also: Abrams, Creighton; Bunker, Ellsworth; Civil Operations and Revolutionary Development Support (CORDS); Colby, William Egan; ENHANCE PLUS, Operation; Jacobson, George D.; Nixon, Richard Milhous; Pacification.

Vô Nguyên Giáp (1911–)

Vietnamese military leader. Widely recognized as a master logistician, Vô Nguyên Giáp also became adept at tactics and strategy. He drew his understanding of military science from many sources, which he welded togther with his own field experiences to create an approach to combat that confounded his enemies.

Giáp joined the Communist Party in 1937. In April 1940 the party ordered him to flee into southern China. There he met Nguyên Âi Quôc, now calling himself Hô Chí Minh. Under Hô's orders, Giáp returned to the mountains of northern Tonkin between 1941 and 1945 and, with his cadre, worked to convert the hill tribes—the Nùng, Thô, Mán Trang, Mán Tiên, Tày [Tai], Dao, Hmong, and others—to the anti-French cause. A follower, Chu Van Tân, became a leader in the first armed resistance organization, the Army for National Salvation. Meanwhile Hô organized a new group, the Viêt Nam Dôc Lâp Dông Minh Hôi (Vietnam Independence League), or Viêt Minh. Its rivals for power included the Dang Dai Viêt, a nationalist middle-class urban group; the Viêt Nam Quôc Dân Dang, an older group founded in 1927 by radical intellectuals; and the Viêt Nam Cách Mang Dông Minh Hôi, founded in 1942 under Chinese sponsorship.

Giáp's Viêt Minh cadres succesfully enlisted support among lowland Vietnamese and hill people. French efforts between 1942 and 1944 to destroy this fledgling movement came to be called "the time of the white terror."

On 22 December 1944, Giáp formed 34 men into the Viêt Nam Tuyên Truyên Giai Phóng Quân (Vietnam Armed Propaganda and Liberation Brigade). First attacks against the French came on 24 December when Giáp's unit struck outposts at Phai Khát and Nà Ngân. During a later attack on Thái Nguyên on 20 August 1945, Giáp learned that the Japanese had surrendered, and he marched his men into Hà Nôi. Between 19 and 30 August, Hô's Viêt Minh grabbed power from the Red River to the Mekong Delta. Giáp became minister of the interior of the new Democratic Republic of Vietnam (DRV) and was later named to the rank of full general and commander of all Viêt Minh military forces.

Military incidents with the French in Tonkin, particularly at Hai Phòng, caused Giáp to issue a national call to arms on 19 December 1946. Retreating in the face of French strength, by early 1947 the Viêt Minh government and Giáp's army were once again hiding in remote northern Vietnam. In the following years, Giáp assembled an army of nearly 300,000 troops and militia and made a series of attacks against French troops and positions, sometimes sustaining savage casualties. In 1953 he launched a drive into Laos, having already gained control of most of central and northern Vietnam outside the coastal lowlands. French military commander Gen. Henri Navarre, seeking a "set-piece" battle with Giáp's forces, chose to commit 10,000 troops to Điên Biên Phu. Giáp secretly brought recently obtained artillery into the surrounding mountains, a development the French considered impossible, massed 50,000 troops, and laid siege for 55 days to French strongpoints in the valley. The French surrendered on 8 May 1954 and, at Geneva, gave up further efforts to control Vietnam north of the 17th parallel.

Giáp also led the military campaign against the Republic of Vietnam (RVN) and the United States during the 1960s and 1970s. Giáp, like Mao, believed that revolutionary warfare against a government passed through three stages: guerrilla warfare, strategic defense, and counteroffensive. Giáp was long concerned that the United States might invade the North and, when he believed his forces strong enough, frequently orchestrated frontal attacks on U.S. positions, as in the Ia Drang Valley (November 1965), at Khe Sanh (January 1968), and in the Têt Offensive (January 1968). Militarily opposed to the latter, he bowed before the greater political influence of Lê Duân, Gen. Nguyên Chí Thanh, and their allies in the Politburo. These individuals faulted Giáp for his reticence to use his units boldly below the 17th parallel and consistently called for increased military action in the South.

Following Hô's death, Giáp shared power with Lê Duân, who controlled domestic affairs, and Pham Van Đông, who presided over the Foreign Ministry. Giáp's goals were to prolong the war, to inflict setbacks to Nixon's policy of Vietnamization, and to impose continuing casualties on U.S. troops. Not until 1970 did Giáp order new offensives, concentrating on the conquest of southern Laos and destabilization of Cambodia's border region.

In 1972, with some dismay because he felt the time was not yet right, Giáp planned his NGUY N HU , or Easter Offensive. The Politburo had called for the offensive, assuming that, with U.S. forces all but withdrawn, the Republic of Vietnam was ripe for attack. Once again Giáp's misgivings were proven correct. Throughout most of the RVN, after initial withdrawals, the Army of the Republic of Vietnam (ARVN) held its positions when buttressed with massive U.S. air strikes. Nixon also ordered extensive bombings of the DRV and mining of Hai Phòng harbor. The PAVN suffered more than 100,000 casualties. Still, when it was over, Giáp's divisions occupied territory never before controlled, and the terms of the 1973 peace agreement did not require their removal.

The Politburo allowed Giáp to retain his post of minister of defense but stripped him of his command of the PAVN and gave it to his chief of staff and longtime disciple, Gen. Van Tiên Dung. Dung led the Hô Chí Minh offensive, the final assault on the South in 1975. Thereafter, Giáp's life consisted of a round of visits to mostly Communist countries. Appointed to head the Ministry of Science and Technology, Giáp played only a supervisory role in the 1978 Vietnamese invasion of Cambodia (which he opposed) and the conflict with China that began in 1979.

—Cecil B. Currey

References: Currey, Cecil B. *Victory at Any Cost. The Genius of Viet Nam's Gen. Vo Nguyen Giap* (1997); Davidson, Phillip B. *Vietnam at War: The History, 1946–1975* (1988); Turley, Gerald H. *The Easter Offensive: The Last American Advisors, Vietnam, 1972* (1985); Van Tiên Dung. *Our Great Spring Victory* (1977); Vô Nguyên Giáp. *Dien Bien Phu* (1962); Vô Nguyên Giáp. *Unforgettable Days* (1978); —, interviews with the author (1988, 1991); *Who's Who in the Socialist Countries* (1978).

See also: *Đâu Tranh*; Điên Biên Phu, Battle of; Easter Offensive (Nguyên Huê Campaign); Hô Chí Minh; Ia Drang, Battle of; Khe Sanh, Battles of; Lê Duân; Navarre, Henri Eugène; Nixon, Richard Milhous; Nguyên Chí Thanh; Pham Van Đông; Têt Offensive: Overall Strategy; Têt Offensive: the Sài Gòn Circle; Transportation Group 559; Van Tiên Dung; Viêt Minh; Vietnam, Democratic Republic of: Army (People's Army of Vietnam [PAVN]).

Vô Trân Chí (?–)

Vietnamese Communist Party (VCP) figure. Little is known about Vô Trân Chí's activities during the Vietnam War except that he was a guerrilla leader in the Sài Gòn area. In 1977 he was elected secretary of the VCP Committee of the 5th District of Hô Chí Minh City. In 1986 he became secretary of the VCP Committee of Hô Chí Minh City, a position he retained through 1996. Chí was promoted to the Politburo in June 1991. A protégé of SRV Premier Vô Van Kiêt, Chí was regarded as a staunch conservative. In June 1996 he was dropped from the Politburo at the Eighth Communist Party Congress.

—Ngô Ngoc Trung

References: Biographical Files, Indo-China Archives, University of California at Berkeley.

See also: Vietnam, Socialist Republic of: 1975 to the Present; Vietnamese Communist Party (VCP); Vô Van Kiêt.

Vô Van Kiêt (1922–)

Leader in the Vietnamese Communist Party (VCP) and the Socialist Republic of Vietnam (SRV). Considered easy-going and charming, Kiêt was regarded as a moderate within the VCP and an advocate of changes based on material incentives, decentralized decision making, and limited free enterprise. He also favored normalization of relations with the United States.

—Ngô Ngoc Trung

References: Biographical Files, Indo-China Archives, University of California at Berkeley.

See also: Pham Hùng; Vietnam, Socialist Republic of: 1975 to the Present; Vietnamese Communist Party (VCP).

Vogt, John W., Jr. (1920–)

U.S. Air Force general. From 1965 to 1968 Vogt served as deputy for plans and operations, Pacific Air Forces in Honolulu, Hawaii. In this capacity he participated in the planning and direction of the air campaign against North Vietnam. In 1972 he was named commander of the Seventh U.S. Air Force in Vietnam, while serving concurrently as deputy commander of Military Assistance Command, Vietnam (MACV). The 1972 Easter bombardment of the North was carried out under his direction. Vogt presided over the withdrawal of U.S. forces from Vietnam through the remainder of 1972 to March 1973, after which his headquarters was moved to Nakhom Phnom Royal Thai Air Force Base.

—Robert G. Mangrum

References: Olson, James S., ed. *Dictionary of the Vietnam War* (1988); Sumners, Harry G. *Vietnam War Almanac* (1985).

See also: Air Power, Role in War; LINEBACKER I, Operation; LINEBACKER II, Operation; Military Assistance Command, Vietnam (MACV); ROLLING THUNDER, Operation; United States: Air Force.

Vu Hông Khanh (1898–1993)

Leader of the Viêt Nam Quôc Dân Đang (VNQDD); real name Vu Van Giang. Khanh was among the first to join the VNQDD, and in the 1930 uprising he commanded the VNQDD force attacking French colonial bases in Hai Phòng City and Kiên An Province. His force failed to take its objectives, and Khanh fled to south China where, with Nguyên Hai Thân, Nghiêm Kê Tô, and others, he helped reorganize the VNQDD.

In August 1945 Khanh directed VNQDD militia units in attacks against Japanese troops in Hà Giang Province and other border areas. In early 1946 he became vice-chairman of the Central Military Commission of the Democratic Republic of Vietnam (DRV), of which Vô Nguyên Giáp was the chairman. Khanh was a cosignatory of the 6 March 1946 preliminary agreement between Hô Chí Minh and French representative Jean Sainteny. Many of his nationalist colleagues were critical of Khanh for this agreement, which they saw as a sellout to the French.

In November 1949 Khanh led three infantry divisions of Vietnamese and Chinese across the border into Vietnam. His troops promptly came under attack by both the Viêt Minh and French Army. Fierce fighting and supply shortages, coupled with an appeal from Bao Dai, chief of state of the newly established State of Vietnam, led Khanh to side with the State of Vietnam. In 1952 he became minister of youth in the cabinet of Premier Nguyên Van Tâm. Khanh did not hold any government post after 1954, but he remained a VNQDD leader in South Vietnam. In June 1975 the Communists sentenced him to prison. Released in 1979, he was kept under house arrest until his death.

—Nguyên Công Luân (Lu Tuân)

References: Cao Thê Dung. *Viêt Nam Huyêt Lê Su* (1996); Hoàng Van Đào. *Viêt Nam Quôc Dân Đang* (1970); Pham Kim Vinh. *The Vietnamese Culture* (1995).

See also: Bao Đai; Hô Chí Minh; Hô-Sainteny Agreement; Nguyên Hai Thân; Pham Duy; Sainteny, Jean; Van Cao; Vô Nguyên Giáp.

Vu Oanh (?–)

Vietnamese Communist Party (VCP) and Socialist Republic of Vietnam (SRV) official. During the Vietnam War, Oanh was political commissar of a division commanded by Gen. Van Tiên Dung, who led the victorious 1975 Hô Chí Minh Campaign. In 1972 Oanh was deputy chief of the VCP Central Committee Organization Department, one of the most important bodies in charge of personnel matters. Oanh apparently was the architect of the SRV's new policy of open-

ing up to the outside world in the wake of political upheaval in the USSR and Eastern Europe.

—Ngô Ngoc Trung

References: Biographical Files, Indo-China Archives, University of California at Berkeley.

See also: Vietnam, Socialist Republic of: 1975 to the Present; Vietnamese Communist Party (VCP).

Vu Quôc Thúc (1920–)

Vietnamese intellectual who participated in Republic of Vietnam (RVN) politics throughout the Vietnam War era. After the 1954 Geneva Agreements, Vu Quôc Thúc and several colleagues founded the first national university in Sài Gòn. He continued teaching at its school of law until the April 1975 defeat of the RVN. He held various important positions, including governor of the central RVN bank, advisor to President Ngô Đình Diêm, head of the RVN Post-War Planning Group, and minister of state in charge of reconstruction and development. His most important contributions during the Vietnam War were his coauthored joint reports with Eugene Staley (1961) and D. E. Lilienthal (1968) on Vietnam postwar reconstruction and development programs, which were submitted to the presidents of the United States.

—Nguyên Bá Long

References: Lilienthal, D. E., and Vu Quôc Thúc. *The Postwar Development of the Republic of Vietnam: Policies and Programs* (1970); Vu Quôc Thúc. *L'Economie communaliste du Vietnam* (1952); Vu Quôc Thúc. "Le Vietnam vainquer et vaincu" (1995).

See also: Ngô Đình Diêm; Staley, Eugene.

VULTURE, Operation (March–April 1954)

Proposed air strike to rescue French military forces trapped at Điên Biên Phu during March and April 1954. On 20 March, French chief of staff Gen. Paul Ely informed U.S. officials that French forces needed American support to hold Điên Biên Phu. Throughout the crisis, U.S. and French military officers developed plans for intervention at Điên Biên Phu—codenamed VULTURE by Navarre's staff. These plans shifted in scope and intensity according to the condition of the French garrison. The general outline called for an air attack by 60 to 100 U.S. B-29 bombers from the Philippines, supported by several hundred jet fighters from U.S. aircraft carriers. A plan to strike Viêt Minh forces in the mountains surrounding Điên Biên Phu was dropped because French radar was inadequate to support close fire. Another strategy called for bombing raids on Viêt Minh bases and supply lines near the Chinese border. On at least one occasion, Admiral Radford suggested the use of nuclear bombs.

French expectations were raised on 29 March when Secretary of State John Foster Dulles said that, since China supported the Viêt Minh with the purpose of dominating Southeast Asia, other nations should meet the threat with "united action." President Eisenhower seconded Dulles's call for united action in a press conference two days later, but he pointedly neither promised nor ruled out direct U.S. assistance. On 3 April, Dulles and Radford met with congressional leaders to seek their support for intervention if the president decided it was necessary. The legislators insisted on three conditions to make congressional approval likely: (1) intervention had to be a united, multinational action including Britain and the British Commonwealth nations; (2) France had to promise to accelerate independence for its Indo-China colonies; and (3) France had to agree not to withdraw from the war once the United States became involved.

Meanwhile in Paris, Ely received a desperate cable from Navarre on 4 April, requesting a U.S. bombing attack on Viêt Minh positions at Điên Biên Phu. The French War Committee that night formally requested immediate intervention. In a 7 April press conference, however, Eisenhower refused comment when asked if the United States would act unilaterally in Indo-China.

On 13 April, Dulles and British Foreign Secretary Anthony Eden issued a communiqué supporting the principle of "collective defense." But as Dulles traveled to Paris, Eden stated in the House of Commons that the statement meant only willingness to examine "possibilities" rather than any specific obligation. Given the restrictions earlier expressed by congressional leaders, there was now no likelihood of U.S. military intervention over Điên Biên Phu.

On 23 April, Bidault received a message from officials in Indo-China that the final battle for Điên Biên Phu had begun. The only alternatives, he informed Dulles, were Operation VULTURE or a cease-fire. That evening, Laniel asked Britain to participate in the united action that was a condition for intervention. Prime Minister Winston Churchill held an emergency meeting of the cabinet, which decided against military involvement in Vietnam, marking the end of serious discussion about Operation VULTURE.

—Kenneth R. Stevens

References: Billings-Yun, Melanie. *Decision against War: Eisenhower and Dien Bien Phu, 1954* (1988); Eden, Anthony. *Full Circle* (1960); Eisenhower, Dwight D. *Mandate for Change, 1953–1956: The White House Years* (1963); Ely, Paul. *L'Indochine dans la Tourmente* (1964); Radford, Arthur W. *From Pearl Harbor to Vietnam: The Memoirs of Admiral Arthur W. Radford* (1980).

See also: Bidault, Georges; Điên Biên Phu, Battle of; Dulles, John Foster; Eden, Anthony; Eisenhower, Dwight David; Ely, Paul Henri Romuald; Geneva Conference and Geneva Accords; Johnson, Lyndon Baines; Laniel, Joseph; Navarre, Henri Eugène; Radford, Arthur W.; Southeast Asia Treaty Organization (SEATO); Taylor, Maxwell Davenport; Twining, Nathan Farragut; Vô Nguyên Giáp.

W

Wallace, George Corley, Jr. (1919–)

U.S. presidential candidate; governor of Alabama. Capitalizing on his stand to preserve "segregation now, segregation tomorrow, segregation forever," Wallace catapulted to the national political scene in the early 1960s. In February 1967 Wallace said, "The Vietnam War is the most important matter facing the American people." He called for a more vigorous pursuit of military victory by bombing the roads and highways leading from Hà Nội to China and mining Hai Phòng Harbor.

Wallace ran unsuccessfully for the presidency in 1968 on the American Independent Party ticket with retired Air Force Gen. Curtis E. LeMay as his running mate. After LeMay refused to rule out the use of nuclear weapons in Vietnam, Wallace sent him on a tour of Vietnam to keep him out of the country until after the election. Wallace excoriated the antiwar movement and warned that any student at any college or university in Alabama who advocated a victory by the Việt Cộng would be expelled.

During his run for the Democratic Party presidential nomination in 1972, Wallace was seriously wounded by a would-be assassin. He won several state primaries but ultimately withdrew from the campaign.

—Earl H. Tilford, Jr.

References: Frady, Marshall. *Wallace* (1972); Lesher, Stephan. *George Wallace: American Populist* (1994); Wallace, George, C., Jr. *Hear Me Out: This Is Where I Stand* (1968).

See also: Elections, U.S.: 1968; LeMay, Curtis Emerson.

Walt, Lewis W. (1913–1989)

U.S. Marine Corps general. In June 1965 Walt assumed command of the 3d Marine Division in Vietnam as a major general, while serving concurrently as commander of III Marine Amphibious Force (MAF). When III MAF was elevated to the first corps-level headquarters in Marine Corps history, Walt was given command and promoted to lieutenant general in 1966; he had under his control U.S. Naval Forces, Vietnam. He also served as senior advisor and coordinator of the Army of the Republic of Vietnam's I Corps, supervising the corps buildup between 1965 and 1967.

Walt insisted on a balance of small-unit patrols, large-unit operations, and a program of pacification that consisted of Marine Combined Action Platoons (CAPs) operating with Vietnamese in the countryside. Walt and the Marines placed much more emphasis on small-unit operations and pacification than did Gen. William Westmoreland in his strategy of large-unit actions.

Walt retired from the Marine Corps in 1971, and in 1976 he published *Strange War, Strange Strategy: A General's Report on Vietnam.*

—Robert G. Mangrum

References: Karnow, Stanley. *Vietnam: A History* (1984); Millet, Allan R. *Semper Fidelis: The History of the United States Marine Corps* (1980); Moskin, J. Robert. *The U.S. Marine Corps Story.* Rev.

Ed. (1982); Olson, James S., ed. *Dictionary of the Vietnam War* (1988); Walt, Lewis W. *Strange War, Strange Strategy: A General's Report on Vietnam* (1976).

See also: Marine Combined Action Platoons (CAPs); United States: Marine Corps; Vietnam, Republic of: Army (ARVN); Westmoreland, William Childs.

War Powers Act (1973)

U.S. congressional effort to limit presidential war-making powers and to ensure more legislative control of the nation's military. The War Powers Resolution of 1973 (Public Law 93-148, 93rd Congress, H.J. Resolution S42, 7 November 1973), simply known as the War Powers Act, requires that the president consult with Congress before military forces are sent into combat abroad, or to areas where hostilities are likely, and to report in writing within 48 hours after troops are deployed. The president must then terminate the use of military force within 60 to 90 days. The deployment can continue for another 60 days, and for another 30 days beyond that if the president certifies to Congress in writing that the safety of the force so requires. Unless Congress authorizes a continuation, through a declaration of war, a concurrent resolution, or other appropriate legislation, the deployment cannot be continued beyond 90 days.

Senator Jacob K. Javits introduced the War Powers Act after the 1970 U.S. invasion of Cambodia. At the time many believed it was a direct result of U.S. experience in Vietnam. Javits in 1973 stated that the act was an effort to learn from the lessons of Vietnam that had cost the United States so heavily in blood, treasure, and morale. Although the act was passed only months after the final U.S. withdrawal, many scholars claim that it was not just a reaction to that conflict but the product of a slow, evolutionary debate on the respective war powers of Congress and the president that had been going on for decades. The act was an attempt by the legislative branch to reassert some authority over the military that it had lost to the president after 1941. The law, passed by Congress (House, 284–135; Senate, 75–18) on 7 November 1973 over the veto of President Nixon, gave more authority to Congress to limit the war-making powers of the chief executive.

Nixon vetoed the bill, arguing that it could imperil the nation in times of crisis and that it granted Congress authority over troop deployments in violation of Article II of the Constitution, which granted such powers to the president. Other critics maintained that the act placed inflexible restrictions on the president's ability to conduct foreign policy. Supporters held that the act served as a necessary restraint on the president's power and inherently compelled communication between the executive and legislative branches in times of emergency. Although many flaws have been found in the act, it has not been amended since passage.

—Clayton D. Laurie

References: Fisher, Louis. *Presidential War Power* (1995); Javits, Jacob K. *Who Makes War: The President versus Congress* (1973);

Stern, Gary M., and Morton Halperin, eds. *The U.S. Constitution and the Power to Go to War: Historical and Current Perspectives* (1994).
See also: Cooper-Church Amendment; Ford, Gerald R.; FREQUENT WIND, Operation; Hatfield-McGovern Amendment; Javits, Jacob K.; *Mayaguez* Incident; Nixon, Richard Milhous; Stennis, John Cornelius.

War Resisters League (WRL)

Pacifist organization; support group for conscientious objectors. The War Resisters League (WRL) was founded in 1932 by Jessie Wallace Hughan as the American branch of the Fellowship of Reconciliation (FOR), which was founded in England in 1914. By 1963, under the leadership of David Dellinger and David McReynolds, the WRL focused its protests on the escalating Vietnam War and Selective Service inductions.

The first major WRL peace demonstration on the Vietnam War issue came on 9 October 1963. On 16 May 1964 the WRL cosponsored a demonstration in New York City at which 12 men burned their draft cards. In 1965 Congress outlawed the burning of draft cards, but on 5 November of that year McReynolds and four others burned their draft cards at a rally in Union Square. McReynolds, classified 4-F, was not arrested.

Between 1964 and 1973, WRL membership grew from 3,000 to 15,000 people. From 1965 through 1983, the WRL's Workshop in Nonviolence produced *WIN*, a widely read "movement" magazine, and published *WRL News*. In late 1967 the WRL organized "Stop the Draft Week." It endorsed "teach-ins" and demonstrations, including the 1971 May Day demonstrations. Because of its growing visibility and antiwar activities, the WRL was the target of Central Intelligence Agency infiltration and periodic seizures by the Internal Revenue Service.

After the Vietnam War, WRL membership again declined, and it turned its attention to issues such as nuclear disarmament and amnesty for draft resisters.

—Gary Kerley

References: DeBenedetti, Charles. *An American Ordeal: The Antiwar Movement of the Vietnam Era* (1990); McReynolds, David. "Pacifists and the Vietnam Antiwar Movement" (1992); Olson, James S., ed. *Dictionary of the Vietnam War* (1988); Wittner, Laurence S. *Rebels Against War: The American Peace Movement, 1941–1960* (1969); Zaroulis, Nancy, and Gerald Sullivan. *Who Spoke Up? American Protest Against the War in Vietnam, 1963–1975* (1984).
See also: Antiwar Movement, United States; Berrigan, Daniel; Conscientious Objectors (COs); Dellinger, David; Draft; Fellowship of Reconciliation (FOR); Muste, Abraham J.

War Zone C and War Zone D

Geographical areas important because of their proximity to Sài Gòn. Gen. William Westmoreland attributes the terms to the HOP TÁC plan of 1964, but several experts mention the earlier existence of these zones as 1950s French designations, People's Army of Vietnam (PAVN) classifications prior to U.S. involvement, or U.S. references prior to 1964.

War Zone C served as the main PAVN approach from Cambodia to Sài Gòn. It included parts of the Hô Chí Minh Trail and elaborate, concealed facilities with command posts, ammunition and supply dumps, and hospitals, some connected by tunnels. Under Communist control before the 1954 partition of Vietnam, War Zone C later served as the headquarters of the Central Office for South Vietnam and therefore was a National Liberation Front stronghold and sanctuary. War Zone C borders ran from Bên Cát due north on the western side of Route 13 to the Cambodian border, then followed the border southwest to Tapang Raboa, from which a west-east arc ran through Tây Ninh City back to Bên Cát. Portions of Tây Ninh, Bình Long, and Bình Duong provinces fell within the zone. The varied terrain included flat, potentially marshy land (dry in summer, muddy in winter), rolling hills nearer Cambodia, dense tropical rainforest, and the landmark Núi Bà Đen (Black Woman) Mountain (elevation 3,235 feet).

War Zone D, with its heavy jungle, rain forest, and elephant grasses, provided the main access from the central part of the country to Sài Gòn. Like Zone C, it also included branches of the Hô Chí Minh Trail and tunnel complexes. Part of a PAVN guerrilla force, Unit 250, appeared in Zone D in October 1957 and within a year had grown to battalion size. In January 1961 the Politburo decision to escalate the war in the South led to a 15 February meeting in War Zone D to unify all armed units into an integrated command known as the People's Liberation Armed Forces (PLAF), more widely known as the Viêt Công. In time the PLAF would name War Zone D "the forbidden zone."

War Zone D borders ran due north from Bên Cát on the eastern side of Route 13 parallel to the border of War Zone C, to Chon Thành at the split of Routes 13 and 14, then northeast and east on Route 14 through Chí Linh and Đông Xoài to Bu Nard; it then ran due east for ten miles, then due south for 25 miles to Thanh Son, then due west for ten miles; after following the Đông Nai River and Route 20 south for a few miles, it went southwest for about ten miles, crossing Route 20 before heading 20 miles due west along 11 degrees east latitude parallel to Route 1 via Biên Hòa (headquarters of III Corps); northwest about ten miles to Phú Cuong to rejoin Route 13 north, parallel to the Iron Triangle, and then north 12 miles back to Bên Cát. War Zone D included portions of Bình Duong, Biên Hòa, Phuoc Long, and Long Khánh provinces.

Forces operating within War Zones C and/or D included the U.S. 1st, 4th, and 25th Infantry Divisions, 11th Armored Cavalry Regiment, 1st Cavalry Division, 196th Infantry Brigade, and 173d Airborne Brigade; the ARVN 5th Division; and the PLAF 9th Division.

The 1st Infantry Division's 1st and 3d Brigades, located at Phuoc Vinh and Lai Khê, respectively, occupied areas vital to PLAF lines of communication. In both Zones C and D, from its first significant battle near Bâu Bàn on 12 November 1965 through its last at Phú Hòa Đông between 15 and 28 September 1969, the 1st Infantry Division participated in operations or battles each year. The 11th Armored Cavalry carried out joint military operations with the 1st Infantry

Division from 8 May 1967 to 12 April 1969. A year later the 11th Armored Cavalry joined the 1st Cavalry Division to conduct Operation MONTANA RAIDER in Zone C. On 9 May 1970 the 11th Armored Cavalry, under the 1st Cavalry Division, moved from its support position in War Zone C into the Fishhook area of Cambodia. The 1st Cavalry Division, in III Corps (III CTZ) in 1969, engaged Communist forces north of the Đông Nai River in War Zone D and took part in a half-dozen major battles in War Zone C, including those of Landing Zones Grant, Carolyn, Jamie, and Ike and Fire Support Bases Becky and Ike.

Major U.S. operations in War Zone C, including EL PASO II, ATTLEBORO, JUNCTION CITY, and YELLOWSTONE, saw the long and costly involvement of the 196th Infantry Brigade; the 173d Airborne Brigade; the 1st, 4th, and 25th Infantry Divisions; and various ARVN units.

Herbicide warfare targeted War Zones C and D heavily. Operations included the initial RANCH HAND test site (1961), BIG PATCH (1964), SHERWOOD FOREST (1965), and PINK ROSE (1966–1967). The latter had two target areas in Zone C and one in Zone D, the third and last effort combining defoliation with incendiaries to produce forest fires.

U.S. Army Special Forces had about a dozen active A camps in War Zone C and a half-dozen in Zone D. In War Zone D, BLACKJACK 31 and HARVEST MOON, which included the first mass Special Forces–led Civilian Irregular Defense Group (CIDG) combat parachute drop of the Vietnam War, stand out as successful 1967 offensive operations utilizing the concepts of the Mobile Guerrilla Force and Mobile Strike Force, respectively.

Gen. Westmoreland stated that operations in War Zones C and D had "shortcomings but probably saved Saigon from enemy control." The constant struggle in these zones between PLAF/PAVN forces and those of the United States and the RVN centered on the control of Sài Gòn, which was crucial to the outcome of the war.

—Paul S. Daum, with Francis Ryan

References: Buckingham, William A., Jr. *Operation Ranch Hand: The Air Force and Herbicides in Southeast Asia, 1961–1971* (1982); Haldane, Robert, ed. *The First Infantry Division in Vietnam, 1965–1970* (1993); Hatch, Gardner, ed. *11th U.S. Cavalry: Blackhorse* (1990); Martin, Robert, ed. *1st Air Cavalry Division: Memoirs of the First Team, Vietnam, August 1965–December 1969* (1995); Palmer, Bruce, Jr. *The 25-Year War: America's Military Role in Vietnam* (1984); Rogers, Bernard William. *Cedar Falls–Junction City: A Turning Point* (1974); Stanton, Shelby L. *The Rise and Fall of an American Army: U.S. Ground Forces in Vietnam, 1965–1973* (1985); Turley, William S. *The Second Indochina War: A Short Political and Military History, 1954–1975* (1986); Westmoreland, William C. *Report on the War in Vietnam (as of 30 June 1968). Part II. Report on Operations in South Vietnam, January 1964–June, 1968* (1968).

See also: ATTLEBORO, Operation; Cambodian Incursion; Civilian Irregular Defense Group (CIDG); COSVN (Central Office for South Vietnam or Trung Uong Cuc Miên Nam); Defoliation; HARVEST MOON, Operation; Hồ Chí Minh Trail; Iron Triangle; JUNCTION CITY, Operation; Mobile Guerrilla Forces (MGF); Mobile Strike Force Commands; National Front for the Liberation of South Vietnam (NFLSV); RANCH HAND, Operation; United States: Army; United States: Special Forces; Vietnam, Democratic Republic of: Army (People's Army of Vietnam [PAVN]); Vietnam, Republic of: Army (ARVN); YELLOWSTONE, Operation.

Ware, Keith L. (1915–1968)

U.S. Army general; commander of the 1st Infantry Division, March–September 1968. Ware reported to Vietnam for assignment as deputy commanding general, I Field Force, Vietnam (IFFV), in December 1967. He then served as deputy commanding general of IIFFV before assuming command of the 1st Infantry Division ("Big Red One"). Ware was an inspirational leader whose dream had been to command the division in combat. On 13 September 1968 Gen. Ware was killed in action when his command helicopter was hit by hostile ground fire and crashed in the jungle southeast of Lôc Ninh. He was the fourth general officer killed in Vietnam.

—John F. Votaw

References: *First Infantry Division in Vietnam.* Vol. 2 (n.d.); *Official Biography of Major General Keith L. Ware* (n.d.)
See also: Casualties; United States: Army.

Warnke, Paul C. (1920–)

General counsel for the U.S. Department of Defense, 1966–1967; assistant secretary of defense for international security affairs, 1967–1969. A staunch opponent of the Vietnam War, Warnke helped convince Secretary of Defense Robert McNamara of its hopelessness and later exerted considerable influence over McNamara's successor, Clark Clifford. With the election of Richard Nixon, Warnke left the Defense Department and returned to the practice of law as a partner in Clifford's firm.

—David Coffey

References: Karnow, Stanley. *Vietnam: A History* (1983); *Who's Who in American Politics, 1996* (1995).
See also: Clifford, Clark M.; McNamara, Robert S.; Westmoreland, William Childs.

Wars of National Liberation

Organized violence from within a state aimed at overthrowing the government and restructuring the state's political—and often its economic and social—order. To some the Vietnam War fit this pattern. The U.S. government, however, took the position that the organized violence came not primarily from within, but from external Communist-sponsored aggression, and was therefore an invasion by an outside power.

From one point of view, many aspects of the Vietnam insurgency are characteristic of a revolutionary war. The National Liberation Front, or Viêt Công (VC), and Central Office for South Vietnam (COSVN) provided an organized, disciplined leadership. Nationalism and communism provided popular ideologies, which challenged perceived American imperialism that many Vietnamese believed had replaced French colonialism. There was considerable popular support for the insurgency, and the VC provided the military forces necessary to wage the conflict.

Washington, however, considered the NLF and COSVN to

be directed and controlled by the Democratic Republic of Vietnam, supported by its larger Soviet and PRC patrons. Mass support for the insurgency was thought to be based somewhat on Communist and nationalist sympathies, but largely forced by VC fear tactics and terrorism. Finally, the military forces necessary to wage the war did not come solely from the South Vietnamese population but were primarily provided by North Vietnamese People's Army of Vietnam regulars, especially after the 1968 Têt Offensive.

—Arthur T. Frame

References: Gaddis, John Lewis. *Russia, The Soviet Union, and the United States: An Interpretive History* (1978); Herring, George C. *America's Longest War: The United States and Vietnam, 1950–1975.* 2d ed. (1986); Lewy, Gunther. *America in Vietnam* (1978).

See also: Containment Policy; COSVN (Central Office for South Vietnam or Trung Uong Cuc Miên Nam); Counterinsurgency Warfare; Domino Theory; Khrushchev, Nikita Sergeyevich; National Front for the Liberation of South Vietnam (NFLSV).

Warships, Allied and Democratic Republic of Vietnam

Excluding submarines, virtually every type of modern combat vessel, from the largest aircraft carriers to the smallest river patrol boats, were used in the Vietnam War. Warships of several lesser navies took part in the conflict, but all were overshadowed by those of the U.S. Navy.

Australia The Australian destroyer H.M.S. *Hobart* of the U.S. Navy Charles F. Adams class provided gunfire support for Allied forces in South Vietnam.

Democratic Republic of Vietnam (DRV) In 1964 the DRV Navy was a coastal force composed of small combatants acquired from the larger Communist powers. Most numerous were tiny Swatow-class motor gunboats, a Chinese-made version of the Soviet P-6. These steel-hulled vessels were powered by diesel engines, had a top speed of 28 knots, and were armed with four 37-mm cannon and depth charges. Swifter were the twelve P-4 motor torpedo boats with their two torpedo tubes. Although their stepped hull made possible a speed of 42 knots, their stability at high speeds was marginal. Three of these vessels were involved in the August 1964 Tonkin Gulf incidents. The DRV Navy received reinforcements in 1967 in the form of four P-6 gunboats. Against these modest additions must be counted the loss of approximately 33 Swatows and P-4s to air strikes during Operation PIERCE ARROW.

Republic of Vietnam (RVN, or South Vietnam) The South Vietnamese Navy was built up from obsolescent small craft donated by the United States. In 1964 it numbered 44 seagoing vessels and more than 200 lesser craft. The best-armed of these warships were five escort patrol craft (PCEs) and 12 motor gunboats (PGMs). As fighting accelerated, the United States transferred to the RVN seven Coast Guard cutters of the Barnegat class and two Edsall-class frigates. By 1972, when Vietnamization had been completed, the RVN Navy numbered about 1,000 craft of varying types. Twenty-seven of its seagoing vessels carried 18,000 refugees to Subic Bay in the Philippines following the final 1975 Communist offensive.

United States Throughout the conflict, the United States possessed the strongest navy in the world. Its backbone was the attack aircraft carrier, the largest type of warship ever constructed. The U.S.S. *Enterprise*, the first nuclear-powered carrier, displaced almost 90,000 tons at full load and was armed with an air group of 90 aircraft.

Escorting the carriers were the Navy's newest surface warships: guided missile cruisers and frigates. Keeping pace with the *Enterprise* was the cruiser *Long Beach*. At 16,602 tons, she was equipped with one Talos and two Terrier missile launchers; her nuclear power plant drove her at 30 knots. While on station in the Tonkin Gulf in May 1968, this ship scored the first hit ever made on an enemy aircraft with guided missiles. In 1972 the cruiser *Chicago*, an 18,777-ton ship converted from a gunship, scored a similar success while providing cover for planes mining Hai Phòng Harbor.

Also operating in the South China Sea were the Navy's new frigates, including the nuclear-powered *Bainbridge*. Usually displacing close to 8,000 tons at full load, these fast ships (over 30 knots) were armed with one or two Terrier missile launchers and often a 5-inch gun. The newest ships of the Belknap class were fitted with the Naval Tactical Data System that allowed them to track hundreds of aircraft simultaneously. On 19 July 1972, one of these vessels, the *Biddle*, while on station in the Gulf of Tonkin, engaged five MiGs and shot down two. Another Belknap-class frigate, the U.S.S. *Sterett*, in an action of 19 April 1972, claimed two MiGs, a Styx antiship missile, and two PT boats.

Gunnery support duties fell to the Navy's senior surface warships, some older than many of their crewmen. Beginning in 1965 they supported friendly troops in South Vietnam and, starting in 1966, bombarded North Vietnamese military forces north of the Demilitarized Zone. Especially valuable in this role were the 8-inch gun cruisers *Newport News* and *St. Paul*, the latter a veteran of World War II and Korea. So scarce were major-caliber rifles on the gunline that the Navy's first guided missile cruisers *Boston* and *Canberra* remained in commission for their two 8-inch forward mounts even when their missile batteries aft were removed. The Cleveland-class missile cruiser conversions were valued more for their 6-inch guns than for their Terrier batteries. The *Boston* fired so many missions during Operation SEA DRAGON that the rifling in her gun barrels was worn virtually smooth. Also reinforcing the bombardment force was the battleship *New Jersey*, brought out of retirement in 1967.

Destroyers—both World War II veterans and newer ships of the Forrest Sherman and Charles F. Adams classes—also performed in the gunnery role, as did newer destroyer escorts of the Claud Jones, Garcia, and Brooke classes. The destroyer types engaged in lengthy fire missions; the *Towers*, for instance, expended 3,266 5-inch shells in July 1966 alone. These extensive bombardments revealed defects in ammunition of the new 5-inch/54-caliber gun, with several ships suffering in-bore explosions. Off Vietnam, the destroyer types also performed plane guard and search-and-rescue duties; radar picket destroyer escorts helped enforce the MARKET TIME patrols.

Smaller warships—as varied as Coast Guard cutters, Asheville-class patrol gunboats, minesweepers, hydrofoils, Swift boats, and Boston Whalers—undertook a host of missions off South Vietnam's coasts and on her rivers.

Essential to the Navy's power projection duty were the fleet's amphibious ships: assault ships, dock landing ships, infantry landing ships, inshore fire support ships, tank and infantry landing ships, transport docks, and others. Backing up the fighting forces was an armada of support craft with designations as varied as aircraft ferry, attack transport, ammunition ship, barracks ship, cargo ship, fleet tug, floating crane, floating drydock, harbor tug, hospital ship, hydrographic survey ship, net-layer, oiler, open lighter, provision ship, refrigerator ship, repair ship, salvage ship, seaplane tender, storeship, tanker, and transport.

—Malcolm Muir, Jr.

References: Friedman, Norman. *U.S. Small Combatants* (1987); Gardiner, Robert, ed. *Conway's All the World's Fighting Ships 1947–1982, Part 1: The Western Powers; Part 2: The Warsaw Pact and Non-Aligned Nations* (1983); *Jane's Fighting Ships* (various editions); U.S. Naval History Division. *Dictionary of American Naval Fighting Ships* (1959–1981).
See also: Aircraft Carriers; Australia; *New Jersey* (BB-62); MARKET TIME, Operation; PIERCE ARROW, Operation; SEA DRAGON, Operation; United States: Navy; Vietnam, Republic of: Navy (VNN).

Washington Special Actions Group (WSAG)

Contingency-planning crisis management board established and chaired by Henry Kissinger. The Washington Special Actions Group (WSAG) was composed of personnel responsible for national security, including the deputy secretaries of the State and Defense Departments, the director of the Central Intelligence Agency (CIA), the chairman of the Joint Chiefs of Staff (JCS), and the assistant to the president for National Security Affairs. In spring 1969 it became Kissinger's vehicle for crisis management.

The WSAG worked on various programs designed to harass North Vietnamese troops in the Cambodian border areas, including air attacks and raids by South Vietnamese forces. When Prince Norodom Sihanouk was overthrown the United States had to decide whether or not to support the Lon Nol government, which was under attack by North Vietnamese forces. In this crisis the WSAG—now augmented by additional staff personnel and sending its documents through formal channels—approved shipment of captured Communist weapons from South Vietnam to Lon Nol's forces and, on 15 April 1970, arranged the transfer of $5 million for the purchase of arms. More important, the WSAG supported President Nixon's subsequent decision to launch the incursion against Communist sanctuaries in Cambodian border areas.

The WSAG met almost daily during the 1972 North Vietnamese Easter Offensive and supported Nixon's decision to mine Hai Phòng Harbor. As Washington moved toward the Paris Accords with the North Vietnamese, the WSAG worked on Operation ENHANCE PLUS in an effort to supply the Republic of Vietnam with sufficient equipment to defend itself when all U.S. troops were withdrawn. The WSAG thus

played a key role in planning, implementing, and advising Nixon on matters related to the national security.

—Claude R. Sasso

References: Johnson, U. Alexis. *Right Hand of Power* (1984); Kalb, Marvin, and Bernard Kalb. *Kissinger* (1974); Kissinger, Henry. *White House Years* (1979).
See also: Cambodia; Cambodian Incursion; ENHANCE PLUS, Operation; Johnson, U. Alexis; Kissinger, Henry Alfred; Nixon, Richard Milhous; Sihanouk, Norodom.

Watergate

Term given to a vast array of abuses of power during Richard Nixon's administration. Watergate is generally considered to have begun with National Security Advisor Henry Kissinger's order, approved by Nixon, to tap the telephone of *New York Times* reporter William Beecher in an attempt to locate the source of Beecher's story on the secret bombing of Cambodia.

White House paranoia over internal leaks to the news media climaxed with the 1971 release to the press of the Pentagon Papers, a top-secret study on the conduct of the war, by one of the study's Defense Department authors. Although nothing in the study compromised his administration, Nixon was incensed by this breach of security and ordered his staff to find the source of the leak. The result was an attempted burglary on 23 June 1972 at the Watergate Hotel complex in Washington, D.C., undertaken to obtain information from the offices of the Democratic National Committee that might be of use in the upcoming presidential campaign. Subsequent attempts to cover up the genesis of this crime, as well as the existence of others committed by the administration, led to the resignation of the president on 8 August 1974.

To many Americans, the Vietnam War and Watergate represented what had gone wrong with American politics in the 1960s. Many agreed with historian Arthur M. Schlesinger, Jr., that the American presidency had become "imperial" in nature. This feeling contributed greatly to the passage of the 1973 War Powers Act, which limited the president's ability to commit troops in times of military crisis without explicit reporting to Congress.

Watergate did, however, play an indirect role in the end of the Vietnam War in 1975. During the negotiations that led to the 1973 cease-fire and withdrawal of U.S. troops from Vietnam, Nixon secretly promised Republic of Vietnam President Nguyên Van Thiêu that, if the North violated the peace, the United States would reenter the conflict and protect Sài Gòn. This promise, more than anything else, led Thiêu to accept the cease-fire. However, thanks to the new mood of Congressional oversight toward the presidency caused largely by Watergate, President Ford was unable to keep Nixon's promise. Despite Thiêu's rather frantic entreaties after the fall of Ban Mê Thuột in March 1975, Ford recognized the volatility of the political situation and never asked for the troops that Thiêu requested.

—John Robert Greene

References: Greene, John Robert. *The Limits of Power: The Nixon and Ford Administrations* (1992); Kutler, Stanley I. *The Wars of*

Watergate: The Last Crisis of Richard Nixon (1990); Schlesinger, Arthur M., Jr. *The Imperial Presidency* (1973).
See also: Ellsberg, Daniel; Ford, Gerald R.; Kissinger, Henry Alfred; Mitchell, John Newton; Nixon, Richard Milhous; Pentagon Papers and Trial; United States: Department of Justice; War Powers Act.

Weathermen

Radical faction of the Students for a Democratic Society (SDS). The Weathermen grew out of an SDS national "war council" held in Austin, Texas, in March 1969, which resolved to promote "armed struggle" as the only way to transform American society. Weathermen agreed with the council's conclusions and in October organized more than 600 people to engage in violent protests in Chicago. That became known as the "Days of Rage." The Weathermen caught the attention of the Federal Bureau of Investigation, particularly because of their reliance on arson and bombings to assault the federal government.

The Weathermen's philosophical foundations were Marxist in nature: militant struggle was the key to striking out against the state and building a revolutionary consciousness among the young, particularly the white working class. The message was antiracist and anti-imperialist; the goal was a radical counterculture that provoked arguments and incited fights within itself and with its opponents. The Weathermen thought that perpetual criticism would force American youth to continually question the political establishment and reverse the corruption of once-democratic American ideals. The radicals believed that most Americans understood their political message and the reasons they considered violent tactics necessary. In fact, an overwhelming number of Americans regarded the Weathermen's activities as criminal and supported efforts by federal law enforcement agencies to end their activities in the early 1970s.

—Tracy R. Szczepaniak

References: Gitlin, Todd. *The Sixties: Years of Hope, Days of Rage* (1987); Jacobs, Harold. *The Weathermen* (1971); Miller, James. *Democracy is in the Streets: From Port Huron to The Siege of Chicago* (1987); O'Neill, William L. *Coming Apart: An Informal History of America in the 1960s* (1971); Viorst, Milton. *Fire in the Streets: America in the 1960s* (1979).
See also: Antiwar Movement, United States; Students for a Democratic Society (SDS); University of Wisconsin Bombing.

Westmoreland, William Childs (1914–)

U.S. Army general; commander of American forces in Vietnam, June 1964–June 1968. Ordered to Vietnam as deputy commander, U.S. Military Assistance Command, Vietnam (MACV), Westmoreland arrived in Vietnam on 27 January 1964. In June he was named to succeed Gen. Paul D. Harkins as commander of MACV. Westmoreland judged the South Vietnamese to lack a "sense of urgency." His own approach to command in Vietnam was to be one of action, not contemplation. In August Westmoreland was promoted to full general; it was now Westmoreland's war.

Westmoreland's strategy of search and destroy seemingly was consistent with the political character of limited war in Vietnam. Search-and-destroy operations were predicated on the assumption that combat in Vietnam had moved from insurgency/guerrilla actions to larger-unit actions. But both Gen. Bruce Palmer, Jr., and Andrew F. Krepinevich, Jr., have written that MACV's assumption that large-unit warfare had supplanted the Communists' small-unit guerrilla-style "hit-and-run" tactics after 1965 was invalid. In 1967 Westmoreland believed that the initiative had firmly switched to the Allies, noting that the VC and the PAVN had lost control over large areas and populations.

The flaw in the U.S. phase (1965–1973) of the war in Vietnam may have been a poorly conceived grand strategy. Grand strategy—the sum of political, economic, military, and other component strategies—is designed to accomplish the purpose of the war. In the most striking way, the chosen military strategy of attrition did not lead directly and resolutely to the political end of the conflict. It is not surprising that Westmoreland and the MACV staff sought a strategic solution to the growing VC/PAVN capability through the application of U.S. technology and firepower. What is surprising is that they believed that an American-style quick fix could win a protracted war. In many ways, pacification—the "other war"—was the more important stepping stone to an Allied victory. American strategists discovered too late that carrying the war to the Communists while attempting to strengthen the South Vietnamese toward national self-sufficiency was like pulling on both ends of a rope simultaneously.

Through it all the Communists had their eyes on the objective—to frustrate and damage the Americans' will to continue the war. Instead of being weakened by attrition, the VC/PAVN seemed to gain in strength and audacity after suffering enormous losses in their 1968 Têt Offensive. It was clear that after the Têt Offensive, the U.S. government, reflecting the impatience and confusion of the American people, began withdrawing the essential moral support and then the resources necessary for victory. It was not entirely Westmoreland's fault, only his misfortune to be the responsible official on the ground in Vietnam. In that regard Harry Summers is probably right that it is unfair to compare Gen. Westmoreland with Gen. Giáp because the PAVN commander enjoyed a unity of command that in the American system of war-fighting was distributed among many civilian and military authorities.

In July 1968 President Johnson recalled Westmoreland from Vietnam and appointed him U.S. Army chief of staff. As his former deputy, Gen. Creighton Abrams, carried on with the gradual hand-off of the war to the unready and sometimes unwilling South Vietnamese, Westmoreland set to work on issues such as the all-volunteer force. In July 1972 Westmoreland retired from the Army after more than 36 years of service. In 1974 he published his memoirs, *A Soldier Reports*.

In January 1982 the Columbia Broadcasting System (CBS) and its journalist Mike Wallace aired a television documentary that accused Gen. Westmoreland and his staff of fudging Communist casualty figures to give the appearance of progress and eventual success in Vietnam. Westmoreland brought a libel suit against CBS that resulted in an out-of-court settlement on 18 February 1985. CBS stood by its documentary but issued a statement that it did not mean to impugn Gen. Westmoreland's patriotism or loyalty "in performing his duties as he saw them."

—John F. Votaw

References: Furgurson, Ernest B. *Westmoreland: The Inevitable General* (1968); Herring, George C. "Westmoreland, William Childs" (1984); Sheehan, Neil. *A Bright Shining Lie: John Paul Vann and America in Vietnam* (1988); —. Interview with the author (1994); —. *A Soldier Reports* (1976); Westmoreland, William C. "Vietnam in Perspective" (1990); Zaffiri, Samuel. *Westmoreland: A Biography of General William C. Westmoreland* (1994).

See also: Abrams, Creighton; Attrition; COWIN Report; Manila Conference; McNamara, Robert S.; Media and the War; Military Assistance Command, Vietnam (MACV); Order of Battle Dispute; Search and Destroy; Sheehan, Cornelius Mahoney (Neil); Têt Offensive: Overall Strategy; Têt Offensive: the Sài Gòn Circle; United States: Army; United States: Involvement in Vietnam, 1965–1968.

Weyand, Frederick C. (1916–)

U.S. Army general; commander II Field Force, Vietnam; last commander of Military Assistance Command, Vietnam (MACV). In 1964 Weyand assumed command of the 25th Infantry Division in Hawaii. He took the division to Vietnam in 1966 and commanded it during Operations CEDAR FALLS and JUNCTION CITY. In March 1967 he became deputy commander of II Field Force and then its commander from July 1967 to August 1968.

As commander of II Field Force, Weyand controlled combat operations inside the Sài Gòn Circle during the 1968 Têt Offensive. In the months leading up to Têt, Weyand's maneuver battalions were increasingly sent to outlying border regions in response to Việt Công (VC) attacks in those areas. But Weyand and his civilian political advisor, John Paul Vann, were suspicious of the increased Communist radio traffic around Sài Gòn and of the lack of contacts by his units in the border.

On 10 January 1968 Weyand convinced General Westmoreland to let him pull more U.S. combat battalions back in around Sài Gòn. As a result there were 27 battalions in the Sài Gòn area, instead of the planned 14, when the Têt attacks came. Weyand's shrewd analysis and subsequent actions unquestionably altered the course of the Têt fighting to the Allies' advantage.

Weyand left Vietnam in 1968 and served as the Army's chief of the Office of Reserve Components until 1969. In 1969 and 1970 he was a military advisor to the Paris peace talks. In April 1970 Weyand returned to Vietnam as deputy commander of MACV, succeeding Gen. Creighton Abrams as MACV commander in July 1972. Weyand presided over the U.S. military withdrawal from Vietnam and folded MACV's flag on 29 March 1973.

After he left Vietnam, Weyand became commander in chief, U.S. Army Pacific, becoming vice-chief of staff of the Army later in 1973 and chief of staff in October 1974. Just before the fall of the Republic of Vietnam (RVN), President Ford sent Weyand to Sài Gòn to assess the situation. Weyand arrived there on 27 March 1975 and delivered the message to President Nguyên Van Thiêu that although the U.S. government would support the RVN to the best of its ability, the United States would not fight in Vietnam again. Upon his return to Washington, Weyand reported—to no avail—that the military situation could not be improved without direct U.S. intervention.

—David T. Zabecki

References: Bell, William G. *Commanding Generals and Chiefs of Staff: 1775–1983* (1983); Oberdorfer, Don. *Tet!* (1971); Palmer, Bruce, Jr. *The 25-Year War: America's Military Role in Vietnam* (1984); Zabecki, David T. "Battle for Saigon" (1989).

See also: Abrams, Creighton; Ford, Gerald R.; Military Assistance Command, Vietnam (MACV); Nguyên Van Thiêu; United States: Army; Vann, John Paul; Westmoreland, William Childs.

Wheeler, Earle G. (1908–1975)

U.S. Army general; chief of staff, 1962–1964; chairman of the Joint Chiefs of Staff (JCS), 1964–1970. Wheeler succeeded Maxwell Taylor as chairman of the JCS in June 1964, after Taylor was appointed ambassador to Vietnam. Wheeler had good political relations with Congress and was fairly close to President Johnson. Nonetheless, as the war progressed, Wheeler was increasingly overshadowed by Secretary of Defense Robert McNamara and his systems analysis "whiz kids." Wheeler worked to smooth over dissenting opinions in JCS recommendations. He believed these opened the door for interference by McNamara and his assistants, resulting in unqualified civilians making military decisions. Unanimity did not produce greater JCS influence, however, and McNamara increasingly made military decisions to a far greater degree than any of his predecessors.

As U.S. involvement in the war grew, the JCS recognized the widening discrepancy between the total force needed to meet worldwide U.S. commitments and the manpower base the political leadership was willing to support. In August 1965 Wheeler and the chiefs proposed an overall strategy for U.S. military operations in Vietnam that centered around three tasks: (1) forcing Hà Nôi to "cease and desist" in the South; (2) defeating the Việt Công in the South; and (3) deterring China from intervening. To support the strategy and rebuild the depleted strategic reserve at home, the JCS urged at least a limited call-up of reserve forces.

The chiefs continually pressed for this overall strategy throughout the war, but their recommendations were never fully accepted. On the other hand, they could clearly see where McNamara's strategy of piecemeal force and graduated response would lead. Wheeler once commented, "Whatever the political merits of [graduated response], we deprived ourselves of the military effects of early weight of effort and shock, and gave the enemy time to adjust to our slow quantitative and qualitative increase of pressure."

Wheeler and the other chiefs failed in one of their most important responsibilities by never directly advising the president that the ad hoc strategy being pursued was sure to fail. Gen. Bruce Palmer suggested that the chiefs were too imbued with the military's characteristic "can-do" attitude, and they did not want to appear disloyal or to be openly challenging civilian authority.

The 1968 Tết Offensive and the siege of Khe Sanh brought the psychological turning point of the war. They also marked a historical low point in the relations between U.S. military leaders and their civilian superiors. President Johnson became obsessed with Khe Sanh and insisted that Wheeler and the chiefs sign a formal declaration of their belief in Gen. William Westmoreland's ability to hold Khe Sanh.

Immediately after the Tết Offensive, Westmoreland remained confident. Wheeler, however, strongly encouraged the Military Assistance Command, Vietnam (MACV) commander to request more troops. Wheeler apparently hoped that another large commitment of forces to Vietnam would finally force Johnson to mobilize the reserves. At that point in the war, members of the JCS were alarmed over the United States' worldwide strategic posture. The only combat-ready division outside of Vietnam was the 82d Airborne Division, and even one of its three brigades was on its way to Vietnam. The once-proud Seventh Army in Europe had been reduced to little more than a replacement holding pool. The chiefs believed the reserve call-up was necessary to restore the military's global strategic posture.

On 23 February 1968, Wheeler flew to Sài Gòn to confer with Westmoreland. He informed the MACV commander of McNamara's impending departure. Wheeler also overstated the likelihood that Westmoreland's long-standing requests to attack Communist sanctuaries in Laos and Cambodia would be approved. The two generals developed a request for an additional 206,000 troops. Back in Washington, however, Wheeler presented the proposal as if Westmoreland were on the verge of defeat unless he was rapidly reinforced.

From that point, Wheeler's influence declined even more. Although he continued to attend all high-level White House meetings on Vietnam, his advice was virtually ignored. Oddly enough, Johnson in July 1968 requested and received congressional approval to extend Wheeler's tenure as JCS chairman for another year. Richard Nixon also requested another one-year extension but did not heed the military advice of Wheeler and the chiefs. Wheeler retired on 2 July 1970, after an unprecedented six years in office.

One positive legacy of the Wheeler years was the lesson of JCS unanimity. Under one of the provisions of the much-heralded 1986 Goldwater-Nichols Defense Reorganization Act, the chairman of the JCS is now required to report all dissenting opinions to the president, and the dissenting service chief is both allowed and obligated to state his views.

—David T. Zabecki

References: Bell, William G. *Commanding Generals and Chiefs of Staff: 1775–1983* (1983); Halberstam, David. *The Best and the Brightest* (1972); Palmer, Bruce, Jr. *The 25-Year War: America's Military Role in Vietnam* (1984); Sheehan, Neil, et al. *The Pentagon Papers* (1971); Webb, Willard J., and Ronald Cole. *The Chairmen of the Joint Chiefs of Staff* (1989); Wheeler, Earle G. *Addresses* (1970).

See also: Johnson, Lyndon Baines; Joint Chiefs of Staff; Khe Sanh, Battles of; McNamara, Robert S.; Military Assistance Command,

Vietnam (MACV); Palmer, Bruce, Jr.; Stennis, John Cornelius; Taylor, Maxwell Davenport; Tết Offensive: Overall Strategy; Tết Offensive: the Sài Gòn Circle; Westmoreland, William Childs.

WHEELER/WALLOWA, Operation
(November 1967–November 1968)

Division-sized Army task force in Quang Nam and Quang Tín Provinces in I Corps. Operation WHEELER/WALLOWA followed Task Force Oregon (TFO), a multibrigade Army force deployed in April 1967, to southern I Corps to blunt an offensive by the People's Army of Vietnam (PAVN) 2d Division and to enable units of the 3d Marine Task Force to relocate to Quang Tri Province. Organized by Maj. Gen. William Rosson, TFO was composed of the 196th Light Infantry Brigade, the 1st Brigade of the 101st Airborne Division, and the 3d Brigade of the 25th Infantry Division (later designated the 3d Brigade, 4th Infantry Division). Shortly after the launching of Operation WHEELER on 11 September, Brig. Gen. Samuel W. Koster assumed command, and on 25 September U.S. Military Assistance Command, Vietnam (MACV) announced that TFO would be reconstituted as the Americal Division (23d Infantry), consisting of the 196th, 198th, and 11th Light Infantry Brigades, and would be headquartered at Chu Lai. The latter two brigades, however, would not arrive in South Vietnam until 22 October and 20 December respectively, and only the 198th would join successor operations to WHEELER early in 1968.

Operation WHEELER had barely begun when the 1st Brigade, 1st Airborne, and two battalions of the 3d Brigade, 4th Infantry, returned to their parent divisions. These units were effectively replaced by the 3d Brigade and Troop B, 1st Squadron, 9th Cavalry, of the 1st Cavalry Division (Airmobile), which on 3 October launched Operation WALLOWA in the northern sector of the Americal Division's area of operation (AO). On 11 November Operations WHEELER and WALLOWA were combined as WHEELER/WALLOWA under Koster's command.

WHEELER/WALLOWA became the code name for a series of sweeping operations throughout Quang Nam and Quang Tín Provinces, from Hôi An south to Tam Ky along Route 1, and west into the Quê Son and Hiệp Đuc Valleys, areas never previously under Allied control. Communist strength proved much greater than anticipated, as four independent PAVN battalions reinforced the PAVN 2d Division.

Until mid-January 1968 the 1st Cavalry's highly mobile 3d Brigade and the 196th Brigade continuously engaged a determined Communist force, which brought down dozens of helicopters in the Hiệp Đuc Valley and mounted regimental-sized attacks against three fire bases in the Quê Son Valley. By 31 January WHEELER/WALLOWA claimed 1,718 Việt Công and 1,585 PAVN troops killed, and more than 600 weapons captured, at a cost of more than 200 American lives.

Just days after the 3d Brigade joined another 1st Cavalry brigade already deployed to Quang Tri Province, the PAVN launched the Tết Offensive, during which the most intensive fighting in the WHEELER/WALLOWA area occurred at the provincial capital of Tam Ky. In February and March 1968 the 3d Brigade of the 82d Airborne Division also came under operational control of the Americal Division, and in late April the 198th Light Infantry Brigade assumed primary responsibility for the remaining six months of the operation. The 198th's 1st Battalion, 6th Infantry distinguished itself in successive battles against the 60th and 70th Main Force Việt Cộng (VC) Battalions at Lo Giang and Op Banh and in 22 days of consecutive fighting against the entire 3d Regiment of the 2d PAVN Division.

Ending on 11 November 1968, one year after it began, WHEELER/WALLOWA claimed 10,020 VC/PAVN killed and 2,053 captured weapons. U.S. casualties were 682 killed and 2,548 wounded. Nevertheless WHEELER/WALLOWA only temporarily halted the threat of the PAVN 2d Division. Quang Nam and Quang Tín defied pacification as thousands of fresh PAVN and VC replacements appeared during 1969.

—John D. Root

References: McCoy, J. W. *Secrets of the Viet Cong* (1992); Stanton, Shelby L. *The Rise and Fall of an American Army: U.S. Ground Forces in Vietnam, 1965–1973* (1985).

See also: Tết Offensive: Overall Strategy; Tết Offensive: the Sài Gòn Circle; United States: Army; Vietnam, Democratic Republic of: Army (People's Army of Vietnam [PAVN]).

White Star

Special Forces teams in Laos. The U.S. military aid program in Laos from 1955 to 1961 was managed by the Programs Evaluation Office (PEO), which was attached to the economic aid mission in Vientiane. In April 1961 the PEO was converted into a full-scale Military Assistance and Advisory Group (MAAG) by presidential decision. At that time several U.S. Army Special Forces teams (called White Star teams) were sent to Laos under the MAAG. The July 1962 Geneva Agreement confirmed the neutrality of Laos, and as early as 23 June the United States withdrew the White Star teams. The number of U.S. military advisors in Laos was steadily reduced, and the last of them were gone by 7 October 1962.

—Arthur J. Dommen

References: Castle, Timothy N. *At War in the Shadow of Vietnam. U.S. Military Aid to the Royal Lao Government, 1955–1975* (1993); Dommen, Arthur J. *Conflict in Laos. The Politics of Neutralization* (1964).

See also: Laos; United States: Special Forces.

Williams, Samuel T. (1896–1984)

U.S. Army general and commander, U.S. Military Assistance and Advisory Group (MAAG), Vietnam, 1955–1960. Williams replaced Gen. John W. O'Daniel as the senior U.S. army officer in Vietnam on 24 October 1955 and eliminated "Indo-China" from the mission title, renaming it the Military Assistance and Advisory Group, Vietnam (MAAG). Williams had a close relationship with Republic of Vietnam President Ngô Đình Diệm and enjoyed the trust of the Diệm government's top-ranking officers. His determination to operate MAAG independent of the U.S. embassy led to

difficulties when Ambassador G. Frederick Reinhardt was superseded by Elbridge Durbrow, who exercised greater control. Personality differences between the two men made the clash bitter.

Under Williams the MAAG prepared for a conventional war. Williams and his staff concentrated on the possibility of a conventional attack by the Democratic Republic of Vietnam. He tended to downgrade the threat posed by the DRV. He was also critical of the organization of the Army of the Republic of Vietnam (ARVN), and he favored eliminating territorial regiments and light units and creating division-size organizations able to cope with a cross-border invasion or internal insurgency. His accompanying defensive strategy, CINCPAC Operation Plan 46A, perceived an enemy drive through the Mekong Valley with the Central Highlands area as the decisive center of operations. Williams was not alarmed by increasing guerrilla activity in the South. Believing that internal security was not the ARVN's principal responsibility, he advocated upgrading militia forces. He also doubted the value of the Michigan State University Advisory Group police and public administration advisors assisting the training of local security personnel. Williams preferred instruction by MAAG personnel.

Williams retired from the service in August 1960 while in Vietnam and was replaced by Gen. Lionel C. McGarr in September. At the time of his departure from Vietnam, Williams expressed confidence in an early American withdrawal.

—Rodney J. Ross

References: Arnold, James R. *The First Domino: Eisenhower, the Military and America's Intervention in Vietnam* (1991); Meyer, Harold J. *Hanging Sam: A Military Biography of General Samuel T. Williams, From Pancho Villa to Vietnam* (1990); Spector, Ronald H. *Advice and Support: The Early Years, 1941–1960* (1983).

See also: Durbrow, Elbridge; Military Assistance and Advisory Group (MAAG), Vietnam; Ngô Đình Diệm; Reinhardt, George Frederick; United States: Involvement in Vietnam, 1954–1965.

Wilson, Harold (1916–1995)

British prime minister, 1964–1970 and 1974–1975. Most of Wilson's time between 1964 and 1970 was spent trying to keep Britain economically viable. With a widening trade deficit and the devalued pound, the government was forced into increasing austerity measures, including military retrenchment. Wilson was unable, and possibly unwilling, to influence U.S. policies in Vietnam. Both the Labour and Conservative parties supported U.S. bombing of North Vietnam following the 1964 Gulf of Tonkin incidents. Privately Wilson wanted an end to the bombing and a negotiated end to the war, and he so informed President Johnson. He was constrained, however, from publicly criticizing U.S. policy by the long-standing special relationship between the two countries and by Washington's role in supporting the pound sterling.

In 1965 Wilson attempted several Vietnam peace initiatives, all of which failed. In early 1966 he endeavored to act as intermediary in setting up talks between Washington and Moscow regarding Vietnam. In his memoirs Wilson noted

Moscow's inability to "exert any real pressure on Hanoi in the face of continuing militant Chinese pressure."

—Spencer C. Tucker

References: Frankel, Joseph. *British Foreign Policy, 1945–1973* (1975); Great Britain, Foreign Office. *Recent Exchanges Concerning Attempts to Promote a Negotiated Settlement of the Conflict in Viet-Nam* (1965); Wilson, Harold K. *A Personal Record. The Labour Government, 1964–1970* (1971).

See also: de Gaulle, Charles André Marie Joseph; Great Britain; Johnson, Lyndon Baines; Kosygin, Aleksei Nikolayevich; SUN-FLOWER, Operation.

Wilson, Thomas Woodrow (1856–1924)

President of the United States, 1913–1921. Wilson led negotiations at Paris following the end of World War I and in that role influenced developments in Southeast Asia. Wilson advanced his plan for international peace in the Fourteen Points. In addition, in his call for a peace-keeping organization, the League of Nations, he set forth the principle of self-determination of peoples.

Wilson's rhetoric inspired the nationalist leader Hô Chí Minh to submit a statement to the 1919 Paris Peace Conference, noting that "all subject peoples are filled with hope by the prospect that an era of right and justice is opening to them." Hô did not demand independence for the French colony but asked for a constitutional government, democratic freedoms, and economic reforms. Although Hô did not gain an audience with Wilson, who seemed concerned only with Europe, this was the first step in his long campaign to gain Indo-Chinese self-determination. The U.S. Senate later rejected Wilson's internationalism, including the Treaty of Versailles and membership in Wilson's cherished League of Nations.

—Brenda J. Taylor

References: Ferrell, Robert H. *Woodrow Wilson and World War I: 1917–1921* (1985); Karnow, Stanley. *Vietnam: A History* (1983).
See also: Hô Chí Minh.

"Wise Men"

Senior advisors to President Johnson on Vietnam policy. Hoping to upgrade his foreign affairs credentials, deflect political criticism, and forge ties with America's foreign policy leadership, Johnson established an informal body of senior advisors that became known as the "Wise Men." They met for the first time in July 1965. Some participants, both past and current officials, had played significant roles in post–World War II policymaking, including establishment of the containment strategy. The group comprised establishment notables: Dean Acheson, George W. Ball, McGeorge Bundy, Douglas Dillon, Cyrus Vance, Arthur Dean, John J. McCloy, Gen. Omar Bradley, Gen. Matthew Ridgway, Gen. Maxwell Taylor, Robert Murphy, Henry Cabot Lodge, Jr., Abe Fortas, and Arthur Goldberg.

The Wise Men assembled again on November 2 1965, a day after Secretary of Defense Robert S. McNamara's personal memorandum to Johnson urging an end to the bombing of North Vietnam, curtailment of U.S. military operations in the Republic of Vietnam, and examination of ground actions aimed at cutting U.S. losses and placing a greater burden on the South Vietnamese. To McNamara's disappointment, Johnson did not share this memorandum with the Wise Men who, with the notable exception of Ball, urged Johnson to press ahead with his current program.

In the wake of the 1968 Têt Offensive, Johnson, prompted by Acheson, again summoned the Wise Men to the State Department. Briefed on 25 March 1968, the group was shocked by extent of damage that the Communist attacks had done to security and pacification programs in the Vietnamese countryside. Following questions about the killed-to-wounded ratio and the remaining force capacity of the National Front for the Liberation of South Vietnam, the gathering was predisposed to admit the war had taken an unfortunate turn. The next day the Wise Men met for the last time. Acheson stated that he no longer believed the United States could reach its goal by military methods. Instead, he favored measures to facilitate a U.S. withdrawal. Acheson's viewpoint, Bundy told a disappointed Johnson, was held by Dean, Vance, Dillon, and Ball. Only Bradley, Taylor, and Murphy thought the administration should take the counsel of the military leadership. Since a majority warned against further escalation, recourse to nuclear weapons, or expansion of the war, disengagement became the unquestioned alternative, a decision Johnson acknowledged only grudgingly.

—Rodney J. Ross

References: Berman, Larry. *Lyndon Johnson's War: The Road to Stalemate in Vietnam* (1989); Herring, George C. *LBJ and Vietnam: A Different Kind of War* (1994); Isaacson, Walter, and Evan Thomas. *The Wise Men* (1987); McNamara, Robert S., with Brian VanDeMark. *In Retrospect. The Tragedy and Lessons of Vietnam* (1995).
See also: Acheson, Dean G.; Ball, George W.; Bradley, Omar Nelson; Bundy, McGeorge; Fortas, Abe; Goldberg, Arthur Joseph; Johnson, Lyndon Baines; Lodge, Henry Cabot, Jr.; McCloy, John Jay; McNamara, Robert S.; Murphy, Robert D.; Ridgway, Matthew B.; Taylor, Maxwell Davenport; Vance, Cyrus Roberts; Wheeler, Earle G.

Women in the War, U.S.

Estimates of the number of U.S. military women serving in Vietnam vary from 7,000 to 21,000, depending on compilation methods and on how the statistical compilers define "serving in Vietnam." Maj. Gen. Jeanne Holm estimated the total number of women service members physically stationed in Vietnam and Thailand at 7,500, including 5,000–6,000 nurses and medical specialists, 500 Army nonmedical personnel, 600 Air Force personnel (more than half officers), less than 50 Navy personnel (all officers), and less than 36 Marines.

A small group of Army and Navy nurses had served in Vietnam and Thailand before 1965, primarily as advisors and trainers of local medical staffs. After the beginning of active U.S. military engagement, larger numbers were deployed to field medical units in combat areas of Vietnam. Air Force nurses were added to the complement in medical evacuation units, as well as in major hospitals at Cam Ranh Bay and other Air Force installations in Vietnam and Thailand.

Line (nonmedical) military women served in various specialties, the most coomon of which were administration (including clerical), personnel, intelligence, information, security, supply, transportation, data processing, training, special services, and law enforcement. The first detachment of Army line women arrived in Sài Gòn in 1967. By midyear approximately 160 enlisted women were stationed in Sài Gòn and Long Bình, and the number would remain approximately constant throughout the war. The first Navy and Marine women also arrived in 1967. Air Force women were assigned to Korat and Takhli in Thailand in 1969. Only in 1970 were enlisted Air Force women assigned to Vietnam itself, at Tân Son Nhut Air Base, although Air Force officers were already in place in Sài Gòn. The proportion of female Air Force officers serving in Southeast Asia, as a percentage of the total officer force, was nearly equal to that of male officers: 7 percent female officers compared with 8 percent male officers.

Eight U.S. military women died in the line of duty during the war. Many women stationed outside the area normally considered the combat theater participated to varying degrees in war operations as flight nurses, medical and line personnel at hospitals receiving casualties in such places as Okinawa and Japan, or line personnel for units whose male personnel were regularly deployed into the theater. Medical evacuation squadrons, for example, operated out of the Philippines, Guam, and as far away as Alaska. Some female personnel in such units were awarded unit decorations such as the Outstanding Unit Award and Presidential Unit Citation for being part of combat units, but never received campaign ribbons and were therefore ineligible for official "Vietnam veteran" status or even membership in the Veterans of Foreign Wars.

A large number of civilian women also served in Vietnam and Thailand as headquarters staff workers or as employees of U.S. government agencies, civilian charitable and relief organizations, and civilian corporations. Red Cross workers served in units based at 28 locations within Vietnam, and United Services Organization (USO) units maintained almost as many centers in country, peaking at 17 centers during 1967–1969.

In November 1993 the Vietnam Women's Memorial was dedicated in Washington, D.C., depicting three nurses and a wounded soldier. The statue honors all women who served during the Vietnam War.

—Phoebe S. Spinrad

References: Holm, Jeanne. *Women in the Military: An Unfinished Revolution*. Rev. ed. (1992); Seeley, Charlotte Palmer, et al., eds. *American Women and the U.S. Armed Forces: A Guide to the Records of Military Agencies in the National Archives Relating to American Women* (1992); Walker, Keith. *A Piece of My Heart: The Stories of Twenty-Six American Women Who Served in Vietnam* (1985)

See also: BABYLIFT, Operation; Medevac; United States: Nurses; United States: Red Cross Recreation Workers; Vietnam Veterans Memorial.

Women in the War, Vietnamese

Twentieth-century Communist leaders could successfully appeal to women as a potential revolutionary class because laws and customs in Vietnam treated all women as inferior to all men. When the Viêt Nam Quôc Dân Đang (VNQDD) was established in 1927, it admitted many women who shared with their male comrades experiences of torture and other hardships under the French. Nguyên Thi Giang and her sister Nguyên Thi Bac inspired generations of Vietnamese women to become activists and soldiers in patriotic movements.

In 1930 the Indo-Chinese Communist Party (ICP) organized the Women's Union as the party organization responsible for political mobilization, education, and representation of Vietnamese women. The Women's Union became an important part of the Viêt Minh, and the Viêt Minh constitution for Vietnam supported women's equality and suffrage. Hà Thi Quê formed the first all-woman guerrilla unit in 1945 to fight the French. Estimates in the early 1950s suggest that more than 800,000 female guerrillas operated in the northern half of the country and about 140,000 in the south. Women commonly participated in community mobilization, intelligence gathering, and transportation of war material.

After the 1954 partition of Vietnam, both governments sought the support of women's groups. Madame Nhu, sister-in-law of Republic of Vietnam (RVN) President Ngô Đình Diêm, formed the Women's Solidarity Movement to oppose public and private immorality. Her volunteer Paramilitary Girls provided firearms, first aid training, and moral instruction for high school–age women. Neither of Madame Nhu's women's groups was very effective, however. Since the French colonial administration and the RVN governments that followed supported the traditional Vietnamese cultural inferiority of women, village women had more incentive to back the revolutionary movement.

The "long-haired army" consisted of women who organized protest demonstrations, rallies, and strikes challenging first the French and then the RVN government. On 17 January 1960, a series of demonstrations by peasant women began in Bên Tre province. Led by Madame Nguyên Thi Đinh, the women protested killing and looting by government troops and forced the removal of troops from a large area of Vinh Bình province. Women formed a significant portion of the National Liberation Front (NLF). About 40 percent of regimental commanders were women. Madame Đinh was a general and was second in command of the Southern insurgents. The women's Movement to Drive Out the American Aggressors set fire to the U.S. library in Sài Gòn, and the same group began a campaign to make life dangerous for GIs on Sài Gòn streets. Women served as spies, gaining access to U.S. military bases as laundresses, peddlers, servants, and secretaries, and they targeted locations for attack. They also participated in the 1968 Têt Offensive.

But female fighting forces represented only a small portion of southern women who supported the Communist movement. The Women's Liberation Association (WLA), formed in March 1961, conducted extensive letter-writing campaigns urging RVN soldiers to desert, led village indoctrination sessions, raised food and delivered it to guerrilla bands, made spiked foot traps, carried ammunition, and dug roadblocks. In 1965 the WLA claimed a membership of 1.2

million. In addition, the NLF retained the old Việt Minh practice of organizing older women into Foster Mother Associations, whose members served as surrogate mothers to young guerrillas away from home. This strategy added the traditional Vietnamese female cultural symbol of the nurturing mother to that of the heroic female leader.

The pre-1954 Vietnamese National Army employed young women in its Women's Auxiliary Personnel Corps. Its members served in clerical and medical jobs in various army units and agencies. Women also staffed the small Social Assistance Service, an organization that helped care for soldiers' dependents. Both organizations had a hierarchical system and pay scale similar to that of the military.

Women also served in the RVN army. The RVN established the Women's Armed Forces Corps (WAFC) in 1964, and its strength increased as the armed forces expanded. The WAFC had an initial complement of 1,800 women, who served mainly in medical or clerical capacities. Three women reached the rank of full colonel. Although these women were not supposed to fight, many proved their bravery under fire. The social assistance branch was a separate service under the administrative management of the Center for Training and Management of the WAFC. Other military service women served in many military branches and large units, including a women's parachutist team. There were also woman officers in the Police Special Group, known as the "Thiên Nga" (the Swans). They ran intelligence nets and infiltrated VC and underground organizations in RVN-controlled areas.

In the DRV the "Three Responsibilities Movement" set defense as a primary task for women, who responded by forming self-defense teams in factories, schools, and villages. Many women became skilled with antiaircraft weapons and downed U.S. aircraft. Although all women in the DRV received military training, including hand-to-hand combat, they were not subject to the draft, and few joined the People's Army of Vietnam (PAVN). Those who did served primarily in support roles as medics, bomb defusers, or supply personnel. Most female members of the PAVN were young women without children. DRV propaganda portrayed women as heroic revolutionaries in the manner of the Trung Sisters and honored women's traditional roles. The DRV's willingness to recognize the contributions of women was one reason for the large number of Vietnamese women actively supporting the revolutionary movement.

—Elizabeth Urban Alexander

References: Eisen, Arlene. *Women and Revolution in Viet Nam* (1984); Mai Thi Tu. *Women in Vietnam* (1978); Pike, Douglas. *Viet Cong: The Organization and Techniques of the National Liberation Front of South Vietnam* (1967); Tetreault, Mary Ann. *Women and Revolution in Viet Nam* (1991).

See also: Lao Đông Party; Ngô Đình Nhu, Madame (Trân Lê Xuân); Nguyên Thi Đinh; Trung Trac and Trung Nhi.

Women Strike for Peace (WSP)

U.S. antiwar organization. Among the most active dissenting organizations during the Vietnam War, Women Strike for Peace's moderate approach effectively communicated the antiwar message to mainstream Americans. Founded by Dagmar Wilson as a nuclear disarmament group in November 1961, WSP achieved notoriety in December 1962, when several of its members deflected red-baiting tactics in testimony before the House Un-American Activities Committee.

Beginning in February 1965, WSP frequently lobbied Washington officials to end the war, sometimes drawing thousands of people for a single effort. WSP also participated in antiwar coalition activities and by 1967 was increasingly involved in draft counseling. Some members visited the Democratic Republic of Vietnam and helped establish communications between U.S. prisoners of war and their families. Tactically, WSP appealed primarily to the nurturing role of traditional motherhood in challenging U.S. foreign policy. Members avoided divisive radical rhetoric and supported amnesty for all war resisters, yet refused to criticize soldiers and veterans. The election of WSP's legislative chairperson Bella Abzug to the House of Representatives in 1970 marked its greatest electoral victory. The organization's influence faded with the war's conclusion.

—Mitchell K. Hall

References: Alonso, Harriet Hyman. *Peace as a Women's Issue: A History of the U.S. Movement for World Peace and Women's Rights* (1993); Swerdlow, Amy. *Women Strike for Peace: Traditional Motherhood and Radical Politics in the 1960s* (1993).

See also: Antiwar Movement, United States; Draft; Prisoners of War, Allied.

X

Xuân Lôc, Battle of (9–23 April 1975)

Last stand of the South Vietnamese military during the Hô Chí Minh Campaign. Xuân Lôc, on National Route 1 near the junction with National Route 20, was a strategic location protecting the Biên Hòa–Long Bình–Sài Gòn area. On 9 April the People's Army of Vietnam (PAVN) IV Corps pushed into the city behind a heavy artillery barrage. Brutal fighting for control of the town lasted for days. The North Vietnamese cut Route 1, forcing reinforcements for the 18th Division to be helicoptered in. But men of the 1st Airborne Brigade were pinned down as they landed at a rubber plantation east of the city. Two more PAVN divisions joined the siege.

Under Gen. Đao's inspired leadership, the 18th ARVN Division and its supporting elements fought courageously against incredible odds, but their fate was sealed without reinforcements. With Communist forces moving in for the kill, an evacuation began on 21 April, the same day that President Nguyên Van Thiêu resigned. By 23 April, the evacuation was complete and the Battle of Xuân Lôc was over. The 18th Division suffered casualties of 30 percent, and their Regional and Popular Forces allies were virtually decimated. During the fighting and the evacuation, RVN air support effectively employed 750 pound cluster bombs (CBUs) and 15,000-pound "daisy cutter" bombs against PAVN troop concentrations. In a final act, a CBU-55 B asphyxiation bomb—the most powerful nonnuclear weapon in the U.S. arsenal—was dropped on Xuân Lôc, killing more than 250 Vietnamese. Never before employed, this bomb depleted the oxygen over a two-acre area and literally sucked air from its victims' lungs. With the fall of Xuân Lôc, the march into Sài Gòn was merely days away.

—Joe P. Dunn

References: Butler, David. *The Fall of Saigon* (1985); Cao Van Vien, General. *The Final Collapse* (1983); Dawson, Alan. *55 Days: The Fall of South Vietnam* (1977); Le Gro, William E. *Vietnam from Cease Fire to Capitulation* (1981); Warner, Denis. *Certain Victory: How Hanoi Won the War* (1978).

See also: Bombs, Dumb; Hô Chí Minh Campaign; Nguyên Van Thiêu; Vietnam, Democratic Republic of: Army (People's Army of Vietnam [PAVN]); Vietnam, Republic of: Army (ARVN).

Xuân Thuy (1912–1985)

Vietnamese revolutionary; foreign minister, Democratic Republic of Vietnam (DRV), 1963–1965; head of Hà Nôi's delegation at the Paris Peace Talks, 1968–1970. As key spokesperson for the DRV at Paris, Thuy insisted on four conditions for peace: a unilateral U.S. withdrawal; recognition of the National Front for the Liberation of South Vietnam; dissolution of the government of the Republic of Vietnam (RVN); and the reunification of Vietnam. The United States, on the other hand, demanded that the DRV end its support of the southern insurrection and withdraw its troops north of the 17th parallel. President Nixon had Henry Kissinger warn Thuy that refusal to compromise on these key issues would lead to increased air attacks against northern targets.

Kissinger also initiated secret meetings with Thuy. On 4 August 1969, Kissinger and Thuy met secretly, but the talks broke down after Thuy refused to accept U.S. conditions and Nixon's ultimatum. Ultimately, Nixon resorted to the policy of Vietnamization to extricate the United States from Vietnam and expanded the air war over North Vietnam and Cambodia in further attempts to force a settlement.

In 1970 the DRV sent Lê Đuc Tho to Paris to replace Thuy, possibly as a result of Hô Chí Minh's death in September 1969 and the diplomatic stalemate in Paris. Thuy accepted the demotion and served as Tho's chief deputy until signing the final accord in January 1973.

—Robert K. Brigham

References: Herring, George C., ed. *The Secret Diplomacy of the Vietnam War: The Negotiating Volumes of the Pentagon Papers* (1983); Kalb, Marvin, and Bernard Kalb. *Kissinger* (1974); Karnow, Stanley. *Vietnam: A History* (1983); Porter, Gareth. *A Peace Denied: The United States, Vietnam, and the Paris Agreement* (1975); Thies, Wallace J. *When Governments Collide: Coercion and Diplomacy in the Vietnam Conflict, 1964–1968* (1980).

See also: Kissinger, Henry Alfred; Lê Đuc Tho; National Front for the Liberation of South Vietnam (NFLSV); Nixon, Richard Milhous; Paris Negotiations; Paris Peace Accords; Poulo Condore (Côn Son).

Yankee Station

Fixed point in international waters off the coast of North Vietnam in the South China Sea (17 degrees 30 minutes north, 108 degrees 30 minutes east). Yankee Station was the staging area for the U.S. Navy's Seventh Fleet Attack Carrier Strike Force (Task Force 77), from which Navy pilots conducted strikes on the Democratic Republic of Vietnam. The carrier force's two primary goals were control of the sea and projection of power ashore.

From Yankee Station, strikes were mounted on specific targets such as railyards or major bridges. From 1965 to 1968 these strikes were part of Operation ROLLING THUNDER. Target times were assigned to both the U.S. Air Force and the Seventh Fleet to facilitate the initial ROLLING THUNDER operation. When the strategy became difficult to coordinate, U.S. planners replaced it by dividing North Vietnam into geographical areas known as "route packages." The new structure lessened interference between Task Force 77 and the Seventh Air Force. In addition it became possible to assign responsibility to each service for target development and analysis, intelligence, and data collection in its own area. For other strike zones (those in Cambodia, Laos, and South Vietnam), Task Force 77 attacks were flown from the carriers of Dixie Station, 100 miles southeast of Cam Ranh Bay.

Part of the so-called Tonkin Gulf Yacht Club, Yankee Station served as a crucial staging area and helped maintain U.S. air and naval superiority during the Vietnam War. However, three of the four deployed carriers—one at Dixie Station and two at Yankee Station—spent a grueling and unacceptable 80 percent of the time at sea, with little time for rest and maintenance.

—J. Nathan Campbell

References: Marolda, Edward J., and G. Wesley Pryce, III. *A Short History of the United States Navy and the Southeast Asia Conflict, 1950–1975* (1984); Nichols, John B., and Barrett Tillman. *On Yankee Station* (1987); Polmar, Norman. "Support by Sea for War in the Air" (1967).
See also: Air Power, Role in War; Aircraft Carriers; ROLLING THUNDER, Operation; United States: Navy.

YELLOWSTONE, Operation

(8 December 1967–24 February 1968)
Military operation in the northwest section of War Zone C. In November 1967 the U.S. Military Assistance Command, Vietnam (MACV) received intelligence that Communist forces were massing on both sides of Vietnam's Cambodian border. MACV decided to launch offensive operations to seal off the area and prevent the Communists from penetrating into the III Corps Tactical Zone. In Operation YELLOW-STONE, the 2d and 3d Brigades of the 25th Infantry ("Tropic Lightning") Division were deployed in War Zone C, principally in the northern half of Tây Ninh Province, with orders to locate and destroy Viêt Công (VC) installations.

Since their arrival in October 1965, units of the 25th

Division had maintained a continuous presence in the Tây Ninh, Bình Duong, and Hâu Nghi provinces west and northwest of Sài Gòn. During the first month of YELLOWSTONE, battalions of the 25th Division encountered frequent mortar attacks on their temporary positions, but ground contact with the VC was sporadic. The operation demonstrated, however, that War Zone C was still being used as a major VC and People's Army of Vietnam (PAVN) logistical base. The most intensive action occurred the night of 1 January 1968, when units of the 271st and 272d VC Regiments mounted a massive assault on the 3d Brigade's principal fire support base, Burt. Following a barrage of machine-gun, recoilless rifle, and rocket grenade fire, VC soldiers charged the base and blasted their way into the perimeter. The result was a savage battle in which the defenders fired "beehive" artillery rounds and called for close-in aerial napalm strikes. Simultaneously, reserves were rushed from other sides of the perimeter. The attack was repelled by dawn. The VC left behind more than 300 dead; U.S. casualties also were heavy, totaling 29 killed and 159 wounded.

Throughout January the 2d Brigade was involved in continuous heavy fighting along the Cambodian border south of Tây Ninh City. The 1968 Têt Offensive erupted while more than half of the 25th Division's maneuver battalions were tied down in YELLOWSTONE and thus unable to provide immediate support to the division's 1st Brigade and Army of the Republic of Vietnam (ARVN) units that became heavily engaged in the area between Sài Gòn and Cu Chi. During and after Têt, intense small-unit fighting continued throughout Tây Ninh Province. Known Communist casualties during Operation YELLOWSTONE totaled 1,254.

—John D. Root

References: Bergerud, Eric M. *The Dynamics of Defeat: The Vietnam War in Hau Nghia Province* (1991); Stanton, Shelby L. *The Rise and Fall of an American Army: U.S. Ground Forces in Vietnam, 1965–1973* (1985).
See also: Cambodia; National Front for the Liberation of South Vietnam (NFLSV); Têt Offensive: Overall Strategy; Têt Offensive: the Sài Gòn Circle; Vietnam, Democratic Republic of: Army (People's Army of Vietnam [PAVN]); War Zone C and War Zone D.

Youth International Party ("Yippies")

Antiwar group founded in 1967 by Jerry Rubin, Abbie Hoffman, Dick Gregory, and Paul Krassner. The name *Yippie* is credited to Krassner, editor of an underground newspaper, *The Realist*. According to Rubin the Yippies were conceived as a joke to scare Americans over age 30, but when authorities began to take the movement's outlandish rhetoric and frivolous behavior seriously, so did Rubin. The movement supposedly sought to create a new myth of the dope-taking, freedom-loving, politically committed activist.

The Yippie movement was soon noted by the conventional media. The Yippies planned a Festival of Life to coincide with the August 1968 Democratic National Convention in

Chicago. In preparation, they held their first "Yip-in" on 22 March 1968 at New York City's Grand Central Station. Acts of vandalism prompted New York police to break up the gathering in what some called a "police riot." Rubin and Hoffman were among those injured.

Rubin hoped to attract 50,000 people to Chicago to launch a demonstration that would end the war. Like other groups, however, they were not given a permit to stay in Lincoln Park because of delays imposed by Mayor Richard Daley, who promised that attempts to disrupt the convention would be met with the full power of local, state, and federal agencies. Trouble began for the Yippies on 25 August 1968, when police refused to allow a flatbed truck into Lincoln Park for a scheduled rock concert. At midnight police moved against an estimated 1,000 people, causing scores of injuries. Three days later, 4,500 protesters gathered in Grant Park, across from the Hilton Hotel, where the Democratic Party leadership was staying. Within hours violence erupted as Chicago police again used massive force to break up the gathering. In March 1969 both Hoffman and Rubin were indicted for their activities during the convention and stood trial as members of the "Chicago Seven." Convicted of crossing state lines to riot and slapped with numerous contempt charges, Hoffman, Rubin, and three others saw their convictions overturned on appeal.

The Yippies gradually declined after 1968, an eclipse furthered by U.S. troop withdrawals from Vietnam that made the antiwar movement increasingly irrelevant. They were present during the 1972 Democratic National Convention at Miami Beach but did not repeat the demonstrations of 1968. Ironically, both Rubin and Hoffman were expelled from the Yippie movement after the 1972 election because of their ages and "establishment" tendencies.

—Clayton D. Laurie

References: Gitlin, Todd. *The Sixties: Years of Hope, Days of Rage* (1987); Matusow, Allen J. *The Unraveling of America* (1984).

See also: Antiwar Movement, United States; Chicago Eight; Dellinger, David; Democratic Party National Convention, 1968; Hayden, Thomas E.; Hoffman, Abbie; McCarthy, Eugene Joseph; Rubin, Jerry; Spring Mobilization to End the War in Vietnam.

Z

Zhou Enlai (Chou En-lai) (1898–1976)

Chinese Communist leader and diplomat. Zhou was instrumental in shaping the Peoples' Republic of China (PRC) policy of recognizing Hô Chí Minh's Democratic Republic of Vietnam (DRV) in 1950. In 1954 Zhou attended the Geneva Conference, where he he supported the continued existence of Cambodia and Laos. The PRC did not want Vietnam to control all of Southeast Asia and preferred instead to work with several smaller, weaker states.

DRV Premier Pham Van Đông was furious that Zhou had supported the West against Vietnam. Zhou was quoted later as complaining that he had been "had" at Geneva. Between 18 and 22 November 1956, he visited the DRV and told Hô Chí Minh that the PRC would increase its support. In a joint communiqué issued after this meeting, the PRC government promised to expand economic, cultural, and technical exchanges with the DRV. Zhou also promised to send Chinese technical experts to North Vietnam.

During the early 1960s, PRC relations with the Soviet Union worsened. In 1965 Zhou Enlai tried to convene an Afro-Asian conference to oppose the USSR. Zhou even undertook an extensive tour of Africa to organize developing countries there. His efforts failed, however, and the PRC's international diplomacy became increasingly isolated. Faced with renewed border tensions with the USSR, Zhou quietly probed U.S. officials to see whether improving Sino-American relations might be used to offset the USSR. Henry Kissinger later described these Chinese inquiries as an "intricate minuet." Upon receiving positive signs from Washington, on 21 April 1971, Zhou invited Kissinger to visit Beijing.

Kissinger's visit led to President Nixon's historic trip to China the following year. As a result of Zhou's diplomatic skills, the PRC and the United States signed the "Shanghai Communiqué" on 28 February 1972. This document opened formal diplomatic relations between the United States and the People's Republic of China and also helped lead to the end of the Vietnam War.

—Bruce Elleman

References: Chai, Winberg. *The Foreign Relations of the People's Republic of China* (1972); Fairbank, John King. *The Great Chinese Revolution, 1800–1985* (1986); Kissinger, Henry. *White House Years* (1979); Lee, Chae-jin. *Zhou Enlai, The Early Years* (1994); MacFarquhar, Roderick. *The Politics of China, 1949–1989* (1993); Wilson, Dick. *Zhou Enlai, A Biography* (1984).
See also: China, People's Republic of (PRC); Geneva Conference and Geneva Accords; Hô Chí Minh; Kissinger, Henry Alfred; Knowland, William F.; Mao Zedong (Mao Tse-tung); Nixon, Richard Milhous; Pham Van Đông; Union of Soviet Socialist Republics (USSR; Soviet Union).

Zorthian, Barry (1920–)

Public affairs officer, U.S. Embassy, Sài Gòn; director, Joint U.S. Public Affairs Office (JUSPAO), Sài Gòn. From 1965 to 1968 Barry Zorthian was the "czar" of information in Sài Gòn. He was the embassy public affairs officer in Sài Gòn when Ambassador Maxwell Taylor named him to head a new Joint U.S. Public Affairs Office (JUSPAO), with responsibility for all psychological warfare operations as well as relations with the news media. Answerable only to the ambassador, Zorthian was able to marshal whatever powers he needed to present the positive side of the Vietnam story. Although the Johnson administration and the Military Assistance Command, Vietnam (MACV) preferred press censorship, Zorthian's view prevailed that censorship was neither necessary, acceptable, nor workable. Zorthian instead established voluntary guidelines and, even as the number of accredited correspondents grew to more than 600 by Têt 1968, there were few serious violations of security.

Zorthian initiated the notorious "5 O'Clock Follies," the daily briefings given by the MACV Office of Information, and provided weekly backgrounders to selected members of the media. Peter Braestrup recalled that while Zorthian had a tendency to "stroke" reporters, he was careful not to mislead them. Less shrewdly, says Neil Sheehan, Zorthian believed that Gen. Westmoreland was correct in his assessment of the war, and he pressed for the fall 1967 expeditions of Westmoreland, Ellsworth Bunker, and Robert Komer to publicize progress being made in Vietnam.

Under Zorthian, civilian and military information operations grew into a large, extremely effective system that provided the American media with what they wanted. After leaving government service in 1969, Zorthian noted that at the beginning of the U.S. buildup there was no accepted doctrine for dealing with the media, and that a government and military accustomed to withholding information was slow to learn that the media provided an opportunity to educate the public. "Without public support," noted Zorthian, "Vietnam could not continue. And public support was ultimately lost." He added that communication with the media must be candid and correspond to reality, something too often not done in Vietnam. In retrospect, Zorthian felt that the public was well served by the press, which, more often than not, was more accurate than the government in their coverage of Vietnam, "at least up until Têt."

—John D. Root

References: Braestrup, Peter. *Big Story* (1978); Hammond, William M. *Public Affairs: The Military and the Media, 1962–1968* (1988); Wyatt, Clarence R. *Paper Soldiers: The American Press and the Vietnam War* (1993); Zorthian, Barry. "The Press and the Government" (1984).
See also: Bunker, Ellsworth; Civilian Operations and Revolutionary Development Support (CORDS); Joint U.S. Public Affairs Office (JUSPAO); Komer, Robert W.; Media and the War; Psychological Warfare Operations (PSYOP); Westmoreland, William Childs.

Zumwalt, Elmo R., Jr. (1920–)

U.S. Navy admiral; commander of U.S. riverine warfare units in South Vietnam, 1968–1970. In September 1968 Zumwalt was detailed to the post of commander, U.S. Naval Forces in Vietnam and the Naval Advisory Group, Vietnam, a position often viewed as a dead-end job—a "brown-water" post in a "blue-water" navy. Zumwalt was tasked with interdicting Communist waterborne logistics traffic in the Mekong Delta, cooperating with Allied ground troops in the area, and turning over the burden of the naval war to the South Vietnamese.

Zumwalt moved with vigor to execute all three charges. To cut Communist logistical support, he supplemented existing MARKET TIME patrols with strikes by small craft (Operation GIANT SLINGSHOT) against supplies coming down the backwaters from Cambodia. To assist Allied soldiers, Zumwalt provided shallow-draft landing craft in support of the U.S. Army's 9th Infantry Division. To execute his command's role in Vietnamization, Zumwalt organized a program dubbed ACTOV (Accelerated Turnover to the Vietnamese), with special emphasis on cooperation between U.S. and South Vietnamese naval personnel. He set a personal example by his close relationship with Commodore Trân Van Chon, the head of the Republic of Vietnam Navy.

Zumwalt's Vietnamese tour ended abruptly on 12 April 1970, when he was summoned to Washington to begin a four-year assignment as chief of naval operations (CNO). Sworn in on 1 July 1970, Zumwalt became the youngest officer to hold the Navy's top job and the rank of full admiral. In his new position Zumwalt turned to larger issues, such as the reform of personnel policies and the Navy's fading ability to confront a rapidly expanding Soviet fleet. Still, as CNO, Zumwalt continued to exert an influence on the Vietnamese struggle, especially during the Easter Offensive of 1972, when he strongly advocated the mining of Hai Phòng harbor. Following the war, Zumwalt became involved as a private citizen in humanitarian concerns related to the Vietnam struggle, managing, for instance, to secure the release from captivity of Trân Van Chon and serving as a spokesman for U.S. servicemen suffering from exposure to the herbicide Agent Orange.

—Malcolm Muir, Jr.

References: Friedman, Norman. "Elmo Russell Zumwalt, Jr." (1980); Reynolds, Clark G. *Famous American Admirals* (1978); Zumwalt, Elmo, Jr. *On Watch: A Memoir* (1976); Zumwalt, Elmo, Jr., Elmo Zumwalt, III, and John Pekkanen. *My Father, My Son* (1986).

See also: MARKET TIME, Operation; Mobile Riverine Force; Nitze, Paul Henry; Riverine Craft; Riverine Warfare; United States: Navy; Vietnam, Republic of: Navy (VNN); Vietnamization.

Introduction to the Documents

Most of the documents in this section pertain to the period of American involvement in Vietnam. This in part results from simple accessibility to the documents themselves. Many U.S. documents have been made available in the publication of the so-called *Pentagon Papers* and under the Freedom of Information Act.

Our primary motivation was to select U.S. documents that show the thinking of officials both in Vietnam and in Washington, D.C., and reflect changes in U.S. policy. Other documents included here should be useful as references by simply spelling out provisions or specific agreements.

Some documents reflect the evolution of French policy, and we have also included writings by principal Communist leaders such as Hô Chí Minh and Vo Nguyên Giáp.

A word on the documents themselves: We have checked as many of these as we could access and have endeavored to present all of them in their original, unedited form. They thus do not have the diacritical marks that appear in the main body of this work. Many have spelling and grammatical errors or appear to be in fragmented form, especially in the cables to and from Sài Gòn.

We hope these documents provide illumination on how government policies evolve. Those researching the vagaries of policies regarding Vietnam will also see how on occasion governments can totally misread the intentions and capabilities of one another.

—Spencer C. Tucker

List of Documents

December 1920
Hô Chí Minh's Speech at the Tours Congress

Chairman: Comrade Indochinese Delegate, you have the floor.

Indochinese Delegate [Nguyen Ai Quoc]: Today, instead of contributing, together with you, to world revolution, I come here with deep sadness to speak as a member of the Socialist Party, against the imperialists who have committed abhorrent crimes on my native land. You all have known that French imperialism entered Indochina half a century ago. In its self-ish interests, it conquered our country with bayonets. Since then we have not only been oppressed and exploited shame-lessly, but also tortured and poisoned pitilessly. Plainly speak-ing, we have been poisoned with opium, alcohol, etc. I cannot, in some minutes, reveal all the atrocities that the predatory capitalists have inflicted on Indochina. Prisons outnumber schools and are always overcrowded with detainees. Any natives having socialist ideas are arrested and sometimes murdered without trial. Such is the so-called justice in Indochina. In that country, the Vietnamese are discriminated against, they do not enjoy safety like Europeans or those hav-ing European citizenship. We have neither freedom of press nor freedom of speech. Even freedom of assembly and free-dom of association do not exist. We have no right to live in other countries or to go abroad as tourists. We are forced to live in utter ignorance and obscurity because we have no right to study. In Indochina the colonialists find all ways and means to force us to smoke opium and drink alcohol to poison and beset us. Thousands of Vietnamese have been led to a slow death or massacred to protect other people's interests.

Comrades, such is the treatment inflicted upon more than 20 million Vietnamese, that is more than half the popu-lation of France. And they are said to be under French pro-tection! The Socialist Party must act practically to support the oppressed natives.

Jean Longuet: I have spoken in favor of the natives.

Indochinese Delegate: Right from the beginning of my speech I have already asked everyone to keep absolute silence. The Party must make propaganda for socialism in all colonial countries. We have realized that the Socialist Party's joining the Third International means that it has practically promised that from now on it will correctly assess the impor-tance of the colonial question. We are very glad to learn that a Standing Delegation has been appointed to study the North Africa question, and, in the near future, we will be very glad if the Party sends one of its members to Indochina to study on-the-spot the questions relating to this country, and the activities which should be carried out there.

[A right-wing delegate had a contradictory opinion.]

Indochinese Delegate: Silence! You for the Parliament!

Chairman: Now all delegates must keep silence! Including those not standing for the Parliament!

Indochinese Delegate: On behalf of the whole of mankind, on behalf of all the Socialist Party's members, both left and right wings, we call upon you! Comrades, save us!

Chairman: Through the applause of approval, the Indochinese Delegate can realize that the whole of the Socialist Party sides with you to oppose the crimes commit-ted by the bourgeois class.

Source: Hô Chí Minh. *Ho Chi Minh: Selected Writings, 1920–1969.* pp. 3–4. Hanoi: Foreign Languages Publishing House, 1977.

18 February 1930
Hô Chí Minh's Appeal Made on the Occasion of the Founding of the Communist Party of Indo-China

Workers, peasants, soldiers, youth, and pupils! Oppressed and exploited compatriots!

Sisters and brothers! Comrades!

Imperialist contradictions were the cause of the 1914–18 World War. After this horrible slaughter, the world was divid-ed into two camps: One is the revolutionary camp including the oppressed colonies and the exploited working class throughout the world. The vanguard force of this camp is the Soviet Union. The other is the counterrevolutionary camp of international capitalism and imperialism whose general staff is the League of Nations.

During this World War, various nations suffered untold losses in property and human lives. The French imperialists were the hardest hit. Therefore, in order to restore the capital-ist forces in France, the French imperialists have resorted to every underhand scheme to intensify their capitalist exploitation in Indochina. They set up new factories to exploit the workers with low wages. They plundered the peas-ants' land to establish plantations and drive them to utter poverty. They levied many heavy taxes. They imposed public loans upon our people. In short, they reduced us to wretched-ness. They increased their military forces, firstly to strangle the Vietnamese revolution, secondly to prepare for a new imperialist war in the Pacific aimed at capturing new colonies, thirdly to suppress the Chinese revolution, fourthly to attack the Soviet Union because the latter helps the revolu-tion of the oppressed nations and the exploited working class. World War II will break out. When it breaks, the French imperialists will certainly drive our people to a more horrible slaughter. If we give them a free hand to prepare for this war, suppress the Chinese revolution, and attack the Soviet Union, if we give them a free hand to stifle the Vietnamese revolu-tion, it is tantamount to giving them a free hand to wipe our race off the earth and drown our nation in the Pacific.

However the French imperialists' barbarous oppression and ruthless exploitation have awakened our compatriots, who have all realized that revolution is the only road to life, without it they will die out piecemeal. This is the reason why the Vietnamese revolutionary movement has grown even stronger with each passing day. The workers refuse to work, the peasants demand land, the pupils strike, the traders boycott. Everywhere the masses have risen to oppose the French imperialists.

The Vietnamese revolution has made the French imperi-alists tremble with fear. On the one hand, they utilize the feudalists and comprador bourgeois in our country to oppress and exploit our people. On the other, they terrorize, arrest, jail, deport, and kill a great number of Vietnamese revolutionaries. If the French imperialists think that they can suppress the Vietnamese revolution by means of terrorist acts, they are utterly mistaken. Firstly, it is because the Vietnamese revolution is not isolated but enjoys the assistance of the world proletarian class in general and of the French working class in particular. Secondly, while the French imperialists are frenziedly carrying out terrorist acts, the Vietnamese Communists, formerly working separately, have now united into a single party, the Communist Party of Indochina, to lead our entire people in their revolution.

Workers, peasants, soldiers, youth, pupils!

Oppressed and exploited compatriots!

The Communist Party of Indochina is founded. It is the party of the working class. It will help the proletarian class to lead the revolution in order to struggle for all the oppressed and exploited people. From now on we must join the Party, help it and follow it in order to implement the following slogans:

1. To overthrow French imperialism, feudalism, and the reactionary Vietnamese capitalist class.

2. To make Indochina completely independent.

3. To establish a worker-peasant and soldier government.

4. To confiscate the banks and other enterprises belonging to the imperialists and put them under the control of the worker-peasant and soldier government.

5. To confiscate the whole of the plantations and property belonging to the imperialists and the Vietnamese reactionary capitalist class and distribute them to poor peasants.

6. To implement the eight-hour working day.

7. To abolish public loans and poll tax. To waive unjust taxes hitting the poor people.

8. To bring back all freedoms to the masses.

9. To carry out universal education.

10. To implement equality between man and woman.

Source: Hô Chí Minh. *Ho Chi Minh: Selected Writings, 1920–1969.* pp. 127–129. Hanoi: Foreign Languages Publishing House, 1977.

15 March 1945
Memorandum of Conversation with President Franklin Roosevelt by Adviser on Caribbean Affairs Charles Taussig [Extract]

The Peoples of East Asia

The President said he was concerned about the brown people in the East. He said that there are 1,100,000,000 brown people. In many Eastern countries, they are ruled by a handful of whites and they resent it. Our goal must be to help them achieve independence—1,100,000,000 potential enemies are dangerous. He said he included the 450,000,000 Chinese in that. He then added, Churchill doesn't understand this.

The President said he thought we might have some difficulties with France in the matter of colonies. I said that I thought that was quite probable and it was also probable the British would use France as a "stalking horse."

I asked the President if he had changed his ideas on French Indochina as he had expressed them to us at the luncheon with Stanley. He said no he had not changed his ideas; that French Indo-China and New Caledonia should be taken from France and put under a trusteeship. The President hesitated a moment and then said—well if we can get the proper pledge from France to assume for herself the obligations of a trustee, then I would agree to France retaining these colonies with the proviso that independence was the ultimate goal. I asked the President if he would settle for self-government. He said no. I asked him if he would settle for dominion status. He said no—it must be independence. He said that is to be the policy and you can quote me in the State Department.

Source: *Foreign Relations of the United States, Diplomatic* Papers (1945). Vol. I, p. 124.

1 August 1945
Telegram from President Harry S Truman to Generalissimo Chiang Kai-shek, Transmitted via Ambassador to China Patrick Hurley

Top secret from the President to Ambassador Hurley.

Please deliver the following message from me to Generalissimo Chiang Kai-shek.

"1. At the Potsdam Conference the Prime Minister of Great Britain and I, in consultation with the Combined Chiefs of Staff, have had under consideration future military operations in Southeast Asia.

"2. On the advice of the Combined Chiefs of Staff we have reached the conclusion that for operational purposes it is desirable to include that portion of French Indo-China lying south of 16° north latitude in the Southeast Asia Command. This arrangement would leave in the China Theater that part of Indo-China which covers the flank of projected Chinese operations in China and would at the same time enable Admiral Mountbatten to develop operations in the southern half of Indo-China.

"3. I greatly hope that the above conclusions will recommend themselves to Your Excellency and that, for the purpose of facilitating operations against the common enemy, Your Excellency will feel able to concur in the proposed arrangements.

"4. I understand that the Prime Minister of Great Britain is addressing a communication to Your Excellency in a similar sense."

Source: *Foreign Relations* (1945). Vol. II, p. 1321.

2 September 1945
Vietnamese Declaration of Independence

"All men are created equal. They are endowed by their Creator with certain inalienable rights; among these are Life, Liberty, and the pursuit of Happiness."

This immortal statement was made in the Declaration of Independence of the United States of America in 1776. In a broader sense, this means: All the peoples on the earth are equal from birth, all the peoples have a right to live, to be happy and free.

The Declaration of the French Revolution made in 1791 on the Rights of Man and the Citizen also states: "All men are born free and with equal rights, and must always remain free and have equal rights."

Those are undeniable truths.

Nevertheless, for more than eighty years, the French imperialists, abusing the standard of Liberty, Equality, and Fraternity, have violated our Fatherland and oppressed our fellow-citizens. They have acted contrary to the ideals of humanity and justice.

In the field of politics, they have deprived our people of every democratic liberty.

They have enforced inhuman laws; they have set up three distinct political regimes in the North, the Center and the South of Vietnam in order to wreck our national unity and prevent our people from being united.

They have built more prisons than schools. They have mercilessly slain our patriots, they have drowned our uprisings in rivers of blood.

They have fettered public opinion, they have practised obscanturism against our people.

To weaken our race they have forced us to use opium and alcohol.

In the field of economics, they have fleeced us to the backbone, impoverished our people, and devastated our land.

They have robbed us of our rice fields, our mines, our forests, and our raw materials. They have monopolized the issuing of bank-notes and the export trade.

They have invented numerous unjustifiable taxes and reduced out people, especially our peasantry, to a state of extreme poverty.

They have hampered the prospering of our national bourgeoisie; they have mercilessly exploited our workers.

In the autumn of 1940, when the Japanese Fascists violated Indochina's territory to establish new bases in their fight against the Allies, the French imperialists went down on their bended knees and handed over our country to them.

Thus, from that date, our people were subjected to the double yoke of the French and the Japanese. Their sufferings and miseries increased. The result was that from the end of last year to the beginning of this year, from Quang Tri Province to the North of Vietnam, more than two million of our fellow-citizens died from starvation. On March 9, the French troops were disarmed by the Japanese. The French colonialists either fled or surrendered showing that not only were they incapable of "protecting" us, but that, in the span of five years, they had twice sold our country to the Japanese.

On several occasions before March 9, the Viet Minh League urged the French to ally themselves with it against the Japanese. Instead of agreeing to this proposal, the French colonialists so intensified their terrorist activities against the Viet Minh members that before fleeing they massacred a great number of our political prisoners detained at Yen Bay and Cao Bang.

Notwithstanding all this, our fellow citizens have always manifested toward the French a tolerant and humane attitude. Even after the Japanese Putsch of March, 1945, the Viet Minh League helped many Frenchmen to cross the frontier, rescued some of them from Japanese jails, and protected French lives and property.

From the autumn of 1940, our country had in fact ceased to be a French colony and had become a Japanese possession.

After the Japanese had surrendered to the Allies, our whole people rose to regain our national sovereignty and to found the Democratic Republic of Viet-Nam.

The truth is that we have wrested our independence from the Japanese and not from the French.

The French have fled, the Japanese have capitulated, Emperor Bao Dai has abdicated. Our people have broken the chains which for nearly a century have fettered them and have independence for the Fatherland. Our people at the same time have overthrown the monarchic regime that has reigned supreme for dozens of centuries. In its place has been established the present Democratic Republic.

For these reasons, we, members of the Provisional Government, representing the whole Vietnamese people, declare that from now on we break off all relations of a colonial character with France; we repeal all the international obligation that France has so far subscribed to on behalf of Viet-Nam, and we abolish all the special rights the French have unlawfully acquired in our Fatherland.

The whole Vietnamese people, animated by a common purpose, are determined to fight to the bitter end against any attempt by the French colonialists to reconquer their country.

We are convinced that the Allied nations, which at Teheran and San Francisco have acknowledged the principles of self-determination and equality of nations, will not refuse to acknowledge the independence of Viet-Nam.

A people who have courageously opposed French domination for more than eighty years, a people who have fought side by side with the Allies against the fascists during these last years, such a people must be free and independent.

For these reasons, we, members of the Provisional Government of the Democratic Republic of Viet-Nam, solemnly declare to the world that Viet-Nam has the right to be a free and independent country—and in fact it is so already. The entire Vietnamese people are determined to mobilize all their physical and mental strength, to sacrifice their lives and property in order to safeguard their independence and liberty.

Source: Hô Chí Minh. *Selected Works (Hanoi, 1960–1962).* Vol. III, pp. 17–21.

17 October 1945

Letter from Hô Chí Minh to President Harry S Truman

Establishment of Advisory Commission for the Far East is heartily welcomed by Vietnamese people in principle stop. Taking into consideration primo the strategical and economical importance of Vietnam secundo the earnest desire which Vietnam deeply feels and has unanimously manifested to cooperate with the other democracies in the establishment and consolidation of world peace and prosperity we wish to call the attention of the Allied nations on the following points colon:

First absence of Vietnam and presence of France in the Advisory Commission leads to the conclusion that France is to represent the Vietnamese people at the Commission stop. Such representation is groundless either de jure or defacto. stop. De jure no alliance exists any more between France and Vietnam colon: Baodai abolished treaties of 1884 and 1863 comma, Baodai voluntarily abdicated to hand over government to Democratic Republican Government comma, Provisional Govemment rectorated [sic] abolishment of treaties of 1884 and 1863 stop. De facto since March ninth France having handed over governing rule to Japan has broken all administrative links with Vietnam, since August 18, 1945, Provisional Government has been a de facto independent government in every respect, recent incidents in Saigon instigated by the French roused unanimous disapproval leading to fight for independence.

Second France is not entitled because she had ignominiously sold Indo China to Japan and betrayed the Allies: Third Vietnam is qualified by Atlantic Charter and subsequent peace agreement and by her goodwill and her unflinching stand for democracy to be represented at the Advisory Commission. Stop. We are convinced that Vietnam at Commission will be able to bring effective contribution to solution of pending problems in Far East whereas her absence would bring forth unstability [sic] and temporary character to solutions otherwise reached. Therefore we express earnest request to take part in Advisory Commission for Far East. Stop. We should be very grateful to your excellency and Premier Attlee Premier Stalin Generalissimo Tchang Kai Shek for the conveyance of our desiderata to the United Nations.

Source: *United States–Vietnam Relations, 1945–1967.* Study Prepared by Department of Defense, printed for the use of House Committee on Armed Services. Book 1, Section 1-C, pp. 73–74. Washington, DC: Government Printing Office, 1971.

6 March 1946
Preliminary Franco–Viêt Minh Convention

1. The French Government recognizes the Vietnamese Republic as a Free State having its own Government, its own Parliament, its own Army, and its own Finances, forming part of the Indochinese Federation and of the French Union....

2. The Vietnamese Government declares itself ready to welcome amicably the French Army when, conforming to international agreements, it relieves the Chinese Troops....

Enclosure to Dispatch No. 366 from Bangkok, April 24, 1947, "Transmitting Documents relative to recent developments in Indo China, received from Dr. Pham Ngoc Thack [sic], Vietnam Under-Secretary of State." F.W. 851.G.00/4-2447, State Department Central Files,

Source: Porter, Gareth, editor. *Vietnam. A History in Documents.* pp. 42–44. New York: New American Library, 1981. Translation of this and all other documents enclosed with this dispatch was done by the Department of State in 1947.

22 November 1946
Telegram from General Jean-Etienne Valluy to Colonel Pierre-Louis Debès

It appears clear that we are up against premeditated aggressions carefully staged by the Vietnamese regular army, which no longer seems to obey its government's orders. Under these circumstances, your commendable attempts at conciliation and division of quarters, as well as the inquiry that I asked you to make are out of season. The moment has come to give a severe lesson to those who have treacherously attacked you. Use all the means at your disposal to make yourself complete master of Haiphong and so bring the Vietnamese army around to a better understanding of the situations.

Source: Ellen J. Hammer. *The Struggle for Indochina, 1940–1955.* Stanford, CA: Stanford University Press, 1966. p. 183.

15 December 1946
Telegram from Hô Chí Minh to French Premier Léon Blum

Occasion your election Presidency French Government,

To show our confidence in you and in people France,

To show our sincere desire fraternal cooperation with French people,

To prove that our only aspiration is independence and territorial integrity of Viet Nam within French Union,

To prove our ardent desire to settle peacefully serious incidents which at present steep our country in blood,

To prove that we have always been prepared to apply loyally agreements signed by our two Governments,

To dispel atmosphere of hostility, reestablish atmosphere of confidence and friendship, and effectively prepare definitive negotiations,

I have the honor to make to you the following concrete proposals:

a) On the Viet Nam side:

1) To invite the evacuated Viet Nam population to return to the cities.

2) To take all necessary measures to assure the return to the cities of the economic life disturbed by the present state of hostility.

3) To put an end to the measures of self-protection taken by the inhabitants of the cities.

4) To assure the return to normalcy of the Hanoi-Langson thoroughfare.

b) On the French side:

1) Return of the French and Viet Nam troops to the positions held before November 20, 1946 at Haiphong and Langson, and withdrawal of the reinforcements recently sent to Tourane, contrary to the agreements.

2) To cease the so-called mopping-up operations and campaigns of repression in Cochin-China and North Annam.

c) On both sides:

1) To start working immediately the agencies contemplated for the application of the Modus-Vivendi, a part of the Commission at Hanoi, another at Saigon, as the country resort of DALAT offers us no conveniences for work.

2) To put an end to all unfriendly propaganda in French and Viet Nam radio-broadcasts and press.

Awaiting the honor of your reply, I beg you to accept the expression of my very high consideration.

Source: *Enclosure to Despatch 366 from Bangkok, April 24, 1947.* In

Porter, Gareth, editor. *Vietnam. A History in Documents*. pp. 57–58. New York: New American Library, 1981.

12 May 1947
DRV Account of Hô Chí Minh–Paul Mus Meeting

President HO and Minister of Foreign Affairs GIAM met with a representative of High Commissioner BOLLAERT in a place not far from Hanoi.

This meeting was most cordial for the representative of the High Commissioner is an old acquaintance of President HO and Minister GIAM.

When the discussion began on the question of the cessation of hostilities, the representative of M. BOLLAERT proposed the following conditions:

1) The Vietnam Government will abstain from all reprisals against pro-French people upon the cessation of hostilities.

2) The Vietnamese troops will surrender all their arms and munitions to France.

3) The French troops have the right to circulate and occupy freely throughout the territory of Vietnam. Vietnamese troops will assemble in spots designated by the French Army.

President HO replied to the first condition: After the last worldwide hostilities, if France took action against Frenchmen who delivered France to Germany, we ought to punish Vietnamese who have decided to deliver our country to a foreign nation. However, we can promise leniency toward these individuals.

To the other conditions, President HO replied:

High Commissioner BOLLAERT is a French democrat and also a patriot. I ask you if High Commissioner BOLLAERT has recognized the act by which the Pétain Government delivered arms and munitions to the German Army, permitted German troops freedom of action in French territory and obliged French troops to assemble in determined positions? Is this an armistice?

At this point in the conversation, the representative of M. BOLLAERT said: In these circumstances, we have nothing more to say to you.

The diplomatic interview thus ended.

President HO then asked the French representative: You certainly know the history of Vietnam

Yes, I have made several studies of it.

In that case, you recall the feats of our ancestors. TRAN HUNG DAO who fought for five years against the Mongol armies and LE LOI who resisted for ten years against the Chinese armies. Well, at the present time, we can resist five years, ten years and more. Our compatriots are firmly decided to unite and to obey the government's orders to resist until independence and unification are obtained.

Source: Translation of Vietnamese-language document distributed by the DRV, in Airgram from U.S. Consul James L. O'Sullivan in Hanoi to the secretary of state, 20 June 1947, 851G,00/6-2047. Diplomatic Papers, National Archives. In Porter, Gareth, editor. *Vietnam. A History in Documents*. New York: New American Library, 1981.

25 July 1950
Hô Chí Minh's Answers to Questions Put by the Press Regarding U.S. Intervention in Indo-China

Question: What is, Mr. President, the present situation of the U.S. imperialists' interventionist policy in Indochina?

Answer: The U.S. imperialists have of late openly interfered in Indochina's affairs. It is with their money and weapons and their instructions that the French colonialists have been waging war in Viet-Nam, Cambodia, and Laos.

However, the U.S. imperialists are intensifying their plot to discard the French colonialists so as to gain complete control over Indochina. That is why they do their utmost to redouble their direct intervention in every field—military, political, and economic. It is also for this reason that the contradictions between them and the French colonialists become sharper and sharper.

Question: What influence does this intervention exert on the Indochinese people?

Answer: The U.S. imperialists supply their henchmen with armaments to massacre the Indochinese people. They dump their goods in Indochina to prevent the development of local handicrafts. Their pornographic culture contaminates the youth in areas placed under their control. They follow the policy of buying up, deluding, and dividing our people. They drag some bad elements into becoming their tools and use them to invade our country.

Question: What measure shall we take against them?

Answer: To gain independence, we, the Indochinese people, must defeat the French colonialists, our number-one enemy. At the same time, we will struggle against the U.S. interventionists. The deeper their interference, the more powerful are our solidarity and our struggle. We will expose their maneuvers before all our people, especially those living in areas under their control. We will expose all those who serve as lackeys for the U.S. imperialists to coerce, deceive, and divide our people.

The close solidarity between the peoples of Viet-Nam, Cambodia, and Laos constitutes a force capable of defeating the French colonialists and the U.S. interventionists. The U.S. imperialists failed in China, they will fail in Indochina.

We are still laboring under great difficulties but victory will certainly be ours.

Source: Hô Chí Minh. *Ho Chi Minh: Selected Writings, 1920–1969*. pp. 199–200. Hanoi: Foreign Languages Publishing House, 1977.

14 January 1954
Report by Vo Nguyên Giáp to Senior Field Commanders on the Điên Biên Phu Campaign [Extract]

Two main objectives:

1. To annihilate an important part of enemy forces.

2. To liberate the whole of the Northwest.

This campaign has a great significance:

a) It will be the greatest positional battle in the annals of our army. Hitherto, we have attacked fortified positions only with forces numbering up to one or two regiments; now we are throwing into action several divisions; we have never before coordinated infantry and artillery action on a large scale; we have succeeded only in capturing positions defended by one or two companies, one battalion at most. This time we shall have to coordinate the action of several branches of the army on a large scale and to annihilate an entrenched camp defended by 13 battalions.

Our victory will mark a big leap forward in the growth of our army, which will have an enormous influence on the future military situation.

b) By annihilating such an important part of enemy forces, by liberating such a wide area, we shall foil the Navarre plan, which is the French and American imperialists' plan for the extension of the war, and shall create conditions for destroying enemy forces on all fronts.

What does this mean, to foil the Navarre plan?

The enemy is seeking to concentrate mobile forces in the delta: we compel him to scatter them in mountain regions where they will be destroyed piecemeal.

He is seeking to increase the size of the puppet army and to bring reinforcements from France: we shall annihilate an important part of his forces to aggravate his manpower crisis beyond retrieve.

He is seeking to pacify the Northern plans and various theatres of operations in the South: our victory at Dien Bien Phu will make it possible for our forces to intensify their action on those various fronts thus creating conditions for the annihilation of important enemy forces and foiling his plans for pacification.

The enemy is seeking to wrest back the initiative; our victory will drive him further to the defensive and will consolidate our offensive situation.

c) From the political point of view, this battle will have a very great influence. On the internal plane, it will consolidate our rear, and ensure the success of the land reform. By winning a victory, the People's Army, which is fighting imperialism by force of arms, will make an effective and glorious complement to the mighty battle being waged in the rear by millions of peasants against feudalism.

This battle is taking place at a time when French imperialism is meeting with numerous difficulties in Vietnam, Laos and Cambodia, when the French people's struggle for an end to the war is increasing and when the struggle of the world's peoples for the defence of peace and an end to the war in Vietnam has reached unequalled designs and will be an important contribution of our army to the defence of world peace.

Source: "Contribution to the History of Dien Bien Phu." *Vietnamese Studies* (Hanoi), No. 3, March 1965, pp. 50–52.

7 April 1954
President Dwight Eisenhower's News Conference

Q. ROBERT RICHARDS, COPLEY PRESS: Mr. President, would you mind commenting on the strategic importance of Indochina to the free world? I think there has been, across the country, some lack of understanding on just what it means to us.

THE PRESIDENT: You have, of course, both the specific and the general when you talk about such things.

First of all, you have the specific value of a locality in its production of materials that the world needs.

Then you have the possibility that many human beings pass under a dictatorship that is inimical to the free world.

Finally, you have broader considerations that might follow what you would call the "falling domino" principle. You have a row of dominoes set up, you knock over the first one, and what will happen to the last one is the certainty that it will go over very quickly. So you could have a beginning of a disintegration that would have the most profound influences.

Now, with respect to the first one, two of the items from this particular area that the world uses are tin and tungsten. They are very important. There are others, of course, the rubber plantations and so on.

Then with respect to more people passing under this domination, Asia, after all, has already lost some 450 million of its peoples to the Communist dictatorship, and we simply can't afford greater losses.

But when we come to the possible sequence of events, the loss of Indochina, of Burma, of Thailand, of the Peninsula, and Indonesia following, now you begin to talk about areas that not only multiply the disadvantages that you would suffer through loss of materials, sources of materials, but now you are talking really about millions and millions and millions of people.

Finally, the geographical position achieved thereby does many things. It turns the so-called island defensive chain of Japan, Formosa, of the Philippines and to the southward; it moves in to threaten Australia and New Zealand.

It takes away, in its economic aspects, that region that Japan must have as a trading area or Japan, in turn, will have only one place in the world to go—that is, toward the Communist areas in order to live.

So, the possible consequences of the loss are just incalculable to the free world.

Source: *Public Papers of the Presidents of the United States. Dwight D. Eisenhower 1954.* pp. 382–383. Washington, DC: Government Printing Office, 1960.

21 July 1954
Final Declaration of the Geneva Conference on Indo-China

1. The Conference takes note of the agreements ending hostilities in Cambodia, Laos, and Vietnam and organizing international control and the supervision of the execution of the provisions of these agreements.

2. The Conference expresses satisfaction at the end of hostilities in Cambodia, Laos, and Vietnam; the Conference expresses its conviction that the execution of the provisions set out in the present declaration and in the agreements of the cessation of hostilities will permit Cambodia, Laos, and Vietnam henceforth to play their part, in full independence and sovereignty, in the peaceful community of nations.

3. The Conference takes note of the declarations made by the Governments of Cambodia and Laos of their intention to adopt measures permitting all citizens to take their place in the national community, in particular by participating in the next general elections, which, in conformity with the consti-

tution of each of these countries, shall take place in the course of the year 1955, by secret ballot and in conditions of respect for fundamental freedoms.

4. The Conference takes note of the clauses in the agreement on the cessation of hostilities in Vietnam prohibiting the introduction into Vietnam of foreign troops and military personnel as well as of all kinds of arms and munitions. The Conference also takes note of the declarations made by the Governments of Cambodia and Laos of their resolution not to request foreign aid, whether in war material, in personnel, or in instructors except for the purpose of the effective defense of their territory and, in the case of Laos, to the extent defined by the agreements of the cessation of hostilities in Laos.

5. The Conference takes note of the clauses in the agreement on the cessation of hostilities in Vietnam to the effect that no military base under the control of a foreign State may be established in the regrouping zones of the two parties, the latter having the obligation to see that the zones allotted to them shall not constitute part of any military alliance and shall not be utilized for the resumption of hostilities or in the service of an aggressive policy. The Conference also takes note of the declarations of the Governments of Cambodia and Laos to the effect that they will not join in any agreement with other States if this agreement includes the obligation to participate in a military alliance not in conformity with the principles of the Charter of the United Nations or, in the case of Laos, with the principles of the agreement on the cessation of hostilities in Laos or, so long as their security is not threatened, the obligation to establish bases on Cambodian or Laotian territory for the military forces of foreign powers.

6. The Conference recognizes that the essential purpose of the agreement relating to Vietnam is to settle military questions with a view to ending hostilities and that the military demarcation line is provisional and should not in any way be interpreted as constituting a political or territorial boundary. The Conference expresses its conviction that the execution of the provisions set out in the present declaration and in the agreement on the cessation of hostilities creates the necessary basis for the achievement in the near future of a political settlement in Vietnam.

7. The Conference declares that, so far as Vietnam is concerned, the settlement of political problems, effected on the basis of respect for the principles of independence, unity, and territorial integrity, shall permit the Vietnamese people to enjoy the fundamental freedoms, guaranteed by democratic institutions established as a result of free general elections by secret ballot. In order to ensure that sufficient progress in the restoration of peace has been made, and that all the necessary conditions obtain for free expression of the national will, general elections shall be held in July 1956 under the supervision of an international commission composed of representatives of the Member States of the International Supervisory Commission, referred to in the agreement on the cessation of hostilities. Consultations will be held on this subject between the competent representative authorities of the two zones from July 20, 1955, onward.

8. The provisions of the agreements on the cessation of hostilities intended to ensure the protection of individuals and of property must be most strictly applied and must, in particular, allow everyone in Vietnam to decide freely in which zone he wishes to live.

9. The competent representative authorities of the North and South zones of Vietnam, as well as the authorities of Laos and Cambodia, must not permit any individual or collective reprisals against persons who had collaborated in any way with one of the parties during the war, or against members of such persons' families.

10. The Conference takes note of the declaration of the Government of the French Republic to the effect that it is ready to withdraw its troops from the territory of Cambodia, Laos, and Vietnam, at the request of the Governments concerned and within periods which shall be fixed by agreement between the parties except in the cases where, by agreement between the two parties, a certain number of French troops shall remain at specified points and for a specified time.

11. The Conference takes note of the declaration of the French Government to the effect that for the settlement of all the problems connected with the re-establishment and consolidation of peace in Cambodia, Laos, and Vietnam, the French Government will proceed from the principle of respect for the independence and sovereignty, unity and territorial integrity of Cambodia, Laos, and Vietnam.

12. In their relations with Cambodia, Laos, and Vietnam, each member of the Geneva Conference undertakes to respect the sovereignty, the independence, the unity, and the territorial integrity of the above-mentioned States, and to refrain from any interference in their internal affairs.

13. The members of the Conference agree to consult one another on any question which may be referred to them by the International Supervisory Commission, in order to study such measures as may prove necessary to ensure that the agreements on the cessation of hostilities in Cambodia, Laos, and Vietnam are respected.

Source: *The Pentagon Papers. The Senator Gravel Edition. The Defense Department of the United States Decisionmaking on Vietnam.* Vol. 1, pp. 279–282. Boston: Beacon Press, n.d.

21 July 1954
Declaration by Walter Bedell Smith to the Geneva Conference

The Government of the United States being resolved to devote its efforts to the strengthening of peace in accordance with the principles and purposes of the United Nations.

Takes note of the Agreements concluded at Geneva on July 20 and 21, 1954 between the (a) Franco-Laotian Command and the Command of the People's Army of Viet-Nam; (b) The Royal Khmer Army Command and the Command of the People's Army of Viet-Nam; (c) Franco-Viet-Namese Command and the Command of the People's Army of Viet-Nam, and of paragraphs 1 to 12 inclusive of the Declaration presented to the Geneva Conference on July 21, 1954.

Declares with regard to the aforesaid Agreements and paragraphs (i) it will refrain from the threat or the use of force to disturb them, in accordance with Article 2 (4) of the

Charter of the United Nations dealing with the obligation of Members to refrain in their international relations from the threat or use of force; and (ii) it would view any renewal of the aggression in violation of the aforesaid agreements with grave concern and as seriously threatening international peace and security.

In connection with this statement in the Declaration concerning free elections in Viet-Nam, my Government wishes to make clear its position which it has expressed in a Declaration made in Washington June 19, 1954, as follows: "In the case of nations now divided against their will, we shall continue to seek to achieve unity through free elections, supervised by the United Nations to ensure that they are conducted fairly."

With respect to the statement made by the Representative of the State of Viet-Nam, the United States reiterates its traditional position that peoples are entitled to determine their own future and that it will not join in any arrangement which would hinder this. Nothing in its declaration just made is intended to or does indicate any departure from this traditional position.

We share the hope that the agreement will permit Cambodia, Laos and Viet-Nam to play their part in full independence and sovereignty, in the peaceful community of nations, and will enable the peoples of that area to determine their own future.

Source: Great Britain, Parliament. *Papers by Command, Documents Relating to British Involvement in the Indochina Conflict, 1945–1965.* p. 86. London: Her Majesty's Stationery Office.

19 July 1955
Message from Hồ Chí Minh and Foreign Minister Pham Van Đông to RVN Chief of State Bao Đai and Prime Minister Ngô Đình Diêm [Extract]

The holding on schedule of the consultative conference by the competent authorities of the North and the South is of great importance, and has a bearing not only on the prospect of the unity of our country but also on the loyal implementation of the Geneva Agreements, and the consolidation of peace in Indo-China and in the world.

Following the June 6, 1955 declaration by the Government of the Democratic Republic of Viet-nam, Saigon Radio on July 16, 1955, made known the "position of the Government of the State of Viet-nam on the problem of general elections for the unification of the national territory". The statement mentioned general elections and reunification but did not touch upon a very important and most realistic issue, that of the meeting of the competent representative authorities of the two zones, of the holding of the consultative conference on the question of general elections and reunification, as provided for by the Geneva Agreements. Moreover there were in the statement things which are untrue and which would not help to create a favourable climate for the convening of the consultative conference.

Our compatriots from the South to the North, irrespective of classes, creeds and political affiliations have deeply at heart the reunification of the country, and are looking forward to

the early convening of the consultative conference and to its good outcome. All the countries responsible for the guarantee of the implementation of the Geneva Agreements and in general all the peace-loving countries in the world are anxious to see that the consultative conference will be held and yield good results and that the reunification of our country will be achieved.

The Government of the Democratic Republic of Viet-nam proposes that you appoint your representatives and that they and ours hold the consultative conference from July 20, 1955 onwards, as provided for by the Geneva Agreements, at a place agreeable to both sides, on the Vietnamese territory, in order to discuss the problem of reunification of our country by means of free general elections all over Viet-nam.

Source: Democratic Republic of Viet-nam Ministry of Foreign Affairs, Press and Information Department. *Documents Related to the Implementation of the Geneva Agreements Concerning Viet-nam* (Hanoi, 1956). pp. 41–44.

9 August 1955
Republic of Vietnam Statement on Reunification

In the last July 1955 broadcast, the Vietnamese national Government has made it clear its position towards the problem of territorial unity.

The Government does not consider itself bound in any respect by the Geneva Agreements which it did not sign.

Once more, the Government reasserts that in any circumstance, it places national interests above all, being resolved to achieve at all cost the obvious aim it is pursuing and eventually to achieve national unity, peace and freedom.

The Viet-Minh leaders have had a note dated July 19 transmitted to the Government, in which they asked for the convening of a consultative conference on general elections. This is just a propaganda move aimed at making the people believe that they are the champions of our territorial unity. Everyone still remembers that last year at Geneva, the Vietnamese Communists boisterously advocated the partition of our territory and asked for an economically self-sufficient area whereas the delegation of the State of Viet-nam proposed an armistice without any partition, not even provisional, with a view to safeguarding the sacred rights of the Vietnamese national and territorial unity, national independence and individual freedom. As the Vietnamese delegation states, the Vietnamese Government then stood for the fulfillment of national aspirations by the means which have been given back to Viet-nam by the French solemn recognition of the independence and sovereignty of Viet-nam, as a legal, independent state.

The policy of the Government remains unchanged. Confronted with the partition of the country, which is contrary to the will of the entire people, the Government will see to it that everybody throughout the country may live free from fear, and completely free from all totalitarian oppression. As a champion of justice, of genuine democracy, the Government always holds that the principle of free general election is a peaceful and democratic means only if, first of all, the freedom to live and freedom of vote is sufficiently guaranteed.

In this connection, nothing constructive can be contemplated in the present situation in the North where, under the rule of the Vietnamese Communists, the citizens do not enjoy democratic freedoms and fundamental human rights.

Source: Democratic Republic of Viet-nam Ministry of Foreign Affairs, Press and Information Department. *Documents Related to the Implementation of the Geneva Agreements Concerning Viet-nam* (Hanoi, 1956). pp. 98–99. (In McMahon, Robert J., ed. *Major Problems in the History of the Vietnam War.* 2nd edition. pp. 131–132. Lexington, MA: D.C. Heath, 1995.)

9 March 1957
Conversation between Presidents Ngô Đình Diêm and Dwight Eisenhower Regarding Additional Aid for the Republic of Vietnam

After introductory remarks by the President praising President Diem for the excellent achievements he has brought about in the last three years in stabilizing the situation in Viet-Nam, President Eisenhower asked President Diem to outline the principal problems he is facing today.

President Diem replied that his country has gone through a very grave and serious crisis and has been able to hold on despite strong pressures from all sides. The principal problem of establishing internal security and building up their defense posture has been achieved to a considerable extent. The principal reason Viet Nam has been able to hold out against these pressures has been because of the sympathy and encouragement given by the United States despite the fact that for a time even some people in the United States did not think that the Diem government could maintain itself.

At the present time Viet-Nam is faced with the possibility of a strong Communist offensive from the Vietminh who have 400 thousand men under arms. Fortunately, however, the Vietminh are faced with serious problems such as high taxes needed to maintain this large force and must have other controls which have caused discontent among the population in the North. Diem feels that Red China is faced with the same problems. They are maintaining a large army which requires heavy taxes and controls over the people, which Diem hopes in the long run will force the Chinese Government to demobilize a considerable portion of their forces and treat the people in a more liberal manner. There is, nevertheless, the possibility that the Vietminh with their large army might try to attack now while they have a superiority in numbers. The Vietminh during the first year after the Geneva Conference did not think it would be necessary to use armed force to take over the South; they thought the government in the South would crumble and they could take over without difficulty. With internal stability in Free Viet-Nam and the build-up of their own armed forces, they have now the possibility of holding out for a few years more during which time Diem reiterated the strain and drain on the economy of the Vietminh may cause them to demobilize some of their forces and adopt a more liberal attitude toward the population….

Diem [stated] that Viet-Nam has attained stability due primarily to the volume of American aid. He pointed out that the magnitude of American aid permitted the US Government to have a large number of advisers and consultants in Viet-Nam who not only can assist Viet-Nam with its problems but also follow closely developments and the use to which aid is placed. In contrast, the small amounts of aid given to other countries, such as 20/30 million dollars, does not permit the US Government to maintain such close control over developments in other countries as is the case in Viet-Nam. Diem pleaded for the maintenance of the present aid level of 250 million dollars a year of which 170 million dollars is allocated for defense purposes. This aid has permitted Viet-Nam to build up its armed strength and thus play an important role in Southeast Asia. If this aid should be cut both the military and economic progress would have to be reduced. This would cause serious repercussions not only in Viet-Nam but among neighboring countries in Southeast Asia who look on Viet-Nam as an example of the good US aid can bring. Any cut would also bring serious political repercussions in Viet-Nam.

Source: McMahon, Robert J., ed. *Major Problems in the History of the Vietnam War.* 2nd edition. pp. 390–391. Lexington, MA: D.C. Heath, 1995.

11 November 1961
Dean Rusk and Robert S. McNamara's Memorandum to President John F. Kennedy [Extracts]

1. United States National Interests in South Viet-Nam.

The deteriorating situation in South Viet-Nam requires attention to the nature and scope of United States national interests in that country. The loss of South Viet-Nam to Communism would involve the transfer of a nation of 20 million people from the free world to the Communist bloc. The loss of South Viet-Nam would make pointless any further discussion about the importance of Southeast Asia to the free world; we would have to face the near certainty that the remainder of Southeast Asia and Indonesia would move to a complete accommodation with Communism, if not formal incorporation with the Communist bloc. The United States, as a member of SEATO, has commitments with respect to South Viet-Nam under the Protocol to the SEATO Treaty. Additionally, in a formal statement at the conclusion session of the 1954 Geneva Conference, the United States representative stated that the United States "would view any renewal of the aggression … with grave concern as seriously threatening international peace and security."

The loss of South Viet-Nam to Communism would not only destroy SEATO but would undermine the credibility of American commitments elsewhere. Further, loss of South Viet-Nam would stimulate bitter domestic controversies in the United States and would be seized upon by extreme elements to divide the country and harass the Administration….

3. The United States' Objective in South Viet-Nam.

The United States should commit itself to the clear objective of preventing the fall of South Viet-Nam to Communism. The basic means for accomplishing this objective must be to put the Government of South Viet-Nam into a position to win its own war against the Guerillas. We must insist that that Government itself take the measures necessary for that purpose in exchange for large-scale United States assistance in the military, economic and political fields. At the same time we must recognize that it will probably not be possible for the GVN to win this war as long as the flow of men and supplies from North Viet-Nam continues unchecked and the guerillas enjoy a safe sanctuary in neighboring territory.

We should be prepared to introduce United States combat forces if that should become necessary for success. Dependent upon the circumstances, it may also be necessary for United States forces to strike at the source of the aggression in North Viet-Nam.

4. The Use of United States Forces in South Viet-Nam.

The commitment of United States forces to South Viet-Nam involves two different categories: (A) Units of modest size required for the direct support of South Viet-Namese military effort, such as communications, helicopter and other forms of airlift, reconnaissance aircraft, naval patrols, intelligence units, etc., and (B) larger organized units with actual or potential direct military missions. Category (A) should be introduced as speedily as possible. Category (B) units pose a more serious problem in that they are much more significant from the point of view of domestic and international political factors and greatly increase the probabilities of Communist bloc escalation. Further, the employment of United States combat forces (in the absence of Communist bloc escalation) involves a certain dilemma: if there is a strong South Viet-Namese effort, they may not be needed; if there is not such an effort, United States forces could not accomplish their mission in the midst of an apathetic or hostile population. Under present circumstances, therefore, the question of injecting United States and SEATO combat forces should in large part be considered as a contribution to the morale of the South Viet-Namese in their own effort to do the principal job themselves.

5. Probable Extent of the Commitment of United States Forces.

If we commit Category (B) forces to South Viet-Nam, the ultimate possible extent of our military commitment in Southeast Asia must be faced. The struggle may be prolonged, and Hanoi and Peiping may overtly intervene. It is the view of the Secretary of Defense and the Joint Chiefs of Staff that, in the light of the logistic difficulties faced by the other side, we can assume that the maximum United States forces required on the ground in Southeast Asia would not exceed six divisions, or about 205,000 men (CINCPAC Plan 32/59 PHASE IV). This would be in addition to local forces and such SEATO forces as may be engaged. It is also the view of the Secretary of Defense and the Joint Chiefs of Staff that our military posture is, or, with the addition of more National Guard or regular Army divisions, can be made, adequate to furnish these forces and support them in action without serious interference with our present Berlin plans....

Recommendations

In the light of the foregoing, the Secretary of State and the Secretary of Defense recommend that:

1. We now take the decision to commit ourselves to the objective of preventing the fall of South Viet-Nam to Communism and that, in doing so, we recognize that the introduction of United States and other SEATO forces may be necessary to achieve this objective. (However, if it is necessary to commit outside forces to achieve the foregoing objective, our decision to introduce United States forces should not be contingent upon unanimous SEATO agreement thereto.)

2. The Department of Defense be prepared with plans for the use of United States forces in South Viet-Nam under one or more of the following purposes:

(a) Use of a significant number of United States forces to signify United States determination to defend South Viet-Nam and to boost South Viet-Nam morale.

(b) Use of substantial United States forces to assist in suppressing Viet Cong insurgency short of engaging in detailed counter-guerrilla operations but including relevant operations in North Viet-Nam.

(c) Use of United States forces to deal with the situation if there is organized Communist military intervention.

3. We immediately undertake the following actions in support of the GVN: ...

(c) Provide the GVN with small craft, including such United States uniformed advisers and operating personnel as may be necessary for quick and effective operations in effecting surveillance and control over coastal waters and inland waterways....

(e) Provide such personnel and equipment as may be necessary to improve the military-political intelligence system beginning at the provincial level and extending upward through the Government and the armed forces to the Central Intelligence Organization.

(f) Provide such new terms of reference, reorganization and additional personnel for United States military forces as are required for increased United States participation in the direction and control of GVN military operations and to carry out the other increased responsibilities which accrue to MAAG under these recommendations....

(i) Provide individual administrators and advisers for insertion into the Governmental machinery of South Viet-Nam in types and numbers to be agreed upon by the two Governments....

5. Very shortly before the arrival in South Viet-Nam of the first increments of United States military personnel and equipment proposed under 3., above, that would exceed the Geneva Accord ceilings, publish the "Jorden report" [by State Department official William J. Jorden and critical of Ngô Đình Diêm] as a United States "white paper," transmitting it as simultaneously as possible to the Governments of all countries with which we have diplomatic relations, including the Communist states.

6. Simultaneous with the publication of the "Jorden report," release an exchange of letters between Diem and the President.

(a) Diem's letter would include: reference to the DRV violations of Geneva Accords as set forth in the October 24 GVN letter to the ICC [International Control Commission] and other documents; pertinent references to GVN statements with respect to its intent to observe the Geneva Accords; reference to its need for flood relief and rehabilitation; reference to previous United States aid and the compliance hitherto by both countries with the Geneva Accords; reference to the USG statement at the time the Geneva Accords were signed; the necessity of now exceeding some provisions of the Accords in view of the DRV violations thereof; the lack of aggressive intent with respect to the DRV; GVN intent to return to strict compliance with the Geneva Accords as soon as the DRV violations ceased; and request for additional United States assistance in framework foregoing policy. The letter should also set forth in appropriate general terms steps Diem has taken and is taking to reform Governmental structure.

(b) The President's reply would be responsive to Diem's request for additional assistance and acknowledge and agree to Diem's statements on the intent promptly to return to strict compliance with the Geneva Accords as soon as DRV violations have ceased....

Source: *United States–Vietnam Relations, 1945–1967.* Book 11, pp. 359–366. Washington, DC: Government Printing Office, 1971.

14 December 1961
President John F. Kennedy's Letter to President Ngô Đình Diêm

Dear Mr. President:

I have received your recent letter in which you described so cogently the dangerous conditions caused by North Vietnam's effort to take over your country. The situation in your embattled country is well known to me and to the American people. We have been deeply disturbed by the assault on your country. our indignation has mounted as the deliberate savagery of the Communist programs of assassination, kidnapping, and wanton violence became clear.

Your letter underlines what our own information has convincingly shown—that the campaign of force and terror now being waged against your people and your Government is supported and directed from outside by the authorities at Hanoi. They have thus violated the provisions of the Geneva Accords designed to ensure peace in Vietnam and to which they bound themselves in 1954.

At that time, the United States, although not a party to the Accords, declared that it "would view any renewal of the aggression in violation of the Agreements with grave concern and as seriously threatening international peace and security." We continue to maintain that view.

In accordance with that declaration, and in response to your request, we are prepared to help the Republic of Vietnam to protect its people and to preserve its independence. We shall promptly increase our assistance to your defense effort as well as help relieve the destruction of the floods which you describe. I have already given the orders to get these programs underway.

The United States, like the Republic of Vietnam, remains devoted to the cause of peace and our primary purpose is to help your people maintain their independence. If the Communist authorities in North Vietnam will stop their campaign to destroy the Republic of Vietnam, the measures we are taking to assist your defense efforts will no longer be necessary. We shall seek to persuade the Communists to give up their attempts to force and subversion. In any case, we are confident that the Vietnamese people will preserve their independence and gain the peace and prosperity for which they have sought so hard and so long.

Source: *Department of State Bulletin*, 1 January 1962.

2 September 1963
President John F. Kennedy's Remarks on the Situation in Vietnam

Mr. Cronkite: Mr. President, the only hot war we've got running at the moment is of course the one in Viet-Nam, and we have our difficulties there, quite obviously.

The President: I don't think that unless a greater effort is made by the Government to win popular support that the war can be won out there. In the final analysis, it is their war. They are the ones who have to win it or lose it. We can help them, we can give them equipment, we can send our men out there as advisers, but they have to win it, the people of Viet-Nam, against the Communists.

We are prepared to continue to assist them, but I don't think that the war can be won unless the people support the effort and, in my opinion, in the last 2 months, the government has gotten out of touch with the people.

The repressions against the Buddhists, we felt, were very unwise. Now all we can do is to make it very clear that we don't think this is the way to win. It is my hope that this will become increasingly obvious to the government, that they will take steps to try to bring back popular support for this very essential struggle.

Mr. Cronkite: Do you think this government still has time to regain the support of the people?

The President: I do. With changes in policy and perhaps with personnel I think it can. If it doesn't make those changes, I would think that the chances of winning it would not be very good.

Mr. Cronkite: Hasn't every indication from Saigon been that President Diem has no intention of changing his pattern?

The President: If he does not change it, of course, that is his decision. He has been there 10 years and, as I say, he has carried this burden when he has been counted out on a number of occasions.

Our best judgment is that he can't be successful on this basis. We hope that he comes to see that, but in the final analysis it is the people and the government itself who have to win or lose this struggle. All we can do is help, and we are making it very clear, but I don't agree with those who say we should withdraw. That would be a great mistake. I know people don't like Americans to be engaged in this kind of an effort. Forty-seven Americans have been killed in combat with the enemy, but this is a very important struggle even though it is far away.

We took all this—made this effort to defend Europe. Now Europe is quite secure. We also have to participate—we may not like it—in the defense of Asia.

Source: McMahon, Robert J., editor. *Major Problems in the History of the Vietnam War.* 2nd ed. pp. 169–170. Lexington, MA: D.C. Haeth, 1995.

25 October 1963

Cable from Ambassador Henry Cabot Lodge to National Security Adviser McGeorge Bundy Discussing Coup Prospects

1. I appreciate the concern expressed by you in ref. a relative to the Gen. Don/Conein relationship, and also the present lack of firm intelligence on the details of the general's plot. I hope that ref. b will assist in clearing up some of the doubts relative to general's plans, and I am hopeful that the detailed plans promised for two days before the coup attempt will clear up any remaining doubts.

2. CAS [Classified American Source-refers to CIA] has been punctilious in carrying out my instructions. I have personally approved each meeting between Gen. Don and Conein who has carried out my orders in each instance explicitly. While I share your concern about the continued involvement of Conein in this matter, a suitable substitute for Conein as the principal contact is not presently available. Conein, as you know, is a friend of some eighteen years' standing with Gen. Don, and General Don has expressed extreme reluctance to deal with anyone else. I do not believe the involvement of another American in close contact with the generals would be productive. We are, however, considering the feasibility of a plan for the introduction of an additional officer as a cut-out between Conein and a designee of Gen. Don for communication purposes only. This officer is completely unwitting of any details of past or present coup activities and will remain so.

3. With reference to Gen Harkins' comment to Gen. Don which Don reports to have referred to a presidential directive and the proposal for a meeting with me, this may have served the useful purpose of allaying the General's fears as to our interest. If this were a provocation, the GVN could have assumed and manufactured any variations of the same theme. As a precautionary measure, however, I of course refused to see Gen. Don. As to the lack of information as to General Don's real backing, and the lack of evidence that any real capabilities for action have been developed, ref. b provides only part of the answer. I feel sure that the reluctance of the generals to provide the U.S. with full details of their plans at this time, is a reflection of their own sense of security and a lack of confidence that in the large American community present in Saigon their plans will not be prematurely revealed.

4. The best evidence available to the Embassy, which I grant you is not as complete as we would like it, is that Gen. Don and the other generals involved with him are seriously attempting to effect a change in the government. I do not believe that this is a provocation by Ngo Dinh Nhu, although we shall continue to assess the planning as well as possible. In the event that the coup aborts, or in the event that Nhu has masterminded a provocation, I believe that our involvement to date through Conein is still within the realm of plausible denial. CAS is perfectly prepared to have me disavow Conein at any time it may serve the national interest.

5. I welcome your reaffirming instructions contained in CAS Washington [cable] 74228. It is vital that we neither thwart a coup nor that we are even in a position where we do not know what is going on.

6. We should not thwart a coup for two reasons. First, it seems at least an even bet that the next government would not bungle and stumble as much as the present one has. Secondly, it is extremely unwise in the long range for us to pour cold water on attempts at a coup, particularly when they are just in their beginning stages. We should remember that this is the only way in which the people in Vietnam can possibly get a change of government. Whenever we thwart attempts at a coup, as we have done in the past, we are incurring very long lasting resentments, we are assuming an undue responsibility for keeping the incumbents in office, and in general are setting ourselves in judgment over the affairs of Vietnam. Merely to keep in touch with this situation and a policy merely limited to "not thwarting" are courses both of which entail some risks but these are lesser risks than either thwarting all coups while they are stillborn or our not being informed of what is happening. All the above is totally distinct from not wanting U.S. military advisors to be distracted by matters which are not in their domain, with which I heartily agree. But obviously this does not conflict with a policy of not thwarting. In judging proposed coups, we must consider the effect on the war effort. Certainly a succession of fights for control of the Government of Vietnam would interfere with the war effort. It must also be said that the war effort has been interfered with already by the incompetence of the present government and the uproar which this has caused.

7. Gen. Don's intention to have no religious discrimination in a future government is commendable and I applaud his desire not to be "a vassal" of the U.S. But I do not think his promise of a democratic election is realistic. This country simply is not ready for that procedure. I would add two other requirements. First, that there be no wholesale purges of personnel in the government. Individuals who were particularly reprehensible could be dealt with later by the regular legal process. Then I would be impractical, but I am thinking of a government which might include Tri Quang and which certainly should include men of the stature of Mr. Buu, the labor leader.

8. Copy to Gen. Harkins.

Source: *United States–Vietnam Relations, 1945–1967.* pp. 590–591. Washington, DC: Government Printing Office, 1971.

1 November 1963

Phone Conversation between Ngo Dinh Diem and Henry Cabot Lodge

DIEM: Some Units have made a rebellion and I want to know, what is the attitude of the U.S.?

LODGE: I do not feel well enough informed to be able to tell you. I have heard the shootings but with all the facts. Also, it is 4: 30 A.M. in Washington and the U.S. Government cannot possibly have a view.

DIEM: But you must have some general ideas. After all, I am Chief of State. I have tried to do my duty. I want to do now what duty and good sense require. I believe in duty above all.

LODGE: You have certainly done your duty. As I told you only this morning, I admire your courage and your great contribution to your country. No one can take away from you the credit for all you have done. Now I am worried about your physical safety. I have a report that those in charge of the current activity offer you and your brother safe conduct out of the country if you resign. Had you heard this?

DIEM: No. (pause) You have my phone number.

LODGE: Yes. If I can do anything for your physical safety, please call me.

DIEM: I am trying to re-establish order. (hangs up)

Source: Vassar College. *The Wars for Viet Nam: 1945 to 1975* (website). http://students.vassar.edu/~vietnam/

5 August 1964
President Johnson's Message to Congress

Last night I announced to the American people that the North Vietnamese regime had conducted further deliberate attacks against U.S. naval vessels operating in international waters, and I had therefore directed air action against gunboats and supporting facilities used in these hostile operations. This air action has now been carried out with substantial damage to the boats and facilities. Two U.S. aircraft were lost in the action.

After consultation with the leaders of both parties in the Congress, I further announced a decision to ask the Congress for a resolution expressing the unity and determination of the United States in supporting freedom and in protecting peace in southeast Asia.

These latest actions of the North Vietnamese regime has given a new and grave turn to the already serious situation in southeast Asia. Our commitments in that area are well known to the Congress. They were first made in 1954 by President Eisenhower. They were further defined in the Southeast Asia Collective Defense Treaty approved by the Senate in February 1955.

This treaty with its accompanying protocol obligates the United States and other members to act in accordance with their constitutional processes to meet Communist aggression against any of the parties or protocol states.

Our policy in southeast Asia has been consistent and unchanged since 1954. I summarized it on June 2 in four simple propositions:

1. America keeps her word. Here as elsewhere, we must and shall honor our commitments.

2. The issue is the future of southeast Asia as a whole. A threat to any nation in that region is a threat to all, and a threat to us.

3. Our purpose is peace. We have no military, political, or territorial ambitions in the area.

4. This is not just a jungle war, but a struggle for freedom on every front of human activity. Our military and economic assistance to South Vietnam and Laos in particular has the purpose of helping these countries to repel aggression and strengthen their independence.

The threat to the free nations of southeast Asia has long been clear. The North Vietnamese regime has constantly sought to take over South Vietnam and Laos. This Communist regime has violated the Geneva accords for Vietnam. It has systematically conducted a campaign of subversion, which includes the direction, training, and supply of personnel and arms for the conduct of guerrilla warfare in South Vietnamese territory. In Laos, the North Vietnamese regime has maintained military forces, used Laotian territory for infiltration into South Vietnam, and most recently carried out combat operations—all in direct violation of the Geneva Agreements of 1962.

In recent months, the actions of the North Vietnamese regime have become steadily more threatening...

As President of the United States I have concluded that I should now ask the Congress, on its part, to join in affirming the national determination that all such attacks will be met, and that the United States will continue in its basic policy of assisting the free nations of the area to defend their freedom.

As I have repeatedly made clear, the United States intends no rashness, and seeks no wider war. We must make it clear to all that the United States is united in its determination to bring about the end of Communist subversion and aggression in the area. We seek the full and effective restoration of the international agreements signed in Geneva in 1954, with respect to South Vietnam, and again in Geneva in 1962, with respect to Laos....

Source: *Department of State Bulletin*, 24 August 1964.

7 August 1964
Joint Resolution of Congress H.J. RES 1445: Tonkin Gulf Resolution

Resolved by the Senate and House of Representatives of the United States of America in Congress assembled, That the Congress approves and supports the determination of the President, as Commander in Chief, to take all necessary measures to repel any armed attack against the forces of the United States and to prevent further aggression.

Sec. 2. The United States regards as vital to its national interest and to world peace and security in southeast Asia. Consonant with the Constitution of the United States and the Charter Of the United Nations and in accordance with its obligations under the Southeast Asia Collective Defense Treaty, the United States is, therefore, prepared, as the President determines, to take all necessary steps, including the use of armed force, to assist any member or protocol state of the Southeast Asia Collective Defense Treaty requesting assistance in defense of its freedom.

Sec. 3. This resolution shall expire when the President shall determine that the peace and security of the area is reasonably assured by international conditions created by action of the United Nations or otherwise, except that it may be terminated earlier by concurrent resolution of the Congress.

Source: *Department of State Bulletin*, 24 August 1964. In McMahon, Robert J., ed. *Major Problems in the History of the Vietnam War.* 2nd edition. p. 209. Lexington, MA: D.C. Heath, 1995.

1965
Robert S. McNamara Recommends Escalation
Introduction

Our objective is to create conditions for a favorable settlement by demonstrating to the VC/DRV that the odds are against their winning. Under present conditions, however, the chances of achieving this objective are small—and the VC are winning now—largely because the ratio of guerrilla to anti-guerrilla forces is unfavorable to the government. With this in mind, we must choose among three courses of action with respect to South Vietnam: (1) Cut our losses and withdraw under the best conditions that can be arranged; (2) continue at about the present level, with US forces limited to, say, 75,000, holding on and playing for the breaks while recognizing that our position will probably grow weaker; or (3) expand substantially the US military pressure against the Viet Cong in the South and the North Vietnamese in the North and at the same time launch a vigorous effort on the political side to get negotiations started. An outline of the third of these approaches follows.

I. Expanded Military Moves

The following military moves should be taken together with the political initiatives in Part II below.

A. Inside South Vietnam. Increase US/SVN military strength in SVN enough to prove to the VC that they cannot win and thus to turn the tide of the war....

B. Against North Vietnam. While avoiding striking population and industrial targets not closely related to the DRV's supply of war material to the VC, we should announce to Hanoi and carry out actions to destroy such supplies and to interdict their flow into and out of North Vietnam....

II. Expanded Political Moves

Together with the above military moves, we should take the following political initiatives in order (a) to open a dialogue with Hanoi, Peking, and the VC looking toward a settlement in Vietnam, (b) to keep the Soviet Union from deepening its military involvement and support of North Vietnam until the time when settlement can be achieved, and (c) to cement the support for US policy by the US public, allies and friends, and to keep international opposition at a manageable level. While our approaches may be rebuffed until the tide begins to turn, they nevertheless should be made....

III. Evaluation of the Above Program

A. Domestic US Reaction. Even though casualties will increase and the war will continue for some time, the United States public will support this course of action because it is a combined military-political program designed and likely to bring about a favorable solution to the Vietnam problem.

B. Communist Reaction to the Expanded Programs.

1. Soviet. The Soviets can be expected to continue to contribute materiel and advisors to the North Vietnamese. Increased US bombing of Vietnam, including targets in Hanoi and Haiphong, SAM [surface-to-air missile] sites and airfields, and mining of North Vietnamese harbors, might oblige the Soviet Union to enter the contest more actively with volunteers and aircraft. This might result in minor encounters between US and Soviet personnel.

2. China. So long as no US or GVN troops invade North Vietnam and so long as no US or GVN aircraft attack Chinese territory, the Chinese probably will not send regular ground forces or aircraft into the war. However, the possibility of a more active Soviet involvement in North Vietnam might precipitate a Chinese introduction of land forces, probably dubbed volunteers, to preclude the Soviets' taking a pre-eminent position in North Vietnam.

3. North Vietnam. North Vietnam will not move towards the negotiating table until the tide begins to turn in the south. When that happens, they may seek to counter it by sending large numbers of men into South Vietnam.

4. Viet Cong. The VC, especially if they continue to take high losses, can be expected to depend increasingly upon the PAVN [People's Army of Vietnam, regular forces of North Vietnam] forces as the war moves into a more conventional phase; but they may find ways of continuing almost indefinitely their present intensive military, guerrilla and terror activities, particularly if reinforced with some regular PAVN units. A key question on the military side is whether POL [petroleum-oil-lubricants], ammunition, and cadres can be cut off and if they are cut off whether this really renders the Viet Cong impotent. A key question on the political side is whether any arrangement acceptable to us would be acceptable to the VC.

C. Estimate of Success

1. Militarily. The success of the above program from a military point of view turns on whether the increased effort stems the tide in the South; that in turn depends on two things—on whether the South Vietnamese hold their own in terms of numbers and fighting spirit, and on whether the US forces can be effective in a quick-reaction reserve role, a role in which they have not been tested. The number of US troops is too small to make a significant difference in the traditional 10-1 government-guerrilla formula, but it is not too small to make a significant difference in the kind of war which seems to be evolving in Vietnam—a "Third Stage" or conventional war in which it is easier to identify, locate and attack the enemy. (South Vietnam has 141 battalions as compared with an estimated equivalent number of VC battalions. The 44 US/3d country battalions mentioned above are the equivalent of 100 South Vietnamese battalions.)

2. Politically. It is frequently alleged that such a large expansion of US military personnel, their expanded military role (which would put them in close contact and offer some degree of control over South Vietnamese citizens), and the inevitable expansion of US voice in the operation of the GVN economy and facilities, command and government services will be unpopular; it is said that they could lead to the rejection of the government which supported this American presence, to an irresistible pressure for expulsion of the Americans, and to the greatly increased saleability of Communist propaganda. Whether these allegations are true, we do not know.

The political initiatives are likely to be successful in the early stages only to demonstrate US good faith; they will pay off toward an actual settlement only after the tide begins to turn (unless we lower our sights substantially). The tide almost certainly cannot begin to turn in less than a few months, and may not for a year or more; the war is one of attrition and will be a long one. Since troops once committed as a practical matter cannot be removed, since US casualties will rise, since we should take call up actions to support the additional forces in Vietnam, the test of endurance may be as much in the United States as in Vietnam.

3. Generally (CIA estimate). Over the longer term we doubt if the Communists are likely to change their basic strategy in Vietnam (i.e., aggressive and steadily mounting insurgency) unless and until two conditions prevail: (1) they are forced to accept a situation in the war in the South which offers them no prospect of an early victory and no grounds for hope that they can simply outlast the US and (2) North Vietnam itself is under continuing and increasingly damaging punitive attack. So long as the Communists think they scent the possibility of an early victory (which is probably now the case), we believe that they will persevere and accept extremely severe damage to the North. Conversely, if North Vietnam itself is not hurting, Hanoi's doctrinaire leaders will probably be ready to carry on the Southern struggle almost indefinitely. If, however, both of the conditions outlined above should be brought to pass, we believe Hanoi probably would, at least for a period of time, alter its basic strategy and course of action in South Vietnam.

Hanoi might do so in several ways. Going for a conference as a political way of gaining a respite from attack would be one. Alternatively it might reduce the level of insurgent activity in the hopes that this would force the US to stop its punishment of the North but not prevent the US and GVN from remaining subject to wearying harassment in the South. Or, Hanoi might order the VC to suspend operations in the hopes that in a period of temporary tranquillity, domestic and international opinion would force the US to disengage without destroying the VC apparatus or the roots of VC strength. Finally, Hanoi might decide that the US/GVN will to fight could still be broken and the tide of war turned back again in favor of the VC by launching a massive PAVN assault on the South. This is a less likely option in the circumstances we have posited, but still a contingency for which the US must be prepared.

Source: McMahon, Robert J., ed. *Major Problems in the History of the Vietnam War.* 2nd edition. pp. 213–216. Lexington, MA: D.C. Heath, 1995.

27 February 1965
"Aggression from the North." State Department White Paper on Vietnam

South Vietnam is fighting for its life against a brutal campaign of terror and armed attack inspired, directed, supplied, and controlled by the Communist regime in Hanoi. This flagrant aggression has been going on for years, but recently the pace has quickened and the threat has now become acute.

The war in Vietnam is a new kind of war, a fact as yet poorly understood in most parts of the world. Much of the confusion that prevails in the thinking of many people, and even governments, stems from this basic misunderstanding. For in Vietnam a totally new brand of aggression has been loosed against an independent people who want to make their way in peace and freedom.

Vietnam is not another Greece, where indigenous guerrilla forces used friendly neighboring territory as a sanctuary.

Vietnam is not another Malaya, where Communist guerrillas were, for the most part, physically distinguishable from the peaceful majority they sought to control.

Vietnam is not another Philippines, where Communist guerrillas were physically separated from the source of their moral and physical support.

Above all, the war in Vietnam is not a spontaneous and local rebellion against the established government.

There are elements in the Communist program of conquest directed against South Vietnam common to each of the previous areas of aggression and subversion. But there is one fundamental difference. In Vietnam a Communist government has set out deliberately to conquer a sovereign people in a neighboring state. And to achieve its end, it has used every resource of its own government to carry out its carefully planned program of concealed aggression. North Vietnam's commitment to seize control of the South is no less total than was the commitment of the regime in North Korea in 1950. But knowing the consequences of the latter's undisguised attack, the planners in Hanoi have tried desperately to conceal their hand. They have failed and their aggression is as real as that of an invading army.

This report is a summary of the massive evidence of North Vietnamese aggression obtained by the Government of South Vietnam. This evidence has been jointly analyzed by South Vietnamese and American experts.

The evidence shows that the hard core of the Communist forces attacking South Vietnam were trained in the North and ordered into the South by Hanoi. It shows that the key leadership of the Vietcong (VC), the officers and much of the cadre, many of the technicians, political organizers, and propagandists have come from the North and operate under Hanoi's direction. It shows that the training of essential military personnel and their infiltration into the South is directed by the Military High Command in Hanoi. In recent months new types of weapons have been introduced in the VC army, for which all ammunition must come from outside sources. Communist China and other Communist states have been the prime suppliers of these weapons and ammunition, and they have been channeled primarily through North Vietnam.

The directing force behind the effort to conqueror South Vietnam is the Communist Party in the North, the Lao Dong (Workers) Party. As in every Communist state, the party is an integral part of the regime itself. North Vietnamese officials have expressed their firm determination to absorb South Vietnam into the Communist world.

Through its Central Committee, which controls the Government of the North, the Lao Dong Party directs the total political and military effort of the Vietcong. The Military High Command in the North trains the military men and sends them into South Vietnam. The Central Research Agency, North Vietnam's central intelligence organization, directs the elaborate espionage and subversion effort...

Under Hanoi's overall direction the Communists have established an extensive machine for carrying on the war within South Vietnam. The focal point is the Central Office for South Vietnam with its political and military subsections and other specialized agencies. A subordinate part of this Central Office is the liberation Front for South Vietnam. The front was formed at Hanoi's order in 1960. Its principle function is to influence opinion abroad and to create the false impression that the aggression in South Vietnam is an indigenous rebellion against the established Government.

For more than 10 years the people and the Government of South Vietnam, exercising the inherent right of self-defense, have fought back against these efforts to extend Communist power south across the 17th parallel. The United States has responded to the appeals of the Government of the Republic of Vietnam for help in this defense of the freedom and independence of its land and its people.

In 1961 the Department of State issued a report called A Threat to the Peace. It described North Vietnam's program to seize South Vietnam. The evidence in that report had been presented by the Government of the Republic of Vietnam to the International Control Commission (ICC). A special report by the ICC in June 1962 upheld the validity of that evidence. The Commission held that there was "sufficient evidence to show beyond reasonable doubt" that North Vietnam had sent arms and men into South Vietnam to carry out subversion with the aim of overthrowing the legal Government there. The ICC found the authorities in Hanoi in specific violation of four provisions of the Geneva Accords of 1954.

Since then, new and even more impressive evidence of Hanoi's aggression has accumulated. The Government of the United States believes that evidence should be presented to its own citizens and to the world. It is important for free men to know what has been happening in Vietnam, and how, and why. That is the purpose of this report...

The record is conclusive. It establishes beyond question that North Vietnam is carrying out a carefully conceived plan of aggression against the South. It shows that North Vietnam has intensified its efforts in the years since it was condemned by the International Control Commission. It proves that Hanoi continues to press its systematic program of armed aggression into South Vietnam. This aggression violates the United Nations Charter. It is directly contrary to the Geneva Accords of 1954 and of 1962 to which North Vietnam is a party. It is a fundamental threat to the freedom and security of South Vietnam.

The people of South Vietnam have chosen to resist this threat. At their request, the United States has taken its place beside them in their defensive struggle.

The United States seeks no territory, no military bases, no favored position. But we have learned the meaning of aggression elsewhere in the post-war world, and we have met it.

If peace can be restored in South Vietnam, the United States will be ready at once to reduce its military involvement. But it will not abandon friends who want to remain free. It will do what must be done to help them. The choice now between peace and continued and increasingly destructive conflict is one for the authorities in Hanoi to make.

Source: *Department of State Bulletin,* 22 March 1965.

1 July 1965
Memorandum for President Lyndon Johnson from Under Secretary of State George Ball

(1) A Losing War: The South Vietnamese are losing the war to the Viet Cong. No one can assure you that we can beat the Viet Cong or even force them to the conference table on our terms, no matter how many hundred thousand white, foreign (U.S.) troops we deploy.

No one has demonstrated that a white ground force of whatever size can win a guerrilla war—which is at the same time a civil war between Asians—in jungle terrain in the midst of a population that refuses cooperation to the white forces (and the South Vietnamese) and thus provides a great intelligence advantage to the other side. Three recent incidents vividly illustrate this point: (a) the sneak attack on the Da Nang Air Base which involved penetration of a defense parameter guarded by 9,000 Marines. This raid was possible only because of the cooperation of the local inhabitants; (b) the B-52 raid that failed to hit the Viet Cong who had obviously been tipped off; (c) the search and destroy mission of the 173rd Air Borne Brigade which spent three days looking for the Viet Cong, suffered 23 casualties, and never made contact with the enemy who had obviously gotten advance word of their assignment.

(2) The Question to Decide: Should we limit our liabilities in South Vietnam and try to find a way out with minimal long-term costs?

The alternative—no matter what we may wish it to be—is almost certainly a protracted war involving an open-ended commitment of U.S. forces, mounting U.S. casualties, no assurance of a satisfactory solution, and a serious danger of escalation at the end of the road.

(3) Need for a Decision Now: So long as our forces are restricted to advising and assisting the South Vietnamese, the struggle will remain a civil war between Asian peoples. Once we deploy substantial numbers of troops in combat it will become a war between the U.S. and a large part of the population of South Vietnam, organized and directed from North Vietnam and backed by the resources of both Moscow and Peiping.

The decision you face now, therefore, is crucial. Once large numbers of U.S. troops are committed to direct combat, they will begin to take heavy casualties in a war they are ill-equipped to fight in a non-cooperative if not downright hostile countryside.

Once we suffer large casualties, we will have started a well-nigh irreversible process. Our involvement will be so great that we cannot—without national humiliation—stop short of achieving our complete objectives. Of the two possibilities I think humiliation would be more likely than the achievement of our objectives—even after we have paid terrible costs.

(4) Compromise Solution: Should we commit U.S. manpower and prestige to a terrain so unfavorable as to give a very large advantage to the enemy—or should we seek a compromise settlement which achieves less than our stated objectives and thus cut our losses while we still have the freedom of maneuver to do so.

(5) Costs of a Compromise Solution: The answer involves a judgment as to the cost to the U.S. of such a compromise settlement in terms of our relations with the countries in the area of South Vietnam, the credibility of our commitments, and our prestige around the world. In my judgment, if we act before we commit a substantial U.S. truce [sic] to combat in South Vietnam we can, by accepting some short-term costs, avoid what may well be a long-term catastrophe. I believe we attended [sic] grossly to exaggerate the costs involved in a compromise settlement. An appreciation of probable costs is contained in the attached memorandum.

(6) With these considerations in mind, I strongly urge the following program:

(a) Military Program

(1) Complete all deployments already announced—15 battalions—but decide not to go beyond a total of 72,000 men represented by this figure.

(2) Restrict the combat role of the American forces to the June 19 announcement, making it clear to General Westmoreland that this announcement is to be strictly construed.

(3) Continue bombing in the North but avoid the Hanoi-Haiphong area and any targets nearer to the Chinese border than those already struck.

(b) Political Program

(1) In any political approaches so far, we have been the prisoners of whatever South Vietnamese government that was momentarily in power. If we are ever to move toward a settlement, it will probably be because the South Vietnamese government pulls the rug out from under us and makes its own deal or because we go forward quietly without advance prearrangement with Saigon.

(2) So far we have not given the other side a reason to believe there is any flexibility in our negotiating approach. And the other side has been unwilling to accept what in their terms is complete capitulation.

(3) Now is the time to start some serious diplomatic feelers looking towards a solution based on some application of a self-determination principle.

(4) I would recommend approaching Hanoi rather than any of the other probable parties, the NLF,—or Peiping. Hanoi is the only one that has given any signs of interest in discussion. Peiping has been rigidly opposed. Moscow has recommended that we negotiate with Hanoi. The NLF has been silent.

(5) There are several channels to the North Vietnamese, but I think the best one is through their representative in Paris, Mai van Bo. Initial feelers of Bo should be directed toward a discussion both of the four points we have put forward and the four points put forward by Hanoi as a basis for negotiation. We can accept all but one of Hanoi's four points, and hopefully we should be able to agree on some ground rules for serious negotiations—including no preconditions.

(6) If the initial feelers lead to further secret, exploratory talks, we can inject the concept of self-determination that would permit the Viet Cong some hope of achieving some of their political objectives through local elections or some other device.

(7) The contact on our side should be handled through a nongovernmental cutout (possibly a reliable newspaper man who can be repudiated).

(8) If progress can be made at this level a basis can be laid for a multinational conference. At some point, obviously, the government of South Vietnam will have to be brought on board, but I would postpone this step until after a substantial feeling out of Hanoi.

(7) Before moving to any formal conference we should be prepared to agree once the conference is started:

(a) The U.S. will stand down its bombing of the North

(b) The South Vietnamese will initiate no offensive operations in the South, and

(c) The DRV will stop terrorism and other aggressive action against the South.

(8) The negotiations at the conference should aim at incorporating our understanding with Hanoi in the form of a multinational agreement guaranteed by the U.S., the Soviet Union and possibly other parties, and providing for an international mechanism to supervise its execution.

Source: *The Pentagon Papers. The Senator Gravel Edition. The Defense Department of the United States Decisionmaking on Vietnam.* Vol. IV, pp. 615–617. Boston: Beacon Press, n.d.

30 November 1965
Memorandum from Secretary of Defense Robert McNamara to President Lyndon Johnson

The Ky "government of generals" is surviving, but not acquiring wide support or generating actions; pacification is thoroughly stalled, with no guarantee that security anywhere is permanent and no indications that able and willing leadership will emerge in the absence of that permanent security. (Prime Minister Ky estimates that his government controls only 25% of the population today and reports that his pacification chief hopes to increase that to 50% two years from now.)

The dramatic recent changes in the situation are on the military side. They are the increased infiltration from the North and the increased willingness of the Communist forces to stand and fight, even in large-scale engagements. The Ia Drang River Campaign of early November is an example. The Communists appear to have decided to increase their forces in SVN both by heavy recruitment in the South (especially in the Delta) and by infiltration of regular NVN forces from the North.... The enemy can be expected to enlarge his present strength of 110 battalion equivalents to more than 150 battalion equivalents by the end of calendar 1966, when hopefully his losses can be made to equal his input.

As for the Communist ability to supply this force, it is estimated that, even taking account of interdiction of routes by air and sea, more than 200 tons of supplies a day can be infiltrated—more than enough, allowing for the extent to which the enemy lives off the land, to support the likely PAVN/VC force at the likely level of operations.

To meet this possible—and in my view likely—Communist buildup, the presently contemplated Phase I forces will not be enough (approx. 220,000 Americans, almost all in place by end of 1965). Bearing in mind the nature of the war, the expected weighted combat force ratio of less than 2-to-1 will not be good enough. Nor will the originally contemplated Phase II addition of 28 more U.S. battalions (112,000 men) be enough; the combat force ratio, even with 32 new SVNese battalions, would still be little better than 2-to-1 at the end of 1966. The initiative which we have held since August would pass to the enemy; we would fall far short of what we expected to achieve in terms of population control and disruption of enemy bases and lines of communications. Indeed, it is estimated that with the contemplated Phase II addition of 28 U.S. battalions, we would be able only to hold our present geographical positions.

2. We have but two options, it seems to me. One is to go now for a compromise solution (something substantially less than the "favorable outcome" I described in my memo of Nov 3) and hold further deployments to a minimum. The other is to stick with our stated objectives and with the war, and provide what it takes in men and materiel. If it is decided not to move now toward a compromise, I recommend that the US both send a substantial number of additional troops and very gradually intensify the bombing of NVN. Amb. Lodge, Wheeler, Sharp and Westmoreland concur in this prolonged course of action, although Wheeler and Sharp would intensify the bombing of the North more quickly.

(recommend up to 74 battalions by end-66: total to approx 400,000 by end-66. And it should be understood that further deployments (perhaps exceeding 200,000) may be needed in 1967.) 3. Bombing of NVN.... over a period of the next six months we gradually enlarge the target system in the northeast (Hanoi-Haiphong) quadrant until, at the end of the period, it includes "controlled" reconnaissance of lines of communication throughout the area, bombing of petroleum storage facilities and power plants, and mining of the harbors. (Left unstruck would be population targets, industrial plants, locks and dams).

4. Pause in bombing NVN. It is my belief that there should be a three- or four-week pause in the program of bombing the North before we either greatly increase our troop deployments to VN or intensify our strikes against the North. (My recommendation for a "pause" is not concurred in by Lodge, Wheeler, or Sharp.) The reasons for this belief are, first, that we must lay a foundation in the minds of the American public and in world opinion for such an enlarged phase of the war and, second, we should give NVN a face-saving chance to stop the aggression. I am not seriously concerned about the risk of alienating the SVNese, misleading Hanoi, or being "trapped" in a pause; if we take reasonable precautions, we can avoid these pitfalls. I am seriously concerned about embarking on a markedly higher level of war in VN without having tried, through a pause, to end the war or at least having made it clear to our people that we did our best to end it.

5. Evaluation. We should be aware that deployments of the kind I have recommended will not guarantee success. U.S. killed-in-action can be expected to reach 1000 a month, and the odds are even that we will be faced in early 1967 with a

"no-decision" at an even higher level. My overall evaluation, nevertheless, is that the best chance of achieving our stated objectives lies in a pause followed, if it fails, by the deployments mentioned above.

Source: *The Pentagon Papers. The Senator Gravel Edition. The Defense Department of the United States Decisionmaking on Vietnam.* Vol. IV, pp. 622–623. Boston: Beacon Press, n.d.

15 February 1967
Letter of Hô Chí Minh to Lyndon Johnson

To His Excellency Mr. Lyndon B. Johnson,
President, United States of America
Your Excellency:

On February 10, 1967, I received your message. This is my reply. Vietnam is thousands of miles away from the United States. The Vietnamese people have never done any harm to the United States. But contrary to the pledges made by its representative at the 1954 Geneva conference, the U.S. has ceaselessly intervened in Vietnam, it has unleashed and intensified the war of aggression in North Vietnam with a view to prolonging the partition of Vietnam and turning South Vietnam into a neocolony and a military base of the United States. For over two years now, the U.S. government has, with its air and naval forces, carried the war to the Democratic Republic of (North) Vietnam, an independent and sovereign country.

The U.S. govenunent has committed war crimes, crimes against peace and against mankind. In South Vietnam, half a million U.S. and satellite troops have resorted to the most inhuman weapons and most barbarous methods of warfare, such as napalm, toxic chemicals and gases, to massacre our compatriots, destroy crops, and raze villages to the ground. In North Vietnam, thousands of U.S. aircraft have dropped hundreds of thousands of tons of bombs, destroying towns, villages, factories, schools. In your message, you apparently deplore the sufferings and destruction in Vietnam. May I ask you: Who has perpetrated these monstrous crimes? It is the United States and satellite troops. The U.S. government is entirely responsible for the extremely serious situation in Vietnam.

The U.S. war of aggression against the Vietnamese people constitutes a challenge to the countries of the socialist camp, a threat to the national independence movement, and a serious danger to peace in Asia and the world.

The Vietnamese people deeply love independence, freedom and peace. But in the face of U.S. aggression, they have risen up, united as one man, fearless of sacrifices and hardships. They are determined to carry on their resistance until they have won genuine independence and freedom and true peace. Our just cause enjoys strong sympathy and support from the peoples of the whole world, including broad sections of the American people.

The U.S. government has unleashed the war of aggression in Vietnam. It must cease this aggression. This is the only way to restoration of peace. The U.S. government must stop definitely and unconditionally its bombing raids and all other acts of war against the Democratic Republic of Vietnam, withdraw from South Vietnam all U.S. and satellite troops, recognize the South Vietnam National Front for Liberation, and let the Vietnamese people settle themselves their own affairs. Such is the basis of the five-point stand of the government of the Democratic Republic of Vietnam, which embodies the essential principles and provision of the 1954 Geneva Agreements on Vietnam; it is the basis of a correct political solution to the Vietnam problem.

In your message you suggested direct talks between the Democratic Republic of Vietnam and the United States. If the U.S. government really wants these talks, it must first of all stop unconditionally its bombing raids and all other acts of war against the Democratic Republic of Vietnam. It is only after the unconditional cessation of U.S. bombing raids and all other acts of war against the Democratic Republic of Vietnam that the Democratic Republic of Vietnam and the U.S. could enter into talks and discuss questions concerning the two sides.

The Vietnamese people will never submit to force, they will never accept talks under threat of bombs.

Our cause is absolutely just. It is to be hoped that the U.S. government will act in accordance with reason.

Sincerely,

Ho Chi Minh

Source: Furr, Grover: Vietnam Home Page (website). http://www.shss.montclair.edu/english/furr/hotolbj.html

21 November 1967

Address by Commander of U.S. Forces in Vietnam General William Westmoreland [Extracts]

Improving Vietnamese Effectiveness

With 1968, a new phase is now starting. We have reached an important point when the end begins to come into view. What is this third phase we are about to enter?

In Phase III, in 1968, we intend to do the following:

Help the Vietnamese Armed Forces to continue improving their effectiveness.

Decrease our advisers in training centers and other places where the professional competence of Vietnamese officers makes this possible.

Increase our advisory effort with the younger brothers of the Vietnamese Army: the Regional Forces and Popular Forces.

Use U.S. and free-world forces to destroy North Vietnamese forays while we assist the Vietnamese to reorganize for territorial security.

Provide the new military equipment to revitalize the Vietnamese Army and prepare it to take on an ever-increasing share of the war.

Continue pressure on North to prevent rebuilding and to make infiltration more costly.

Turn a major share of frontline DMZ defense over to the Vietnamese Army.

Increase U.S. support in the rich and populated delta.

Help the Government of Viet-Nam single out and destroy the Communist shadow government.

Continue to isolate the guerrilla from the people.

Help the new Vietnamese government to respond to popular aspirations and to reduce and eliminate corruption.

Help the Vietnamese strengthen their policy forces to enhance law and order.

Open more roads and canals.

Continue to improve the Vietnamese economy and standard of living.

The Final Phase

Now for phase IV—the final phase. That period will see the conclusion of our plan to weaken the enemy and strengthen our friends until we become progressively superfluous. The object will be to show the world that guerrilla warfare and invasion do not pay as a new means of Communist aggression.

I see phase IV happening as follows:

Infiltration will slow.

The Communist infrastructure will be cut up and near collapse.

The Vietnamese Government will prove its stability, and the Vietnamese Army will show that it can handle Viet Cong.

The Regional Forces and Popular Forces will reach a higher level of professional performance.

U.S. units can begin to phase down as the Vietnamese Army is modernized and develops its capacity to the fullest.

The military physical assets, bases and ports, will be progressively turned over to the Vietnamese.

The Vietnamese will take charge of the final mopping up of the Viet Cong (which will probably last several years). The U.S., at the same time, will continue the developmental help envisaged by the President for the community of Southeast Asia.

You may ask how long phase III will take, before we reach the final phase. We have already entered part of phase III. Looking back on phases I and II, we can conclude that we have come a long way.

I see progress as I travel all over Viet-Nam.

I see it in the attitudes of the Vietnamese.

I see it in the open roads and canals.

I see it in the new crops and the new purchasing power of the farmer.

I see it in the increasing willingness of the Vietnamese Army to fight North Vietnamese units and in the victories they are winning.

Parenthetically, I might say that the U.S. press tends to report U.S. actions; so you may not be as aware as I am of the victories won by South Vietnamese forces.

The enemy has many problems:

He is losing control of the scattered population under his influence.

He is losing credibility with the population he still controls.

He is alienating the people by his increased demands and taxes, where he can impose them.

He sees the strength of his forces steadily declining.

He can no longer recruit in the South to any meaningful extent; he must plug the gap with North Vietnamese.

His monsoon offensives have been failuraes.

He was dealt a mortal blow by the installation of a freely elected representative government.

And he failed in his desperate effort to take the world's headlines from the inauguration by a military victory.

Lastly, the Vietnamese Army is on the road to becoming a competent force. Korean troops in Viet-Nam provide a good example for the Vietnamese. Fifteen years ago the Koreans themselves had problems now ascribed to the Vietnamese. The Koreans surmounted these problems, and so can and will the Vietnamese....

We are making progress. We know you want an honorable and early transition to the fourth and last phase. So do your sons and so do I.

It lies within our grasp—the enemy's hopes are bankrupt. With your support we will give you a success that will impact not only on South Viet-Nam but on every emerging nation in the world.

Source: *Department of State, Bulletin,* 11 December 1967. In Porter, Gareth, editor. *Vietnam. A History in Documents.* pp. 352–364. New York: New American Library, 1981.

27 February 1968
Report of Chairman of the Joint Chiefs of Staff General Earle G. Wheeler on the Situation in Vietnam [Extracts]

1. The Chairman, JCS and party visited SVN on 23, 24 and 25 February. This report summarizes the impressions and facts developed through conversations and briefings at MACV and with senior commanders throughout the country.

2. Summary

—The current situation in Vietnam is still developing and fraught with opportunities as well as dangers.

—There is no question in the mind of MACV that the enemy went all out for a general offensive and general uprising and apparently believed that he would succeed in bringing the war to an early successful conclusion.

—The enemy failed to achieve this initial objectives but is continuing his effort. Although many of his units were badly hurt, the judgment is that he has the will and the capability to continue.

—Enemy losses have been heavy; he has failed to achieve his prime objectives of mass uprisings and capture of a large number of the capital cities and towns. Morale in enemy units which were badly mauled or where the men were oversold the idea of a decisive victory at TET probably has suffered severely. However, with replacements, his indoctrination system would seem capable of maintaining morale at a generally adequate level. His determination appears to be unshaken.

—The enemy is operating with relative freedom in the countryside, probably recruiting heavily and no doubt infiltrating NVA units and personnel. His recovery is likely to be rapid; his supplies are adequate; and he is trying to maintain the momentum of his winter-spring offensive.

—The structure of the GVN held up but its effectiveness has suffered.

—The RVNAF held up against the initial assault with gratifying, and in a way, surprising strength and fortitude. However, ARVN is now in a defensive posture around towns and cities and there is concern about how well they will bear up under sustained pressure.

—The initial attack nearly succeeded in a dozen places, and defeat in those places was only averted by the timely reaction of US forces. In short, it was a very near thing.

—There is no doubt that the RD Program has suffered a severe set back.

—RVNAF was not badly hurt physically—they should recover strength and equipment rather quickly (equipment in 2–3 months—strength in 3–6 months). Their problems are more psychological than physical.

—US forces have lost none of their pre-TET capability.

—MACV has three principal problems. First, logistic support north of Danang is marginal owing to weather, enemy interdiction and harassment and the massive deployment of US forces into the DMZ/Hue area. Opening Route 1 will alleviate this problem but takes a substantial troop commitment. Second, the defensive posture of ARVN is permitting the VC to make rapid inroads in the formerly pacified countryside. ARVN, in its own words, is in a dilemma as it cannot afford another enemy thrust into the cities and towns and yet if it remains in a defensive posture against this contingency, the countryside goes by default. MACV is forced to devote much of its troop strength to this problem. Third, MACV has been forced to deploy 50% of all US maneuver battalions into I Corps, to meet the threat there, while stripping the rest of the country of adequate reserves. If the enemy synchronizes an attack against Khe Sanh/Hue-Quang Tri with an offensive in the Highlands and around Saigon while keeping the pressure on throughout the remainder of the country, MACV will be hard pressed to meet adequately all threats. Under these circumstances, we must be prepared to accept some reverses.

—For these reasons, General Westmoreland has asked for a 3 division–15 tactical fighter squadron force. This force would provide him with a theater reserve and an offensive capability which he does not now have.

3. The situation as it stands today:

a. Enemy capabilities

(1) The enemy has been hurt badly in the populated lowlands, but is practically intact elsewhere. He committed over 67,000 combat maneuver forces plus perhaps 25% or 17,000 more impressed men and boys, for a total of about 84,000. He lost 40,000 killed, at least 3,000 captured, and perhaps 5,000 disabled or died of wounds. He had peaked his force total to about 240,000 just before TET, by hard recruiting, infiltration, civilian impressment, and drawdowns on service and guerrilla personnel. So he has lost about one fifth of his total strength. About two-third of his trained, organized unit strength can continue offensive action. He is probably infiltrating and recruiting heavily in the countryside while allied forces are securing the urban areas. (Discussions of strengths and recruiting are in paragraphs 1, 2 and 3 of Enclosure (1)). The enemy has adequate munitions, stockpiled in-country and available through the DMZ, Laos, and Cambodia, to support major attacks and countrywide pressure; food procurement may be a problem. (Discussion is in paragraph 6 Enclosure (1)). Besides strength losses, the enemy now has morale and training problems which currently limit combat

effectiveness of VC guerrilla, main and local forces. (Discussions of forces are in paragraphs 2, 5, Enclosure (1)).

(a) I Corps Tactical Zone: Strong enemy forces in the northern two provinces threaten Quang Tri and Hue cities, and US positions at the DMZ. Two NVA divisions threaten Khe Sanh. Eight enemy battalion equivalents are in the Danang-Hoi An area. Enemy losses in I CTZ have been heavy, with about 13,000 killed; some NVA as well as VC units have been hurt badly. However, NVA replacements in the DMZ area can offset these losses fairly quickly. The enemy has an increased artillery capability at the DMZ, plus some tanks and possibly even a limited air threat in I CTZ.

(b) II Corps Tactical Zone: The 1st NVA Division went virtually unscathed during TET offensive, and represents a strong threat in the western highlands. Seven combat battalion equivalents threaten Dak To. Elsewhere in the highlands, NVA units have been hurt and VC units chopped up badly. On the coast, the 3rd NVA Division had already taken heavy losses just prior to the offensive. The 5th NVA Division, also located on the coast, is not in good shape. Local force strength in coastal II CTZ had dwindled long before the offensive. The enemy's strength in II CTZ is in the highlands where enemy troops are fresh and supply lines short.

(c) III CTZ: Most of the enemy's units were used in the TET effort, and suffered substantial losses. Probably the only major unit to escape heavy losses was the 7th NVA Division. However, present dispositions give the enemy the continuing capability of attacking the Saigon area with 10 to 11 combat effective battalion equivalents. His increased movement southward of supporting arms and infiltration of supplies has further developed his capacity for attacks by fire.

(d) IV Corps Tactical Zone: All enemy forces were committed in IV Corps, but losses per total strength were the lightest in the country. The enemy continues to be capable of investing or attacking cities throughout the area.

(2) New weapons or tactics:

We may see heavier rockets and tube artillery, additional armor, and the use of aircraft, particularly in the I CTZ. The only new tactic in view is infiltration and investment of cities to create chaos, to demoralize the people, to discredit the government, and to tie allied forces to urban security....

4. What does the future hold?

a. Probable enemy strategy. (Reference paragraph 7b, Enclosure (1)). We see the enemy pursuing a reinforced offensive to enlarge his control throughout the country and keep pressures on the government and allies. We expect him to maintain strong threats in the DMZ area, at Khe Sanh, in the highlands, and at Saigon, and to attack in force when conditions seem favorable. He is likely to try to gain control of the country's northern provinces. He will continue efforts to encircle cities and province capitals to isolate and disrupt normal activities, and infiltrate them to create chaos. He will seek maximum attrition of RVNAF elements. Against US forces, he will emphasize attacks by fire on airfields and installations, using assaults and ambushes selectively. His central objective continues to be the destruction of the Government of SVN and its armed forces. As a minimum he

hopes to seize sufficient territory and gain control of enough people to support establishment of the groups and committees he proposes for participation in an NLF dominated government.

b. MACV Strategy:

(1) MACV believes that the central thrust of our strategy now must be to defeat the enemy offensive and that if this is done well, the situation overall will be greatly improved over the pre-TET condition.

(2) MACV accepts the fact that its first priority must be the security of Government of Vietnam in Saigon and provincial capitals. MACV describes its objectives as:

—First, to counter the enemy offensive and to destroy or eject the NVA invasion force in the north.

—Second, to restore security in the cities and towns.

—Third, to restore security in the heavily populated areas of the countryside.

—Fourth, to regain the initiative through offensive operations.

c. Tasks:

(1) Security of Cities and Government. MACV recognizes that US forces will be required to reinforce and support RVNAF in the security of cities, towns and government structure. At this time, 10 US battalions are operating in the environs of Saigon. It is clear that this task will absorb a substantial portion of US forces.

(2) Security in the Countryside. To a large extent the VC now control the countryside. Most of the 54 battalions formerly providing security for pacification are now defending district or province towns. MACV estimates that US forces will be required in a number of places to assist and encourage the Vietnamese Army to leave the cities and towns and reenter the country. This is especially true in the Delta.

(3) Defense of the borders, the DMZ and the northern provinces. MACV considers that it must meet the enemy threat in I Corps Tactical Zone and has already deployed there slightly over 50% of all US maneuver battalions. US forces have been thinned out in the highlands, notwithstanding an expected enemy offensive in the early future.

(4) Offensive Operations. Coupling the increased requirement for the cities and subsequent reentry into the rural areas, and the heavy requirement for defense of the I Corps Zone, MACV does not have adequate forces at this time to resume the offensive in the remainder of the country, nor does it have adequate reserves against the contingency of simultaneous large-scale enemy offensive action throughout the country.

5. Force Requirements:

a. Forces currently assigned to MACV, plus the residual Program Five forces yet to be delivered, are inadequate in numbers and balance to carry out the strategy and to accomplish the tasks described above in the proper priority. To contend with, and defeat, the new enemy threat, MACV has stated requirements for forces over the 525,000 ceiling imposed by Program Five. The add-on requested totals 206,756 spaces for a new proposed ceiling of 731,756, with all forces being deployed into country by the end of CY 68. Principal forces included in the add-on are three division equivalents, 15 tactical fighter squadrons and augmentation for current Navy programs. MACV desires that these additional forces be delivered in three packages as follows:

(1) Immediate Increment, Priority One: To be deployed by 1 May 68.Major elements include one brigade of the 5th Mechanized Division with a mix of one infantry, one armored and one mechanized battalion; the Fifth Marine Division (less RLT-26); one armored cavalry regiment; eight tactical fighter squadrons; and a groupment of Navy units to augment on-going programs.

(2) Immediate Increment, Priority Two: To be deployed as soon as possible but prior to 1 Sep. 68. Major elements include the remainder of the 5th Mechanized Division, and four tactical fighter squadrons. It is desirable that the ROK Light Division be deployed within this time frame.

Follow-On Increment: To be deployed by the end of CY 68. Major elements include one infantry division, three tactical fighter squadrons, and units to further augment Navy Programs.

Source: Document declassified by Department of Defense, no date shown. In McMahon, Robert J., ed. *Major Problems in the History of the Vietnam War.* 2nd edition. pp. 344–347. Lexington, MA: D.C. Heath, 1995.

31 March 1968
Television Address by President Lyndon Johnson

Good evening, my fellow Americans. Tonight I want to speak to you of peace in Viet-Nam and Southeast Asia.

No other question so preoccupies our people. No other dream so absorbs the 250 million human beings who live in that part of the world. No other goal motivates American policy in Southeast Asia.

For years, representatives of our Government and others have traveled the world seeking to find a basis for peace talks.

Since last September, they have carried the offer that I made public at San Antonio.

That offer was this: that the United States would stop its bombardment of North Viet-Nam when that would lead promptly to productive discussions—and that we would assume that North Viet-Nam would not take military advantage of our restraint.

Hanoi denounced this offer, both privately and publicly. Even while the search for peace was going on, North Viet-Nam rushed their preparations for a savage assault on the people, the Government, and the allies of South Viet-Nam.

Their attack—during the Tet holidays—failed to achieve its principal objectives.

It did not collapse the elected government of South Viet-Nam or shatter its army, as the Communists had hoped.

It did not produce a "general uprising" among the people of the cities, as they had predicted.

The Communists were unable to maintain control of any of the more than 30 cities that they attacked. And they took very heavy casualties.

But they did compel the South Vietnamese and their allies to move certain forces from the countryside into the cities. They caused widespread disruption and suffering. Their attacks, and the battles that followed, made refugees of half a million human beings.

The Communists may renew their attack any day. They are, it appears, trying to make 1968 the year of decision in South Viet-Nam—the year that brings, if not final victory or defeat, at least a turning point in the struggle.

This much is clear: If they do mount another round of heavy attacks, they will not succeed in destroying the fighting power of South Viet-Nam and its allies.

But tragically, this is also clear: Many men—on both sides of the struggle—will be lost. A nation that has already suffered 20 years of warfare will suffer once again. Armies on both sides will take new casualties. And the war will go on.

There is no need for this to be so.

There is no need to delay the talks that could bring an end to this long and this bloody war.

Tonight I renew the offer I made last August—to stop the bombardment of North Viet-Nam. We ask that talks begin promptly, that they be serious talks on the substance of peace. We assume that during those talks Hanoi will not take advantage of our restraint.

We are prepared to move immediately toward peace through negotiations. So tonight, in the hope that this action will lead to early talks, I am taking the first step to deescalate the conflict. We are reducing—substantially reducing—the present level of hostilities. And we are doing so unilaterally and at once.

Tonight I have ordered our aircraft and our naval vessels to make no attacks on North Viet-Nam, except in the area north of the demilitarized zone where the continuing enemy buildup directly threatens Allied forward positions and where the movements of their troops and supplies are clearly related to that threat.

The area in which we are stopping our attacks includes almost 90 percent of North Viet-Nam's population and most of its territory. Thus there will be no attacks around the principal populated areas or in the food-producing areas of North Viet-Nam.

Even this very limited bombing of the North could come to an early end if our restraint is matched by restraint in Hanoi. But I cannot in good conscience stop all bombing so long as to do so would immediately and directly endanger the lives of our men and our allies. Whether a complete bombing halt becomes possible in the future will be determined by events.

Our purpose in this action is to bring about a reduction in the level of violence that now exists.

It is to save the lives of brave men and to save the lives of innocent women and children. It is to permit the contending forces to move closer to a political settlement.

And tonight I call upon the United Kingdom and I call upon the Soviet Union, as cochairmen of the Geneva conferences and as permanent members of the United Nations Security Council, to do all they can to move from the unilateral act of deescalation that I have just announced toward genuine peace in Southeast Asia.

Now, as in the past, the United States is ready to send its representatives to any forum, at any time, to discuss the means of bringing this ugly war to an end.

I am designating one of our most distinguished Americans, Ambassador Averell Harriman, as my personal representative for such talks. In addition, I have asked Ambassador Llewellyn Thompson, who returned from Moscow for consultation, to be available to join Ambassador Harriman at Geneva or any other suitable place just as soon as Hanoi agrees to a conference.

I call upon President Ho Chi Minh to respond positively and favorably to this new step toward peace.

But if peace does not come now through negotiations, it will come when Hanoi understands that our common resolve is unshakable and our common strength is invincible.

Tonight, we and the other allied nations are contributing 600,000 fighting men to assist 700,000 South Vietnamese troops in defending their little country.

Our presence there has always rested on this basic belief: The main burden of preserving their freedom must be carried out by them—by the South Vietnamese themselves.

We and our allies can only help to provide a shield behind which the people of South Viet-Nam can survive and can grow and develop. On their efforts—on their determinations and resourcefulness—the outcome will ultimately depend....

The actions that we have taken since the beginning of the year to reequip the South Vietnamese forces; to meet our responsibilities in Korea, as well as our responsibilities in Viet-Nam; to meet price increases and the cost of activating and deploying Reserve forces; to replace helicopters and provide the other military supplies we need—all of these actions are going to require additional expenditures.

The tentative estimate of those additional expenditures is $2.5 billion in this fiscal year and $2.6 billion in the next fiscal year.

These projected increases in expenditures for our national security will bring into sharper focus the Nation's need for immediate action, action to protect the prosperity of the American people and to protect the strength and the stability of our American dollar.

On many occasions I have pointed out that without a tax bill or decreased expenditures next year's deficit would again be around $20 billion. I have emphasized the need to set strict priorities in our spending. I have stressed that failure to act—and to act promptly and decisively—would raise very strong doubts throughout the world about America's willingness to keep its financial house in order.

Yet Congress has not acted. And tonight we face the sharpest financial threat in the post-war era—a threat to the dollar's role as the keystone of international trade and finance in the world....

One day, my fellow citizens, there will be peace in Southeast Asia.

It will come because the people of Southeast Asia want it—those whose armies are at war tonight and those who, though threatened, have thus far been spared.

Peace will come because Asians were willing to work for it—and to sacrifice for it—and to die by the thousands for it.

But let it never be forgotten: Peace will come also because America sent her sons to help secure it.

It has not been easy—far from it. During the past 4-1/2 years, it has been my fate and my responsibility to be Commander in Chief. I lived daily and nightly with the cost of this war. I know the pain that it has inflicted. I know perhaps better than anyone the misgivings that it has aroused.

Throughout this entire long period, I have been sustained by a single principle: that what we are doing now in Viet-Nam is vital not only to the security of Southeast Asia, but it is vital to the security of every American.

Surely we have treaties which we must respect. Surely we have commitments that we are going to keep. Resolutions of the Congress testify to the need to resist aggression in the world and in Southeast Asia.

But the heart of our involvement in South Viet-Nam—under three different Presidents, three separate administrations—has always been America's own security.

And the larger purpose of our involvement has always been to help the nations of Southeast Asia become independent and stand alone, self-sustaining as members of a great world community—at peace with themselves and at peace with all others.

With such an Asia, our country—and the world—will be far more secure than it is tonight.

I believe that a peaceful Asia is far nearer to reality because of what America has done in Viet-Nam. I believe that the men who endure the dangers of battle—fighting there for us tonight—are helping the entire world avoid far greater conflicts, far wider wars, far more destruction, than this one.

The peace that will bring them home some day will come. Tonight I have offered the first in what I hope will be a series of mutual moves toward peace.

I pray that it will not be rejected by the leaders of North Viet-Nam. I pray that they will accept it as a means by which the sacrifices of their own people may be ended. And I ask your help and your support, my fellow citizens, for this effort to reach across the battlefield toward an early peace....

Throughout my entire public career I have followed the personal philosophy that I am a free man, an American, a public servant, and a member of my party, in that order always and only.

For 37 years in the service of our nation, first as a Congressman, as a Senator and as Vice President and now as your President, I have put the unity of the people first. I have put it ahead of any divisive partisanship.

And in these times as in times before, it is true that a house divided against itself by the spirit of faction, of party, of region, of religion, of race, is a house that cannot stand.

There is division in the American house now. There is divisiveness among us all tonight. And holding the trust that is mine, as President of all the people, I cannot disregard the peril to the progress of the American people and the hope and the prospect of peace for all peoples.

So I would ask all Americans, whatever their personal

interests or concern, to guard against divisiveness and all its ugly consequences.

Fifty-two months and 10 days ago, in a moment of tragedy and trauma, the duties of this Office fell upon me. I asked then for your help and God's, that we might continue America on its course, binding up our wounds, healing our history, moving forward in new unity, to clear the American agenda and to keep the American commitment for all of our people.

United we have kept that commitment. United we have enlarged that commitment.

Through all time to come, I think America will be a stronger nation, a more just society, and a land of greater opportunity and fulfillment because of what we have all done together in these years of unparalleled achievement.

Our reward will come in the life of freedom, peace, and hope that our children will enjoy through ages ahead.

What we won when all of our people united just must not now be lost in suspicion, distrust, selfishness, and politics among any of our people.

Believing this as I do, I have concluded that I should not permit the Presidency to become involved in the partisan divisions that are developing in this political year.

With America's sons in the fields far away, with America's future under challenge right here at home, with our hopes and the world's hopes for peace in the balance every day, I do not believe that I should devote an hour or a day of my time to any personal partisan causes or to any duties other than the awesome duties of this Office—the Presidency of your country.

Accordingly, I shall not seek, and I will not accept, the nomination of my party for another term as your President.

But let men everywhere know, however, that a strong, a confident, and a vigilant America stands ready tonight to seek an honorable peace—and stands ready tonight to defend an honored cause—whatever the price, whatever the burden, whatever the sacrifices that duty may require.

Thank you for listening.

Good night and God bless all of you.

Source: *Department of State Bulletin*, April 15, 1968, pp. 481–486.

14 May 1969
Television Address by President Richard M. Nixon [Extract]

This brings us, then, to the matter of negotiations.

We must recognize that peace in Vietnam cannot be achieved overnight. A war which has raged for so many years will require detailed negotiations and cannot be settled at a single stroke.

What kind of a settlement will permit the South Vietnamese people to determine freely their own political future? Such a settlement will require the withdrawal of all non-South Vietnamese forces from South Vietnam and procedures for political choice that give each significant group in South Vietnam a real opportunity to participate in the political life of the nation.

To implement these principles, I reaffirm now our willingness to withdraw our forces on a specified timetable. We ask only that North Vietnam withdraw its forces from South Vietnam, Cambodia and Laos into North Vietnam, also in accordance with a timetable.

We include Cambodia and Laos to ensure that these countries would not be used as bases for a renewed war. The Cambodian border is only 35 miles from Saigon: the Laotian border is only 25 miles from Hue.

Our offer provides for a simultaneous start on withdrawal by both sides: agreement on a mutually acceptable timetable; and for the withdrawal to be accomplished quickly.

If North Vietnam wants to insist that it has no forces in South Vietnam, we will no longer debate the point-provided that its forces cease to be there, and that we have reliable assurances that they will not return.

The North Vietnamese delegates have been saying in Paris that political issues should be discussed along with military issues, and that there must be a political settlement in the South. We do not dispute this, but the military withdrawal involves outside forces, and can therefore be properly negotiated by North Vietnam and the United States, with the concurrence of its allies. The political settlement is an internal matter, which ought to be decided among the South Vietnamese themselves and not imposed by outside powers. However, if our presence at these political negotiations would be helpful, and if the South Vietnamese concerned agreed, we would be willing to participate, along with the representatives of Hanoi if that were also desired.

Recent statements by President Thieu have gone far toward opening the way to a political settlement. He has publicly declared his government's willingness to discuss a political solution with the National Liberation Front and has offered free elections. His was a dramatic step forward, a reasonable offer that could lead to a settlement. The South Vietnamese Government has offered to talk without preconditions. I believe that the other side should also be willing to talk without preconditions.

The South Vietnamese Government recognizes, as we do, that a settlement must permit all persons and groups that are prepared to renounce the use of force to participate freely in the political life of South Vietnam. To be effective, such a settlement would require two things: First, a process that would allow the South Vietnamese people to express their choice; and second, a guarantee that this process would be a fair one.

We do not insist on a particular form of guarantee. The important thing is that the guarantees should have the confidence of the South Vietnamese people, and that they should be broad enough and strong enough to protect the interests of all major South Vietnamese groups.

This, then, is the outline of the settlement that we seek to negotiate in Paris. Its basic terms are very simple: Mutual withdrawal of non-South Vietnamese forces from South Vietnam, and free choice for the people of South Vietnam. I believe that the long-term interests of peace require that we insist on no less, and that the realities of the situation require that we seek no more.

Programs and Alternatives

To make very concrete what I have said, I propose the following measures, which seem to me consistent with the principles of all parties. These proposals are made on the basis of full consultation with President Thieu.

—As soon as agreement can be reached, all non-South Vietnamese forces would begin withdrawals from South Vietnam.

—Over a period of 12 months, by agreed-upon stages, the major portions of all U.S., Allied and other non-South Vietnamese forces would be withdrawn. At the end of this 12-month period, the remaining U.S., Allied and other non-South Vietnamese forces would move into designated base areas and would not engage in combat operations.

—The remaining U.S. and Allied forces would move to complete their withdrawals as the remaining North Vietnam forces were withdrawn and returned to North Vietnam.

—An international supervisory body, acceptable to both sides, would be created for the purpose of verifying withdrawals, and for any other purposes agreed upon between the two sides.

—This international body would begin operating in accordance with an agreed timetable, and would participate in arranging supervised ceasefires.

—As soon as possible after the international body was functioning, elections would be held under agreed procedures and under the supervision of the international body.

—Arrangements would be made for the earliest possible release of prisoners of war on both sides.

—All parties would agree to observe the Geneva Accords of 1954 regarding Vietnam and Cambodia, and the Laos Accords of 1962.

I believe this proposal for peace is realistic, and takes account of the legitimate interests of all concerned. It is consistent with President Thieu's six points. It can accommodate the various programs put forth by the other side. We and the Government of South Vietnam are prepared, to discuss its details with the other side. Secretary Rogers is now in Saigon and will be discussing with President Thieu how, together, we may put forward these proposed measures most usefully in Paris. He will, as well, be consulting with our other Asian allies on these measures while on his Asian trip. However, I would stress that these proposals are not offered on a take-it-or-leave-it basis. We are quite willing to consider other approaches consistent with our principles.

We are willing to talk about anybody's program—Hanoi's four points, the NLF's 10 points—provided it can be made consistent with the few basic principles I have set forth here.
Source: Committee on Foreign Relations, U.S. Senate, *Background Information Relating to Southeast Asia and Vietnam*. 7th rev. ed. December 1974, pp. 345–347.

30 April 1970
President Richard Nixon's Speech on Cambodia
Good evening, my fellow Americans.

Ten days ago, in my report to the Nation on Viet-Nam, I announced a decision to withdraw an additional 150,000 Americans from Viet-Nam over the next year. I said then that I was making that decision despite our concern over increased enemy activity in Laos, in Cambodia, and in South Viet-Nam.

At that time, I warned that if I concluded that increased enemy activity in any of these areas endangered the lives of Americans remaining in Viet-Nam, I would not hesitate to take strong and effective measures to deal with that situation.

Despite that warning, North Viet-Nam has increased its military aggression in all these areas, and particularly in Cambodia.

After full consultation with the National Security Council, Ambassador Bunker, General Abrams, and my other advisers, I have concluded that the actions of the enemy in the last 10 days clearly endanger the lives of Americans who are in Viet-Nam now and would constitute an unacceptable risk to those who will be there after withdrawal of another 150,000.

To protect our men who are in Viet-Nam and to guarantee the continued success of our withdrawal and Vietnamization programs, I have concluded that the time has come for action.

Tonight I shall describe the actions of the enemy, the actions I have ordered to deal with that situation, and the reasons for my decision.

Cambodia, a small country of 7 million people, has been a neutral nation since the Geneva agreement of 1954—an agreement, incidentally, which was signed by the Government of North Viet-Nam.

American policy since then has been to scrupulously respect the neutrality of the Cambodian people. We have maintained a skeleton diplomatic mission of fewer than 15 in Cambodia's capital, and that only since last August. For the previous 4 years, from 1965 to 1969, we did not have any diplomatic mission whatever in Cambodia. And for the past 5 years, we have provided no military assistance whatever and no economic assistance to Cambodia.

North Viet-Nam, however, has not respected that neutrality.

For the past 5 years ... North Viet-Nam has occupied military sanctuaries all along the Cambodian frontier with South Viet-Nam. Some of these extend up to 20 miles into Cambodia. The sanctuaries ... are on both sides of the border. They are used for hit-and-run attacks on American and South Vietnamese forces in South Viet-Nam.

These Communist-occupied territories contain major base camps, training sites, logistics facilities, weapons and ammunition factories, airstrips, and prisoner of war compounds.

For 5 years neither the United States nor South Viet-Nam has moved against these enemy sanctuaries, because we did not wish to violate the territory of a neutral nation. Even after the Vietnamese Communists began to expand these sanctuaries 4 weeks ago, we counseled patience to our South Vietnamese allies and imposed restraints on our own commanders.

In contrast to our policy, the enemy in the past 2 weeks has stepped up his guerrilla actions, and he is concentrating his main forces in these sanctuaries ... where they are building up to launch massive attacks on our forces and those of South Viet-Nam.

North Viet-Nam in the last 2 weeks has stripped away all pretense of respecting the sovereignty or the neutrality of Cambodia. Thousands of their soldiers are invading the country from the sanctuaries; they are encircling the Capital of Phnom Penh. Coming from these sanctuaries . . . they have moved into Cambodia and are encircling the Capital.

Cambodia, as a result of this, has sent out a call to the United States, to a number of other nations, for assistance. Because if this enemy effort succeeds, Cambodia would become a vast enemy staging area and a springboard for attacks on South Viet-Nam along 600 miles of frontier, a refuge where enemy troops could return from combat without fear of retaliation.

North Vietnamese men and supplies could then be poured into that country, jeopardizing not only the lives of our own men but the people of South Viet-Nam as well. . . .

In cooperation with the armed forces of South Viet-Nam, attacks are being launched this week to clean out major enemy sanctuaries on the Cambodian-Viet-Nam border.

A major responsibility for the ground operations is being assumed by South Vietnamese forces. For example, the attacks in several areas . . . are exclusively South Vietnamese ground operations under South Vietnamese command, with the United States providing air and logistical support.

There is one area, however . . . where I have concluded that a combined American and South Vietnamese operation is necessary.

Tonight American and South Vietnamese units will attack the headquarters for the entire Communist military operation in South Viet-Nam. This key control center has been occupied by the North Vietnamese and Viet Cong for 5 years in blatant violation of Cambodia's neutrality.

This is not an invasion of Cambodia. The areas in which these attacks will be launched are completely occupied and controlled by North Vietnamese forces. Our purpose is not to occupy the areas. Once enemy forces are driven out of these sanctuaries and once their military supplies are destroyed, we will withdraw.

These actions are in no way directed at the security interests of any nation. Any government that chooses to use these actions as a pretext for harming relations with the United States will be doing so on its own responsibility and on its own initiative, and we will draw the appropriate conclusions.

Now, let me give you the reasons for my decision.

A majority of the American people, a majority of you listening to me, are for the withdrawal of our forces from Viet-Nam. The action I have taken tonight is indispensable for the continuing success of that withdrawal program.

A majority of the American people want to end this war rather than to have it drag on interminably. The action I have taken tonight will serve that purpose.

A majority of the American people want to keep the casualties of our brave men in Viet-Nam at an absolute minimum. The action I take tonight is essential if we are to accomplish that goal.

We take this action not for the purpose of expanding the war into Cambodia, but for the purpose of ending the war in Viet-Nam and winning the just peace we all desire. We have made and we will continue to make every possible effort to end this war through negotiation at the conference table rather than through more fighting on the battlefield. . . .

My fellow Americans, we live in an age of anarchy, both abroad and at home. We see mindless attacks on all the great institutions which have been created by free civilizations in the last 500 years. Even here in the United States, great universities are being systematically destroyed. Small nations all over the world find themselves under attack from within and from without.

If, when the chips are down, the world's most powerful nation, the United States of America, acts like a pitiful, helpless giant, the forces of totalitarianism and anarchy will threaten free nations and free institutions throughout the world.

It is not our power but our will and character that is being tested tonight. The question all Americans must ask and answer tonight is this: Does the richest and strongest nation in the history of the world have the character to meet a direct challenge by a group which rejects every effort to win a just peace, ignores our warning, tramples on solemn agreements, violates the neutrality of an unarmed people, and uses our prisoners as hostages?

If we fail to meet this challenge, all other nations will be on notice that despite its overwhelming power the United States, when a real crisis comes, will be found wanting.

During my campaign for the Presidency, I pledged to bring Americans home from Viet-Nam. They are coming home.

I promised to end this war. I shall keep that promise.

I promised to win a just peace. I shall keep that promise.

We shall avoid a wider war. But we are also determined to put an end to this war. . . .

No one is more aware than I am of the political consequences of the action I have taken. It is tempting to take the easy political path: to blame this war on previous administrations and to bring all of our men home immediately, regardless of the consequences, even though that would mean defeat for the United States; to desert 18 million South Vietnamese people who have put their trust in us and to expose them to the same slaughter and savagery which the leaders of North Viet-Nam inflicted on hundreds of thousands of North Vietnamese who chose freedom when the Communists took over North Viet-Nam in 1954; to get peace at any price now, even though I know that a peace of humiliation for the United States would lead to a bigger war or surrender later.

I have rejected all political considerations in making this decision.

Whether my party gains in November is nothing compared to the lives of 400,000 brave Americans fighting for our country and for the cause of peace and freedom in Viet-Nam. Whether I may be a one-term President is insignificant compared to whether by our failure to act in this crisis the United States proves itself to be unworthy to lead the forces of freedom in this critical period in world history. I would rather be a one-term President and do what I believe is right than to be a two-term President at the cost of seeing America become a second-rate power and to see this nation accept the first defeat in its proud 190-year history.

Committee on Foreign Relations, U.S. Senate, *Background Information Relating to Southeast Asia and Vietnam* (7th rev. ed), December 1974, pp. 412–414.

Source: Porter, Gareth, editor. *Vietnam. A History in Documents.* pp. 392–394. New York: New American Library, 1981.

8 May 1972
President Richard Nixon's Address to the Nation [Extract]

It is plain then that what appears to be a choice among three courses of action for the United States is really no choice at all. The killing in this tragic war must stop. By simply getting out, we would only worsen the bloodshed. By relying solely on negotiations, we would give an intransigent enemy the time he needs to press his aggression on the battlefield.

There is only one way to stop the killing. That is to keep the weapons of war out of the hands of the international outlaws of North Vietnam.

… I therefore concluded that Hanoi must be denied the weapons and supplies it needs to continue the aggression. In full coordination with the Republic of Vietnam, I have ordered the following measures which are being implemented as I am speaking to you.

All entrances to North Vietnamese ports will be mined, to prevent access to these ports and North Vietnamese naval operations from these ports. United States forces have been direct to take appropriate measures within the internal and claimed territorial waters of North Vietnam to interdict the delivery of supplies. Rail and all other communications will be cut off to the maximum extent possible. Air and naval strikes against military targets in North Vietnam will continue.

These actions are not directed against any other nation. Countries with ships presently in North Vietnamese ports have already been notified that their ships will have three daylight periods to leave in safety. After that time, the mines will become active and any ships attempting to leave or enter these ports will do so at their own risk.

These actions I have ordered will cease when the following conditions are met:

First, all American prisoners of war must be returned.

Second, there must be an internationally supervised cease-fire throughout Indochina.

Once prisoners of war are released, once the internationally supervised cease-fire has begun, we will stop all acts of force throughout Indochina, and at that time we will proceed with a complete withdrawal of all American forces from Vietnam within 4 months.

Now these terms are generous terms. They are terms which would not require surrender and humiliation on the part of anybody. They would permit the United States to withdraw with honor. They would end the killing. They would bring our POW's home. They would allow negotiations on a political settlement between the Vietnamese themselves. They would permit all the nations which have suffered in this long war—Cambodia, Laos, North Vietnam, South Vietnam—to turn at last to the urgent works of healing and of peace. They deserve immediate acceptance by North Vietnam.

Source: Committee on Foreign Relations, U.S. Senate, *Background Information Relating to Southeast Asia and Vietnam.* 7th rev. ed. December 1974, p. 473.

5 January 1973
Letter from President Richard Nixon to President Nguyên Van Thiêu

This will acknowledge your letter of December 20, 1972.

There is nothing substantial that I can add to my many previous messages, including my December 17 letter, which clearly stated my opinions and intentions. With respect to the question of North Vietnamese troops, we will again present your views to the Communists as we have done vigorously at every other opportunity in the negotiations. The result is certain to be once more the rejection of our position. We have explained to you repeatedly why we believe the problem of North Vietnamese troops is manageable under the agreement, and I see no reason to repeat all the arguments.

We will proceed next week in Paris along the lines that General [Alexander] Haig explained to you. Accordingly, if the North Vietnamese meet our concerns on the two outstanding substantive issues in the agreement, concerning the DMZ and the method of signing, and if we can arrange acceptable supervisory machinery, we will proceed to conclude the settlement. The gravest consequences would then ensue if your government chose to reject the agreement and split off from the United States. As I said in my December 17 letter, "I am convinced that your refusal to join us would be an invitation to disaster—to the loss of all that we together have fought for over the past decade. It would be inexcusable above all because we will have lost a just and honorable alternative."

As we enter this new round of talks, I hope that our countries will now show a united front. It is imperative for our common objectives that your government take no further actions that complicate our task and would make more difficult the acceptance of the settlement by all parties. We will keep you informed of the negotiations in Paris through daily briefings of Ambassador Lam.

I can only repeat what I have so often said: The best guarantee for the survival of South Vietnam is the unity of our two countries which would be gravely jeopardized if you persist in your present course. The actions of our Congress since its return have clearly borne out the many warnings we have made.

Should you decide, as I trust you will, to go with us, you have my assurance of continued assistance in the post-settlement period and that we will respond with full force should the settlement be violated by North Vietnam. So once more I conclude with an appeal to you to close ranks with us.

Source: Document released by Dr. Nguyun Tiên Hung, former Prime Minister of Planning under President Thiêu, at press conference in Washington, D.C., 30 April 1975. Porter, Gareth, editor. *Vietnam. A History in Documents.* p 424. New York: New American Library, 1981.

27 January 1973

Paris Peace Agreement

The Parties participating in the Paris Conference on Viet-Nam,

With a view to ending the war and restoring peace in Viet-Nam on the basis of respect for the Vietnamese people's fundamental national rights and the South Vietnamese people's right to self-determination, and to contributing to the consolidation of peace in Asia and the world.

Have agreed on the following provisions and undertake to respect and to implement them:

Chapter I The Vietnamese People's Fundamental National Rights

Article 1. The United States and all other countries respect the independence, sovereignty, unity, and territorial integrity of Viet-Nam as recognized by the 1954 Geneva Agreements on Viet-Nam.

Chapter II Cessation of Hostilities—Withdrawal of Troops

Article 2. A cease-fire shall be observed throughout South Viet-Nam as of 2400 hours G.M.T., on January 27, 1973.

At the same hour, the United States will stop all its military activities against the territory of the Democratic Republic of Viet-Nam by ground, air and naval forces, wherever they may be based, and end the mining of the territorial waters, ports, harbors, and waterways of the Democratic Republic of Viet-Nam. The United States will remove, permanently deactivate or destroy all the mines in the territorial waters, ports, harbors, and waterways of North Viet-Nam as soon as this Agreement goes into effect.

The complete cessation of hostilities mentioned in this Article shall be durable and without limit of time.

Article 3. The parties undertake to maintain the cease-fire and to ensure a lasting and stable peace.

As soon as the cease-fire goes into effect:

a. The United States forces and those of the other foreign countries allied with the United States and the Republic of Viet-Nam shall remain in-place pending the implementation of the plan of troop withdrawal. The Four-Party Joint Military Commission described in Article 16 shall determine the modalities.

b. The armed forces of the two South Vietnamese parties shall remain in-place. The Two-Party Joint Military Commission described in Article 17 [not included here] shall determine the areas controlled by each party and the modalities of stationing.

c. The regular forces of all services and arms and the irregular forces of the parties in South Viet-Nam shall stop all offensive activities against each other and shall strictly abide by the following stipulations:

—All acts of force on the ground, in the air, and on the sea shall be prohibited;

—All hostile acts, terrorism and reprisals by both sides will be banned.

Article 4. The United States will not continue its military involvement or intervene in the internal affairs of South Viet-Nam.

Article 5. Within sixty days of the signing of this Agreement, there will be a total withdrawal from South Viet-Nam of troops, military advisers, and military personnel, including technical military personnel and military personnel associated with the pacification program, armaments, munitions, and war material of the United States and those of the other foreign countries mentioned in Article 3 (a). Advisers from the above-mentioned countries to all paramilitary organizations and the police force will also be withdrawn within the same period of time.

Article 6. The dismantlement of all military bases in South Viet-Nam of the United States and of the other foreign countries mentioned in Article 3 (a) shall be completed within sixty days of the signing of this Agreement.

Article 7. From the enforcement of the cease-fire to the formation of the government provided for in Article 9 (b) and 14 of this Agreement, the two South Vietnamese parties shall not accept the introduction of troops, military advisers, and military personnel including technical military personnel, armaments, munitions, and war material into South Viet-Nam.

The two South Vietnamese parties shall be permitted to make periodic replacement of armaments, munitions and war material which have been destroyed, damaged, worn out or used up after the cease-fire, on the basis of piece-for-piece, of the same characteristics and properties, under the supervision of the Joint Military Commission of the two South Vietnamese parties and of the International Commission of Control and Supervision.

Chapter III The Return of Captured Military Personnel and Foreign Civilians, and Captured and Detained Vietnamese Civilian Personnel

Article 8

a. The return of captured military personnel and foreign civilians of the parties shall be carried out simultaneously with and completed not later than the same day as the troop withdrawal mentioned in Article 5. The parties shall exchange complete lists of the above-mentioned captured military personnel and foreign civilians on the day of the signing of this Agreement.

b. The Parties shall help each other to get information about those military personnel and foreign civilians of the parties missing in action, to determine the location and take care of the graves of the dead so as to facilitate the exhumation and repatriation of the remains, and to take any such other measures as may be required to get information about those still considered missing in action.

c. The question of the return of Vietnamese civilian personnel captured and detailed in South Viet-Nam will be resolved by the two South Vietnamese parties on the basis of the principles of Article 21 (b) of the Agreement on the Cessation of Hostilities in Viet-Nam of July 20, 1954. The two South Vietnamese parties will do so in a spirit of national reconciliation and concord, with a view to ending hatred and enmity, in order to ease suffering and to reunite families. The two South Vietnamese parties will do their utmost to resolve this question within ninety days after the cease-fire comes into effect.

Chapter IV The Exercise of the South Vietnamese People's Right to Self-Determination

Article 9. The Government of the United States of America and the Government of the Democratic Republic of Viet-Nam undertake to respect the following principles for the exercise of the South Vietnamese people's right to self-determination:

a. The South Vietnamese people's right to self-determination is sacred, inalienable, and shall be respected by all countries.

b. The South Vietnamese people shall decide themselves the political future of South Viet-Nam through genuinely free and democratic general elections under international supervision.

c. Foreign countries shall not impose any political tendency or personality on the South Vietnamese people.

Article 10. The two South Vietnamese parties undertake to respect the cease-fire and maintain peace in South Viet-Nam, settle all matters of contention through negotiations, and avoid all armed conflict.

Article 11. Immediately after the cease-fire, the two South Vietnamese parties will:

—achieve national reconciliation and concord, end hatred and enmity, prohibit all acts of reprisal and discrimination against individuals or organizations that have collaborated with one side or the other;

—ensure the democratic liberties of the people: personal freedom, freedom of speech, freedom of the press, freedom of meeting, freedom of organization, freedom of political activities, freedom of belief, freedom of movement, freedom of residence, freedom of work, right to property ownership, and right to free enterprise.

Article 12

a. Immediately after the cease-fire, the two South Vietnamese parties shall hold consultations in a spirit of national reconciliation and concord, mutual respect, and mutual non-elimination to set up a National Council of National Reconciliation and Concord of three equal segments. The Council shall operate on the principle of unanimity. After the National Council of National Reconciliation and Concord has assumed its functions, the two South Vietnamese parties will consult about the formation of councils at lower levels. The two South Vietnamese parties shall sign an agreement on the internal matters of South Viet-Nam as soon as possible and do their utmost to accomplish this within ninety days after the cease-fire comes into effect, in keeping with the South Vietnamese people's aspirations for peace, independence and democracy.

b. The National Council of National Reconciliation and Concord shall have the task of promoting the two South Vietnamese parties' implementation of this Agreement, achievement of national reconciliation and concord and ensurance of democratic liberties. The National Council of National Reconciliation and Concord will organize the free and democratic general elections provided for in Article 9 (b) and decide the procedures and modalities of these general elections. The institutions for which the general elections are to be held will be agreed upon through consultations between the two South Vietnamese parties. The National Council of National Reconciliation and Concord will also decide the procedures and modalities of such local elections as the two South Vietnamese parties agree upon.

Article 13. The question of Vietnamese armed forces in South Viet-Nam shall be settled by the two South Vietnamese parties in a spirit of national reconciliation and concord, equality and mutual respect, without foreign interference, in accordance with the postwar situation. Among the questions to be discussed by the two South Vietnamese parties are steps to reduce their military effectives and to demobilize the troops being reduced. The two South Vietnamese parties will accomplish this as soon as possible.

Article 14. South Viet-Nam will pursue a foreign policy of peace and independence. It will be prepared to establish relations with all countries irrespective of their political and social systems on the basis of mutual respect for independence and sovereignty and accept economic and technical aid from any country with no political conditions attached. The acceptance of military aid by South Viet-Nam in the future shall come under the authority of the government set up after the general elections in South Viet-Nam provided for in Article 9 (b).

Chapter V The Reunification of Viet-Nam and the Relationship Between North and South Viet-Nam

Article 15. The reunification of Viet-Nam shall be carried out step by step through peaceful means on the basis of discussions and agreements between North and South Viet-Nam, without coercion or annexation by either party, and without foreign interference. The time for reunification will be agreed upon by North and South Viet-Nam.

Pending reunification:

a. The military demarcation line between the two zones at the 17th parallel is only provisional and not a political or territorial boundary, as provided for in paragraph 6 of the Final Declaration of the 1954 Geneva Conference.

b. North and South Viet-Nam shall respect the Demilitarized Zone on either side of the Provisional Military Demarcation Line.

c. North and South Viet-Nam shall promptly start negotiations with a view to reestablishing normal relations in various fields. Among the questions to be negotiated are the modalities of civilian movement across the Provisional Military Demarcation Line.

d. North and South Viet-Nam shall not join any military alliance or military bloc and shall not allow foreign powers to maintain military bases, troops, military advisers, and military personnel on their respective territories, as stipulated in the 1954 Geneva Agreements on Viet-Nam.

Source: *United States Treaties and Other International Agreements*, Vol. 24. In McMahon, Robert J., ed. *Major Problems in the History of the Vietnam War.* 2nd edition. pp. 565–569. Lexington, MA: D.C. Heath, 1995.

7 November 1973
Excerpts from the War Powers Resolution

... The President in every possible instance shall consult with Congress before introducing United States Armed Forces into hostilities or into situations where imminent involvement in hostilities is clearly indicated by the circumstances, and after every such introduction shall consult regularly with the Congress until United States Armed Forces are no longer engaged in hostilities or have been removed from such situations.

§ 1543. Reporting Requirement

(a) Written report; time of submission; circumstances necessitating submission; information reported

In the absence of a declaration of war, in any case in which United States Armed Forces are introduced—

(1) into hostilities or into situations where imminent involvement in hostilities is clearly indicated by the circumstances;

(2) into the territory, airspace or waters of a foreign nation, while equipped for combat, except for deployments which relate solely to supply, replacement, repair or training of such forces; or

(3) in numbers which substantially enlarge United States Armed Forces equipped for combat already located in a foreign nation; the President shall submit within 48 hours to the Speaker of the House of Representatives and to the President, pro tempore of the Senate a report, in writing, setting forth—

(A) the circumstances necessitating the introduction of United States Armed Forces;

(B) the constitutional and legislative authority under which such introduction took place; and

(C) the estimated scope and duration of the hostilities or involvement.

(b) Other information reported

The President shall provide such other information as the Congress may request in the fulfillment of its constitutional responsibilities with respect to committing the Nation to war and to the use of United States Armed Forces abroad.

(c) Periodic reports; semiannual requirement

Whenever United States Armed Forces are introduced into hostilities or into any situation described in subsection (a) of this section, the President shall, so long as such armed forces continue to be engaged in such hostilities or situation, report to the Congress periodically on the status of such hostilities or situation as well as on the scope and duration of such hostilities or situation, but in no event shall he report to the Congress less often than once every six months.

§ 1544. Congressional action

(a) Transmittal of report and referral to Congressional Committees; joint request for convening Congress

Each report submitted pursuant to section 1543(a)(1) of this title shall be transmitted to the Speaker of the House of Representatives and to the President pro tempore of the Senate on the same calendar day. Each report so transmitted shall be referred to the Committee on International Relations of the House of Representatives and to the Committee on Foreign Relations of the Senate for appropriate action. If, when the report is transmitted, the Congress has adjourned sine die or has adjourned for any period in excess of three calendar days, the Speaker of the House of Representatives and the President pro tempore of the Senate, if they deem it advisable (or if petitioned by at least 30 percent of the membership of their respective Houses) shall jointly request the President to convene Congress in order that it may consider the report and take appropriate action pursuant to this section.

(b) Termination of use of United States Armed Forces; exceptions; extension period

Within sixty calendar days after a report is submitted or is required to be submitted pursuant to section 1543(a)(1) of this title, whichever is earlier, the President shall terminate any use of United States Armed Forces with respect to which such report was submitted (or required to be submitted), unless the Congress (1) has declared war or has enacted a specific authorization for such use of United States Armed Forces, (2) has extended by law such sixty-day period, or (3) is physically unable to meet as a result of an armed attack upon the United States. Such sixty-day period shall be extended for not more than an additional thirty days if the President determines and certifies to the Congress in writing that unavoidable military necessity respecting the safety of United States Armed Forces requires the continued use of such armed forces in the course of bringing about a prompt removal of such forces.

(c) Concurrent resolution for removal by President of United States Armed Forces

Notwithstanding subsection (b) of this section, at any time that United States Armed Forces are engaged in hostilities outside the territory of the United States, its possessions and territories without a declaration of war or specific statutory authorization, such forces shall be removed by the President if the Congress so directs by concurrent resolution.

Source: Moss, George Donelson, editor. *A Vietnam Reader. Sources and Essays.* p. 169. Englewood Cliffs, NJ: Prentice Hall, 1991.

Bibliography

Abegglen, James C. *Sea Change: Pacific Asia as the New World-Industrial Center.* New York: Free Press, 1994.

Abramson, Rudy. *Spanning the Century: The Life of W. Averell Harriman 1891–1986.* New York: William Morrow, 1992.

Acheson, Dean. *Present at the Creation: My Years at the State Department.* New York: W. W. Norton, 1969.

Adair, Gilbert. *Hollywood's Vietnam.* London: Proteus, 1981.

Adams, Larry. *Walter Lippmann.* Boston: Twayne, 1977.

Adams, Sam. "Vietnam Cover-Up: Playing War with Numbers." *Harper's Magazine* (May 1975).

——. *War of Numbers: An Intelligence Memoir.* South Royalton, VT: Steerforth Press, 1994.

Adamson, Judith. *Graham Greene: The Dangerous Edge.* New York: St. Martin's Press, 1990.

Adee, Michael J. "American Civil Religion and the Presidential Rhetoric of Jimmy Carter." In *The Presidency and Domestic Policies of Jimmy Carter.* Westport, CT: Greenwood Press, 1994.

Adler, Bill. *The Generals: The New American Heroes.* New York: Avon Books, 1991.

Agnew, Spiro T. *Go Quietly . . . or Else.* New York: William Morrow, 1980.

Alan, Louis. *The End of the War in Asia.* London: Hart-Davis MacGibbon, 1976.

Alexander, Charles C. *Holding the Line: The Eisenhower Era, 1952–1961.* Bloomington: Indiana University Press, 1975.

Alexander, Joseph H., and Merrill L. Bartlett. "Amphibious Warfare and the Vietnam War." In *Sea Soldiers in the Cold War. Amphibious Warfare, 1945–1991.* Annapolis, MD: Naval Institute Press, 1994.

Alford, Elisée. *Le Père Louis de la Trinité, Admiral Thierry d'Argenlieu.* Paris: Desclée de Brouwer, 1969.

Allen, Leslie. "The Wall." *American Heritage* (February/March 1995): 92–103.

Almquist, Leann G. *Joseph Alsop and American Foreign Policy: The Journalist as Advocate.* Lanham, MD: University Press of America, 1993.

Alonso, Harriet Hyman. *Peace As A Women's Issue: A History of the U.S. Movement for World Peace and Women's Rights.* Syracuse, NY: Syracuse University Press, 1993.

Alsop, Joseph W., with Adam Platt. *"I've Seen the Best of It": Memoirs.* New York: W. W. Norton, 1992.

Alvarez, Everett, Jr., and Anthony S. Pitch. *Chained Eagle.* New York: Dell, 1989.

Alvarez, Everett, Jr., with Samuel A. Schreiner, Jr. *Code of Conduct.* New York: Donald I. Fine, 1991.

Ambrose, Stephen E. *Eisenhower.* Vol. 2. *President and Elder Statesman.* New York: Simon & Schuster, 1984.

——. *Nixon: Ruin and Recovery 1973–1990.* New York: Simon & Schuster, 1991.

——. *Nixon: The Triumph of a Politician 1961–1972.* New York: Simon & Schuster, 1989.

——. *Rise to Globalism: American Foreign Policy since 1938.* 6th rev. ed. New York: Penguin Books, 1991.

Ameringer, Charles D. *U.S. Foreign Intelligence: The Secret Side of American History.* Lexington, MA: Lexington Books, 1990.

Andersen, Christopher. *Citizen Jane: The Turbulent Life of Jane Fonda.* New York: Henry Holt, 1990.

Anderson, David L. *Trapped by Success: The Eisenhower Administration and Vietnam, 1953–1961.* New York: Columbia University, 1991.

Anderson, David L., ed. *Shadow on the White House: Presidents and the Vietnam War, 1945–1975.* Lawrence: University Press of Kansas, 1993.

Anderson, Patrick. *The President's Men.* Garden City, NY: Anchor Books, 1968.

Andrade, Dale. *Ashes to Ashes: The Phoenix Program and the Vietnam War.* Lexington, MA: D. C. Heath, 1990.

Andrews, Deborah. *The Annual Obituary, 1989.* Detroit: St. James Press, 1992.

Anson, Robert S. *McGovern: A Biography.* New York: Holt, Rinehart and Winston, 1972.

Appy, Christian G. *Working Class War: American Combat Soldiers and Vietnam.* Chapel Hill: University of North Carolina Press, 1993.

Arkin, William M., et al.., eds. *Encyclopedia of the U.S. Military.* New York: Hallinger, 1990.

Arlen, Michael. *Living Room War.* New York: Viking Books, 1969.

Arnett, Peter. *Live from the Battle Field: From Vietnam to Baghdad.* New York: Simon & Schuster, 1994.

Arnold, James R. *Armor.* The Illustrated History of the Vietnam War. New York: Bantam Books, 1987.

——. *The First Domino. Eisenhower, The Military, and America's Intervention in Vietnam.* New York: William Morrow, 1991.

Asher, Herbert B. *Presidential Elections & American Politics.* Pacific Grove, CA: Brooks/Cole, 1992.

Asprey, Robert B. *War in the Shadows: The Guerrilla in History.* New York: William Morrow, 1994.

Aster, Sidney, *Anthony Eden.* New York: St. Martin's Press, 1976.

Austin, Anthony. *The President's War: The Story of the Tonkin Gulf Resolution and How the Nation Was Trapped in Vietnam.* Philadelphia: J. B. Lippincott, 1971.

Bac Ky Hà Đê Su Tích (History of Red River Dikes in North Vietnam). Translation into modern Vietnamese by Hà Ngọc Xuyên. Sài Gòn: Bộ Quốc Gia Giáo, 1963.

Bailey, Jonathan B. A. *Field Artillery and Firepower.* Oxford, UK: Military Press, 1987.

Bailey, Lois Esther. *Jules Ferry and French Indo-China.* Madison: University of Wisconsin, 1946.

Bain, Chester A. *Vietnam: The Roots of Conflict.* Englewood Cliffs, NJ: Prentice-Hall, 1967.

Ball, George W. *The Past Has Another Pattern: Memoirs.* New York: W. W. Norton, 1982.

Bannan, John F., and Rosemary S. Bannan. *Law, Morality, and Vietnam: The Peace Militants and the Courts.* Bloomington: University of Indiana Press, 1974.

Baritz, Loren. *Backfire: A History of How American Culture Led Us into Vietnam and Made Us Fight the Way We Did.* New York: William Morrow, 1985.

Barrett, David M. *Uncertain Warriors: Lyndon Johnson and His Vietnam Advisers.* Lawrence: University Press of Kansas, 1993.

Barry, John. "The Very Model of a Political General: On Duty with Powell, from Vietnam to the Gulf." *Newsweek* (11 September 1995), pp. 25–26.

Baskir, Lawrence M., and William A. Strauss. *Chance and Circumstance: The Draft, The War, and The Vietnam Generation.* New York: Alfred A. Knopf, 1978.

Bass, Thomas A. *Vietnamerica: The War Comes Home.* New York: Soho Press, 1996.

Bassford, Christopher. *Clausewitz in English: The Reception of Clausewitz in Britain and America 1815–1945.* New York: Oxford University Press, 1994.

Beau, Paul. *Situation de L'Indo-Chine de 1902 à 1907.* Saigon: Imprimerie Commerciale Marcellin Rey, 1908.

Becker, Elizabeth. *When the War Was Over: Cambodia's Revolution and the Voices of Its People.* New York: Simon & Schuster, 1986.

Beckett, Brian. *The Illustrated History of the Viet Nam War.* New York: Gallery Books, 1985.

Beichman, Arnold. "Study in Academic Freedom." *New York Times Magazine,* 19 December 1965.

Beidler, Philip D. *American Literature and The Experience of Vietnam.* Athens: University of Georgia Press, 1982.

——— . *Re-Writing America: Vietnam Authors in Their Generation.* Athens: University of Georgia Press, 1991.

Bell, Dana. *Vietnam Warbirds in Action.* London: Arms and Armour Press, 1986.

Bell, David S., Douglas Johnson, and Peter Morris. *Biographical Dictionary of French Political Leaders since 1870.* New York: Simon & Schuster, 1990.

Bell, J. Bower. *The Myth of the Guerrilla: Revolutionary Theory and Malpractice.* New York: Alfred A. Knopf, 1971.

Bell, Kenneth H. *100 Missions North.* Washington, DC: Brassey's, 1993.

Bell, William G. *Commanding Generals and Chiefs of Staff: 1775–1983.* Washington, DC: U.S. Army Center of Military History, 1983.

Benjamin, Milton R., and Brinkley, Paul Rogers. "Farewell to Phnom Penh." *Newsweek* (2 April 1975): 27.

Berent, Mark. *Steel Tiger.* New York: Putnam, 1990

Beresford, Melanie. *Vietnam: Politics, Economics and Society.* Marxist Regimes Series, edited by Bogdan Szajkowski. New York: Pinter, 1988.

Bergen, John D. *Military Communications: A Test for Technology.* Washington, DC: U.S. Army Center of Military History, 1986.

Berger, Carl, ed. *The United States Air Force in South East Asia 1961–1973.* Washington, DC: U.S. Government Printing Office, 1984.

Berger, Graenum. *Not So Silent an Envoy: A Biography of Ambassador Samuel David Berger.* New Rochelle, NY: John Washburn Bleeker Hampton, 1992.

Bergerud, Eric M. *The Dynamics of Defeat: The Vietnam War in Hau Nghia Province.* Boulder, CO: Westview Press, 1991.

——— . *Red Thunder, Tropic Lightning: The World of a Combat Division in Vietnam.* San Francisco: Westview Press, 1993.

Bergonzi, Bernard. "Graham Greene." In *British Writers, Supplement 1.* New York: Charles Scribner's Sons, 1987, pp. 1–20.

Berman, Harvey P. "The Agent Orange Payment Program." *Law and Contemporary Problems* (Autumn 1990): 49–60.

Berman, Larry. *Lyndon Johnson's War: The Road to Stalemate in Vietnam.* New York: W. W. Norton, 1989.

——— . *Planning a Tragedy: The Americanization of the War in Vietnam.* New York: W. W. Norton, 1982.

Berman, William C. *William Fulbright and the Vietnam War: The Dissent of a Political Realist.* Kent, OH: Kent State University Press, 1988.

Bernstein, S. *Histoire du parti radical.* Paris: Presses de la Foundation Nationale des Sciences Politiques, 1980–1982.

Berrigan, Daniel. *No Bars to Manhood.* Garden City, NY: Doubleday, 1970.

Bidault, Georges. *Resistance: The Political Biography of Georges Bidault.* Translated by M. Sinclair. New York: Praeger, 1967.

Bigeard, Marcel. *Pour une parcelle de gloire.* Paris: Plon, 1975.

Billings-Yun, Melanie. *Decision against War: Eisenhower and Dien Bien Phu.* New York: Columbia University Press, 1988.

Bills, Scott L., ed. *Kent State/May 4: Echoes through a Decade.* Kent, OH: Kent State University Press, 1982.

Binkin, Martin, Mark J. Eitelberg, et al. *Blacks in the Military.* Washington, DC: Brookings Institution, 1982.

Biographical Dictionary of French Political Leaders since 1870, edited by David S. Bell, Douglas Johnson, and Peter Morris. New York: Simon & Schuster, 1990.

Biographical Files, Indo-China Archives, University of California at Berkeley.

Bird, Kai. *The Chairman: John J. McCloy and the Making of the American Establishment.* New York: Simon & Schuster, 1992.

Bishop, Chris, and Ian Drury, eds. *Combat Guns: An Illustrated Encyclopedia of 20th Century Firearms.* Secaucus, NJ: Chartwell Books, 1987.

Blackburn, Robert M. *Mercenaries and Lyndon Johnson's "More Flags."* Jefferson, NC: McFarland, 1994.

Blackwelder, Donald I. *The Long Road to Desert Storm and Beyond: The Development of Precision Guided Bombs.* Maxwell Air Force Base, AL: Air University Press, 1993.

Blair, Anne E. *Lodge in Vietnam: A Patriot Abroad.* New Haven, CT: Yale University Press, 1995.

Blaker, Michael, ed. *Development Assistance to Southeast Asia: The U.S. and Japanese Approaches.* New York: Columbia University, East Asian Institute, 1984.

Blaufarb, Douglas S. *The Counterinsurgency Era: U.S. Doctrine and Performance 1950 to Present.* New York: Free Press, 1977.

Blum, Léon. *Léon Blum, chef de gouvernement.* Paris: A. Colin, 1967.

Boettcher, Thomas D. *Vietnam, The Valor and the Sorrow.* Boston: Little, Brown, 1985.

Bole, Albert G., Jr., and K. Kobata. *An Examination of the Measurements of the Hamlet Evaluation System.* Newport, RI: Naval War College, 1975.

Bolton, Michael, and Kevin Sim. *Four Hours in My Lai.* New York: Viking, 1992.

Bonds, Ray, ed. *The Vietnam War: The Illustrated History of the Conflict in Southeast Asia.* New York: Crown, 1983.

Bongard, David L. "Brown, George Scratchley." In *The Harper Encyclopedia of Military Biography.* New York: Harper Collins, 1992.

Booth, Michael T. *Paratrooper: The Life of General James M. Gavin.* New York: Simon & Schuster, 1994.

Bothwell, Robert, Ian Drummond, and John English. *Canada since 1945: Power, Politics, and Provincialism.* Toronto: University of Toronto Press, 1981.

Boudarel, Georges, ed. *La bureaucratic au Vietnam.* Paris: L'Hartmattan, 1983.

Bowers, Peter M., and Gordon Swanborough. *United States Military Aircraft since 1909.* Washington, DC: Smithsonian Institution Press, 1989.

——— . *United States Navy Aircraft since 1911.* New York: Funk & Wagnalls, 1968.

Bowers, Ray L. *The United States Air Force in Southeast Asia: Tactical Aircraft.* Washington, DC: Office of Air Force History, 1983.

Bowles, Chester B. *Promises to Keep: My Years in Public Life, 1941–1969.* New York: Harper & Row, 1971.

Boyd, Andrew. *Fifteen Men on a Powder Keg: A History of the U.N. Security Council.* New York: Stein & Day, 1971.

Bradley, Omar N. *A Soldier's Story.* New York: Holt, Rinehart and Winston, 1951.

Brady, Patrick H. "When I Have Your Wounded." *Army* (June 1989): 64–72.

Braestrup, Peter. *Big Story: How the American Press and Television Reported and Interpreted the Crisis of Tet 1968 in Vietnam and Washington.* New Haven, CT: Yale University Press, 1977.

Brands, H. W. *Cold Warriors: Eisenhower's Generation and American Foreign Policy.* New York: Columbia University Press, 1988.

——— . *India and the United States: The Cold Peace.* Boston: Twayne, 1990.

Brandt, Ed. *The Last Voyage of USS Pueblo.* New York: W. W. Norton, 1969.

Brandt, Willy. *People and Politics. The Years 1960–1973.* Translated by J. Maxwell Brownjohn. Boston: Little, Brown, 1978.

Brecht, Stephan. *The Bread and Puppet Theatre.* New York: Routledge, 1988.

Brende, Joel Osler, and Erwin Randolph Parson. *Vietnam Veterans: The Road to Recovery.* New York: Plenum Press, 1985.

Brewin, Bob, and Sydney Shaw. *Vietnam on Trial: Westmoreland vs. CBS.* New York: Atheneum, 1987.

Brigham, Erwin R. "Pacification Measurement." *Military Review* (May 1970): 47–54.

Brinkley, Douglas, ed. *Dean Acheson and the Making of U.S. Foreign Policy.* New York: St. Martin's Press, 1993.

Broadwater, Jeff. *Adlai Stevenson and American Politics, The Odyssey of a Cold War Liberal.* New York: Twayne, 1994.

Bromage, Bernard. *Molotov: The Story of an Era.* London: Peter Owen, 1961.

Brown, Anthony Cave. *The Last Hero: Wild Bill Donovan.* New York: Vintage Books, 1982.

Brown, Holmes, and Don Luce. *Hostages of War: Saigon's Political Prisoners.* Washington, DC: Indochina Mobile Education Project, 1973.

Brown, Sam, and Len Ackland, eds. *Why Are We Still in Vietnam?* New York: Random House, 1970.

Browne, Malcolm. *The New Face of War.* New York: Bobbs-Merrill, 1965.

Brunn, Geoffrey. *Clemenceau.* Cambridge, MA: Harvard University Press, 1943.

Bucher, Lloyd M., with Mark Rascovich. *Bucher: My Story.* Garden City, NY: Doubleday, 1970.

Buckingham, William A., Jr. *Operation Ranch Hand: The Air Force and Herbicides in Southeast Asia, 1961–1971.* Washington, DC: Office of Air Force History, 1982.

Buckley, Kevin. "General Abrams Deserves a Better War." *New York Times Magazine,* 5 October 1969.

Bùi Diêm. "Reflections on the Vietnam War: The Views of a Vietnamese on Vietnamese-American Misconceptions." In *Looking Back on the Vietnam War,* edited by William Head and Lawrence Grinter. Westport, CT: Greenwood, 1993.

Bùi Diêm and David Chanoff. *In The Jaws of History.* Boston: Houghton Mifflin, 1987.

Bùi Quang Tung. "Cuôc Khoi Nghia Hai Bà Trung Duoi Mat Su Gia." (The Two Trung Ladies' Uprising in Historians' Eyes). In *Ðai Hoc* (Huê University), No. 10 (July 1959): 1–16.

Bunker, Ellsworth. *The Bunker Papers: Reports to the President from Vietnam, 1967–1973,* edited by Douglas Pike. Berkeley: University of California Institute for East Asian Studies, 1990.

Burchett, Wilfred G. *At the Barricades.* New York: Times Books, 1981.

——. *The Furtive War: The United States in Vietnam and Laos.* New York: International Publishers, 1963.

—— G. *Vietnam: The Inside Story of the Guerrilla War.* New York: International Publishers, 1965.

Burgess, Patricia, ed. *The Annual Obituary 1986.* Chicago: St. James Press, 1989.

Burkard, Dick J. *Military Airlift Command: Historical Handbook, 1941–1984.* Scott Air Force Base, IL: Military Airlift Command, 1984.

Burner, David. *The Torch is Passed.* 1st ed. New York: Athenum, 1984.

Bury, J. P. T. *Napoleon III and the Second Empire.* London: English Universities Press, 1964.

Bush, George, with Victor Gold. *Looking Forward.* New York: Doubleday, 1987.

Butler, David. *The Fall of Saigon.* New York: Simon & Schuster, 1985.

Butler, Deborah A. *American Women Writers on Vietnam.* New York: Garland, 1990.

Butterfield, Fox. *China: Alive in the Bitter Sea.* New York: Times Books, 1982.

Buttinger, Joseph. *The Smaller Dragon: A Political History of Vietnam.* New York: Praeger, 1958.

——. *Vietnam: A Dragon Embattled.* New York: Praeger, 1967.

——. *Vietnam: A Political History.* New York: Praeger, 1968.

Buzzanco, Robert. *Masters of War: Military Dissent and Politics in the Vietnam Era.* Cambridge, MA: Cambridge University Press, 1996.

Cable, James. *The Geneva Conference of 1954 on Indochina.* New York: St. Martin's Press, 1986.

Cable, Larry. *Conflict of Myths: The Development of American Counterinsurgency Doctrine and the Vietnam War.* New York: New York University Press, 1988.

——. *Unholy Grail: The U.S. and the Wars in Vietnam, 1965–68.* London: Routledge, 1991.

Cady, John F. *The Roots of French Imperialism in Eastern Asia.* Ithaca, NY: Cornell University Press, 1954.

Caldwell, Malcolm, and Lek Tan, *Cambodia in the Southeast Asian War.* New York: Monthly Review Press, 1973.

Callison, Charles S. *Land-to-the-Tiller in the Mekong Delta.* Lanham, MD: University Press of America, 1983.

Callot, E.-F. *Le M.R.P., Origine, structure, doctrine, programme et action politique.* Paris: M. Rivière, 1978.

Cameron, Dan. "The Trials of Peter Saul." *Arts Magazine* (January 1990).

Camp, Norman M., Robert H. Stretch, and William C. Marshall. *Stress, Strain, and Vietnam: An Annotated Bibliography of Psychiatric and Social Sciences Literature.* New York: Greenwood Press, 1988.

Cannon, Lou. *President Reagan: The Role of a Lifetime.* New York: Simon & Schuster, 1991.

Cao Thê Dung. *Viêt Nam Huyêt Lê Su.* New Orleans, LA: Ðông Huong, 1996.

Cao Van Viên. *The Final Collapse.* Indochina Monographs. Washington, DC: U.S. Army Center of Military History, 1982.

——. "Leadership." In *Indochina Monographs.* Washington, DC: U.S. Army Center of Military History, 1981.

Cao Van Viên and Dong Van Khuyen, *Reflections on the Vietnam War.* Indochina Monographs. Washington, DC: U.S. Army Center of Military History, 1980.

Cao Van Viên, et al. *The U.S. Advisor.* Washington, DC: U.S. Army Center of Military History, 1980.

Cargas, Harry. "Daniel Berrigan: The Activist as Poet." *Laurel Review,* no. 9 (1969): 11–17.

Carlson, Elof Axel. "International Symposium on Herbicides in the Vietnam War." *Bioscience* (September 1983): 507–512.

Carney, Timothy Michael. *Communist Party Power in Kampuchea (Cambodia).* Ithaca, NY: Cornell Southeast Asia Program, Data Paper No. 106, January 1977.

Carter, Jimmy. *Keeping Faith: Memoirs of a President.* New York: Bantam Books, 1982.

Caruthers, Lawrence H. "Characteristics and Capabilities of Enemy Weapons." *The Field Artilleryman* (September 1970): 11–24.

Case of Pvt. Robert R. Garwood, USMC. Final Report, Report to the Assistant Secretary of Defense for Command, Control, Communication and Intelligence, June 1993.

Castelli, Leo. *James Rosenquist: The Big Paintings.* New York: Leo Castelli Gallery, 1994.

Castle, Timothy N. *At War in the Shadow of Vietnam. U.S. Military Aid to the Royal Lao Government, 1955–1975.* New York: Columbia University Press, 1993.

Catroux, Général [Georges]. *Deux Actes du Drame Indochinois.* Paris: Plon, 1959.

Cecil, Paul. *Herbicidal Warfare: The Ranch Hand Project in Vietnam.* New York: Praeger, 1986.

Chafe, William H. *Never Stop Running: Allard Lowenstein and the Struggle to Save American Liberalism.* New York: Basic Books, 1993.

Chai, Winberg. *The Foreign Relations of the People's Republic of China.* New York: Capricorn Books, 1972.

Chan, Sucheng. *Hmong Means Free: Life in Laos and America.* Philadelphia: Temple University Press, 1994.

Chanda, Nayan. *Brother Enemy.* New York: Harcourt Brace Jovanovich, 1986.

Chandler, David P. *Brother Number One: A Political Biography of Pol Pot.* Boulder, CO: Westview Press, 1992.

——. *The Tragedy of Cambodian History: Politics, War and Revolution since 1945.* New Haven, CT: Yale University Press, 1991.

Chandler, Robert W. *War of Ideas: U.S. Propaganda Campaign in Vietnam.* Boulder, CO: Westview Press, 1981.

Chant, Christopher, ed. *How Weapons Work.* London: Marshall Cavendish, 1976.

Charlton, Michael, and Anthony Moncrieff. *Many Reasons Why: The American Involvement in Vietnam.* New York: Hill & Wang, 1978.

Chary, M. Srinivas. *The Eagle and the Peacock: U.S. Foreign Policy toward India since Independence.* Westport, CT: Greenwood Press, 1995.

Chen, King G. *China's War with Vietnam, 1979.* Stanford, CA: Hoover Institution, 1987.

Chesneaux, Jean. *Contribution à L'Histoire de la Nation Vietnamienne.* Paris: Editions Sociales, 1955.

Chiang Kai-shek. *Soviet Russia in China*. New York: Farrar, Straus and Giroux, 1957.

Chi-kin Lo. *China's Policy toward Territorial Disputes*. New York: Routledge, 1989.

Chomsky, Noam. *American Power and the New Mandarins*. New York: Pantheon, 1969.

——. "Vietnam and United States Global Strategy (1973)." In *The Chomsky Reader*, edited by James Peck. New York: Pantheon, 1987.

Christienne, Charles, and Pierre Lissarague. *A History of French Military Aviation*. Translated by Francis Klanka. Washington, DC: Smithsonian Press, 1986.

Chuev, Feliks. *Molotov Remembers*. Paris: YMCA Press, 1980.

Ciabatari, Jane. "Senator Harkin Returns to the Tiger Cages of Con Son." *Parade* (8 October 1995): 19.

Cima, Ronald, ed. *Vietnam: A Country Study*. Washington, DC: U.S. Government Printing Office, 1989.

Cincinnatus [Cecil B. Currey]. *Self-Destruction: The Disintegration and Decay of the United States Army during the Vietnam Era*. New York: W. W. Norton, 1981.

Cinna, Ronald J., ed. *Vietnam: A Country Study*. Washington, DC: U.S. Government Printing Office, 1989.

Clark, Jeffrey J. *Advise and Support: The Final Years, The U.S. in Vietnam*. Washington, DC: U.S. Government Printing Office, 1988.

Clausewitz, Carl von. *On War*. Edited and translated by Michael Howard and Per Paret. Princeton, NJ: Princeton University Press, 1976.

Clayton, Anthony. *Three Marshals Who Saved France: Leadership after Trauma*. London: Brassey's, 1992.

Clifford, Clark, with David Holbrooke. *Counsel to the President: A Memoir*. New York: Random House, 1991.

Clodfelter, Mark. *The Limits of Air Power: The American Bombing of North Vietnam*. New York: Free Press, 1989.

Coedes, Georges. *The Making of South East Asia*. Translated by H. M. Wright. Berkeley: University of California Press, 1966.

Coffee, Thomas M. *Iron Eagle: The Turbulent Life of General Curtis E. LeMay*. New York: Crown, 1986.

Cohen, Richard M., and Jules Witcover. *A Heartbeat Away: The Investigation and Resignation of Vice President Spiro T. Agnew*. New York: Viking, 1974.

Cohen, Stephen F. *Sovieticus*. New York: W. W. Norton, 1985.

Cohen, Steven, ed. *The Soviet Union since Stalin*. Bloomington: University of Indiana Press, 1980.

Colby, William. *Honorable Men: My Life in the CIA*. New York: Simon & Schuster, 1978.

Colby, William, with James McCargar. *Lost Victory: A Firsthand Account of America's Sixteen-Year Involvement in Vietnam*. Chicago: Contemporary Books, 1989.

Cole, Robert H., Lorna S. Jaffe, Walter S. Poole, and Willard J. Webb. *The Chairmanship of the Joint Chiefs of Staff*. Washington, DC: Office of the Chairman of the Joint Chiefs of Staff, 1995.

Coleman, J. D. *Incursion*. New York: St. Martin's Press, 1991.

Collins, James Lawton, Jr. *The Development and Training of the South Vietnamese Army, 1950–1972*. Washington, DC: U.S. Army Center of Military History, 1975.

——. *Lightning Joe: An Autobiography*. Baton Rouge: Louisiana State University Press, 1979.

Colton, Joel. *Léon Blum. Humanist in Politics*. New York: Alfred A. Knopf, 1966.

Coming to Terms: American Plays and the Vietnam War. New York: Theatre Communications Group, 1985.

Command after Action Report, "Kingfisher." Headquarters, 2d Battalion, 4th Marines, 3d Marine Division, September–October 1967. Washington, DC: History and Museum Division, Marine Corps Historical Center.

Conboy, Kenneth, and Kenneth Bowra. *The War in Cambodia 1970–75*. Men-at Arms Series. London: Osprey, 1989.

Condit, Kenneth W. *The History of the Joint Chiefs of Staff: The Joint Chiefs of Staff and National Policy*. Vol. 2, *1947–1949*. Wilmington, DE: Michael Glazier, 1979.

Condominas, George. *We Have Eaten the Forest: The Story of a Montagnard Village in the Central Highlands of Vietnam*, translated by Adrienne Foulke. New York: Hill & Wang, 1977.

Congressional Quarterly. *Congress and the Nation*. Vol. 7, *1985–1988*. Washington, DC: Congressional Quarterly, 1990.

Congressional Quarterly Almanac. 102d Congress. 2d Session. Vol. 48, 1992. Washington, DC: Congressional Quarterly, 1993.

Congressional Quarterly Weekly Reports. Washington: Congressional Quarterly Press, 1973.

Converse, Philip E., Warren E. Miller, Jerrold G. Rusk, and Arthur C. Wolfe. "Continuity and Change in American Politics: Parties and Issues in the 1968 Election." *American Political Science Review* 63 (December 1969): 1083–1105.

Cooney, John. *The American Pope: The Life and Times of Francis Cardinal Spellman*. New York: Times Books, 1984.

Cooper, Chester. *The Lost Crusade: America in Vietnam*. Rev. Ed. New York: Dodd, Mead, 1973.

Cordell, Helen, compiler. *Laos*. World Bibliographical Series, Vol. 133. Santa Barbara, CA: Clio Press, 1991.

Corson, William R. *The Betrayal*. New York: W. W. Norton, 1968.

Crimson, Fred W. *U.S. Military Tracked Vehicles*. Osceola, WI: Motor Books International, 1992.

Croizat, Victor. *The Brown Water Navy: The River and Coastal War in Indochina and Vietnam, 1940–1972*. Dorset, United Kingdom: Blandford Press, 1984.

——. "Vietnamese Naval Forces: Origin of the Species." *U.S. Naval Institute Proceedings* (February 1973): 48–58.

Crosswell, D. K. R. *The Chief of Staff: The Military Career of General Walter Bedell Smith*. New York: Greenwood Press, 1991.

Crouch, Harold. *The Army and Politics in Indonesia*. Rev. ed. Ithaca, NY: Cornell University Press, 1988.

Crozier, Brian. *The Man Who Lost China, The First Full Biography of Chiang Kai-shek*. New York: Charles Scribner's Sons, 1976.

Cummings, Richard. *The Pied Piper: Allard K. Lowenstein and the Liberal Dream*. New York: Grove Press, 1985.

Cunningham, Randy. *Fox Two*. Mesa, AZ: Champlin Fighter Museum Publications, 1984.

Current Biography 1951. Edited by Anna Rothe. New York: H. W. Wilson, 1952.

Current Biography Yearbook 1961. New York: H. W. Wilson, 1961.

Current Biography Yearbook 1968. New York: H. W. Wilson, 1969.

Current Biography Yearbook 1974. New York: H. W. Wilson, 1975.

Current Biography Yearbook 1978. New York: H. W. Wilson, 1978.

Current Biography Yearbook, 1995. New York: H. W. Wilson, 1995.

Currey, Cecil B. "Bao Dai: The Last Emperor." *Viet Nam Generation*, 6, no. 1–2 (1994): 199–206.

——. *Edward Lansdale. The Unquiet American*. Boston: Houghton Mifflin, 1988.

——. *Victory at Any Cost. The Genius of Viet Nam's Gen. Vo Nguyen Giap*. New York: Brassey's, 1996.

Cutler, Thomas J. *Brown Water, Black Berets: Coastal and Riverine Warfare in Vietnam*. Annapolis, MD: Naval Institute Press, 1988.

Dacy, Douglas C. *The Fiscal System of Wartime Vietnam*. Arlington, VA: Institute for Defense Analysis, 1969.

Dalglish, Carol. *Refugees from Vietnam*. London: Macmillan, 1989.

Dallek, Robert. *F.D.R. and American Diplomacy*. New York: Oxford University Press, 1979.

——. *Lone Star Rising: Lyndon Johnson and His Times, 1908–1960*. New York: Oxford University Press, 1991.

Dalloz, Jacques. *The War in Indo-China, 1945–1954*. Translated by Josephine Bacon. Savage, MD: Barnes & Noble, 1990.

Đào Duy Anh. *Việt Nam Van Hóa Su Cuong (An Outline History of Vietnamese Culture)*. Sài Gòn: Bôn Phuong, 1961.

Đào Trinh Nhât. *Phan Đình Phùng*. Sài Gòn: Tân Viêt, 1950.

David, Heather. *Operation Rescue*. New York: Pinnacle Books, 1970.

Davidson, Phillip B. *Secrets of the Vietnam War*. Novato, CA: Presidio Press, 1990.

———. *Vietnam at War, the History: 1946–1975*. Novato, CA: Presidio Press, 1988.

Davies, S. Gethyn. *Central Banking in South and East Asia*. Hong Kong: Hong Kong University Press, 1960.

Davis, Gordon M. "Dewey Canyon: All Weather Classic." *Marine Corps Gazette* (July 1969): 32–40.

Dawson, Alan. *55 Days: The Fall of South Vietnam*. New York: Prentice-Hall, 1977.

de Gaulle, Charles. *The War Memoirs of Charles de Gaulle*. Vol. 3, *Salvation, 1944–1946*. Translated by Richard Howard. New York: Simon & Schuster, 1960.

Dean, Bashford. *American and German Helmets and Body Armor of World War I and Body Armor in Modern Warfare*. Baltimore, MD: Gateway Printing, 1980.

DeBenedetti, Charles, and Charles Chatfield. *An American Ordeal: The Antiwar Movement of the Vietnam Era*. Syracuse, NY: Syracuse University Press, 1990.

DeBonis, Steven. *Children of the Enemy: Oral Histories of Vietnamese Amerasians and Their Mothers*. Jefferson, NC: McFarland, 1995.

Decoux, Jean. *A la Barre de l'Indochine*. Paris: Plon, 1952.

DeForest, Orrin, and David Chanoff. *Slow Burn: The Rise and Fall of American Intelligence in Vietnam*. New York: Simon & Schuster, 1990.

Deleon, Peter. *The Laser-Guided Bomb: Case History of a Development*. R-13121-PR. Santa Monica, CA: RAND, 1974.

Dellinger, David. *Revolutionary Non-Violence*. New York: Doubleday, 1971.

———. *Vietnam Revisited: Covert Action to Invasion to Reconstruction*. Boston: South End Press, 1986.

DeLoach, Cartha D. "Deke." *Hoover's FBI: The Inside Story by Hoover's Trusted Lieutenant*. Washington, DC: Regnery, 1995.

Denton, Jeremiah A., Jr., with Ed Brandt. *When Hell Was in Session*. New York: Reader's Digest Press, 1976.

Depoe, Stephen. *Arthur M. Schlesinger, Jr., and the Ideological History of American Liberalism*. Tuscaloosa: University of Alabama, 1994.

DeRose, David J. "Drama." In *Vietnam War Literature*, 3d ed., edited by John Newman. Metuchen, NJ: Scarecrow Press, 1996.

Devéria, G. *Histoire des Relations de la Chine avec L'Annam-Viêtnam du XVIe au XIXe Siècle*. Paris: Ernest Leroux, 1880.

Devillers, Philippe. *Histoire du Viêt-Nam de 1940 à 1952*. Paris: Editions du Seuil, 1952.

Di Mona, Joseph. *Great Court-Martial Cases*. New York: Grosset & Dunlap, 1972.

Dickerson, Sharon Lewis. "American Red Cross Women in Vietnam." In *Celebration of Patriotism and Courage: Dedication of the Vietnam Women's Memorial*. Washington, DC: Vietnam Women's Memorial Project, 1993.

Dickson, Paul. *The Electronic Battlefield*. Bloomington: Indiana University Press, 1976.

Dictionary of American Biography. New York: Charles Scribner's Sons, 1988.

Dietz, Terry. *Republicans and Vietnam, 1961–1968*. Westport, CT: Greenwood Press, 1986.

Dinh Tan Tho. *Pacification*. Washington, DC: U.S. Army Center of Military History, 1980.

"Diplomat with Aggressive Style." *The New York Times*, 12 July 1973.

Dittmar, Linda, and Gene Michaud, eds. *From Hanoi to Hollywood: The Vietnam War in American Film*. New Brunswick, NJ: Rutgers University Press, 1990.

Divine, Robert A. *Eisenhower and the Cold War*. New York: Oxford University Press, 1981.

Divine, Robert A., ed. *The Johnson Years*. Austin: University of Texas Press, 1981.

Đoàn Van Toai. *The Vietnam Gulag*. New York: Simon & Schuster, 1986.

Dobrynin, Anatoly. *In Confidence*. Edited by Lawrence Malkin. New York: Times Books/Random House, 1995.

Doleman, Edgar D. Jr., and the editors of Boston Publishing Company. *Tools of War*. The Vietnam Experience, edited by Robert Manning. Boston: Boston Publishing, 1984.

Dommen, Arthur J. *Conflict in Laos. The Politics of Neutralization*. New York: Praeger, 1964.

———. *Laos: Keystone of Indochina*. Boulder, CO: Westview Press, 1985.

Donahue, James C. *Mobile Guerrilla Forces with the Special Forces in War Zone D*. Annapolis, MD: Naval Institute Press, 1996.

Dong Van Khuyen. *The Republic of Vietnam Armed Forces*. Washington, DC: U.S. Army Center of Military History, 1980.

———. *The RVNAF*. Washington, DC: U.S. Army Center of Military History, 1980.

Donlon, Roger H. C., and Warren Rogers. *Outpost of Freedom*. New York: McGraw-Hill, 1965.

Donovan, David. *Once a Warrior King*. New York: Ballantine, 1985.

Donovan, Robert J. *Nemesis: Truman and Johnson in the Coils of War in Asia*. New York: St. Martin's/Marek, 1984.

Donovan, William Joseph. *Papers*. United States Army Military History Institute, Army War College, Carlisle Barracks, Carlisle, PA.

Dorland, Peter, and James Nanney. *Dust Off: Army Aeromedical Evacuation in Vietnam*. Washington, DC: U.S. Army Center of Military History, 1982.

Dougan, Clark, David Fulghum, and the editors of Boston Publishing Company. *The Fall of the South*. The Vietnam Experience, edited by Robert Manning. Boston: Boston Publishing, 1985.

Dougan, Clark, Samuel Lipsman, and the editors of Boston Publishing Company. *A Nation Divided*. The Vietnam Experience, edited by Robert Manning. Boston: Boston Publishing, 1984.

Dougan, Clark, Stephen Weiss, and the editors of Boston Publishing Company. *Nineteen Sixty-Eight*. The Vietnam Experience, edited by Robert Manning. Boston: Boston Publishing, 1983.

Doumer, Paul. *Situation de l'Indo-Chine, 1897–1901*. Hà Nôi: F. H. Schneider, 1902.

———. *L'Indochine française (Souvenirs)*. Paris: Vuibert, 1930.

Doyle, Edward, Samuel Lipsman, Terrence Maitland, and the editors of Boston Publishing Company. *The North*. The Vietnam Experience, edited by Robert Manning. Boston: Boston Publishing, 1986.

Doyle, Robert C. *Voices from Captivity: Interpreting the American POW Narrative*. Lawrence: University Press of Kansas, 1994.

Dreyfus, Gilbert. "Napalm and Its Effects on Human Beings." In *Against the Crime of Silence*, edited by John Duffett. Flanders, NJ: O'Hare Books, 1968, pp. 374–381.

Duiker, William J. *The Communist Road to Power in Vietnam*. Boulder, CO: Westview Press, 1981.

———. *Historical Dictionary of Vietnam*. Metuchen, NJ: Scarecrow Press, 1989.

———. *The Rise of Nationalism in Vietnam, 1900–1911*. Ithaca, NY: Cornell University Press, 1976.

———. *U.S. Containment Policy and the Conflict in Indochina*. Stanford, CA: Stanford University Press, 1994.

———. "Waging Revolutionary War: The Evolution of Hanoi's Strategy in the South, 1959–1965." In *The Vietnam War: Vietnamese and American Perspectives*, edited by Jayne S. Werner and Luu Doan Huynh. Armonk, NY: M. E. Sharpe, 1993.

Dulles, Allen. *The Craft of Intelligence*. New York: Harper & Row, 1963.

Duncan, Philip, and Christine Lawrence, eds. *Congressional Quarterly's Politics in America: The 104th Congress*. Washington, DC: CQ Press, 1995.

Duncanson, Dennis J. *Government and Revolution in Vietnam*. New York: Oxford University Press, 1968.

Dunlop, John B. *The Rise of Russia and the Fall of the Soviet Empire.* Princeton, NJ: Princeton University Press, 1993.

Dunlop, Richard. *Donovan, America's Master Spy.* Chicago: Rand McNally, 1982.

Dunn, Carroll H. *Base Development in South Vietnam, 1965–1970.* Washington, DC: U.S. Government Printing Office, 1972.

Dunn, Joe P. "The Vietnam War and the POWs/MIAs." In *Teaching the Vietnam War: Resources and Assessments.* Los Angeles: Center for the Study of Armament and Disarmament, California State University–LA, 1990.

Dunn, Peter M. *The First Vietnam War.* New York: St. Martin's Press, 1985.

Dunnavent, R. Blake. "SEALORDS: The Riverine Interdiction Campaign in Vietnam." Master's thesis, Texas Tech University, 1992.

Dunstan, Simon. *Flak Jackets: 20th Century Military Body Armor.* London: Osprey, 1984.

——. *Vietnam Choppers: Helicopters in Battle, 1950–1975.* London: Osprey, 1988.

——. *Vietnam Tracks: Armor in Battle, 1945–1975.* Novato, CA: Presidio Press, 1982.

Dupuis, Jean. *Les Origines de la Question du Tonkin.* Paris: Challamel, 1886.

Dupuy, Trevor N., Curt Johnson, and David L. Bongard. *The Harper Encyclopedia of Military Biography.* New York: HarperCollins, 1992.

Dutt, Ashok J., ed. *Southeast Asia: Realm of Contrasts.* 3d rev. ed. Boulder, CO: Westview Press, 1985.

Dwyer, Denis J., ed. *South East Asian Development.* New York: Wiley/Longman, 1990.

Ebert, James R. *A Life in a Year: The American Infantryman in Vietnam 1965–1972.* Novato, CA: Presidio Press, 1993.

Eckhardt, George S. *Command and Control, 1950–1969.* Washington, DC: U.S. Army Center of Military History, 1974.

Eden, Anthony. *Full Circle.* Boston: Houghton Mifflin, 1960.

Edmonds, Robin. *Soviet Foreign Policy: The Brezhnev Years.* New York: Oxford University Press, 1983.

Eisele, Albert. *Almost to the Presidency: A Biography of Two American Politicians.* Blue Earth, MN: Piper, 1972.

Eisen, Arlene. *Woman and Revolution in Vietnam.* London: Zed Books, 1984.

Eisenhower, Dwight D. *The White House Years.* 2 vols. New York: Doubleday, 1963–1965.

Elleman, Bruce. "Sino-Soviet Relations and the February 1979 Sino-Vietnamese Conflict." Paper presented at "After the Cold War: Reassessing Vietnam." symposium at the Center for the Study of the Vietnam Conflict, Texas Tech University, Lubbock, Texas, April 1996.

Elliff, John T. *Crime, Dissent, and the Attorney General: The Justice Department in the 1960s.* Beverly Hills, CA: Sage Publications, 1971.

Ellsberg, Daniel. *Papers on the War.* New York: Simon & Schuster, 1972.

Ely, Paul. *L'Indochine dans la Tourmente.* Paris: Librairie Plon, 1964.

——. *Mémoires. L'Indochine dans la Tourmente.* Paris: Plon, 1964.

Emering, Edward. *Orders, Decorations and Badges of the Socialist Republic of Vietnam and the National Front for the Liberation of South Vietnam.* Atglen, PA: Schiffer, 1997.

Emery, Robert F. *The Financial Institutions of Southeast Asia.* New York: Praeger, 1970.

English, John. *The Worldly Years: The Life of Lester Pearson.* Toronto: Vintage Books, 1992.

Enthoven, Alain C., and K. Wayne Smith. *How Much Is Enough? Shaping the Defense Program, 1961–69.* New York: Harper & Row, 1971.

Epstein, Jason. *The Great Conspiracy Trial.* New York: Random House, 1970.

Eschmann, Karl J. *Linebacker: The Untold Story of the Air Raids over North Vietnam.* New York: Ivy Books, 1989.

Esper, George, and the Associated Press. *The Eyewitness History of the Vietnam War, 1961–1975.* New York: Ballantine Books, 1983.

Etcheson, Craig. *The Rise and Fall of Democratic Kampuchea.* Boulder, CO: Westview Press, 1984.

Facts on File 1991. New York: Facts on File, 1991.

Fairbank, John King. *The Great Chinese Revolution, 1800–1985.* New York: Harper & Row, 1986.

Fall, Bernard B. *Hell in a Very Small Place: The Siege of Dien Bien Phu.* New York: J. B. Lippincott, 1966.

——. *Last Reflections on a War.* Garden City, NY: Doubleday, 1967.

——. "The Political-Religious Sects of Viet-Nam." *Pacific Affairs* 28 (September 1955): 235–253.

——. *Street without Joy.* Harrisburg, PA: Stackpole, 1961.

——. *The Two Viet Nams. A Political and Military Analysis.* 2nd rev. ed. New York: Praeger, 1967.

——. *Viet-Nam Witness 1953–66.* New York: Praeger, 1966.

Fauvet, Jacques. *La Quatrième République.* Paris: Fayard, 1959.

Fenn, Charles. *Ho Chi Minh: A Biographical Introduction.* New York: Charles Scribner's Sons, 1973.

Fenn, Jeffery. "Vietnam: The Dramatic Response." In *Tell Me Lies about Vietnam,* edited by Alf Louvre and Jeffrey Walsh. Milton Keynes, UK: Open University Press, 1988.

Ferber, Michael, and Staughton Lynd. *The Resistance.* Boston: Beacon Press, 1971.

Ferrell, Robert H. *Woodrow Wilson and World War I: 1917–1921.* New York: Harper & Row, 1985.

Figley, Charles R., and Seymour Leventman, eds. *Strangers at Home: Vietnam Veterans since the War.* New York: Praeger, 1980.

Findling, John E. *Dictionary of American Diplomatic History.* Westport, CT: Greenwood Press, 1980.

Fineman, Daniel. *A Special Relationship; The United States and Military Government in Thailand, 1947–1958.* Honolulu: University of Hawaii Press, 1997.

Finn, James. *Protest: Pacifism and Politics.* New York: Random House, 1967.

First Infantry Division in Vietnam. Vol. 2, 1 May 1967–31 Dec 1968. Vietnam: 1st Infantry Division, nd.

Fishel, Wesley R. *Vietnam: Anatomy of a Conflict.* Itasca, IL: F. E. Peacock, 1968.

Fishel, Wesley R., ed. *Problems of Freedom; South Vietnam since Independence.* East Lansing: Michigan State University Press, 1961.

Fisher, Charles A. *Southeast Asia: A Social, Economic and Political Geography.* New York: E. P. Dutton, 1966.

Fisher, Louis. *Presidential War Power.* Lawrence: University of Kansas, 1995.

Fite, Gilbert C. *Richard B. Russell Jr., Senator From Georgia.* Chapel Hill: University of North Carolina Press, 1991.

FitzGerald, Frances. *Fire in the Lake: The Vietnamese and the Americans in Vietnam.* Boston: Little, Brown, 1972.

Flynn, George Q. *The Draft, 1940–1973.* Lawrence: University Press of Kansas, 1993.

——. *Lewis B. Hershey: Mr. Selective Service.* Chapel Hill: University of North Carolina Press, 1985.

Fontaine, Ray. *The Dawn of Free Vietnam.* Brownsville, TX: Pan American Business Services, 1992.

Foote, Joseph, ed. *The Presidential Nominating Conventions 1968.* Washington, DC: Congressional Quarterly Service, 1968.

Ford, Carey. *Donovan of OSS.* Boston: Little, Brown, 1970.

Ford, Gerald R. *A Time to Heal.* New York: Harper & Row, 1979.

Fourcade, Marie-Madeleine. *Noah's Ark: A Memoir of Struggle and Resistance.* New York: E. P. Dutton, 1974.

Frady, Marshall. *Wallace.* New York: New American Library, 1972.

Francillon, René J. *Lockheed Aircraft since 1913.* London: Putnam, 1982.

——. *McDonnell Douglas Aircraft since 1920.* London: Putnam, 1979.

——. *Tonkin Gulf Yacht Club: U.S. Carrier Operations off Vietnam.* Annapolis, MD: Naval Institute Press, 1988.

Francillon, Rene, and Mick Roth. *Douglas B-66 Destroyer.* Arlington, TX: Aerofax, 1988.

Frankel, Joseph. *British Foreign Policy, 1945–1973.* New York: Oxford University Press, 1975.

Frankel, Max. "Ky Tells 6 Allies at Manila Talks Civil Rule Is Near." *The New York Times,* 25 October 1966.

——. "Manila Talks End." *The New York Times,* 26 October 1966.

Franklin, H. Bruce. *M.I.A. or Mythmaking in America.* Brooklyn, NY: Lawrence Hill Books, 1992.

Frantz, Douglas, and David MacKean. *Friends in High Places. The Rise and Fall of Clark Clifford.* Boston: Little, Brown, 1995.

Fried, Richard M. *Nightmare in Red: The McCarthy Era in Perspective.* New York: Oxford University Press, 1990.

Friedman, Norman. "Elmo Russell Zumwalt, Jr." In *The Chiefs of Naval Operations,* edited by Robert W. Love, Jr. Annapolis, MD: Naval Institute Press, 1980.

——. *U.S. Aircraft Carriers: An Illustrated Design History.* Annapolis, MD: Naval Institute Press, 1983.

——. *U.S. Small Combatants.* Annapolis, MD: Naval Institute Press, 1987.

Fulghum, David, Terrence Maitland, and the editors of Boston Publishing Company. *South Vietnam on Trial: Mid-1970 to 1972.* The Vietnam Experience, edited by Robert Manning. Boston: Boston Publishing, 1984.

Fulton, William B. *Riverine Operations, 1966–1969.* Washington, DC: Vietnam Studies, Office of the Chief of Military History, 1985.

Furgurson, Ernest B. *Westmoreland: The Inevitable General.* Boston: Little, Brown, 1968.

Futrell, Robert F. *The United States Air Force in Southeast Asia: The Advisory Years to 1965.* Washington, DC: Office of Air Force History, 1981.

Gabriel, Richard A., and Paul L. Savage. *Crisis in Command: Mismanagement in the Army.* New York: Hill & Wang, 1978.

Gaddis, John Lewis. *Russia, The Soviet Union, and the United States: An Interpretive History.* New York: John Wiley & Sons, 1978.

——. *Strategies of Containment: A Critical Appraisal of Postwar American National Security Policy.* New York: Oxford University Press, 1982.

Gaffen, Fred. *Unknown Warriors: Canadians in the Vietnam War.* Toronto: Dundurn Press, 1990.

Gaillard, Jean-Michel. *Jules Ferry.* Paris: Fayard, 1989.

Galbraith, John Kenneth. *A Life in Our Times.* Boston: Houghton Mifflin, 1981.

Galvin, John R. *Air Assault: The Development of Airmobile Warfare.* New York: Hawthorn Books, 1969.

Gardiner, Robert, ed. *Conway's All the World's Fighting Ships 1947–1982.* Annapolis, MD: Naval Institute Press, 1983.

Garfinkle, Adam. *Telltale Hearts: The Origins and Impact of the Vietnam Antiwar Movement.* New York: St. Martin's Press, 1995.

Garnier, Francis. *Voyage d'exploration en Indochine.* Paris: Editions la Découverte, 1985.

Garver, John W. *Foreign Relations of the People's Republic of China.* Englewood Cliffs, NJ: Prentice-Hall, 1993.

Garza, Hedda. *Joan Baez.* New York: Chelsea House, 1991.

Gaspar, Charles J. "The Search for Closure: Vietnam War Literature and the Vietnam Veterans Memorial." *War, Literature, and the Arts* (Spring 1989): 19–34.

Gatzke, Hans W. *Germany and the United States. "A Special Relationship?"* Cambridge, MA: Harvard University Press, 1980.

Gavin, James M. *On to Berlin: Battles of an Airborne Commander, 1943–1946.* New York: Viking Press, 1978.

Gelb, Leslie H., with Richard K. Betts. *The Irony of Vietnam: The System Worked.* Washington, DC: Brookings Institution, 1979.

Gelman, H. *The Brezhnev Politburo.* Ithaca, NY: Cornell University Press, 1984.

"General Historical Records." National Archives Branch Depository, Records of the United States Army, Vietnam (USARV), RG 472. Headquarters, U.S. Army, Vietnam, Special Services Agency (Provisional), Entertainment Branch, College Park, MD.

Genovese, Michael A. *The Nixon Presidency: Power and Politics in Turbulent Times.* New York: Greenwood Press, 1990.

Gerassi, John. *North Vietnam: A Documentary.* Indianapolis, IN: The Bobbs-Merrill, 1968.

Gerhardt, James M. *The Draft and Public Policy.* Columbus: Ohio State University Press, 1971.

Gerson, Louis L. *John Foster Dulles.* New York: Cooper Square, 1968.

Gheddo, Piero. *The Cross and the Bo Tree: Catholics and Buddhists in Vietnam.* New York: Sheed and Ward, 1970.

Gibbons, William Conrad. *The U.S. Government and the Vietnam War, Parts 1–3.* Princeton, NJ: Princeton University Press, 1986.

Gibson, James William. *The Perfect War: Technowar in Vietnam.* Boston: Atlantic Monthly Press, 1986.

Gilman, Owen W., and Lorrie Smith, eds. *America Rediscovered: Critical Essays on Literature and Film of the Vietnam War.* New York: Garland, 1990.

Ginsburg, Gordon A. *The Lavelle Case: Crisis in Integrity.* Maxwell Air Force Base, AL: Air University, 1974.

Gioglio, Gerald R. *Days of Decision: An Oral History of Conscientious Objectors in the Military during the Vietnam War.* Trenton, NJ: Broken Rifle Press, 1989.

Gitlin, Todd. *The Sixties: Years of Hope, Days of Rage.* New York: Bantam Books, 1987.

Glister, Herman L. *The Air War in Southeast Asia: Case Studies of Selected Campaigns.* Maxwell Air Force Base, AL: Air University Press, 1993.

Goff, Stanley, and Robert Sanders, with Clark Smith. *Brothers: Black Soldiers in the Nam.* Novato, CA: Presidio Press, 1982.

Goldman, Eric F. *The Tragedy of Lyndon Johnson.* New York: Alfred A. Knopf, 1969.

Goldstein, Joseph, Burke Marshall, and Jack Schwartz. *The My Lai Massacre and Its Cover-Up: Beyond the Reach of the Law?* New York: Free Press, 1976.

Goldwater, Barry N. *The Conscience of a Conservative.* New York: Victor, 1960.

Goodman, Allan E. *The Lost Peace: America's Search for a Negotiated Settlement of the Vietnam War.* Stanford, CA: Hoover Institute Press, 1978.

——. *The Search for a Negotiated Settlement of the Vietnam War.* Berkeley: Institute of East Asian Studies, 1986.

Goodwin, Doris Kearns. *Lyndon Johnson and the American Dream.* New York: Harper & Row, 1976.

Goold-Adams, Richard. *The Time of Power: A Reappraisal of John Foster Dulles.* London: Weidenfeld and Nicolson, 1962.

Gordon, William A. *The Fourth of May: Killings and Coverups at Kent State.* Buffalo, NY: Prometheus Books, 1990.

Gormly, James L. *From Potsdam to the Cold War.* Wilmington, DE: Scholarly Resources, 1990.

Gotera, Vince. *Radical Visions: Poetry by Vietnam Veterans.* Athens: University of Georgia Press, 1994.

Gough, Michael. *Dioxin, Agent Orange.* New York: Plenum, 1986.

Gould, James W. *The United States and Malaysia.* The American Foreign Policy Library Series. Cambridge, MA: Harvard University Press, 1969.

Goulden, Steven L. *Political Profiles: The Johnson Years.* New York: Facts on File, 1976.

Granatstein, J. L., with Norman Hillmer. *For Better or For Worse: Canada and the United States to the 1990s.* Toronto: Copp Clark Pittman, 1991.

Grant, Zalin. *Facing the Phoenix: The CIA and the Political Defeat of the United States in Vietnam.* New York: W. W. Norton, 1991.

——. *Survivors.* New York: W. W. Norton, 1975.

Gras, Yvres. *Histoire de La Guerre d'Indochine.* Paris: Editions Denoël, 1992.

Gravel, Mike. *Citizen Power: A People's Platform.* New York: Holt, Rinehart and Winston, 1972.

——. *Introduction to The Pentagon Papers: The Senator Gravel Edition.* Boston: Beacon Press, 1972.

Great Britain, Foreign Office. *Recent Exchanges Concerning Attempts to Promote a Negotiated Settlement of the Conflict in Viet-Nam.* London: H. M. Stationery Office, 1965.

Greene, John Robert. *The Limits of Power: The Nixon and Ford Administrations*. Bloomington: University of Indiana Press, 1992.

——. *The Presidency of Gerald R. Ford*. Lawrence: University Press of Kansas, 1995.

Gregory, Barry. *Vietnam Helicopter Handbook*. Wellingborough, Northants England: Patrick Stephens, 1988.

Groom, Winston, and Duncan Spencer. *Conversations with the Enemy*. New York: Putnam, 1983.

Gropman, Alan L. *Air Power and the Airlift Evacuation of Kham Duc*. U.S. Air Force Southeast Asia Monograph Series, Vol. 5, Monograph 7. Washington, DC: Office of Air Force History, 1985.

Gross, Charles J. "A Different Breed of Cats: The Air National Guard and the 1968 Reserve Mobilizations." *Air University Review* (January–February 1983): 94–95.

——. *Militiaman, Volunteer, and Professional: The Air National Guard and the American Military Tradition*. Washington, DC: National Guard Bureau, 1996.

——. *Prelude to the Total Force: The Air National Guard, 1943–1969*. Washington, DC: Office of Air Force History, 1985.

Gruening, Ernest. *Many Battles: The Autobiography of Ernest Gruening*. New York: Liveright, 1973.

Gruner, Elliott. *Prisoners of Culture: Representing the Vietnam POW*. New Brunswick, NJ: Rutgers University Press, 1993.

Guhin, Michael. *John Foster Dulles: A Statesman and His Times*. New York: Columbia University Press, 1972.

Guilhaume, Philippe. *Jules Ferry*. Paris: Albin Michel, 1992.

Guilmartin, John F. *A Very Short War: The Mayaguez and the Battle of Koh Tang*. College Station: Texas A&M University Press, 1995.

Guizot, François. *Mémoires pour servir à l'histoire de mon temps*. Paris: Nichel Levy Frères, 1872.

Gunston, Bill. *The Illustrated Encyclopedia of the World's Modern Military Aircraft*. New York: Crescent Books, 1978.

Gurney, Gene. *Vietnam: The War in the Air*. New York: Crown, 1985.

Hà Mai Việt. "Famous Generals of the Republic of Việt Nam Armed Forces" (in Vietnamese). Unpublished manuscript.

Hackworth, David H., and Julie Sherman. *About Face: The Odyssey of an American Warrior*. New York: Simon & Schuster, 1989.

Hagan, Kenneth J. *This People's Navy: The Making of American Sea Power*. New York: Free Press, 1991.

Haig, Alexander. *Inner Circles*. New York: Warner Books, 1992.

Halberstam, David. *The Best and the Brightest*. New York: Random House, 1973.

——. "Diem Asks Peace in Religious Crisis." *The New York Times*, 12 June 1963.

——. *Ho*. New York: Fawcett, 1971.

——. *The Making of a Quagmire*. Rev. ed. New York: Knopf, 1987.

Haldane, Robert, ed. *The First Infantry Division in Vietnam, 1965–1970*. Paducah, KY: Turner, 1993.

Haldeman, H. R., with Joseph DiMina. *The Ends of Power*. New York: Times Books, 1978.

——. *The Haldeman Diaries: Inside the Nixon White House*. New York: Putnam, 1994.

Hall, Mitchell K. *Because of Their Faith: CALCAV and Religious Opposition to the Vietnam War*. New York: Columbia University Press, 1990.

——. "Clergy and Laymen Concerned about Vietnam: A Study of Opposition to the Vietnam War." Ph.D. dissertation, University of Kentucky, 1987.

Hallin, Daniel C. *The "Uncensored War": The Media and Vietnam*. Berkeley: University of California Press, 1986.

Halperin, Morton H. *Bureaucratic Politics and Foreign Policy*. Washington, DC: Brookings Institution, 1974.

——. *National Security Policy-Making*. Lexington, MA: D. C. Heath, 1975.

Halperin, Morton H., et al. *The Lawless State: The Crimes of the U.S. Intelligence Agencies*. New York: Penguin Books, 1976.

Halstead, Fred. *Out Now! A Participant's Account of the American Movement against the Vietnam War*. New York: Monad Press, 1978.

Hamel, Bernard. *Sihanouk et le Drame Cambodgien*. Paris: Editions L'Harmattan, 1993.

Hamilton-Merritt, Jane. *Tragic Mountains: The Hmong, the Americans, and the Secret Wars for Laos, 1942–1992*. Bloomington: Indiana University Press, 1993.

Hammer, Ellen J. *A Death in November: America in Vietnam, 1963*. New York: E. P. Dutton, 1987.

——. *The Struggle for Indochina*. Stanford, CA: Stanford University Press, 1954.

Hammond, William M. *Public Affairs: The Military and the Media, 1962–1968*. Washington, DC: Center of Military History, 1988.

Hanak, Walter, ed. *The United States Air Force in Southeast Asia—Aces and Aerial Victories, 1965–1973*. Washington, DC: Office of Air Force History, 1976.

Hannah, Norman, B. *The Key to Failure: Laos and the Vietnam War*. New York: Madison Books, 1987.

Hanoi Hannah. Audiotape of interview by Janet Gardner and Paul Camacho. Boston: William F. Joiner Center for the Study of War and Its Social Consequences, 1987.

Hardy, Gordon, Arnold R. Isaacs, MacAlister Brown, and the editors of Boston Publishing Company. *Pawns of War: Cambodia and Laos*. The Vietnam Experience, edited by Robert Manning. Boston: Boston Publishing, 1987.

Harris, David. *Dreams Die Hard*. New York: St. Martin's Press, 1982.

——. *I Shoulda Been Home Yesterday*. New York: Delacorte Press, 1976.

Harris, Richard. *Justice: The Crisis of Law, Order, and Freedom in America*. New York: E. P. Dutton, 1970.

Harrison, James Pinckney. *The Endless War: Vietnam's Struggle for Independence*. New York: McGraw-Hill, 1982.

——. *The Long March to Power*. New York: Praeger, 1972.

Hatch, Gardner, ed. *11th U.S. Cavalry: Blackhorse*. Paducah, KY: Turner, 1990.

Havens, Thomas R. *Fire Across the Sea: The Vietnam War and Japan 1965–1975*. Princeton, NJ: Princeton University Press, 1987.

Hay, John H., Jr. *Tactical and Materiel Innovations*. Vietnam Studies. Washington, DC: U.S. Government Printing Office, 1974.

Hayden, Tom. *Reunion: A Memoir*. New York: Random House, 1988.

Hayes, James R. "The War Within: Dissent in the Military with an Emphasis on Vietnam." Ph.D. Dissertation, University of Connecticut, 1975.

Head, William, and Lawrence Grinter, eds. *Looking Back on the Vietnam War: A 1990s Perspective on the Decisions, Combat, and Legacies*. Westport, CT: Greenwood Press, 1993.

Heaton, Leonard, Carl Hughes, Harold Rosegay, George Fisher, and Robert E. Feighny. "Military Surgical Practices of the United States Army in Viet Nam." *Current Problems in Surgery* (November 1966).

Heiser, Joseph M. *A Soldier Supporting Soldiers*. Washington, DC: U.S. Army Center of Military History, 1991.

——. *Vietnam Studies: Logistic Support*. Washington, DC: Department of the Army, 1974.

Helling, Philip H. *Vietnam in American Literature*. Boston: Tawyne, 1990.

Hemery, Daniel. *Ho Chi Minh: de l'Indochine au Vietnam*. Paris: Gallimard, 1990.

Hendin, Herbert, and Ann Pollinger Haas. *Wounds of War: The Psychological Aftermath of Combat in Vietnam*. New York: Basic Books, 1984.

Hendrick, James P. Papers. Harry S Truman Library, Independence, MO.

Hentoff, Nat. *The Essays of A. J. Muste*. New York: Simon & Schuster, 1967.

Herbert, Anthony B., with James T. Wooten. *Soldier*. New York: Holt, Rinehart and Winston, 1973.

Herbert, Paul H. *Deciding What Has to Be Done: General William E. DePuy and the 1976 Edition of FM 100–5, Operations*. Leavenworth Papers, No. 16. Fort Leavenworth, KS: Combat Studies Institute, 1988.

Herman, Edward S., and F. Brodhead. *Demonstration Elections—U.S.—Staged Elections in the Dominican Republic, Vietnam, and El Salvador.* Boston: South End Press, 1984.

Herman, Gary, and David Downing. *Jane Fonda: All-American Anti-Heroine.* New York: Quick Fox, 1980.

Herman, Judith Lewis. *Trauma and Recovery.* New York: Basic Books, 1992.

Herr, Michael. *Dispatches.* New York: Alfred A. Knopf, 1977.

Herring, George C. *America's Longest War: The U.S. and Vietnam, 1950–1975,* 2d ed. New York: Alfred A. Knopf, 1986

——— . *LBJ and Vietnam: A Different Kind of War.* Austin: University of Texas Press, 1994.

——— . "Westmoreland, William Childs." In *Dictionary of American Military Biography,* edited by Roger Spiller. Westport, CT: Greenwood Press, 1984, pp. 1179–1183.

Herring, George C., ed. *The Secret Diplomacy of the Vietnam War: The Negotiating Volumes of the Pentagon Papers.* Austin: University of Texas Press, 1983.

Herrington, Stuart A. *Peace with Honor?* Novato, CA: Presidio Press, 1983.

——— . *Silence Was a Weapon: The Vietnam War in the Villages.* Novato, CA: Presidio Press, 1982.

Hersh, Burton. *The Old Boys: The American Elite and the Origins of the CIA.* New York: Charles Scribner's Sons, 1992.

Hersh, Seymour M. *Cover-Up: The Army's Secret Investigation of the Massacre at My Lai 4.* New York: Random House, 1972.

——— . *My Lai 4: A Report on the Massacre and Its Aftermath.* New York: Random House, 1970.

——— . *The Price of Power: Kissinger in the Nixon White House.* New York: Summit, 1983.

Herz, Martin F. "Conclusions." In Audrey Bracey. *Resolution of the Dominican Crisis, 1965: A Study in Mediation.* Washington, DC: Institute for the Study of Diplomacy, Georgetown University, 1980.

Herzog, Arthur. *McCarthy for President.* New York: Viking, 1969.

Herzog, Tobey C. *Vietnam War Stories: Innocence Lost.* New York: Routledge, 1992.

Herzstein, Robert E. *Henry R. Luce: A Political Portrait of the Man Who Created the American Century.* New York: Macmillan, 1994.

Heyn, Pia Christine. "The Role of Army Combat Medics in the Viet Nam War, 1965–1971." Master's thesis, Georgia State University, 1994.

Hickey, Gerald C. *Free in the Forest: Ethnohistory of the Vietnamese Central Highlands, 1954–1976.* New Haven, CT: Yale University Press, 1982.

——— . *Shattered World: Adaptation and Survival among Vietnam's Highland Peoples during the Vietnam War.* Philadelphia: University of Pennsylvania Press, 1993.

——— . *Sons of the Mountains: Ethnohistory of the Vietnamese Central Highlands to 1954.* New Haven, CT: Yale University Press, 1982.

——— . *Village in Vietnam.* New Haven, CT: Yale University Press, 1964.

Hiebert, Murray. "Ex-Communist Official Turns into Vocal Critic." *Far Eastern Economic Review* 156 (2 December 1993).

Higham, Charles. *The Archaeology of Mainland Southeast Asia.* New York: Cambridge University Press, 1989.

Hilgartner, P. L. "Amphibious Doctrine in Vietnam." In *The Marines in Vietnam, 1954–1973: An Anthology and Annotated Bibliography,* edited by Peter L. Hilgartner. Washington, DC: U.S. Government Printing Office, 1974. Originally published in *Marine Corps Gazette* (January 1969), 28–31.

Hilsman, Roger. *American Guerrilla.* Washington, DC: Brassey's, 1990.

——— . *To Move a Nation: The Politics of Foreign Policy in the Administration of John F. Kennedy.* Garden City, NY: Doubleday, 1967.

Historical Dictionary of the Third French Republic, 1870—1940. Edited by Patrick H. Hutton. New York: Greenwood Press, 1986.

History of the August Revolution. Hà Nôi: Foreign Languages Publishing House, 1972.

Hitch, Charles J. *Decision Making for Defense.* Berkeley: University of California Press, 1965.

Hixson, Walter L. *George F. Kennan: Cold War Iconoclast.* New York: Columbia University Press, 1990.

Hô Chí Minh. *Ho Chi Minh on Revolution: Selected Writings, 1920–1966.* New York: Signet Books, 1967.

Hoa Bang. *Quang Trung Nguyên Huê: Anh Hùng Dân Tôc (1788–1792) (Quang Trung Nguyen Hue, Our National Hero).* Sài Gòn: Bôn Phuong tái ban, 1950.

Hoa Hao Buddhism. *Bibliography and Teaching of Prophet Huynh-Phu-So.* Santa Fe Spring, CA: Overseas Office, Hoa Hao Buddhism Church, 1983.

Hoàng Ngoc Lung. *General Offensives of 1968–69.* Washington, DC: U.S. Army Center of Military History, 1981.

Hoang Sa and Truong Sa Archipelagoes (Paracels and Spratlys). Hà Nôi: Vietnam Courrier, 1981.

Hoàng Van Chí. *From Colonialism to Communism.* New York: Praeger, 1966.

Hoàng Van Đào. *Viêt Nam Quôc Dân Đang.* Sài Gòn: Published by the author, 1970; reprinted in the United States.

Hoàng Van Hoan. *A Drop in the Ocean: Hoang van Hoan's Revolutionary Reminiscences.* Beijing: Foreign Language Press, 1988.

Hobart, F. W. A. *Pictorial History of the Machinegun.* New York: Drake, 1972.

Hogg, Ian V. *The Complete Machinegun: 1885 to the Present.* New York: Exeter, 1979.

Holm, Jeanne. *Women in the Military: An Unfinished Revolution.* Rev. ed. Novato, CA: Presidio Press, 1992.

Honey, P. J. *Communism in North Vietnam.* Cambridge, MA: M.I.T. Press, 1962.

Hooper, Edwin B. *United States Naval Power in a Changing World.* New York: Praeger, 1988.

Hooper, Edwin B., Dean Allard, and Oscar Fitzgerald. *The United States Navy and the Vietnam Conflict.* Vol. 1, *The Setting of the Stage to 1959.* Washington, DC: U.S. Government Printing Office, 1976.

Hoopes, Townsend. *The Devil and John Foster Dulles.* Boston: Little, Brown, 1973.

——— . *The Limits of Intervention.* New York: David McKay, 1969.

Hopkins, George W. "From Naval Pauper to Naval Power: The Development of Charleston's Metropolitan-Military Complex." In *The Martial Metropolis: U.S. Cities in War and Peace,* edited by Roger W. Lotchin. New York: Praeger, 1984.

Hopkins, J. C., and Sheldon A. Goldberg. *The Development of the Strategic Air Command, 1946–1986: The Fortieth Anniversary History.* Offutt Air Force Base, NE: Office of the Historian, Headquarters Strategic Air Command, 1986.

Hosmer, Stephen T., Konrad Kellen, and Brian M. Jenkins. *The Fall of South Vietnam: Statements by Vietnamese Military and Civilian Leaders.* New York: Crane, Russak, 1980.

Howes, Craig. *Voices of the Vietnam POWs: Witnesses to Their Fight.* New York: Oxford University Press, 1993.

Hoyt, Edwin F. *Airborne: The History of American Parachute Forces.* New York: Stein & Day, 1979.

Hsiao, Lisa, "Project 100,000: The Great Society's Answer to Military Manpower Needs in Vietnam." *Vietnam Generation—A White Man's War: Race Issues and Vietnam* 1, No. 2 (Spring 1989): 14–37.

Hsü, Immanuel C. Y. *The Rise of Modern China.* New York: Oxford University Press, 1995.

Hu Pu-yu. *The Military Exploits and Deeds of President Chiang Kai-shek.* Taipei, Taiwan: Chung Wu Publishing, 1971.

Huynh Kim Khánh. *Vietnamese Communism, 1925–1945.* Ithaca, NY: Cornell University Press, 1982.

Hubbell, John G., et al. *P.O.W.: A Definitive History of the American Prisoner of War Experience in Vietnam, 1964–1973.* New York: Reader's Digest Press, 1976.

Humphrey, Hubert H. *The Education of a Public Man: My Life and Politics.* New York: Doubleday, 1976.

Hunt, Richard A. *Pacification: The American Struggle for Vietnam's Hearts and Minds.* Boulder, CO: Westview Press, 1995.

Hutton, Patrick H., ed. *Historical Dictionary of the Third French Republic, 1870–1940.* Westport, CT: Greenwood Press, 1986.

Huynh Kim Khanh. "The Vietnamese August Revolution Reinterpreted." *Journal of Asian Studies* 30, no. 4. (August 1971): 761–782.

——. *Vietnamese Communism, 1925–1945.* Ithaca, NY: Cornell University Press, 1982.

Hymoff, Edward. *The First Air Cavalry Division, Vietnam.* New York: M. W. Lads, 1967.

International Who's Who 1976–1977. London: Europa Publications, 1977.

International Who's Who, 1983–1984. London: Europa Publications, 1983.

Irish, Kent R. *Information Manual for Vegetation Control in Southeast Asia.* Frederick, MD: Department of the Army, 1969.

Irving, R. E. M. *Christian Democracy in France.* London: Allen & Unwin, 1973.

——. *The First Indochina War.* London: Croom-Helm, 1975.

Isaacs, Arnold R. *Without Honor: Defeat in Vietnam and Cambodia.* Baltimore: Johns Hopkins Press, 1983.

Isaacson, Walter. *Kissinger: A Biography.* New York: Simon & Schuster, 1992.

Isaacson, Walter, and Evan Thomas. *The Wise Men: Six Friends and the World They Made.* New York: Simon & Schuster, 1986.

Jackson, John Hampden. *Clemenceau and the Third Republic.* New York: Macmillan, 1948.

Jackson, Kenneth T., ed. *Dictionary of American Biography.* Suppl. 9, 1971–1975. New York: Charles Scribner's Sons, 1994.

Jacobs, Harold, ed. *Weathermen.* Berkeley: Ramparts Press, 1970.

James, D. Clayton. *The Years of MacArthur.* Vol. 3. *Triumph and Disaster, 1945–1964.* Boston: Houghton Mifflin, 1985.

James, Doug. *Cronkite: His Life and Times.* Brentwood, TN: JM Press, 1991.

Jamieson, Neil R. *Understanding Vietnam.* Berkeley: University of California Press, 1993.

Jane's Fighting Ships, 1976–1977. London: Jane's Publishing, 1977.

Janis, Irving L. *Groupthink.* Boston: Houghton Mifflin, 1982.

Jason, Philip K., ed. *Fourteen Landing Zones: Approaches to Vietnam War Literature.* Iowa City: University of Iowa Press, 1991.

Javits, Jacob K., with Donald Kellerman. *Who Makes War: The President versus Congress.* New York: William Morrow, 1970.

Javits, Jacob K., with Rafael Steinberg. *Javits: The Autobiography of a Public Man.* Boston: Houghton Mifflin, 1981.

Jenkins, E. F. *A History of the French Navy. From Its Beginnings to the Present Day.* Annapolis, MD: Naval Institute Press, 1973.

Jensen-Stevenson, Monika. *Spite House; The Last Secret of the War in Vietnam.* New York: W. W. Norton, 1997.

Jensen-Stevenson, Monika, and William Stevenson. *Kiss the Boys Goodbye: How the United States Betrayed Its Own POWs in Vietnam.* New York: Plume, 1991.

Jessup, John K., ed. *The Ideas of Henry Luce.* New York: Athenaeum, 1969.

Johnson, Chalmers. *Autopsy on People's Wars.* Berkeley: University of California Press, 1973.

Johnson, Douglas W. J. *Guizot: Aspects of French History, 1787–1874.* Toronto: University of Toronto Press, 1963.

Johnson, Harold K. *Challenge: Compendium of Army Accomplishment: A Report by the Chief of Staff: July 1964–April 1968.* Washington, DC: Department of the Army, 1 July 1968.

Johnson, Haynes. *Sleepwalking through History: America in the Reagan Years.* New York: W. W. Norton, 1991.

Johnson, Lawrence H., III. *Winged Sabers: The Air Cavalry in Vietnam, 1965–1973.* Harrisburg, PA: Stackpole, 1990.

Johnson, Lyndon B. *The Vantage Point: Perspectives on the Presidency, 1963–1969.* New York: Holt, Rinehart and Winston, 1971.

Johnson, U. Alexis, with Jef Olivarius McAllister. *The Right Hand of Power.* Englewood Cliffs, NJ: Prentice-Hall, 1984.

Jones, James. *Viet Journal.* New York: Delacorte Press, 1973.

Kahin, George M. *Intervention: How America Became Involved in Vietnam.* New York: Alfred A. Knopf, 1986.

Kahin, George M., and John Lewis. *The United States in Vietnam: An Analysis in Depth of the History of America's Involvement in Vietnam.* New York: Delta, 1967.

Kalb, Marvin, and Bernard Kalb. *Kissinger.* Boston: Little, Brown, 1974.

Kalisch, Phillip A., and Beatrice Kalisch. *The Advance of American Nursing,* 3d ed. Boston: Little, Brown, 1994.

Kalman, Laura. *Abe Fortas: A Biography.* New Haven, CT: Yale University Press, 1990.

Kamps, Charles T., Jr. *The History of the Vietnam War.* New York: Exeter Books, 1987.

Kaplan, Fred. "Scientists at War: The Birth of the RAND Corporation." *American Heritage* (June/July 1983): 49–64.

——. *The Wizards of Armageddon.* New York: Simon & Schuster, 1983.

Kaplan, Hyman R. *Coast Guard in Vietnam.* Washington, DC: U.S. Coast Guard, Public Information Division, 1971.

Karnow, Stanley. *Vietnam: A History.* New York: Viking Press, 1983.

——. *Vietnam: A History.* Rev. Ed. New York: Penguin Books, 1991

Katcher, Philip. *The American Soldier: U.S. Armies in Uniform, 1755 to the Present.* New York: Military Press, 1990.

——. *Armies of the Vietnam War, 1962–1975.* London: Osprey Publishing, 1980.

Kattenburg, Paul. *The Vietnam Trauma in American Foreign Policy, 1945–75.* New Brunswick, NJ: Transaction Books, 1980.

Kaufman, Burton I. *The Korean War: Challenges in Crisis, Credibility, and Command.* Philadelphia: Temple University Press, 1986.

Kearns, Doris. *Lyndon Johnson and the American Dream.* New York: Harper & Row, 1976.

Keating, Susan Katz. *Prisoners of Hope: Exploiting the POW/MIA Myth in America.* New York: Random House, 1994.

Keely, Francis J. *U.S. Army Special Forces, 1961–1971.* Washington, DC: U.S. Government Printing Office, 1973.

Kellner, Kathleen. "Broker of Power: General Lyman L. Lemnitzer." Ph.D. dissertation, Kent State University, 1987.

Kelly, Francis J. *The Green Berets in Vietnam 1961–71.* Washington, DC: Brassey's, 1991.

——. *U.S. Army Special Forces, 1961–1971.* Washington, DC: Department of the Army, 1973.

Kelly, George A. *Lost Soldiers: The French Army and Empire in Crisis, 1947–1962.* Cambridge, MA: M.I.T. Press, 1965.

Kennan, George F. *American Diplomacy, 1900–1950.* Chicago: University of Chicago Press, 1951.

——. *Memoirs, 1925–1950.* Boston: Little, Brown, 1967.

——. *Memoirs, 1950–1963.* New York: Pantheon, 1983.

——. "The Sources of Soviet Conduct." *Foreign Affairs* 25 (July 1947): 566–582.

Kennedy, Stephen J. *Battlefield Protection of the Soldier through his Clothing/Equipment System.* Natick, MA: U.S. Army Natick Lab, 1969.

Khieu Samphan. *Cambodia's Economy and Industrial Development.* Translated by Laura Summers. Ithaca, NY: Cornell Southeast Asia Program, Data Paper No. 111, March 1979.

Khrushchev, Nikita S. *Khrushchev Remembers.* Boston: Little, Brown, 1971.

Kiêm Đat. *Chiên Tranh Viêt Nam (The Vietnam War).* Glendale, CA: Đai Nam, 1982.

Kiernan, Ben. *Burchett Reporting the Other Side of the World, 1939–1983.* London: Quartet, 1986.

——. *How Pol Pot Came to Power.* London: Verso Books, 1985.

Kilian, Robert. *History and Memories: Naval Infantryman in Indochina.* Paris: Berger-Levrault, 1948.

Kim, Young C., ed. *The Southeast Asian Economic Miracle.* New Brunswick, NJ: Transaction, 1995.

Kimery, Anthony. "John Kerry: The Senate's Rising Voice for Veterans." *VVA Veteran*, Vol. 10, No. 10 (October 1990): 1, 13–16.

Kimnel, Michael. *Home from the War: Vietnam Veterans, Neither Victims Nor Executioners.* New York: Simon & Schuster, 1973.

———. *Thought Reform and the Psychology of Totalism: A Study of "Brainwashing" in China.* New York: W. W. Norton, 1961.

King, Peter, ed. *Australia's Vietnam: Australia in the Second Indo-China War.* Boston: Allen & Unwin, 1983.

Kinnard, Douglas. *The Certain Trumpet: Maxwell Taylor & The American Experience in Vietnam.* Washington, DC: Brassey's, 1991.

———. *The War Managers.* Hanover, NH: University Press of New England, 1977.

Kinnard, Harry W. O. "A Victory in the Ia Drang: The Triumph of a Concept." *Army* 17 (September 1967): 71–91.

Kirk, Donald. "Presidential Campaign Politics: The Uncontested 1971 Election." In *Electoral Politics in South Vietnam*, edited by John C. Donnell and C. A. Joiner. Lexington, MA: D. C. Heath, 1974.

———. *Wider War: The Struggle for Cambodia, Thailand and Laos.* New York: Praeger, 1971.

Kirkpatrick, Lyman D., Jr. *The Real CIA.* New York: Macmillan, 1968.

Kirkpatrick, Sandra. "Battle Casualty." *American Journal of Nursing* (July 1968).

Kissinger, Henry A. *Diplomacy.* New York: Simon & Schuster, 1994.

———. *White House Years.* Boston: Little, Brown, 1979.

———. *Years of Upheaval.* Boston: Little, Brown, 1982.

Koburger, Charles W., Jr. *The French Navy in Indochina.* New York: Praeger, 1991.

Koh, Byung Chul. *The Foreign Policy of North Korea.* New York: Praeger, 1969.

Kolko, Gabriel. *Anatomy of a War: Vietnam, the United States, and the Modern Historical Experience.* New York: Pantheon, 1985.

Komer, Robert W. *Bureaucracy at War: U.S. Performance in the Vietnam Conflict.* Boulder, CO: Westview Press, 1986.

———. "Impact of Pacification on Insurgency in South Vietnam." *Journal of International Affairs* 25 (1971): 48–69.

Korb, Lawrence J. *The Joint Chiefs of Staff: The First Twenty-Five Years.* Bloomington: Indiana University Press, 1976.

Kraslow, David, and Stuart H. Loory. *The Secret Search for Peace in Vietnam.* New York: Random House, 1968.

Krepinevich, Andrew F., Jr. *The Army and Vietnam.* Baltimore: Johns Hopkins University Press, 1986.

Krulak, Victor H. *First to Fight.* Annapolis, MD: U.S. Naval Institute Press, 1984.

Kulka, Richard A., et al., eds. *National Vietnam Veterans Readjustment Study: Tables of Findings and Technical Appendices.* New York: Brunner/Mazel, 1990.

———. *Trauma and the Vietnam War Generation: Report of Findings of the National Vietnam Veterans Readjustment Study.* New York: Brunner/Mazel, 1990.

Kutler, Stanley I. *The Wars of Watergate: The Last Crisis of Richard Nixon.* New York: Alfred A. Knopf, 1990.

Kutler, Stanley I., ed. *Encyclopedia of the Vietnam War.* New York: Simon & Schuster, 1996.

Kux, Dennis. *Estranged Democracies, 1941–1991: India and the United States.* Washington, DC: Sage, 1994.

Lacouture, Jean. *De Gaulle. The Rebel, 1890–1944.* Translated by Patrick O'Brian. New York: W. W. Norton, 1990.

———. *Ho Chi Minh: A Political Biography.* New York: Random House, 1968.

———. *Pierre Mendès-France,* translated by George Holoch. New York: Holmes & Meier, 1984.

Lafont, Pierre-Bernard. "Les Frontieres en Mer de Chine Meridionale." In *Les Frontieres du Vietnam: Histoire des Frontieres de la Peninsule Indochinoise.* Paris: L'Harmattan, 1989.

Lake, Anthony, ed. *The Vietnam Legacy: The War, American Society and the Future of American Foreign Policy.* New York: Council on Foreign Relations, 1976.

Lake, Anthony, I. M. Destler, and Leslie H. Gelb. *Our Own Worst Enemy: The Unmaking of American Foreign Policy.* New York: Simon & Schuster, 1984.

Lamb, Christopher Jon. *Belief Systems and Decision Making in the Mayaguez Crisis.* Gainesville: University of Florida Press, 1988.

Lamson, Peggy. *Speaking of Galbraith: A Personal Portrait.* New York: Ticknor & Fields, 1991.

Laniel, Joseph. *Jours de Gloire et Jours Cruels (1908–1958).* 1971.

Lankford, Nelson D. *The Last American Aristocrat: The Biography of Ambassador David K. E. Bruce.* Boston: Little, Brown, 1996.

Lanning, Michael L. *Vietnam at the Movies.* New York: Fawcett Columbine, 1994.

Lanning, Michael L., and Dan Cragg. *Inside the VC and the NVA.* New York: Ballantine Books, 1992.

Lansdale, Edward G. *In the Midst of Wars: An American's Mission to Southeast Asia.* New York: Harper & Row, 1972.

Larsen, Stanley Robert, and James Lawton Collins, Jr. *Allied Participation in Vietnam.* Washington, DC: U.S. Government Printing Office, 1975.

Larzelere, Alex. *The Coast Guard at War. Vietnam, 1965–1975.* Annapolis, MD: Naval Institute Press, 1997.

Lavalle, A. J. C. *Air Power and the 1972 Spring Invasion.* U.S. Air Force Southeast Asia Monograph Series Vol. 2, Monograph 3. Washington, DC: Office of Air Force History, 1985.

Lavelle, A. J. C., ed. *The Tale of Two Bridges and the Battle for the Skies over North Vietnam.* Washington, DC: U.S. Government Printing Office, 1976.

Lê Duân. "Under the Glorious Party Banner, for Independence, Freedom, and Socialism, Let Us Advance and Achieve New Victories." *Nhân Dân* (Hà Nôi), 14 February 1970; translated in JUSPAO (Sài Gòn), *Viet Nam Documents and Research Notes* No. 77 (April 1970), p. 14.

Le Gro, William E. *Vietnam from Cease Fire to Capitulation.* Washington, DC: U.S. Army Center of Military History, 1981.

Lê Huu Muc. *Huân Dich Thâp Diêu: Thánh Du Cua Vua Thánh Tô, Diên Nghia Cua Vua Duc Tông (Ten Moral Maxims: Imperial Teachings by Emperor Thanh To and Translation into Nom by Emperor Tu Duc).* Sài Gòn: Phu Quôc Vu Khanh Đac Trách Van Hoa, 1971.

Lê Kim Ngân. *Tô Chuc Chính Quyên Trung Uong Duoi Triêu Lê Thánh Tông, 1460–1497 (Organization of the Central Government under Le Thanh Tong, 1460–1497).* Sài Gòn: Bô Quôc Gia Giáo Duc, 1963.

Le Prestre, P. "European Defense Community." In *Historical Dictionary of the French Fourth and Fifth Republics, 1946–1991,* edited by Wayne Northcutt. Westport, CT: Greenwood Press, 1992.

Lê Thanh Khôi. *Histoire de Viêt Nam des origines à 1858.* Paris: Sudestasie, 1981.

———. *Le Viet Nam: Histoire et Civilisation.* Paris: Editions de Minuit, 1955.

Leary, William M. "The CIA and the 'Secret' War in Laos: The Battle for Skyline Ridge, 1971–1972." *Journal of Military History* 59 (July 1995): 505–517.

Lebar, Frank, Gerald C. Hickey, and John Musgrave. *Ethnic Groups of Mainland Southeast Asia.* New Haven, CT: Human Relations Area Files Press, 1964.

Lee, Chae-jin. *Zhou Enlai, The Early Years.* Stanford, CA: Stanford University Press, 1994.

LeGro, William E. "The Enemy's Jungle Cover Was No Match for the Finding Capabilities of the Army's Radio Research Units." *Vietnam* 3 (June 1990): 12–20.

LeMay, Curtis E. *America Is in Danger.* New York: Funk & Wagnalls, 1968.

LeMay, Curtis E., with MacKinlay Kantor. *Mission with LeMay: My Story.* New York: Doubleday, 1965.

Lemish, Michael G. *War Dogs: Canines in Combat.* Washington: Brassey's, 1996.

Lesher, Stephan. *George Wallace: American Populist*. Reading, MA: Addison-Wesley, 1994.

Leslie, Jacques. *The Mark: A War Correspondent's Memoir of Vietnam and Cambodia*. New York: Four Walls Eight Windows, 1995.

Levant, Victor. *Quiet Complicity: Canadian Involvement in the Vietnam War*. Toronto: Between the Lines, 1986.

Levie, Howard S. " Maltreatment of Prisoners of War in Vietnam." *Boston University Law Review* 48 (1968): 323–359.

———. "Weapons of Warfare." In *Law and Responsibility in Warfare: The Vietnam Experience*, edited by Peter D. Trooboff. Chapel Hill: University of North Carolina, 1975.

Lewin, Isaac. *War on War*. New York: Shengold, 1969.

Lewinski, Jorge. *The Camera at War*. New York: Simon & Schuster, 1978.

Lewis, Judy, ed. *Minority Cultures of Laos: Kammu, Lua', Lahu, Hmong, and Iu-Mien*. Rancho Cordova, CA: Folsom Cordova Unified School District, 1992.

Lewis, Lloyd B. *The Tainted War: Culture and Identity in Vietnam War Narratives*. Westport, CT: Greenwood Press, 1985.

Lewy, Guenter. *America in Vietnam*. New York: Oxford University Press, 1978.

Li Zhisui. *The Private Life of Chairman Mao*. New York: Random House, 1994.

Lichtenstein, Nelson, ed. *Political Profiles: The Johnson Years*. New York: Facts on File, 1976.

Lifton, Robert J. *Home from the War: Vietnam Veterans, Neither Victims nor Executioners*. New York: Simon & Schuster, 1973.

Lilienthal, D. E., and Vu Quôc Thúc. *The Postwar Development of the Republic of Vietnam: Policies and Programs*. New York: Praeger, 1970.

Linderer, Gary. "The 101st Airborne Division: The Vietnam Experience." In *101st Airborne Division: Screaming Eagles*, edited by Robert J. Martin. Paducah, KY: Turner, 1995.

Lippard, Lucy R. *A Different War: Vietnam in Art*. Seattle: Real Comet Press, 1990.

Lippman, Walter. *The Cold War: A Study in U.S. Foreign Policy*. New York: Harper & Row, 1947.

Lipsman, Samuel, Stephen Weiss, and the editors of Boston Publishing Company. *The False Peace, 1972–1974*. The Vietnam Experience, edited by Robert Manning. Boston: Boston Publishing, 1985.

Littauer, Raphael, and Norman Uphoff, ed. *The Air War in Indochina*. Boston: Beacon Press, 1971

Litwak, Robert S. *Détente and the Nixon Doctrine: American Foreign Policy and the Pursuit of Stability, 1969–1976*. Cambridge, MA: Cambridge University Press, 1984.

Locher, Frances Carol, ed. *Contemporary Authors*. Vols. 73–76. Detroit: Gale Research, 1978.

Lockhart, Greg. *Nation in Arms: The Origins of the People's Army of Vietnam*. Sydney: Allen & Unwin, 1989.

Logue, William. *Léon Blum: The Formative Years, 1872–1914*. DeKalb: Northern Illinois University Press, 1973.

Loh, Pichon. *The Early Chiang Kai-shek*. New York: Columbia University Press, 1971.

Lomperis, Timothy J. *The War Everyone Lost—and Won: America's Intervention in Viet Nam's Twin Struggles*. Rev. ed. Washington, DC: CQ Press, 1993.

Lomperis, Timothy J., and John Clark Pratt. *Reading The Wind: The Literature of the Vietnam War*. Durham, NC: Duke University Press, 1987.

Longmire, R. A. *Soviet Relations with South-East Asia: An Historical Survey*. London: Keegan Paul International, 1989.

Louvre, Alf. "The Reluctant Historians: Sontag, Mailer, and American Culture Critics in the 1960's." *Prose Studies* (May 1986): 47–61.

Love, Robert W., Jr. *History of the U.S. Navy*. Vol. 2, *1942–1991*. Harrisburg, PA: Stackpole, 1992.

Lucas, Jim Griffing. *Agnew: Profile in Conflict*. New York: Award, 1970.

Luce, Don, and John Sommer. *Viet Nam: The Unheard Voices*. Ithaca, NY: Cornell University Press, 1969.

Luskin, John. *Lippmann, Liberty, and the Press*. Tuscaloosa: University of Alabama, 1972.

Lynd, Alice, ed. *We Won't Go: Personal Accounts of War Objectors*. Boston: Beacon Press, 1968.

Lyttle, Bradford. *The Chicago Anti-Vietnam War Movement*. Chicago: Midwest Pacifist Center, 1988.

MacFarquhar, Roderick. *The Politics of China, 1949–1989*. New York: Cambridge University Press, 1993.

Maclean, Donald. *British Foreign Policy: The Years since Suez, 1956–1968*. New York: Stein & Day, 1970.

Maclear, Michael. *The Ten Thousand Day War: Vietnam, 1945–1975*. New York: St. Martin's Press, 1981.

MacMillan, James F. *Napoleon III*. London: Longman, 1991.

MacPherson, Myra. *Long Time Passing. Vietnam and the Haunted Generation*. New York: Doubleday, 1984.

Mai Thi Tu. *Women in Vietnam*. Hanoi: Foreign Languages Publishing House, 1978.

Mailer, Norman. *The Armies of the Night*. New York: New American Library, 1968.

———. *Miami and the Siege of Chicago: An Informal History of the Republican and Democratic Conventions of 1968*. New York: New American Library, 1968.

Maitland, Terrence, Peter McInerney, and the editors of Boston Publishing Company. *A Contagion of War*. The Vietnam Experience, edited by Robert Manning. Boston: Boston Publishing, 1983.

Malia, Martin. *The Soviet Tragedy*. New York: Free Press, 1994.

Malo, Jean Jacques, and Tony Williams. *Vietnam War Films: Over 600 Feature, Made-for-TV, Pilot and Short Movies, 1939–1992*. Jefferson, NC: McFarland, 1994.

Manchester, William. *American Caesar: Douglas MacArthur, 1880–1964*. London: Arrow Books, 1978.

Maneli, Mieczyslaw. *The War of the Vanquished*. New York: Harper & Row, 1969.

Mangold, Thomas. *The Tunnels of Cu Chi*. New York: Random House, 1985.

Marks, Frederick W., III. *Power and Peace: The Diplomacy of John Foster Dulles*. Westport, CT: Praeger, 1993.

Marolda, Edward J. *By Sea, Air, and Land: An Illustrated History of the U.S. Navy and the War in Southeast Asia*. Washington, DC: Naval Historical Center, 1994.

Marolda, Edward J., and Oscar P. Fitzgerald. *The United States Navy and the Vietnam Conflict*. Vol. 2: *From Military Assistance to Combat, 1959–1965*. Washington, DC: Naval Historical Center, 1986.

Marolda, Edward J., and G. Wesley Pryce III. *A Short History of the United States Navy and the Southeast Asia Conflict, 1950–1975*. Washington, DC: Naval Historical Center, 1984.

Marr, David G. *Vietnam 1945: The Quest for Power*. Berkeley: University of California Press, 1996.

———. *Vietnam: World Bibliographical Series*. Oxford: Clio Press, 1992.

———. *Vietnamese Anticolonialism, 1885–1925*. Berkeley: University of California, 1971.

———. *Vietnamese Tradition on Trial, 1920–1945*. Berkeley: University of California Press, 1981.

Marr, David G., and Christine White, eds. *Postwar Vietnam: Dilemmas in Socialist Development*. Ithaca, NY: Cornell University Southeast Asia Program, 1988.

Marshall, Kathryn. *In the Combat Zone*. New York: Penguin Books, 1987.

Marshall, S. L. A. *Battles in the Monsoon: Campaigning in the Central Highlands Vietnam, Summer 1966*. New York: William Morrow, 1967.

———. *Bird*. New York: Cowles, 1968.

———. *Bringing Up the Rear: A Memoir*. San Raphael, CA: Presidio Press, 1979.

———. *The Fields of Bamboo*. New York: Dial Press, 1967

———. *Men against Fire*. New York: William Morrow, 1947.

——— . *Vietnam: Three Battles*. New York: Da Capo Press, 1982.

Martin, John Bartlow. *Adlai Stevenson and the World*. Garden City, NY: Doubleday, 1978.

——— . *Adlai Stevenson of Illinois*. Garden City, NY: Doubleday, 1977.

Martin, Robert, ed. *1st Air Cavalry Division: Memoirs of the First Team, Vietnam, August 1965–December 1969*. Paducah, KY: Turner, 1995.

Mason, Todd. *Perot: An Unauthorized Biography*. Homewood, IL: Business One Irwin, 1990.

Matthews, Ronald. *The Death of the Fourth Republic*. New York: Praeger, 1954.

Matusow, Allen J. *The Unraveling of America: A History of Liberalism in the 1960s*. New York: Harper & Row, 1984.

Maurois, André. *Lyautey*. New York: D. Appleton, 1931.

Mayers, David. *George Kennan and the Dilemmas of US Foreign Policy*. New York: Oxford University Press, 1988.

Mazzeo, Donatella, and Chiara Silvi Antonini. *Monuments of Civilization: Ancient Cambodia*. New York: Grosset & Dunlap, 1978.

McAleavy, Henry. *Black Flags in Vietnam. The Story of a Chinese Intervention*. New York: Macmillan, 1968.

McCarthy, Eugene. *The Year of the People*. New York: Doubleday, 1969.

McClintock, Michael. *Instruments of Statecraft: U.S. Guerrilla Warfare, Counterinsurgency, and Counter-Terrorism, 1940–1990*. New York: Pantheon Books, 1992.

McClintock, Robert. "The River War in Indochina." *U.S. Naval Institute Proceedings* (December 1954), 1303–1311.

McCloy, John J. *The Challenge to American Foreign Policy*. Cambridge, MA: Harvard University Press, 1953.

McConnell, Malcolm. *Inside Hanoi's Secret Archives*. New York: Simon & Schuster, 1995.

McCoy, Alfred. *The Politics of Heroin*. New York: Lawrence Hill Books, 1991.

McCoy, J. W. *Secrets of the Viet Cong*. New York: Hippocrene Books, 1992.

McCullough, David. *Truman*. New York: Simon & Schuster, 1992.

McKahin, George McT. *Intervention: How America Became Involved in Vietnam*. New York: Alfred A. Knopf, 1986.

McLellan, David S. *Cyrus Vance*. Vol. 20, *The American Secretaries of State and Their Diplomacy*, edited by Robert H. Ferrell. Totawa, NJ: Rowman & Allanheld, 1985.

——— . *Dean Acheson: The State Department Years*. New York: Dodd, Mead, 1976.

McMahon, Robert J. *Cold War on the Periphery: The United States, India, and Pakistan*. New York: Columbia University Press, 1994.

McMaster, H. R. *Dereliction of Duty: Lyndon Johnson, Robert McNamara, The Joint Chiefs of Staff, and the Lies That Led to Vietnam*. New York: HarperCollins, 1997.

McNamara, Robert S., with Brian VanDeMark. *In Retrospect, the Tragedy and Lessons of Vietnam*. New York: Times Books, 1995.

McNeill, Ian. *The Team: Australian Army Advisers in Vietnam 1962–1972*. Canberra: Australian War Memorial, 1984.

McReynolds, David. "Pacifists and the Vietnam Antiwar Movement." In *Give Peace A Chance: Explaining the Vietnam Antiwar Movement*, edited by Melvin Small and William D. Hoover. Syracuse, NY: Syracuse University Press, 1992, pp. 53–70.

Meconis, Charles. *With Clumsy Grace: The American Catholic Left, 1961–1975*. New York: Continuum, 1979.

Medvedev, R. A., and A. A. Medvedev. *Khrushchev*. New York: W. W. Norton, 1978.

Meisler, Jurg. "Koh Chang. The Unknown Battle. Franco-Thai War of 1940–41." *World War II Investigator* (London, England) II, no. 14 (1989), 26–34.

Meisner, Maurice. *Mao's China: A History of the People's Republic*. New York: Free Press, 1977.

Melson, Charles D., and Curtis G. Arnold. *U.S. Marines in Vietnam, 1954–1973. An Anthology and Annotated Bibliography*. Washington, DC: Headquarters, U.S. Marine Corps, 1985.

Mendès-France, Pierre, and Gabriel Ardant. *Economics and Action*. New York: Columbia University Press, 1955.

Merry, Robert W. *Taking on the World: Joseph and Stewart Alsop—Guardians of the American Century*. New York: Viking, 1996.

Meyer, Harold J. *Hanging Sam: A Military Biography of General Samuel T. Williams*. Denton: University of North Texas Press, 1990.

Middleton Drew, ed. *Air War—Vietnam*. New York: Arno Press, 1978.

Miles, Donna. "A Real Hero: Col. Nick Rowe Assassinated in the Philippines." *Soldiers* (June 1989): 24–25.

Miller, Arthur H., Warren E. Miller, Alden S. Raine, and Thad A. Brown. "A Majority Party in Disarray: Policy Polarization in the 1972 Election." *American Political Science Review* (September 1976): 753–778.

Miller, David. "Giap's Army." *War Monthly* 28 (July 1976): 26–33.

Miller, James. *Democracy Is in the Streets: From Port Huron to The Siege of Chicago*. New York: Simon & Schuster, 1987.

Miller, Kenn. *Tiger the Lurp Dog*. Boston: Little, Brown, 1983.

Millet, Allan R. *Semper Fidelis: The History of the United States Marine Corps*. New York: Macmillan, 1980.

Minear, Larry. "Private Aid and Public Policy: A Case Study." *IndoChina Issues* (June 1988): 1–8.

Miscamble, Wilson D. *George F. Kennan and the Making of American Foreign Policy, 1947–1950*. Princeton, NJ: Princeton University Press, 1992.

Misra, Kalidas. "Print-Journalism and Vietnam: Shifting Perspectives." *Indian Journal of American Studies* 15, no. 2 (1985): 105–111.

Mitchell, Tom, ed. *DogMan* (Vietnam Dog Handlers Association newsletter) 1, no. 1 (March 1994); 3, no. 2 (March 1996).

Mitford, Jessica. *The Trial of Dr. Spock*. New York: Alfred A. Knopf, 1969.

Moeller, Susan D. *Shooting War: Photography and the American Experience of Combat*. New York: Basic Books, 1989.

Moise, Edwin E. *Land Reform in China and North Vietnam: Consolidating the Revolution at the Village Level*. Chapel Hill: University of North Carolina Press, 1983.

——— . *Tonkin Gulf and the Escalation of the Vietnam War*. Chapel Hill: University of North Carolina Press, 1996.

——— . "Why Westmoreland Gave Up." *Pacific Affairs* 58, no. 4 (Winter 1985–1986): 663–673.

Momeyer, William W. *Airpower in Three Wars*. Washington, DC: U.S. Government Printing Office, 1978.

Montero, Darrel. *Vietnamese Americans: Patterns of Resettlement and Socioeconomic Adaptations in the United States*. Boulder, CO: Westview Press, 1979.

Mooney, James L., ed. *Dictionary of American Naval Fighting Ships*. Washington, DC: U.S. Navy Department, 1959.

Mooney, Louise, ed. *The Annual Obituary 1992*. Detroit: St. James Press, 1993.

Moore, Harold G., and Joseph Galloway. *We Were Soldiers Once . . . and Young: Ia Drang, The Battle That Changed the War in Vietnam*. New York: Random House, 1992.

Mordal, Jacques. *Marine Indochine*. Paris: Amiot-Dumont, 1953.

Mordal, Jacques, and Gabriel Auphan. *La Marine Française pendant la Deuxième Guerre Mondiale*. Paris: Hachette, 1958.

Mordant, Eugène. *Au Service de la France en Indochine, 1941–1945*. Sài Gòn: IFOM, 1950.

Morella, Joe, Edward Epstein, and Eleanor Clark. *The Amazing Careers of Bob Hope*. New Rochelle, NY: Arlington House, 1973.

Morgan, Edward P. *The 60s Experience: Hard Lessons about Modern America*. Philadelphia: Temple University Press, 1991.

Morgan, Joseph G. *The Vietnam Lobby; The American Friends of Vietnam, 1955–1975*. Chapel Hill: University of North Carolina Press, 1997.

Moritz, Charles, ed. *Current Biography 1980*. New York: H. W. Wilson, 1980.

——— . *Current Biography Yearbook 1967*. New York: H. W. Wilson, 1967.

——— . *Current Biography Yearbook 1983*. New York: H. W. Wilson, 1983.

——— . *Current Biography Yearbook 1984*. New York: H. W. Wilson, 1984.

——— . *Current Biography Yearbook 1988*. New York: H. W. Wilson, 1988.

Morris, Roger. *Haig*. New York: Playboy Press, 1982.

—— . *Uncertain Greatness: Henry Kissinger and American Foreign Policy*. New York: Harper & Row, 1977.

Morrison, Wilbur H. *The Elephant and the Tiger: The Full Story of the Vietnam War*. New York: Hippocrene Books, 1990.

Morrocco, John. *Rain of Fire: Air War, 1969–1973*. The Vietnam Experience, edited by Robert Manning. Boston: Boston Publishing, 1985.

—— . *Thunder from Above: Air War, 1941–1968*. The Vietnam Experience, edited by Robert Manning. Boston: Boston Publishing, 1984.

Moskin, J. Robert. *The U.S. Marine Corps Story*. Rev. Ed. New York: McGraw-Hill, 1982.

Mosley, Leonard. *Dulles: A Biography of Eleanor, Allen, and John Foster Dulles and Their Family Network*. New York: Dial Press, 1978.

Moss, George Donelson. *Vietnam: An American Ordeal*. Englewood Cliffs, NJ: Prentice-Hall, 1990.

Moyers, Bill D. *Listening to America: A Traveller Rediscovers His Country*. New York: Harper's Magazine Press, 1971.

Moynihan, Daniel P. *Maximum Feasible Misunderstanding: Community Action in the War on Poverty*. New York: Free Press, 1970.

Mrozek, Donald J. "Nathan F. Twining: New Dimensions, a New Look." In *Makers of the Modern Air Force*, edited by John L. Frisbee. Washington, DC: Pergamon-Brassey's, 1989.

Muir, Malcolm, Jr. *Black Shoes and Blue Water: Surface Warfare in the United States Navy, 1945–1975*. Washington, DC: Naval Historical Center, 1996.

—— . *The Iowa Class Battleships*. Poole, Dorset, UK: Blandford Press, 1987.

Mullins, William S., ed. *A Decade of Progress: The United States Army Medical Department: 1959–1969*. Washington, DC: Office of the Surgeon General, 1971.

Murphy, Bruce Allen. *Fortas; The Rise and Ruin of a Supreme Court Justice*. New York: William Morrow, 1988.

Murphy, Edward F. *Dak Tô: The 173rd Airborne Brigade in South Vietnam's Central Highlands, June–November 1967*. Novato, CA: Presidio Press, 1993.

Murphy, Robert D. *Diplomat among Warriors*. New York: Doubleday, 1964.

Nalty, Bernard C. *Air Power and the Fight for Khe Sanh*. Washington, DC: Office of Air Force History, 1973.

—— . *Strength for the Fight: A History of Black Americans in the Military*. New York: Free Press, 1986.

National Guard Association of the United States. *The Abrams Doctrine: Then, Now and in the Future*. Washington, DC: National Guard Association, 1994.

National Guard Bureau. *A NGB Activity Input to Project Corona Harvest on Air National Guard Support of U.S. Air Force Operations in Southeast Asia, 1954 to March 31, 1968*. Vol. I. Washington, DC: National Guard Bureau, 1970.

Naval Air Systems Command. *Antitank Bomb Cluster Mk 20, Mods 2, 3, 4 and 6 and Antipersonnel/Antimateriel Bomb Cluster CBU-59/B*. NAVAIR 11–5A-3. Washington, DC: U.S. Government Printing Office, 1975.

"Naval Facilities Engineering Command History, 1965–1974." Vol. 2. Report Symbol OPNAV 5750–1. Washington, DC, NAVFAC Historian's Office, 1975, unpublished.

Navarre, Henri. *Agonie de l'Indochine, 1953–1954*. Paris: Plon, 1956.

Neel, Spurgeon. *Medical Support of the U.S. Army in Vietnam, 1965–1972*. Washington, DC: U.S. Army Center of Military History, 1973.

Newman, Edgar L. *Historical Dictionary of France from the 1815 Restoration to the Second Empire*. New York: Greenwood Press, 1987.

Newman, John. *Vietnam War Literature*, 3d ed. Metuchen, NJ: Scarecrow Press, 1996.

—— . *Vietnam War Literature: An Annotated Bibliography of Imaginative Works about Americans Fighting in Vietnam*. Metuchen, NJ: Scarecrow Press, 1988.

Newman, John M. *JFK and Vietnam: Deception, Intrigue, and the Struggle for Power*. New York: Warner Books, 1992.

Ngô Quang Truong. *The Easter Offensive of 1972*. Washington, DC: U.S. Government Printing Office, 1980.

—— . *Territorial Forces*. Washington, DC: U.S. Army Center of Military History, 1981.

Ngô Vinh Hai. "Postwar Vietnam: Political Economy." In *Coming to Terms: Indochina, the United States, and the War*, edited by Douglas Allen and Ngô Vinh Long. Boulder, CO: Westview Press, 1991, pp. 65–88.

Nguyên Cao Ky. *Twenty Years and Twenty Days*. New York: Stein & Day, 1976.

Nguyên Đuc Phuong. *Nhung Trân Đánh Lich Su Trong Chiên Tranh Viet Nam 1963–1975*. Glendale, CA: Đai Nam, 1993.

Nguyên Đình Hòa. *Language in Vietnamese Society*. Carbondale, IL: Asia Books, 1980.

Nguyên Duy Hinh. *Vietnamization and the Cease-Fire*. Washington, DC: U.S. Army Center of Military History, 1980.

Nguyen Huyen Anh. *Viêt Nam Danh Nhân Tu Điên (Dictionary of Vietnamese Great Men and Women)*. Houston: Zieleks, 1990.

Nguyên Khac Kham. "Vietnamese National Language and Modern Vietnamese Literature." *East Asian Cultural Studies* (Tokyo) 15, no. 1–4 (1976): 177–194.

Nguyên Khac Ngu. *Đai Cuong Vê Các Đang Phái Chính Tri Viêt Nam (Overview of Political Parties in Vietnam)*. Montreal: Tu Sách Nghiên Cuu Su Đia, 1989.

—— . *Nhung Ngày Cuôi Cung Cua Viêt Nam Công Hòa (The Last Days of the Republic of Vietnam)*. Montreal: Nhom Nghiên Cuu Su Đia, 1979.

Nguyên Khac Viên. *The Long Resistance, 1858–1975*. Ha Noi: Foreign Language Publishing House, 1975.

—— . *Vietnam: A Long History*. Hà Nôi: Foreign Languages Publishing House, 1987.

Nguyên Long. *After Saigon Fell*. Berkeley: University of California Press, 1981.

Nguyên Long Thanh Nam. *Phât Giáo Hòa Hao Trong Dòng Lich Su Dân Tôc*. Santa Fe Spring, CA: Tâp San Duoc Tu Bi, 1991.

Nguyên Thê Anh. "Introduction à la connaissance de la peninsule indochinoise: Le Viet Nam." In *Tuyên Tâp Ngôn Ngu Van Tu*. Campbell, CA: Dòng Viêt, 1993.

—— . *Viêt Nam Duoi Thoi Pháp Đô Hô (Vietnam under French Domination)*. Sài Gòn: Lua Thiêng, 1970.

Nguyen Thi Đinh. *No Other Road to Take: Memoir of Mrs. Nguyen Thi Dinh*. Ithaca, NY: Cornell Southeast Asia Studies Program, 1976.

Nguyên Tiên Hang and Jerrold L. Schechter. *The Palace File*. New York: Harper & Row, 1986.

Nguyên Van Ban. *Giac Co Đen: Môt Ông Cu Già 90 Tuôi Kê Truyên (The Black Flags Pirates, as Told by a Ninety-year-old Man)*. Hà Nôi: Trung Bac Thu Xã, 1941.

Nguyên Van Canh. "Thanh Niên Và Các Phong Trào Chông Pháp Thoi Cân Đai (1900–1945)." In *Tuyên Tâp Ngôn Ngo Và Van Hoc Viêt Nam— Essays on Vietnamese Language and Literature*, No. 2, Fascicle II. San Jose, CA: Mekong-Tynan, 1994, pp. 491–505.

—— . *Vietnam under Communism, 1975–1982*. Stanford, CA: Hoover Institute Press, 1983.

Nichols, John B., and Barrett Tillman. *On Yankee Station: The Naval Air War over Vietnam*. Annapolis, MD: Naval Institute Press, 1987.

Nixon, Richard M. *No More Vietnams*. New York: Avon Books, 1985.

—— . *RN: The Memoirs of Richard Nixon*. New York: Grosset & Dunlap, 1978.

Nolan, Keith William. *Into Cambodia: Spring Campaign, Summer Offensive, 1970*. Novato, CA: Presidio Press, 1990.

—— . *Into Laos: The Story of Dewey Canyon II/Lam Son 719*. Novato, CA: Presidio Press, 1986.

—— . *The Magnificent Bastards: The Joint Army-Marine Defense of Dong Ha, 1968*. Novato, CA: Presidio Press, 1994.

—— . *Operation Buffalo: U.S.M.C. Fight for the DMZ*. New York: Dell, 1991.

Nordeen, Lon O. Jr. *Air Warfare in the Missile Age*. Washington, DC: Smithsonian Institution Press, 1985.

Norman, Elizabeth M. "A Study of Female Military Nurses in Vietnam during the War Years 1965–1973." *Journal of Nursing History* (November 1986).

Norris, Margot. "Painting Vietnam Combat: The Art of Leonard Cutrow." *Michigan Quarterly Review* (Spring 1989).

Northcutt, Wayne. ed. *Historical Dictionary of the French Fourth and Fifth Republics, 1946–1991.* Westport, CT: Greenwood Press, 1992.

O'Ballance, Edgar. *The Wars in Vietnam, 1954–1980.* New York: Hippocrene Books, 1981.

O'Neill, William L. *Coming Apart: An Informal History of America in the 1960s.* New York: Times Books, 1971.

O'Reilly, Kenneth. *"Racial Matters." The FBI's Secret File on Black America 1960–1972.* New York: Free Press, 1989.

Oakley, Meredith L. *On the Make: The Rise of Bill Clinton.* Washington, DC: Regnery Publishing, Inc., 1994.

Oates, Stephen B. *Let The Trumpet Sound: The Life of Martin Luther King, Jr.* New York: Harper & Row, 1982.

Oberdorfer, Don. *Tet!* Garden City, NY: Doubleday, 1971.

Office of Information Management and Statistics. *Data on Vietnam Era Veterans.* Washington, DC: Veterans Administration, 1983.

Olson, James S., ed. *Dictionary of the Vietnam War.* New York: Greenwood Press, 1988.

Olson, James S., and Randy Roberts. *Where the Domino Fell: America and Vietnam, 1945 to 1990.* New York: St. Martin's Press, 1991.

Ortiz, Elizabeth. "The Mekong Project of Vietnam." *Far Eastern Economic Review* XXV (6 November 1958): 596–597.

Osborne, Milton. *River Road to China: The Mekong River Expedition, 1866–73.* New York: Liveright, 1975.

Osborne, Milton. *Southeast Asia: An Illustrated History.* 5th ed. Sydney: Allen & Unwin, 1990.

——— . *Strategic Hamlets in Vietnam.* Data Paper 55. Ithaca, NY: Cornell University Southeast Asia Program, April 1965.

Ott, David E. *Field Artillery, 1954–1973.* Vietnam Studies Series. Washington, DC: Department of the Army, 1975.

"Our Man in Vientiane." *The Washington Post,* 1 October 1972.

Outline History of the Vietnam Workers' Party, 1930–1975. Hanoi: Foreign Languages Publishing House, 1978.

Oye, Kenneth A. "The Domain of Choice: International Constraints and Carter Administration Foreign Policy." In *Eagle Entangled: U.S. Foreign Policy in a Complex World,* edited by Kenneth A. Oye. New York: Longman, 1979.

Page, Benjamin I., and Richard A. Brody. "Policy Voting and the Electoral Process: The Vietnam War Issue." *American Political Science Review* 66 (September 1972): 979–995.

Palmer, Bruce, Jr. *The 25-Year War: America's Military Role in Vietnam.* Lexington: University Press of Kentucky, 1984.

Palmer, Dave Richard. *Readings in Current Military History.* West Point, NY: Department of Military Art and Engineering, U.S. Military Academy, 1969.

——— . *The Summons of the Trumpet: U.S.-Vietnam in Perspective.* San Rafael, CA: Presidio Press, 1977.

Palmer, Gregory. *The McNamara Strategy and the Vietnam War: Program Budgeting in the Pentagon, 1960–1968.* Westport, CT: Greenwood Press, 1978.

Pao-min Chang. *Beijing, Hanoi, and the Overseas Chinese.* Berkeley: University of California Press, 1982.

Paret, Peter. *French Revolutionary Warfare from Indochina to Algeria. The Analysis of a Political and Military Doctrine.* New York: Praeger, 1964.

Patti, Archimedes L. A. *Why Viet Nam? Prelude to America's Albatross.* Berkeley: University of California Press, 1980.

Pearson, Lester B. *Mike: The Memoirs of the Right Honourable Lester B. Pearson.* New York: Quadrangle Books, 1972.

Pearson, Willard. *The War in the Northern Provinces 1966–1968.* Washington, DC: U.S. Army Center of Military History, 1975.

Peers, William R. *The My Lai Inquiry.* New York: W. W. Norton, 1979.

Peers, William R., and Dean Brelis. *Behind the Burma Road: The Story of America's Most Successful Guerrilla Force.* Boston: Little, Brown, 1963.

Pentagon Papers as Published by The New York Times. New York: Bantam Books, 1971.

Pentagon Papers: The Defense Department History of United States Decisionmaking on Vietnam. Boston: Beacon Press, 1971–1972.

Persico, Joseph. *The Imperial Rockefeller.* New York: Simon & Schuster, 1982.

Personalities of the South Vietnam Liberation Movement. Tran Phu: Foreign Relations Commission of the South Vietnam National Front for Liberation, 1965.

Pham Cao Duong. *Lich Su Dân Tôc Viêt Nam, Quyên I: Thoi Ky Lâp Quôc (History of the Vietnamese People, Vol. I: The Making of the Nation).* Fountain Valley, CA: Truyên Thông Viêt, 1987.

——— . *Vietnamese Peasants under French Domination (1861–1945).* Lanham, MD: University Press of America, 1985.

Pham Duy. *Hôi K˝ (Memoirs).* Midway City, CA: PDC Musical Productions, 1991.

Pham Kim Vinh. *The Vietnamese Culture.* Solana Beach, CA: PM Enterprises, 1995.

Pham Van Son. *Viêt Su Toàn Thu.* Sài Gòn: Thu Lâm Ân Thu Quán, 1960; reprinted at Glendale, CA: Dainamco, n.d.

Pham Van Son and Le Van Duong, eds. *The Viet Cong Tet Offensive.* Saigon: Republic of Vietnam Armed Forces, 1969.

Phan Khoang. *Viêt Nam Pháp Thuôc Su: 1862–1945 (The History of Vietnam under French Rule, 1862–1945).* Sài Gòn: Phu Quôc Vu Khanh Đac Trách Van Hoa), 1971.

Phan Quang Đán. "From the Homeland to Overseas . . . ." *Viet Marketing and Business Report* 16 (Oct/Nov/Dec 1994): 3–4.

Phan Trân Chuc. *Vua Hàm Nghi.* Hà Nôi: Chinh Ky, 1951.

Phelps, J. Alfred. *Chappie. America's First Black Four Star General. The Life and Times of Daniel James, Jr.* Novato, CA: Presidio Press, 1991.

Pierce, J. A., et al., eds. *LORAN: Long Range Navigation.* Massachusetts Institute of Technology Radiation Laboratory Series, edited by Louis N. Ridenour. New York: McGraw-Hill, 1948.

Pike, Douglas, ed. *The Bunker Papers: Reports to the President from Vietnam, 1967–1973.* Berkeley, CA: Institute of East Asian Studies, 1990.

——— . *A History of Vietnamese Communism, 1923–1978.* Stanford, CA: Hoover Institute Press, 1978.

——— . *PAVN: People's Army of Vietnam.* Novato, CA: Presidio Press, 1986.

——— . *The Viet-Cong Strategy of Terror.* Saigon: U.S. Mission South Vietnam, 1971.

——— . *Viet Cong: The Organization and Techniques of the National Liberation Front of South Vietnam.* Cambridge, MA: M.I.T. Press, 1966.

——— . *Vietnam and the Soviet Union: Anatomy of an Alliance.* Boulder, CO: Westview Press, 1987.

Pimlott, J. C. "Armour in Vietnam." In *Armoured Warfare,* edited by J. P. Harris and F. H. Toase. New York: St. Martin's Press, 1990.

——— . *Vietnam: The Decisive Battles.* New York: Macmillan, 1990.

Pisor, Robert. *The End of the Line: The Siege of Khe Sanh.* New York: W. W. Norton, 1982.

Ploger, Robert R. *U.S. Army Engineers, 1965–1970.* Washington, DC: U.S. Government Printing Office, 1974.

Police Organizations. Springfield, IL: Charles C Thomas, 1973.

Polmar, Norman. "Support by Sea for War in the Air." *Aerospace International* (July–August 1967), III: 29–31.

Polmar, Norman, and Floyd D. Kennedy, Jr. *Military Helicopters of the World: Military Rotary-Wing Aircraft since 1917.* Annapolis, MD: Naval Institute Press, 1981.

Ponchaud, François. *Cambodia Year Zero.* Translated by Nancy Amphoux. New York: Holt, Rinehart & Winston, 1978.

Popkin, Samuel L. *The Rational Peasant: The Political Economy of Rural Society in Vietnam.* Berkeley: University of California Press, 1979.

Porch, Douglas. *The French Foreign Legion*. New York: HarperCollins, 1991.

Porter, Gareth. *A Peace Denied: The United States, Vietnam, and the Paris Agreement*. Bloomington: Indiana University Press, 1975.

——. *Vietnam: A History in Documents*. New York: New American Library, 1981.

——. *Vietnam: The Definitive Documentation of Human Decisions*. Stanfordville, NY: Earl M. Coleman, 1979.

——. *Vietnam: The Politics of Bureaucratic Socialism*. Ithaca, NY: Cornell University Press, 1993.

Posner, Gerald. *Citizen Perot: His Life and Times*. New York: Random House, 1996.

Post, Ken. *Revolution, Socialism and Nationalism in Viet Nam*. Brookfield, VT: Darmouth, 1989–94.

Powell, Colin. *My American Journey*. New York: Random House, 1995.

Power, T. *Jules Ferry and the Renaissance of French Imperialism*. New York: King's Crown Press, 1944.

Powers, Thomas. *The Man Who Kept the Secrets: Richard Helms and the CIA*. New York: Alfred A. Knopf, 1979.

Prados, John. *Presidents' Secret Wars: CIA and Pentagon Covert Operations from World War II through Iranscam*. New York: William Morrow, 1988.

——. *The Sky Would Fall. Operation Vulture: The U.S. Bombing Mission in Indochina, 1954*. New York: Dial Press, 1983.

——. "We Are Spiritual in the Material World: The Rise of Buddhist Activism in South Vietnam." *VVA Veteran* 15, No. 2 (February 1995): 1, 23–24, 40–41.

Prados, John, and Ray W. Stubbe. *Valley of Decision: The Siege of Khe Sanh*. Boston: Houghton Mifflin, 1991.

Pratt, John Clark. *Vietnam Voices*. New York: Viking Press, 1984.

President's Commission on Campus Unrest. *Report of the President's Commission on Campus Unrest*. New York: Arno Press, 1970.

Preston, Anthony. "The Naval War in Vietnam." In *The Vietnam War: An Almanac*, edited by John S. Bowman. New York: World Almanac Publications, 1985.

Prevost, M., and Roman D. Amat, eds. *Dictionnaire de Biographie Française*. Paris: Librairie Letouzey et Ané, 1951.

Prochnau, William. "If There's a War, He's There." *New York Times Magazine* (3 March 1991).

——. *Once upon a Distant War: Young War Correspondents and the Early Vietnam Battles*. New York: Random House, 1995.

"Projects CHECO and Corona Harvest: Keys to the Air Force's Southeast Asia Memory Bank." *Aerospace Historian* (June 1986): 114–120.

Puller, Lewis B. *Fortunate Son: The Autobiography of Lewis B. Puller, Jr*. New York: Bantam Books, 1991.

Puryear, Edgar F., Jr. *George S. Brown. General, U. S. Air Force: Destined For Stars*. Novato, CA: Presidio Press, 1983.

Quincy, Keith. *Hmong: History of a People*. Cheney: Eastern Washington University Press, 1988.

Quôc Su Quán. *Quôc Triêu Chánh Biên Toát Yêu (A Summary of the History of Our Current Dynasty)*. Sài Gòn: Nhom Nghiên Cuu Su Ðia, 1971.

Race, Jeffrey. *War Comes to Long An: Revolutionary Conflict in a Vietnamese Province*. Berkeley: University of California Press, 1972.

Radford, Arthur W. *From Pearl Harbor to Vietnam: The Memoirs of Admiral Arthur W. Radford*, edited by Stephen Jurika, Jr. Stanford, CA: Hoover Institute Press, 1980.

Radvanyi, Janos. *Delusion and Reality: Gambits, Hoaxes, and Diplomatic One-Upmanship in Vietnam*. South Bend, IN: Gateway Editions, 1978.

Rainwater, Lee, and W. L. Yancey. *The Moynihan Report and the Politics of Controversy*. Cambridge, MA: MIT Press, 1967.

Randle, Robert F. *Geneva 1954: The Settlement of the Indochinese War*. Princeton, NJ: Princeton University Press, 1969.

Ranelegh, John. *The Agency: The Rise and Decline of the CIA*. New York: Simon & Schuster, 1986.

Ranney, Austin. *Curing the Mischiefs of Faction*. Berkeley: University of California Press, 1975.

Rappaport, Doreen. *Tinker vs. Des Moines: Student Rights on Trial*. New York: HarperCollins, 1993.

Rausa, Rosario. *Gold Wings, Blue Sea: A Naval Aviator's Story*. Annapolis, MD: Naval Institute Press, 1980.

Rawlings, Stuart. *The IVS Experience from Algeria to Vietnam*. Washington, DC: International Voluntary Services, 1992.

Reclus, Maurice. *Ferry le Tonkinois; recit historique*. Paris: Oeuvres Libres, 1946.

Reeves, Richard. *President Kennedy: Profile of Power*. New York: Simon & Schuster, 1993.

Reinberg, Linda. *In the Field: The Language of the Vietnam War*. New York: Facts on File, 1991.

Reynolds, Clark G. *Famous American Admirals*. New York: Van Nostrand Reinhold, 1978.

Ridgway, Matthew. *Soldier: The Memoirs of Matthew B. Ridgway*. New York: Harper and Brothers, 1956.

Risner, Robinson. *The Passing of the Night: My Seven Years As a Prisoner of the North Vietnamese*. New York: Random House, 1973.

Robbins, Christopher. *Air America*. New York: Putnam, 1979.

——. *The Ravens*. New York: Crown, 1987.

Robinson, Anthony, Anthony Preston, and Ian V. Hogg. *Weapons of the Vietnam War*. New York: Gallery Books, 1983.

Robinson, Jo Ann Ooiman. *Abraham Went Out: A Biography of A. J. Muste*. Philadelphia, PA: Temple University Press, 1981.

Rogers, Bernard William. *Cedar Falls–Junction City: A Turning Point*. Vietnam Studies Series. Washington, DC: Department of the Army, 1974.

Rosa, Joseph G., and Robin May. *An Illustrated History of Guns and Small Arms*. London: Peerage Books, 1984.

Rosenbaum, David E. "Moratorium Organizer." *The New York Times*, 16 October 1969.

Ross, Douglas. *In the Interests of Peace: Canada and Vietnam, 1954–1973*. Toronto: University of Toronto Press, 1984.

Rosser-Owen, David. *Vietnam Weapons Handbook*. Wellingborough, Northants, England: Patrick Stephens, 1986.

Rostow, Eugene V. *Law, Power, and the Pursuit of Peace*. Lincoln: University of Nebraska Press, 1968.

——. *Toward Managed Peace: The National Security Interests of the United States, 1759 to the Present*. New Haven, CT: Yale University Press, 1993.

Rostow, Walt W. *The Diffusion of Power, 1957–1972: An Essay in Recent History*. New York: Macmillan, 1972.

Roth, David. *Sacred Honor: A Biography of Colin Powell*. San Francisco: Harper, 1993.

Rothwell, Victor. *Anthony Eden: A Political Biography, 1931–57*. Manchester, UK: Manchester University Press, 1992.

Routledge, Howard, and Phyllis Routledge. *In the Presence of Mine Enemies, 1965–1973: A Prisoner at War*. London: Collins, 1974.

Rowan, Stephen A. *They Wouldn't Let Us Die: The Prisoners of War Tell Their Story*. Middle Village, NY: Jonathan David, 1973.

Rowe, James N. *Five Years to Freedom*. Boston: Little, Brown, 1971.

Rowny, Edward L. *It Takes One to Tango*. Washington, DC: Brassey's, 1992.

Roy, Jules. *The Battle of Dienbienphu*. New York: Harper & Row, 1965.

Rubin, Jerry. *Do It! Scenarios of the Revolution*. New York: Simon & Schuster, 1970.

Rubin, Jonathan. *The Barking Deer*. New York: George Braziller, 1974.

Rudenstine, David. *The Day the Presses Stopped: A History of the Pentagon Papers Case*. Berkeley: University of California Press, 1996.

Rusk, Dean. *As I Saw It*. New York: W. W. Norton, 1990.

Ruskin, Marcus G., and Bernard B. Fall. *The Vietnam Reader: Articles and Documents on American Foreign Policy and the Viet-Nam Crisis*. New York: Vintage Books, 1965.

Russell, Lee. E. *Armies of the Vietnam War,* 2d ed. London: Osprey, 1983.

Rust, William J., et al. *Kennedy in Vietnam: American Vietnam Policy, 1960–1963.* New York: Charles Scribner's Sons, 1985.

Saal, Harve. *MACV–Studies and Observations Group (SOG).* Milwaukee: Jones Techno-Comm, 1990.

Sabattier, Gabriel. *Le Destin de l'Indochine: Souvenirs et documents, 1941–1951.* Paris: Plon, 1952.

Safer, Morley. "Prescott's War." *American Heritage* (February-March 1991).

Sagan, Ginette, and Stephen Denney. *Violations of Human Rights in the Socialist Republic of Vietnam.* Palo Alto, CA: Aurora Foundation, 1983.

Sainteny, Jean. *Histoire d'une Paix Manquée: Indochine, 1945–1947.* Paris: Amiot-Dumont, 1953.

—— . *Ho Chi Minh and His Vietnam: A Personal Memoir.* Chicago: Cowles, 1972.

Sakwa, Richard. *Gorbachev and His Reforms 1985–1990.* New York: Prentice-Hall, 1991.

Salan, Raoul. *Indochine Rouge: le Message d'Ho Chi Minh.* Paris: Presses de la Cité, 1975.

—— . *Le Sens d'un Engagement, 1899–1946.* Paris: Presses de la Cité, 1970.

—— . *Mémoires: Fin d'un Empire, "Le Viet-Minh Mon Adversaire" October 1946–October 1954.* Paris: Presses de la Cité, 1954.

Sale, Kirkpatrick. *SDS.* New York: Random House, 1973.

Salisbury, Harrison. *Behind the Lines: Hanoi, December 23, 1966–January 7, 1967.* New York: Harper & Row, 1967.

—— . *A Journey for Our Times: A Memoir.* New York: Harper & Row, 1983.

—— . *A Time of Change: A Reporter's Tale of Our Time.* New York: Harper & Row, 1988.

—— . *Without Fear or Favor: The New York Times and Its Times.* New York: Harper & Row, 1980.

Sandler, Stanley. *"Cease Resistance: It's Good For You." A History of U.S. Army Combat Psychological Operations.* Fort Bragg, NC: U.S. Army Special Operations Command, n.d.

Sansom, Robert L. *The Economics of Insurgency in the Mekong Delta.* Cambridge, MA: MIT Press, 1970.

SarDesai, D. R. *Indian Foreign Policy in Cambodia, Laos, and Vietnam 1947–1964.* Berkeley: University of California Press, 1968.

—— . *Southeast Asia: Past and Present.* 2d rev. ed. Boulder, CO: Westview Press, 1989.

—— . *Vietnam: The Struggle for National Identity.* Boulder, CO: Westview Press, 1992.

Sarraut, Albert. *Grandeur et servitude coloniales.* Paris: Editions du Sagittaire, 1931.

—— . *La Mise en valeur des colonies françaises.* Paris: Payot, 1923.

Savada, Andrea Matles, ed. *Laos: A Country Study.* Washington, DC: Federal Research Division, Library of Congress, 1995.

Scadato, Anthony. *Bob Dylan.* New York: Grosset & Dunlap, 1971.

Scales, Robert H., Jr. *Firepower in Limited War.* 2nd ed. Novato, CA: Presidio Press, 1995.

Schaffer, Howard B. *Chester Bowles: New Dealer in the Cold War.* Cambridge, MA: Harvard University Press, 1993.

Schandler, Herbert Y. *The Unmaking of a President: Lyndon Johnson and Vietnam.* Princeton, NJ: Princeton University Press, 1977.

Schardt, Arlie, et al. *Amnesty? The Unsettled Question of Vietnam.* Lawrence, MA: Sun River Press, 1973.

Schemmer, Benjamin F. "Requiem for a Warrior: Col. Arthur D. "Bull" Simons." *Armed Forces Journal International* (November 1979): 44–46.

Schemmer, Benjamin F. *The Raid.* New York: Harper & Row, 1976.

Schlesinger, Arthur M., Jr. *The Imperial Presidency.* Boston: Houghton Mifflin, 1973.

—— . *Robert Kennedy and His Times.* Boston: Houghton Mifflin, 1978.

Schlight, John. *The Air War in South Vietnam: The Years of the Offensive, 1965–1968.* Washington, DC: Office of Air Force History, 1988.

—— . *The United States Air Force in Southeast Asia: The War in South Vietnam, The Years of the Offensive, 1965–1968.* Washington, DC: Office of Air Force History, 1988.

Schnell, Jonathan. *The Village of Ben Suc.* New York: Alfred A. Knopf, 1967.

Schoenbaum, Thomas J. *Waging Peace and War.* New York: Simon & Schuster, 1988.

Schoenebaum, Eleanora W., ed. *Political Profiles: The Eisenhower Years.* New York: Facts on File, 1980.

—— . *Political Profiles: The Nixon/Ford Years.* New York: Facts on File, 1979.

Schrag, Peter. *Test of Loyalty: Daniel Ellsberg and the Rituals of Secret Government.* New York: Simon & Schuster, 1974.

Schreadley, R. L. *From the Rivers to the Sea: The United States Navy in Vietnam.* Annapolis, MD: Naval Institute Press, 1992.

Schrock, J. L. *Minority Groups in the Republic of Vietnam.* Washington, DC: U.S. Government Printing Office, 1966.

Schultz, Clifford J., II, et al. "American Involvement in Vietnam, Part II: Prospects for U.S. Business in a New Era." *Business Horizons* 38, no. 6 (March–April 1995): 21–28.

Schultz, John. *The Chicago Conspiracy Trial.* Rev. ed. New York: Da Capo, 1993.

Schulzinger, Robert. *Henry Kissinger: Doctor of Diplomacy.* New York: Columbia University Press, 1989.

Schumacher, F. Carl, Jr., and George C. Wilson. *Bridge of No Return: The Ordeal of the U.S.S. Pueblo.* New York: Harcourt Brace Jovanovich, 1971.

Schurmann, Franz, P. D. Scott, and R. Zelnik. *The Politics of Escalation in Vietnam.* New York: Fawcett, 1966.

Schwarzkopf, H. Norman. *It Doesn't Take A Hero.* New York: Bantam Books, 1992.

Scigliano, Robert. *South Vietnam: Nation under Stress.* Boston: Houghton Mifflin, 1963.

Scott, Wilbur J. *The Politics of Readjustment: Vietnam Veterans since the War.* New York: Aldine de Gruyter, 1993.

Scoville, Thomas W. *Reorganizing for Pacification Support.* Washington, DC: U.S. Army Center of Military History, 1982.

Scruggs, Jan C., and Swerdlow, Joel. *To Heal a Nation.* New York: Harper & Row, 1985.

Seagrave, Sterling. *Soldiers of Fortune.* Alexandria, VA: Time-Life Books, 1981.

Seale, Bobby. *A Lonely Rage.* New York: Times Books, 1968.

Searle, William, ed. *Search and Clear: Critical Responses to Selected Literature and Films of the Vietnam War.* Bowling Green, OH: Popular Press, 1988.

Secord, Richard, with Jay Wurts. *Honored and Betrayed. Irangate, Covert Affairs, and the Secret War in Laos.* New York: John Wiley & Sons, 1992.

Seeley, Charlotte Palmer, et al., eds. *American Women and the U.S. Armed Forces: A Guide to the Records of Military Agencies in the National Archives Relating to American Women.* Washington, DC: National Archives and Records Administration, 1992.

Selden, Mark. *The Yenan Way in Revolutionary China.* Cambridge, MA: Harvard University Press, 1971.

Senate Committee on Veterans' Affairs. *Medal of Honor Recipients 1863–1978.* 96th Cong. Washington, DC: U.S. Government Printing Office, 1979.

Shafer, D. Michael. *Deadly Paradigms: The Failure of U.S. Counterinsurgency Policy.* Princeton, NJ: Princeton University Press, 1988.

Shagegg, S. Stephen. *Whatever Happened to Goldwater?* New York: Holt, Rinehart and Winston, 1965.

Shaplen, Robert. *The Road From War: Vietnam, 1965–1970.* New York: Harper & Row, 1970.

Shapley, Deborah. *Promise and Power: The Life and Times of Robert McNamara.* Boston: Little, Brown, 1993.

Share, Michael. "The Chinese Community in South Vietnam during the Second Indochina War." *Journal of Third World Studies* (Fall 1994): 240–265.

Sharp, U. S. G. "Report on Air and Naval Campaigns against North Vietnam and Pacific Command-Wide Support of the War, June 1964–July 1968." In *Report on the War in Vietnam*. Washington, DC: U.S. Government Printing Office, 1969.

——. *Strategy for Defeat: Vietnam in Retrospect*. San Rafael, CA: Presidio Press, 1978.

Sharp, U. S. G., and W. C. Westmoreland. *Report on the War in Vietnam*. Washington, DC: U.S. Government Printing Office, 1969.

Shawcross, William. *Sideshow: Kissinger, Nixon and the Destruction of Cambodia*. New York: Simon & Schuster, 1979.

Sheehan, Neil. *A Bright Shining Lie: John Paul Vann and America in Vietnam*. New York: Random House, 1988.

Sheehan, Neil, et al. *The Pentagon Papers as Published by* The New York Times. New York: Bantam Books, 1971.

Shelden, Michael. *Graham Greene: The Man Within*. London: Heinemann, 1994.

Shelton, Robert. *No Direction Home: The Life and Music of Bob Dylan*. New York: Beech Tree Books, 1986.

Shenon, Philip. "Air Warfare: The Broadcaster Once Known to GIs as Hanoi Hannah Has No Regrets." *Fort-Worth Star Telegram*, 26 November 1994.

——. "Boat People Prefer Death To Homeland." *The New York Times*, 16 March 1995.

Sheppard, Don. *"Riverine": A Brown Water Sailor in the Delta, 1967*. Novato, CA: Presidio Press, 1992.

Sherrill, Robert. *The Last Kennedy*. New York: Dial Press, 1976.

Shore, Moyers S., II. *The Battle for Khe Sanh (1969)*. Washington, DC: U.S. Marine Corps, 1977.

Short, Anthony. *The Origins of the Vietnam War*. London: Longman, 1989.

Shoup, Gen. David M. "The New American Militarism." *Atlantic Monthly* (April 1969).

Shulimson, Jack, and Charles M. Johnson, USMC. *U.S. Marines in Vietnam, 1965, The Landing and the Buildup*. Washington, DC: U.S. Government Printing Office, 1978.

Sievers, Allen M. *The Mystical World of Indochina: Culture and Economic Development in Conflict*. Baltimore: Johns Hopkins University Press, 1974.

Sigler, David Burns. *Vietnam Battle Chronology: U.S. Army and Marine Corps Combat Operations, 1965–1973*. Jefferson, NC: McFarland, 1992.

Simmons, Edwin H. "Marine Corps Operations in Vietnam, 1965–1966." In *The Marines in Vietnam, 1954–1973: An Anthology and Annotated Bibliography*, 2d ed. Washington, DC: History and Museums Division, Headquarters, U.S. Marine Corps, 1985.

——. *The United States Marines, 1775–1975*. New York: Viking Press, 1976.

Simpson, Charles M. *Inside the Green Berets*. Novato, CA: Presidio Press, 1983.

Simpson, Howard R. *Dien Bien Phu: The Epic Battle America Forgot*. Washington, DC: Brassey's, 1994.

Singlaub, John K., with Malcolm McConnell. *Hazardous Duty: An American Soldier in the Twentieth Century*. New York: Summit Books, 1991.

Small, Melvin. *Johnson, Nixon, and the Doves*. New Brunswick, NJ: Rutgers University Press, 1988.

Smith, Charles R. *High Mobility and Standdown, 1969*. Vol. 6 in *U.S. Marines in Vietnam*. Washington, DC: History and Museums Division, U.S. Marine Corps, 1988.

Smith, Gaddis. *Dean Acheson*. New York: Cooper Square, 1972.

Smith, Harvey H., et al. *Area Handbook for South Vietnam*. Washington, DC: U.S. Government Printing Office, 1967.

Smith, Herbert L. *Landmine and Countermine Warfare: Vietnam, 1964–1969*. Vol. 9. Washington, DC: Engineer Agency for Resource Inventories, 1972.

Smith, Jay H. *Anything, Anywhere, Anytime: An Illustrated History of the Military Airlift Command, 1941–1991*. Scott Air Force Base, IL: Headquarters, Military Airlift Command, Office of History, 1991.

Smith, R. B. *An International History of the Vietnam War*. New York: St. Martin's Press, 1985.

Smith, Ralph Harris. *OSS: The Secret History of America's First Central Intelligence Agency*. Berkeley: University of California Press, 1972.

Smith, W. H. B. *Small Arms of the World*, 10th ed. Harrisburg, PA: Stackpole, 1973.

Smith, W. H. C. *Napoleon III*. New York: St. Martin's Press, 1972.

Smith, Winnie. *American Daughter Gone to War*. New York: William Morrow, 1992.

Snepp, Frank. *Decent Interval*. New York: Random House, 1977.

Sobel, Lester A., ed. *South Vietnam: U.S.-Communist Confrontation in Southeast Asia, Vol. 5, 1970*. New York: Facts on File, 1973.

Solberg, Carl. *Hubert Humphrey: A Biography*. New York: W. W. Norton, 1984.

Solomon, Zahava. *Combat Stress Reaction*. New York: Plenum Press, 1993.

Sonnenberg, Stephen M., Arthur S. Blank, Jr., and John A. Talbott, eds. *The Trauma of War: Stress and Recovery in Vietnam Veterans*. Washington, DC: American Psychiatric Press, 1985.

Sorley, Lewis. "Creighton Abrams and Active-Reserve Integration in Wartime." *Parameters* (Summer 1991): 35–50.

——. *Thunderbolt: General Creighton Abrams and the Army of His Times*. New York: Simon & Schuster, 1992.

Spanier, John and Steven W. Hook. *American Foreign Policy since World War II*. 13th ed. Washington, DC: CQ Press, 1995.

Spector, Ronald H. *Advice and Support. The Early Years. The U.S. Army in Vietnam*. Washington, DC: U.S. Army Center of Military History, 1983.

——. *After Tet: The Bloodiest Year in Vietnam*. New York: Macmillan, 1993.

Spence, Jonathan D. *The Search for Modern China*. New York: W. W. Norton, 1990.

Spencer, Dao, ed. *Directory of U.S. NGOs Vietnam Programs*. New York: U.S. NGO Forum on Viet Nam, Cambodia and Laos, 1992.

Spofford, Tim. *Lynch Street: The May 1970 Slayings at Jackson State College*. Kent, OH: Kent State University Press, 1988.

Sridharan, Kripa. *The ASEAN Region in India's Foreign Policy*. Brookfield, VT: Dartmouth, 1996.

Staaveren, Jacob Van. *The United States Air Force in Southeast Asia: Interdiction in Southern Laos, 1960–1968*. Washington, DC: Center for Air Force History, 1993.

Stanton, Shelby L. *Anatomy of a Division: 1st Cav in Vietnam*. Novato, CA: Presidio Press, 1987.

——. *Green Berets at War*. Novato, CA: Presidio Press, 1985.

——. *Rangers at War: Combat Recon in Vietnam*. New York: Orion, 1992.

——. *The Rise and Fall of an American Army: U.S. Army Ground Forces in Vietnam, 1965–1973*. Novato, CA: Presidio Press, 1985.

——. *Vietnam Order of Battle*. Washington, DC: U. S. News & World Report Books, 1981.

Starr, Paul. *The Discarded Army: Veterans after Vietnam*. New York: Charterhouse, 1973.

Starry, Donn A. *Armored Combat in Vietnam*. New York: Bobbs-Merrill, 1980.

——. *Mounted Combat in Vietnam*. Washington, DC: U.S. Army Center of Military History, 1978.

Steel, Ronald. *Walter Lippmann and the American Century*. Boston: Little, Brown, 1980.

Stein, Herbert. *Presidential Economics: The Making of Economic Policy from Roosevelt to Reagan and Beyond*. New York: Simon & Schuster, 1984.

Stephanson, Anders. *George Kennan and the Art of Foreign Policy*. Cambridge, MA: Harvard University Press, 1989.

Stern, Gary M., and Morton Halperin, ed. *The U.S. Constitution and the Power to Go to War: Historical and Current Perspectives*. Westport, CT: Greenwood Press, 1994.

Stevens, Richard Linn. *The Trail: A History of the Ho Chi Minh Trail and the Role of Nature in the War in Viet Nam*. New York: Garland, 1993.

Stevenson, Charles A. *The End of Nowhere: American Policy Towards Laos since 1954*. Boston: Beacon Press, 1972.

Stillwell, Paul. *Battleship New Jersey: An Illustrated History*. Annapolis, MD: Naval Institute Press, 1986.

Stockdale, James. *A Vietnam Experience: Ten Years of Reflection.* Stanford, CA: Hoover Institution Press, 1984.

Stockdale, James, and Sybil Stockdale. *In Love and War: The Story of a Family's Ordeal and Sacrifice during the Vietnam Years.* New York: Harper & Row, 1984.

Stockholm International Peace Research Institute. *Anti-personnel Weapons.* London: Taylor & Francis, 1978.

——. *Incendiary Weapons.* Cambridge, MA: M.I.T. Press, 1975.

Stoessinger, John. *Henry Kissinger: The Anguish of Power.* New York: W. W. Norton, 1976.

Stolfi, Russel H. *Mine and Countermine Warfare in Recent History.* Report No. 1582. Aberdeen Proving Ground, MD: U.S. Army Ballistic Research Laboratories, 1972.

Stone, I. F. *Polemics and Prophecies, 1967–1970: A Non-Conformist History of Our Times.* Boston: Little, Brown, 1989.

Strassfeld, Robert. "The Vietnam War on Trial: The Court-Martial of Dr. Howard B. Levy." *Wisconsin Law Review* (1994): 839–963.

Straub, Deborah A. "Halberstam, David." In *Contemporary Authors,* edited by Ann Evory and Linda Metzger. New Revision Series, vol 10. Detroit: Gale, 1983, pp. 215–218.

Stuart-Fox, Martin, and Mary Kooyman. *Historical Dictionary of Laos.* Asian Historical Dictionaries No. 6. Metuchen, NJ: Scarecrow Press, 1992.

Stuckey, Col. John D., and Col. Joseph H. Pistorius. *Mobilization of the Army National Guard and Army Reserve: Historical Perspective and the Vietnam War.* Carlisle Barracks, PA: Strategic Studies Institute, U.S. Army War College, 15 November 1984.

Sturken, Marita. "The Wall, the Screen, and the Image: The Vietnam Veterans Memorial." *Representations* 35 (1991): 118–142.

Sullivan, Marianna P. *France's Vietnam Policy: A Study in French-American Relations.* Westport, CT: Greenwood Press, 1978.

Sullivan, William H. *Obbligato, 1939–1979: Notes on a Foreign Service Career.* New York: W. W. Norton, 1984.

Summers, Harry G. *On Strategy: A Critical Analysis of the Vietnam War.* Novato, CA: Presidio Press, 1982.

——. *On Strategy: The Vietnam War in Context.* Carlisle Barracks, PA: U.S. Army War College, Strategic Studies Institute, 1981.

——. *Vietnam War Almanac.* New York: Facts on File, 1985.

Sumrall, Robert F. *Iowa Class Battleships: Their Design, Weapons & Equipment.* Annapolis, MD: Naval Institute Press, 1988.

Supreme Court Justices: Illustrated Biographies. Washington, DC: Congressional Quarterly, 1993.

Sutherland, Ian D. W. *1952/1982. Special Forces of the United States Army.* San Jose, CA: R. James Bender, 1990.

Swerdlow, Amy. *Women Strike for Peace: Traditional Motherhood and Radical Politics in the 1960s.* Chicago: University of Chicago Press, 1993.

Sylvester, John, and Frank Foster, *The Decorations and Medals of the Republic of Vietnam.* Fountain Inn, SC: MOA Press, 1995.

Taboulet, Georges. "Les origines immédiates de l'intervention de la France en Indochine (1857–1858)." *Revue d'histoire des colonies françaises* 344 (1954–1955): 281–302.

Tâm Vu (Trân Van Giàu). "People's War Against Special War." *Vietnamese Studies* No. 11, 1967.

Taylor, John M. *General Maxwell Taylor: The Sword and the Pen.* New York: Doubleday, 1989.

Taylor, Keith W. *The Birth of Vietnam.* Berkeley: University of California Press, 1983.

Taylor, Maxwell D. *Responsibility and Response.* New York: Harper & Row, 1967.

——. *Swords and Plowshares.* New York: W. W. Norton, 1972.

——. *The Uncertain Trumpet.* New York: Harper & Row, 1960.

Taylor, Milton C. "South Vietnam: Lavish Aid, Limited Progress." *Pacific Affairs* XXXIV (1961): 242–256.

Taylor, Telford. *Nuremberg and Vietnam: An American Tragedy.* Chicago: Quadrangle Books, 1970.

Telfer, Gary L., Lane Rogers, and Keith Fleming. *U.S. Marines in Vietnam: Fighting the North Vietnamese, 1967.* Washington, DC: History and Museums Division, Headquarters, U.S. Marine Corps, 1984.

Terrill, Ross. *Mao: A Biography.* New York: Harper & Row, 1980.

Terzani, Tiziano. *Giai Phong: The Fall and Liberation of Saigon.* New York: St. Martin's Press, 1976.

Tetreault, Mary Ann. *Women and Revolution in Viet Nam.* East Lansing: Michigan State University, 1991.

Thakur, Ramesh. *Peacekeeping in Vietnam: Canada, India, Poland, and the International Commission.* Edmonton: University of Alberta Press, 1984.

Thayer, Carlyle A. "Political Reform in Viet Nam: Doi Moi and the Emergence of Civil Society." In *The Development of Civil Society in Communist Systems,* edited by Robert F. Miller. Sydney: Allen & Unwin, 1992.

——. *War by Other Means: National Liberation and Revolution in Viet-Nam, 1954–60.* Sydney: Allen & Unwin, 1989.

Thayer, Thomas. *How to Analyze a War without Fronts.* Boulder, CO: Westview Press, 1985.

Theis, Wallace J. *When Governments Collide: Coercion and Diplomacy in the Vietnam Conflict, 1964–1968.* Berkeley: University of California Press, 1980.

Thompson, Charles. *Bob Hope.* London: Thames Methuen, 1981.

Thompson, James Clay. *Rolling Thunder: Understanding Policy and Program Failure.* Chapel Hill: University of North Carolina Press, 1979.

Thompson, Julian. *The Lifeblood of War: Logistics in Armed Conflict.* London: Brassey's, 1991.

Thompson, Kenneth, ed. *The Kennedy Presidency: Seventeen Intimate Perspectives of John F. Kennedy.* Lanham, MD: University Press of America, 1985.

Thompson, Robert. *Defeating Communist Insurgency: The Lessons of Malaya and Vietnam.* New York: Praeger, 1966.

——. *No Exit from Vietnam.* New York: D. McKay, 1969.

Thompson, Virginia. *French Indo-China.* New York: Macmillan, 1937.

"320 Vow to Help Draft Resisters." *New York Times,* September 27, 1967, p. 13.

Tilford, Earl H., Jr. *A History of U.S. Air Force Search and Rescue in Southeast Asia, 1961–1975.* Washington, DC: Office of Air Force History, 1980.

——. *Crosswinds: The Air Force Setup in Vietnam.* College Station: Texas A&M University Press, 1993.

——. *Setup: What The Air Force Did in Vietnam and Why.* Maxwell Air Force Base, AL: Air University Press, 1991.

——. *The USAF Search and Rescue in Southeast Asia.* Washington, DC: Office of Air Force History, 1992.

Tinberg, Robert. *The Nightingale's Song.* New York: Simon & Schuster, 1995.

Tolson, John J. *Airmobility, 1961–1971.* Washington, DC: Department of the Army, 1973.

Tourison, Sedgwick D. *Project Alpha: Washington's Secret Military Operations in North Vietnam.* New York: St. Martin's Press, 1997.

Towers, Edwin L. *Hope for Freedom: Operation Thunderhead.* La Jolla, CA: Lane & Associates, 1981.

Truong Buu Lâm. *Resistance, Rebellion, and Revolution: Popular Movements in Vietnamese History.* Singapore: Institute of Southeast Asian Studies, 1984.

Truong Nhu Tang. *A Viet Cong Memoir: An Inside Account of the Vietnam War and Its Aftermath.* New York: Vintage Books, 1985.

Trân Đình Tho. *The Cambodian Incursion.* Washington, DC: U.S. Army Center of Military History, 1983.

——. *Pacification.* Washington, DC: U.S. Army Center of Military History, 1980.

Trân Trong Kim. *Viêt Nam Su Luoc (Outline of Vietnamese History).* Sài Gòn: Bô Giáo Duc, Trung Tâm Hoc Liêu, 1971.

Trân Van Đôn. *Our Endless War: Inside Vietnam.* Novato, CA: Presidio Press, 1978.

Trân Van Giàu, and Lê Van Chât. *The South Vietnam Liberation National Front.* Hà Nôi: Foreign Languages Publishing House, 1962.

Trần Van Trà. *Vietnam: History of the Bulwark B2 Theatre*. vol. 5, *Concluding the 30-Years War* (in Vietnamese). Hồ Chí Minh City: Van Nghê, 1982. Translated in *Southeast Asia Report* 1247, no. 82783 (2 February 1983).

Tregaskis, Richard. *Southeast Asia: Building the Bases*. Washington, DC: U.S. Government Printing Office, 1975.

Trotta, Liz. *Fighting for Air: In the Trenches with Television News*. Columbia: University of Missouri Press, 1991.

Troy, Thomas F. *Donovan and the CIA*. Frederick, MD: Aletheia Books, 1981.

Truong-Chinh Selected Writings. Hà Nôi: Gioi Publishers, 1994.

Tsai Maw-Kuey. *Les Chinois au Sud-Vietnam*. Paris: Bibliotheque Nationale, 1968.

Tulich, Eugene N. *The United States Coast Guard in Southeast Asia during the Vietnam Conflict*. Washington, DC: U.S. Coast Guard, Public Affairs Division, 1986.

Tull, Theresa. "Broadening the Base: South Vietnamese Elections, 1967–71." In *Electoral Politics in South Vietnam*, edited by John C. Donnell and C. A. Joiner. Lexington, MA: D. C. Heath, 1974.

Turley, G. H. *The Easter Offensive*. Novato, CA: Presidio Press, 1985.

Turley, William S. *The Second Indochina War: A Short Political and Military History, 1954–1975*. Boulder, CO: Westview Press, 1986.

Turley, William S., and Mark Selden, eds. *Reinventing Vietnamese Socialism: Doi moi in Comparative Perspective*. Boulder, CO: Westview Press, 1993.

U Thant. *View from the UN: The Memoirs of U Thant*. Garden City, NY: Doubleday, 1978.

U.S. Air Force Special Study, Headquarters Strategic Air Command. "Activity Input to Project Corona Harvest-Arc Light Operations, 1 Jan 65–31 Mar 68." (Declassified 31 May 1990).

U.S. Army. *Body Armor for the Individual Soldier. DA PAM 21–54*. Washington, DC: U.S. Government Printing Office, 1965.

——— . *Bombs and Bomb Components. TM9–1325–200*. Washington, DC: U.S. Government Printing Office, 1966.

——— . *Field Artillery Cannon Gunnery*. Field Manual 6–40. Washington, DC: Headquarters, Department of the Army.

——— . *FM 6–40 Field Artillery Cannon Gunnery*. Washington, DC: U.S. Government Printing Office, 1967.

——— . *40-mm Grenade Launchers M203 and M79*. FM-23–31. Washington, DC: U.S. Government Printing Office, 1972.

——— . Military maps: Sheet 6441 II, "A SAP." Series L 7014, edition 3-TPC (29 ETB), prepared by 29th Engr Bn U.S. Army, 1970, printed by 29th Engr Bn (BT) April 1971; and Sheet 6441 IV, Series L 7014, "A LUOI" [A LUOI], edition 3-TPC. U.S. Army Topographic Command, September 1970.

——— . *The My Lai Massacre and Its Cover-Up: Beyond the Reach of Law? The Peers Commission Report*. New York: Free Press, 1976.

——— . Official Biography of Major General Keith L. Ware, nd.

——— . Special Operations Command, Directorate of History and Archives, Fort Bragg, NC.

U.S. Army Foreign Service and Technology Center. *Mines and Booby Traps*. (Translation of *Minas E Armadilhas*.) Washington, DC: Department of the Army, 1969.

U.S. Army Materiel Command. *Grenades (U). Engineering Design Handbook*. AMCP 706–240. Washington, DC: U.S. Government Printing Office, 1967.

U.S. Council of Economic Advisors. *Economic Report of the President*. Washington, DC: U.S. Government Printing Office, various issues.

U.S. Department of the Air Force. *61st Military Airlift Wing History, Dec 65–Jan 66*. Maxwell Air Force Base, AL: Air Force Historical Research Agency, n.d.

——— . *Military Airlift Command History, Jul 65–Jan 66*. Maxwell Air Force Base, AL: Air Force Historical Research Agency, n.d.

U.S. Department of State. *Foreign Relations of the United States, 1952–1954*. Vol. XVI, *The Geneva Conference*. U.S. Department of State Publication 9167. Washington, DC: U.S. Government Printing Office, 1981, pp. 1500–1501, 1505–1546.

U.S. Department of State, Bureau of Public Affairs. *Indochinese Refugees*. Washington, DC: U.S. Government Printing Office, 1981.

U.S. House Select Committee on Hunger. *Three Asian Countries in Crisis: Afghanistan, Vietnam, and the Philippines*. 100th Cong., 2d sess., serial 100–27. Washington, DC: U.S. Government Printing Office, 1988.

U.S. Marine Corps Base Quantico. *Vietcong Mine Warfare*. Quantico, VA: Department of the Navy, 1966.

U.S. Naval History Division. *Dictionary of American Naval Fighting Ships*. Washington, DC: U.S. Government Printing Office, 1959–1981.

U.S. Senate. Committee on Foreign Relations. *U.S. Involvement in the Overthrow of Diem, 1963*. Washington, DC: U.S. Government Printing Office, 1972.

——— . *Report of the Select Committee on POW/MIA Affairs*. 103d Cong., 1st sess. Washington, DC: U.S. Government Printing Office, 1993.

Uhlig, Frank, Jr., ed. *Vietnam: The Naval Story*. Annapolis: Naval Institute Press, 1986.

Ungar, Sanford J. *FBI*. Boston: Little, Brown, 1976.

——— . *The Papers & the Papers: An Account of the Legal and Political Battle over the Pentagon Papers*. New York: E. P. Dutton, 1972; reprint, New York: Columbia University Press, 1988.

Unger, Irwin. *The Movement: A History of the American New Left, 1959–1972*. New York: Dodd, Mead, 1974.

United Nations. *Napalm and Other Incendiary Weapons and All Aspects of Their Possible Use: Report of the Secretary-General*. New York: United Nations, 1973.

United Nations High Commissioner for Refugees. *Resettlement Section: Statistics Concerning Indochinese in East and South East Asia*. Geneva: United Nations, 1995.

United States–Vietnam Relations, 1945–1967: Study Prepared by the Department of Defense. Washington, DC: U.S. Government Printing Office, 1971.

"U.S. Electronic Espionage: A Memoir." *Ramparts* (August 1972): 35–50.

Uy Ban Khoa Hoc Xa Hôi Viêt Nam. *Lich Su Viêt Nam, tâp I (History of Vietnam, vol. 1)*. Hà Nôi: Nhà Xuât Ban Khoa Hoc Xa Hôi, 1971.

Van Tân, Nguyên Linh, Lê Van Lân, Nguyên Đông Chi, Hoàng Hung. *Thoi Đai Hùng Vuong: Lich Su, Kinh Tê, Chính Tri, Van Hóa, Xã Hôi (The Hùng Vuong Era: History, Economy, Politics, Society)*. Hà Nôi: Nhà Xuât Ban Khoa Hoc Xã Hôi, 1976.

Van Tiên Dung. *Our Great Spring Victory*. New York: Monthly Review Press, 1977.

Vu Ky. *Luân Cuong Vê Van Hóa Viêt Nam*. Brussels: Trung Tâm Van Hóa Xã Hôi Viêt Nam, 1995.

Vu Quôc Thúc. *L'Economie communaliste du Vietnam*. Hà Nôi: Press Universitaire du Vietnam, 1952.

Vu Thu Hiên. *Đêm Giua Ban Ngày*. Westminster, CA: Van Nghê, 1997.

Van Devanter, Lynda. *Home before Morning*. New York: Warner Books, 1984.

Van Vleet, Clarke, and William J. Armstrong. *United States Naval Aviation, 1910–1980*. Washington, DC: U.S. Government Printing Office, 1980.

Vance, Cyrus. *Hard Choices: Critical Years in America's Foreign Policy*. New York: Simon & Schuster, 1983.

VanDeMark, Brian. *Into the Quagmire: Lyndon Johnson and the Escalation of the Vietnam War*. New York: Oxford University Press, 1991.

Vang Pao, Maj. Gen. Speech delivered at the Vietnam Seminar, Texas Tech University, Lubbock, Texas, 18 April 1996.

Verger, Paul, et al. "Correlation between Dioxin Levels in Adipose Tissue and Estimated Exposure to Agent Orange in South Vietnamese Residents." *Environmental Research* (May 1994): 226–243.

Viên Khao Cô Hoc, Uy Ban Khoa Hoc Xã Hôi Viêt Nam. *Nhung Phát Hiên Moi Vê Khao Cô Hoc Nam 1984 (New Archaeological Discoveries in 1984)*. Thành Phô Hồ Chí Minh, 1985

Viet Chung. "Recent Findings on the Tay Son Insurgency." *Vietnamese Studies* 81 (1985): 30–62.

Vietnam Revisited. Videotape of interview with Ngô Thi Trinh; "Hanoi Hannah on Vietnam." West Lafayette, IN: Purdue University, Public Affairs Video Archives, 1992.

Vietnam: A Television History. Videotape produced by WGBH TV, Boston. New York: Sony, 1983.

Vietnam: The Ten Thousand Day War. Videotape produced by Michael Mclear. Los Angeles: Embassy Home Entertainment, 1987.

The Vietnam Veteran in Contemporary Society: Collected Materials Pertaining to Young Veterans. Washington, DC: U.S. Government Printing Office, 1972.

Viorst, Milton. *Fire in the Streets: America in the 1960s*. New York: Simon & Schuster, 1979.

Vo Long Te. *Les Archipels de Hoang-Sa et de Truong-Sa Selon Les Anciens ouvrages de l'Histoire et de Geographie*. Sài Gòn: Ministere de la Culture, de l'Education et de la Jeunesse, 1974.

Vô Nguyên Giáp. *Big Victory, Great Task*. New York: Praeger Press, 1968.

———. *Dien Bien Phu*. Hà Nôi: Foreign Languages Publishing House, 1962.

———. *People's War People's Army: The Viet Cong Insurrection Manual for Underdeveloped Countries*. New York: Praeger, 1967.

———. *Unforgettable Days*. Hà Nôi: Foreign Languages Publishing House, 1978.

———. *Unforgettable Months and Years*. Translated by Mai Elliott. Ithaca, NY: Cornell University Press, 1975.

Wagner-Pacifici, Robin, and Barry Schwartz. "The Vietnam Veterans Memorial: Commemorating a Difficult Past." *American Journal of Sociology* (September 1991): 376–420.

Walker, Daniel. *Rights in Conflict: Chicago's Seven Brutal Days*. New York: Grosset & Dunlap, 1968.

Walker, Keith. *A Piece of My Heart: The Stories of Twenty-Six American Women Who Served in Vietnam*. New York: Ballantine Books, 1985.

Walsh, Jeffrey, and James Aulich, eds. *Vietnam Images: War and Representation*. New York: St. Martin's Press, 1989.

Walt, Lewis W. *Strange War, Strange Strategy: A General's Report on Vietnam*. New York: Funk & Wagnalls, 1976.

Walton, Richard J. *Cold War and Counter-Revolution: The Foreign Policy of John F. Kennedy*. New York: Viking, 1972.

———. *The Remnants of Power: The Last Tragic Years of Adlai Stevenson*. New York: Coward-McCann, 1968.

Warner, Denis. *Certain Victory: How Hanoi Won the War*. Kansas City, MO: Sheed Andrews and McMeel, 1978.

———. *The Last Confucian*. London: Angus & Robertson, 1964.

Warner, Roger. *Back Fire: The CIA's Secret War in Laos and Its Link to the War in Vietnam*. New York: Simon & Schuster, 1995.

Watson, David R. *Georges Clemenceau: A Political Biography*. New York: David McKay, 1974.

Webb, Willard J., and Ronald Cole. *The Chairmen of the Joint Chiefs of Staff*. Washington, DC: Historical Division, Joint Chiefs of Staff, 1989.

Weber, Mike. *Grenades!* Ontario, Canada: Unit Nine, 1979.

Weiss, Stephen, Clark Dougan, David Fulghum, Denis Kennedy, and the editors. *Vietnam Experience: A War Remembered*. The Vietnam Experience, edited by Robert Manning. Boston: Boston Publishing, 1986.

Wells, Robert, ed. *The Invisible Enemy: Boobytraps in Vietnam*. Miami, FL: J. Flores Publications, 1992.

Wells, Tom. *The War Within: America's Battle Over Vietnam*. Berkeley: University of California Press, 1994.

Wenke, Joseph. *Mailer's America*. Hanover, NH: University Press of New England, 1987.

Werth, Alexander. *The Strange History of Mendès-France and the Great Struggle over French North Africa*. London: Barrie Books, 1957.

West, F. J. *The Village*. Madison: University of Wisconsin Press, 1985.

———. *Small Unit Action in Vietnam, Summer 1966*. Washington, DC: Historical Branch, G-3 Division, U.S. Marine Corps Headquarters, 1967.

Westmoreland, William C. *A Soldier Reports*. Garden City, NY: Doubleday, 1976.

———. "Report on Operations in South Vietnam, January 1964–June 1968." In *Report on the War in Vietnam*. Washington, DC: U.S. Government Printing Office, 1969.

Wheeler, Earle G. *Addresses*. Washington, DC: U.S. Government Printing Office, 1970.

White, Theodore H. *The Making of the President, 1968*. New York: Atheneum, 1969.

———. *The Making of the President, 1972*. New York: Atheneum, 1973.

Whitfield, Danny J. *Historical and Cultural Dictionary of Vietnam*. Metuchen, NJ: Scarecrow Press, 1976.

Whitfield, Stephen J. "The Stunt Man: Abbie Hoffman (1936–1989)." In *Sights on the Sixties*, edited by Barbara L. Tischler. New Brunswick, NJ: Rutgers University Press, 1992, pp. 103–119.

Who Was Who in America with World Notables, 1985–1989. Wilmette, IL: Macmillan Directory Division, 1989.

Who Was Who in America with World Notables, 1989–1993. Chicago: Marquis Who's Who, 1993.

Who's Who in America, 1968–1969. New Providence, NJ: Marquis, 1969.

Who's Who in America, 1980–1981. Chicago: Marquis, 1981.

Who's Who in America, 1984–1985. New Providence, NJ: Marquis, 1984.

Who's Who in America, 1993. New Providence, NJ: Marquis, 1994.

Who's Who in America, 1997. New Providence, NJ: Marquis, 1996.

Who's Who in American Politics, 1995–1996. New Providence, NJ: R. R. Bowker, 1995.

Who's Who in North Vietnam. Washington, DC: Office of External Research, U.S. Department of State, 1972.

Who's Who in the Socialist Countries. New York: Saur, 1978.

Who's Who in Vietnam. Sài Gòn: Vietnam Press Agency, 1967–1968.

Who's Who in the World, 1984–1985. Chicago: Marquis, 1989.

Wiesner, Louis A. *Victims and Survivors: Displaced Persons and Other War Victims in Viet-Nam, 1954–1975*. New York: Greenwood Press, 1988.

Willbanks, James H. *Thiet Giap! The Battle of An Loc, April 1972*. Fort Leavenworth, KS: Combat Studies Institute, 1993.

Williams, Frederick D. *SLAM: The Influence of S. L. A. Marshall on the United States Army*. Fort Monroe, VA: U.S. Army Training and Doctrine Command, 1990.

Williams, J. E. D. *From Sails to Satellites: The Origin and Development of Navigational Science*. New York: Oxford University Press, 1992.

Williams, Michael. *Vietnam at the Crossroads*. London: Pinter, 1992.

Williams, Michael W., ed. *The African American Encyclopedia*. New York: Marshall Cavendish, 1993.

Williams, William Appleman, ed. *America in Vietnam: A Documentary History*. Garden City, NY: Anchor Press, 1985.

Wilson, Dick. *Zhou Enlai, A Biography*. New York: Viking Press, 1984.

Wilson, George C. *Mud Soldiers: Life Inside the New American Army*. New York: Collier Books, 1989.

Wilson, Harold K. *A Personal Record. The Labour Government, 1964–1970*. Boston: Little, Brown, 1971.

Wilson, James C. *Vietnam in Prose and Film*. Jefferson, NC: McFarland, 1982.

Wintle, Justin. *The Vietnam Wars*. New York: St. Martin's Press, 1991.

Wirtz, James. *The Tet Offensive: Intelligence Failure in War*. Ithaca, NY: Cornell University Press, 1991.

Wittman, Sandra M. *Writing about Vietnam: A Bibliography of the Vietnam Conflict*. Boston: G. K. Hall, 1989.

Wittner, Laurence S. *Rebels Against War: The American Peace Movement, 1941–1960*. New York: Columbia University Press, 1969.

Wolf, Richard I., ed. *The United States Air Force Basic Documents on Roles and Missions*. Washington, DC: Office of Air Force History, 1987.

Wolfe, William. "Health Status of Air Force Veterans Occupationally Exposed to Herbicides in Vietnam." *JAMA* 264 (10 October 1990): 1824–1832.

Woodby, Sylvia. *Gorbachev and the Decline of Ideology in Soviet Foreign Policy*. Boulder, CO: Westview Press, 1989.

Woods, Randall Bennett. "Dixie's Dove: J. William Fulbright, the Vietnam

War, and the American South." *The Journal of Southern History* 60, no. 3 (August 1994): 533–552.

Woodside, Alexander B. *Community and Revolution in Modern Vietnam.* Boston: Houghton Mifflin, 1976.

———. *Vietnam and the Chinese Model: A Comparative Study of Nguyen and Ch'ing Government in the First Half of the Nineteenth Century.* Cambridge, MA: Harvard University Press, 1971.

Woodward, Bob, and Carl Bernstein. *The Final Days.* New York: Simon & Schuster, 1976.

Woodward, Ernest L. *Three Studies in European Conservatism: Metternich, Guizot, the Catholic Church in the Nineteenth Century.* Hamden, CT: Archon Books, 1963.

Wunderlin, Clarence E., Jr. "Paradox of Power: Infiltration, Coastal Surveillance, and the United States Navy in Vietnam, 1965–1968." *The Journal of Military History* 53 (July 1989): 275–289.

Wyatt, Clarence R. *Paper Soldiers: The American Press and the Vietnam War.* Chicago: University of Chicago Press, 1993.

Yang Dao. *Hmong at the Turning Point.* Minneapolis: WorldBridge Associates, 1993.

Yoder, Edwin M., Jr. *Joe Alsop's Cold War: A Study of Journalistic Influence and Intrigue.* Chapel Hill: University of North Carolina Press, 1995.

Young, A. L., and G. M. Reggiani, eds. *Agent Orange and Its Associated Dioxin.* Amsterdam: Elsevier, 1988.

Young, Kenneth T. *The 1954 Geneva Conference.* New York: Greenwood Press, 1968.

Young, Marilyn B. *The Vietnam Wars, 1945–1990.* New York: HarperCollins, 1991.

Young, Stephen. "How North Vietnam Won the War" (interview with former Colonel Bui Tin). *The Wall Street Journal,* 3 August 1995.

Zabecki, David T. "Battle for Saigon." *Vietnam* (Summer 1989): 19–25.

Zaffiri, Samuel. *Hamburger Hill.* New York: Pocket Books, 1988.

———. *Westmoreland.* New York: William Morrow, 1994

Zaroulis, Nancy, and Gerald Sullivan. *Who Spoke Up: American Protest Against the War in Vietnam, 1963–1975.* New York: Henry Holt, 1985.

Zasloff, Joseph J., and MacAlister Brown. *Apprentice Revolutionaries: The Communist Movement in Laos, 1930–1985.* Stanford, CA: Hoover Institution Press, 1986.

Zasloff, Joseph J., and Leonard Unger, eds. *Laos: Beyond the Revolution.* London: Macmillan, 1991.

Zinn, Howard. *The Twentieth Century: A People's History.* New York: Harper & Row, 1984.

Zito, Tom. "Old Soldier's Media Battle; Colonel Herbert's War with CBS." *The Washington Post,* 1 October 1979.

Zorthian, Barry. "The Press and the Government." In *Vietnam Reconsidered: Lessons from a War,* edited by Harrison Salisbury. New York: Harper & Row, 1984.

Zumbro, Ralph. *Tank Sergeant.* New York: Pocket Books, 1988.

Zumwalt, Elmo, Jr. *On Watch: A Memoir.* New York: Quadrangle Books, 1976.

Zumwalt, Elmo, Jr., Elmo Zumwalt, III, and John Pekkanen. *My Father, My Son.* New York: Macmillan, 1986.

576 Index

Đình Diêm overthrow, 162, 290; specific people, 48, 83, 146, 147, 196, 200, 201, 216, 263, 279, 347, 361, 488. *See also* Dulles, John Foster; Rostow, Walt Whitman; Rusk, Dean

U.S. strategy/policy, 1–2, 86, 172, 356, 387; air power controversy, 7, 234, 276, 277, 418; and Chinese/Soviet intervention possibility, 215, 233, 358, 359, 370, 383; declaration of war absence, 31, 151, 278–279, 361; and DRV-NLF control issue, 174, 285; enclave strategy, 121–122, 373, 392; flexible response policy, 132, 197, 230, 255, 391, 424; Krulak/Mendenhall mission, 216, 263; and Operation ROLLING THUNDER, 358; PROVN study, 195, 213, 426, 427; RAND Corporation, 346–347; secrecy, 54, 131, 159, 164, 171; SIGMA I/II war games, 376. *See also* attrition strategy; body count; counterinsurgency warfare; critics of U.S. strategy/policy; massive retaliation policy; pacification; reserve forces policy; search and destroy; U.S. bombing of North Vietnam; U.S. post-Tết policy reassessment

U.S. troop withdrawals, 23, 76, 84, 112, 138, 211, 212, 217, 278, 306, 426–427; and Abrams, 2, 217; and aircraft carriers, 9; and antiwar movement, 19, 493; and armor warfare, 22; Bradley on, 46; Bruce on, 48; and Cambodian incursion, 57, 59, 307; Clifford on, 78; and Hamburger Hill, 160; Katzenbach on, 200–201; McGovern demands, 117; Midway Island Conference, 265–266; and Montagnards, 67; and 1972 elections, 116; Operation JEFFERSON GLENN, 194; and Operation MARKET TIME, 250; and Operation MENU, 264, 265; and Paris Peace Accords, 134, 317, 318; and Phoenix Program, 329. *See also* antiwar movement; critics of U.S. strategy

United States v. Seeger, 82

U.S. v. U.S. District Court for the Eastern District of Michigan (1972), 421

U.S.-Chinese relations, 63, 83, 194, 212–213, 255, 429, 464; Nixon rapprochement, 70, 210, 211, 248, 307, 341, 494

U.S.-RVN summits: Guam Conference (1967), 155; Honolulu Conference (1966), 180, 295, 303, 314, 392, 457; Midway Island Conference (1969), 265–266

U.S.-SRV relations, 15, 347, **429–430**; and boat people, 63, 464; Bush administration, 52, 121, 466; Carter administration, 63, 464–465; Clinton administration, 52, 78, 121, 273, 324, 430, 466; embargo, **121**, 139, 252, 429, 430, 465; POW/MIA issue, 52, 224, 272–273, 296, 429–430, 465; reconstruction aid, 272, 429, 432, 464; and Vietnamese invasion/occupation of Cambodia, 63, 121, 429, 430, 464–465

United Struggle Front for the Liberation of Oppressed Races. *See* FULRO

University of California, 18

University of Michigan, 19

University of Wisconsin bombing, **436**

Unknown Soldier, 468

Uông Bí thermal power plant strike, 9

USAID. *See* U.S. Agency for International Development

USARVIS (U.S. Army, Vietnam, Installation

Stockade) (Long Bình Jail), **437–438**

USIA. *See* U.S. Information Agency

USO (United Service Organizations), 436, 489

USSR (Union of Soviet Socialist Republics). *See* Soviet Union

UTAH, Operation (1966), **438**

U-Tapao Airfield (Thailand), 56, 233, 249, 400

Utter, Leon, 438

Vinh Thuy. *See* Bao Đai

VA. *See* Veterans Administration

VAL-4 (Navy Attack Light Squadron 4) ("Black Ponies"), 145, 370

Valdez, Juan, 143

Valeriano, Napoleon, 365

Valluy, Jean-Etienne, 92, 188, 439, **439**, 446, 447

Vàm Co River, 13, 372

Vân Đình. *See* Vo Nguyen Giáp

Van Cao, **439**, 471

Van Devanter, Lynda, 338, 468

Van Tiên Dung, 34, 175, **439**, 450, 476

Van Xuân, 243

Vance, Cyrus Roberts, 63, 316, **439–440**, 488

Vang Pao, 222, 223, 348, *751–752*. *See also* Hmong; Laos

Vann, John Paul, 19–20, 23, 165, 186, 375, **440**, 485

Vaught, James B., 96

VCI. *See* Viêt Cong Infrastructure

VCP. *See* Đang Công San Viêt Nam

VDHA. *See* Vietnam Dog Handlers Association

Vê Quôc Đoàn, 412

vedette patrouille, 137–138

vertical replenishment, 9

Vessey, John W., 2, 272–273, 296, **440–441**, 465

Vet Centers, 232, 335, 467

veterans, 77, 109, 170, 342, 489; art/literature, 25, 108, 128, 130, 332–333, 468. *See also* Vietnam Veterans Against the War

Veterans Administration (VA), 77, 232, 260, 335

Vientiane (Laos), 222

Vientiane Agreement (1973), 6, 36, 94, 222, **441**

Vientiane Protocol (1973), **441**

Viêt Cong. *See* People's Liberation Armed Forces; Viêt Cong Infrastructure

Viêt Cong Infrastructure (VCI), 2, 74, 313, 396–397, 427, 475; and specific operations, 37, 42, 65–66, 124, 247. *See also* Phoenix Program

Viêt Kiêu (overseas Vietnamese), 50, 443

Viêt Minh (Viêt Nam Đôc Lâp Đông Minh Hôi), 85, 173, 285, 289, 297, 416, **441–442**; and Bình Xuyên, 39, 228; casualties, 64, 190; Chinese support, 70, 101; and Devillers, 99; land policy, 219; and Laos, 221; and Pathet Lao, 319; specific people, 50, 185, 294, 301, 325, 411; "Tiên Quân Ca," 439; and U.S. agencies, 66, 106; and women, 489; and World War II, 151, 309–310. *See also* August Revolution; Geneva Accords (1954); Hô Chí Minh; Indo-China War; Office of Strategic Services; post-World War II Vietnamese conflict (1945–1946)

Viêt Nam Đôc Lâp Đông Minh Hôi (Vietnamese Independence League). *See* Viêt Minh

Viêt Nam Cách Mênh Đông Minh Hôi (VNCMDMH), 297, 443, 477

Viêt Nam Duy Tân Hôi (Association for Modernization of Vietnam), 88

Viêt Nam Phuc Quôc Hôi. *See* Viêt Nam Quang

Phuc Hôi

Viêt Nam Quang Phuc Hôi (Association for the Restoration of Viet Nam), 88, 111, 326

Viêt Nam Quôc Dân Đang (Vietnam National Party) (VNQDĐ), 141, 181, 300–301, 302, **442–443**, 471; Nguyên Hai Thân, 242, 297, 477; women, 301, 489; Yên Bái Uprising (1930), 301, 442–443. *See also* Hô-Sainteny Agreement

Viêt Nam Thanh Niên Cách Mang Đông Chí Hôi (Vietnam Revolutionary Youth Association), 173, **443**, 469–470

Viêt Nam Tuyên Truyên Giai Phóng Quân (Vietnam Armed Propaganda and Liberation Brigade), 475

Viêt Thanh Nguyên, 332

Viêt Trì, 90, 178

Vietnam Armed Propaganda and Liberation Brigade. *See* Viêt Nam Tuyên Truyên Giai Phóng Quân

Vietnam Day Committee, 284, 362

Vietnam Day Protest (1965), 19, 246

Vietnam, Democratic Republic of (DRV), 73, 99, 213–214, 222, 360, 394, **446–450**; air defense, 6, 374, 450–451; Chinese recognition, 189, 415, 447, 494; economy, 359–360, 447–448; land policy, 4–5, 219, 221, 411, 447–448, 472; music/films, 129, 439, 471, 471–472; Sài Gòn Military Mission destabilization/sabotage operations, 67, 81, 220, 227, 365; Soviet relations with, 215–216, 414–415, 448; U.S. antiwar movement visits, 33, 37, 132, 165, 243, 280, 490. *See also* August Revolution; Chinese military aid to DRV; DRV-NLF control issue; People's Army of Vietnam; Soviet military aid to DRV

Vietnam Dog Handlers Association (VDHA), 61

Vietnam Information Group (VIG), **467**

Vietnam Moratorium Committee, 48

Vietnam National Party. *See* Viêt Nam Quôc Dân Đang

Vietnam Patrol Force. *See* MARKET TIME, Operation

Vietnam, Republic of (RVN), **454–458**; Adams reports, 3; and Armed Forces Radio and Television Network, 280; and atrocities, 29; Buddhist protests (1964), 49, 171, 268, 269, 408, 456; Bùi Diêm, 50; constitution (1964), 171, 269, 456; constitution (1967), 118, 155, 180, 295, 457; corruption, 34, 67, 69–70, 72, 86, 120, 250, 295, 300, 304; coup attempt (1965), 325; Duong Van Đuc coup attempt (1964), 110; High National Council, 171–172, 327; and HOP TAC, 181, 313; labor unions, 60, 258; Manila Conference, 247; Military Revolutionary Council, 110, 171, 198, 269, 299; Montagnard opposition, 66; music, 471–472; National Leadership Council ("Young Turks"), 172, 198, 269, 285–286, 294, 303, 408, 456; Nguyên Khánh coup (1964), 110, 161–162, 171, 229, 236, 269, 294, 456; and Poulo Condore, 272–273, 336, 402; triumvirate (National Provisional Steering Committee) (1964), 110, 171, 269, 285–286, 294; U.S. bombing, 7, 417; Vu Quôc Thúc, 477; Vung Tau Charter, 299. *See also* Ngô Đình Diêm government; Nguyên Van Thiêu; RVN elections; RVN fall (1975); *specific people*

Vietnam Restoration Society. *See* Viêt Nam